Contents

First published in 1991 by

Philip's, a division of Octopus Publishing Group Ltd,
2-4 Heron Quays, London E14 4JP

www.philips-maps.co.uk

Fourteenth edition 2005 First impression 2005

Ordnance Survey® This product includes mapping data licensed from Ordnance Survey®, with the permission of the Controller of Her Majesty's Stationery Office © Crown copyright 2005. All rights reserved. Licence number 100011710

This product includes mapping data licensed from Ordnance Survey of Northern Ireland® reproduced by permission of the Chief Executive, acting on behalf of the Controller of Her Majesty's Stationery Office. © Crown Copyright 2005 Permit No 50343

The mapping on page 132 and the town plans of Edinburgh and London are based on mapping data licenced from Ordnance Survey with the permission of the Controller of Her Majesty's Stationery Office. © Crown Copyright 2005. All rights reserved. Licence number 100011710.

The maps of Ireland on pages 18 to 21 and the town plan of Dublin are based on Ordnance Survey Ireland by permission of the Government Permit Number 7978 © Ordnance Survey Ireland and Government of Ireland, and Ordnance Survey Northern Ireland on behalf of the Controller of Her Majesty's Stationery Office © Crown Copyright 2005 Permit Number 50343

Cartography by Philip's. Copyright © Philip's 2005

Printed and bound in Spain by Cayfosa-Quebecor

Cover photograph: The Europa Bridge carries the E45 motorway through the Brenner Pass between Innsbruck and Bolzano. 71 A6

Aflo Foto Agency / Alamy

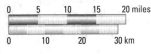

	Motorway – tunnel, under construction
	Toll motorway
	Pre-pay motorway
	Main through route
	Other major route
	Other road
25 50	European road number, motorway number
55	National road number
56	Distances – in kilometres
	International boundary, national boundary
LE HAVRE	Car ferry and destination
⨯ ✈ 1089	Mountain pass, international airport, height – in metres
	National park

Town – population

MOSKVA ▣	5 million +	Ikast ○	10000–20000
BERLIN ▣	2–5 million	Skjern ○	5000–10000
MINSK ▣	1–2 million	Lillesand ○	0–5000
Oslo ◉	500000–1 million		
Århus ◉	200000–500000		
Turku ◉	100000–200000		
Gävle ○	50000–100000		
Nybro ○	20000–50000		

Scale 1: 4 250 000
approximately 67 miles to 1 inch

0   20   40   60   80 miles

0   40   80   120 km

Legend to road maps pages 18–120

7 8 ◇	Motorway with junctions – full, restricted access services tunnel, under construction
	Toll motorway
	Pre-pay motorway – A CH CZ H SK 'Vignette' must be purchased before travel, see pages II–IV
	Principal trunk highway – single / dual carriageway tunnel, under construction
	Other main highway – single / dual carriageway tunnel, under construction
	Other important road
	Other road
E25 A49	European road number, motorway number
135	National road number
Col Bayard 1248	Mountain pass
	Scenic route, gradient – arrow points uphill
143	Distances – in kilometres major
28	minor
	Principal railway tunnel
Nápoli 15:30	Ferry route with journey time – hours:minutes Short ferry route
	International boundary
	National boundary
✈	Airport
⛪	Ancient monument
⚓	Beach
⛫	Castle or house
⌂	Cave
	National park
	Natural park
✦	Other place of interest
❀	Park or garden
✝	Religious building
⛷	Ski resort
1754▲	Spot height
Verona	Town of tourist interest

Pages 18–110 and 120
Scale 1: 1 000 000
approximately 16 miles to 1 inch

0   5   10   15   20 miles

0   10   20   30 km

Pages 111–119
Scale 1: 2 000 000
approximately 32 miles to 1 inch

0   10   20   30   40 miles

0   10   20   30   40   50   60 km

Driving regulations

A national vehicle identification plate is always required when taking a vehicle abroad.

It is important for your own safety and that of other drivers to fit headlamp converters or beam deflectors when taking a right-hand drive car to a country where driving is on the right (every country in Europe except the UK and Ireland). When the headlamps are dipped on a right-hand drive car, the lenses of the headlamps cause the beam to shine upwards to the left – and so, when driving on the right, into the eyes of oncoming motorists.

The symbols used are:

⩚	Motorway
⩘	Dual carriageway
⩗	Single carriageway
🚘	Surfaced road
🚗	Unsurfaced / gravel road
🏔	Urban area
◎	Speed limit in kilometres per hour (kph)
🩱	Seat belts
👶	Children
♀	Blood alcohol level
△	Warning triangle
⊞	First aid kit
⚕	Spare bulb kit
↑	Fire extinguisher
€	Motorcycle helmet
⊖	Minimum driving age
🖥	Additional documents required
▯	Mobile phones
★	Other information

All countries require that you carry a driving licence, green card/insurance documentation, registration document or hire certificate, and passport.

The penalties for infringements of regulations vary considerably from one country to another. In many countries the police have the right to impose on-the-spot fines (you should always request a receipt for any fine paid). Penalties can be severe for serious infringements, particularly for drinking when driving which in some countries can lead to immediate imprisonment. Insurance is important, and you may be forced to take out cover at the frontier if you cannot produce acceptable proof that you are insured.

Please note that driving regulations often change.

Andorra (AND)

◎	⩚	⩘	⩗	🏔
	n/a	90	90	50

- 🩱 Compulsory in front seats
- 👶 Over 10 only allowed in front seats if over 150cm
- ♀ 0.05%
- △ Compulsory
- ⊞ Recommended
- ⚕ Compulsory
- ↑ Recommended
- € Compulsory for all riders
- ⊖ 18 (16-18 accompanied)
- ▯ Use not permitted whilst driving

Austria (A)

◎	⩚	⩘	⩗	🏔
	130	100	100	50
If towing trailer under 750kg				
	100	100	100	50
If towing trailer over 750kg				
	100	100	80	50

- 🩱 Compulsory in front seats and rear seats
- 👶 Under 14 and under 150cm in front seats only in child safety seat; under 14 and over 150cm, must wear adult seat belt
- ♀ 0.05%
- △ Compulsory
- ⊞ Compulsory
- ⚕ Recommended
- ↑ Recommended
- € Compulsory for all riders
- ⊖ 18 (16 for mopeds)
- 🖥 Third party insurance
- ▯ Use permitted only with hands-free speaker system
- ★ If you intend to drive on motorways or expressways, a motorway vignette must be purchased at the border. These are available for 10 days, 2 months or 1 year.
- ★ Dipped headlights must be used at all times on motorbikes.

Belarus (BY)

◎	⩚	⩘	⩗	🏔
	110	90	90	60
If towing trailer under 750kg				
	90	70	70	

Vehicle towing another vehicle 50 kph limit

- 🩱 Compulsory in front seats, and rear seats if fitted
- 👶 Under 12 in front seats only in child safety seat
- ♀ 0.5
- △ Compulsory
- ⊞ Compulsory

Belgium (B)

◎	⩚	⩘	⩗	🏔
	120*	120	90	50

*Minimum speed of 70kph on motorways

◎	⩚	⩘	⩗	🏔
If towing trailer				
	90	90	60	50

- 🩱 Compulsory in front and rear seats
- 👶 Under 12 in front seats only in child safety seat
- ♀ 0.05%
- △ Compulsory
- ⊞ Compulsory
- ⚕ Recommended
- ↑ Compulsory
- € Compulsory for all riders
- ⊖ 18 (16 for mopeds)
- 🖥 Third party insurance
- ▯ Use only allowed with hands-free kit

Bulgaria (BG)

◎	⩚	⩘	⩗	🏔
	120	80	80	50-60
If towing trailer				
	100	70	70	50

- 🩱 Compulsory in front seats; advised in rear
- 👶 Under 12 not allowed in front seats
- ♀ 0.00%
- △ Compulsory
- ⊞ Compulsory
- ⚕ Recommended
- ↑ Compulsory
- € Compulsory for all riders
- ⊖ 18
- 🖥 Driving licence with translation or international driving permit, third party insurance
- ▯ Use only allowed with hands-free kit
- ★ Fee at border

Croatia (HR)

◎	⩚	⩘	⩗	🏔
	130	80	80	50
If towing				
	110	80	80	50

- 🩱 Compulsory if fitted
- 👶 Under 12 not allowed in front seats
- ♀ 0.05%
- △ Compulsory
- ⊞ Compulsory
- ⚕ Compulsory
- € Compulsory for all riders
- ⊖ 18
- ▯ Use only allowed with hands-free kit

Czech Republic (CZ)

◎	⩚	⩘	⩗	🏔
	130	130	90	50
If towing				
	80	80	80	50

- 🩱 Compulsory in front seats and, if fitted, in rear
- 👶 Under 12 or under 150cm not allowed in front seats
- ♀ 0.00%
- △ Compulsory
- ⊞ Compulsory
- ⚕ Compulsory
- € Compulsory for all riders
- ⊖ 18 (16 for motorcycles under 125 cc)
- 🖥 International driving permit
- ▯ Use only allowed with hands-free kit
- ★ Vignette needed for motorway driving, available for 1 year, 60 days, 15 days. Toll specific to lorries introduced 2006.

Denmark (DK)

◎	⩚	⩘	⩗	🏔
	110/130	80	80	50
If towing				
	80	70	70	50

- 🩱 Compulsory in front seats and, if fitted, in rear
- 👶 Under 3 not allowed in front seat except in a child safety seat; in rear, 3 to 7 years in a child safety seat or on a booster cushion
- ♀ 0.05%
- △ Compulsory
- ⊞ Recommended
- ⚕ Recommended
- ↑ Recommended
- € Compulsory for all riders
- ⊖ 18
- 🖥 Third party insurance

Estonia (EST)

◎	⩚	⩘	⩗	🏔
	n/a	90	70	50

- 🩱 Compulsory in front seats and if fitted in rear seats
- 👶 Under 12 not allowed in front seats; under 7 must have child safety seat in rear
- ♀ 0.00%
- △ Compulsory
- ⊞ Compulsory
- ⚕ Recommended
- ↑ Compulsory
- € Compulsory for all riders
- ⊖ 18 (16 for motorcycles, 14 for mopeds)
- 🖥 International driving permit recommended
- ▯ Use only allowed with hands-free kit

Finland (FIN)

◎	⩚	⩘	⩗	🏔
	120	100	80	30-60
If towing				
	80	80	80	30-60

If towing a vehicle by rope, cable or rod, max speed limit 60 kph.

Maximum of 80 kph for vans and lorries

Speed limits are often lowered in winter

- 🩱 Compulsory in front and rear
- 👶 Children must travel with a safety belt or in special child's seat
- ♀ 0.05%
- △ Compulsory
- ⊞ Recommended
- ⚕ Recommended
- ↑ Recommended
- € Compulsory for all riders
- ⊖ 18
- 🖥 Third party insurance
- ▯ Use only allowed with hands-free kit
- ★ Dipped headlights must be used at all times

France (F)

◎	⩚	⩘	⩗	🏔
	130	110	90	50
On wet roads				
	110	90	80	50

50kph on all roads if fog reduces visibility to less than 50m. Licence will be lost and driver fined for exceeding speed limit by over 40kph

Andorra (also see top — Recommended entries continued)

- ⚕ Recommended
- ↑ Compulsory
- € Compulsory for all riders
- ⊖ 18 (16 for motorbikes)
- 🖥 Third party insurance; visa (ensure it's specific to driving); vehicle technical check stamp; international driving permit
- ▯ Use only allowed with hands-free kit

- Compulsory in front seats and, if fitted, in rear
- Under 10 not allowed in front seats unless in approved safety seat facing backwards; in rear, if 4 or under, must have a child safety seat (rear facing if up to 9 months); if 5 to 10 may use a booster seat with suitable seat belt
- 0.05%
- Compulsory unless hazard warning lights are fitted; compulsory for vehicles over 3,500kgs or towing a trailer
- Recommended
- Recommended
- Compulsory for all riders
- 18 (16 for light motorcycles, 14 for mopeds)
- Use not permitted whilst driving
- Tolls on motorways

Germany (D)

	🚤	⚠	▲	🏭
⏱	*	*	100	50
If towing				
⏱	*	*	80	50

*no limit, 130 kph recommended

- Compulsory
- Children under 12 and under 150cm must have a child safety seat, in front and rear
- 0.05%
- Compulsory
- Compulsory
- Recommended
- Recommended
- Compulsory for all riders
- 18 (motorbikes: 16 if not more than 125cc and limited to 11 kW)
- Third party insurance
- Use permitted only with hands-free kit – also applies to drivers of motorbikes and bicycles
- Motorcyclists must use dipped headlights at all times.

Greece (GR)

	🚤	⚠	▲	🏭
⏱	120	110	110	50
If towing				
⏱	90	70	70	40

- Compulsory in front seats and, if fitted, in rear
- Under 12 not allowed in front seats except with suitable safety seat; under 10 not allowed in front seats
- 0.025%
- Compulsory
- Compulsory
- Recommended
- Compulsory

- Compulsory for all riders
- 18 (16 for low cc motorcycles)
- Third party insurance
- Use only allowed with hands-free kit

Hungary (H)

	🚤	⚠	▲	🏭
⏱	130	110	90	50
If towing				
⏱	80	70	70	50

- Compulsory in front seats and if fitted in rear seats
- Under 12 or under 140cm not allowed in front seats
- 0.00%
- Compulsory
- Compulsory
- Compulsory
- Recommended
- Compulsory for all riders
- 18
- Third party insurance
- Use only allowed with hands-free kit
- All motorways are toll and operate the vignette system, tickets are available for 4 days, 10 days, 1 month, 1 year
- Dipped headlights are compulsory during daylight hours (cars exempted in built-up areas)

Iceland (IS)

	🚤	🚗	🚙	🏭
⏱	n/a	90	80	50

- Compulsory in front and rear seats
- Under 12 or under 140cm not allowed in front seats
- 0.00%
- Compulsory
- Compulsory
- Compulsory
- Compulsory for all riders
- 18
- Third party insurance
- Use only allowed with hands-free kit
- Headlights are compulsory at all times
- Highland roads are not suitable for ordinary cars
- Driving off marked roads is forbidden

Ireland (IRL)

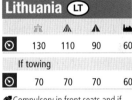

	🚤	⚠	▲	🏭
⏱	120	100	80	50
If towing				
⏱	80	80	80	50

- Compulsory in front seats and if fitted in rear seats. Driver responsible for ensuring passengers under 17 comply.
- Under 4 not allowed in front seats unless in a child safety seat or other suitable restraint
- 0.08%
- Recommended
- Recommended
- Recommended
- Recommended
- Compulsory for all riders
- 17 (16 for motorbikes up to 125cc; 18 for over 125cc; 18 for lorries; 21 bus/minibus)
- Third party insurance; international driving permit for non-EU drivers
- No specific legislation
- Driving is on the left

Italy (I)

	🚤	⚠	▲	🏭
⏱	130	110	90	50
If towing				
⏱	80	70	70	50

- Compulsory in front seats and, if fitted, in rear
- Under 12 not allowed in front seats except in child safety seat; children under 3 must have special seat in the back
- 0.08%
- Compulsory
- Recommended
- Compulsory
- Recommended
- Compulsory for all motorcyclists
- 18 (14 for mopeds, 16 for up to 125cc, 20 for up to 350cc)
- International Driving Licence unless you have photocard licence
- Use only allowed with hands-free kit

Latvia (LV)

	🚤	⚠	▲	🏭
⏱	n/a	90	90	50
If towing				
⏱	n/a	80	80	50

In residential areas limit is 20kph

- Compulsory in front seats and if fitted in rear
- If under 150cm must use child restraint in front and rear seats
- 0.05%
- Compulsory

- Compulsory
- Recommended
- Compulsory
- Compulsory for all riders
- 18 (14 for mopeds, 16 for up to 125cc, 21 for up to 350cc)
- International driving permit if licence is not in accordance with Vienna Convention
- Use only allowed with hands-free kit
- Dipped headlights must be used at all times all year round
- Cars and minibuses under 3.5 tonnes must have winter tyres from 1Dec-1Mar

Lithuania (LT)

	🚤	⚠	▲	🏭
⏱	130	110	90	60
If towing				
⏱	70	70	70	60

- Compulsory in front seats and if fitted in rear seats
- Under 12 not allowed in front seats unless in a child safety seat
- 0.04%
- Compulsory
- Compulsory
- Recommended
- Compulsory
- Compulsory for all riders
- 18 (14 for mopeds)
- Visa
- No legislation
- Dipped headlights must be used day and night from Nov to Mar (all year for motorcyclists) and from 1 to 7 Sept

Luxembourg (L)

	🚤	⚠	▲	🏭
⏱	130/110	90	90	50
If towing				
⏱	90	75	75	50

- Compulsory
- Under 12 or 150cm not allowed in front seats unless in a child safety seat; under 12 must have child safety seat or belt in rear seats
- 0.08%
- Compulsory
- Recommended
- Recommended
- Recommended

- Compulsory for all riders
- 18 (16 for mopeds)
- Third party insurance
- Use permitted only with hands-free speaker system
- Motorcyclists must use dipped headlights at all times.

Macedonia (MK)

	🚤	⚠	▲	🏭
⏱	120	100	60	60
If towing				
⏱	80	70	50	50

- Compulsory in front seats; compulsory if fitted in rear seats
- Under 12 not allowed in front seats
- 0.05%
- Compulsory
- Compulsory
- Compulsory
- Recommended
- Compulsory for all riders
- 18 (mopeds 16)
- International driving permit; visa
- No legislation

Moldova (MD)

	🚤	⚠	▲	🏭
⏱	90	90	60	60

- Compulsory in front seats
- Under 12 not allowed in front seats
- 0.00%
- Compulsory
- Compulsory
- Compulsory
- Recommended
- Compulsory for all riders
- 18 (mopeds 16)
- Visa
- No legislation

Netherlands (NL)

	🚤	⚠	▲	🏭
⏱	120	80	80	50

- Compulsory in front seats and, if fitted, rear
- Under 12 not allowed in front seats except in child restraint; in rear, 0-3 child safety restraint, 4-12 child restraint or seat belt
- 0.5%
- Recommended
- Recommended
- Recommended
- Recommended
- Compulsory for all riders

- 18 (16 for mopeds)
- Third party insurance
- Use only allowed with hands-free kit

Norway (N)

90	80	80	50
If towing trailer with brakes			
80	80	80	50
If towing trailer without brakes			
60	60	60	50

- Compulsory in front seats and, if fitted, in rear
- Under 4 must have child restraint; over 4 child restraint or seat belt
- 0.02%
- Compulsory
- Recommended
- Recommended
- Recommended
- Compulsory for all riders
- 18 (16 mopeds, heavy vehicles 18/21)
- Use only allowed with hands-free kit
- Dipped headlights must be used at all times
- Tolls apply on some bridges, tunnels and access roads into major cities

Poland (PL)

130	110	90	50-60*

50kph 06.00-22.00 60kph 23.00-05.00

If towing			
80*	80	60	30

*40kph minimum; 20kph in residential areas

- Compulsory in front seats and, if fitted, in rear
- Under 12 not allowed in front seats unless in a child safety seat or the child is 150cm tall
- 0.02%
- Compulsory
- Recommended
- Recommended
- Compulsory
- Compulsory for all riders
- 18 (mopeds and motorbikes – 16)
- International permit (recommended)
- Use only allowed with hands-free kit
- Between 1 Nov and 1 Mar dipped headlights must be used day and night

Portugal (P)

120*	100	90	50
If towing			
100*	90	80	50

*40kph minimum; 90kph maximum if licence held under 1 year

- Compulsory in front seats; compulsory if fitted in rear seats
- Under 3 not allowed in front seats unless in a child seat; 3 – 12 not allowed in front seats except in approved restraint system
- 0.05%. Imprisonment for 0.12% or more
- Compulsory
- Recommended
- Recommended
- Recommended
- Compulsory for all riders
- 18 (motorcycles under 50cc 16)
- Use only allowed with hands-free kit
- Tolls on motorways

Romania (RO)

Cars			
120	90	90	50
Vehicles seating eight persons or more			
90	80	80	50
Motorcycles			
100	80	80	50

Jeep-like vehicles: 70kph outside built-up areas but 60kph in all areas if diesel

- Compulsory in front seats and, if fitted, in rear
- Under 12 not allowed in front seats
- 0.00%
- Recommended
- Compulsory
- Recommended
- Recommended
- Compulsory for all riders
- 18 (16 for mopeds)
- Visa (only if stay over 30 days for EU citizens); third party insurance
- Use only allowed with hands-free kit
- Tolls on Bucharest to Constanta motorway and bridges over Danube

Russia (RUS)

130	120	110	60

- Compulsory in front seats
- Under 12 not allowed in front seats
- 0.00%
- Compulsory
- Compulsory
- Recommended
- Compulsory
- Compulsory
- 18
- International driving licence with translation; visa
- No legislation

Serbia and Montenegro (SCG)

120	100	80	60

- Compulsory in front and rear seats
- Under 12 not allowed in front seats
- 0.05%
- Compulsory
- Compulsory
- Recommended
- Compulsory
- Compulsory
- 18 (16 for motorbikes less than 125cc; 14 for mopeds)
- International driving permit; visa
- No legislation
- Tolls on motorways and some primary roads
- All types of fuel available at petrol stations
- 80km/h speed limit if towing a caravan

Slovak Republic (SK)

130	90	90	60

- Compulsory in front seats and, if fitted, in rear
- Under 12 not allowed in front seats unless in a child safety seat
- 0.0
- Compulsory
- Compulsory
- Compulsory
- Recommended
- Compulsory for motorcyclists
- 18 (15 for mopeds)
- International driving permit

- Use only allowed with hands-free kit
- Tow rope recommended
- Vignette required for motorways, car valid for 1 year, 30 days, 7 days; lorry vignettes carry a higher charge.

Slovenia (SLO)

130	100*	90*	50
If towing			
80	80*	80*	50

*70kph in urban areas

- Compulsory in front seats and, if fitted, in rear
- Under 12 only allowed in the front seats with special seat; babies must use child safety seat
- 0.05%
- Compulsory
- Compulsory
- Compulsory
- Recommended
- Compulsory for all riders
- 18 (motorbikes up to 125cc – 16, up to 350cc – 18)
- Use only allowed with hands-free kit
- Dipped headlights must be used at all times

Spain (E)

120	100	90	50
If towing			
80	80	70	50

- Compulsory in front seats and if fitted in rear seats
- Under 12 not allowed in front seats except in a child safety seat
- 0.05% (0.03% if vehicle over 3,500 kgs or carries more than 9 passengers, and in first two years of driving licence)
- Two compulsory (one for in front, one for behind)
- Recommended
- Compulsory in adverse weather conditions
- Recommended
- Compulsory for all riders
- 18 (18/21 heavy vehicles; 18 for motorbikes over 125cc; 16 for motorbikes up to 125cc; 14 for mopeds up to 75cc)
- Third party insurance
- Use only allowed with hands-free kit
- Tolls on motorways

Sweden (S)

110	90	70	50
If towing trailer with brakes			
80	80	70	50

- Compulsory in front and rear seats
- Under 7 must have safety seat or other suitable restraint
- 0.02%
- Compulsory
- Recommended
- Recommended
- Recommended
- Compulsory for all riders
- 18
- Third party insurance
- No legislation
- Dipped headlights must be used at all times

Switzerland (CH)

120	100	80	50/30
If towing up to 1 tonne			
80	80	80	50/30
If towing over 1 tonne			
80	80	60	50/30

- Compulsory in front and, if fitted, in rear
- Under 7 not allowed in front seats unless in child restraint; between 7 and 12 must use child restraint or seatbelt
- 0.05%
- Compulsory
- Recommended
- Recommended
- Recommended
- Compulsory for all riders
- 18 (mopeds up to 50cc – 14)
- Third party insurance
- Use only allowed with hands-free kit
- Motorways are all toll and a vignette must be purchased at the border. Can also be purchased online at www.swisstravelsystem.com/uk/, by phone on 020 7292 1550 or freephone 00800 10020030. The vignette costs £18.50 and is valid for one calendar year.

Turkey (TR)

120	90	90	50
If towing			
70	70	70	40

- Compulsory in front seats
- Under 12 not allowed in front seats
- 0.05%

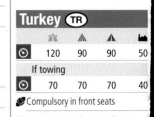

Ski resorts

The resorts listed are popular ski centres, therefore road access to most is normally good and supported by road clearing during snow falls. However, mountain driving is never predictable and drivers should make sure they take suitable snow chains as well as emergency provisions and clothing. Listed for each resort are: the atlas page and grid square; the altitude; the number of lifts; the season start and end dates; the nearest town (with its distance in km) and the telephone number of the local tourist information centre ('00' prefix required for calls from the UK).

Left column (driving regulation symbols)

△ Two compulsory (one in front, one behind)

␣ Compulsory

🦺 Compulsory

🔺 Compulsory

☀ Compulsory for all riders (except on freight motorcycles)

⊖ 18

📖 International driving permit advised; note that Turkey is in both Europe and Asia

📵 Use only allowed with hands-free kit

★ Tow rope and tool kit must be carried

Ukraine (UA)

	🏠	🛣	🛤	📶
⊘	130	90	90	60
If towing				
⊘	80	80	80	60

Speed limit in pedestrian zone 20 kph

🚗 Compulsory in front and rear seats

🧒 Under 12 not allowed in front seats

🍷 0.0%

△ Compulsory

␣ Compulsory

🦺 Optional

🔺 Compulsory

☀ Compulsory for all riders

⊖ 18 – cars; 16 motorbikes

📖 International driving permit; visa

📵 No legislation

★ Tow rope and tool kit recommended

United Kingdom (GB)

	🏠	🛣	🛤	📶
⊘	112	112	96	48
If towing				
⊘	96	96	80	48

🚗 Compulsory in front seats and if fitted in rear seats

🧒 Under 3 not allowed in front seats except with appropriate restraint, and in rear must use child restraint if available; 3–12 and under 150cm must use appropriate restraint or seat belt in front seats, and in rear if available

🍷 0.08%

△ Recommended

␣ Recommended

🦺 Recommended

🔺 Recommended

☀ Compulsory for all riders

⊖ 17 (16 for mopeds)

📵 Use only allowed with hands-free kit

Andorra

Pyrenees

Pas de la Casa / Grau Roig 91 A4 2640m 31 lifts Dec–May •Andorra La Vella (30km) ☎+376 801060 🖥www.pasgrau.com *Access via Envalira Pass (2407m), highest in Pyrenees, snow chains essential.*

Austria

Alps

A 24-hour driving conditions information line is provided by the Tourist Office of Austria www.austria.info +43 1 588 660

Bad Gastein 72 A3 1002m 51 lifts Dec–Apr •Bad Hofgastein (6km) ☎+43 6434 85044 🖥www.skigastein.at *Snow report: +43 6432 64555.*

Bad Hofgastein 72 A3 860m 51 lifts Dec–Apr •Salzburg (90km) ☎+43 6432 33930 🖥www.badhofgastein.com

Bad Kleinkirchheim 72 B3 1100m 32 lifts Dec–Apr •Villach (35km) ☎+43 4240 8212 🖥www.badkleinkirchheim.com *Snowfone:+43 4240 8222. Near Ebene Reichenau.*

Ehrwald 71 A5 1000m 22 lifts Dec–Apr •Imst (30km) ☎+43 5678 20000208 🖥www.tiscover.at/ehrwald *Weather report: +43 5673 3329*

Innsbruck 71 A6 574m 75 lifts Dec–Apr •Innsbruck ☎+43 5125 9850 🖥www.innsbruck-tourismus.com *Motorway normally clear. The motorway through to Italy and through the Arlberg Tunnel West to Austria are both toll roads.*

Ischgl 71 A5 1400m 42 lifts Dec–May •Landeck (25km) ☎+43 5444 52660 🖥www.ischgl.com *Car entry to resort prohibited between 2200hrs and 0600hrs.*

Kaprun 72 A2 800m, 56 lifts Jan–Dec •Zell am See (10km) ☎+43 6542 7700 🖥www.zellkaprun.at *Snowfone:+43 6547 73684.*

Kirchberg in Tyrol 72 A2 860m 59 lifts Dec–Apr •Kitzbühel (6km) ☎+43 5357 2309 🖥www.kirchberg.at *Easily reached from Munich International Airport (120 km)*

Kitzbühel 72 A2 800m 59 lifts Dec–Apr •Wörgl (40km) ☎+43 5356 777 🖥www.kitzbuehel.com

Lech/Oberlech 71 A5 1450m 84 lifts Dec–Apr •Bludenz (50km) ☎+43 5583 21610 🖥www.Lech.at *Roads normally cleared but keep chains accessible because of altitude. Road conditions report tel +43 5583 1515.*

Mayrhofen 72 A1 630m 29 lifts Dec–Apr •Jenbach (35km) ☎+43 5285 67600 🖥www.mayrhofen.at *Chains rarely required.*

Obertauern 72 A3 1740m 27 lifts Nov–May •Radstadt (20km) ☎+43 6456 7252 🖥www.top-obertauern.com *Roads normally cleared but chains accessibility recommended. Camper vans and caravans not allowed; park these in Radstadt*

Saalbach Hinterglemm 72 A2 1003m 52 lifts Dec–Apr •Zell am See (19km) ☎+43 6541 6800 68 🖥www.saalbach. com *Both village centres are pedestrianised and there is a good ski bus service during the daytime*

St Anton am Arlberg 71 A5 1304m 84 lifts Nov–May •Innsbruck (104km) ☎+43 5446 22690 🖥www.stantonamarlberg.com *Snow report tel +43 5446 2565*

Schladming 72 A3 2708m 86 lifts Nov–Apr •Schladming ☎+43 3687 22777 🖥www.schladming.com

Serfaus 71 A5 1427m 53 lifts Dec–Apr •Landeck (30km) ☎+43 5476 62390 🖥www.serfaus.com *Cars banned from village, use world's only 'hover' powered underground railway.*

Sölden 71 B6 1377m, 32 lifts all year •Imst (50km) ☎+43 5254 5100 🖥www.soelden.com *Roads normally cleared but snow chains recommended because of altitude. The route from Italy and the south over the Timmelsjoch via Obergurgl is closed in the winter and anyone arriving from the south should use the Brenner Pass motorway. Snow information tel +43 5254 2666.*

Zell am See 72 A2 758m 57 lifts Dec–Mar •Zell am See ☎+43 6542 7700 🖥www.zellkaprun.at *Snowfone +43 6542 73694 Low altitude, therefore good access and no mountain passes to cross.*

Zell im Zillertal (Zell am Ziller) 72 A1 580m 47 lifts Dec–Apr •Jenbach (25km) ☎+43 5282 2281 🖥www.tiscover.at/ zell *Snowfone +43 5282 716526.*

Zürs 71 A5 1720m 84 lifts Dec–May •Bludenz (30km) ☎+43 5583 2245 🖥www.lech.at *Roads normally cleared but keep chains accessible because of altitude. Village has garage with 24-hour self-service gas/petrol, breakdown service and wheel chains supply.*

France

Alps

Alpe d'Huez 79 A5 1860m 87 lifts Dec–Apr •Grenoble (63km) ☎+33 4 76 11 44 44 🖥www.alpedhuez.com *Snow chains may be required on access road to resort. Road report tel +33 4 76 11 44 50.*

Avoriaz 70 B1 2277m 38 lifts Dec–May •Morzine (14km) ☎+33 4 50 74 02 11 🖥www.avoriaz.com *Chains may be required for access road from Morzine. Car free resort, park on edge of village. Horse-drawn sleigh service available.*

Chamonix-Mont-Blanc 70 C1 1035m 49 lifts Nov–May •Martigny (38km) ☎+33 4 50 53 00 24 🖥www.chamonix.com

Chamrousse 79 A4 1700m 26 lifts Dec–Apr •Grenoble (30km) ☎+33 4 76 89 92 65 🖥www.chamrousse.com *Roads normally cleared, keep chains accessible because of altitude.*

Châtel 70 B1 2200m 40 lifts Dec–Apr •Thonon Les Bains (35km) ☎+33 4 50 73 22 44 🖥www.chatel.com

Courchevel 70 C1 1850m 185 lifts Dec–Apr •Moûtiers (23km) ☎+33 4 79 08 00 29 🖥www.courchevel.com *Roads normally cleared but keep chains accessible. Traf-*

fic 'discouraged' within the four resort bases. Traffic info: +33 4 79 37 73 37.

Flaine 70 B1 1800m 74 lifts Dec–Apr •Cluses (25km) ☎+33 4 50 90 80 01 🖥www.flaine.com *Keep chains accessible for D6 from Cluses to Flaine. Car access for depositing luggage and passengers only. 1500-space car park outside resort. Near Sixt-Fer-á-Cheval.*

La Clusaz 69 C6 1100m 55 lifts Dec–Apr •Annecy (32km) ☎+33 4 50 32 65 00 🖥www.laclusaz.com *Roads normally clear but keep chains accessible for final road from Annecy.*

La Plagne 70 C1 2100m 110 lifts Dec–Apr Moûtiers (32km) ☎+33 4 79 09 79 79 🖥www.la-plagne.com *Ten different centres up to 2100m altitude. Road access via Bozel, Landry or Aime normally cleared.*

Les Arcs 70 C1 2600m 77 lifts Dec–Apr •Bourg-St-Maurice (15km) ☎+33 4 79 07 12 57 🖥www.lesarcs.com *Three base areas up to 2000 metres; keep chains accessible. Pay parking at edge of each base resort.*

Les Carroz d'Araches 70 B1 1140m 74 lifts Dec–Apr •Cluses (13km) ☎+33 4 50 90 00 04 🖥www.lescarroz.com

Les Deux-Alpes 79 B5 1650m 63 lifts Dec–May •Grenoble (75km) ☎+33 4 76 79 22 00 🖥www.les2alpes.com *Roads normally cleared, however snow chains recommended for D213 up from valley road (N91).*

Les Gets 70 B1 1172m 53 lifts Dec–May •Cluses (18km) ☎+33 4 50 75 80 80 🖥www.lesgets.com

Les Ménuires 69 C6 1815m 197 lifts Dec–Apr •Moûtiers (27km) ☎+33 4 79 00 73 00 🖥www.lesmenuires.com *Keep chains accessible for N515A from Moûtiers.*

Les Sept Laux 69 C6 1350m, 29 lifts Dec–Apr •Grenoble (38km) ☎+33 4 76 08 17 86 🖥www.les7laux.com *Roads normally cleared, however keep chains accessible for mountain road up from the A41 motorway. Near St Sorlin d'Arves.*

Megève 69 C6 2350m 117 lifts Dec–Apr •Sallanches (12km) ☎+33 4 50 21 27 28 🖥www.megeve.com *Horse-drawn sleigh rides available.*

Méribel 69 C6 1400m 197 lifts Dec–May •Moûtiers (18km) ☎+33 4 79 08 60 01 🖥www.meribel.com *Keep chains accessible for 18km to resort on D90 from Moûtiers.*

To the best of the Publisher's knowledge the information in this table was correct at the time of going to press. No responsibility can be accepted for any errors or their consequences.

Morzine 70 B1 1000m 217 lifts, Dec–May •Thonon-Les-Bains (30km) +33 4 50 74 72 72 www.morzine.com

Pra Loup 79 B5 1600m 53 lifts Dec–Apr •Barcelonnette (10km) +33 4 92 84 10 04 www.praloup.com *Roads normally cleared but chains accessibility recommended.*

Risoul 79 B5 1850m 58 lifts Dec–Apr •Briançon (40km) +33 4 92 46 02 60 www.risoul.com *Keep chains accessible. Near Guillestre.*

St Gervais 70 C1 850m 121 lifts Dec–Apr +33 4 50 47 76 08 www.st-gervais.com

Serre-Chevalier 79 B5 1350m 79 lifts Dec–May •Briançon (10km) +33 4 92 24 98 98 www.serre-chevalier.com *Made up of 13 small villages along the valley road, which is normally cleared.*

Tignes 70 C1 2100m 97 lifts Jan–Dec +33 4 79 40 04 40 www.tignes.net *Keep chains accessible because of altitude. Parking information tel +33 4 79 06 39 45.*

Val d'Isère 70 C1 1850m 97 lifts Nov–May •Bourg-St-Maurice (30km) +33 4 79 06 06 60 www.valdisere.com *Roads normally cleared but keep chains accessible.*

Val Thorens 69 C6 2300m 197 lifts Nov–May •Moûtiers (37km) +33 4 79 00 08 08 www.valthorens.com *Chains essential – highest ski resort in Europe. Obligatory paid parking on edge of resort.*

Valloire 69 C6 1430m 36 lifts Dec–May •Modane (20km) +33 4 79 59 03 96 www.valloire.net *Road normally clear up to the Col du Galbier, to the south of the resort, which is closed from 1st November to 1st June.*

Valmeinier 69 C6 2600m 32 lifts Dec–Apr •St Michel de Maurienne (47km) +33 4 79 59 53 69 www.valmeinier.com *Access from north on N9 / N902. Col du Galbier, to the south of the resort closed from 1st November to 1st June. Near Valloire.*

Valmorel 69 C6 1400m 55 lifts Dec–Apr •Moûtiers (15km) +33 4 79 09 85 55 www.valmorel.com *Near St Jean-de-Belleville.*

Vars Les Claux 79 B5 1850m 58 lifts Dec–Apr •Briançon (40km) +33 4 92 46 51 31 www.vars-ski.com *Four base resorts up to 1850 metres. Keep chains accessible. Road and weather information tel +33 4 36 68 02 05 and +33 4 91 78 78 78. Snowfone +33 492 46 51 04*

Villard-de-Lans 79 A4 1050m 29 lifts Dec–Apr •Grenoble (32km) +33 4 76 95 10 38 www.villard-de-lans.com

Pyrenees

Font-Romeu 91 A5 1800m 33 lifts Dec–Apr •Perpignan (87km) +33 4 68 30 68 30 www.fontromeu.com *Roads normally cleared but keep chains accessible.*

St Lary-Soulan 830m 32 lifts Dec–Apr •Tarbes (75km) +33 5 62 39 50 81 www.saintlary.com *Access roads constantly cleared of snow.*

Vosges

La Bresse-Hohneck 900m 20 lifts Dec–Mar •Cornimont (6km) +33 3 29 25 41 29 www.labresse-remy.com .

Germany

Alps

Garmisch-Partenkirchen 71 A6 702m 38 lifts Dec–Apr •Munich (95km) +49 8821 180 700 www.garmisch-partenkirchen.de *Roads usually clear, chains rarely needed.*

Oberaudorf 62 C3 483m 21 lifts Dec–Apr •Kufstein (15km) +49 8033 301 20 www.oberaudorf.de *Motorway normally kept clear. Near Bayrischzell.*

Oberstdorf 71 A5 815m 31 lifts Dec–Apr •Sonthofen (15km) +49 8322 7000 www.oberstdorf.de *Snow information on tel +49 8322 3035 or 1095 or 5757.*

Rothaargebirge

Winterberg 51 B4 700m 55 lifts Dec–Mar •Brilon (30km) +49 2981 925 00 www.winterberg.de *Roads usually cleared, chains rarely required.*

Greece

Central Greece

Mountain Parnassos: Kelaria-Fterolakka 116 D4 1750–1950m 14 lifts Dec–Apr •Amfiklia Kelaria +30 22340 22694, Ftorolakka 22340 22373 www.parnassos-eot.gr

Mountain Parnassos: Gerondovrahos 116 D4 1800–2390m 3 lifts Dec–Apr •Amfiklia +30 29444 70371

Ipiros

Mountain Pindos: Karakoli 116 C3 1350–1700m 1 lift Dec–Mar •Metsovo +30 26560 41333

Mountain Pindos: Profitis Ilias 116 C3 1500–1700m 3 lifts Dec–Mar •Metsovo +30 26560 41095

Peloponnisos

Mountain Helmos: Kalavrita Ski Centre 117 D4 1650–2340m 7 lifts Dec–Mar •Kalavrita +30 26920 244541 www.kalavrita-ski.gr/en/default.asp

Mountain Menalo: Oropedio Ostrakinos 117 E4 1600m 3 lifts Dec–Mar •Tripoli +30 27960 22227

Macedonia

Mountain Falakro: Agio Pneuma 116 A6 1720m 3 lifts Dec–Mar •Drama +30 25210 62224 www.falakro.gr

Mountain Vasilitsa: Vasilitsa 116 B3 1750m 2 lifts Dec–Mar •Konitsa +30 24620 84850 www.vasilitsa.com

Mountain Vermio: Seli 116 B4 1500m 4 lifts Dec–Mar •Kozani +30 23310 26237

Mountain Vermio: Tria-Pente Pigadia 116 B3 1420–2005m 4 lifts Dec–Mar •Ptolemaida +30 23320 44446

Mountain Verno: Vigla 116 B3 1650–2000m 3 lifts Dec–Mar •Florina +30 23850 22354

Mountain Vrondous: Lailias 116 A5 1847m 3 lifts Dec–Mar •Serres +30 23210 62400

Thessalia

Mountain Pilio: Agriolefkes 116 C5 1500m 4 lifts Dec–Mar •Volos +30 24280 73719

Italy

Alps

Bardonecchia 1312m 24 lifts Dec–Apr •Bardonecchia +39 122 99137 Snowfone +39 122 907778 www.goski.com/rit/bardon.htm *Resort reached through the 11km Frejus tunnel from France, roads normally cleared.*

Bórmio 71 B5 1225m 16 lifts Dec–Apr •Tirano (40km) +39 342 903300 www.bormio.com *Tolls payable in Ponte del Gallo Tunnel, open 0800hrs–2000hrs.*

Breuil-Cervinia 2050m 73 lifts Jan–Dec •Aosta (54km) +39 166 940986 www.breuil-cervinia.it *Snow chains strongly recommended. Bus from Milan airport.*

Courmayeur 70 C1 1224m 27 lifts Dec–Apr •Aosta (40km) +39 165 842370 www.courmayeur.com *Access through the Mont Blanc tunnel from France. Roads constantly cleared.*

Limone Piemonte 80 B1 1050m 29 lifts Dec–Apr •Cuneo (27km) +39 171 925280 www.limonepiemonte.it *Roads normally cleared, chains rarely required. Snow report tel +39 171 926254.*

Livigno 71 B5 1816m 33 lifts Dec–May •Zernez (CH) (27km) +39 342 052200 www.aptlivigno.it *Keep chains accessible. La Drosa Tunnel from Zernez, Switzerland, is open only from 0800hrs to 2000hrs.*

Sestrière 79 B5 2035m 91 lifts Dec–Apr •Oulx (22km) +39 122 755444 www.sestriere.it *One of Europe's highest resorts; although roads are normally cleared, chains should be accessible.*

Appennines

Roccaraso – Aremogna 103 B7 1285m 31 lifts Dec–Apr •Castel di Sangro (7km) +39 864 62210 www.roccaraso.net

Dolomites

Andalo – Fai della Paganella 71 B5 1042m 22 lifts Dec–Apr •Trento (40km) www.paganella.net +39 461 585588

Arabba 72 B1 2500m 30 lifts Dec–Apr •Brunico (45km) +39 436 780019 www.arabba.it *Roads normally cleared but keep chains accessible.*

Cortina d'Ampezzo 1224m 48 lifts Dec–Apr •Belluno (72km) +39 436 866252 www.cortinadampezzo.it *Access from north on route 51 over the Cimabanche Pass may require chains.*

Corvara (Alta Badia) 1568m 54 lifts Dec–Apr •Brunico (38km) +39 471 836176 www.altabadia.it/inverno *Roads normally clear but keep chains accessible.*

Madonna di Campiglio 71 B5 1550m 60 lifts Dec–Apr •Trento (60km) +39 465 447501 www.campiglio.net *Roads normally cleared but keep chains accessible.*

Moena di Fassa (Sorte/Ronchi) 1184m 29 lifts Dec–Apr •Bolzano (40km) +39 462 602466 www.dolomitisuperski.com

Passo del Tonale 1883m 30 lifts Dec–Aug •Breno (50km) +39 364 903838 www.adamelloski.com *Located on high mountain pass; keep chains accessible.*

Selva di Val Gardena/Wolkenstein Groden 1563m 82 lifts Dec–Apr •Bolzano (40km) +39 471 792277 www.valgardena.it *Roads normally cleared but keep chains accessible.*

Norway

Hemsedal 32 B5 650m 16 lifts Nov–May •Honefoss (150km) +47 32 055030 www.hemsedal.com *Be prepared for extreme weather conditions.*

Trysil (Trysilfjellet) 34 A4 465m 24 lifts Nov–May •Elverum (100km) +47 62 451000 www.trysil.com *Be prepared for extreme weather conditions.*

Slovakia

Chopok 65 B5 2024m 21 lifts Nov–May •Jasna +421 48 991505 www.jasna.sk

Donovaly 65 B5 1360m 15 lifts Nov–May •Ruzomberok +421 48 4199900 www.parksnow.sk

Martinske Hole 65 A4 1456m 7 lifts Nov–May •Zilina +421 41 500 3429 www.martinskehole.sk

Plejsy 65 B6 912m 8 lifts Nov–May •Krompachy +421 53 447 1121 www.plejsy.com

Strbske Pleso 65 A6 1915m 8 lifts Nov–May •Poprad +421 52 449 2343 www.parksnow.sk/tatry-leto

Rohace 65 A5 1450m 4 lifts Nov–May •Liptovsky Mikulas +421 43 5395320

Slovenia

Julijske Alpe

Kanin 72 B3 2289m 6 lifts Dec–May •Bovec +386 5 3841 919 www.bovec.si

Kobla 72 B3 1480m 6 lifts Dec–Apr •Bohinjska Bistrica +386 4 5747 100 www.bohinj.si/kobla

Kranjska Gora 72 B3 1620m 20 lifts Dec–Apr •Kranjska Gora +386 4 588 1768 www.kranjska-gora.si

Vogel 72 B3 1800m 9 lifts Dec–Apr •Bohinjska Bistrica +386 4 5724 236 www.bohinj.si/vogel

Kawiniske Savinjske Alpe

Krvavec 73 B4 1970m 13 lifts Dec–May •Kranj +386 4 2525 930 www.rtc-krvavec.si

Pohorje

Rogla 73 B5 1517m 11 lifts Dec–May •Slovenska Bistrica +386 3 757 6000 www.unior.si/slo/turizem

Spain

Baqueira/Beret 90 A3 1500m 24 lifts Dec–Apr •Viella (15km) +34 973 649010 www.baqueira.es *Roads normally clear but keep chains accessible. Snowfone tel +34 973 639025. Near Salardú.*

Sistema Penibetico

Sierra Nevada 100 B2 2102m 21 lifts Dec–May •Granada (32km) +34 958 249100 www.sierranevadaski.com *Access road designed to be avalanche safe and is snow cleared. Snowfone +34 958 249119.*

Sweden

Idre Fjäll 115 F9 710m 30 lifts Oct–May •Mora (140km) +46 253 41000 www.idrefjall.se *Be prepared for extreme weather conditions.*

Sälen 34 A5 360m 101 lifts Nov–Apr •Malung (70km) +46 280 86070 www.salen.se, www.salenfjallen.se *Be prepared for extreme weather conditions.*

Switzerland

Adelboden 70 B2 1353m 50 lifts Dec–Apr •Frutigen (15km) +41 33 673 80 80 www.adelboden.ch

Arosa 71 B4 1800m 16 lifts Dec–Apr •Chur (30km) +41 81 378 70 20 www.arosa.ch *Roads cleared but keep chains accessible because of high altitude (1800m).*

Crans Montana 70 B2 1500m 35 lifts Dec–Apr, Jul-Oct •Sierre (15km) +41 27 485 04 04 www.crans-montana.ch *Roads normally cleared, however keep chains accessible for ascent from Sierre.*

Davos 71 B4 1560m 54 lifts Nov–Apr •Davos +41 81 415 21 21 www.davos.ch

Engelberg 70 B3 1000m 26 lifts Nov–Jun •Luzern (39km) +41 41 639 77 77 www.engelberg.ch *Straight access road normally cleared.*

Flums (Flumserberg) 71 A4 1400m 17 lifts Dec–Apr •Buchs (25km) +41 81 720 18 18 www.flumserberg.com *Roads normally cleared, but 1000-metre vertical ascent; keep chains accessible.*

Grindelwald 1034m 30 lifts Dec–Apr •Interlaken (20km) +41 33 854 12 12 www.grindelwald.ch

Gstaad – Saanenland 1050m 66 lifts Dec–Apr •Gstaad +41 33 748 81 81 www.gstaad.ch

Klosters 71 B4 1191m 61 lifts Dec–Apr •Davos (10km) +41 81 410 20 20 www.klosters.ch

Leysin 1263m 19 lifts Dec–Apr •Aigle (6km) +41 24 494 22 44 www.leysin.ch

Mürren 1650m 37 lifts Dec–Apr •Interlaken (18km) +41 33 856 86 86 www.wengen-muerren.ch *No road access. Park in Strechelberg (1500 free places) and take the two-stage cable car.*

Nendaz 1365m 91 lifts Nov–Apr •Sion (16km) +41 27 289 55 89 www.nendaz.ch *Roads normally cleared, however keep chains accessible for ascent from Sion. Near Vex.*

Saas-Fee 1800m 25 lifts Jan–Dec •Brig (35km) +41 27 958 18 58 www.saas-fee.ch *Roads normally cleared but keep chains accessible because of altitude.*

St Moritz 71 B4 1856m 58 lifts Nov–May •Chur (89km) +41 81 837 33 33 www.stmoritz.ch *Roads normally cleared but keep chains accessible because of altitude.*

Samnaun 71 B5 1846m 42 lifts Dec–May •Scuol (30km) +41 81 868 58 58 www.samnaun.ch *Roads normally cleared but keep chains accessible.*

Verbier 1500m 95 lifts Nov–May, Jun-Jul •Martigny (27km) +41 27 775 38 88 www.verbier.ch *Roads normally cleared.*

Villars 1253m 37 lifts Nov–Apr, Jun-Jul •Montreux (35km) +41 24 495 32 32 www.villars.ch *Roads normally cleared but keep chains accessible for ascent from N9. Near Bex.*

Wengen 1270m 37 lifts Dec–Apr •Interlaken (12km) +41 33 855 14 14 www.wengen-muerren.ch *No road access. Park at Lauterbrunnen and take mountain railway.*

Zermatt 1620m 73 lifts all year •Brig (42km) +41 27 966 81 00 www.zermatt.ch *Cars not permitted in resort, park in Täsch (3km) and take shuttle train.*

Turkey

North Anatolian Mountains

Uludag 118 B4 2543m 14 lifts Dec–March •Bursa (36km) +90 224 254 22 74 www.goski.com/rtur/uludag.htm

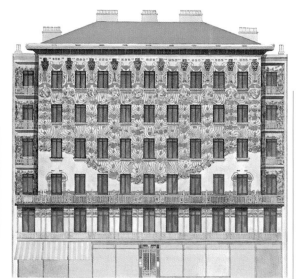

Maholicahaus, Vienna, Austria

Albania Shqipëria

www.albanian.com

Berat
Fascinating old town with picturesque Ottoman Empire buildings and traditional Balkan domestic architecture. 105 C5

Tirana Tiranë
Capital of Albania. Skanderbeg Square has main historic buildings. Also: 18c Haxhi Ethem Bey Mosque; Art Gallery (Albanian); National Museum of History. Nearby: medieval Krujë; Roman monuments. 105 B5

Austria Österreich

www.austria-tourism.at

Bregenz
Lakeside town bordering Germany, Liechtenstein, Switzerland. Locals, known as Vorarlbergers, have their own dialect. St Martinsturm 17th century tower, 17th century town hall, Kunsthaus Bregenz gallery of modern art, Vorarlberger Landesmuseum, Festspielhaus www.bregenz.ws 71 A4

Graz
University town, seat of imperial court to 1619. Historic centre around Hauptplatz. Imperial monuments: Burg; mausoleum of Ferdinand II; towers of 16c schloss; 17c Schloss Eggenburg. Also: 16c Town Hall; Zeughaus; 15c cathedral. Museums: Old Gallery (Gothic, Flemish); New Gallery (good 19–20c).
www.graztourismus.at 73 A5

Innsbruck
Old town is reached by Maria-Theresien-Strasse with famous views. Buildings: Goldenes Dachl (1490s); 18c cathedral; remains of Hofburg imperial residence; 16c Hofkirche (tomb of Maximilian I).
www.innsbruck.info 71 A6

Krems
On a hill above the Danube, medieval quarter has Renaissance mansions. Also: Gothic Piaristenkirche; Wienstadt Museum.
www.krems.at 63 B6

Linz
Port on the Danube. Historic buildings are concentrated on Hauptplatz below the imperial 15c schloss. Notable: Baroque Old Cathedral; 16c Town Hall; New Gallery.
www.linz.at 63 B5

Melk
Set on a rocky hill above the Danube, the fortified abbey is the greatest Baroque achievement in Austria – particularly the Grand Library and abbey church. www.stiftmelk.at 63 B6

Salzburg
Set in subalpine scenery, the town was associated with powerful 16-17c prince-archbishops. The 17c cathedral has a complex of archiepiscopal buildings: the Residence and its gallery (excellent 16–19c); the 13c Franciscan Church (notable altar). Other sights: Mozart's birthplace; the Hohensalzburg fortress; the Collegiate Church of St Peter (cemetery, catacombs); scenic views from Mönchsberg and Hettwer Bastei. The Grosse Festspielhaus runs the Salzburg festival. www.2.salzburg.info 62 C4

Salzkammergut
Natural beauty with 76 lakes (Wolfgangersee, Altersee, Gosausee, Traunsee, Grundlsee) in mountain scenery. Attractive villages (St Wolfgang) and towns (Bad Ischl, Gmunden) include Hallstatt, famous for Celtic remains.
www.salzkammergut.at 63 C4

Vienna Wien
Capital of Austria. The historic centre lies within the Ring. Churches: Gothic St Stephen's Cathedral; 17c Imperial Vault; 14c Augustine Church; 14c Church of the Teutonic Order (treasure); 18c Baroque churches (Jesuit Church, Franciscan Church, St Peter, St Charles). Imperial residences: Hofburg; Schönbrunn. Architecture of Historicism on Ringstrasse (from 1857). Art Nouveau: Station Pavilions, Postsparkasse, Looshaus, Majolicahaus. Exceptional museums: Art History Museum (antiquities, old masters); Cathedral and Diocesan Museum (15c); Academy of Fine Arts (Flemish); Belvedere (Gothic, Baroque, 19–20c).
www.wien.gv.at 64 B2

Belgium Belgique

www.visitbelgium.com

Antwerp Antwerpen
City with many tall gabled Flemish houses on the river. Heart of the city is Great Market with 16–17c guildhouses and Town Hall. 14–16c Gothic cathedral has Rubens paintings. Rubens also at the Rubens House and his burial place in St Jacob's Church. Excellent museums: Mayer van den Berg Museum (applied arts); Koninklijk Museum of Fine Arts (Flemish, Belgian).
www.visitantwerp.be 49 B5

Bruges Brugge
Well-preserved medieval town with narrow streets and canals. Main squares: the Market with 13c Belfort and covered market; the Burg with Basilica of the Holy Blood and Town Hall. The Groeninge Museum and Memling museum in St Jans Hospital show 15c Flemish masters. The Onze Lieve Vrouwekerk has a famous *Madonna and Child* by Michelangelo
www.brugge.be 49 B4

Brussels Bruxelles
Capital of Belgium. The Lower Town is centred on the enormous Grand Place with Hôtel de Ville and rebuilt guildhouses. Symbols of the city include the 'Manneken Pis' and Atomium (giant model of a molecule). The 13c Notre Dame de la Chapelle is the oldest church. The Upper Town contains: Gothic cathedral; Neoclassical Place Royale; 18c King's Palace; Royal Museums of Fine Arts (old and modern masters). Also: much Art Nouveau (Victor Horta Museum, Hôtel Tassel, Hôtel Solvay); Place du Petit Sablon and Place du Grand Sablon; 19c Palais de Justice.
www.brusselsinternational.be 49 C5

Ghent Gent
Medieval town built on islands surrounded by canals and rivers. Views from Pont St-Michel. The Graslei and Koornlei quays have Flemish guild houses. The Gothic cathedral has famous Van Eyck altarpiece. Also: Belfort; Cloth Market; Gothic Town Hall; Gravensteen. Museums: Bijloke Museum in beautiful abbey (provincial and applied art); Museum of Fine Arts (old masters). www.gent.be 49 B4

Namur
Reconstructed medieval citadel is the major sight of Namur, which also has a cathedral and provincial museums.
www.namur.be 49 C5

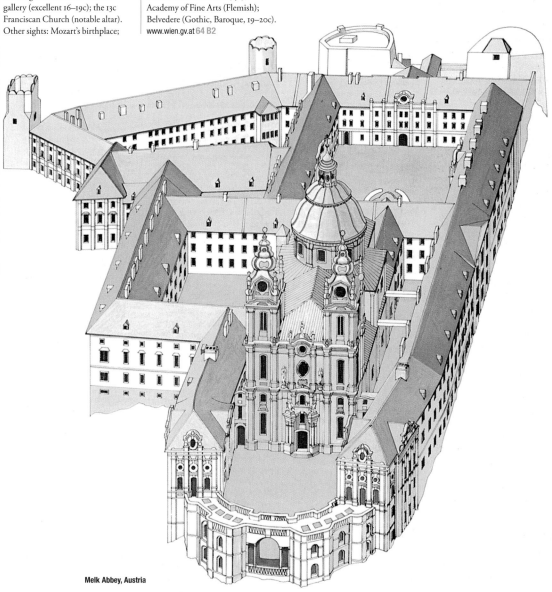

Melk Abbey, Austria

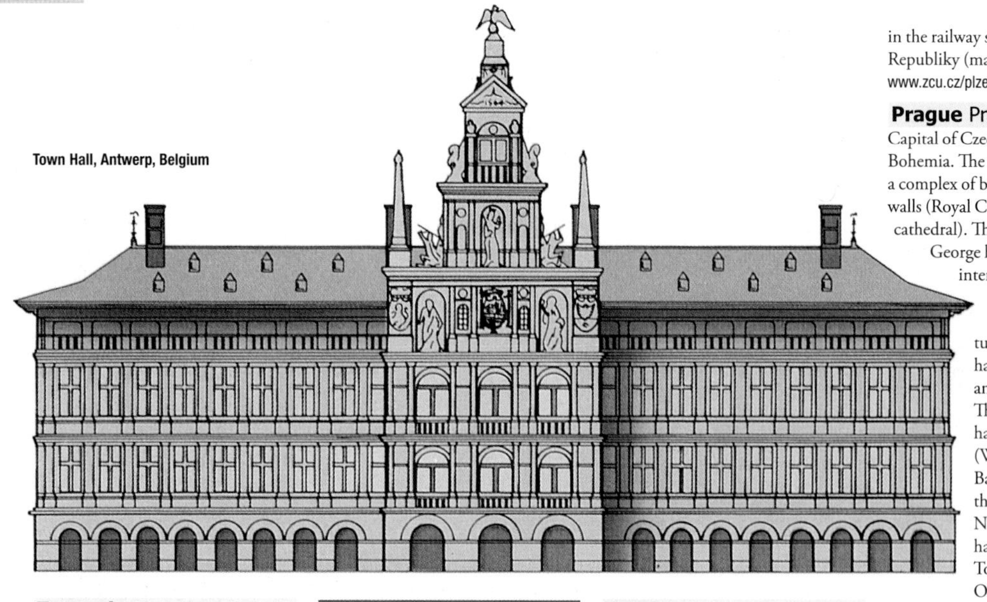

Town Hall, Antwerp, Belgium

Tournai

The Romanesque-Gothic cathedral is Belgium's finest (much excellent art). Fine Arts Museum has a good collection (15–20c). www.tournai.be 49 C4

Bulgaria Bulgariya

www.bulgariatravel.org

Black Sea Coast

Beautiful unspoiled beaches (Zlatni Pyasŭtsi). The delightful resort Varna is popular. Nesebŭr is famous for Byzantine churches. Also: Danube Delta in Hungary. 11 E9

Koprivshtitsa

Beautiful village known both for its half-timbered houses and links with the April Rising of 1876. Six house museums amongst which the Lyutov House and the Oslekov House, plus the birthplaces of Georgi Benkovski, Dimcho Debelyanov, Todor Kableshkov, and Lyuben Karavelov.

Plovdiv

City set spectacularly on three hills. The old town has buildings from many periods: 2c Roman stadium and amphitheatre; 14c Dzumaiya Mosque; 19c Koyumdjioglu House and Museum (traditional objects). Nearby: Bačkovo Monastery (frescoes). www.plovdiv.org 11 E8

Rila

Bulgaria's finest monastery, set in the most beautiful scenery of the Rila mountains. The church is richly decorated with frescoes.

Sofia Sofiya

Capital of Bulgaria. Sights: exceptional neo-Byzantine cathedral; Church of St Sofia; 4c rotunda of St George (frescoes); Byzantine Boyana Church (frescoes) on panoramic Mount Vitoša. Museums: National Historical Museum (particularly for Thracian artefacts); National Art Gallery (icons, Bulgarian art). www.sofia.bg/en 11 E7

Veliko Tŭrnovo

Medieval capital with narrow streets. Notable buildings: House of the Little Monkey; Hadji Nicoli Inn; ruins of medieval citadel; Baudouin Tower; churches of the Forty Martyrs and of SS Peter and Paul (frescoes); 14c Monastery of the Transfiguration. www.veliko-tarnovo.net 11 E8

Croatia Hrvatska

www.croatia.hr

Dalmatia Dalmacija

Exceptionally beautiful coast along the Adriatic. Among its 1185 islands, those of the Kornati Archipelago and Brijuni Islands are perhaps the most spectacular. Along the coast are several attractive medieval and Renaissance towns, most notably Dubrovnik, Split, Šibenik, Trogir, Zadar. www.dalmacija.net 83 B4

Dubrovnik

Surrounded by medieval and Renaissance walls, the city's architecture dates principally from 15–16c. Sights: many churches and monasteries including Church of St Vlah and Dominican monastery (art collection); promenade street of Stradun, Dubrovnik Museums; Renaissance Rector's Palace; Onofrio's fountain; Sponza Palace. The surrounding area has some 80 16c noblemen's summer villas. www.dubrovnik-online.com 105 A4

Islands of Croatia

There are over 1,000 islands off the coast of Croatia among which there is Brač, known for its white marble and the beautiful beaches of Bol (www.bol.hr); Hvar (www.hvar.hr) is beautifully green with fields of lavender, marjoram, rosemary, sage and thyme; Vis (www.tz-vis.hr) has the beautiful towns of Komiža and Vis Town, with the Blue Cave on nearby Biševo. 83–84

Istria Istra

Peninsula with a number of ancient coastal towns (Rovinj, Poreč, Pula, Piran in Slovene Istria) and medieval hill-top towns (Motovun). Pula has Roman monuments (exceptional 1c amphitheatre). Poreč has narrow old streets; the mosaics in 6c Byzantine basilica of St Euphrasius are exceptional. See also Slovenia. www.istra.com 82 A2

Plitvička Jezera

Outstandingly beautiful world of water and woodlands with 16 lakes and 92 waterfalls interwoven by canyons. www.np-plitvicka-jezera.hr 83 B4

Split

Most notable for the exceptional 4c palace of Roman Emperor Diocletian, elements of which are incorporated into the streets and buildings of the town itself. The town also has a cathedral (11c baptistry) and a Franciscan monastery. www.split.hr 83 C5

Trogir

The 13–15c town centre is surrounded by medieval city walls. Romanesque-Gothic cathedral includes the chapel of Ivan the Blessed. Dominican and Benedictine monasteries house art collections. www.trogir-online.com 83 C5

Zagreb

Capital city of Croatia with cathedral and Archbishop's Palace in Kaptol and to the west Gradec with Baroque palaces. Donji Grad is home to the Archaological Museum, Art Pavilion, Museum of Arts and Crafts, Ethnographic Museum, Mimara Museum and National Theatre. www.zagreb-touristinfo.hr 73 C5

Czech Republic
Česka Republica

www.czech.cz

Brno

Capital of Moravia. Sights: Vegetable Market and Old Town Hall; Capuchin crypt decorated with bones of dead monks; hill of St Peter with Gothic cathedral; Mies van der Rohe's buildings (Bata, Avion Hotel, Togendhat House). Museums: UPM (modern applied arts); Pražáků Palace (19c Czech art). www.brno.cz 64 A2

České Budějovice

Famous for Budvar beer, the medieval town is centred on náměstí Přemysla Otokara II. The Black Tower gives fine views. Nearby: medieval Český Krumlov. www.c-budejovice.cz 63 B5

Kutná Hora

A town with strong silver mining heritage shown in the magnificent Cathedral of sv Barbara which was built by the miners. See also the ossuary with 40,000 complete sets of bones moulded into sculptures and decorations. www.kutnohorsko.cz 53 D5

Olomouc

Well-preserved medieval university town of squares and fountains. The Upper Square has the Town Hall. Also: 18c Holy Trinity; Baroque Church of St Michael. www.olomoucko.cz 64 A3

Plzeň

Best known for Plzeňský Prazdroj (Pilsener Urquell), beer has been brewed here since 1295. An industrial town with eclectic architecture shown in the railway stations and the namesti Republiky (main square). www.zcu.cz/plzen 63 A4

Prague Praha

Capital of Czech Republic and Bohemia. The Castle Quarter has a complex of buildings behind the walls (Royal Castle; Royal Palace; cathedral). The Basilica of St George has a fine Romanesque interior. The Belvedere is the best example of Renaissance architecture. Hradčani Square has aristocratic palaces and the National Gallery. The Little Quarter has many Renaissance (Wallenstein Palace) and Baroque mansions and the Baroque Church of St Nicholas. The Old Town has its centre at the Old Town Square with the Old Town Hall (astronomical clock), Art Nouveau Jan Hus monument and Gothic Týn church. The Jewish quarter has 14c Staranova Synagogue and Old Jewish Cemetery. The Charles Bridge is famous. The medieval New Town has many Art Nouveau buildings and is centred on Wenceslas Square. www.prague.cz 53 C4

Spas of Bohemia

Spa towns of Karlovy Vary (Carlsbad), Márianske Lázně (Marienbad) and Frantiskovy Lázně (Franzenbad). 52 C2

Denmark Danmark

www.visitdenmark.com

Århus

Second largest city in Denmark with a mixture of old and new architecture that blends well, Århus has been dubbed the culture capital of Denmark with the Gothic Domkirke; Latin Quarter; 13th Century Vor Frue Kirke; Den Gamle By, open air museum of traditional Danish life; ARoS, Århus Art Museum. www.visitaarhus.com 39 C3

Copenhagen København

Capital of Denmark. Old centre has fine early 20c Town Hall. Latin Quarter has 19c cathedral. 18c Kastellet has statue of the Little Mermaid nearby. The 17c Rosenborg Castle was a royal residence, as was the Christianborg (now government offices). Other popular sights: Nyhavn canal; Tivoli Gardens. Excellent art collections: Ny Carlsberg Glypotek; State Art Museum; National Museum. www.visitcopenhagen.dk 41 D2

Hillerød

Frederiksborg is a fine red-brick Renaissance castle set among three lakes. 41 D2

Roskilde

Ancient capital of Denmark. The marvellous cathedral is a burial place of the Danish monarchy. The Viking Ship Museum houses the remains of five 11c Viking ships excavated in the 1960s. www.visitroskilde.com 39 D5

Estonia Eesti

www.visitestonia.com

Kuressaare

Main town on the island of Saaremaa with the 14c Kuressaare Kindlus. www.kuressaare.ee 6 B7

Pärnu

Sea resort with an old town centre. Sights: 15c Red Tower; neoclassical Town Hall; St Catherine's Church. www.parnu.ee 6 B8

Tallinn

Capital of Estonia. The old town is centred on the Town Hall Square. Sights: 15c Town Hall; Toompea Castle; Three Sisters houses. Churches: Gothic St Nicholas; 14c Church of the Holy Spirit; St Olaf's Church. www.tallinn.ee 6 B8

Tartu

Historic town with 19c university. The Town Hall Square is surrounded by neoclassical buildings. Also: remains of 13c cathedral; Estonian National Museum. www.tartu.ee 7 B9

Finland Suomi

www.virtualfinland.fi

Finnish Lakes

Area of outstanding natural beauty covering about one third of the country with thousands of lakes, of which Päijänne and Saimaa are the most important. Tampere, industrial centre of the region, has numerous museums, including the Sara Hildén Art Museum (modern). Savonlinna has the medieval Olavinlinna Castle. Kuopio has the Orthodox and Regional Museums. 3 E27

Helsinki

Capital of Finland. The 19c neoclassical town planning between the Esplanade and Senate Square includes the Lutheran cathedral. There is also a Russian Orthodox cathedral. The Constructivist Stockmann Department Store is the largest in Europe. The main railway station is Art Nouveau. Gracious 20c buildings in Mannerheimintie avenue include Finlandiatalo by Alvar Aalto. Many good museums: Art Museum of the Ateneum (19–20c); National Museum; Museum of Applied Arts; Helsinki City Art Museum (modern Finnish); Open Air Museum (vernacular architecture); 18c fortress of Suomenlinna has several museums. www.hel.fi 7 A8

Lappland (Finnish)

Vast unspoiled rural area. Lappland is home to thousands of nomadic Sámi living in a traditional way. The capital, Rovaniemi, was rebuilt after WWII; museums show Sámi history and culture. Nearby is the Arctic Circle with the famous Santa Claus Village. Inari is a centre of Sámi culture. See also Norway and Sweden. www.laplandfinland.com 113

France

www.franceguide.com

Albi

Old town with rosy brick architecture. The vast Cathédrale Ste-Cécile (begun 13c) holds some good art. The Berbie Palace houses the Toulouse-Lautrec museum. www.mairie-albi.fr 77 C5

Alps

Grenoble, capital of the French Alps, has a good 20c collection in the Museum of Painting and Sculpture. The Vanoise Massif has the greatest number of resorts (Val d'Isère, Courchevel). Chamonix has spectacular views on Mont Blanc, France's and Europe's highest peak. www.thealps.com 69 C5

Amiens
France's largest Gothic cathedral has beautiful decoration. The Museum of Picardy has unique 16c panel paintings. www.amiens.fr **58 A3**

Arles
Ancient, picturesque town with Roman relics (1c amphitheatre), 11c cathedral, Archaeological Museum (Roman art). www.ville-arles.fr **78 C3**

Avignon
Medieval papal capital (1309–77) with 14c walls and many ecclesiastical buildings. Vast Palace of the Popes has stunning frescoes. The Little Palace has fine Italian Renaissance painting. The 12–13c Bridge of St Bénézet is famous. www.ot-avignon.fr **78 C3**

Bourges
The Gothic Cathedral of St Etienne, one of the finest in France, has a superb sculptured choir. Also notable is the House of Jacques Coeur. www.bourgestourisme.com **68 A2**

Burgundy Bourgogne
Rural wine region with a rich Romanesque, Gothic and Renaissance heritage. The 12c cathedral in Autun and 12c basilica in Vézelay have fine Romanesque sculpture. Monasteries include 11c L'Abbaye de Cluny (ruins) and L'Abbaye de Fontenay. Beaune has beautiful Gothic Hôtel-Dieu and 15c Nicolas Rolin hospices. www.burgundy-tourism.com **69 B4**

Brittany Bretagne
Brittany is famous for cliffs, sandy beaches and wild landscape. It is also renowned for megalithic monuments (Carnac) and Celtic culture. Its capital, Rennes, has the Palais de Justice and good collections in the Museum of Brittany (history) and Museum of Fine Arts. Also: Nantes; St-Malo. www.brittany-bretagne.com **56–57**

Caen
City with two beautiful Romanesque buildings: Abbaye aux Hommes; Abbaye aux Dames. The château has two museums (15–20c painting; history). The *Bayeux Tapestry* is displayed in nearby Bayeux. www.ville-caen.fr **57 A5**

Carcassonne
Unusual double-walled fortified town of narrow streets with an inner fortress. The fine Romanesque Church of St Nazaire has superb stained glass. www.carcassonne.org **77 C5**

Chartres
The 12–13c cathedral is an exceptionally fine example of Gothic architecture (Royal Doorway, stained glass, choir screen). The Fine Arts Museum has a good collection. www.chartres.com **58 B2**

Loire Valley
The Loire Valley has many 15–16c châteaux built amid beautiful scenery by French monarchs and members of their courts. Among the most splendid are Azay-le-Rideau, Chenonceaux and Loches. Also: Abbaye de Fontévraud. www.lvo.com **67 A5**

Clermont-Ferrand
The old centre contains the cathedral built out of lava and Romanesque basilica. The Puy de Dôme and Puy de Sancy give spectacular views over some 60 extinct volcanic peaks (*puys*). www.ville-clermont-ferrand.fr **68 C3**

Colmar
Town characterised by Alsatian half-timbered houses. The Unterlinden Museum has excellent German religious art including the famous Isenheim altarpiece. The Dominican church also has a fine altarpiece. www.ot-colmar.fr **60 B3**

Corsica Corse
Corsica has a beautiful rocky coast and mountainous interior. Napoleon's birthplace of Ajaccio has: Fesch Museum with Imperial Chapel and a large collection of Italian art; Maison Bonaparte; cathedral. Bonifacio, a medieval town, is spectacularly set on a rock over the sea. www.visit-corsica.com **102**

Côte d'Azur
The French Riviera is best known for its coastline and glamorous resorts. There are many relics of artists who worked here: St-Tropez has Musée de l'Annonciade; Antibes has 12c Château Grimaldi with the Picasso Museum; Cagnes has the Renoir House and Mediterranean Museum of Modern Art; St-Paul-de-Vence has the excellent Maeght Foundation and Matisse's Chapelle du Rosaire. Cannes is famous for its film festival. Also: Marseille, Monaco, Nice. www.cote.azur.fr **79 C6**

Dijon
Great 15c cultural centre. The Palais des Ducs et des Etats is the most notable monument and contains the Museum of Fine Arts. Also: the Charterhouse of Champmol. www.dijon-tourism.com **69 A5**

Disneyland Paris
Europe's largest theme park follows in the footsteps of its famous predecessors in the United States. www.disneylandparis.com **59 B3**

Le Puy-en-Velay
Medieval town bizarrely set on the peaks of dead volcanoes. It is dominated by the Romanesque cathedral (cloisters). The Romanesque chapel of St-Michel is dramatically situated on the highest rock. www.ot-lepuyenvelay.fr **78 A2**

Lyon
France's third largest city has an old centre and many museums including the Museum of the History of Textiles and the Museum of Fine Arts (old masters). www.lyon-france.com **69 C4**

Marseilles Marseille
Second lagest city in France. Spectacular views from the 19c Notre-Dame-de-la-Garde. The Old Port has 11–12c Basilique St Victor (crypt, catacombs). Cantini Museum has major collection of 20c French art. Château d'If was the setting of Dumas' *The Count of Monte Cristo*. www.marseille-tourisme.com **79 C4**

Mont-St-Michel
Gothic pilgrim abbey (11–12c) set dramatically on a steep rock island rising from mud flats and connected to the land by a road covered by the tide. The abbey is made up of a complex of buildings. www.e-mont-saint-michel.com **57 B4**

Nancy
A centre of Art Nouveau. The 18c Place Stanislas was constructed by dethroned Polish king Stanislas. Museums: School of Nancy Museum (Art Nouveau furniture); Fine Arts Museum. www.ot-nancy.fr **60 B2**

Nantes
Former capital of Brittany, with the 15c Château des ducs de Bretagne. The cathedral has a striking interior. www.nantes-tourisme.com **66 A3**

Nice
Capital of the Côte d'Azur, the old town is centred on the old castle on the hill. The seafront includes the famous 19c Promenade des Anglais. The aristocratic quarter of the Cimiez Hill has the Marc Chagall Museum and the Matisse Museum. Also: Museum of Modern and Contemporary Art (especially neo-Realism and Pop Art). www.nicetourism.com **79 C6**

Paris
Capital of France, one of Europe's most interesting cities. The Île de la Cité area, an island in the River Seine has the 12–13c Gothic Notre Dame (wonderful stained glass) and La Sainte-Chapelle (1240–48), one of the jewels of Gothic art. The Left Bank area: Latin Quarter with the famous Sorbonne university; Museum of Cluny housing medieval art; the Panthéon; Luxembourg Palace and Gardens; Montparnasse, interwar artistic and literary centre; Eiffel Tower; Hôtel des Invalides with Napoleon's tomb. Right Bank: the great boulevards (Avenue des Champs-Élysées joining the Arc de Triomphe and Place de la Concorde); 19c Opéra Quarter; Marais, former aristocratic quarter of elegant mansions (Place des Vosges); Bois de Boulogne, the largest park in Paris; Montmartre, centre of 19c bohemianism, with the Basilique Sacré-Coeur.

The Church of St Denis is the first gothic church and the mausoleum of the French monarchy. Paris has three of the world's greatest art collections: The Louvre (to 19c, *Mona Lisa*), Musée d'Orsay (19–20c) and National Modern Art Museum in the Pompidou Centre. Other major museums include: Orangery Museum; Paris Museum of Modern Art; Rodin Museum; Picasso Museum. Notable cemeteries with graves of the famous: Père-Lachaise, Montmartre, Montparnasse. Near Paris are the royal residences of Fontainebleau and Versailles. www.paris.fr **58 B3**

Pyrenees
Beautiful unspoiled mountain range. Towns include: delightful sea resorts of St-Jean-de-Luz and Biarritz; Pau, with access to the Pyrenees National Park; pilgrimage centre Lourdes. www.pyrenees-online.fr **76-77**

Reims
Together with nearby Epernay, the centre of champagne production. The 13c Gothic cathedral is one of the greatest architectural achievements in France (stained glass by Chagall). Other sights: Palais du Tau with cathedral sculpture, 11c Basilica of St Rémi; cellars on Place St-Niçaise and Place des Droits-des-Hommes. www.reims-tourisme.com **59 A5**

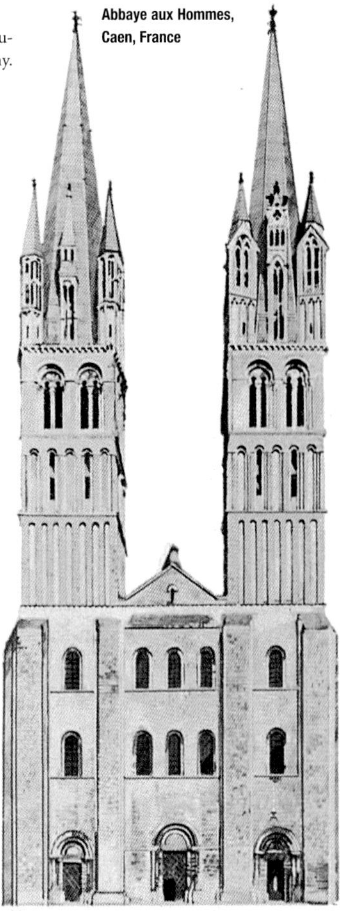
Abbaye aux Hommes, Caen, France

Rouen
Old centre with many half-timbered houses and 12–13c Gothic cathedral and the Gothic Church of St Maclou with its fascinating remains of a dance macabre on the former cemetery of Aître St-Maclou. The Fine Arts Museum has a good collection. www.mairie-rouen.fr **58 A2**

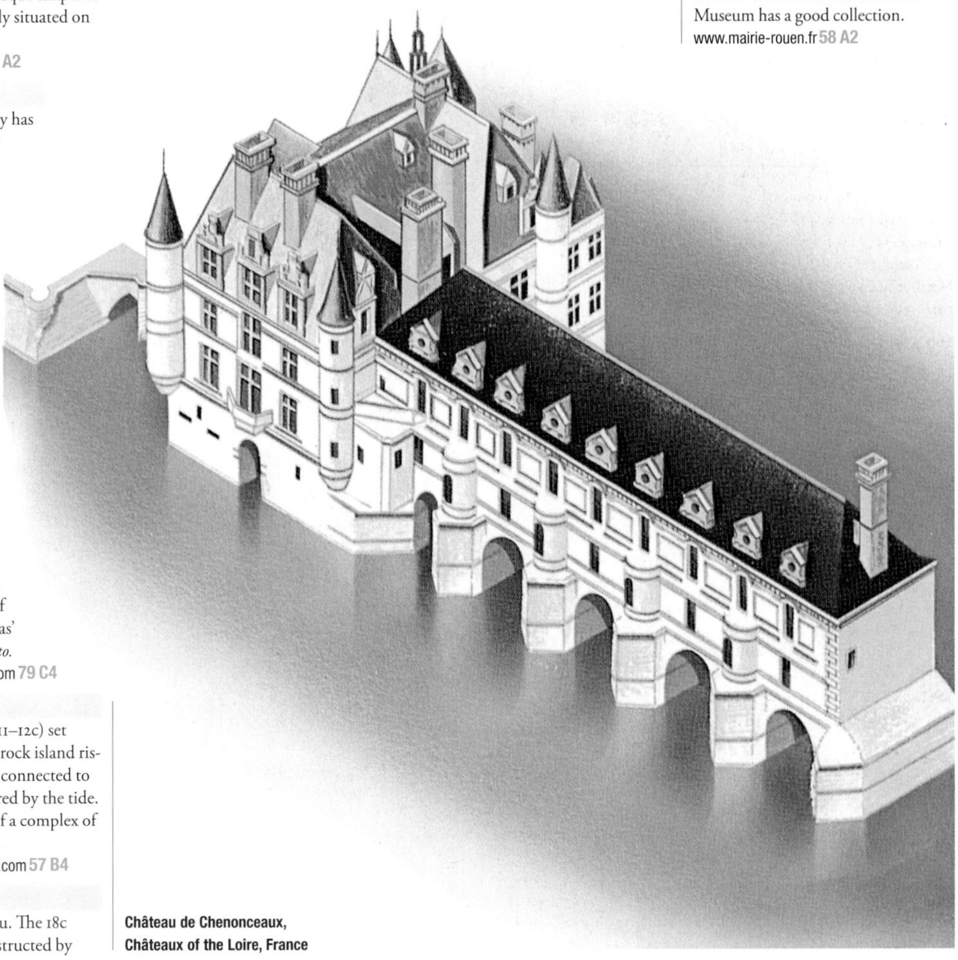
Château de Chenonceaux, Châteaux of the Loire, France

St-Malo

Fortified town (much rebuilt) in a fine coastal setting. There is a magnificent boat trip along the river Rance to Dinan, a splendid well-preserved medieval town. www.saint-malo.fr **57 B3**

Strasbourg

Town whose historic centre includes a well-preserved quarter of medieval half-timbered Alsatian houses, many of them set on the canal. The cathedral is one of the best in France. The Palais Rohan contains several museums. www.strasbourg.fr **60 B3**

Toulouse

Medieval university town characterised by flat pink brick (Hôtel Assézat). The Basilique St Sernin, the largest Romanesque church in France, has many art treasures. Marvellous Church of the Jacobins holds the body of St Thomas Aquinas. www.ot-toulouse.fr **77 C4**

Tours

Historic town centred on Place Plumereau. Good collections in the Guilds Museum and Fine Arts Museum. www.tours.fr **67 A5**

Versailles

Vast royal palace built for Louis XIV, primarily by Mansart, set in large formal gardens with magnificent fountains. The extensive and much-imitated state apartments include the famous Hall of Mirrors and the exceptional Baroque chapel. www.chateauversailles.fr **58 B3**

Vézère Valley Caves

A number of prehistoric sites, most notably the cave paintings of Lascaux (some 17,000 years old), now only seen in a duplicate cave, and the cave of Font de Gaume. The National Museum of Prehistory is in Les Eyzies. www.leseyzies.com **77 B4**

Germany Deutschland

www.germany-tourism.de

Northern Germany

Aachen

Once capital of the Holy Roman Empire. Old town around the Münsterplatz with magnificent cathedral. An exceptionally rich treasure is in the Schatzkammer. The Town Hall is on the medieval Market. www.aachen.de **50 C2**

Berlin

Capital of Germany. Sights include: the Kurfürstendamm avenue; Brandenburg Gate, former symbol of the division between East and West Germany; Tiergarten; Unter den Linden; 19c Reichstag. Berlin has many excellent art and history collections. Museum Island includes: Pergamon Museum (classical antiquity, Near and Far East, Islam); Bode Museum (Egyptian, Early Christian, Byzantine and European); Old National Gallery (19–20c German). Dahlem Museums: Picture Gallery (13–18c); Sculpture Collection (13–19c); Prints and Drawings Collection; Die Brücke Museum (German Expressionism). Tiergarten Museums: New National Gallery (19–20c); Decorative Arts Museum; Bauhaus Archive. In the Kreuzberg area: Berlin Museum; Grupius Building with Jewish Museum and Berlin Gallery; remains of Berlin Wall and Checkpoint Charlie House. Schloss Charlottenburg houses a number of collections including the National Gallery's Romantic Gallery; the Egyptian Museum is nearby. www.berlin-tourist-information.de **45 C5**

Cologne Köln

Ancient city with 13–19c cathedral (rich display of art). In the old town are the Town Hall and many Romanesque churches (Gross St Martin, St Maria im Kapitol, St Maria im Lyskirchen, St Ursula, St Georg, St Severin, St Pantaleon, St Apostolen). Museums: Diocesan Museum (religious art); Roman-German Museum (ancient history); Wallraf-Richartz/Ludwig Museum (14–20c art). www.koeln.de **50 C2**

Dresden

Historic centre with a rich display of Baroque architecture. Major buildings: Castle of the Electors of Saxony; 18c Hofkirche; Zwinger Palace with fountains and pavilions (excellent old masters); Albertinum with excellent Gallery of New Masters; treasury of Grünes Gewölbe. The Baroque-planned New Town contains the Japanese Palace and Schloss Pillnitz. www.dresden.de **53 B3**

Frankfurt

Financial capital of Germany. The historic centre around the Römerberg Square has 13–15c cathedral, 15c Town Hall, Gothic St Nicholas Church, Saalhof (12c chapel). Museums: Museum of Modern Art (post-war); State Art Institute. www.frankfurt.de **51 C4**

Hamburg

Port city with many parks, lakes and canals. The Kunsthalle has Old Masters and 19-20c German art. Buildings: 19c Town Hall; Baroque St Michael's Church. www.hamburg-tourismus.de **44 B2**

Hildesheim

City of Romanesque architecture (much destroyed). Principal sights: St Michael's Church; cathedral (11c interior, sculptured doors, St Anne's Chapel); superb 15c Tempelhaus on the Market Place. www.hildesheim.de **51 A5**

Lübeck

Beautiful old town built on an island and characterised by Gothic brick architecture. Sights: 15c Holsten Gate; Market with the Town Hall and Gothic brick St Mary's Church; 12–13c cathedral; St Ann Museum. www.luebeck-tourism.de **44 B2**

Mainz

The Electoral Palatinate schloss and Market fountain are Renaissance. Churches: 12c Romanesque cathedral; Gothic St Steven's (with stained glass by Marc Chagall). www.mainz.de **50 C4**

Marburg

Medieval university town with the Market Place and Town Hall, St Elizabeth's Church (frescoes, statues, 13c shrine), 15–16c schloss. www.marburg.de **51 C4**

Münster

Historic city with well-preserved Gothic and Renaissance buildings: 14c Town Hall; Romanesque-Gothic cathedral. The Westphalian Museum holds regional art. www.munster.de **50 B3**

Potsdam

Beautiful Sanssouci Park contains several 18–19c buildings including: Schloss Sanssouci; Gallery (European masters); Orangery; New Palace; Chinese Teahouse. www.potsdam.de **45 C5**

Rhein Valley Rheintal

Beautiful 80km gorge of the Rhein Valley between Mainz and Koblenz with rocks (Loreley), vineyards (Bacharach, Rüdesheim), white medieval towns (Rhens, Oberwesel) and castles. Some castles are medieval (Marksburg, Rheinfels, island fortress Pfalzgrafenstein) others were built or rebuilt in the 19c (Stolzenfels, Rheinstein). www.rheintal.de **50 C3**

Weimar

The Neoclassical schloss, once an important seat of government, now houses a good art collection. Church of SS Peter and Paul has a Cranach masterpiece. Houses of famous people: Goethe, Schiller, Liszt. The famous Bauhaus was founded at the School of Architecture and Engineering. www.weimar.de **52 C1**

Southern Germany

Alpine Road Deutsche Alpenstrasse

German Alpine Road in the Bavarian Alps, from Lindau on Bodensee to Berchtesgaden. The setting for 19c fairy-tale follies of Ludwig II of Bavaria (Linderhof, Hohenschwangau,

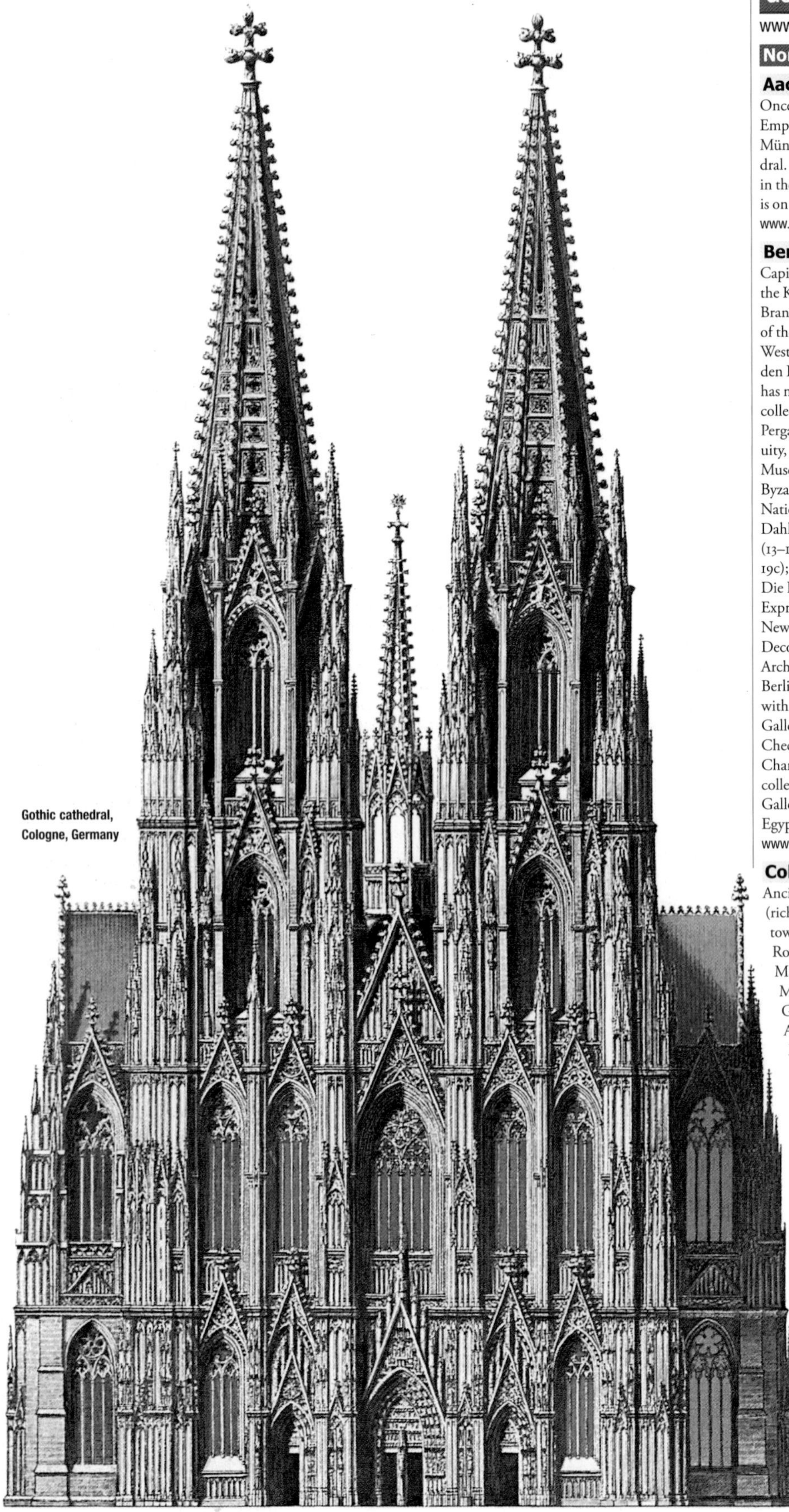

Gothic cathedral, Cologne, Germany

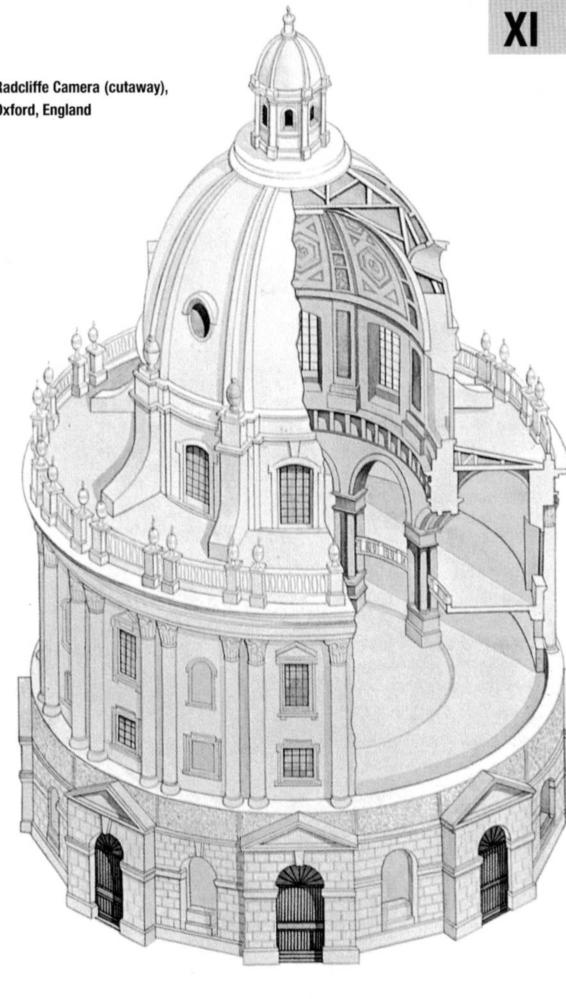

Neuschwanstein), charming old villages (Oberammergau) and Baroque churches (Weiss, Ottobeuren). Garmisch-Partenkirchen has views on Germany's highest peak, the Zugspitze. www.deutsche-alpenstrasse.de **62 C2**

Augsburg
Attractive old city. The Town Hall is one of Germany's finest Renaissance buildings. Maximilianstrasse has several Renaissance houses and Rococo Schaezler Palace (good art collection). Churches: Romanesque-Gothic cathedral; Renaissance St Anne's Church. The Fuggerei, founded 1519 as an estate for the poor, is still in use. www.augsburg.de **62 B1**

Bamberg
Well-preserved medieval town. The island, connected by two bridges, has the Town Hall and views of Klein Venedig. Romanesque-Gothic cathedral (good art) is on an exceptional square of Gothic, Renaissance and Baroque buildings – Alte Hofhalttung; Neue Residenz with State Gallery (German masters); Ratstube. www.bamberg.info **62 A1**

Black Forest Schwarzwald
Hilly region between Basel and Karlsruhe, the largest and most picturesque woodland in Germany, with the highest summit, Feldberg, lake resorts (Titisee), health resorts (Baden-Baden) and clock craft (Triberg). Freiburg is regional capital. www.schwarzwald.de **61 B4**

Freiburg
Old university town with system of streams running through the streets. The Gothic Minster is surrounded by the town's finest buildings. Two towers remain of the medieval walls. The Augustine Museum has a good collection. www.freiburg.de **60 C3**

Heidelberg
Germany's oldest university town, majestically set on the banks of the river and romantically dominated by the ruined schloss. The Gothic Church of the Holy Spirit is on the Market Place with the Baroque Town Hall. Other sights include the 16c Knight's House and the Baroque Morass Palace with a museum of Gothic art. www.heidelberg.de **61 A4**

Lake Constance Bodensee
Lake Constance, with many pleasant lake resorts. Lindau, on an island, has numerous gabled houses. Birnau has an 18c Rococo church. Konstanz (Swiss side) has the Minster set above the Old Town. www.bodensee.de **61 C5**

Munich München
Old town centred on the Marienplatz with 15c Old Town Hall and 19c New Town Hall. Many richly decorated churches: St Peter's (14c tower); Gothic red-brick cathedral; Renaissance St Michael's (royal portraits on the façade); Rococo St Asam's. The Residenz palace consists of seven splendid buildings holding many art objects. Schloss Nymphenburg has a palace, park, botanical gardens and four beautiful pavilions. Superb museums: Old Gallery (old masters), New Gallery (18–19c), Lenbachhaus (modern German). Many famous beer gardens. www.muenchen.de **62 B2**

Nuremberg Nürnberg
Beautiful medieval walled city dominated by the 12c Kaiserburg. Romanesque-Gothic St Sebaldus Church and Gothic St Laurence Church are rich in art. On Hauptmarkt is the famous 14c Schöner Brunnen. Also notable is 15c Dürer House. The German National Museum has excellent German medieval and Renaissance art. www.nuernberg.de **62 A2**

Regensburg
Medieval city set majestically on the Danube. Views from 12c Steinerne Brücke. Churches: Gothic cathedral; Romanesque St Jacob's; Gothic St Blaisius; Baroque St Emmeram. Other sights: Old Town Hall (museum); Haidplatz; Schloss Thurn und Taxis; State Museum. www.regensburg.de **62 A3**

Romantic Road
Romantische Strasse
Romantic route between Aschaffenburg and Füssen, leading through picturesque towns and villages of medieval Germany. The most popular section is the section between Würzburg and Augsburg, centred on Rothenburg ob der Tauber. Also notable are Nördlingen, Harburg Castle, Dinkelsbühl, Creglingen. www.romantischestrasse.de **61 A6**

Rothenburg ob der Tauber
Attractive medieval walled town with tall gabled and half-timbered houses on narrow cobbled streets. The Market Place has Gothic-Renaissance Town Hall, Rattrinke-stubbe and Gothic St Jacob's Church (altarpiece). www.rothenburg.de **61 A6**

Speyer
The 11c cathedral is one of the largest and best Romanesque buildings in Germany. 12c Jewish Baths are well-preserved. www.speyer.de **61 A4**

Stuttgart
Largely modern city with old centre around the Old Schloss, Renaissance Alte Kanzlei, 15c Collegiate Church and Baroque New Schloss. Museums: Regional Museum; post-modern State Gallery (old masters, 20c German). The 1930s Weissenhofsiedlung is by several famous architects. www.stuttgart.de **61 B5**

Trier
Superb Roman monuments: Porta Nigra; Aula Palatina (now a church); Imperial Baths; amphitheatre. The Regional Museum has Roman artefacts. Also, Gothic Church of Our Lady; Romanesque cathedral. www.trier.de **60 A2**

Ulm
Old town with half-timbered gabled houses set on a canal. Gothic 14–19c minster has tallest spire in the world (161m). www.tourismus.ulm.de **61 B5**

Würzburg
Set among vineyard hills, the medieval town is centred on the Market Place with the Rococo House of the Falcon. The 18c episcopal princes' residence (frescoes) is magnificent. The cathedral is rich in art. Work of the great local Gothic sculptor, Riemenschneider, is in Gothic St Mary's Chapel, Baroque New Minster, and the Mainfränkisches Museum. www.wuerzburg.de **61 A5**

Great Britain
www.visitbritain.com

England

Bath
Elegant spa town with notable 18c architecture: Circus, Royal Crescent, Pulteney Bridge, Assembly Rooms; Pump Room. Also: well-preserved Roman baths; superb Perpendicular Gothic Bath Abbey. Nearby: Elizabethan Longleat House; exceptional 18c landscaped gardens at Stourhead. www.visitbath.co.uk **29 B5**

Brighton
Resort with a sea-front of Georgian, Regency and Victorian buildings with the Palace Pier, and an old town of narrow lanes. The main sight is the 19c Royal Pavilion in Oriental styles. www.brighton.co.uk **31 D3**

Bristol
Old port city with the fascinating Floating Harbour. Major sights include Gothic 13–14c Church of St Mary Redcliffe and 19c Clifton Suspension Bridge. www.visitbristol.co.uk **29 B5**

Cambridge
City with university founded in the early 13c. Peterhouse (1284) is the oldest college. Most famous colleges were founded in 14–16c: Queen's, King's (with the superb Perpendicular Gothic 15–16c King's College Chapel), St John's (with famous 19c Bridge of Sighs), Trinity, Clare, Gonville and Caius, Magdalene. Museums: excellent Fitzwilliam Museum (classical, medieval, old masters). Kettle's Yard (20c British). www.visitcambridge.org **30 B4**

Canterbury
Medieval city and old centre of Christianity. The Norman-Gothic cathedral has many sights and was a major medieval pilgrimage site (as related in Chaucer's *Canterbury Tales*). St Augustine, sent to convert the English in 597, founded St Augustine's Abbey, now in ruins. www.canterbury.co.uk **31 C5**

Chatsworth
One of the richest aristocratic country houses in England (largely 17c) set in a large landscaped park. The palatial interior has some 175 richly furnished rooms and a major art collection. www.chatsworth-house.co.uk **27 B4**

Chester
Charming medieval city with complete walls. The Norman-Gothic cathedral has several abbey buildings. www.visitchester.co.uk **26 B3**

Cornish Coast
Scenic landscape of cliffs and sandy beaches (the north being a popular surfing destination) with picturesque villages (Fowey, Mevagissey). St Ives has the Tate Gallery with work of the St Ives Group. The island of St Michael's Mount holds a priory. www.cornwalltouristboard.co.uk **28 C2**

Dartmoor
Beautiful wilderness area in Devon with tors and its own breed of wild pony as well as free-ranging cattle and sheep. www.dartmoor-npa.gov.uk **28 C4**

Durham
Historic city with England's finest Norman cathedral and a castle, both placed majestically on a rock above the river. www.durham.gov.uk **27 A4**

Eden Project
Centre showing the diversity of plant life on the planet, built in a disused clay pit. Two biomes, one with Mediterranean and Southern African focus and the larger featuring a waterfall, river and tropical trees plants and flowers. Outdoors also features plantations including bamboo and tea. www.edenproject.com **28 C3**

Hadrian's Wall
Built to protect the northernmost border of the Roman Empire in the 2c AD, the walls originally extended some 120km with castles every mile and 16 forts. Best-preserved walls around Hexam; forts at Housesteads and Chesters. www.hadrians-wall.org **25 C5**

Lake District
Beautiful landscape of lakes (Windermere, Coniston) and England's high peaks (Scafell Pike, Skiddaw, Old Man), famous for its poets, particularly Wordsworth. www.lake-district.gov.uk **26 A2**

Leeds Castle
One of the oldest and most romantic English castles, standing in the middle of a lake. Most of the present appearance dates from 19c. www.leeds-castle.com **31 C4**

Lincoln
Old city perched on a hill with narrow streets, majestically dominated by the Norman-Gothic cathedral and castle. www.visitlincolnshire.com **27 B5**

Liverpool
City on site of port founded in 1207 and focused around 1846 Albert Dock, now a heritage attraction. Croxteth Hall and Country Park; Speke Hall; Sudley House; Royal Liver Building; Liverpool Cathedral; Walker Art Gallery; University of Liverpool Art Gallery. www.visitliverpool.com **26 B3**

London
Capital of UK and Europe's largest city. To the east of the medieval heart of the city – now the largely modern financial district and known as the City of London – is the Tower of London (11c White Tower, Crown Jewels) and 1880s Tower Bridge. The popular heart of the city and its entertainment is the West End, around Piccadilly Circus, Leicester Square and Trafalgar Square (Nelson's Column). Many sights of political and royal power: Whitehall (Banqueting House, 10 Downing Street, Horse Guards); Neo-Gothic Palace of Westminster (Houses of Parliament) with Big Ben; The Mall leading to Buckingham Palace (royal residence, famous ceremony of the Changing of the Guard). Numerous churches include: 13–16c Gothic Westminster Abbey (many tombs, Henry VII's Chapel); Wren's Baroque St Paul's Cathedral, St Mary-le-Bow, spire of St Bride's, St Stephen Walbrook. Museums of world fame: British Museum (prehistory, oriental and classical antiquity, medieval); Victoria and Albert Museum (decorative arts); National Gallery (old masters to 19c); National Portrait Gallery (historic and current British portraiture); Tate – Britain and Modern; Science Museum; Natural History Museum. Madame Tussaud's waxworks museum is hugely popular. Other sights include: London Eye, Kensington Palace; Greenwich with Old Royal Observatory (Greenwich meridian), Baroque Royal Naval College, Palladian Queen's House; Tudor Hampton Court Palace; Syon House. Nearby: Windsor Castle (art collection, St George's Chapel). www.visitlondon.com **31 C3**

Longleat
One of the earliest and finest Elizabethan palaces in England. The

Radcliffe Camera (cutaway), Oxford, England

palace is richly decorated. Some of the grounds have been turned into a pleasure park, with the Safari Park, the first of its kind outside Africa. www.longleat.co.uk 29 B5

Manchester
Founded on a Roman settlement of 79AD and a main player in the Industrial Revolution. Victorian Gothic Town Hall; Royal Exchange; Cathedral. Many museums including Imperial War Museum North, Lowry Centre and Manchester Art Gallery. www.visitmanchester.com 26 B3

Newcastle
A key player in the Industrial Revolution with 12th century cathedral and many museums as well as strong railway heritage. www.visitnewcastle.co.uk 25 D6

Norwich
Medieval quarter has half-timbered houses. 15c castle keep houses a museum and gallery. Many medieval churches include the Norman-Gothic cathedral. www.visitnorwich.co.uk 30 B5

Oxford
Old university city. Earliest colleges date from 13c: University College; Balliol; Merton. 14–16c colleges include: New College; Magdalen; Christ Church (perhaps the finest). Other buildings: Bodleian Library; Radcliffe Camera; Sheldonian Theatre; cathedral. Good museums: Ashmolean Museum (antiquity to 20c); Museum of Modern Art; Christ Church Picture Gallery (14–17c). Nearby: outstanding 18c Blenheim Palace. www.visitoxford.org 31 C2

Petworth
House (17c) with one of the finest country-house art collections (old masters), set in a huge landscaped park. www.nationaltrust.org.uk 31 D3

Salisbury
Pleasant old city with a magnificent 13c cathedral built in an unusually unified Gothic style. Nearby: Wilton House. www.visitsalisburyuk.com 29 B6

Stonehenge
Some 4000 years old, one of the most famous and haunting Neolithic monuments in Europe. Many other Neolithic sites are nearby. www.english-heritage.org.uk 29 B6

Stourhead
Early 18c palace famous for its grounds, one of the finest examples of neoclassical landscaped gardening, consisting of a lake surrounded by numerous temples. www.nationaltrust.org.uk 29 B5

Stratford-upon-Avon
Old town of Tudor and Jacobean half-timbered houses, famed as the birth and burial place of William Shakespeare. Nearby: Warwick Castle. www.shakespeare-country.co.uk 29 A6

Wells
Charming city with beautiful 12–16c cathedral (west facade, scissor arches, chapter house, medieval clock). Also Bishop's Palace; Vicar's Close. 29 B5

Winchester
Historic city with 11–16c cathedral (tombs of early English kings). Also: 13c Great Hall; Winchester College; St Cross almshouses. www.visitwinchester.co.uk 29 B6

York
Attractive medieval city surrounded by well-preserved walls with magnificent Gothic 13–15c Minster. Museums: York City Art Gallery (14–19c); Jorvik Viking Centre. Nearby: Castle Howard. www.york-tourism.co.uk 27 B4

Scotland

Edinburgh
Capital of Scotland, built on volcanic hills. The medieval Old Town is dominated by the castle set high on a volcanic rock (Norman St Margaret's Chapel, state apartments, Crown Room). Holyrood House (15c and 17c) has lavishly decorated state apartments and the ruins of Holyrood Abbey (remains of Scottish monarchs). The 15c cathedral has the Crown Spire and Thistle Chapel. The New Town has good Georgian architecture (Charlotte Square, Georgian House). Excellent museums: Scottish National Portrait Gallery, National Gallery of Scotland; Scottish National Gallery of Modern Art. www.edinburgh.org 25 C4

Glamis Castle
In beautiful, almost flat landscaped grounds, 14c fortress, rebuilt 17c, gives a fairy-tale impression. www.glamis-castle.co.uk 25 B5

Glasgow
Scotland's largest city, with centre around George Square and 13–15c Gothic cathedral. The Glasgow School of Art is the masterpiece of Charles Rennie Mackintosh. Fine art collections: Glasgow Museum and Art Gallery; Hunterian Gallery; Burrell Collection. www.seeglasgow.com 24 C3

Loch Ness
In the heart of the Highlands, the lake forms part of the scenic Great Glen running from Inverness to Fort William. Famous as home of the fabled Loch Ness Monster (exhibition at Drumnadrochit). Nearby: ruins of 14–16c Urquhart Castle. www.loch-ness-scotland.com 23 D4

Wales

Caernarfon
Town dominated by a magnificent 13c castle, one of a series built by Edward I in Wales (others include Harlech, Conwy, Beaumaris, Caerphilly). www.visitcaernarfon.com 26 B1

Cardiff
Capital of Wales, most famous for its medieval castle, restored 19c in Greek, Gothic and Oriental styles. Also: National Museum and Gallery. www.visitcardiff.info 29 B4

Greece Ellas
www.gnto.gr

Athens Athina
Capital of Greece. The Acropolis, with 5c BC sanctuary complex (Parthenon, Propylaia, Erechtheion, Temple of Athena Nike), is the greatest architectural achievement of antiquity in Europe. The Agora was a public meeting place in ancient Athens. Plaka has narrow streets and small Byzantine churches (Kapnikarea). The Olympeum was the largest temple in Greece. Also: Olympic Stadium; excellent collections of ancient artefacts (Museum of Cycladic and Ancient Greek Art; Acropolis Museum; National Archeological Museum; Benaki Museum). www.athens.gr 117 E5

Corinth Korinthos
Ancient Corinth (ruins), with 5c BC Temple of Apollo, was in 44 BC made capital of Roman Greece by Julius Caesar. Set above the city, the Greek-built acropolis hill of Acrocorinth became the Roman and Byzantine citadel (ruins). 117 E4

Crete Kriti
Largest Greek island, Crete was home to the great Minoan civilization (2800–1100 BC). The main relics are the ruined Palace of Knossos and Malia. Gortys was capital of the Roman province. Picturesque Rethimno has narrow medieval streets, a Venetian fortress and a former Turkish mosque. Matala has beautiful beaches and famous caves cut into cliffs. Iraklio (Heraklion), the capital, has a good Archeological Museum. 117 G7

Delphi
At the foot of the Mount Parnassos, Delphi was the seat of the Delphic Oracle of Apollo, the most important oracle in Ancient Greece. Delphi was also a political meeting place and the site of the Pythian Games. The Sanctuary of Apollo consists of: Temple of Apollo, led to by the Sacred Way; Theatre; Stadium. The museum has a display of objects from the site (5c BC Charioteer). www.delphi.gr 116 D4

Epidavros
Formerly a spa and religious centre focused on the Sanctuary of Asclepius (ruins). The enormous 4c BC theatre is probably the finest of all ancient theatres. www.ancientepidavros.org 117 E5

Greek Islands
Popular islands with some of the most beautiful and spectacular beaches in Europe. The many islands are divided into various groups and individual islands: The major groups are the Kiklades and Dodekanisa in the Aegean Sea, the largest islands are Kerkyra (Corfu) in the Ionian Sea and Kriti. 116-117

Meteora
The tops of bizarre vertical cylinders of rock and towering cliffs are the setting for 14c Cenobitic monasteries, until recently only accessible by baskets or removable ladders. Mega Meteoro is the grandest and set on the highest point. Roussánou has the most extraordinary site. Varlaám is one of the oldest and most beautiful, with the Ascent Tower and 16c church with frescoes. Aghiou Nikolaou also has good frescoes. 116 C3

Mistras
Set in a beautiful landscape, Mistras is the site of a Byzantine city, now in ruins, with palaces, frescoed churches, monasteries and houses. 117 E4

Mount Olympus
Oros Olymbos
Mount Olympus, mythical seat of the Greek gods, is the highest, most dramatic peak in Greece. 116 B4

Mycenae Mikines
The citadel of Mycenae prospered between 1950 BC and 1100 BC and consists of the royal complex of Agamemnon: Lion Gate, royal burial site, Royal Palace, South House, Great Court. 117 E4

Olympia
In a stunning setting, the Panhellenic Games were held here for a millennium. Ruins of the sanctuary of Olympia consist of the Doric temples of Zeus and Hera and the vast Stadium. There is also a museum (4c BC figure of Hermes). 117 E3

Rhodes
One of the most attractive islands with wonderful sandy beaches. The city of Rhodes has a well-preserved medieval centre with the Palace of the Grand Masters and the Turkish Süleymaniye Mosque 119 F2

Salonica Thessaloniki
Largely modern city with Byzantine walls and many fine churches: 8c Aghia Sofia; 11c Panaghia Halkeo; 14c Dodeka Apostoli; 14c Aghios Nikolaos Orfanos; 5c Aghios Dimitrios (largest in Greece, 7c Mosaics). www.thessalonikicity.gr 116 B4

Hungary Magyarorszàg
www.hungarytourism.hu

Balaton
The 'Hungarian sea', famous for its holiday resorts: Balatonfüred, Tihany, Badasconytomaj, Keszthely. www.balaton.hu 74 B2

Budapest
Capital of Hungary on River Danube, with historic area centring on the Castle Hill of Buda district. Sights include: Matthias church; Pest district with late 19c architecture, centred on Ferenciek tere; neo-Gothic Parliament Building on river; Millennium Monument. The Royal Castle houses

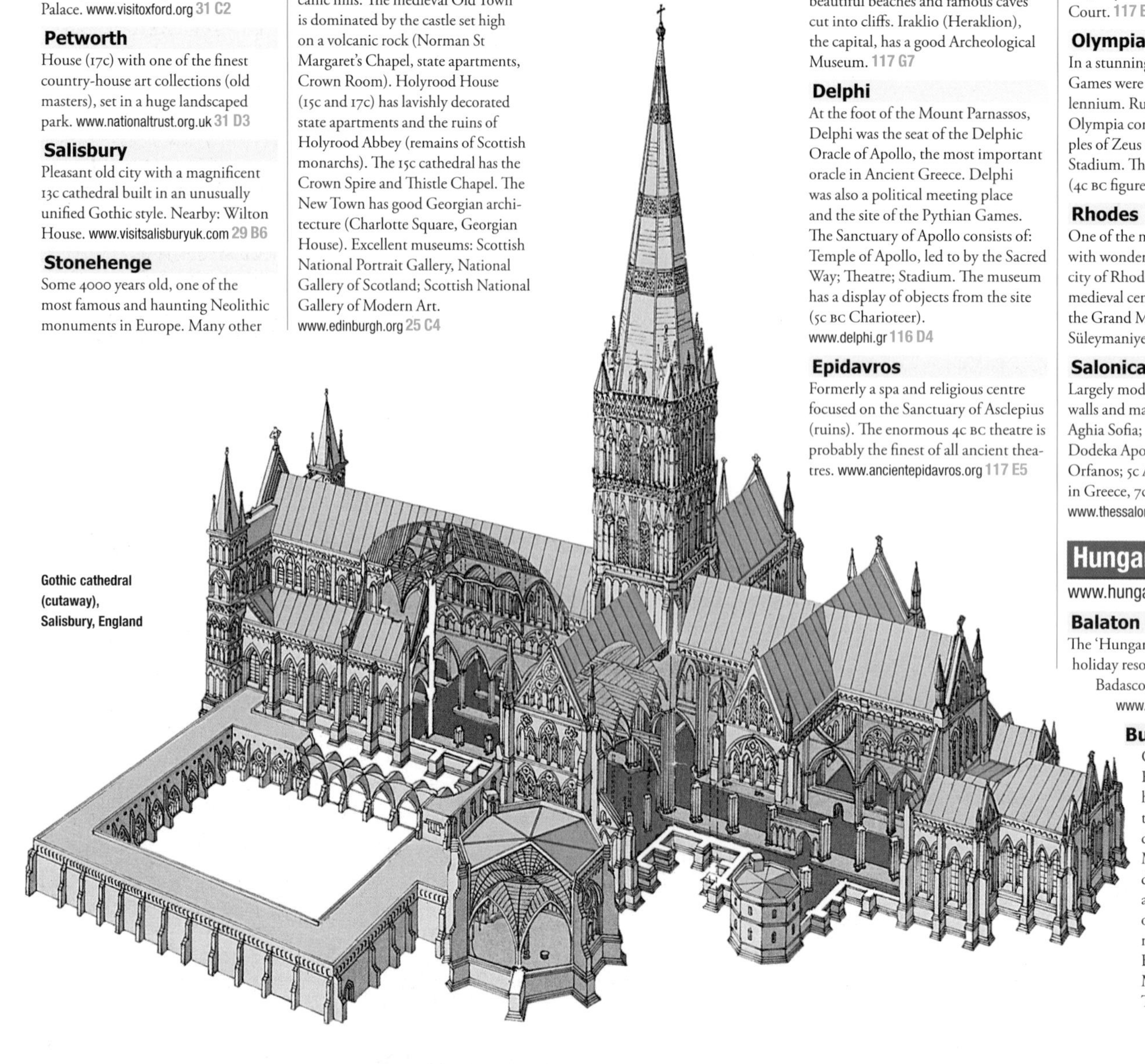

Gothic cathedral
(cutaway),
Salisbury, England

a number of museums: Hungarian National Gallery, Budapest History Museum; Ludwig Collection. Other museums: National Museum of Fine Arts (excellent Old and Modern masters); Hungarian National Museum (Hungarian history). Famous for public thermal baths: Király and Rudas baths, both made under Turkish rule; Gellért baths, the most visited. www.budapestinfo.hu **75 A4**

Esztergom
Medieval capital of Hungary set in scenic landscape. Sights: Hungary's largest basilica (completed 1856); royal palace ruins. www.esztergom.hu **65 C4**

Pécs
Attractive old town with Europe's fifth oldest university (founded 1367). Famous for Turkish architecture (Mosque of Gazi Kasim Pasha, Jakovali Hassan Mosque). www.pecs.hu **74 B3**

Sopron
Beautiful walled town with many Gothic and Renaissance houses. Nearby: Fertöd with the marvellous Eszergázy Palace. www.sopron.hu **64 C2**

Ireland
www.ireland.travel.ie
www.discovernorthernireland.com

Northern Ireland

Antrim Coast
Spectacular coast with diverse scenery of glens (Glenarm, Glenariff), cliffs (Murlough Bay) and the famous Giant's Causeway, consisting of some 40,000 basalt columns. Carrickefergus Castle is the largest and best-preserved Norman castle in Ireland. www.northantrim.com **19 A5**

Belfast
Capital of Northern Ireland. Sights: Donegall Square with 18c Town Hall; neo-Romanesque Protestant cathedral; University Square; Ulster Museum (European painting). www.gotobelfast.com **19 B6**

Giant's Causeway
Spectacular and unique rock formations in the North Antrim coast, formed by volcanic activity 50–60 million years ago. World Heritage Site. www.northantrim.com **19 A5**

Republic of Ireland

Aran Islands
Islands with spectacular cliffs and notable pre-Christian and Christian sights, especially on Inishmore. www.visitaranislands.com **18 B3**

Cashel
Town dominated by the Rock of Cashel (61m) topped by ecclesiastical ruins including 13c cathedral; 15c Halls of the Vicars; beautiful Romanesque 12c Cormac's Chapel (fine carvings). www.connemar-tourism.org **21 B4**

Connemara
Beautiful wild landscape of mountains, lakes, peninsulas and beaches. Clifden is the capital. www.connemar-tourism.org **18 C1**

Cork
Pleasant city with its centre along St Patrick's Street and Grand Parade lined with fine 18c buildings. Churches: Georgian St Anne's Shandon (bell tower); 19c cathedral. www.corkcorp.ie **20 C3**

County Donegal
Rich scenic landscape of mystical lakes and glens and seascape of cliffs (Slieve League cliffs are the highest in Europe). The town of Donegal has a finely preserved Jacobean castle. www.donegaldirect.ie **18 B3**

Dublin
Capital of Ireland. City of elegant 18c neoclassical and Georgian architecture with gardens and parks (St Stephen's Green, Merrion Square with Leinster House – now seat of Irish parliament). City's main landmark, Trinity College (founded 1591), houses in its

Old Library fine Irish manuscripts (7c Book of Durrow, 8c Book of Kells). Two Norman cathedrals: Christ Church; St Patrick's. Other buildings: originally medieval Dublin Castle with State Apartments; James Gandon's masterpieces: Custom House; Four Courts. Museums: National Museum (Irish history); National Gallery (old masters, Impressionists, Irish painting); Guinness Brewery Museum; Dublin Writers' Museum (Joyce, Wilde, Yeats and others). www.visitdublin.com **19 C5**

Glendalough
Impressive ruins of an important early Celtic (6c) monastery with 9c cathedral, 12c St Kevin's Cross, oratory of St Kevin's Church. www.wicklow.com/glendalough **21 A5**

Kilkenny
Charming medieval town, with narrow streets dominated by 12c castle (restored 19c). The 13c Gothic cathedral has notable tomb monuments. www.kilkenny.ie **21 B4**

Newgrange
One of the best passage graves in Europe, the massive 4500-year-old tomb has stones richly decorated with patterns. www.knowth.com/newgrange **19 C5**

Ring of Kerry
Route around the Iveragh peninsula with beautiful lakes (Lough Leane), peaks overlooking the coastline and islands (Valencia Island, Skelling). Also: Killarney; ruins of 15c Muckross Abbey. www.ringofkerrytourism.com **20 B2**

Italy Italia
www.enit.it

Northern Italy

Alps
Wonderful stretch of the Alps running from the Swiss and French borders to Austria. The region of Valle d'Aosta is one of the most popular ski regions, bordered by the highest peaks of the Alps. www.thealps.com **70-71**

Arezzo
Beautiful old town set on a hill dominated by 13c cathedral. Piazza Grande is surrounded by medieval and Renaissance palaces. Main sight: Piero della Francesca's frescoes in the choir of San Francesco. www.arezzocitta.com **81 C5**

Assisi
Hill-top town that attracts crowds of pilgrims to the shrine of St Francis of Assisi at the Basilica di San Francesco, consisting of two churches, Lower and Upper, with superb frescoes (particularly Giotto's in the Upper). www.assisi.com **82 C1**

Bologna
Elegant city with oldest university in Italy. Historical centre around Piazza Maggiore and Piazza del Nettuno with the Town Hall, Palazzo del Podestà, Basilica di San Petronio. Other churches: San Domenico; San Giacomo Maggiore. The two towers (one incomplete) are symbols of the city. Good collection in the National Gallery (Bolognese). www.commune.bologna.it/bolognaturismo **81 B5**

Dolomites Dolomiti
Part of the Alps, this mountain range spreads over the region of Trentino-Alto Adige, with the most picturesque scenery between Bolzano and Cortina d'Ampezzo. www.dolomiti.it **72 B1**

Ferrara
Old town centre around Romanesque-Gothic cathedral and Palazzo Communale. Also: Castello Estenese; Palazzo Schifanoia (frescoes); Palazzo dei Diamanti housing Pinacoteca Nazionale. www.ferraraturismo.it **81 B5**

Florence Firenze
City with exceptionally rich medieval and Renaissance heritage. Piazza del Duomo has:13–15c cathedral (first dome since antiquity); 14c campanile;

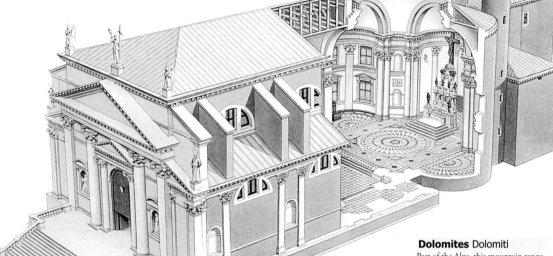

Il Redentore, Venice, Italy

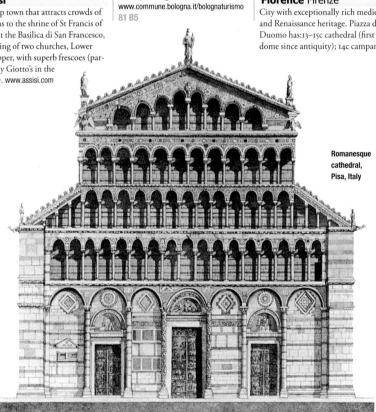

Romanesque cathedral, Pisa, Italy

11c baptistry (bronze doors). Piazza della Signoria has: 14c Palazzo Vecchio (frescoes); Loggia della Signoria (sculpture); 16c Uffizi Gallery with one of the world's greatest collections (13–18c). Other great paintings: Museo di San Marco; Palatine Gallery in 15–16c Pitti Palace surrounded by Boboli Gardens. Sculpture: Cathedral Works Museum; Bargello Museum; Academy Gallery (Michelangelo's *David*). Among many other Renaissance palaces: Medici-Riccardi; Rucellai; Strozzi. The 15c church of San Lorenzo has Michelangelo's tombs of the Medici. Many churches have richly frescoed chapels: Santa Maria Novella, Santa Croce, Santa Maria del Carmine. The 13c Ponte Vecchio is one of the most famous sights. www.firenzeturismo.it 81 C5

Italian Lakes

Beautiful district at the foot of the Alps, most of the lakes with holiday resorts. Many lakes are surrounded by aristocratic villas (Maggiore, Como, Garda). 70-71

Mantua Mántova

Attractive city surrounded by three lakes. Two exceptional palaces: Palazzo Ducale (Sala del Pisanello; Camera degli Sposi, Castello San Giorgio); luxurious Palazzo Tè (brilliant frescoes). Also: 15c Church of Sant'Andrea; 13c law courts. www.mantova.com 71 C5

Milan Milano

Modern city, Italy's fashion and design capital (Corso and Galleria Vittoro Emmanuelle II). Churches include: Gothic cathedral (1386–1813), the world's largest (4c baptistry); Romanesque St Ambrose; 15c San Satiro; Santa Maria delle Grazie with Leonardo da Vinci's *Last Supper* in the convent refectory. Great art collections, Brera Gallery, Ambrosian Library, Museum of Contemporary Art. Castello Sforzesco (15c, 19c) also has a gallery. The famous La Scala theatre opened in 1778. Nearby: monastery at Pavia. www.milaninfotourist.com 71 C4

Padua Pádova

Pleasant old town with arcaded streets. Basilica del Santo is a place of pilgrimage to the tomb of St Anthony. Giotto's frescoes in the Scrovegni chapel are exceptional. Also: Piazza dei Signori with Palazzo del Capitano; vast Palazzo della Ragione; church of the Eremitani (frescoes). www.turismopadova.it 72 C1

Parma

Attractive city centre, famous for Correggio's frescoes in the Romanesque cathedral and church of St John the Evangelist, and Parmigianino's frescoes in the church of Madonna della Steccata. Their works are also in the National Gallery. www.commune.parma.it 81 B4

Perúgia

Hill-top town centred around Piazza Quattro Novembre with the cathedral, Fontana Maggiore and Palazzo dei Priori. Also: Collegio di Cambio (frescoes); National Gallery of Umbria; many churches. www.perugiaonline.com 82 C1

Pisa

Medieval town centred on the Piazza dei Miracoli. Sights: famous Romanesque Leaning Tower, Romanesque cathedral (excellent façade, Gothic pulpit); 12–13c Baptistry; 13c Camposanto cloistered cemetery (fascinating 14c frescoes). www.commune.pisa.it 81 C4

Ravenna

Ancient town with exceptionally well-preserved Byzantine mosaics. The finest are in 5c Mausoleo di Galla Placidia and 6c Basilica di San Vitale. Good mosaics also in the basilicas of Sant'Apollinare in Classe and Sant'Apollinare Nuovo. www.turismo.ravenna.it 82 B1

Siena

Outstanding 13–14c medieval town centred on beautiful Piazza del Campo with Gothic Palazzo Publico (frescoes of secular life). Delightful Romanesque-Gothic Duomo (Libreria Piccolomini, baptistry, art works). Many other richly decorated churches. Fine Sienese painting in Pinacoteca Nazionale and Museo dell'Opera del Duomo. www.terresiena.it 81 C5

Turin Torino

City centre has 17-18c Baroque layout dominated by twin Baroque churches. Also: 15c cathedral (holds Turin Shroud); Palazzo Reale; 18c Superga Basilica; Academy of Science with two museums (Egyptian antiquities; European painting). www.commune.torino.it 80 A1

Urbino

Set in beautiful hilly landscape, Urbino's heritage is mainly due to the 15c court of Federico da Montefeltro at the magnificent Ducal Palace (notable Studiolo), now also a gallery. www.turismo.pesaurbino.it 82 C1

Venice Venezia

Stunning old city built on islands in a lagoon, with some 150 canals. The Grand Canal is crossed by the famous 16c Rialto Bridge and is lined with elegant palaces (Gothic Ca'd'Oro and Ca'Foscari, Renaissance Palazzo Grimani, Baroque Rezzonico). The district of San Marco has the core of the best known sights and is centred on Piazza San Marco with 11c Basilica di San Marco (bronze horses, 13c mosaics); Campanile (exceptional views) and Ducal Palace (connected with the prison by the famous Bridge of Sighs). Many churches (Santa Maria Gloriosa dei Frari, Santa Maria della Salute, Redentore, San Giorgio Maggiore, San Giovanni e Paolo) and scuole (Scuola di San Rocco, Scuola di San Giorgio degli Schiavoni) have excellent works of art. The Gallery of the Academy houses superb 14–18c Venetian art. The Guggenheim Museum holds 20c art. http://english.comune.venezia.it 72 C2

Verona

Old town with remains of 1c Roman Arena and medieval sights including the Palazzo degli Scaligeri; Arche Scaligere; Romanesque Santa Maria Antica; Castelvecchio; Ponte Scaliger. The famous 14c House of Juliet has associations with *Romeo and Juliet*. Many churches with fine art works (cathedral; Sant'Anastasia; basilica di San Zeno Maggiore). www.tourism.verona.it 71 C6

Vicenza

Beautiful town, famous for the architecture of Palladio, including the Olympic Theatre (extraordinary stage), Corso Palladio with many of his palaces, and Palazzo Chiericati. Nearby: Villa Rotonda, the most influential of all Palladian buildings. www.vicenzae.org 71 C6

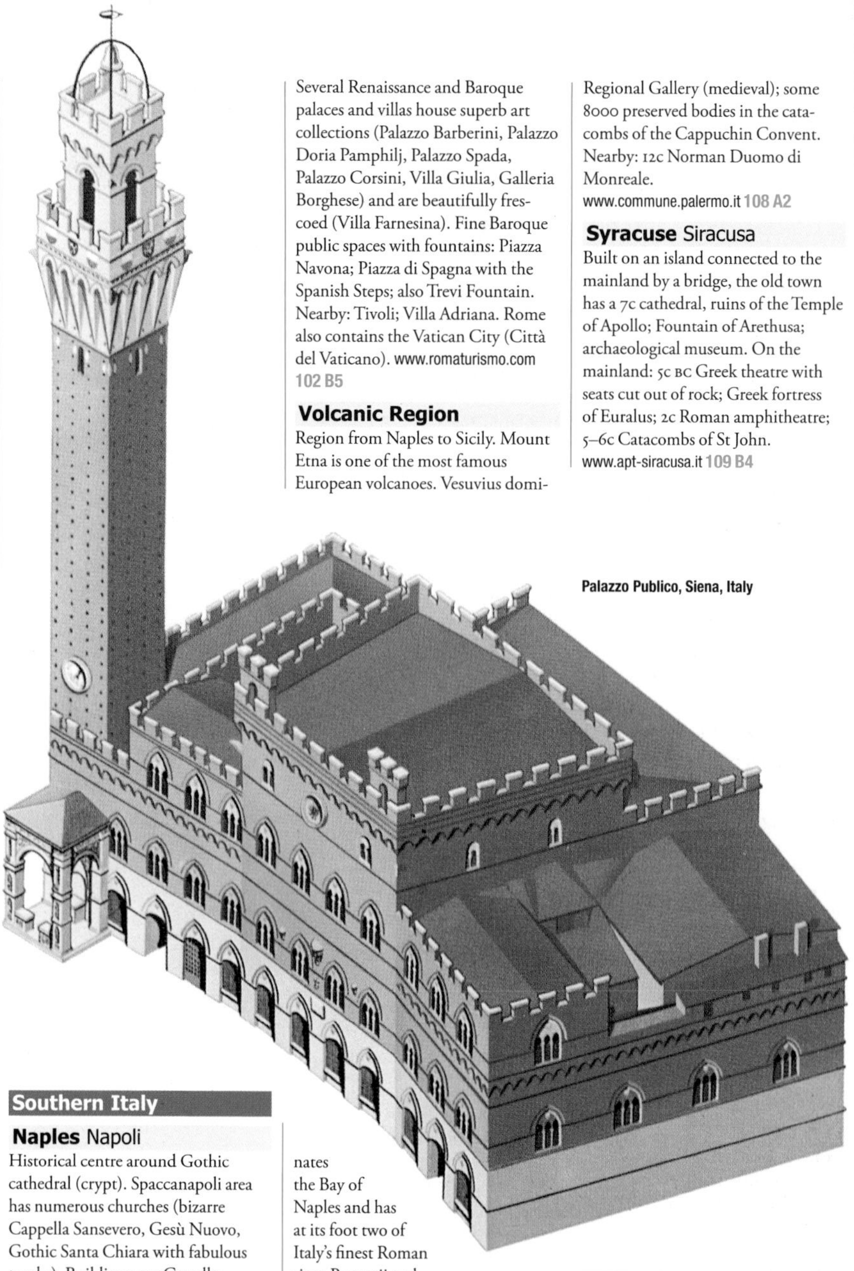

Palazzo Publico, Siena, Italy

Several Renaissance and Baroque palaces and villas house superb art collections (Palazzo Barberini, Palazzo Doria Pamphilj, Palazzo Spada, Palazzo Corsini, Villa Giulia, Galleria Borghese) and are beautifully frescoed (Villa Farnesina). Fine Baroque public spaces with fountains: Piazza Navona; Piazza di Spagna with the Spanish Steps; also Trevi Fountain. Nearby: Tivoli; Villa Adriana. Rome also contains the Vatican City (Città del Vaticano). www.romaturismo.com 102 B5

Volcanic Region

Region from Naples to Sicily. Mount Etna is one of the most famous European volcanoes. Vesuvius domi-

Southern Italy

Naples Napoli

Historical centre around Gothic cathedral (crypt). Spaccanapoli area has numerous churches (bizarre Cappella Sansevero, Gesù Nuovo, Gothic Santa Chiara with fabulous tombs). Buildings: 13c Castello Nuovo; 13c Castel dell'Ovo; 15c Palazzo Cuomo. Museums: National Archeological Museum (artefacts from Pompeii and Herculaneum); National Museum of Capodimonte (Renaissance painting). Nearby: spectacular coast around Amalfi; Pompeii; Herculaneum. www.inaples.it 103 C7

Orvieto

Medieval hill-top town with a number of monuments including the Romanesque-Gothic cathedral (façade, frescoes). www.commune.orvieto.tr.it 82 D1

Rome Roma

Capital of Italy, exceptionally rich in sights from many eras. Ancient sights: Colosseum; Arch of Constantine; Trajan's Column; Roman and Imperial fora; hills of Palatino and Campidoglio (Capitoline Museum shows antiquities); Pantheon; Castel Sant' Angelo; Baths of Caracalla). Early Christian sights: catacombs (San Calisto, San Sebastiano, Domitilla); basilicas (San Giovanni in Laterano, Santa Maria Maggiore, San Paolo Fuori le Mura). Rome is known for richly decorated Baroque churches: il Gesù, Sant'Ignazio, Santa Maria della Vittoria, Chiesa Nuova. Other churches, often with art treasures: Romanesque Santa Maria in Cosmedin, Gothic Santa Maria Sopra Minerva, Renaissance Santa Maria del Popolo, San Pietro in Vincoli.

nates the Bay of Naples and has at its foot two of Italy's finest Roman sites, Pompeii and Herculaneum, both destroyed by its eruption in 79AD. Stromboli is one of the beautiful Aeolian Islands.

Sardinia Sardegna

Sardinia has some of the most beautiful beaches in Italy (Alghero). Unique are the nuraghi, some 7000 stone constructions (Su Nuraxi, Serra Orios), the remains of an old civilization (1500–400 BC). Old towns include Cagliari and Sássari. www.sardi.it 110

Sicily Sicilia

Surrounded by beautiful beaches and full of monuments of many periods, Sicily is the largest island in the Mediterranean. Taormina with its Greek theatre has one of the most spectacular beaches, lying under the mildly active volcano Mount Etna. Also: Agrigento; Palermo, Siracusa. www.regione.sicilia.it/turismo/web_turismo 108-109

Agrigento

Set on a hill above the sea and famed for the Valley of the Temples. The nine originally 5c BC Doric temples are Sicily's best-preserved Greek remains. www.agrigento-sicilia.it 108 B2

Palermo

City with Moorish, Norman and Baroque architecture, especially around the main squares (Quattro Canti, Piazza Pretoria, Piazza Bellini). Sights: remains of Norman palace (12c Palatine Chapel); Norman cathedral;

Regional Gallery (medieval); some 8000 preserved bodies in the catacombs of the Cappuchin Convent. Nearby: 12c Norman Duomo di Monreale. www.commune.palermo.it 108 A2

Syracuse Siracusa

Built on an island connected to the mainland by a bridge, the old town has a 7c cathedral, ruins of the Temple of Apollo; Fountain of Arethusa; archaeological museum. On the mainland: 5c BC Greek theatre with seats cut out of rock; Greek fortress of Euralus; 2c Roman amphitheatre; 5–6c Catacombs of St John. www.apt-siracusa.it 109 B4

Latvia Latvija

www.lv

Riga

Well-preserved medieval town centre around the cathedral. Sights: Riga Castle; medieval Hanseatic houses; Great Guild Hall; Gothic Church of St Peter; Art Nouveau buildings in the New Town. Nearby: Baroque Rundale Castle. www.riga.lv 6 C8

Lithuania Lietuva

www.tourism.lt

Vilnius

Baroque old town with fine architecture including: cathedral; Gediminas Tower; university complex; Archbishop's Palace; Church of St Anne. Also: remains of Jewish life; Vilnius Picture Gallery (16–19c regional); Lithuanian National Museum. www.vilnius.lt 7 D8

Luxembourg

www.ont.lu

Luxembourg

Capital of Luxembourg, built on a rock with fine views. Old town is around the Place d'Armes. Buildings: Grand Ducal Palace; fortifications of Rocher du Bock; cathedral. Museum of History and Art holds an excellent regional collection. www.ont.lu 60 A2

Macedonia Makedonija

www.macedonia.org

Skopje
Historic town with Turkish citadel, fine 15c mosques, oriental bazaar, ancient bridge. Superb Byzantine churches nearby.
www.skopjeonline.com.mk 10 E6

Ohrid
Old town, beautifully set by a lake, with houses of wood and brick, remains of a Turkish citadel, many churches (two cathedrals; St Naum south of the lake). www.ohrid.org.mk 116 A2

Malta

www.visitmalta.com

Valletta
Capital of Malta. Historic walled city, founded in 16c by the Maltese Knights, with 16c Grand Master's Palace and a richly decorated cathedral. 107 C5

Monaco

www.visitmonaco.com

Monaco
Major resort area in a beautiful location. Sights include: Monte Carlo casino, Prince's Palace at Monaco-Ville; 19c cathedral; oceanographic museum. www.visitmonaco.com 80 C1

The Netherlands
Nederland

www.visitholland.com

Amsterdam
Capital of the Netherlands. Old centre has picturesque canals lined with distinctive elegant 17–18c merchants' houses. Dam Square has 15c New Church and Royal Palace. Other churches include Westerkerk. The Museumplein has three world-famous museums: Rijksmuseum (several art collections including 15–17c painting); Van Gogh Museum; Municipal Museum (art from 1850 on). Other museums: Anne Frank House; Jewish Historical Museum; Rembrandt House. www.visitamsterdam.nl 42 C1

Westerkerk,
Amsterdam,
Netherlands

Delft
Well-preserved old Dutch town with gabled red-roofed houses along canals. Gothic churches: New Church; Old Church. Famous for Delftware (two museums). www.delft.nl 49 A5

The Hague Den Haag
Seat of Government and of the royal house of the Netherlands. The 17c Mauritshuis houses the Royal Picture Gallery (excellent 15–18c Flemish and Dutch). Other good collections: Prince William V Gallery; Hesdag Museum; Municipal Museum www.denhaag.nl 49 A5

Haarlem
Many medieval gabled houses centred on the Great Market with 14c Town Hall and 15c Church of St Bavon. Museums: Frans Hals Museum; Teylers Museum. www.haarlem.nl 42 C1

Het Loo
Former royal palace and gardens set in a vast landscape (commissioned by future Queen of England, Mary Stuart). www.paleishetloo.nl 50 A1

Keukenhof
Landscaped gardens, planted with bulbs of many varieties, are the largest flower gardens in the world. www.keukenhof.nl 49 A5

Leiden
University town of beautiful gabled houses set along canals. The Rijksmuseum Van Oudheden is Holland's most important home to archaeological artefacts from the Antiquity. The 16c Hortus Botanicus is one of the oldest botanical gardens in Europe. The Cloth Hall with van Leyden's *Last Judgement*. www.leidenpromotie.nl 49 A5

Rotterdam
The largest port in the world. The Boymans-van Beuningen Museum has a huge and excellent decorative and fine art collection (old and modern). Nearby: 18c Kinderdijk with 19 windmills. www.rotterdam.nl 49 B5

Utrecht
Delightful old town centre along canals with the Netherlands' oldest university and Gothic cathedral. Good art collections: Central Museum; National Museum. www.utrecht.nl 49 A6

Norway Norge

www.norway.no

Bergen
Norway's second city in a scenic setting. The Quay has many painted wooden medieval buildings. Sights: 12c Romanesque St Mary's Church; Bergenhus fortress with 13c Haakon's Hall; Rosenkrantztårnet; Grieghallen; Rasmus Meyer Collection (Norwegian art); Bryggens Museum. www.visitbergen.com 32 B2

Lappland (Norwegian)
Vast land of Finnmark is home to the Sámi. Nordkapp is the northern point of Europe. Also Finland, Sweden. www.lappland.no 113

Norwegian Fjords
Beautiful and majestic landscape of deep glacial valleys filled by the sea. The most thrilling fjords are between Bergen and Ålesund. www.fjords.com 32 & 114

Oslo
Capital of Norway with a modern centre. Buildings: 17c cathedral; 19c city hall, 19c royal palace; 19c Stortinget (housing parliament); 19c University; 13c Akershus (castle); 12c Akerskirke (church). Museums: National Gallery; Munch Museum; Viking Ship Museum; Folk Museum (reconstructed buildings). www.visitoslo.com 34 C2

Stavkirker
Wooden medieval stave churches of bizarre pyramidal structure, carved with images from Nordic mythology. Best preserved in southern Norway.

Tromsø
Main arctic city of Norway with a university and two cathedrals. www.destinasjontromso.no 112 C8

Trondheim
Set on the edge of a fjord, a modern city with the superb Nidaros cathedral (rebuilt 19c). Also: Stiftsgaard (royal residence); Applied Arts Museum. www.trondheim.com 114 D7

Poland Polska

www.poland.pl

Częstochowa
Centre of Polish Catholicism, with the 14c monastery of Jasna Góra a pilgrimage site to the icon of the Black Madonna for six centuries. 55 C4

Gdańsk
Medieval centre with: 14c Town Hall (state rooms); Gothic brick St Mary's Church, Poland's largest; Long Market has fine buildings (Artus Court); National Art Museum. www.gdansk.pl 47 A4

Kraków
Old university city, rich in architecture, centred on superb 16c Marketplace with Gothic-Renaissance Cloth Hall containing the Art Gallery (19c Polish), Clock Tower, Gothic red-brick St Mary's Church (altarpiece). Czartoryski Palace has city's finest art collection. Wawel Hill has the Gothic cathedral and splendid Renaissance Royal Palace. The former Jewish ghetto in Kazimierz district has 16c Old Synagogue, now a museum. www.krakow.pl 55 C4

Poznań
Town centred on the Old Square with Renaissance Town Hall and Baroque mansions. Also: medieval castle; Gothic cathedral; National Museum (European masters). www.plot.poznan.pl 46 C2

Tatry
One of Europe's most delightful mountain ranges with many beautiful ski resorts (Zakopane). Also in Slovakia. 65 A5

Warsaw Warszawa
Capital of Poland, with many historic monuments in the Old Town with the Royal Castle (museum) and Old Town Square surrounded by reconstructed 17–18c merchants' houses. Several churches including: Gothic cathedral; Baroque Church of the Nuns of Visitation. Richly decorated royal palaces and gardens: Neoclassical Łazienki Palace; Baroque palace in Wilanów. The National Museum has Polish and European art. www.warsawtour.pl 55 A5

Wrocław
Historic town centred on the Market Square with 15c Town Hall and man-sions. Churches: Baroque cathedral; St Elizabeth; St Adalbert. National Museum displays fine art. Vast painting of Battle of Racławice is specially housed. www.wroclaw.pl 54 B2

Portugal

www.visitportugal.pt

Alcobaça
Monastery of Santa Maria, one of the best examples of a Cistercian abbey, founded in 1147 (exterior 17–18c). The church is Portugal's largest (14c tombs). 92 B1

Algarve
Modern seaside resorts among picturesque sandy beaches and rocky coves (Praia da Rocha). Old towns: Lagos; Faro. www.rtalgarve.pt 98 B2

Batalha
Abbey is one of the masterpieces of French Gothic and Manueline architecture (tombs, English Perpendicular chapel, unfinished pantheon). 92 B2

Braga
Historic town with cathedral and large Archbishop's Palace. www.cm-braga.com.pt 87 C2

Coimbra
Old town with narrow streets set on a hill. The Romanesque cathedral is particularly fine (portal). The university (founded 1290) has a fascinating Baroque library. Also: Museum of Machado de Castro; many monasteries and convents. 92 A2

Évora
Centre of the town, surrounded by walls, has narrow streets of Moorish character and medieval and Renaissance architecture. Churches: 12–13c Gothic cathedral; São Francisco with a chapel decorated with bones of some 5000 monks; 15c Convent of Dos Lóis. The Jesuit university was founded in 1559. Museum of Évora holds fine art (particularly Flemish and Portugese). 92 C3

Guimarães
Old town with a castle with seven towers on a vast keep. Churches: Romanesque chapel of São Miguel; São Francisco. Alberto Sampaio Museum and Martins Sarmento Museum are excellent. 87 C2

Lisbon Lisboa
Capital of Portugal. Baixa is the Neoclassical heart of Lisbon with the Praça do Comércio and Rossío squares. São Jorge castle (Visigothic, Moorish, Romanesque) is surrounded by the medieval quarters. Bairro Alto is famous for *fado* (songs). Monastery of Jerónimos is exceptional. Churches: 12c cathedral; São Vicente de Fora; São Roque (tiled chapels); Torre de Belém; Convento da Madre de Deus. Museums: Gulbenkian Museum (ancient, oriental, European), National Museum of Antique Art (old masters), Modern Art Centre; Azulejo Museum (decorative tiles). Nearby: palatial monastic complex Mafra; royal resort Sintra. www.cm-lisboa.pt 92 C1

Porto
Historic centre with narrow streets. Views from Clérigos Tower. Churches: São Francisco; cathedral. Soares dos Reis Museum holds fine and decorative arts (18–19c). The suburb of Vila Nova de Gaia is the centre for port wine. www.portoturismo.pt 87 C2

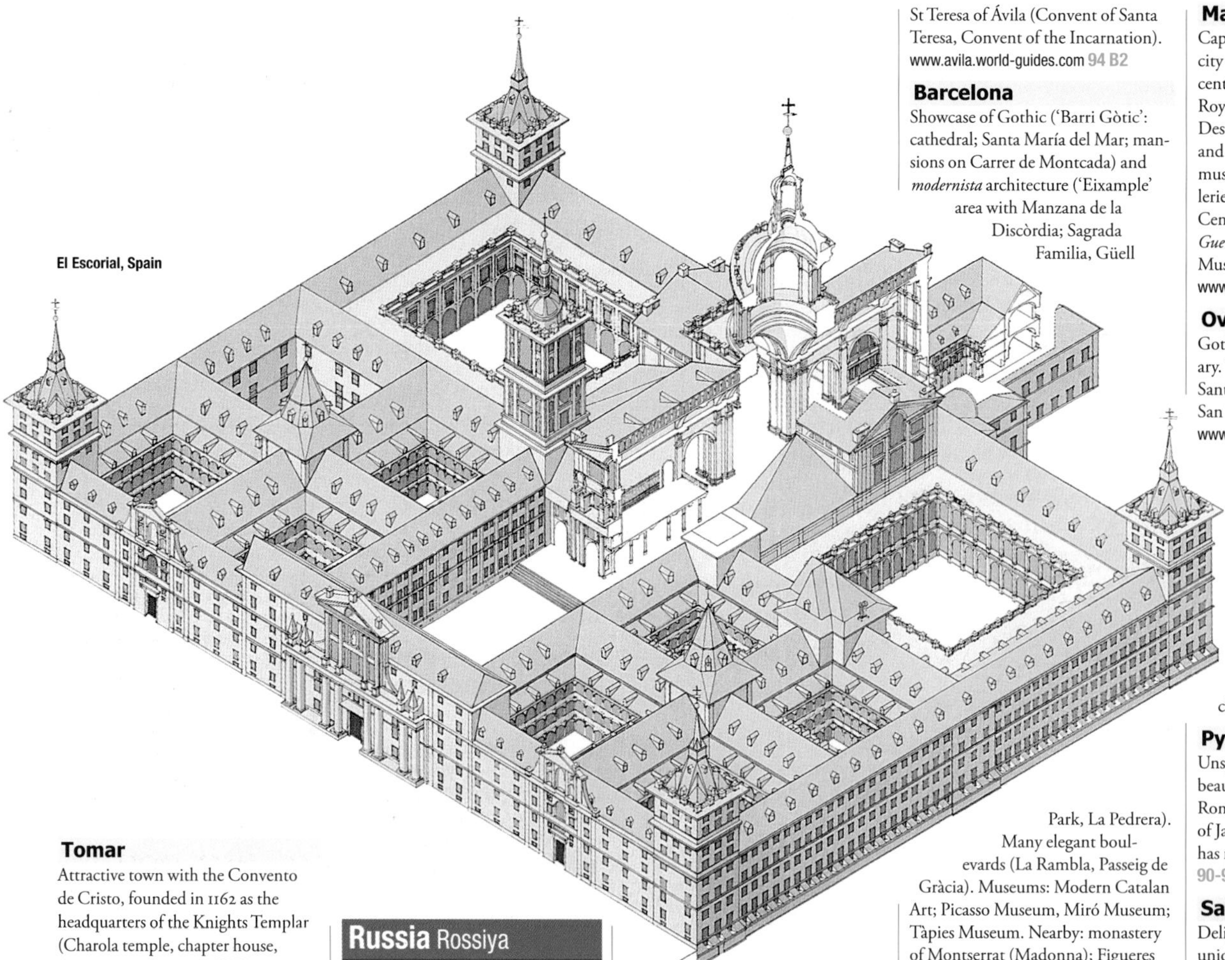

El Escorial, Spain

Tomar

Attractive town with the Convento de Cristo, founded in 1162 as the headquarters of the Knights Templar (Charola temple, chapter house, Renaissance cloisters). 92 B2

Romania

www.turism.ro

Bucovina

Beautiful region in northern Romanian Moldova renowned for a number of 15–16c monasteries and their fresco cycles. Of particular note are Moldovita, Voroneţ and Suceviţa. 11 C8

Bucharest Bucureşti

Capital of Romania with the majority of sites along the Calea Victoriei and centring on Piaţa Revoluţiei with 19c Romanian Athenaeum and 1930s Royal Palace housing the National Art Gallery. The infamous 1980s Civic Centre with People's Palace is a symbol of dictatorial aggrandisement. www.bucuresti.ro 11 D9

Carpathian Mountains Carpaţii

The beautiful Carpathian Mountains have several ski resorts (Sinaia) and peaks noted for first-rate mountaineering (Făgăraşuiui, Rodnei). Danube Delta Europe's largest marshland, a spectacular nature reserve. Travel in the area is by boat, with Tulcea the starting point for visitors. The Romanian Black Sea Coast has a stretch of resorts (Mamaia, Eforie) between Constanţa and the border, and well-preserved Roman remains in Histria. 11 C8

Transylvania Transilvania

Beautiful and fascinating scenic region of medieval citadels (Timişoara, Sibiu) provides a setting for the haunting image of the legendary Dracula (Sighişoara, Braşov, Bran Castle). Cluj-Napoca is the main town. 11 C7

Russia Rossiya

www.russia.com

Moscow Moskva

Capital of Russia, with many monuments. Within the Kremlin's red walls are: 15c Cathedral of the Dormition; 16c Cathedral of the Archangel; Cathedral of the Annunciation (icons), Armour Palace. Outside the walls, Red Square has the Lenin Mausoleum and 16c St Basil's Cathedral. There are a number of monasteries (16c Novodevichi). Two superb museums: Tretiakov Art Gallery (Russian); Pushkin Museum of Fine Art (European). Kolomenskoe, once a royal summer retreat, has the Church of the Ascension. The VDNKh is a symbol of the Stalinist era. www.moscow-guide.ru 7 D14

Novgorod

One of Russia's oldest towns, centred on 15c Kremlin with St Sophia Cathedral (iconostasis, west door). Two other cathedrals: St Nicholas; St George. Museum of History, Architecture and Art has notable icons and other artefacts. www.novgorod.ru 7 B11

Petrodvorets

Grand palace with numerous pavilions (Monplaisir) set in beautiful parkland interwoven by a system of fountains, cascades and waterways connected to the sea. www.petrodvorets.ru 7 B10

Pushkin

(Tsarskoye Selo) Birthplace of Alexander Pushkin, with the vast Baroque Catherine Palace – splendid state apartments, beautiful gardens and lakes. www.pushkin-town.net 7 B11

Saint Petersburg Sankt Peterburg

Founded in 1703 with the SS Peter and Paul Fortress and its cathedral by Peter the Great, and functioning as seat of court and government until 1918. Many of the most famous sights are around elegant Nevski Prospekt. The Hermitage, one of the world's largest and finest art collections is housed in five buildings including the Baroque Winter and Summer palaces. The Mikhailovsky Palace houses the Russian Museum (Russian art). Other sights: neoclassical Admiralty; 19c St Isaac's Cathedral and St Kazan Cathedral; Vasilievsky Island with 18c Menshikov Palace; Alexander Nevsky Monastery; 18c Smolny Convent. www.spb.ru 7 B11

Sergiev Posad

(Zagorsk) Trinity St Sergius monastery with 15c cathedral. www.musobl.divo.ru 7 C15

Serbia & Montenegro Srbija i Crna Gora

www.serbia-tourism.org;
www.visit-montenegro.com

Belgrade Beograd

Capital of Serbia & Montenegro. The largely modern city is set between the Danube and Sava rivers. The National Museum holds European art. To the south there are numerous fascinating medieval monasteries, richly embellished with frescoes. www.belgradetourism.org.yu 85 B5

Spain España

www.spaintour.com

Ávila

Medieval town with 2km-long 11c walls. Pilgrimage site to shrines to St Teresa of Ávila (Convent of Santa Teresa, Convent of the Incarnation). www.avila.world-guides.com 94 B2

Barcelona

Showcase of Gothic ('Barri Gòtic': cathedral; Santa María del Mar; mansions on Carrer de Montcada) and *modernista* architecture ('Eixample' area with Manzana de la Discòrdia; Sagrada Familia, Güell Park, La Pedrera). Many elegant boulevards (La Rambla, Passeig de Gràcia). Museums: Modern Catalan Art; Picasso Museum, Miró Museum; Tàpies Museum. Nearby: monastery of Montserrat (Madonna); Figueres (Dali Museum). www.barcelonaturisme.com 91 B5

Burgos

Medieval town with Gothic cathedral, Moorish-Gothic Royal Monastery and Charterhouse of Miraflores. www.burgos.es 88 B3

Cáceres

Medieval town surrounded by originally Moorish walls and with several aristocratic palaces with solars. www.caceres.es 93 B4

Córdoba

Capital of Moorish Spain with a labyrinth of streets and houses with tile-decorated patios. The 8–10c Mezquita is the finest mosque in Spain. A 16c cathedral was added at the centre of the building and a 17c tower replaced the minaret. The old Jewish quarter has 14c synagogue www.cordoba.es 100 B1

El Escorial

Immense Renaissance complex of palatial and monastic buildings and mausoleum of the Spanish monarchs. www.patrimonionacional.es/escorial/escorial.htm 94 B2

Granada

The Alhambra was hill-top palace-fortress of the rulers of the last Moorish kingdom and is the most splendid example of Moorish art and architecture in Spain. The complex has three principal parts: Alcazaba fortress (11c); Casa Real palace (14c, with later Palace of Carlos V); Generalife gardens. Also: Moorish quarter; gypsy quarter; Royal Chapel with good art in the sacristy. www.granadatur.com 100 B2

León

Gothic cathedral has notable stained glass. Royal Pantheon commemorates early kings of Castile and León. 88 B1

Madrid

Capital of Spain, a mainly modern city with 17–19c architecture at its centre around Plaza Mayor. Sights: Royal Palace with lavish apartments; Descalzas Reales Convent (tapestries and other works); Royal Armoury museum. Spain's three leading galleries: Prado (15–18c); Queen Sofia Centre (20c Spanish, Picasso's *Guernica*); Thyssen-Bornemisza Museum (medieval to modern). www.munimadrid.es 94 B3

Oviedo

Gothic cathedral with 12c sanctuary. Three Visigoth (9c) churches: Santullano, Santa María del Naranco, San Miguel de Lillo. www.ayto-oviedo.es 88 A1

Palma

Situated on Mallorca, the largest and most beautiful of the Balearic islands, with an impressive Gothic cathedral. www.a-palma.es 97 B2

Picos de Europa

Mountain range with river gorges and peaks topped by Visigothic and Romanesque churches. 88 A2

Pyrenees

Unspoiled mountain range with beautiful landscape and villages full of Romanesque architecture (cathedral of Jaca). The Ordesa National Park has many waterfalls and canyons. 90-91

Salamanca

Delightful old city with some uniquely Spanish architecture: Renaissance Plateresque is famously seen on 16c portal of the university (founded 1215); Baroque Churrigueresque on 18c Plaza Mayo; both styles at the Convent of San Esteban. Also: Romanesque Old Cathedral; Gothic-Plateresque New Cathedral; House of Shells. www.salamanca.com 94 B1

Santiago di Compostela

Medieval city with many churches and religious institutions. The famous pilgrimage to the shrine of St James the Apostle ends here in the magnificent cathedral, originally Romanesque with many later elements (18c Baroque façade). www.santiagoturismo.com 86 B2

Segovia

Old town set on a rock with a 1c Roman aqueduct. Also: 16c Gothic cathedral; Alcázar (14–15c, rebuilt 19c); 12-sided 13c Templar church of Vera Cruz. www.viasegovia.com 94 B2

Seville Sevilla

City noted for festivals and flamenco. The world's largest Gothic cathedral (15c) retains the Orange Court and minaret of a mosque. The Alcazar is a fine example of Moorish architecture. The massive 18c tobacco factory, now part of the university, was the setting for Bizet's *Carmen*. Barrio de Santa Cruz is the old Jewish quarter with narrow streets and white houses. Casa de Pilatos (15–16c) has a fine domestic patio. Hospital de la Caridad has good Spanish painting. Nearby: Roman Italica with amphitheatre. www.sevilla.org 99 B5

Tarragona

The city and its surroundings have some of the best-preserved Roman heritage in Spain. Also: Gothic cathedral (cloister); Archaeological Museum. www.tarragona.es 91 B4

Toledo

Historic city with Moorish, Jewish and Christian sights. The small 11c mosque of El Cristo de la Luz is one of the earliest in Spain. Two synagogues have been preserved: Santa María la Blanca; El Tránsito. Churches: San Juan de los Reyes; Gothic cathedral (good artworks). El Greco's *Burial of the Count of Orgaz* is in the Church of Santo Tomé. More of his works are in the El Greco house and, with other art, in Hospital de Santa Cruz. www.toledo.es **94 C2**

Valencia

The old town has houses and palaces with elaborate façades. Also: Gothic cathedral and Lonja de la Seda church. www.comunitatvalenciana.com **96 B2**

Zaragoza

Town notable for Moorish architecture (11c Aljafería Palace). The Basilica de Nuestra Señora del Pilar, one of two cathedrals, is highly venerated. www.zaragoza-ciudad.com **90 B2**

Slovenia Slovenija

www.slovenia-tourism.si

Istria Istra

Two town centres, Koper and Piran, with medieval and Renaissance squares and Baroque palaces. See also Croatia. www.slo-istra.com **72 C3**

Julian Alps Julijske Alpe

Wonderfully scenic section of the Alps with lakes (Bled, Bohinj), deep valleys (Planica, Vrata) and ski resorts (Kranjska Gora, Bohinjska Bistrica). **72 B3**

Karst Caves

Numerous caves with huge galleries, extraordinary stalactites and stalagmites, and underground rivers. The most spectacular are Postojna (the most famous, with Predjamski Castle nearby) and Škocjan. www.postojnska-jama.si **73 C4**

Ljubljana

Capital of Slovenia. The old town, dominated by the castle (good views), is principally between Prešeren Square and Town Hall (15c, 18c), with the Three Bridges and colonnaded market. Many Baroque churches (cathedral, St Jacob, St Francis, Ursuline) and palaces (Bishop's Palace, Seminary, Gruber Palace). Also: 17c Križanke church and monastery complex; National Gallery and Modern Gallery show Slovene art. www.ljubljana.si **73 B4**

Slovakia Slovenska Republika

www.slovenska-republika.com

Bratislava

Capital of Slovakia, dominated by the castle (Slovak National Museum, good views). Old Town centred on the Main Square with Old Town Hall and Jesuit Church. Many 18–19c palaces (Mirbach Palace, Pálffy Palace, Primate's Palace), churches (Gothic cathedral, Corpus Christi Chapel) and museums (Slovak National Gallery). www.bratislava.sk **64 B3**

Košice

Charming old town with many Baroque and neoclassical buildings and Gothic cathedral. www.kosice.sk **10 B6**

Spišské Podhradie

Region, east of the Tatry, full of picturesque medieval towns (Levoča, Kežmarok, Prešov) and architectural monuments (Spišský Castle). **65 A6**

Tatry

Beautiful mountain region. Poprad is an old town with 19c villas. Starý Smokovec is a popular ski resort. See also Poland. www.tatry.sk **65 A5**

Sweden Sverige

www.sweden.se

Abisko

Popular resort in the Swedish part of Lapland set in an inspiring landscape of lakes and mountains. www.abisko.nu **112 D7**

Gothenburg Göteborg

Largest port in Sweden, the historic centre has 17–18c Dutch architectural character (Kronhuset). The Art Museum has interesting Swedish works. www.goteborg.com **38 B4**

Gotland

Island with Sweden's most popular beach resorts (Ljugarn) and unspoiled countryside with churches in Baltic Gothic style (Dahlem, Bunge). Visby is a pleasant walled medieval town. www.gotland.se **37 E5**

Lappland (Swedish)

Swedish part of Lappland with 18c Arvidsjaur the oldest preserved Sámi village. Jokkmokk is a Sámi cultural centre, Abisko a popular resort in fine scenery. Also Finland, Norway. www.lappland.se **112-113**

Lund

Charming university city with medieval centre and a fine 12c Romanesque cathedral (14c astronomical clock, carved tombs). www.lund.se **41 D3**

Malmö

Old town centre set among canals and parks dominated by a red-brick castle (museums) and a vast market square with Town Hall and Gothic Church of St Peter. www.malmo.se **41 D3**

Mora

Delightful village on the shores of Siljan Lake in the heart of the Dalarna region, home to folklore and traditional crafts. www.mora.se **36 A1**

Stockholm

Capital of Sweden built on a number of islands. The Old Town is largely on three islands with 17–18c houses, Baroque Royal Castle (apartments and museums), Gothic cathedral, parliament. Riddarholms church has tombs of the monarchy. Museums include: Modern Gallery (one of world's best modern collections); Nordiska Museet (cultural history); open-air Skansen (Swedish houses). Baroque Drottningholm Castle is the residence of the monarchy. www.stockholm.se **37 C5**

Swedish Lakes

Beautiful region around the Vättern and Vänern Lakes. Siljan Lake is in the Dalarna region where folklore and crafts are preserved (Leksand, Mora, Rättvik). **35 D5**

Uppsala

Appealing university town with a medieval centre around the massive Gothic cathedral. www.uppsala.se **36 C4**

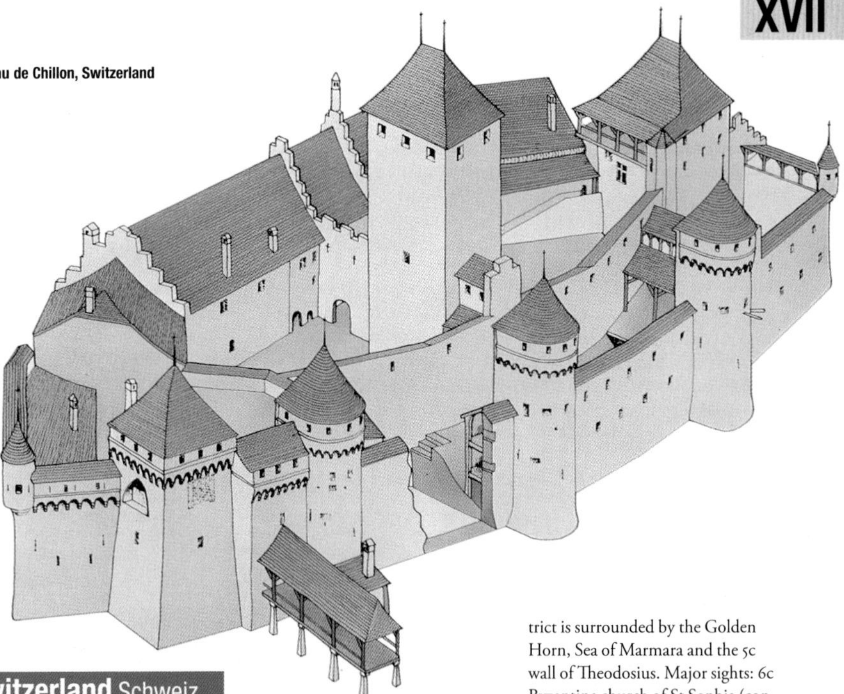

Château de Chillon, Switzerland

Switzerland Schweiz

www.myswitzerland.com

Alps

The most popular Alpine region is the Berner Oberland with the town of Interlaken a starting point for exploring the large number of picturesque peaks (Jungfrau). The valleys of the Graubünden have famous ski resorts (Davos, St Moritz). Zermatt lies below the highest and most recognizable Swiss peak, the Matterhorn. www.thealps.com **70 B2**

Basle Basel

Medieval university town with Romanesque-Gothic cathedral (tomb of Erasmus). Superb collections: Art Museum; Museum of Contemporary Art. www.baseltourismus.ch **70 A2**

Bern

Capital of Switzerland. Medieval centre has fountains, characteristic streets (Spitalgasse) and tower-gates. The Bärengraben is famed for its bears. Also: Gothic cathedral; good Fine Arts Museum. www.berne.ch **70 B2**

Geneva Genève

Wonderfully situated on the lake with the world's highest fountain. The historic area is centred on the Romanesque cathedral and Place du Bourg du Four. Excellent collections: Art and History Museum; Museum of Modern Art in 19c Petit Palais. On the lake shore: splendid medieval Château de Chillon. www.geneva-tourism.ch **69 B6**

Interlaken

Starting point for excursions to the most delightful part of the Swiss Alps, the Bernese Oberland, with Grindelwald and Lauterbrunnen – one of the most thrilling valleys leading up to the ski resort of Wengen with views on the Jungfrau. www.interlakentourism.ch **70 B2**

Lucerne Luzern

On the beautiful shores of Vierwaldstättersee, a charming medieval town of white houses on narrow streets and of wooden bridges (Kapellbrücke, Spreuerbrücke). It is centred on the Kornmarkt with the Renaissance Old Town Hall and Am Rhyn-Haus (Picasso collection). www.luzern.org **70 A3**

Zürich

Set on Zürichsee, the old quarter is around Niederdorf with 15c cathedral. Gothic Fraumünster has stained glass by Chagall. Museums: Swiss National Museum (history); Art Museum (old and modern masters); Bührle Foundation (Impressionists, Post-impressionists). www.zuerich.ch **70 A3**

Turkey Türkiye

www.tourismturkey.org

Istanbul

Divided by the spectcular Bosphorus, the stretch of water that separates Europe from Asia, the historic district is surrounded by the Golden Horn, Sea of Marmara and the 5c wall of Theodosius. Major sights: 6c Byzantine church of St Sophia (converted first to a mosque in 1453 and then a museum in 1934); 15c Topkapi Palace; treasury and Archaeological Museum; 17c Blue Mosque; 19c Bazaar; 16c Süleymaniye Mosque; 12c Kariye Camii; European district with Galata Tower and 19c Dolmabahçe Palace. www.istanbul.com **118 A3**

Ukraine Ukraina

www.ukraine.com

Kiev Kyïv

Capital of Ukraine, known for its cathedral (11c, 17c) with Byzantine frescoes and mosaics. The Monastery of the Caves has churches, monastic buildings and catacombs. www.uazone.net/kiev **11 A11**

Vatican City Città del Vaticano

www.vatican.va

Vatican City Città del Vaticano

Independent state within Rome. On Piazza San Pietro is the 15–16c Renaissance-Baroque Basilica San Pietro (Michelangelo's dome and *Pietà*), the world's most important Roman Catholic church. The Vatican Palace contains the Vatican Museums with many fine art treasures including Michelangelo's frescoes in the Sistine Chapel. www.vatican.va **102 B5**

The facade of Basilica San Pietro, Vatican City

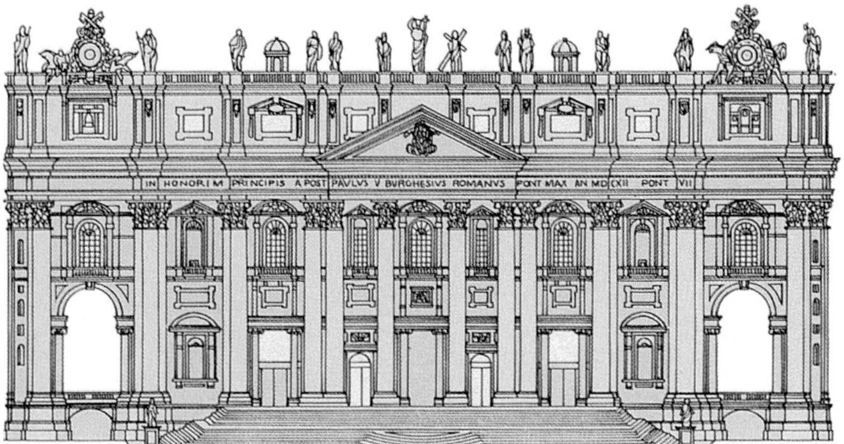

History and culture of Europe

The following definitions describe some of the key terms in the timeline below.

Aegean civilization Bronze Age cultures, chiefly Minoan (on Crete, at its height c.1700BC–c.1100BC) and Mycenaean (at its height c.1580BC–c.1120BC).

Baroque Style of art and architecture which at its best was a blend of light, colour, and movement calculated to overwhelm through emotional appeal. Buildings were heavily decorated with ornament and free-standing sculpture. Baroque became increasingly complex and florid. The term is often used to describe the period in history as well as the style.

Byzantine Empire Christian, Greek-speaking, Eastern Roman Empire that outlasted the Western Empire by nearly 1000 years. The area of the Byzantine Empire varied greatly, and its history from c.600 was marked by continual military crisis and recovery.

Carolingian period Cultural revival in France and Italy beginning under the encouragement of Charlemagne, who gathered notable educators and artists to his court at Aachen.

Counter-Reformation Revival of the Roman Catholic Church in Europe, beginning as a reaction to the Reformation. The reforms were largely conservative, trying to remove many of the abuses of the late medieval church and win new prestige for the papacy. The Council of Trent (1545-63) generated many of the key decisions and doctrines.

Dark Ages Term that at one time historians used to imply cultural and economic backwardness, but now is used mainly to indicate our ignorance of the period due to lack of historical evidence.

Enlightenment (Age of Reason) Philosophical movement that influenced many aspects of 18th-century society. It was inspired by the scientific and philosophical revolutions of the late 17th century and stressed the use of reason and the rational side of human nature.

Gothic Architecture and painting characterized by the pointed arch and ribbed vault. Religious in inspiration, its greatest expression was the cathedral. Gothic sculpture was elegant and more realistic than Romanesque. The Gothic style was also well expressed in manuscript illumination.

High Renaissance Brief period regarded as the height of Italian (particularly Roman) Renaissance art, brought to an end by the sack of Rome by the troops of Charles V.

Historicism, 19th-century Revival of past architectural styles. Ancient Greek and Gothic forms predominated, though buildings were constructed in a wide range of styles, including Renaissance, Romanesque and baroque.

Holy Roman Empire Empire centred on Germany, which aimed to echo ancient Rome. It was founded when Otto I was crowned in Rome (some date it from the coronation of Charlemagne). The Emperor claimed to be the worldly sovereign of Christendom ruling in co-operation with

BC

1500

c.1250-1200 Trojan War

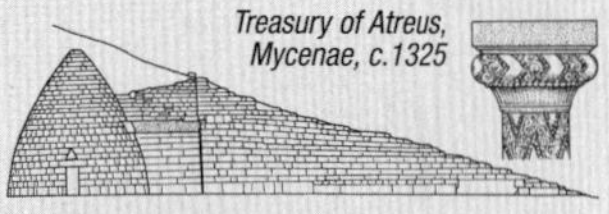

Treasury of Atreus, Mycenae, c.1325

1000

776 First Olympic Games held in Greece

753 Traditional date for the foundation of Rome by Romulus and Remus

c.750 *Odyssey* and *Iliad* complete in known forms

582?-500? Pythagoras

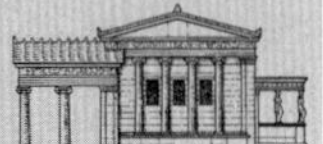

Erechtheion, part of the Acropolis, Athens, 421-405

500

336-323 Alexander the Great's campaigns

218 Hannibal crosses Alps with elephants

58-51 Romans conquer Gaul

43 Romans invade Britain

428?-347? Plato

384-322 Aristotle

356-323 Alexander the Great

c.140 *Venus de Milo* sculpted

100-44 Julius Caesar

69-30 Cleopatra

63BC-14AD Augustus

AD

37-68 Nero

c.58 St Paul's Letter to the Corinthians

79 Vesuvius erupts burying Pompeii and Herculaneum

75-80 Coliseum built in Rome

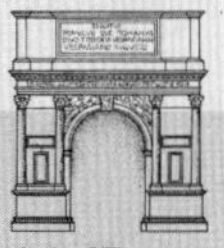

Arch of Titus, Rome, 81

53-117 Trajan

100

101–2, 105–6 Trajan's Dacian campaigns (recounted on Trajan's Column)

Pantheon, Rome, 120-124

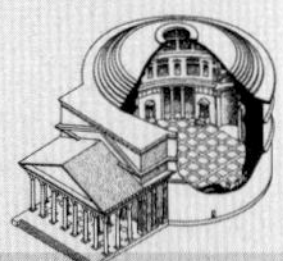

121-126 Hadrian's wall built across northern England

121-180 Marcus Aurelius

200

245-313 Diocletian

c.274-337 Constantine the Great

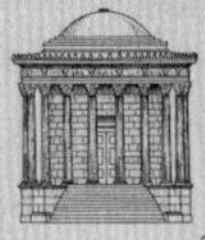

Temple of Vesta, Rome, 205

285 Roman Empire first split – Rome in the West and Byzantium (Constantinople) in the East

300

313 Edict of Milan: tolerance of Christianity in Empire

330 Constantinople founded

391 Christianity official religion of Roman Empire

395 Final division of Roman Empire into E and W

313-315 Arch of Constantine

c.329-379 St Basil

354-430 St Augustine

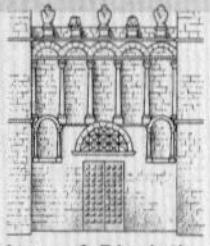

Palace of Diocletian, Split, Croatia, c.300

400

410 Visigoths sack Rome

455 Vandals sack Rome

476 Last Western Roman emperor overthrown

465-511 Clovis I, Frankish (Merovingian) king

483-565 Justinian I, ruler in first Byzantine Golden Age

San Apollinare Nuovo, Ravenna, Italy, detail of apse mosaic, 6th century

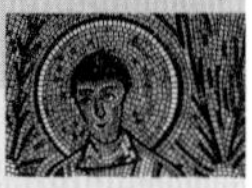

500

527–530 Slavs cross Danube

c.550 Major outbreak of bubonic plague in Europe

c.550 Height of Byzantine power and art

532-37 Church of Santa Sophia (Hagia Sophia) built in Constantinople

532-37 Church of San Vitale, Ravenna, built

San Apollinare in Classe, Ravenna, Italy, begun 532

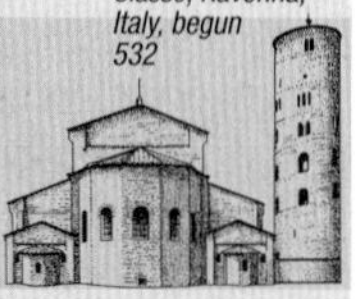

600

603 Slavs invade Balkans

c.679–1018 First Bulgarian Empire

700

711-718 Muslims invade Spain

732 Franks defeat Muslims in Spain, preventing further conquests

742-814 Charlemagne

790-800 Palatine Chapel at Aachen

Great Mosque, Cordoba, Spain, detail of arches, begun 785

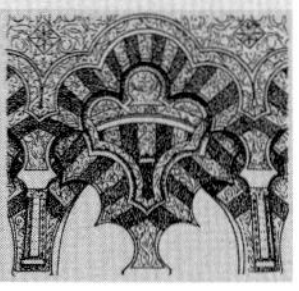

800

800 Charlemagne crowned Emperor by Pope

835-71 Danes establish settlements in England

c.860 Vikings raiders reach Mediterranean

Period bars:

- Bronze age to **c.1000**
- Aegean civilization to **c.1200**
- **c1000** Ancient Greek civilisation **c.27**
- **c.753** Early Romans **c.500**
- **c.500** Rise of Roman power **c.27**
- **c.900** Etruscans **c.500**
- **c.800** Carthaginian power **146**
- **27BC** Pax Romana **AD180**
- **27BC** Imperial Rome **AD476**
- **285** Byzantine empire **1453**
- **c.150** Major Slavic invasions of eastern Europe **c.900**
- **180** Germanic (barbarian) tribes invade Roman empire **476**
- **476** Middle Ages **c.1400**
- **476** Dark Ages **c.1000**
- **c.481** Frankish power in western Europe **962**
- **c.800** Vikings raid…

900

911 Vikings take control of Normandy

962 Holy Roman Empire founded

972 Hungarian state established

912-973 Otto I, first Holy Roman Emperor

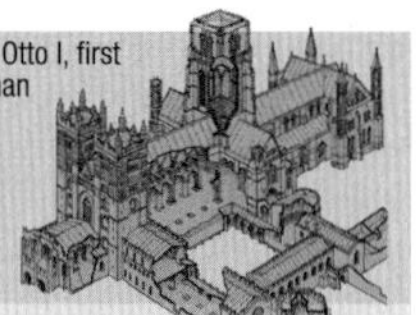

1000

1054 Church splits into Roman Catholic and Eastern Orthodox

1066 Norman conquest of England begins

1094 El Cid takes Valencia from the Moors

1050 Work begins on St Marks, Venice

1063 Pisa Romanesque cathedral started

Durham Cathedral, England, 1093-c.1130

Worms Cathedral, Germany, c.1110-81

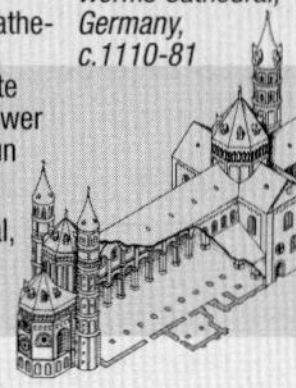

1100

1130 Normans take control of Sicily, having conquered much of southern Italy

1186–1393 Second Bulgarian Empire

c.1077-97 White Tower of the Tower of London begun

1140 First gothic cathedral, St Denis near Paris, begun

1200

1204 Fourth Crusade and sack of Constantinople

1209-1229 Wars against Albigensians in France

1209 St Francis of Assisi establishes rules for Franciscans

1194-1250 Frederick II Barbarossa Holy Roman Emperor and King of Sicily

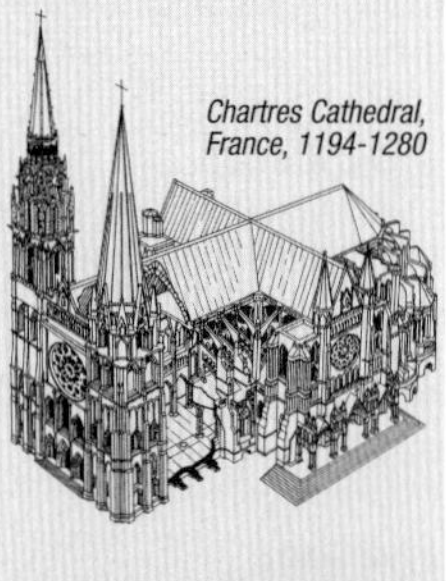

Chartres Cathedral, France, 1194-1280

1236 Christian forces take Córdoba from Moors

1237-1241 Tartar Golden Horde ravage Russia and much of north-east Europe

1350

Angel Choir, Lincoln Cathedral, England, 1256-1280

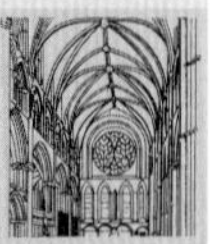

1265-1321 Dante Alighieri

c.1266-1337 Giotto

1261-1431 Paleologue age in Byzantium

1265 First English parliament in Westminster Hall, London

1271 Marco Polo's first visit to China

1282 Sicilian Vespers massacre of French in Sicily

c.1290 Invention of spectacles

1291 Swiss Confederation formed

Salisbury Cathedral, England, 1220-1380

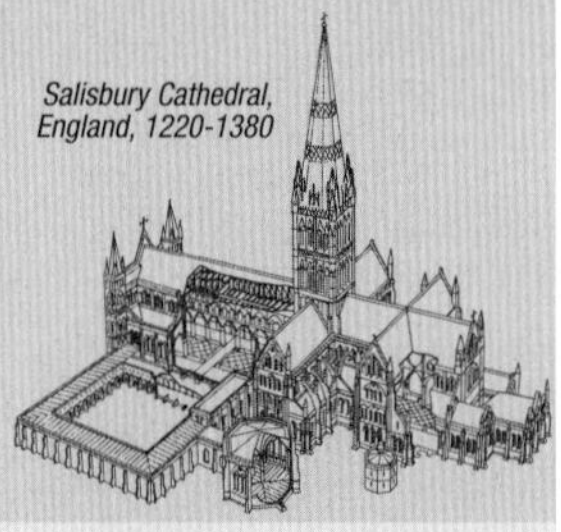

1300

c.1300 Gunpowder appears in Europe

1309-77 Papacy moves from Rome to Avignon

1304-74 Francesco Petrarch

1309 Doge's Palace, Venice, started

1313-1321 Dante works on the *Divine Comedy*

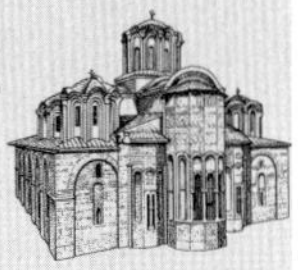

Church of the Holy Apostles, Salonica, Greece, an Orthodox continuation of the Byzantine style, 1312-15

1347-50 Worst outbreaks of plague (the Black Death), which kill about a quarter of Europe's population

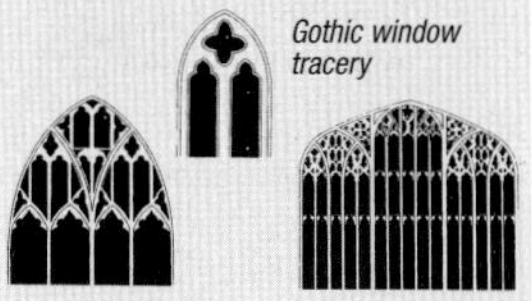

Gothic window tracery

Period bars:

- **476** Middle Ages **c.1400**
- **476** Dark Ages **c.1000**
- **285** Byzantine empire **1453**
- **c.1000** Romanesque **c.1180**
- **c.800** Vikings raid many parts of Europe **c.1050**
- **1096** Crusades **1291**
- **c.1135** Gothic period **c.1450**
- **1337** Hundred Years War…

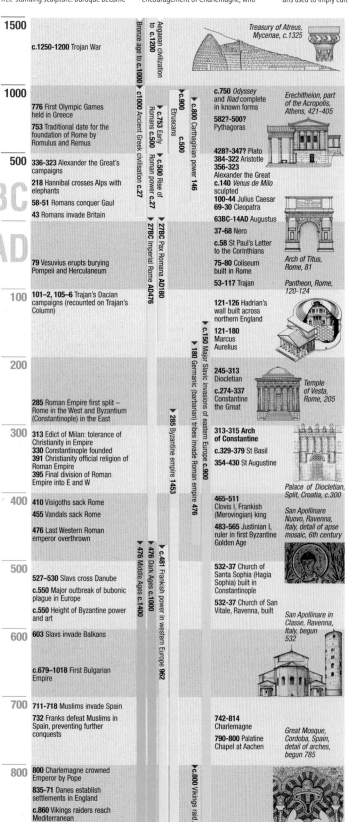

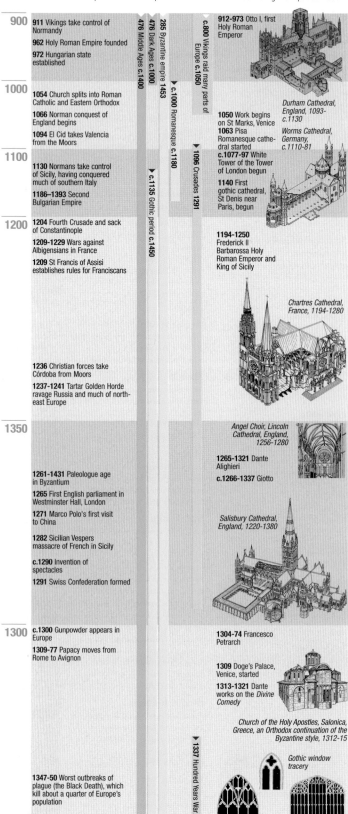

the Pope. After 1648 the Empire became a loose confederation, containing hundreds of virtually independent states. It was abolished by Napoleon I.

Imperial Rome Period of Roman history starting when Augustus declared himself emperor, ending the Roman republic. Most of the empire had already been conquered.

International Gothic Style of painting characterized by naturalistic detail, elegant elongated figures and jewel-like colour.

Mannerism Loose term applied to the art and architecture of Italy between the High Renaissance and the Baroque. A self-conscious style, it aimed to exceed earlier work in emotional impact. Painting is characterized by elongated figures in distorted poses,

often using lurid colours.

Middle Ages Period between the disintegration of the Roman Empire and the Renaissance. The Middle Ages were, above all, the age of the Christian church and of the social structure known as the feudal system.

Modern art Loose term that describes painting and sculpture that breaks from traditions going back to the Renaissance. There have been many movements, including fauvism, cubism, surrealism and expressionism.

Neoclassicism Movement in art and architecture that grew out of the Enlightenment. Exponents admired and imitated the order and clarity of ancient Greek and Roman art.

Pax Romana Period when ancient Rome was so powerful that its authority could not be challenged by outside forces and peace was maintained in the empire.

Reformation Sixteenth-century movement that sought reform of the Catholic Church and resulted in the development of Protestantism. The starting date is often given as 1517, when Martin Luther nailed his 95 theses to the door of the Schlosskirche in Wittenburg, Germany, protesting against abuses of the clergy. In Zurich, the Reformation was led by Ulrich Zwingli and then by John Calvin.

Renaissance Period of rapid cultural and economic development. An important element in this was humanism, which involved

a revival of interest in classical learning and emphasis on the philosophical and moral importance of the human individual. There was a great flowering of all the arts. Architectural and artistic style emerged in Italy and was heavily influenced by Greek and Roman models and by humanism. There was development of perspective, increasing use of secular and pagan subjects, a rise of portraiture, constant experimentation, and growing concern for the expression of the individual artist. The ideas spread and were emulated with national variations.

Rococo Playful, light style of art, architecture and decoration that developed from baroque. Rococo brought to interior decoration swirls, scrolls, shells and arabesques.

It was also applied to furniture, porcelain and silverware.

Romanesque Medieval architectural style preceding gothic. It was characterized by heavy round arches and massive walls, often decorated with carving or, originally, painted scenes.

Romanticism Movement that valued individual experience and intuition, rather than the orderly, structured universe of neoclassicism. An emphasis on nature was also a characteristic. In music, the term refers to the rather later period from c.1800–1910.

1350

1353 First Ottoman (Turkish) invasion of Europe	
1378-81 War of Chioggia – Venice takes control of Mediterranean	
1378-1417 Great Schism in the Papacy between Rome and Avignon	
1389 Battle of Kosovo - Turks gain firm foothold in the Balkans	

- 476 Middle Ages c.1400
- 285 Byzantine empire 1453
- c.1135 Gothic period c.1450
- c.1370 International Gothic style c.1450
- 1337 Hundred Years War between England and Franc 1453

1353 Giovanni Boccaccio writes the *Decameron*

Church of the Holy Cross, Schwabish-Gemund, Germany, begun c.1350

1377-1446 Filippo Brunelleschi
1378-1455 Lorenzo Ghiberti
1386-1466 Donatello
1387/1400-55 Fra Angelico
c.1390-1441 Jan van Eyck
1386-1400 Geoffrey Chaucer's *Canterbury Tales*

1400

c.1400 onward Full plate armour begins to be used instead of chain main	
1414 Discovery of Vitruvius' ancient treatise on architecture	
1415 Introduction of oil paints by Jan and Hubert van Eyck in the Netherlands	
1434-94 Medici family gain power in Florence	
1431 Joan of Arc executed at Rouen	
c.1440 Gutenberg invents moveable type allowing large-scale printing	

- c.1400 Renaissance c.1600

c.1400-1464 Rogier van der Weyden
1401-c1428 Masaccio

Foundling Hospital, Florence, Italy, from 1429

1404-72 Leon Battista Alberti
1415-92 Piero della Francesca
c.1420 Work begins on dome of Florence Cathedral

Town Hall, Louvain, Belgium, 1448-63

1434 Van Eyck paints the *Arnolfini Marriage*
c.1445-1510 Sandro Botticelli
c.1450-1516 Hieronymus Bosch

1450

1453 Turks capture Constantinople	
1479 Aragon and Castile unite to become Spain	
1479 Start of Spanish Inquisition	
1492 Christopher Columbus reaches the Americas; Spanish and Portuguese colonization begins	
1494 Spanish take Granada, the last Moorish stronghold	
1499 Portuguese discover sea route to India	

- c.1450 Late Gothic period c.1550

1452-1519 Leonardo da Vinci
1466?-1536 Erasmus of Rotterdam

St Georges Chapel, Windsor Castle, England, 1481-1528

1471-1528 Albrecht Dürer
1475-1564 Michelangelo Buonarotti
1473-1543 Nicolaus Copernicus
1483-1512 Raphael Sanzio

- c.1480 Great age of European discovery c.1580

c.1487-1576 Titian
1492/9-1546 Giuliano Romano

St Maria Novella, Florence, Italy, from 1458

1497/8-1543 Hans Holbein the Younger
c.1480 Botticelli paints *The Birth of Venus*

- 1495 High Renaissance c.1550

1500

1506 Antique statue of the Laocöon discovered near Rome, sparking increased interest in the forms of Hellenistic sculpture	
1517 Martin Luther publishes his 95 Theses in Wittenberg	
1522 Magellan's expedition completes circumnavigation of the globe	
1527 Sack of Rome by Imperial troops	
1541 John Calvin founds church in Geneva	
1543 Copernicus publishes idea that Earth revolves around the Sun	

- 1517 High Renaissance 1527
- 1517 Reformation c.1600
- c.1480 Great age of European discovery c.1580
- c.1520 Mannerism c.1610

1500 Bosch paints *The Garden of Earthly Delights*

Palazzo Strozzi, Florence, Italy, from 1490

1503 Leonardo da Vinci paints *Mona Lisa*
1504 Michelangelo sculpts *David*
1506 St Peter's, Rome, begun on Bramante's plan

Bibliotecha Laurenziana, door to library, Florence, Italy, from 1524

1508-1512 Michelangelo paints Sistine Chapel
1508-80 Andrea Palladio
1513 Machiavelli's *The Prince*
1541-1614 El Greco
1547 Ivan IV (the Terrible) Tsar of Russia

1550

1545-63 Council of Trent	
1562 Netherlands revolt against Spanish rule	
1562-98 Wars of Religion in France; end with religious tolerance under Edict of Nantes	
1557-82 Livonia War between Sweden and its Baltic neighbours	
1571 Ottoman Turk navy defeated by Holy League at Battle of Lepanto	
1572 St Bartholomew's Day Massacre in Paris	
1572-1648 Dutch revolt against Spanish rule	
1581 Independence of United Provinces (Netherlands)	
1588 English fleet defeats Spanish Armada	

- c.1400 Renaissance c.1600
- 1545 Counter Reformation 1648
- c.1520 Mannerism c.1610
- c.1480 Great age of European discovery c.1580

1558-1603 Elizabeth I Queen of England
1564-1616 William Shakespeare
1571-1610 Michelangelo Merisi da Caravaggio
1573-1652 Inigo Jones
1577-1640 Peter Paul Rubens
1581/5-1666 Frans Hals
1594-1665 Nicolas Poussin
1598-1680 Gianlorenzo Bernini
1599-1660 Diego Velazquez
1599-1641 Sir Anthony Van Dyck
1598-1666 Françoise Mansart

Palace of Charles V, Granada, Spain, detail, begun 1526

S. Georgio Maggiore, Venice, Italy, begun 1566

1600

1607 First English colony in North America at Jamestown	
1618 Defenestration of Prague starts Thirty Years' War	
1630 Sweden enters Thirty Year's War	
1635 Peace of Prague ends German involvement in Thirty Years' War	
1635 France enters Thirty Years' War	
1642-5 English Civil War	
1648 Treaty of Westphalia ends Thirty Years' War	
1649 Execution of Charles I of England	

- c.1600 Baroque c.1750
- 1618 Thirty Years' War 1648

1600-92 Claude Lorraine
1603 *Hamlet* written by Shakespeare
1606-69 Rembrandt van Rijn
1624 Frans Hals paints *The Laughing Cavalier*
1624 Palace of Versailles started
1627-1725 Peter I, the Great, of Russia
1632-75 Jan Vermeer
1632-1723 Sir Christopher Wren
1633 Galileo tried for heresy
1642 Rembrandt paints *The Night Watch*

Mauritzhuis, The Hague, Netherlands, c.1633

1650

1652-3, 1665-7, 1672-4 1st, 2nd and 3rd Anglo-Dutch wars	
1660 Restoration of English monarchy	
1666 Great Fire of London	
1671 Spain and United Provinces ally against France	
1671 Hungarian Revolt and Reign of Terror	
1682 Spain and Holy Roman Empire ally against France	
1683 Turks besiege Vienna	
1685 Edict of Nantes revoked and Huguenots leave France	
1689 English Parliament passes Bill of Rights	
1699 Habsburgs recover Hungary from Turks	

1661 Louis XIV takes power in France
1667 John Milton, *Paradise Lost*
1667-70 Main façade of Louvre
1687 Isaac Newton publishes *Principia Mathematica*
1696 Peter I, the Great, becomes Tsar of Russia
1696-1770 Giovanni Battista Tiepolo

S. Carlo alle Quatro Fontane, Rome, Italy, detail, begun 1633

Troja Palace, Prague, Czech Republic, 1679-96

1700

1700-21 Great Northern War between Sweden and Russia and its allies	
1702-1713 War of Spanish Succession (ends with Peace of Utrecht)	
1703 St Petersburg founded	
1704 "Grand Alliance" of Holland, England and Austria defeat France at Blenheim	
1707 Act of Union between England and Scotland	
1730 Methodism founded by John and Charles Wesley	
1740-86 Prussia under Frederick the Great	
1740-8 War of Austrian Succession	

- c.1700 Rococo c.1750
- c.1700 Age of Enlightenment 1789
- c.1730 Gothic Revival c.1780

1719 Daniel Defoe, *Robinson Crusoe*
1720 J.S.Bach *Brandenburg Concertos*
1726 Jonathan Swift, *Gulliver's Travels*
1728-92 Robert Adam
1742 Handel's *Messiah*
1746-1828 Goya
1748-1825 Jacques-Louis David
1749-1832 Johann Wolfgang von Goethe

Baroque interior, St John Nepomuk, Munich, Germany, 1732-46

Amalienburg Palace, near Munich, Rococo detail and decoration, 1734

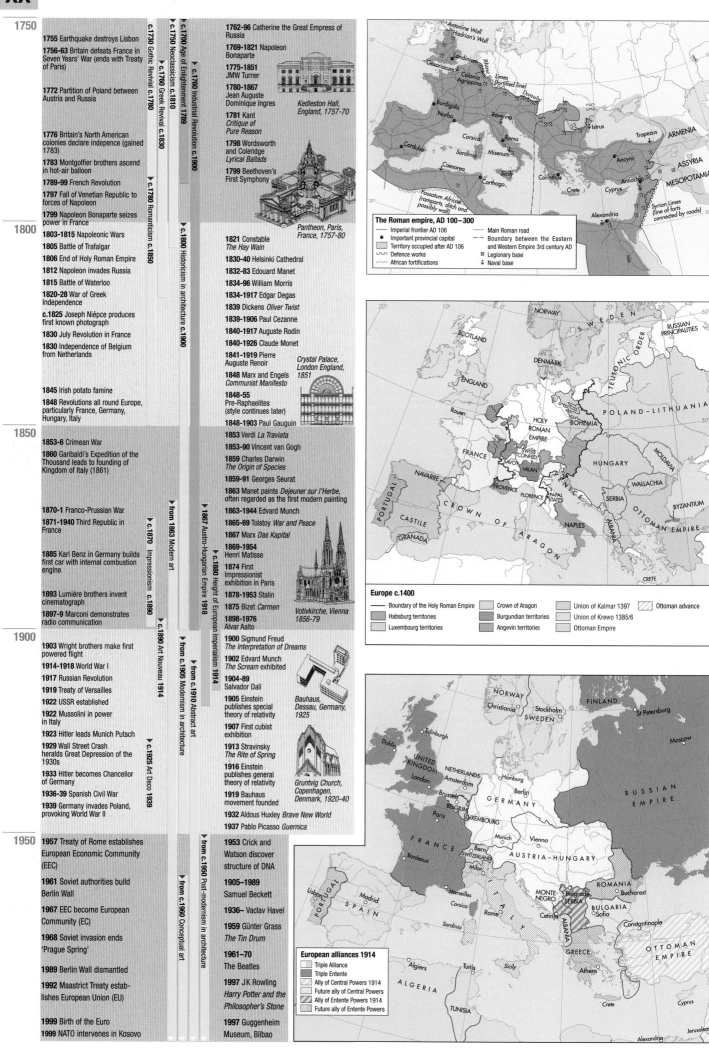

1750

1755 Earthquake destroys Lisbon

1756-63 Britain defeats France in Seven Years' War (ends with Treaty of Paris)

1772 Partition of Poland between Austria and Russia

1776 Britain's North American colonies declare indepence (gained 1783)

1783 Montgolfier brothers ascend in hot-air balloon

1789-99 French Revolution

1797 Fall of Venetian Republic to forces of Napoleon

1799 Napoleon Bonaparte seizes power in France

1800

1803-1815 Napoleonic Wars

1805 Battle of Trafalgar

1806 End of Holy Roman Empire

1812 Napoleon invades Russia

1815 Battle of Waterloo

1820-28 War of Greek Independence

c.1825 Joseph Niépce produces first known photograph

1830 July Revolution in France

1830 Independence of Belgium from Netherlands

1845 Irish potato famine

1848 Revolutions all round Europe, particularly France, Germany, Hungary, Italy

1850

1853-6 Crimean War

1860 Garibaldi's Expedition of the Thousand leads to founding of Kingdom of Italy (1861)

1870-1 Franco-Prussian War

1871-1940 Third Republic in France

1885 Karl Benz in Germany builds first car with internal combustion engine

1893 Lumiére brothers invent cinematograph

1897-9 Marconi demonstrates radio communication

1900

1903 Wright brothers make first powered flight

1914-1918 World War I

1917 Russian Revolution

1919 Treaty of Versailles

1922 USSR established

1922 Mussolini in power in Italy

1923 Hitler leads Munich Putsch

1929 Wall Street Crash heralds Great Depression of the 1930s

1933 Hitler becomes Chancellor of Germany

1936-39 Spanish Civil War

1939 Germany invades Poland, provoking World War II

1950

1957 Treaty of Rome establishes European Economic Community (EEC)

1961 Soviet authorities build Berlin Wall

1967 EEC become European Community (EC)

1968 Soviet invasion ends 'Prague Spring'

1989 Berlin Wall dismantled

1992 Maastrict Treaty establishes European Union (EU)

1999 Birth of the Euro

1999 NATO intervenes in Kosovo

---

c.1730 Gothic Revival c.1780

c.1760 Greek Revival c.1830

c.1780 Neoclassicism c.1810

c.1780 Romanticism c.1850

c.1870 Impressionism c.1890

c.1890 Art Nouveau 1914

c.1925 Art Deco 1939

---

c.1700 Age of Enlightenment 1789

c.1760 Industrial Revolution c.1900

c.1800 Historicism in architecture c.1900

from 1863 Modern art

from c.1905 Modernism in architecture

from c.1910 Abstract art

from c.1950 Post-modernism in architecture

from c.1960 Conceptual art

1867 Austro-Hungarian Empire 1918

c.1880 Height of European imperialism 1914

1762-96 Catherine the Great Empress of Russia

1769-1821 Napoleon Bonaparte

1775-1851 JMW Turner

1780-1867 Jean Auguste Dominique Ingres

1781 Kant Critique of Pure Reason

1798 Wordsworth and Coleridge Lyrical Ballads

1799 Beethoven's First Symphony

1821 Constable The Hay Wain

1830-40 Helsinki Cathedral

1832-83 Edouard Manet

1834-96 William Morris

1834-1917 Edgar Degas

1839 Dickens Oliver Twist

1839-1906 Paul Cezanne

1840-1917 Auguste Rodin

1840-1926 Claude Monet

1841-1919 Pierre Auguste Renoir

1848 Marx and Engels Communist Manifesto

1848-55 Pre-Raphaelites (style continues later)

1848-1903 Paul Gauguin

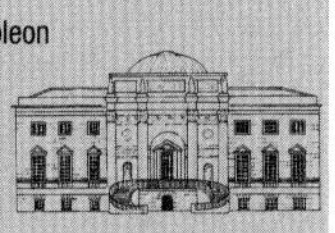

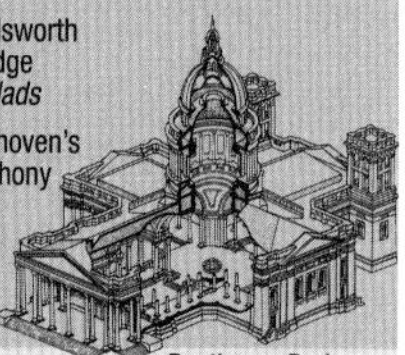

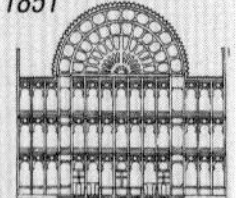

1853 Verdi La Traviata

1853-90 Vincent van Gogh

1859 Charles Darwin The Origin of Species

1859-91 Georges Seurat

1863 Manet paints Dejeuner sur l'Herbe, often regarded as the first modern painting

1863-1944 Edvard Munch

1865-69 Tolstoy War and Peace

1867 Marx Das Kapital

1869-1954 Henri Matisse

1874 First Impressionist exhibition in Paris

1878-1953 Stalin

1875 Bizet Carmen

1898-1976 Alvar Aalto

1900 Sigmund Freud The Interpretation of Dreams

1902 Edvard Munch The Scream exhibited

1904-89 Salvador Dali

1905 Einstein publishes special theory of relativity

1907 First cubist exhibition

1913 Stravinsky The Rite of Spring

1916 Einstein publishes general theory of relativity

1919 Bauhaus movement founded

1932 Aldous Huxley Brave New World

1937 Pablo Picasso Guernica

1953 Crick and Watson discover structure of DNA

1905–1989 Samuel Beckett

1936– Vaclav Havel

1959 Günter Grass The Tin Drum

1961–70 The Beatles

1997 JK Rowling Harry Potter and the Philosopher's Stone

1997 Guggenheim Museum, Bilbao

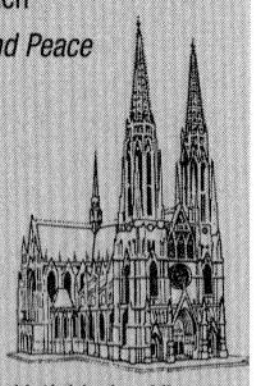

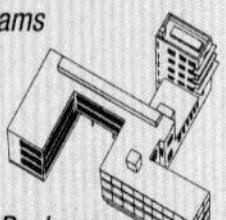

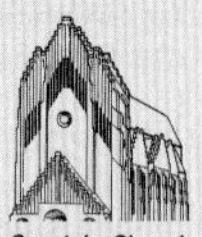

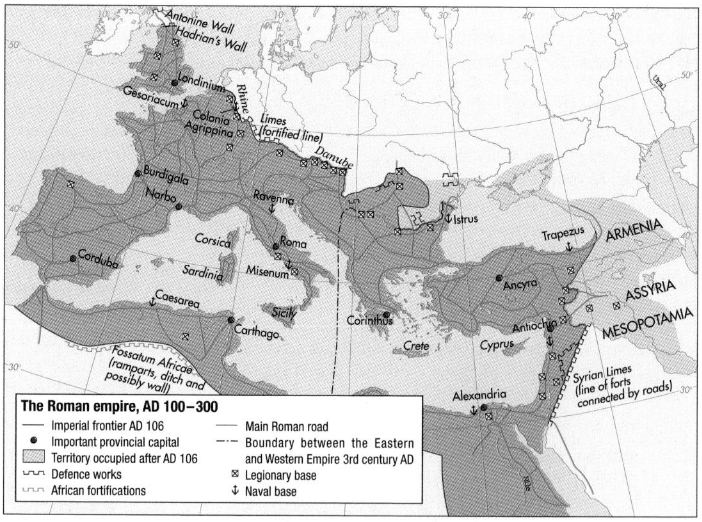

Kedleston Hall, England, 1757-70

Pantheon, Paris, France, 1757-80

Crystal Palace, London England, 1851

Votivkirche, Vienna 1856-79

Bauhaus, Dessau, Germany, 1925

Gruntvig Church, Copenhagen, Denmark, 1920-40

The Roman empire, AD 100–300
- Imperial frontier AD 106
- Important provincial capital
- Territory occupied after AD 106
- Defence works
- African fortifications
- Main Roman road
- Boundary between the Eastern and Western Empire 3rd century AD
- Legionary base
- Naval base

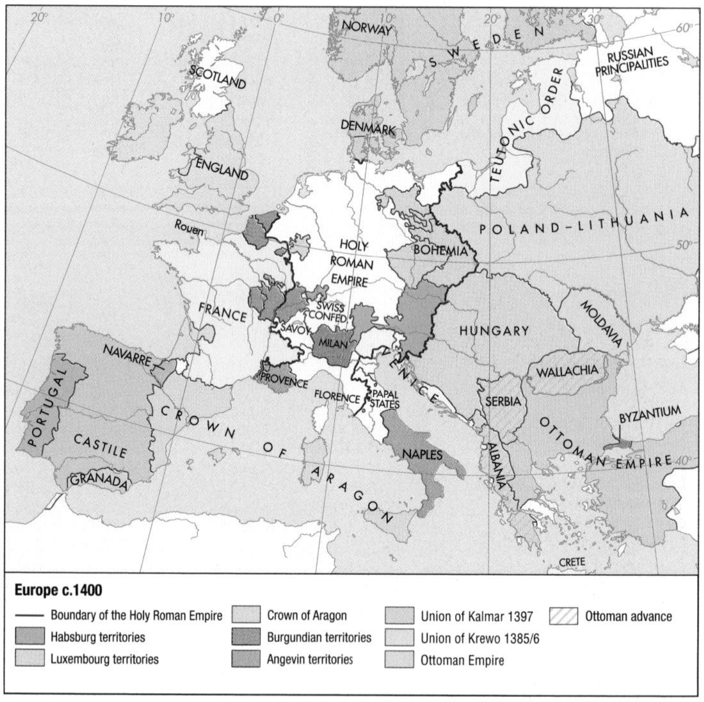

Europe c.1400
- Boundary of the Holy Roman Empire
- Habsburg territories
- Luxembourg territories
- Crown of Aragon
- Burgundian territories
- Angevin territories
- Union of Kalmar 1397
- Union of Krewo 1385/6
- Ottoman Empire
- Ottoman advance

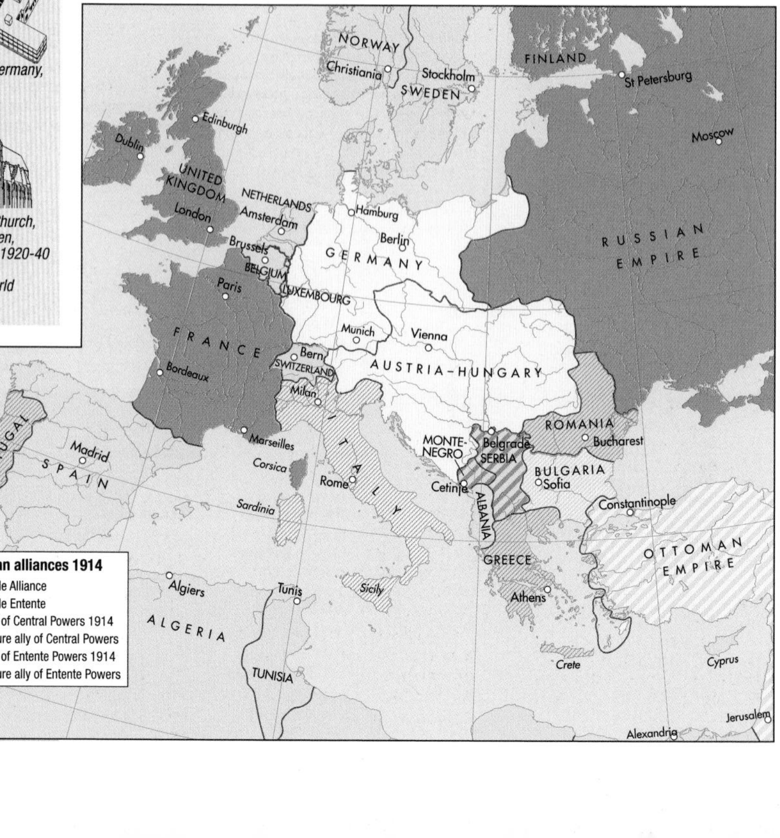

European alliances 1914
- Triple Alliance
- Triple Entente
- Ally of Central Powers 1914
- Future ally of Central Powers
- Ally of Entente Powers 1914
- Future ally of Entente Powers

European politics and economics

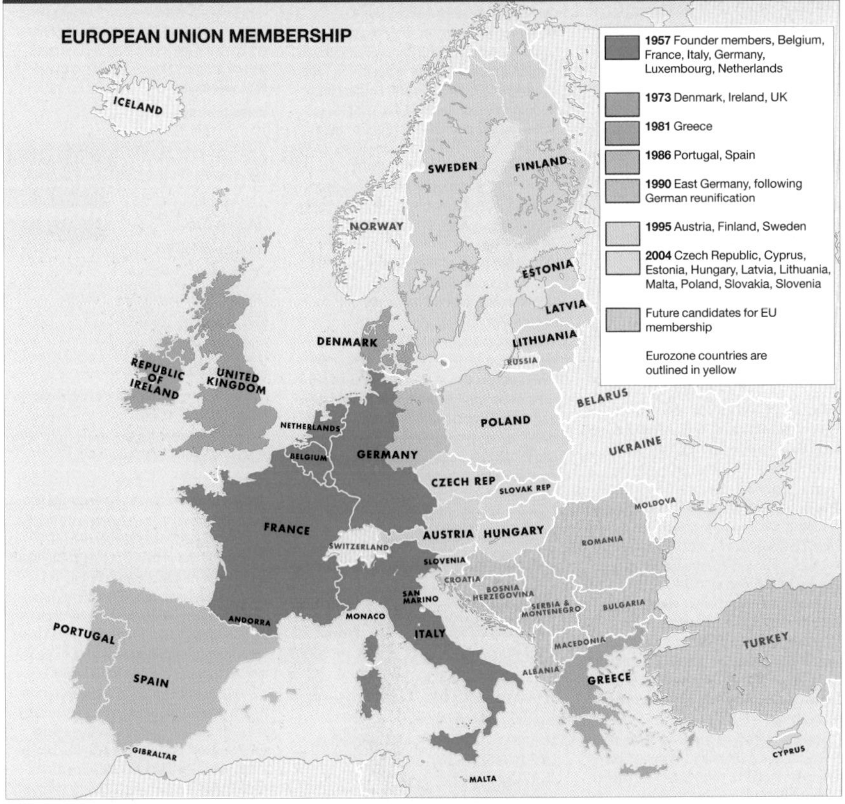
EUROPEAN UNION MEMBERSHIP
1957 Founder members, Belgium, France, Italy, Germany, Luxembourg, Netherlands
1973 Denmark, Ireland, UK
1981 Greece
1986 Portugal, Spain
1990 East Germany, following German reunification
1995 Austria, Finland, Sweden
2004 Czech Republic, Cyprus, Estonia, Hungary, Latvia, Lithuania, Malta, Poland, Slovakia, Slovenia
Future candidates for EU membership
Eurozone countries are outlined in yellow
ICELAND
SWEDEN
FINLAND
NORWAY
ESTONIA
LATVIA
LITHUANIA
RUSSIA
DENMARK
REPUBLIC OF IRELAND
UNITED KINGDOM
BELARUS
POLAND
NETHERLANDS
BELGIUM
GERMANY
UKRAINE
CZECH REP
SLOVAK REP
MOLDOVA
FRANCE
AUSTRIA
HUNGARY
SWITZERLAND
ROMANIA
SLOVENIA
CROATIA
BOSNIA HERZEGOVINA
SAN MARINO
SERBIA & MONTENEGRO
BULGARIA
ANDORRA
MONACO
PORTUGAL
ITALY
MACEDONIA
TURKEY
ALBANIA
GREECE
SPAIN
GIBRALTAR
CYPRUS
MALTA

Albania *Shqipëria*

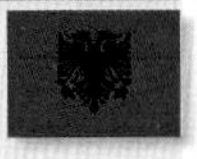

Area 28,748 sq km (11,100 sq miles)
Population 3,582,205
Capital Tirana / Tiranë (300,000)
Languages Albanian (official), Greek
GDP 2002 US$4,400
Currency Lek = 100 Quindars
Government multiparty republic
Head of state President Alfred Moisiu, 2002
Head of government Prime Minister Fatos Nano, Socialist Party, 2002
Events Government wishes to sign an association accord with the EU but has been told that political and economic reforms must progress further before this can happen. Preliminary results for the General Election were declared on 14 July 2005, with Sali Berisha's Democratic Party in the lead, but the incumbent Socialist Party protested the result.
Economy 56% of the workforce are engaged in agriculture. Private ownership of land has been encouraged since 1991. Crops include fruits, maize, olives, potatoes, sugar beet, vegetables, and wheat. Livestock farming is also important. Chromite, copper, and nickel are exported. Other resources include oil, brown coal and hydroelectricity.
Website www.parlament.al

Andorra *Principat d'Andorra*

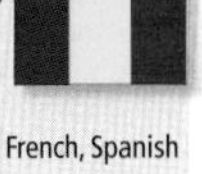

Area 468 sq km (181 sq miles)
Population 69,150
Capital Andorra la Vella (22,000)
Languages Catalan (official), French, Spanish
GDP 2002 US$19,000
Currency Euro = 100 cents
Government independent state and co-principality
Head of state co-princes: Joan Enric Vives Sicilia, Bishop of Urgell, 2003 and Jacques Chirac (see France), 1995
Head of government Chief Executive Albert Pintat, 2005
Events In 1993 a new democratic constitution was adopted that reduced the roles of the President of France and the Bishop of Urgell to purely constitutional figureheads.
Economy The main sources of income include agriculture; the sale of water and hydroelectricity to Catalonia; tourism, particularly skiing.
Website www.andorra.ad

Austria *Österreich*

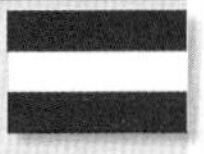

Area 83,859 sq km (32,377 sq miles)
Population 8,188,000
Capital Vienna / Wien (1,560,000)
Languages German (official)
GDP 2002 US$27,900
Currency Euro = 100 cents
Government federal republic
Head of state President Heinz Fischer, Social Democrats, 2004
Head of government Federal Chancellor Wolfgang Schüssel, People's Party, 2000
Events In general elections in 1999, the extreme right Freedom Party, under Jörg Haider, made gains at the expense of the Social Democrats. He subsequently resigned as leader. People's Party electoral win in 2002 wasn't sufficient to form a government so a new government coalition was formed with the Freedom Party after failure of talks with the Social Democrats and the Greens. As a result Chancellor Schüssel is widely deemed to have moved to the right having introduced the toughest asylum laws in Europe. Freedom Party suffered heavy losses in the European elections of June 2004. In July 2004 President Fischer's predecessor Thomas Klestil died of a heart attack one day before Heinz Fischer was due to take his place. The Freedom Party split in April 2005 when its former leader Jörg Haider left to set up the Alliance for Austria's Future.
Economy Austria is a wealthy nation which, despite plenty of hydroelectric power, is dependent on the import of fossil fuels. Austria's leading economic activity is the manufacture of metals. Dairy and livestock farming are the principal agricultural activities. Tourism is an important industry.
Website www.austria.gv.at/e/

Belarus

Area 207,600 sq km (80,154 sq miles)
Population 10,322,151
Capital Minsk (1,677,000)
Languages Belarussian, Russian (both official)
GDP 2002 US$8,700
Currency Belarussian rouble = 100 kopek
Government Republic
Head of state President Alexander Lukashenko, 1994
Head of government Prime Minister Sergei Sidorsky, 2003
Events Belarus was very badly contaminated by the Chernobyl disaster in April 1986, lying as it does just to the north of the reactor. Belarus is a founder member of the CIS, of which Minsk is the administrative centre. In 1997, despite opposition from nationalists, Belarus signed a Union Treaty with Russia, committing it to integration with Russia. Currency union scheduled for 2008. As a result of a referendum in 1996 the president increased his power at the expense of parliament. He was re-elected in 2001 though the elections were widely deemed undemocratic by western observers and his rule is seen as a dictatorship. A referendum in October 2004 showed popular support for the abolition of the rule preventing Lukashenko from standing for a third term. However, there were similar accusations of widespread fraud in both that and the general elections held at the same time.
Economy Belarus has faced problems in the transition to a free-market economy. In 1995 an agreement with Russia enabled Belarus to receive subsidised fuel. Relationships between Belarus and Russia became strained in 2004 when the Russian Foreign Ministry accused Lukashenka of protectionism and pursuing policies detrimental to economic development. Agriculture, especially meat and dairy farming, is important.
Website http://government.by/eng/sovmin/index.htm

Belgium *Belgique*

Area 30,528 sq km (11,786 sq miles)
Population 10,289,088
Capital Brussels/Bruxelles (136,000)
Languages Dutch, French, German (all official)
GDP 2002 US$29,200
Currency Euro = 100 cents
Government federal constitutional monarchy
Head of state King Albert II, 1993
Head of government Prime Minister Guy Verhofstadt, Flemish Liberal Democrats, 1999
Events In 1993 Belgium adopted a federal system of government, each of the regions having its own parliament. The socialist and liberal parties have two thirds of the seats in parliament, each main party is split into two – one half for the Flemish and one half for the Walloons.
Economy Belgium is a major trading nation. The leading activity is manufacturing and products include steel and chemicals. Agriculture employs only 3% of the workforce, but the country is mostly self-sufficient. Barley and wheat are the chief crops, but the most valuable activities are dairy farming and livestock rearing.
Website www.belgium.be

Bosnia-Herzegovina *Bosna i Hercegovina*

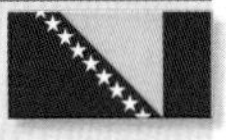

Area 51,197 sq km (19,767 sq miles)
Population 3,989,000
Capital Sarajevo (529,000)
Languages Serbian/Croatian
GDP 2002 US$1,900
Currency Convertible Marka = 100 convertible pfenniga
Government federal republic
Head of state Chairman of the Presidency Ivo Miro Jovic, Croatian Democratic Union, 2005
Head of government Chairman of the Council of Ministers Adnan Terzic, Muslim Party of Democratic Action, 2002
Events In 1992 a referendum approved independence from the Yugoslav federation. The Bosnian Serb population was against independence and in the resulting war occupied over two-thirds of the land. Croat forces seized other parts of the country. The 1995 Dayton Peace Accord ended the war and set up the Bosnian Muslim/Croat Federation and the Bosnian Serb Republic, each with their own president, government, parliament, military and police, there is also a central Bosnian government and rotating presidency the other members of which are Sulejman Tihic (Muslim Party of Democratic Action) and Borislav Paravac (Serb Democratic Party). The office of High Representative has the power to impose decision where the authorities are unable to agree or where political or economic interests are affected. In 2005, Paddy Ashdown sacked Ivo Jovic's predecessor Dragan Covic. Eufor troops took over from the NATO-led force as peacekeepers in 2004.
Economy Excluding Macedonia, Bosnia was the least developed of the former republics of Yugoslavia. Currently receiving substantial aid, though this will be reduced.
Website www.fbihvlada.gov.ba

Bulgaria *Bulgariya*

Area 110,912 sq km (42,822 sq miles)
Population 7,537,929
Capital Sofia (1,139,000)
Languages Bulgarian (official), Turkish
GDP 2002 US$6,500
Currency Lev = 100 stotinki
Government multiparty republic
Head of state President Georgi Purvanov, Bulgarian Socialist Party, 2002
Head of government Prime Minister Simeon Saxe-Coburg-Gotha, National Movement for Simeon II, 2001
Events In 1990 the first non-communist president for 40 years, Zhelyu Zhelev, was elected. A new constitution in 1991 saw the adoption of free-market reforms. Former king Simeon Saxe-Coburg-Gotha was the first ex-monarch in post-communist eastern Europe to return to power. He leads a coalition government, has gained membership of NATO for Bulgaria and signed an accession treaty with the EU in April 2005 allowing for EU membership in 2007 subject to reforms being satisfactory. Parliament voted in early 2005 to withdraw troops from Iraq by the end of 2005. Elections in June 2005 were inclusive. Sergei Stanishev's Socialist Party was originally asked to form a government but after parliament rejected his choice of ministers, the president asked the NMS to form a coalition.
Economy Bulgaria is a lower-middle-income developing country, faced with a difficult transition to a market economy. Manufacturing is the leading economic activity but has outdated technology. The main products are chemicals, metals, machinery and textiles. Mineral reserves include molybdenum. Wheat and maize are the main crops. The valleys of the Maritsa are ideal for winemaking, plums and tobacco. Tourism is increasing rapidly.
Website www.president.bg/en

Croatia *Hrvatska*

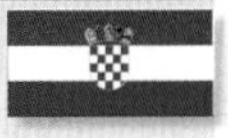

Area 56,538 sq km (21,829 sq miles)
Population 4,422,000
Capital Zagreb (779,000)
Languages Croatian
GDP 2002 US$ 9,800
Currency Kuna = 100 lipas
Government multiparty republic
Head of state President Stjepan Mesic, 2000
Head of government Prime Minister Ivo Sanader, Croatian Democratic Union, 2003
Events A 1991 referendum voted overwhelmingly in favour of independence. Serb-dominated areas took up arms to remain in the federation. Serbia armed Croatian Serbs, war broke out between Serbia and Croatia, and Croatia lost much territory. In 1992 United Nations peacekeeping troops were deployed. In 1995 Croatian government forces occupied Krajina and 150,000 Serbs fled. Following the Dayton Peace Accord of 1995, Croatia and Yugoslavia established diplomatic relations. An agreement between the Croatian government and Croatian Serbs provided for the eventual reintegration of Krajina into Croatia in 1998. PM Sanader leads a minority government with the support of many smaller parties. Croatia is a partner-country with NATO and applied for EU membership in 2003. The start-date for accession talks has been postponed because of the lack of progress in arresting some war crimes suspects, particularly Gen Ante Gotvina.
Economy The wars have badly disrupted Croatia's relatively prosperous economy. Croatia has a wide range of manufacturing industries, such as steel, chemicals, oil refining, and wood products. Agriculture is the principal employer. Crops include maize, soya beans, sugar beet and wheat.
Website www.croatia.hr

Czech Republic *Česka Republica*

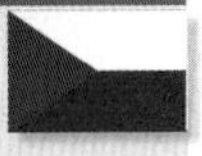

Area 78,864 sq km (30,449 sq miles)
Population 10,249,000
Capital Prague/Praha (1,193,000)
Languages Czech (official), Moravian
GDP 2002 US$15,300
Currency Czech Koruna = 100 haler
Government multiparty republic
Head of state President Václav Klaus, 2003
Head of government Prime Minister Jiri Paroubek, Czech Social Democratic Party, 2005
Events Free elections were held in 1990, resulting in the re-election of Vaclav Havel. In 1992 the government agreed to the secession of the Slovak Republic, and on 1 January 1993 the Czech Republic was created. The Czech Republic was granted full membership of NATO in 1999 and joined the EU in May 2004. The coalition government has a small majority and is formed of Social Democrats and an alliance of Christian Democrats and Freedom Union. The country still experiences problems of discrimination against the Roma. The opposition Civic Democratic Party with their agenda of not ceding too much power to the EU were the winners in the European elections of June 2004, as a result of which Prime Minister Vladimir Spidla resigned, to be replaced by Stanislav Gross, who then resigned in April 2005 over a financial scandal.
Economy The country has deposits of coal, uranium, iron ore, magnesite, tin and zinc. Industries include chemicals, beer, iron and steel, and machinery. Private ownership of land is gradually being restored. Agriculture employs 12% of the workforce. Livestock raising is important. Crops include grains, fruit, and hops for brewing. Prague is now a major tourist destination.
Website www.czech.cz

Denmark *Danmark*

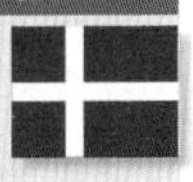

Area 43,094 sq km (16,638 sq miles)
Population 5,384,000
Capital Copenhagen / København (499,000)
Languages Danish (official)
GDP 2002 US$28,900
Currency Krone = 100 øre
Government parliamentary monarchy
Head of state Queen Margrethe II, 1972
Head of government Prime Minister Anders Fogh Rasmussen, Venstre (Left) Party, 2001

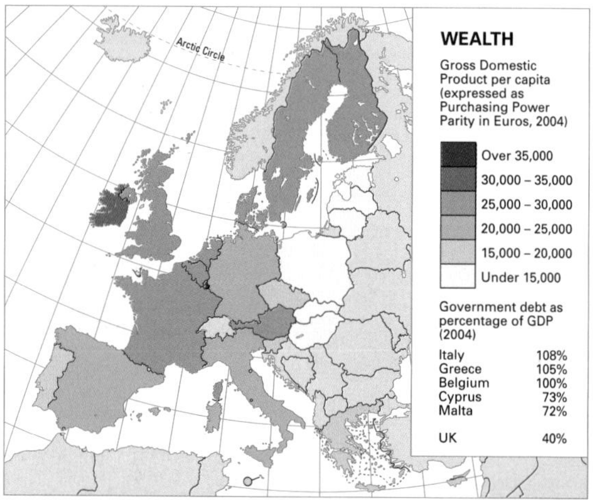

WEALTH

Gross Domestic Product per capita (expressed as Purchasing Power Parity in Euros, 2004)

- Over 35,000
- 30,000 – 35,000
- 25,000 – 30,000
- 20,000 – 25,000
- 15,000 – 20,000
- Under 15,000

Government debt as percentage of GDP (2004)

Italy	108%
Greece	105%
Belgium	100%
Cyprus	73%
Malta	72%
UK	40%

Events In 1992 Denmark rejected the Maastricht Treaty, but reversed the decision in a 1993 referendum. In 1998 the Amsterdam Treaty was ratified by a further referendum. Currency pegged to Euro but still independent. The government is a coalition formed with the Conservative Party. Anti-immigration policies are backed by the well-supported far-right Danish People's Party. Rasmussen wants a second referendum on the Euro. The opposition Social Democrats were clear winners in the European elections of June 2004, though this could be down to opposition to the government's support for the war in Iraq, and snap elections in February 2005 gave Rasmussen's Venstre Party a second term in power.
Economy Danes enjoy a high standard of living. Denmark is self-sufficient in oil and natural gas. Products include furniture, electrical goods and textiles. Services, including tourism, form the largest sector (63% of GDP). Farming employs only 4% of the workforce but is highly productive. Fishing is also important.
Website www.denmark.dk

Estonia *Eesti*

Area 45,100 sq km (17,413 sq miles)
Population 1,408,556
Capital Tallinn (418,000)
Languages Estonian (official), Russian
GDP 2002 US$11,000
Currency Kroon = 100 sents
Government multiparty republic
Head of state President Arnold Rüütel, Estonian People's Union, 2001
Head of government Prime Minister Andrus Ansip, Reform Party 2005
Events coalition between the centre-right Reform Party, the centre-left Centre Party and the centre-left People's Party. The previous coalition broken up when Juhan Parts resigned after a vote of no confidence in his justice minister's proposed anti-corruption measures.
Economy Privatisation and free-trade reforms have increased foreign investment and trade with the EU. Chief natural resources are oil shale and forests. Manufactures include petrochemicals, fertilisers and textiles. Agriculture and fishing are important. Barley, potatoes and oats are major crops.
Website www.riik.ee/en

Finland *Suomi*

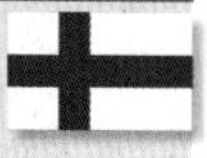

Area 338,145 sq km (130,557 sq miles)
Population 5,190,000
Capital Helsinki (549,000)
Languages Finnish, Swedish (both official)
GDP 2002 US$25,800
Currency Euro = 100 cents
Government multiparty republic
Head of state President Tarja Kaarina Halonen, 2000
Head of government Prime Minister Matti Vanhanen, Centre Party, 2003
Events In 1986 Finland became a member of EFTA, and in 1995 joined the EU. A new constitution was established in March 2000. A coalition was set up between the Social Democrats and the Swedish Peoples' Party after a close election result in 2003.
Economy Forests are Finland's most valuable resource, with wood and paper products accounting for 35% of exports. Engineering, shipbuilding and textile industries have grown. Also a leading light in the telecoms industry. Farming employs 9% of the workforce. Livestock and dairy farming are the chief activities.
Website www.government.fi

France

Area 551,500 sq km (212,934 sq miles)
Population 60,181,000
Capital Paris (2,152,000)
Languages French (official), Breton, Occitan
GDP 2002 US$26,000
Currency Euro = 100 cents
Government multiparty republic
Head of state President Jacques Chirac, Assembly for the Republic, 1995
Head of government Prime Minister Dominique de Villepin, Democratie Liberale, 2005
Events In 2002 voter apathy led to FN leader Jean-Marie Le Pen reaching second round of voting in presidential elections above Lionel Jospin, who resigned as PM after the presidential elections which Jacques Chirac won with 82% of the vote. As a result of their opposition to the 2003 war in Iraq France and Germany have forged closer ties while relations with the UK and the US have been put under some strain. The US believes that France is being ungrateful for their assistance in WWII some 60 years before. The opposition Socialist Party were clear victors in the European elections of June 2004. The resounding 'no' vote in the referendum on the European constitution in May 2005 led both to the resignation of PM Jean-Pierre Raffarin and further decline in the relationship between Jacques Chirac and Tony Blair over the UK's rebate and Common Agricultural Policy subsidies for French farmers.
Economy France is a leading industrial nation. It is the world's fourth-largest manufacturer of cars. Industries include chemicals and steel. It is the leading producer of farm products in western Europe. Livestock and dairy farming are vital sectors. It is the world's second-largest producer of cheese and wine. Tourism is a major industry.
Website www.elysee.fr

Germany *Deutschland*

Area 357,022 sq km (137,846 sq miles)
Population 82,398,000
Capital Berlin (3,387,000)
Languages German (official)
GDP 2002 US$26,200
Currency Euro = 100 cents
Government federal multiparty republic
Head of state President Horst Köhler, Christian Democratic Union, 2004
Head of government Chancellor Angela Merkel, CDU in coalition with SPD, 2005
Events Germany is a major supporter of the European Union, and former chancellor Helmut Kohl was the driving force behind the creation of the Euro. During 2002, state elections in the former German Democratic Republic saw massive losses for the Social Democrats. As a result of their opposition to the 2003 war in Iraq Germany and France have forged closer ties. Economy not as strong as before as the many still heading West from the East exacerbate the imbalance. The European constitution was ratified by Parliament. In July 2005, Schröder triggered early general elections. Subject to ratification the CDU and SPD formed a coalition in mid-October, with the SPD holding eight seats and the CDU six.
Economy Germany is one of the world's greatest economic powers. Services form the largest economic sector. Machinery and transport equipment account for 50% of exports. It is the world's third-largest car producer. Other major products: ships, iron, steel, petroleum, tyres. It has the world's second-largest lignite mining industry. Other minerals: copper, potash, lead, salt, zinc, aluminium. Germany is the world's second-largest producer of hops and beer, and fifth-largest of wine. Other products: cheese and milk, barley, rye, pork.
Website www.deutschland.de

Greece *Ellas*

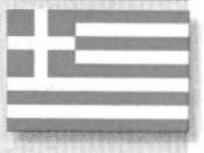

Area 131,957 sq km (50,948 sq miles)
Population 10,665,000
Capital Athens / Athina (772,000)
Languages Greek (official)
GDP 2002 US$19,100
Currency Euro = 100 cents
Government multiparty republic
Head of state President Karolos Papoulias, Panhellenic Socialist Movement (PASOK), 2005
Head of government Prime Minister Costas Karamanlis, New Democracy Party, 2004
Events In 1981 Greece joined the EU and Andreas Papandreou became Greece's first socialist prime minister, 1981-89 and 1993-96. PM Costas Karamanlis is the nephew of former Greek president Constantine Karamanlis. The issue of Cyprus is still contentious in Greece's relations with Turkey, with the southern two-thirds still being Greek Cypriot and no agreement on unification yet reached. In July 2004 Greece unexpectedly won the European football championships. The 28th Olympiad took place in Greece in August 2004. Karolos Papoulias was nominated President by the PM in 2005.
Economy Greece is one of the poorest members of the European Union. Manufacturing is important. Products: textiles, cement, chemicals, metallurgy. Minerals: lignite, bauxite, chromite. Farmland covers 33% of Greece, grazing land 40%. Major crops: tobacco, olives, grapes, cotton, wheat. Livestock are raised. Shipping and tourism are also major sectors.
Website www.greece.gr

Hungary *Magyarorszàg*

Area 93,032 sq km (35,919 sq miles)
Population 10,045,000
Capital Budapest (1,825,000)
Languages Hungarian (official)
GDP 2002 US$13,300
Currency Forint = 100 filler
Government multiparty republic
Head of state President Laszlo Solyom, 2005
Head of government Prime Minister Ferenc Gyurcsany
Events In 1990 multiparty elections were won by the conservative Democratic Forum. In 1999 Hungary joined NATO. Former PM Peter Medgyessy narrowly avoided having to resign in 2002 when he admitted to having worked for the secret services in the late 70s/early 80s, but denied working for the KGB. He oversaw Hungary's accession to the European Union in May 2004 but resigned later in the year after arguments over a cabinet reshuffle with coalition co-members the Free Democrats. Gyurcsany is a multi-millionaire and pro free enterprise, but also supports welfare for the needy. Hungary still has problems with discrimination against the Roma community, though in the European elections of 2004 a member of this ethnic group was elected for the first time. Hungary is aiming to adopt the Euro in 2010.
Economy Since the early 1990s, Hungary has adopted market reforms and privatisation programmes. The economy has suffered from the collapse in exports to the former Soviet Union and Yugoslavia. The manufacture of machinery and transport is the most valuable sector. Hungary's resources include bauxite, coal and natural gas. Major crops include grapes for wine-making, maize, potatoes, sugar beet and wheat. Tourism is a growing sector.
Website www.magyarorszag.hu/angol

Iceland *Island*

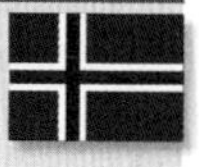

Area 103,000 sq km (39,768 sq miles)
Population 280,798
Capital Reykjavik (108,000)
Languages Icelandic
GDP 2002 US$30,200
Currency Krona = 100 aurar
Government multiparty republic
Head of state President Olafur Ragnar Grimsson, 1996
Head of government Prime Minister Halldor Asgrimsson, Progressive Party, 2004
Events In 1944, a referendum decisively voted to sever links with Denmark, and Iceland became a fully independent republic. In 1946 it joined NATO. The USA maintained military bases on Iceland after WWII. In 1970 Iceland joined the European Free Trade Association. The extension of Iceland's fishing limits in 1958 and 1972 precipitated the "Cod War" with the UK. In 1977, the UK agreed not to fish within Iceland's 370km fishing limits. The continuing US military presence remains a political issue. David Oddson leader of the Independence Party stood down as PM in September 2004 and the leader of coalition partner the Progressive Party Halldor Asgrimsson took over the premiership.
Economy Fishing and fish processing are major industries, accounting for 80% of Iceland's exports. Barely 1% of the land is used to grow crops, and 23% is used for grazing sheep and cattle. Iceland is self-sufficient in meat and dairy products. Vegetables and fruits are grown in greenhouses. Manufacturing – aluminium, cement, electrical equipment and fertilizers. Geothermal power is an important energy source. Overfishing is an economic problem.
Website http://government.is

Ireland, Republic of
Eire

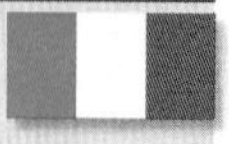

Area 70,273 sq km (27,132 sq miles)
Population 3,924,000
Capital Dublin (482,000)
Languages Irish, English (both official)
GDP 2002 US$29,300
Currency Euro = 100 cents
Government multiparty republic
Head of state President Mary McAleese, 1997
Head of government Taoiseach Bertie Ahern, Fianna Fáil, 1997
Events The Anglo-Irish Agreement (1985) gave Ireland a consultative role in the affairs of Northern Ireland. Following a 1995 referendum, divorce was legalised. Abortion remains a contentious political issue. In 1997 elections Bertie Ahern became taoiseach and Mary McAleese became president. In the Good Friday Agreement of 1998 the Irish Republic gave up its constitutional claim to Northern Ireland and a North-South Ministerial Council was established. Sinn Fein got its first seats in the European elections of June 2004.
Economy Ireland has benefited greatly from its membership of the European Union. Grants have enabled the modernisation of farming, which employs 14% of the workforce. Major products include cereals, cattle and dairy products, sheep, sugar beet and potatoes. Fishing is important. Traditional sectors, such as brewing, distilling and textiles, have been supplemented by high-tech industries, such as electronics. Tourism is the most important component of the service industry.
Website www.irlgov.ie

Italy *Italia*

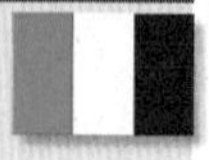

Area 301,318 sq km (116,338 sq miles)
Population 57,998,000
Capital Rome / Roma (2,460,000)
Languages Italian (official)
GDP 2002 US$25,100
Currency Euro = 100 cents
Government multiparty republic
Head of state President Carlo Ciampi, 1997
Head of government Silvio Berlusconi, Forza Italia, 2001
Events In 2001 Silvio Berlusconi won the general election as leader of the Casa della Libertà coalition. In 2003 he was tried for matters relating to his business affairs in the 1980s, however the trial was halted when parliament approved a law giving serving prime ministers immunity from prosecution. This law was subsequently thrown out and Berlusconi's trial restarted in April 2004, and he was acquitted in December of that year. In April 2005, his centre-right coalition fell after poor results in regional elections and he resigned, but bounced back just a few days later with a substantially unchanged coalition. The close relationship between media and politics is a point of contention due to Berlusconi's ownership of a media empire.
Economy Italy's main industrial region is the north-western triangle of Milan, Turin and Genoa. It is the world's eighth-largest car and steel producer. Machinery and transport equipment account for 37% of exports. Agricultural production is important. Italy is the world's largest producer of wine. Tourism is a vital economic sector.
Website www.enit.it

Latvia *Latvija*

Area 64,589 sq km (24,942 sq miles)
Population 2,349,000
Capital Riga (793,000)
Languages Latvian (official), Russian
GDP 2002 US$8,900
Currency Lats = 100 santimi
Government multiparty republic
Head of state President Vaira Vike-Freiberga, 1999
Head of government Prime Minister Aigars Kalvitis, People's Party, 2004
Events In 1993 Latvia held its first multiparty elections. President Vaira Vike-Freiberga was re-elected for a second four-year term in June 2003. Latvia became a member of NATO in March 2004 and of the EU in May 2004. People applying for citizenship are now required to pass a Latvian language test, which has caused much upset amongst the one third of the population who are Russian speakers. As a result many are without citizenship, much like their compatriots in Estonia. PM Indulis Emsis was chosen as a result of the resignation of his predecessor just before Latvia's accession to the EU. Only one party in the three-party governing coalition won a seat in the European elections of June 2004, but the turnout was low, as across all countries. After the resignation of the ruling minority coalition in October 2004 following rejection of Indulis Emsis' budget for 2005, a new 4-party coalition was approved by parliament in December.
Economy Latvia is a lower-middle-income country. The country has to import many of the materials needed for manufacturing. Latvia produces only 10% of the electricity it needs, and the rest has to be imported from Belarus, Russia and Ukraine. Manufactures include electronic goods, farm machinery and fertiliser. Farm exports include beef, dairy products and pork.
Website www.lv

Liechtenstein

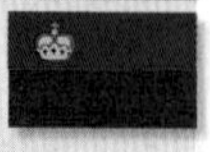

Area 157 sq km (61 sq miles)
Population 33,000
Capital Vaduz (5,000)
Languages German (official)
GDP 2002 US$25,000
Currency Swiss franc = 100 centimes
Government independent principality
Head of state Prince Alois, 2004
Head of government Prime Minister Otmar Hasler, Progressive Citizens Party, 2001
Events Independent principality in western central Europe in a currency and customs union with Switzerland. Women finally got the vote in 1984. The principality joined the UN in 1990. In 2003 the people voted in a referendum to give Prince Hans Adam II new political powers thus rendering the country Europe's only absolute monarchy with the prince having power of veto over the government. Its status as a tax haven has been criticised as it has been alleged that many billions are laundered there each year, the law has therefore been reformed to ensure that anonymity is no longer permitted when opening a bank account. In August 2004 Prince Hans Adam II transferred the day-to-day running of the country to his son Prince Alois, though he did not abdicate and remains titular head of state. Following elections in 2005, the government is made up of 3 ministers from the Progressive Citizens Party and 2 from the People's Union.
Economy Liechtenstein is the fourth-smallest country in the world and one of the richest per capita. Since 1945 it has rapidly developed a specialised manufacturing base. The major part of state revenue is derived from international companies attracted by low taxation rates. Tourism is increasingly important.
Website www.liechtenstein.li

Lithuania *Lietuva*

Area 65,200 sq km (25,173 sq miles)
Population 3,593,000
Capital Vilnius (578,000)
Languages Lithuanian (official), Russian, Polish
GDP 2002 US$8,400
Currency Litas = 100 centai
Government multiparty republic
Head of state President Valdas Adamkus, 2004
Head of government Prime Minister Algirdas Mykolas Brazauskas, Social Democratic Party, 2001
Events The Soviet Union recognised Lithuania as independent in September 1991. In 1993 Soviet troops completed their withdrawal. Valdas Adamkus regained the presidency from Rolandus Paksas after the latter was impeached in April 2004 after being found guilty of leaking classified material and unlawfully granting citizenship to a Russian businessman who had funded his election campaign. His successor was also his predecessor. Lithuania joined NATO in March 2004 and the EU in May 2004. In June 2004 Lithuania fixed the value of the Litas against the Euro with a view to joining in 2007.
Economy Lithuania is a developing country. It is dependent on Russian raw materials. Manufacturing is the most valuable export sector: major products include chemicals, electronic goods and machine tools. Dairy and meat farming and fishing are also important activities.
Website www.lithuania.lt

Luxembourg

Area 2,586 sq km (998 sq miles)
Population 454,000
Capital Luxembourg (77,000)
Languages Luxembourgian / Letzeburgish (official), French, German
GDP 2002 US$44,900
Currency Euro = 100 cents
Government constitutional monarchy (or grand duchy)
Head of state Grand Duke Henri, 2000
Head of government Prime Minister Jean-Claude Juncker, Christian Social People's Party, 1995
Events Following 1994 elections, the Christian Social People's Party (CD) and the Luxembourg Socialist Workers' Party (SOC) formed a coalition government, which lasted until 1999 and was followed by a 5-year coalition with the Democratic Party. Grand Duke Jean abdicated in favour of his son Prince Henri in October 2000. In general elections in 2004, the CD held on to power, again in coalition with the SOC. In 2005 the people voted for the European constitution.
Economy There are rich deposits of iron ore, and Luxembourg is a major producer of iron and steel. Other industries include chemicals, textiles, tourism, banking and electronics. Farmers raise cattle and pigs. Major crops include cereals, fruits and grapes for winemaking. The city of Luxembourg is a major centre of European administration and finance. Its strict laws on secrecy in banking have meant that tax evasion and fraud are prevalent.
Website www.luxembourg.lu

Former Yugoslav Republic of Macedonia *Makedonija*

Area 25,713 sq km (9,927 sq miles)
Population 2,063,000
Capital Skopje (430,000)
Languages Macedonian (official), Albanian
GDP 2002 US$5,100
Currency Denar = 100 deni
Government multiparty republic
Head of state President Branko Crvenkovski, Social Democrat Union, 2004
Head of government Vlado Buckovski, Social Democrats, 2004
Events In 1993 the UN accepted the new republic as a member. In 2001 there was an uprising of rebels demanding greater rights for the ethnic Albanian population. A peace deal was eventually brokered by the late president Boris Trajkovski leading to a new constitution acknowledging the rights of ethnic Albanians. Still retains the FYR prefix due to Greek fears that the names implies territorial ambitions towards the Greek region named Macedonia. President Branko Crvenovski was elected in April 2004 as a result of the death in a plane crash of Boris Trajkovski. He aims to continue the improvement of the country with EU membership as the goal. The government is a coalition of Social Democrat Union and Democratic Union for Integration (Albanian community). In August 2004, proposed expansion of rights and local autonomy for Albanians provoked riots by Macedonian nationalists, but the ensuing referendum was rendered invalid by a low turnout and the measures went through.
Economy Macedonia is a developing country. The poorest of the six former republics of Yugoslavia, its economy was devastated by UN trade damaged by sanctions against Yugoslavia and by the Greek embargo. The GDP is increasing each year and successful privatisation in 2000 boosted the country's reserves to over $700 Million. Manufactures, especially metals, dominate exports. Agriculture employs 17% of the workforce. Major crops include cotton, fruits, maize, tobacco and wheat.
Website www.gov.mk/english

Malta

Area 316 sq km (122 sq miles)
Population 400,420
Capital Valetta (9,000)
Languages Maltese, English (both official)
GDP 2002 US$17,200
Currency Maltese lira = 100 cents
Government multiparty republic
Head of state President Edward Fenech Adami, Christian Democratic Nationalist Party, 2004
Head of government Prime Minister Lawrence Gonzi, Christian Democratic Nationalist Party, 2004
Events In 1990 Malta applied to join the EU. In 1997 the newly elected Malta Labour Party pledged to rescind the application. The Christian Democratic Nationalist Party, led by the pro-European Edward Fenech Adami, regained power in 1998 elections. Malta joined the EU in May 2004.
Economy Malta is an upper-middle-income developing country. Machinery and transport equipment account for more than 50% of exports. Malta's historic naval dockyards are now used for commercial shipbuilding and repair. The state-owned Malta Drydocks is Malta's leading industry. Manufactures include chemicals, electronic equipment and textiles. The largest sector is services, especially tourism. The main crops are barley, fruits, vegetables and wheat. Privatisation of state-controlled companies and liberalisation of markets is still a contentious issue.
Website www.gov.mt

Moldova

Area 33,851 sq km (13,069 sq miles)
Population 4,439,000
Capital Chisinau (658,000)
Languages Moldovan / Romanian (official)
GDP 2002 US$2,600
Currency Leu = 100 bani
Government multiparty republic
Head of state President Vladimir Voronin, Communist Party, 2001
Head of government Prime Minister Vasile Tarlev, Communist Party, 2001
Events In 1994 a referendum rejected reunification with Romania and Parliament voted to join the CIS. A new constitution established a presidential parliamentary republic. In 2001 Vladimir Voronin was elected president. The Transnistria region mainly inhabited by Russian and Ukrainian speakers declared independence from Moldova in 1990 fearing the impact of closer ties with Romania, this independence has never been recognised. Withdrawal of Russian troops from Transnistria still planned but repeatedly falters. Relations with Moscow have cooled in the last few years and Voronin is now actively seeking ties with the west.
Economy Moldova is a lower-middle-income developing economy. Agriculture is important and major products include fruits and grapes for wine-making. Farmers also raise livestock, including dairy cattle and pigs. Moldova has to import materials and fuels for its industries. Major manufactures include agricultural machinery and consumer goods. Exports include food, wine, tobacco, textiles and footwear.
Website www.parliament.md/en.html

Monaco

Area 1.5 sq km (0.6 sq miles)
Population 30,000
Capital Monaco-Ville
Languages French (official), Italian, Monegasque
GDP 2002 US$27,000
Currency Euro = 100 cents
Government principality
Head of state Prince Albert II, 2005
Head of government Minister of State Patrick Leclerque, 2000
Events Monaco has been ruled by the Grimaldi family since the end of the 13th century and been under the protection of France since 1860.
Economy The chief source of income is tourism, attracted by the casinos of Monte Carlo. There is some light industry, including printing, textiles and postage stamps. Also a major banking centre, residents live tax free. The state has been accused of tolerating money laundering.
Website www.monaco.gouv.mc

The Netherlands *Nederland*

Area 41,526 sq km (16,033 sq miles)
Population 16,151,000
Capital Amsterdam (729,000); administrative capital 's-Gravenhage (The Hague) (440,000)
Languages Dutch (official), Frisian
GDP 2002 US$ 27,200
Currency Euro = 100 cents
Government constitutional monarchy
Head of state Queen Beatrix, 1980
Head of government Prime Minister Jan Pieter Balkenende, Christian Democrats, 2002
Events In 2002 Pim Fortuyn, leader of right wing anti-immigrant party Lijst Pim Fortuyn was assassinated. Subsequently Wim Kok lost power to Jan Peter Balkenende who formed a coalition cabinet with the Democrats-66 and VVD (Peoples' Party for Freedom and Democracy). Like the French, the Dutch voters rejected the proposed European constitution in 2005.
Economy The Netherlands has prospered through its close European ties. Private enterprise has successfully combined with progressive social policies. It is highly industrialised. Products include aircraft, chemicals, electronics and machinery. Natural resources include natural gas. Agriculture is intensive and mechanised, employing only 5% of the workforce. Dairy farming is the leading agricultural activity. Major products are cheese, barley, flowers and bulbs.
Website www.holland.com

Norway *Norge*

Area 323,877 sq km (125,049 sq miles)
Population 4,546,000
Capital Oslo (513,000)
Languages Norwegian (official), Lappish, Finnish
GDP 2002 US$33,000
Currency Krone = 100 øre
Government constitutional monarchy
Head of state King Harald V, 1991
Head of government Prime Minister Jens Stoltenberg, Labour, 2005
Events In referenda in 1972 and 1994 Norway rejected joining the EU. A centre-left coalition, the Labour-led 'Red-Green Alliance' won closely contested elections in September 2005.
Economy Norway has one of the world's highest standards of living. Its chief exports are oil and natural gas. Norway is the world's eighth-largest producer of crude oil. Per capita, Norway is the world's largest producer of hydroelectricity. Major manufactures include petroleum products, chemicals, aluminium, wood pulp and paper. The chief farming activities are dairy and meat production, but Norway has to import food. Norway has the largest fish catch in Europe after Russia and continues with whaling despite opposition and the fact that it contravenes the International Whaling Commission ban on whaling.
Website www.norge.no

Poland *Polska*

Area 323,250 sq km (124,807 sq miles)
Population 38,623,000
Capital Warsaw / Warszawa (1,615,000)

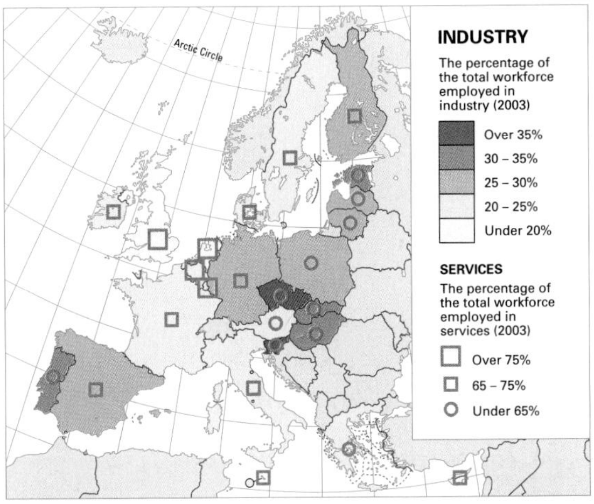

Languages Polish (official)
GDP 2002 US$9,700
Currency Zloty = 100 groszy
Government multiparty republic
Head of state President Aleksander Kwasniewski, Alliance of the Democratic Left (SdRP/SLD), 1995
Head of government Prime Minister Marek Belka, Alliance of the Democratic Left (SdRP/SLD), 2004
Events In 1996 Poland joined the OECD. Poland joined NATO in 1999 and the EU in May 2004. Marek Belka took over as PM on the resignation of Leszek Miller, but then suffered a vote of no-confidence, which he managed to overturn in a subsequent second vote, and pledged to remain in the role until elections in September 2005. Poland sent about 2,000 troops to Iraq in support of the US, the bulk of whom are due to be withdrawn in 2006. In the European elections of June 2004 the ruling party came fifth in a very low turnout of only 20%.
Economy Of the workforce, 27% is employed in agriculture and 37% in industry. Poland is the world's fifth-largest producer of lignite and seventh-largest producer of bituminous coal. Copper ore is also a vital resource. Manufacturing accounts for 24% of exports. Poland is the world's fifth-largest producer of ships. Agriculture remains important. Major crops include barley, potatoes and wheat. Economic growth is slowly returning.
Website www.poland.pl

Portugal

Area 88,797 sq km (34,284 sq miles)
Population 10,102,000
Capital Lisbon / Lisboa (663,000)
Languages Portuguese (official)
GDP 2002 US$19,400
Currency Euro = 100 cents
Government multiparty republic
Head of state President Jorge Sampaio, Socialist Party, 1996
Head of government Jose Socrates, Socialist Party, 2005
Events In 1986 Portugal joined the EU. In 2002 the Social Democrat Party won the election and formed a coalition government with the Popular Party. The opposition Socialist Party were clear victors in European elections of June 2004, a result attributed in part to the ruling party's support for the war in Iraq. Portugal hosted the Euro 2004 football championships in summer 2004. PM Barroso was chosen as president of EU Commission in July 2004 and consequently resigned his premiership. President Sampaio chose Lisbon mayor Pedro Santana Lopes to succeed him. The leader of the Socialists Eduardo Ferro Rodrigues then resigned in protest saying Sampaio should have ordered elections. In the general election in February 2005, the Socialists won an outright majority under their new leader Jose Socrates.
Economy Portugal's commitment to the EU has seen the economy emerge from recession. Manufacturing accounts for 33% of exports. Textiles, footwear and clothing are major exports. Portugal is the world's fifth-largest producer of tungsten and eighth-largest producer of wine. Olives, potatoes and wheat are also grown. Tourism is very important.
Website www.portugal.gov.pt

Romania

Area 238,391 sq km (92,042 sq miles)
Population 22,272,000
Capital Bucharest / Bucuresti (2,016,000)
Languages Romanian (official), Hungarian
GDP 2002 US$7,600
Currency Romanian leu = 100 bani
Government multiparty republic
Head of state Traian Basescu, 2004
Head of government Calin Tariceanu, 2004
Events A new constitution was introduced in 1991. Ion Iliescu, a former communist official, was re-elected in 2000, but barred from standing again in 2004, when he was replaced by Traian Basescu. Tariceanu's government is a centrist coalition. Romania joined NATO in March 2004 and signed its EU accession treaty in April 2005 and could become a member in 2007, depending on the pace of reform. The Romany minority still suffers from discrimination.
Economy Industry accounts for 40% of GDP. Oil, natural gas and antimony are the main mineral resources. Agriculture employs 29% of the workforce. Romania is the world's second-largest producer of plums (after China) and ninth-largest producer of wine. Other major crops include maize and cabbages. Economic reform is slow.
Website www.gov.ro/engleza/index.php

Russia *Rossiya*

Area 17,075,000 sq km (6,592,800 sq miles)
Population 144,526,000
Capital Moscow / Moskva (9,700,000)
Languages Russian (official), and many others
GDP 2002 US$8,297
Currency Russian rouble = 100 kopeks
Government federal multiparty republic
Head of state President Vladimir Putin, 2000
Head of government Prime Minister Mikail Fradkov, 2003
Events In 1992 the Russian Federation became a co-founder of the CIS. A new Federal Treaty was signed between the central government and the autonomous republics within the Russian Federation, Chechnya refused to sign and declared independence. In December 1993 a new democratic constitution was adopted. From 1994 to 1996, Russia fought a costly civil war in Chechnya which flared up again in 1999. Having supported the US-led campaign against terrorism in 2002 a NATO-Russian Council was formed with an eye on terrorism policy. Russia did not support the war in Iraq of 2003. Now reliant on world oil prices to keep its economy from crashing. Tycoons who have capitalised on the change to a capitalist system find themselves under criminal investigation. Putin re-elected March 2004, much criticism in the west of media bias towards him that left opponents little opportunity to broadcast their views, this also applied to parliamentary elections of December 2003. Putin has a very high level of control over parliament and appointed the PM Mikhail Fradkov. The only privately owned national television station was closed in 2003. Moscow-backed Chechen president Akhmet Kadryov assassinated in May 2004. In September 2004 Chechen separatists stormed a school in North Ossetia taking over 1000 children and adults hostage. Hundreds died when bombs were set off and a gun battle ensued.

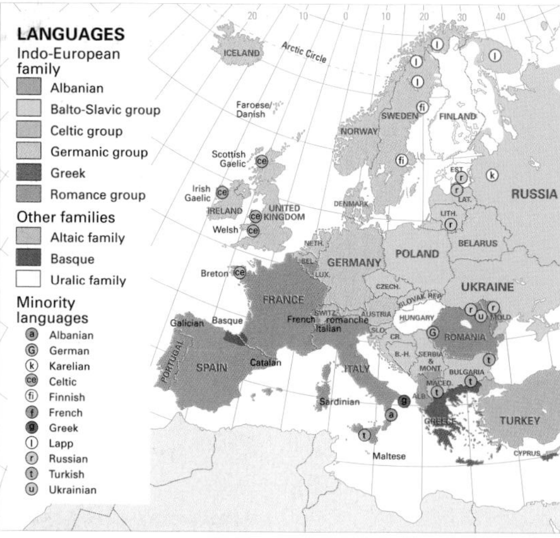
LANGUAGES
Indo-European family
Albanian
Balto-Slavic group
Celtic group
Germanic group
Greek
Romance group
Other families
Altaic family
Basque
Uralic family
Minority languages
a Albanian
G German
k Karelian
ce Celtic
fi Finnish
f French
g Greek
l Lapp
r Russian
t Turkish
u Ukrainian
20
10
0
10
20
30
40
ICELAND
Arctic Circle
Faroese/ Danish
NORWAY
SWEDEN
FINLAND
Scottish Gaelic
Irish Gaelic
IRELAND
UNITED KINGDOM
Welsh
DENMARK
EST.
LAT.
LITH.
RUSSIA
BELARUS
POLAND
NETH.
BEL.
GERMANY
LUX.
Breton
CZECH.
SLOVAK REP.
UKRAINE
FRANCE
SWITZ.
AUSTRIA
HUNGARY
MOLD.
French
romanche
Italian
Galician
Basque
SLO.
CR.
ROMANIA
PORTUGAL
SPAIN
Catalan
B.-H.
SERBIA & MONT.
BULGARIA
ITALY
MACED.
ALB.
Sardinian
GREECE
TURKEY
Maltese
CYPRUS

Economy In 1993 mass privatisation began. By 1996, 80% of the Russian economy was in private hands. A major problem remains the size of Russia's foreign debt. Industry employs 46% of the workforce and contributes 48% of GDP. Mining is the most valuable activity. Russia is the world's leading producer of natural gas and nickel, the second largest producer of aluminium and phosphates. and the third-largest of crude oil, lignite and brown coal. Light industries are growing in importance. Most farmland is still government-owned or run as collectives, with important products barley, oats, rye, potatoes, beef and veal.
Website http://president.kremlin.ru/eng/

San Marino

Area 61 sq km (24 sq miles)
Population 28,119
Capital San Marino (5,000)
Languages Italian (official)
GDP 2002 US$34,600
Currency Euro = 100 cents
Government multiparty republic
Head of state co-Captains Regent: Fausta Simona Morganti, Cesare Antonio Gasperoni
Events World's smallest republic and perhaps Europe's oldest state, San Marino's links with Italy led to the adoption of the Euro. Its 60-member Great and General Council is elected every five years and headed by two captains-regent, who are elected by the council every six months.
Economy The economy is largely agricultural. Tourism is vital to the state's income. Also a tax haven used by many non-residents. Income also from stamps and coins.
Website www.omniway.sm

Serbia & Montenegro *Srbija i Crna Gora*

Area 102,173 sq km (39,449 sq miles)
Population 10,656,000
Capital Belgrade / Beograd (1,594,000)
Languages Serbian (official), Albanian
GDP 2002 US$2,200
Currency Dinar = 100 paras (Serbia), Euro = 100 cents (Montenegro)
Government federal republic
Head of state President of Serbia & Montenegro Svetozvar Marovic, Democratic Party of Socialists, 2003; President of Serbia Boris Tadic, Democratic Party, 2004; President of Montenegro Filip Vujanovic, 2003
Head of government Prime Minister of Serbia Vojislav Kostunica, Democratic Party of Serbia, 2004; Prime Minister of Montenegro Milo Djukanovic, Democratic Party of Socialists, 2002
Events In 1989 Slobodan Milosevic became president of Serbia and called for the creation of a "Greater Serbia". Serbian attempts to dominate the Yugoslav federation led to the secession of Slovenia and Croatia (with whom Serbia fought a brief war) in 1991 and to Bosnia-Herzegovina's declaration of independence in March 1992. In April 1992 Serbia and Montenegro announced the formation of a new Yugoslav federation and invited Serbs in Croatia and Bosnia-Herzegovina to join. Serbian aid to the Bosnian Serb campaign of "ethnic cleansing" in the civil war in Bosnia led the UN to impose sanctions on Serbia, Milosevic severed support for the Bosnian Serbs. In 1995 Milosevic signed the Dayton Peace Accord, which ended the Bosnian war. In 1997 Milosevic became president of Yugoslavia. In 1998 fighting erupted in Kosovo between Albanian nationalists and Serbian security forces. In 1999, following the forced expulsion of Albanians from Kosovo, NATO bombed Yugoslavia, forcing withdrawal of Serbian forces from Kosovo. Kostunica won the elections of September 2000, but Milosevic refused to hand over power. After a week of civil unrest and increased support for Kostunica, Milosevic was finally ousted. A constitutional charter for the union of Serbia and Montenegro was agreed in December 2002. There is a federal presidency with federal foreign and defence ministries, but the two republics are semi-independent states in charge of their own economies. This arrangement will remain for a minimum of three years. Kosovo is legally part of Serbia, but is an international protectorate. The position of president in Serbia was left vacant between January 2003 and June 2004 after Milan Milutinovic surrendered to the war crimes tribunal in The Hague. The Serbian government must govern in coalition with small parties as well as relying on the support of Slobodan Milosovic's Socialist Party. Although no longer controlled by Milosovic, such co-operation could impact on the continuing extradition of war crimes suspects to The Hague. In early 2005 the Montenegrin leadership suggested dissolving the Union early – to allow for quicker reform and improve EU membership prospects – but this was rejected by the Serbs.
Economy The lower-middle income economy was devastated by war and economic sanctions. Industrial production collapsed. Natural resources include bauxite, coal and copper. There is some oil and natural gas. Manufacturing includes aluminium, cars, machinery, plastics, steel and textiles. Agriculture is important.
Website www.info.gov.yu; www.serbia-tourism.org; www.montenegro.yu

Slovakia *Slovenska Republika*

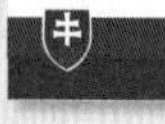

Area 49,012 sq km (18,923 sq miles)
Population 5,430,000
Capital Bratislava (449,000)
Languages Slovak (official), Hungarian
GDP 2002 US$12,400
Currency Koruna = 100 halierov
Government multiparty republic
Head of state President Ivan Gasparovic, 2004
Head of government Prime Minister Mikulás Dzurinda, Democratic & Christian Union, 1998
Events In 1993 the Slovak Republic became a sovereign state, breaking peaceably from the Czech Republic, with whom it maintains close relations. In 1996 the Slovak Republic and Hungary ratified a treaty confirming their borders and stipulating basic rights for the 560,000 Hungarians in Slovakia. Mikulás Dzurinda of Democratic & Christian Union heads centre right coalition made up of ethnic Hungarians – Magyar Koalicio Partja, Christian Democrats and ANO – Allianca Noveno Obcana (New Citizens' Alliance). Slovakia joined NATO in March 2004 and the EU in May 2004. There is still a problem with the Romany population being deprived. The 17% turn-out for the European elections in June 2004 was the lowest of all 25 members.
Economy The transition from communism to private ownership has been painful with industrial output falling, unemployment and inflation rising. In 1995 the privatisation programme was suspended. Manufacturing employs 33% of the workforce. Bratislava and Košice are the chief industrial cities. Major products include ceramics, machinery and steel. Farming employs 12% of the workforce. Crops include barley and grapes. Tourism is growing.
Website www.slovakia.org

Slovenia *Slovenija*

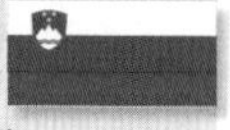

Area 20,256 sq km (7,820 sq miles)
Population 1,936,000
Capital Ljubljana (264,000)
Languages Slovene
GDP 2002 US$19,200
Currency Tolar = 100 stotin
Government multiparty republic
Head of state President Janez Drnovsek, Liberal Democrats of Slovenia, 2002
Head of government Prime Minister Janez Jansa, Slovenian Democratic Party, 2004
Events In 1990 Slovenia declared itself independent, which led to brief fighting between Slovenes and the federal army. In 1992 the EU recognised Slovenia's independence. Janez Drnovsek was elected president in December 2002 and immediately stepped down as prime minister. Slovenia joined NATO in March 2004 and the EU in May 2004. In June 2004 the value of the Tolar was fixed against the Euro with a view to joining in 2007. Their reputation as a liberal nation has been somewhat scarred by the recent referendum overturning a parliamentary bill that restored citizenship of Slovenia to resident nationals of other former Yugoslav countries. The 2004 general election resulted in a coalition government of the Slovenian Democratic Party, New Slovenia, the People's Party and the Democratic Party of Pensioners.
Economy The transformation of a centrally planned economy and the fighting in other parts of former Yugoslavia have caused problems for Slovenia. Manufacturing is the leading activity. Major manufactures include chemicals, machinery, transport equipment, metal goods and textiles. Major crops include maize, fruit, potatoes and wheat.
Website www.gov.si

Spain *España*

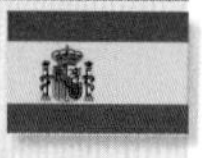

Area 497,548 sq km (192,103 sq miles)
Population 40,217,000
Capital Madrid (2,939,000)
Languages Castilian Spanish (official), Catalan, Galician, Basque
GDP 2002 US$21,200
Currency Euro = 100 cents
Government constitutional monarchy
Head of state King Juan Carlos, 1975
Head of government Prime Minister Jose Luis Rodriguez Zapatero, Socialist Party, 2004
Events From 1959 the militant Basque organization ETA waged a campaign of terror but announced a ceasefire in 1998. Basque separatist party Batasuna was permanently banned in 2003 as it is thought to be the political wing of ETA. In March 2004 terrorist bombs exploded in Madrid killing 191 people, this was deemed to be the work of al Qaeda, though the then government were keen to persuade the people that it was the work of ETA. The country went to the polls three days later and voted Aznar out, largely seen as a reaction to his support of the US in Iraq and the sending of troops which was to blame for the bombing some three days earlier. The new PM subsequently withdrew all troops from Iraq. Although the ruling Socialist Party are short of a majority, Zapatero has pledged to govern through dialogue with others rather than form a coalition. In a referendum in 2005, Spanish voters voted for the proposed European constitution.
Economy Spain has rapidly transformed from a largely poor, agrarian society into a prosperous industrial nation. Agriculture now employs only 10% of the workforce. Spain is the world's third-largest wine producer. Other crops include citrus fruits, tomatoes and olives. Industries: cars, ships, chemicals, electronics, metal goods, steel, textiles.
Website www.la-moncloa.es/

Sweden *Sverige*

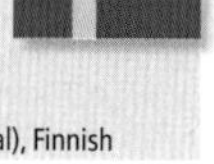

Area 449,964 sq km (173,731 sq miles)
Population 8,878,000
Capital Stockholm (744,000)
Languages Swedish (official), Finnish
GDP 2002 US$26,000
Currency Swedish krona = 100 ore
Government constitutional monarchy
Head of state King Carl XVI Gustaf, 1973
Head of government Prime Minister Göran Persson, Social Democratic Workers' Party (SSA), 1996
Events In 1995 Sweden joined the European Union. Göran Persson was re-elected in 2002. The cost of maintaining Sweden's extensive welfare services has become a major political issue. In September 2003 Sweden was shocked by the murder of popular minister Anna Lindh (a pro-Euro campaigner), thus reigniting discussion over the relaxed attitude to security. Days later Sweden said no to the Euro. Brand new Euro-sceptic party Junilistan (June List) came third in the European elections, exceeding all expectations and underlining Swedish ambivalence towards Europe.
Economy Sweden is a highly developed industrial country. It has rich iron ore deposits, but other industrial materials are imported. Steel is a major product, used to manufacture aircraft, cars, machinery and ships. Forestry and fishing are important. Livestock and dairy farming are valuable activities; crops include barley and oats.
Website www.sweden.gov.se

Switzerland *Schweiz*

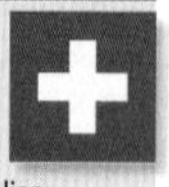

Area 41,284 sq km (15,939 sq miles)
Population 7,319,000
Capital Bern (124,000)
Languages French, German, Italian, Romansch (all official)
GDP 2002 US$32,000
Currency Swiss Franc = 100 centimes
Government federal republic
Head of state President Samuel Schmid, 2005
Events Priding itself on their neutrality, Swiss voters rejected membership of the UN in 1986 and the EU in 1992 and 2001. However, Switzerland finally became a partner country of NATO in 1997 and joined the UN in 2002. The federal council is made up of seven federal ministers from whom the president is chosen on an annual basis. Prior to 2003 the allocation of posts was fixed between Free Democrats (2), Social Democrats (2), Christian Democrats (2) and Swiss People's Party (SVP) (1), however this changed after the elections of 2003 when the SVP increased their share of the vote to 28%, thereby becoming the largest party. The allocation was subsequently changed (after much debate) with the SVP taking an extra seat and the Christian Democrats losing one.
Economy Switzerland is wealthy and industrialised. Manufactures include chemicals, electrical equipment, machinery, precision instruments, watches and textiles. Livestock raising, notably dairy farming, is the chief agricultural activity. Tourism is important, and Swiss banks attract worldwide investment.
Website www.gov.ch

Turkey *Türkiye*

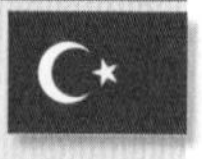

Area 774,815 sq km (299,156 sq miles)
Population 68,109,000
Capital Ankara (2,984,000)
Languages Turkish (official), Kurdish
GDP 2002 US$7,300
Currency New Turkish lira = 100 kurus
Government multiparty republic
Head of state President Ahmet Necdet Sezer, 2000
Head of government Prime Minister Recep Tayyip Erdogan, Justice and Development Party (AK), 2002
Events Civil unrest between Turkish forces and the Kurdistan Workers Party (PKK) in the 1980s and 1990s. In 1999 the PKK leader Ocalan was sentenced to death, since commuted to life imprisonment on the abolition of the death penalty. The PKK changed their name to Congress for Freedom and Democracy in Kurdistan (KADEK) and say they want to campaign peacefully for Kurdish rights, but in September 2003 they ended a four year ceasefire with the aim of increasing pressure on the government to listen to Kurdish demands. Membership of the EU is an aim but Turkey's record on human rights needs to improve before this can happen, along with a resolution to the Cyprus issue. Although by ratifying a customs union with the EU, Turkey has admitted the economic existence of southern Cyprus, it has not done so politically; however, EU leaders agreed in principle in September 2005 to start accession talks the following month. The president is interested in greater freedom of expression. The PM is leader of the Islamist Justice & Development Party, though claims to be committed to secularism.
Economy Turkey is a lower-middle income developing country. Agriculture employs 47% of the workforce. Turkey is a leading producer of citrus fruits, barley, cotton, wheat, tobacco and tea. It is a major producer of chromium and phosphate fertilisers. Tourism is a vital source of foreign exchange. In January 2005, the New Turkish lira was introduced at a rate of 1 to 1,000,000 old Turkish lira.
Website www.tourismturkey.org

Ukraine *Ukraina*

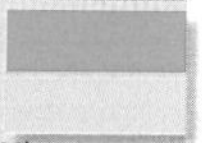

Area 603,700 sq km (233,088 sq miles)
Population 48,055,000
Capital Kiev / Kyyiv (2,590,000)
Languages Ukrainian (official), Russian
GDP 2002 US$4,500
Currency Hryvna = 100 kopiykas
Government multiparty republic
Head of state President Viktor Yushchenko, 2005
Head of government Prime Minister Yulia Tymoshenko, 2005
Events The Chernobyl disaster of 1986 contaminated large areas of Ukraine. Leonid Kuchma was elected president in 1994. He continued the policy of establishing closer ties with the West and sped up the pace of privatisation. There are continuing disputes over the the powers of the Crimean legislature. Ukraine is pushing for membership of NATO though reforms are required before this can happen. The election of November 2004 was thrown into turmoil after opposition presidential candidate Yushchenko was poisoned with dioxins and the result was declared as a victory for former PM, and pro-Russian, Viktor Yanukovich leading to accusations of electoral fraud and widespread demonstrations. After 10 days the Supreme Court declared the vote invalid and the elections were re-run, resulting in victory for the pro-west Yushchenko. In September 2005, bitter in-fighting, widespread accusations of corruption and lack of progress on economic reform led Mr Yushchenko to sack the entire cabinet and appoint Yuri Yekhanurov as acting Prime Minister, subject to parliamentary approval.
Economy Ukraine is a lower-middle-income economy. Agriculture is important. It is the world's leading producer of sugar beet, the second-largest producer of barley, and a major producer of wheat. Ukraine has extensive raw materials, including coal (though many mines are exhausted), iron ore and manganese ore. Ukraine is reliant on oil and natural gas imports. Ukraine's debt to Russia has been partly offset by allowing Russian firms majority shares in many industries.
Website www.mfa.gov.ua/eng/

United Kingdom

Area 241,857 sq km (93,381 sq miles)
Population 60,095,000
Capital London (8,089,000)
Languages English (official), Welsh (also official in Wales), Gaelic
GDP 2002 US$25,500
Currency Sterling (pound) = 100 pence
Government constitutional monarchy
Head of state Queen Elizabeth II, 1952
Head of government Prime Minister Tony Blair, Labour Party, 1997
Events The United Kingdom of Great Britain and Northern Ireland is a union of four countries – England, Northern Ireland, Scotland and Wales. In 1997 referenda on devolution saw Scotland and Wales gain their own legislative assemblies. The Scottish assembly was given tax-varying power. The Good Friday Agreement of 1998 offered the best chance of peace in Northern Ireland for a generation. In 2005 the IRA announced a permanent cessation of hostilities. Tony Blair controversially gave full support to Bush over the war in Iraq in 2003. The 2005 general election resulted in a reduced majority for Labour. Widespread delight at London's winning the 2012 Olympics was shattered the following day when four suicide bombers hit the city's transport network killing 57 people.
Economy The UK is a major industrial and trading nation. The economy has become more service-centred and high-technology industries have grown in importance. A producer of oil, petroleum products, natural gas, potash, salt and lead. Agriculture employs only 2% of the workforce. Financial services and tourism are the leading service industries.
Website www.parliament.uk

1:4 250 000 map pages

Calais

	Dublin ▶ Göteborg = 477 km
548	**Dublin**
726 346	**Edinburgh**
575 1123 1301	**Frankfurt**
1342 477 176 1067	**Göteborg**
760 477 1486 485 582	**Hamburg**

000 = ⛴

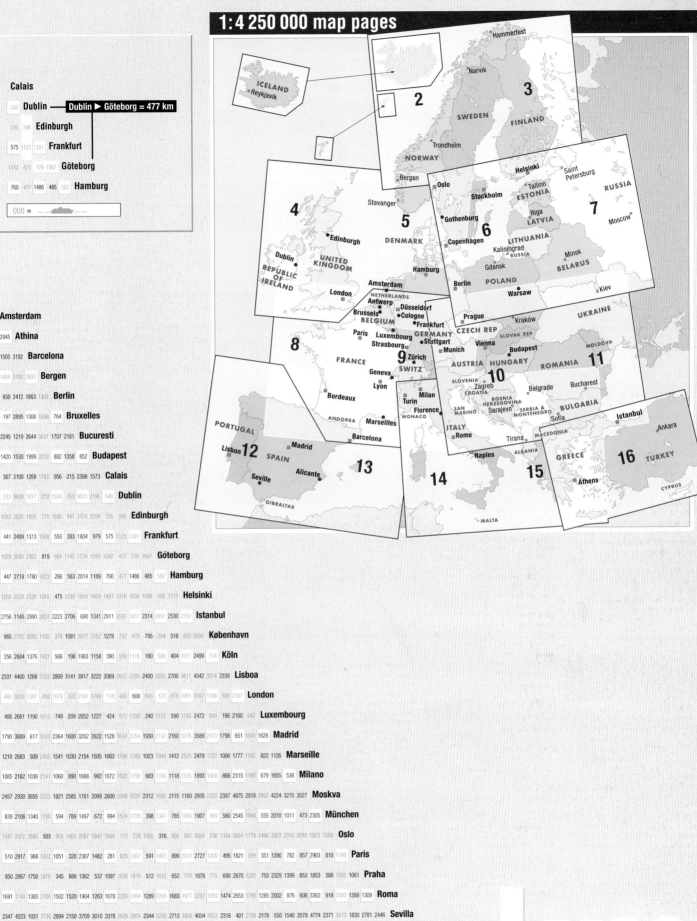

Amsterdam

2945 **Athina**

1505 3192 **Barcelona**

1484 3742 2803 **Bergen**

650 2412 1863 1309 **Berlin**

197 2895 1308 1586 764 **Bruxelles**

2245 1219 2644 3037 1707 2181 **Bucuresti**

1420 1530 1999 2212 882 1358 852 **Budapest**

367 3100 1269 1783 956 215 2398 1573 **Calais**

533 3630 1817 270 1504 763 3021 2196 548 **Dublin**

1093 3826 1995 176 1696 941 3124 2299 726 346 **Edinburgh**

441 2499 1313 1508 550 383 1804 979 575 1123 1301 **Frankfurt**

1029 3080 2362 819 668 1145 1734 1510 1342 477 176 1067 **Göteborg**

447 2719 1780 1023 286 563 2014 1189 760 477 1486 485 582 **Hamburg**

1560 2539 2338 1063 475 1239 1834 1009 1431 1318 1236 1598 505 1113 **Helsinki**

2756 1145 2990 3653 2223 2706 690 1341 2911 3537 3657 2314 2891 2530 2350 **Istanbul**

965 2782 2090 1103 370 1081 2077 1252 1278 752 479 795 284 518 803 2593 **København**

256 2684 1376 1427 566 198 1983 1158 390 938 1116 180 986 404 1517 2499 714 **Köln**

2331 4460 1268 3723 2869 3141 3917 3222 2069 2617 2795 2400 3282 2700 3817 4342 3014 2339 **Lisboa**

480 3200 1387 458 1074 333 2591 118 430 608 693 122 878 1991 3107 1188 508 2187 **London**

406 2661 1190 1613 749 209 2052 1227 424 972 1150 240 1172 590 1703 2472 900 186 2160 542 **Luxembourg**

1790 3809 617 3183 2364 1600 3262 2622 1528 1634 2254 1930 2742 2160 3276 3589 2473 1798 651 1646 1628 **Madrid**

1210 2683 509 2435 1541 1030 2154 1505 1063 1588 1789 1023 1994 1412 2525 2479 1722 1006 1777 1182 822 1126 **Marseille**

1085 2182 1038 2141 1060 890 1668 992 1072 1620 1796 683 1700 1118 1993 1428 868 2315 1190 679 1655 538 **Milano**

2457 2930 3655 2223 1821 2585 1761 2099 2800 3348 3526 2312 1685 2115 1160 2605 2325 2387 4875 2918 3267 4224 3270 3027 **Moskva**

839 2106 1340 1788 594 789 1497 672 994 1524 1720 398 1347 765 1069 1907 969 580 2545 1094 555 2010 1011 473 2305 **München**

1347 3372 2680 503 960 1463 2667 1842 1660 773 729 1385 316 900 697 3089 590 1304 3604 1778 1490 3063 2312 2018 1823 1559 **Oslo**

510 2917 988 1922 1051 320 2307 1482 281 829 1007 591 1481 899 2012 2727 1209 495 1821 399 351 1280 782 857 2903 810 1799 **Paris**

950 2067 1750 1675 345 888 1362 537 1097 1635 1816 512 1013 652 770 1878 715 690 2870 1205 753 2329 1399 853 1853 388 1305 1061 **Praha**

1691 1140 1385 2706 1502 1520 1904 1263 1678 2265 2404 1289 1977 2237 1993 1474 2653 1796 1285 2002 876 606 3362 918 2583 1389 1309 **Roma**

2347 4223 1031 3736 2894 2150 3709 3010 2078 2626 2804 2344 3295 2713 3826 4034 3023 2318 401 2196 2178 550 1540 2078 4774 2371 3613 1830 2781 2446 **Sevilla**

2206 828 2453 3103 1673 2156 391 790 2361 3087 1764 2341 1980 1800 550 2043 1949 3706 2461 1922 3037 1929 1443 2252 1367 2632 2177 1328 1687 3484 **Sofiya**

1393 3418 2726 1063 1096 1509 2713 1888 1673 2254 1699 1431 505 945 167 3185 590 1350 3650 1824 1536 3100 2268 2064 1228 1600 530 1845 1351 2629 3659 2679 **Stockholm**

1256 2128 2366 1909 606 1350 1473 648 1542 2110 2268 1136 1274 886 361 1989 956 1152 3480 1680 1345 2960 2015 1469 1245 996 1506 1677 616 1853 3397 1439 1612 **Warszawa**

1168 1772 1856 1970 640 1114 1067 242 1308 1954 2034 731 1308 947 1088 1583 1010 916 3100 1524 993 2473 1353 818 2137 430 1600 1240 295 1126 2876 1033 1646 727 **Wien**

816 2426 1030 1938 863 619 1810 985 804 1352 1530 464 1497 915 589 2296 922 410 1647 699 292 2552 303 1815 592 691 898 2061 1173 1851 1307 743 **Zürich**

km

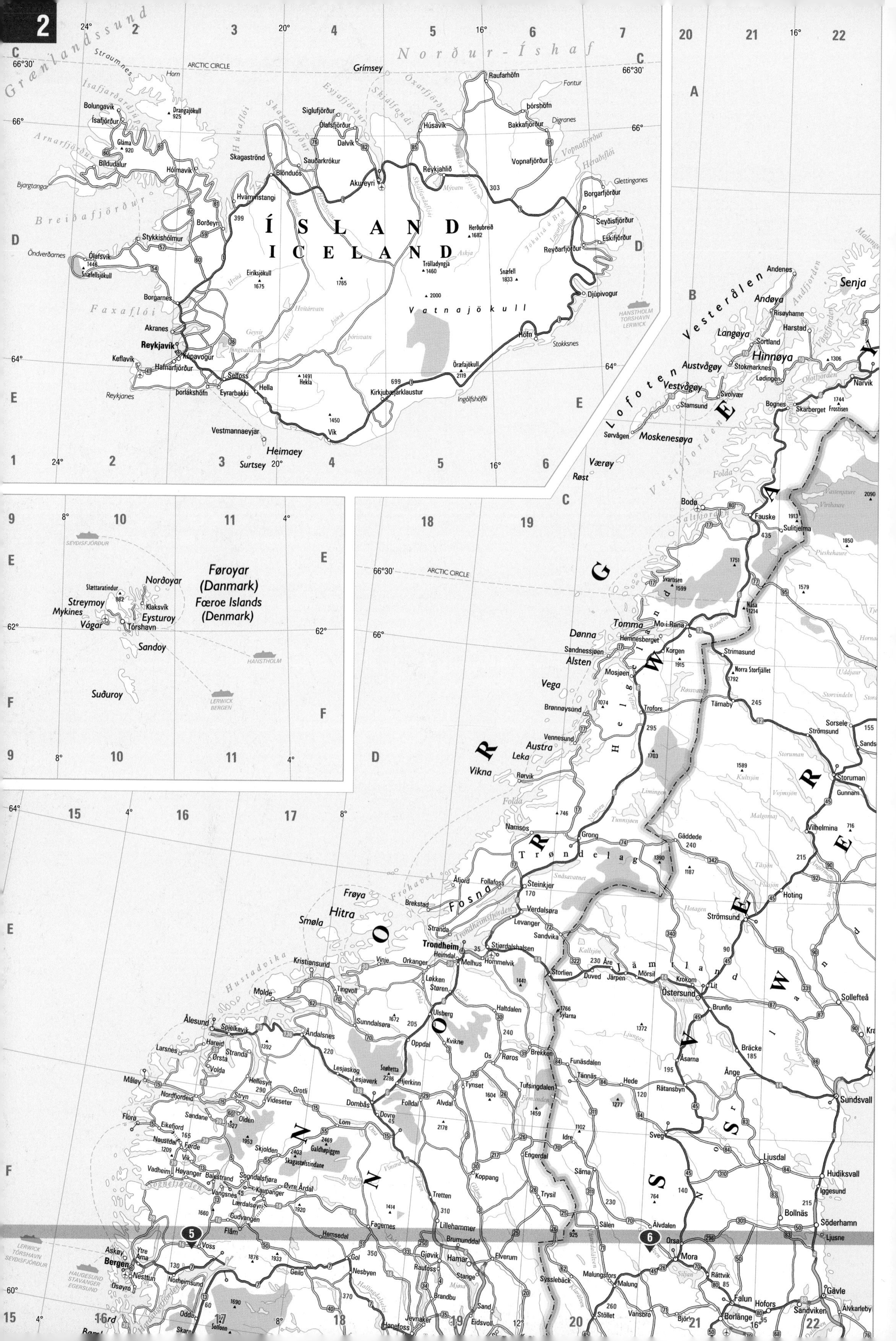

Norður-Íshaf
Grænlandssund
ARCTIC CIRCLE
Grímsey
ÍSLAND
ICELAND
Vatnajökull
Reykjavík
Kópavogur
Hafnarfjörður
Keflavík
Akranes
Borgarnes
Selfoss
Hella
Vík
Heimaey
Surtsey
Vestmannaeyjar
Akureyri
Húsavík
Raufarhöfn
Þórshöfn
Bakkafjörður
Vopnafjörður
Seyðisfjörður
Eskifjörður
Reyðarfjörður
Djúpivogur
Höfn
Kirkjubæjarklaustur
Ísafjörður
Bolungavík
Bíldudalur
Hólmavík
Stykkishólmur
Ólafsvík
Blönduós
Skagaströnd
Sauðárkrókur
Siglufjörður
Ólafsfjörður
Dalvík
Reykjahlíð
Mývatn
Askja
Herðubreið 1682
Trölladyngja 1460
Snæfell 1833
Öræfajökull 2119
Hekla 1491
Faxaflói
Breiðafjörður
Føroyar (Danmark)
Faeroe Islands (Denmark)
Streymoy
Eysturoy
Norðoyar
Vágar
Mykines
Sandoy
Suðuroy
Tórshavn
Klaksvík
Slættaratindur 882
HANSTHOLM
LERWICK BERGEN
SEYÐISFJÖRÐUR
Lofoten
Vesterålen
Senja
Andøya
Hinnøya
Langøya
Austvågøy
Vestvågøy
Moskenesøya
Værøy
Røst
Narvik
Harstad
Sortland
Stokmarknes
Svolvær
Bodø
Fauske
Sulitjelma
Mo i Rana
Mosjøen
Brønnøysund
Sandnessjøen
Namsos
Grong
Steinkjer
Trondheim
Stjørdalshalsen
Kristiansund
Molde
Ålesund
Åndalsnes
Røros
Lillehammer
Hamar
Gjøvik
Bergen
Voss
Flåm
Førde
Florø
Måløy
Galdhøpiggen 2469
Snøhetta 2286
NORGE
NORWAY
SVERIGE
SWEDEN
Trøndelag
Helgeland
Jämtland
Östersund
Storlien
Åre
Strömsund
Sundsvall
Hudiksvall
Söderhamn
Gävle
Falun
Borlänge
Mora
Orsa
Sveg
Storuman
Vilhelmina
Tärnaby
Sorsele
Sollefteå
Ljusdal
Bollnäs
Hofors
Sandviken

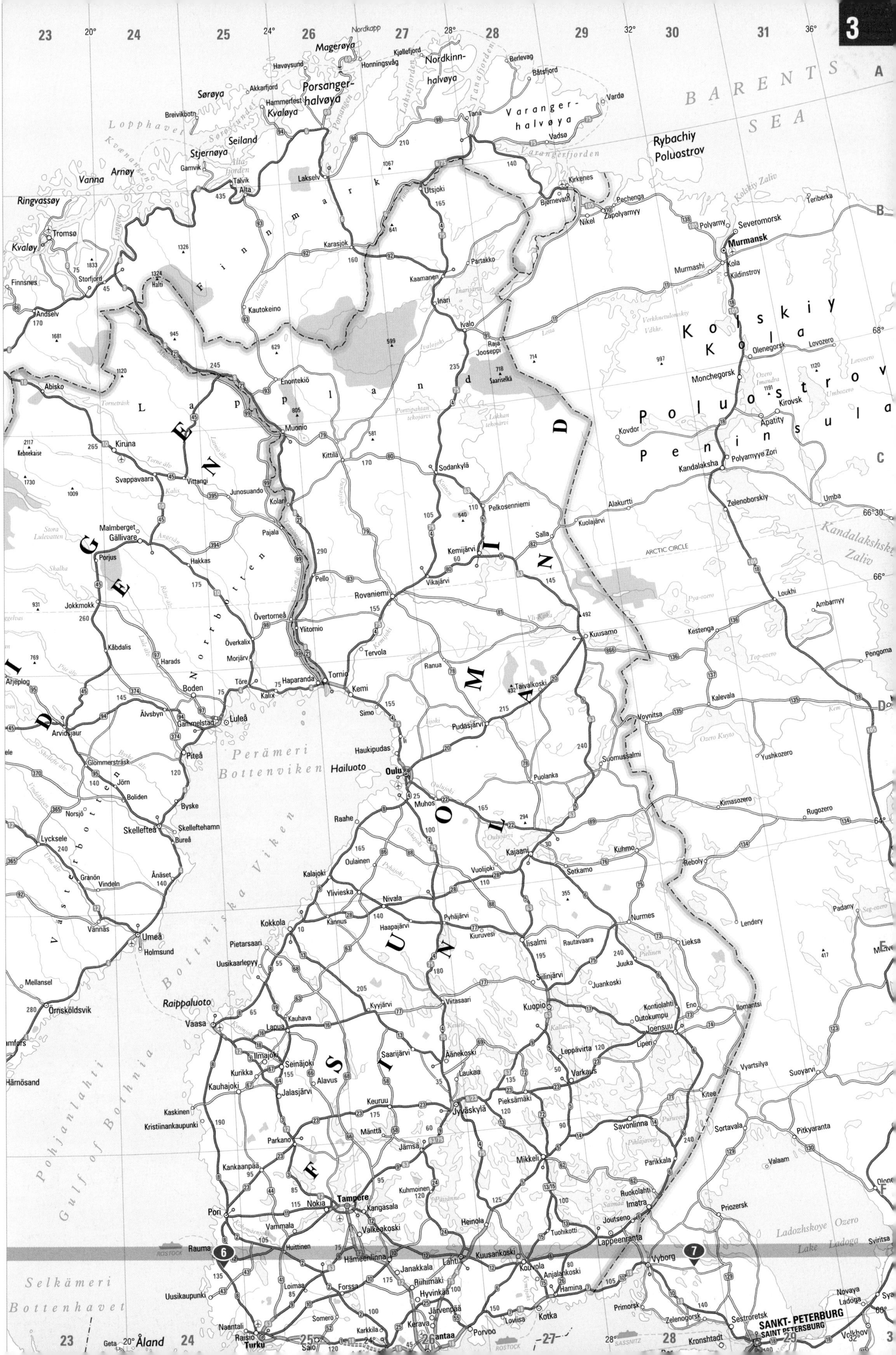
BARENTS SEA
Nordkapp
Magerøya
Havøysund
Honningsvåg
Kjøllefjord
Nordkinn-halvøya
Berlevag
Båtsfjord
Porsanger-halvøya
Sørøya
Akkarfjord
Hammerfest
Kvaløya
Vardø
Varanger-halvøya
Vadsø
Varangerfjorden
Tana
Breivikbotn
Loppha vet
Seiland
Stjernøya
Gamvik
Talvik
Alta
Arnøy
Vanna
Ringvassøy
Tromsø
Kvaløy
Storfjord
Finnsnes
Andselv
Lakselv
Karasjok
Utsjoki
Kirkenes
Bjørnevatn
Pechenga
Nikel
Zapolyarnyy
Rybachiy Poluostrov
Polyarny
Severomorsk
Murmansk
Kola
Kildinstroy
Murmashi
Teriberka
Kolskiy Zaliv
Finnmark
Halti
Kautokeino
Kaamanen
Partakko
Inari
Inarijärvi
Ivalo
Raja Jooseppi
Saariselkä
Enontekiö
Lappland
Abisko
Kebnekaise
Kiruna
Svappavaara
Vittangi
Junosuando
Muonio
Kittilä
Sodankylä
Pelkosenniemi
Kolari
Pajala
Malmberget
Gällivare
Porjus
Hakkas
Salla
Kuolajärvi
Alakurtti
Kemijärvi
Vikajärvi
Pello
Rovaniemi
Jokkmokk
Övertorneå
Ylitornio
Överkalix
Morjärvi
Harads
Kåbdalis
Arjeplog
Boden
Töre
Kalix
Haparanda
Tornio
Kemi
Tervola
Ranua
Kuusamo
Taivalkoski
Simo
Pudasjärvi
Ii
Haukipudas
Luleå
Gammelstad
Älvsbyn
Arvidsjaur
Piteå
Glommersträsk
Jörn
Boliden
Norsjö
Byske
Skellefteå
Skelleftehamn
Bureå
Lycksele
Granön
Vindeln
Ånäset
Vännäs
Umeå
Holmsund
Mellansel
Örnsköldsvik
Härnösand
Perämeri
Bottenviken
Hailuoto
Oulu
Muhos
Raahe
Oulainen
Kalajoki
Ylivieska
Nivala
Haapajärvi
Pyhäjärvi
Kiuruvesi
Vuolijoki
Kajaani
Sotkamo
Kuhmo
Puolanka
Suomussalmi
Nurmes
Lieksa
Iisalmi
Rautavaara
Juuka
Siilinjärvi
Juankoski
Kuopio
Kontiolahti
Outokumpu
Eno
Joensuu
Ilomantsi
Liperi
Kokkola
Kannus
Pietarsaari
Uusikaarlepyy
Vaasa
Raippaluoto
Lapua
Kauhava
Kyyjärvi
Viitasaari
Saarijärvi
Äänekoski
Laukaa
Ilmajoki
Seinäjoki
Kurikka
Kauhajoki
Alavus
Jalasjärvi
Kaskinen
Kristiinankaupunki
Keuruu
Jyväskylä
Pieksämäki
Leppävirta
Varkaus
Kitee
Parkano
Mänttä
Jämsä
Savonlinna
Mikkeli
Kankaanpää
Pori
Nokia
Tampere
Kangasala
Vammala
Valkeakoski
Kuhmoinen
Heinola
Ruokolahti
Imatra
Joutseno
Lappeenranta
Rauma
Huittinen
Hämeenlinna
Janakkala
Lahti
Kuusankoski
Kouvola
Anjalankoski
Hamina
Kotka
Loviisa
Porvoo
Riihimäki
Hyvinkää
Järvenpää
Kerava
Vantaa
Forssa
Loimaa
Uusikaupunki
Somero
Karkkila
Naantali
Raisio
Turku
Salo
Åland
Selkämeri
Bottenhavet
Pohjanlahti
Gulf of Bothnia
Botnis ka Viken
SUOMI
FINLAND
SVERIGE
Norrbotten
Västerbotten
Kolskiy Poluostrov
Kola Peninsula
Monchegorsk
Olenegorsk
Lovozero
Kirovsk
Apatity
Kovdor
Polyarnyye Zori
Kandalaksha
Zelenoborskiy
Umba
Kandalakshskiy Zaliv
ARCTIC CIRCLE
Loukhi
Ambarnyy
Kestenga
Pongoma
Kalevala
Voynitsa
Yushkozero
Kimasozero
Rugozero
Reboly
Lendery
Padany
Vyartsilya
Suoyarvi
Sortavala
Pitkyaranta
Valaam
Priozersk
Ladozhskoye Ozero
Lake Ladoga
Svirtsa
Vyborg
Primorsk
Zelenogorsk
Sestroretsk
Kronshtadt
SANKT-PETERBURG
SAINT PETERSBURG
Novaya Ladoga
ROSTOCK
SASSNITZ

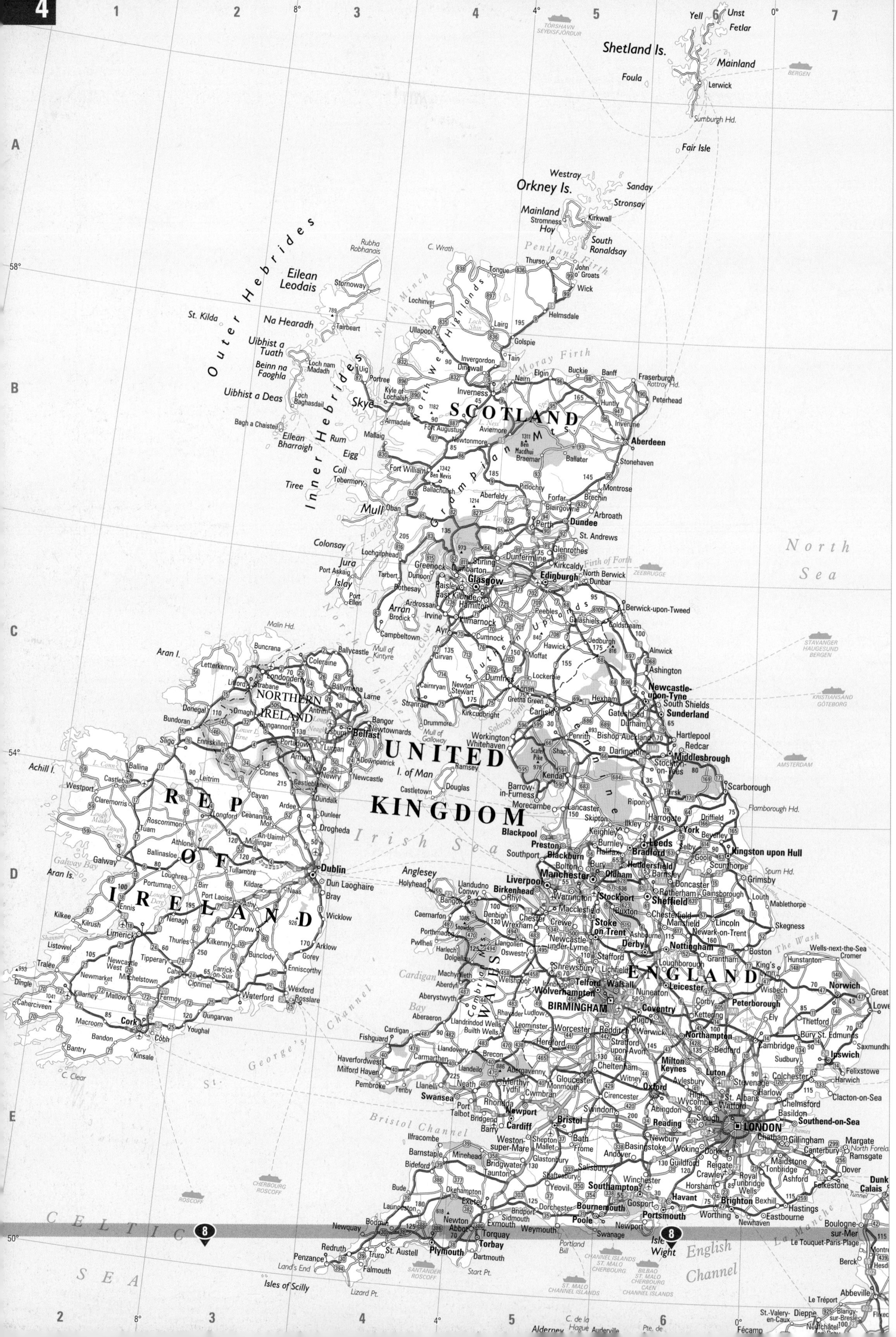
Shetland Is.
Orkney Is.
Outer Hebrides
Inner Hebrides
SCOTLAND
Grampian Mts.
North West Highlands
Southern Uplands
NORTHERN IRELAND
UNITED KINGDOM
REP OF IRELAND
ENGLAND
WALES
Cambrian Mts.
Pennines
North Sea
Irish Sea
Celtic Sea
English Channel
La Manche
Bristol Channel
St. George's Channel
Cardigan Bay
Moray Firth
Pentland Firth
Firth of Forth
North Minch
North Channel
The Wash
Galway Bay
I. of Man
Anglesey
Isle of Wight
Isles of Scilly
LONDON
BIRMINGHAM
Edinburgh
Glasgow
Aberdeen
Dundee
Inverness
Belfast
Dublin
Cork
Limerick
Galway
Newcastle-upon-Tyne
Sunderland
Middlesbrough
Leeds
Bradford
Manchester
Liverpool
Sheffield
Nottingham
Leicester
Coventry
Cardiff
Swansea
Bristol
Southampton
Portsmouth
Plymouth
Bournemouth
Brighton
Norwich
Kingston upon Hull
York
Dover
Calais
TÓRSHAVN SEYÐISFJÖRÐUR
BERGEN
ZEEBRUGGE
STAVANGER HAUGESUND BERGEN
KRISTIANSAND GÖTEBORG
AMSTERDAM
CHERBOURG ROSCOFF
ROSCOFF
SANTANDER ROSCOFF
CHANNEL ISLANDS ST. MALO CHERBOURG
ST. MALO CHANNEL ISLANDS
BILBAO ST. MALO CHERBOURG CAEN CHANNEL ISLANDS
1 2 3 4 5 6 7
A B C D E
58° 54° 50°
8° 4° 0°

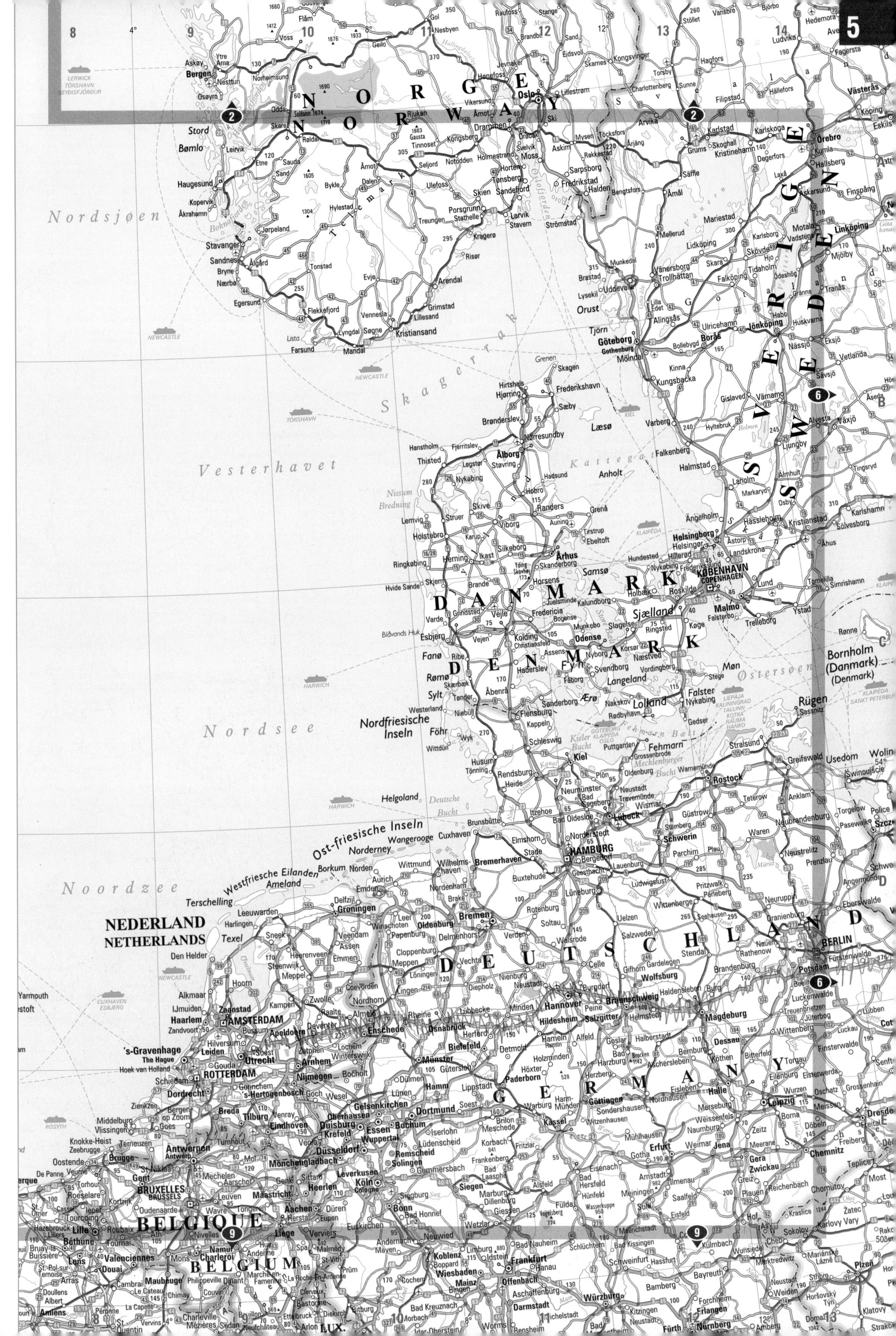
NORGE
NORWAY
SVERIGE
SWEDEN
DANMARK
DENMARK
DEUTSCHLAND
GERMANY
NEDERLAND
NETHERLANDS
BELGIQUE
BELGIUM
Nordsjøen
Vesterhavet
Nordsee
Noordzee
Skagerrak
Kattegat
Østersøen
Nordfriesische Inseln
Ost-friesische Inseln
Westfriesische Eilanden
Deutsche Bucht
Bornholm (Danmark) (Denmark)
Bergen
Oslo
Stavanger
Kristiansand
Drammen
Göteborg
Gothenburg
Malmö
Helsingborg
Jönköping
Örebro
Linköping
København
Copenhagen
Århus
Ålborg
Odense
Esbjerg
Kiel
Hamburg
Lübeck
Rostock
Bremen
Bremerhaven
Hannover
Berlin
Potsdam
Magdeburg
Braunschweig
Leipzig
Dresden
Chemnitz
Erfurt
Kassel
Göttingen
Dortmund
Essen
Düsseldorf
Köln
Bonn
Frankfurt
Wiesbaden
Mainz
Würzburg
Nürnberg
Amsterdam
Rotterdam
Utrecht
's-Gravenhage
The Hague
Antwerpen
Bruxelles
Brussels
Gent
Brugge
Lille
Liège
Namur
Charleroi
Groningen
Enschede
Osnabrück
Münster
Bielefeld
Schwerin
Flensburg
Rügen
Fehmarn
Helgoland
Sylt
Texel
Lolland
Falster
Sjælland
Fyn
Langeland
Læsø
Anholt
Samsø
Orust
Tjörn

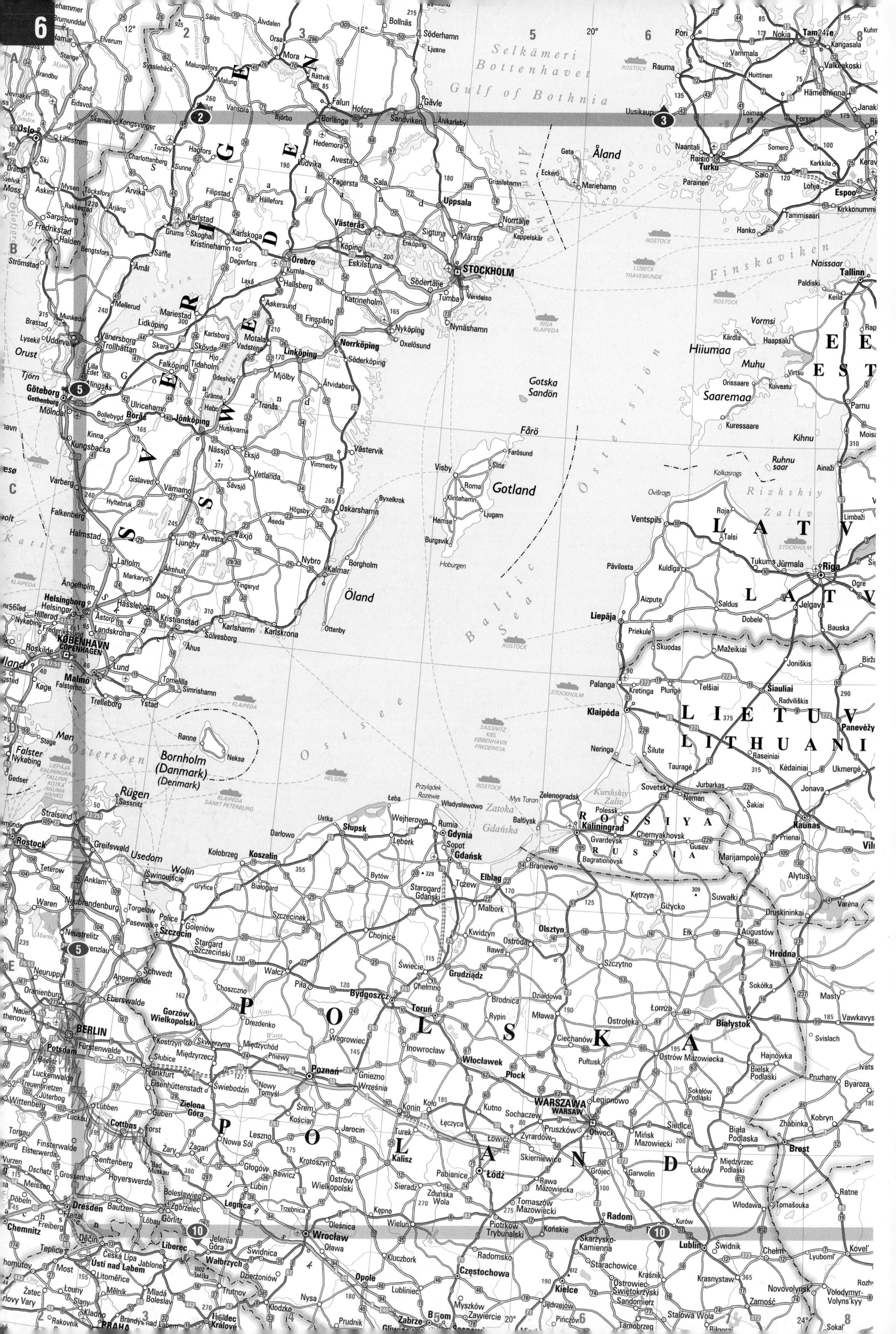
Selkämeri
Bottenhavet
Gulf of Bothnia
Åland
Finskaviken
SVERIGE
SWEDEN
STOCKHOLM
Uppsala
Västerås
Örebro
Norrköping
Linköping
Jönköping
Göteborg
Gothenburg
Helsingborg
Malmö
KØBENHAVN
COPENHAGEN
Gotland
Öland
Bornholm
(Danmark)
(Denmark)
Gotska Sandön
Saaremaa
Hiiumaa
Tallinn
Turku
Espoo
LATVIJA
LATVIA
Riga
LIETUVA
LITHUANIA
Kaunas
Klaipėda
ROSSIYA
RUSSIA
Kaliningrad
POLSKA
POLAND
WARSZAWA
WARSAW
Gdańsk
Gdynia
Poznań
Łódź
Wrocław
Kraków
Szczecin
Bydgoszcz
Toruń
Lublin
Białystok
BERLIN
Rostock
Dresden
Rügen
Ostsee
Baltic Sea
Östersjön
Kattegat
Zatoka Gdańska
Rizhskiy Zaliv
Hrodna
Brest

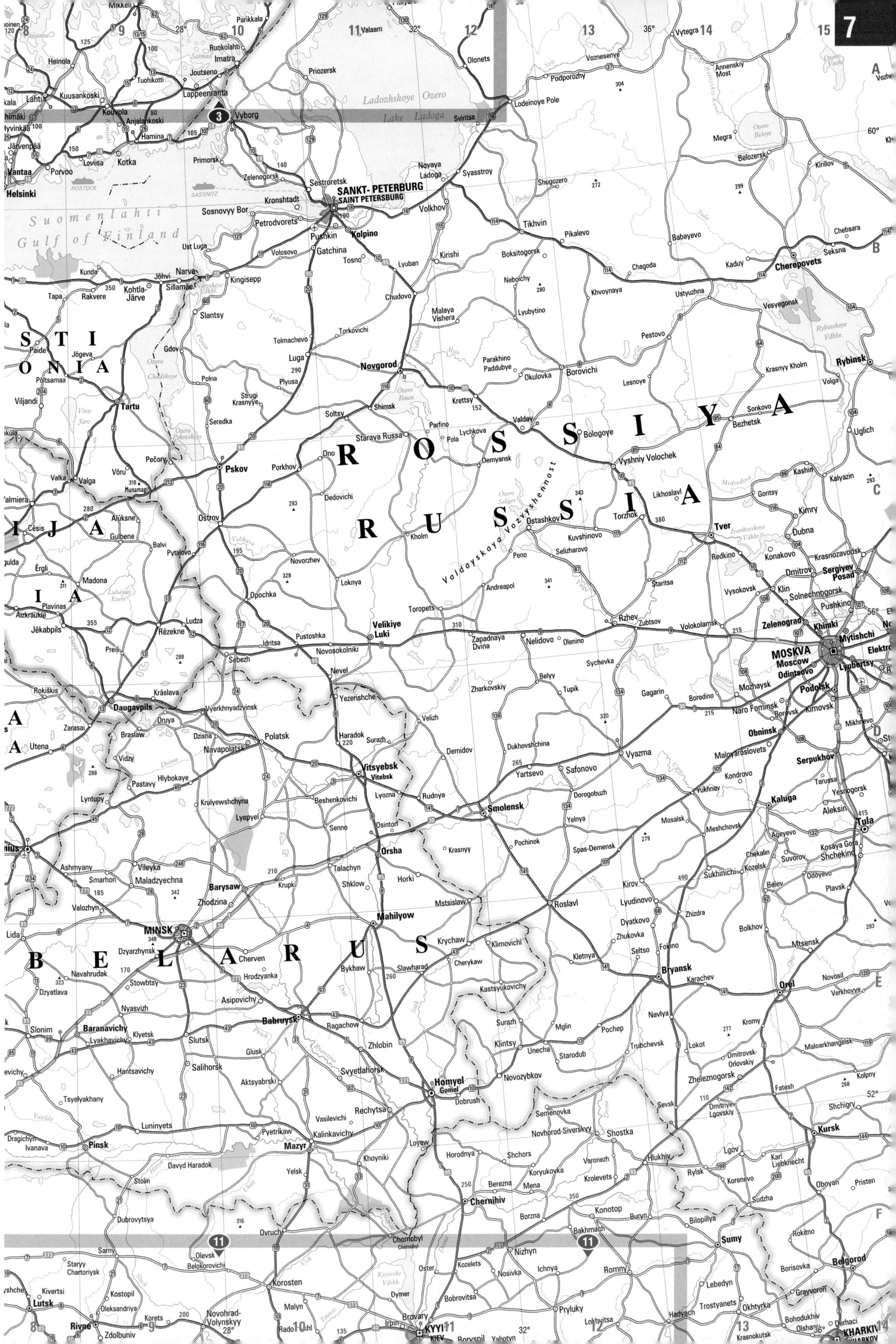
ROSSIYA
RUSSIA
BELARUS
Helsinki
Vantaa
Porvoo
Lahti
Kouvola
Kotka
Hamina
Lappeenranta
Imatra
Vyborg
Suomenlahti
Gulf of Finland
Ladozhskoye Ozero
Lake Ladoga
Sestroretsk
SANKT-PETERBURG
SAINT PETERSBURG
Kronshtadt
Petrodvorets
Pushkin
Kolpino
Gatchina
Volkhov
Tikhvin
Lodeinoye Pole
Podporozhy
Vytegra
Belozersk
Kirillov
Cherepovets
Rybinsk
Narva
Kingisepp
Sillamäe
Kohtla-Järve
Rakvere
Tartu
Paide
Viljandi
Valga
Valka
Pskov
Ostrov
Luga
Novgorod
Staraya Russa
Valday
Bologoye
Vyshniy Volochek
Torzhok
Tver
Ostashkov
Valdayskaya Vozvyshennost
Velikiye Luki
Nelidovo
Rzhev
Volokolamsk
Klin
Dubna
Zelenograd
Khimki
Mytishchi
MOSKVA
Moscow
Odintsovo
Lyubertsy
Podolsk
Obninsk
Serpukhov
Kaluga
Tula
Orel
Kursk
Belgorod
Bryansk
Roslavl
Smolensk
Vyazma
Safonovo
Yartsevo
Vitsyebsk
Vitebsk
Orsha
Mahilyow
Babruysk
Homyel
Gomel
Rechytsa
Mazyr
Pinsk
Baranavichy
MINSK
Barysaw
Maladzyechna
Polatsk
Navapolatsk
Daugavpils
Rēzekne
Jēkabpils
Chernihiv
Sumy
Shostka
Konotop
Chornobyl
Chernobyl
Korosten
Lutsk
Rivne
Novohrad-Volynskyy
KYYIV
KIEV
Brovary
Pryluky
Romny
Okhtyrka
Hadyach
KHARKIV

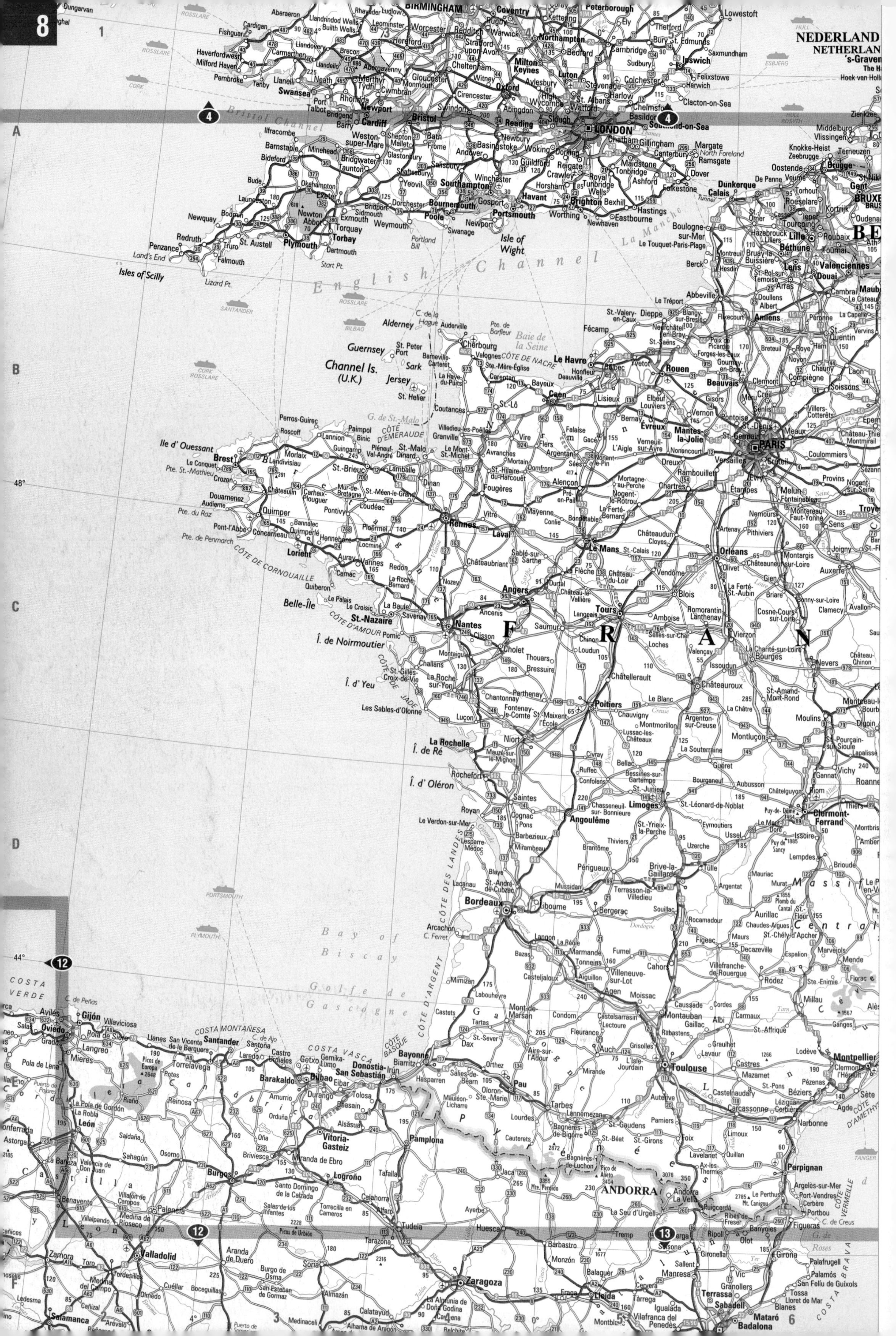
BIRMINGHAM
LONDON
Bristol
Cardiff
Swansea
Plymouth
Southampton
Portsmouth
Brighton
Bournemouth
Oxford
Reading
Cambridge
Ipswich
Dover
Isle of Wight
Isles of Scilly
Bristol Channel
English Channel
La Manche
Channel Is.
(U.K.)
Alderney
Guernsey
Jersey
NEDERLAND
NETHERLAND
PARIS
Rouen
Le Havre
Caen
Amiens
Lille
Calais
Brest
Rennes
Nantes
Angers
Tours
Orléans
Le Mans
Poitiers
La Rochelle
Limoges
Bordeaux
Toulouse
Montpellier
Perpignan
Clermont-Ferrand
FRANCE
Massif Central
Bay of Biscay
Golfe de Gascogne
Pyrénées
ANDORRA
Bilbao
Santander
Oviedo
Gijón
León
Burgos
Valladolid
Zaragoza
Pamplona
Donostia-San Sebastián
Vitoria-Gasteiz
Logroño
Lleida
Girona
Sabadell
Badalona

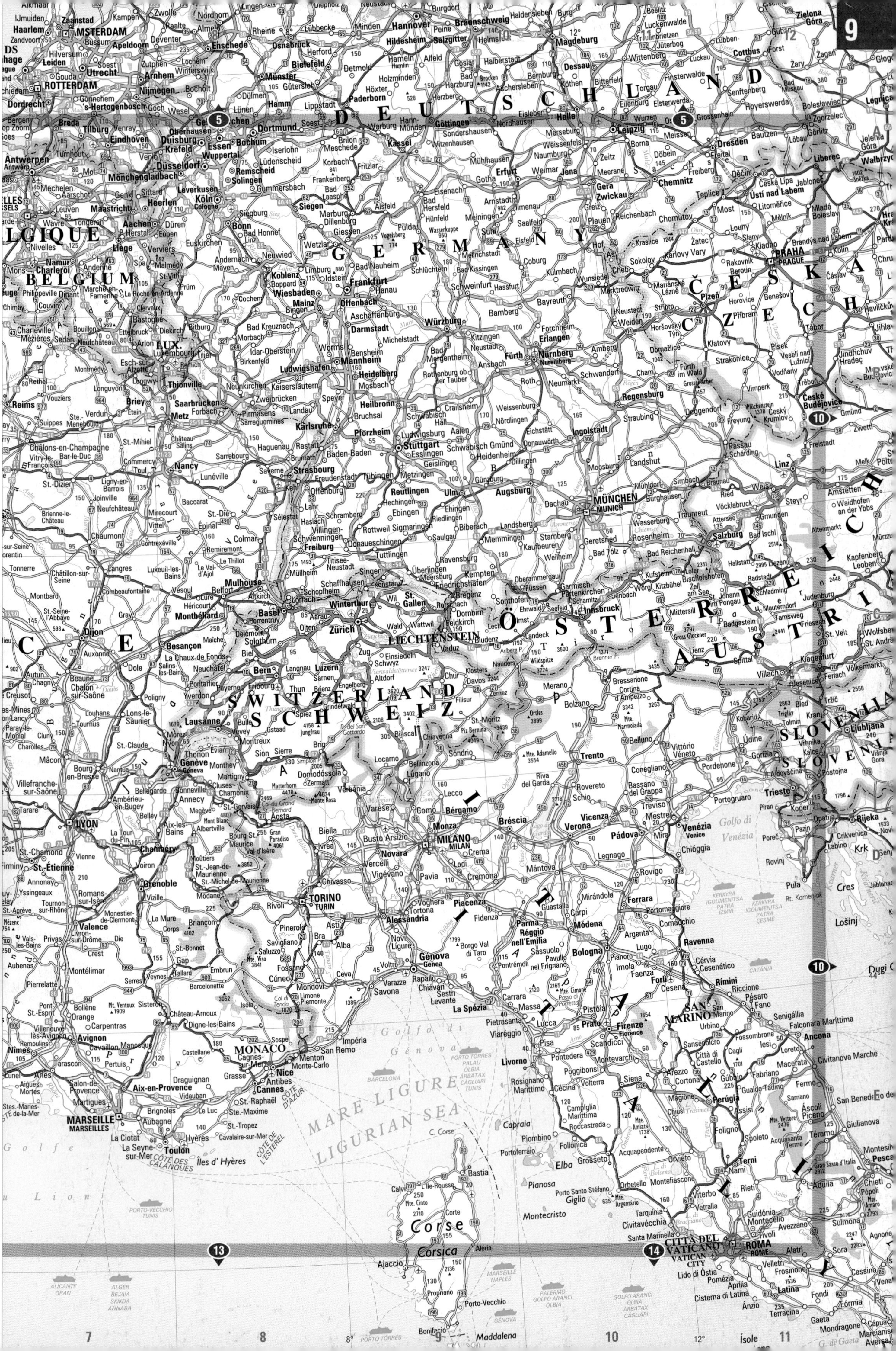
DEUTSCHLAND
GERMANY
BELGIQUE
BELGIUM
LUX.
ČESKÁ
CZECH
ÖSTERREICH
AUSTRIA
SWITZERLAND
SCHWEIZ
LIECHTENSTEIN
SLOVENIJA
SLOVENIA
ITALIA
ITALY
MONACO
SAN MARINO
CITTÀ DEL VATICANO
VATICAN CITY
MARE LIGURE
LIGURIAN SEA
Golfo di Genova
Golfo di Venézia
Corse
Corsica
Elba
Capraia
Pianosa
Montecristo
Giglio
AMSTERDAM
ROTTERDAM
Haarlem
Utrecht
Arnhem
Nijmegen
Dordrecht
's-Hertogenbosch
Breda
Tilburg
Eindhoven
Antwerpen
Mechelen
Leuven
Liège
Maastricht
Aachen
Charleroi
Namur
Nivelles
Mons
Hannover
Braunschweig
Magdeburg
Osnabrück
Bielefeld
Münster
Dortmund
Essen
Duisburg
Düsseldorf
Mönchengladbach
Köln
Cologne
Bonn
Koblenz
Wiesbaden
Mainz
Frankfurt
Offenbach
Darmstadt
Mannheim
Heidelberg
Ludwigshafen
Karlsruhe
Stuttgart
Kassel
Göttingen
Halle
Leipzig
Dresden
Chemnitz
Zwickau
Erfurt
Jena
Gera
Weimar
Würzburg
Bamberg
Bayreuth
Erlangen
Nürnberg
Fürth
Regensburg
Ingolstadt
Augsburg
München
MUNICH
Ulm
Freiburg
Saarbrücken
Kaiserslautern
Trier
Luxembourg
Metz
Nancy
Strasbourg
Mulhouse
Basel
Zürich
Bern
Luzern
Lausanne
Genève
Geneva
St. Gallen
Winterthur
Innsbruck
Salzburg
Linz
Passau
Praha
PRAGUE
Plzeň
Liberec
Ústí nad Labem
České Budějovice
Karlovy Vary
Ljubljana
Trieste
Rijeka
Reims
Dijon
Besançon
Lyon
Grenoble
Chambéry
St.-Étienne
Valence
Avignon
Nîmes
Aix-en-Provence
Marseille
MARSEILLES
Toulon
Cannes
Nice
Antibes
Menton
Monte-Carlo
San Remo
Torino
TURIN
Milano
MILAN
Genova
Bergamo
Brescia
Verona
Vicenza
Pádova
Venézia
Venice
Trento
Bolzano
Parma
Modena
Bologna
Ferrara
Ravenna
Rimini
Pisa
Livorno
Lucca
Firenze
Florence
Siena
Perúgia
Ancona
Roma
ROME
Bastia
Ajaccio
Corte
Porto-Vecchio

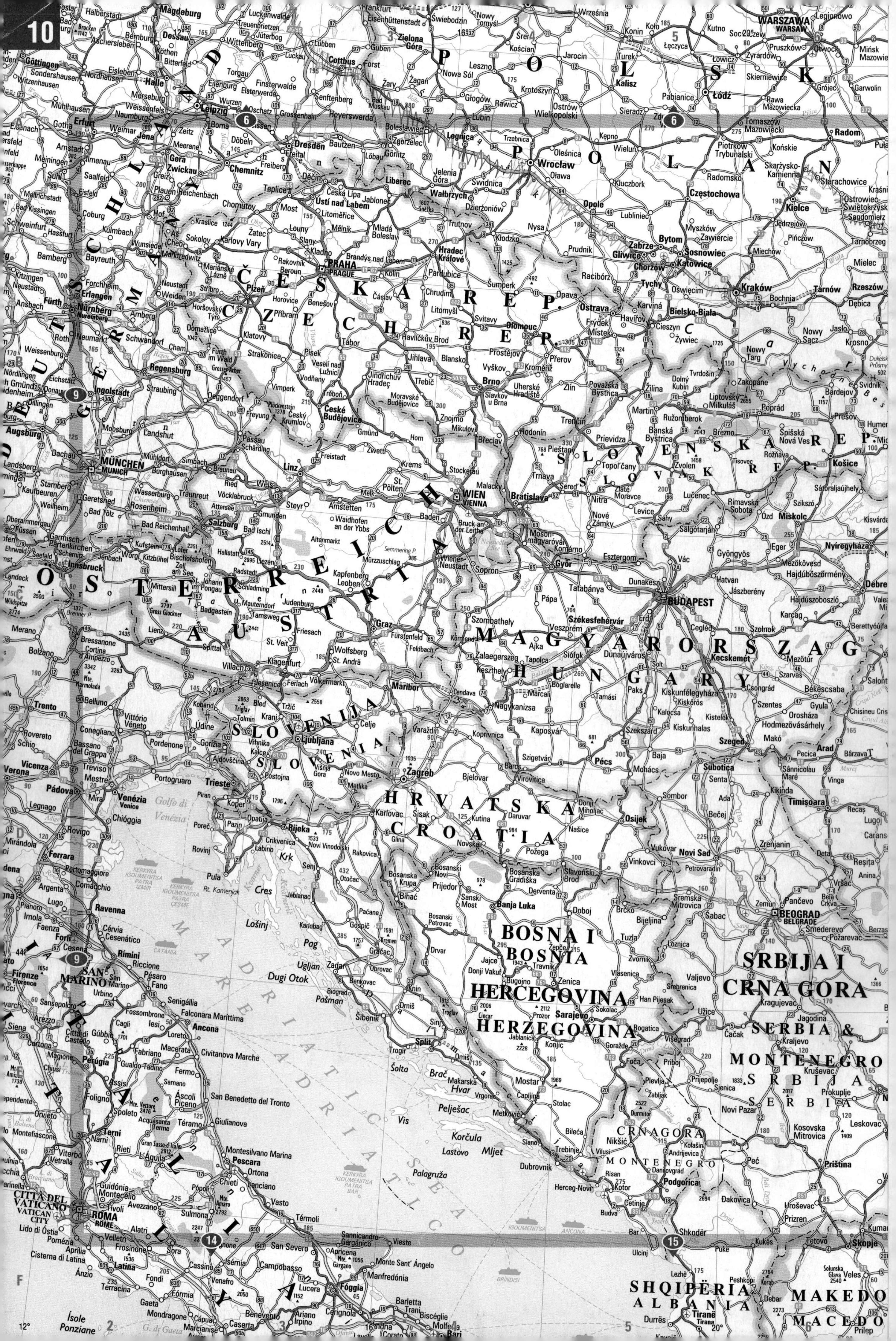
DEUTSCHLAND
GERMANY
POLSKA
POLAND
ČESKÁ REP.
CZECH REP.
ÖSTERREICH
AUSTRIA
SLOVENSKÁ REP.
SLOVAKIA
MAGYARORSZÁG
HUNGARY
SLOVENIJA
SLOVENIA
HRVATSKA
CROATIA
BOSNA I HERCEGOVINA
BOSNIA HERZEGOVINA
SRBIJA I CRNA GORA
SERBIA & MONTENEGRO
SRBIJA
SERBIA
CRNA GORA
MONTENEGRO
SHQIPËRIA
ALBANIA
MAKEDO
MACEDO
ITALIA
ITALY
MARE ADRIATICO
ADRIATIC SEA
Golfo di Venézia
Magdeburg
Leipzig
Dresden
Chemnitz
Erfurt
Nürnberg
Nuremberg
Regensburg
Ingolstadt
Augsburg
MÜNCHEN
MUNICH
Salzburg
Innsbruck
Linz
WIEN
VIENNA
Graz
Klagenfurt
Villach
PRAHA
PRAGUE
Plzeň
Brno
Ostrava
Olomouc
České Budějovice
Liberec
Ústí nad Labem
Hradec Králové
Pardubice
Wrocław
Opole
Katowice
Kraków
Łódź
WARSZAWA
WARSAW
Częstochowa
Kielce
Radom
Poznań
Zielona Góra
Legnica
Bratislava
Trnava
Nitra
Žilina
Banská Bystrica
Košice
Prešov
BUDAPEST
Győr
Székesfehérvár
Miskolc
Debrecen
Nyíregyháza
Kecskemét
Szeged
Pécs
Ljubljana
Maribor
Zagreb
Rijeka
Osijek
Split
Zadar
Dubrovnik
Banja Luka
Sarajevo
Mostar
Tuzla
Novi Sad
BEOGRAD
BELGRADE
Subotica
Niš
Priština
Podgorica
Skopje
Tirane
Timişoara
Arad
Trieste
Venézia
Venice
Pádova
Verona
Vicenza
Trento
Bolzano
Ferrara
Bologna
Ravenna
Rímini
Ancona
Perúgia
Firenze
Florence
SAN MARINO
Pescara
Foggia
Bari
CITTÀ DEL VATICANO
VATICAN CITY
ROMA
ROME
Latina
Chieti
L'Áquila
Térmoli
6
9
14
15

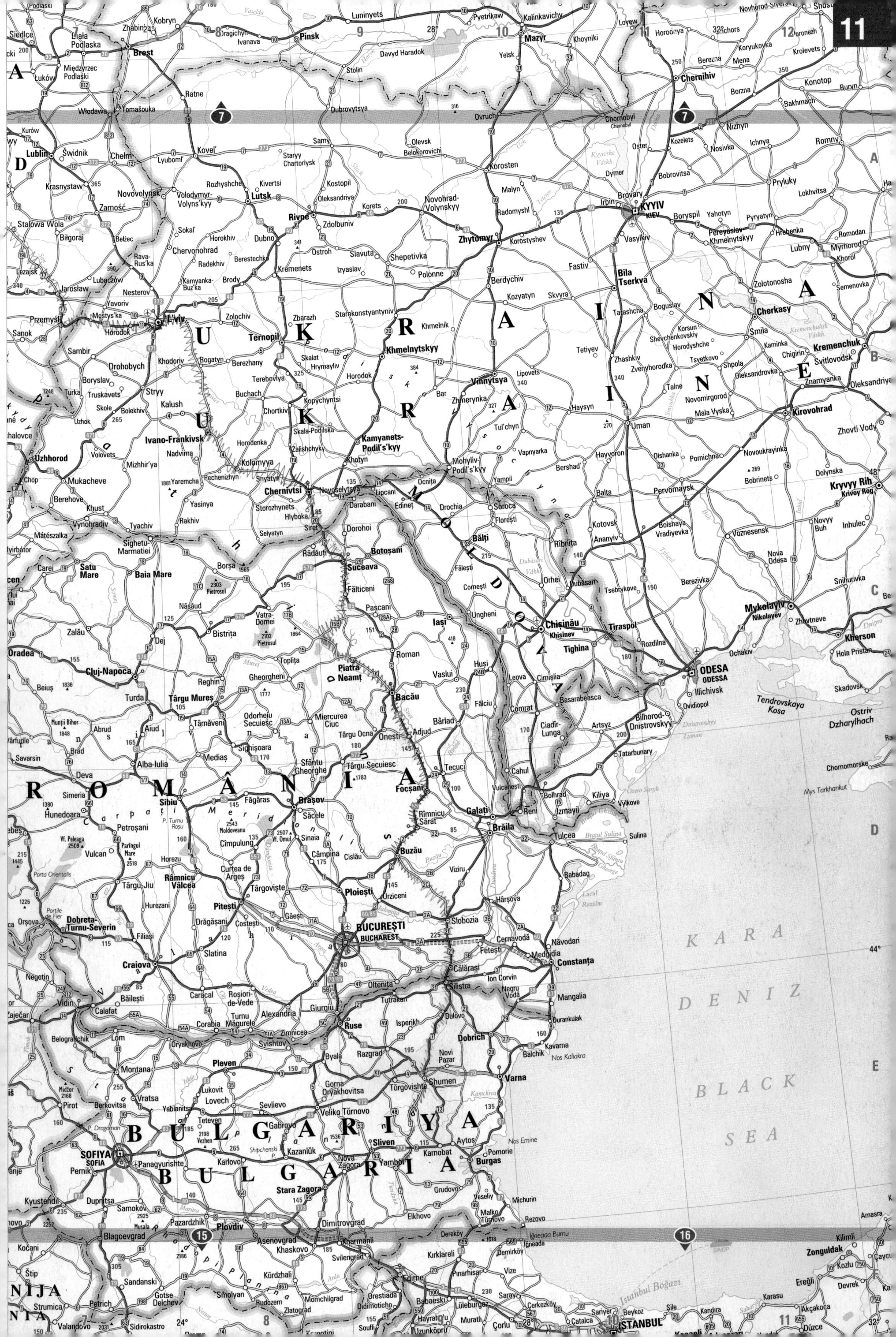
UKRAINA
UKRAÏNA
MOLDOVA
ROMÂNIA
BULGARIYA
BULGARIA
KARA DENIZ
BLACK SEA
KYYIV
KIEV
ODESA
CHIŞINĂU
BUCUREŞTI
BUCHAREST
SOFIYA
SOFIA
ISTANBUL
Brest
Pinsk
Mazyr
Lublin
Lutsk
Rivne
Zhytomyr
Chernihiv
L'viv
Ternopil
Khmelnytskyy
Vinnytsya
Cherkasy
Kremenchuk
Kirovohrad
Uman
Bila Tserkva
Kamyanets-Podil's'kyy
Chernivtsi
Ivano-Frankivsk
Uzhhorod
Mukacheve
Bălţi
Tiraspol
Tighina
Mykolayiv
Nikolayev
Kherson
Kryvyy Rih
Krivoy Rog
Suceava
Botoşani
Iaşi
Piatra Neamţ
Bacău
Cluj-Napoca
Oradea
Baia Mare
Satu Mare
Târgu Mureş
Sibiu
Braşov
Galaţi
Brăila
Tulcea
Constanţa
Buzău
Ploieşti
Piteşti
Craiova
Râmnicu Vâlcea
Focşani
Dobreta-Turnu-Severin
Ruse
Varna
Burgas
Pleven
Shumen
Dobrich
Stara Zagora
Plovdiv
Vratsa
Montana
Vidin
Edirne
Kırklareli
Zonguldak
Tendrovskaya Kosa
Ostriv Dzharylhach
Istanbul Boğazı

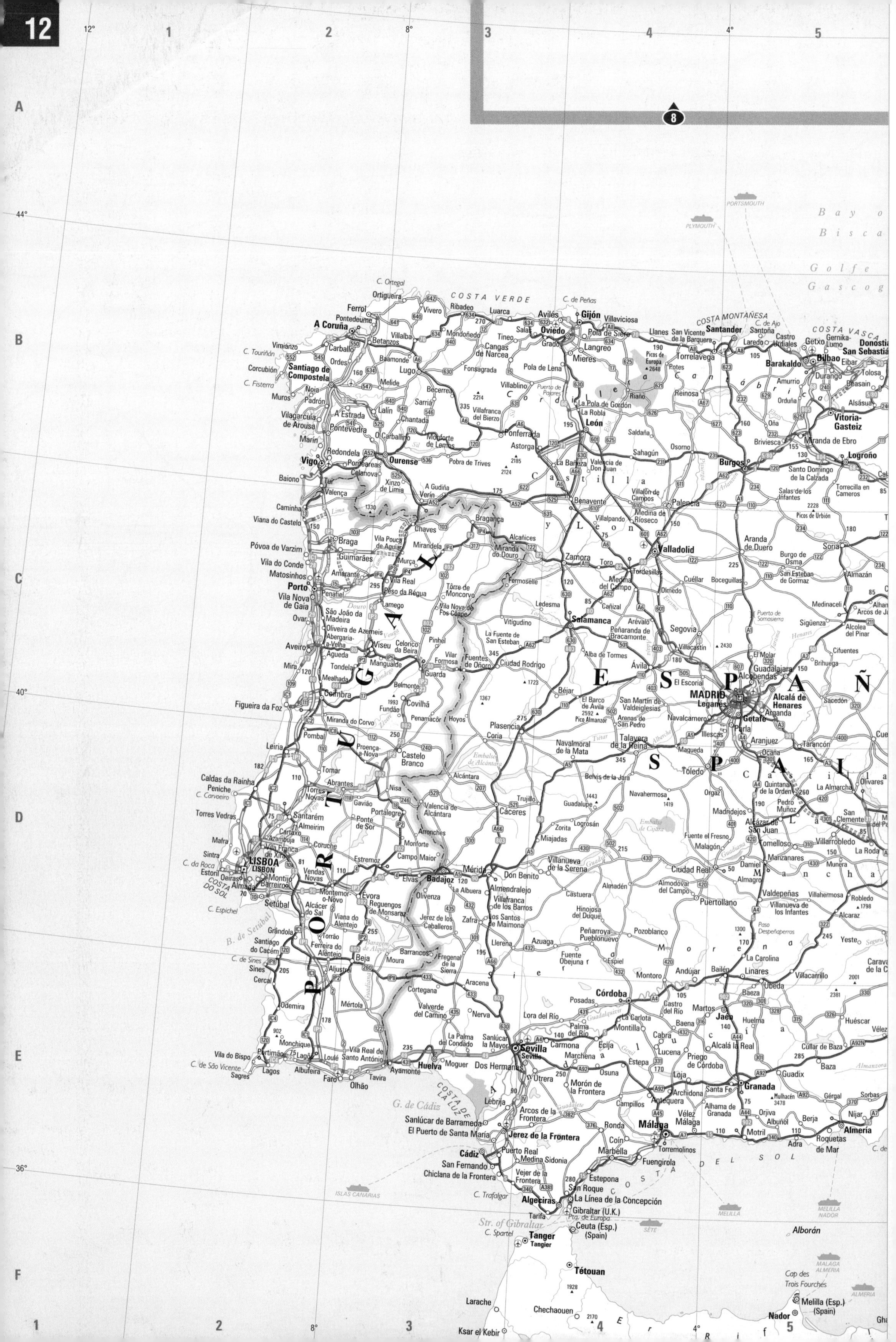

Bay of Biscay
Golfe de Gascogne
PORTSMOUTH
PLYMOUTH
COSTA VERDE
COSTA MONTAÑESA
COSTA VASCA
C. Ortegal
C. de Peñas
A Coruña
Ferrol
Santiago de Compostela
Lugo
Oviedo
Gijón
Avilés
Santander
Bilbao
Donostia
Vitoria-Gasteiz
Pontevedra
Vigo
Ourense
León
Burgos
Logroño
Palencia
Valladolid
Zamora
Salamanca
Segovia
Soria
Ávila
MADRID
Toledo
Alcalá de Henares
Guadalajara
Cáceres
Badajoz
Mérida
Ciudad Real
Córdoba
Sevilla
Huelva
Cádiz
Jerez de la Frontera
Málaga
Granada
Jaén
Almería
Algeciras
Gibraltar (U.K.)
Ceuta (Esp.) (Spain)
Tanger Tangier
Tétouan
Melilla (Esp.) (Spain)
Nador
Alborán
Str. of Gibraltar
G. de Cádiz
COSTA DE LA LUZ
COSTA DEL SOL
Braga
Porto
Vila Nova de Gaia
Aveiro
Viseu
Coimbra
Leiria
Castelo Branco
Santarém
LISBOA LISBON
Setúbal
Évora
Beja
Faro
Lagos
Sagres
C. de São Vicente
B. de Setúbal
PORTUGAL
ESPAÑA SPAIN
Cordillera Cantábrica
Castilla y León
Castilla La Mancha
Sierra Morena
Picos de Europa 2648
Mulhacén 3478
ISLAS CANARIAS
MELILLA
MALAGA ALMERIA

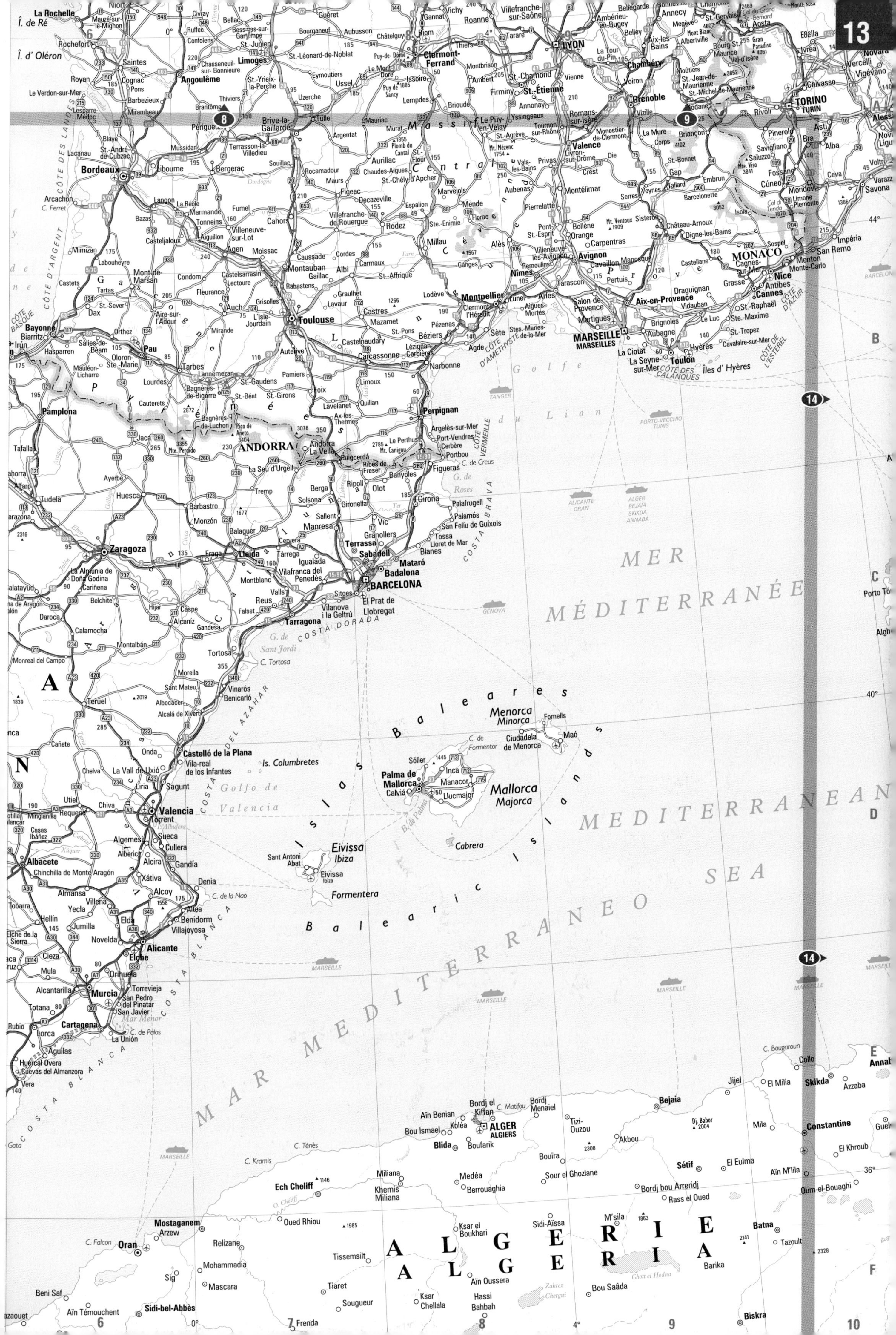
La Rochelle
Î. de Ré
Î. d' Oléron
Rochefort
Saintes
Royan
Cognac
Angoulême
Limoges
Guéret
Vichy
Roanne
Villefranche-sur-Saône
LYON
Annecy
Chambéry
Aosta
Ivrea
Novara
Vercelli
Clermont-Ferrand
St.-Étienne
Grenoble
TORINO
TURIN
Périgueux
Brive-la-Gaillarde
Tulle
Le Puy-en-Velay
Valence
Massif Central
Bordeaux
Arcachon
Bergerac
Libourne
Cahors
Rodez
Aurillac
Mende
Millau
Alès
Avignon
Nîmes
Montpellier
Arles
Aix-en-Provence
MARSEILLE
MARSEILLES
Toulon
Cannes
Nice
MONACO
Menton
Monte-Carlo
San Remo
Imperia
Savona
Cuneo
Gap
Digne-les-Bains
Montélimar
Agen
Montauban
Albi
Toulouse
Castres
Carcassonne
Narbonne
Béziers
Perpignan
Mont-de-Marsan
Bayonne
Biarritz
Pau
Tarbes
Lourdes
Dax
Gascogne
Pyrénées
Pamplona
ANDORRA
Andorra La Vella
Figueras
Girona
Lleida
Zaragoza
Huesca
Tudela
Teruel
Tarragona
Reus
BARCELONA
Badalona
Mataró
Sabadell
Terrassa
Manresa
Vic
Tortosa
Castelló de la Plana
Valencia
Sagunt
Albacete
Alicante
Elche
Murcia
Cartagena
Lorca
Águilas
Benidorm
Alcoy
Dénia
Gandía
Aragón
Cataluña
Valencia
Côte d'Argent
Côte Basque
Côte Vermeille
Costa Brava
Costa Dorada
Costa del Azahar
Costa Blanca
Golfe du Lion
Golfo de Valencia
Îles d' Hyères
Menorca
Minorca
Maó
Ciudadela de Menorca
Mallorca
Majorca
Palma de Mallorca
Cabrera
Eivissa
Ibiza
Formentera
Islas Baleares
Balearic Islands
MER MÉDITERRANÉE
MEDITERRANEAN SEA
MAR MEDITERRANEO
Is. Columbretes
ALGER
ALGIERS
Blida
Bejaia
Jijel
Skikda
Annaba
Constantine
Sétif
Batna
Biskra
Médéa
Ech Cheliff
Mostaganem
Oran
Sidi-bel-Abbès
Mascara
Relizane
Tiaret
ALGÉRIE
ALGERIA
Chott el Hodna
MARSEILLE
GENOVA
TANGER
PORTO-VECCHIO
TUNIS
ALICANTE
ORAN
ALGER
BEJAIA
SKIKDA
ANNABA
BARCELONA
8
9
14
6
7
8
9
10
0°
4°
44°
40°
36°
B
C
D
E
F

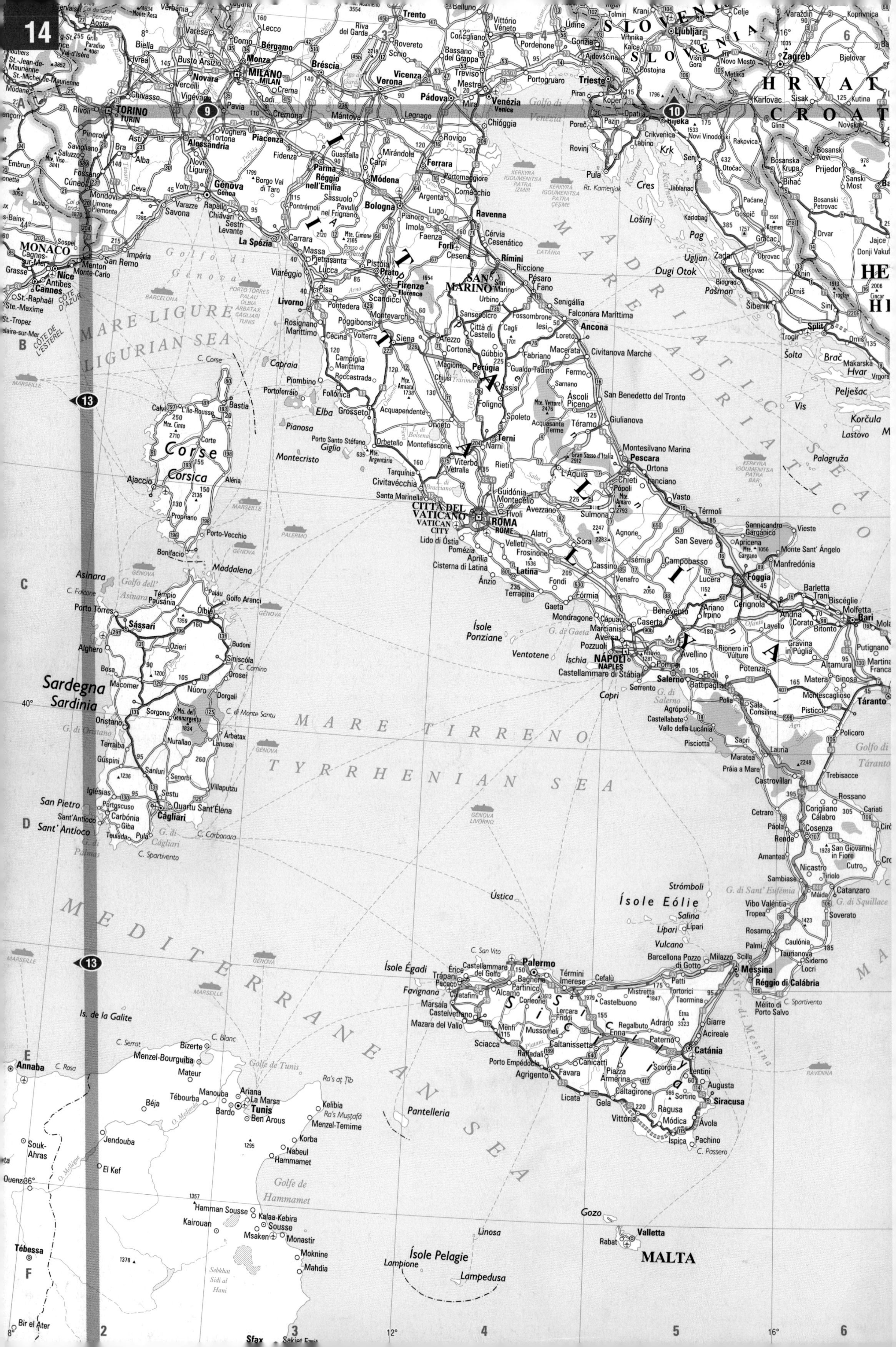
SLOVENIJA
SLOVENIA
HRVATSKA
CROATIA
ITALIA
ITALY
MONACO
Corse
Corsica
Sardegna
Sardinia
Sicilia
MALTA
MARE LIGURE
LIGURIAN SEA
MARE ADRIATICO
ADRIATIC SEA
MARE TIRRENO
TYRRHENIAN SEA
MEDITERRANEAN SEA
Golfo di Genova
Golfo di Venézia
Golfo di Táranto
G. di Squillace
G. di Sant' Eufémia
G. di Salerno
G. di Gaeta
G. di Oristano
G. di Cágliari
G. di Palmas
Golfo dell' Asinara
Golfe de Tunis
Golfe de Hammamet
CÔTE D'AZUR
CÔTE DE L'ESTEREL
Torino
Turin
Milano
Milan
Génova
Genoa
Venézia
Venice
Trento
Trieste
Bologna
Firenze
Florence
Pisa
Livorno
Siena
Perúgia
Ancona
Pescara
SAN MARINO
CITTÀ DEL VATICANO
VATICAN CITY
ROMA
ROME
NÁPOLI
NAPLES
Salerno
Bari
Fóggia
Táranto
Potenza
Cosenza
Catanzaro
Messina
Réggio di Calábria
Palermo
Catánia
Siracusa
Agrigento
Trápani
Marsala
Cágliari
Sássari
Olbia
Nuoro
Oristano
Ajaccio
Bastia
Bonifacio
Porto-Vecchio
Nice
Cannes
Antibes
Menton
Monte-Carlo
San Remo
La Spézia
Parma
Módena
Ferrara
Ravenna
Rímini
Verona
Vicenza
Pádova
Bréscia
Bérgamo
Udine
Ljubljana
Zagreb
Rijeka
Split
Zadar
Pula
Tunis
Bizerte
Sousse
Kairouan
Annaba
Valletta
Gozo
Rabat
Ísole Eólie
Ísole Égadi
Ísole Pelagie
Ísole Ponziane
Strómboli
Lípari
Vulcano
Salina
Ústica
Pantelleria
Linosa
Lampedusa
Lampione
Capri
Íschia
Elba
Capraia
Giglio
Montecristo
Pianosa
Asinara
Maddalena
Is. de la Galite
C. Corse
C. Passero
C. Spartivento
C. Carbonara
C. San Vito
C. Bon
C. Serrat
C. Rosa
Mte. Cinto 2710
Gran Sasso d'Italia 2912
Mte. Amaro 2793
Etna 3323
Mte. Cimone 2165
Mte. Vettore 2476
Mte. Amiata 1738
Mti. del Gennargentu 1834
KERKYRA
IGOUMENITSA
PATRA
IZMIR
ÇEŞME
CATÁNIA
MARSEILLE
BARCELONA
PORTO TORRES
PALAU
OLBIA
ÁRBATAX
CÁGLIARI
TUNIS
PALERMO
GÉNOVA
LIVORNO
RAVENNA
9
10
13
A
B
C
D
E
F
2
3
4
5
6
12°
16°
40°
44°
36°

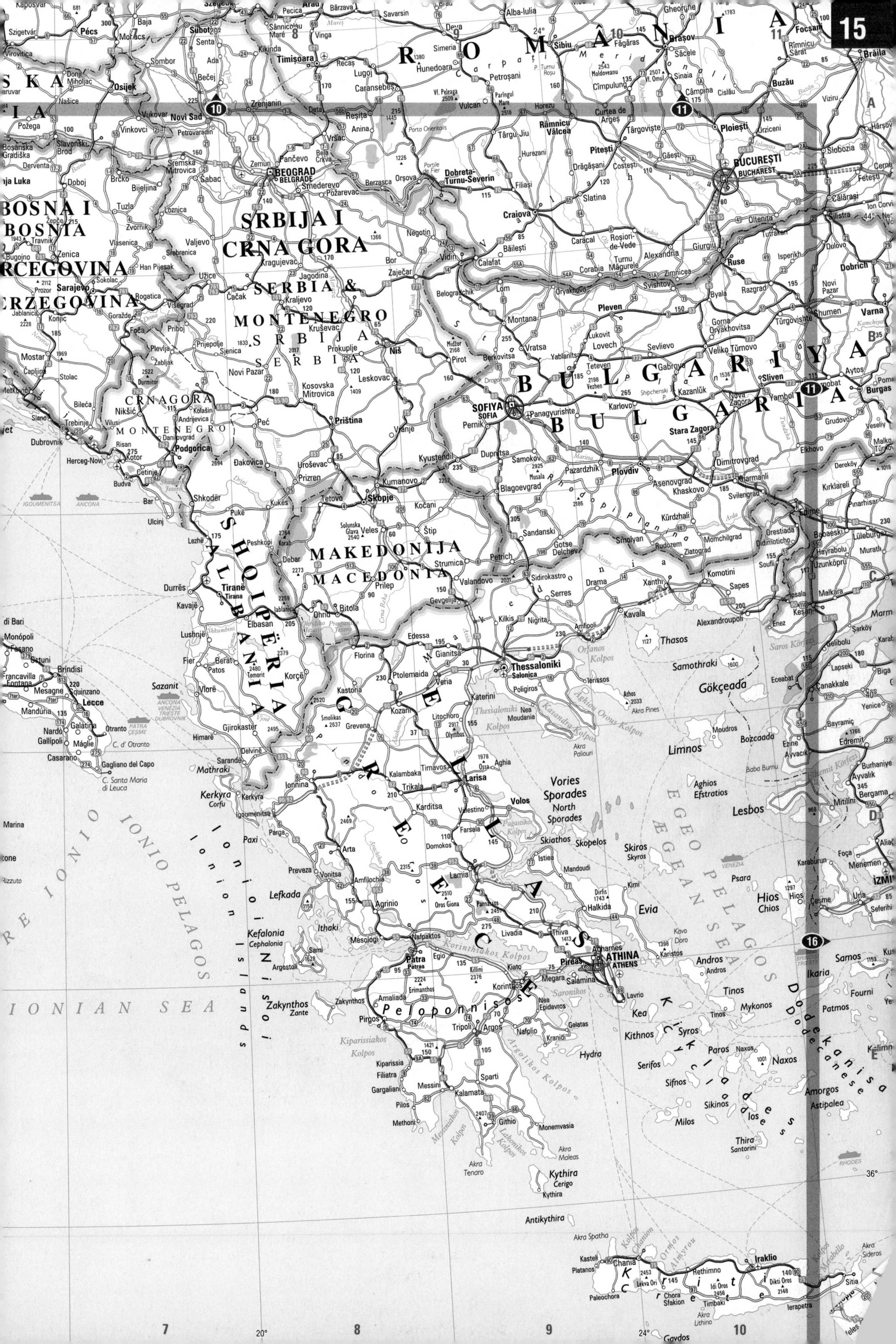
ROMÂNIA
BULGARIYA
BULGARIA
SRBIJA I CRNA GORA
SERBIA & MONTENEGRO
SRBIJA
SERBIA
CRNAGORA
MONTENEGRO
BOSNA I HERCEGOVINA
MAKEDONIJA
MACEDONIA
SHQIPËRIA
ALBANIA
GREECE
BUCUREŞTI
BUCHAREST
BEOGRAD
BELGRADE
SOFIYA
SOFIA
Skopje
Tiranë
Thessaloniki
ATHINA
ATHENS
Sarajevo
Podgorica
Priština
Novi Sad
Niš
Craiova
Timişoara
Braşov
Ploieşti
Constanţa
Varna
Burgas
Plovdiv
Ruse
Pleven
Stara Zagora
Edirne
Patra
Larisa
Volos
Iraklio
Chania
Kerkyra
Corfu
Kefalonia
Zakynthos
Lefkada
Peloponnisos
Limnos
Lesbos
Hios
Samos
Evia
Thasos
Samothraki
Gökçeada
Kythira
Kiklades
Dodekanisa
Dodecanese
Vories Sporades
North Sporades
Karpaţi Meridionali
Stara Planina
Rhodopi Planina
IONIAN SEA
IONIO PELAGOS
Ionioi Nisoi
Ionian Islands
EGEO PELAGOS
AEGEAN SEA
Thermaikos Kolpos
Saronikos Kolpos
Argolikos Kolpos
Korinthiakos Kolpos
Lecce
Brindisi
7
8
9
10
11
20°
24°
36°

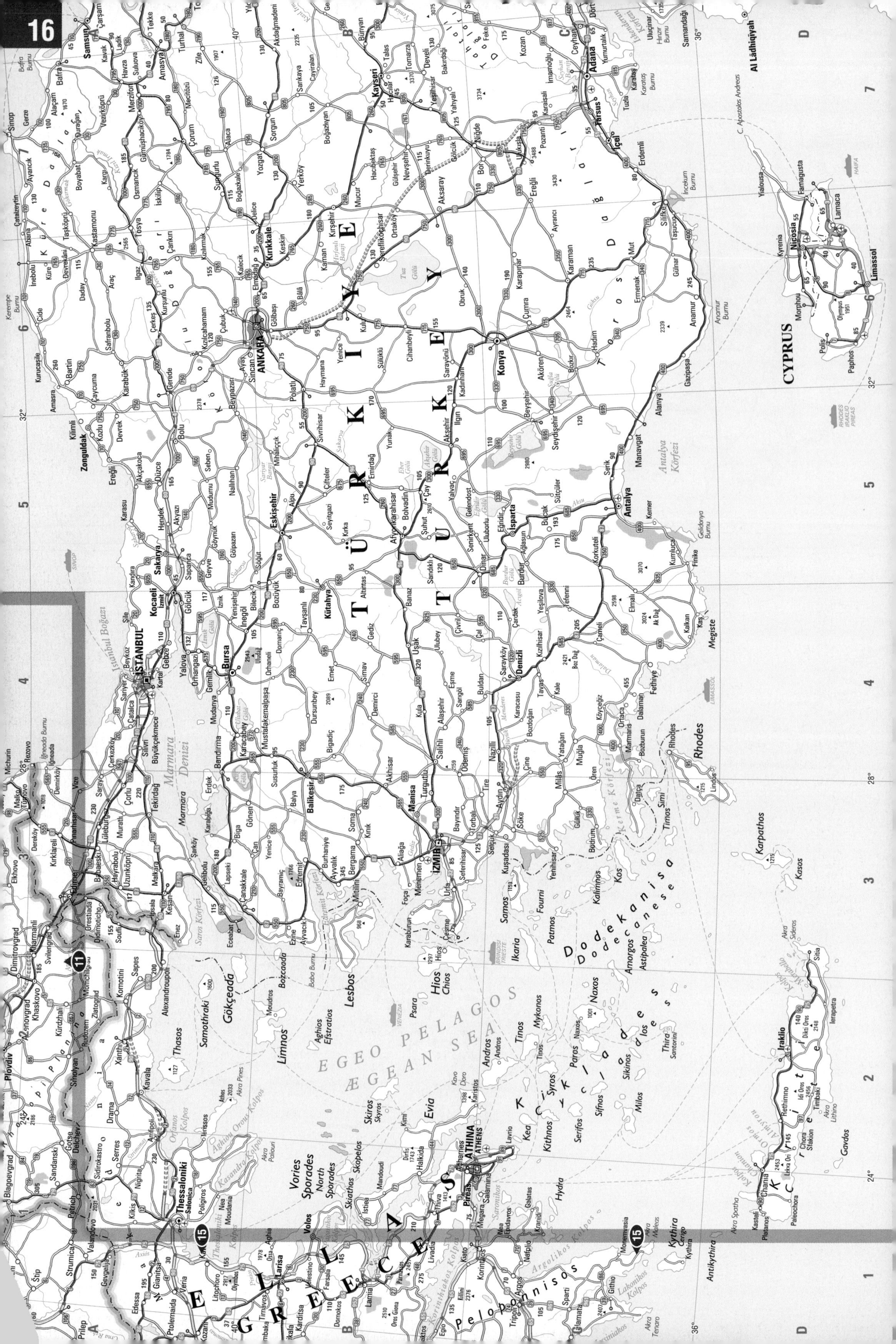
TÜRKIYE
TURKEY
GREECE
ELLAS
CYPRUS
ANKARA
ISTANBUL
IZMIR
ATHINA
ATHENS
Thessaloniki
Bursa
Konya
Antalya
Adana
Kayseri
Eskişehir
Samsun
Sinop
Zonguldak
Denizli
Nicosia
Limassol
Larnaca
Famagusta
Iraklio
Rhodes
Lesbos
Limnos
Thasos
Samothraki
Gökçeada
Bozcaada
Samos
Ikaria
Naxos
Paros
Milos
Kos
Karpathos
Kasos
Evia
Skiros
Kythira
Peloponnisos
EGEO PELAGOS
ÆGEAN SEA
Marmara Denizi
Dodekanisa
Dodecanese
Kiklades
Antalya Körfezi
Toros Dağları
Küre Dağları
Köroğlu Dağları
Al Ladhiqiyah
D

Key to road map pages

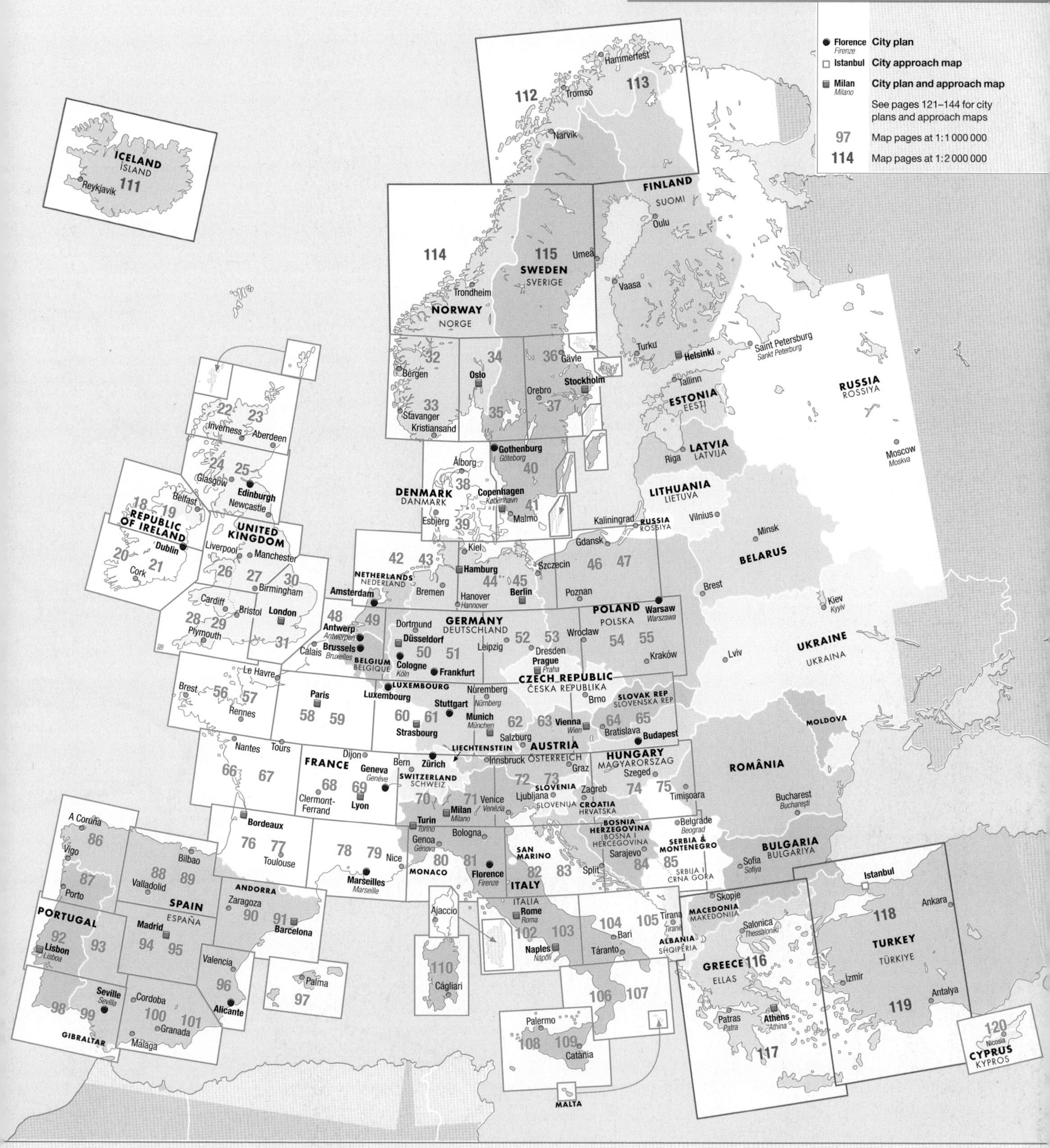

● Florence *Firenze* City plan
□ Istanbul City approach map
■ Milan *Milano* City plan and approach map

See pages 121–144 for city plans and approach maps

97 Map pages at 1:1 000 000

114 Map pages at 1:2 000 000

ICELAND
ÍSLAND
111
Reykjavík

112
Hammerfest
Tromsø
113
Narvik

FINLAND
SUOMI

114
115
SWEDEN
SVERIGE
Oulu

Umeå

NORWAY
NORGE
Trondheim
Vaasa

32
34
36
Gävle
Turku
Helsinki
Saint Petersburg
Sankt Peterburg

Bergen
Oslo
Örebro
Stockholm

RUSSIA
ROSSIYA

33
35
37
Stavanger
Kristiansand

ESTONIA
EESTI

Tallinn

22
23
Inverness
Aberdeen

38
Ålborg
Gothenburg
Göteborg
40
Riga

LATVIA
LATVIJA

Moscow
Moskva

24
25
Glasgow
Edinburgh
Newcastle

DENMARK
DANMARK
Copenhagen
København
41
Malmö

LITHUANIA
LIETUVA

Minsk

18
19
Belfast
REPUBLIC
OF IRELAND

Esbjerg
39
Kiel

Kaliningrad
RUSSIA
ROSSIYA
Vilnius

20
21
Dublin
Cork
Liverpool
Manchester
26
27
30
Birmingham

42
43
Hamburg
Bremen
44
45
Berlin
Gdansk
Szczecin
46
47

BELARUS

Brest

28
29
Cardiff
Bristol
London
31
Plymouth

NETHERLANDS
NEDERLAND
Amsterdam
48
49
Antwerp
Antwerpen
Brussels
Bruxelles
Calais

GERMANY
DEUTSCHLAND
Dortmund
Düsseldorf
50
51
Cologne
Köln
Frankfurt
Leipzig
52
53
Dresden

POLAND
POLSKA
Wrocław
54
55
Kraków
Warsaw
Warszawa
Poznan

UKRAINE
UKRAINA
Lviv
Kiev
Kyiv

56
57
Le Havre
Brest
Rennes
Paris
58
59

LUXEMBOURG
Luxembourg
Nüremberg
Nürnberg
Stuttgart
60
61
Munich
München
Strasbourg

CZECH REPUBLIC
ČESKA REPUBLIKA
Prague
Praha
Brno

62
63
Vienna
Wien
SLOVAK REP
SLOVENSKA REP
64
65
Bratislava
Budapest

MOLDOVA

66
67
Nantes
Tours
Dijon
FRANCE
68
69
Geneva
Genève
Clermont-
Ferrand
Lyon

Bern
Zürich
SWITZERLAND
SCHWEIZ
LIECHTENSTEIN
Innsbruck
AUSTRIA
ÖSTERREICH
Salzburg
Graz

70
71
Venice
Venézia
72
73
SLOVENIA
SLOVENIJA
Ljubljana
Zagreb
CROATIA
HRVATSKA
74
75
Timişoara

HUNGARY
MAGYARORSZÁG
Szeged

ROMÂNIA

Bucharest
Bucureşti

86
A Coruña
Vigo
Bordeaux
76
77
Toulouse
78
79
Nice
Genoa
Génova
80
81
Turin
Torino
MONACO
Milan
Milano
Bologna
Florence
Firenze
82
83
Split
84
85
Belgrade
Beograd
BOSNIA
HERZEGOVINA
BOSNA I
HERCEGOVINA
Sarajevo
SERBIA &
MONTENEGRO
SRBIJA I
CRNA GORA

BULGARIA
BULGARIYA
Sofia
Sofiya

Istanbul

87
Porto
88
89
Bilbao
Valladolid
Marseilles
Marseille
ANDORRA
Zaragoza
90
91
Barcelona
SAN
MARINO
ITALY
ITALIA

MACEDONIA
MAKEDONIJA
Salonica
Thessaloniki

118
Ankara
TURKEY
TÜRKIYE

PORTUGAL
Lisbon
Lisboa
92
93
Madrid
94
95
SPAIN
ESPAÑA
Valencia
96
Rome
Roma
102
103
104
105
Bari
Naples
Nápoli
Táranto
Tirana
Tiranë
ALBANIA
SHQIPËRIA
GREECE
ELLAS
116

Izmir

119
Antalya

98
99
Seville
Sevilla
Cordoba
100
101
Granada
Alicante
110
Cágliari
97
Palma
106
107
Palermo
108
109
Catánia
Patras
Patra
Athens
Athína
117
Skopje
120
Nicosia
CYPRUS
KYPROS

GIBRALTAR
Málaga

MALTA

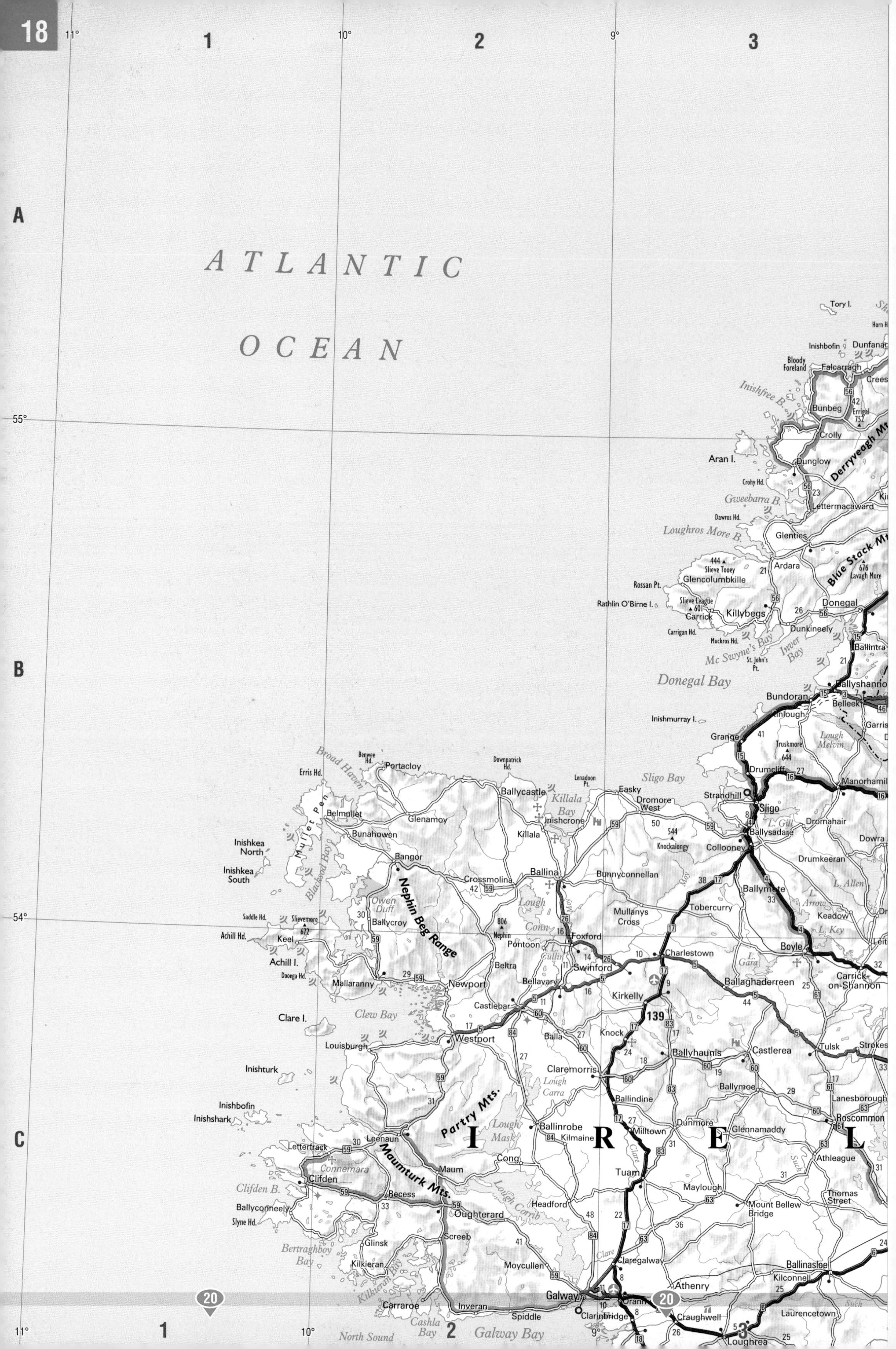

A

ATLANTIC

OCEAN

Tory I.

Horn H.

Inishbofin Dunfanag

Bloody
Foreland Falcarragh

Grees

Inishfree B. Bunbeg 42

Errigal
752

55°

Aran I. Crolly

Dunglow Derryveagh Mt

Crohy Hd. 56

Gweebarra B. 23 Lettermacaward Ki

Dawros Hd.

Loughros More B. Glenties

444 ▲ Ardara Blue Stock Mt 676 ▲

Slieve Tooey 21 Lavagh More

Rossan Pt. Glencolumbkille

Slieve League

Rathlin O'Birne I. ▲601 Donegal

Carrick Killybegs 26

Carrigan Hd. Dunkineely 15

Muckros Hd. Ballintra

B

Mc Swyne's Bay Inver Bay 21 Ballyshannon

St. John's
Pt. 15 13 7 Belleek 46

Donegal Bay Bundoran Garris

Kinlough

Inishmurray I. Grange 41 Lough
Melvin

Truskmore
644

Sligo Bay 15 Drumcliff 27 Manorhamil

Benwee
Hd. Downpatrick
Hd. Easky Strandhill 16 Sligo

Broad Haven Portacloy Lenadoon
Pt. Dromore
West Dromahair

Erris Hd. Ballycastle Killala
Bay Inishcrone 59 50 59 L. Gill

Belmullet Glenamoy Killala H 544 Ballysadare Dowra

Bunahowen Knockalongy Collooney

Inishkea
North Crossmolina Ballina Bunnyconnellan 38 17 Ballymote L. Allen

Mullet Pen. Bangor 42 59 Lough 33 L. Arrow

Inishkea
South Owen
Duff Conn 26 Mullanys
Cross Keadow L. Key

Saddle Hd. Slievemore 30 806 16 Tobercurry 17

54° 672 Ballycroy Nephin Foxford Boyle Leit

Achill Hd. Keel Nephin Beg Range Pontoon L. Gara 32

Achill I. Beltra Cullin 14 26 10 Charlestown

Dooega Hd. 29 59 Swinford 17 Ballaghaderreen 25 Carrick-
on-Shannon

Mallaranny Newport Bellavary 11 9

Clare I. Castlebar 5 16 Kirkelly 44 Tulsk

Clew Bay 17 5 60 Balla 139 Knock Ballyhaunis Castlerea Strokes

Westport 84 27 24 18 H

Louisburgh 27 Claremorris 60 19 Ballymoe 29 Lanesborough

Inishturk Lough
Carra Ballindine 83 61 60 Roscommon

59 Ballinrobe 61 Glennamaddy

Inishbofin 31 Lough
Mask 84 Kilmaine 27 Milltown Dunmore 31 Athleague

Inishshark Letterfrack 30 Leenaun I R E L

Connemara 59 Maumturk Mts. Cong 84 Mount Bellew 31 Thomas
Street

Clifden 59 Maum Tuam Maylough Bridge

Clifden B. Recess Headford 63 24

Ballyconneely 33 Oughterard 48 22 36 Ballinasloe

Slyne Hd. 59 Screeb 84 Kilconnel

Bertraghboy
Bay Glinsk 41 Moycullen Clare Claregalway Laurencetown

Kilkieran Clarinbridge 5

Carraroe Inveran Spiddle Galway Athenry Craughwell 6 Loughrea

North Sound Cashla
Bay Galway Bay

11° 10° 9°

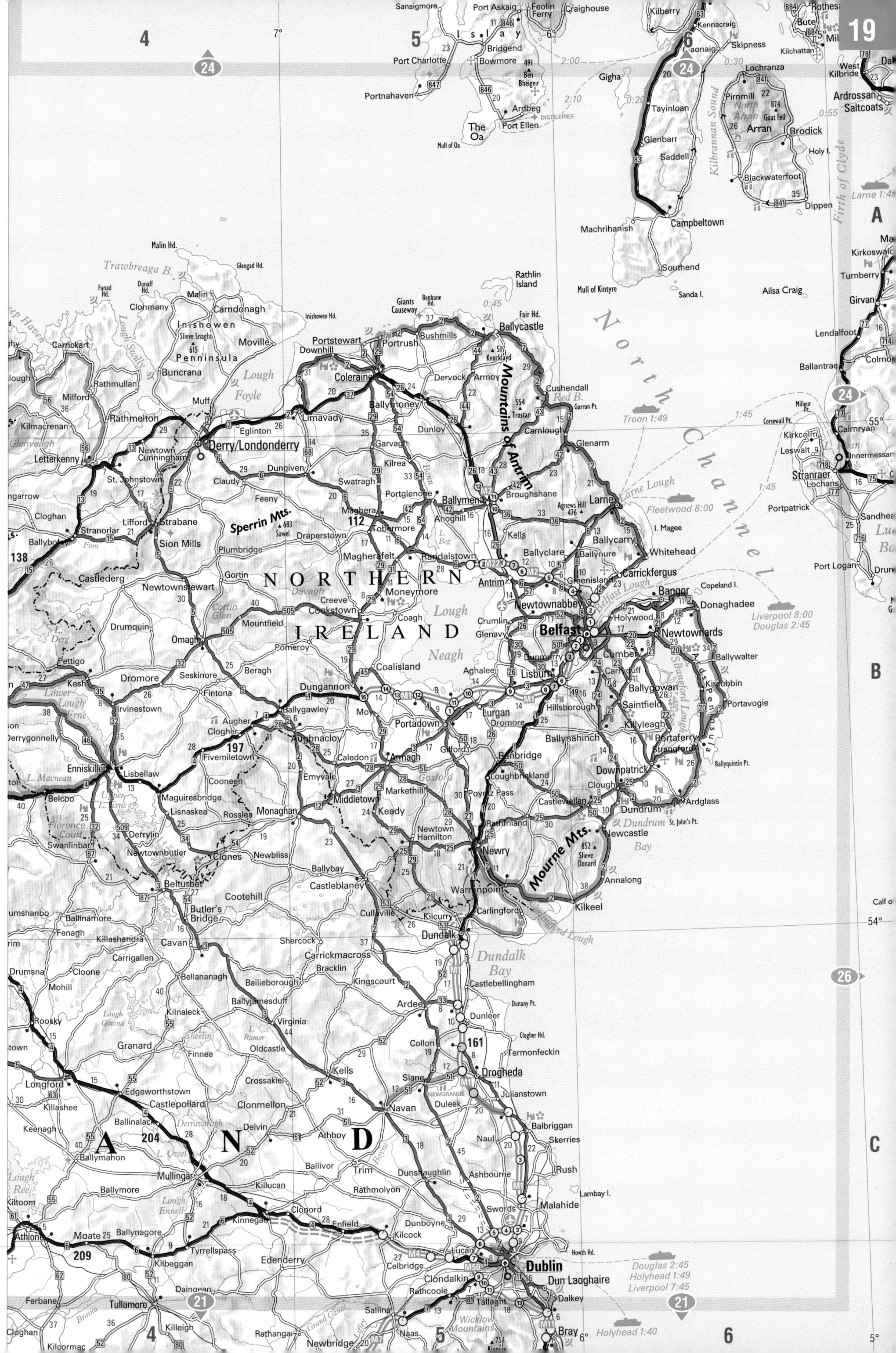

4
5
6
7°
6°
5°
55°
54°
A
B
C
Islay
Sanaigmore
Port Askaig
Feolin Ferry
Craighouse
Bridgend
Port Charlotte
Bowmore
Ben Bheigeir
Portnahaven
Ardbeg
Port Ellen
DISTILLERIES
The Oa
Mull of Oa
Kilberry
Kennacraig
Claonaig
Skipness
Lochranza
Gigha
Tayinloan
Glenbarr
Saddell
Kilbrannan Sound
Pirnmill
North Arran
Goat Fell
Arran
Brodick
Holy I.
Blackwaterfoot
Dippen
Firth of Clyde
Machrihanish
Campbeltown
Southend
Mull of Kintyre
Sanda I.
Ailsa Craig
Rothesay
Bute
Millport
Kilchattan
West Kilbride
Ardrossan
Saltcoats
Larne 1:45
Kirkoswald
Turnberry
Girvan
Lendalfoot
Ballantrae
Colmonell
Milleur Pt.
Corsewall Pt.
Cairnryan
Kirkcolm
L. Ryan
Leswalt
Innermessan
Stranraer
Lochans
Portpatrick
Sandhead
Luce Bay
Port Logan
Drummore
Troon 1:49
Fleetwood 8:00
Liverpool 8:00
Douglas 2:45
North Channel
Malin Hd.
Glengad Hd.
Trawbreaga B.
Fanad Hd.
Dunaff Hd.
Malin
Clonmany
Carndonagh
Inishowen Hd.
Inishowen Penninsula
Slieve Snaght
Lough Swilly
Carrickart
Moville
Buncrana
Rathmullan
Lough Foyle
Milford
Muff
Rathmelton
Eglinton
Kilmacrenan
Derry/Londonderry
Glenveagh
Letterkenny
Newtown Cunningham
St. Johnstown
Claudy
Dungiven
Feeny
Lifford
Strabane
Stranorlar
Ballybofey
Cloghan
Sion Mills
Sperrin Mts.
Sawel
Plumbridge
Draperstown
Castlederg
Newtownstewart
Gortin
Cortin Glen
Drumquin
Omagh
Mountfield
L. Derg
Rathlin Island
Giants Causeway
Benbane Hd.
Fair Hd.
Ballycastle
Portstewart
Portrush
Bushmills
Downhill
Coleraine
Knocklayd
Dervock
Armoy
Mountains of Antrim
Cushendall
Red B.
Garron Pt.
Trostan
Ballymoney
Limavady
Dunloy
Carnlough
Glenarm
Garvagh
Kilrea
Swatragh
Portglenone
Ballymena
Broughshane
Agnews Hill
Larne
Larne Lough
Maghera
Ahoghill
Tobermore
Kells
I. Magee
Ballycarry
Whitehead
Ballyclare
Ballynure
Magherafelt
Randalstown
L. Beg
Carrickfergus
Greenisland
Belfast Lough
Antrim
Copeland I.
Bangor
Donaghadee
NORTHERN IRELAND
Davagh
Moneymore
Creeve
Cookstown
Newtownabbey
Crumlin
Holywood
Lough Neagh
Coagh
Glenavy
Belfast
Newtownards
Pomeroy
Dunmurry
Comber
Ballywalter
Beragh
Seskinore
Coalisland
Carryduff
Aghalee
Lisburn
Ballygowan
Kircubbin
Pettigo
Dromore
Fintona
Kesh
Lower Lough Erne
Irvinestown
Dungannon
Moy
Ballygawley
Lurgan
Hillsborough
Saintfield
Killyleagh
Strangford Lough
Ards Peninsula
Portavogie
Augher
Clogher
Aughnacloy
Portadown
Derrygonnelly
Fivemiletown
Caledon
Armagh
Gilford
Ballynahinch
Portaferry
Strangford
Ballyquintin Pt.
Enniskillen
Lisbellaw
Banbridge
Cooneen
Emyvale
Gosford
Loughbrickland
Downpatrick
L. Macnean
Belcoo
Upper L. Erne
Maguiresbridge
Middletown
Markethill
Poyntz Pass
Clough
Castlewellan
Ardglass
Lisnaskea
Rosslea
Monaghan
Keady
Dundrum
Dundrum Bay
St. John's Pt.
Florence Court
Rathfriland
Newcastle
Swanlinbar
Derrylin
Newtown Hamilton
Newry
Mourne Mts.
Slieve Donard
Newtownbutler
Clones
Newbliss
Ballybay
Annalong
Belturbet
Castleblaney
Warrenpoint
Cootehill
Carlingford
Kilkeel
Carlingford Lough
Drumshanbo
Ballinamore
Butler's Bridge
Cullaville
Kilcurry
Fenagh
Killashandra
Cavan
Shercock
Dundalk
Carrigallen
Carrickmacross
Dundalk Bay
Bracklin
Drumsna
Cloone
Bellananagh
Bailieborough
Kingscourt
Castlebellingham
Mohill
Ballyjamesduff
Ardee
Dunany Pt.
Roosky
Lough Gowna
Kilnaleck
L. Sheelin
L. Ramor
Virginia
Dunleer
Oldcastle
Clogher Hd.
Granard
Finnea
Collon
Termonfeckin
Longford
Edgeworthstown
Crossakiel
Kells
Slane
Drogheda
Killashee
Castlepollard
Clonmellon
Newgrange
Duleek
Julianstown
Keenagh
Ballinalack
L. Derravaragh
Delvin
Navan
Balbriggan
Athboy
Naul
Skerries
Ballymahon
L. Owel
Boyne
Lough Ree
Mullingar
Ballivor
Trim
Dunshaughlin
Ashbourne
Rush
Ballymore
Killucan
Rathmolyon
Lambay I.
Kiltoom
Lough Ennell
Clonard
Malahide
Kinnegad
Enfield
Dunboyne
Swords
Athlone
Moate
Ballynagore
Kilcock
Tyrrellspass
Edenderry
Lucan
Howth Hd.
Kilbeggan
Celbridge
Dublin
Clondalkin
Dun Laoghaire
Daingean
Rathcoole
Tallaght
Dalkey
Douglas 2:45
Holyhead 1:49
Liverpool 7:45
Ferbane
Tullamore
Sallins
Brosna
Grand Canal
Wicklow Mountains
Cloghan
Killeigh
Kilcormac
Rathangan
Naas
Newbridge
Liffey
Kippure
Bray
Holyhead 1:40
ANDD
24
21
26

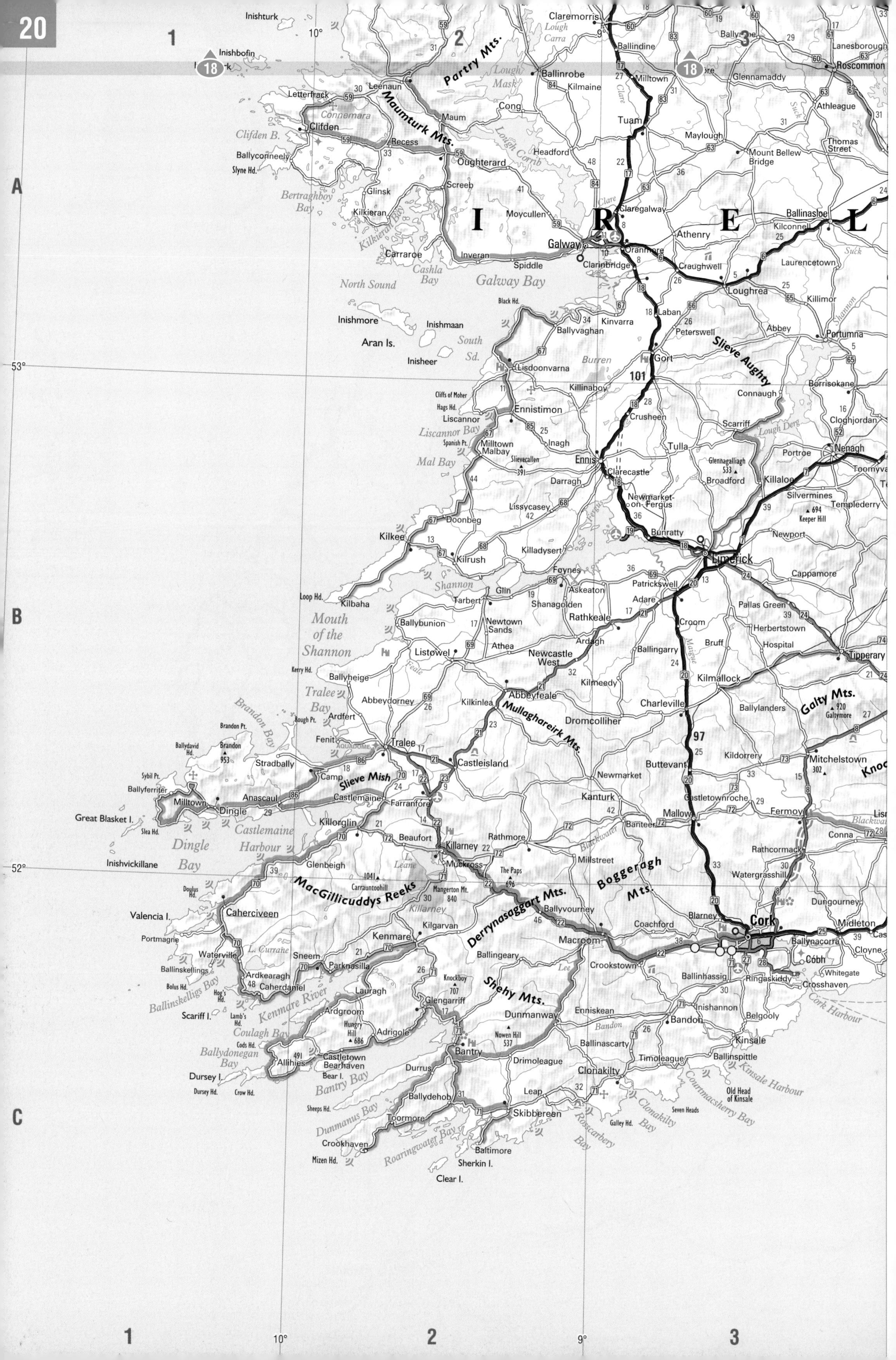
I R E L
Inishturk
Inishbofin
Claremorris
Lough Carra
Partry Mts.
Lough Mask
Ballinrobe
Kilmaine
Ballindine
Milltown
Glennamaddy
Roscommon
Lanesborough
Athleague
Letterfrack
Leenaun
Maumturk Mts.
Connemara
Clifden
Clifden B.
Maum
Cong
Tuam
Recess
Lough Corrib
Headford
Maylough
Mount Bellew Bridge
Thomas Street
Ballyconneely
Slyne Hd.
Oughterard
Screeb
Glinsk
Bertraghboy Bay
Kilkieran
Kilkieran Bay
Moycullen
Claregalway
Ballinasloe
Kilconnell
Athenry
Galway
Oranmore
Clarinbridge
Craughwell
Carraroe
Inveran
Spiddle
Cashla Bay
North Sound
Galway Bay
Laurencetown
Loughrea
Killimor
Black Hd.
Kinvarra
Laban
Peterswell
Abbey
Portumna
Inishmore
Inishmaan
Aran Is.
Inisheer
South Sd.
Ballyvaghan
Slieve Aughty
Lisdoonvarna
Burren
Gort
Killinaboy
Connaugh
Borrisokane
Cliffs of Moher
Hags Hd.
Ennistimon
Liscannor
Liscannor Bay
Spanish Pt.
Milltown Malbay
Inagh
Crusheen
Scarriff
Lough Derg
Cloghjordan
Mal Bay
Slievecallen
Ennis
Clarecastle
Darragh
Tulla
Glennagalliagh
Broadford
Killaloe
Portroe
Nenagh
Toomyvara
Silvermines
Keeper Hill
Templederry
Newmarket-on-Fergus
Lissycasey
Doonbeg
Kilkee
Kilrush
Killadysert
Bunratty
Limerick
Newport
Foynes
Askeaton
Patrickswell
Cappamore
Shannon
Loop Hd.
Kilbaha
Glin
Tarbert
Shanagolden
Adare
Rathkeale
Pallas Green
Mouth of the Shannon
Ballybunion
Newtown Sands
Croom
Herbertstown
Listowel
Athea
Ardagh
Newcastle West
Ballingarry
Bruff
Hospital
Tipperary
Kerry Hd.
Feale
Ballyheige
Kilmeedy
Kilmallock
Tralee Bay
Abbeydorney
Kilkinlea
Abbeyfeale
Charleville
Galty Mts.
Galtymore
Ballylanders
Mullaghareirk Mts.
Dromcolliher
Brandon Bay
Brandon Pt.
Rough Pt.
Ardfert
Brandon
Ballydavid Hd.
Fenit
Aquadome
Tralee
Castleisland
Kildorrery
Buttevant
Mitchelstown
Sybil Pt.
Stradbally
Camp
Slieve Mish
Newmarket
Ballyferriter
Milltown
Dingle
Anascaul
Castlemaine
Farranfore
Kanturk
Castletownroche
Great Blasket I.
Slea Hd.
Killorglin
Mallow
Fermoy
Banteer
Blackwater
Conna
Dingle Bay
Castlemaine Harbour
Beaufort
Killarney
Rathmore
Inishvickillane
Glenbeigh
L. Leane
Muckross
Millstreet
Rathcormack
MacGillicuddys Reeks
Carrauntoohill
Mangerton Mt.
The Paps
Boggeragh Mts.
Watergrasshill
Doulus Hd.
Killarney
Derrynasaggart Mts.
Ballyvourney
Dungourney
Valencia I.
Caherciveen
Kilgarvan
Coachford
Blarney
Cork
Midleton
Portmagne
Kenmare
Macroom
Ballynacorra
Cloyne
Waterville
L. Currane
Sneem
Ballingeary
Crookstown
Cobh
Ballinskellings
Parknasilla
Ballinhassig
Whitegate
Ardkearagh
Caherdaniel
Knockboy
Shehy Mts.
Ringaskiddy
Crosshaven
Bolus Hd.
Ballinskelligs Bay
Hog's Hd.
Lauragh
Glengarriff
Inishannon
Cork Harbour
Kenmare River
Scariff I.
Lamb's Hd.
Ardgroom
Dunmanway
Enniskean
Bandon
Belgooly
Coulagh Bay
Hungry Hill
Adrigole
Nowen Hill
Cods Hd.
Ballydonegan Bay
Allihies
Castletown Bearhaven
Bantry
Ballinascarty
Kinsale
Bear I.
Durrus
Drimoleague
Timoleague
Ballinspittle
Kinsale Harbour
Dursey I.
Bantry Bay
Clonakilty
Dursey Hd.
Crow Hd.
Leap
Old Head of Kinsale
Courtmacsherry Bay
Ballydehob
Clonakilty Bay
Seven Heads
Sheeps Hd.
Dunmanus Bay
Toormore
Skibbereen
Rosscarbery Bay
Galley Hd.
Roaringwater Bay
Crookhaven
Baltimore
Mizen Hd.
Sherkin I.
Clear I.

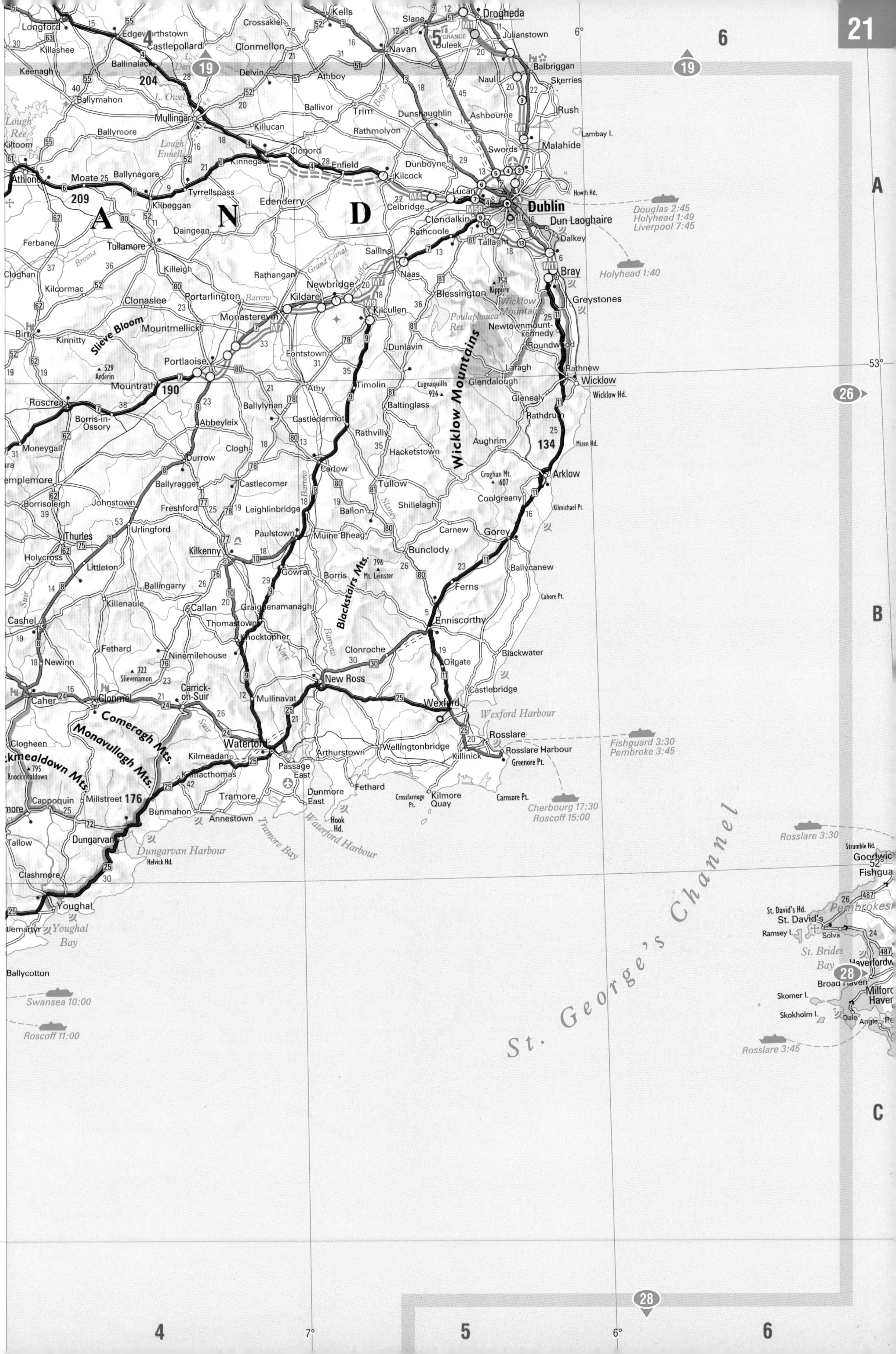

Longford
Edgeworthstown
Castlepollard
Crossakiel
Kells
Slane
Drogheda
Julianstown
Killashee
Ballinalack
Clonmellon
Navan
Duleek
Balbriggan
Skerries
Keenagh
Delvin
Athboy
Naul
Ballymahon
Ballivor
Trim
Dunshaughlin
Ashbourne
Rush
Mullingar
Killucan
Lough Ree
Lough Ennell
L. Owel
Ballymore
Rathmolyon
Swords
Malahide
Lambay I.
Kiltoom
Clonard
Enfield
Kinnegad
Dunboyne
Kilcock
Athlone
Moate
Ballynagore
Tyrrellspass
Lucan
Howth Hd.
Kilbeggan
Edenderry
Celbridge
Dublin
Dun Laoghaire
Clondalkin
Douglas 2:45
Holyhead 1:49
Liverpool 7:45
A N D
Rathcoole
Dalkey
Ferbane
Tullamore
Daingean
Tallaght
Sallins
Brosna
Grand Canal
Bray
Holyhead 1:40
Clogham
Killeigh
Rathangan
Naas
Kilcormac
Newbridge
Liffey
Blessington
Kippure
Portarlington
Barrow
Kildare
Greystones
Clonaslee
Wicklow Mountains
Monasterevin
Kilcullen
Poulaphouca Res.
Slieve Bloom
Mountmellick
Newtownmount-kennedy
Birr
Kinnitty
Fontstown
Dunlavin
Roundwood
Portlaoise
Arderin
Laragh
Rathnew
Wicklow
Wicklow Hd.
Lugnaquilla
Glendalough
Timolin
Mountrath
Athy
Glenealy
Roscrea
Ballylynan
Baltinglass
Borris-in-Ossory
Castledermot
Rathdrum
Abbeyleix
Rathvilly
Aughrim
Mizen Hd.
Moneygall
Clogh
Hacketstown
Durrow
Carlow
Croghan Mt.
Arklow
Templemore
Ballyragget
Castlecomer
Tullow
Coolgreany
Borrisoleigh
Johnstown
Freshford
Leighlinbridge
Ballon
Shillelagh
Kilmichael Pt.
Slaney
Urlingford
Paulstown
Muine Bheag
Carnew
Gorey
Thurles
Kilkenny
Bunclody
Holycross
Littleton
Gowran
Borris
Mt. Leinster
Ballycanew
Blackstairs Mts.
Ballingarry
Ferns
Killenaule
Callan
Graiguenamanagh
Cahore Pt.
Cashel
Thomastown
Enniscorthy
Knocktopher
Nore
Fethard
Ninemilehouse
Clonroche
Blackwater
Newinn
Slievenamon
Oilgate
New Ross
Carrick-on-Suir
Castlebridge
Caher
Clonmel
Mullinavat
Wexford
Comeragh Mts.
Suir
Wexford Harbour
Monavullagh Mts.
Rosslare
Clogheen
Waterford
Arthurstown
Wellingtonbridge
Fishguard 3:30
Pembroke 3:45
Knockmealdown Mts.
Kilmeadan
Passage East
Killinick
Rosslare Harbour
Greenore Pt.
Knockmealdown
Kilmacthomas
Fethard
Dunmore East
Cappoquin
Millstreet
Tramore
Crossfarnoge Pt.
Kilmore Quay
Carnsore Pt.
Cherbourg 17:30
Roscoff 15:00
Bunmahon
Annestown
Hook Hd.
Tallow
Dungarvan
Tramore Bay
Waterford Harbour
Dungarvan Harbour
Helvick Hd.
Rosslare 3:30
Strumble Hd.
Goodwic
Fishgua
Clashmore
Youghal
Youghal Bay
St. David's Hd.
St. David's
Pembrokesh
Ramsey I.
Solva
St. Brides Bay
Haverfordw
Broad Haven
Milforc Haver
Ballycotton
Skomer I.
Skokholm I.
Dale
Angle
Swansea 10:00
Roscoff 11:00
Rosslare 3:45
St. George's Channel
A
B
C
4
5
6
7°
6°
53°
52°
19
26
28

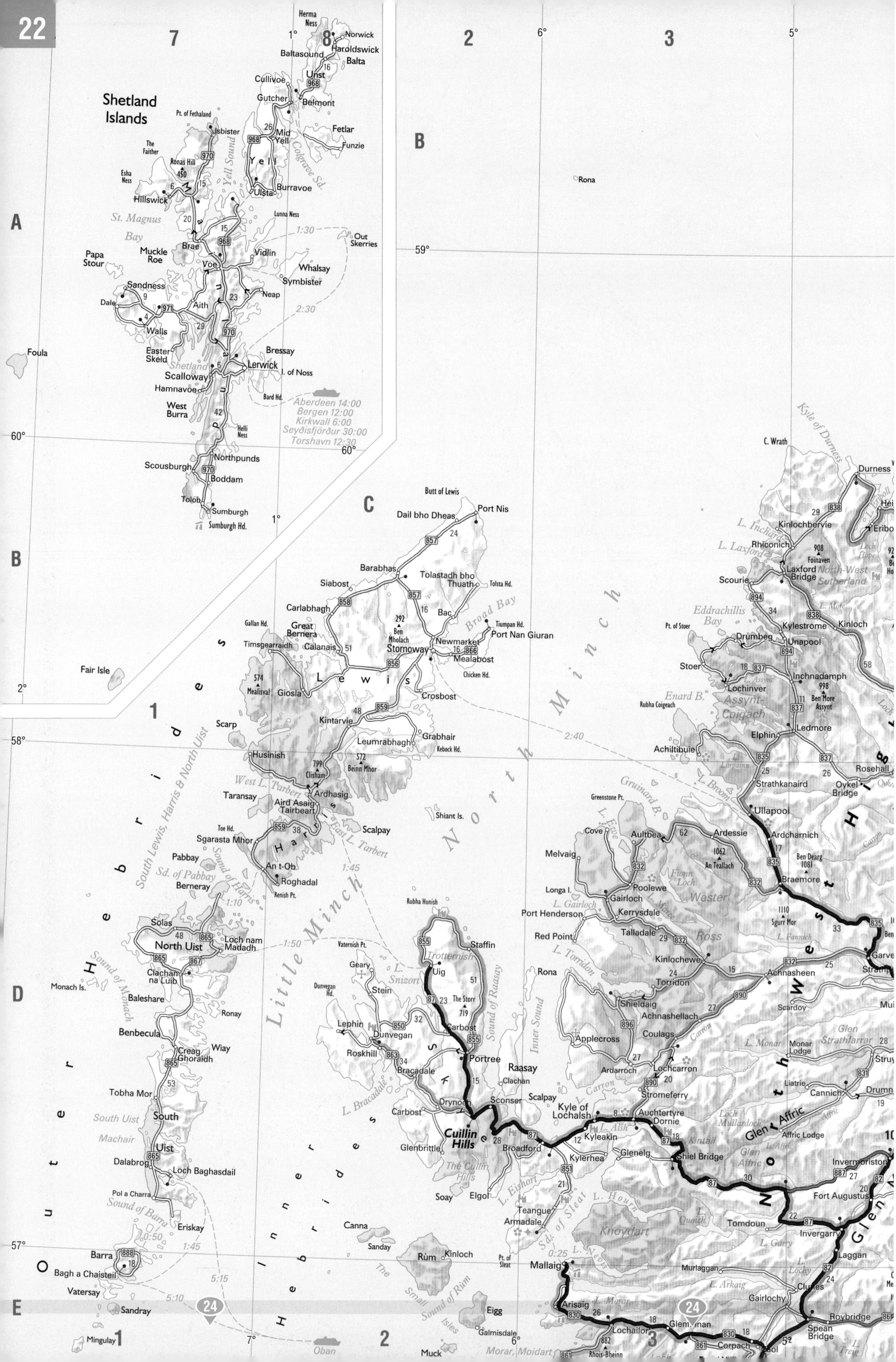
Shetland Islands
Herma Ness
Norwick
Haroldswick
Baltasound
Balta
Unst
Cullivoe
Gutcher
Belmont
Pt. of Fethaland
Isbister
Mid Yell
Yell
Fetlar
Funzie
Colgrave Sd.
Yell Sound
The Faither
Ronas Hill
Esha Ness
Hillswick
Ulsta
Burravoe
St. Magnus Bay
Lunna Ness
Out Skerries
Papa Stour
Muckle Roe
Brae
Vidlin
Whalsay
Symbister
Voe
Sandness
Dale
Aith
Neap
Walls
Foula
Easter Skeld
Bressay
Lerwick
I. of Noss
Scalloway
Hamnavoe
West Burra
Bard Hd.
Aberdeen 14:00
Bergen 12:00
Kirkwall 6:00
Seyðisfjörður 30:00
Torshavn 12:30
Helli Ness
Northpunds
Scousburgh
Boddam
Toab
Sumburgh
Sumburgh Hd.
Fair Isle
Rona
Butt of Lewis
Port Nis
Dail bho Dheas
Barabhas
Siabost
Tolastadh bho Thuath
Tolsta Hd.
Carlabhagh
Gallan Hd.
Great Bernera
Ben Mholach
Broad Bay
Tiumpan Hd.
Port Nan Giuran
Timsgearraidh
Calanais
Stornoway
Newmarket
Mealabost
Chicken Hd.
Lewis
Mealisval
Giosla
Crosbost
Scarp
Kintarvie
Grabhair
Leumrabhagh
Kebock Hd.
Husinish
Clisham
Beinn Mhor
Ardhasig
West L. Tarbert
Taransay
Aird Asaig
Tairbeart
Shiant Is.
Toe Hd.
Sgarasta Mhor
Harris
Scalpay
East L. Tarbert
Pabbay
Sd. of Pabbay
Sound of Harris
An t-Ob
Roghadal
Renish Pt.
Berneray
South Lewis, Harris & North Uist
North Minch
Little Minch
Rubha Hunish
Solas
North Uist
Loch nam Madadh
Vaternish Pt.
Staffin
Trotternish
Geary
L. Snizort
Uig
Clachan na Luib
Monach Is.
Sound of Monach
Baleshare
Dunvegan Hd.
Stein
The Storr
Sound of Raasay
Inner Sound
Ronay
Lephin
Dunvegan
Carbost
Benbecula
Wiay
Creag Ghoraidh
Roskhill
Portree
Raasay
Bracadale
Clachan
Tobha Mor
L. Bracadale
Sconser
Scalpay
Carbost
Drynoch
South Uist
South Uist Machair
Cuillin Hills
The Cuillin Hills
Glenbrittle
Broadford
Kyle of Lochalsh
Kyleakin
Kylerhea
Dalabrog
Loch Baghasdail
Soay
Elgol
L. Eishort
Pol a Charra
Sound of Barra
Eriskay
Teangue
Armadale
Sd. of Sleat
Canna
Sanday
Rùm
Kinloch
Pt. of Sleat
Mallaig
Barra
Bagh a Chaisteil
Vatersay
Sandray
Mingulay
The Small Isles
Sound of Rùm
Eigg
Galmisdale
Muck
Oban
Morar, Moidart
Outer Hebrides
Inner Hebrides
C. Wrath
Kyle of Durness
Durness
L. Eriboll
Kinlochbervie
L. Inchard
Rhiconich
L. Laxford
Foinaven
Laxford Bridge
Scourie
North-West Sutherland
Eddrachillis Bay
Kylestrome
Kinloch
L. More
Pt. of Stoer
Drumbeg
Unapool
Stoer
Inchnadamph
L. Assynt
Lochinver
Ben More Assynt
Enard B.
Rubha Coigeach
Assynt-Coigach
Ledmore
Elphin
Achiltibuie
L. Lurgainn
Rosehall
Strathkanaird
L. Broom
Oykel Bridge
Gruinard B.
Greenstone Pt.
Ullapool
L. Ewe
Cove
Aultbea
Ardessie
Ardcharnich
Melvaig
An Teallach
Ben Dearg
Fionn Loch
Poolewe
Braemore
Longa I.
Gairloch
L. Gairloch
L. Maree
Wester Ross
Port Henderson
Kerrysdale
Sgurr Mor
L. Fannich
Red Point
Talladale
Kinlochewe
L. Torridon
Achnasheen
Rona
Torridon
Shieldaig
Achnashellach
Scardoy
Applecross
Coulags
L. Monar
Monar Lodge
Glen Strathfarrar
Lochcarron
Ardarroch
Liatrie
Cannich
Stromeferry
L. Carron
Auchtertyre
Dornie
Loch Mullardoch
Glen Affric
Affric Lodge
L. Alsh
Kintail
Glenelg
Shiel Bridge
Invermoriston
Fort Augustus
L. Hourn
Knoydart
L. Quoich
Tomdoun
Invergarry
L. Garry
L. Nevis
Laggan
Murlaggan
L. Arkaig
L. Lochy
Clunes
Gairlochy
Arisaig
L. Morar
Glenfinnan
Lochailort
Spean Bridge
Roybridge
Corpach
Rhois-Bheinn
North West Highlands
Glen More
1:30
2:30
2:40
1:45
1:10
1:50
0:50
5:15
5:10
0:25
7
8
2
3
1
A
B
C
D
E
22
24
24

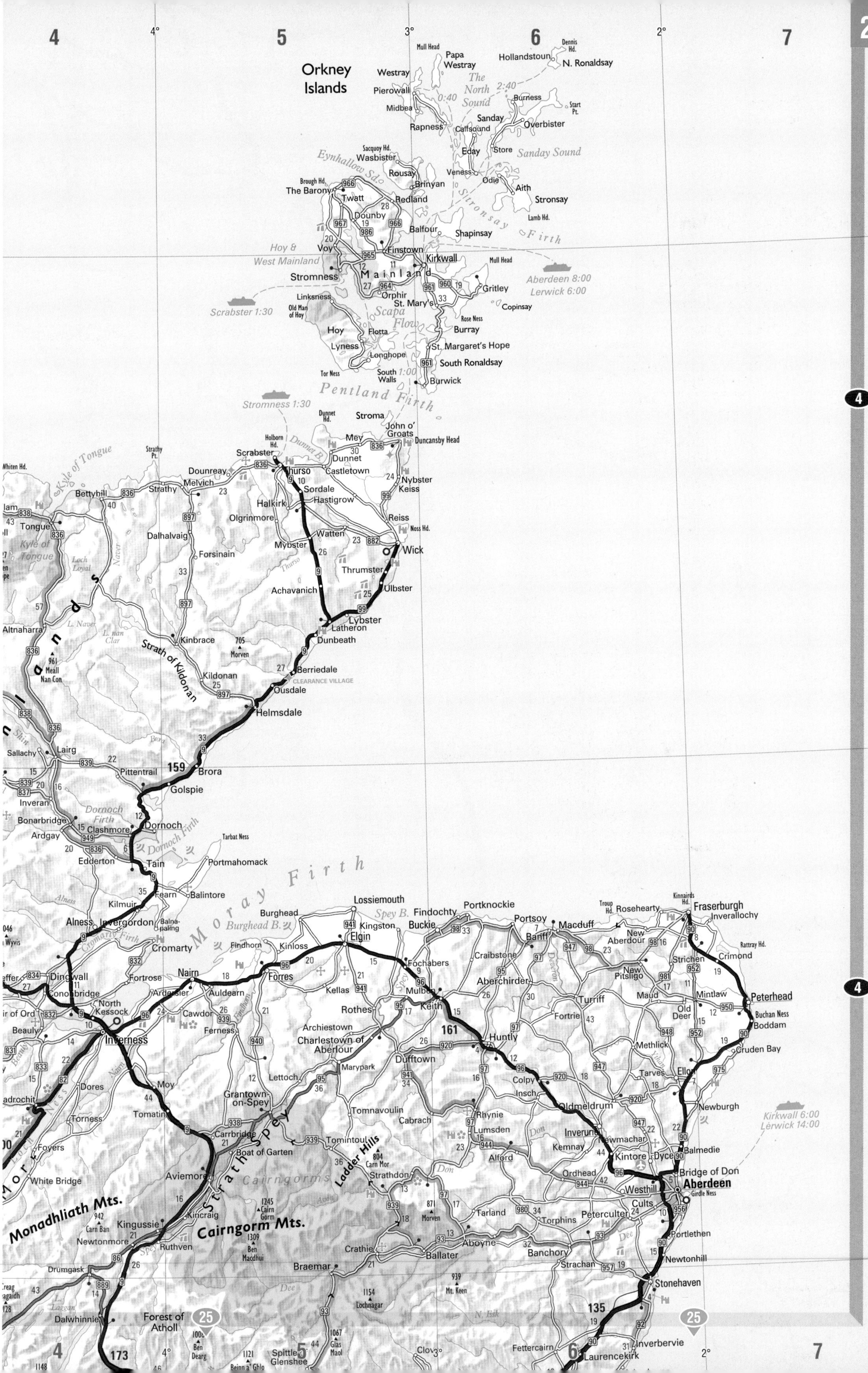

4
5
6
7
4°
3°
2°
B
C
D
E
59°
58°
57°
Orkney Islands
Mull Head
Papa Westray
Hollandstoun
Dennis Hd.
N. Ronaldsay
Westray
Pierowall
Midbea
The North Sound
0:40
2:40
Burness
Start Pt.
Sanday
Overbister
Rapness
Calfsound
Eday
Store
Sanday Sound
Sacquoy Hd.
Wasbister
Eynhallow Sd.
Rousay
Veness
Brough Hd.
The Barony
Twatt
Brinyan
Odie
Aith
Stronsay
Redland
Dounby
Stronsay Firth
Lamb Hd.
Balfour
Shapinsay
Hoy & West Mainland
Voy
Finstown
Kirkwall
Mull Head
Stromness
Mainland
Gritley
Aberdeen 8:00
Lerwick 6:00
Linksness
Orphir
St. Mary's
Copinsay
Scrabster 1:30
Old Man of Hoy
Scapa Flow
Rose Ness
Burray
Hoy
Flotta
Lyness
St. Margaret's Hope
Longhope
South Ronaldsay
Tor Ness
South Walls
1:00
Burwick
Pentland Firth
Stromness 1:30
Dunnet Hd.
Stroma
John o' Groats
Duncansby Head
Holborn Hd.
Mey
Dunnet B.
Dunnet
Strathy Pt.
Scrabster
Thurso
Castletown
Kyle of Tongue
Whiten Hd.
Dounreay
Melvich
Nybster
Keiss
Bettyhill
Strathy
Sordale
Halkirk
Hastigrow
Tongue
Olgrinmore
Reiss
Noss Hd.
Dalhalvaig
Watten
Mybster
Wick
Kyle of Tongue
Loch Loyal
Forsinain
Thurso
Thrumster
Ulbster
Achavanich
Lybster
Latheron
Altnaharra
L. Naver
L. nan Clar
Kinbrace
705 Morven
Dunbeath
Strath of Kildonan
961 Meall Nan Con
Berriedale
CLEARANCE VILLAGE
Kildonan
Ousdale
Helmsdale
Shin
Lairg
Sallachy
Brora
Pittentrail
159
Golspie
Inveran
Dornoch Firth
Bonarbridge
Clashmore
Dornoch
Ardgay
Tarbat Ness
Edderton
Tain
Portmahomack
Moray Firth
Fearn
Balintore
Kilmuir
Lossiemouth
Burghead
Spey B.
Findochty
Portknockie
Troup Hd.
Rosehearty
Kinnairds Hd.
Fraserburgh
Inverallochy
Alness
Invergordon
Balnapaling
Burghead B.
Kingston
Buckie
Portsoy
Macduff
Cromarty Firth
Cromarty
Findhorn
Kinloss
Elgin
Banff
New Aberdour
Rattray Hd.
Crimond
Craibstone
Strichen
Fochabers
New Pitsligo
Dingwall
Fortrose
Nairn
Forres
Aberchirder
Conon Bridge
Ardersier
Auldearn
Kellas
Mulben
Keith
Turriff
Maud
Mintlaw
Peterhead
North Kessock
Cawdor
Rothes
Fortrie
Old Deer
Buchan Ness
Boddam
Beauly
Inverness
Ferness
Archiestown
161
Charlestown of Aberlour
Huntly
Methlick
Cruden Bay
Marypark
Dufftown
Tarves
Ellon
Dores
Lettoch
Moy
Colpy
Insch
Grantown-on-Spey
Tomnavoulin
Oldmeldrum
Newburgh
Kirkwall 6:00
Lerwick 14:00
Torness
Tomatin
Cabrach
Rhynie
Lumsden
Inverurie
Newmachar
Carrbridge
Strath Spey
Tomintoul
Kemnay
Foyers
Boat of Garten
Ladder Hills
804 Carn Mor
Alford
Kintore
Dyce
Balmedie
Strathdon
Don
Bridge of Don
White Bridge
Aviemore
Cairngorms
Ordhead
Westhill
Aberdeen
Girdle Ness
Monadhliath Mts.
1245 Cairn Gorm
871 Morven
Cults
Kincraig
Tarland
Torphins
Peterculter
942 Carn Ban
Kingussie
Cairngorm Mts.
Portlethen
Newtonmore
Ruthven
1309 Ben Macdhui
Crathie
Ballater
Aboyne
Banchory
Drumgask
Braemar
Strachan
Newtonhill
939 Mt. Keen
Stonehaven
1154 Lochnagar
Dalwhinnie
Forest of Atholl
N. Esk
135
1067 Glas Maol
Fettercairn
Inverbervie
173
1121 Beinn a' Ghlo
Spittle of Glenshee
Laurencekirk
Clova

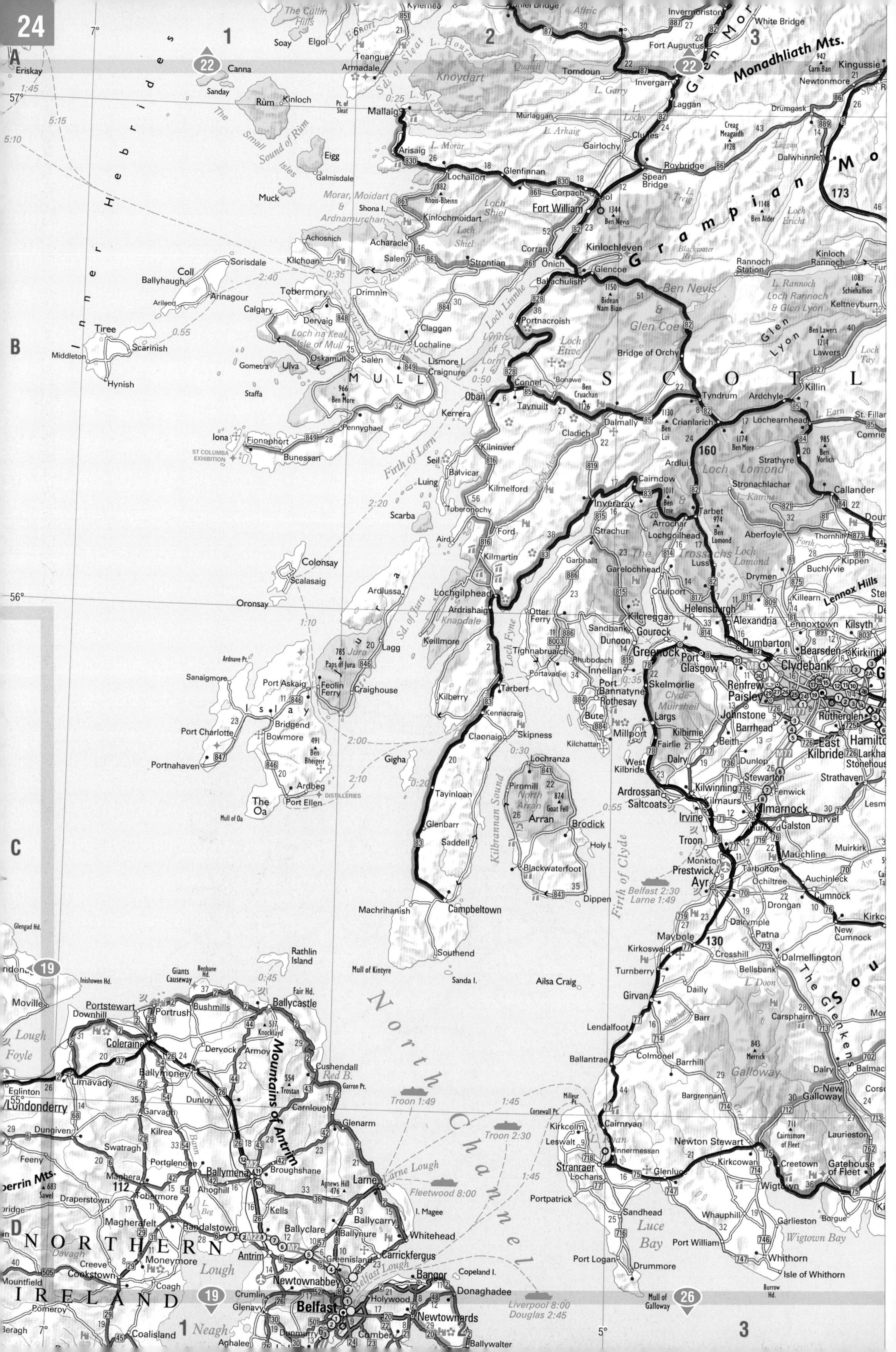
Inner Hebrides
Eriskay
Canna
Sanday
Rùm
Kinloch
The Small Isles
Sound of Rum
Eigg
Galmisdale
Muck
Soay
Elgol
The Cuillin Hills
Teangue
Armadale
Pt. of Sleat
Sd. of Sleat
Mallaig
Knoydart
L. Nevis
L. Hourn
L. Morar
Arisaig
Lochailort
Rhois-Bheinn
Morar, Moidart & Ardnamurchan
Shona I.
Kinlochmoidart
Glenfinnan
Corpach
Fort William
Ben Nevis
Loch Shiel
Acharacle
Salen
Achosnich
Kilchoan
Strontian
Corran
Onich
Kinlochleven
Glencoe
Ballachulish
Coll
Sorisdale
Ballyhaugh
Arileod
Arinagour
Tiree
Scarinish
Middleton
Hynish
Tobermory
Drimnin
Calgary
Dervaig
Loch na Keal
Isle of Mull
Sound of Mull
Claggan
Lochaline
Oskamull
Salen
Ulva
Gometra
Staffa
MULL
Ben More
Lismore I.
Craignure
Loch Linnhe
Portnacroish
Connel
Oban
Taynuilt
Kerrera
Iona
Fionnphort
Pennyghael
Bunessan
ST COLUMBA EXHIBITION
Firth of Lorn
Kilninver
Seil
Balvicar
Luing
Kilmelford
Scarba
Toberonochy
Aird
Ford
Kilmartin
Colonsay
Scalasaig
Oronsay
Ardlussa
Lochgilphead
Ardrishaig
Knapdale
Keillmore
Jura
Sd. of Jura
Paps of Jura
Lagg
Craighouse
Feolin Ferry
Ardnave Pt.
Sanaigmore
Port Askaig
Islay
Bridgend
Bowmore
Port Charlotte
Portnahaven
Ben Bheigeir
Ardbeg
Port Ellen
DISTILLERIES
The Oa
Mull of Oa
Gigha
Kilberry
Tarbert
Kennacraig
Claonaig
Skipness
Tayinloan
Glenbarr
Saddell
Kilbrannan Sound
Campbeltown
Machrihanish
Southend
Mull of Kintyre
Sanda I.
Lochranza
Pirnmill
North Arran
Goat Fell
Arran
Brodick
Holy I.
Blackwaterfoot
Dippen
Firth of Clyde
Belfast 2:30
Larne 1:49
Ailsa Craig
North Channel
Rathlin Island
Invermoriston
White Bridge
Fort Augustus
Glen More
Monadhliath Mts.
Kingussie
Carn Ban
Newtonmore
Tomdoun
L. Quoich
Invergarry
L. Garry
Laggan
Drumgask
Creag Meagaidh
L. Laggan
Dalwhinnie
Murlaggan
L. Arkaig
L. Lochy
Gairlochy
Clunes
Spean Bridge
Roybridge
L. Treig
Ben Alder
Loch Ericht
Grampian Mountains
Blackwater Res.
Rannoch Station
Kinloch Rannoch
L. Rannoch
Schiehallion
Loch Rannoch & Glen Lyon
Keltneyburn
Ben Nevis & Glen Coe
Bidean Nam Bian
Loch Etive
Bridge of Orchy
Glen Lyon
Ben Lawers
Lawers
Loch Tay
Bonawe
Ben Cruachan
SCOTLAND
Tyndrum
Ardchyle
Killin
Dalmally
Crianlarich
Ben Lui
Cladich
Lochearnhead
L. Earn
St. Fillans
Comrie
Ben More
Ben Vorlich
Strathyre
Ardlui
Loch Lomond
Stronachlachar
L. Katrine
Callander
Cairndow
Inveraray
Ben Ime
Arrochar
Tarbet
Ben Lomond
Aberfoyle
Strachur
Lochgoilhead
The Trossachs
Loch Lomond
Luss
Thornhill
Forth
Buchlyvie
Kippen
Garbhallt
Garelochhead
Drymen
Killearn
Lennox Hills
Coulport
Helensburgh
Alexandria
Lennoxtown
Kilsyth
Otter Ferry
Sandbank
Kilcreggan
Gourock
Dunoon
Dumbarton
Bearsden
Kirkintilloch
Tighnabruaich
Rhubodach
Innellan
Greenock
Port Glasgow
Clydebank
Glasgow
Renfrew
Paisley
Rutherglen
Hamilton
Portavadie
Port Bannatyne
Rothesay
Bute
Skelmorlie
Clyde-Muirsheil
Largs
Johnstone
Barrhead
East Kilbride
Larkhall
Stonehouse
Millport
Kilchattan
Kilbirnie
Fairlie
Beith
Dalry
Dunlop
West Kilbride
Stewarton
Strathaven
Ardrossan
Saltcoats
Kilwinning
Kilmaurs
Fenwick
Kilmarnock
Irvine
Galston
Darvel
Lesmahagow
Troon
Hurlford
Muirkirk
Mauchline
Monkton
Prestwick
Tarbolton
Ayr
Ochiltree
Auchinleck
Cumnock
Drongan
Dalrymple
New Cumnock
Maybole
Patna
Kirkoswald
Crosshill
Dalmellington
Turnberry
Bellsbank
L. Doon
The Glenkens
Girvan
Dailly
Barr
Carsphairn
Lendalfoot
Stinchar
Ballantrae
Colmonell
Barrhill
Merrick
Galloway
Dalry
New Galloway
Bargrennan
Cairnsmore of Fleet
Laurieston
Corsewall Pt.
Milleur Pt.
Kirkcolm
L. Ryan
Leswalt
Cairnryan
Innermessan
Newton Stewart
Stranraer
Lochans
Glenluce
Kirkcowan
Creetown
Gatehouse of Fleet
Wigtown
Portpatrick
Sandhead
Luce Bay
Whauphill
Garlieston
Borgue
Port William
Wigtown Bay
Port Logan
Drummore
Whithorn
Isle of Whithorn
Mull of Galloway
Burrow Hd.
Troon 1:49
Troon 2:30
Fleetwood 8:00
Liverpool 8:00
Douglas 2:45
Glengad Hd.
Inishowen Hd.
Giants Causeway
Benbane Hd.
Fair Hd.
Ballycastle
Portstewart
Portrush
Bushmills
Downhill
Moville
Lough Foyle
Coleraine
Knocklayd
Dervock
Armoy
Mountains of Antrim
Cushendall
Red B.
Garron Pt.
Trostan
Limavady
Ballymoney
Dunloy
Eglinton
Londonderry
Garvagh
Carnlough
Glenarm
Dungiven
Kilrea
Swatragh
Feeny
Portglenone
Ballymena
Broughshane
Sperrin Mts.
Sawel
Maghera
Tobermore
Draperstown
Ahoghill
Agnews Hill
Larne
Larne Lough
Kells
I. Magee
Magherafelt
Randalstown
Ballyclare
Ballycarry
Ballynure
Whitehead
NORTHERN IRELAND
Davagh
Antrim
Moneymore
Lough Neagh
Greenisland
Carrickfergus
Belfast Lough
Creeve
Cookstown
Newtownabbey
Bangor
Copeland I.
Mountfield
Coagh
Crumlin
Donaghadee
Pomeroy
Glenavy
Belfast
Holywood
Newtownards
Beragh
Coalisland
Dunmurry
Comber
Aghalee
Ballywalter

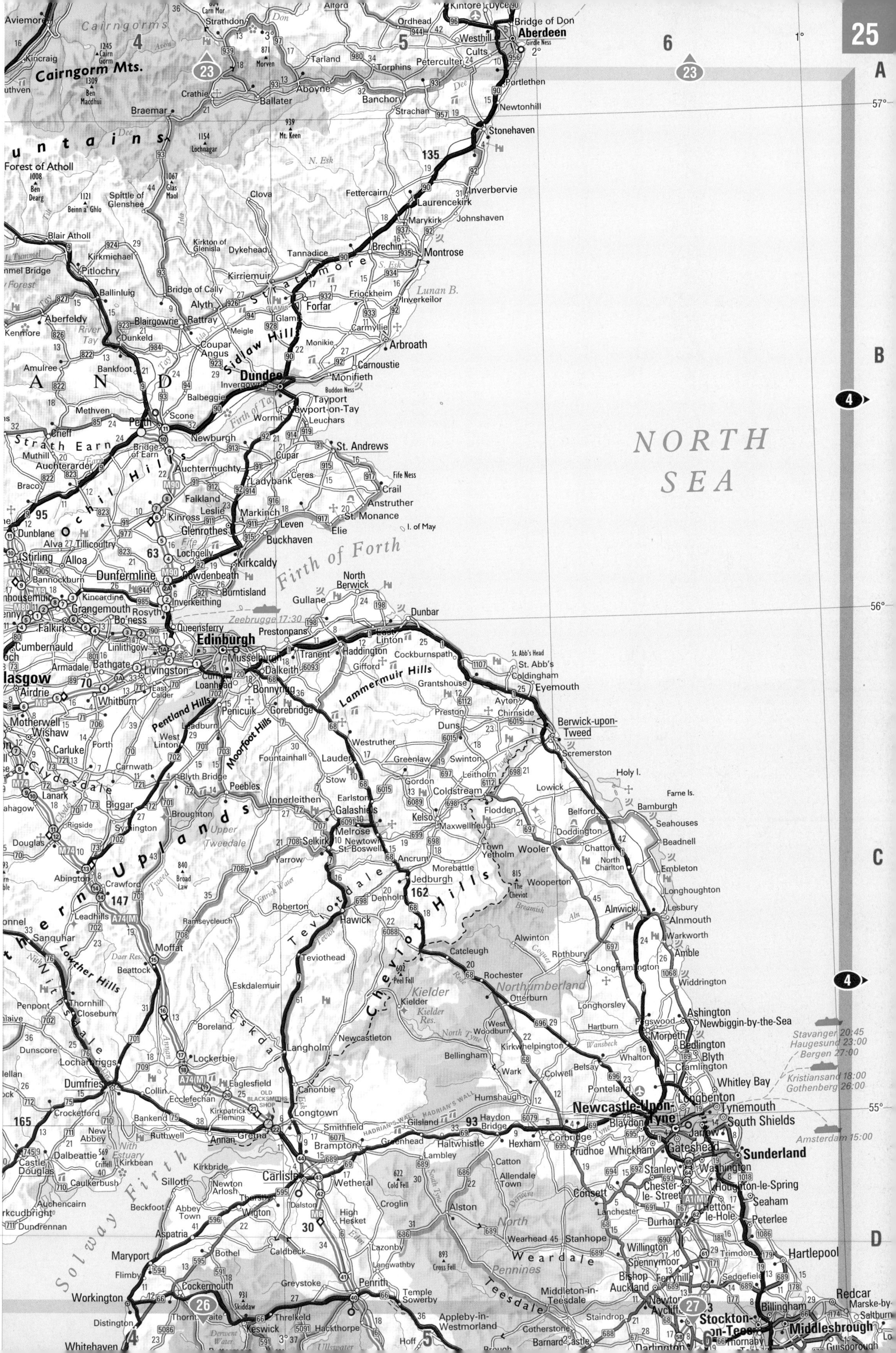
Aberdeen
Stonehaven
Inverbervie
Laurencekirk
Montrose
Brechin
Forfar
Arbroath
Carnoustie
Dundee
Perth
St. Andrews
Cupar
Kirkcaldy
Glenrothes
Dunfermline
Stirling
Falkirk
Edinburgh
Musselburgh
Haddington
North Berwick
Dunbar
Eyemouth
Berwick-upon-Tweed
Galashiels
Melrose
Kelso
Jedburgh
Hawick
Selkirk
Peebles
Moffat
Lockerbie
Dumfries
Annan
Gretna
Langholm
Carlisle
Penrith
Keswick
Cockermouth
Workington
Whitehaven
Maryport
Wigton
Hexham
Newcastle-Upon-Tyne
Gateshead
Tynemouth
South Shields
Sunderland
Durham
Hartlepool
Stockton-on-Tees
Middlesbrough
Redcar
Alnwick
Morpeth
Blyth
Whitley Bay
Bamburgh
Holy I.
Farne Is.
Cairngorm Mts.
Cairngorms
Grampian Mountains
Sidlaw Hills
Ochil Hills
Pentland Hills
Moorfoot Hills
Lammermuir Hills
Cheviot Hills
Southern Uplands
Lowther Hills
Teviotdale
Eskdale
Nithsdale
Strathmore
Strath Earn
Clydesdale
Northumberland
Kielder
North Pennines
Weardale
Teesdale
Solway Firth
Firth of Forth
Firth of Tay
NORTH SEA
Zeebrugge 17:30
Stavanger 20:45
Haugesund 23:00
Bergen 27:00
Kristiansand 18:00
Gothenberg 26:00
Amsterdam 15:00
HADRIAN'S WALL
57°
56°
55°
1°
2°
3°
A
B
C
D
4
5
6
23
26
27

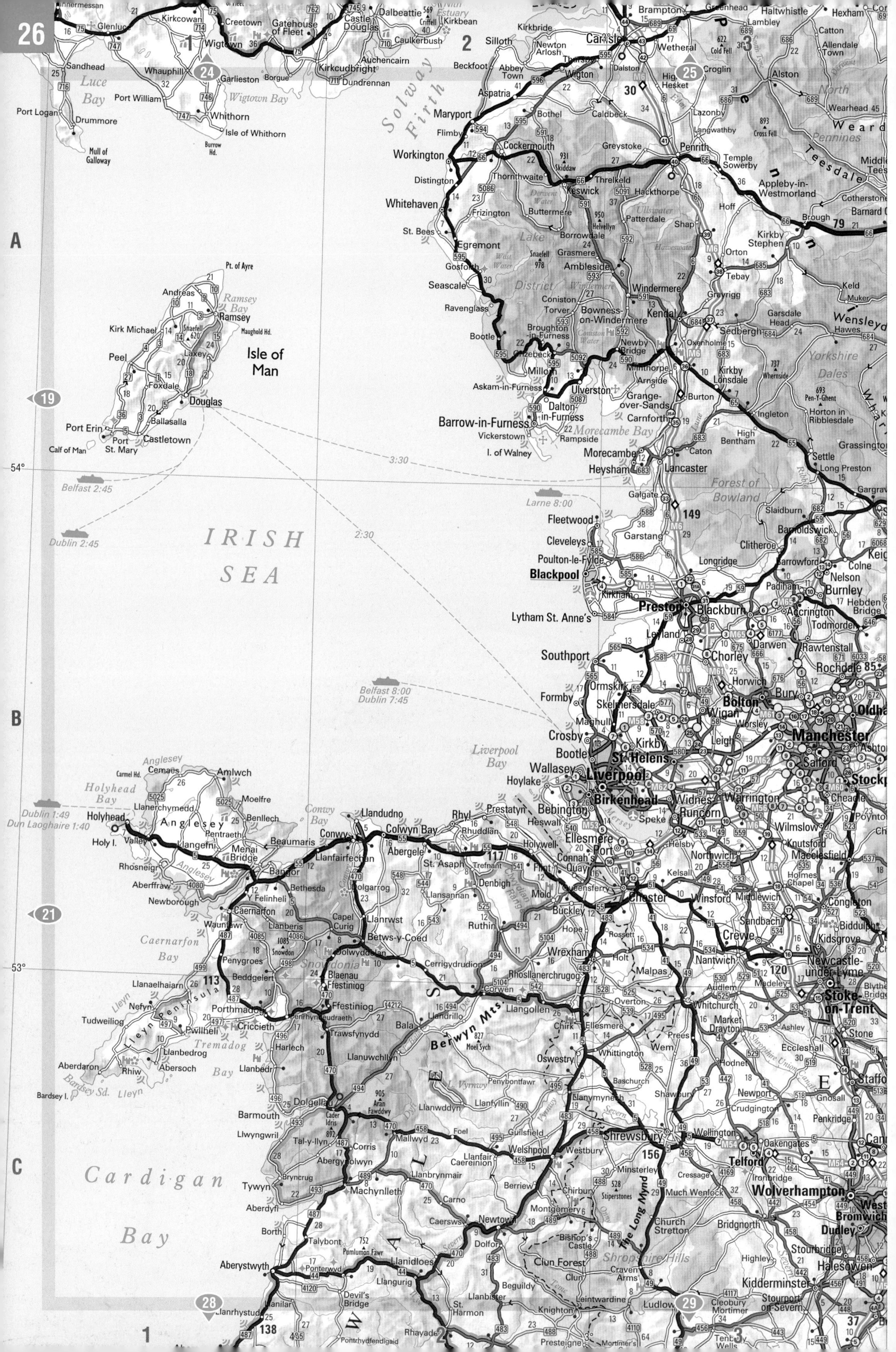

Glenluce
Kirkcowan
Wigtown
Creetown
Gatehouse of Fleet
Castle Douglas
Dalbeattie
Criffell
Kirkbean
Caulkerbush
Auchencairn
Kirkcudbright
Dundrennan
Borgue
Garlieston
Whauphill
Sandhead
Luce Bay
Port William
Wigtown Bay
Port Logan
Drummore
Whithorn
Isle of Whithorn
Burrow Hd.
Mull of Galloway
Kirkbride
Silloth
Newton Arlosh
Carlisle
Brampton
Greenhead
Haltwhistle
Hexham
Lambley
Catton
Allendale Town
Wetheral
Cold Fell
Croglin
Alston
Beckfoot
Abbey Town
Thursby
Wigton
Dalston
High Hesket
Aspatria
Solway Firth
Maryport
Bothel
Caldbeck
Lazonby
North Pennines
Wearhead
Weardale
Flimby
Langwathby
Cross Fell
Workington
Cockermouth
Greystoke
Penrith
Temple Sowerby
Teesdale
Distington
Thornthwaite
Skiddaw
Threlkeld
Hackthorpe
Appleby-in-Westmorland
Keswick
Whitehaven
Frizington
Derwent Water
Buttermere
Ullswater
Patterdale
Helvellyn
Shap
Hoff
Cotherstone
Brough
Barnard Castle
St. Bees
Egremont
Lake District
Borrowdale
Grasmere
Haweswater
Kirkby Stephen
Orton
Gosforth
Wast Water
Scafell
Ambleside
Tebay
Seascale
Windermere
Grayrigg
Keld
Muker
Ravenglass
Coniston
Torver
Bowness-on-Windermere
Kendal
Garsdale Head
Hawes
Wensleydale
Sedbergh
Bootle
Broughton-in-Furness
Coniston Water
Oxenholme
Yorkshire Dales
Whernside
Kirkby Lonsdale
Newby Bridge
Millom
Milnthorpe
Arnside
Askam-in-Furness
Ulverston
Grange-over-Sands
Burton
Pen-Y-Ghent
Horton in Ribblesdale
Dalton-in-Furness
Carnforth
Ingleton
Barrow-in-Furness
Vickerstown
Rampside
Morecambe Bay
High Bentham
Grassington
I. of Walney
Morecambe
Caton
Settle
Long Preston
Heysham
Lancaster
Forest of Bowland
Galgate
Slaidburn
Pt. of Ayre
Andreas
Ramsey Bay
Ramsey
Maughold Hd.
Kirk Michael
Snaefell
Isle of Man
Peel
Laxey
Foxdale
Douglas
Ballasalla
Port Erin
Port St. Mary
Castletown
Calf of Man
Belfast 2:45
Dublin 2:45
3:30
2:30
Larne 8:00
IRISH SEA
Fleetwood
Garstang
Cleveleys
Barnoldswick
Clitheroe
Poulton-le-Fylde
Longridge
Barrowford
Colne
Nelson
Blackpool
Padiham
Burnley
Kirkham
Preston
Blackburn
Accrington
Hebden Bridge
Lytham St. Anne's
Todmorden
Leyland
Darwen
Rawtenstall
Southport
Chorley
Rochdale
Ormskirk
Horwich
Bury
Formby
Skelmersdale
Bolton
Wigan
Oldham
Maghull
Worsley
Crosby
Kirkby
Leigh
Manchester
Bootle
St Helens
Salford
Liverpool Bay
Wallasey
Liverpool
Hoylake
Birkenhead
Widnes
Warrington
Stockport
Bebington
Runcorn
Cheadle
Heswall
Speke
Wilmslow
Ellesmere Port
Helsby
Knutsford
Northwich
Macclesfield
Connah's Quay
Kelsall
Holmes Chapel
Queensferry
Chester
Winsford
Middlewich
Congleton
Sandbach
Biddulph
Crewe
Kidsgrove
Nantwich
Newcastle-under-Lyme
Stoke-on-Trent
Audlem
Madeley
Whitchurch
Market Drayton
Stone
Eccleshall
Prees
Wem
Hodnet
Stafford
Shawbury
Newport
Gnosall
Crudgington
Penkridge
Wellington
Oakengates
Telford
Cannock
Ironbridge
Wolverhampton
West Bromwich
Much Wenlock
Dudley
Bridgnorth
Stourbridge
Halesowen
Kidderminster
Stourport-on-Severn
Cleobury Mortimer
Highley
Tenbury Wells
Anglesey
Carmel Hd.
Cemaes
Amlwch
Holyhead Bay
Moelfre
Benllech
Llanerchymedd
Dublin 1:49
Dun Laoghaire 1:40
Holyhead
Holy I.
Valley
Llangefni
Pentraeth
Beaumaris
Conwy Bay
Llandudno
Menai Bridge
Rhosneigr
Bangor
Conwy
Colwyn Bay
Rhyl
Prestatyn
Rhuddlan
Abergele
St. Asaph
Llanfairfechan
Aberffraw
Bethesda
Dolgarrog
Trefnant
Denbigh
Flint
Holywell
Mold
Newborough
Y Felinheli
Caernarfon
Llanrwst
Llansannan
Ruthin
Buckley
Capel Curig
Llanberis
Waunfawr
Betws-y-Coed
Hope
Caernarfon Bay
Snowdon
Dolwyddelan
Wrexham
Penygroes
Rossett
Holt
Beddgelert
Snowdonia
Blaenau Ffestiniog
Cerrigydrudion
Malpas
Rhosllanerchrugog
Llanaelhaiarn
Corwen
Overton
Nefyn
Lleyn Peninsula
Porthmadog
Ffestiniog
Llangollen
Tudweiliog
Pwllheli
Criccieth
Penrhyndeudraeth
Llandrillo
Bala
Chirk
Ellesmere
Trawsfynydd
Harlech
Berwyn Mts.
Moel Sych
Whittington
Llanbedrog
Tremadog Bay
Llanuwchllyn
Oswestry
Aberdaron
Rhiw
Abersoch
Llanbedr
L. Vyrnwy
Penybontfawr
Baschurch
Bardsey Sd.
Bardsey I.
Dolgellau
Aran Fawddwy
Llanwddyn
Llanfyllin
Llanymynech
Barmouth
Cader Idris
Shrewsbury
Llwyngwril
Foel
Guilsfield
Mallwyd
Welshpool
Westbury
Tal-y-llyn
Corris
Llanfair Caereinion
Aberllefenni
Minsterley
Cressage
Cardigan Bay
Tywyn
Bryncrug
Machynlleth
Llanbrynmair
Berriew
Chirbury
Stiperstones
The Long Mynd
Carno
Aberdyfi
Montgomery
Church Stretton
Caersws
Newtown
Borth
Talybont
Dolfor
Bishop's Castle
Pumlumon Fawr
Llanidloes
Clun Forest
Shropshire Hills
Aberystwyth
Ponterwyd
Clun
Craven Arms
Llangurig
Beguildy
Llanbister
Leintwardine
Devil's Bridge
St. Harmon
Knighton
Ludlow
Llanrhystud
Llanilar
Rhayader
Presteigne
Mortimer's Cross
Pontrhydfendigaid
WALES
ENGLAND
Pennines

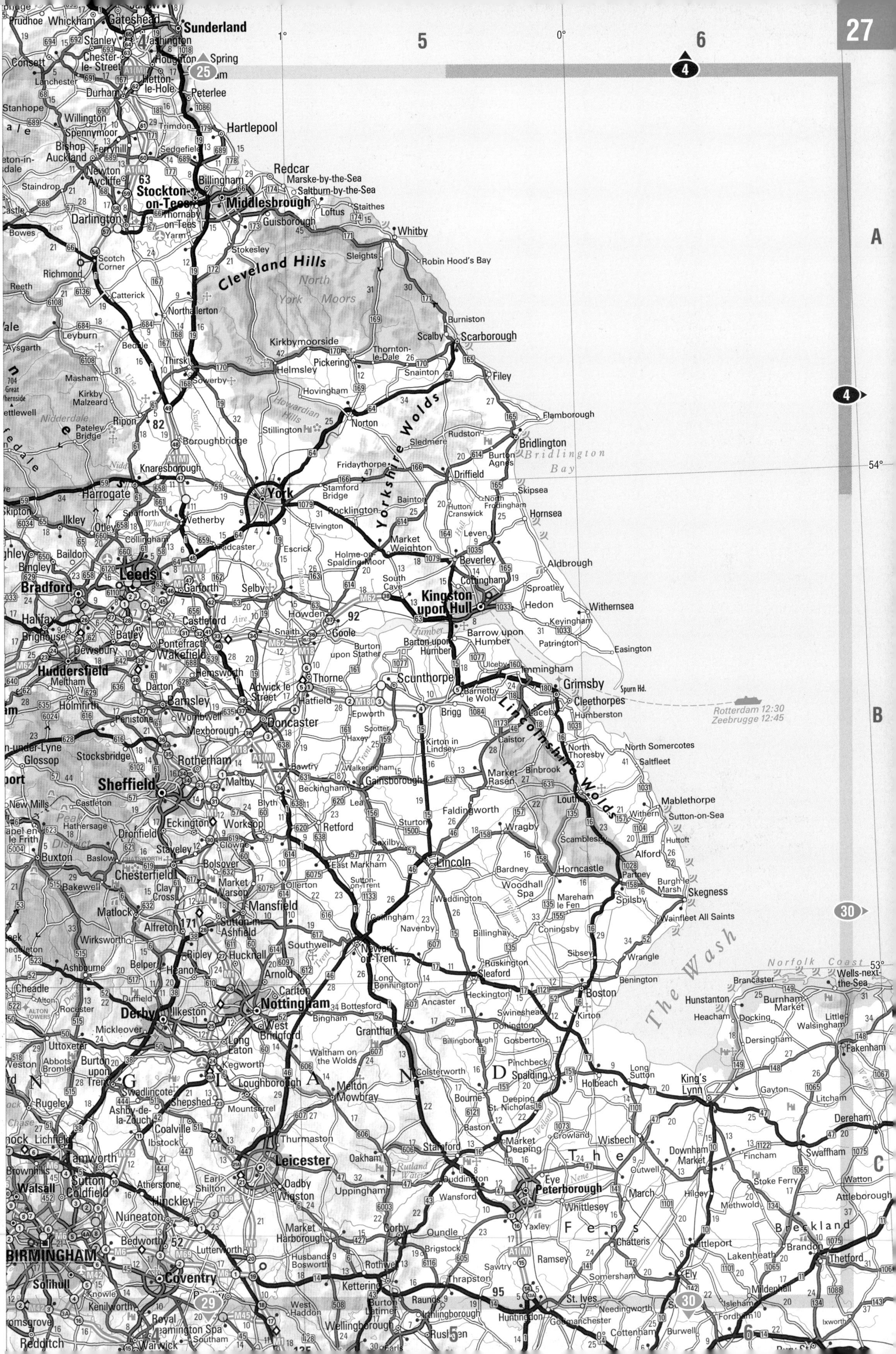
Sunderland
Gateshead
Washington
Stanley
Consett
Chester-le-Street
Houghton
Spring
Peterlee
Durham
Hetton-le-Hole
Stanhope
Willington
Spennymoor
Hartlepool
Bishop Auckland
Ferryhill
Sedgefield
Trimdon
Newton Aycliffe
Billingham
Redcar
Marske-by-the-Sea
Saltburn-by-the-Sea
Staindrop
Stockton-on-Tees
Middlesbrough
Staithes
Loftus
Darlington
Thornaby on Tees
Yarm
Guisborough
Whitby
Bowes
Richmond
Scotch Corner
Stokesley
Sleights
Robin Hood's Bay
Cleveland Hills
North York Moors
Reeth
Catterick
Northallerton
Burniston
Leyburn
Scalby
Scarborough
Aysgarth
Bedale
Kirkbymoorside
Thornton-le-Dale
Pickering
Thirsk
Helmsley
Snainton
Masham
Sowerby
Filey
Kirkby Malzeard
Hovingham
Howardian Hills
Flamborough
Nidderdale
Pateley Bridge
Ripon
Stillington
Norton
Yorkshire Wolds
Bridlington
Sledmere
Rudston
Boroughbridge
Burton Agnes
Bridlington Bay
Knaresborough
Fridaythorpe
Driffield
Harrogate
York
Stamford Bridge
Skipsea
Skipton
Spofforth
Wetherby
Baintor
Hutton Cranswick
North Frodingham
Hornsea
Ilkley
Otley
Pocklington
Elvington
Collingham
Tadcaster
Escrick
Market Weighton
Leven
Baildon
Bingley
Holme-on-Spalding-Moor
Beverley
Aldbrough
Leeds
Bradford
Garforth
Selby
South Cave
Cottingham
Sproatley
Kingston upon Hull
Hedon
Withernsea
Halifax
Castleford
Howden
Brighouse
Batley
Pontefract
Snaith
Goole
Keyingham
Dewsbury
Wakefield
Barrow upon Humber
Patrington
Barton upon Humber
Burton upon Stather
Easington
Huddersfield
Hemsworth
Meltham
Darton
Thorne
Ulceby
Immingham
Adwick le Street
Scunthorpe
Grimsby
Holmfirth
Barnsley
Hatfield
Barnetby le Wold
Spurn Hd.
Cleethorpes
Wombwell
Penistone
Epworth
Brigg
Humberston
Doncaster
Rotterdam 12:30
Zeebrugge 12:45
Mexborough
Caistor
Kirton in Lindsey
North Thoresby
North Somercotes
Stocksbridge
Rotherham
Glossop
Bawtry
Walkeringham
Saltfleet
Gainsborough
Market Rasen
Binbrook
Lincolnshire Wolds
Sheffield
Maltby
Beckingham
Louth
Mablethorpe
New Mills
Castleton
Blyth
Lea
Faldingworth
Withern
Sutton-on-Sea
Hathersage
Peak District
Eckington
Worksop
Retford
Sturton
Wragby
Scamblesby
Chapel en le Frith
Dronfield
Huttoft
Buxton
Staveley
Clowne
Saxilby
Alford
Baslow
Bolsover
East Markham
Lincoln
Bardney
Horncastle
Partney
Chesterfield
Market Warsop
Sutton-on-Trent
Woodhall Spa
Burgh le Marsh
Skegness
Bakewell
Clay Cross
Ollerton
Waddington
Mareham le Fen
Spilsby
Matlock
Mansfield
Gollingham
Navenby
Coningsby
Wainfleet All Saints
Alfreton
Sutton-in-Ashfield
Billinghay
Wirksworth
Southwell
Newark-on-Trent
Sibsey
Wrangle
The Wash
Hucknall
Ripley
Ruskington
Sleaford
Norfolk Coast
Belper
Heanor
Arnold
Ashbourne
Long Bennington
Benington
Brancaster
Wells-next-the-Sea
Carlton
Heckington
Boston
Hunstanton
Burnham Market
Cheadle
Alton Towers
Duffield
Nottingham
Bottesford
Ancaster
Swineshead
Kirton
Heacham
Docking
Walsingham
Rocester
Derby
Ilkeston
West Bridgford
Bingham
Grantham
Donington
Little
Mickleover
Long Eaton
Billingborough
Gosberton
Dersingham
Fakenham
Uttoxeter
Waltham on the Wolds
Pinchbeck
Spalding
Weston
Abbots Bromley
Burton upon Trent
Kegworth
Colsterworth
Long Sutton
King's Lynn
Holbeach
Swadlincote
Loughborough
Melton Mowbray
Bourne
Gayton
Litcham
Rugeley
Ashby-de-la-Zouch
Shepshed
Mountsorrel
Deeping St. Nicholas
Dereham
Coalville
Thurmaston
Lichfield
Ibstock
Oakham
Stamford
Market Deeping
Crowland
Wisbech
Downham Market
Fincham
Swaffham
Tamworth
Leicester
Rutland Water
Outwell
Brownhills
Sutton Coldfield
Atherstone
Earl Shilton
Oadby
Wigston
Uppingham
Duddington
Eye
Peterborough
Stoke Ferry
Watton
Walsall
Hinckley
Wansford
March
Hilgay
Methwold
Attleborough
Whittlesey
Nuneaton
Market Harborough
Corby
Oundle
Yaxley
The Fens
Breckland
BIRMINGHAM
Bedworth
Lutterworth
Brigstock
Chatteris
Littleport
Lakenheath
Brandon
Thetford
Husbands Bosworth
Rothwell
Sawtry
Ramsey
Coventry
Thrapston
Somersham
Ely
Mildenhall
Solihull
Knowle
Kettering
Kenilworth
West Haddon
Raunds
St. Ives
Needingworth
Isleham
Fordham
Ixworth
Royal Leamington Spa
Burton Latimer
Irthlingborough
Huntingdon
Godmanchester
Bromsgrove
Wellingborough
Rushden
Cottenham
Burwell
Redditch
Warwick
Southam
A
B
C
4
5
6
1°
0°
54°
53°
England

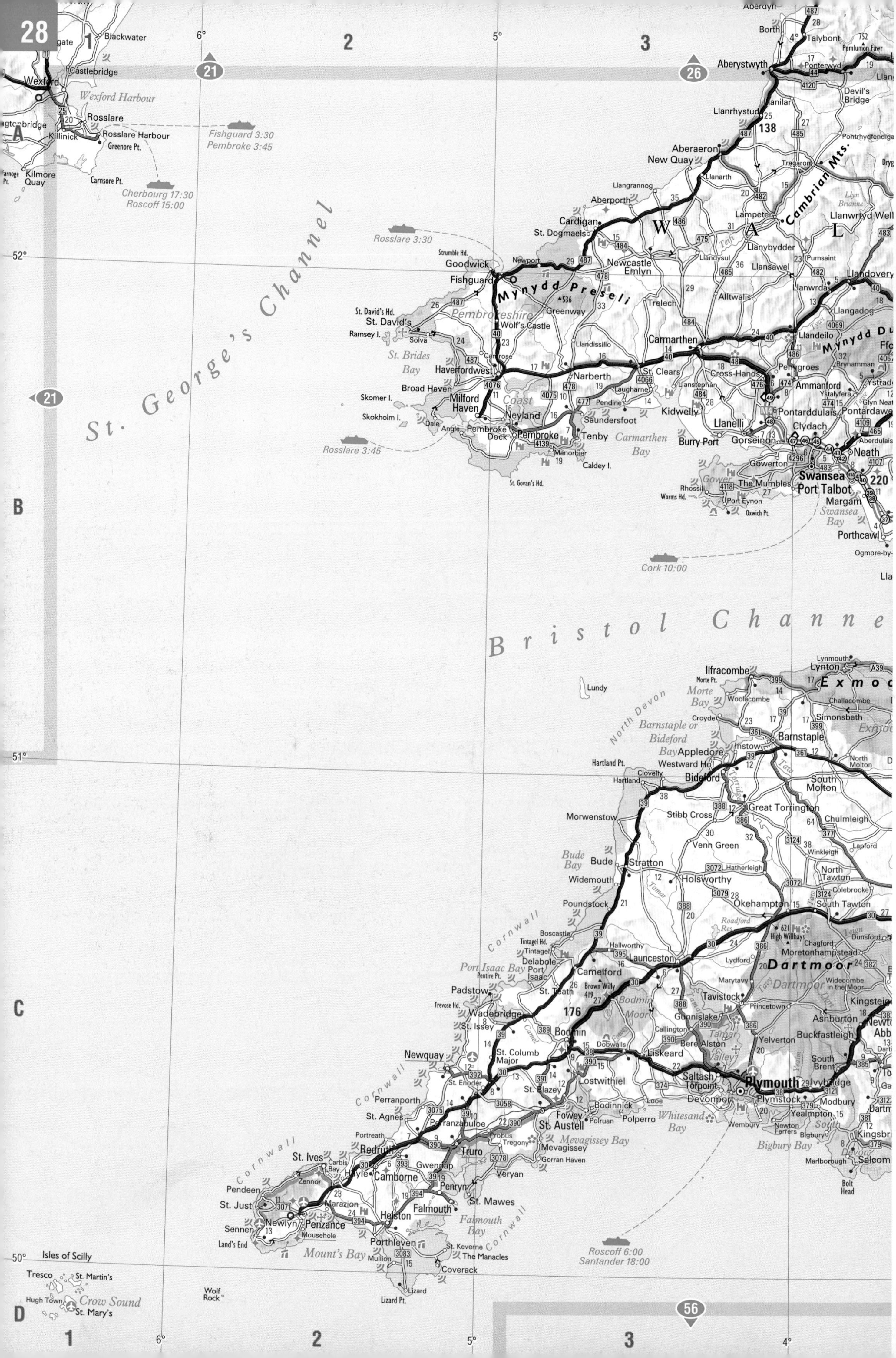
St. George's Channel
Bristol Channel
Wexford
Wexford Harbour
Castlebridge
Blackwater
Rosslare
Rosslare Harbour
Killinick
Greenore Pt.
Kilmore Quay
Carnsore Pt.
Fishguard 3:30
Pembroke 3:45
Cherbourg 17:30
Roscoff 15:00
Rosslare 3:30
Rosslare 3:45
Cork 10:00
Roscoff 6:00
Santander 18:00
Aberystwyth
Borth
Talybont
Ponterwyd
Devil's Bridge
Llanrhystud
Aberaeron
New Quay
Llanarth
Llangrannog
Aberporth
Cardigan
St. Dogmaels
Cambrian Mts.
Tregaron
Lampeter
Llanybydder
Llandysul
Newcastle Emlyn
Llansawel
Pumsaint
Llandovery
Llanwrtyd Wells
WALES
Strumble Hd.
Goodwick
Fishguard
Newport
Mynydd Preseli
Greenway
St. David's Hd.
St. David's
Ramsey I.
Solva
Pembrokeshire Coast
Wolf's Castle
St. Brides Bay
Haverfordwest
Camrose
Broad Haven
Milford Haven
Skomer I.
Skokholm I.
Dale
Angle
Pembroke Dock
Pembroke
Neyland
Narberth
St. Clears
Laugharne
Pendine
Saundersfoot
Tenby
Manorbier
Caldey I.
St. Govan's Hd.
Carmarthen Bay
Carmarthen
Trelech
Alltwalis
Llandissilio
Llanstephan
Kidwelly
Cross Hands
Llanelli
Burry Port
Gorseinon
Pontarddulais
Ammanford
Llandeilo
Llangadog
Mynydd Du
Clydach
Pontardawe
Neath
Swansea
Port Talbot
Gower
The Mumbles
Rhossili
Worms Hd.
Port Eynon
Oxwich Pt.
Margam
Swansea Bay
Porthcawl
Ogmore-by-Sea
Lundy
Ilfracombe
Lynmouth
Lynton
Exmoor
Morte Pt.
Morte Bay
Woolacombe
Croyde
Barnstaple
Simonsbath
Challacombe
North Devon
Barnstaple or Bideford Bay
Appledore
Instow
Westward Ho!
Hartland Pt.
Hartland
Clovelly
Bideford
Great Torrington
South Molton
North Molton
Chulmleigh
Morwenstow
Stibb Cross
Venn Green
Winkleigh
Lapford
Bude Bay
Bude
Stratton
Widemouth
Holsworthy
Hatherleigh
North Tawton
Colebrooke
Okehampton
South Tawton
Poundstock
Roadford Res.
High Willhays
Chagford
Moretonhampstead
Dartmoor
Boscastle
Tintagel Hd.
Tintagel
Delabole
Hallworthy
Launceston
Lydford
Camelford
Port Isaac Bay
Pentire Pt.
Port Isaac
St. Teath
Brown Willy
Bodmin Moor
Padstow
Trevose Hd.
Wadebridge
St. Issey
Bodmin
Tavistock
Gunnislake
Callington
Princetown
Widecombe in the Moor
Ashburton
Buckfastleigh
Newton Abbot
Kingsteignton
Newquay
St. Columb Major
Dobwalls
Liskeard
Bere Alston
Tamar Valley
Yelverton
South Brent
St. Enoder
Lostwithiel
Saltash
Torpoint
Plymouth
Devonport
Plymstock
Ivybridge
Modbury
Yealmpton
Wembury
Newton Ferrers
Bigbury
Bigbury Bay
Kingsbridge
Salcombe
Marlborough
Bolt Head
Perranporth
St. Agnes
Perranzabuloe
St. Blazey
Bodinnick
Fowey
Polruan
Polperro
Looe
Whitesand Bay
St. Austell
Mevagissey Bay
Mevagissey
Gorran Haven
Probus
Tregony
Truro
Veryan
Portreath
Redruth
Camborne
Gwennap
Penryn
St. Ives
Carbis Bay
Hayle
Zennor
Pendeen
St. Just
Marazion
Newlyn
Penzance
Mousehole
Sennen
Land's End
Mount's Bay
Helston
Falmouth
Falmouth Bay
St. Mawes
Porthleven
Mullion
St. Keverne
The Manacles
Coverack
Lizard
Lizard Pt.
Isles of Scilly
Tresco
St. Martin's
Hugh Town
St. Mary's
Crow Sound
Wolf Rock
Cornwall
Devon

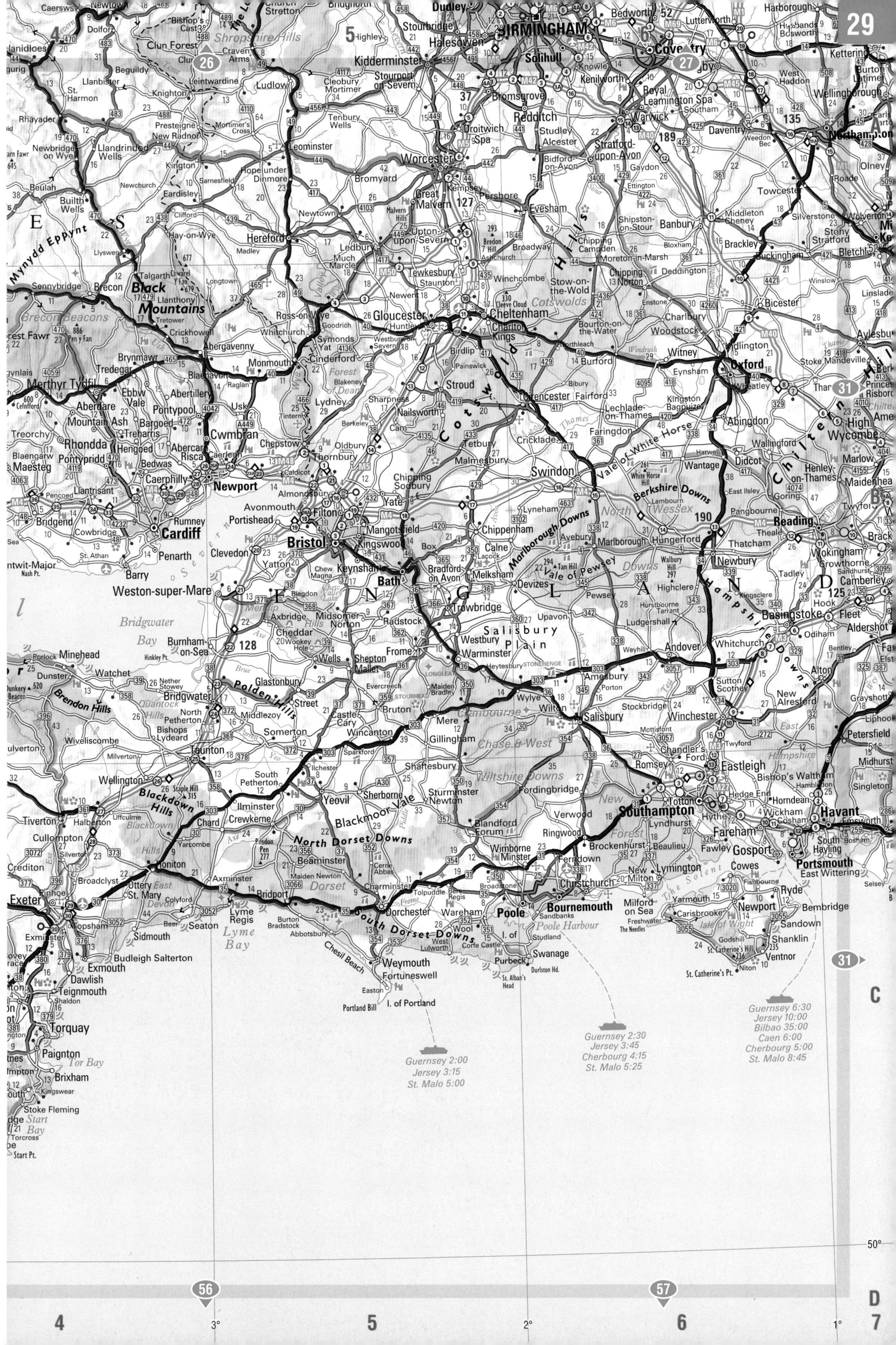
Dudley
BIRMINGHAM
Coventry
Solihull
Bedworth
Lutterworth
Harborough
Kettering
Stourbridge
Halesowen
Kidderminster
Stourport-on-Severn
Cleobury Mortimer
Bromsgrove
Redditch
Kenilworth
Royal Leamington Spa
Warwick
Southam
Daventry
Wellingborough
Northampton
West Haddon
Droitwich Spa
Studley
Alcester
Stratford-upon-Avon
Bidford-on-Avon
Gaydon
Worcester
Great Malvern
Kempsey
Pershore
Evesham
Upton-upon-Severn
Tewkesbury
Ledbury
Much Marcle
Bredon Hill
Broadway
Chipping Campden
Shipston-on-Stour
Banbury
Middleton Cheney
Brackley
Towcester
Buckingham
Stony Stratford
Wolverton
Bletchley
Olney
Winchcombe
Stow-on-the-Wold
Moreton-in-Marsh
Chipping Norton
Deddington
Bicester
Cheltenham
Gloucester
Newent
Ross-on-Wye
Hereford
Leominster
Ludlow
Tenbury Wells
Bromyard
Kington
Presteigne
New Radnor
Knighton
Clun Forest
Craven Arms
Shropshire Hills
Church Stretton
Bishop's Castle
Llanidloes
Rhayader
Llandrindod Wells
Newbridge on Wye
Builth Wells
Hay-on-Wye
Brecon
Black Mountains
Brecon Beacons
Abergavenny
Crickhowell
Monmouth
Merthyr Tydfil
Aberdare
Mountain Ash
Ebbw Vale
Tredegar
Pontypool
Cwmbran
Usk
Chepstow
Caerphilly
Newport
Cardiff
Penarth
Barry
Bridgend
Maesteg
Rhondda
Pontypridd
Llantrisant
Cowbridge
Forest of Dean
Cinderford
Lydney
Stroud
Nailsworth
Cirencester
Fairford
Tetbury
Malmesbury
Cotswolds
Cotswold Hills
Charlton Kings
Northleach
Burford
Witney
Woodstock
Charlbury
Oxford
Kidlington
Eynsham
Abingdon
Wheatley
Thame
Aylesbury
Princes Risborough
High Wycombe
Chiltern Hills
Marlow
Henley-on-Thames
Maidenhead
Reading
Wokingham
Crowthorne
Camberley
Fleet
Aldershot
Basingstoke
Hook
Odiham
Wallingford
Didcot
Wantage
Goring
Pangbourne
Thatcham
Newbury
Hungerford
Lambourn
Berkshire Downs
Vale of White Horse
Faringdon
Lechlade-on-Thames
Cricklade
Swindon
Marlborough
Marlborough Downs
Avebury
Chippenham
Calne
Lacock
Melksham
Devizes
Vale of Pewsey
Pewsey
Bradford on Avon
Trowbridge
Westbury
Warminster
Salisbury Plain
Upavon
Ludgershall
Andover
Whitchurch
Highclere
Hampshire Downs
Bristol
Kingswood
Mangotsfield
Filton
Yate
Chipping Sodbury
Thornbury
Avonmouth
Portishead
Clevedon
Yatton
Keynsham
Bath
Chew Magna
Weston-super-Mare
Burnham-on-Sea
Bridgwater Bay
Axbridge
Cheddar
Wells
Midsomer Norton
Radstock
Frome
Shepton Mallet
Glastonbury
Street
Bridgwater
Polden Hills
Quantock Hills
Minehead
Watchet
Dunster
Brendon Hills
Wiveliscombe
Taunton
Wellington
Blackdown Hills
Tiverton
Cullompton
Crediton
Exeter
Exmouth
Dawlish
Teignmouth
Torquay
Paignton
Brixham
Tor Bay
Start Bay
Lyme Bay
Honiton
Ottery St. Mary
Sidmouth
Budleigh Salterton
Axminster
Seaton
Lyme Regis
Bridport
Chard
Crewkerne
Ilminster
Yeovil
Sherborne
Somerton
Castle Cary
Wincanton
Bruton
Mere
Gillingham
Shaftesbury
Sturminster Newton
Blackmoor Vale
North Dorset Downs
Beaminster
Dorchester
South Dorset Downs
Weymouth
Fortuneswell
I. of Portland
Portland Bill
Chesil Beach
Wareham
Poole
Poole Harbour
Bournemouth
Christchurch
Swanage
Wimborne Minster
Blandford Forum
Cranborne Chase & West Wiltshire Downs
Fordingbridge
Ringwood
Verwood
Wilton
Salisbury
Amesbury
Stockbridge
Winchester
Romsey
Eastleigh
Southampton
Totton
Lyndhurst
New Forest
Hythe
Fawley
Fareham
Gosport
Portsmouth
Havant
Petersfield
Alton
New Alresford
Lymington
New Milton
Milford on Sea
Isle of Wight
Newport
Cowes
Ryde
Sandown
Shanklin
Ventnor
Yarmouth
The Needles
St. Catherine's Pt.
Guernsey 2:00
Jersey 3:15
St. Malo 5:00
Guernsey 2:30
Jersey 3:45
Cherbourg 4:15
St. Malo 5:25
Guernsey 6:30
Jersey 10:00
Bilbao 35:00
Caen 6:00
Cherbourg 5:00
St. Malo 8:45
E N G L A N D
50°
3°
2°
1°
4
5
6
7
C
D
26
27
31
56
57

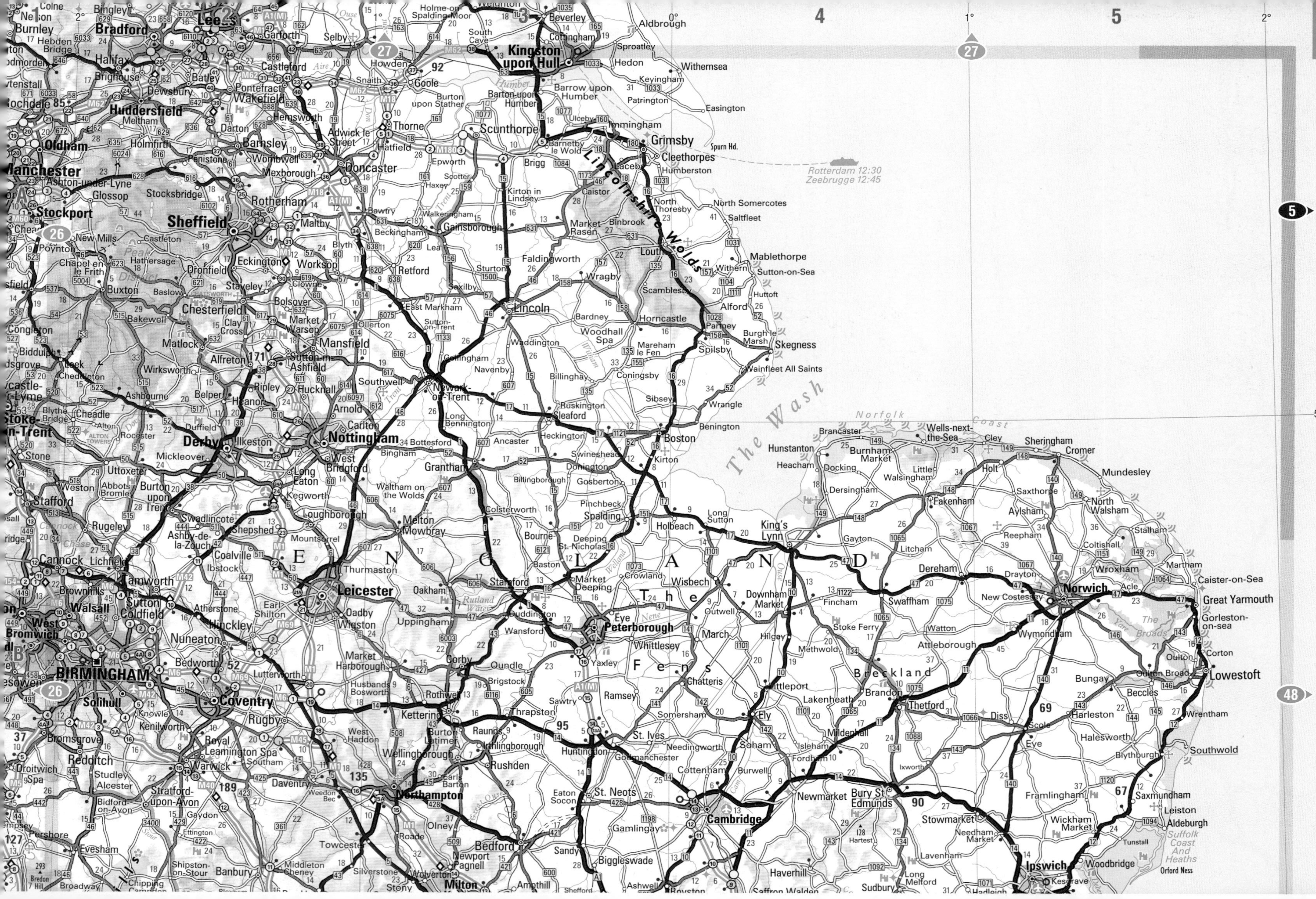
A
B
4
5
27
5
48
26
53°
Rotterdam 12:30
Zeebrugge 12:45
Spurn Hd.
The Wash
Norfolk Coast
Lincolnshire Wolds
E N G L A N D
The Fens
Breckland
The Broads
Suffolk Coast And Heaths
Peak District
Bradford
Leeds
Burnley
Halifax
Huddersfield
Oldham
Manchester
Stockport
Sheffield
Rotherham
Barnsley
Doncaster
Wakefield
Pontefract
Castleford
Dewsbury
Selby
Goole
Howden
Scunthorpe
Kingston upon Hull
Beverley
Cottingham
Aldbrough
Withernsea
Hedon
Patrington
Easington
Immingham
Grimsby
Cleethorpes
Humberston
North Somercotes
Saltfleet
Mablethorpe
Sutton-on-Sea
Louth
Alford
Skegness
Wainfleet All Saints
Spilsby
Horncastle
Woodhall Spa
Coningsby
Lincoln
Gainsborough
Market Rasen
Brigg
Retford
Worksop
Chesterfield
Mansfield
Newark-on-Trent
Sleaford
Boston
Grantham
Nottingham
Derby
Buxton
Bakewell
Matlock
Leek
Stoke-on-Trent
Stafford
Burton upon Trent
Loughborough
Melton Mowbray
Leicester
Oakham
Stamford
Spalding
Peterborough
Wisbech
King's Lynn
Hunstanton
Wells-next-the-Sea
Sheringham
Cromer
Mundesley
Fakenham
Holt
Dereham
Swaffham
Norwich
Great Yarmouth
Caister-on-Sea
Gorleston-on-sea
Lowestoft
Beccles
Bungay
Southwold
Halesworth
Aldeburgh
Leiston
Saxmundham
Woodbridge
Orford Ness
Ipswich
Stowmarket
Bury St. Edmunds
Newmarket
Thetford
Diss
Attleborough
Wymondham
Ely
Cambridge
Huntingdon
St. Neots
St. Ives
March
Chatteris
Ramsey
Kettering
Corby
Wellingborough
Northampton
Bedford
Rugby
Coventry
Nuneaton
Hinckley
Tamworth
Lichfield
Walsall
West Bromwich
BIRMINGHAM
Solihull
Redditch
Warwick
Royal Leamington Spa
Stratford-upon-Avon
Evesham
Banbury
Daventry
Towcester
Haverhill
Sudbury
Saffron Walden
Royston
Biggleswade
Milton

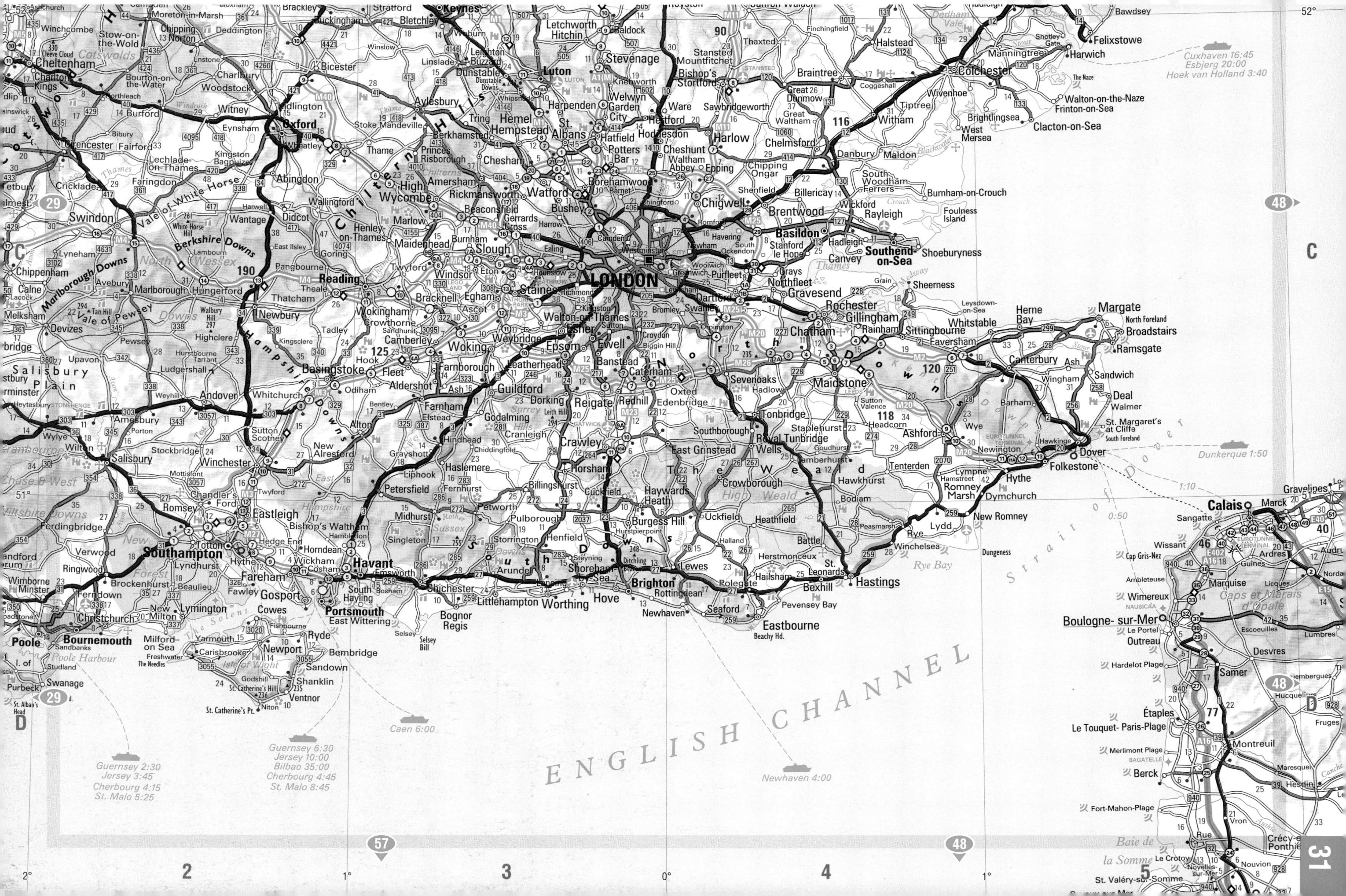
ENGLISH CHANNEL
Strait of Dover
LONDON
Oxford
Reading
Southampton
Portsmouth
Brighton
Hastings
Dover
Folkestone
Canterbury
Margate
Ramsgate
Maidstone
Chelmsford
Colchester
Harwich
Felixstowe
Southend-on-Sea
Luton
Stevenage
Swindon
Salisbury
Winchester
Guildford
Crawley
Eastbourne
Bournemouth
Poole
Calais
Boulogne-sur-Mer
Étaples
Le Touquet-Paris-Plage
Montreuil
Berck
North Downs
South Downs
The Weald
Chiltern Hills
Salisbury Plain
Isle of Wight
Cuxhaven 16:45
Esbjerg 20:00
Hoek van Holland 3:40
Dunkerque 1:50
Newhaven 4:00
Caen 6:00
Guernsey 6:30
Jersey 10:00
Bilbao 35:00
Cherbourg 4:45
St. Malo 8:45
Guernsey 2:30
Jersey 3:45
Cherbourg 4:15
St. Malo 5:25
31

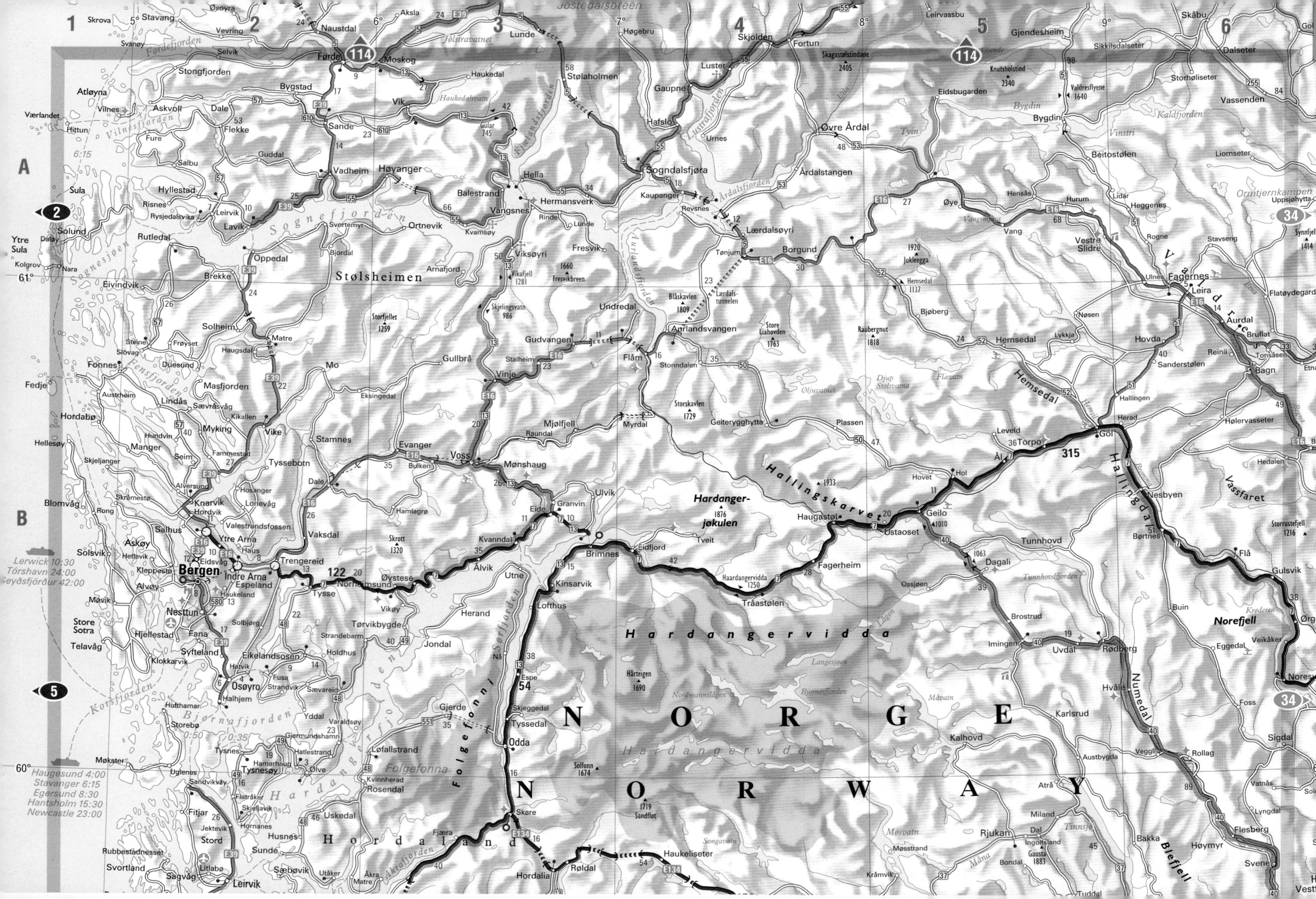
NORGE
NORWAY
Hardangervidda
Hardangerjøkulen
1876
Hallingskarvet
Hallingdal
Hemsedal
Numedal
Valdres
Stølsheimen
Folgefonna
Hordaland
Norefjell
Blefjell
Vassfaret
Jostedalsbreen
Sognefjorden
Aurlandsfjorden
Lustrafjorden
Årdalsfjorden
Hardangerfjorden
Sørfjorden
Bjørnafjorden
Korsfjorden
Fensfjorden
Førdefjorden
Bergen
Voss
Førde
Sogndalsfjøra
Lærdalsøyri
Fagernes
Gol
Geilo
Odda
Flåm
Aurlandsvangen
Gudvangen
Eidfjord
Ulvik
Norheimsund
Rjukan
Nesbyen
Lerwick 10:30
Tórshavn 24:00
Seyðisfjörður 42:00
Haugesund 4:00
Stavanger 6:15
Egersund 8:30
Hantsholm 15:30
Newcastle 23:00
Skagastølstindane 2405
Knutsholstind 2340
Gausta 1883
Hårteigen 1690
Sandfløt 1719
Solfonn 1674

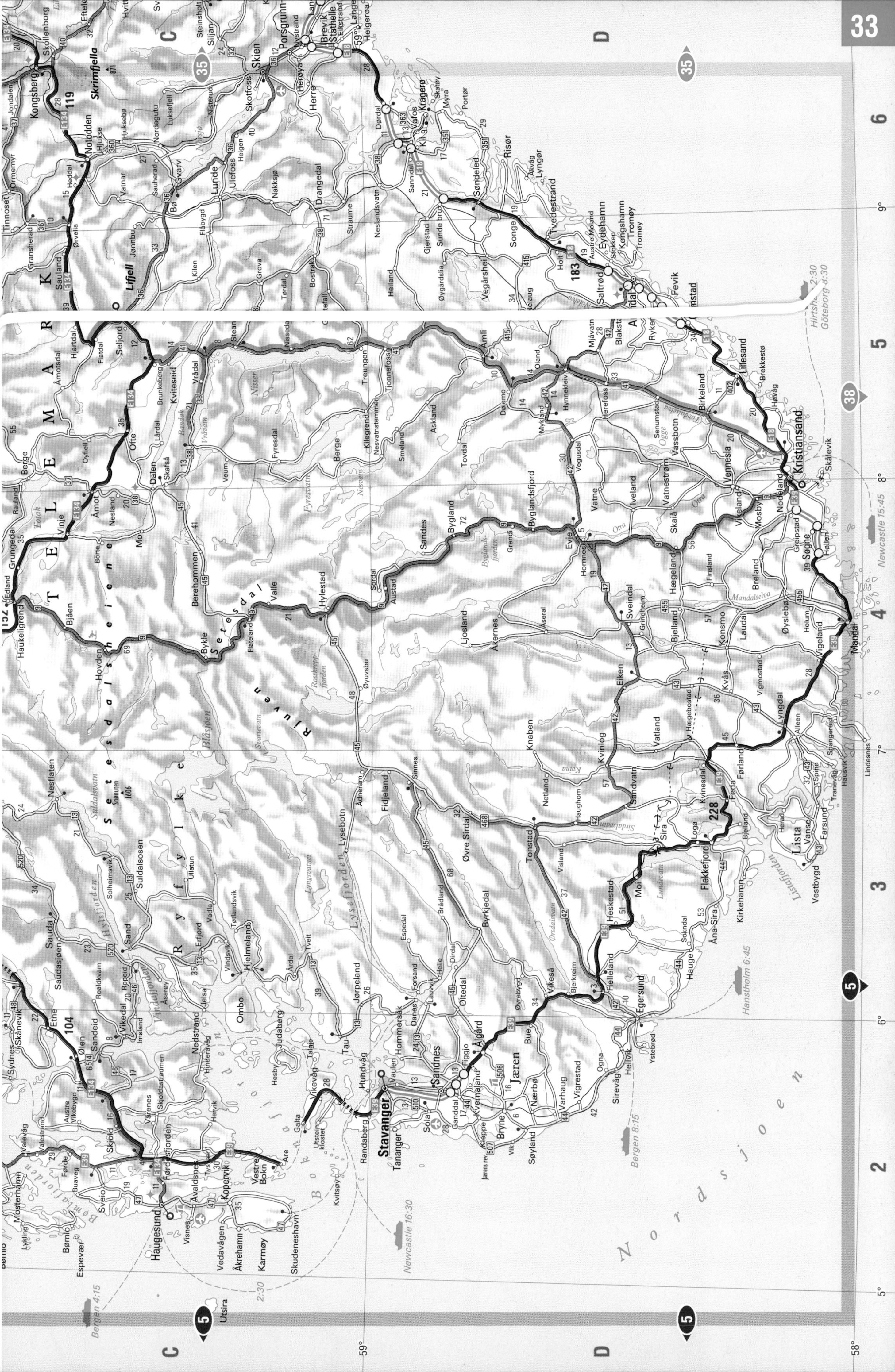

TELEMARK
Ryfylke
Setesdal
Setesdalsheiene
Rjuven
Jæren
Lista
Nordsjøen
Boknafjorden
Kristiansand
Stavanger
Haugesund
Sandnes
Egersund
Flekkefjord
Mandal
Arendal
Grimstad
Lillesand
Tvedestrand
Risør
Kragerø
Skien
Porsgrunn
Notodden
Kongsberg
Dalen
Bykle
Valle
Evje
Sauda
Søgne
Vennesla
Newcastle 16:30
Newcastle 15:45
Hanstholm 6:45
Bergen 8:15
Bergen 4:15
Hirtshals 2:30
Göteborg 8:30

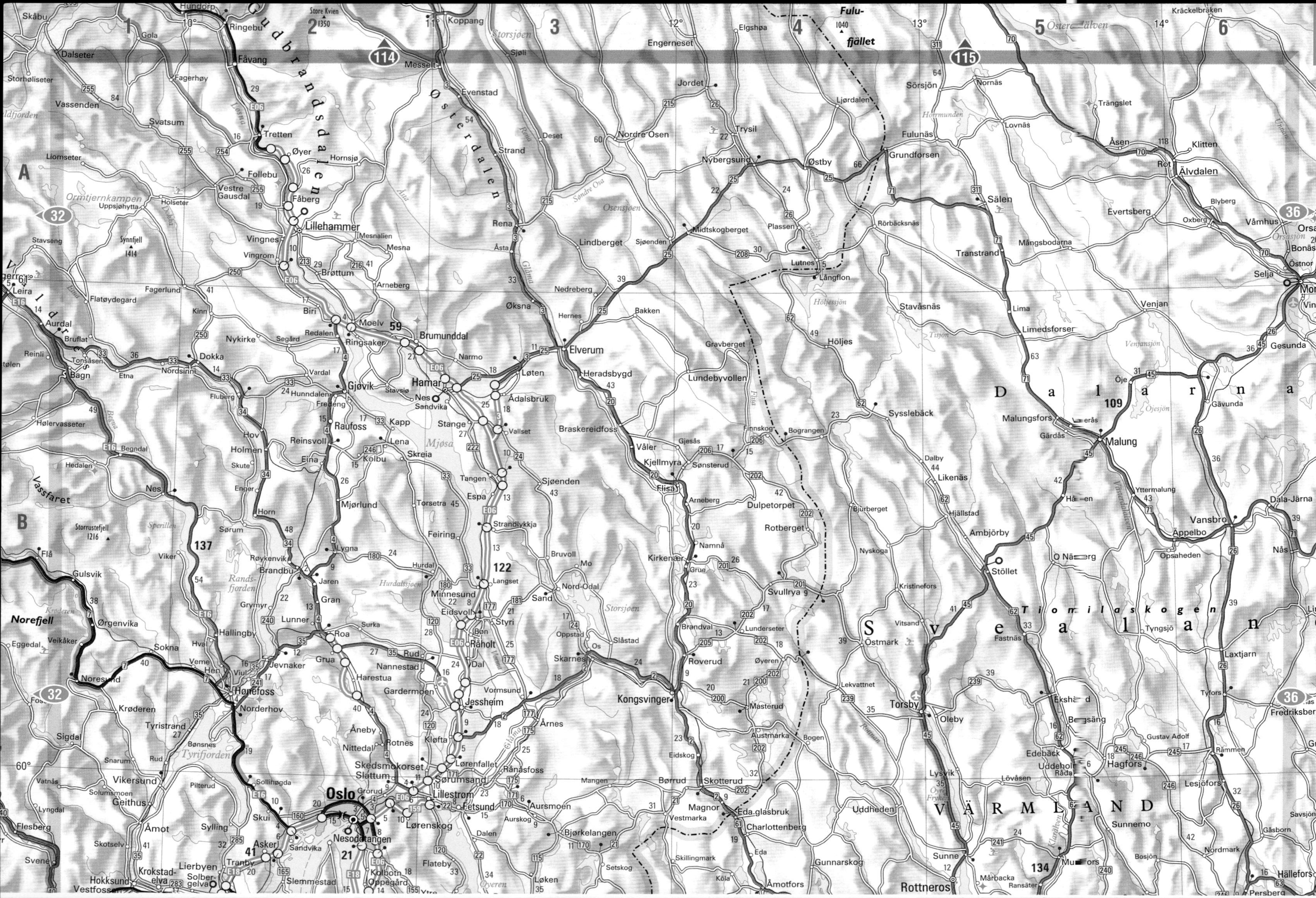
Gudbrandsdalen
Østerdalen
Dalarna
Svealand
VÄRMLAND
Tiomilaskogen
Fulu-fjället
Lillehammer
Hamar
Gjøvik
Elverum
Kongsvinger
Oslo
Lillestrøm
Hønefoss
Mora
Malung
Torsby
Sälen
Trysil
Älvdalen
Rena
Mjøsa
Tyrifjorden
Siljan
Hagfors
Sunne
Rottneros
Vansbro
Stöllet
Brumunddal
Moelv
Jessheim
Eidsvoll
Charlottenberg
Eda glasbruk
Flisa
Kirkenær
Sysslebäck
Asker
Sandvika
Fåvang
Ringebu
Tretten
Øyer
Dokka
Raufoss
Gran
Jevnaker
Koppang
Evenstad
Nybergsund
Grundforsen
Transtrand
Orsa
Hällefors

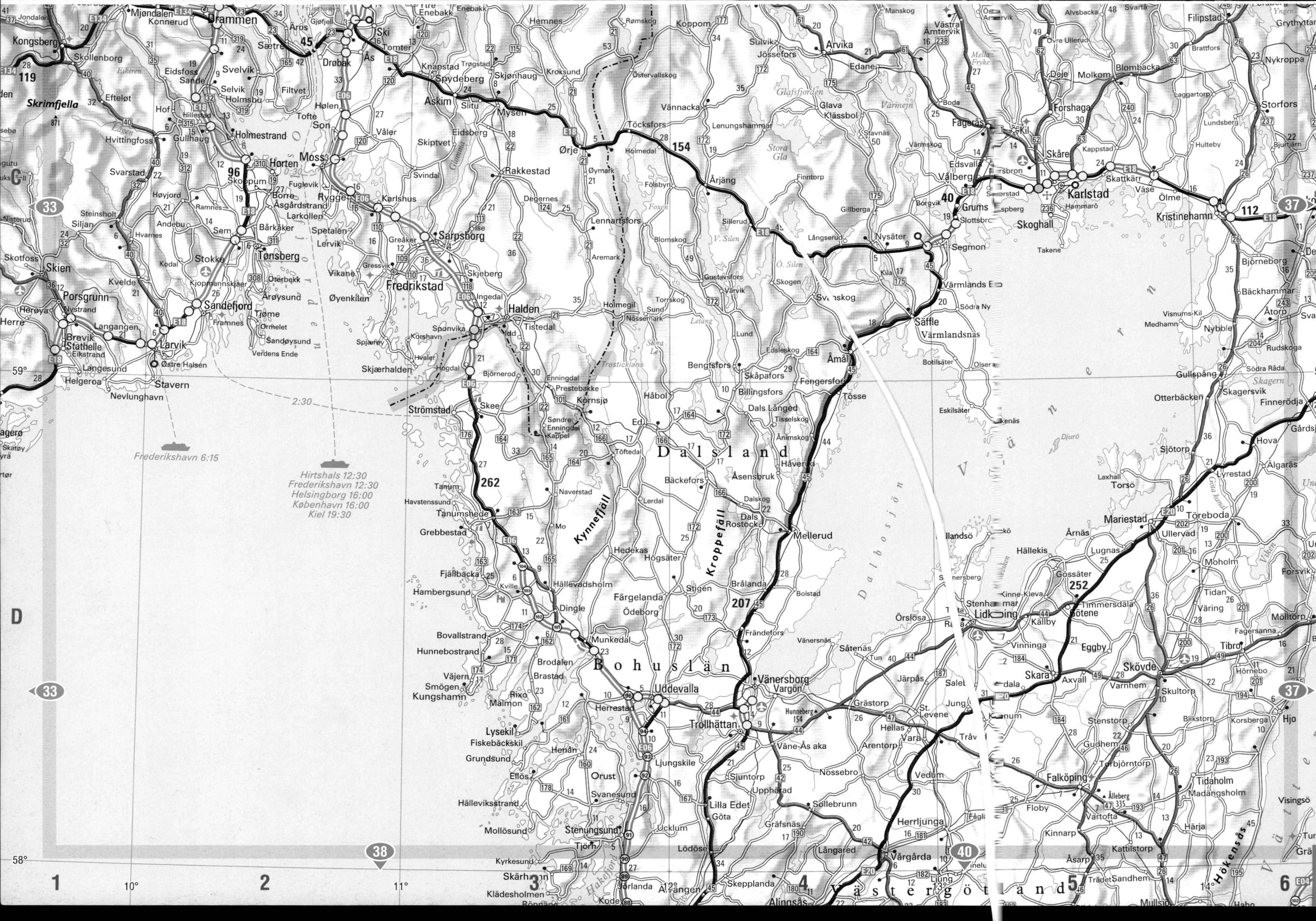
Dalsland
Bohuslän
Västergötland
Vänern
Dalbosjön
Kynnefjäll
Kroppefjäll
Skrimfjella
Drammen
Kongsberg
Skien
Porsgrunn
Larvik
Sandefjord
Tønsberg
Horten
Holmestrand
Moss
Sarpsborg
Fredrikstad
Halden
Askim
Mysen
Spydeberg
Ski
Drøbak
Rakkestad
Ørje
Töcksfors
Årjäng
Arvika
Säffle
Åmål
Mellerud
Grums
Karlstad
Kristinehamn
Skoghall
Forshaga
Kil
Fagerås
Strömstad
Tanumshede
Grebbestad
Fjällbacka
Lysekil
Uddevalla
Vänersborg
Trollhättan
Stenungsund
Kungshamn
Smögen
Orust
Lidköping
Mariestad
Skövde
Skara
Falköping
Tidaholm
Hjo
Götene
Vara
Vårgårda
Alingsås
Herrljunga
Frederikshavn 6:15
Hirtshals 12:30
Frederikshavn 12:30
Helsingborg 16:00
København 16:00
Kiel 19:30
2:30
59°
58°
10°
11°
12°
14°
1
2
3
4
5
6
C
D
33
37
38
40

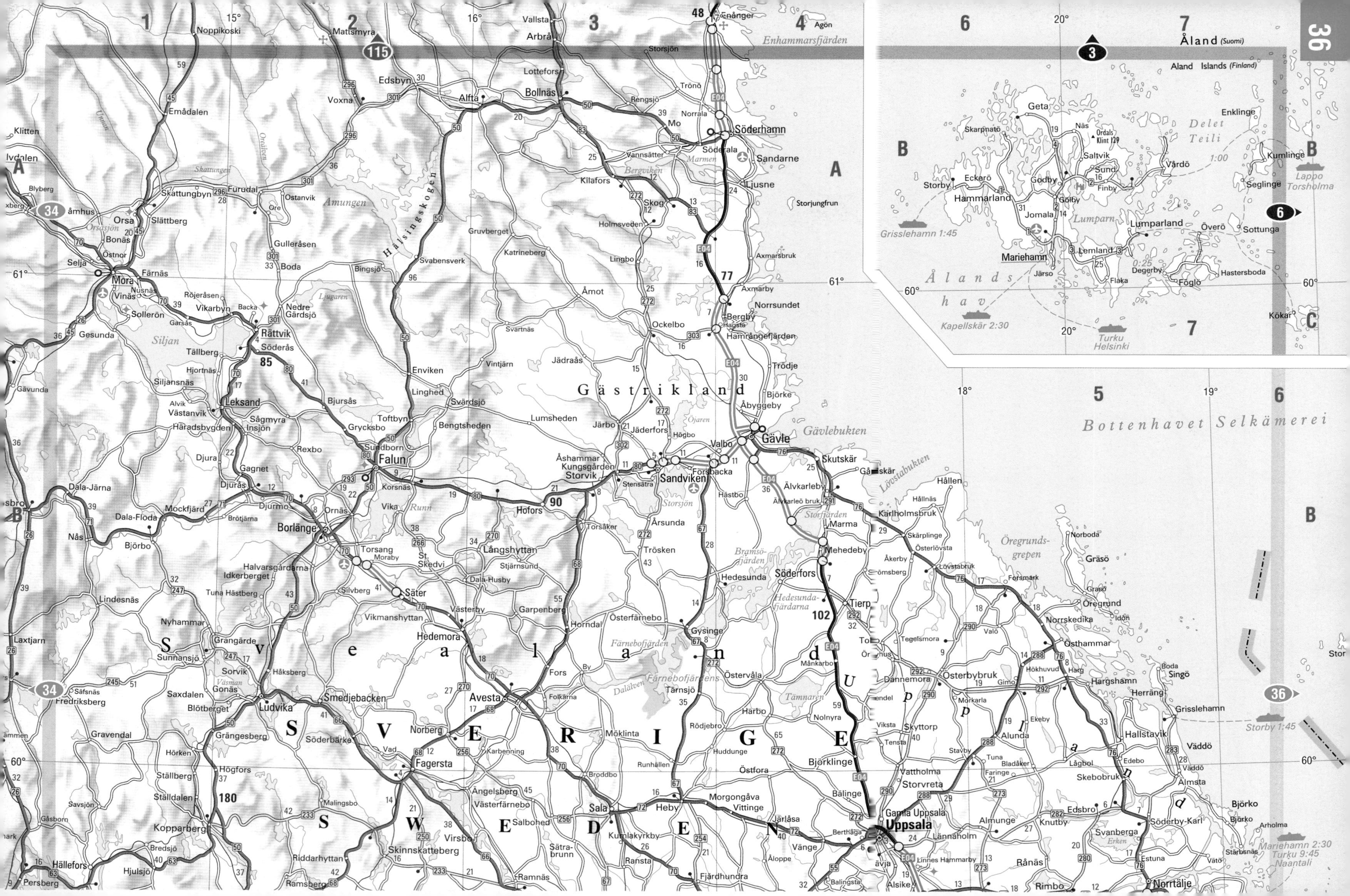

Åland (Suomi)
Aland Islands (Finland)
Delet
Teili
Lumparn
Ålands hav
Grisslehamn 1:45
Kapellskär 2:30
Turku Helsinki
Mariehamn
Jomala
Hammarland
Eckerö
Geta
Saltvik
Sund
Vårdö
Lumparland
Lemland
Föglö
Kökar
Kumlinge
Sottunga
Bottenhavet Selkämerei
Gävlebukten
Öregrunds-grepen
Gävle
Söderhamn
Bollnäs
Edsbyn
Alfta
Mora
Orsa
Rättvik
Leksand
Falun
Borlänge
Ludvika
Hedemora
Avesta
Sala
Uppsala
Tierp
Östhammar
Norrtälje
Sandviken
Hofors
Fagersta
Kopparberg
Hällefors
Smedjebacken
Säter
Siljan
Gästrikland
Uppland
SVERIGE
SWEDEN
Hälsingskogen
Storby 1:45
Mariehamn 2:30
Turku 9:45
Naantali

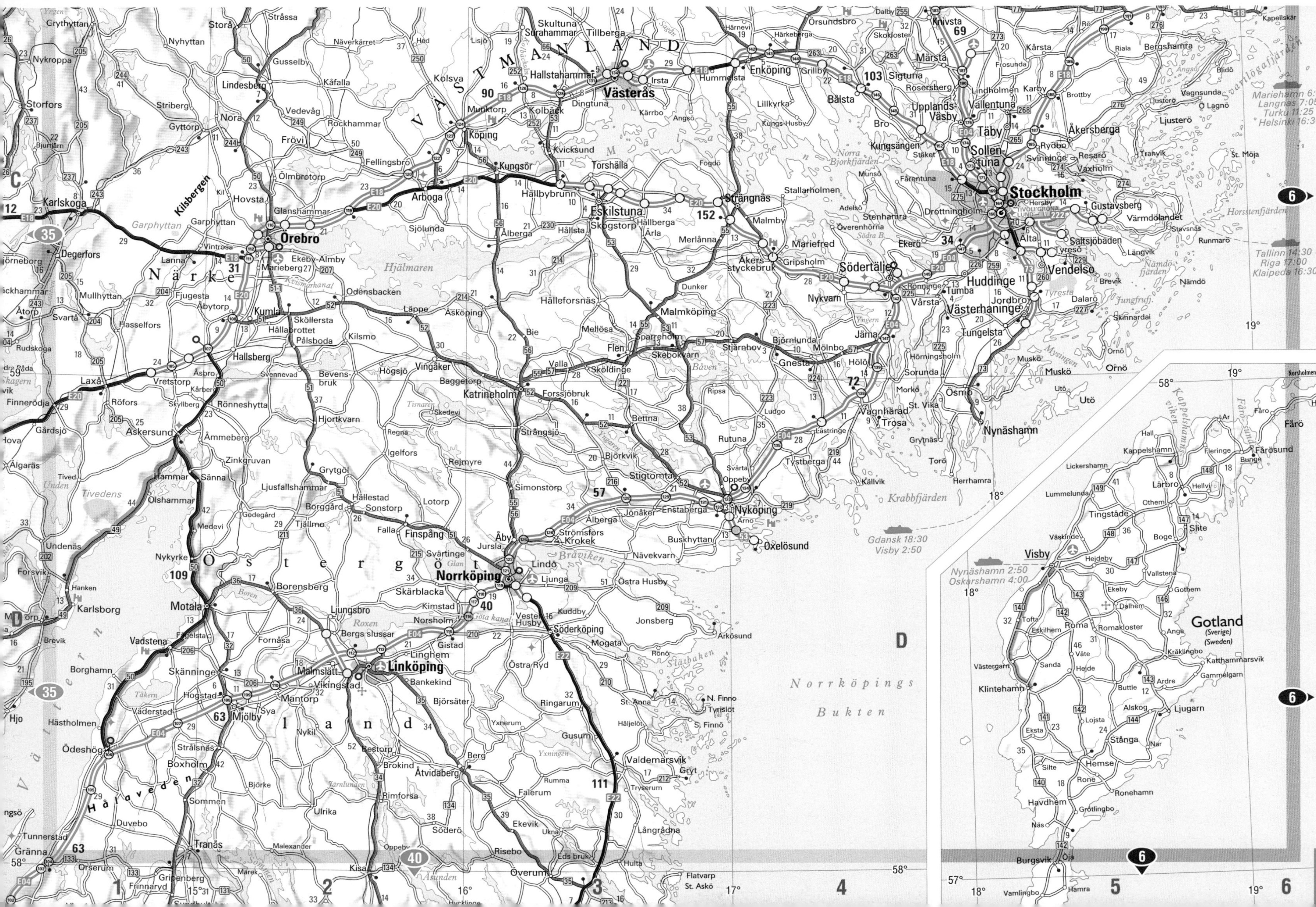
Stockholm
Västerås
Örebro
Norrköping
Linköping
Eskilstuna
Nyköping
Södertälje
Strängnäs
Enköping
Köping
Arboga
Katrineholm
Motala
Mjölby
Vadstena
Karlskoga
Lindesberg
Kumla
Hallsberg
Finspång
Flen
Nynäshamn
Visby
Gotland
(Sverige)
(Sweden)
Fårö
Slite
Klintehamn
Hemse
Burgsvik
Sigtuna
Märsta
Bålsta
Huddinge
Västerhaninge
Åtvidaberg
Söderköping
Valdemarsvik
Kisa
Tranås
Gränna
Ödeshög
Askersund
Trosa
Oxelösund
Hjälmaren
Norrköpings
Bukten
Krabbfjärden
Västmanland
Närke
Östergötland
Mariehamn 6:15
Langnas 7:05
Turku 11:25
Helsinki 16:30
Tallinn 14:30
Riga 17:00
Klaipeda 16:30
Gdansk 18:30
Visby 2:50
Nynäshamn 2:50
Oskarshamn 4:00

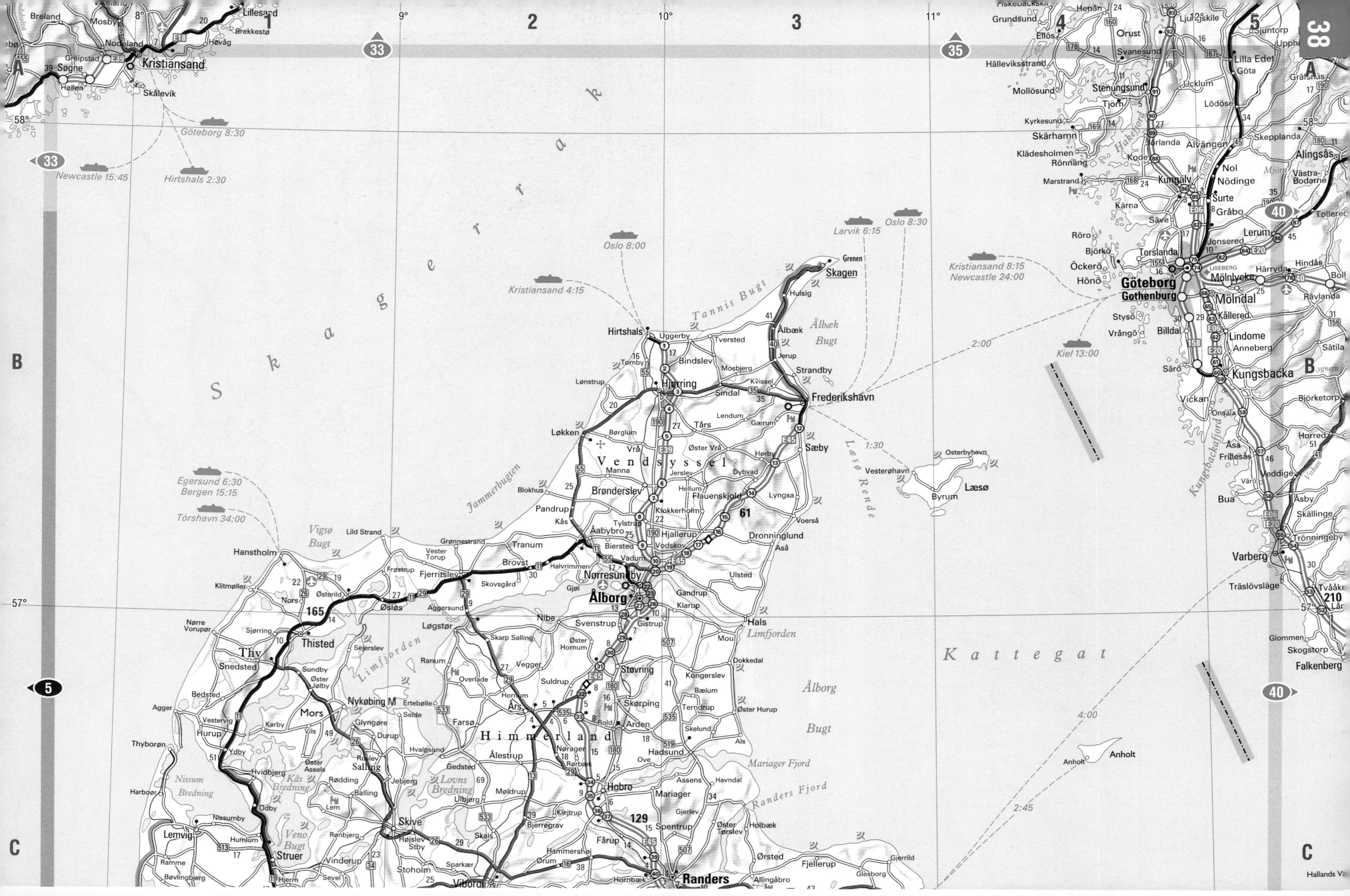
Kristiansand
Søgne
Lillesand
Skålevik
Göteborg 8:30
Newcastle 15:45
Hirtshals 2:30
Skagerrak
Oslo 8:00
Kristiansand 4:15
Larvik 6:15
Oslo 8:30
Kristiansand 8:15
Newcastle 24:00
Kiel 13:00
Egersund 6:30
Bergen 15:15
Tórshavn 34:00
Grenen
Skagen
Tannis Bugt
Ålbæk Bugt
Hirtshals
Hjørring
Sindal
Frederikshavn
Sæby
Løkken
Vendsyssel
Brønderslev
Læsø
Læsø Rende
Vesterøhavn
Østerbyhavn
Byrum
Jammerbugten
Vigsø Bugt
Hanstholm
Thisted
Thy
Fjerritslev
Nørresundby
Ålborg
Limfjorden
Hals
Mors
Nykøbing M
Himmerland
Års
Hobro
Skive
Struer
Lemvig
Viborg
Randers
Mariager Fjord
Randers Fjord
Ålborg Bugt
Kattegat
Anholt
Göteborg
Gothenburg
Mölndal
Kungsbacka
Kungälv
Stenungsund
Orust
Alingsås
Lerum
Varberg
Falkenberg
Kungsbackafjord
Hakefjord
2:00
1:30
4:00
2:45

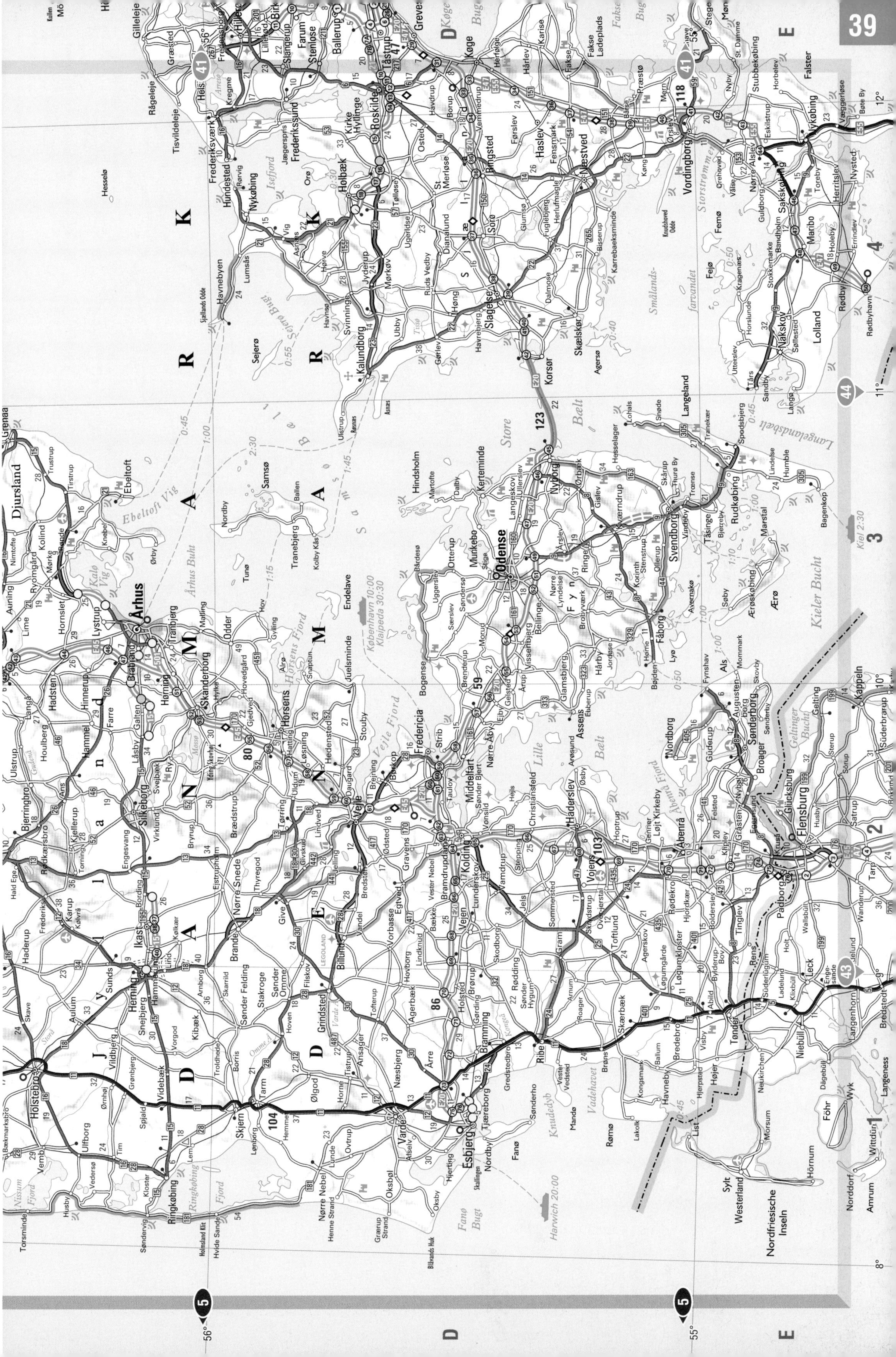
D A N M A R K
Djursland
Jylland
Sjælland
Fyn
Århus
Odense
Esbjerg
Vejle
Kolding
Fredericia
Horsens
Silkeborg
Herning
Holstebro
Ringkøbing
Skjern
Varde
Ribe
Haderslev
Åbenrå
Sønderborg
Tønder
Flensburg
Niebüll
Svendborg
Nyborg
Fåborg
Middelfart
Assens
Kerteminde
Slagelse
Korsør
Kalundborg
Holbæk
Roskilde
Køge
Ringsted
Næstved
Sorø
Vordingborg
Nakskov
Maribo
Nykøbing
Rødbyhavn
Lolland
Falster
Langeland
Ærø
Als
Samsø
Fanø
Rømø
Sylt
Föhr
Amrum
Nordfriesische Inseln
Store Bælt
Lille Bælt
Kieler Bucht
Smålands-farvandet
Horsens Fjord
Vejle Fjord
Ringkøbing Fjord
Nissum Fjord
Ebeltoft Vig
Århus Bugt
Isefjord
Køge Bugt
Fakse Bugt
Harwich 20:00
København 10:00
Klaipeda 30:30
Kiel 2:30
56°
55°
8°
9°
10°
11°
12°
D
E
1
2
3
4
5
41
43
44

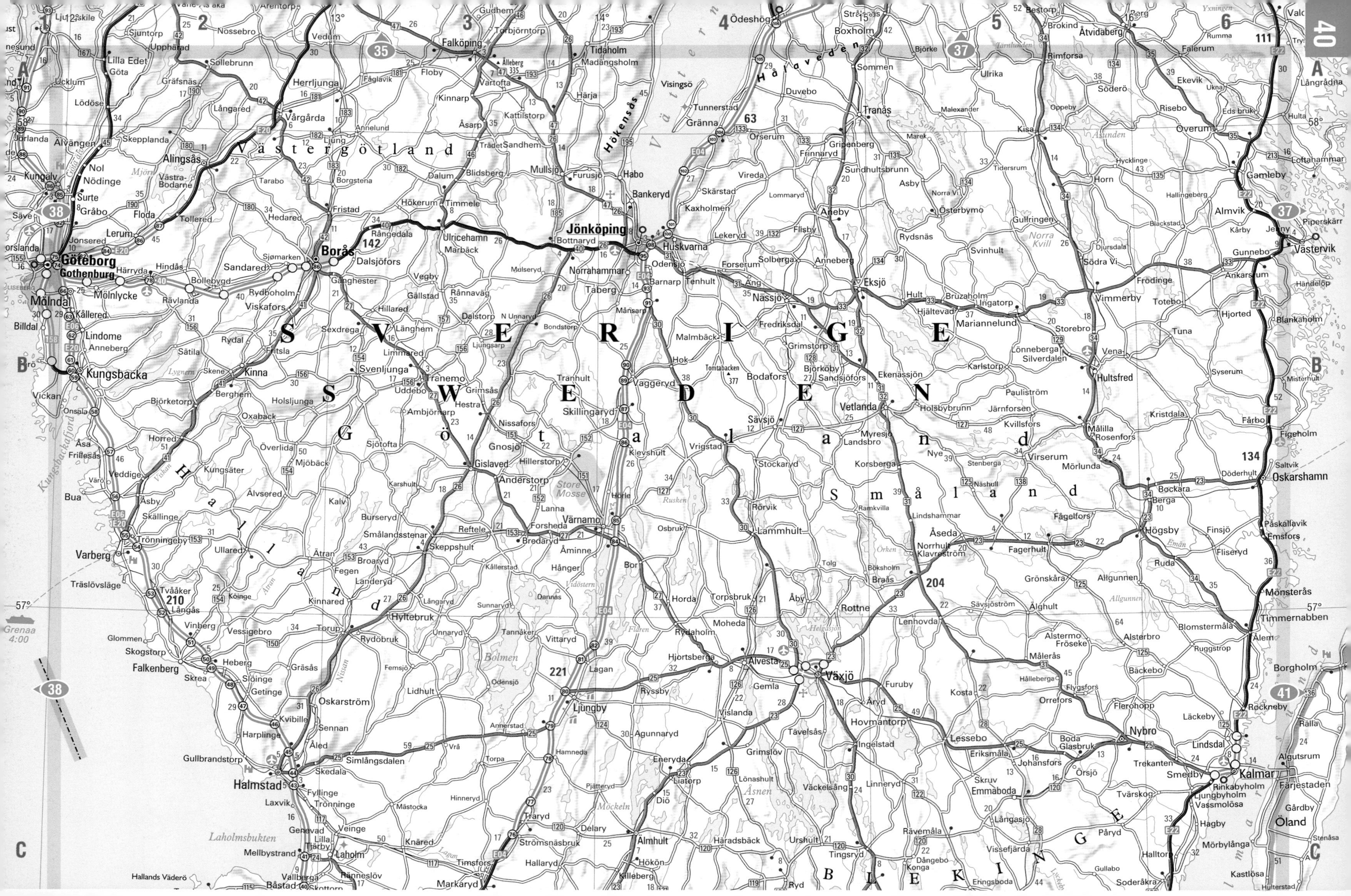
S V E R I G E
S W E D E N
Västergötland
Småland
Halland
Götaland
BLEKINGE
Vättern
Hökensås
Hålaveden
Göteborg
Gothenburg
Mölndal
Kungsbacka
Borås
Jönköping
Huskvarna
Växjö
Kalmar
Öland
Halmstad
Falkenberg
Varberg
Alingsås
Falköping
Tidaholm
Gränna
Tranås
Eksjö
Nässjö
Vetlanda
Värnamo
Ljungby
Alvesta
Vimmerby
Hultsfred
Oskarshamn
Västervik
Åtvidaberg
Gislaved
Ulricehamn
Nybro
Lessebo
Emmaboda
Laholm
Markaryd
Älmhult
Tingsryd
Mönsterås
Borgholm
Färjestaden
Kungälv
Lerum
Mölnlycke
Sävsjö
Hylteburk
Laholmsbukten
Kungsbackafjord
Grenaa 4:00
57°

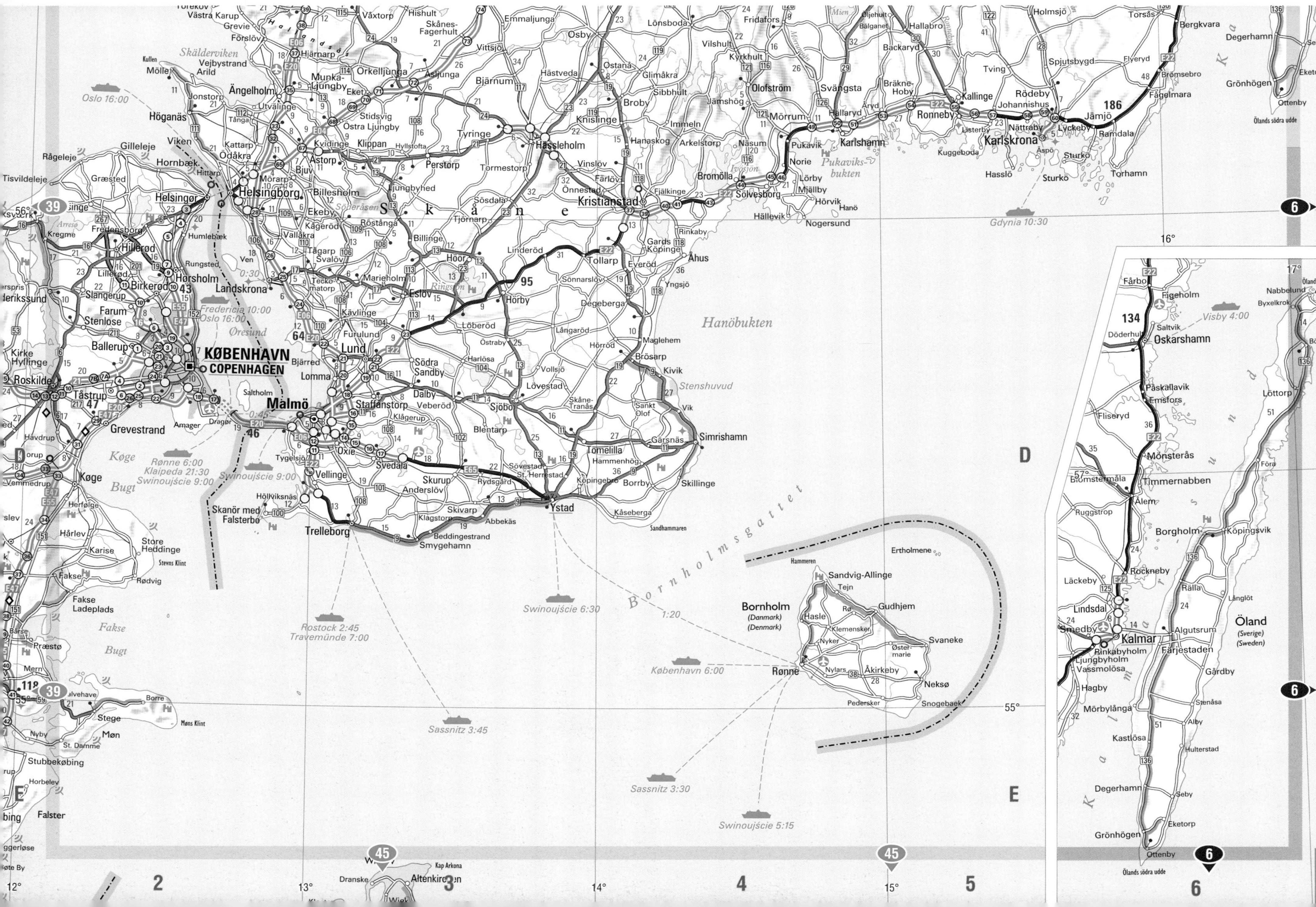
Skåne
Hanöbukten
Øresund
Køge Bugt
Fakse Bugt
Bornholmsgattet
Kalmarsund
KØBENHAVN
COPENHAGEN
Malmö
Helsingborg
Helsingør
Landskrona
Lund
Trelleborg
Ystad
Simrishamn
Kristianstad
Hässleholm
Sölvesborg
Karlshamn
Ronneby
Karlskrona
Kalmar
Oskarshamn
Öland
(Sverige)
(Sweden)
Bornholm
(Danmark)
(Denmark)
Rønne
Nexø
Svaneke
Gudhjem
Sandvig-Allinge
Hasle
Åkirkeby
Ertholmene
Höganäs
Ängelholm
Eslöv
Hörby
Höör
Sjöbo
Tomelilla
Svedala
Skurup
Staffanstorp
Kävlinge
Lomma
Bjärred
Skanör med Falsterbo
Roskilde
Hillerød
Køge
Grevestrand
Ballerup
Fakse
Stege
Møn
Falster
Borgholm
Färjestaden
Mönsterås
Nybro
Gdynia 10:30
Oslo 16:00
Fredericia 10:00
Oslo 16:00
Rønne 6:00
Klaipeda 21:30
Swinoujście 9:00
Rostock 2:45
Travemünde 7:00
Sassnitz 3:45
Swinoujście 6:30
København 6:00
Sassnitz 3:30
Swinoujście 5:15
Visby 4:00
56°
55°
57°
12°
13°
14°
15°
16°
17°
B
C
D
E
2
3
4
5
6
7

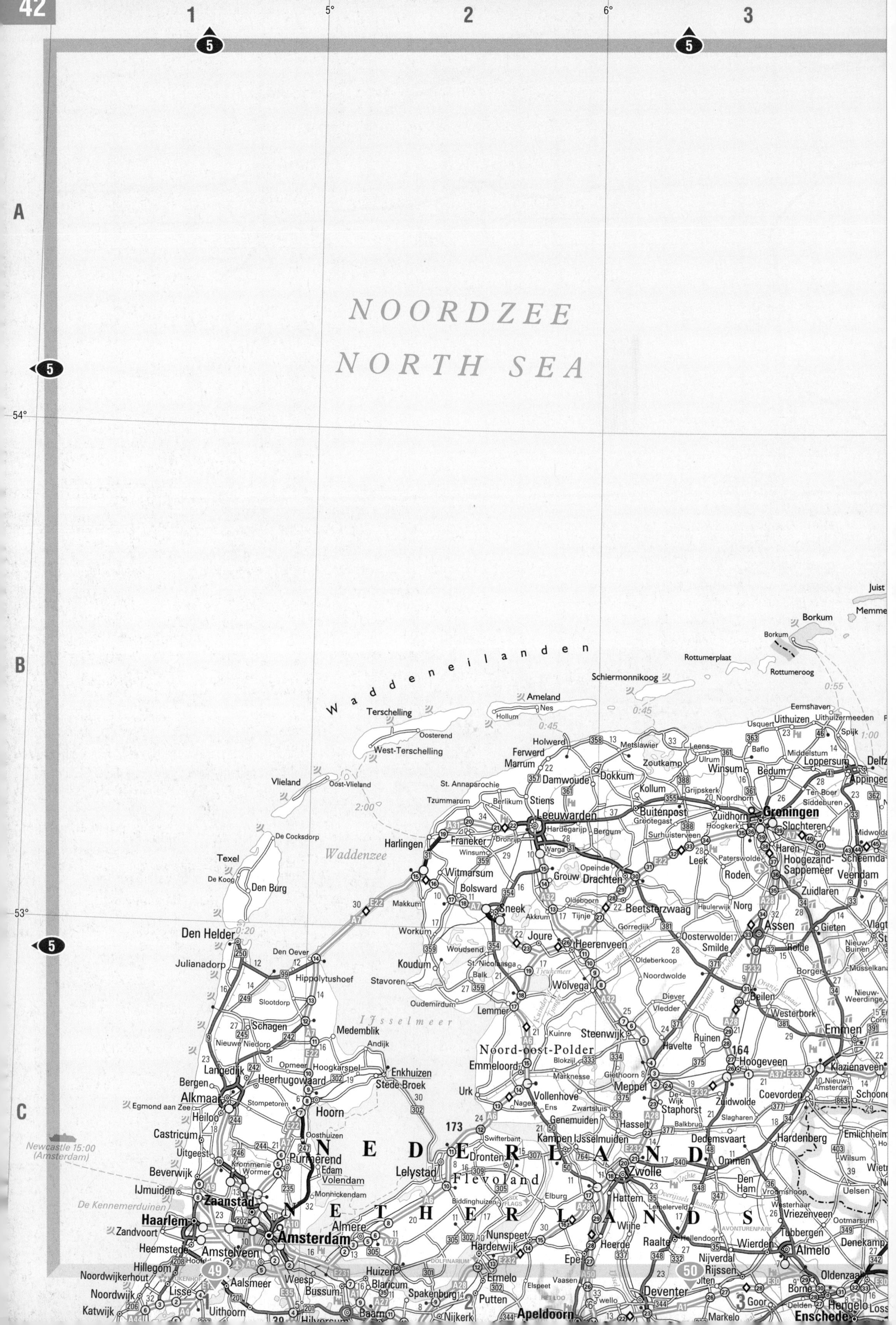
NOORDZEE
NORTH SEA
Waddeneilanden
Waddenzee
IJsselmeer
NEDERLAND
NETHERLANDS
Flevoland
Noord-oost-Polder
Texel
Vlieland
Terschelling
Ameland
Schiermonnikoog
Rottumerplaat
Rottumeroog
Borkum
Juist
Den Helder
Den Burg
De Cocksdorp
Harlingen
Leeuwarden
Franeker
Sneek
Drachten
Heerenveen
Groningen
Assen
Emmen
Hoogeveen
Meppel
Zwolle
Kampen
Dronten
Lelystad
Almere
Amsterdam
Haarlem
Zaanstad
Alkmaar
Hoorn
Enkhuizen
Purmerend
Edam
Volendam
Amstelveen
Hilversum
Apeldoorn
Deventer
Almelo
Hengelo
Enschede
Harderwijk
Ermelo
Nijkerk
Lemmer
Urk
Emmeloord
Steenwijk
Coevorden
Hardenberg
Veendam
Winschoten
Newcastle 15:00 (Amsterdam)
De Kennemerduinen
0:20
0:45
0:55
2:00
1:00
173
164
49
50
5
1
2
3
A
B
C
5°
6°
53°
54°

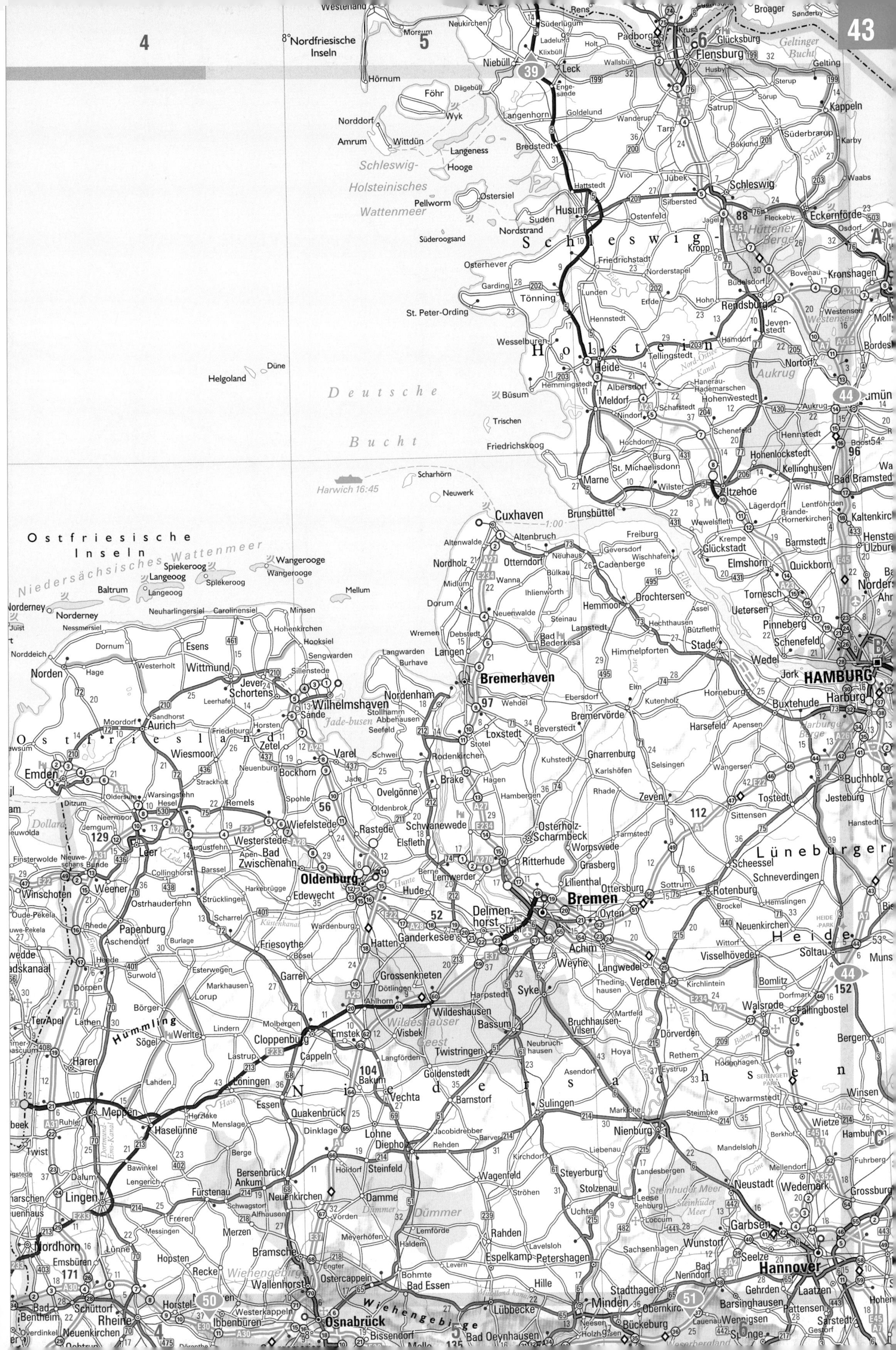
4
5
6
Nordfriesische Inseln
Westerland
Morsum
Hörnum
Föhr
Wyk
Dagebüll
Norddorf
Amrum
Wittdün
Langeness
Hooge
Schleswig-Holsteinisches Wattenmeer
Pellworm
Ostersiel
Suden
Nordstrand
Süderoogsand
Neukirchen
Süderlügum
Rens
Ladelund
Klixbüll
Niebüll
Leck
Holt
Wallsbüll
Padborg
Kruså
Glücksburg
Flensburg
Broager
Sønderby
Geltinger Bucht
Gelting
Husby
Sterup
Sörup
Kappeln
Satrup
Wanderup
Tarp
Langenhorn
Goldelund
Enge-Sande
Bredstedt
Süderbrarup
Karby
Böklund
Viöl
Jübek
Schleswig
Schlei
Waabs
Hattstedt
Husum
Silberstedt
Ostenfeld
Jagel
Fleckeby
Eckernförde
Hüttener Berge
Osdorf
Schleswig-Holstein
Kropp
Friedrichstadt
Norderstapel
Osterhever
Garding
Tönning
St. Peter-Ording
Lunden
Erfde
Hohn
Büdelsdorf
Rendsburg
Bovenau
Kronshagen
Jevenstedt
Westensee
Hennstedt
Hamdorf
Wesselburen
Tellingstedt
Heide
Nord-Ostsee Kanal
Nortorf
Aukrug
Bordesholm
Hemmingstedt
Albersdorf
Hanerau-Hademarschen
Hohenwestedt
Neumünster
Büsum
Meldorf
Schafstedt
Nindorf
Trischen
Schenefeld
Hennstedt
Boostedt
Friedrichskoog
Hochdonn
Burg
Hohenlockstedt
Deutsche Bucht
Helgoland
Düne
Scharhörn
Neuwerk
Harwich 16:45
St. Michaelisdonn
Marne
Wilster
Itzehoe
Kellinghusen
Bad Bramstedt
Wrist
Lägerdorf
Lentföhrden
Brande-Hornerkirchen
Kaltenkirchen
Cuxhaven
Brunsbüttel
Wewelsfleth
Krempe
Glückstadt
Barmstedt
Henstedt-Ulzburg
Altenwalde
Altenbruch
Freiburg
Geversdorf
Wischhafen
Ostfriesische Inseln
Niedersächsisches Wattenmeer
Wangerooge
Spiekeroog
Langeoog
Baltrum
Norderney
Juist
Mellum
Nordholz
Otterndorf
Neuhaus
Cadenberge
Elmshorn
Quickborn
Midlum
Wanna
Bülkau
Ihlienworth
Tornesch
Norderstedt
Uetersen
Dorum
Neuenwalde
Steinau
Hemmoor
Drochtersen
Assel
Pinneberg
Neuharlingersiel
Carolinensiel
Minsen
Nessmersiel
Hohenkirchen
Hooksiel
Sengwarden
Norddeich
Dornum
Esens
Wremen
Debstedt
Bad Bederkesa
Lamstedt
Hechthausen
Bützfleth
Schenefeld
Stade
Wedel
Langwarden
Burhave
Langen
Himmelpforten
Norden
Hage
Westerholt
Wittmund
Sillenstede
Jever
Schortens
Leerhafe
Wilhelmshaven
Bremerhaven
Jork
HAMBURG
Elm
Horneburg
Buxtehude
Harburg
Nordenham
Stollhamm
Abbehausen
Sande
Jade-busen
Seefeld
Wehdel
Ebersdorf
Kutenholz
Bremervörde
Sandhorst
Moordorf
Aurich
Friedeburg
Horsten
Zetel
Loxstedt
Beverstedt
Harsefeld
Apensen
Harburger Berge
Ostfriesland
Wiesmoor
Neuenburg
Bockhorn
Varel
Schwei
Stotel
Rodenkirchen
Gnarrenburg
Kuhstedt
Karlshöfen
Selsingen
Wangersen
Buchholz
Emden
Strackholt
Jade
Brake
Hagen
Ovelgönne
Oldenbrok
Hambergen
Rhade
Zeven
Tostedt
Jesteburg
Oldersum
Warsingsfehn
Spohle
Neermoor
Hesel
Remels
Rastede
Schwanewede
Osterholz-Scharmbeck
Sittensen
Hanstedt
Dollard
Jemgum
Wiefelstede
Elsfleth
Tarmstedt
Worpswede
Ditzum
Leer
Westerstede
Augustfehn
Bad Zwischenahn
Ritterhude
Grasberg
Lüneburger Heide
Finsterwolde
Nieuweschans
Bunde
Barssel
Oldenburg
Berne
Lemwerder
Lilienthal
Scheessel
Collinghorst
Hunte
Hude
Ottersberg
Sottrum
Schneverdingen
Winschoten
Weener
Ostrhauderfehn
Harkebrügge
Edewecht
Bremen
Rotenburg
Oude-Pekela
Strücklingen
Delmenhorst
Oyten
Brockel
Hemslingen
Rhede
Scharrel
Küstenkanal
Wardenburg
Stuhr
Neuenkirchen
HEIDE-PARK
Papenburg
Aschendorf
Burlage
Friesoythe
Hatten
Ganderkesee
Achim
Langwedel
Wittorf
Visselhövede
Soltau
Munster
Bösel
Weyhe
Verden
Kirchlinteln
Bomlitz
Heede
Esterwegen
Garrel
Grossenkneten
Dötlingen
Thedinghausen
Dorfmark
Fallingbostel
Surwold
Markhausen
Lorup
Ahlhorn
Wildeshausen
Harpstedt
Syke
Martfeld
Walsrode
Dörpen
Börger
Lathen
Hümmling
Werlte
Sögel
Lindern
Molbergen
Cloppenburg
Emstek
Wildeshauser Geest
Visbek
Bassum
Bruchhausen-Vilsen
Dörverden
Bergen
Ter Apel
Lastrup
Cappeln
Twistringen
Neubruchhausen
Hoya
Rethem
Haren
Langförden
Goldenstedt
Eystrup
Hodenhagen
SERENGETI PARK
Lahden
Löningen
Bakum
Vechta
Asendorf
Essen
Barnstorf
Sulingen
Niedersachsen
Meppen
Herzlake
Quakenbrück
Markloh
Steimbke
Schwarmstedt
Winsen
Ruhle
Haselünne
Menslage
Dinklage
Lohne
Jacobidrebber
Nienburg
Wietze
Twist
Diepholz
Rehden
Barver
Berge
Dortmund-Ems-Kanal
Liebenau
Mandelsloh
Hambühren
Bawinkel
Bersenbrück
Ankum
Holdorf
Steinfeld
Kirchdorf
Landesbergen
Mellendorf
Fuhrberg
Dalum
Lengerich
Wagenfeld
Steyerberg
Neustadt
Wedemark
Großburgwedel
Lingen
Fürstenau
Neuenkirchen
Damme
Ströhen
Stolzenau
Steinhuder Meer
Schwagstorf
Alfhausen
Dümmer
Leese
Rehburg
Loccum
Garbsen
Vorden
Freren
Merzen
Lemförde
Rahden
Uchte
Nordhorn
Messingen
Meyerhöfen
Haldem
Lavelsloh
Sachsenhagen
Wunstorf
Seelze
Hannover
Emsbüren
Lünne
Hopsten
Bramsche
Espelkamp
Petershagen
Bad Nenndorf
Recke
Wiehengebirge
Engter
Levern
Hille
Ostercappeln
Bohmte
Bad Essen
Stadthagen
Gehrden
Laatzen
Wallenhorst
Minden
Obernkirchen
Barsinghausen
Pattensen
Bad Bentheim
Schüttorf
Horstel
Westerkappeln
Lübbecke
Neesen
Lauenau
Wennigsen
Sarstedt
Bentheim
Rheine
Ibbenbüren
Osnabrück
Bückeburg
Holzhausen
Springe
Neuenkirchen
Ochtrup
Bissendorf
Melle
Bad Oeynhausen
Weserbergland
Gestorf
Hohen
39
44
50
51
88
96
56
97
112
129
52
104
152
171
135
A
B
C
E45
A7
A23
A27
A28
A29
A31
A1
A30
A33
A352
E22
E37
E234
E233
E30
A210
A215
A261
A270

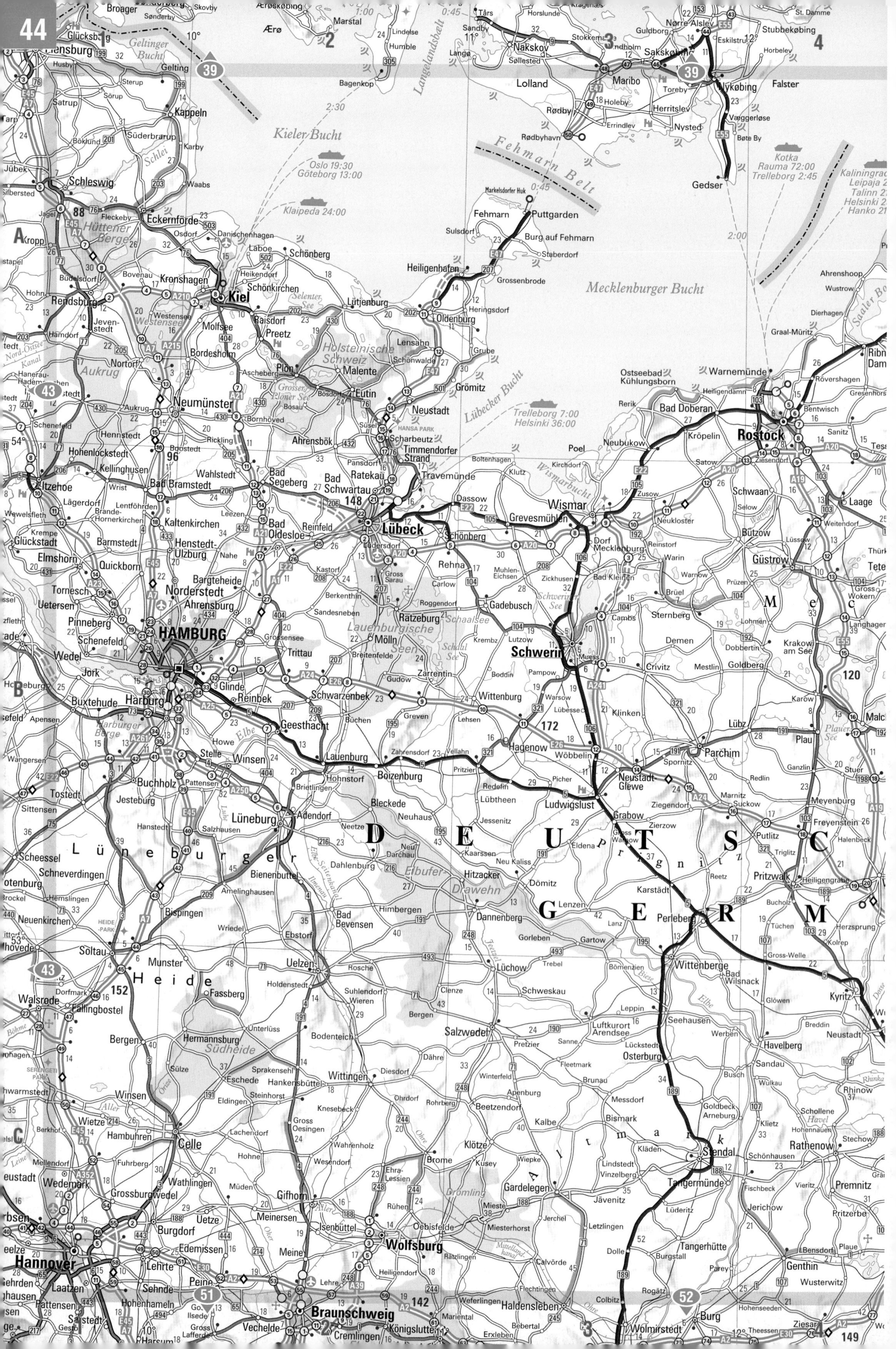
Flensburg
Schleswig
Kappeln
Eckernförde
Kiel
Rendsburg
Neumünster
Itzehoe
Plön
Eutin
Lütjenburg
Oldenburg
Heiligenhafen
Fehmarn
Puttgarden
Burg auf Fehmarn
Neustadt
Bad Segeberg
Bad Oldesloe
Lübeck
Travemünde
Ratzeburg
Mölln
Elmshorn
Pinneberg
Norderstedt
Ahrensburg
HAMBURG
Harburg
Buxtehude
Stade
Geesthacht
Lauenburg
Winsen
Buchholz
Lüneburg
Soltau
Uelzen
Celle
Gifhorn
Wolfsburg
Braunschweig
Hannover
Peine
Lehrte
Burgdorf
Salzwedel
Wittingen
Gardelegen
Stendal
Tangermünde
Haldensleben
Wolmirstedt
Burg
Genthin
Rathenow
Havelberg
Kyritz
Wittenberge
Perleberg
Pritzwalk
Ludwigslust
Hagenow
Schwerin
Gadebusch
Wismar
Grevesmühlen
Bad Doberan
Rostock
Warnemünde
Güstrow
Bützow
Parchim
Lübz
Plau
Neustadt Glewe
Dömitz
Hitzacker
Dannenberg
Lüchow
Lolland
Maribo
Nakskov
Nykøbing
Falster
Gedser
Rødbyhavn
Ærø
Marstal
Kieler Bucht
Fehmarn Belt
Mecklenburger Bucht
Lübecker Bucht
Lüneburger Heide
Altmark
DEUTSCHLAND
GERMANY
Elbe
Prignitz
Holsteinische Schweiz
Lauenburgische Seen
Schweriner See
Oslo 19:30
Göteborg 13:00
Klaipeda 24:00
Trelleborg 7:00
Helsinki 36:00
Kotka
Rauma 72:00
Trelleborg 2:45
39
43
51
52
120
149

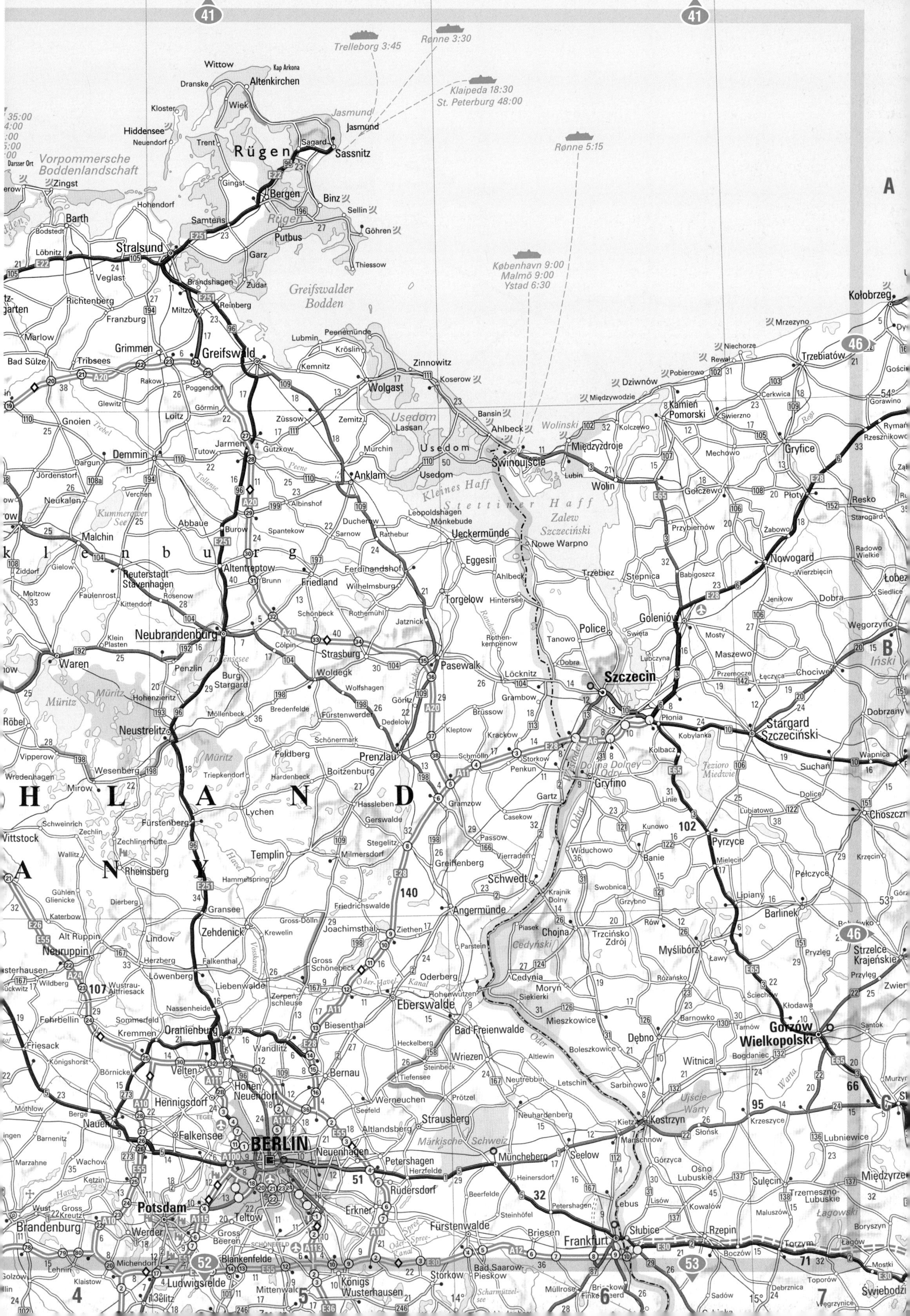

4
13°
5
14°
6
15°
7
41
Trelleborg 3:45
Rønne 3:30
Klaipeda 18:30
St. Peterburg 48:00
Rønne 5:15
København 9:00
Malmö 9:00
Ystad 6:30
Wittow
Kap Arkona
Dranske
Altenkirchen
Wiek
Kloster
Hiddensee
Neuendorf
Jasmund
Sagard
Sassnitz
Rügen
Trent
Gingst
Bergen
Binz
Sellin
Göhren
Putbus
Samtens
Garz
Thiessow
Zudar
Vorpommersche Boddenlandschaft
Darsser Ort
Zingst
Barth
Bodstedt
Hohendorf
Löbnitz
Stralsund
Veglast
Brandshagen
Reinberg
Greifswalder Bodden
Richtenberg
Franzburg
Miltzow
Marlow
Grimmen
Greifswald
Bad Sülze
Tribsees
Lubmin
Peenemünde
Kröslin
Kemnitz
Zinnowitz
Wolgast
Koserow
Rakow
Poggendorf
Glewitz
Görmin
Loitz
Züssow
Zemitz
Lassan
Usedom
Bansin
Ahlbeck
Świnoujście
Gnoien
Trebel
Jarmen
Gützkow
Tutow
Demmin
Dargun
Peene
Anklam
Jördenstorf
Verchen
Kleines Haff
Stettiner Haff
Zalew Szczeciński
Neukalen
Kummerower See
Albinshof
Leopoldshagen
Mönkebude
Abbaue
Burow
Spantekow
Ducherow
Sarnow
Rathebur
Ueckermünde
Nowe Warpno
Malchin
Altentreptow
Ferdinandshof
Eggesin
Ahlbeck
Trzebież
Ziddorf
Gielow
Reuterstadt Stavenhagen
Brunn
Friedland
Wilhelmsburg
Torgelow
Hintersee
Moltzow
Faulenrost
Kittendorf
Rosenow
Schönbeck
Rothemühl
Jatznick
Neubrandenburg
Klein Plasten
Cölpin
Strasburg
Rothenkempenow
Police
Tanowo
Waren
Penzlin
Tollensesee
Woldegk
Pasewalk
Löcknitz
Dobra
Szczecin
Müritz
Burg Stargard
Hohenzieritz
Wolfshagen
Bredenfelde
Göritz
Grambow
Röbel
Möllenbeck
Fürstenwerder
Dedelow
Brüssow
Neustrelitz
Schönermark
Kleptow
Krackow
Vipperow
Feldberg
Prenzlau
Schmölln
Storkow
Penkun
Wredenhagen
Wesenberg
Boitzenburg
Triepkendorf
Hardenbeck
Gryfino
Dolina Dolnej Odry
Mirow
Hassleben
Gramzow
Gartz
Schweinrich
Zechlin
Lychen
Gerswalde
Casekow
Wittstock
Fürstenberg
Zechlinerhütte
Stegelitz
Passow
Wallitz
Rheinsberg
Templin
Milmersdorf
Vierraden
Widuchowo
Greiffenberg
Hammelspring
Schwedt
Krajnik Dolny
Swobnica
Gühlen Glienicke
Dierberg
Friedrichswalde
Angermünde
Gransee
Gross-Dölln
Katerbow
Joachimsthal
Ziethen
Piasek
Chojna
Trzcińsko Zdrój
Alt Ruppin
Zehdenick
Krewelin
Lindow
Cedyński
Neuruppin
Herzberg
Falkenthal
Gross Schönebeck
Parstein
Cedynia
Moryń
Oderberg
Wildberg
Wustrau-Altfriesack
Löwenberg
Liebenwalde
Zerpenschleuse
Eberswalde
Hohenwutzen
Siekierki
Mieszkowice
Fehrbellin
Sommerfeld
Kremmen
Oranienburg
Nassenheide
Biesenthal
Bad Freienwalde
Friesack
Königshorst
Wandlitz
Heckelberg
Wriezen
Altlewin
Boleszkowice
Bernau
Steinbeck
Tiefensee
Neutrebbin
Letschin
Börnicke
Velten
Hohen Neuendorf
Hennigsdorf
Werneuchen
Prötzel
Sarbinowo
Möthlow
Berge
Nauen
Seefeld
Strausberg
Neuhardenberg
Kostrzyn
Kietz
Falkensee
Altlandsberg
Märkische Schweiz
Barnenitz
BERLIN
Neuenhagen
Müncheberg
Seelow
Manschnow
Marzahne
Wachow
Petershagen
Herzfelde
Heinersdorf
Ketzin
Rüdersdorf
Beerfelde
Górzyca
Ośno Lubuskie
Potsdam
Wust
Gross Kreutz
Erkner
Steinhöfel
Petershagen
Lebus
Lisów
Brandenburg
Werder
Teltow
Gross Beeren
Fürstenwalde
Briesen
Słubice
Frankfurt
Rzepin
Michendorf
Blankenfelde
Schönefeld
Lehnin
Klaistow
Ludwigsfelde
Königs Wusterhausen
Storkow
Bad Saarow-Pieskow
Scharmützelsee
Müllrose
Finkenheerd
Mittenwalde
Zossen
Mostki
Świebodzin
Kołobrzeg
Mrzeżyno
Niechorze
Rewal
Pobierowo
Trzebiatów
Dziwnów
Międzywodzie
Wolinski
Kamień Pomorski
Cerkwica
Gorawino
Kołczewo
Świerzno
Międzyzdroje
Lubin
Wolin
Mechowo
Gryfice
Rymań
Rzesznikowo
Golczewo
Płoty
Resko
Przybiernów
Żabowo
Starogard
Radowo Wielkie
Nowogard
Wierzbięcin
Stepnica
Babigoszcz
Łobez
Siedlice
Goleniów
Jenikow
Dobra
Święta
Mosty
Węgorzyno
Lubczyna
Maszewo
Iński
Przemocze
Łęczyca
Chociwel
Płonia
Kobylanka
Stargard Szczeciński
Dobrzany
Kolbacz
Jezioro Miedwie
Wapnica
Suchań
Linie
Dolice
Lubiatowo
Choszczno
Kunowo
Banie
Pyrzyce
Mielęcin
Krzęcin
Pełczyce
Grzybno
Lipiany
Barlinek
Rów
Myślibórz
Łąwy
Strzelce Krajeńskie
Przyłęg
Różańsko
Ściechów
Kłodawa
Zwierzyn
Barnowko
Tarnów
Gorzów Wielkopolski
Santok
Dębno
Witnica
Bogdaniec
Murzynowo
Ujście Warty
Warta
Krzeszyce
Słońsk
Lubniewice
Sulęcin
Trzemeszno-Lubuskie
Międzyrzecz
Maluszów
Łagowski
Kowalów
Boryszyn
Łagów
Torzym
Boczów
Debrznica
Toporów
Sadów
Węgrzynice
H L A N D
A N Y
k l e n b u r g
A
B
C
46
52
53

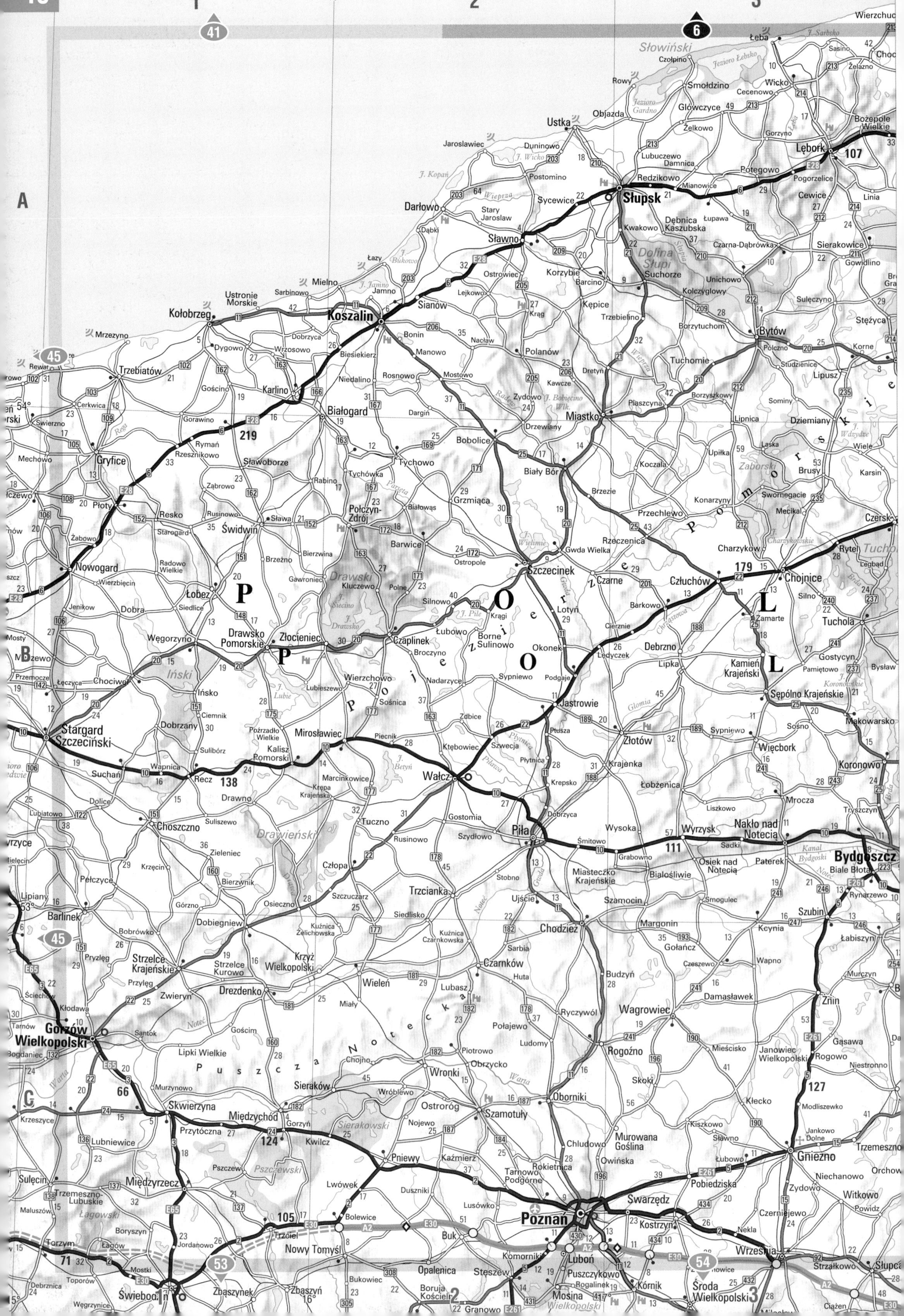
1
2
3
16°
17°
41
6
45
53
54
A
B
C
Słowiński
Łeba
Czołpino
Jezioro Łebsko
Rowy
Smołdzino
Główczyce
Ustka
Objazda
Jarosławiec
Duninowo
J. Wicko
Postomino
J. Kopań
Darłowo
Wieprza
Stary Jarosław
Sycewice
Słupsk
Redzikowo
Mianowice
Potęgowo
Lębork
Dębnica Kaszubska
Łupawa
Kwakowo
Sławno
Dąbki
J. Bukowo
Łazy
Dolina Słupi
Suchorze
Czarna-Dąbrówka
Sierakowice
Mielno
J. Jamno
Jamno
Sarbinowo
Ustronie Morskie
Kołobrzeg
Koszalin
Sianów
Lejkowo
Ostrowiec
Korzybie
Barcino
Kępice
Trzebielino
Unichowo
Kołczygłowy
Borzytuchom
Bytów
Mrzezyno
Rewal
Trzebiatów
Dygowo
Wrzosowo
Dobrzyca
Biesiekierz
Bonin
Manowo
Nacław
Polanów
Tuchomie
Karlino
Gościno
Niedalino
Rosnowo
Mostowo
Zydowo
J. Bobięcino Wlk.
Kawcze
Dretyń
Miastko
Piaszczyna
Borzyszkowy
Lipnica
Dziemiany
Cerkwica
Białogard
Dargiń
Drzewiany
Gorawino
Rymań
Rzesznikowo
Bobolice
Biały Bór
Koczała
Płoty
Gryfice
Sławoborze
Tychowo
Tychówka
Rąbino
Grzmiąca
Brzezie
Konarzyny
Przechlewo
Połczyn-Zdrój
Białowąs
Resko
Rusinowo
Sława
Świdwin
Starogard
Barwice
Rzeczenica
Charzykowy
Czersk
Nowogard
Radowo Wielkie
Brzeżno
Bierzwnik
Drawski
Kluczewo
Ostropole
Gwda Wielka
Szczecinek
Czarne
Człuchów
Chojnice
Wierzbięcin
Łobez
Gawroniec
Polne
Silnowo
Kłączno
J. Pile
Lotyń
Barkowo
Zamarte
Tuchola
Jeników
Dobra
Siedlice
Drawsko Pomorskie
Złocieniec
Czaplinek
Łubowo
Borne Sulinowo
Okonek
Debrzno
Lipka
Kamień Krajeński
Węgorzyno
Broczyno
Ińsko
Wierzchowo
Nadarzyce
Sypniewo
Podgaje
Jastrowie
Sępólno Krajeńskie
Stargard Szczeciński
Chociwel
Ciemnik
Dobrzany
Sulibórz
Pożrzadło Wielkie
Kalisz Pomorski
Mirosławiec
Piecnik
Zdbice
Szwecja
Płytnica
Złotów
Więcbork
Koronowo
Suchań
Wapnica
Recz
Drawno
Marcinkowice
Krępa Krajeńska
Wałcz
Krajenka
Łobżenica
Mrocza
Dolice
Choszczno
Suliszewo
Drawieński
Tuczno
Rusinowo
Gostomia
Szydłowo
Piła
Wysoka
Wyrzysk
Nakło nad Notecią
Bydgoszcz
Zieleniec
Krzęcin
Pełczyce
Człopa
Stobno
Miasteczko Krajeńskie
Białośliwie
Osiek nad Notecią
Szubin
Lipiany
Barlinek
Osieczno
Szczuczarz
Trzcianka
Ujście
Szamocin
Margonin
Chodzież
Dobiegniew
Kuźnica Żelichowska
Siedlisko
Kuźnica Czarnkowska
Gołańcz
Kcynia
Łabiszyn
Strzelce Krajeńskie
Krzyż Wielkopolski
Czarnków
Wapno
Budzyń
Drezdenko
Zwierzyn
Wieleń
Lubasz
Damasławek
Żnin
Kłodawa
Gorzów Wielkopolski
Santok
Gościm
Połajewo
Ryczywół
Wągrowiec
Lipki Wielkie
Piotrowo
Obrzycko
Rogoźno
Mieścisko
Janowiec Wielkopolski
Puszcza Notecka
Chojno
Wronki
Sieraków
Skoki
Kłecko
Gąsawa
Rogowo
Skwierzyna
Ostroróg
Szamotuły
Oborniki
Międzychód
Przytóczna
Kwilcz
Nojewo
Sierakowski
Murowana Goślina
Gniezno
Pniewy
Kaźmierz
Tarnowo Podgórne
Rokietnica
Owińska
Lubniewice
Międzyrzecz
Pszczew
Lwówek
Duszniki
Swarzędz
Pobiedziska
Zbąszyń
Nowy Tomyśl
Buk
Poznań
Kostrzyn
Września
Opalenica
Stęszew
Luboń
Komorniki
Puszczykowo
Środa Wielkopolska
Świebodzin
Zbąszynek
Bukowiec
Mosina
Kórnik
Słupca
Pomorskie
Pojezierze
POLLPOO

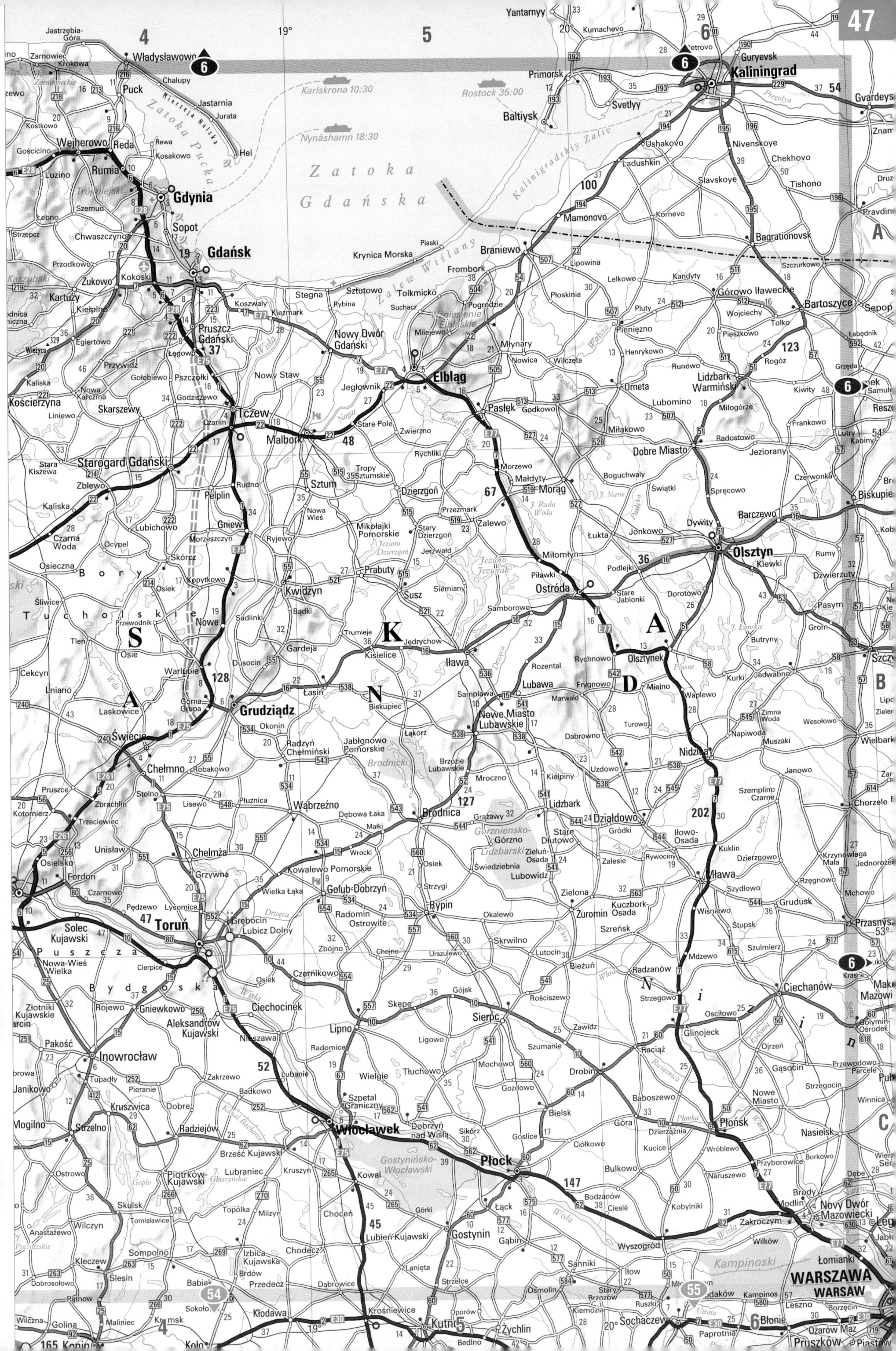
Zatoka Gdańska
Zatoka Pucka
Mierzeja Helska
Kaliningradskiy Zaliv
Zalew Wiślany
Karlskrona 10:30
Rostock 35:00
Nynäshamn 18:30
Władysławowo
Jastrzębia Góra
Puck
Jastarnia
Jurata
Hel
Wejherowo
Reda
Rumia
Gdynia
Sopot
Gdańsk
Kartuzy
Żukowo
Pruszcz Gdański
Tczew
Malbork
Kościerzyna
Skarszewy
Starogard Gdański
Pelplin
Gniew
Sztum
Kwidzyn
Nowe
Świecie
Chełmno
Grudziądz
Toruń
Chełmża
Golub-Dobrzyń
Wąbrzeźno
Brodnica
Rypin
Lipno
Ciechocinek
Aleksandrów Kujawski
Inowrocław
Kruszwica
Strzelno
Mogilno
Radziejów
Włocławek
Kowal
Gostynin
Płock
Sierpc
Lubień Kujawski
Kutno
Żychlin
Kłodawa
Koło
Konin
Krynica Morska
Nowy Dwór Gdański
Elbląg
Frombork
Braniewo
Tolkmicko
Pasłęk
Młynary
Orneta
Morąg
Ostróda
Iława
Susz
Prabuty
Lubawa
Nowe Miasto Lubawskie
Olsztyn
Olsztynek
Dobre Miasto
Lidzbark Warmiński
Bartoszyce
Górowo Iławeckie
Pieniężno
Biskupiec
Nidzica
Działdowo
Lidzbark
Mława
Żuromin
Ciechanów
Płońsk
Raciąż
Drobin
Bielsk
Wyszogród
Sochaczew
Zakroczym
Nowy Dwór Mazowiecki
Łomianki
WARSZAWA
WARSAW
Błonie
Pruszków
Ożarów Maz.
Kaliningrad
Guryevsk
Svetlyy
Baltiysk
Primorsk
Yantarnyy
Mamonovo
Ladushkin
Ushakovo
Bagrationovsk
Gvardeysk
Bory Tucholskie
Puszcza Bydgoska
Kaszuby
Kampinoski
Jezioro Jeziorak
Jezioro Gopło

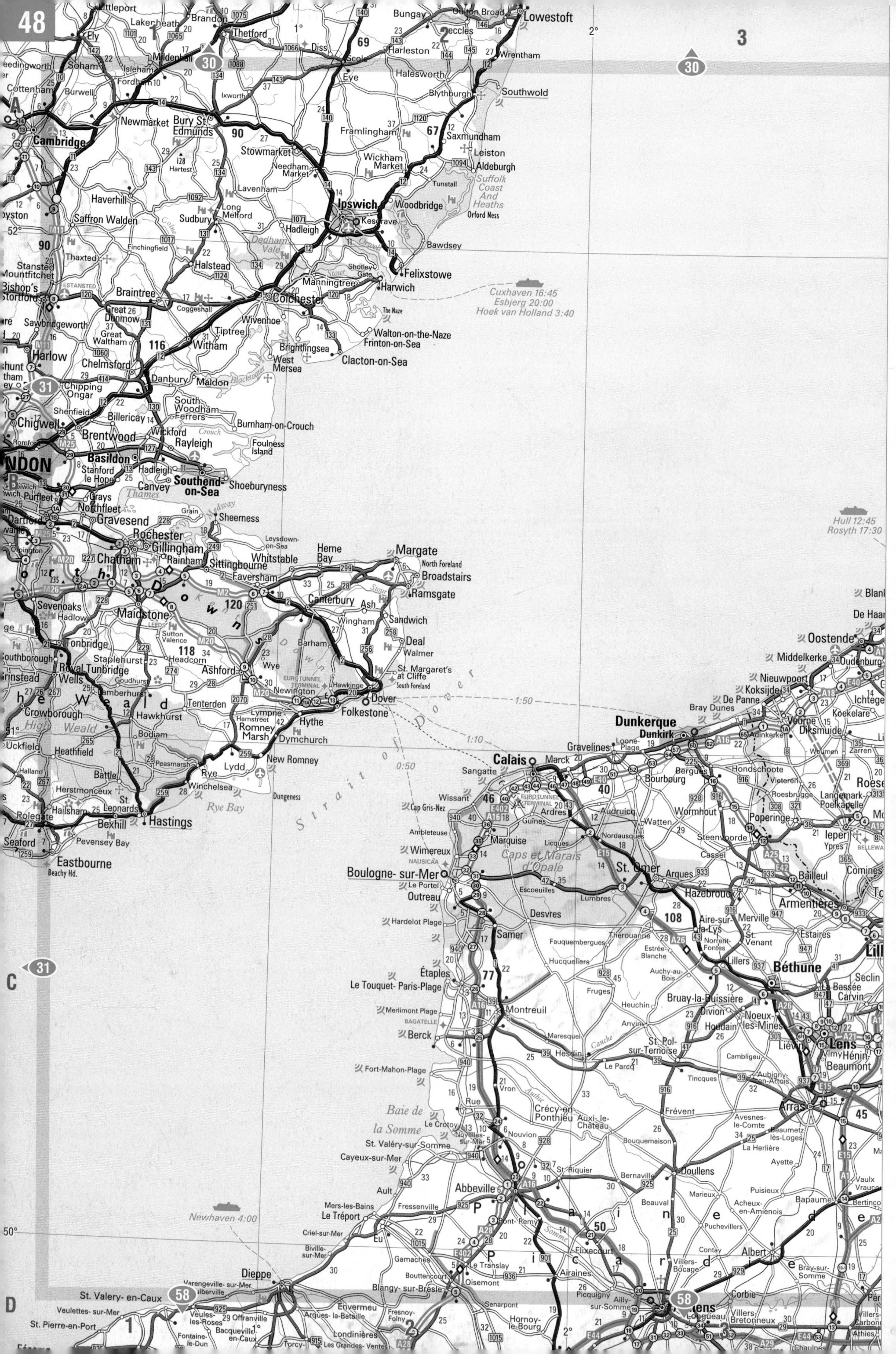
Littleport
Ely
Lakenheath
Brandon
Thetford
Mildenhall
Soham
Isleham
Fordham
Newmarket
Bury St. Edmunds
Cambridge
Cottenham
Burwell
Diss
Scole
Eye
Bungay
Oulton Broad
Lowestoft
Beccles
Harleston
Halesworth
Wrentham
Southwold
Blythburgh
Ixworth
Stowmarket
Needham Market
Framlingham
Wickham Market
Saxmundham
Leiston
Aldeburgh
Tunstall
Suffolk Coast And Heaths
Orford Ness
Woodbridge
Ipswich
Kesgrave
Felixstowe
Bawdsey
Haverhill
Saffron Walden
Lavenham
Long Melford
Sudbury
Hadleigh
Hartest
Dedham Vale
Finchingfield
Thaxted
Halstead
Manningtree
Shotley Gate
Harwich
Stansted Mountfitchet
Bishop's Stortford
Braintree
Coggeshall
Colchester
Great Dunmow
Sawbridgeworth
Great Waltham
Wivenhoe
Tiptree
Witham
Brightlingsea
West Mersea
Walton-on-the-Naze
Frinton-on-Sea
Clacton-on-Sea
The Naze
Harlow
Chelmsford
Chipping Ongar
Danbury
Maldon
Blackwater
South Woodham Ferrers
Burnham-on-Crouch
Crouch
Shenfield
Billericay
Chigwell
Brentwood
Wickford
Rayleigh
Romford
Foulness Island
Basildon
Stanford le Hope
Hadleigh
Southend-on-Sea
Shoeburyness
Canvey
Grays
Purfleet
Northfleet
Thames
Grain
Medway
Dartford
Gravesend
Sheerness
Rochester
Gillingham
Chatham
Rainham
Leysdown-on-Sea
Whitstable
Herne Bay
Margate
North Foreland
Broadstairs
Ramsgate
Sittingbourne
Faversham
Canterbury
Stour
Ash
Sandwich
Wingham
Sevenoaks
Hadlow
Maidstone
Leeds
Sutton Valence
North Downs
Barham
Deal
Walmer
Tonbridge
Staplehurst
Headcorn
Ashford
Wye
St. Margaret's at Cliffe
South Foreland
Royal Tunbridge Wells
Goudhurst
Lamberhurst
Hawkinge
Eurotunnel Terminal
Newington
Dover
Folkestone
The Weald
Crowborough
Hawkhurst
Tenterden
Hamstreet
Lympne
Hythe
Romney Marsh
Dymchurch
High Weald
Uckfield
Heathfield
Bodiam
Peasmarsh
Rye
Lydd
New Romney
Winchelsea
Dungeness
Rye Bay
Battle
Herstmonceux
Hailsham
St. Leonards
Hastings
Bexhill
Polegate
Seaford
Pevensey Bay
Eastbourne
Beachy Hd.
LONDON
Cuxhaven 16:45
Esbjerg 20:00
Hoek van Holland 3:40
Hull 12:45
Rosyth 17:30
Strait of Dover
1:50
1:10
0:50
Newhaven 4:00
Oostende
Blankenberge
De Haan
Middelkerke
Oudenburg
Nieuwpoort
Koksijde
De Panne
Bray Dunes
Veurne
Diksmuide
Koekelare
Ichtegem
Dunkerque
Dunkirk
Adinkerke
Gravelines
Loon-Plage
Calais
Marck
Sangatte
Wissant
Cap Gris-Nez
Eurotunnel Terminal
Guînes
Ardres
Audruicq
Bourbourg
Bergues
Hondschoote
Wormhout
Watten
Poperinge
Ieper
Ypres
Langemark-Poelkapelle
Roeselare
Ambleteuse
Marquise
Wimereux
Nausicaa
Boulogne-sur-Mer
Le Portel
Outreau
Licques
Nordausques
Caps et Marais d'Opale
St. Omer
Arques
Steenvoorde
Cassel
Hazebrouck
Bailleul
Armentières
Comines
Escoeuilles
Lumbres
Desvres
Hardelot Plage
Samer
Aire-sur-la-Lys
Merville
Estaires
Thérouanne
Fauquembergues
Norrent-Fontes
St. Venant
Lillers
Béthune
Estrée-Blanche
Hucqueliers
Auchy-au-Bois
Étaples
Le Touquet-Paris-Plage
Fruges
Bruay-la-Buissière
Divion
Noeux-les-Mines
Houdain
Liévin
Lens
Seclin
La Bassée
Carvin
Vimy
Hénin-Beaumont
Merlimont Plage
Bagatelle
Montreuil
Berck
Heuchin
Anvin
Maresquel
Canche
Hesdin
St. Pol-sur-Ternoise
Le Parcq
Cambligneul
Aubigny-en-Artois
Tincques
Fort-Mahon-Plage
Vron
Authie
Rue
Crécy-en-Ponthieu
Auxi-le-Château
Frévent
Arras
Baie de la Somme
Le Crotoy
Noyelles-sur-Mer
Nouvion
Avesnes-le-Comte
Beaumetz-lès-Loges
La Herlière
Bouquemaison
St. Valéry-sur-Somme
Cayeux-sur-Mer
St. Riquier
Doullens
Bernaville
Ayette
Ault
Abbeville
Beauval
Marieux
Puisieux
Acheux-en-Amiénois
Bapaume
Mers-les-Bains
Le Tréport
Fressenville
Pont-Remy
Somme
Puchevillers
Criel-sur-Mer
Biville-sur-Mer
Eu
Picardie
Flixecourt
Contay
Albert
Bray-sur-Somme
Gamaches
Le Translay
Airaines
Villers-Bocage
Dieppe
Varengeville-sur-Mer
Bouttencourt
Oisemont
Blangy-sur-Bresle
Picquigny
Ailly-sur-Somme
Corbie
Amiens
Longueau
Villers-Bretonneux
St. Valery-en-Caux
Veulettes-sur-Mer
St. Pierre-en-Port
Veules-les-Roses
Offranville
Bacqueville-en-Caux
Fontaine-le-Dun
Envermeu
Arques-la-Bataille
Fresnoy-Folny
Senarpont
Hornoy-le-Bourg
Londinières
Torcy
Les Grandes-Ventes
Chaulnes
Athies

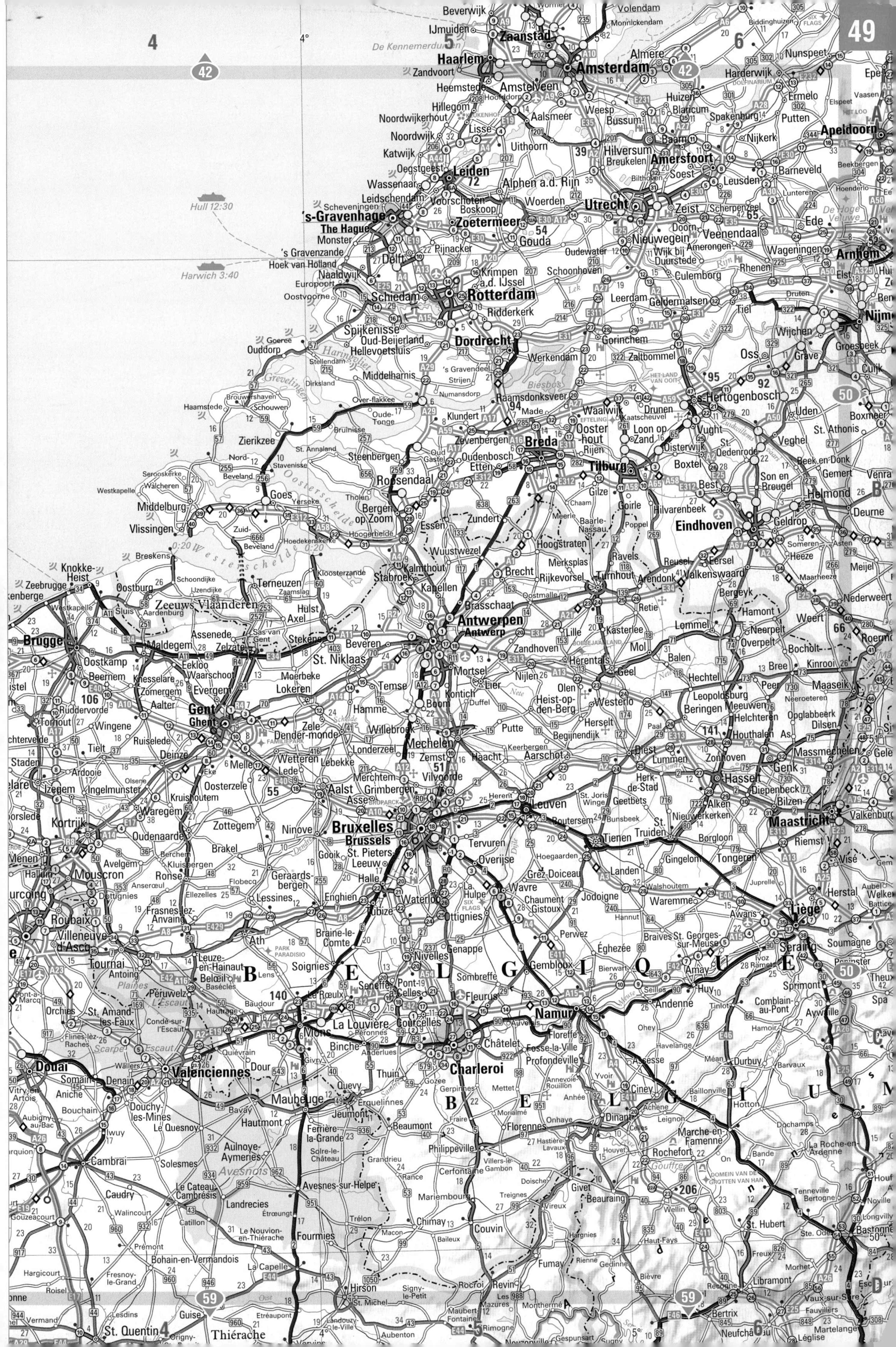
Amsterdam
Haarlem
Zaanstad
Beverwijk
IJmuiden
Volendam
Monnickendam
Zandvoort
Almere
Harderwijk
Nunspeet
Amstelveen
Hilversum
Amersfoort
Apeldoorn
Leiden
's-Gravenhage
The Hague
Zoetermeer
Utrecht
Gouda
Delft
Rotterdam
Schiedam
Dordrecht
Arnhem
Nijmegen
Ede
Veenendaal
Oss
's-Hertogenbosch
Breda
Tilburg
Eindhoven
Helmond
Roosendaal
Bergen op Zoom
Goes
Middelburg
Vlissingen
Terneuzen
Brugge
Gent
Ghent
Antwerpen
Antwerp
Mechelen
Leuven
Bruxelles
Brussels
Aalst
Kortrijk
Mouscron
Roubaix
Tournai
Mons
La Louvière
Charleroi
Namur
Liège
Maastricht
Hasselt
Genk
Tienen
Wavre
Waterloo
Valenciennes
Douai
Cambrai
Maubeuge
Dinant
Bastogne
St. Quentin
Hull 12:30
Harwich 3:40
B E L G I Q U E
B E L G I U M
42
50
59

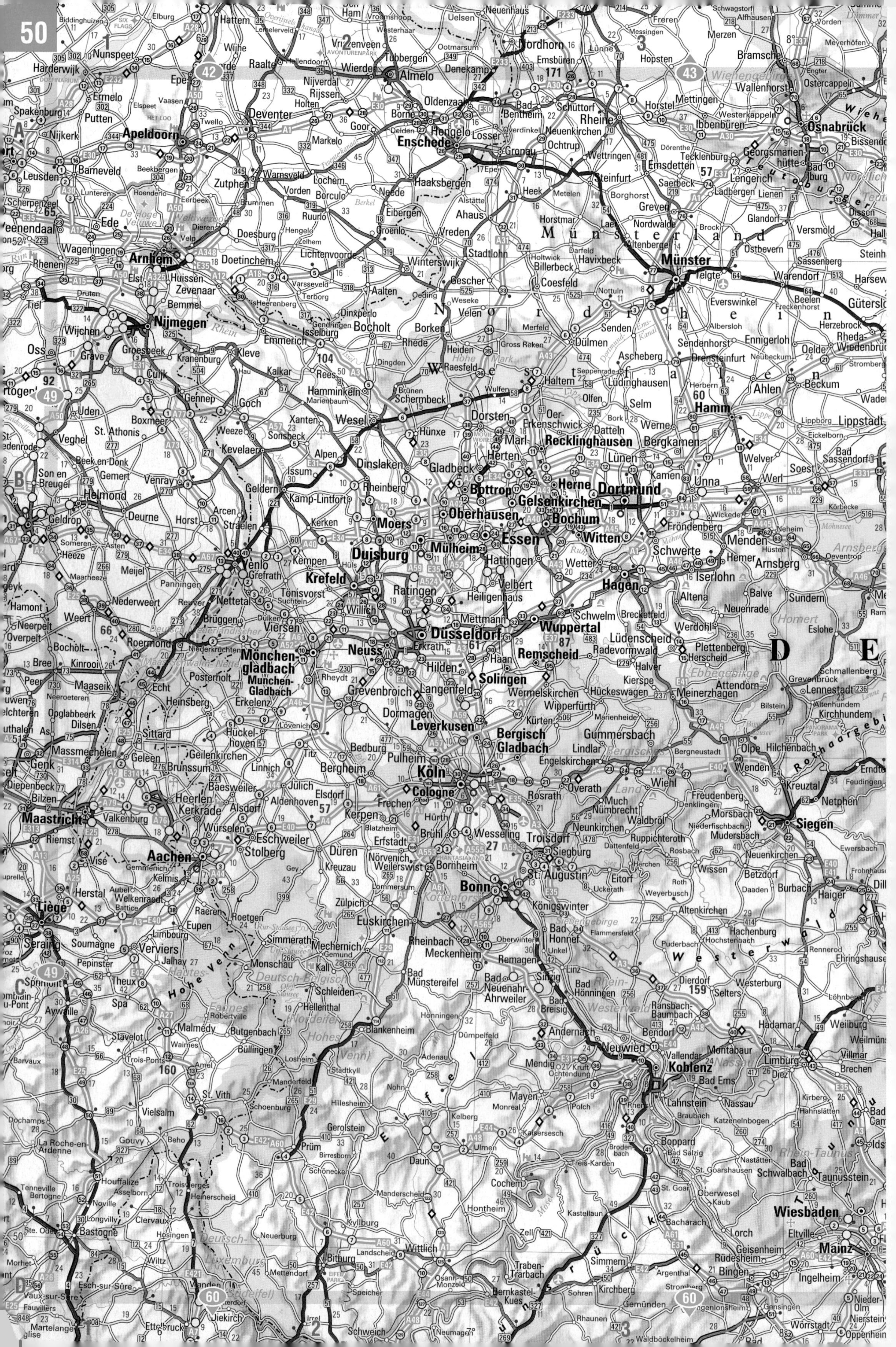
Apeldoorn
Arnhem
Nijmegen
Enschede
Almelo
Hengelo
Osnabrück
Münster
Münsterland
Nordrhein-Westfalen
Duisburg
Krefeld
Moers
Oberhausen
Bottrop
Gelsenkirchen
Essen
Bochum
Dortmund
Herne
Recklinghausen
Witten
Hagen
Wuppertal
Remscheid
Solingen
Mülheim
Düsseldorf
Neuss
Mönchengladbach
Leverkusen
Bergisch Gladbach
Köln
Cologne
Bonn
Aachen
Maastricht
Liège
Siegen
Koblenz
Wiesbaden
Mainz
Hamm
Venlo
Eifel
Westerwald
Hunsrück
Sauerland
D
E

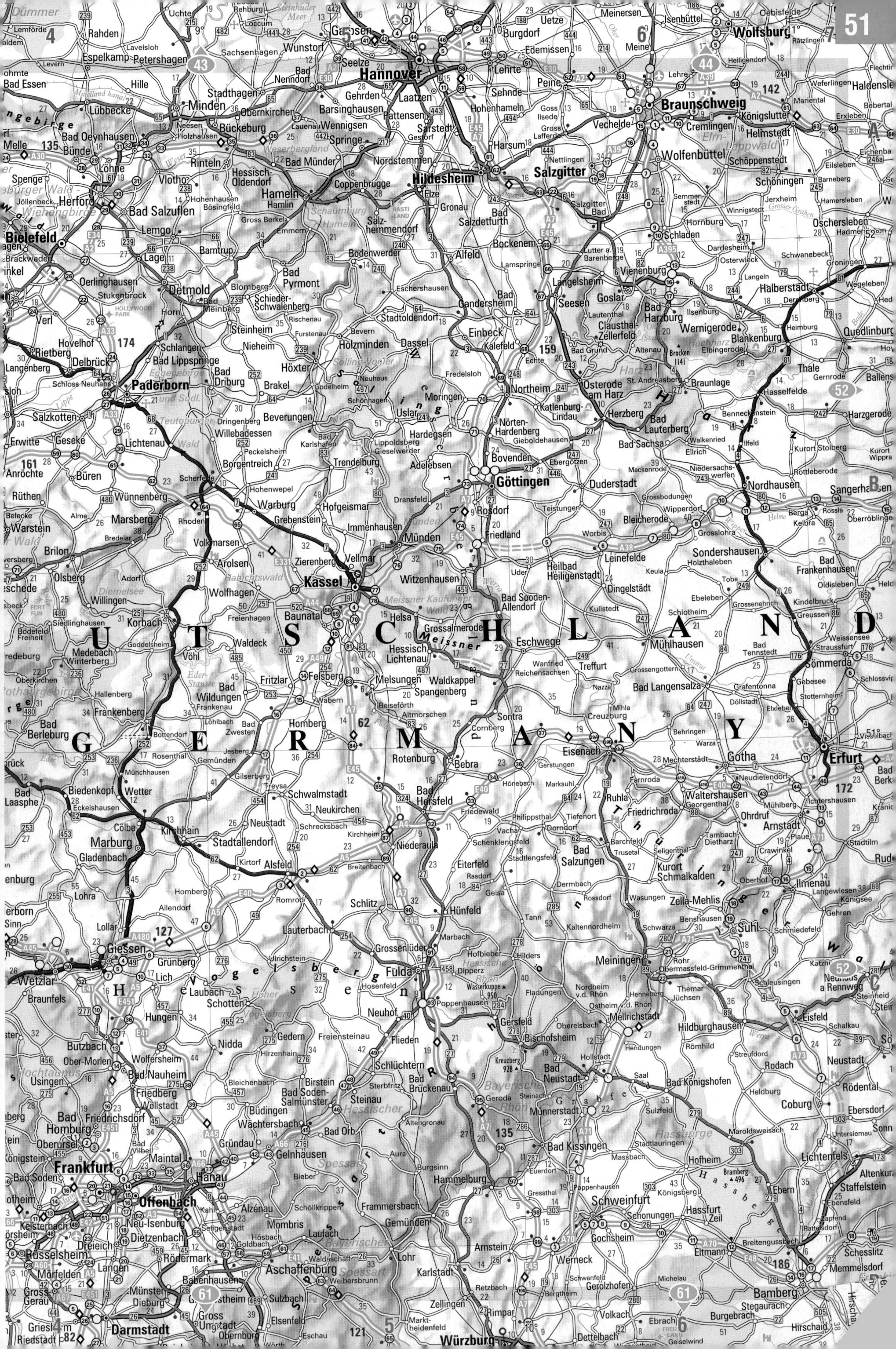
Hannover
Wolfsburg
Braunschweig
Minden
Bielefeld
Herford
Bad Salzuflen
Detmold
Paderborn
Hameln
Hildesheim
Salzgitter
Wolfenbüttel
Helmstedt
Goslar
Halberstadt
Quedlinburg
Wernigerode
Göttingen
Northeim
Kassel
Höxter
Holzminden
Warburg
Marsberg
Korbach
Arolsen
Mühlhausen
Nordhausen
Sondershausen
Eisenach
Gotha
Erfurt
Sömmerda
Bad Hersfeld
Fulda
Marburg
Giessen
Wetzlar
Frankfurt
Offenbach
Hanau
Darmstadt
Aschaffenburg
Würzburg
Schweinfurt
Bad Kissingen
Bamberg
Coburg
Meiningen
Suhl
Ilmenau
Arnstadt
D E U T S C H L A N D
G E R M A N Y

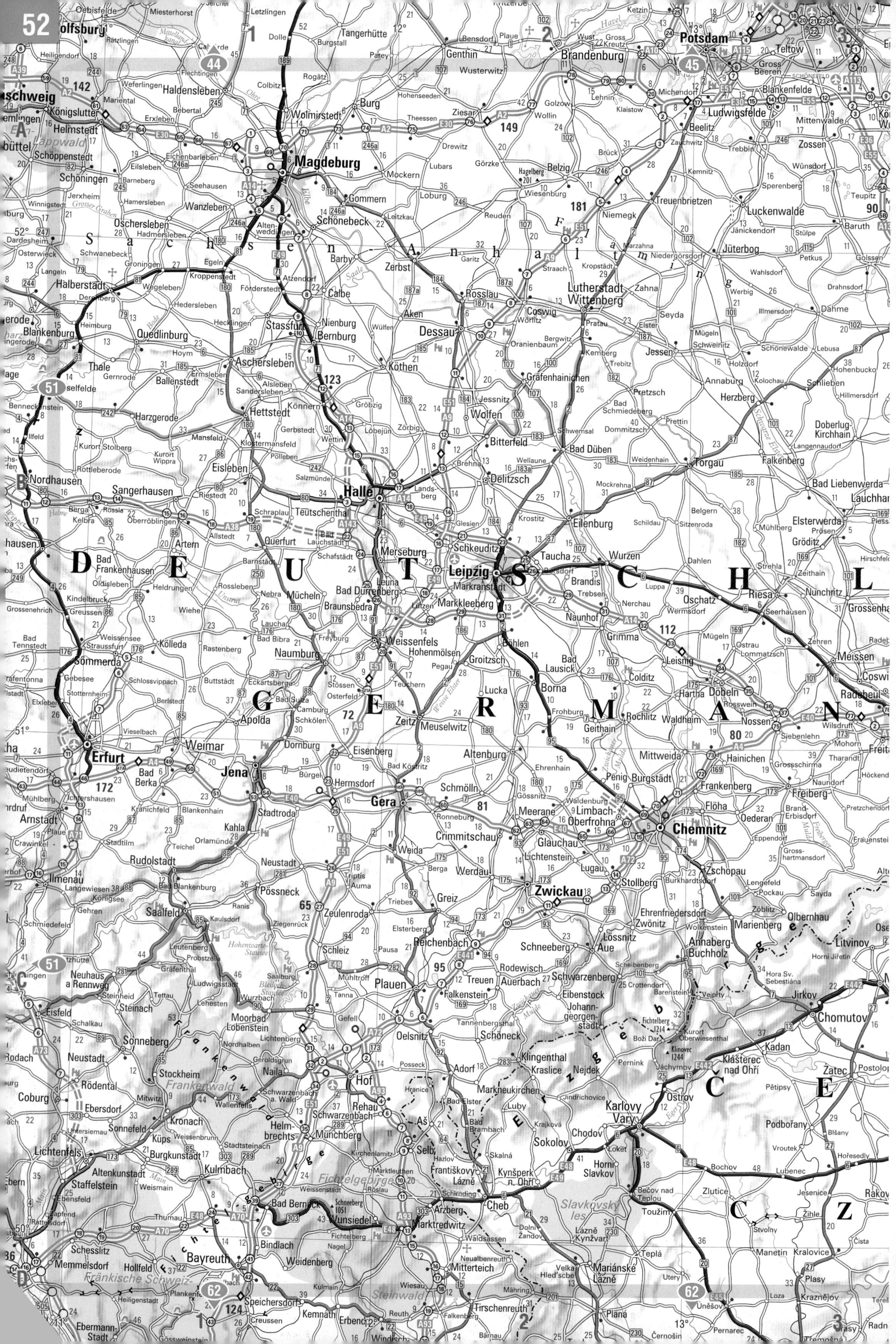

Wolfsburg · Potsdam · Teltow · Gross Beeren · Brandenburg · Ludwigsfelde · Beelitz · Michendorf · Blankenfelde · Zossen · Wünsdorf

Königslutter · Helmstedt · Schöppenstedt · Schöningen · Haldensleben · Wolmirstedt · Burg · Genthin · Wusterwitz · Genthin

Magdeburg · Gommern · Loburg · Belzig · Treuenbrietzen · Niemegk · Luckenwalde · Jüterbog · Baruth

Oschersleben · Hadmersleben · Wanzleben · Schönebeck · Barby · Zerbst · Rosslau · Lutherstadt Wittenberg · Zahna · Herzberg

Halberstadt · Quedlinburg · Aschersleben · Staßfurt · Nienburg · Bernburg · Köthen · Aken · Dessau · Coswig · Jessen · Schweinitz

Thale · Ballenstedt · Hettstedt · Könnern · Zörbig · Wolfen · Bitterfeld · Bad Düben · Torgau · Bad Liebenwerda · Elsterwerda

Nordhausen · Sangerhausen · Eisleben · Salzmünde · Halle · Landsberg · Delitzsch · Eilenburg · Wurzen · Gröditz · Riesa

Bad Frankenhausen · Artern · Querfurt · Merseburg · Schkeuditz · Leipzig · Taucha · Brandis · Oschatz · Meissen · Radebeul

Sömmerda · Kölleda · Naumburg · Bad Dürrenberg · Markranstädt · Markkleeberg · Naunhof · Grimma · Leisnig · Döbeln · Nossen

Erfurt · Weimar · Apolda · Bad Sulza · Weissenfels · Hohenmölsen · Zeitz · Borna · Colditz · Rochlitz · Waldheim · Freital

Jena · Bad Berka · Dornburg · Eisenberg · Altenburg · Geithain · Penig · Burgstädt · Mittweida · Hainichen · Freiberg

Stadtroda · Hermsdorf · Gera · Schmölln · Meerane · Glauchau · Limbach-Oberfrohna · Chemnitz · Oederan · Flöha

Rudolstadt · Kahla · Neustadt · Triptis · Ronneburg · Crimmitschau · Werdau · Lichtenstein · Lugau · Stollberg · Zschopau

Saalfeld · Pössneck · Zeulenroda · Greiz · Zwickau · Zwönitz · Ehrenfriedersdorf · Marienberg · Olbernhau · Litvínov

Neuhaus a. Rennweg · Gräfenthal · Schleiz · Triebes · Reichenbach · Schneeberg · Aue · Annaberg-Buchholz · Jirkov

Eisfeld · Lobenstein · Lichtenberg · Plauen · Rodewisch · Auerbach · Schwarzenberg · Eibenstock · Hora Sv. Šebestiána · Chomutov

Sonneberg · Naila · Oelsnitz · Schöneck · Klingenthal · Kraslice · Johanngeorgenstadt · Kláštarec nad Ohří · Kadaň

Neustadt · Stockheim · Hof · Adorf · Markneukirchen · Karlovy Vary · Sokolov · Ostrov · Podbořany · Žatec

Coburg · Rödental · Kronach · Schwarzenbach · Rehau · Aš · Bad Elster · Chodov · Loket · Bečov nad Teplou · Pětipsy

Lichtenfels · Burgkunstadt · Kulmbach · Münchberg · Selb · Cheb · Františkovy Lázně · Kynšperk nad Ohří · Žlutice

Staffelstein · Altenkunstadt · Stadtsteinach · Marktredwitz · Arzberg · Waldsassen · Lázně Kynžvart · Mariánské Lázně · Teplá

Bayreuth · Bindlach · Bad Berneck · Wunsiedel · Mitterteich · Tirschenreuth · Pla ná · Stříbro

Speichersdorf · Kemnath · Erbendorf · Windischeschenbach · Mähring · Úněšov

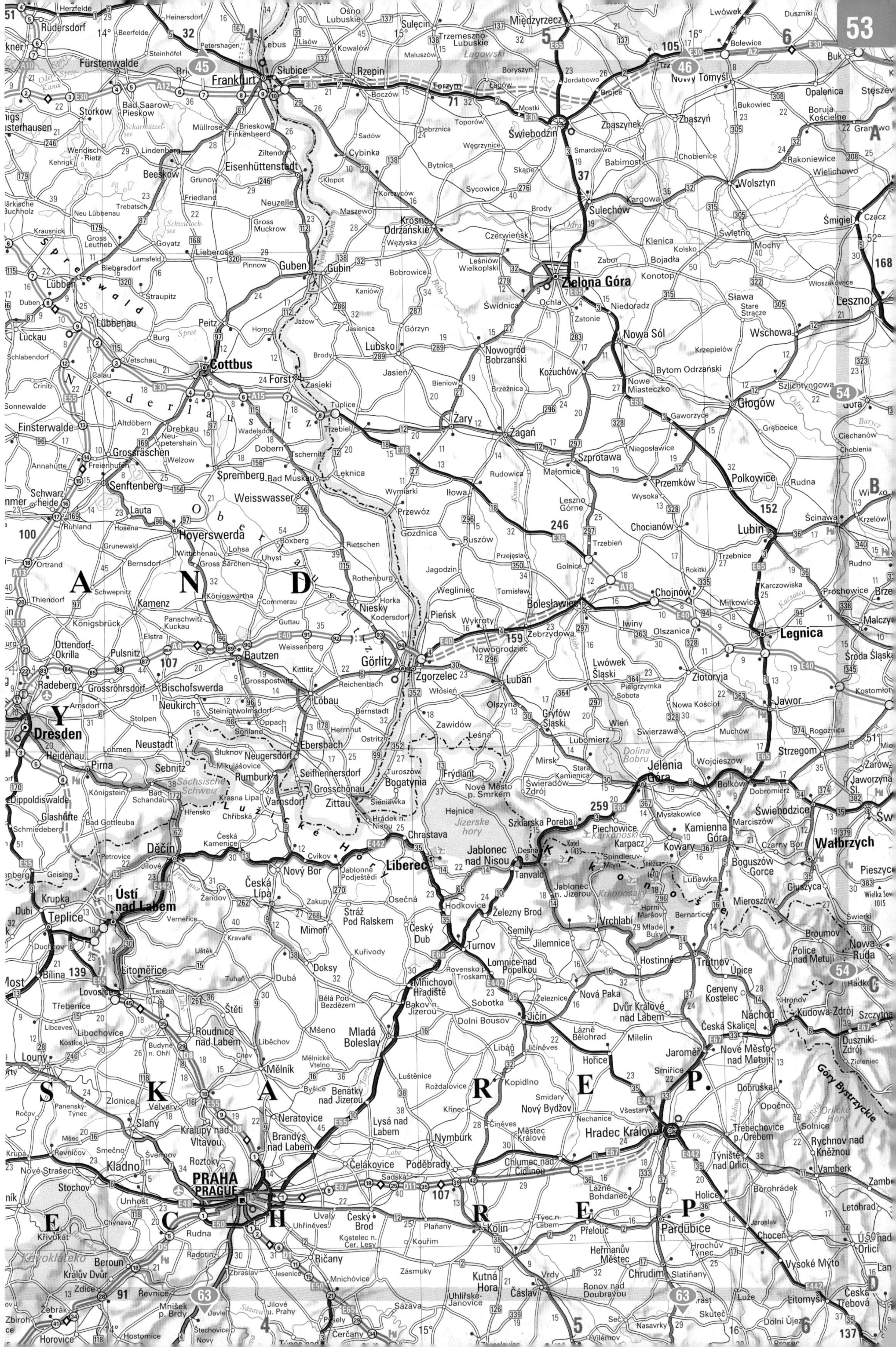
Frankfurt
Słubice
Fürstenwalde
Eisenhüttenstadt
Świebodzin
Zbąszynek
Wolsztyn
Sulechów
Zielona Góra
Krosno Odrzańskie
Guben
Gubin
Lübben
Lübbenau
Cottbus
Forst
Nowa Sól
Leszno
Wschowa
Głogów
Żary
Żagań
Szprotawa
Polkowice
Lubin
Spremberg
Senftenberg
Weisswasser
Hoyerswerda
Chojnów
Legnica
Bolesławiec
Kamenz
Bautzen
Görlitz
Zgorzelec
Lubań
Złotoryja
Jawor
Radeberg
Bischofswerda
Löbau
Dresden
Pirna
Zittau
Jelenia Góra
Wałbrzych
Děčín
Liberec
Jablonec nad Nisou
Ústí nad Labem
Teplice
Česká Lípa
Turnov
Trutnov
Litoměřice
Mladá Boleslav
Jičín
Náchod
Mělník
Hradec Králové
Kladno
PRAHA
PRAGUE
Nymburk
Poděbrady
Kolín
Pardubice
Kutná Hora
Chrudim
Beroun
Čáslav
Česká Třebová
Spreewald
Niederlausitz
Oberlausitz
Lužické Hory
Krkonoše
Góry Bystrzyckie
SACHSEN
ČESKÁ REPUBLIKA

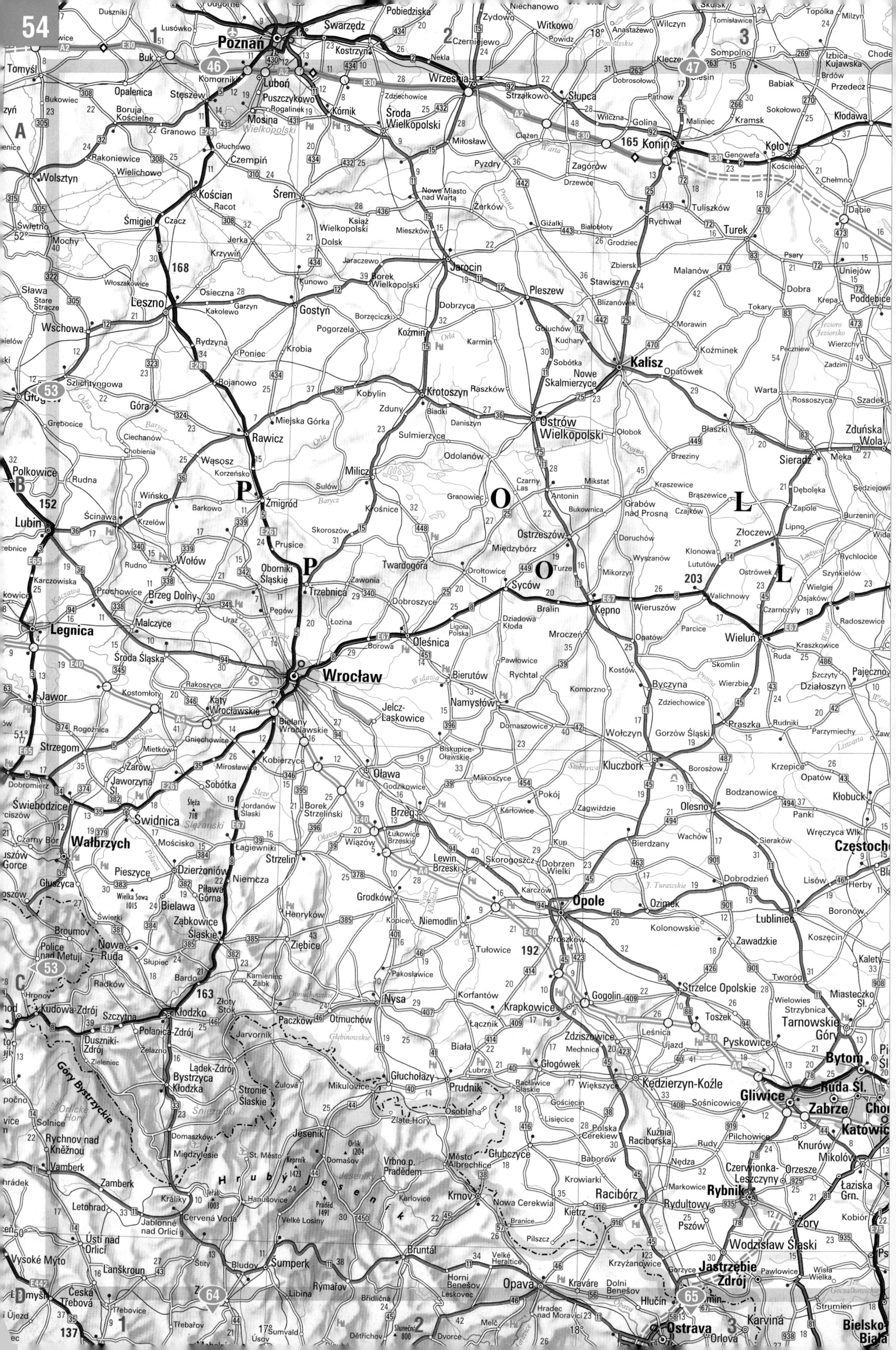
P O L
P O L
Poznań
Swarzędz
Pobiedziska
Niechanowo
Witkowo
Wilczyn
Skulsk
Topólka
Milzyn
Dusznik
Lusówko
Buk
Tomyśl
Komorniki
Luboń
Kostrzyn
Nekla
Czerniejewo
Powidz
Anastazewo
Tomisławice
Sompolno
Izbica Kujawska
Brdów
Przedecz
Babiak
Opalenica
Stęszew
Puszczykowo
Rogalinek
Kórnik
Zdziechowice
Środa Wielkopolski
Września
Strzałkowo
Słupca
Dobrosołowo
Kleczew
Ślesin
Patnów
Golina
Wilczna
Maliniec
Kramsk
Sokołowo
Kłodawa
Bukowiec
Boruja Kościelne
Mosina Wielkopolski
Granowo
Głuchowo
Czempiń
Rakoniewice
Wielichowo
Miłosław
Ciążeń
Konin
Genowefa
Koło
Kościelec
Pyzdry
Zagórów
Drzewce
Chełmno
Wolsztyn
Kościan
Racot
Śrem
Nowe Miasto nad Wartą
Żerków
Tuliszków
Dąbie
Książ Wielkopolski
Śmigiel
Czacz
Jerka
Krzywiń
Dolsk
Mieszków
Giżałki
Białobłoty
Grodziec
Rychwał
Turek
Świętno
Mochy
Jaraczewo
Jarocin
Psary
Uniejów
Kunowo
Borek Wielkopolski
Zbiersk
Stawiszyn
Malanów
Dobra
Sława
Stare Strącze
Włoszakowice
Osieczna
Leszno
Kakolewo
Garzyn
Gostyń
Borzęciczki
Dobrzyca
Pleszew
Blizanówek
Tokary
Krępa
Poddębice
Wschowa
Pogorzela
Koźmin
Karmin
Gołuchów
Kuchary
Morawin
Jezioro Jeziorsko
Rydzyna
Poniec
Krobia
Sobótka
Nowe Skalmierzyce
Kalisz
Opatówek
Koźminek
Pęczniew
Wierzchy
Zadzim
Szlichtyngowa
Bojanowo
Kobylin
Krotoszyn
Raszków
Warta
Szadek
Głogów
Góra
Miejska Górka
Zduny
Biadki
Daniszyn
Ostrów Wielkopolski
Ołobok
Błaszki
Rossoszyca
Zduńska Wola
Grębocice
Ciechanów
Chobienia
Rawicz
Sulmierzyce
Odolanów
Brzeziny
Sieradz
Męka
Polkowice
Rudna
Wąsosz
Korzeńsko
Milicz
Czarny Las
Mikstat
Kraszewice
Sędziejowice
Wińsko
Barkowo
Żmigród
Sułów
Barycz
Krośnice
Granowiec
Antonin
Grabów nad Prosną
Brąszewice
Czajków
Dębołęka
Zapole
Lubin
Ścinawa
Krzelów
Skoroszów
Bukownica
Burzenin
Lipno
Prusice
Ostrzeszów
Międzybórz
Doruchów
Złoczew
Wolów
Rudno
Oborniki Śląskie
Twardogóra
Drołtowice
Turze
Wyszanów
Klonowa
Lututów
Rychłocice
Szynkielów
Karczowiska
Prochowice
Brzeg Dolny
Trzebnica
Zawonia
Syców
Bralin
Mikorzyn
Ostrówek
Wielgie
Osjaków
Legnica
Malczyce
Uraz
Pęgów
Dobroszyce
Łozina
Ligota Polska
Dziadowa Kłoda
Kępno
Wieruszów
Walichnowy
Czarnożyły
Radoszewice
Środa Śląska
Oleśnica
Borowa
Mroczeń
Opatów
Parcice
Wieluń
Kraszkowice
Wrocław
Bierutów
Pawłowice
Rychtal
Kostów
Skomlin
Ruda
Pajęczno
Jawor
Rakoszyce
Kostomłoty
Kąty Wrocławskie
Namysłów
Komorzno
Byczyna
Wierzbie
Działoszyn
Szczyty
Rogoźnica
Bielany Wrocławskie
Jelcz-Laskowice
Zdziechowice
Strzegom
Mietków
Gniechowice
Domaszowice
Wołczyn
Gorzów Śląski
Praszka
Rudniki
Parzymiechy
Żarów
Mirosławice
Kobierzyce
Biskupice-Oławskie
Kluczbork
Borosów
Krzepice
Opatów
Dobromierz
Jaworzyna Śl.
Sobótka
Ślęza
Ślęże
Oława
Godzikowice
Makoszyce
Pokój
Olesno
Bodzanowice
Kłobuck
Świebodzice
Świdnica
Jordanów Śląski
Borek Strzeliński
Brzeg
Karłowice
Zagwiździe
Panki
Wręczyca Wlk.
Czarny Bór
Wałbrzych
Mościsko
Łagiewniki
Wiązów
Łukowice Brzeskie
Kup
Wachów
Bierdzany
Sieraków
Częstochowa
Gorce
Pieszyce
Dzierżoniów
Niemcza
Strzelin
Lewin Brzeski
Skorogoszcz
Dobrzeń Wielki
Dobrodzień
Lisów
Herby
Głuszyca
Wielka Sowa
Bielawa
Piława Górna
Grodków
Karczów
Opole
Ozimek
Boronów
Broumov
Ząbkowice Śląskie
Henryków
Kopice
Niemodlin
J. Turawskie
Kolonowskie
Lubliniec
Police nad Metují
Nowa Ruda
Ziębice
Tułowice
Proszków
Zawadzkie
Koszęcin
Słupiec
Bardo
Kamieniec Ząbkowicki
Pakosławice
Kalety
Radków
Hronov
Złoty Stok
J. Otmuchowskie
Nysa
Korfantów
Krapkowice
Gogolin
Strzelce Opolskie
Tworóg
Miasteczko Śl.
Kudowa-Zdrój
Szczytna
Kłodzko
Paczków
Otmuchów
Łącznik
Zdzieszowice
Toszek
Wielowieś
Strzybnica
Tarnowskie Góry
Duszniki-Zdrój
Polanica-Zdrój
Javorník
J. Głębinowskie
Biała
Leśnica
Ujazd
Pyskowice
Bytom
Żelazno
Lądek-Zdrój
Mechnica
Góry Bystrzyckie
Zieleniec
Bystrzyca Kłodzka
Stronie Śląskie
Żulová
Mikulovice
Głuchołazy
Prudnik
Lubrza
Racławice Śląskie
Głogówek
Większyce
Kędzierzyn-Koźle
Gliwice
Ruda Śl.
Zabrze
Orlické Hory
Śnieżnicki
Osoblaha
Gościęcin
Sośnicowice
Solnice
Zlaté Hory
Lisięcice
Polska Cerekiew
Kuźnia Raciborska
Katowice
Rychnov nad Kněžnou
Domaszków
Jeseník
Orlík
Domašov
Keprník
Vrbno p. Pradědem
Město Albrechtice
Głubczyce
Baborów
Rudy
Pilchowice
Knurów
Mikołów
Vamberk
Międzylesie
St. Město
Hrubý Jeseník
Nędza
Czerwionka-Leszczyny
Orzesze
Žamberk
Králíky
Jeřáb
Hanušovice
Praděd
Karlovice
Krnov
Krowiarki
Racibórz
Rybnik
Łaziska Grn.
Letohrad
Jablonné nad Orlicí
Červená Voda
Velké Losiny
Nowa Cerekwia
Kietrz
Rydułtowy
Kobiór
Ústí nad Orlicí
Branice
Pszów
Żory
Pilszcz
Wodzisław Śląski
Vysoké Mýto
Lanškroun
Štíty
Bludov
Šumperk
Bruntál
Velké Heraltice
Krzyżanowice
Jastrzębie Zdrój
Pawłowice
Wisła Wielka
Jez. Goczałkowickie
Litomyšl
Česká Třebová
Horní Benešov
Leskovec
Opava
Kravaře
Dolní Benešov
Gorzyce
Libina
Rýmařov
Břidličná
Hradec nad Moravicí
Hlučín
Karviná
Strumień
Bielsko-Biała
Třebovice
Třebařov
Šumvald
Úsov
Dětřichov
Sluneční
Melč
Dvorce
Ostrava
Orlová
Ujezd

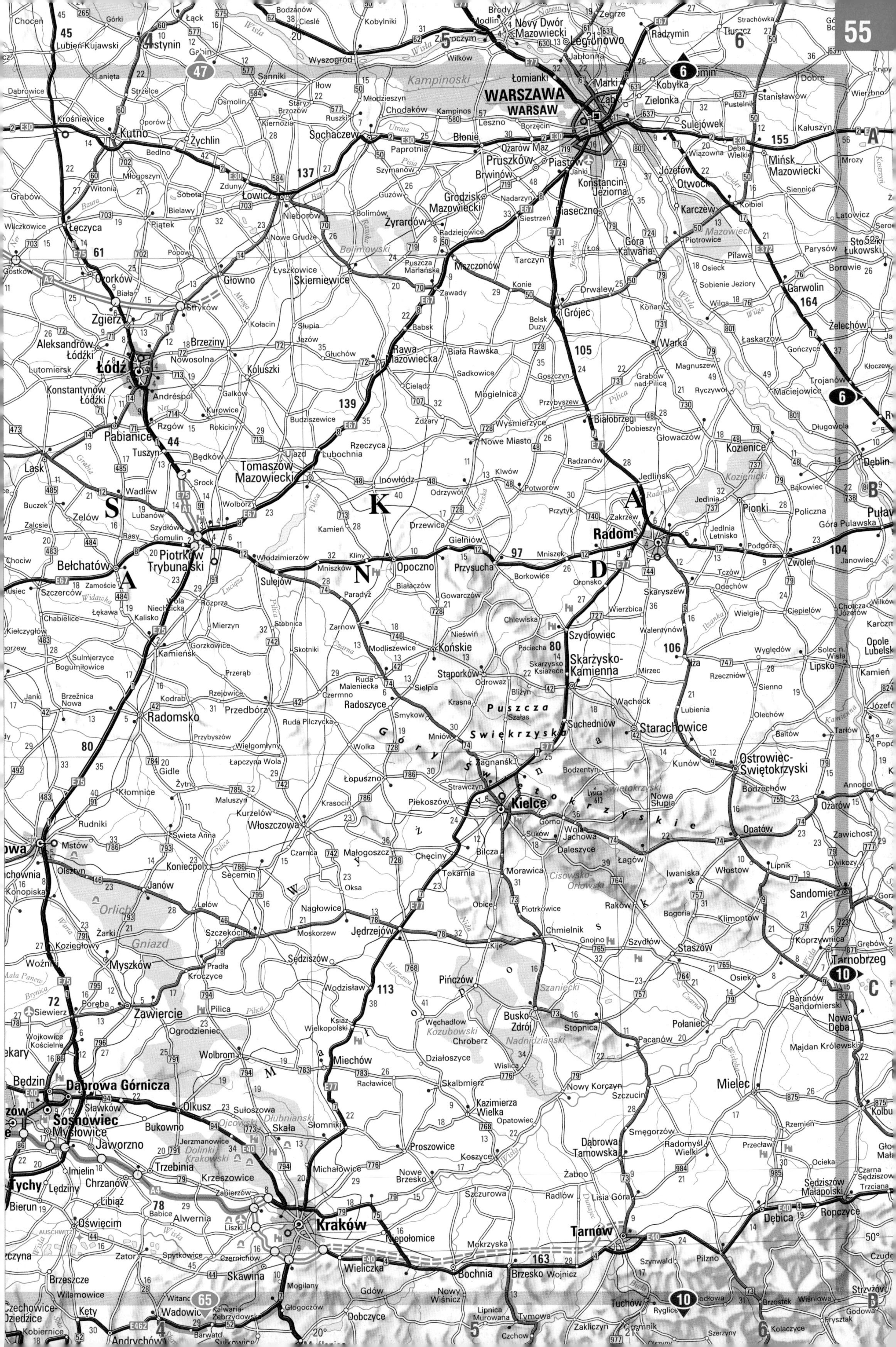
WARSZAWA
WARSAW
Łódź
Radom
Kielce
Kraków
Tarnów
Piotrków Trybunalski
Częstochowa
Sosnowiec
Dąbrowa Górnicza
Będzin
Mysłowice
Jaworzno
Tychy
Oświęcim
Kutno
Łowicz
Skierniewice
Sochaczew
Żyrardów
Grodzisk Mazowiecki
Pruszków
Piaseczno
Legionowo
Nowy Dwór Mazowiecki
Otwock
Mińsk Mazowiecki
Garwolin
Dęblin
Puławy
Kozienice
Grójec
Białobrzegi
Rawa Mazowiecka
Tomaszów Mazowiecki
Opoczno
Końskie
Skarżysko-Kamienna
Starachowice
Ostrowiec Świętokrzyski
Opatów
Sandomierz
Tarnobrzeg
Mielec
Dębica
Ropczyce
Bochnia
Brzesko
Wieliczka
Niepołomice
Proszowice
Miechów
Jędrzejów
Pińczów
Busko Zdrój
Staszów
Połaniec
Olkusz
Zawiercie
Myszków
Radomsko
Bełchatów
Pabianice
Zgierz
Zduńska Wola
Włoszczowa
Chęciny
Kampinoski
Puszcza Świękrzyska
Góry Świętokrzyskie
Wyżyna Małopolska
Kozienicki
Mazowiecki
Bolimowski
E30
E67
E75
E77
E40
E371
E372
E462
A1
A2
A4
MAZOWIECKIE
ŁÓDZKIE
ŚWIĘTOKRZYSKIE
MAŁOPOLSKIE
Wisła
Pilica
Nida
50°
51°

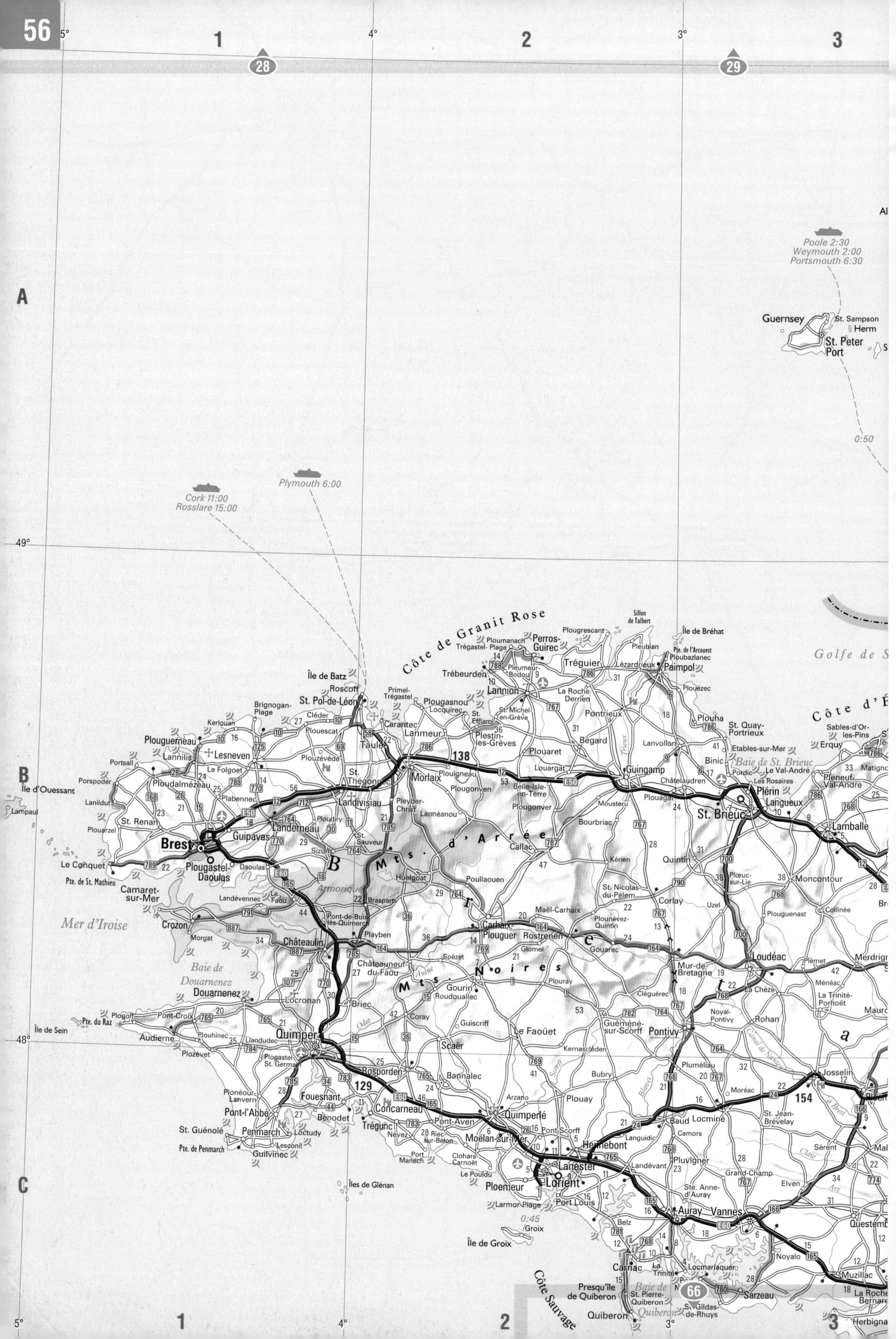

5°
1
4°
2
3°
3
28
29
A
B
C
49°
48°
Poole 2:30
Weymouth 2:00
Portsmouth 6:30
Guernsey
St. Sampson
Herm
St. Peter Port
0:50
Cork 11:00
Rosslare 15:00
Plymouth 6:00
Côte de Granit Rose
Golfe de S
Côte d'É
Sillon de Talbert
Île de Bréhat
Plougrescant
Pleubian
Pte. de l'Arcouest
Ploubazlanec
Perros-Guirec
Ploumanach
Trégastel-Plage
Tréguier
Lézardrieux
Paimpol
Trébeurden
Lannion
Pleumeur-Bodou
La Roche Derrien
Pontrieux
Ploëzec
Plouha
St. Quay-Portrieux
Sables-d'Or-les-Pins
Erquy
Île de Batz
Roscoff
St. Pol-de-Léon
Primel-Trégastel
Plougasnou
Locquirec
St. Efflam
St. Michel-en-Grève
Plestin-les-Grèves
Brignogan-Plage
Kerlouan
Cléder
Plouescat
Carantec
Lanmeur
Taulé
Bégard
Lanvollon
Etables-sur-Mer
Binic
Baie de St. Brieuc
Pordic
Le Val-André
Les Rosaires
Pléneuf-Val-André
Matignon
Plouguerneau
Lesneven
Lannilis
Le Folgoet
Portsall
Porspoder
Ploudalmézeau
Plabennec
Plouzévédé
St. Thégonnec
Morlaix
Plouigneau
138
Plouaret
Louargat
Guingamp
Châtelaudren
Plérin
Langueux
St. Brieuc
Lamballe
Île d'Ouessant
Lampaul
Lanildut
Landivisiau
Plougonven
Belle-Isle-en-Terre
Plougonver
Mousteru
Plouagat
St. Renan
Plouarzel
Brest
Guipavas
Landerneau
Ploudiry
Pleyber-Christ
Lannéanou
Bourbriac
Le Conquet
Pte. de St. Mathieu
Plougastel-Daoulas
Daoulas
Sizun
St. Sauveur
Mts. d'Arrée
Callac
Quintin
Kérien
Plœuc-sur-Lie
Moncontour
Camaret-sur-Mer
Landévennec
Le Faou
Huelgoat
Poullaouen
St. Nicolas-du-Pélem
Corlay
Collinée
Plouguenast
Mer d'Iroise
Crozon
Morgat
Armorique
Brasparts
Pont-de-Buis-lès-Quimerch
Carhaix-Plouguer
Maël-Carhaix
Plounévez-Quintin
Rostrenen
Uzel
Châteaulin
Playben
Glomel
Gouarec
Loudéac
Plémet
Merdrignac
Baie de Douarnenez
Douarnenez
Châteauneuf-du-Faou
Spézet
Mts. Noires
Mur-de-Bretagne
Aulne
Gourin
Roudouallec
Plouray
Cléguérec
La Chèze
Ménéac
La Trinité-Porhoët
Locronan
Pte. du Raz
Plogoff
Pont-Croix
Île de Sein
Audierne
Plouhinec
Quimper
Briec
Coray
Guiscriff
Le Faouët
Guémené-sur-Scorff
Pontivy
Noyal-Pontivy
Rohan
Canal de Nantes
Plozévet
Llandudec
Plogastel-St. Germain
Odet
Scaër
Kernascléden
Pluméliau
Josselin
Rosporden
Bannalec
Bubry
Moréac
154
Ploërmel
Ploneour-Lanvern
Pont-l'Abbé
Fouesnant
Bénodet
Concarneau
129
Quimperlé
Arzano
Plouay
Baud
Locminé
St. Jean-Brévelay
St. Guénolé
Pte. de Penmarch
Penmarch
Loctudy
Lesconil
Guilvinec
Trégunc
Névez
Pont-Aven
Riec-sur-Bélon
Port Manech
Clohars-Carnoët
Moëlan-sur-Mer
Pont Scorff
Hennebont
Languidic
Camors
Sérent
Le Pouldu
Lanester
Lorient
Landévant
Pluvigner
Grand-Champ
Elven
Îles de Glénan
Ploemeur
Larmor-Plage
Port Louis
Ste. Anne-d'Auray
Auray
Vannes
Questembert
0:45
Groix
Île de Groix
Belz
Noyalo
Carnac
La Trinité
Locmariaquer
Sarzeau
Muzillac
Côte Sauvage
Presqu'île de Quiberon
Baie de Quiberon
St. Pierre-Quiberon
Quiberon
66
St. Gildas-de-Rhuys
La Roche Bernard
Herbignac
E50
E60

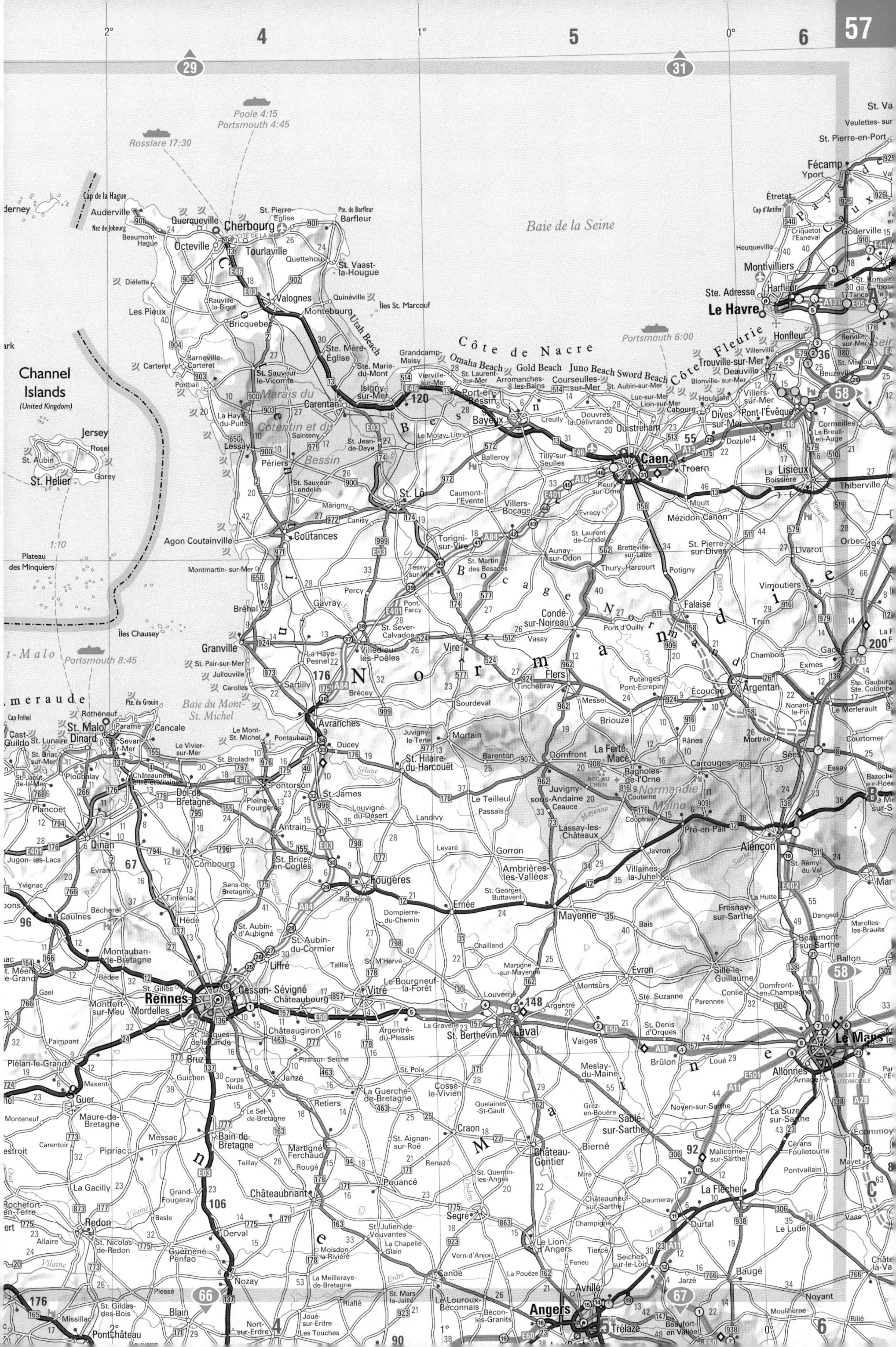
Channel Islands
(United Kingdom)
Jersey
St. Helier
St. Aubin
Gorey
Rosel
Plateau des Minquiers
Îles Chausey
Baie de la Seine
Baie du Mont-St. Michel
Côte de Nacre
Côte Fleurie
Omaha Beach
Gold Beach
Juno Beach
Sword Beach
Utah Beach
Poole 4:15
Portsmouth 4:45
Rosslare 17:30
Portsmouth 6:00
Portsmouth 8:45
Cap de la Hague
Cherbourg
Querqueville
Octeville
Tourlaville
Barfleur
St. Vaast-la-Hougue
Valognes
Les Pieux
Bricquebec
Montebourg
Ste. Mère-Église
Carteret
Barneville-Carteret
St. Sauveur-le-Vicomte
Carentan
Isigny-sur-Mer
Lessay
Périers
Marais du Cotentin et du Bessin
Coutances
Agon Coutainville
Bréhal
Granville
Gavray
Villedieu-les-Poêles
St. Lô
Bayeux
Port-en-Bessin
Arromanches-les-Bains
Courseulles-sur-Mer
Ouistreham
Caen
Troarn
Cabourg
Houlgate
Dives-sur-Mer
Deauville
Trouville-sur-Mer
Honfleur
Pont-l'Évêque
Lisieux
Le Havre
Harfleur
Montivilliers
Ste. Adresse
Étretat
Fécamp
Yport
Goderville
St. Pierre-en-Port
Veulettes-sur
Villers-Bocage
Aunay-sur-Odon
Thury-Harcourt
Falaise
Vire
Condé-sur-Noireau
Flers
Tinchebray
Argentan
Écouché
Vimoutiers
Livarot
Orbec
Thiberville
Sées
Alençon
Le Merlerault
Avranches
Pontorson
St. Malo
Dinard
Cancale
Dinan
Dol-de-Bretagne
Combourg
Fougères
Mortain
St. Hilaire-du-Harcouët
Domfront
La Ferté-Macé
Bagnoles-de-l'Orne
Carrouges
Mayenne
Ernée
Pré-en-Pail
Rennes
Cesson-Sévigné
Vitré
Laval
Château-Gontier
Sablé-sur-Sarthe
La Flèche
Le Mans
Allonnes
Ancenis
Angers
Trélazé
Avrillé
Segré
Châteaubriant
Craon
Bain-de-Bretagne
Redon
Nozay
Blain
Pontchâteau
Derval
Guer
Montfort-sur-Meu
Évron
Sillé-le-Guillaume
Beaumont-sur-Sarthe
Fresnay-sur-Sarthe
Bocage
Normandie
Bretagne
Maine
Mayenne
Pays de Caux
Émeraude
Baugé
Durtal
Le Lude

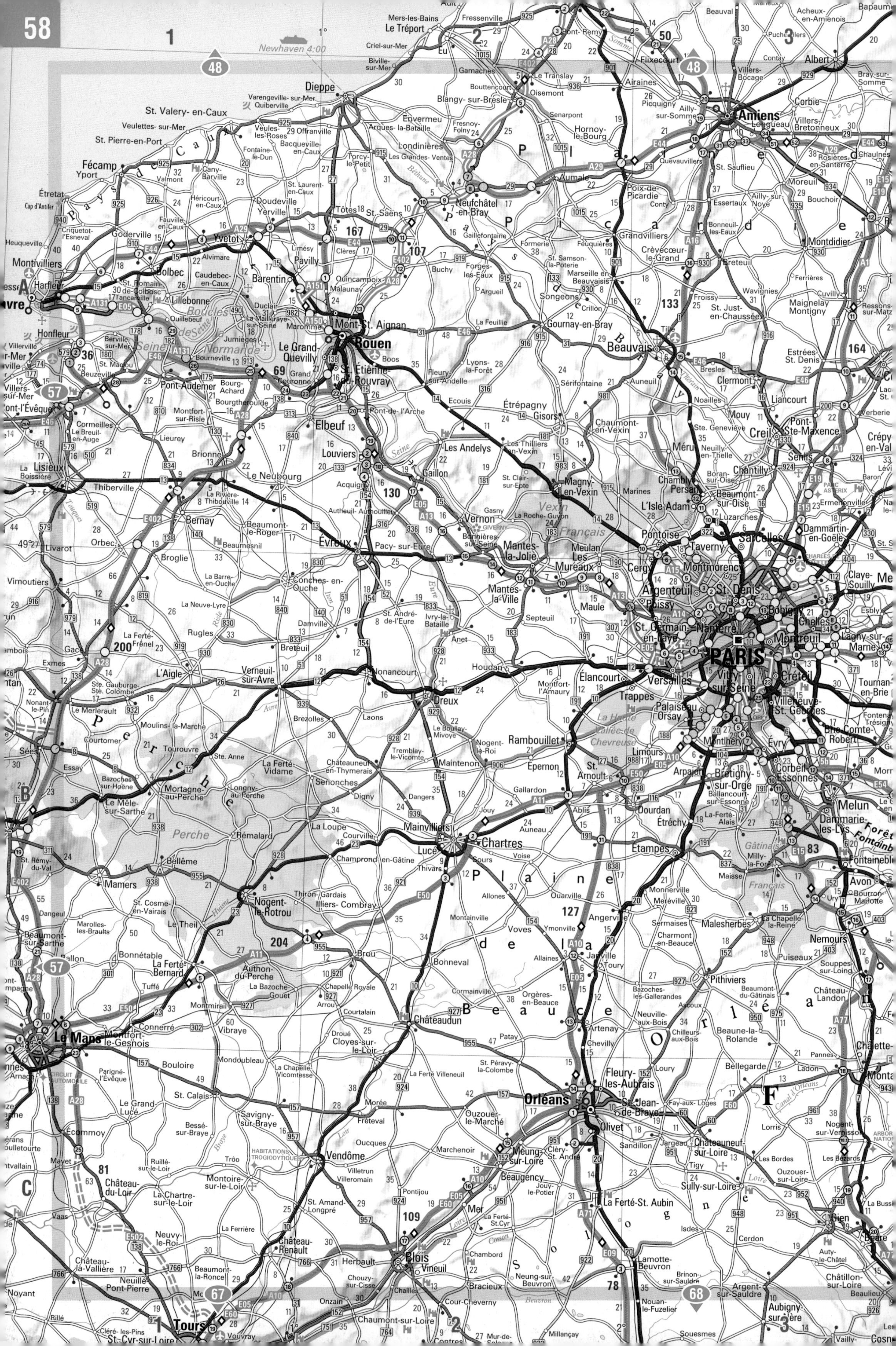

PARIS

Rouen · Amiens · Beauvais · Le Havre · Dieppe · Le Tréport · Fécamp · Étretat

Évreux · Chartres · Dreux · Mantes-la-Jolie · Versailles · Pontoise · Creil · Senlis · Clermont · Montdidier

Le Mans · Nogent-le-Rotrou · Châteaudun · Orléans · Blois · Vendôme · Tours · Chartres

Lisieux · Bernay · Verneuil-sur-Avre · L'Aigle · Mortagne-au-Perche · Bellême · Mamers · La Ferté-Bernard

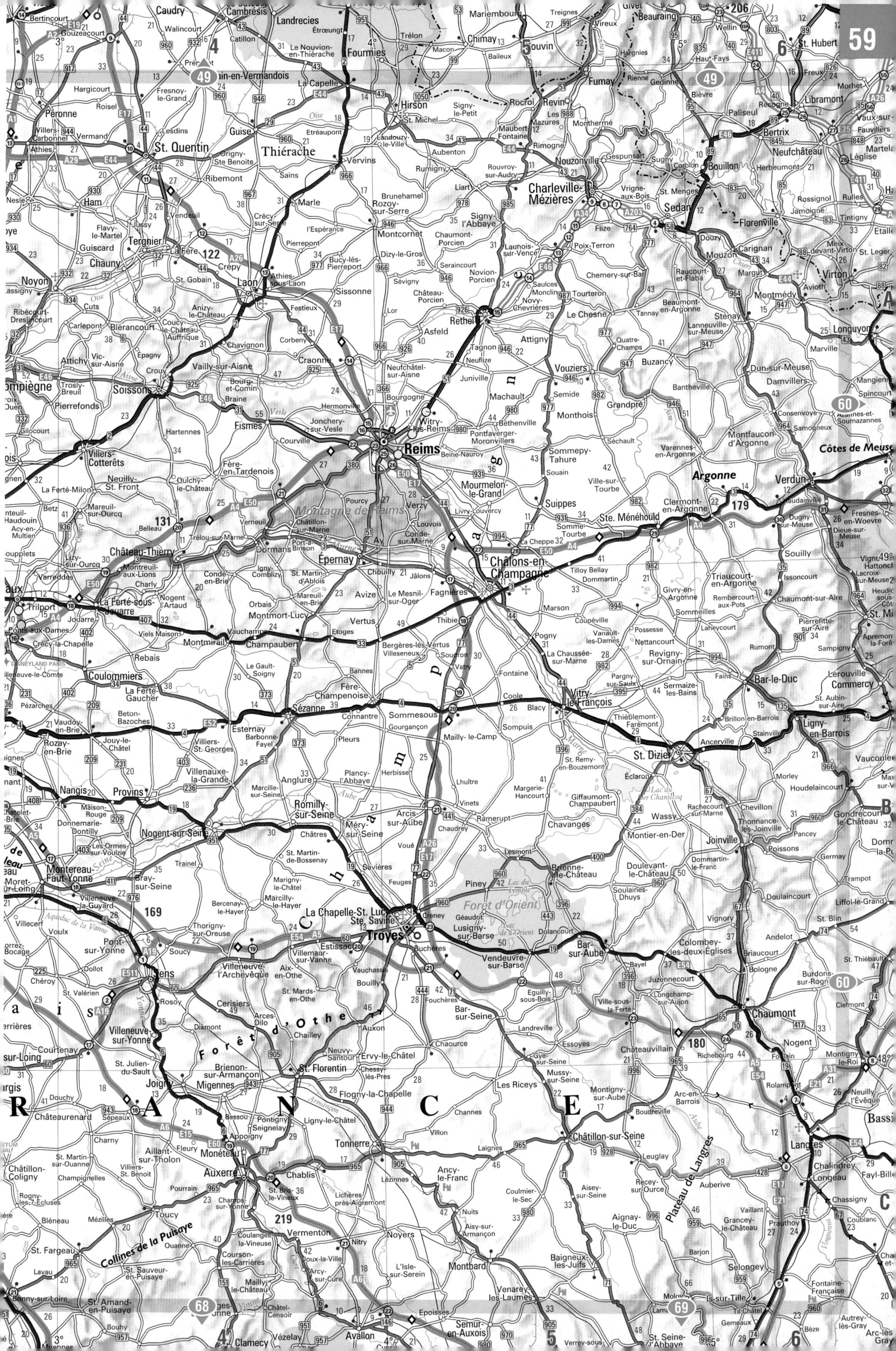
Thiérache
Champagne
Argonne
Côtes de Meuse
Montagne de Reims
Forêt d'Orient
Forêt d'Othe
Plateau de Langres
Collines de la Puisaye
FRANCE
Cambrésis
Caudry
Landrecies
Fourmies
Chimay
Givet
Couvin
Beauraing
St. Hubert
Libramont
Neufchâteau
Bertrix
Bouillon
Florenville
Virton
Rocroi
Revin
Fumay
Charleville-Mézières
Sedan
Carignan
Montmédy
Stenay
Longuyon
Hirson
La Capelle
Vervins
Guise
St. Quentin
Péronne
Ham
Tergnier
La Fère
Chauny
Noyon
Laon
Crépy
Soissons
Compiègne
Villers-Cotterêts
La Ferté-Milon
Fismes
Rethel
Vouziers
Grandpré
Reims
Épernay
Châlons-en-Champagne
Ste. Ménéhould
Verdun
Dun-sur-Meuse
Varennes-en-Argonne
Bar-le-Duc
Commercy
Ligny-en-Barrois
St. Dizier
Vitry-le-François
Château-Thierry
La Ferté-sous-Jouarre
Montmirail
Coulommiers
Sézanne
Provins
Nangis
Nogent-sur-Seine
Romilly-sur-Seine
Arcis-sur-Aube
Montereau-Faut-Yonne
Sens
Troyes
La Chapelle-St. Luc
Ste. Savine
Bar-sur-Aube
Joinville
Chaumont
Langres
Bar-sur-Seine
Brienne-le-Château
Villeneuve-sur-Yonne
Joigny
St. Florentin
Tonnerre
Chablis
Auxerre
Toucy
Montbard
Avallon
Semur-en-Auxois
Châtillon-sur-Seine
Venarey-les-Laumes
Clamecy
Vézelay
Courtenay
St. Fargeau
Bléneau
Châtillon-Coligny
Bonny-sur-Loire

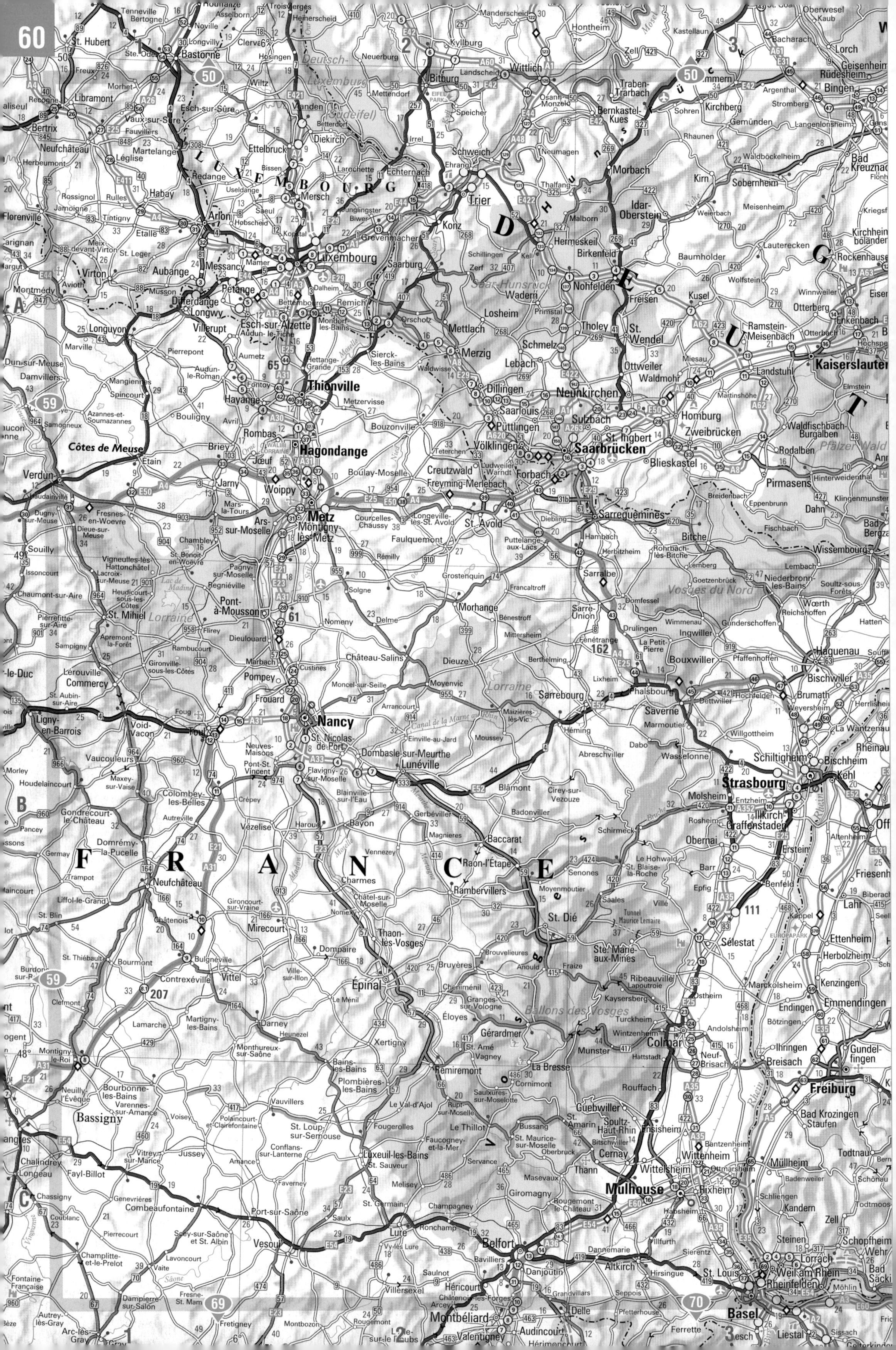
LUXEMBOURG
Luxembourg
Bastogne
Arlon
Esch-sur-Alzette
Diekirch
Echternach
Trier
Wittlich
Bitburg
Saarburg
Saarbrücken
Saarlouis
Neunkirchen
Homburg
Zweibrücken
Pirmasens
Kaiserslautern
Idar-Oberstein
Bad Kreuznach
Bingen
Rüdesheim
Sarreguemines
Forbach
St. Avold
Thionville
Hagondange
Metz
Nancy
Toul
Lunéville
Verdun
Longwy
Longuyon
Pont-à-Mousson
St. Mihiel
Commercy
Sarrebourg
Saverne
Haguenau
Wissembourg
Strasbourg
Kehl
Sélestat
Colmar
Mulhouse
Freiburg
Basel
St. Louis
Lörrach
Belfort
Montbéliard
Épinal
St. Dié
Remiremont
Vesoul
Neufchâteau
Vittel
Contrexéville
Mirecourt
Baccarat
Gérardmer
Luxeuil-les-Bains
Bitche
Haguenau
Offenburg
Lahr
Emmendingen
Müllheim
F R A N C E
D E U T S C H L A N D
V O S G E S
Ballons des Vosges
Vosges du Nord
Lorraine
Côtes de Meuse
Pfälzer Wald
Saar-Hunsrück
Deutsch-Luxemburg (Südeifel)
Hunsrück
Rhein
Mosel
Moselle
Saône
50
59
65
61
69
70
162
111
207

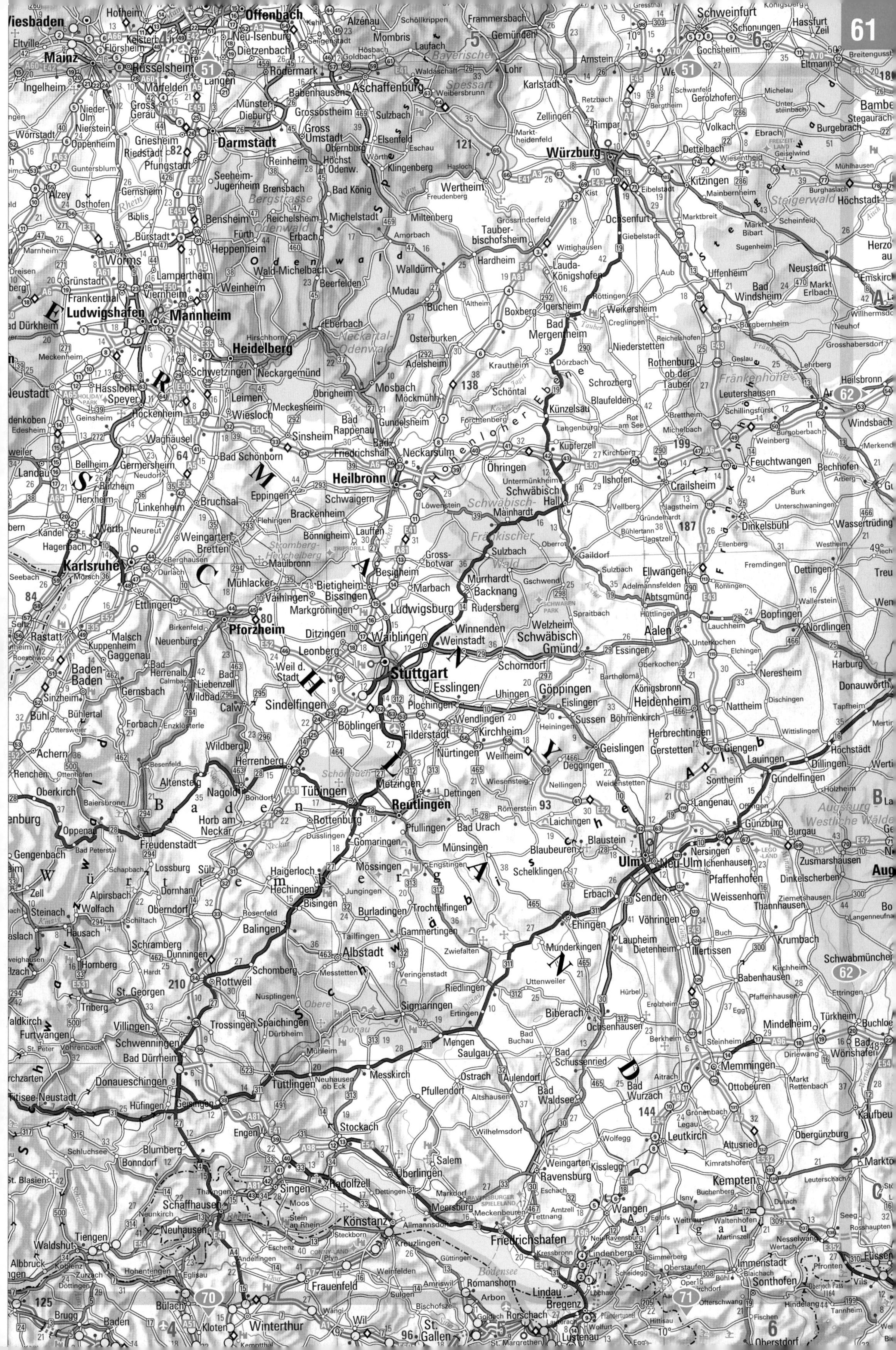
Wiesbaden
Mainz
Offenbach
Aschaffenburg
Darmstadt
Schweinfurt
Würzburg
Worms
Ludwigshafen
Mannheim
Heidelberg
Heilbronn
Karlsruhe
Pforzheim
Stuttgart
Esslingen
Ludwigsburg
Waiblingen
Böblingen
Sindelfingen
Tübingen
Reutlingen
Göppingen
Schwäbisch Gmünd
Schwäbisch Hall
Aalen
Heidenheim
Ulm
Neu-Ulm
Baden-Baden
Rastatt
Offenburg
Freudenstadt
Rottweil
Villingen
Schwenningen
Tuttlingen
Sigmaringen
Biberach
Ravensburg
Friedrichshafen
Konstanz
Singen
Schaffhausen
Winterthur
St. Gallen
Bregenz
Lindau
Kempten
Memmingen
Nördlingen
Dinkelsbühl
Rothenburg ob der Tauber
Ansbach
Bad Mergentheim
Crailsheim
Ellwangen
Günzburg
Spessart
Odenwald
Bergstrasse
Steigerwald
Frankenhöhe
Hohenloher Ebene
Schwäbisch-Fränkischer Wald
Schwäbische Alb
Baden-Württemberg
Bayern
Schwarzwald
Bodensee
Allgäu
Donau
Neckar
Main
Rhein

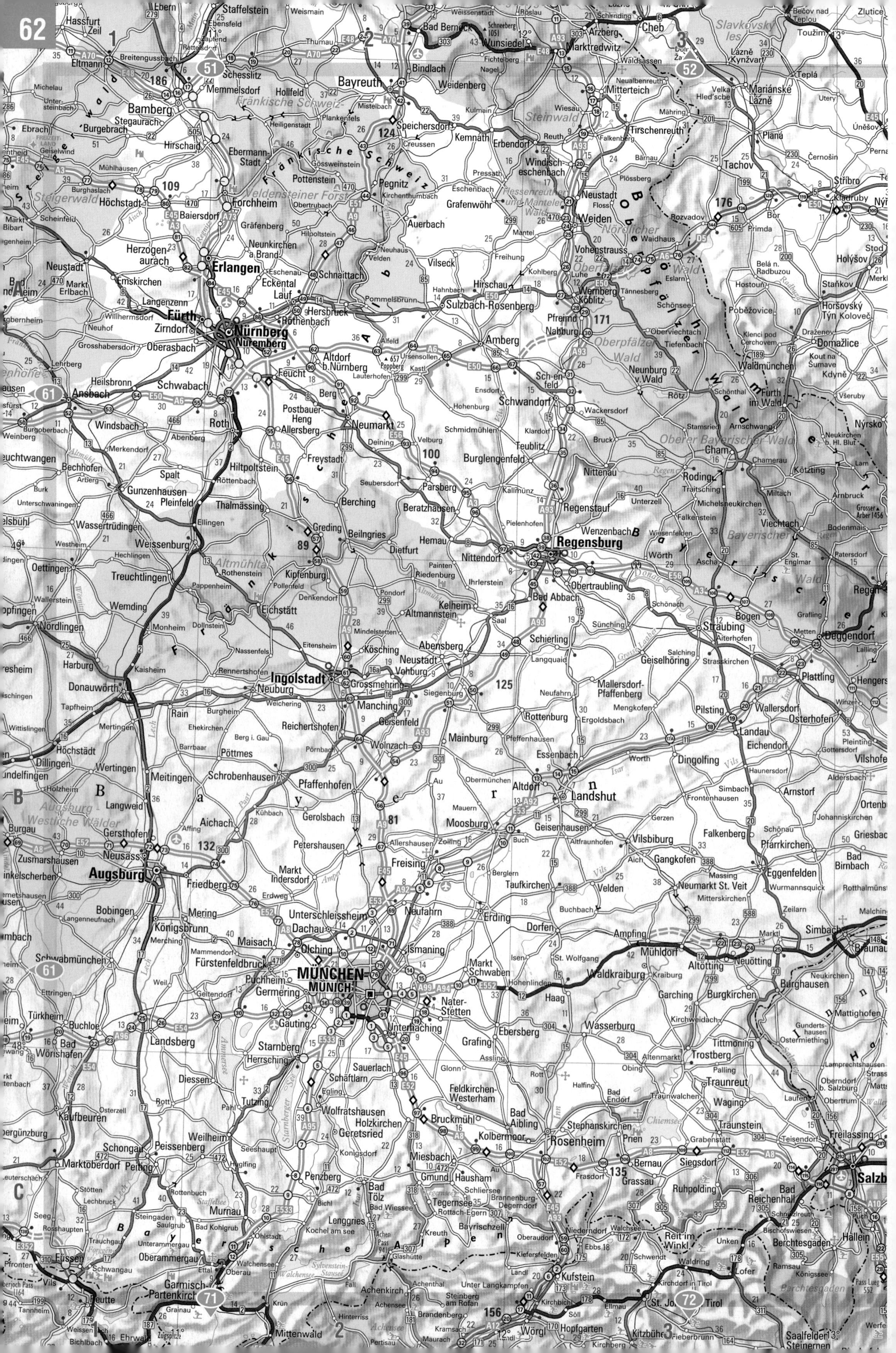
Bamberg
Bayreuth
Erlangen
Fürth
Nürnberg
Nuremberg
Ansbach
Schwabach
Roth
Neumarkt
Amberg
Weiden
Regensburg
Ingolstadt
Eichstätt
Kelheim
Straubing
Deggendorf
Landshut
Freising
Dachau
Augsburg
MÜNCHEN
MUNICH
Rosenheim
Kufstein
Füssen
Garmisch-Partenkirchen
Mittenwald
Cheb
Marktredwitz
Wunsiedel
Mariánské Lázně
Tachov
Domažlice
Cham
Donauwörth
Nördlingen
Weissenburg
Gunzenhausen
Landsberg
Kaufbeuren
Starnberg
Wasserburg
Traunstein
Freilassing
Burghausen
Altötting
Mühldorf
Erding
Fränkische Schweiz
Steigerwald
Steinwald
Oberpfälzer Wald
Oberer Bayerischer Wald
Bayerischer Wald
Fränkische Alb
Bayerische Alpen
Chiemsee
Ammersee
Starnberger See
Donau
Isar
Inn
Bayern

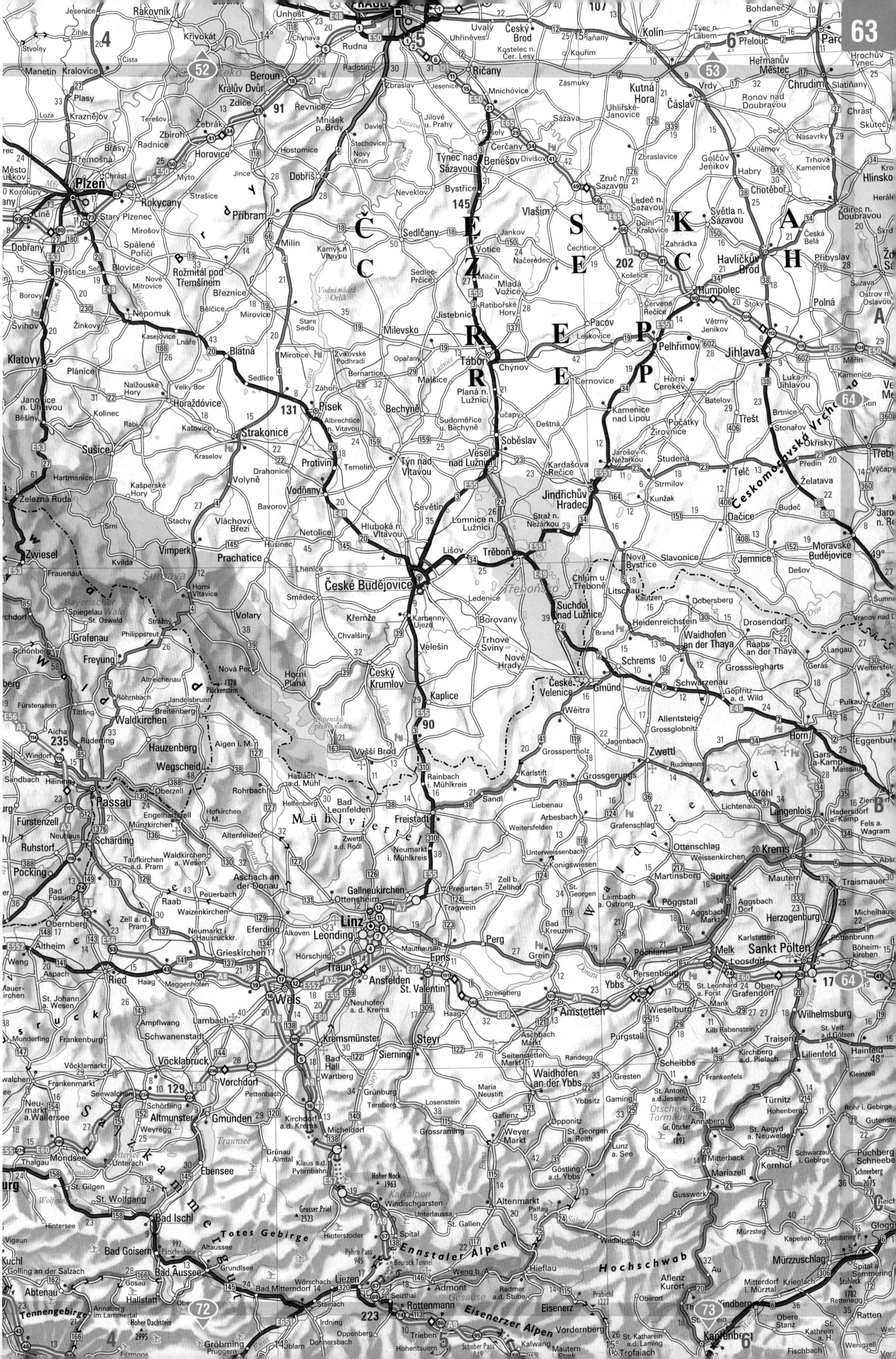
Praha
Rakovník
Beroun
Kolín
Kutná Hora
Čáslav
Chrudim
Plzeň
Rokycany
Příbram
Benešov
Vlašim
Havlíčkův Brod
Humpolec
Pelhřimov
Jihlava
Tábor
Písek
Strakonice
Klatovy
Sušice
Milevsko
Jindřichův Hradec
Třeboň
České Budějovice
Český Krumlov
Prachatice
Vimperk
Telč
Dačice
Moravské Budějovice
Zwiesel
Passau
Freistadt
Linz
Wels
Steyr
Enns
Amstetten
Melk
Krems
Sankt Pölten
Zwettl
Horn
Gmünd
Waidhofen an der Thaya
Vöcklabruck
Gmunden
Bad Ischl
Liezen
Mariazell
Kapfenberg
Ried
Schärding
Č E S K É
Č E S K O M O R A V S K Á V R C H O V I N A
Mühlviertel
Waldviertel
Totes Gebirge
Ennstaler Alpen
Hochschwab
Eisenerzer Alpen
Salzkammergut
Šumava
Bayerischer Wald

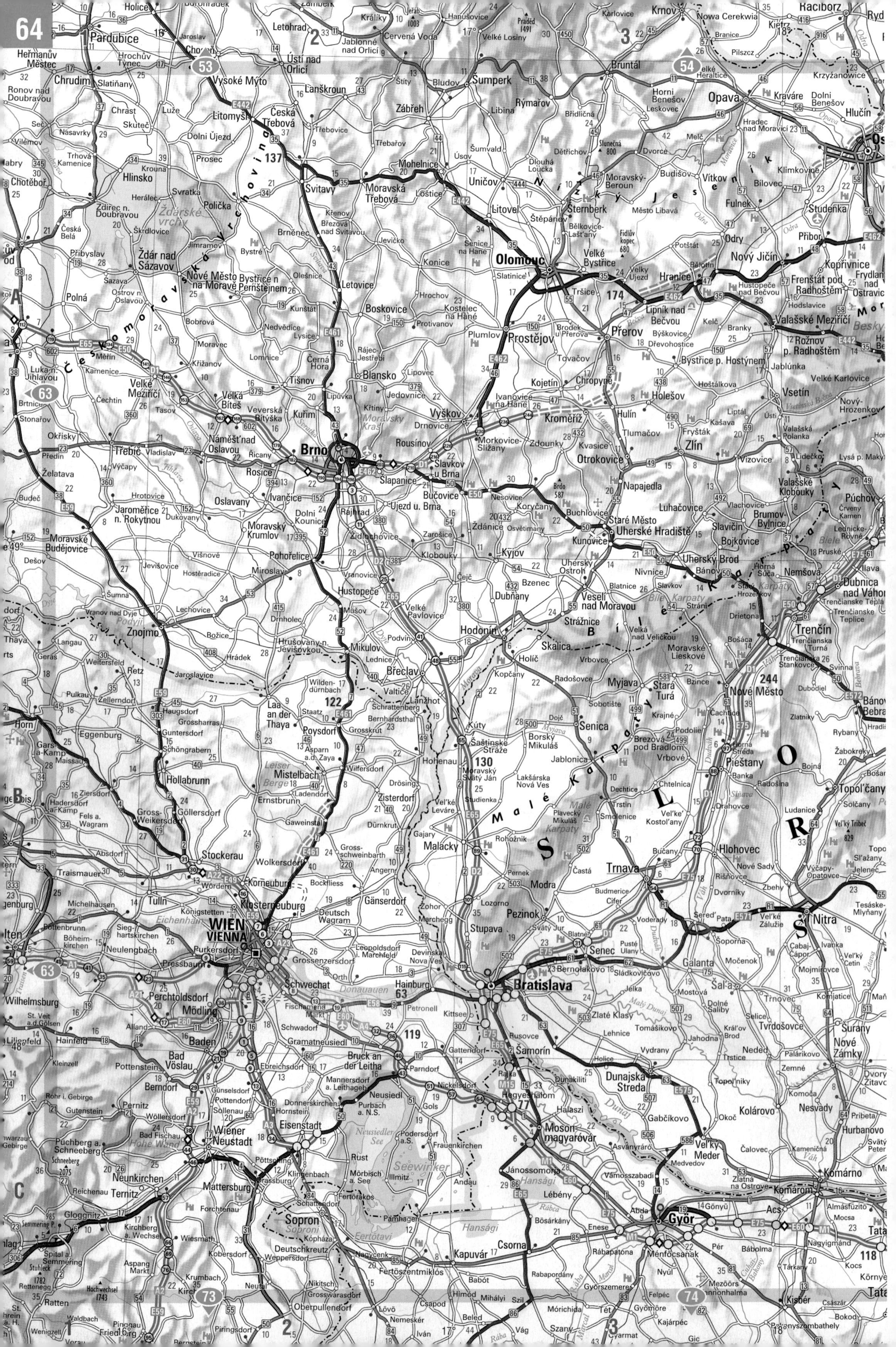
Pardubice
Heřmanův Městec
Chrudim
Holice
Choceň
Vysoké Mýto
Ústí nad Orlicí
Letohrad
Jablonné nad Orlicí
Králíky
Červená Voda
Hanušovice
Velké Losiny
Praděd 1491
Krnov
Karlovice
Nowa Cerekwia
Racibórz
Kietrz
Branice
Pilszcz
Krzyżanowice
Bruntál
Velké Heraltice
Opava
Kravaře
Dolní Benešov
Hlučín
Ostrava
Hradec nad Moravicí
Ronov nad Doubravou
Slatiňany
Hrochův Týnec
Chrast
Skuteč
Luže
Litomyšl
Česká Třebová
Lanškroun
Štíty
Bludov
Šumperk
Zábřeh
Rýmařov
Libina
Horní Benešov
Leskovec
Břidličná
Nasavrky
Dolní Újezd
Třebovice
Třebařov
Mohelnice
Šumvald
Úsov
Dlouhá Loučka
Dětřichov
Slunečná 800
Dvorce
Melč
Budišov
Vítkov
Klimkovice
Bílovec
Trhová Kamenice
Hlinsko
Krouna
Prosec
Svitavy
Moravská Třebová
Loštice
Uničov
Litovel
Šternberk
Moravský Beroun
Město Libavá
Fulnek
Studénka
Chotěboř
Svratka
Polička
Heralec
Ždárské vrchy
Zdírec n. Doubravou
Škrdlovice
Česká Belá
Přibyslav
Žďár nad Sázavou
Jimramov
Bystré
Brněnec
Křenov
Březová nad Svitavou
Jevíčko
Konice
Senice na Hané
Olomouc
Štěpánov
Bělkovice-Lašťany
Fidlův kopec 680
Velké Bystřice
Potštát
Odry
Příbor
Nový Jičín
Kopřivnice
Frenštát pod Radhoštěm
Frýdlant nad Ostravicí
Nízký Jeseník
Českomoravská vrchovina
Sázava
Ostrov n. Oslavou
Nové Město na Moravě
Bystřice n. Pernštejnem
Olešnice
Letovice
Kunštát
Boskovice
Hrochov
Kostelec na Hané
Slatinice
Velký Újezd
Tršice
Hranice
Bělotín
Hustopeče nad Bečvou
Hodslavice
Polná
Bobrová
Nedvědice
Lysice
Protivanov
Plumlov
Prostějov
Brodek u Přerova
Přerov
Lipník nad Bečvou
Kelč
Branky
Valašské Meziříčí
Rožnov p. Radhoštěm
Beskydy
Měřín
Moravec
Křižanov
Lomnice
Rájec-Jestřebí
Černá Hora
Blansko
Tovačov
Kojetín
Chropyně
Býškovice
Dřevohostice
Bystřice p. Hostýnem
Jablůnka
Velké Karlovice
Luka n. Jihlavou
Kamenice
Velké Meziříčí
Velká Bíteš
Tišnov
Lipovec
Jedovnice
Ivanovice na Hané
Holešov
Hošťálkova
Vsetín
Nový Hrozenkov
Čechtín
Brtnice
Stonařov
Tasov
Veverská Bítýška
Kuřim
Lipůvka
Křtiny
Moravský Kras
Vyškov
Drnovice
Kroměříž
Hulín
Tlumačov
Fryšták
Kašava
Liptál
Valašská Polanka
Okříšky
Třebíč
Vladislav
Náměšť nad Oslavou
Řícany
Brno
Rousínov
Slavkov u Brna
Morkovice-Slížany
Zdounky
Kvasice
Otrokovice
Zlín
Vizovice
Lidečko
Lysá p. Makytou
Předín
Výčapy
Rosice
Šlapanice
Bučovice
Nesovice
Brdo 587
Napajedla
Luhačovice
Valašské Klobouky
Púchov
Želatava
Hrotovice
Oslavany
Ivančice
Újezd u. Brna
Rajhrad
Koryčany
Buchlovice
Ždánice
Osvětimany
Staré Město
Uherské Hradiště
Kunovice
Slavičín
Bojkovice
Brumov-Bylnice
Červený Kameň
Lednické Rovné
Budeč
Jaroměřice n. Rokytnou
Dukovany
Moravský Krumlov
Dolní Kounice
Židlochovice
Zarošice
Klobouky
Kyjov
Uherský Ostroh
Uherský Brod
Bánov
Horná Súča
Nemšová
Pruské
Ilava
Dubnica nad Váhom
Moravské Budějovice
Dešov
Jevišovice
Višňové
Hostěradice
Pohořelice
Miroslav
Vranovice
Hustopeče
Čejč
Bzenec
Dubňany
Veselí nad Moravou
Blatnice
Nivnice
Slavkov
Strání
Drietoma
Trenčianske Teplá
Trenčianske Teplice
Trenčín
Šumná
Vranov nad Dyjí
Podyjí
Lechovice
Znojmo
Božice
Drnholec
Mušov
Velké Pavlovice
Podivín
Hodonín
Strážnice
Velká nad Veličkou
Skalica
Bílé Karpaty
Moravské Lieskové
Bošáca
Trenčianska Turná
Trenčianska Stankovce
Svinná
Thaya
Langau
Geras
Weitersfeld
Retz
Hrádek
Hrušovany n. Jevišovkou
Mikulov
Lednice
Břeclav
Holíč
Vrbovce
Jaroslavice
Wildendürnbach
Valtice
Lanžhot
Kopčany
Radošovce
Myjava
Stará Turá
Bzince
Nové Mesto
Dubodiel
Bánovce nad Bebravou
Pulkau
Zellerndorf
Haugsdorf
Laa an der Thaya
Schrattenberg
Sobotište
Senica
Krajné
Čachtice
Zlatníky
Horn
Eggenburg
Grossharras
Guntersdorf
Staatz
Bernhardsthal
Poysdorf
Grosskrut
Kúty
Šaštínske Stráže
Dojč
Borský Mikuláš
Podolie
Brezová pod Bradlom
Vrbové
Rybany
Gars am Kamp
Maissau
Schöngrabern
Asparn a.d. Zaya
Wilfersdorf
Hohenau
Jablonica
Piešťany
Banka
Radošina
Bojná
Žabokreky
Hollabrunn
Leiser Berge
Mistelbach
Ladendorf
Drösing
Moravský Svätý Ján
Lakšárska Nová Ves
Studienka
Chtelnica
Dechtice
Topoľčany
Zistersdorf
Veľké Leváre
Trstín
Drahovce
Ziersdorf
Hadersdorf a. Kamp
Fels a. Wagram
Göllersdorf
Gross-Weikersdorf
Ernstbrunn
Gaweinstal
Dürnkrut
Gajary
Malé Karpaty
Plavecký Mikuláš
Smolenice
Veľké Kostoľany
Ludanice
Solčany
Veľký Tribeč 829
Malacky
Rohožník
Hlohovec
Nové Sady
Absdorf
Stockerau
Wolkersdorf
Gross-schweinbarth
Bučany
Trnava
Šľažany
Výčapy-Opatovce
Jelenec
Traismauer
Korneuburg
Angern
Pernek
Častá
Modra
Rišňovce
Dvorníky
Zbehy
Tulln
Königstetten
Wördern
Bockfliess
Budmerice
Cífer
Michelhausen
Klosterneuburg
Gänserndorf
Deutsch Wagram
Zohor
Marchegg
Lozorno
Pezinok
Voderady
Sereď
Pata
Veľké Zálužie
Nitra
Tesárske Mlyňany
Eichenhain
Sieghartskirchen
Böheimkirchen
WIEN
VIENNA
Stupava
Svätý Jur
Blatné
Pusté Úľany
Šoporňa
Ivanka
Neulengbach
Purkersdorf
Leopoldsdorf i. Marchfeld
Devínska Nová Ves
Senec
Galanta
Močenok
Cabaj-Čápor
Veľký Cetín
Pressbaum
Grossenzersdorf
Orth
Hainburg
Bernolákovo
Sládkovičovo
Šaľa
Mojmírovce
Perchtoldsdorf
Schwechat
Donauauen
Petronell
Bratislava
Jelka
Mostová
Trnovec
Komjatice
Wilhelmsburg
Mödling
Fischamend Markt
Kittsee
Zlaté Klasy
Dolné Saliby
Selice
Tvrdošovce
St. Veit a.d. Gölsen
Alland
Schwadorf
Lehnice
Tomášikovo
Kráľov Brod
Šurany
Lilienfeld
Hainfeld
Baden
Gramatneusiedl
Rusovce
Vydrany
Jahodná
Neded
Palárikovo
Nové Zámky
Kleinzell
Pottenstein
Bad Vöslau
Ebreichsdorf
Bruck an der Leitha
Gattendorf
Šamorín
Holice
Trstice
Zemné
Dvory nad Žitavou
Berndorf
Mannersdorf a. Leithageb.
Parndorf
Rajka
Dunakiliti
Dunajská Streda
Topoľníky
Rohr i. Gebirge
Gutenstein
Pernitz
Günselsdorf
Pottendorf
Neusiedl
Nickelsdorf
Hegyeshalom
Halászi
Komoča
Kolárovo
Nesvady
Pribeta
Wöllersdorf
Sollenau
Donnerskirchen
Hornstein
Purbach a. N.S.
Gols
Gabčíkovo
Okoč
Hurbanovo
Bad Fischau
Hohe Wand
Wiener Neustadt
Eisenstadt
Neusiedler See
Podersdorf a.S.
Frauenkirchen
Mosonmagyaróvár
Ásványráró
Veľký Meder
Čalovec
Kameničná
Svätý Peter
Puchberg a. Schneeberg
Schneeberg 2075
Pöttsching
Rust
Seewinkel
Medvedov
Komárno
Neunkirchen
Mattersburg
Klingenbach
Mörbisch a. See
Illmitz
Andau
Jánossomorja
Hanság
Vámosszabadi
Zlatná na Ostrove
Komárom
Reichenau
Ternitz
Forchtenau
Fertőrákos
Schattendorf
Lébény
Gönyű
Ács
Almásfüzitő
Gloggnitz
Semmering P.
Kirchberg a. Wechsel
Sopron
Fertőtavi
Pamhagen
Hansági
Bősárkány
Abda
Győr
Mocsa
Tata
Spital a. Semmering
Stuhleck 1782
Wiesmath
Kobersdorf
Deutschkreutz
Weppersdorf
Kópháza
Nagycenk
Fertőszentmiklós
Kapuvár
Csorna
Enese
Rábapatona
Ménfőcsanak
Pér
Bábolna
Nagyigmánd
Kocs
Rettenegg
Aspang Markt
Krumbach
Hochwechsel 1743
Kirchschlag
Nikitsch
Grosswarasdorf
Babót
Rabapordány
Győrszemere
Nyúl
Mezőörs
Pannonhalma
Tárkány
Kisbér
Császár
Ratten
Neutal
Oberpullendorf
Lövő
Csapod
Himód
Mihályi
Szil
Mórichida
Tét
Gyömöre
Felpéc
Bokod
St. Jakob i. Walde
Waldbach
Pinggau
Friedberg
Wenigzell
Piringsdorf
Nemeskér
Beled
Vág
Szany
Kajárpéc
Gyarmat
Gic
Pápateszér
Iván
Bakonyszombathely
Rába
Marcal
Karpaty
Biele Karpaty
Malý Dunaj
Dunaj
Váh
Morava
Dyje
Odra
Bečva
Svratka
Jihlava
Oslava
Rábca
Dudváh
Bebrava
Žitava
Nitra
Leitha
Traisen
Thaya
Čierna voda
Bílé Karpaty
Malé Karpaty
Moravský Kras
Slovensko
S
L
O
R

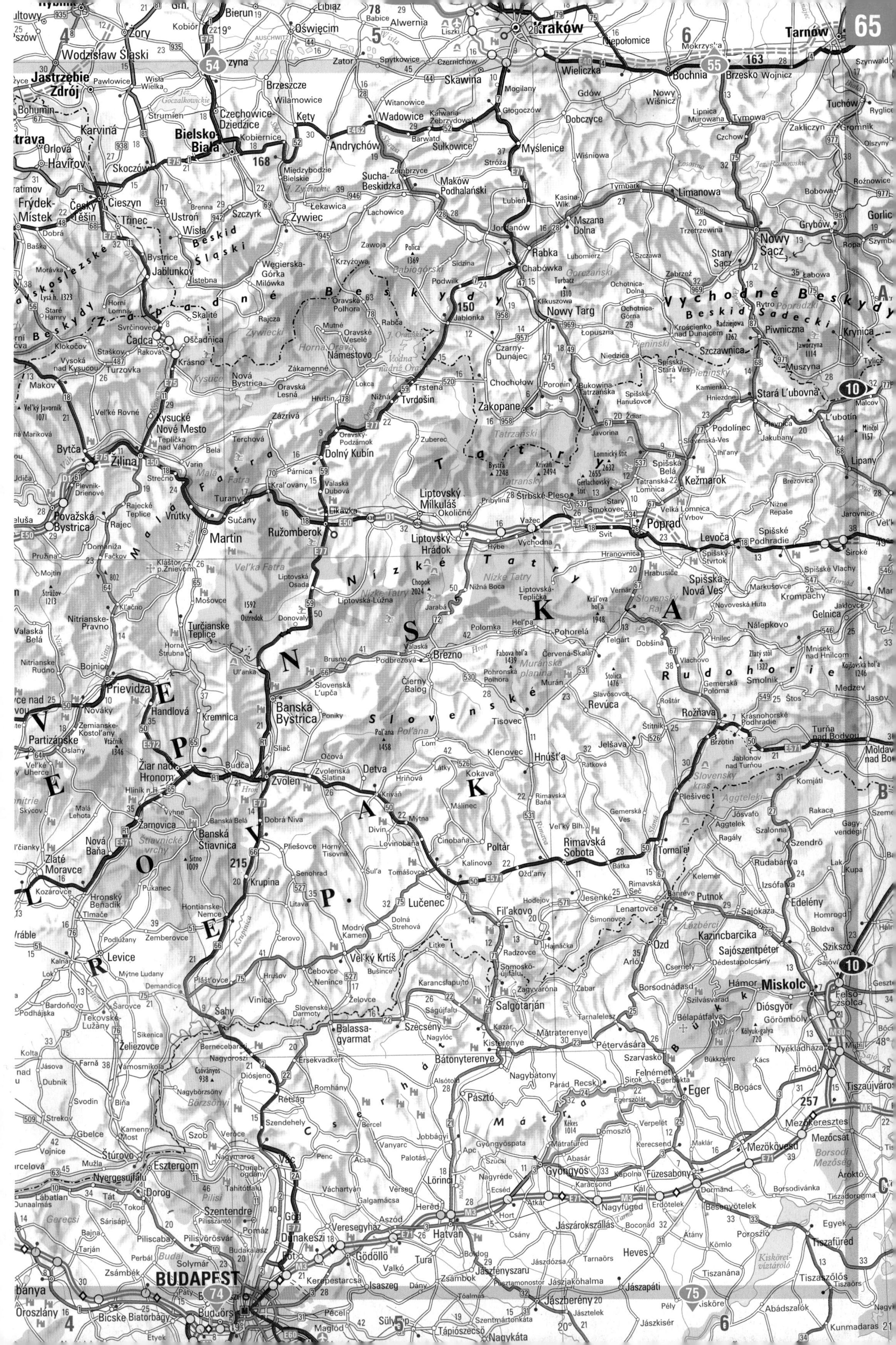

Kraków
Oświęcim
Bieruń
Żory
Wodzisław Śląski
Jastrzębie Zdrój
Tarnów
Niepołomice
Wieliczka
Bochnia
Brzesko
Skawina
Zator
Wadowice
Kalwaria-Zebrzydowska
Myślenice
Dobczyce
Andrychów
Kęty
Czechowice-Dziedzice
Bielsko-Biała
Skoczów
Cieszyn
Český Těšín
Frýdek-Místek
Havířov
Karviná
Orlová
Třinec
Ustroń
Wisła
Szczyrk
Żywiec
Sucha-Beskidzka
Maków Podhalański
Limanowa
Tymbark
Mszana Dolna
Rabka
Jordanów
Chabówka
Nowy Targ
Nowy Sącz
Stary Sącz
Grybów
Gorlice
Krynica
Piwniczna
Muszyna
Szczawnica
Zakopane
Beskid Śląski
Zapadné Beskydy
Vychodné Beskydy
Beskid Sądecki
Jabłonka
Babiogórski
Čadca
Kysucké Nové Mesto
Bytča
Žilina
Považská Bystrica
Martin
Vrútky
Ružomberok
Dolný Kubín
Námestovo
Tvrdošín
Trstená
Liptovský Mikuláš
Liptovský Hrádok
Štrbské Pleso
Poprad
Kežmarok
Levoča
Spišská Nová Ves
Stará Ľubovňa
Lipany
Gelnica
Malá Fatra
Veľká Fatra
Vysoké Tatry
Tatry
Nízke Tatry
Chopok 2024
Gerlachovský štít 2655
Lomnický štít 2632
Kriváň 2494
Bystrá 2248
Kráľova hoľa 1948
Slovenský Raj
Slovenské Rudohorie
Brezno
Banská Bystrica
Zvolen
Detva
Kremnica
Handlová
Prievidza
Bojnice
Partizánske
Žiar nad Hronom
Žarnovica
Banská Štiavnica
Nová Baňa
Zlaté Moravce
Levice
Krupina
Lučenec
Poltár
Rimavská Sobota
Revúca
Rožňava
Tornaľa
Hnúšťa
Tisovec
Veľký Krtíš
Fiľakovo
Šahy
Štúrovo
Esztergom
Szob
Vác
Dorog
Szentendre
Budapest
Budaörs
Gödöllő
Hatvan
Gyöngyös
Eger
Mezőkövesd
Miskolc
Kazincbarcika
Ózd
Putnok
Salgótarján
Balassagyarmat
Pásztó
Mátra
Bükk
Cserhát
Börzsöny
Füzesabony
Jászberény
Tiszaújváros
Tiszafüred
Abádszalók
Heves
Slovensko
Republika

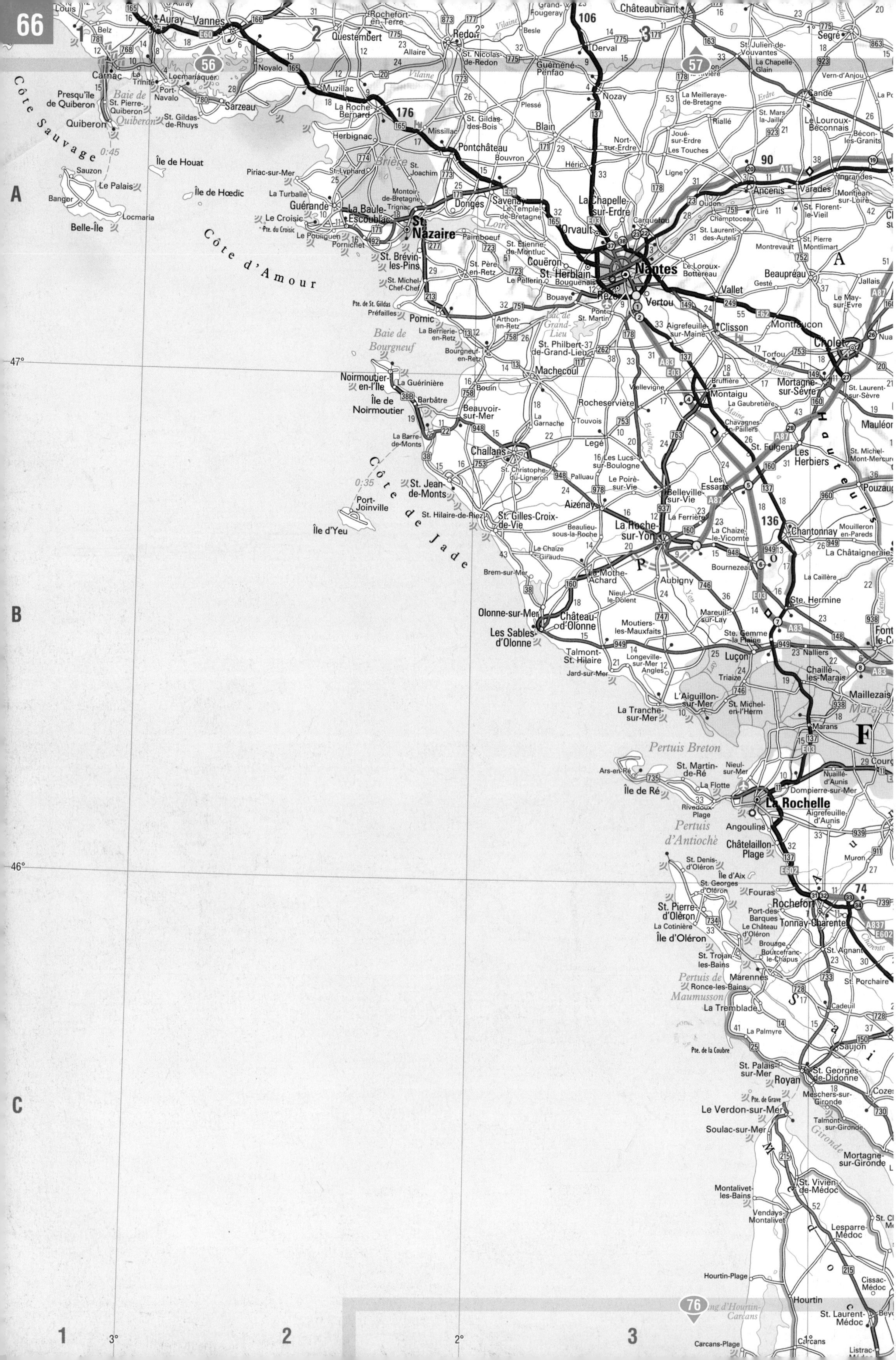
Côte Sauvage
Côte d'Amour
Côte de Jade
Presqu'île de Quiberon
Baie de Quiberon
Quiberon
Carnac
Auray
Vannes
Sarzeau
Muzillac
La Roche-Bernard
Questembert
Redon
Rochefort-en-Terre
Châteaubriant
Derval
Guémené-Penfao
Nozay
Blain
Pontchâteau
Herbignac
Guérande
Le Croisic
La Baule-Escoublac
Pornichet
St. Nazaire
Donges
Savenay
St. Brevin-les-Pins
Paimboeuf
Couëron
St. Herblain
Orvault
La Chapelle-sur-Erdre
Carquefou
Nantes
Rezé
Vertou
Bouguenais
Ancenis
Varades
Segré
Candé
Vallet
Clisson
Beaupréau
Montfaucon
Cholet
Mortagne-sur-Sèvre
Montaigu
Les Herbiers
Pornic
Préfailles
Baie de Bourgneuf
Bourgneuf-en-Retz
Machecoul
Noirmoutier-en-l'Île
Île de Noirmoutier
Barbâtre
La Guérinière
Beauvoir-sur-Mer
Challans
St. Jean-de-Monts
Port-Joinville
Île d'Yeu
St. Hilaire-de-Riez
St. Gilles-Croix-de-Vie
Aizenay
La Roche-sur-Yon
Olonne-sur-Mer
Les Sables-d'Olonne
Château-d'Olonne
Talmont-St. Hilaire
Luçon
La Tranche-sur-Mer
L'Aiguillon-sur-Mer
Marans
Pertuis Breton
Île de Ré
St. Martin-de-Ré
La Rochelle
Pertuis d'Antioche
Châtelaillon-Plage
Île d'Oléron
St. Pierre-d'Oléron
Rochefort
Tonnay-Charente
Marennes
La Tremblade
Royan
St. Georges-de-Didonne
Le Verdon-sur-Mer
Soulac-sur-Mer
Montalivet-les-Bains
Lesparre-Médoc
Hourtin
St. Laurent-Médoc
Carcans
Belle-Île
Le Palais
Île de Houat
Île de Hœdic
56
57
76
A
B
C
1
2
3
47°
46°
3°
2°

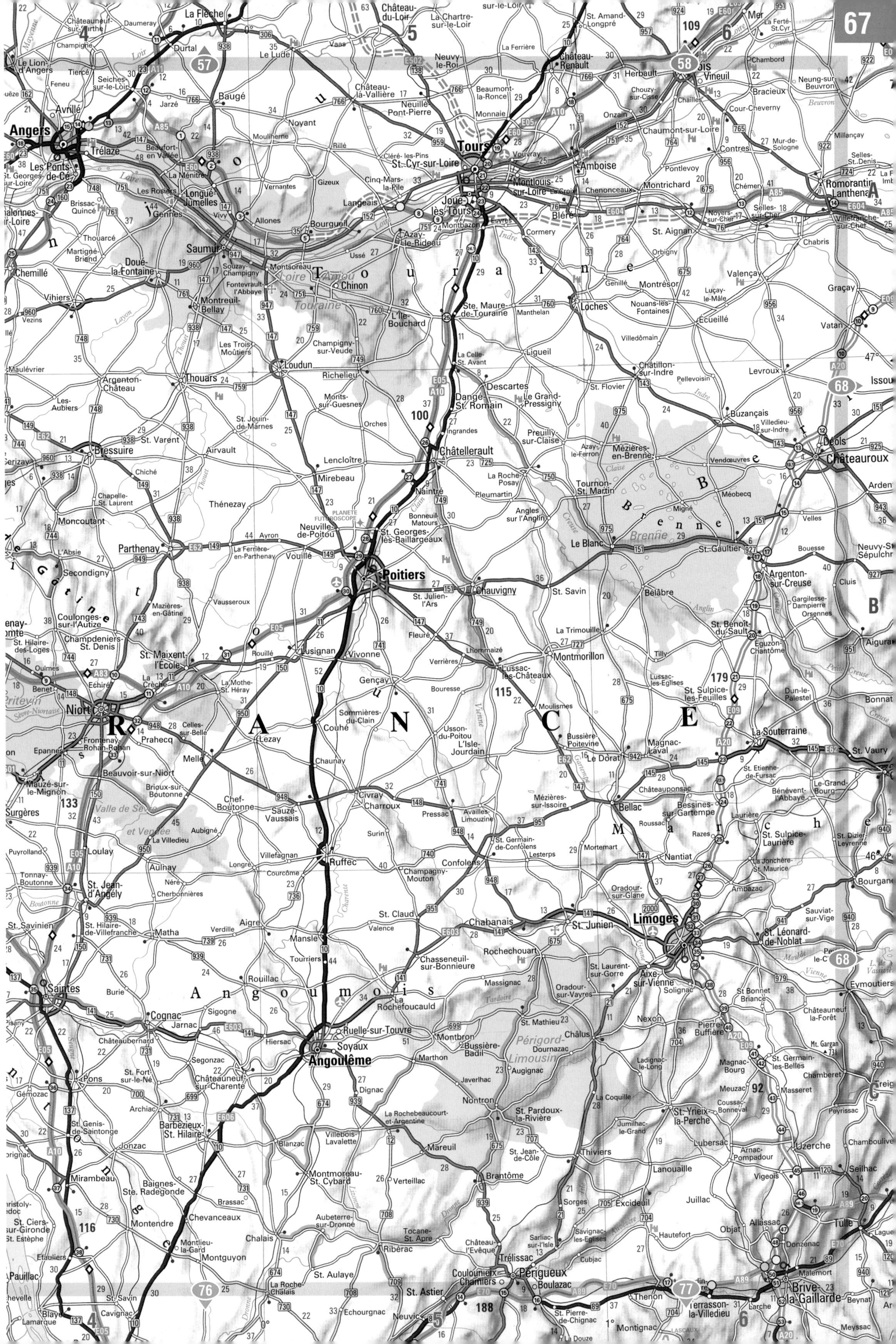
La Flèche
Château-du-Loir
La Chartre-sur-le-Loir
St. Amand-Longpré
Mer
Durtal
Le Lude
Château-Renault
Blois
Angers
Trélaze
Les Ponts-de-Cé
Baugé
Noyant
Tours
St.-Cyr-sur-Loire
Vouvray
Amboise
Montlouis-sur-Loire
Joué-lès-Tours
Chenonceaux
Montrichard
Romorantin-Lanthenay
Saumur
Doué-la-Fontaine
Chinon
Azay-le-Rideau
Loches
Bourgueil
Langeais
Longué-Jumelles
Montreuil-Bellay
Loudun
Richelieu
L'Île-Bouchard
Ste. Maure-de-Touraine
Valençay
Chemillé
Vihiers
Thouars
Argenton-Château
Bressuire
Parthenay
Airvault
Châtellerault
Descartes
Le Grand-Pressigny
Châtillon-sur-Indre
Buzançais
Déols
Châteauroux
Levroux
Vatan
Mirebeau
Lencloître
Neuville-de-Poitou
Poitiers
Chauvigny
St. Savin
Le Blanc
Tournon-St. Martin
Mézières-en-Brenne
Argenton-sur-Creuse
St.-Gaultier
Brenne
Niort
St. Maixent-l'École
Lusignan
Vivonne
Gençay
Montmorillon
Lussac-les-Châteaux
St. Benoît-du-Sault
Éguzon-Chantôme
La Souterraine
Le Dorat
Bellac
Magnac-Laval
Bessines-sur-Gartempe
Melle
Couhé
Civray
Charroux
Ruffec
Confolens
Limoges
St. Junien
Chabanais
Rochechouart
Aixe-sur-Vienne
St. Léonard-de-Noblat
Eymoutiers
Surgères
St. Jean-d'Angély
Matha
Saintes
Cognac
Jarnac
Angoulême
Soyaux
La Rochefoucauld
Montbron
Châlus
Nontron
St. Yrieix-la-Perche
Uzerche
Pons
Barbezieux-St. Hilaire
Jonzac
Mirambeau
Montmoreau-St. Cybard
Brantôme
Thiviers
Périgueux
Ribérac
Montguyon
Blaye
St. Astier
Terrasson-la-Villedieu
Brive-la-Gaillarde
Tulle
F R A N C E
A n g o u m o i s
T o u r a i n e
M a r c h e
B e r r y
S a i n t o n g e

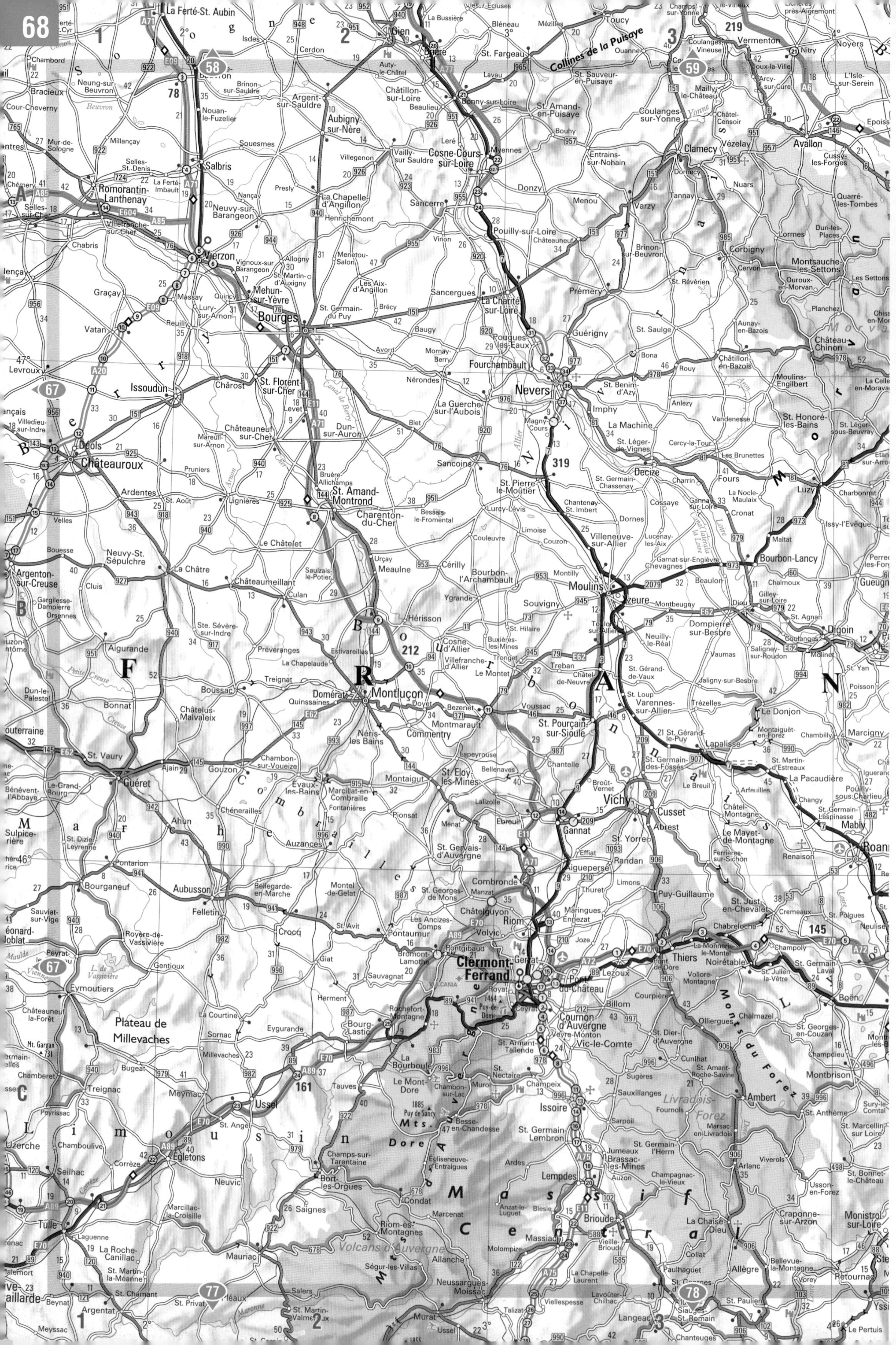
La Ferté-St. Aubin
Gien
Briare
Toucy
Collines de la Puisaye
St. Fargeau
Vermenton
Noyers
Chambord
Bracieux
Cour-Cheverny
Neung-sur-Beuvron
Lamotte-Beuvron
Argent-sur-Sauldre
Aubigny-sur-Nère
Châtillon-sur-Loire
St. Amand-en-Puisaye
Coulanges-sur-Yonne
Clamecy
Vézelay
Avallon
Salbris
Romorantin-Lanthenay
Cosne-Cours-sur-Loire
Sancerre
La Chapelle-d'Angillon
Henrichemont
Donzy
Varzy
Pouilly-sur-Loire
Vierzon
Mehun-sur-Yèvre
Bourges
La Charité-sur-Loire
Prémery
Corbigny
Montsauche-les-Settons
Château-Chinon
Graçay
Vatan
Issoudun
Levroux
Châteauroux
Déols
St. Florent-sur-Cher
Châteauneuf-sur-Cher
Dun-sur-Auron
Fourchambault
Nevers
La Guerche-sur-l'Aubois
Imphy
La Machine
Decize
Moulins-Engilbert
St. Honoré-les-Bains
Luzy
Sancoins
St. Pierre-le-Moûtier
St. Amand-Montrond
Lignières
Ardentes
Argenton-sur-Creuse
La Châtre
Châteaumeillant
Cérilly
Bourbon-l'Archambault
Moulins
Yzeure
Dompierre-sur-Besbre
Bourbon-Lancy
Digoin
Aigurande
Boussac
Montluçon
Domérat
Commentry
Montmarault
St. Pourçain-sur-Sioule
Varennes-sur-Allier
Lapalisse
Le Donjon
Guéret
Gouzon
Évaux-les-Bains
Chénerailles
Aubusson
Felletin
Gannat
Vichy
Cusset
Roanne
Riom
Châtelguyon
Volvic
Clermont-Ferrand
Thiers
Billom
Cournon-d'Auvergne
Vic-le-Comte
Monts du Forez
Plateau de Millevaches
Bourganeuf
Eymoutiers
La Bourboule
Le Mont-Dore
Issoire
Ambert
Livradois-Forez
Ussel
Egletons
Meymac
Mts. Dore
Massif Central
Bort-les-Orgues
Brioude
La Chaise-Dieu
Craponne-sur-Arzon
Tulle
Mauriac
Volcans d'Auvergne
Allanche
Neussargues-Moissac
Argentat
Langeac
Yssingeaux
Montbrison
Boën
Puy de Dôme
Puy de Sancy
Monts du Cantal
B o u r b o n n a i s
C o m b r a i l l e s
L i m o u s i n
A u v e r g n e
B e r r y
N i v e r n a i s
M o r v a n
58
59
67
77
78
1
2
3
4
A
B
C

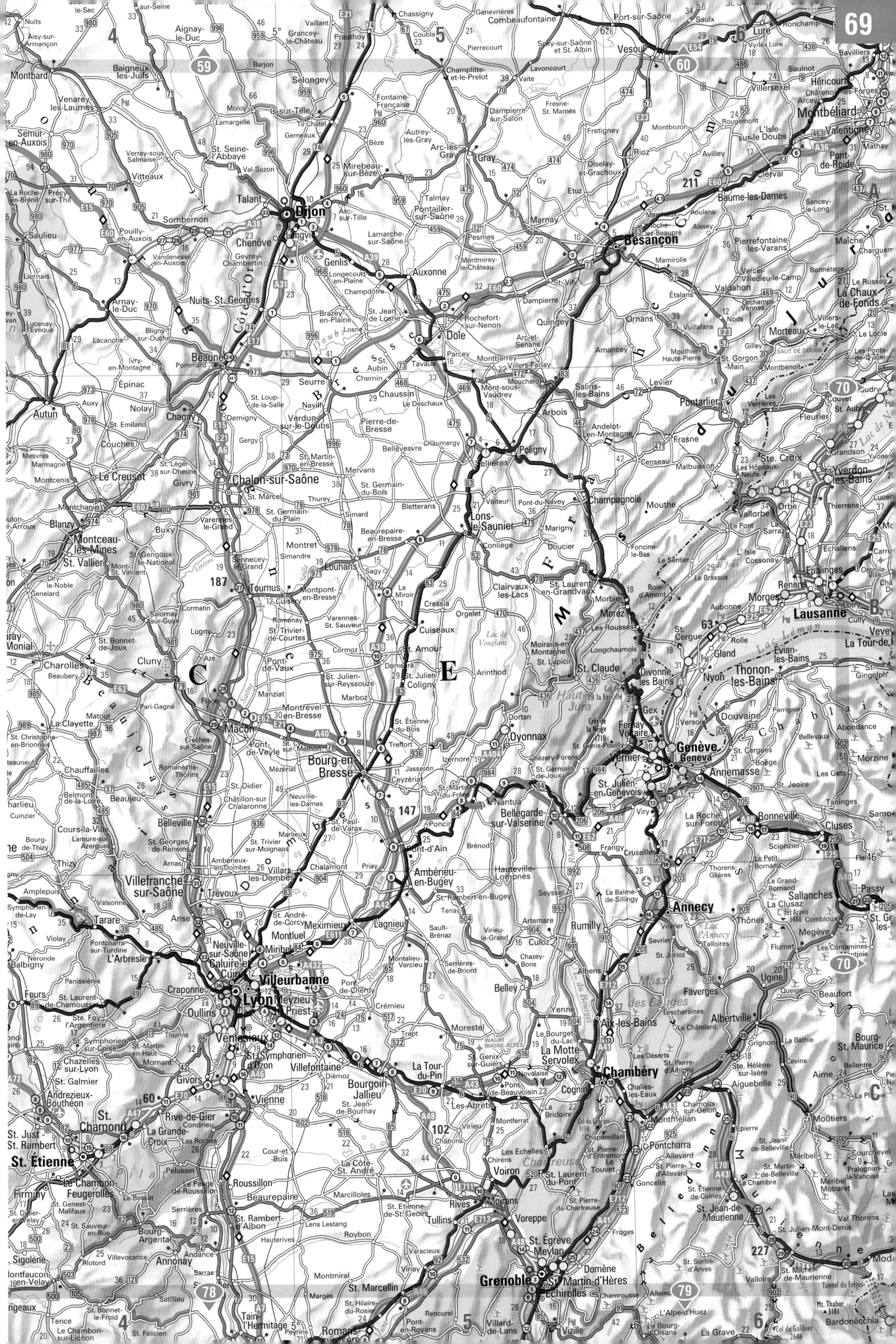

Nuits
Aisy-sur-Armançon
Montbard
Aignay-le-Duc
Baigneux-les-Juifs
Venarey-les-Laumes
Semur-en-Auxois
Vitteaux
Précy-sous-Thil
Saulieu
Pouilly-en-Auxois
Sombernon
Arnay-le-Duc
Liernais
Lucenay-l'Evêque
Autun
Épinac
Nolay
Couches
Le Creusot
Montceau-les-Mines
St. Vallier
Blanzy
Montchanin
Charolles
Paray-le-Monial
La Clayette
Chauffailles
Cluny
Tournus
Mâcon
Chalon-sur-Saône
Chagny
Beaune
Pommard
Nuits-St. Georges
Gevrey-Chambertin
Chenôve
Dijon
Talant
Longvic
Genlis
Auxonne
Is-sur-Tille
Selongey
Grancey-le-Château
Prauthoy
Chassigny
Coublanc
Champlitte-et-le-Prelot
Fontaine-Française
Mirebeau-sur-Bèze
Gray
Arc-lès-Gray
Autrey-lès-Gray
Dampierre-sur-Salon
Combeaufontaine
Port-sur-Saône
Vesoul
Scey-sur-Saône et St. Albin
Lure
Ronchamp
Héricourt
Montbéliard
Valentigney
Villersexel
Rougemont
L'Isle-sur-le Doubs
Clerval
Baume-les-Dames
Rioz
Marnay
Pesmes
Besançon
Ornans
Quingey
Dole
Tavaux
St. Jean de Losne
Seurre
Verdun-sur-le-Doubs
Pierre-de-Bresse
Chaussin
Mont-sous-Vaudrey
Arbois
Poligny
Salins-les-Bains
Levier
Pontarlier
Morteau
La Chaux-de-Fonds
Valdahon
Vercel-Villedieu-le-Camp
Pierrefontaine-les-Varans
Maîche
Sellières
Lons-le-Saunier
Champagnole
Louhans
Montret
Cuiseaux
St. Amour
St. Julien
Orgelet
Clairvaux-les-Lacs
St. Laurent-en-Grandvaux
Morez
Les Rousses
St. Claude
Moirans-en-Montagne
Oyonnax
Nantua
Bourg-en-Bresse
Pont-de-Vaux
Montrevel-en-Bresse
Ambérieu-en-Bugey
Pont-d'Ain
Meximieux
Villars-les-Dombes
Trévoux
Villefranche-sur-Saône
Belleville
Tarare
L'Arbresle
Lyon
Villeurbanne
Vénissieux
Oullins
Givors
Vienne
Rive-de-Gier
St. Chamond
St. Étienne
Firminy
Annonay
Roussillon
Beaurepaire
Bourgoin-Jallieu
La Tour-du-Pin
Les Abrets
Voiron
Moirans
Voreppe
Tullins
Rives
Grenoble
Meylan
St. Martin-d'Hères
Échirolles
Vizille
St. Marcellin
Romans
Tain-l'Hermitage
Chambéry
La Motte-Servolex
Aix-les-Bains
Annecy
Rumilly
Belley
Bellegarde-sur-Valserine
Gex
Ferney-Voltaire
Genève
Geneva
Annemasse
Thonon-les-Bains
Évian-les-Bains
Bonneville
Cluses
Sallanches
Megève
Albertville
Ugine
Moûtiers
Bourg-St. Maurice
St. Jean-de-Maurienne
Modane
Bardonècchia
Lausanne
Morges
Renens
Nyon
Yverdon-les-Bains
Grandson
Vallorbe
Orbe
Ste. Croix
Vevey
La Tour-de-Peilz
Côte-d'Or
Bresse
Dombes
Beaujolais
Monts du Jura
Lac Léman
Chablais
Massif des Bauges
Chartreuse
Belledonne
Maurienne
Pilat
Haut-Jura

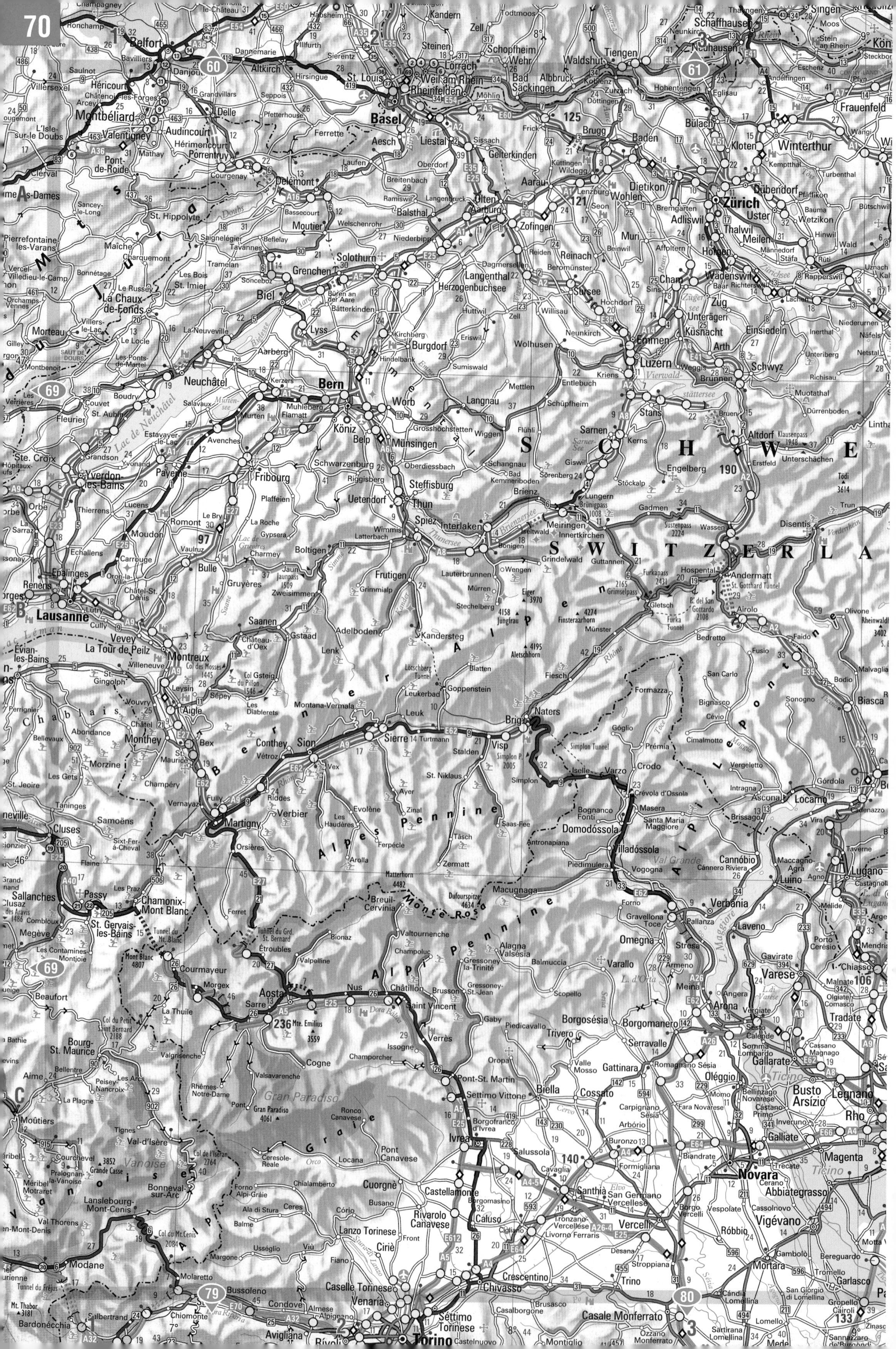

Belfort
Montbéliard
Basel
Lörrach
Weil am Rhein
Rheinfelden
St. Louis
Altkirch
Delle
Porrentruy
Delémont
Liestal
Aarau
Olten
Zofingen
Brugg
Baden
Waldshut
Tiengen
Schaffhausen
Neuhausen
Singen
Winterthur
Frauenfeld
Bülach
Kloten
Zürich
Dübendorf
Uster
Dietikon
Wohlen
Adliswil
Thalwil
Meilen
Horgen
Wädenswil
Rapperswil
Zug
Cham
Luzern
Emmen
Schwyz
Stans
Sarnen
Altdorf
Einsiedeln
Solothurn
Grenchen
Biel
Langenthal
Herzogenbuchsee
Burgdorf
Lyss
Bern
Köniz
Worb
Münsingen
Thun
Spiez
Interlaken
Brienz
Meiringen
Langnau
La Chaux-de-Fonds
Le Locle
Neuchâtel
Lac de Neuchâtel
Yverdon-les-Bains
Payerne
Fribourg
Murten
Romont
Bulle
Gruyères
Lausanne
Renens
Vevey
Montreux
Lac Léman
Évian-les-Bains
Aigle
Monthey
Martigny
Sion
Sierre
Visp
Brig
Naters
Zermatt
Saas-Fee
Verbier
Gstaad
Saanen
Adelboden
Kandersteg
Grindelwald
Lauterbrunnen
Wengen
Andermatt
Airolo
Biasca
Locarno
Ascona
Lugano
Chiasso
Mendrisio
Domodóssola
Verbania
Stresa
Arona
Varese
Gallarate
Busto Arsízio
Legnano
Novara
Vercelli
Biella
Ivrea
Aosta
Courmayeur
Chamonix-Mont Blanc
Sallanches
Cluses
Morzine
Bourg-St. Maurice
Moûtiers
Val-d'Isère
Modane
Bardonècchia
Susa
Rivoli
Torino
Chivasso
Casale Monferrato
Mortara
Vigévano
Abbiategrasso
Magenta
S C H W E I Z
S W I T Z E R L A N D
Berner Alpen
Alpes Pennine
Alpi Pennine
Alpi Lepontine
Alpi Graie
Monte Rosa
Gran Paradiso
Vanoise
Jura
Matterhorn 4482
Mont Blanc 4807
Eiger 3970
Jungfrau 4158
Finsteraarhorn 4274
Simplon Tunnel
St. Gotthard Tunnel
L. Maggiore
60
61
69
79
80

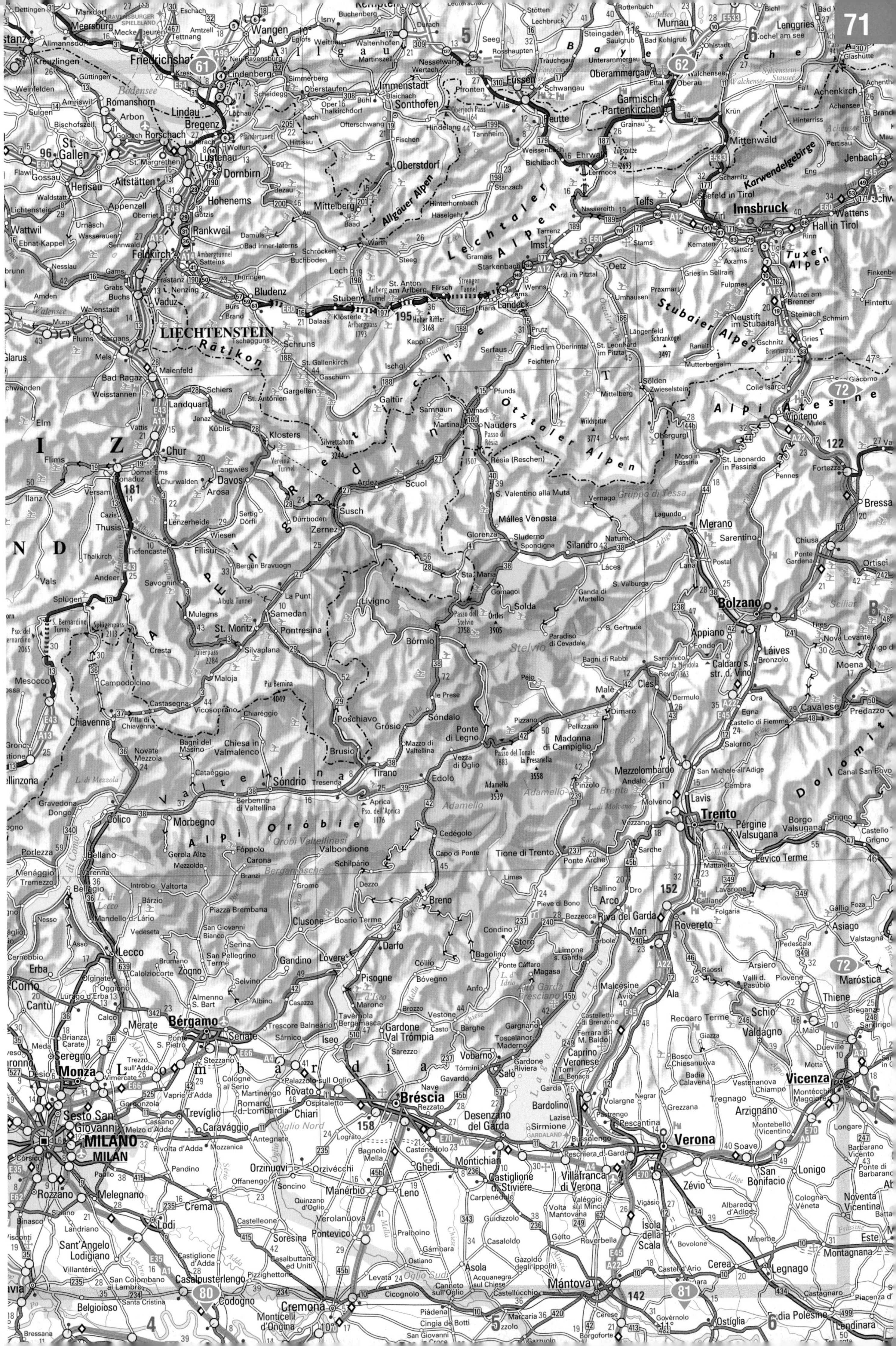
Meersburg
Friedrichshafen
Wangen
Allgäu
Kempten
Isny
Immenstadt
Sonthofen
Oberstdorf
Nesselwang
Füssen
Schwangau
Reutte
Murnau
Oberammergau
Garmisch-Partenkirchen
Mittenwald
Zugspitze
Bayerische
Lenggries
Achenkirch
Jenbach
Karwendelgebirge
Innsbruck
Hall in Tirol
Wattens
Telfs
Zirl
Seefeld in Tirol
Scharnitz
Lermoos
Ehrwald
Nassereith
Imst
Landeck
Zams
St. Anton am Arlberg
Lech
Warth
Lechtaler Alpen
Allgäuer Alpen
Mittelberg
Bodensee
Lindau
Bregenz
Lindenberg
Dornbirn
Lustenau
Hohenems
Götzis
Rankweil
Feldkirch
Bludenz
Schruns
LIECHTENSTEIN
Vaduz
Rätikon
St. Gallen
Rorschach
Romanshorn
Kreuzlingen
Herisau
Gossau
Appenzell
Altstätten
Wattwil
Buchs
Sargans
Walensee
Bad Ragaz
Landquart
Chur
Klosters
Davos
Arosa
Flims
Thusis
Tiefencastel
Filisur
Bergün
Savognin
Splügen
Mesocco
Bellinzona
Albula Tunnel
St. Moritz
Samedan
Pontresina
Silvaplana
Maloja
Piz Bernina
Poschiavo
Brusio
Tirano
Zernez
Susch
Scuol
Samnaun
Nauders
Ötztaler Alpen
Sölden
Obergurgl
Wildspitze
Stubaier Alpen
Neustift im Stubaital
Matrei am Brenner
Brennerpass
Tuxer Alpen
Alpi Atesine
Vipiteno
Fortezza
Bressanone
Merano
Bolzano
Silandro
Málles Venosta
Glorenza
Sta. Maria
Livigno
Bórmio
Passo dello Stelvio
Ortles
Solda
Stelvio
Sóndalo
Grósio
Sóndrio
Valtellina
Morbegno
Chiavenna
Colico
Alpi Oróbie
Lecco
Bellágio
Como
Cantù
Erba
Monza
MILANO
MILAN
Sesto San Giovanni
Rozzano
Melegnano
Lodi
Crema
Bérgamo
Seriate
Trevíglio
Caravággio
Chiari
Rovato
Iseo
Lóvere
Brescia
Desenzano del Garda
Sirmione
Salò
Lago di Garda
Riva del Garda
Arco
Rovereto
Trento
Pérgine Valsugana
Levico Terme
Lavis
Mezzolombardo
Tione di Trento
Madonna di Campiglio
Adamello
Passo del Tonale
Ponte di Legno
Edolo
Breno
Darfo
Clusone
Cles
Malè
Egna
Cavalese
Predazzo
Moena
Ortisei
Dolomiti
Asiago
Thiene
Schio
Valdagno
Vicenza
Verona
Bussolengo
Peschiera del Garda
Villafranca di Verona
Mántova
Cremona
Codogno
Casalpusterlengo
Soave
San Bonifacio
Lonigo
Legnago
Este
Montagnana
Ostíglia
Lendinara
Badia Polésine
Castiglione d. Stiviere
Montichiari
Ghedi
Leno
Manérbio
Orzinuovi
Soncino
Pizzighettone
Ísola della Scala
Cerea
Zévio
Noventa Vicentina
Marostica
Feltre
Lombardia
Grigioni

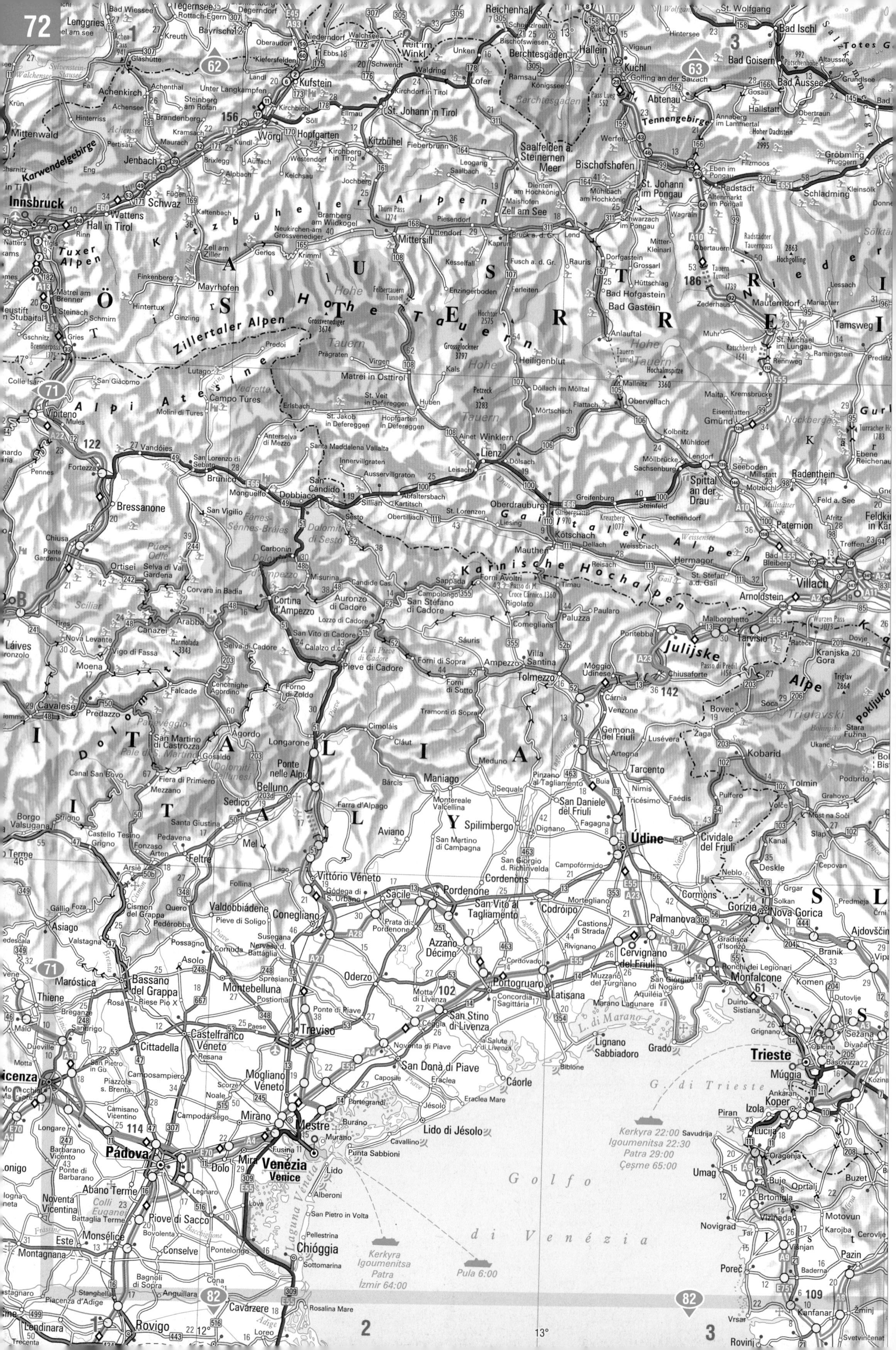

Lenggries
Bad Wiessee
Tegernsee
Reichenhall
St. Wolfgang
Bad Ischl
Kreuth
Achenkirch
Kufstein
Lofer
Berchtesgaden
Hallein
Kuchl
Bad Goisern
Bad Aussee
Totes Gebirge
Mittenwald
Walchensee
Karwendelgebirge
Achensee
Wörgl
Söll
Ellmau
St. Johann in Tirol
Kitzbühel
Hopfgarten
Fieberbrunn
Saalfelden a. Steinernen Meer
Bischofshofen
St. Johann im Pongau
Abtenau
Tennengebirge
Werfen
Hallstatt
Gröbming
Schladming
Radstadt
Jenbach
Schwaz
Innsbruck
Hall in Tirol
Wattens
Kitzbüheler Alpen
Zell am See
Mittersill
Saalbach
Dienten am Hochkönig
Wagrain
Altenmarkt im Pongau
Tuxer Alpen
Zell am Ziller
Gerlos
Krimml
Mayrhofen
Bruck a. d. Gr.
Lend
Rauris
Dorfgastein
Bad Hofgastein
Bad Gastein
Obertauern
Mauterndorf
Tamsweg
St. Michael im Lungau
Ö S T E R R E I C H
Hohe Tauern
Zillertaler Alpen
Grossvenediger 3674
Grossglockner 3797
Heiligenblut
Matrei in Osttirol
Alpi Atesine
Vipiteno
Campo Túres
Brenner
Steinach
Gries
Kals
Döllach im Mölltal
Mallnitz
Obervellach
Gmünd
Spittal an der Drau
Lienz
Winklern
Millstatt
Radenthein
Seeboden
Bressanone
Brunico
Dobbiaco
San Cándido
Sillian
Oberdrauburg
Kötschach
Mauthen
Gailtaler Alpen
Hermagor
Villach
Arnoldstein
Paternion
Bad Bleiberg
Karnische Hochalpen
Fortezza
Ortisei
Selva di Val Gardena
Corvara in Badia
Canazei
Marmolada 3343
Arabba
Cortina d'Ampezzo
Misurina
Auronzo di Cadore
Sappada
San Stéfano di Cadore
Paluzza
Tarvisio
Malborghetto
Pontebba
Julijske Alpe
Kranjska Gora
Triglav 2864
Bovec
Kobarid
Tolmin
Bolzano
Moena
Cavalese
Predazzo
Vigo di Fassa
Pieve di Cadore
Calalzo d. C.
San Vito di Cadore
Ampezzo
Villa Santina
Tolmezzo
Móggio Udinese
Chiusaforte
Venzone
Gemona del Friuli
Tarcento
Cividale del Friuli
Dolomiti
Agordo
San Martino di Castrozza
Fiera di Primiero
Longarone
Belluno
Feltre
Borgo Valsugana
Maniago
Aviano
Spilimbergo
San Daniele del Friuli
Údine
Vittório Véneto
Conegliano
Sacile
Pordenone
Codróipo
Palmanova
Gorizia
Nova Gorica
Asiago
Bassano del Grappa
Maróstica
Thiene
Montebelluna
Castelfranco Véneto
Treviso
Oderzo
Motta di Livenza
Portogruaro
Latisana
Cervignano del Friuli
Monfalcone
Aquiléia
Grado
Lignano Sabbiadoro
Trieste
Múggia
Koper
Izola
Piran
Vicenza
Pádova
Mestre
Venezia
Venice
Lido
Chióggia
San Donà di Piave
Jésolo
Lido di Jésolo
Cáorle
Golfo di Venézia
G. di Trieste
Kerkyra 22:00
Igoumenitsa 22:30
Patra 29:00
Çesme 65:00
Kerkyra
Igoumenitsa
Patra
İzmir 64:00
Pula 6:00
Abano Terme
Piove di Sacco
Monsélice
Este
Montagnana
Rovigo
Cavárzere
Umag
Novigrad
Poreč
Rovinj
Buzet
Pazin
Motovun
Kanfanar
Sežana
I T A L I A
Y
S L
I s t
13°
46°
47°
1
2
3
62
63
71
82

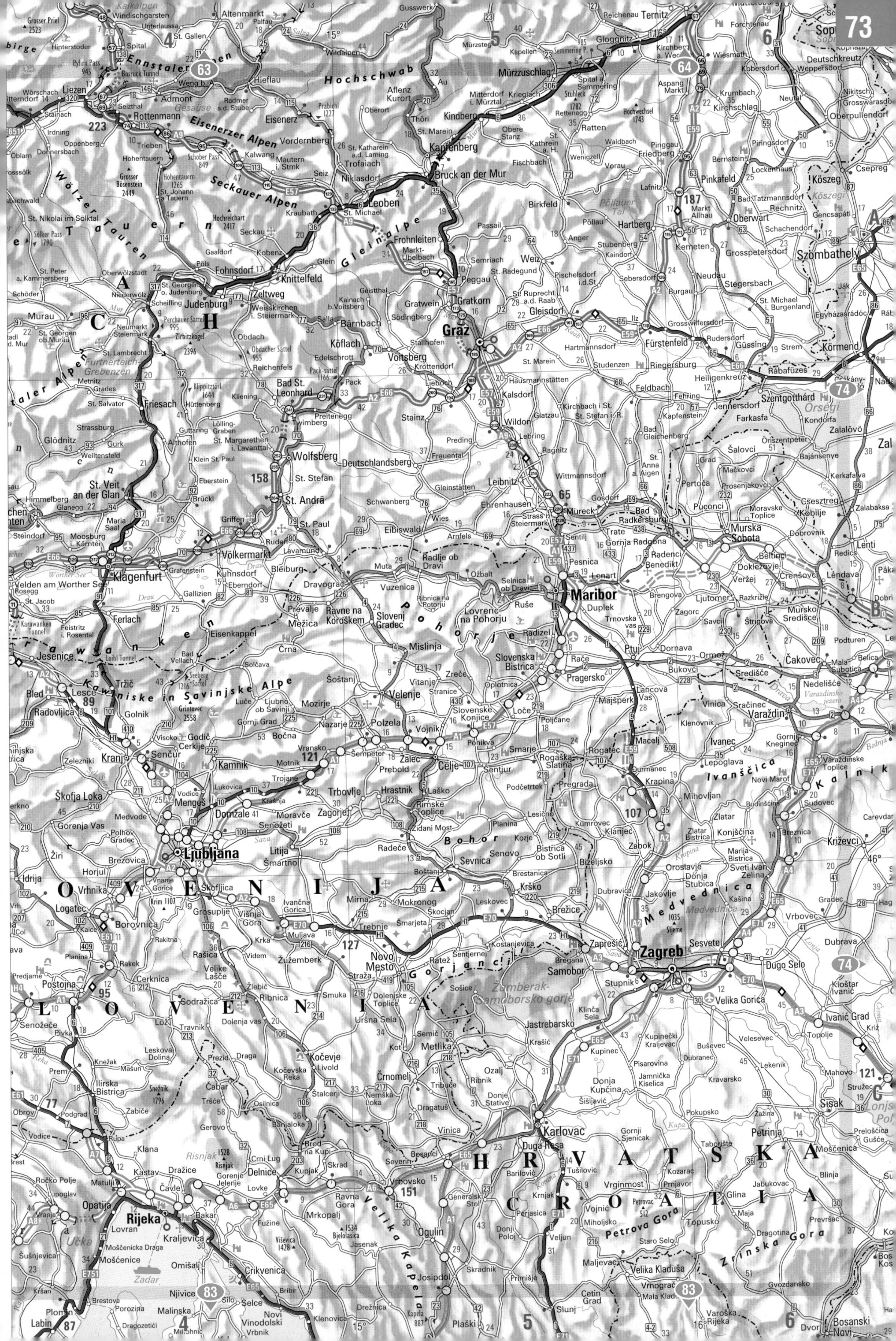
Ennstaler Alpen
Hochschwab
Eisenerzer Alpen
Seckauer Alpen
Wölzer Tauern
Gleinalpe
Pohorje
Karawanken
Kamniško-Savinjske Alpe
Ivanščica
Kalnik
Medvednica
Gorjanci
Bohor
Žumberak-Samoborsko gorje
Velika Kapela
Petrova Gora
Zrinska Gora
Učka
Risnjak
Pöllauer Tal
Windischgarsten
Altenmarkt
Gusswerk
Reichenau
Ternitz
Gloggnitz
Liezen
Admont
Hieflau
Eisenerz
Mürzzuschlag
Kindberg
Kapfenberg
Bruck an der Mur
Rottenmann
Trofaiach
Leoben
Mautern i. Stmk
Niklasdorf
St. Michael
Frohnleiten
Birkfeld
Friedberg
Pinkafeld
Hartberg
Oberwart
Köszeg
Szombathely
Weiz
Gleisdorf
Fürstenfeld
Körmend
Judenburg
Fohnsdorf
Knittelfeld
Zeltweg
Murau
Köflach
Voitsberg
Bärnbach
Graz
Gratkorn
Peggau
Kalsdorf
Wildon
Leibnitz
Feldbach
Riegersburg
Jennersdorf
Szentgotthárd
Rábafüzes
Güssing
Friesach
Bad St. Leonhard
Wolfsberg
St. Andrä
Deutschlandsberg
Stainz
Eibiswald
Mureck
Bad Radkersburg
St. Veit an der Glan
Klagenfurt
Völkermarkt
Velden am Worther See
Ferlach
Bleiburg
Dravograd
Ravne na Koroškem
Slovenj Gradec
Maribor
Ptuj
Murska Sobota
Lendava
Čakovec
Varaždin
Ormož
Slovenska Bistrica
Pragersko
Velenje
Celje
Žalec
Rogaška Slatina
Krapina
Jesenice
Bled
Radovljica
Tržič
Kranj
Kamnik
Domžale
Škofja Loka
Ljubljana
Trbovlje
Zagorje
Hrastnik
Litija
Sevnica
Krško
Brežice
Zaprešić
Zagreb
Samobor
Sesvete
Dugo Selo
Velika Gorica
Vrbovec
Križevci
Ivanić Grad
Sisak
Jastrebarsko
Karlovac
Duga Resa
Ogulin
Slunj
Novo Mesto
Metlika
Črnomelj
Kočevje
Ribnica
Grosuplje
Vrhnika
Logatec
Idrija
Postojna
Cerknica
Ilirska Bistrica
Rijeka
Opatija
Matulji
Kastav
Bakar
Kraljevica
Crikvenica
Delnice
Vrbovsko
Petrinja
Glina
Topusko
Velika Kladuša
Labin
Novi Vinodolski
Senj
Omišalj
Njivice
Malinska
SLOVENIJA
SLOVENIA
HRVATSKA
CROATIA
CH
Sava
Drava
Mur
Kupa
Krapina
Zadar
46°
15°
63
64
65
74
83
87
89
95
107
121
127
151
158
187
223

MAGYAR HUNG

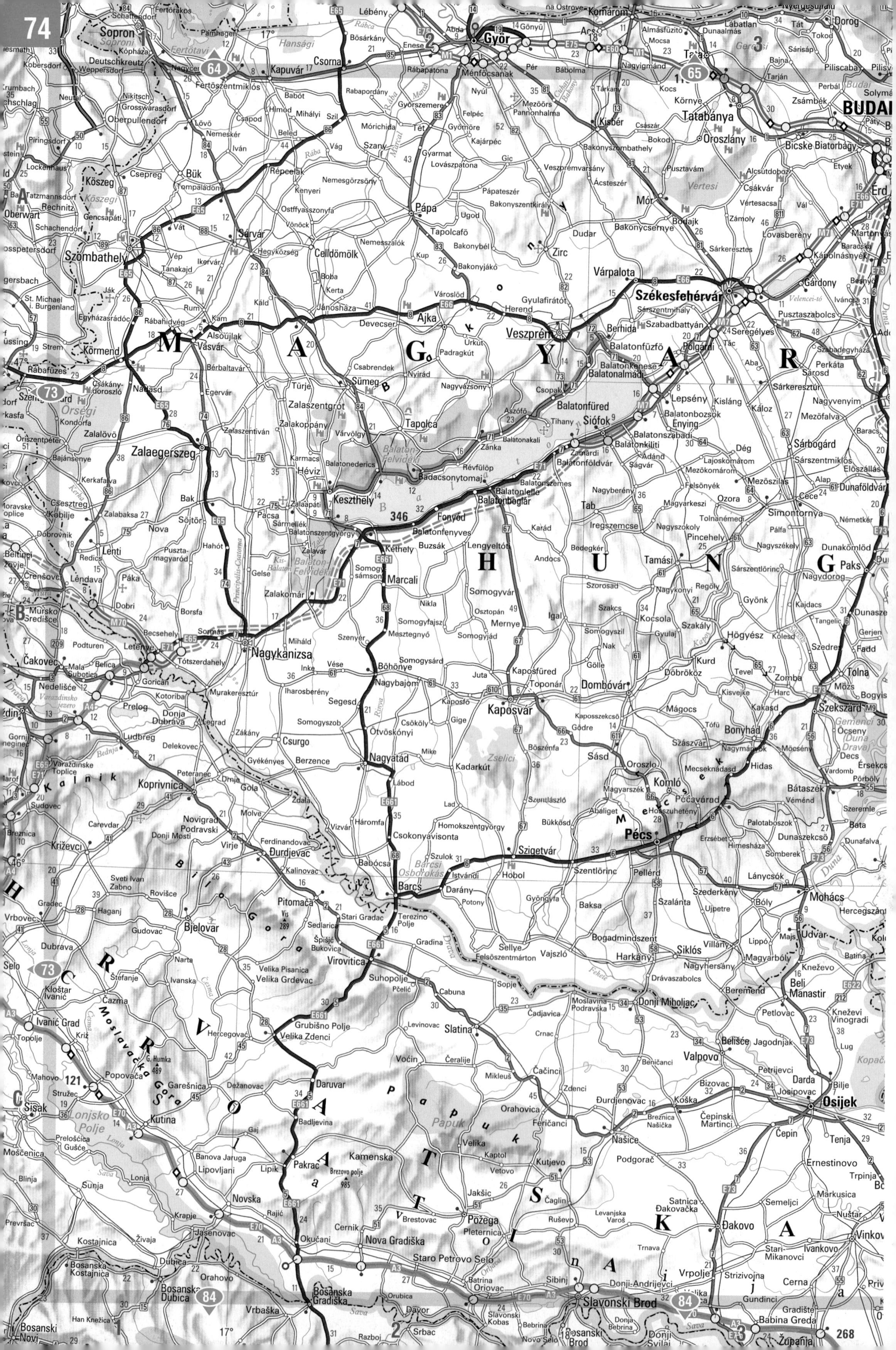

Sopron · Győr · Komárom · Tatabánya · BUDA

Szombathely · Pápa · Veszprém · Székesfehérvár

Körmend · Zalaegerszeg · Keszthely · Siófok · Balatonfüred

Nagykanizsa · Marcali · Kaposvár · Dombóvár · Pécs · Szekszárd

Koprivnica · Bjelovar · Virovitica · Barcs · Szigetvár · Mohács · Osijek

Sisak · Kutina · Daruvar · Pakrac · Požega · Slavonski Brod

HRVATSKA

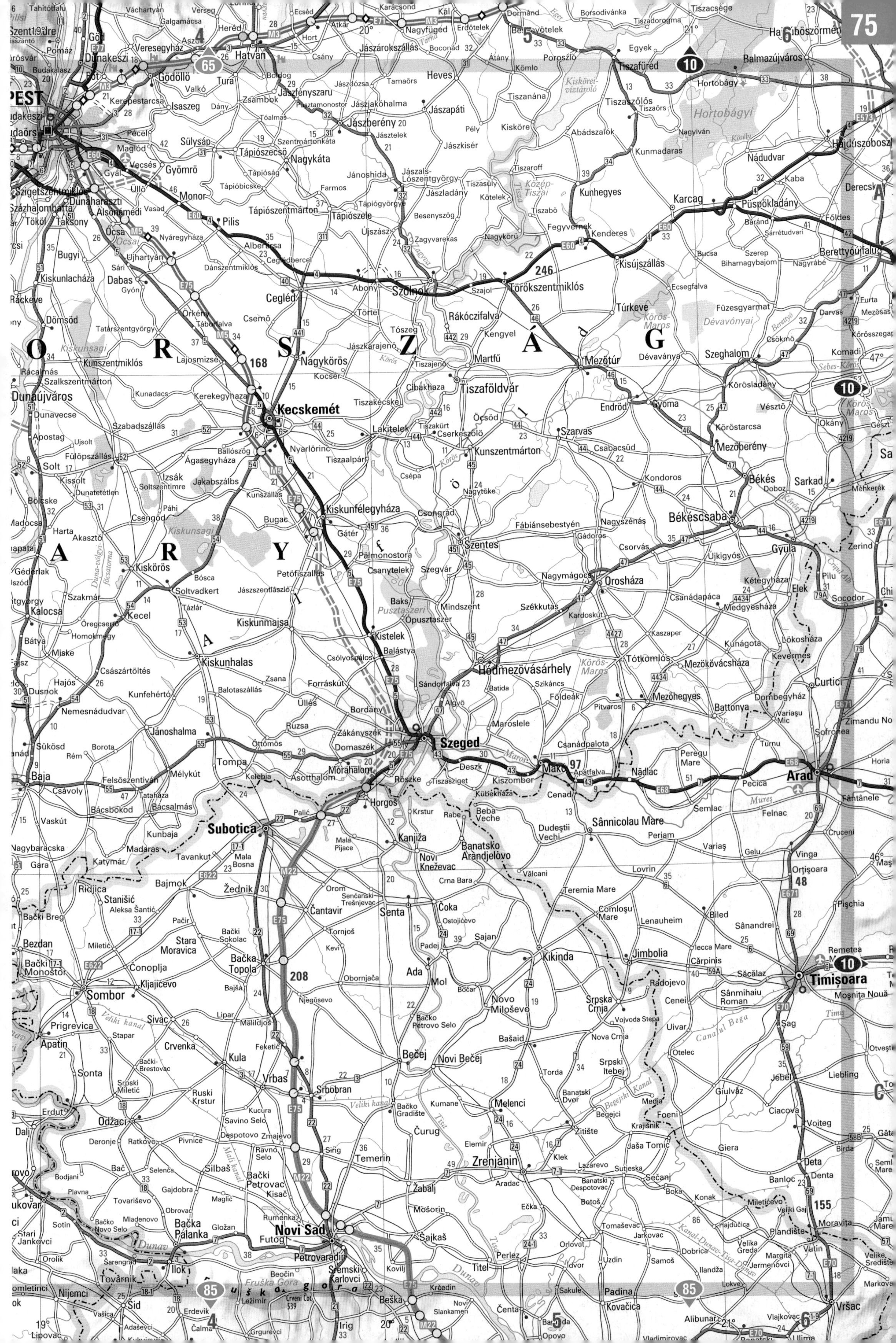

O R S Z Á G

...A R Y

PEST

Dunakeszi · Gödöllő · Hatvan · Aszód · Veresegyház · Fót

Kecskemét · Cegléd · Nagykőrös · Nagykáta · Jászberény · Heves · Tiszafüred · Balmazújváros · Hajdúszoboszló · Derecske · Berettyóújfalu

Szolnok · Törökszentmiklós · Túrkeve · Mezőtúr · Karcag · Püspökladány · Szeghalom · Komádi

Kiskunfélegyháza · Csongrád · Szentes · Kunszentmárton · Szarvas · Mezőberény · Békés · Békéscsaba · Gyula · Sarkad

Kiskunhalas · Kiskunmajsa · Kistelek · Hódmezővásárhely · Orosháza · Mezőhegyes · Battonya · Arad

Baja · Mórahalom · **Szeged** · Makó · Nădlac · Pecica · Nagykörös

Subotica · Horgoš · Kanjiža · Sânnicolau Mare · Jimbolia · **Timişoara**

Sombor · Bačka Topola · Senta · Kikinda · Zrenjanin · Vršac

Odžaci · Kula · Vrbas · Bečej · Novi Bečej

Novi Sad · Petrovaradin · Sremski Karlovci · Beška

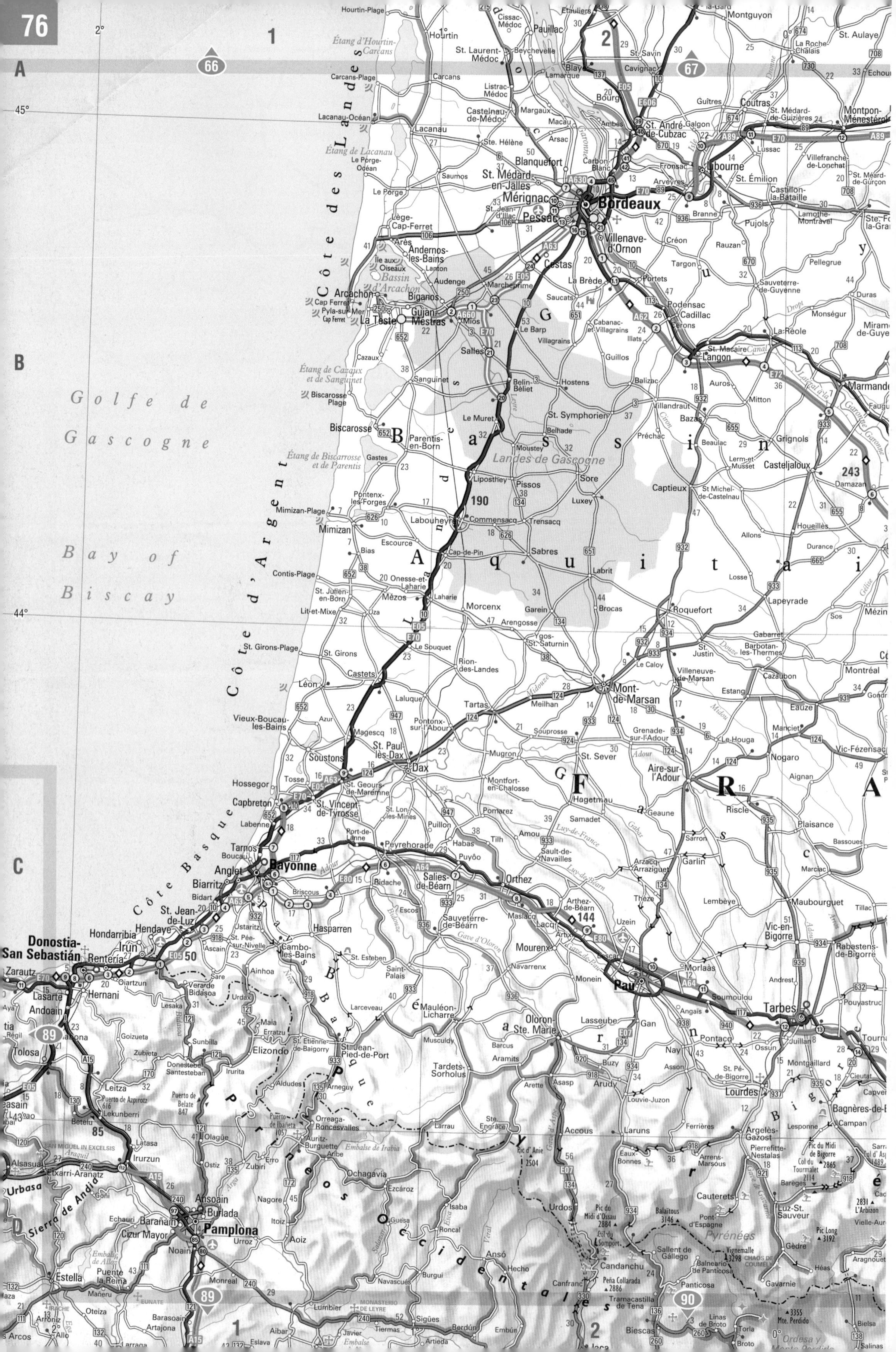
Golfe de Gascogne
Bay of Biscay
Côte des Landes
Côte d'Argent
Côte Basque
Landes de Gascogne
Aquitaine
Pyrénées Occidentales
Bordeaux
Mérignac
Pessac
Arcachon
Bassin d'Arcachon
Biscarosse
Mimizan
Mont-de-Marsan
Dax
Bayonne
Biarritz
Anglet
St. Jean-de-Luz
Hendaye
Irún
Donostia-San Sebastián
Pau
Tarbes
Lourdes
Orthez
Oloron-Ste. Marie
Pamplona
Libourne
Langon
Marmande
Casteljaloux
Aire-sur-l'Adour
Hagetmau
Sierra de Andía
Pic du Midi d'Ossau
Pic du Midi de Bigorre
Col du Tourmalet
Balaitous
Vignemale
Mte. Perdido
Ordesa y Monte Perdido

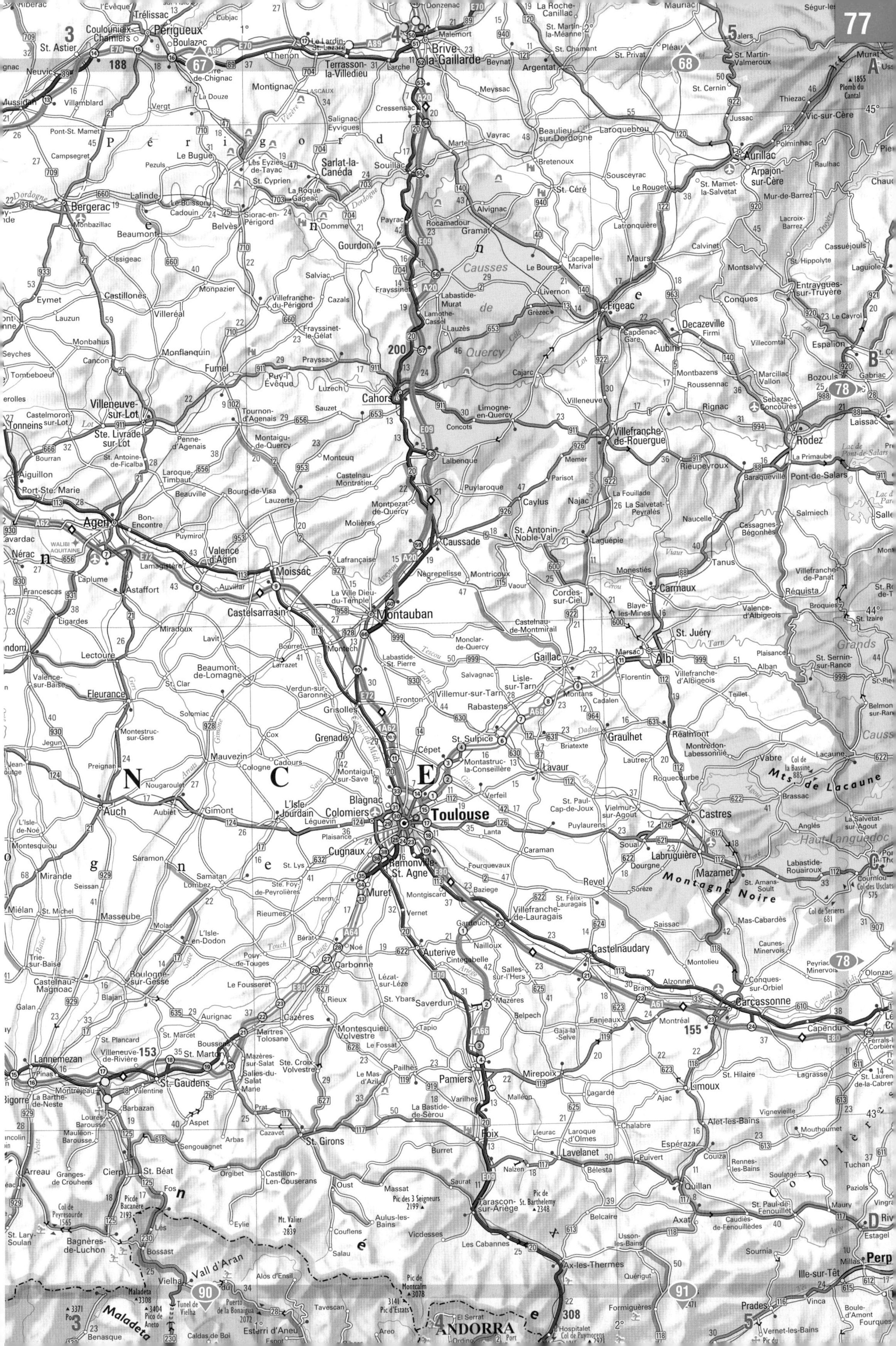
Périgueux
Boulazac
St. Astier
Coulounieix-Chamiers
Trélissac
Neuvic
Mussidan
Terrasson-la-Villedieu
Brive-la-Gaillarde
Malemort
Donzenac
Beynat
Argentat
St. Chamant
St. Privat
Pléaux
St. Martin-Valmeroux
Salers
Murat
Plomb du Cantal
Thiezac
Vic-sur-Cère
St. Cernin
Jussac
Aurillac
Arpajon-sur-Cère
Polminhac
St. Mamet-la-Salvetat
Mur-de-Barrez
Lacroix-Barrez
Cassuéjouls
Laguiole
St. Hippolyte
Montsalvy
Calvinet
Entraygues-sur-Truyère
Le Cayrol
Espalion
Bozouls
Gabriac
Conques
Villecomtal
Marcillac-Vallon
Sebazac-Concourès
Rodez
Laissac
La Primaube
Pont-de-Salars
Baraqueville
Rieupeyroux
Lac de Pont-de-Salars
Salmiech
Cassagnes-Bégonhès
Naucelle
Tanus
Villefranche-de-Panat
Réquista
Broquiès
St. Izaire
Carmaux
Monestiés
Valence-d'Albigeois
Albi
St. Juéry
Alban
Plaisance
St. Sernin-sur-Rance
Grands Causses
Belmon-sur-Rance
Lacaune
Mts de Lacaune
Col de la Bassine
Vabre
Brassac
Anglès
La Salvetat-sur-Agout
Haut-Languedoc
Labastide-Rouairoux
Mazamet
Montagne Noire
St. Amans-Soult
Col des Usclats
Col de Serieres
Mas-Cabardès
Caunes-Minervois
Peyriac-Minervois
Olonzac
Conques-sur-Orbiel
Carcassonne
Capendu
Ferrals-les-Corbières
Lagrasse
St. Laurent-de-la-Cabrerisse
Corbières
Mouthoumet
Vignevieille
Alet-les-Bains
Limoux
St. Hilaire
Tuchan
Paziols
Maury
Rennes-les-Bains
Soulatgé
Couiza
Espéraza
Quillan
Puivert
St. Paul-de-Fenouillet
Caudiès-de-Fenouillèdes
Axat
Estagel
Millas
Perpignan
Ille-sur-Têt
Vinca
Prades
Boule-d'Amont
Fourques
Vernet-les-Bains
Pic du Canigou
Quérigut
Usson-les-Bains
Formiguères
Ax-les-Thermes
Belcaire
Bélesta
Lavelanet
Laroque-d'Olmes
Lieurac
Foix
Tarascon-sur-Ariège
Pic de St. Barthelemy
Les Cabannes
Vicdessos
L'Hospitalet
Col de Puymorens
El Serrat
ANDORRA
Pic de Montcalm 3078
Pic d'Estats 3141
Tavescan
Areo
Esterri d'Aneu
Caldas de Boi
Puerto de la Bonaigua 2072
Tunel de Vielha
Vielha
Vall d'Aran
Bossost
Les
Fos
St. Béat
Cierp
Bagnères-de-Luchon
St. Lary-Soulan
Col de Peyresourde 1565
Picde Bacanère 2193
Pico de Aneto 3404
Maladeta
Benasque
Arreau
Granges-de Crouhens
Mauleon-Barousse
Loures-Barousse
Barbazan
Montréjeau
Lannemezan
La Barthe-de-Neste
Valentine
St.-Gaudens
Villeneuve-de-Rivière
St. Martory
Boussens
Mazères-sur-Salat
Salies-du-Salat
Mane
Aspet
Arbas
Sengouagnet
Orgibet
Castillon-en-Couserans
St. Girons
Oust
Massat
Aulus-les-Bains
Couflens
Salau
Pic des 3 Seigneurs 2199
Mt. Valier 2839
Saurat
Burret
La Bastide-de-Sérou
Varilhes
Pamiers
Mirepoix
Malléon
Lagarde
Chalabre
Ajac
Fanjeaux
Belpech
Mazères
Saverdun
Le Fossat
Pailhès
Le Mas-d'Azil
Tapio
Montesquieu-Volvestre
Ste. Croix-Volvestre
Prat
Cazavet
Rieux
St. Ybars
Lézat-sur-Lèze
Cazères
Martres Tolosane
Aurignac
St. Marcet
St. Plancard
Blajan
Boulogne-sur-Gesse
Castelnau-Magnoac
Galan
Trie-sur-Baïse
Masseube
L'Isle-en-Dodon
Molas
Pouy-de-Touges
Le Fousseret
Carbonne
Noé
Bérat
Auterive
Cintegabelle
Nailloux
Gardouch
Salles-sur-l'Hers
Villefranche-de-Lauragais
St. Félix-Lauragais
Revel
Sorèze
Saissac
Castelnaudary
Bram
Alzonne
Montolieu
Montréal
Dourgne
Labruguière
Soual
Castres
Puylaurens
Vielmur-sur-Agout
St. Paul-Cap-de-Joux
Caraman
Lanta
Fourquevaux
Baziège
Montgiscard
Vernet
Muret
Ramonville-St. Agne
Toulouse
Blagnac
Colomiers
Léguevin
Plaisance
Cugnaux
St. Lys
Ste. Foy-de-Peyrolières
Lherm
Rieumes
Samatan
Lombez
Saramon
Gimont
L'Isle-Jourdain
Aubiet
Auch
Mirande
Seissan
Montesquiou
L'Isle-de-Noé
Miélan
St. Michel
Jegun
Preignac
Montestruc-sur-Gers
Fleurance
Valence-sur-Baïse
Condom
Lectoure
Miradoux
St. Clar
Solomiac
Mauvezin
Cologne
Cadours
Cox
Grenade
Montaigut-sur-Save
Beaumont-de-Lomagne
Lavit
Larrazet
Bourret
Verdun-sur-Garonne
Grisolles
Fronton
Villemur-sur-Tarn
Bouloc
Cépet
St. Sulpice
Montastruc-la-Conseillère
Verfeil
Lavaur
Rabastens
Lisle-sur-Tarn
Salvagnac
Gaillac
Montans
Cadalen
Graulhet
Briatexte
Réalmont
Lautrec
Roquecourbe
Montredon-Labessonnié
Florentin
Marsac
Villefranche-d'Albigeois
Teillet
Castelnau-de-Montmirail
Cordes-sur-Ciel
Vaour
Blaye-les-Mines
Monclar-de-Quercy
Labastide-St. Pierre
Montech
Montauban
Castelsarrasin
La Ville Dieu-du-Temple
Moissac
Auvillar
Valence-d'Agen
Lamagistère
Astaffort
Laplume
Nérac
Francescas
Ligardes
Agen
Bon-Encontre
Layrac
Puymirol
Beauville
Bourg-de-Visa
Lauzerte
Montaigu-de-Quercy
Tournon-d'Agenais
Penne-d'Agenais
Villeneuve-sur-Lot
Ste. Livrade-sur-Lot
St. Antoine-de-Ficalba
Laroque-Timbaut
Castelmoron-sur-Lot
Tonneins
Aiguillon
Port-Ste. Marie
Bourran
Fumel
Monflanquin
Villeréal
Castillonès
Eymet
Lauzun
Monbahus
Cancon
Tombeboeuf
Seyches
Monpazier
Beaumont
Issigeac
Bergerac
Lalinde
Le Buisson
Cadouin
Belvès
Siorac-en-Périgord
Monbazillac
Le Bugue
Les Eyzies-de-Tayac
St. Cyprien
Périgord
Sarlat-la-Canéda
La Roque-Gageac
Domme
Souillac
Salignac-Eyvigues
Montignac
Lascaux
Thenon
Vergt
Pezuls
Campsegret
Pont-St. Mamet
Villamblard
Rouffignac
Cressensac
Martel
Vayrac
Beaulieu-sur-Dordogne
Bretenoux
Laroquebrou
Meyssac
Sousceyrac
Le Rouget
St. Céré
Latronquière
Maurs
Lacapelle-Marival
Le Bourg
Gramat
Alvignac
Rocamadour
Payrac
Gourdon
Salviac
Cazals
Frayssinet
Labastide-Murat
Lamothe-Cassel
Lauzès
Causses de Quercy
Livernon
Grèzec
Figeac
Capdenac-Gare
Decazeville
Firmi
Aubin
Montbazens
Roussennac
Rignac
Villeneuve
Cajarc
Limogne-en-Quercy
Concots
Villefranche-de-Rouergue
Memer
Parisot
Najac
La Fouillade
La Salvetat-Peyralès
Caylus
St. Antonin-Noble-Val
Laguépie
Puylaroque
Lalbenque
Montcuq
Castelnau-Montratier
Montpezat-de-Quercy
Molières
Caussade
Lafrançaise
Nègrepelisse
Montricoux
Cahors
Luzech
Prayssac
Puy-l'Évêque
Sauzet
Frayssinet-le-Gélat
Villefranche-du-Périgord
Walibi Aquitaine

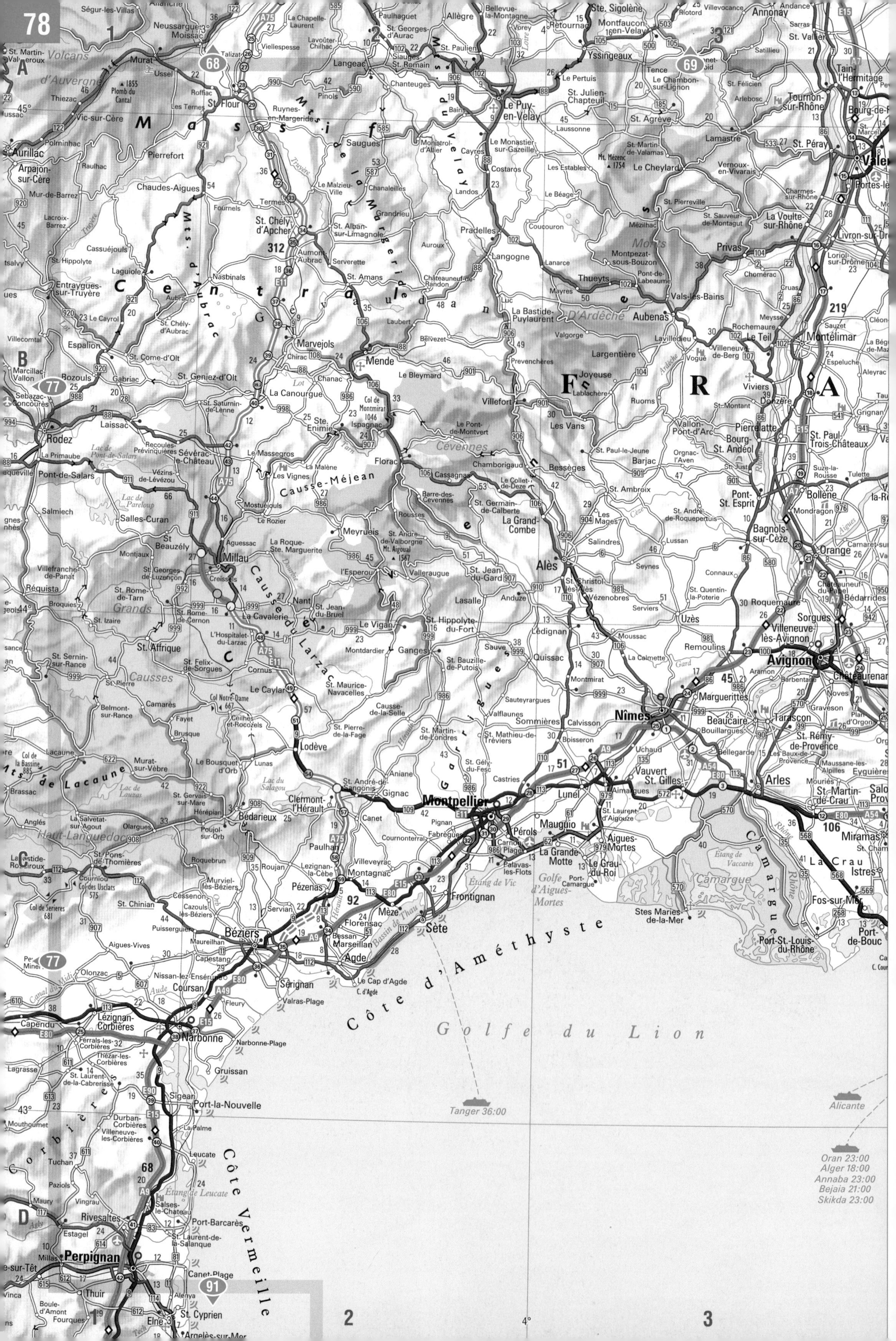
Ségur-les-Villas
Neussargues-Moissac
Murat
Ussel
Volcans d'Auvergne
Plomb du Cantal
Thiezac
Vic-sur-Cère
Aurillac
Arpajon-sur-Cère
Polminhac
Pierrefort
St. Flour
Massif Central
Chaudes-Aigues
Raulhac
Mur-de-Barrez
Lacroix-Barrez
Cassuéjouls
St. Hippolyte
Laguiole
Entraygues-sur-Truyère
Nasbinals
Aubrac
Mts. d'Aubrac
St. Chély-d'Aubrac
Le Cayrol
Espalion
St. Come-d'Olt
Bozouls
Gabriac
St. Geniez-d'Olt
Marcillac-Vallon
Sebazac-Concourès
Rodez
Laissac
La Primaube
Pont-de-Salars
Lac de Pont-de-Salars
Sévérac-le-Château
Recoules-Prévinquières
Vézins-de-Lévézou
Salmiech
Salles-Curan
Lac de Pareloup
St. Beauzély
Montjaux
Millau
Aguessac
Creissels
Villefranche-de-Panat
Réquista
St. Rome-de-Tarn
Broquiès
St. Izaire
St. Affrique
St. Sernin-sur-Rance
St. Félix-de-Sorgues
Causses
Belmont-sur-Rance
Camarès
Col Notre-Dame
Fayet
Brusque
Ceilhes-et-Rocozels
Lacaune
Mts. de Lacaune
Murat-sur-Vèbre
Le Bousquet-d'Orb
Lac du Salagou
Brassac
Lac de Laouzas
St. Gervais-sur-Mare
Hérépian
Bédarieux
La Salvetat-sur-Agout
Anglès
Olargues
Haut-Languedoc
Poujol-sur-Orb
La Bastide-Rouairoux
St. Pons-de-Thomières
Roquebrun
Courniou
Col des Usclats
Murviel-lès-Béziers
Cessenon
Col de Serieres
St. Chinian
Cazouls-lès-Béziers
Puisserguier
Aigues-Vives
Maureilhan
Béziers
Capestang
Olonzac
Nissan-lez-Enserune
Canal du Midi
Coursan
Aude
Capendu
Lézignan-Corbières
Fleury
Narbonne
Narbonne-Plage
Ferrals-les-Corbières
Thézan-les-Corbières
Lagrasse
St. Laurent-de-la-Cabrerisse
Gruissan
Sigean
Port-la-Nouvelle
Mouthoumet
Durban-Corbières
Villeneuve-les-Corbières
La Palme
Corbières
Tuchan
Leucate
Paziols
Vingrau
Étang de Leucate
Maury
Salses-le-Château
Rivesaltes
Agly
Estagel
Port-Barcarès
St. Laurent-de-la-Salanque
Millas
Perpignan
Canet-Plage
Thuir
Boule-d'Amont
Fourques
Elne
St. Cyprien
Alenya
Argelès-sur-Mer
Côte Vermeille
Langeac
Paulhaguet
St. Georges-d'Aurac
Allègre
La Chapelle-Laurent
Lavoûte-Chilhac
Siaugues-St. Romain
Chanteuges
Pinols
Ruynes-en-Margeride
Mts. de la Margeride
Saugues
Monistrol-d'Allier
Le Malzieu-Ville
Chanaleilles
Termes
Fournels
St. Chély-d'Apcher
St. Alban-sur-Limagnole
Grandrieu
Aumont-Aubrac
Serverette
St. Amans
Auroux
Châteauneuf-de-Randon
Laubert
Marvejols
Chirac
Mende
Chanac
La Canourgue
St. Saturnin-de-Lenne
Le Bleymard
Col de Montmirat
Ste. Enimie
Ispagnac
Le Massegros
Les Vignes
La Malène
Causse-Méjean
Florac
Mostuéjouls
Le Rozier
Meyrueis
La Roque-Ste. Marguerite
Mt. Aigoual
Causse du Larzac
Nant
St. Jean-du-Bruel
La Cavalerie
L'Hospitalet-du-Larzac
Cornus
Le Caylar
Le Vigan
Montdardier
Ganges
St. Maurice-Navacelles
Causse-de-la-Selle
St. Pierre-de-la-Fage
Lodève
Lunas
St. André-de-Sangonis
Clermont-l'Hérault
Gignac
Aniane
Canet
Paulhan
Lezignan-la-Cèbe
Montagnac
Pézenas
Servian
Florensac
Bessan
Marseillan
Agde
Le Cap d'Agde
Sérignan
Valras-Plage
Mèze
Bassin de Thau
Sète
Frontignan
Villeveyrac
Montpellier
Pignan
Cournonterral
Fabrègues
Palavas-les-Flots
Pérols
Carnon Plage
Mauguio
La Grande-Motte
Lunel
Castries
Étang de Vic
Golfe d'Aigues-Mortes
Le Grau-du-Roi
Aigues-Mortes
Port-Camargue
Côte d'Améthyste
Golfe du Lion
Tanger 36:00
Le Puy-en-Velay
Mts. du Velay
Vorey
Bellevue-la-Montagne
St. Paulien
Le Monastier-sur-Gazeille
Cayres
Costaros
Landos
Pradelles
Langogne
Le Bouchet
Coucouron
Le Béage
Les Estables
Mt. Mézenc
Laussonne
Lanarce
Thueyts
Mayres
La Bastide-Puylaurent
Le Pont-de-Montvert
Cévennes
Villefort
Prévenchères
Les Vans
Chamborigaud
Le Collet-de-Dèze
Bessèges
Cassagnas
Barre-des-Cévennes
St. Germain-de-Calberte
La Grand-Combe
Rousses
Valleraugue
L'Esperou
St. Jean-du-Gard
Lasalle
Anduze
St. Hippolyte-du-Fort
Alès
St. Christol-lès-Alès
Vézenobres
Lédignan
Sauve
Quissac
St. Bauzille-de-Putois
Garrigues
Sauteyrargues
Valflaunes
St. Martin-de-Londres
St. Mathieu-de-Tréviers
St. Gély-du-Fesc
Sommières
Calvisson
Boisseron
Montmirat
Nîmes
Uchaud
Vauvert
St. Gilles
Aimargues
St. Laurent-d'Aigouze
Yssingeaux
Retournac
Ste. Sigolène
Montfaucon-en-Velay
Riotord
Annonay
Tence
Le Chambon-sur-Lignon
St. Julien-Chapteuil
St. Agrève
Le Pertuis
St. Martin-de-Valamas
Le Cheylard
Lamastre
Vernoux-en-Vivarais
St. Pierreville
St. Sauveur-de-Montagut
Mézilhac
Montpezat-sous-Bouzon
Pont-de-Labeaume
Monts du Vivarais
Privas
Vals-les-Bains
Aubenas
Largentière
Joyeuse
Lablachère
Ruoms
Vallon-Pont-d'Arc
Barjac
St. Paul-le-Jeune
St. Ambroix
Les Mages
Salindres
Lussan
Seynes
St. Quentin-la-Poterie
Uzès
Serviers
Moussac
La Calmette
Remoulins
Marguerittes
Beaucaire
Bouillargues
Bellegarde
Arles
Tarascon
St. Rémy-de-Provence
Maussane-les-Alpilles
Les Baux-de-Provence
St. Martin-de-Crau
La Crau
Camargue
Étang de Vaccarès
Stes Maries-de-la-Mer
Port-St.-Louis-du-Rhône
Fos-sur-Mer
Port-de-Bouc
Istres
Miramas
Eyguières
Graveson
Avignon
Villeneuve-lès-Avignon
Châteaurenard
Roquemaure
Sorgues
Bédarrides
Châteauneuf-du-Pape
Orange
Bagnols-sur-Cèze
Pont-St. Esprit
Mondragon
Bollène
Suze-la-Rousse
St. Paul-Trois-Châteaux
Pierrelatte
Bourg-St. Andéol
Donzère
Viviers
Le Teil
Montélimar
Villeneuve-de-Berg
Rochemaure
Meysse
Cruas
Chomérac
La Voulte-sur-Rhône
Livron-sur-Drôme
Loriol-sur-Drôme
Charmes-sur-Rhône
St. Péray
Tournon-sur-Rhône
Tain-l'Hermitage
St. Vallier
Andance
Sarras
Satillieu
St. Félicien
Arlebosc
Alicante
Oran 23:00
Alger 18:00
Annaba 23:00
Bejaia 21:00
Skikda 23:00
FRANCE

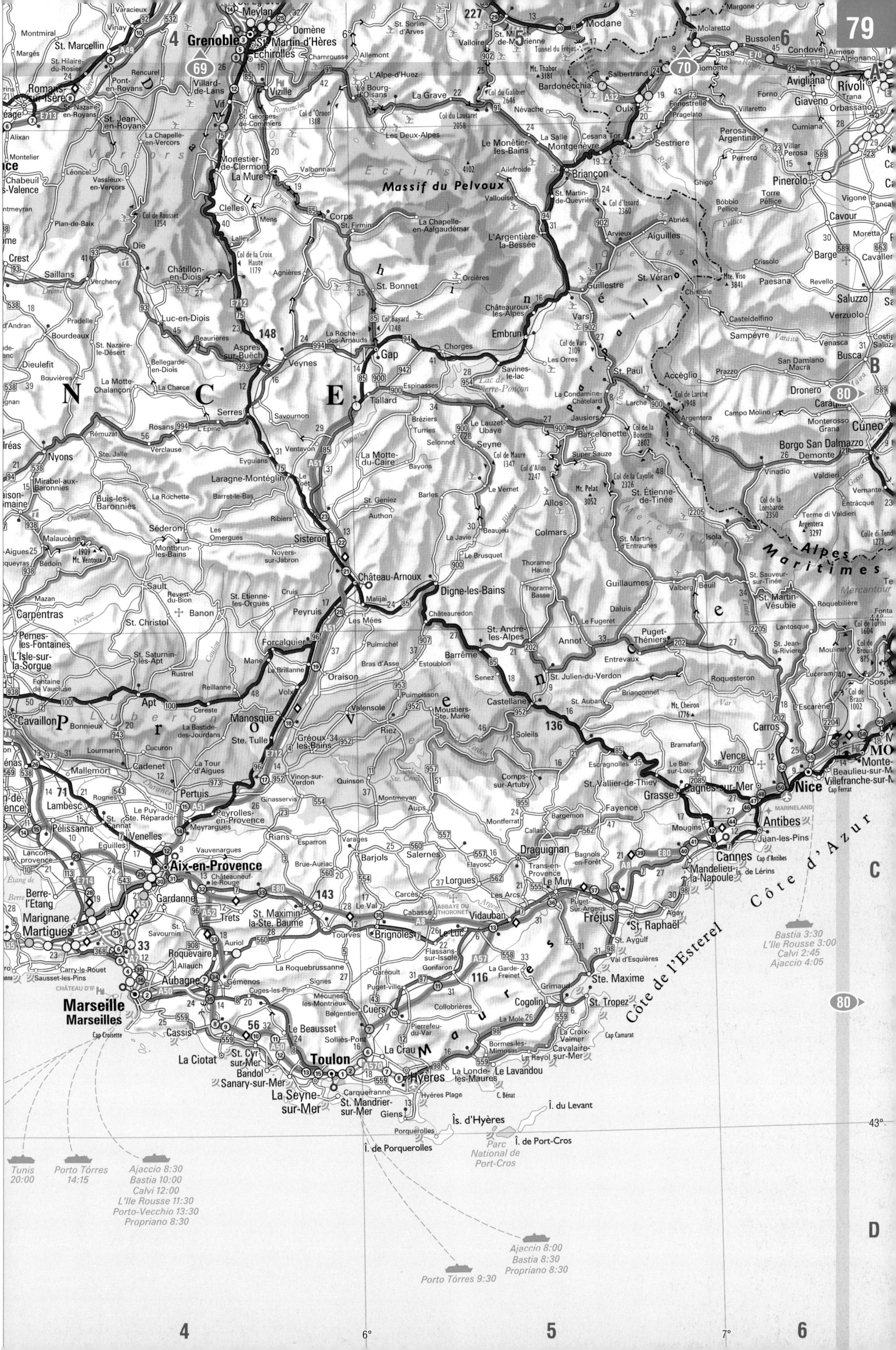
Grenoble
Meylan
St. Martin-d'Hères
Echirolles
Modane
Valloire
Bardonècchia
Susa
Rívoli
Pinerolo
Briançon
Massif du Pelvoux
Ecrins
Vercors
Gap
Embrun
Guillestre
Barcelonette
Digne-les-Bains
Sisteron
Château-Arnoux
Forcalquier
Manosque
Apt
Cavaillon
Carpentras
Nyons
Die
Crest
Dronero
Cúneo
Saluzzo
Alpes Maritimes
Castellane
Grasse
Nice
Cannes
Antibes
Fréjus
St. Raphaël
Draguignan
Brignoles
Aix-en-Provence
Marseille
Marseilles
Martigues
Aubagne
Toulon
Hyères
La Ciotat
Cassis
St. Tropez
Ste. Maxime
Côte d'Azur
Côte de l'Esterel
Î. du Levant
Îs. d'Hyères
Î. de Port-Cros
Î. de Porquerolles
Parc National de Port-Cros
Tunis 20:00
Porto Tórres 14:15
Ajaccio 8:30
Bastia 10:00
Calvi 12:00
L'Ile Rousse 11:30
Porto-Vecchio 13:30
Propriano 8:30
Ajaccio 8:00
Bastia 8:30
Propriano 8:30
Porto Tórres 9:30
Bastia 3:30
L'Ile Rousse 3:00
Calvi 2:45
Ajaccio 4:05
43°
6°
7°
4
5
6
A
B
C
D
69
70
80

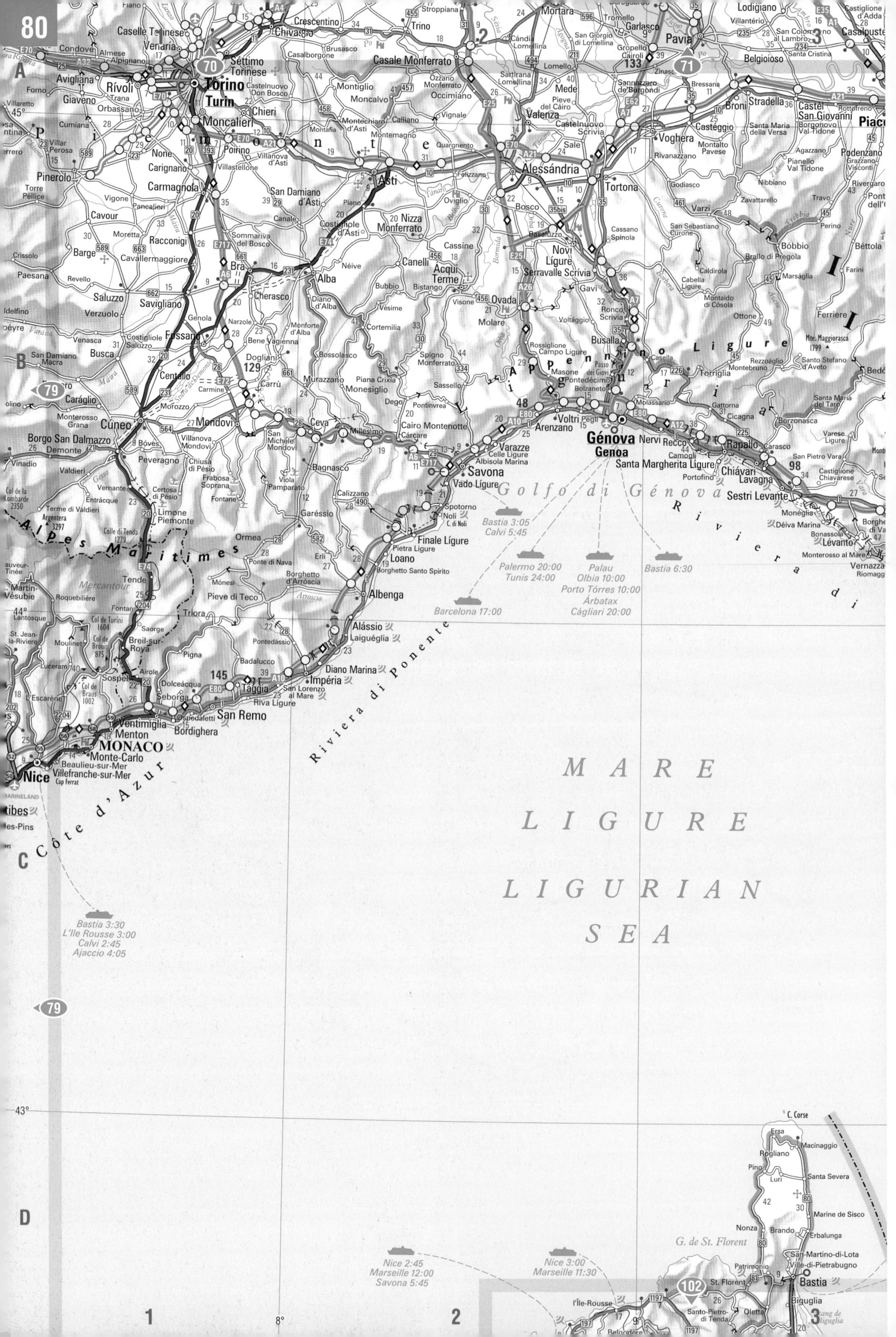
Torino
Turin
Moncalieri
Chieri
Rívoli
Pinerolo
Carmagnola
Asti
Alessándria
Casale Monferrato
Valenza
Tortona
Voghera
Pavia
Stradella
Piacenza
Alba
Bra
Savigliano
Saluzzo
Fossano
Cúneo
Mondovì
Ceva
Acqui Terme
Ovada
Novi Lígure
Serravalle Scrívia
Génova
Genoa
Nervi
Recco
Camogli
Rapallo
Santa Margherita Ligure
Portofino
Chiávari
Lavagna
Sestri Levante
Bóbbio
Varazze
Savona
Vado Lígure
Finale Lígure
Loano
Albenga
Alássio
Diano Marina
Impéria
Sanremo
San Remo
Bordighera
Ventimiglia
Menton
MONACO
Monte-Carlo
Beaulieu-sur-Mer
Villefranche-sur-Mer
Nice
Golfo di Génova
Riviera di Ponente
Riviera di Levante
Côte d'Azur
Alpes Maritimes
Piemonte
Appennino Ligure
MARE LIGURE
LIGURIAN SEA
Bastia 3:05
Calvi 5:45
Palermo 20:00
Tunis 24:00
Palau
Olbia 10:00
Porto Tórres 10:00
Árbatax
Cágliari 20:00
Bastia 6:30
Barcelona 17:00
Bastia 3:30
L'Ile Rousse 3:00
Calvi 2:45
Ajaccio 4:05
Nice 2:45
Marseille 12:00
Savona 5:45
Nice 3:00
Marseille 11:30
C. Corse
Macinaggio
Rogliano
Santa Severa
Marine de Sisco
Erbalunga
G. de St. Florent
St. Florent
Bastia
Biguglia
l'Île-Rousse
45°
44°
43°
8°
A
B
C
D
1
2
3
70
71
79
102

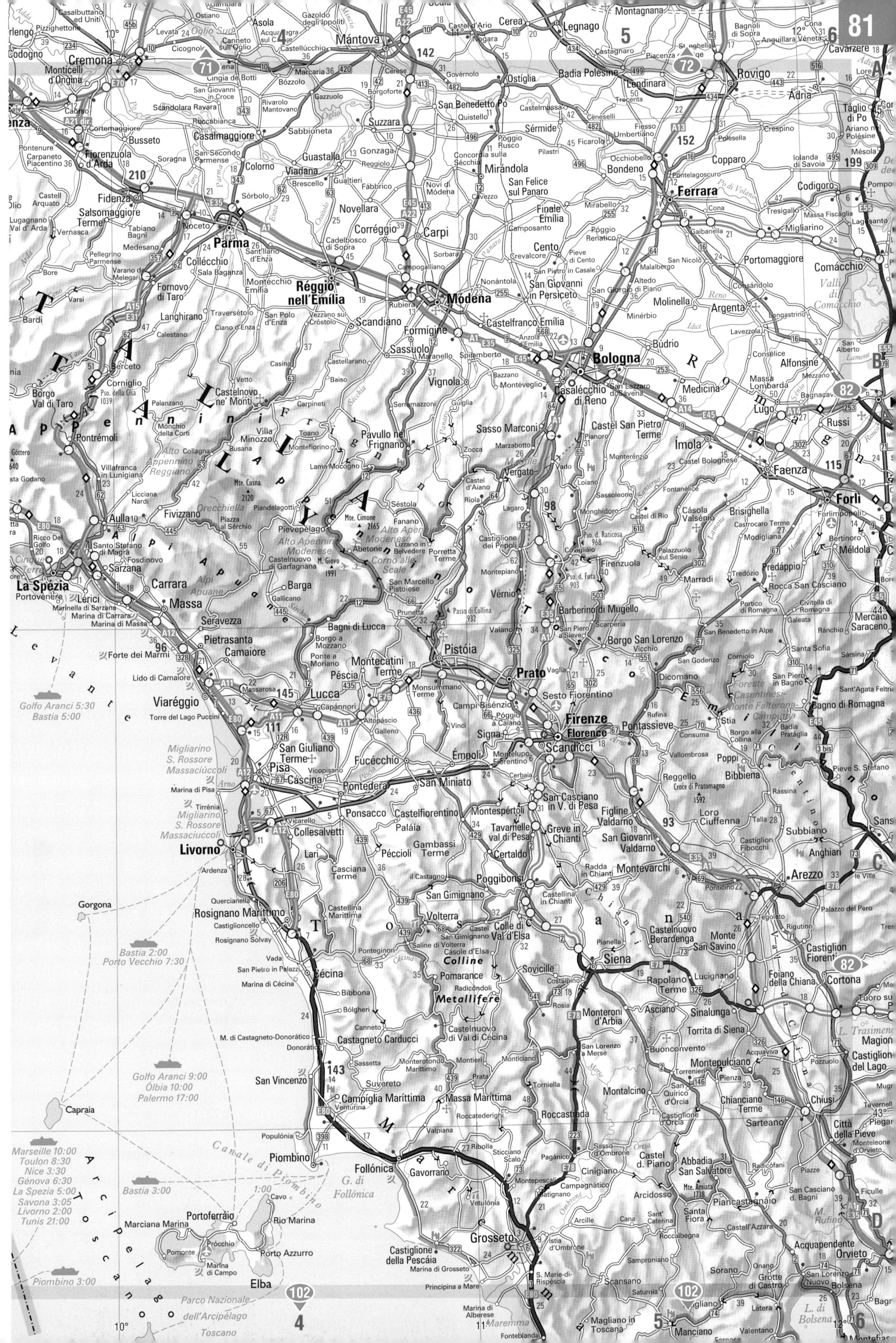

Cremona
Codogno
Casalbuttano ed Uniti
Pizzighettone
Monticelli d'Ongina
Asola
Mantova
Cerea
Legnago
Montagnana
Castagnaro
Badia Polesine
Lendinara
Rovigo
Adria
Cavarzere
Taglio di Po
Ariano nel Polésine
Mésola
Codigoro
Comácchio
Valli di Comácchio
Ostíglia
Governolo
Borgoforte
San Benedetto Po
Suzzara
Sabbioneta
Casalmaggiore
Busseto
Fiorenzuola d'Arda
Cortemaggiore
Fidenza
Salsomaggiore Terme
Noceto
Parma
Colorno
Guastalla
Gonzaga
Viadana
Novellara
Corréggio
Carpi
Concordia sulla Sécchia
Mirándola
San Felice sul Panaro
Finale Emília
Sérmide
Bondeno
Ferrara
Copparo
Portomaggiore
Cento
San Giovanni in Persiceto
Réggio nell'Emília
Módena
Castelfranco Emília
Bologna
Casalécchio di Reno
San Lazzaro di Sàvena
Medicina
Molinella
Argenta
Búdrio
Imola
Castel San Pietro Terme
Castel Bolognese
Lugo
Faenza
Forlì
Russi
Alfonsine
Massa Lombarda
Brisighella
Predáppio
Méldola
Sassuolo
Formígine
Maranello
Vignola
Scandiano
Langhirano
Collécchio
Fornovo di Taro
Bardi
Berceto
Borgo Val di Taro
Pontrémoli
Aulla
Villafranca in Lunigiana
Castelnovo ne' Monti
Pavullo nel Frignano
Sasso Marconi
Vergato
Sestola
Fanano
Pievepelago
Abetone
Mte. Cimone 2165
Mte. Cusna 2120
Fivizzano
Sarzana
La Spézia
Portovenere
Lérici
Carrara
Massa
Seravezza
Pietrasanta
Camaiore
Forte dei Marmi
Viaréggio
Lucca
Bagni di Lucca
Barga
Castelnuovo di Garfagnana
Porretta Terme
Pistóia
Montecatini Terme
Péscia
Prato
Firenze
Florence
Sesto Fiorentino
Scandicci
Empoli
Fucécchio
San Miniato
Pisa
Cascina
Pontedera
Livorno
Collesalvetti
Rosignano Maríttimo
Cécina
Volterra
San Gimignano
Poggibonsi
Colle di Val d'Elsa
Siena
Montevarchi
Arezzo
Figline Valdarno
San Giovanni Valdarno
Pontassieve
Borgo San Lorenzo
Firenzuola
Marradi
Barberino di Mugello
Poppi
Bibbiena
Cortona
Castiglion Fiorentino
Montepulciano
Chiusi
Sinalunga
Montalcino
Chianciano Terme
Città della Pieve
Orvieto
Acquapendente
Bolsena
L. di Bolsena
Grosseto
Castiglione della Pescáia
Follónica
Piombino
Campíglia Maríttima
San Vincenzo
Massa Maríttima
Roccastrada
Portoferraio
Elba
Capraia
Gorgona
Marciana Marina
Rio Marina
Porto Azzurro
Arcipelago Toscano
Canale di Piombino
G. di Follónica
Colline Metallifere
Mte. Amiata 1738
Abbadia San Salvatore
Piancastagnáio
Manciano
Magliano in Toscana
Scansano
Orbetello
Golfo Aranci 5:30
Bastia 5:00
Bastia 2:00
Porto Vecchio 7:30
Golfo Aranci 9:00
Ólbia 10:00
Palermo 17:00
Marseille 10:00
Toulon 8:30
Nice 3:30
Génova 6:30
La Spezia 5:00
Savona 3:05
Livorno 2:00
Tunis 21:00
Bastia 3:00
Piombino 3:00
Parco Nazionale dell'Arcipélago Toscano

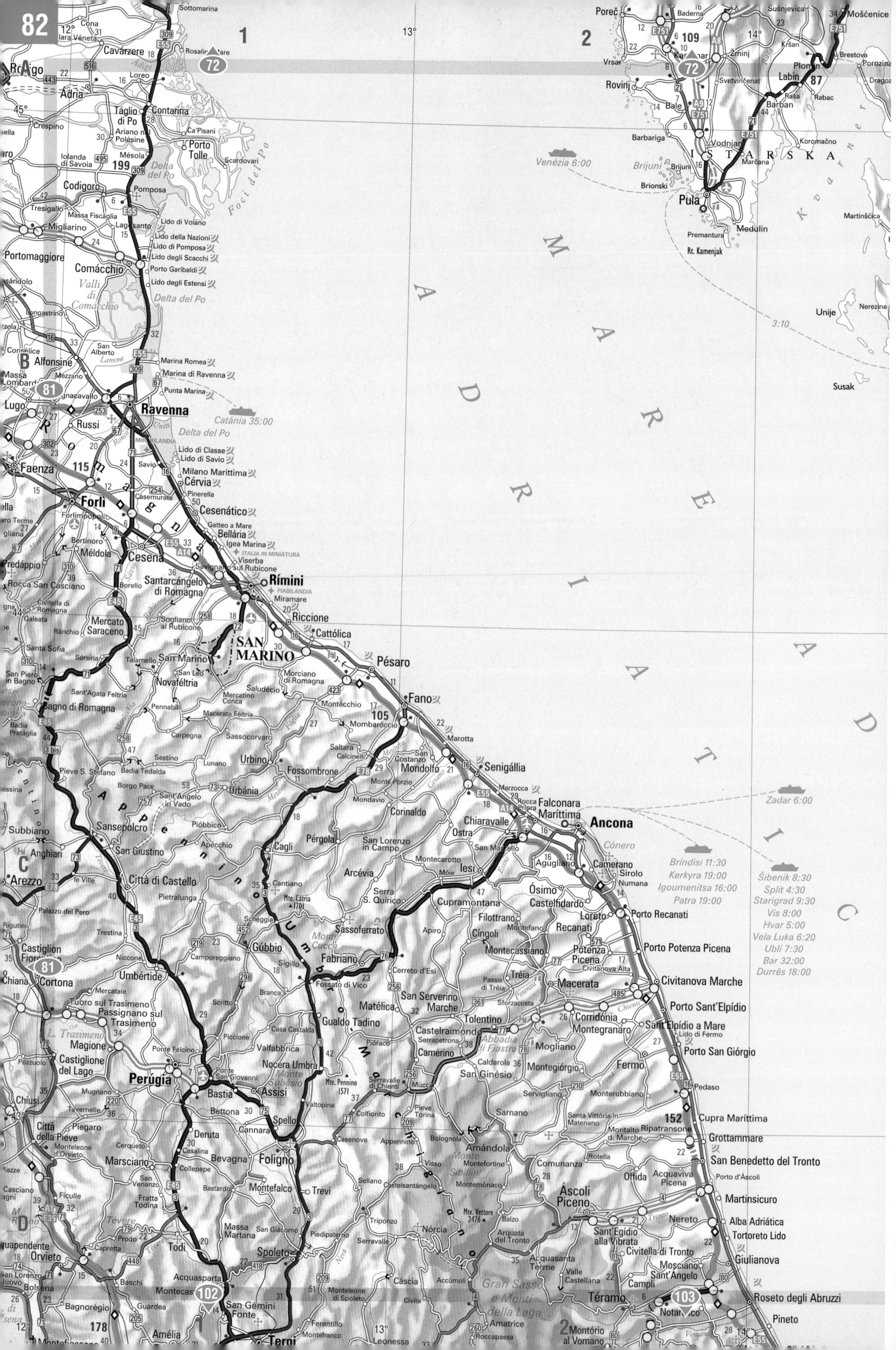
1
2
13°
14°
12°
A
B
C
D
Sottomarina
Cona
Cavarzere
Rosalina Mare
72
Adria
Loreo
Rovigo
Contarina
Táglio di Po
Ariano nel Polésine
Ca'Pisani
Porto Tolle
Scardovari
Mésola
Iolanda di Savoia
Delta del Po
Codigoro
Pomposa
Foci del Po
Tresigallo
Massa Fiscáglia
Lagosanto
Migliarino
Lido di Volano
Lido delle Nazioni
Lido di Pomposa
Lido degli Scacchi
Porto Garibaldi
Lido degli Estensi
Portomaggiore
Comácchio
Valli di Comácchio
Longastrino
Conselice
Alfonsine
San Alberto
Marina Romea
Marina di Ravenna
Punta Marina
Massa Lombarda
Bagnacavallo
Lugo
Ravenna
Russi
Catánia 35:00
Lido di Classe
Lido di Savio
Milano Marittima
Cérvia
Pinerella
Cesenático
Faenza
Forlì
Forlimpopoli
Bertinoro
Méldola
Cesena
Gatteo a Mare
Bellária
Igea Marina
Italia in Miniatura
Viserba
Savignano sul Rubicone
Predáppio
Rocca San Casciano
Santarcángelo di Romagna
Rímini
Fiabilandia
Miramare
Riccione
Civitella di Romagna
Galeata
Mercato Saraceno
Sogliano al Rubicone
Cattólica
Santa Sofia
Sársina
San Marino
SAN MARINO
Pésaro
Novaféltria
San Leo
Morciano di Romagna
San Piero in Bagno
Bagno di Romagna
Sant'Agata Feltria
Saludécio
Mercatino Conca
Fano
Pennabilli
Montécchio
Macerata Féltria
Mombaróccio
Badia Pratáglia
Carpegna
Sassocorvaro
Marotta
Sestino
Lunano
Urbino
Saltara
Calcinelli
Fossombrone
San Costanzo
Mondolfo
Senigállia
Pieve S. Stefano
Badia Tedalda
Borgo Pace
Sant'Angelo in Vado
Urbánia
Monte Porzio
Mondavio
Corinaldo
Marzocca
Falconara Maríttima
Rocca Priora
Ancona
Sansepolcro
Piobbico
Chiaravalle
Ostra
Subbiano
Anghiari
San Giustino
Apécchio
Cagli
Pérgola
San Lorenzo in Campo
Montecarotto
San Marcello
Agugliano
Camerano
Cónero
Sirolo
Numana
Arezzo
Città di Castello
Cantiano
Arcévia
Móie
Iesi
Ósimo
Castelfidardo
Loreto
Porto Recanati
Palazzo del Pero
Pietralunga
Mte. Cátria 1701
Serra S. Quírico
Cupramontana
Filottrano
Recanati
Trestina
Schéggia
Sassoferrato
Monte Cucco
Apiro
Cíngoli
Montefano
Montecassiano
Potenza Picena
Porto Potenza Picena
Castiglion Fiorentino
Niccone
Camporeggiano
Gúbbio
Fabriano
Cerreto d'Esi
Tréia
Passo di Tréia
Civitanova Alta
Civitanova Marche
Cortona
Umbértide
Sigillo
Fossato di Vico
Macerata
Mercatale
Branca
Matélica
San Severino Marche
Sforzacosta
Porto Sant'Elpídio
Tuoro sul Trasimeno
Passignano sul Trasimeno
Scritto
Gualdo Tadino
Tolentino
Corridónia
Sant'Elpídio a Mare
Lido di Fermo
L. Trasimeno
Magione
Piccione
Casa Castalda
Castelraimondo
Serrapetrona
Abbadia di Fiastra
Montegranaro
Porto San Giórgio
Castiglione del Lago
Ponte Felcino
Valfabbrica
Pióraco
Camerino
Mogliano
Fermo
Pozzuolo
Perúgia
Ponte San Giovanni
Nocera Umbra
Monte Subásio
Mte. Pennino 1571
Serravalle di Chienti
Múccia
Caldarola
San Ginésio
Montegiórgio
Pedaso
Chiusi
Mugnano
Bastia
Assisi
Colfiorito
Servigliano
Monterubbiano
Tavernelle
Bettona
Spello
Valtopina
Pieve Torina
Sarnano
Santa Vittória in Matenano
Cupra Maríttima
Città della Pieve
Piegaro
Monteleone d'Orvieto
Cerqueto
Deruta
Cannara
Casenove
Appennino
Bolognola
Amándola
Montalto d. Marche
Ripatransone
Grottammare
Casalina
Collepepe
Marsciano
Bevagna
Foligno
Visso
Monte Sibillini
Montefortino
Comunanza
Rotella
San Benedetto del Tronto
San Venanzo
Bastardo
Montefalco
Trevi
Sellano
Castelsantángelo
Montemónaco
Offida
Acquaviva Picena
Porto d'Ascoli
Ficulle
Fratta Todina
Ascoli Piceno
Martinsicuro
Tévere
Prodo
Massa Martana
San Giácomo
Tripozzo
Nórcia
Mte. Vettore 2476
Balzo
Arquata del Tronto
Sant'Egídio alla Vibrata
Nereto
Alba Adriática
Tortoreto Lido
Orvieto
Capretta
Todi
Spoleto
Piedipaterno
Serravalle
Civitella di Tronto
Giulianova
Acquasanta Terme
Mosciano Sant'Angelo
Baschi
Acquasparta
Valle Castellana
Campli
Bolsena
Bagnorégio
Guardea
Montecastrilli
102
San Gémini Fonte
Cáscia
Accúmoli
Gran Sasso e Monti della Laga
Téramo
103
Notaresco
Roseto degli Abruzzi
Pineto
Amélia
Terni
Ferentillo
Montefranco
Monteleone di Spoleto
Civita
Leonessa
Amatrice
Roccapassa
Montório al Vomano
Poreč
Baderna
Sušnjevica
Mošćenice
Vrsar
Kanfanar
Žminj
Kršan
Brestova
Plomin
Labin
Porozina
Rovinj
Svetvinčenat
Rabac
Raša
Barban
Bale
Barbariga
Vodnjan
Koromačno
Marčana
ISTARSKA
Venézia 6:00
Brijuni
Brionski
Pula
Medulin
Premantura
Rt. Kamenjak
Martinšćica
Kvarner
MARE ADRIATICO
Unije
Nerezine
Susak
3:10
Zadar 6:00
Bríndisi 11:30
Kerkyra 19:00
Igoumenitsa 16:00
Patra 19:00
Šibenik 8:30
Split 4:30
Starigrad 9:30
Vis 8:00
Hvar 5:00
Vela Luka 6:20
Ubli 7:30
Bar 32:00
Durrës 18:00
Appennino Umbro Marchigiano
Romagna
E45
E55
E78
E751
A14
A8
A9

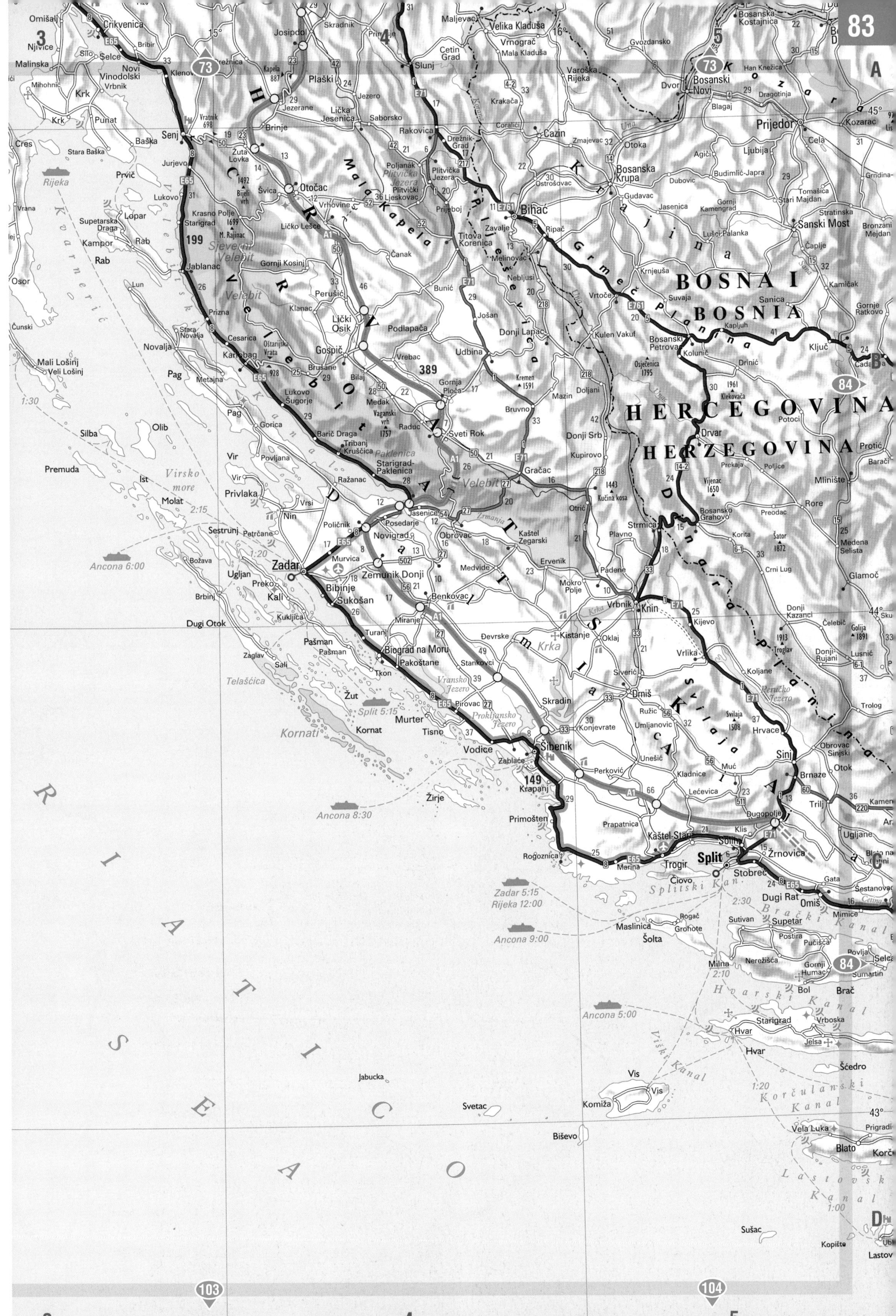
HRVATSKA
BOSNA I HERCEGOVINA
BOSNIA HERZEGOVINA
MARE ADRIATICO
Krajina
Grmeč Planina
Velebit
Velebitski Kanal
Kvarnerić
Mala Kapela
Plješevica
Dinara
Svilaja
Kozara
Dalmacija
Kornati
Rijeka
Crikvenica
Novi Vinodolski
Krk
Senj
Otočac
Plitvička Jezera
Gospić
Karlobag
Pag
Novalja
Mali Lošinj
Rab
Zadar
Nin
Biograd na Moru
Benkovac
Knin
Drniš
Šibenik
Vodice
Primošten
Trogir
Kaštel-Stari
Split
Solin
Sinj
Omiš
Brač
Hvar
Vis
Komiža
Bihać
Cazin
Velika Kladuša
Bosanska Krupa
Bosanski Novi
Bosanski Petrovac
Drvar
Ključ
Sanski Most
Prijedor
Bosansko Grahovo
Glamoč
Livno
Ancona 6:00
Ancona 8:30
Ancona 9:00
Ancona 5:00
Zadar 5:15
Rijeka 12:00
Split 5:15
Lastovski Kanal
Korčulanski Kanal
Hvarski Kanal
Viški Kanal
Brački Kanal
Splitski Kan.
Virsko more
Jabucka
Svetac
Biševo
Sušac
Vela Luka
Blato
Kopište
Lastovo
15°
16°
45°
44°
43°

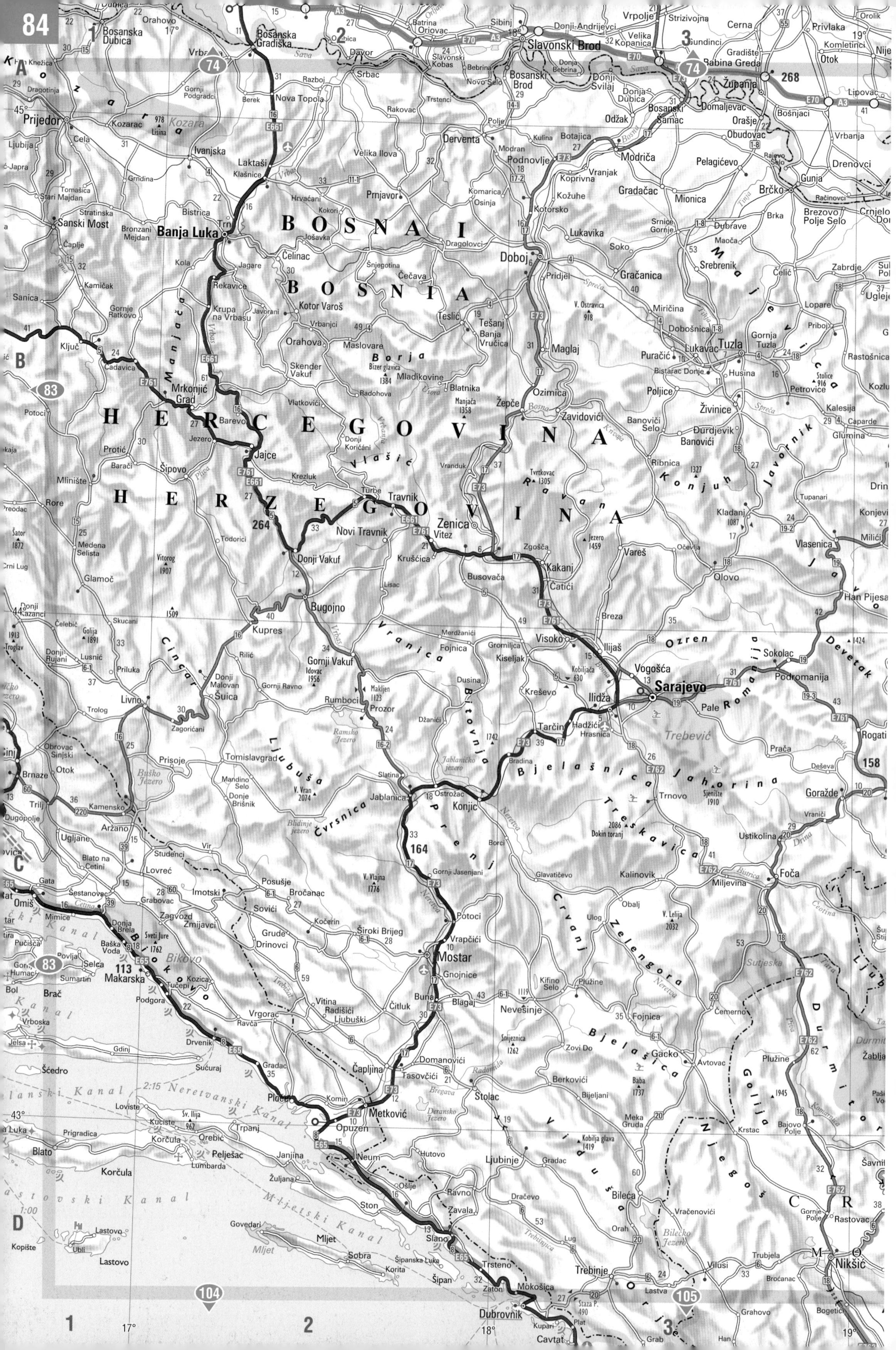
BOSNA I HERCEGOVINA
BOSNIA HERZEGOVINA
Bosanska Dubica
Bosanska Gradiška
Slavonski Brod
Bosanski Brod
Slavonski Kobas
Srbac
Nova Topola
Prijedor
Kozarac
Kozara
Ivanjska
Laktaši
Klašnice
Derventa
Modriča
Bosanski Šamac
Odžak
Orašje
Županja
Babina Greda
Gunja
Brčko
Gradačac
Prnjavor
Sanski Most
Banja Luka
Čelinac
Kotor Varoš
Teslić
Tešanj
Doboj
Gračanica
Srebrenik
Tuzla
Lukavac
Živinice
Banovići
Kladanj
Ključ
Mrkonjić Grad
Jajce
Šipovo
Kupres
Donji Vakuf
Travnik
Novi Travnik
Vitez
Zenica
Žepče
Maglaj
Zavidovići
Kakanj
Visoko
Vareš
Olovo
Vlasenica
Han Pijesak
Sokolac
Ilijaš
Vogošća
Sarajevo
Ilidža
Hadžići
Pale
Trebević
Jahorina
Bjelašnica
Treskavica
Trnovo
Goražde
Foča
Kalinovik
Bugojno
Gornji Vakuf
Fojnica
Kiseljak
Kreševo
Prozor
Konjic
Jablanica
Livno
Tomislavgrad
Glamoč
Posušje
Imotski
Široki Brijeg
Mostar
Čitluk
Ljubuški
Čapljina
Stolac
Nevesinje
Gacko
Bileća
Trebinje
Ljubinje
Neum
Metković
Ploče
Makarska
Omiš
Brač
Korčula
Lastovo
Mljet
Pelješac
Ston
Slano
Dubrovnik
Cavtat
Nikšić
Plužine
Čvrsnica
Prenj
Vranica
Vlašić
Ljubuša
Cincar
Crvanj
Zelengora
Bjelašica
Durmitor
Golija
Njegoš
Orjen
Ozren
Romanija
Devetak
Javornik
Konjuh
Majevica
Neretvanski Kanal
Mljetski Kanal
Korčulanski Kanal
Lastovski Kanal
Sava
Neretva
Drina
Bosna
Vrbas
E70
E73
E661
E761
E762
E65
A3
74
83
104
105
158
164
264
268
113
1
2
3
A
B
C
D
17°
18°
19°
43°
45°

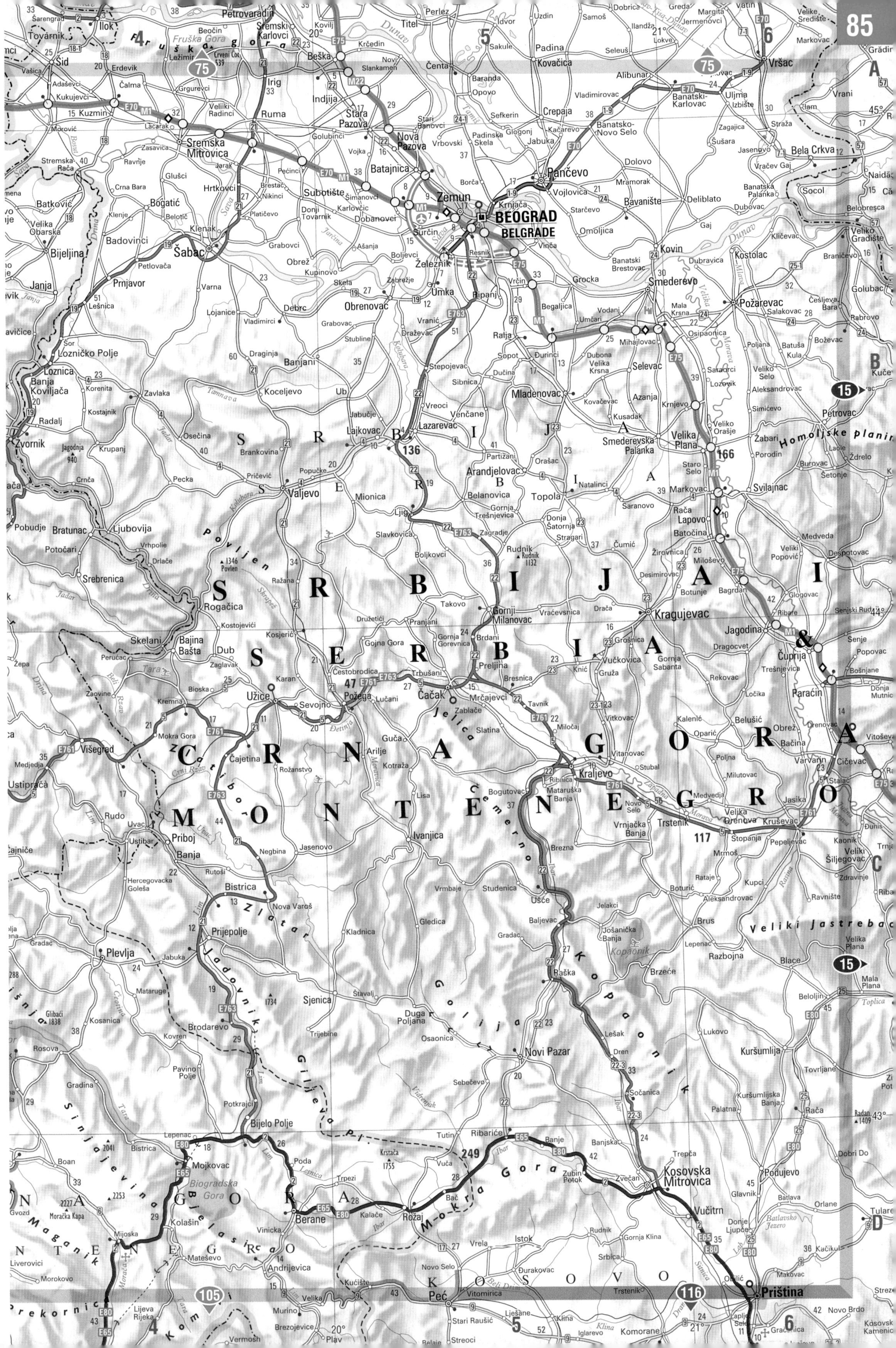

S R B I J A
S E R B I A
C R N A G O R A
M O N T E N E G R O
K O S O V O
BEOGRAD
BELGRADE
Novi Sad
Petrovaradin
Sremski Karlovci
Ilok
Šid
Zemun
Pančevo
Smederevo
Požarevac
Vršac
Bela Crkva
Kovin
Obrenovac
Šabac
Sremska Mitrovica
Ruma
Inđija
Stara Pazova
Nova Pazova
Batajnica
Bijeljina
Zvornik
Loznica
Valjevo
Ljubovija
Bratunac
Srebrenica
Lazarevac
Mladenovac
Arandjelovac
Topola
Smederevska Palanka
Velika Plana
Kragujevac
Jagodina
Ćuprija
Paraćin
Svilajnac
Gornji Milanovac
Čačak
Užice
Požega
Bajina Bašta
Kraljevo
Trstenik
Kruševac
Vrnjačka Banja
Višegrad
Priboj
Prijepolje
Nova Varoš
Ivanjica
Sjenica
Novi Pazar
Raška
Kosovska Mitrovica
Vučitrn
Priština
Peć
Rožaj
Berane
Bijelo Polje
Pljevlja
Mojkovac
Kolašin
Andrijevica
Plav
Kuršumlija
Podujevo
Brus
Blace
Fruška Gora
Homoljske planine
Povljen
Zlatar
Zlatibor
Jelica
Čemerno
Golija
Kopaonik
Mokra Gora
Jadovnik
Sinjajevina
Bjelasica
Veliki Jastrebac
Dunav
Sava
Drina
Morava
Ibar
Lim
Tara
Kolubara
E70
E75
E761
E763
E65
E80
M1
75
105
116
15

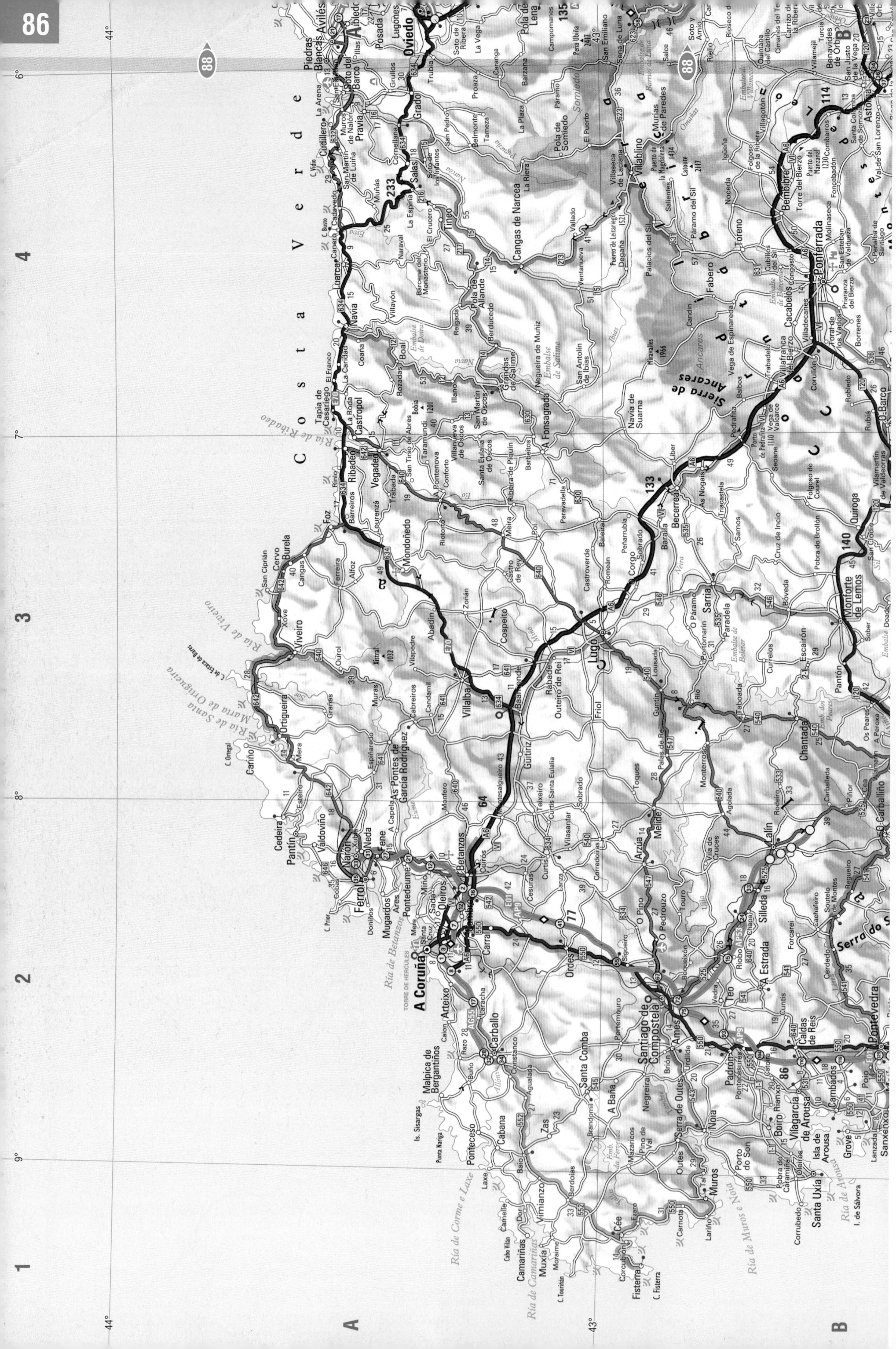

Costa Verde
A Coruña
Ferrol
Lugo
Santiago de Compostela
Pontevedra
Oviedo
Ponferrada
Monforte de Lemos
Vilagarcía de Arousa
Sierra de Ancares
Ría de Betanzos
Ría de Corme e Laxe
Ría de Camariñas
Ría de Muros e Noia
Ría de Arousa
Ría de Ribadeo
Ría de Viveiro
Ría de Santa María de Ortigueira
Fisterra
Muxía
Carballo
Betanzos
Viveiro
Ribadeo
Luarca
Navia
Mondoñedo
Villalba
Sarria
Chantada
Lalín
Silleda
A Estrada
Padrón
Noia
Muros
Cambados
Sanxenxo
Cangas de Narcea
Tineo
Villablino
Astorga
Bembibre
44°
43°
6°
7°
8°
9°
1
2
3
4
A
B

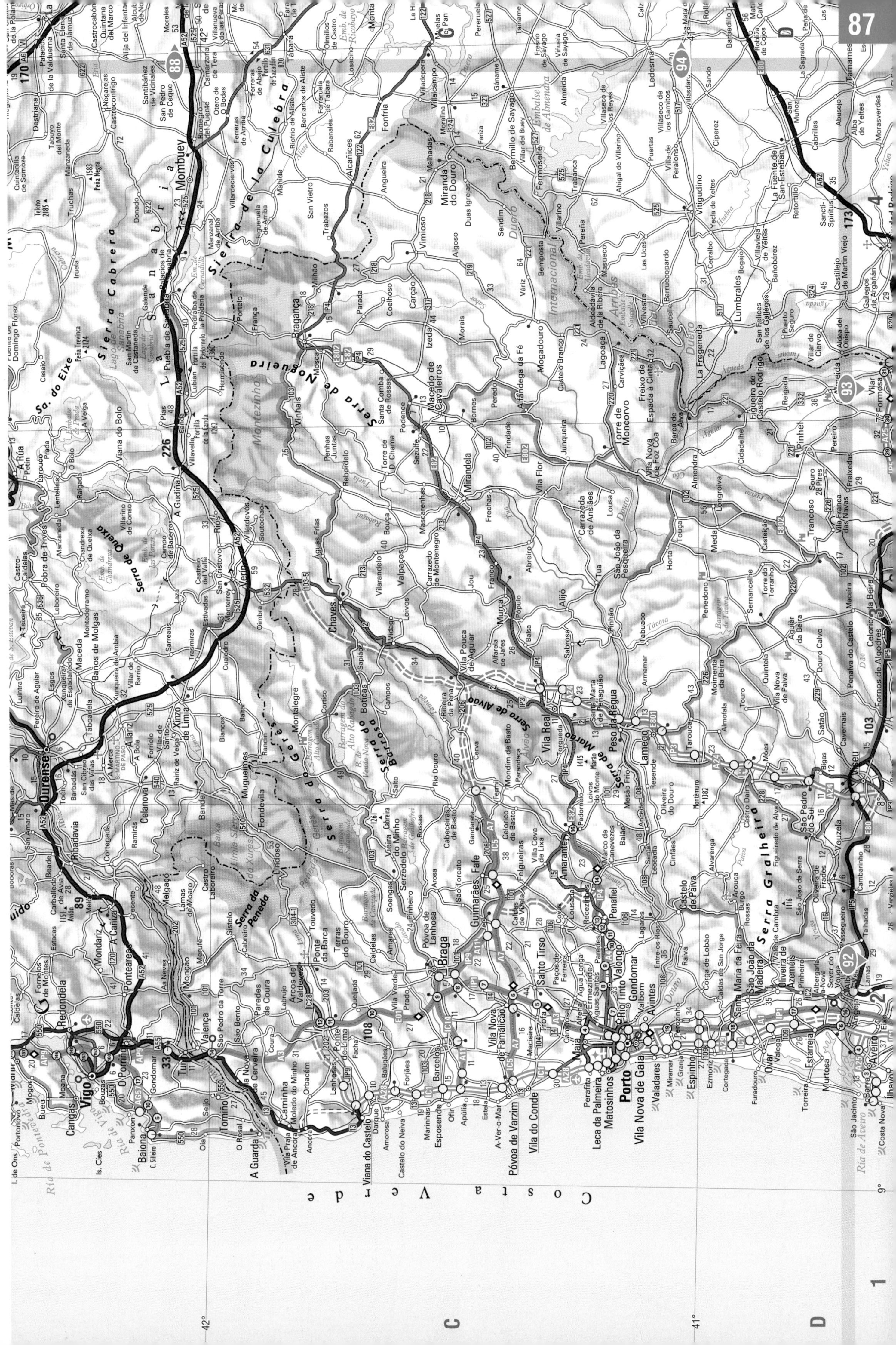

Costa Verde
Vigo
Ourense
Porto
Braga
Bragança
Chaves
Vila Real
Viana do Castelo
Guimarães
Mirandela
Lamego
Peso da Régua
Aveiro
Viseu
Vila Nova de Gaia
Matosinhos
Póvoa de Varzim
Vila do Conde
Barcelos
Valença
Tui
Redondela
Pontevedra
Mombuey
Puebla de Sanabria
Verín
Xinzo de Limia
Ribadavia
Celanova
Miranda do Douro
Macedo de Cavaleiros
Torre de Moncorvo
Vitigudino
Lumbrales
Espinho
Ovar
Serra da Peneda
Serra do Gerês
Serra do Alvão
Serra do Marão
Serra da Nogueira
Serra de Queixa
Serra Cabrera
Sierra de la Culebra
Serra do Barroso
Serra Gralheira
Sa. do Eixe
Duero
Douro
Arribes
Internacional

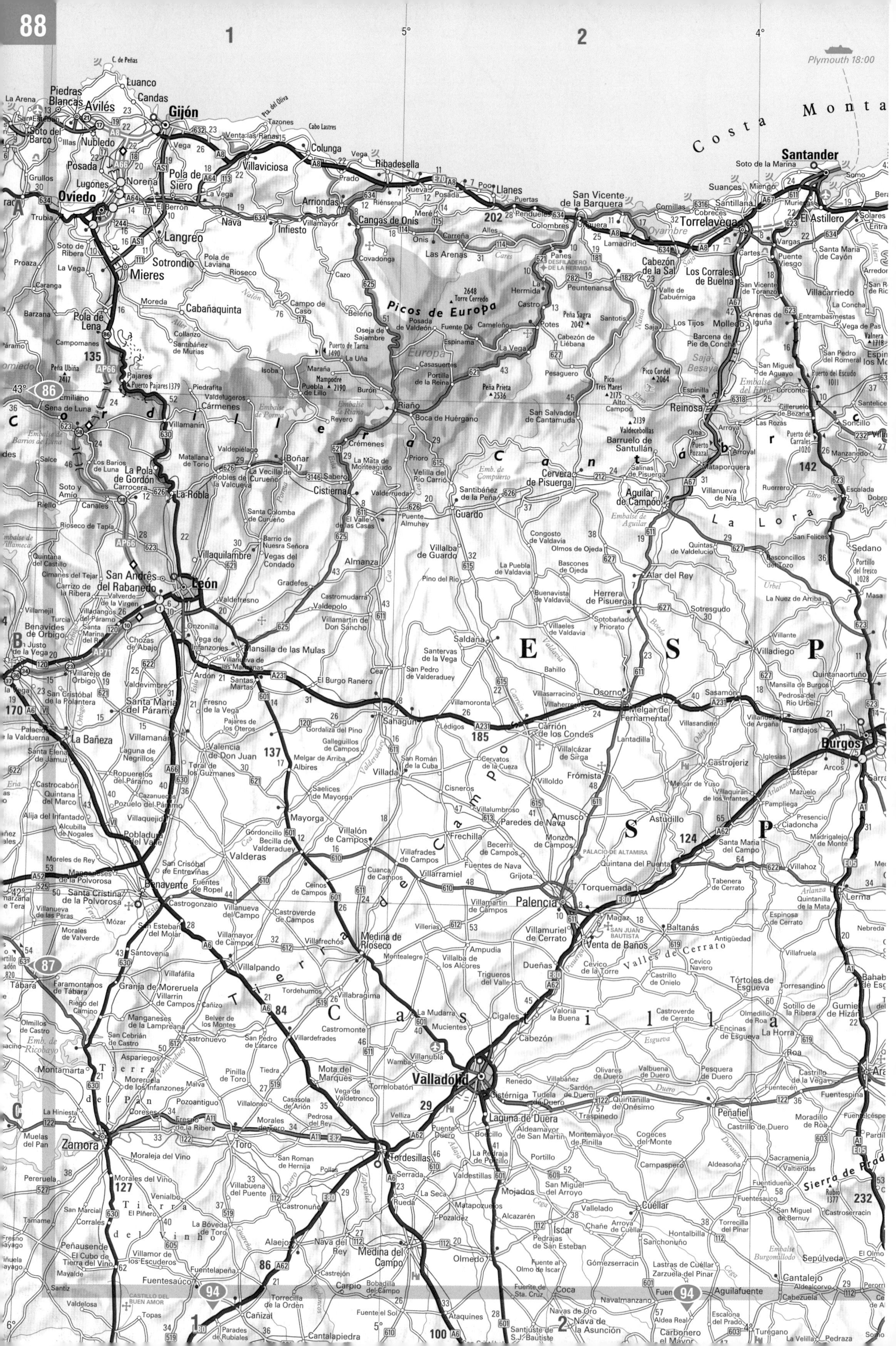
1
2
Plymouth 18:00
Costa Monta
Santander
Gijón
Avilés
Oviedo
Luanco
Candas
Piedras Blancas
La Arena
San Esteban
Soto del Barco
Nubledo
Posada
Noreña
Lugones
Pola de Siero
Villaviciosa
Colunga
Ribadesella
Llanes
Tazones
Cabo Lastres
C. de Peñas
Venta las Ranas
Vega
Prado
Nueva
Posada
Poo
Arriondas
Cangas de Onís
Infiesto
Nava
Langreo
Mieres
Sotrondio
Trubia
Proaza
Soto de Ribera
La Vega
Pola de Laviana
Rioseco
Caranga
Barzana
Moreda
Cabañaquinta
Pola de Lena
Campomanes
Collanzo
Santibáñez de Murias
Campo de Caso
Beleño
Covadonga
Cazo
Picos de Europa
Torre Cerredo 2648
Posada de Valdeón
Fuente Dé
Camaleño
Espinama
La Vega
Oseja de Sajambre
Puerto de Tarna 1490
La Uña
Isoba
Maraña
Mampodre 2190
Puebla de Lillo
Burón
Casasuertes
Portilla de la Reina
Peña Prieta 2536
Riaño
Boca de Huérgano
Embalse de Riaño
Reyero
Crémenes
Prioro
Velilla del Río Carrión
Peña Ubiña 2417
Pajares
Puerto Pajares 1379
Piedrafita
Valdelugueros
Cármenes
Villamanín
Emiliano
Sena de Luna
Embalse de Barrios de Luna
Cordillera Cantábrica
Los Barrios de Luna
La Pola de Gordón
La Robla
Matallana de Torío
Robles de la Valcueva
La Vecilla de Curueño
Boñar
Sabero
Cistierna
La Mata de Monteagudo
Valderrueda
Soto y Amío
Carrocera
Canales
Riello
Rioseco de Tapia
Quintana del Castillo
Cimanes del Tejar
Carrizo de la Ribera
San Andrés del Rabanedo
León
Villaquilambre
Barrio de Nuesta Señora
Vegas del Condado
Santa Colomba de Curueño
Gradefes
Almanza
Valdefresno
Valverde de la Virgen
Villadangos del Páramo
Santa Marina del Rey
Benavides de Orbigo
Hospital de Orbigo
Turcia
Chozas de Abajo
Onzonilla
Vega de Infanzones
Mansilla de las Mulas
Villanueva de las Manzanas
Villarejo de Orbigo
Valdevimbre
Ardón
Santas Martas
San Justo de la Vega
La Bañeza
Santa María del Páramo
Villamañán
Fresno de la Vega
Pajares de los Oteros
Valencia de Don Juan
Toral de los Guzmanes
Laguna de Negrillos
Roperuelos del Páramo
Pozuelo del Páramo
Villaquejida
Pobladura del Valle
Santa Elena de Jamuz
Castrocabón
Quintana del Marco
Alija del Infantado
Alcubilla de Nogales
Moreles de Rey
Manganeses de la Polvorosa
Benavente
Santa Cristina de la Polvorosa
Castrogonzalo
Fuentes de Ropel
San Cristóbal de Entreviñas
San Esteban del Molar
Santovenia
Villafáfila
Granja de Moreruela
Villarrín de Campos
Manganeses de la Lampreana
Tábara
Faramontanos de Tábara
Riego del Camino
Olmillos de Castro
Embalse de Ricobayo
San Cebrián de Castro
Montamarta
Tierra del Pan
La Hiniesta
Muelas del Pan
Zamora
Moraleja del Vino
Pereruela
Morales del Vino
Tierra del Vino
Venialbo
El Piñero
Corrales
San Marcial
Tamame
Peñausende
El Cubo de Tierra del Vino
Mayalde
Villamor de los Escuderos
Fuentesaúco
Fuentelapeña
Santiz
Valdelosa
Topas
Cañizal
Torrecilla de la Orden
Castillo del Buen Amor
Parades de Rubiales
Cantalapiedra
Toro
Fresno de la Ribera
Coreses
Pozoantiguo
Villalonso
Morales de Toro
Pinilla de Toro
Tiedra
Mota del Marqués
Villardefrades
San Pedro de Latarce
Belver de los Montes
Castronuevo
Villalpando
Cañizo
Tordehumos
Villabrágima
Tierra de Campos
Medina de Rioseco
Montealegre
Villafrechós
Villamayor de Campos
Castroverde de Campos
Villanueva del Campo
Valderas
Gordoncillo
Becilla de Valderaduey
Villalón de Campos
Mayorga
Saelices de Mayorga
Melgar de Arriba
Albires
Sahagún
Gordaliza del Pino
Galleguillos de Campos
El Burgo Ranero
Cea
San Pedro de Valderaduey
Villamoronta
Lédigos
San Román de la Cuba
Villada
Cervatos de la Cueza
Cisneros
Villalumbroso
Paredes de Nava
Frechilla
Becerril de Campos
Fuentes de Nava
Villafrades de Campos
Cuenca de Campos
Villarramiel
Ceinos de Campos
Villamartín de Campos
Villerías
Ampudia
Villalba de los Alcores
Trigueros del Valle
Dueñas
Cigales
Cabezón
La Mudarra
Mucientes
Castromonte
Villanubla
Wamba
Valladolid
Renedo
Cistérniga
Laguna de Duero
Tudela de Duero
Villabáñez
Sardón de Duero
Quintanilla de Onésimo
Traspinedo
Olivares de Duero
Valbuena de Duero
Pesquera de Duero
Peñafiel
Aldeamayor de San Martín
Boecillo
La Pedraja de Portillo
Portillo
Montemayor de Pinilla
Cogeces del Monte
Campaspero
Tordesillas
Torrelobatón
Vega de Valdetronco
Casasola de Arión
Pedrosa del Rey
Velliza
Puente Duero
San Roman de Hornija
Pollos
Serrada
Villabuena del Puente
Castronuño
Rueda
La Seca
Valdestillas
Matapozuelos
Pozaldez
Mojados
San Miguel del Arroyo
Alcazarén
Vallelado
Cuéllar
Íscar
Pedrajas de San Esteban
Chañe
Arroyo de Cuéllar
Hontalbilla
Sanchonuño
Alaejos
Nava del Rey
Medina del Campo
Olmedo
Fuente al Olmo de Íscar
Gómezserracín
Lastras de Cuéllar
Zarzuela del Pinar
Castrejón
Carpio
Bobadilla del Campo
Fuente el Sol
Ataquines
Fuente de Sta. Cruz
Coca
Navas de Oro
Nava de la Asunción
Santiuste de S.J. Bautiste
Navalmanzano
Aldea Real
Escalona del Prado
Carbonero el Mayor
Turégano
Fuentepelayo
Aguilafuente
Cantalejo
Cabezuela
Sepúlveda
Valtiendas
Sacramenia
Fuentidueña
Fuentesauco
San Miguel de Bernuy
Castroserracín
Torrecilla del Pinar
Sierra de Pradales
Rubio 1377
Aldeasoña
Castrillo de Duero
Moradillo de Roa
Fuentespina
Fuentecén
Castrillo de la Vega
Roa
La Horra
Encinas de Esgueva
Castroverde de Cerrato
Olmedillo de Roa
Sotillo de la Ribera
Gumiel de Hizán
Torresandino
Tórtoles de Esgueva
Castrillo de Onielo
Cevico de la Torre
Cevico Navero
Valles de Cerrato
Baltanás
Antigüedad
Venta de Baños
San Juan Bautista
Magaz
Villamuriel de Cerrato
Palencia
Torquemada
Tabenera de Cerrato
Quintana del Puente
Palacio de Altamira
Monzón de Campos
Amusco
Astudillo
Grijota
Frómista
Villoldo
Villalcázar de Sirga
Carrión de los Condes
Villasarracino
Villaherreros
Osorno
Bahillo
Saldaña
Santervas de la Vega
Villaeles de Valdavia
Sotobañado y Priorato
Herrera de Pisuerga
Buenavista de Valdavia
Bascones de Ojeda
Olmos de Ojeda
La Puebla de Valdavia
Congosto de Valdavia
Villalba de Guardo
Pino del Río
Guardo
Puente Almuhey
El Valle de las Casas
Santibáñez de la Peña
Cervera de Pisuerga
Embalse de Compuerto
Salinas de Pisuerga
Aguilar de Campóo
Embalse de Aguilar
Alar del Rey
Quintas de Valdelucio
La Lora
Sotresgudo
Melgar de Fernamental
Lantadilla
Villasandino
Castrojeriz
Melgar de Yuso
Villaquirán de los Infantes
Santa María del Campo
Villahoz
Mazuelo
Pampliega
Presencio
Ciadoncha
Madrigalejo de Monte
Estépar
Arcos
Burgos
Tardajos
Villanueva de Argaño
Iglesias
Pedrosa del Río Urbel
Mansilla de Burgos
Sasamón
Villadiego
Villante
Quintanaortuño
La Nuez de Arriba
Basconcillos del Tozo
Urbel
Portillo del fresco 1028
Sedano
San Felices
Masa
Escalada
Dobro
Ruerrero
Villanueva de Nía
Mataporquera
Arroyal
Puerto Pozazal
Olea
Arroya
Puerto de Carrales 1020
Manzanedo
Soncillo
Las Rozas
Cilleruelo de Bezana
Corconte
Puerto del Escudo 1011
San Miguel de Aguayo
Embalse del Ebro
Reinosa
Espinilla
Barruelo de Santullán
Valdecebollas 2139
Alto Campóo
Pico Tres Mares 2175
Pico Cordel 2064
Pesaguero
San Salvador de Cantamuda
Cabezón de Liébana
Peña Sagra 2042
Potes
Castro
La Hermida
Desfiladero de la Hermida
Panes
Puentenansa
Santotís
Saja
Los Tijos
Molledo
Barcena de Pie de Concha
Arenas de Iguña
Los Corrales de Buelna
Cabezón de la Sal
Valle de Cabuérniga
Lamadrid
Torrelavega
Oyambre
Unquera
Colombres
Pendueles
San Vicente de la Barquera
Comillas
Cobreces
Santillana
Suances
Miengo
Soto de la Marina
Muriedas
El Astillero
Somo
Solares
Vargas
Cartes
Puente Viesgo
Santa María de Cayón
Villacarriedo
San Vicente de Toranzo
Entrambasmestas
Vega de Pas
Valnera 1718
San Pedro del Romeral
La Concha
Arredondo
Alles
Carreña
Las Arenas
Onís
Meré
Riénsena
Villamayor
Cares
Lerma
Quintanilla de la Mata
Espinosa de Cerrato
Villafruela
Nebreda
Bahabón de Esgueva
Castilla
Europa
Saja-Besaya
Embalse Burgomillodo
El Olmo
España
Tierra de Campos

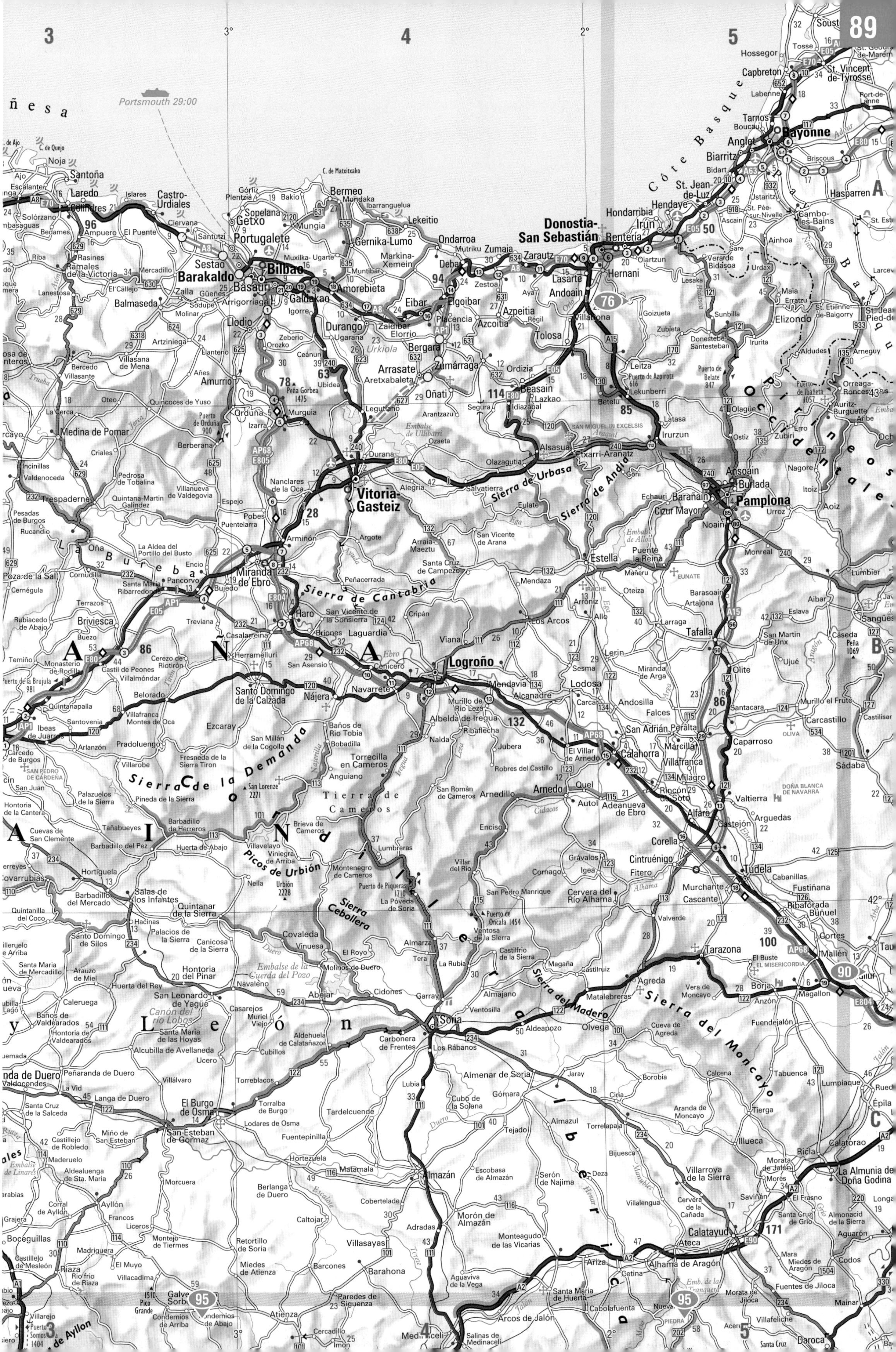

3
4
5
Portsmouth 29:00
Côte Basque
Hossegor
Capbreton
Labenne
Tarnos
Boucau
Bayonne
Anglet
Biarritz
Bidart
St. Jean-de-Luz
Hendaye
Hondarribia
Irún
Donostia-San Sebastián
Rentería
Hernani
Oiartzun
St. Vincent-de-Tyrosse
Port-de-Lanne
Briscous
Hasparren
Cambo-les-Bains
Ustaritz
St. Pée-sur-Nivelle
Ascain
Sare
Ainhoa
Vera de Bidasoa
Urdax
Lesaka
Maia
Erratzu
Elizondo
St. Etienne-de-Baigorry
St. Jean-Pied-de-Port
Arneguy
Aldudes
Irurita
Sunbilla
Donestebe-Santesteban
Goizueta
Zubieta
Leitza
Puerto de Azpirotz
Lekunberri
Puerto de Belate
Orreaga-Roncesvalles
Puerto de Ibañeta
Auritz-Burguette
Aribe
Erro
Zubiri
Olagüe
Ostiz
Latasa
Irurzun
Betelu
Nagore
Itoiz
Aoiz
Ansoain
Burlada
Pamplona
Barañain
Cizur Mayor
Echauri
Noain
Urroz
Monreal
Lumbier
Aibar
Sangüesa
Eslava
Cáseda
Peña 1069
San Martin de Unx
Ujué
Olite
Tafalla
Barasoain
Artajona
Larraga
Miranda de Arga
Murillo el Fruto
Carcastillo
Castilisar
Santacara
Caparroso
Marcilla
Villafranca
Milagro
Peralta
Falces
San Adrián
Andosilla
Calahorra
Rincón de Soto
Alfaro
Castejón
Valtierra
Arguedas
Corella
Cintruénigo
Fitero
Tudela
Murchante
Cascante
Cabanillas
Fustiñana
Ribaforada
Buñuel
Cortes
Mallén
Borja
Magallon
Anzón
Tarazona
El Buste
Vera de Moncayo
Agreda
Matalebreras
Olvega
Cueva de Agreda
Fuendejalón
Tabuenca
Lumpiaque
Épila
Calatorao
Ricla
Morata de Jalón
La Almunia de Doña Godina
Morés
Saviñán
El Frasno
Santa Cruz de Grío
Almonacid de la Sierra
Aguarón
Calatayud
Ateca
Alhama de Aragón
Cetina
Ariza
Mara
Miedes de Aragón
Codos
Fuentes de Jiloca
Morata de Jiloca
Villafeliche
Daroca
Mainar
Emb. de la Tranquera
Nuévalos
Santa María de Huerta
Cabolafuente
Arcos de Jalón
Salinas de Medinaceli
Medinaceli
Bardallur
Sierra del Moncayo
Sierra del Madero
Illueca
Tierga
Aranda de Moncayo
Calcena
Borobia
Ciria
Torrelapaja
Bijuesca
Villarroya de la Sierra
Cervera de la Cañada
Villalengua
Deza
Serón de Najima
Almazul
Jaray
Gómara
Almenar de Soria
Tejado
Escobasa de Almazán
Monteagudo de las Vicarias
Morón de Almazán
Almazán
Adradas
Aguaviva de la Vega
Lubia
Cubo de la Solana
Los Rábanos
Soria
Garray
Ventosilla
Almajano
Aldeapozo
Carbonera de Frentes
Aldehuela de Calatañazor
Cidones
Abejar
Molinos de Duero
Embalse de la Cuerda del Pozo
Navaleno
Covaleda
Vinuesa
El Royo
Tera
Almarza
La Rubia
Castilfrío de la Sierra
Magaña
Castilruiz
Sierra Cebollera
Puerto de Piqueras 1710
La Póveda de Soria
Ventosa de la Sierra
Puerto de Oncala 1454
San Pedro Manrique
Cervera del Río Alhama
Cornago
Igea
Grávalos
Villar del Río
Enciso
Arnedillo
Arnedo
Quel
Autol
Adeanueva de Ebro
Aldeanueva de Ebro
El Villar de Arnedo
San Román de Cameros
Robres del Castillo
Jubera
Ribafrecha
Nalda
Albelda de Iregua
Murillo de Río Leza
Alcanadre
Mendavia
Lodosa
Sesma
Lerín
Carcar
Los Arcos
Arróniz
Allo
Oteiza
Estella
Mañeru
Puente la Reina
Eunate
Irache
Embalse de Alloz
Mendaza
Viana
Logroño
Navarrete
Cenicero
Laguardia
Cripán
Briones
San Vicente de la Sonsierra
Haro
Casalarreina
Herramelluri
San Asensio
Nájera
Santo Domingo de la Calzada
Villalmóndar
Cerezo de Riotirón
Castil de Peones
Belorado
Ezcaray
Baños de Río Tobía
Bobadilla
Torrecilla en Cameros
Anguiano
San Millán de la Cogolla
Fresneda de la Sierra Tirón
Pradoluengo
Villafranca Montes de Oca
Tierra de Cameros
Brieva de Cameros
Lumbreras
Villavelayo
Viniegra de Arriba
Montenegro de Cameros
Picos de Urbión
Urbión 2228
Neila
San Lorenzo 2271
Sierra de la Demanda
Pineda de la Sierra
Barbadillo de Herreros
Tañabueyes
Huerta de Abajo
Barbadillo del Pez
Palazuelos de la Sierra
Villarobe
Ibeas de Juarros
Santovenia
Arlanzón
Carcedo de Burgos
San Pedro de Cardeña
San Juan
Hontoria de la Cantera
Cuevas de San Clemente
Covarrubias
Hortiguela
Barbadillo del Mercado
Salas de los Infantes
Quintanar de la Sierra
Hacinas
Palacios de la Sierra
Canicosa de la Sierra
Santo Domingo de Silos
Quintanilla del Coco
Arauzo de Miel
Santa María de Mercadillo
Huerta del Rey
Hontoria del Pinar
San Leonardo de Yagüe
Casarejos
Muriel Viejo
Cañón del río Lobos
Santa María de las Hoyas
Caleruega
Baños de Valdearados
Hontoria de Valdearados
Alcubilla de Avellaneda
Ucero
Cubillos
Peñaranda de Duero
Aranda de Duero
Villálvaro
Torreblacos
La Vid
Langa de Duero
Santa Cruz de la Salceda
El Burgo de Osma
Torralba de Burgo
Lodares de Osma
San Esteban de Gormaz
Castillejo de Robledo
Miño de San Esteban
Maderuelo
Aldealuenga de Sta. Maria
Tardelcuende
Fuentepinilla
Hortezuela
Matamala
Berlanga de Duero
Cobertelade
Caltojar
Villasayas
Barahona
Barcones
Retortillo de Soria
Miedes de Atienza
Montejo de Tiermes
Morcuera
Ayllón
Francos
Liceros
Corral de Ayllón
Madriguera
El Muyo
Villacadima
Riaza
Riofrío de Riaza
Boceguillas
Castillejo de Mesleón
Grajera
Galve de Sorbe
Pico Grande 1510
Condemios de Arriba
Condemios de Abajo
Atienza
Paredes de Sigüenza
Cercadillo
Imón
Puerto Somosierra 1404
de Ayllon
Villarejo
Sierra de Urbasa
Sierra de Andía
Sierra de Cantabria
Alsasua
Etxarri-Aranatz
Olazagutia
Salvatierra
Eulate
Arraia-Maeztu
Santa Cruz de Campezo
San Vicente de Arana
Peñacerrada
Argote
Armiñón
Vitoria-Gasteiz
Alegría
Nanclares de la Oca
Durana
Embalse de Ullibarri
Ozaeta
Arantzazu
Legutiano
Murguia
Izarra
Orduña
Puerto de Orduña 900
Berberana
Amurrio
Llodio
Arrigorriaga
Basauri
Bilbao
Barakaldo
Sestao
Portugalete
Getxo
Santurtzi
Sopelana
Plentzia
Górliz
Bakio
Mungia
Bermeo
Mundaka
Ibarranguelua
Ea
Lekeitio
C. de Matxitxako
Gernika-Lumo
Muxilka-Ugarte
Markina-Xemein
Amorebieta
Galdakao
Durango
Zaldibar
Elorrio
Eibar
Elgoibar
Placencia
Bergara
Arrasate
Aretxabaleta
Oñati
Zumárraga
Ordizia
Beasain
Lazkao
Idiazábal
Segura
Tolosa
Villabona
Andoain
Lasarte
Azpeitia
Azcoitia
Zarautz
Zumaia
Zestoa
Deba
Mutriku
Ondarroa
Gueñes
Zalla
Sodupe
Balmaseda
Artziniega
Villasana de Mena
Orozko
Zeberio
Igorre
Ceánuri
Peña Gorbea 1475
Ubidea
Urkiola
Castro-Urdiales
Islares
Ciervana
Laredo
Colindres
Santoña
Noja
C. de Quejo
Ampuero
Rasines
Ramales de la Victoria
Medina de Pomar
Trespaderne
Quintana-Martin Galindez
Espejo
Pobes
Puentelarra
Miranda de Ebro
Bujedo
Pancorvo
Santa María Ribarredonda
La Bureba
Briviesca
Poza de la Sal
Treviño
A Ñ A
E S P A Ñ A
Castilla y León
Sistema Ibérico
Pirineos Occidentales
Pays Basque
A
B
C
3°
2°
42°

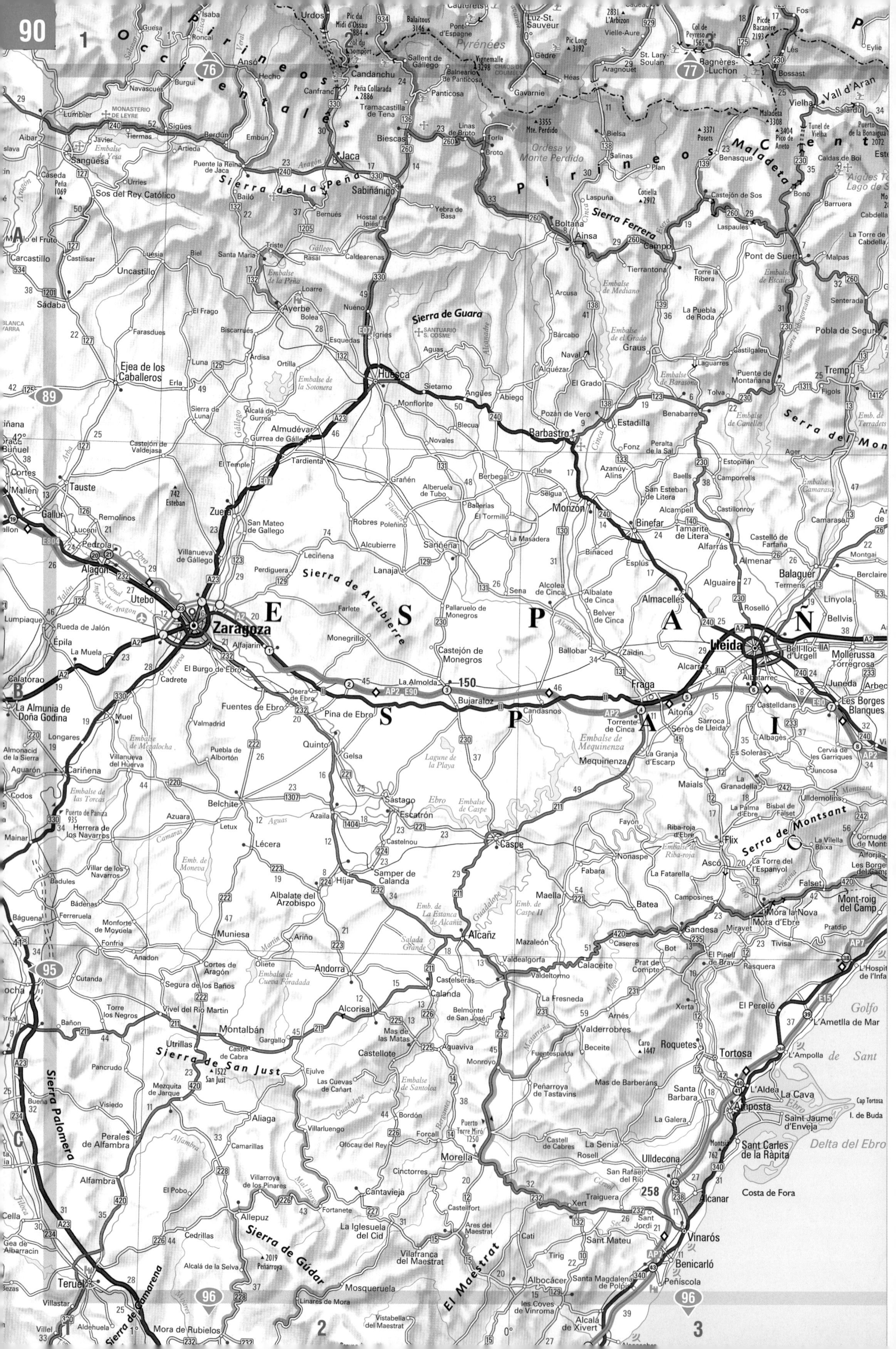
Pirineos Occidentales
Pyrénées
Pirineos Centrales
Maladeta
Sierra de la Peña
Sierra Ferrera
Sierra de Guara
Sierra de Alcubierre
Sierra de San Just
Sierra Palomera
Sierra de Gúdar
El Maestrat
Serra de Montsant
Serra del Montsec
Golfo de Sant Jordi
Delta del Ebro
E S P A Ñ A
Urdos
Pic du Midi d'Ossau 2884
Col du Somport
Cauterets
Luz-St.-Sauveur
Pont d'Espagne
Balaïtous 3146
Vignemalle 3298
Gèdre
Gavarnie
Héas
Pic Long 3192
2831 L'Arbizon
Vielle-Aure
St. Lary-Soulan
Aragnouet
Col de Peyresourde 1565
Bagnères-de-Luchon
Pic de Bacanère 2193
Fos
Eylie
Les
Bossost
Vall d'Aran
Vielha
Salardú
Túnel de Vielha
Puerto de la Bonaigua 2072
Maladeta 3308
3404 Pico de Aneto
Caldas de Boi
Aigües Tortes
Lago de S.
Isaba
Roncal
Guesa
Ansó
Hecho
Candanchu
Canfranc
Peña Collarada 2886
Sallent de Gállego
Balneario de Panticosa
Panticosa
Tramacastilla de Tena
Biescas
Linas de Broto
Torla
Broto
3355 Mte. Perdido
Ordesa y Monte Perdido
Bielsa
Salinas
Plan
3371 Posets
Benasque
Castejón de Sos
Laspaules
Bono
Barruera
Cabdella
La Torre de Cabdella
Pont de Suert
Malpas
Senterada
Pobla de Segur
Tremp
Figols
Navascués
Burgui
Lumbier
Monasterio de Leyre
Tiermas
Sigües
Berdún
Embún
Javier
Embalse de Yesa
Sangüesa
Artieda
Aibar
Puente la Reina de Jaca
Jaca
Sabiñánigo
Caseda
Peña 1069
Urriés
Sos del Rey Católico
Bailó
Bernués
Hostal de Ipiés
Yebra de Basa
Boltaña
Aínsa
Laspuña
Cotiella 2912
Campo
Tierrantona
Torre la Ribera
Embalse de Escales
Mallo el Fruto
Carcastillo
Castiliscar
Luesia
Biel
Santa María
Triste
Rasal
Caldearenas
Embalse de la Peña
Uncastillo
Loarre
Ayerbe
Bolea
Sádaba
Nueno
El Frago
Esquedas
Igriés
Santuario S. Cosme
Arcusa
Embalse de Mediano
La Puebla de Roda
Bárcabo
Embalse de el Grado
Graus
Naval
Castigaleu
Laguarres
Puente de Montañana
Farasdues
Biscarrués
Ardisa
Ortilla
Aguas
Alquézar
El Grado
Embalse de Barasona
Tolva
Ejea de los Caballeros
Luna
Erla
Embalse de la Sotonera
Huesca
Sietamo
Angües
Abiego
Pozán de Vero
Estadilla
Benabarre
Embalse de Canelles
Sierra de Luna
Alcalá de Gurrea
Almudévar
Monflorite
Blecua
Barbastro
Fonz
Peralta de la Sal
Estopiñán
Ager
Emb. de Terradets
Castejón de Valdejasa
Gurrea de Gállego
Novales
Tardienta
El Temple
Grañén
Berbegal
Ilche
Azanúy-Alins
Baells
Camporrells
Embalse Camarasa
742 Esteban
Alberuela de Tubo
Ballerias
Selgua
San Esteban de Litera
Castillonroy
Alcampell
Tauste
Mallén
Cortes
Buñuel
Remolinos
Zuera
Robres
Poleñino
El Tormillo
Monzón
Binéfar
Tamarite de Litera
Camarasa
Gallur
Luceni
Pedrola
San Mateo de Gallego
Alcubierre
Sariñena
La Masadera
Binaced
Alfarrás
Castelló de Farfaña
Montgai
Alagón
Villanueva de Gállego
Leciñena
Perdiguera
Lanaja
Sena
Esplús
Almenar
Balaguer
Berclaire
Termens
Utebo
Canal Imperial de Aragón
Pallaruelo de Monegros
Alcolea de Cinca
Albalate de Cinca
Belver de Cinca
Almacelles
Alguaire
Rosselló
Linyola
Bellvis
Lumpiaque
Rueda de Jalón
Farlete
Zaragoza
Épila
La Muela
Monegrillo
Castejón de Monegros
Ballobar
Zaidín
Lleida
Bell-lloc d'Urgell
Mollerussa
Torregrosa
Alfajarín
Calatorao
El Burgo de Ebro
Cadrete
La Almolda
Osera de Ebro
Bujaraloz
Candasnos
Fraga
Alcarràs
Albatàrrec
Juneda
Arbeca
La Almunia de Doña Godina
Fuentes de Ebro
Pina de Ebro
Torrente de Cinca
Aitona
Seròs
Sarroca de Lleida
Castelldans
Les Borges Blanques
Muel
Valmadrid
Embalse de Mezalocha
Quinto
Gelsa
Laguna de la Playa
Embalse de Mequinenza
Mequinenza
La Granja d'Escarp
Almonacid de la Sierra
Longares
Puebla de Albortón
L'Albagés
Es Soleras
Cervià de les Garrigues
Juncosa
Aguarón
Cariñena
Villanueva del Huerva
Codos
Embalse de las Torcas
Puerto de Paniza 935
Belchite
Sástago
Escatrón
Embalse de Caspe
Maials
La Granadella
Ulldemolins
Montsant
Herrera de los Navarros
Azuara
Letux
Azaila
Castelnou
Caspe
Fayón
Riba-roja d'Ebre
Embalse de Riba-roja
La Palma d'Ebre
Bisbal de Falset
Flix
Cornudella de Montsant
La Vilella Baixa
Mainar
Lécera
Emb. de Moneva
Hijar
Samper de Calanda
Nonaspe
Fabara
Ascó
La Torre de l'Espanyol
Alforja
Les Borges del Camp
Villar de los Navarros
Badules
Albalate del Arzobispo
Maella
La Fatarella
Falset
Mont-roig del Camp
Bádenas
Báguena
Ferreruela
Monforte de Moyuela
Emb. de la Estanca de Alcañiz
Emb. de Caspe II
Batea
Camposines
Móra la Nova
Móra d'Ebre
Muniesa
Fonfría
Ariño
Salada Grande
Alcañiz
Mazaleón
Caseres
Gandesa
Miravet
Pratdip
Tivissa
Anadón
Cortes de Aragón
Oliete
Embalse de Cueva Foradada
Andorra
Valdealgorfa
Calaceite
Prat de Comte
Bot
El Pinell de Bray
Rasquera
L'Hospitalet de l'Infant
Cutanda
Segura de los Baños
Castelserás
Valdeltormo
Torre los Negros
Vivel del Río Martín
Calanda
Belmonte de San José
La Fresneda
Xerta
El Perelló
Baños
Montalbán
Alcorisa
Mas de las Matas
Arnés
Valderrobres
L'Ametlla de Mar
Utrillas
Castel de Cabra
Gargallo
Castellote
Aguaviva
Fuentespalda
Beceite
Caro 1447
Roquetes
Tortosa
L'Ampolla
Pancrudo
1522 San Just
Ejulve
Monroyo
Peñarroya de Tastavins
Mas de Barberáns
Santa Bàrbara
L'Aldea
La Cava
Cap Tortosa
I. de Buda
Mezquita de Jarque
Las Cuevas de Cañart
Embalse de Santolea
Buena
Visiedo
Aliaga
Villarluengo
Bordón
Puerto Torre Miró 1250
La Galera
Amposta
Sant Jaume d'Enveja
Perales de Alfambra
Camarillas
Olocau del Rey
Forcall
Castell de Cabres
La Sénia
Rosell
Ulldecona
Montsià 762
Sant Carles de la Ràpita
Alfambra
Villarroya de los Pinares
Cantavieja
Cinctorres
Morella
San Rafael del Río
Alcanar
Costa de Fora
El Pobo
Fortanete
Castellfort
Traiguera
Xert
Allepuz
La Iglesuela del Cid
Ares del Maestrat
Cati
Sant Jordi
Vinaròs
Cella
Cedrillas
Sant Mateu
Gea de Albarracín
2019 Peñarroya
Vilafranca del Maestrat
Tirig
Benicarló
Alcalá de la Selva
Albocàsser
Santa Magdalena de Polpís
Peñíscola
Teruel
Mosqueruela
les Coves de Vinromà
Villastar
Linares de Mora
Vistabella del Maestrat
Alcalà de Xivert
Aldehuela
Mora de Rubielos
Sierra de Camarena
Villel
76
77
89
95
96
258
150
1
2
3
A
B
C

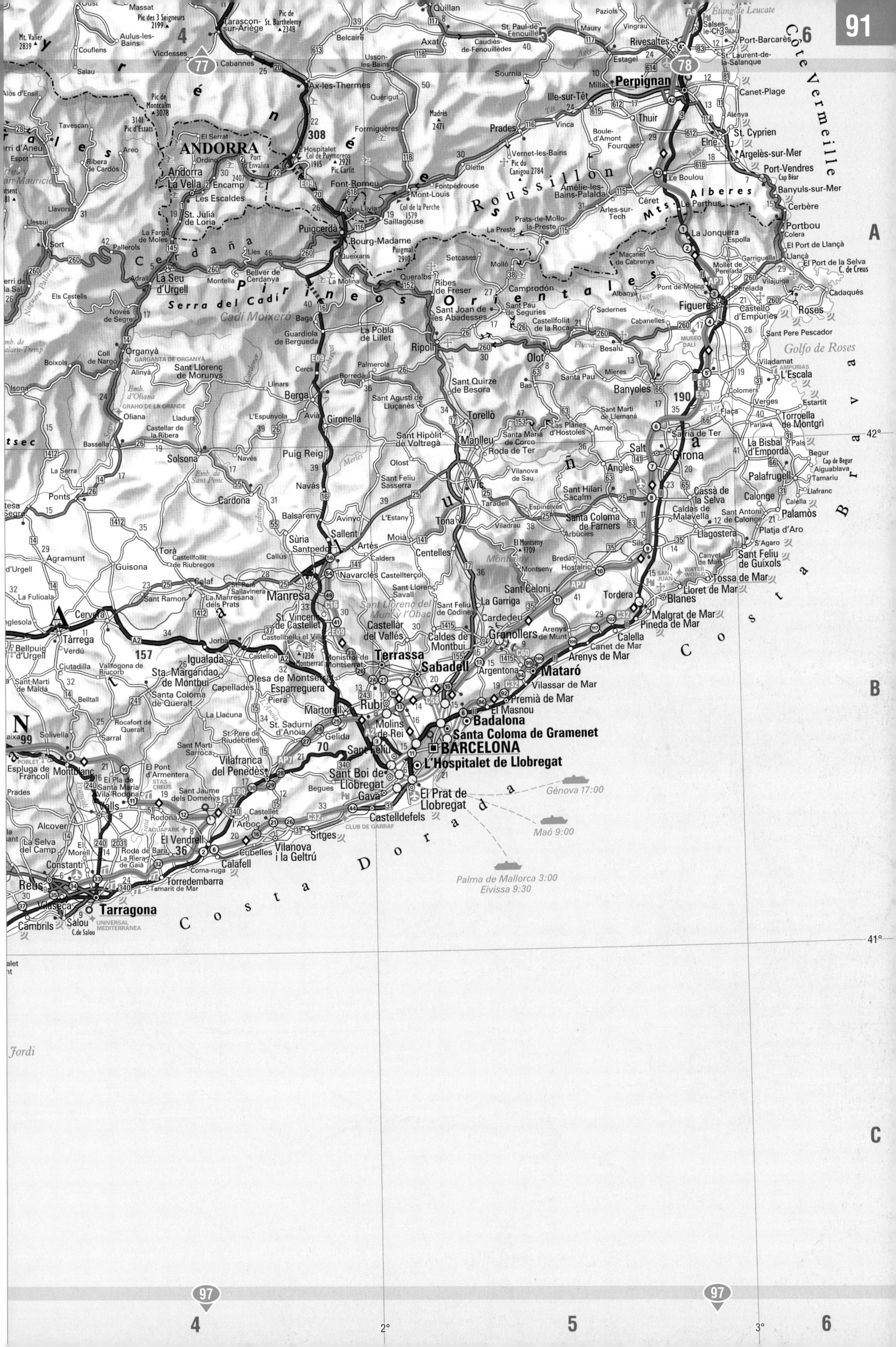
Massat
Pic des 3 Seigneurs 2199
Tarascon-sur-Ariège
Pic de St. Barthelemy 2348
Quillan
Paziols
Étang de Leucate
Mt. Valier 2839
Aulus-les-Bains
Couflens
Vicdessos
Cabannes
Belcaire
Axat
Caudiès-de-Fenouillèdes
St. Paul-de-Fenouillet
Maury
Vingrau
Rivesaltes
Salses-le-Château
Port-Barcarès
Estagel
St. Laurent-de-la-Salanque
Côte Vermeille
Salau
Usson-les-Bains
Ax-les-Thermes
Sournia
Millas
Perpignan
Canet-Plage
Alos d'Ensil
Pic de Montcalm 3078
3141 Pic d'Estats
Quérigut
Madrès 2471
Ille-sur-Têt
Thuir
Tavescan
Formiguères
Prades
Vinca
Boule-d'Amont
Fourques
Alenya
St. Cyprien
Elne
Argelès-sur-Mer
Esterri d'Aneu
Espot
Areo
Ribera de Cardós
El Serrat
ANDORRA
Ordino
Port d'Envalira
L'Hospitalet
Col de Puymorens 1915
2921 Pic Carlit
Vernet-les-Bains
Pic du Canigou 2784
Le Boulou
Port-Vendres
Cap Béar
Banyuls-sur-Mer
Andorra La Vella
Encamp
Les Escaldes
Font-Romeu
Mont-Louis
Fontpédrouse
Olette
Roussillon
Amélie-les-Bains-Palalda
Céret
Mts. Alberes
Le Perthus
Cerbère
Llavorsí
St. Julià de Loria
Llívia
Col de la Perche 1579
Saillagouse
Arles-sur-Tech
Prats-de-Mollo-la-Preste
La Preste
Portbou
Colera
Llessui
La Farga de Moles
Puigcerdà
Bourg-Madame
La Jonquera
Espolla
El Port de Llançà
Sort
Pallerols
Cerdaña
Lles
Queixans
Puigmal 2910
Setcases
Maçanet de Cabrenys
Garriguella
Llançà
El Port de la Selva
C. de Creus
Adrall
La Seu d'Urgell
Montella
Bellver de Cerdanya
La Molina
Queralbs
Ribes de Freser
Molló
Camprodón
Mollet de Peralada
Peralada
Vilajuïga
Cadaqués
Els Castells
Serra del Cadí
Pirineos Orientales
Cadí Moixeró
Sant Joan de les Abadesses
Sant Pau de Segúries
Castellfollit de la Roca
Albanya
Pont de Molins
Figueres
Castelló d'Empúries
Roses
Noves de Segre
Baga
Guardiola de Bergueda
La Pobla de Lillet
Ripoll
Sadernes
Cabanelles
Besalú
Museo Dalí
Sant Pere Pescador
Golfo de Roses
Organyà
Garganta de Organyà
Coll de Nargó
Boixols
Sant Llorenç de Morunys
Cercs
Palmerola
Borredà
Olot
Santa Pau
Mieres
Banyoles
Viladamat
Ampurias
L'Escala
Isona
Alinyà
Llinars
Berga
Sant Quirze de Besora
Bas
Colomers
Emb. d'Oliana
Grabo de la Grande
Oliana
Lladurs
L'Espunyola
Avià
Gironella
Sant Agustí de Lluçanès
Torelló
Sant Martí de Llemaná
Amer
Verges
Estartit
Flaçà
Torroella de Montgrì
Castellar de la Ribera
Sant Hipòlit de Voltregà
Manlleu
Santa Maria de Corco
Las Planes d'Hostoles
Sarrià de Ter
Parlavà
Bassella
Solsona
Navès
Puig Reig
Roda de Ter
Salt
Girona
La Bisbal d'Empordà
Pals
42°
La Serra
Emb. de Sant Ponç
Olost
Vilanova de Sau
Anglès
Begur
Cap de Begur
Aiguablava
Tamariu
Ponts
Cardona
Navás
Sant Feliu Sasserra
Vic
Sant Hilari Sacalm
Cassà de la Selva
Palafrugell
Llafranc
Calella
Calonge
Palamós
Balsareny
L'Estany
Taradell
Espinelves
Santa Coloma de Farners
Caldas de Malavella
Sant Antoni de Calonge
Platja d'Aro
Agramunt
Torà
Castellfollit de Riubregos
Súria
Santpedor
Sallent
Avinyo
Moià
Tona
Viladrau
Arbúcies
El Montseny 1709
Sils
Llagostera
S'Agaro
Sant Feliu de Guíxols
Costa Brava
Guisona
Callús
Artés
Calders
Centelles
Breda
Hostalric
Canyet de Mar
Tossa de Mar
La Fuliola
Calaf
St. Pere Sallavinera
Navarcles
Castellterçol
Sant Llorenç Savall
Montseny
Sant Celoni
Water World
San Juan
Lloret de Mar
Cervera
Sant Ramon
La Manresana dels Prats
Manresa
Sant Llorenç del Munt y l'Obac
Sant Feliu de Codines
La Garriga
Cardedeu
Tordera
Blanes
Malgrat de Mar
Pineda de Mar
Tàrrega
Bellpuig d'Urgell
Verdú
Jorba
St. Vicenç de Castellet
Castellbell i el Vilar
Castellar del Vallés
Caldes de Montbui
Granollers
Arenys de Munt
Calella
Canet de Mar
Arenys de Mar
Costa
Ciutadilla
Vallfogona de Riucorb
Igualada
Castellolí
Montserrat 1236
Monistrol de Montserrat
Terrassa
Sabadell
Argentona
Mataró
Vilassar de Mar
Sant Martí de Maldà
Belltall
Sta. Margarida de Montbui
Capellades
Olesa de Montserrat
Esparreguera
Premià de Mar
El Masnou
Santa Coloma de Queralt
La Llacuna
Piera
Martorell
Rubí
Badalona
Santa Coloma de Gramenet
Rocafort de Queralt
Sarral
St. Sadurní d'Anoia
Gelida
Molins de Rei
Sant Feliu
BARCELONA
L'Hospitalet de Llobregat
Solivella
St. Pere de Riudebitlles
Sant Martí Sarroca
Poblet
Espluga de Francolí
Montblanc
El Pont d'Armentera
Vilafranca del Penedès
Sant Boi de Llobregat
Gava
Begues
El Prat de Llobregat
Génova 17:00
Prades
El Pla de Santa Maria
Vila-Rodona
Stas Creus
Sant Jaume dels Domenys
Valls
Rodonà
Castellet
L'Arboç
Castelldefels
Club de Garraf
Maó 9:00
Alcover
La Selva del Camp
El Morell
Aquapark
Roda de Barà
La Riera de Gaià
El Vendrell
Cubelles
Vilanova i la Geltrú
Sitges
Costa Dorada
Constantí
Coma-ruga
Calafell
Torredembarra
Tamarit de Mar
Palma de Mallorca 3:00
Eivissa 9:30
Reus
Vilaseca
Tarragona
Cambrils
Salou
C. de Salou
Universal Mediterranea
41°
Jordi
A
B
C
4
5
6
2°
3°
77
78
97
97

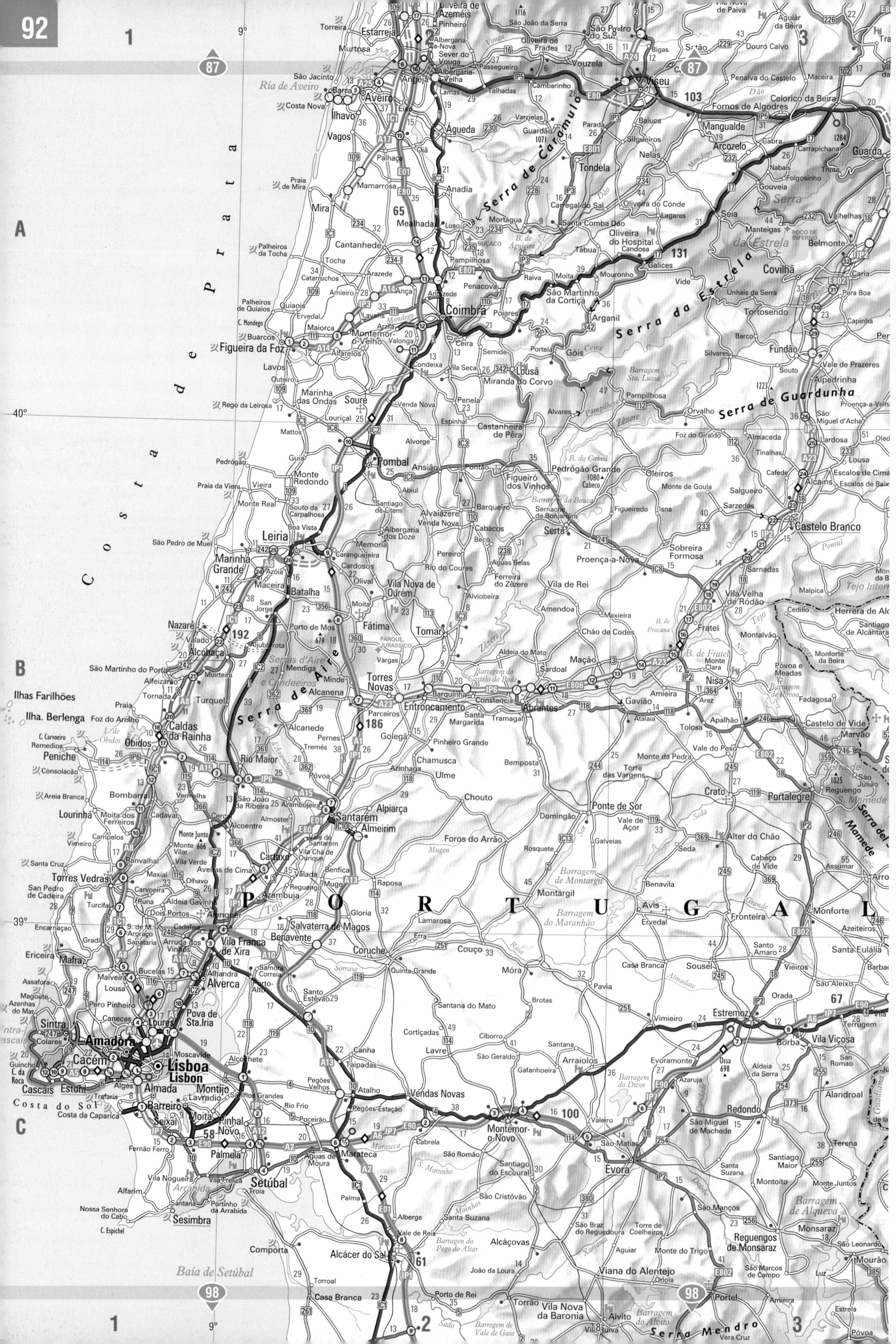
PORTUGAL
Costa de Prata
Ria de Aveiro
Serra do Caramulo
Serra da Estrela
Serra de Guardunha
Serras d'Aire e Candeeiros
Serra de Aire
Costa do Sol
Baía de Setúbal
Serra Mendro
Ilhas Farilhões
Ilha. Berlenga
Aveiro
Ílhavo
Vagos
Águeda
Viseu
Mangualde
Guarda
Tondela
Mira
Mealhada
Cantanhede
Coimbra
Figueira da Foz
Montemor-o-Velho
Lousã
Miranda do Corvo
Arganil
Seia
Gouveia
Covilhã
Belmonte
Fundão
Soure
Pombal
Leiria
Marinha Grande
Batalha
Fátima
Ourém
Tomar
Nazaré
Alcobaça
Caldas da Rainha
Óbidos
Peniche
Torres Novas
Entroncamento
Abrantes
Castelo Branco
Sertã
Proença-a-Nova
Vila Velha de Ródão
Nisa
Portalegre
Marvão
Castelo de Vide
Ponte de Sor
Santarém
Almeirim
Rio Maior
Cartaxo
Azambuja
Torres Vedras
Lourinhã
Vila Franca de Xira
Benavente
Coruche
Alverca
Mafra
Ericeira
Sintra
Cascais
Estoril
Amadora
Cacém
Lisboa
Lisbon
Almada
Barreiro
Montijo
Seixal
Palmela
Setúbal
Sesimbra
Vendas Novas
Montemor-o-Novo
Estremoz
Elvas
Vila Viçosa
Borba
Redondo
Évora
Arraiolos
Reguengos de Monsaraz
Alcácer do Sal
Viana do Alentejo
Portel
Vila Nova da Baronia
Alvito
1
2
3
A
B
C
87
98
9°
40°
39°

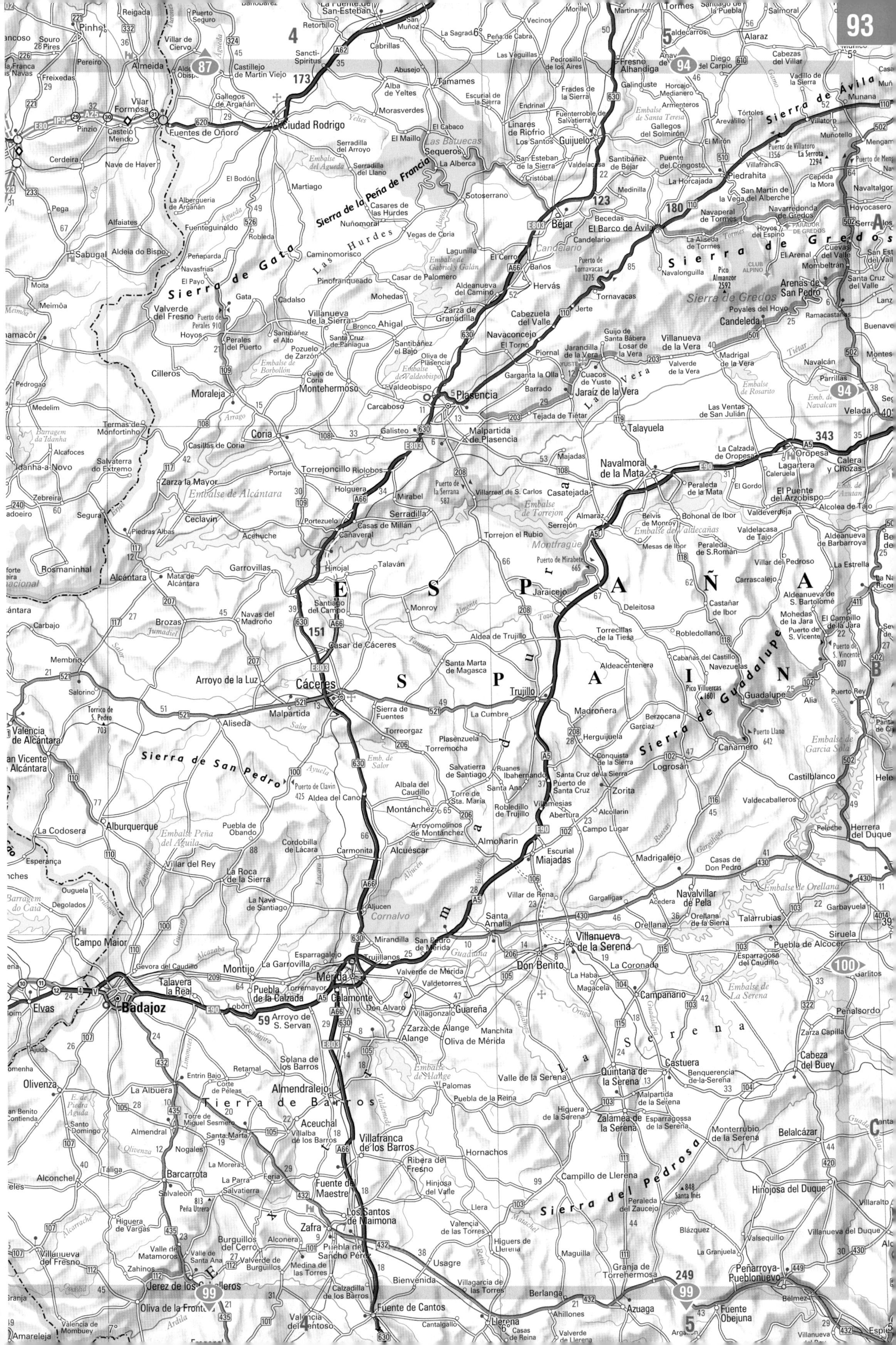

E S P A Ñ A
Ciudad Rodrigo
Almeida
Fuentes de Oñoro
Sabugal
Sierra de Gata
Sierra de la Peña de Francia
Las Batuecas
La Alberca
Las Hurdes
Béjar
Guijuelo
El Barco de Ávila
Piedrahita
Sierra de Ávila
Sierra de Gredos
Arenas de San Pedro
Candeleda
Jaraíz de la Vera
La Vera
Plasencia
Hervás
Moraleja
Coria
Navalmoral de la Mata
Oropesa
Embalse de Alcántara
Alcántara
Garrovillas
Monfragüe
Embalse de Torrejón
Jaraicejo
Trujillo
Cáceres
Arroyo de la Luz
Malpartida
Valencia de Alcántara
Sierra de San Pedro
Alburquerque
Guadalupe
Sierra de Guadalupe
Logrosán
Zorita
Miajadas
Montánchez
Castilblanco
Herrera del Duque
Embalse de Orellana
Navalvillar de Pela
Villanueva de la Serena
Don Benito
Mérida
Montijo
Badajoz
Elvas
Campo Maior
Olivenza
Almendralejo
Tierra de Barros
Guareña
Campanario
La Serena
Castuera
Cabeza del Buey
Zalamea de la Serena
Embalse de La Serena
Sierra del Pedrosa
Hinojosa del Duque
Peñarroya-Pueblonuevo
Belalcázar
Azuaga
Llerena
Fuente de Cantos
Zafra
Los Santos de Maimona
Jerez de los Caballeros
Barcarrota
Oliva de la Frontera
Fuente Obejuna
87
94
99
100

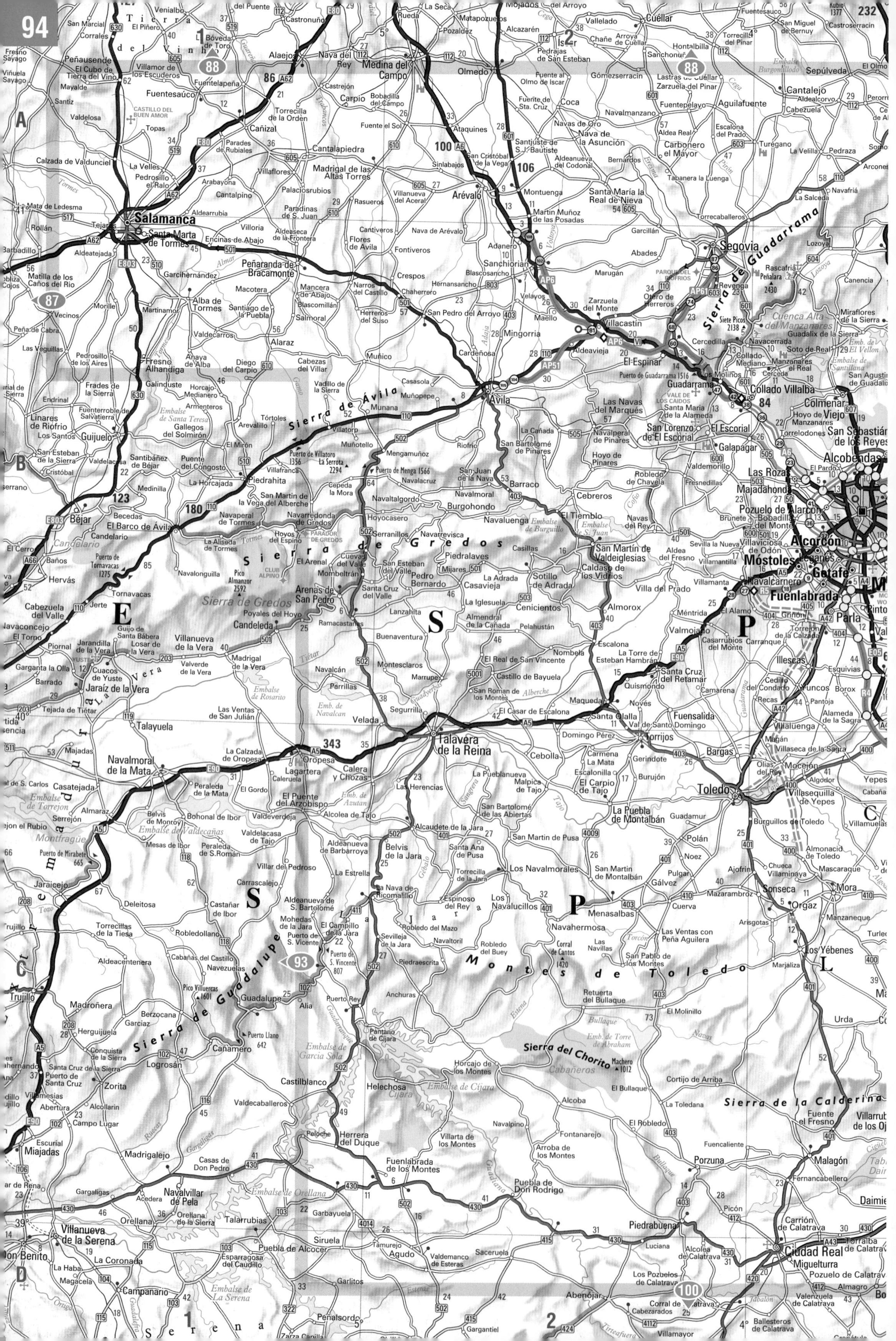
Salamanca
Santa Marta de Tormes
Medina del Campo
Cuéllar
Olmedo
Sepúlveda
Arévalo
Segovia
Sierra de Guadarrama
Peñaranda de Bracamonte
Alba de Tormes
Ávila
Sierra de Ávila
Guadarrama
Collado Villalba
San Lorenzo de El Escorial
Alcobendas
Las Rozas
Majadahonda
Pozuelo de Alarcón
Alcorcón
Móstoles
Getafe
Fuenlabrada
Parla
Béjar
El Barco de Ávila
Piedrahita
Sierra de Gredos
Arenas de San Pedro
Candeleda
Jaraíz de la Vera
Navalmoral de la Mata
Oropesa
Talavera de la Reina
Torrijos
Toledo
Illescas
Sonseca
Orgaz
Mora
Los Yébenes
Montes de Toledo
Sierra de Guadalupe
Guadalupe
Trujillo
Logrosán
Zorita
Miajadas
Castilblanco
Herrera del Duque
Sierra del Chorito
Sierra de la Calderina
Malagón
Piedrabuena
Ciudad Real
Miguelturra
Villanueva de la Serena
Don Benito
Campanario
Siruela
Agudo
Abenójar
Almadén

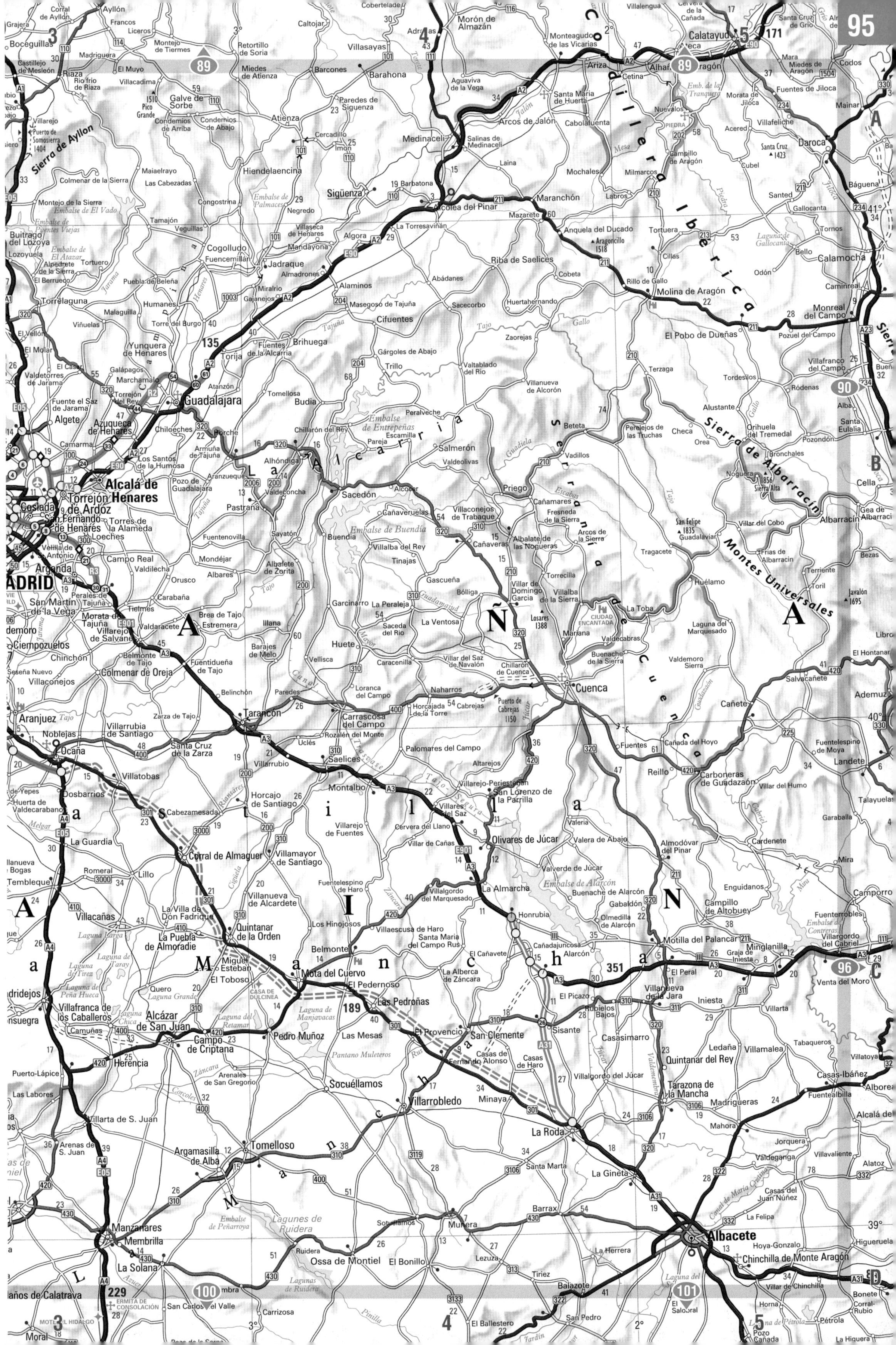
Cordillera Ibérica
Sierra de Ayllón
Sierra de Albarracín
Montes Universales
Serranía de Cuenca
La Alcarria
Castilla La Mancha
Ayllón
Riaza
Boceguillas
Atienza
Sigüenza
Medinaceli
Arcos de Jalón
Ariza
Calatayud
Daroca
Alcolea del Pinar
Maranchón
Molina de Aragón
Monreal del Campo
Calamocha
Jadraque
Cogolludo
Brihuega
Cifuentes
Torija
Guadalajara
Alcalá de Henares
Torrejón de Ardoz
Coslada
San Fernando de Henares
Arganda
Madrid
Pastrana
Sacedón
Priego
Beteta
Albarracín
Cuenca
Huete
Tarancón
Aranjuez
Ocaña
Colmenar de Oreja
Chinchón
Saelices
Carrascosa del Campo
Cañete
Landete
Motilla del Palancar
Minglanilla
Quintanar de la Orden
Mota del Cuervo
Belmonte
Honrubia
Alarcón
San Clemente
Las Pedroñas
Pedro Muñoz
Campo de Criptana
Alcázar de San Juan
Herencia
Madridejos
Consuegra
Villafranca de los Caballeros
Tomelloso
Socuéllamos
Villarrobledo
La Roda
Argamasilla de Alba
Manzanares
Membrilla
La Solana
Munera
Ossa de Montiel
El Bonillo
La Gineta
Albacete
Chinchilla de Monte Aragón
Tarazona de la Mancha
Quintanar del Rey
Casas-Ibáñez
Madrigueras
Mahora
Embalse de Entrepeñas
Embalse de Buendía
Embalse de Alarcón
Embalse de Contreras
Lagunas de Ruidera
89
90
96
100
101

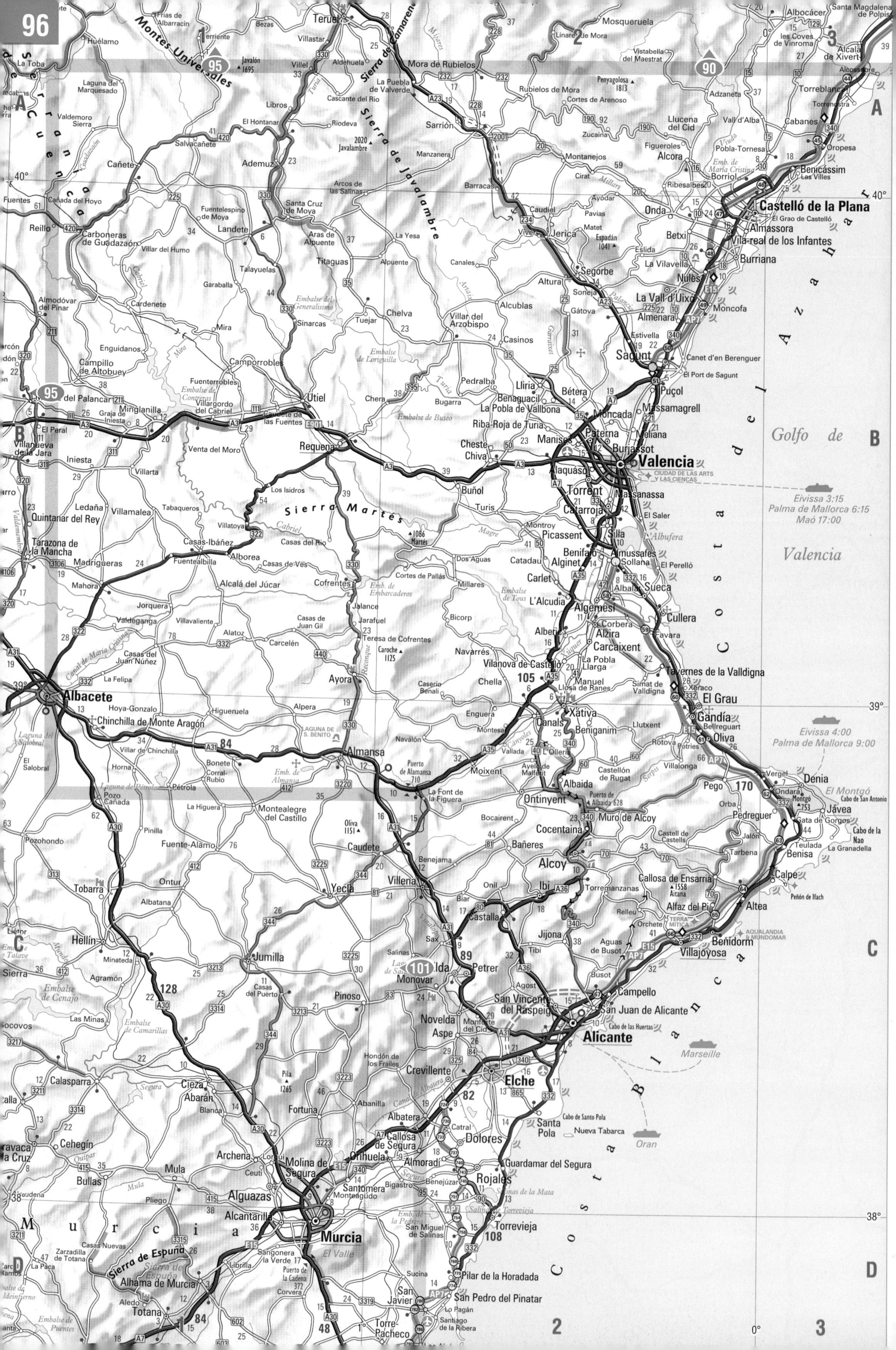

Teruel
Montes Universales
Frías de Albarracín
Huélamo
La Toba
Serranía de Cuenca
Javalón 1695
Mosqueruela
Linares de Mora
Vistabella del Maestrat
Albocàcer
Santa Magdalena de Polpis
Les Coves de Vinromà
Alcalà de Xivert
Alcossebre
Torreblanca
Torrenostra
Cabanes
Oropesa
Benicàssim
Las Villes
Mora de Rubielos
Rubielos de Mora
Penyagolosa 1813
Adzaneta
Cortes de Arenoso
Zucaina
Llucena del Cid
Vall d'Alba
Figueroles
Pobla-Tornesa
Alcora
Emb. de María Cristina
Borriol
Ribesalbes
Castelló de la Plana
El Grao de Castelló
Almassora
Vila-real de los Infantes
Burriana
Onda
Betxi
Eslida
La Vilavella
Nules
Moncofa
La Vall d'Uixó
Almenara
Estivella
Sagunt
Canet d'en Berenguer
El Port de Sagunt
Puçol
Massamagrell
Meliana
Burjassot
Valencia
Ciudad de las Artes y las Ciencias
Golfo de Valencia
Costa del Azahar
Eivissa 3:15
Palma de Mallorca 6:15
Maó 17:00
Villastar
Villel
Aldehuela
La Puebla de Valverde
Cascante del Río
Sierra de Camarena
Sierra de Javalambre
Sarrión
Riodeva
2020 Javalambre
Manzanera
Libros
El Hontanar
Salvacañete
Ademuz
Cañete
Laguna del Marquesado
Valdemoro Sierra
Arcos de las Salinas
Santa Cruz de Moya
Fuentelespino de Moya
Landete
Carboneras de Guadazaón
Villar del Humo
Aras de Alpuente
La Yesa
Titaguas
Alpuente
Talayuelas
Garaballa
Cardenete
Embalse del Generalísimo
Sinarcas
Tuejar
Chelva
Villar del Arzobispo
Alcublas
Casinos
Montanejos
Cirat
Barracas
Caudiel
Ayódar
Pavías
Matet
Espadán 1041
Viver
Jérica
Canales
Segorbe
Altura
Soneja
Gátova
Almodóvar del Pinar
Mira
Enguídanos
Campillo de Altobuey
Camporrobles
Embalse de Loriguilla
Fuenterrobles
Embalse de Contreras
Villargordo del Cabriel
Caudete de las Fuentes
Utiel
Chera
Pedralba
Bugarra
Llíria
Bétera
Benaguacil
La Pobla de Vallbona
Riba-Roja de Turia
Moncada
Paterna
Manises
Cheste
Chiva
Embalse de Buseo
Requena
Venta del Moro
Minglanilla
Graja de Iniesta
El Peral
Villanueva de la Jara
Iniesta
Villarta
Los Isidros
Sierra Martés
1086 Martés
Buñol
Turis
Alaquàs
Torrent
Catarroja
Massanassa
El Saler
L'Albufera
Montroy
Picassent
Silla
Benifaió
Almussafes
Sollana
El Perelló
Alginet
Catadau
Dos Aguas
Carlet
Sueca
Albalat
L'Alcudia
Algemesí
Cullera
Corbera
Alzira
Favara
Carcaixent
Alberic
La Pobla Llarga
Tavernes de la Valldigna
Xeraco
Simat de Valldigna
Manuel
Llosa de Ranes
Vilanova de Castelló
El Grau
Gandía
Bellreguart
Oliva
Xàtiva
Benigánim
Llutxent
Rotova
Potries
Pego
Vergel
Dénia
Ondara
El Montgó
Montgó 753
Cabo de San Antonio
Jávea
Gata de Gorgos
Cabo de la Nao
Teulada
Benisa
La Granadella
Calpe
Peñón de Ifach
Altea
Benidorm
Aqualandia & Mundomar
Terra Mítica
Villajoyosa
Eivissa 4:00
Palma de Mallorca 9:00
Quintanar del Rey
Tabaqueros
Villamalea
Ledaña
Villatoya
Tarazona de la Mancha
Casas-Ibáñez
Casas del Río
Madrigueras
Fuentealbilla
Alborea
Casas de Ves
Cofrentes
Cortes de Pallás
Millares
Embalse de Tous
Emb. de Embarcaderos
Mahora
Alcalá del Júcar
Jorquera
Jalance
Jarafuel
Bicorp
Valdeganga
Villavaliente
Alatoz
Casas de Juan Gil
Carcelén
Teresa de Cofrentes
Caroche 1125
Navarrés
Casas del Juan Núñez
Canal de María Cristina
La Felipa
Albacete
Ayora
Chella
Caserío Benali
Enguera
Montesa
Canals
Hoya-Gonzalo
Higueruela
Alpera
Chinchilla de Monte Aragón
Laguna de S. Benito
Navalón
Vallada
L'Olleria
Ayelo de Malferit
Castellón de Rugat
Villalonga
Laguna del Salobral
El Salobral
Villar de Chinchilla
Bonete
Corral-Rubio
Horna
Pétrola
Laguna de Pétrola
Almansa
Emb. de Almansa
Puerto de Almansa 710
Moixent
Albaida
Puerto de Albaida 628
Ontinyent
La Font de la Figuera
Pozo Cañada
La Higuera
Montealegre del Castillo
Oliva 1151
Bocairent
Muro de Alcoy
Cocentaina
Orba
Pedreguer
Jalón
Tarbena
Castell de Castells
Pinilla
Pozohondo
Fuente-Álamo
Caudete
Benejama
Bañeres
Alcoy
Callosa de Ensarrià
Aitana 1558
Alfaz del Pi
Relleu
Orxeta
Tobarra
Ontur
Albatana
Yecla
Villena
Biar
Onil
Ibi
Torremanzanas
Castalla
Jijona
Tibi
Aguas de Busot
Busot
Campello
Liétor
Hellín
Minateda
Agramón
Embalse de Talave
Sierra
Embalse de Cenajo
Jumilla
Salinas
Sax
Elda
Petrer
Monovar
Agost
San Vicente del Raspeig
San Juan de Alicante
Alicante
Cabo de las Huertas
Marseille
Casas del Puerto
Pinoso
Novelda
Monforte del Cid
Aspe
Las Minas
Embalse de Camarillas
Socovos
Hondón de los Frailes
Crevillente
Elche
Pila 1265
Calasparra
Cieza
Abarán
Blanca
Fortuna
Abanilla
Canal de Albatera
Albatera
Cabo de Santo Pola
Santa Pola
Nueva Tabarca
Oran
Cehegín
Caravaca de la Cruz
Archena
Lorquí
Ceutí
Molina de Segura
Callosa de Segura
Orihuela
Catral
Dolores
Almoradí
Guardamar del Segura
Costa Blanca
Bullas
Mula
Santomera
Monteagudo
Bigastro
Benejúzar
Rojales
Salinas de la Mata
Salinas de Torrevieja
Torrevieja
Emb. de la Pedrera
San Miguel de Salinas
Pliego
Alguazas
Alcantarilla
Murcia
El Valle
Murcia
Casas Nuevas
Sierra de Espuña
Zarzadilla de Totana
La Paca
Librilla
Sangonera la Verde
Puerto de la Cadena 372
Corvera
Alhama de Murcia
Aledo
Totana
Embalse de Puentes
Sucina
Pilar de la Horadada
San Javier
San Pedro del Pinatar
Lo Pagán
Santiago de la Ribera
Torre-Pacheco
A
B
C
D
1
2
3
40°
39°
38°
0°

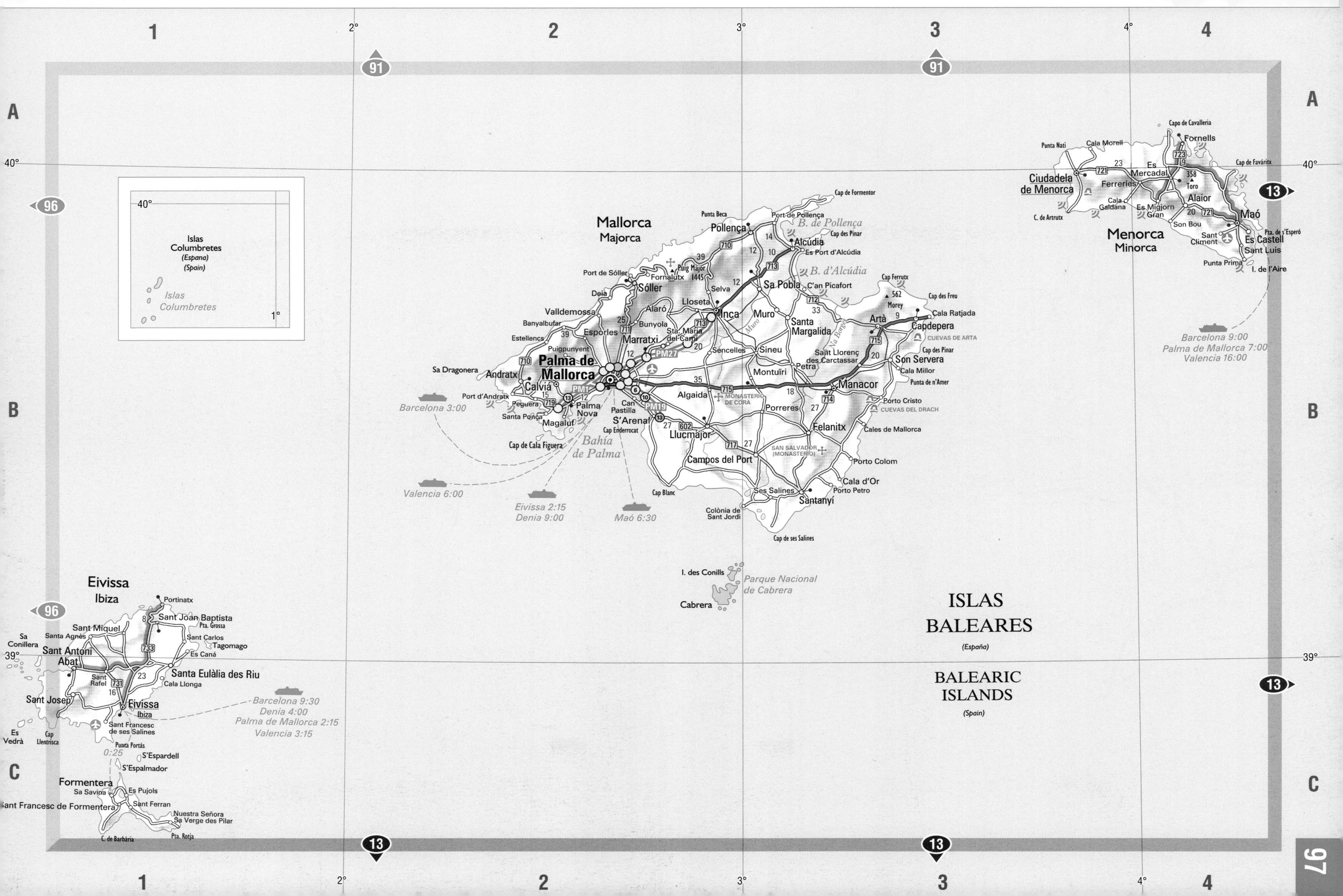

ISLAS BALEARES
(España)
BALEARIC ISLANDS
(Spain)
Mallorca
Majorca
Menorca
Minorca
Eivissa
Ibiza
Formentera
Islas Columbretes
(Espana)
(Spain)
Palma de Mallorca
Inca
Manacor
Sóller
Pollença
Alcúdia
Sa Pobla
Artà
Capdepera
Cala Ratjada
Son Servera
Felanitx
Llucmajor
Campos del Port
Santanyí
Ses Salines
Colònia de Sant Jordi
Andratx
Calvià
Valldemossa
Deia
Bunyola
Marratxi
Muro
Sineu
Santa Margalida
Algaida
Porreres
Petra
Montuïri
Lloseta
Selva
Alaró
Esporles
Magaluf
Palma Nova
S'Arenal
Can Pastilla
Puig Major 1445
Cap de Formentor
B. de Pollença
B. d'Alcúdia
Bahía de Palma
Sa Dragonera
Parque Nacional de Cabrera
Cabrera
I. des Conills
Cap de ses Salines
Ciudadela de Menorca
Ferreries
Es Mercadal
Alaior
Maó
Es Castell
Sant Luis
Fornells
Es Migjorn Gran
Son Bou
Sant Climent
Punta Prima
I. de l'Aire
Cap de Favàritx
Capo de Cavalleria
Punta Nati
Cala Morell
C. de Artrutx
Toro 358
Eivissa
Ibiza
Sant Antoni Abat
Sant Josep
Sant Miquel
Sant Joan Baptista
Santa Eulàlia des Riu
Sant Carlos
Sant Rafel
Sant Francesc de ses Salines
Portinatx
Tagomago
Es Canà
Cala Llonga
Santa Agnès
Sa Conillera
Es Vedrà
Cap Llentrisca
Punta Portás
S'Espardell
S'Espalmador
Sa Savina
Es Pujols
Sant Ferran
Sant Francesc de Formentera
Nuestra Señora Sa Verge des Pilar
C. de Barbària
Pta. Rotja
Barcelona 3:00
Valencia 6:00
Eivissa 2:15
Denia 9:00
Maó 6:30
Barcelona 9:00
Palma de Mallorca 7:00
Valencia 16:00
Barcelona 9:30
Denia 4:00
Palma de Mallorca 2:15
Valencia 3:15
0:25

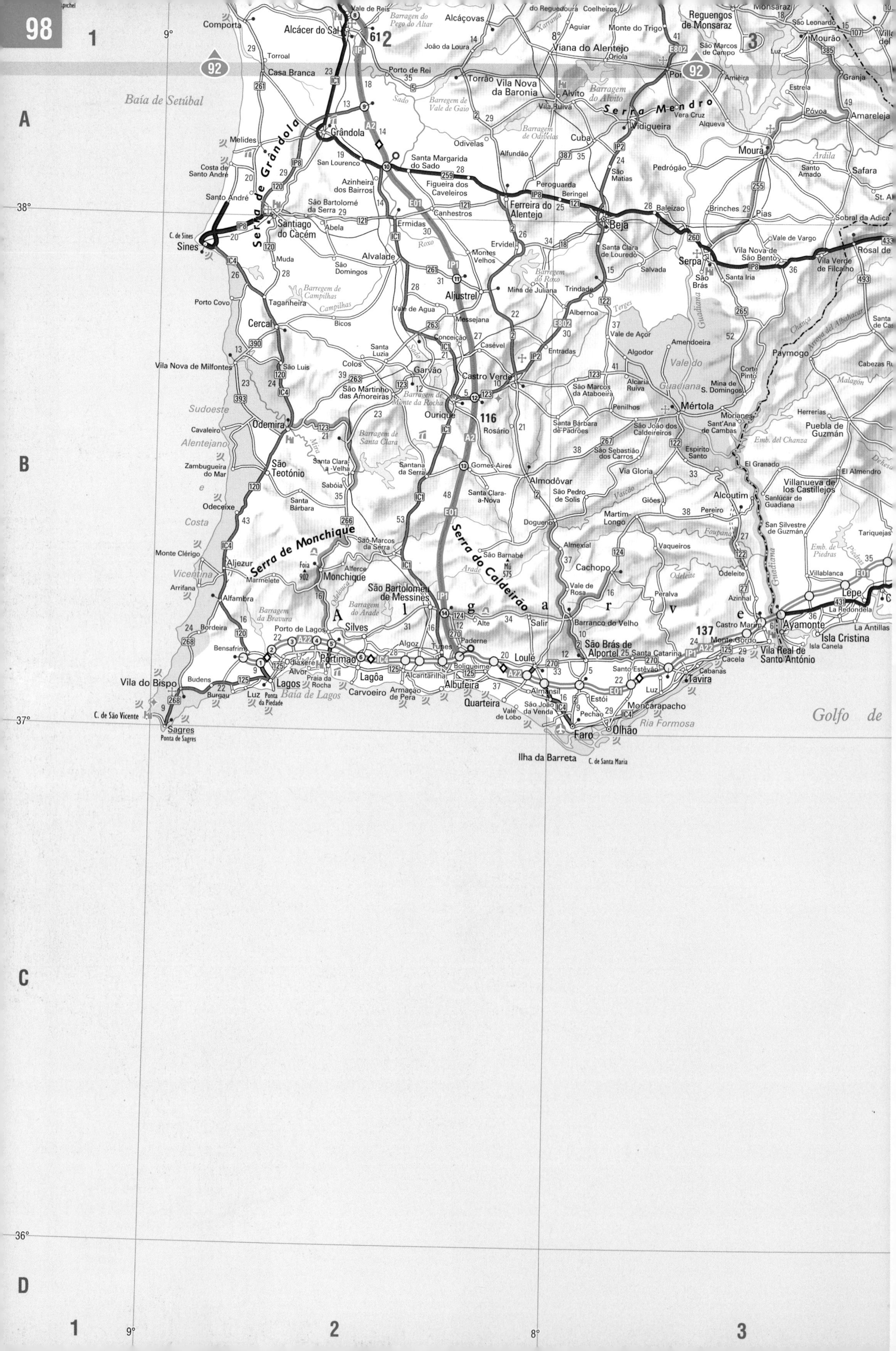
1
2
3
A
B
C
D
9°
8°
38°
37°
36°
92
61
116
137
Baía de Setúbal
Comporta
Alcácer do Sal
Vale de Reis
Barragem do Pego do Altar
Alcáçovas
Reguengos de Monsaraz
Monsaraz
São Leonardo
Mourão
Torroal
Casa Branca
Porto de Rei
João da Loura
Torrão
Vila Nova da Baronia
Viana do Alentejo
Aguiar
Monte do Trigo
Oriola
Alvito
Barragem do Alvito
São Marcos de Campo
Amieira
Granja
Estrela
Póvoa
Amareleja
Barragem de Vale de Gaio
Sado
Serra Mendro
Vila Ruiva
Vidigueira
Vera Cruz
Alqueva
Grândola
Serra de Grândola
Melides
Costa de Santo André
Santo André
San Lourenço
Santa Margarida do Sado
Odivelas
Barragem de Odivelas
Alfundão
Cuba
Moura
Ardila
Santo Amado
Safara
Pedrógão
Azinheira dos Bairros
Figueira dos Caveleiros
Peroguarda
Beringel
São Matias
São Bartolomé da Serra
Santiago do Cacém
Ferreira do Alentejo
Canhestros
Beja
Baleizão
Brinches
Pias
Sobral da Adica
St. Al
C. de Sines
Sines
Abela
Ermidas
Roxo
Ervidel
Montes Velhos
Santa Clara de Louredo
Salvada
Serpa
Vale de Vargo
Vila Nova de São Bento
Vila Verde de Filcalho
Rosal de
Santa Iria
São Brás
Muda
São Domingos
Alvalade
Aljustrel
Barragem do Roxo
Mina de Juliana
Trindade
Porto Covo
Taganheira
Barregem de Campilhas
Campilhas
Vale de Agua
Messejana
Albernoa
Terges
Bicos
Cercal
Conceição
Casével
Vale de Açor
Amendoeira
Chança
Arroyo del Albahacar
Santa
Vila Nova de Milfontes
São Luis
Santa Luzia
Colos
Garvão
Castro Verde
Entradas
Algodor
Vale do Guadiana
Guadiana
Paymogo
Corte Pinto
Cabezas Ru
São Martinho das Amoreiras
Barragem de Monte da Rocha
Ourique
São Marcos da Atabueira
Alcaria Ruiva
Mina de S. Domingos
Malagón
Sudoeste
Alentejano
Cavaleiro
Odemira
Mira
Barragem de Santa Clara
Rosário
Santa Bárbara de Padrões
Penilhos
Mértola
Moriones
Sant'Ana de Cambas
Herrerías
Puebla de Guzmán
São Sebastião dos Carros
São João dos Caldeireiros
Espírito Santo
Emb. del Chanza
Zambugueira do Mar
São Teotónio
Santa Clara-a-Velha
Santana da Serra
Gomes Aires
Almodôvar
Via Gloria
El Granado
El Almendro
Sabóia
Santa Clara-a-Nova
São Pedro de Solis
Vascão
Alcoutim
Villanueva de los Castillejos
Sanlúcar de Guadiana
Odeceixe
Costa
Santa Bárbara
Giões
Pereiro
Martim-Longo
Doguenos
Serra do Caldeirão
San Silvestre de Guzmán
Foupana
Tariquejas
Monte Clérigo
Serra de Monchique
São Marcos da Serra
São Barnabé
Almexial
Vaqueiros
Emb. de Piedras
Aljezur
Vicentina
Foia 902
Alferce
Mu 575
Arade
Cachopo
Odeleite
Villablanca
Arrifana
Marmelete
Monchique
Odelouca
São Bartolomeu de Messines
Vale de Rosa
Peralva
Lepe
Alfambra
Barragem da Bravura
Barragem do Arade
Algarve
Alte
Salir
Barranco do Velho
Azinhal
La Redondela
Ayamonte
Castro Marim
Bordeira
Porto de Lagos
Silves
Paderne
São Brás de Alportel
Monte Gordo
Isla Cristina
Las Antillas
Isla Canela
Bensafrim
Algoz
Tunes
Loulé
Santa Catarina
Cacela
Vila Real de Santo António
Odiáxere
Portimão
Alvor
Boliqueime
Santo Estêvão
Cabanas
Tavira
Vila do Bispo
Budens
Burgau
Lagos
Praia da Rocha
Lagôa
Alcantarilha
Albufeira
Almansil
Estói
Luz
Baía de Lagos
Luz
Ponta da Piedade
Carvoeiro
Armação de Pera
Quarteira
Vale de Lobo
São João da Venda
Pechão
Moncarapacho
C. de São Vicente
Sagres
Ponta de Sagres
Faro
Olhão
Ria Formosa
Golfo de
Ilha da Barreta
C. de Santa Maria

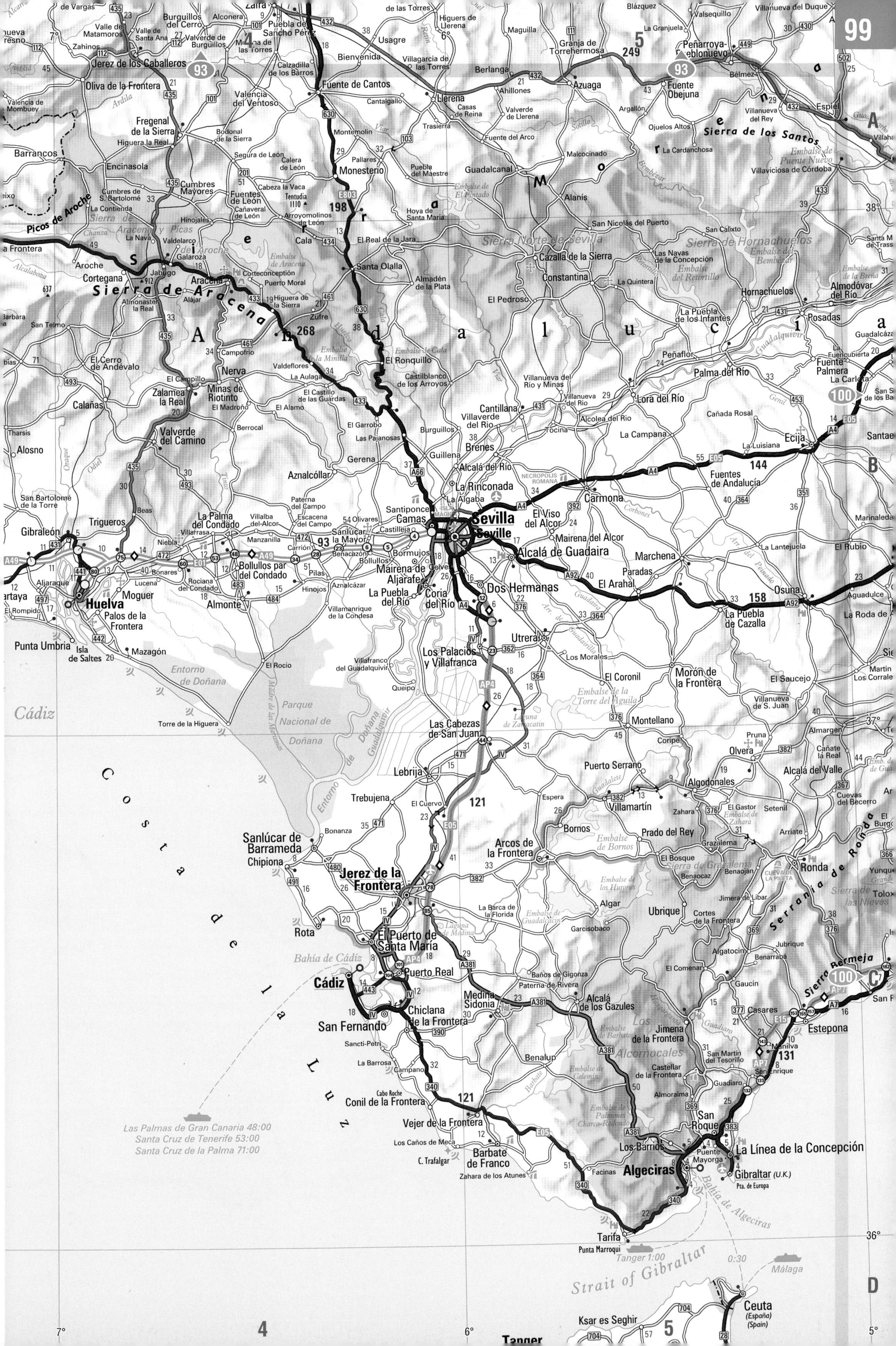
Jerez de los Caballeros
Oliva de la Frontera
Fregenal de la Sierra
Higuera la Real
Barrancos
Encinasola
Cumbres Mayores
Cumbres de S. Bartolomé
Fuentes de León
Segura de León
Calera de León
Monesterio
Fuente de Cantos
Bienvenida
Usagre
Llerena
Azuaga
Berlanga
Granja de Torrehermosa
Peñarroya-Pueblonuevo
Fuente Obejuna
Bélmez
Espiel
Villaviciosa de Córdoba
Sierra de los Santos
Picos de Aroche
Aroche
Cortegana
Aracena
Sierra de Aracena
Santa Olalla
Cala
El Real de la Jara
Almadén de la Plata
Guadalcanal
Alanís
Cazalla de la Sierra
Constantina
San Nicolás del Puerto
Sierra Norte de Sevilla
Sierra de Hornachuelos
Hornachuelos
Almodóvar del Río
Posadas
Palma del Río
Lora del Río
Peñaflor
Fuente Palmera
La Carlota
Écija
Nerva
Minas de Riotinto
Zalamea la Real
Valverde del Camino
Calañas
El Cerro de Andévalo
Alosno
Aznalcóllar
El Ronquillo
Castilblanco de los Arroyos
Cantillana
Villaverde del Río
Brenes
Guillena
Gerena
Alcalá del Río
La Rinconada
Carmona
Fuentes de Andalucía
El Viso del Alcor
Mairena del Alcor
Sevilla
Seville
Camas
Santiponce
Sanlúcar la Mayor
Mairena de Aljarafe
Alcalá de Guadaira
Dos Hermanas
Coria del Río
La Puebla del Río
Marchena
Paradas
El Arahal
Osuna
La Puebla de Cazalla
Utrera
Los Palacios y Villafranca
Morón de la Frontera
El Coronil
Montellano
Las Cabezas de San Juan
Lebrija
Trebujena
Olvera
Algodonales
Puerto Serrano
Villamartín
Bornos
Prado del Rey
Arcos de la Frontera
Grazalema
Sierra de Grazalema
Ronda
Serranía de Ronda
Ubrique
Cortes de la Frontera
Jimena de la Frontera
Los Alcornocales
Gibraleón
Trigueros
La Palma del Condado
Bollullos par del Condado
Almonte
Moguer
Huelva
Palos de la Frontera
Punta Umbría
Isla de Saltes
Mazagón
El Rocío
Entorno de Doñana
Parque Nacional de Doñana
Torre de la Higuera
Cádiz
Costa de la Luz
Sanlúcar de Barrameda
Chipiona
Rota
Jerez de la Frontera
El Puerto de Santa María
Bahía de Cádiz
Puerto Real
San Fernando
Chiclana de la Frontera
Medina Sidonia
Alcalá de los Gazules
Sancti-Petri
Conil de la Frontera
Vejer de la Frontera
Barbate de Franco
Los Caños de Meca
C. Trafalgar
Zahara de los Atunes
Benalup
Tarifa
Punta Marroquí
Algeciras
Los Barrios
San Roque
La Línea de la Concepción
Gibraltar (U.K.)
Pta. de Europa
Bahía de Algeciras
Estepona
Manilva
Casares
Sierra Bermeja
Strait of Gibraltar
Tanger 1:00
0:30
Málaga
Ceuta (España) (Spain)
Ksar es Seghir
Tanger
Las Palmas de Gran Canaria 48:00
Santa Cruz de Tenerife 53:00
Santa Cruz de la Palma 71:00
A
B
C
D
4
5
7°
6°
5°
38°
37°
36°

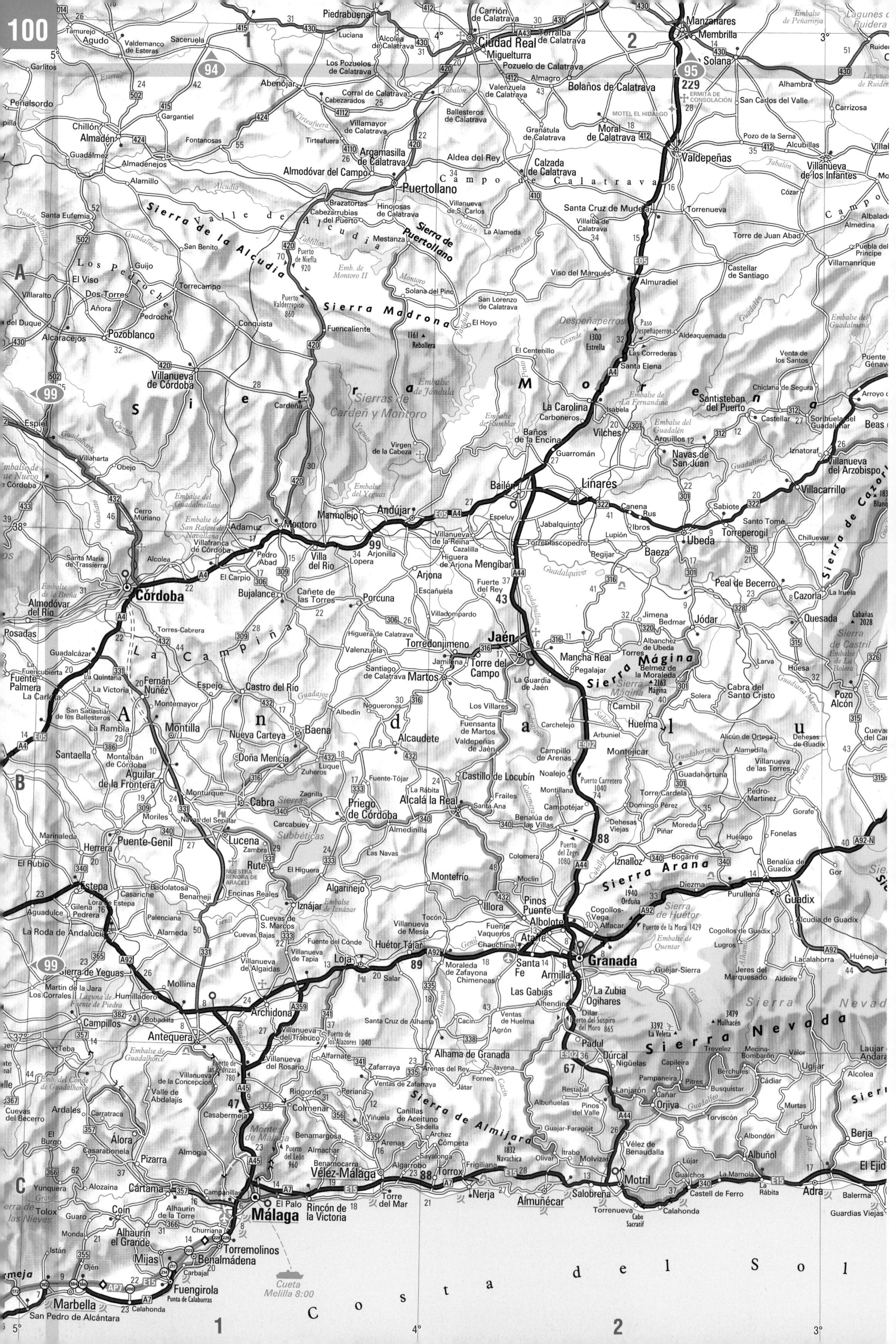
Piedrabuena
Carrión de Calatrava
Ciudad Real
Miguelturra
Torralba de Calatrava
Manzanares
Membrilla
La Solana
Embalse de Peñarroya
Lagunes de Ruidera
Tamurejo
Agudo
Valdemanco de Esteras
Saceruela
Luciana
Alcolea de Calatrava
Los Pozuelos de Calatrava
Pozuelo de Calatrava
Almagro
Bolaños de Calatrava
Alhambra
Garlitos
Abenójar
Corral de Calatrava
Cabezarados
Valenzuela de Calatrava
Ermita de Consolación
Motel el Hidalgo
San Carlos del Valle
Carrizosa
Peñalsordo
Gargantiel
Villamayor de Calatrava
Ballesteros de Calatrava
Moral de Calatrava
Chillón
Almadén
Fontanosas
Tirteafuera
Granátula de Calatrava
Pozo de la Serna
Alcubillas
Guadalmez
Almadenejos
Argamasilla de Calatrava
Aldea del Rey
Calzada de Calatrava
Valdepeñas
Villanueva de los Infantes
Almodóvar del Campo
Puertollano
Campo de Calatrava
Alamillo
Brazatortas
Hinojosas de Calatrava
Villanueva de S. Carlos
Santa Cruz de Mudela
Torrenueva
Cózar
Villalba de Calatrava
Santa Eufemia
Valle de Alcudia
Cabezarrubias del Puerto
Sierra de Puertollano
Mestanza
La Alameda
Torre de Juan Abad
Almedina
Albaladejo
Sierra de la Alcudia
San Benito
Puerto de Niefla 920
Emb. de Montoro II
Puebla del Príncipe
Villamanrique
Los Pedroches
Guijo
El Viso
Viso del Marqués
Almuradiel
Castellar de Santiago
Villaralto
Dos-Torres
Torrecampo
Añora
Pedroche
Puerto Valderrepiso 860
Sierra Madrona
Solana del Pino
San Lorenzo de Calatrava
El Hoyo
Despeñaperros
1300 Estrella
Paso Despeñaperros
Aldeaquemada
Embalse del Guadalmena
del Duque
Conquista
Alcaracejos
Pozoblanco
Fuencaliente
1161 Rebollera
El Centenillo
Las Correderas
Santa Elena
Venta de los Santos
Puente Génave
Villanueva de Córdoba
Sierras de Cardeña y Montoro
Embalse de Jándula
Sierra Morena
La Carolina
Carboneros
Isabela
Embalse de La Fernandina
Santisteban del Puerto
Chiclana de Segura
Arroyo del Ojanco
Cardeña
Embalse de Rumblar
Baños de la Encina
Vilches
Embalse del Guadalén
Arquillos
Castellar
Sorihuela del Guadalimar
Beas de Segura
Espiel
Villaharta
Obejo
Virgen de la Cabeza
Guarromán
Navas de San Juan
Iznatoraf
Villanueva del Arzobispo
Embalse de Puente Nuevo
Embalse del Guadalmellato
Embalse del Yeguas
Bailén
Linares
Villacarrillo
Sierra de Cazorla
Cerro Muriano
Embalse de San Rafael de Navallana
Adamuz
Villafranca de Córdoba
Montoro
Marmolejo
Andújar
Espeluy
Jabalquinto
Canena
Rus
Ibros
Sabiote
Torreperogil
Santo Tomé
Chilluevar
Alcolea
Pedro Abad
Villa del Río
Lopera
Arjonilla
Villanueva de la Reina
Cazalilla
Higuera de Arjona
Mengíbar
Torreblascopedro
Lupión
Begíjar
Baeza
Úbeda
Santa María de Trassierra
Córdoba
El Carpio
Bujalance
Cañete de las Torres
Porcuna
Arjona
Escañuela
Fuerte del Rey
Guadalquivir
Peal de Becerro
Cazorla
La Iruela
Embalse de la Breña
Almodóvar del Río
Villadompardo
Jimena
Bedmar
Jódar
Quesada
Cabañas 2028
Posadas
Torres-Cabrera
La Campiña
Higuera de Calatrava
Torredonjimeno
Jaén
Albanchez de Ubeda
Sierra de Castril
Guadalcázar
Valenzuela
Mancha Real
Torres
Embalse de La Bolera
Fuente Palmera
La Carlota
Fuencubierta
La Quintana
La Victoria
Fernán Núñez
Espejo
Santiago de Calatrava
Martos
Jamilena
Torre del Campo
La Guardia de Jaén
Pegalajar
Sierra Mágina
Belmez de la Moraleda
2163 Mágina
Larva
Huesa
Cabra del Santo Cristo
Pozo Alcón
Montemayor
San Sebastián de los Ballesteros
La Rambla
Castro del Río
Noguerones
Los Villares
Solera
Cambil
Albedín
Fuensanta de Martos
Carchelejo
Huelma
Alicún de Ortega
Dehesas de Guadix
Cuevas del Campo
Montilla
Nueva Carteya
Baena
Alcaudete
Valdepeñas de Jaén
Arbuniel
Montejícar
Alamedilla
Santaella
Montalbán de Córdoba
Doña Mencía
Luque
Zuheros
Campillo de Arenas
Noalejo
Guadahortuna
Villanueva de las Torres
Aguilar de la Frontera
Fuente-Tójar
Castillo de Locubín
Puerto Carretero 1040
Torre Cardela
Pedro-Martínez
Monturque
Cabra
Sierras Subbéticas
Zagrilla
Priego de Córdoba
La Rábita
Alcalá la Real
Frailes
Santa Ana
Montillana
Domingo Pérez
Gorafe
Moriles
Navas del Sepillar
Carcabuey
Almedinilla
Benalúa de las Villas
Campotéjar
Dehesas Viejas
Moreda
Piñar
Fonelas
Marinaleda
Herrera
Puente-Genil
Lucena
Zambra
Las Navas
Puerto del Zegrí 1080
Colomera
Iznalloz
Bogarre
Huélago
Benalúa de Guadix
Gor
El Rubio
Rute
Nuestra Señora de Araceli
El Higuera
Montefrío
Moclín
Sierra Arana
Estepa
Casariche
Badolatosa
Benamejí
Encinas Reales
Algarinejo
Pinos Puente
1940 Orduña
Diezma
Purullena
Guadix
Aguadulce
Gilena
Lora de Estepa
Pedrera
Palenciana
Iznájar
Embalse de Iznájar
Tocón
Illora
Cogollos-Vega
Sierra de Huétor
Alfacar
Puerto de la Mora 1429
Alcudia de Guadix
La Roda de Andalucía
Alameda
Cuevas de S. Marcos
Cuevas Bajas
Villanueva de Mesía
Fuente Vaqueros
Albolote
Atarfe
Chauchina
Embalse de Quéntar
Cogollos de Guadix
Lugros
Fuente del Conde
Huétor Tájar
Granada
Huéneja
Sierra de Yeguas
Villanueva de Tapia
Loja
Santa Fe
Armilla
Güéjar-Sierra
Lacalahorra
Villanueva de Algaidas
Salar
Moraleda de Zafayona
Chimeneas
Jeres del Marquesado
Aldeire
Martín de la Jara
Los Corrales
Laguna de Fuente de Piedra
Humilladero
Mollina
Las Gabias
La Zubia
Ogíjares
Alhendín
Sierra Nevada
Campillos
Bobadilla
Archidona
Santa Cruz de Alhama
Cacín
Ventas de Huelma
Agrón
Dílar
Puerto del Suspiro del Moro 865
3479 Mulhacén
3392 La Veleta
Teba
Antequera
Villanueva del Trabuco
Puerto de los Alazores 1040
Alhama de Granada
Padul
Dúrcal
Nigüelas
Trevelez
Mecina-Bombarón
Válor
Laujar de Andarax
Embalse de Guadalhorce
Puerto de las Pedrizas 780
Villanueva del Rosario
Alfarnate
Zafarraya
Arenas del Rey
Jayena
Capileira
Pampaneira
Bérchules
Ugíjar
Emb. del Conde de Guadalhorce
Villanueva de la Concepción
Ventas de Zafarraya
Fornes
Játar
Restábal
Lanjarón
Pitres
Busquístar
Cádiar
Alcolea
Valle de Abdalajís
Riogordo
Periana
Sierra de Almijara
Albuñuelas
Pinos del Valle
Cáñar
Órgiva
Ardales
Carratraca
Casabermeja
Colmenar
Alfarnatejo
Yunquera
Canillas de Aceituno
Sedella
Guajar-Faragüit
Torviscón
Murtas
Turón
Cuevas del Becerro
El Burgo
Álora
Montes de Málaga
Benamargosa
Almáchar
Archez
Cómpeta
Albondón
Berja
Casarabonela
Puerto del León 960
Arenas
Sayalonga
1832 Navachica
Ítrabo
Olívar
Molvízar
Vélez de Benaudalla
Albuñol
Pizarra
Almogía
Benamocarra
Algarrobo
Frigiliana
Lújar
Gualchos
La Mamola
El Ejido
Alozaina
Cártama
Campanillas
Vélez-Málaga
Torrox
Nerja
Almuñécar
Salobreña
Motril
Castell de Ferro
La Rábita
Adra
Balerma
Tolox
Coín
Alhaurín de la Torre
El Palo
Rincón de la Victoria
Torre del Mar
Torrenueva
Cabo Sacratif
Calahonda
Guardias Viejas
Sierra de las Nieves
Guaro
Málaga
Alhaurín el Grande
Monda
Churriana
Torremolinos
Istán
Mijas
Benalmádena
Ojén
Carbajal
Cueta Melilla 8:00
Costa del Sol
Fuengirola
Punta de Calaburras
Marbella
Calahonda
San Pedro de Alcántara

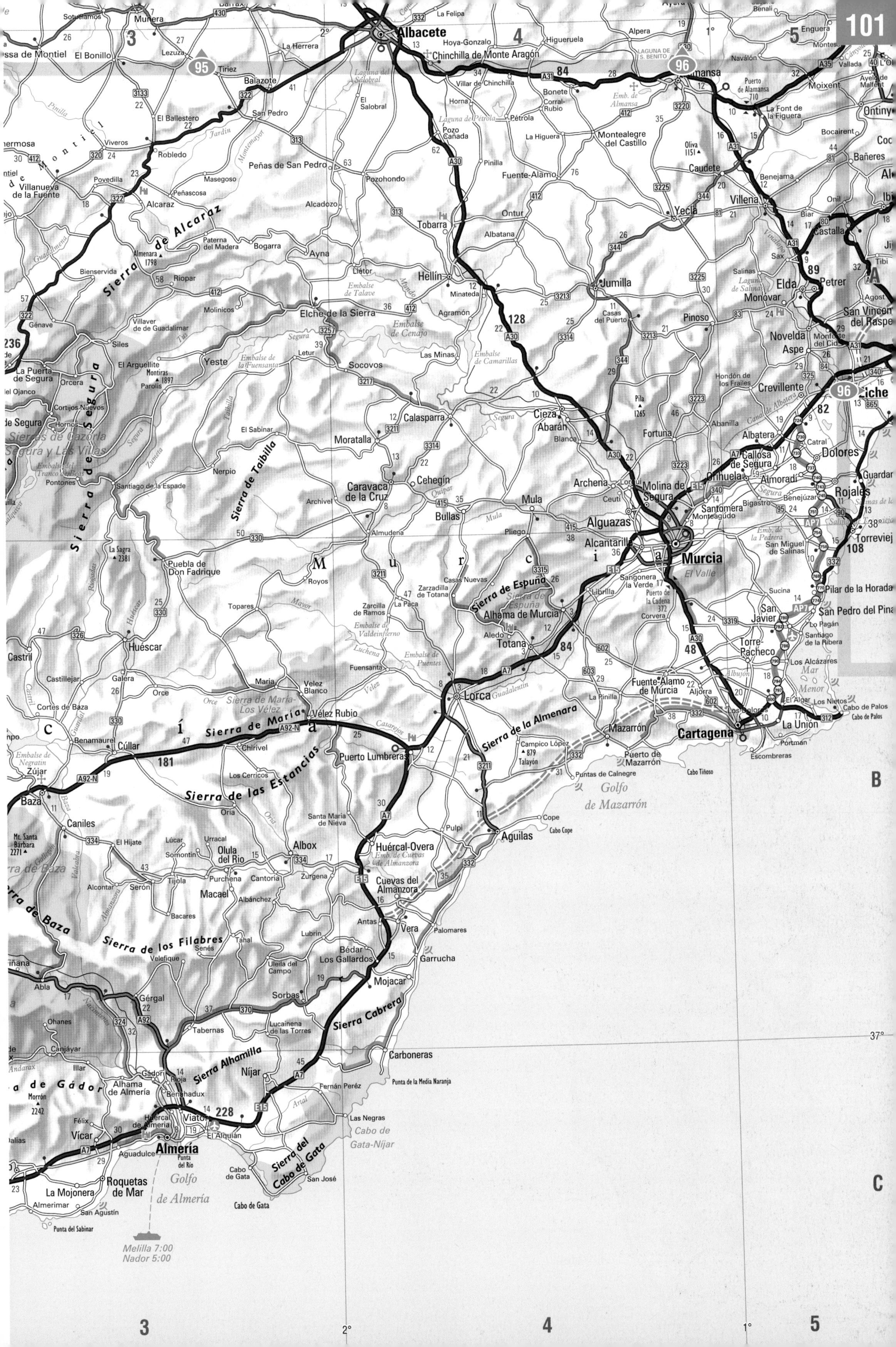

Albacete
Hoya-Gonzalo
Chinchilla de Monte Aragón
Higueruela
Alpera
Almansa
Enguera
Montesa
Navalón
Vallada
Moixent
Ontinyent
Munera
Sotuélamos
El Bonillo
Lezuza
Tiriez
Balazote
La Herrera
Villar de Chinchilla
Bonete
Corral-Rubio
Emb. de Almansa
Puerto de Almansa
La Font de la Figuera
El Ballestero
San Pedro
El Salobral
Laguna del Salobral
Horna
Pozo Cañada
Laguna del Pétrola
Pétrola
La Higuera
Montealegre del Castillo
Oliva 1151
Caudete
Bocairent
Bañeres
Viveros
Robledo
Peñas de San Pedro
Pinilla
Fuente-Álamo
Benejama
Villena
Yecla
Onil
Biar
Castalla
Povedilla
Villanueva de la Fuente
Masegoso
Peñascosa
Alcaraz
Pozohondo
Alcadozo
Ontur
Tobarra
Albatana
Sierra de Alcaraz
Almenara 1798
Paterna del Madera
Bogarra
Ayna
Liétor
Hellín
Minateda
Jumilla
Salinas
Sax
Elda
Petrer
Monóvar
Bienservida
Riopar
Molinicos
Embalse de Talave
Agramón
Casas del Puerto
Pinoso
Novelda
Aspe
Monforte del Cid
Villaver de Guadalimar
Elche de la Sierra
Embalse de Cenajo
Génave
Siles
Letur
Socovos
Las Minas
Embalse de Camarillas
El Arguellite
Montiras 1897
Parolis
Yeste
Embalse de la Fuensanta
La Puerta de Segura
Orcera
Hondón de los Frailes
Crevillente
Elche
Cortijos Nuevos
Hornos
Calasparra
Cieza
Abarán
Blanca
Pila 1265
Fortuna
Abanilla
Albatera
Catral
Dolores
Sierras de Cazorla Segura y Las Villas
Embalse del Tranco de Beas
Pontones
El Sabinar
Moratalla
Callosa de Segura
Almoradí
Orihuela
Guardamar
Rojales
Sierra de Segura
Nerpio
Sierra de Taibilla
Santiago de la Espada
Caravaca de la Cruz
Cehegín
Archena
Molina de Segura
Ceutí
Lorquí
Mula
Bullas
Santomera
Monteagudo
Bigastro
Benejúzar
Archivel
Almudena
Pliego
Alguazas
Alcantarilla
Murcia
El Valle
Torrevieja
San Miguel de Salinas
Emb. de la Pedrera
La Sagra 2381
Puebla de Don Fadrique
Royos
Casas Nuevas
Sierra de Espuña
Zarzadilla de Totana
Sangonera la Verde
Puerto de la Cadena 372
Librilla
Alhama de Murcia
Corvera
Sucina
Pilar de la Horadada
San Pedro del Pinatar
San Javier
Lo Pagán
Santiago de la Ribera
Topares
Zarcilla de Ramos
La Paca
Embalse de Valdeinfierno
Aledo
Totana
Torre-Pacheco
Los Alcázares
Mar Menor
Castril
Huéscar
Castillejar
Galera
Orce
María
Velez Blanco
Fuensanta
Embalse de Puentes
Lorca
Fuente-Álamo de Murcia
Aljorra
La Pinilla
El Algar
Los Nietos
Cabo de Palos
La Unión
Cortes de Baza
Sierra de María-Los Vélez
Vélez Rubio
Sierra de María
Sierra de la Almenara
Mazarrón
Cartagena
Portman
Escombreras
Benamaurel
Cúllar
Chirivel
Puerto Lumbreras
Campico López 879
Talayón
Puerto de Mazarrón
Cabo Tiñoso
Embalse de Negratín
Zújar
Los Cerricos
Sierra de las Estancias
Puntas de Calnegre
Golfo de Mazarrón
Baza
Caniles
Oria
Santa María de Nieva
Cope
Cabo Cope
Mt. Santa Bárbara 2271
El Hijate
Lúcar
Urracal
Somontín
Olula del Río
Albox
Pulpí
Águilas
Huércal-Overa
Emb. de Cuevas del Almanzora
Sierra de Baza
Alcontar
Serón
Tíjola
Purchena
Cantoria
Zurgena
Cuevas del Almanzora
Macael
Albánchez
Bacares
Antas
Vera
Palomares
Sierra de los Filabres
Tahal
Lubrín
Senés
Velefique
Bédar
Los Gallardos
Garrucha
Uleila del Campo
Abla
Gérgal
Mojácar
Sorbas
Ohanes
Tabernas
Lucainena de las Torres
Sierra Cabrera
Canjáyar
Carboneras
Illar
Gádor
Rioja
Sierra Alhamilla
Níjar
Sierra de Gádor
Alhama de Almería
Benahadux
Fernán Pérez
Punta de la Media Naranja
Morrón 2242
Huércal de Almería
Viator
Félix
Vícar
El Alquián
Las Negras
Cabo de Gata-Níjar
Almería
Aguadulce
Punta del Río
Golfo de Almería
Sierra del Cabo de Gata
Cabo de Gata
San José
Roquetas de Mar
La Mojonera
Almerimar
San Agustín
Punta del Sabinar
Melilla 7:00
Nador 5:00
37°
2°
1°
3
4
5
B
C

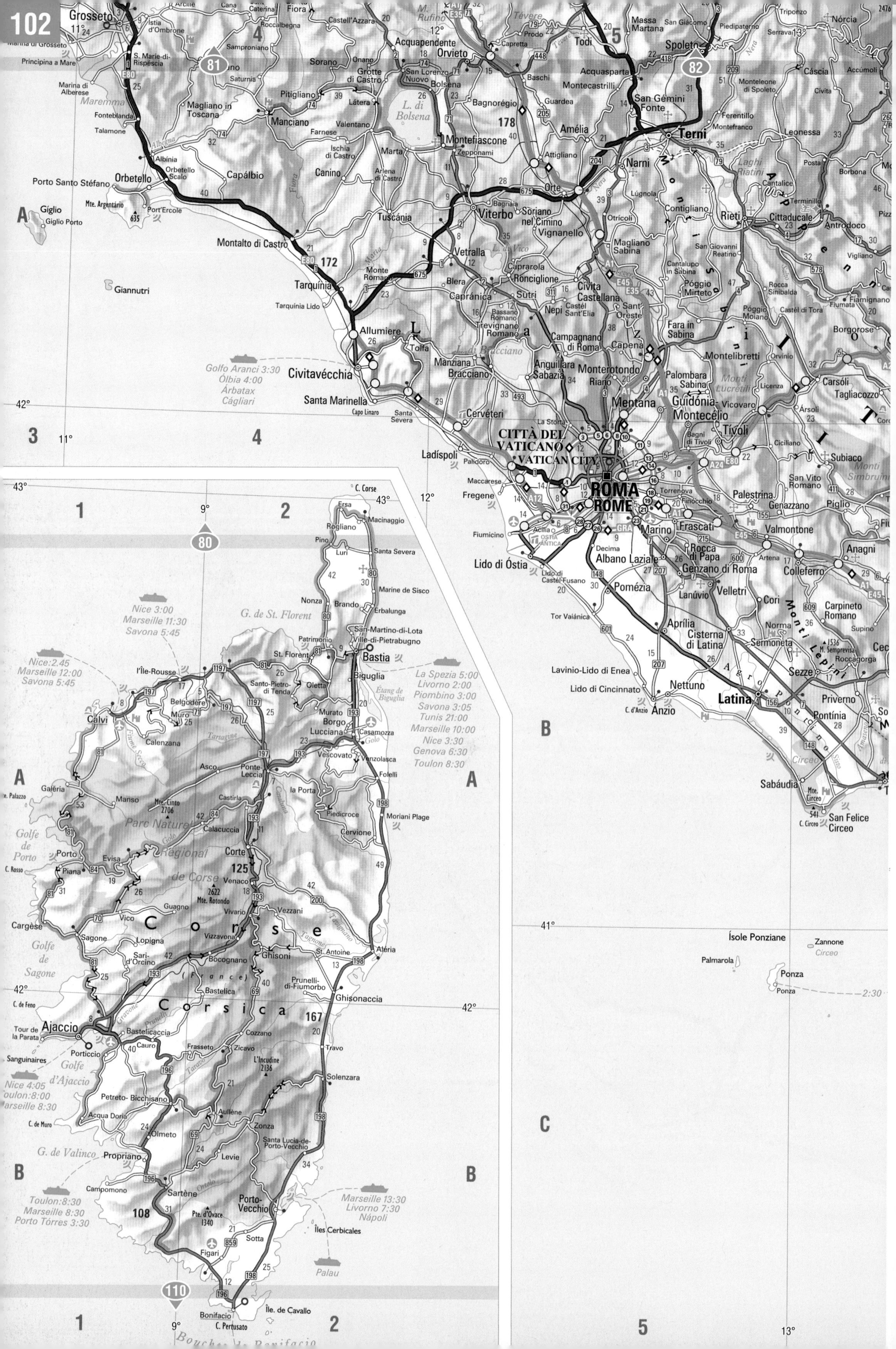
Grosseto
Marina di Grosseto
Principina a Mare
Marina di Alberese
Maremma
Fonteblanda
Talamone
Albinia
Orbetello
Orbetello Scalo
Porto Santo Stéfano
Mte. Argentário
Port'Ercole
Giglio
Giglio Porto
Giannutri
Capálbio
Magliano in Toscana
Manciano
Pitigliano
Sorano
Saturnia
Sampronianо
Roccalbegna
Castell'Azzara
Acquapendente
Onano
Grotte di Castro
San Lorenzo Nuovo
Bolsena
L. di Bolsena
Látera
Valentano
Farnese
Ischia di Castro
Canino
Arlena di Castro
Marta
Montefiascone
Zepponami
Tuscánia
Montalto di Castro
Tarquínia
Tarquínia Lido
Monte Romano
Viterbo
Bagnaia
Soriano nel Cimino
Vignanello
Vetralla
L. di Vico
Caprarola
Ronciglione
Blera
Capránica
Sutri
Nepi
Civita Castellana
Castél Sant'Elia
Bassano Romano
Trevignano Romano
L. di Bracciano
Manziana
Bracciano
Anguillara Sabazia
Campagnano di Roma
Allumiere
Tolfa
Civitavécchia
Santa Marinella
Capo Linaro
Santa Severa
Cerveteri
Ladíspoli
Palidoro
Maccarese
Fregene
Fiumicino
Acilia
Ostia Antica
Lido di Óstia
Lido di Castél Fusano
Tor Vaiánica
Decima
Pomézia
Albano Laziale
Marino
Frascati
Rocca di Papa
Genzano di Roma
Lanúvio
Velletri
Aprília
Cisterna di Latina
Latina
Lavinio-Lido di Enea
Lido di Cincinnato
Nettuno
Anzio
C. d'Anzio
Sabáudia
Mte. Circeo
San Felice Circeo
C. Circeo
Pontínia
Priverno
Sezze
Sermoneta
Norma
Cori
Carpineto Romano
Roccagorga
M. Semprevisa
Monti Lepini
Agro Pontino
Colleferro
Artena
Valmontone
Anagni
Genazzano
Palestrina
Píglio
San Vito Romano
Subiaco
Monti Simbruini
Tívoli
Bagni di Tivoli
Guidónia-Montecélio
Palombara Sabina
Monti Lucrétili
Vicovaro
Licenza
Ársoli
Carsóli
Tagliacozzo
Mentana
Monterotondo
Riano
Capena
Fara in Sabina
Montelibretti
Sant'Oreste
Póggio Mirteto
Cantalupo in Sabina
Magliano Sabina
Otrícoli
Orte
Attigliano
Amélia
Narni
Terni
Rieti
Cittaducale
Contigliano
Antrodoco
Leonessa
Spoleto
Todi
Orvieto
Massa Martana
Acquasparta
San Gémini Fonte
Montecastrilli
Bagnorégio
Guardea
Baschi
Ferentillo
Montefranco
Cáscia
Nórcia
Monteleone di Spoleto
CITTÀ DEL VATICANO
VATICAN CITY
ROMA
ROME
Golfo Aranci 3:30
Ólbia 4:00
Árbatax
Cágliari
Ísole Ponziane
Zannone
Palmarola
Ponza
C. Corse
Ersa
Macinaggio
Rogliano
Pino
Luri
Santa Severa
Marine de Sisco
Nonza
Brando
Erbalunga
G. de St. Florent
San-Martino-di-Lota
Ville-di-Pietrabugno
Patrimonio
St. Florent
Bastia
Biguglia
Étang de Biguglia
Oletta
Santo-Pietro-di Tenda
L'Île-Rousse
Belgodère
Calvi
Calenzana
Muro
Asco
Ponte-Leccia
Murato
Borgo
Lucciana
Casamozza
Vescovato
Venzolasca
Folelli
la Porta
Piedicroce
Cervione
Moriani Plage
Galéria
Manso
Mte. Cinto
Parc Naturel Régional de Corse
Castirla
Calacuccia
Corte
Venaco
Mte. Rotondo
Vivario
Vezzani
Evisa
Golfe de Porto
Porto
Piana
C. Rosso
Cargèse
Guagno
Vico
Sagone
Golfe de Sagone
Lopigna
Sari-d'Orcino
Vizzavona
Bocognano
Ghisoni
St. Antoine
Aléria
Prunelli-di-Fiumorbo
Ghisonaccia
Bastelica
Corse
Corsica
(France)
C. de Feno
Tour de la Parata
Ajaccio
Sanguinaires
Golfe d'Ajaccio
Porticcio
Bastelicaccia
Cauro
Frasseto
Zicavo
Cozzano
L'Incudine
Travo
Solenzara
Petreto-Bicchisano
Acqua Doria
C. de Muro
Aullène
Olmeto
Zonza
G. de Valinco
Propriano
Santa Lucia-de-Porto-Vecchio
Levie
Campomoro
Sartène
Pte. d'Ovace
Porto-Vecchio
Îles Cerbicales
Figari
Sotta
Bonifacio
C. Pertusato
Île. de Cavallo
Bouches de Bonifacio
Nice 3:00
Marseille 11:30
Savona 5:45
Nice 2:45
Marseille 12:00
Savona 5:45
La Spezia 5:00
Livorno 2:00
Piombino 3:00
Savona 3:05
Tunis 21:00
Marseille 10:00
Nice 3:30
Genova 6:30
Toulon 8:30
Nice 4:05
Toulon 8:00
Marseille 8:30
Toulon 8:30
Marseille 8:30
Porto Tórres 3:30
Marseille 13:30
Livorno 7:30
Nápoli
Palau
42°
43°
41°
9°
11°
12°
13°

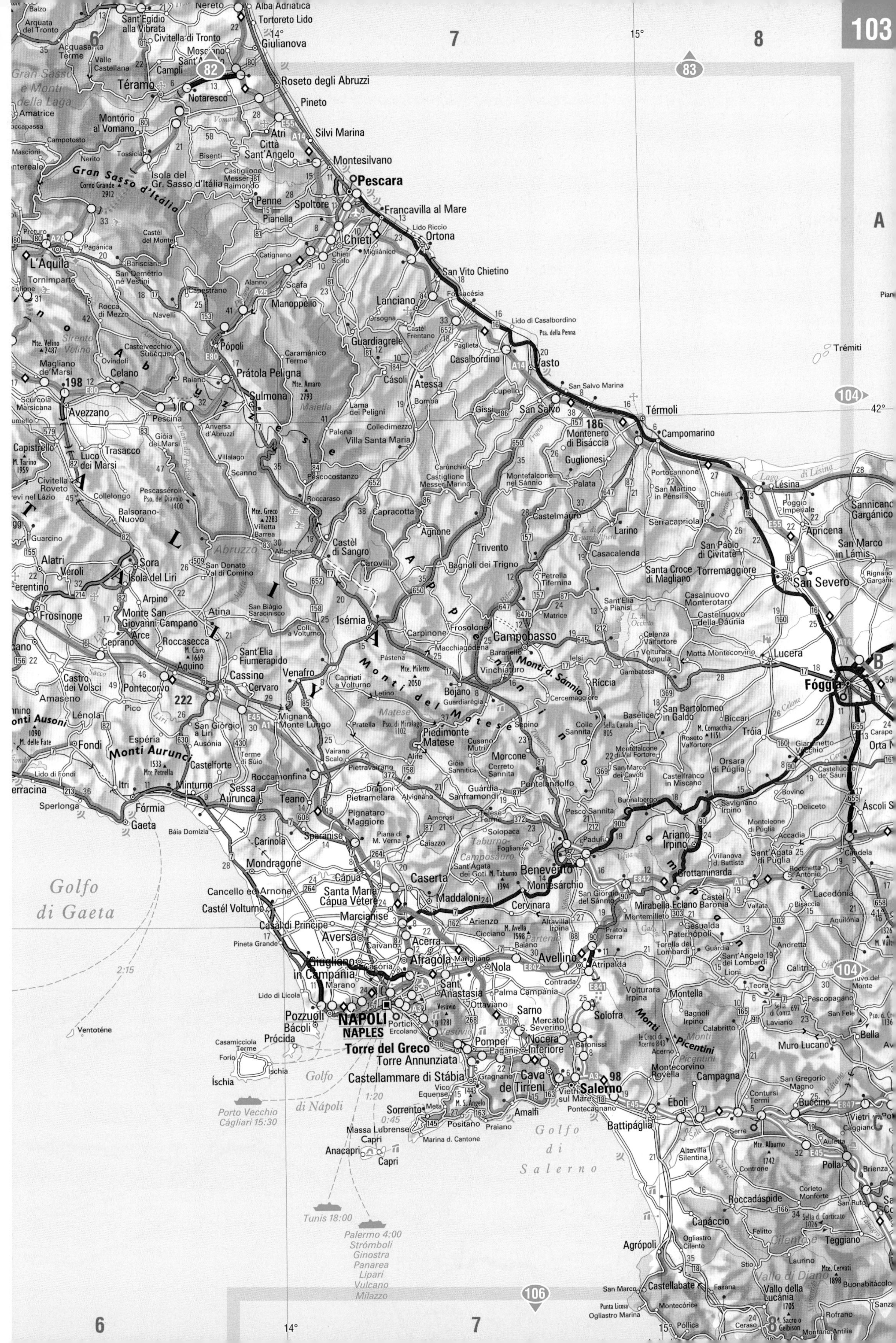

Pescara
L'Aquila
Téramo
Giulianova
Roseto degli Abruzzi
Pineto
Silvi Marina
Montesilvano
Francavilla al Mare
Chieti
Ortona
San Vito Chietino
Lanciano
Vasto
San Salvo
Térmoli
Campomarino
Lésina
Trémiti
Sulmona
Avezzano
Celano
Pópoli
Prátola Peligna
Guardiagrele
Atessa
Casalbordino
Gran Sasso d'Itália
Abruzzo
Maiella
Scanno
Pescasséroli
Roccaraso
Castèl di Sangro
Agnone
Trivento
Isérnia
Campobasso
Larino
San Severo
Lucera
Fóggia
Sora
Frosinone
Cassino
Venafro
Pontecorvo
Fondi
Formia
Gaeta
Terracina
Sperlonga
Itri
Minturno
Monti Aurunci
Golfo di Gaeta
Ventoténe
Mondragone
Cápua
Caserta
Maddaloni
Benevento
Ariano Irpino
Avellino
Aversa
Afragola
Nola
Napoli
Naples
Pozzuoli
Bácoli
Prócida
Íschia
Torre del Greco
Torre Annunziata
Castellammare di Stábia
Pompei
Sorrento
Positano
Amalfi
Capri
Anacapri
Golfo di Nápoli
Salerno
Cava de' Tirreni
Battipáglia
Éboli
Golfo di Salerno
Agrópoli
Capáccio
Vallo della Lucánia
Teggiano
Polla
Vallo di Diano
Monti Picentini
Monti d. Sánnio
Monti del Matese
Appennino
Porto Vecchio
Cágliari 15:30
Tunis 18:00
Palermo 4:00
Strómboli
Ginostra
Panarea
Lípari
Vulcano
Milazzo
82
83
104
106
6
7
8
A
B
C
14°
15°
42°

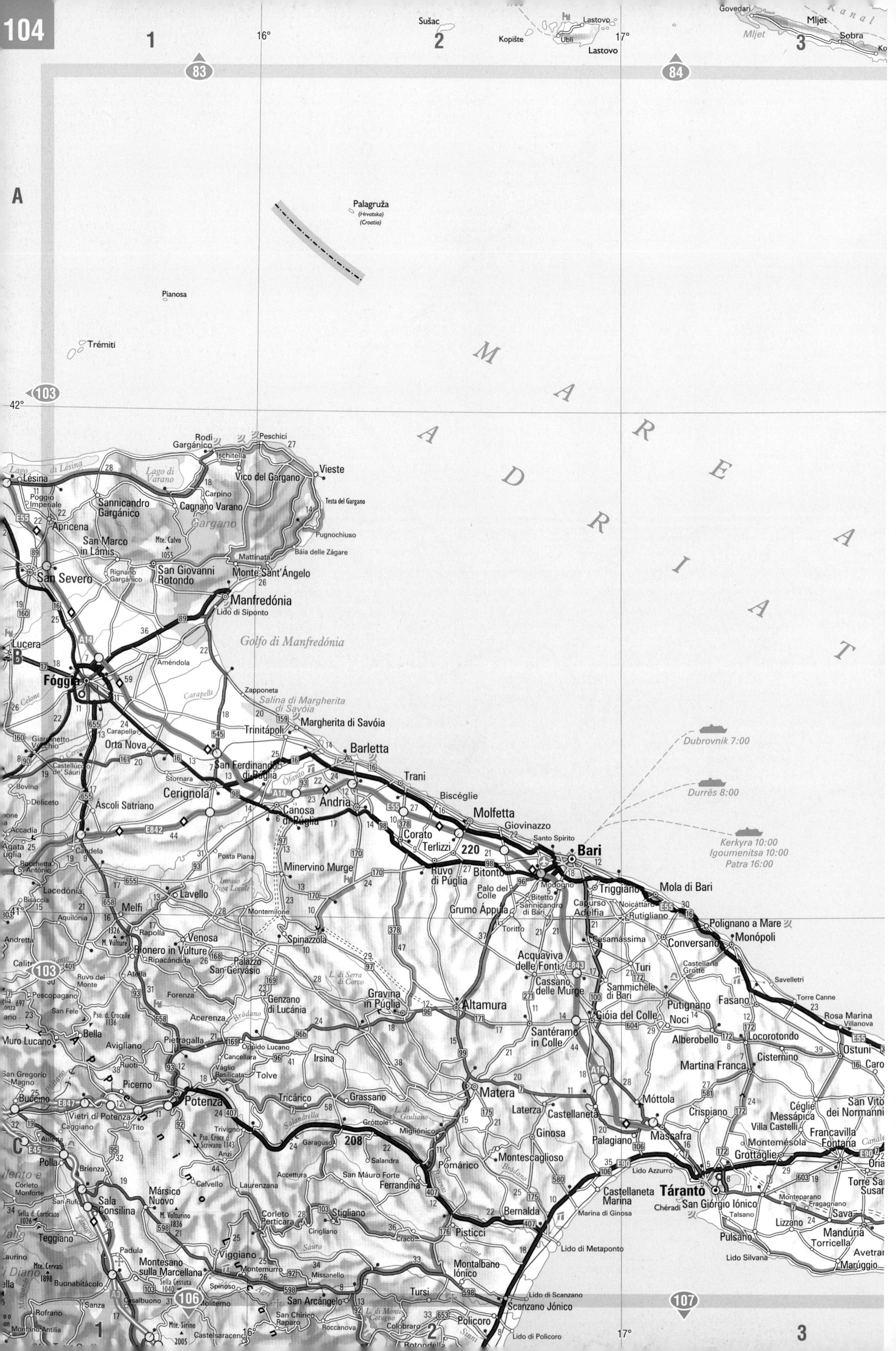
1
2
3
A
B
C
16°
17°
42°
83
84
103
106
107
Sušac
Lastovo
Kopište
Ubli
Govedari
Mljet
Sobra
Kanal
Palagruža
(Hrvatska)
(Croatia)
Pianosa
Trémiti
MARE ADRIATICO
Dubrovnik 7:00
Durrës 8:00
Kerkyra 10:00
Igoumenitsa 10:00
Patra 16:00
Rodi Gargánico
Peschici
Ischitella
Lago di Lésina
Lésina
Lago di Varano
Vico del Gargano
Vieste
Carpino
Testa del Gargano
Poggio Imperiale
Sannicandro Gargánico
Cagnano Varano
Gargano
Apricena
Pugnochiuso
San Marco in Lámis
Mte. Calvo 1055
Báia delle Zágare
Mattinata
San Severo
Rignano Gargánico
San Giovanni Rotondo
Monte Sant'Ángelo
Manfredónia
Lido di Siponto
Lucera
Golfo di Manfredónia
Améndola
Fóggia
Celone
Carapelle
Zapponeta
Salina di Margherita di Savóia
Margherita di Savóia
Trinitápoli
Carapelle
Giardinetto Vecchio
Orta Nova
Barletta
Castelluccio de' Sauri
San Ferdinando di Púglia
Stornara
Trani
Bovino
Cerignola
Ófanto
Bisceglie
Deliceto
Áscoli Satriano
Andria
Canosa di Púglia
Molfetta
Accadia
Giovinazzo
Corato
Terlizzi
Santo Spirito
Bari
Candela
Posta Piana
Ruvo di Púglia
Bitonto
Rocchetta S. Antonio
Minervino Murge
Modugno
Triggiano
Mola di Bari
Lacedónia
Invaso Diga Locone
Palo del Colle
Bitetto
Bisáccia
Lavello
Grumo Áppula
Sannicandro di Bari
Capurso
Noicáttaro
Aquilónia
Melfi
Montemilone
Adelfia
Rutigliano
Polignano a Mare
Andretta
Rapolla
Venosa
Spinazzola
Toritto
Casamássima
Conversano
Monópoli
M. Vúlture 1326
Rionero in Vúlture
Ripacándida
Palazzo San Gervásio
Acquaviva delle Fonti
Turi
Castellana Grotte
Savelletri
Calitri
Atella
Ruvo del Monte
L. di Serra di Corvo
Cassano delle Murge
Sammichele di Bari
Torre Canne
Pescopagano
Forenza
Gravina in Púglia
Altamura
Putignano
Fasano
Genzano di Lucánia
Noci
Rosa Marina
Villanova
San Fele
Pso. d. Crocelle 1136
Acerenza
Bradano
Gióia del Colle
Santéramo in Colle
Alberobello
Locorotondo
Muro Lucano
Bella
Pietragalla
Oppido Lucano
Ostuni
Avigliano
Cancellara
Irsina
Cisternino
Ruoti
Váglio Basilicata
Tolve
Martina Franca
Carovigno
San Gregorio Magno
Picerno
Matera
Buccino
Potenza
Tricárico
Grassano
Móttola
Céglie Messápica
San Vito dei Normanni
Vietri di Potenza
Tito
Laterza
Castellaneta
Crispiano
Villa Castelli
Caggiano
Trivigno
Salandrella
L. di S. Giuliano
Gróttole
Miglionico
Massafra
Francavilla Fontana
Auletta
Pso. Croce d. Scrivano 1143
Anzi
Garaguso
Ginosa
Palagiano
Monteméscola
Polla
Salandra
Montescaglioso
Grottáglie
Oria
Brienza
Accettura
San Máuro Forte
Pomárico
Lido Azzurro
Calvello
Ferrandina
Bradano
Torre Santa Susanna
Corleto Monforte
Laurenzana
Castellaneta Marina
Táranto
Márisco Nuovo
Chéradi
San Giórgio Iónico
Monteparano
Fragagnano
Sala Consilina
Bernalda
Marina di Ginosa
Sava
M. Volturino 1836
Corleto Perticara
Stigliano
Talsano
Lizzano
Mandúria
Sella d. Corticato 1026
Teggiano
Cirigliano
Pisticci
Pulsano
Torricella
Craco
Cavone
Padula
Viggiano
Sáuro
Lido di Metaponto
Lido Silvana
Avetrana
Montesano sulla Marcellana
Montemurro
Missanello
Montalbano Iónico
Marúggio
Mte. Cervati 1898
Buonabitácolo
Sella Cessuta 1040
Spinoso
Agri
Tursi
Casalbuono
Moliterno
San Arcángelo
L. di Monte Cotugno
Lido di Scanzano
Scanzano Jónico
Sanza
Rofrano
San Chirico Raparo
Colobraro
Policoro
Montano Antilia
Mte. Sirino 2005
Roccanova
Castelsaraceno
Sinni
Rotondella
Lido di Policoro
Appennino Lucano
Tánagro
Vallo di Diano
E45
E55
E90
E842
E843
E847
A3
A14
220
208

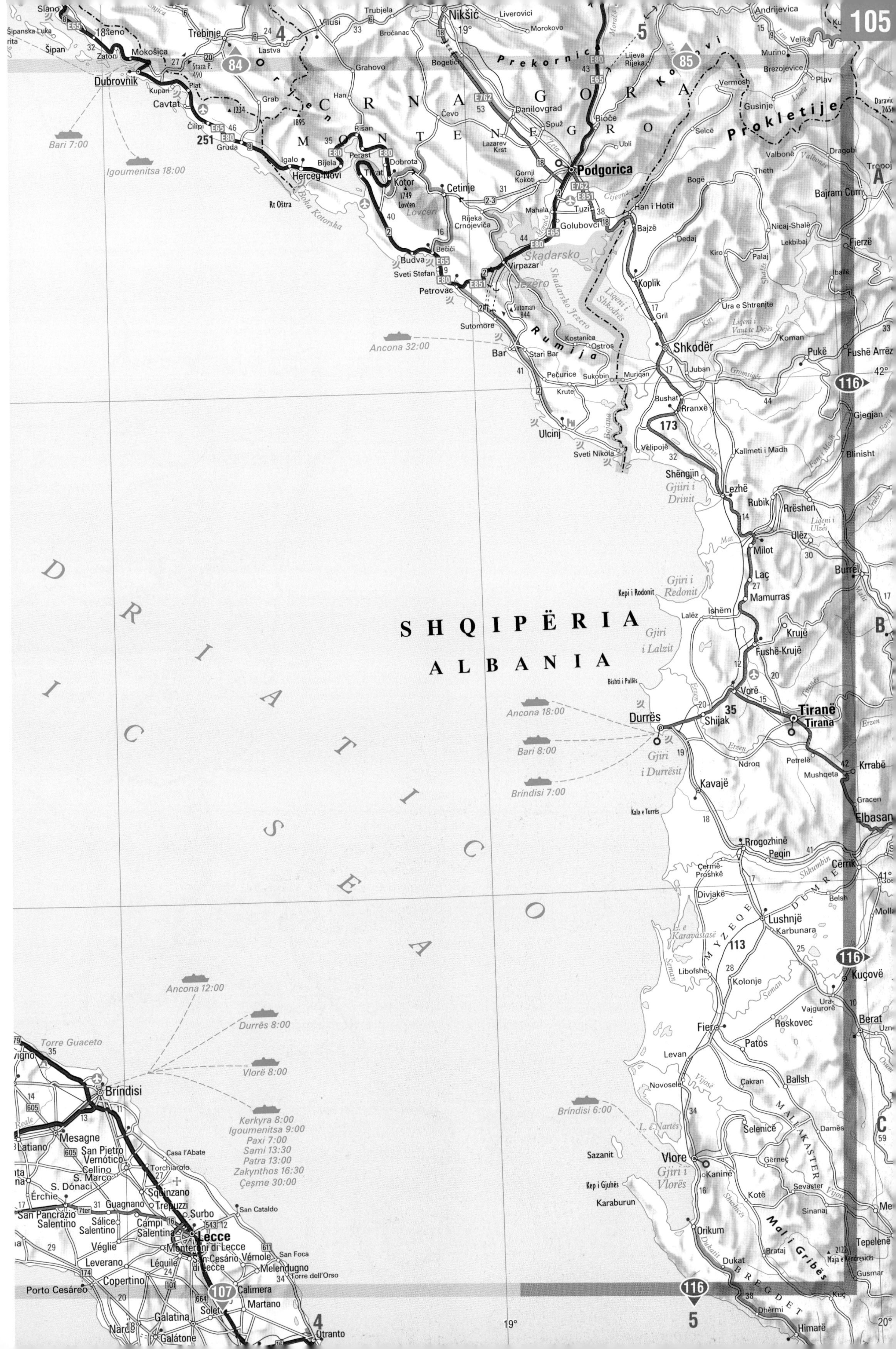

CRNA GORA
MONTENEGRO
SHQIPËRIA
ALBANIA
ADRIATICO
ADRIATIC SEA
Prekornica
Prokletije
Orjen
Rumija
Mali Gribës
Malakaster
Myzeqe
Dumre
Bregdet
Slano
Šipanska Luka
Šipan
Zaton
Dubrovnik
Kupari
Cavtat
Čilipi
Gruda
Mokošica
Trebinje
Lastva
Grab
Vilusi
Grahovo
Trubjela
Broćanac
Nikšić
Liverovici
Morokovo
Bogetići
Han
Risan
Perast
Dobrota
Igalo
Bijela
Herceg-Novi
Tivat
Kotor
Lovćen
Rt Oštra
Boka Kotorska
Čevo
Cetinje
Danilovgrad
Spuž
Lazarev Krst
Gornji Kokoti
Bioče
Ubli
Lijeva Rijeka
Podgorica
Tuzi
Mahala
Golubovci
Rijeka Crnojevića
Budva
Bečići
Sveti Stefan
Petrovac
Virpazar
Skadarsko Jezero
Sutomore
Sutoman
Bar
Stari Bar
Kostanica
Ostros
Pečurice
Sukobin
Muriqan
Krute
Ulcinj
Sveti Nikola
Bojana
Andrijevica
Velika
Murino
Brezojevice
Plav
Vermosh
Gusinje
Selcë
Valbonë
Dragobi
Theth
Bogë
Han i Hotit
Bajzë
Dedaj
Kiro
Palaj
Nicaj-Shalë
Lekbibaj
Bajram Curri
Fierzë
Koplik
Gril
Ura e Shtrenjte
Liqeni i Shkodrës
Liqeni i Vaut te Dejës
Shkodër
Juban
Koman
Pukë
Fushë Arrëz
Bushat
Rranxë
Velipojë
Kallmeti i Madh
Gjegjan
Blinisht
Shëngjin
Gjiri i Drinit
Lezhë
Rubik
Rrëshen
Liqeni i Ulzës
Ulëz
Milot
Burrel
Laç
Mamurras
Kepi i Rodonit
Gjiri i Redonit
Lalëz
Ishëm
Gjiri i Lalzit
Krujë
Fushë-Krujë
Bishti i Pallës
Vorë
Tiranë
Tirana
Durrës
Shijak
Gjiri i Durrësit
Ndroq
Petrelë
Mushqeta
Krrabë
Kavajë
Gracen
Elbasan
Kala e Turrës
Rrogozhinë
Peqin
Cërrik
Çermë-Proshkë
Divjakë
Belsh
Lushnjë
Karbunara
L. e Karavastasë
Libofshë
Kolonje
Kuçovë
Ura-Vajgurore
Berat
Fier
Roskovec
Patos
Levan
Novoselë
Çakran
Ballsh
Selenicë
Damës
L. e Nartës
Sazanit
Vlore
Kaninë
Gjiri i Vlorës
Kep i Gjuhës
Karaburun
Gërneç
Sevaster
Kotë
Sinanaj
Orikum
Brataj
Tepelenë
Maja e Kendrevicës
Dukat
Gusmar
Kuç
Dhërmi
Himarë
Torre Guaceto
Brindisi
Mesagne
Latiano
San Pietro Vernótico
Cellino
S. Marco
S. Dónaci
Casa l'Abate
Torchiarolo
Érchie
Guagnano
Squinzano
Trepuzzi
San Pancrazio Salentino
Sálice Salentino
Surbo
San Cataldo
Campi Salentina
Lecce
Véglie
Monteroni di Lecce
Leverano
Léquile
San Cesário di Lecce
Vérnole
San Foca
Melendugno
Torre dell'Orso
Copertino
Porto Cesáreo
Calimera
Martano
Soleto
Galatina
Nardò
Galátone
Otranto
Bari 7:00
Igoumenitsa 18:00
Ancona 32:00
Ancona 18:00
Bari 8:00
Bríndisi 7:00
Ancona 12:00
Durrës 8:00
Vlorë 8:00
Kerkyra 8:00
Igoumenitsa 9:00
Paxi 7:00
Sami 13:30
Patra 13:00
Zakynthos 16:30
Çeşme 30:00
Bríndisi 6:00
84
85
116
107
4
5
A
B
C
19°
20°
42°
41°

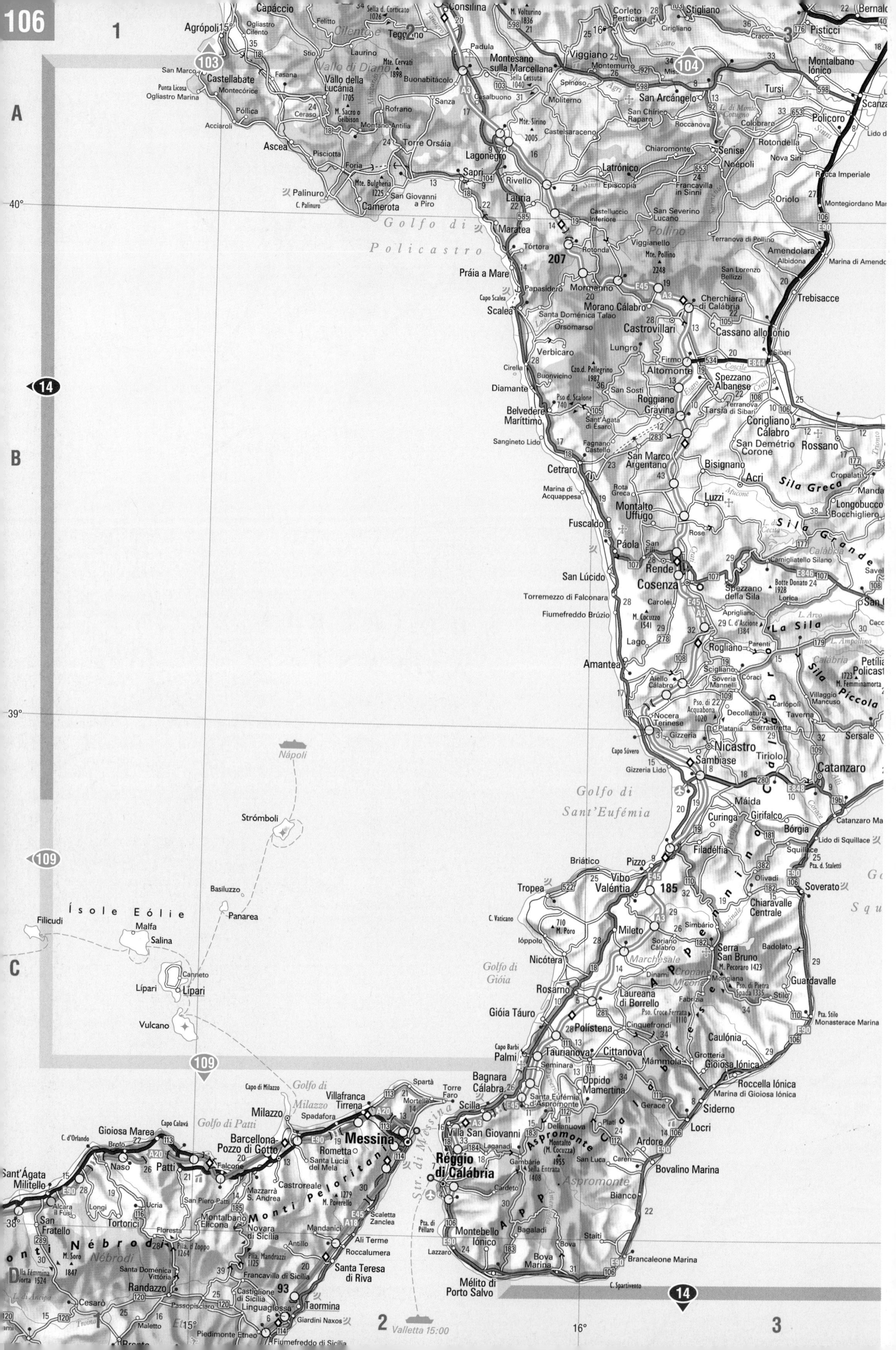

Capáccio
Agrópoli
Ogliastro Cilento
Laurino
Teggiano
Consilina
Padula
M. Volturino 1836
Montesano sulla Marcellana
Corleto Perticara
Stigliano
Viggiano
Montemurro
Cirigliano
Pisticci
Bernalda
Montalbano Iónico
Castellabate
San Marco
Punta Licosa
Ogliastro Marina
Montecórice
Póllica
Acciaroli
Vallo della Lucánia
Mte. Cervati 1898
Buonabitácolo
Sanza
Casalbuono
Sella Cessuta 1040
Spinoso
Moliterno
San Arcángelo
San Chírico Raparo
Roccanova
L. di Monte Cotugno
Colobraro
Tursi
Scanzano
Policoro
Lido di Policoro
Rofrano
M. Sacro o Gelbison 1705
Ceraso
Montano Antilia
Torre Orsáia
Ascea
Pisciotta
Mte. Sirino 2005
Castelsaraceno
Lagonegro
Chiaromonte
Senise
Noépoli
Rotondella
Nova Siri
Foria
Sapri
Rivello
Latrónico
Episcopia
Francavilla in Sinni
Rocca Imperiale
Palinuro
C. Palinuro
Mte. Bulgheria 1225
Camerota
San Giovanni a Piro
Lauria
Castelluccio Inferiore
San Severino Lucano
Oriolo
Montegiordano Marina
40°
Golfo di Policastro
Maratea
Pollino
Tórtora
Rotonda
Viggianello
Mte. Pollino 2248
Terranova di Pollino
Amendolara
Albidona
Marina di Amendolara
Práia a Mare
207
San Lorenzo Bellizzi
Papasidero
Mormanno
Capo Scalea
Scalea
Morano Cálabro
Cerchiara di Calábria
Trebisacce
Santa Doménica Talao
Orsomarso
Castrovillari
Cassano allo Iónio
Verbicaro
Lungro
Cirella
Firmo
Sibari
Czo.d. Pellegrino 1987
Altomonte
Buonvicino
Diamante
San Sosti
Spezzano Albanese
Pso d. Scalone 740
Roggiano Gravina
Terranova
Tarsia di Sibari
Belvedere Maríttimo
Sant'Ágata di Ésaro
Corigliano Cálabro
Rossano
Sangineto Lido
Fagnano Castello
San Demétrio Corone
San Marco Argentano
Bisignano
Cetraro
Acri
Sila Greca
Cropalati
Mandatoriccio
Marina di Acquappesa
Rota Greca
Luzzi
Longobucco
Bocchigliero
Montalto Uffugo
Fuscaldo
Rose
Sila Grande
Páola
San Fili
Camigliatello Silano
Rende
San Lúcido
Cosenza
Botte Donato 1928
Spezzano della Sila
Lorica
Torremezzo di Falconara
Carolei
Aprigliano
Fiumefreddo Brúzio
M. Cocuzzo 1541
C. d'Ascione 1384
La Sila
L. Arvo
L. Ampollino
Lago
Parenti
Rogliano
Amantea
Scigliano
Soveria Mannelli
Cotronei
Petília Policastro
1723 M. Femminamorta
Sila Piccola
Aiello Cálabro
Villaggio Mancuso
Pso. di Acquabona 1020
Decollatura
Carlópoli
Taverna
39°
Nocera Terinese
Platania
Serrastretta
Sersale
Nápoli
Gizzeria
Nicastro
Capo Súvero
Sambiase
Tiriolo
Gizzeria Lido
Catanzaro
Golfo di Sant'Eufémia
Máida
Girifalco
Catanzaro Marina
Curinga
Bórgia
Strómboli
Lido di Squillace
Squillace
Pta. d. Staletti
Filadélfia
Briático
Pizzo
Vibo Valéntia
185
Olivadi
Tropea
Soverato
Basiluzzo
Chiaravalle Centrale
Ísole Eólie
Filicudi
Malfa
Salina
Panarea
C. Vaticano
M. Poro 710
Mileto
Simbário
Iòppolo
Soriano Cálabro
Serra San Bruno
Badolato
Nicótera
Marchesale
Dinami
M. Pecoraro 1423
Canneto
Lípari
Golfo di Gióia
Rosarno
Mongiana
Pso. di Pietra Spada 1335
Guardavalle
Stilo
Laureana di Borrello
Fabrízia
Gióia Táuro
Pso. Croce Ferrata 1110
Cinquefrondi
Pta. Stilo
Monasterace Marina
Vulcano
Polístena
Caulónia
Capo Barbi
Palmi
Taurianova
Cittanova
Seminara
Mámmola
Grotteria
Gioiosa Iónica
109
Capo di Milazzo
Golfo di Milazzo
Spartà
Bagnara Cálabra
Oppido Mamertina
Roccella Iónica
Marina di Gioiosa Iónica
Villafranca Tirrena
Torre Faro
Mortelle
Scilla
Santa Eufémia d'Aspromonte
Milazzo
Spadafora
Golfo di Patti
Capo Calavá
Gioiosa Marea
Messina
Villa San Giovanni
Delianuova
Gerace
Siderno
Locri
C. d'Orlando
Brolo
Barcellona-Pozzo di Gotto
Rometta
Aspromonte
Laganadi
Reggio di Calábria
Montalto (M. Cocuzza) 1955
Ardore
Sant'Ágata Militello
Naso
Patti
Falcone
Santa Lucia del Mela
Gambárie
Sella Entrata 1408
San Luca
Careri
Bovalino Marina
Castroreale
Alcara li Fusi
Ucria
San Piero Patti
Mazzarrà S. Andrea
Monti Peloritani
M. Poverello 1279
Cardeto
Bianco
38°
San Fratello
Longi
Tortorici
Montalbano Elicona
Scaletta Zanclea
Floresta
Monti Nébrodi
Novara di Sicília
Mandanici
Pta. di Péllaro
Montebello Iónico
Bagaladi
Bova
Staiti
Plla. d. Zoppo 1264
Antillo
Ali Terme
M. Soro 1847
Plla. Mandrazzi 1125
Roccalumera
Lazzaro
Bova Marina
Brancaleone Marina
Santa Doménica Vittória
Francavilla di Sicília
Santa Teresa di Riva
Randazzo
Castiglione di Sicília
Mélito di Porto Salvo
C. Spartivento
Cesarò
Passopisciaro
Linguaglossa
Taormina
Maletto
Giardini Naxos
Valletta 15:00
Piedimonte Etneo
Fiumefreddo di Sicília
15°
16°

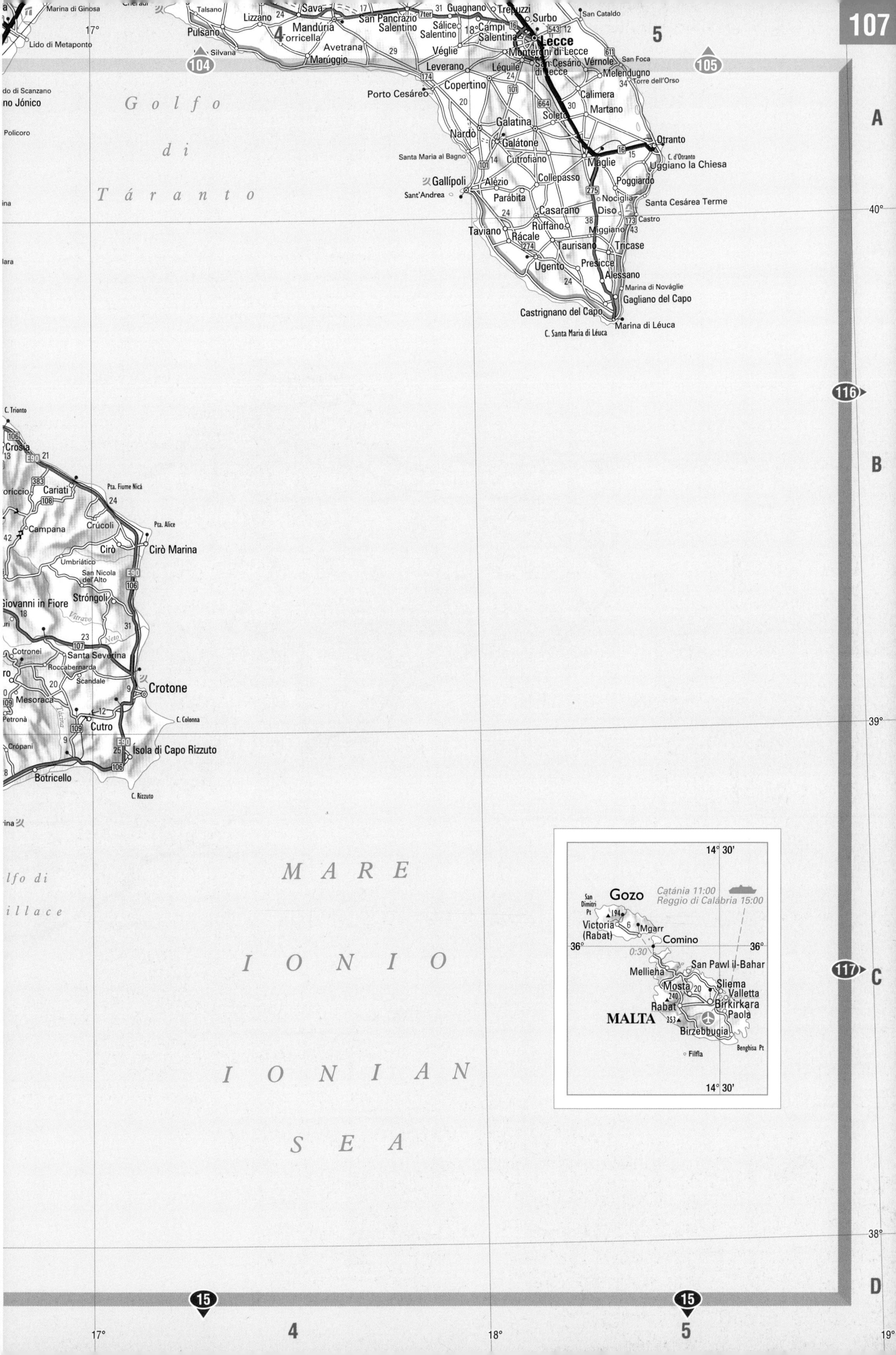
Golfo di Táranto
MARE IONIO
IONIAN SEA
Marina di Ginosa
Lido di Metaponto
Talsano
Pulsano
Silvana
Lizzano
Sava
Mandúria
Torricella
Avetrana
Marúggio
San Pancrázio Salentino
Guagnano
Trepuzzi
Surbo
San Cataldo
Sálice Salentino
Campi Salentina
Lecce
Véglie
Leverano
Monteroni di Lecce
Léquile
San Cesário di Lecce
Vérnole
San Foca
Melendugno
Torre dell'Orso
Porto Cesáreo
Copertino
Calimera
Martano
Soleto
Galatina
Nardò
Galátone
Otranto
Maglie
C. d'Otranto
Uggiano la Chiesa
Santa Maria al Bagno
Cutrofiano
Gallípoli
Sant'Andrea
Alézio
Collepasso
Poggiardo
Parábita
Nociglia
Santa Cesárea Terme
Casarano
Diso
Castro
Taviano
Ruffano
Miggiano
Rácale
Taurisano
Tricase
Ugento
Presicce
Alessano
Marina di Nováglie
Gagliano del Capo
Castrignano del Capo
Marina di Léuca
C. Santa Maria di Léuca
Policoro
C. Trionto
Crosia
Cariati
Pta. Fiume Nicá
Campana
Crúcoli
Pta. Alice
Cirò
Cirò Marina
Umbriático
San Nicola dell'Alto
Stróngoli
Giovanni in Fiore
Vitravo
Neto
Cotronei
Santa Severina
Roccabernarda
Scandale
Crotone
Mesoraca
Petronà
Cutro
C. Colonna
Crópani
Ísola di Capo Rizzuto
Botricello
C. Rizzuto
Gozo
San Dimitri Pt
Victoria (Rabat)
Mgarr
Comino
Catánia 11:00
Reggio di Calábria 15:00
San Pawl il-Bahar
Mellieha
Mosta
Sliema
Valletta
Birkirkara
Rabat
Paola
MALTA
Birzebbugia
Benghisa Pt
Filfla
14° 30'
36°
17°
18°
19°
40°
39°
38°
A
B
C
D
4
5
104
105
116
117
15

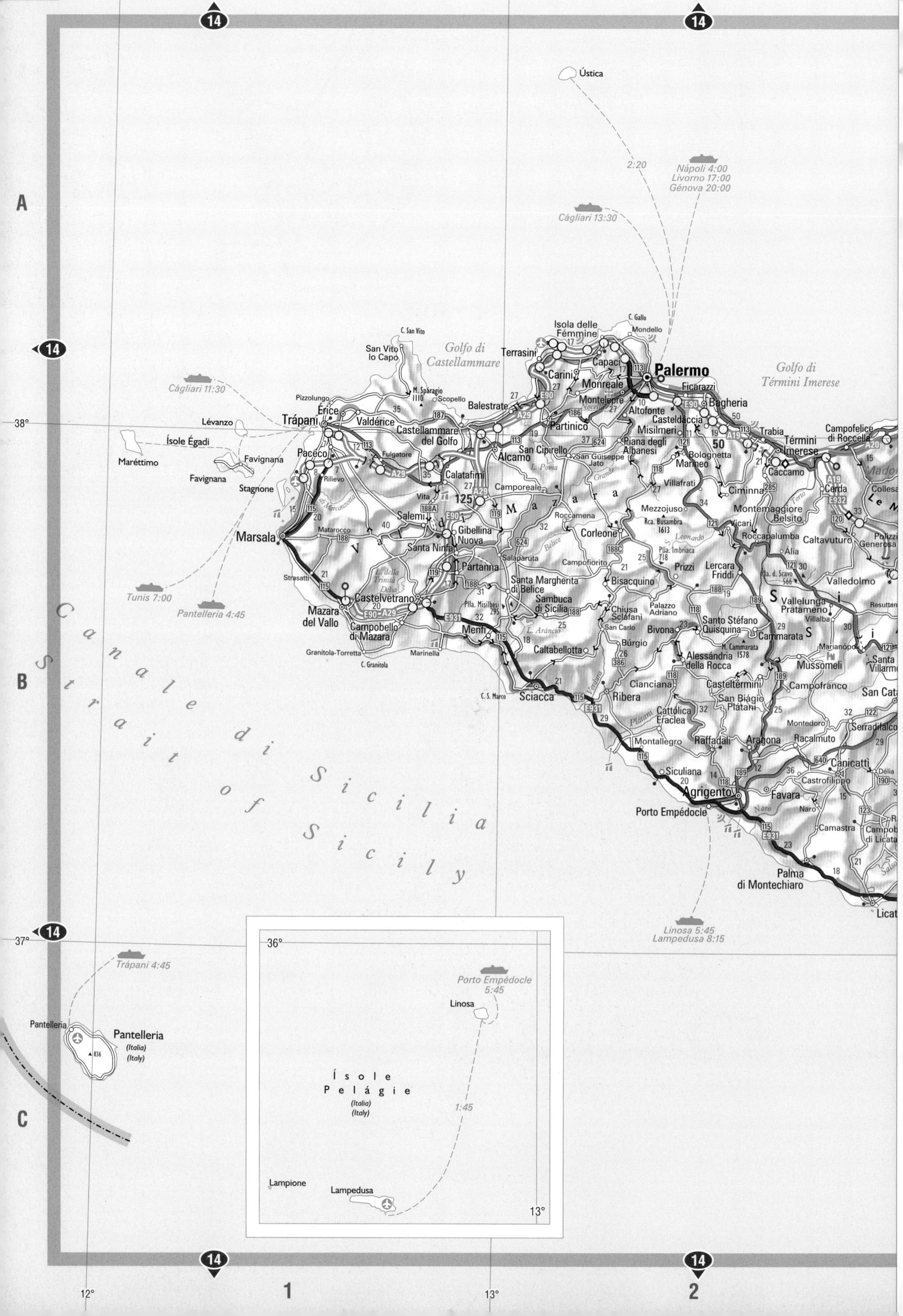
12°
1
13°
2
14
A
B
C
Ústica
2:20
Nápoli 4:00
Livorno 17:00
Génova 20:00
Cágliari 13:30
Cágliari 11:30
Isola delle Fémmine
C. Gallo
Mondello
C. San Vito
San Vito lo Capo
Golfo di Castellammare
Terrasini
Capaci
Carini
Palermo
Golfo di Términi Imerese
Monreale
Montelepre
Ficarazzi
Bagheria
Altofonte
Casteldáccia
Misilmeri
M. Spárágio 1110
Scopello
Pizzolungo
Érice
Trápani
Valdérice
Balestrate
Partinico
Castellammare del Golfo
Lévanzo
Ísole Égadi
Maréttimo
Favignana
Paceco
Fulgatore
Alcamo
San Cipirello
San Guiseppe Jato
Piana degli Albanesi
Marineo
Bolognetta
Trabia
Términi Imerese
Campofelice di Roccella
Cáccamo
Cerda
Stagnone
Rilievo
Calatafimi
Vita
Camporeale
Villafrati
Ciminna
Montemaggiore Belsito
Salemi
Mazara
Roccamena
Mezzojuso
Rca. Busambra 1613
Corleone
Vicari
Roccapalumba
Caltavuturo
Marsala
Matarocco
Gibellina Nuova
Santa Ninfa
Salaparuta
Campofiorito
Prizzi
Lercara Friddi
Ália
Partanna
Strasatti
Santa Margherita di Belice
Bisacquino
Valledolmo
Castelvetrano
Mazara del Vallo
Campobello di Mazara
Sambuca di Sicília
Chiusa Sclàfani
Palazzo Adriano
Vallelunga Pratameno
Tunis 7:00
Pantelleria 4:45
Granitola-Torretta
C. Granitola
Marinella
Menfi
Caltabellotta
San Carlo
Bivona
Santo Stéfano Quisquina
Cammarata
Búrgio
Alessándria della Rocca
M. Cammarata 1578
Mussomeli
Sciacca
C. S. Marco
Ribera
Cianciana
Casteltérmini
San Biágio Plátani
Campofranco
Cattólica Eraclea
Montallegro
Raffadali
Aragona
Racalmuto
Serradifalco
Montedoro
Canicattì
Castrofilippo
Siculiana
Agrigento
Favara
Naro
Porto Empédocle
Camastra
Palma di Montechiaro
Canale di Sicilia
Strait of Sicily
Linosa 5:45
Lampedusa 8:15
37°
38°
Trápani 4:45
Pantelleria
(Italia)
(Italy)
36°
Porto Empédocle 5:45
Linosa
Ísole Pelágie
1:45
Lampione
Lampedusa

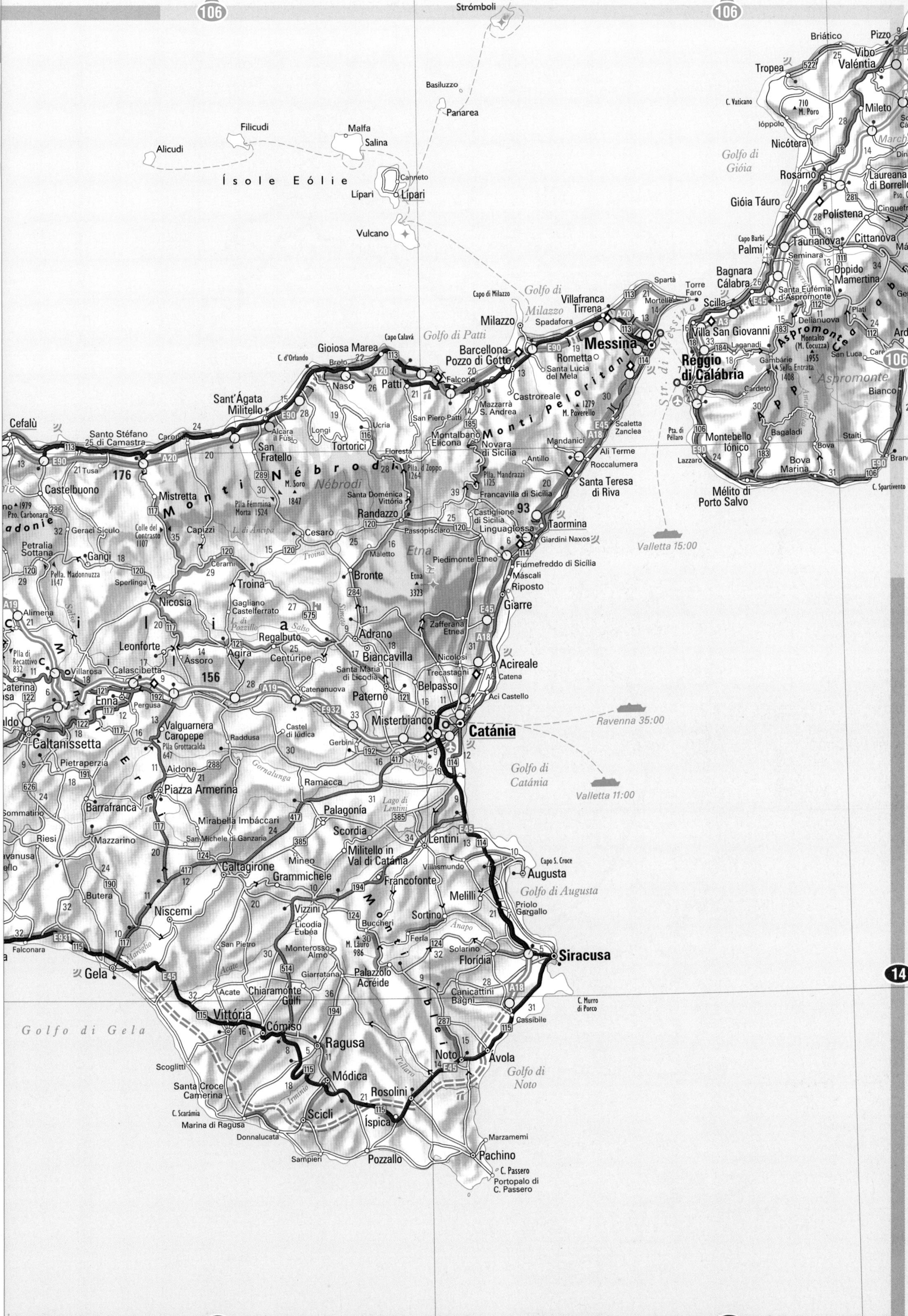
Nápoli
Strómboli
Basiluzzo
Panarea
Filicudi
Alicudi
Malfa
Salina
Ísole Eólie
Canneto
Lípari
Vulcano
Capo di Milazzo
Golfo di Milazzo
Milazzo
Villafranca Tirrena
Spadafora
Capo Calavà
Golfo di Patti
Gioiosa Marea
C. d'Orlando
Brolo
Patti
Naso
Falcone
Barcellona-Pozzo di Gotto
Messina
Rometta
Santa Lucia del Mela
Castroreale
Mazzarrà S. Andrea
Monti Peloritani
M. Poverello 1279
Scaletta Zanclea
Mandanici
Ali Terme
Roccalumera
Santa Teresa di Riva
Antillo
Sant'Ágata Militello
Cefalù
Santo Stéfano di Camastra
Caronia
Alcara li Fusi
San Fratello
Longi
Tortorici
Ucria
San Piero Patti
Montalbano Elicona
Novara di Sicilia
Floresta
Plla. d. Zoppo 1264
Plla. Mandrazzi 1125
Francavilla di Sicilia
Monti Nébrodi
Nébrodi
M. Soro 1847
Castelbuono
Tusa
Mistretta
Plla Fémmina Morta 1524
Santa Doménica Vittória
Randazzo
Castiglione di Sicilia
Linguaglossa
Taormina
Giardini Naxos
Pzo. Carbonara 1979
Madonie
Geraci Sículo
Colle del Contrasto 1107
Capizzi
L. di Ancipa
Cesarò
Passopisciaro
Petralia Sottana
Gangi
Pella. Madonnuzza 1147
Sperlinga
Cerami
Troina
Maletto
Etna
Piedimonte Etneo
Fiumefreddo di Sicília
Máscali
Riposto
Bronte
Etna 3323
Giarre
Nicosia
Gagliano Castelferrato
L. di Pozzillo
Salso
Simeto
Adrano
Zafferana Etnea
Alimena
Leonforte
Regalbuto
Agira
Assoro
Centúripe
Biancavilla
Nicolosi
Acireale
Trecastagni
Aci Catena
Pila di Recattivo 832
Villarosa
Calascibetta
Santa Maria di Licodia
Belpasso
Aci Castello
Caterina
Enna
Pergusa
Catenanuova
Paternò
Misterbianco
Catánia
Caltanissetta
Valguarnera Caropepe
Plla Grottacalda 647
Raddusa
Castel di Iúdica
Gerbini
Pietraperzia
Aidone
Gornalunga
Piazza Armerina
Ramacca
Golfo di Catánia
Barrafranca
Lago di Lentini
Palagonía
Sommatino
Riesi
Mazzarino
Mirabella Imbáccari
San Michele di Ganzaria
Scordia
Lentini
Militello in Val di Catánia
Mineo
Caltagirone
Grammichele
Villasmundo
Capo S. Croce
Augusta
Golfo di Augusta
Francofonte
Melilli
Priolo Gargallo
Butera
Niscemi
Vizzini
Licodia Eubea
Buccheri
Sortino
Monti Iblei
Anapo
Ferla
Solarino
Floridia
Siracusa
Falconara
Gela
San Pietro
Monterosso Almo
M. Lauro 986
Giarratana
Palazzolo Acréide
Canicattini Bagni
Acate
Chiaramonte Gulfi
Vittória
Cómiso
Ragusa
Golfo di Gela
C. Murro di Porco
Cassibile
Avola
Noto
Golfo di Noto
Tellaro
Irminio
Scoglitti
Santa Croce Camerina
Módica
Rosolini
C. Scarámia
Marina di Ragusa
Scicli
Íspica
Donnalucata
Marzamemi
Pachino
Sampieri
Pozzallo
C. Passero
Portopalo di C. Passero
Ravenna 35:00
Valletta 15:00
Valletta 11:00
Briático
Pizzo
Vibo Valéntia
Tropea
C. Vaticano
M. Poro 710
Mileto
Soriano Cálabro
Ióppolo
Nicótera
Golfo di Gióia
Rosarno
Laureana di Borrello
Gióia Táuro
Polístena
Cinquefrondi
Taurianova
Cittanova
Capo Barbi
Palmi
Seminara
Oppido Mamertina
Bagnara Cálabra
Santa Eufémia d'Aspromonte
Delianuova
Sparta
Torre Faro
Mortelle
Scilla
Villa San Giovanni
Aspromonte
Montalto (M. Cucuzza) 1955
Reggio di Calábria
Laganadi
Gambárie
Sella Entrata 1408
San Luca
Ardore
Bovalino
Str. di Messina
Cardeto
Bianco
Pta. di Péllaro
Montebello Iónico
Bagaladi
Staiti
Lazzaro
Bova
Bova Marina
Brancaleone Marina
Mélito di Porto Salvo
C. Spartivento
Calabria

3 4 5

B

C

15° 16° 37° 38°

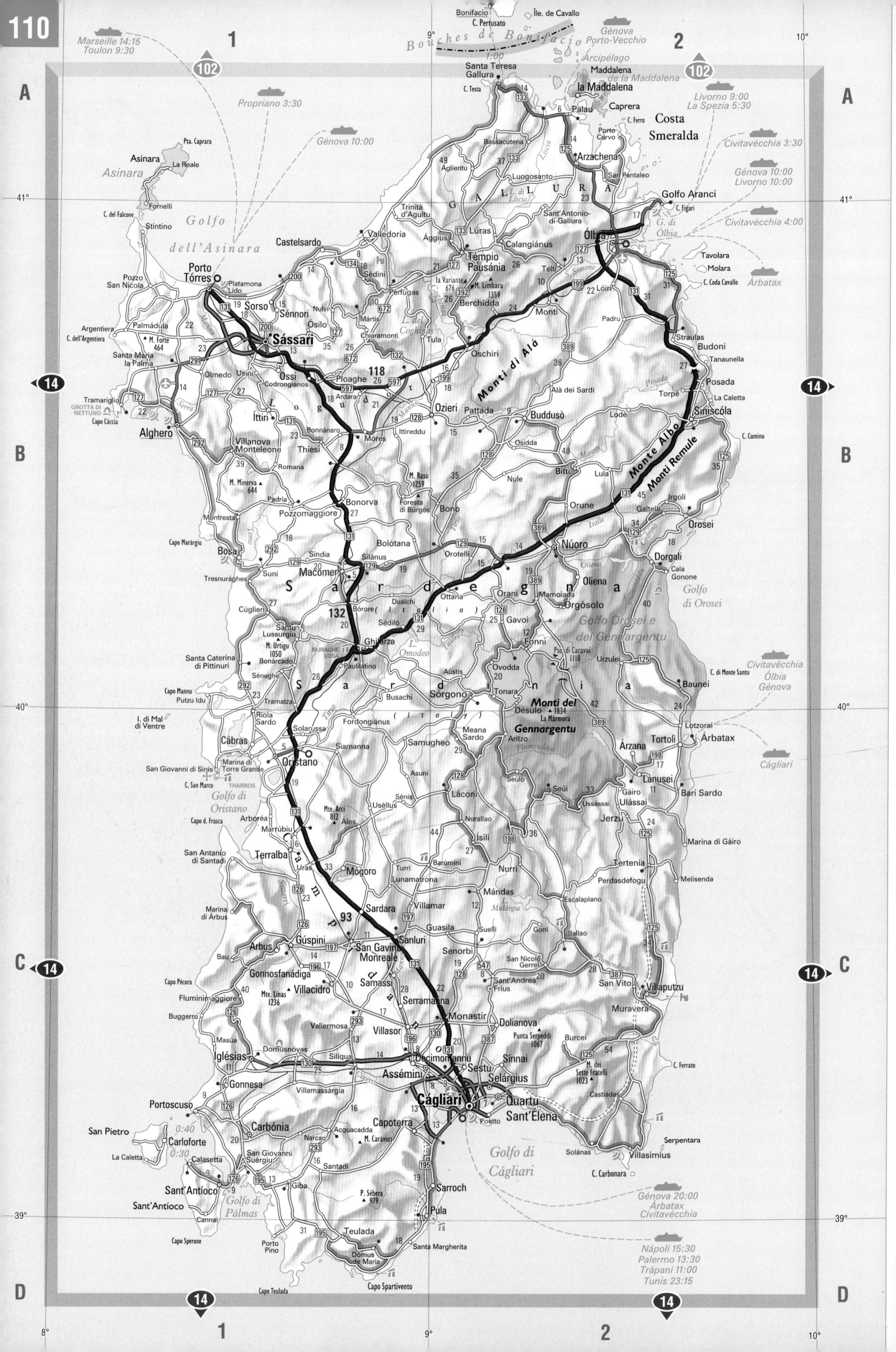
Bonifacio
Île. de Cavallo
C. Pertusato
Bouches de Bonifacio
Génova
Porto-Vecchio
Marseille 14:15
Toulon 9:30
Santa Teresa Gallura
Arcipélago de la Maddalena
Maddalena
la Maddalena
Caprera
Palau
C. Testa
Propriano 3:30
Livorno 9:00
La Spezia 5:30
Costa Smeralda
Porto Cervo
C. Ferro
Arzachena
Civitavécchia 3:30
Génova 10:00
Livorno 10:00
Génova 10:00
Pta. Caprara
Asinara
La Reale
Fornelli
C. del Falcone
Stintino
Golfo dell'Asinara
Bassacutena
Aglientu
Luogosanto
G A L L U R A
San Pantaleo
Golfo Aranci
C. Figari
G. di Ólbia
Civitavécchia 4:00
Trinità d'Agultu
Sant'Antonio-di-Gallura
Ólbia
Castelsardo
Valledoria
Ággius
Lúras
Calangiánus
Tavolara
Molara
C. Coda Cavallo
Árbatax
Porto Tórres
Pozzo San Nicola
Platamona Lido
Sédini
Tempio Pausánia
Telti
Lóiri
Sorso
Sénnori
Pérfugas
La Variante 676
M. Limbara 1359
Berchidda
Monti
Padru
Argentiera
C. dell'Argentiera
Palmádula
M. Forte 464
Sássari
Ósilo
Nulvi
Mártis
Chiaramonti
L. del Coghinas
Tula
Oschiri
Straulas
Budoni
Tanaunella
Santa Maria la Palma
Olmedo
Usini
Ossi
Codrongianos
Ploaghe
Monti di Alá
Posada
Torpè
La Caletta
Tramariglio
GROTTA DI NETTUNO
Capo Cáccia
Alghero
Íttiri
Ardara
Ozieri
Pattada
Alà dei Sardi
Buddusò
Lodè
Siniscóla
C. Comino
Bonnánaro
Thiesi
Mores
Ittireddu
Osidda
Villanova Monteleone
Romana
Monte Albo
Monti Remule
M. Minerva 644
M. Rasu 1259
Foresta di Burgos
Bono
Nule
Bitti
Lula
Irgoli
Galtellì
Orosei
Padria
Pozzomaggiore
Bonorva
Orune
Montresta
Capo Marárgiu
Bosa
Sindia
Bolótana
Silánus
Orotelli
Núoro
Dorgali
Cala Gonone
Golfo di Orosei
Tresnurághes
Suni
Macomer
Oliena
S a r d e g n a
Mamoiada
Orgósolo
Orani
Ottana
Cúglieri
Borore
Dualchi
Sédilo
Gavoi
Golfo Orosei e del Gennargentu
Santu Lussurgiu
M. Urtigu 1050
NURAGHE LOSA
Ghilarza
L. Omodeo
Fonni
Pso. di Caravai 1118
Urzulei
Civitavécchia
Ólbia
Génova
C. di Monte Santu
Santa Caterina di Pittinuri
Bonárcado
Paulilátino
Ovodda
Baunei
Séneghe
Áustis
Tonara
Capo Mannu
Putzu Idu
Tramatza
Busachi
Sórgono
Monti del Gennargentu
Désulo
La Mármora 1834
I. di Mal di Ventre
Riola Sardo
Fordongiánus
Meana Sardo
Lotzorai
Tortolì
Árbatax
Aritzo
Solarussa
Cábras
Siamanna
Samugheo
Árzana
Oristano
Marina di Torre Grande
San Giovanni di Sinis
THARROS
C. San Marco
Golfo di Oristano
Cágliari
Lanusei
Sèulo
Seùi
Asuni
Láconi
Gáiro
Ulássai
Bari Sardo
Capo d. Frasca
Arboréa
Sénis
Usellus
Mte. Arci 812
Áles
Ussássai
Jerzu
Marrúbiu
Nurallao
Ísili
Marina di Gáiro
San Antonio di Santadi
Terralba
Uras
Barúmini
Turri
Mógoro
Lunamatrona
Nurri
Tertenia
Perdasdefogu
Melisenda
Mándas
Escalaplano
Marina di Árbus
Sardara
Villamar
Guasila
Suelli
Goni
Ballao
Árbus
Gúspini
San Gavino Monreale
Sanluri
Senorbì
Bau
San Nicolò Gerrei
Gonnosfanádiga
Samassi
Sant'Andrea Frius
San Vito
Villaputzu
Capo Pécora
Fluminimaggiore
Mte. Linas 1236
Villacidro
Serramanna
Muravera
Buggerru
Vallermosa
Villasor
Monastir
Dolianova
Punta Serpeddì 1067
Burcei
Masúa
Iglésias
Domusnóvas
Siliqua
Decimomannu
Sestu
Sínnai
M. dei Sette Fratelli 1023
C. Ferrato
Gonnesa
Assémini
Selárgius
Villamassárgia
Quartu Sant'Elena
Castiadas
Portoscuso
Carbónia
Acquacadda
Capoterra
Poetto
San Pietro
Carloforte
Narcao
M. Caràvius
Golfo di Cágliari
Serpentara
Villasimíus
Solánas
La Caletta
Calasetta
San Giovanni Suérgiu
Santadi
C. Carbonara
Sant'Antíoco
Giba
Sarroch
Golfo di Pálmas
P. Sébera 979
Génova 20:00
Árbatax
Civitavécchia
Cannai
Pula
Capo Sperone
Porto Pino
Teulada
Santa Margherita
Nápoli 15:30
Palermo 13:30
Trápani 11:00
Tunis 23:15
Domus de Maria
Capo Teulada
Capo Spartivento
C a m p i d a n o
S a r d i n i a
(I t a l i a)
(I t a l y)

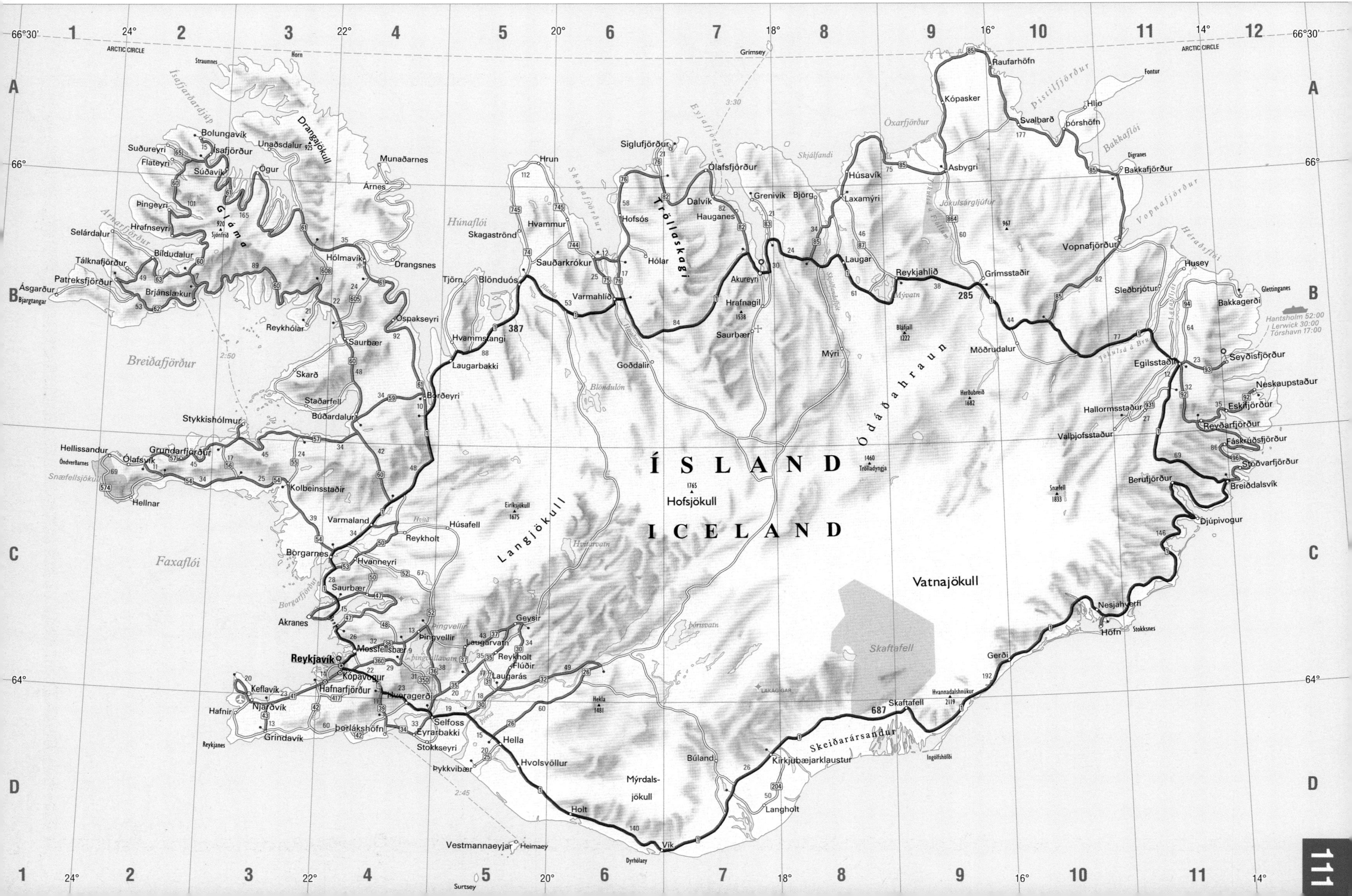
ÍSLAND
ICELAND
Vatnajökull
Hofsjökull
Langjökull
Mýrdals-
jökull
Ódáðahraun
Tröllaskagi
Gláma
Drangajökull
Skeiðarársandur
Skaftafell
Breiðafjörður
Faxaflói
Húnaflói
Skagafjörður
Eyjafjörður
Skjálfandi
Öxarfjörður
Þistilfjörður
Bakkaflói
Vopnafjörður
Héraðsflói
Ísafjarðardjúp
Arnarfjörður
Borgarfjörður
Reykjavík
Kópavogur
Hafnarfjörður
Keflavík
Njarðvík
Grindavík
Hafnir
Reykjanes
Mossfellsbær
Hveragerði
Selfoss
Eyrarbakki
Stokkseyri
Þorlákshöfn
Hella
Hvolsvöllur
Holt
Vík
Dyrhólaey
Vestmannaeyjar
Heimaey
Surtsey
Þykkvibær
Búland
Kirkjubæjarklaustur
Langholt
Skaftafell
Hvannadalshnúkur
2119
Ingólfshöfði
Gerði
Höfn
Stokksnes
Nesjahverfi
Djúpivogur
Breiðdalsvík
Berufjörður
Stöðvarfjörður
Fáskrúðsfjörður
Reyðarfjörður
Eskifjörður
Neskaupstaður
Seyðisfjörður
Egilsstaðir
Hallormsstaður
Valþjofsstaður
Bakkagerði
Glettinganes
Husey
Sleðbrjótur
Vopnafjörður
Bakkafjörður
Digranes
Þórshöfn
Hlio
Fontur
Svalbarð
Raufarhöfn
Kópasker
Asbygri
Grimsstaðir
Möðrudalur
Reykjahlíð
Mývatn
Laugar
Húsavík
Laxamýri
Björg
Grenivík
Akureyri
Hrafnagil
Saurbær
Mýri
Goðdalir
Ólafsfjörður
Dalvík
Hauganes
Siglufjörður
Hofsós
Hólar
Grímsey
Sauðárkrókur
Varmahlíð
Hrun
Hvammur
Skagaströnd
Blönduós
Tjörn
Hvammstangi
Laugarbakki
Borðeyri
Ospakseyri
Drangsnes
Munaðarnes
Árnes
Hólmavík
Ögur
Unaðsdalur
Horn
Straumnes
Bolungavík
Ísafjörður
Súðavík
Suðureyri
Flateyri
Þingeyri
Hrafnseyri
Selárdalur
Bíldudalur
Tálknafjörður
Patreksfjörður
Brjánslækur
Ásgarður
Bjargtangar
Reykhólar
Saurbær
Skarð
Staðarfell
Búðardalur
Stykkishólmur
Grundarfjörður
Ólafsvík
Hellissandur
Öndverðarnes
Snæfellsjökull
Hellnar
Kolbeinsstaðir
Varmaland
Borgarnes
Hvanneyri
Saurbær
Akranes
Reykholt
Húsafell
Þingvellir
Laugarvatn
Geysir
Reykholt
Flúðir
Laugarás
Hekla
1481
Eiríksjökull
1675
Herðubreið
1682
Bláfjall
1222
Snæfell
1833
Trölladyngja
1460
Lakagígar
Þórisvatn
Hvítárvatn
Blöndulón
ARCTIC CIRCLE
Hantsholm 52:00
Lerwick 30:00
Tórshavn 17:00

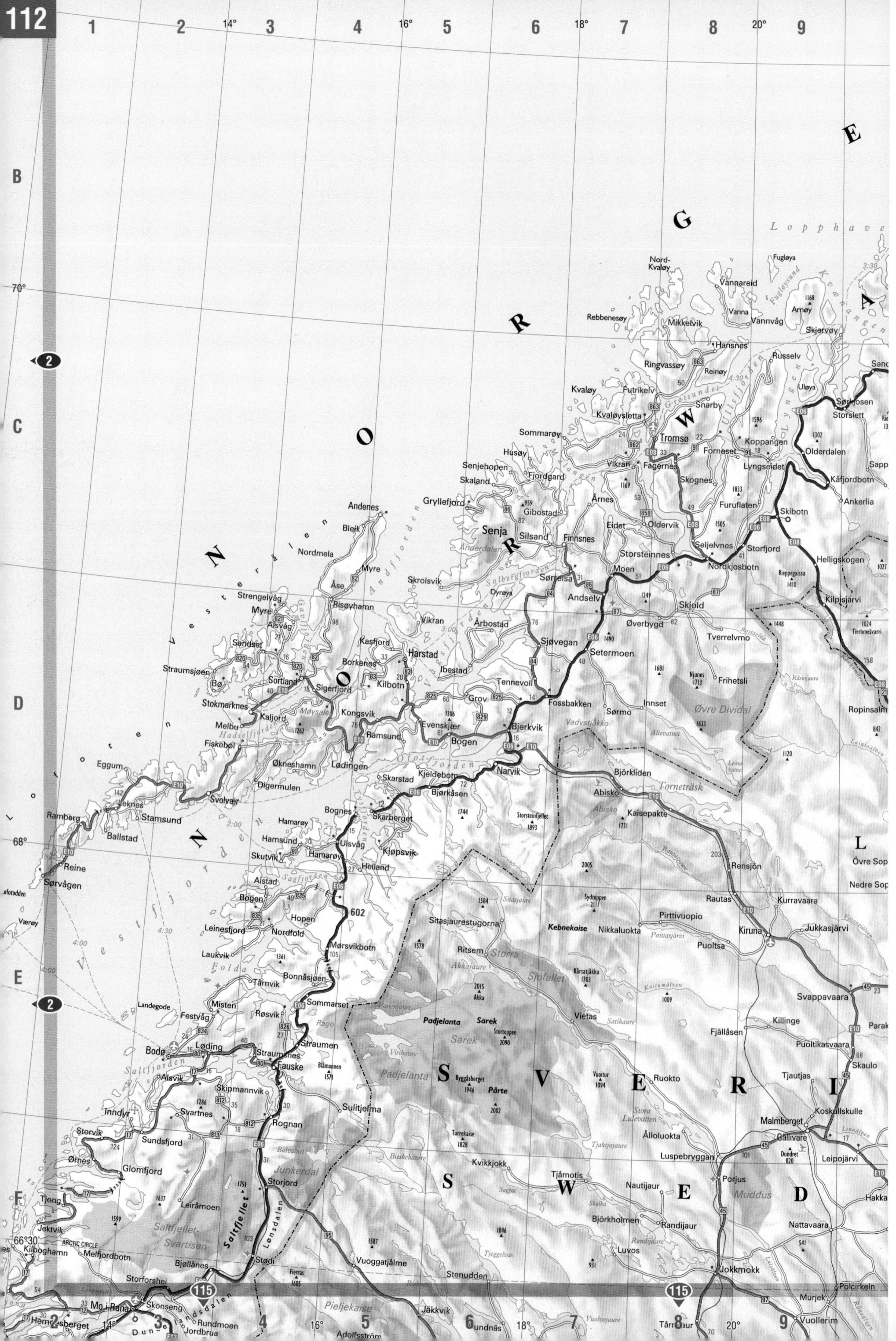

1 2 3 4 5 6 7 8 9
14° 16° 18° 20°
B
C
D
E
F
70°
68°
66°30'
NORGE
NORWAY
SVERIGE
SWEDEN
L
Lopphavet
Vesterålen
Lofoten
Vestfjorden
Andfjorden
Ofotfjorden
Tysfjorden
Sagfjorden
Folda
Saltfjorden
Hadselfjorden
Malangen
Solbergfjorden
Ullsfjorden
Lyngen
Kvænangen
Fugløysund
Grøtsundet
Nord-Kvaløy
Fugløya
Vannareid
Vanna
Vannvåg
Arnøy
Skjervøy
Rebbenesøy
Mikkelvik
Hansnes
Ringvassøy
Reinøy
Russelv
Kvaløy
Futrikelv
Snarby
Uløya
Sørkjosen
Storslett
Kvaløysletta
Tromsø
Sommarøy
Koppangen
Forneset
Olderdalen
Husøy
Vikran
Fagernes
Lyngseidet
Senjehopen
Fjordgard
Skognes
Kåfjordbotn
Skaland
Furuflaten
Ankerlia
Gryllefjord
Gibostad
Årnes
Oldervik
Skibotn
Andenes
Senja
Silsand
Finnsnes
Eidet
Bleik
Storsteinnes
Seljelvnes
Storfjord
Nordmela
Helligskogen
Myre
Moen
Nordkjosbotn
Åse
Skrolsvik
Sørreisa
Dyrøya
Andselv
Skjold
Kilpisjärvi
Strengelvåg
Bisøyhamn
Alsvåg
Vikran
Årbostad
Øverbygd
Sandset
Kasfjord
Harstad
Sjøvegan
Tverrelvmo
Straumsjøen
Borkenes
Ibestad
Setermoen
Bø
Sortland
Sigerfjord
Kilbotn
Tennevoll
Frihetsli
Stokmarknes
Kongsvik
Grov
Fossbakken
Innset
Melbu
Kaljord
Møysalen
Evenskjær
Bjerkvik
Sørmo
Øvre Dividal
Ropinsalmi
Fiskebøl
Ramsund
Bogen
Vadvetjåkko
Altevatnet
Eggum
Økneshamn
Lødingen
Narvik
Björkliden
Skarstad
Kjeldebotn
Abisko
Torneträsk
Digermulen
Bjørkåsen
Leknes
Stamsund
Svolvær
Kaisepakte
Ramberg
Ballstad
Bognes
Skarberget
Storsteinfjellet
Hamarøy
Hamsund
Ulsvåg
Kjøpsvik
Reine
Skutvik
Helland
Rensjön
Øvre Sop
Sørvågen
Alstad
Nedre Sop
Lofotodden
Bogen
Sitasjaure
Sydtoppen
Rautas
Kurravaara
Værøy
Hopen
Sitasjaurestugorna
Kebnekaise
Nikkaluokta
Pirttivuopio
Kiruna
Jukkasjärvi
Leinesfjord
Nordfold
Ritsem
Storra Sjöfallet
Puoltsa
Laukvik
Mørsvikbotn
Akkajaure
Kårsatjåkka
Kaitumälven
Bonnåsjøen
Tårnvik
Akka
Svappavaara
Landegode
Misten
Røsvik
Sommarset
Vietas
Satihaure
Festvåg
Padjelanta
Sarek
Killinge
Parak
Rago
Stortoppen
Fjällåsen
Bodø
Løding
Straumen
Puoltikasvaara
Straumsnes
Fauske
Blåmannen
Ryggåsberget
Pårte
Vuoitur
Ruokto
Skaulo
Alsvik
Tjautjas
Skipmannvik
Sulitjelma
Stora Lulevatten
Koskullskulle
Inndyr
Svartnes
Rognan
Malmberget
Storvik
Sundsfjord
Tarrekaise
Ålloluokta
Gällivare
Balvatnet
Tjaktjajaure
Luspebryggan
Dundret
Leipojärvi
Ørnes
Glomfjord
Junkerdal
Bieskehávrre
Kvikkjokk
Tjåmotis
Porjus
Tjong
Storjord
Nautijaur
Muddus
Hakka
Leiråmoen
Saltfjellet
Lønsdalen
Saggat
Skalka
Björkholmen
Randijaur
Nattavaara
Jektvik
Saltfjellet-Svartisen
Arctic Circle
Kilboghamn
Melfjordbotn
Tjeggelvas
Luvos
Bjøllånes
Stødi
Vuoggatjålme
Jokkmokk
Storforshei
Fierras
Stenudden
Polcirkeln
Mo i Rana
Skonseng
Dunderlandsdalen
Pieljekaise
Jäkkvik
Murjek
Hemnesberget
Rundmoen
Jordbrua
Adolfsström
Gundnäs
Tårrajaur
Vuollerim
Vuolvojaure
Lulealven
Råneälven
Kalixälven
Linaälven
Vittangiälven
Lainioälven
Rautasjaure
E6
E8
E10
E45
115
2

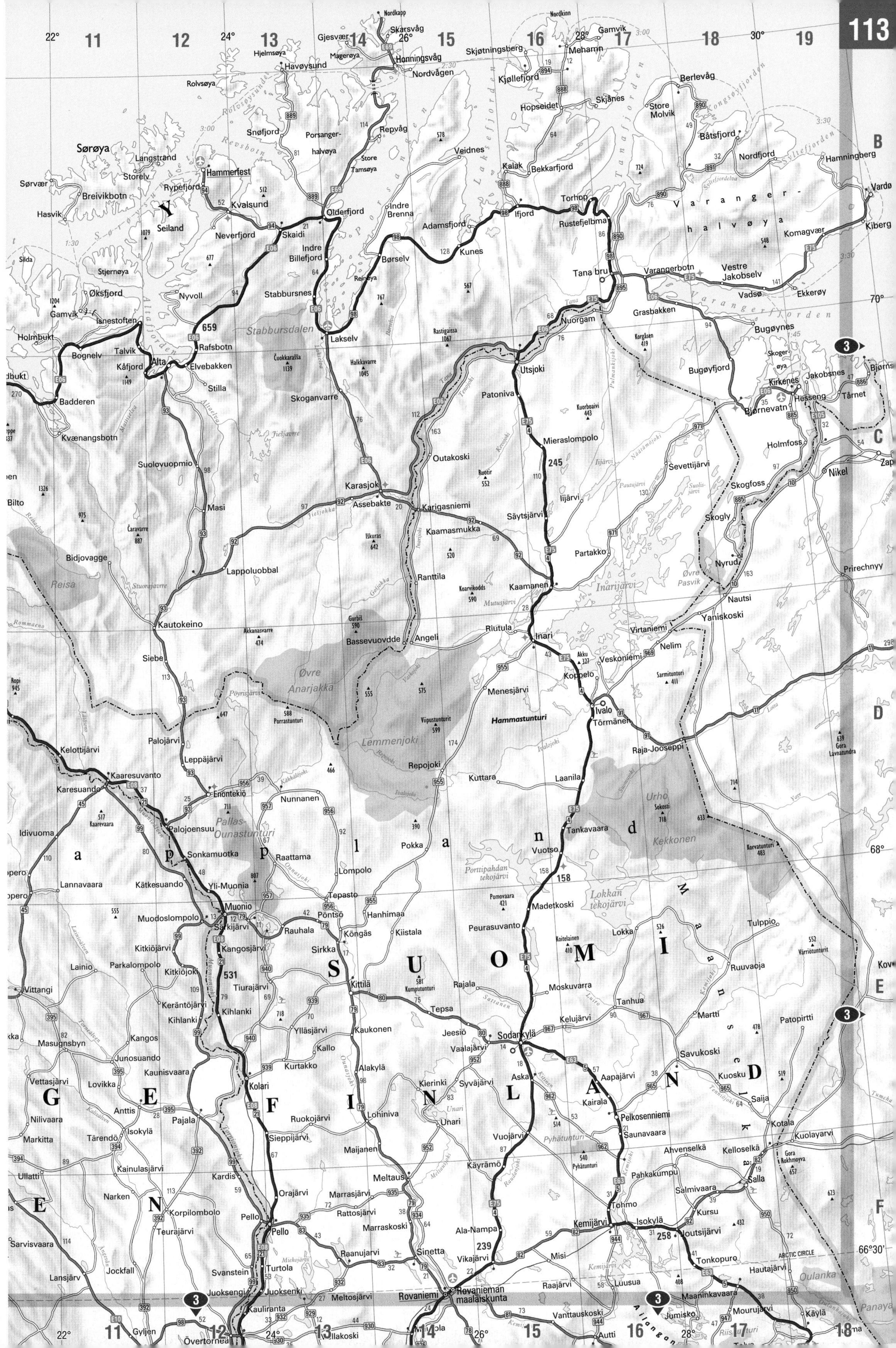

Nordkapp
Nordkinn
Skarsvåg
Gjesvær
Hjelmsøya
Magerøya
Honningsvåg
Havøysund
Nordvågen
Rolvsøya
Skjøtningsberg
Mehamn
Gamvik
Kjøllefjord
Berlevåg
Hopseidet
Skjånes
Store Molvik
Snøfjord
Porsanger-halvøya
Repvåg
Sørøya
Langstrand
Hammerfest
Storelv
Sørvær
Breivikbotn
Hasvik
Rypefjord
Kvalsund
Seiland
Neverfjord
Skaidi
Olderfjord
Store Tamsøya
Veidnes
Kalak
Bekkarfjord
Båtsfjord
Nordfjord
Hamningberg
Vardø
Indre Brenna
Adamsfjord
Ifjord
Torhop
Rustefjelbma
Varanger-halvøya
Kiberg
Komagvær
Stjernøya
Silda
Indre Billefjord
Børselv
Kunes
Tana bru
Varangerbotn
Vestre Jakobselv
Vadsø
Ekkerøy
Øksfjord
Gamvik
Isnestoften
Nyvoll
Stabbursnes
Reinøya
Nuorgam
Grasbakken
Bugøynes
Varangerfjorden
Holmbukt
Stabbursdalen
Lakselv
Rastigaissa
Talvik
Bognelv
Kåfjord
Alta
Rafsbotn
Elvebakken
Stilla
Čuokkarašša
Halkkavarre
Utsjoki
Skogerøya
Bugøyfjord
Kirkenes
Jakobsnes
Bjørnevatn
Hesseng
Tårnet
Badderen
Skoganvarre
Patoniva
Kvænangsbotn
Holmfoss
Zapolyarnyy
Mieraslompolo
Outakoski
Suoloyuopmio
Sevettijärvi
Nikel
Karasjok
Assebakte
Karigasniemi
Skogfoss
Masi
Iijärvi
Säytsjärvi
Skogly
Bilto
Kaamasmukka
Bidjovagge
Čaravarre
Iškuras
Partakko
Nyrud
Reisa
Lappoluobbal
Ranttila
Koarvikodds
Kaamanen
Inarijärvi
Øvre Pasvik
Prirechnyy
Nautsi
Kautokeino
Angeli
Gurbiš
Bassevuovdde
Riutula
Inari
Yaniskoski
Virtaniemi
Nelim
Akkanasvarre
Siebe
Øvre Anarjakka
Veskoniemi
Akku
Koppelo
Sarmitunturi
Ropi
Menesjärvi
Ivalo
Törmänen
Hammastunturi
Viipustunturit
Porrastunturi
Lemmenjoki
Raja-Jooseppi
Palojärvi
Kelottijärvi
Leppäjärvi
Repojoki
Gora Lavnatundra
Kaaresuvanto
Karesuando
Enontekiö
Kuttara
Laanila
Nunnanen
Urho Kekkonen
Sokosti
Palojoensuu
Pallas-Ounastunturi
Idivuoma
Kaarevaara
Tankavaara
Korvatunturi
Pokka
Lappland
Sonkamuotka
Raattama
Vuotso
Porttipahdan tekojärvi
Lokkan tekojärvi
Lannavaara
Kätkesuando
Yli-Muonio
Lompolo
Tepasto
Muonio
Pomovaara
Madetkoski
Muodoslompolo
Särkijärvi
Rauhala
Pöntsö
Hanhimaa
Köngäs
Kiistala
Peurasuvanto
Tulppio
Kitkiöjärvi
Kangosjärvi
Sirkka
Koitelainen
Lokka
Värriötunturi
Lainio
Parkalompolo
Kitkiöjoki
Suomi
Kittilä
Kumputunturi
Rajala
Ruuvaoja
Tiurajärvi
Moskuvarra
Vittangi
Keräntöjärvi
Kihlanki
Tepsa
Tanhua
Patopirtti
Masugnsbyn
Kangos
Ylläsjärvi
Kaukonen
Jeesiö
Sodankylä
Kelujärvi
Martti
Junosuando
Kallo
Vaalajärvi
Kaunisvaara
Kurtakko
Alakylä
Savukoski
Vettasjärvi
Lovikka
Kolari
Kierinki
Syväjärvi
Aapajärvi
Kuosku
Saija
Sverige
Finland
Nilivaara
Anttis
Pajala
Lohiniva
Ruokojärvi
Unari
Kairala
Pelkosenniemi
Markitta
Tärendö
Isokylä
Sieppijärvi
Vuojärvi
Saunavaara
Kotala
Kuolayarvi
Maijanen
Pyhätunturi
Ahvenselkä
Kelloselkä
Gora Rokhmoyva
Ullatti
Kainulasjärvi
Kardis
Meltaus
Käyrämö
Pahkakumpu
Salla
Narken
Korpilombolo
Orajärvi
Marrasjärvi
Salmivaara
Teurajärvi
Pello
Rattosjärvi
Tohmo
Kursu
Sarvisvaara
Marraskoski
Ala-Nampa
Kemijärvi
Isokylä
Joutsijärvi
Raanujärvi
Sinetta
Vikajärvi
Misi
Tonkopuro
Arctic Circle
Hautajärvi
Lansjärvi
Jockfall
Svanstein
Turtola
Oulanka
Juoksengi
Juoksenki
Meltosjärvi
Rovaniemi
Rovaniemen maalaiskunta
Raajärvi
Luusua
Maaninkavaara
Kauliranta
Vanttauskoski
Jumisko
Mourujärvi
Käylä
Gyljen
Övertorneå
Ollakoski
Autti
Aljangan
Panaya
22°
24°
26°
28°
30°
70°
68°
66°30'
11
12
13
14
15
16
17
18
19
B
C
D
E
F

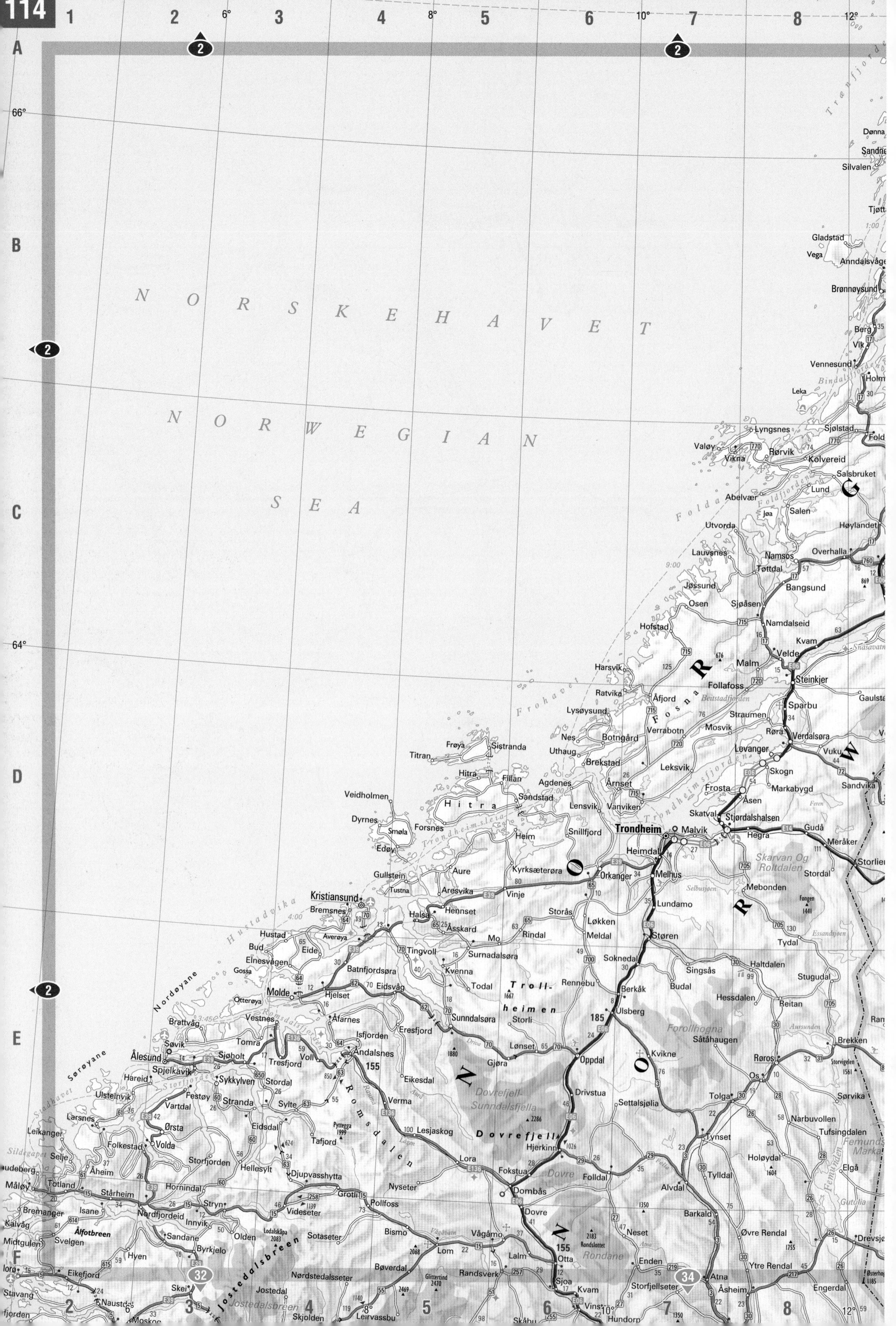
NORSKEHAVET
NORWEGIAN SEA
NORGE
66°
64°
6°
8°
10°
12°
Trænfjorden
Dønna
Sandnessjøen
Silvalen
Tjøtta
Gladstad
Vega
Anndalsvåg
Brønnøysund
Berg
Vik
Vennesund
Holm
Bindalsfjorden
Leka
Lyngsnes
Sjølstad
Foldereid
Valøy
Vikna
Rørvik
Kolvereid
Salsbruket
Lund
Abelvær
Foldfjorden
Folda
Jøa
Salen
Høylandet
Utvorda
Lauvsnes
Namsos
Overhalla
Tøttdal
Bangsund
Jøssund
Osen
Sjøåsen
Namdalseid
Hofstad
Kvam
Velde
Snåsavatnet
Harsvik
Malm
Steinkjer
Follafoss
Fosna
Ratvika
Åfjord
Beitstadfjorden
Gaulstad
Lysøysund
Sparbu
Straumen
Verrabotn
Mosvik
Røra
Verdalsøra
Frohavet
Frøya
Sistranda
Nes
Botngård
Titran
Uthaug
Levanger
Vuku
Brekstad
Leksvik
Skogn
Hitra
Fillan
Agdenes
Årnset
Frosta
Markabygd
Sandvika
Veidholmen
Sandstad
Lensvik
Vanviken
Trondheimsfjorden
Åsen
Dyrnes
Smøla
Forsnes
Trondheimsleia
Skatval
Stjørdalshalsen
Heim
Snillfjord
Trondheim
Malvik
Gudå
Edøy
Hegra
Meråker
Heimdal
Storlien
Aure
Kyrksæterøra
Orkanger
Skarvan Og Roltdalen
Gullstein
Tustna
Melhus
Stordal
Selbusjøen
Mebonden
Kristiansund
Aresvika
Vinje
Bremsnes
Hustadvika
Lundamo
Halsa
Hennset
Storås
Løkken
Averøya
Åsskard
Rindal
Meldal
Støren
Hustad
Eide
Mo
Tydal
Essandsjøen
Bud
Tingvoll
Surnadalsøra
Elnesvågen
Soknedal
Singsås
Haltdalen
Gossa
Batnfjordsøra
Kvenna
Budal
Stugudal
Nordøyane
Molde
Hjelset
Eidsvåg
Todal
Rennebu
Berkåk
Trollheimen
Hessdalen
Otterøya
Reitan
Brattvåg
Vestnes
Åfarnes
Romsdalsfjorden
Sunndalsøra
Storli
Ulsberg
Forollhogna
Eresfjord
Isfjorden
Såtåhaugen
Brekken
Søvik
Tomra
Ålesund
Sjøholt
Andalsnes
Kvikne
Lønset
Gjøra
Oppdal
Røros
Sørøyane
Spjelkavik
Tresfjord
Voll
Storvigelen
Hareid
Sykkylven
Stordal
Eikesdal
Os
Storfjorden
Romsdalen
Ulsteinvik
Festøy
Stranda
Verma
Drivstua
Dovrefjell
Sunndalsfjella
Tolga
Sørvika
Vartdal
Sylte
Settalsjølia
Larsnes
Ørsta
Eidsdal
Pyttegga
Lesjaskog
Dovrefjell
Narbuvollen
Tufsingdalen
Leikanger
Volda
Tafjord
Hjerkinn
Tynset
Folkestad
Femunden
Sildegapet
Selje
Storfjorden
Hellesylt
Lora
Holøydal
Elgå
Åheim
Djupvasshytta
Fokstua
Dovre
Folldal
Tylldal
Måløy
Totland
Stårheim
Hornindal
Grotli
Nyseter
Dombås
Alvdal
Gutulia
Bremanger
Isane
Nordfjordeid
Stryn
Videseter
Pollfoss
Dovre
Barkald
Kalvåg
Innvik
Olden
Lodalskåpa
Sotaseter
Bismo
Vågåmo
Neset
Øvre Rendal
Drevsjø
Ålfotbreen
Svelgen
Sandane
Vågåvatn
Rondslottet
Rondane
Byrkjelo
Lom
Lalm
Otta
Enden
Ytre Rendal
Hyen
Eikefjord
Nordstedalsseter
Bøverdal
Glittertind
Randsverk
Sjoa
Storfjellseter
Atna
Engerdal
Jostedal
Jostedalsbreen
Skei
Kvam
Åsheim
Stavang
Naustdal
Leirvassbu
Vinstra
Skjolden
Moskog
Skåbu
Hundorp
Førde
Florø
Udeberg
Midtgulen
1880
2286
1026
1667
1441
1604
1350
1755
2183
2083
2469
2470
1139
1561
1185
1140
E39
E136
E6
E14
70
65

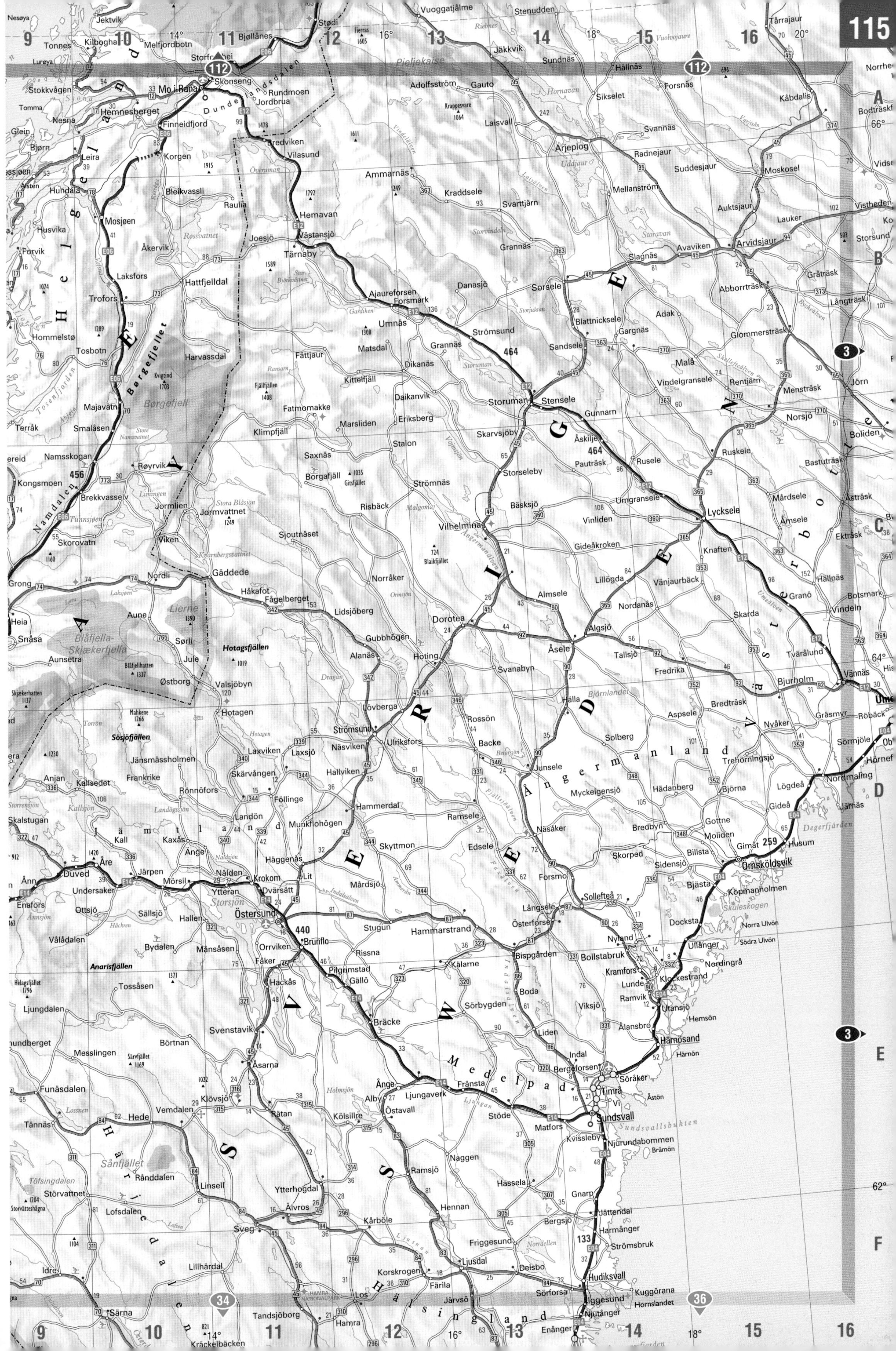

9
10
11
12
13
14
15
16
A
B
C
D
E
F
14°
16°
18°
20°
66°
64°
62°
112
3
34
36
Nesøya
Jektvik
Tonnes
Kilboghamn
Melfjordbotn
Bjøllånes
Stødi
Vuoggatjålme
Stenudden
Tårrajaur
Lurøya
Storforshei
Fierras
Pieljekaise
Jäkkvik
Sundnäs
Hällnäs
Norrhe
Stokkvågen
Mo i Rana
Skonseng
Dunderlandsdalen
Rundmoen
Jordbrua
Adolfsström
Gauto
Hornavan
Forsnäs
Kåbdalis
Tomma
Hemnesberget
Sjona
Krappesvare
Sikselet
Bodträskf
Nesna
Finneidfjord
Laisvall
Svannäs
Glein
Bjørn
Leira
Korgen
Bredviken
Vilasund
Arjeplog
Radnejaur
Moskosel
Vidse
Sjøen
Alsten
Hundåla
Bleikvassli
Raulia
Överuman
Ammarnäs
Kraddsele
Uddjaur
Mellanström
Suddesjaur
Hemavan
Svarttjärn
Auktsjaur
Vistheden
Husvika
Mosjøen
Røssvatnet
Joesjö
Västansjö
Storvindeln
Storavan
Lauker
Ko
Storsund
Forvik
Åkervik
Tärnaby
Grannäs
Slagnäs
Avaviken
Arvidsjaur
Laksfors
Hattfjelldal
Björkvattnet
Sorsele
Abborrträsk
Gråträsk
Ajaureforsen
Forsmark
Danasjö
Långträsk
Trofors
Gardiken
Umnäs
Blattnicksele
Adak
Hommelstø
Børgefjellet
Gargnäs
Glommersträsk
Tosbotn
Matsdal
Grannäs
Strömsund
Sandsele
Harvassdal
Fättjaur
Ransarn
Storuman
Malå
Skellefteälven
Tosenfjorden
Kvigtind
Dikanäs
Rentjärn
Jörn
Fjällfjällen
Kittelfjäll
Vindelgranselet
Mensträsk
Majavatn
Børgefjell
Daikanvik
Storuman
Stensele
Gunnarn
Fatmomakke
Norsjö
Terråk
Smalåsen
Store Namsvatnet
Klimpfjäll
Marsliden
Eriksberg
Skarvsjöby
Åskilje
Boliden
Stalon
Ruskele
Ruselle
Bastuträsk
Ereid
Namsskogan
Røyrvik
Saxnäs
Pauträsk
Borgafjäll
Gitsfjället
Storselebу
Kongsmoen
Brekkvasselv
Limingen
Strömnäs
Mårdsele
Aström
Namdalen
Tunnsjøen
Jormlien
Stora Blåsjön
Risbäck
Malgomaj
Bäsksjö
Umgransele
Lycksele
Jormvattnet
Vilhelmina
Vinliden
Åmsele
Skorovatn
Sjoutnäset
Ekträsk
Viken
Kvarnbergsvattnet
Gideåkroken
Knaften
Ångermanälven
Blaikfjället
Gäddede
Nordli
Lillögda
Vänjaurbäck
Hällnäs
Grong
Laksjøen
Norråker
Håkafot
Fågelberget
Ormsjön
Almsele
Umeälven
Granö
Botsmark
Luru
Lierne
Lidsjöberg
Nordanås
Vindeln
Heia
Aune
Dorotea
Algsjö
Skarda
Snåsa
Bläfjella-Skjækerfjella
Sørli
Hotagsfjällen
Gubbhögen
Åsele
Tallsjö
Tvärålund
Aunsetra
Jule
Alanäs
Hoting
Svanabyn
Fredrika
Vännäs
Blåfjellhatten
Østborg
Valsjöbyn
Dragan
Björnlandet
Bjurholm
Umeå
Skjækerhatten
Hotagen
Lövberga
Hälla
Bredträsk
Röbäck
Mahkene
Torrön
Rossön
Aspsele
Gräsmyr
Sösjöfjällen
Strömsund
Ulriksfors
Backe
Nyåker
Sörmjöle
Obb
Laxviken
Laxsjö
Näsviken
Solberg
Hörnefors
Anjan
Jänsmässholmen
Skärvången
Hallviken
Junsele
Trehörningsjö
Kallsedet
Frankrike
Föllinge
Ångermanland
Nordmaling
Storrensjön
Rönnöfors
Landögssjön
Myckelgensjö
Hädanberg
Björna
Lögdeå
Kallsjön
Hammerdal
Ramsele
Gideå
Järnäs
Skalstugan
Landön
Munkflohögen
Näsåker
Bredbyn
Gottne
Degerfjärden
Jämtland
Kall
Kaxås
Skyttmon
Edsele
Moliden
Gimåt
Husum
Åre
Änge
Naldsjön
Häggenås
Mårdsjö
Skorped
Billsta
Örnsköldsvik
Ånn
Duved
Järpen
Mörsil
Nälden
Krokom
Lit
Forsmo
Sidensjö
Bjästa
Köpmanholmen
Undersåker
Ytteran
Dvärsätt
Ammerån
Indalsälven
Sollefteå
Skuleskogen
Enafors
Storsjön
Långsele
Docksta
Norra Ulvön
Ottsjö
Sällsjö
Östersund
Hallen
Stugun
Hammarstrand
Österforse
Nyland
Södra Ulvön
Håckren
Brunflo
Ullånger
Vålådalen
Bydalen
Orrviken
Rissna
Bispgården
Bollstabruk
Nordingrå
Månsåsen
Kramfors
Klockestrand
Anarisfjällen
Fåker
Pilgrimstad
Kälarne
Lunde
Helagsfjället
Tossåsen
Hackås
Gällö
Boda
Ramvik
Utansjö
Sörbygden
Viksjö
Hemsön
Ljungdalen
Bräcke
Liden
Ålansbro
Härnösand
Svenstavik
Indal
Härnön
Börtnan
Bergeforsen
Söråker
Medelpad
Messlingen
Särvfjället
Åsarna
Ånge
Fränsta
Timrå
Åstön
Funäsdalen
Klövsjö
Alby
Ljungaverk
Vi
Holmsjön
Ljungan
Lossnen
Hede
Vemdalen
Rätan
Kölsillre
Östavall
Stöde
Sundsvall
Sundsvallsbukten
Tännäs
Matfors
Kvissleby
Njurundabommen
Härjedalen
Brämön
Sånfjället
Naggen
Töfsingdalen
Rånddalen
Ramsjö
Hälsingland
Hassela
Gnarp
Störvattnet
Storvätteshågna
Linsell
Ytterhogdal
Jättendal
Lofsdalen
Hennan
Harmånger
Älvros
Kårböle
Bergsjö
Sveg
Ljusnan
Friggesund
Norrdellen
Strömsbruk
Lillhärdal
Ljusdal
Delsbo
Hudiksvall
Idre
Korskrogen
Färila
Sörforsa
Kuggörana
Iggesund
Hornslandet
Hamra Nationalpark
Los
Järvsö
Njutånger
Särna
Tandsjöborg
Hamra
Enånger
Kräckelbäcken

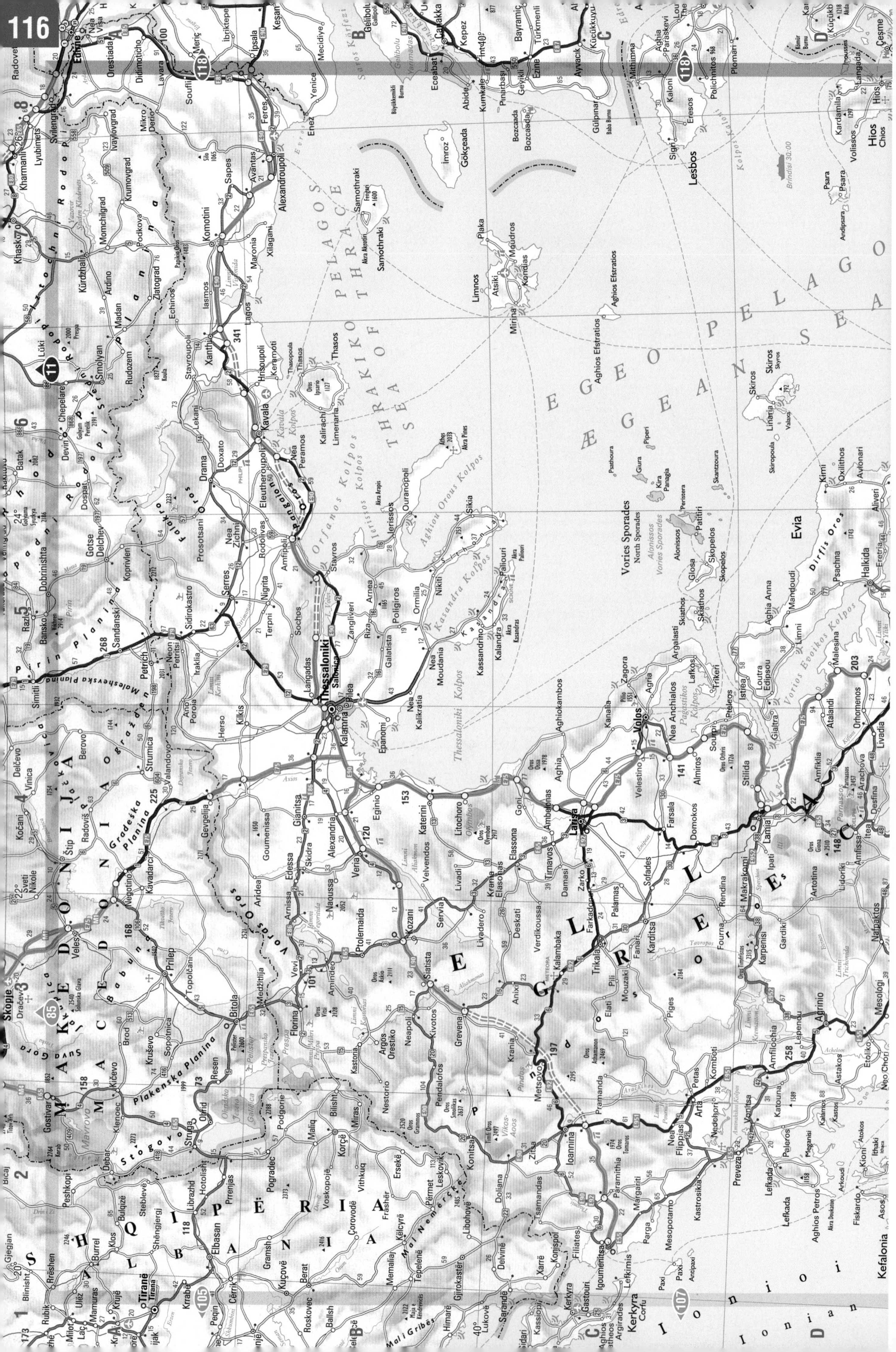
Thessaloniki
Salonica
Kavala
Drama
Serres
Komotini
Xanthi
Alexandroupoli
Larisa
Volos
Lamia
Trikala
Kozani
Veria
Katerini
Ioannina
Arta
Preveza
Igoumenitsa
Kerkyra
Corfu
Lefkada
Kefalonia
Agrinio
Mesologi
Karpenisi
Amfissa
Halkida
Evia
Skopje
Bitola
Prilep
Ohrid
Struga
Veles
Štip
Tiranë
Tirana
Elbasan
Korçë
Berat
Gjirokastër
Sarandë
Kardzhali
Smolyan
Kharmanli
Svilengrad
Edirne
Keşan
İpsala
Gelibolu
Çanakkale
Eceabat
Ayvacık
Limnos
Mirina
Samothraki
Thasos
Lesbos
Skiros
Skiathos
Skopelos
Alonissos
Vories Sporades
North Sporades
Gökçeada
Bozcaada
Hios
Psara
MACEDONIA
SHQIPËRIA
ALBANIA
GREECE
THRAKIKO PELAGOS
THRACIAN SEA
EGEO PELAGO
AEGEAN SEA
Thermaikos Kolpos
Kasandra
Sithonia
Mal i Nemërçkë
Pindos
Olymbos
Parnassos
Rodopi
Pirin Planina
Plakenska Planina
Babuna
Gradeska Planina

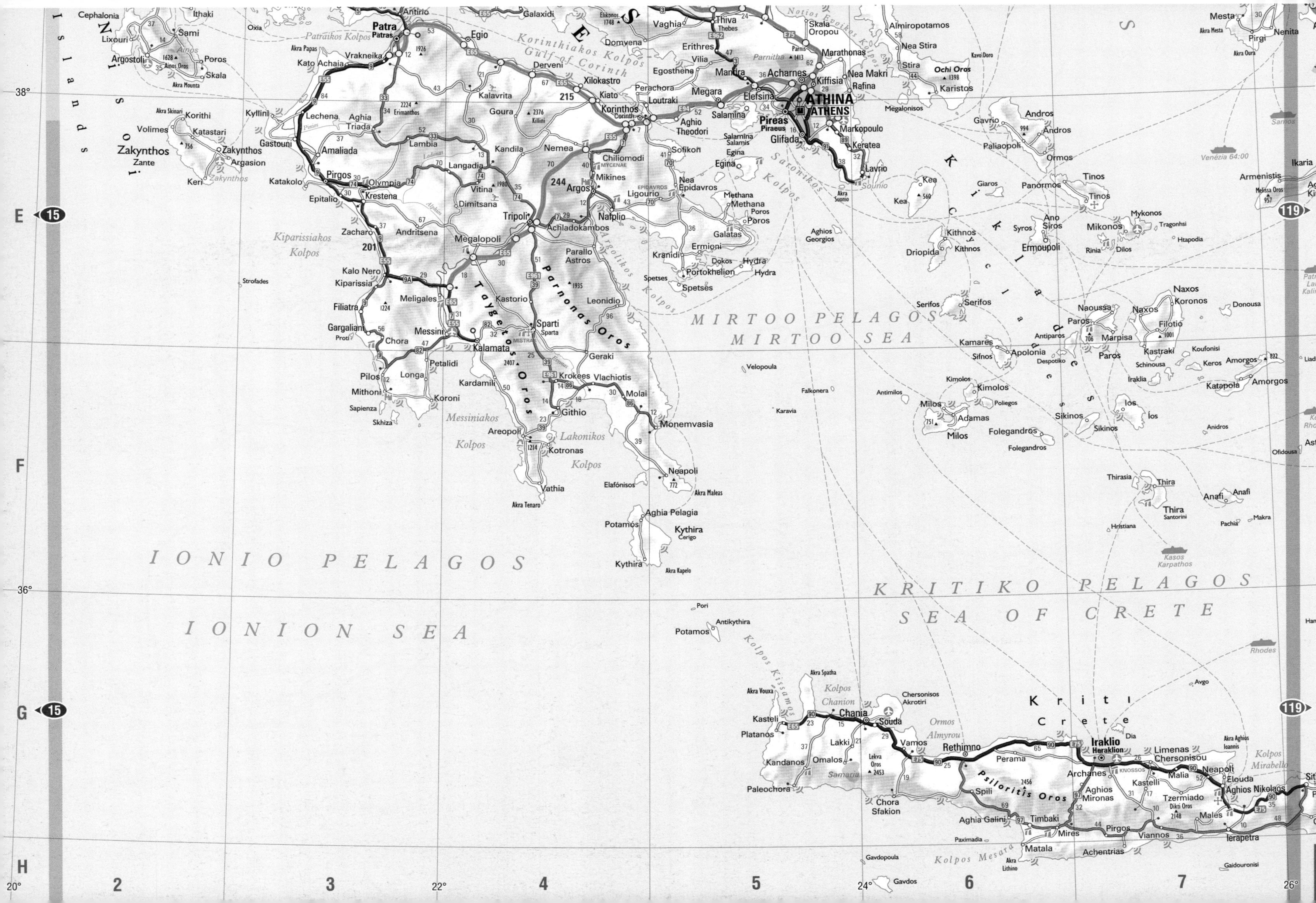
Ionian Islands
Cephalonia
Ithaki
Lixouri
Sami
Argostoli
Poros
Skala
Ainos Oros
Akra Mounta
Zakynthos
Zante
Volimes
Korithi
Katastari
Argasion
Keri
Akra Skinari
Oxia
Patra
Patras
Patraikos Kolpos
Akra Papas
Kato Achaia
Vrakneika
Antirio
Egio
Galaxidi
Korinthiakos Kolpos
Gulf of Corinth
Derveni
Xilokastro
Kiato
Korinthos
Corinth
Kalavrita
Goura
Killini
Erimanthos
Kyllini
Lechena
Aghia Triada
Gastouni
Amaliada
Pirgos
Katakolo
Epitalio
Olympia
Krestena
Lambia
Kandila
Langadia
Vitina
Dimitsana
Tripoli
Megalopoli
Andritsena
Zacharo
Kiparissiakos Kolpos
Kalo Nero
Kiparissia
Filiatra
Gargaliani
Proti
Strofades
Meligales
Messini
Kalamata
Chora
Pilos
Mithoni
Sapienza
Skhiza
Petalidi
Longa
Koroni
Messiniakos Kolpos
Kardamili
Areopoli
Vathia
Akra Tenaro
Kotronas
Lakonikos Kolpos
Githio
Krokees
Vlachiotis
Molai
Monemvasia
Neapoli
Akra Maleas
Elafónisos
Aghia Pelagia
Potamos
Kythira
Cerigo
Akra Kapelo
Taygetos Oros
Parnonas Oros
Sparti
Sparta
Mistras
Kastorio
Geraki
Leonidio
Parallo Astros
Achladokambos
Argos
Nafplio
Mikines
Mycenae
Chiliomodi
Nemea
Ligourio
Epidavros
Nea Epidavros
Sofikon
Argolikos Kolpos
Kranidi
Portokhelion
Spetses
Ermioni
Dokos
Hydra
Galatas
Poros
Methana
Egina
Saronikos Kolpos
Salamina
Salamis
Aghio Theodori
Loutraki
Perachora
Megara
Egosthena
Vilia
Erithres
Mandra
Elefsina
Acharnes
Pireas
Piraeus
Glifada
ATHINA
ATHENS
Kiffisia
Marathonas
Parnitha
Parnis
Thiva
Thebes
Vaghia
Domvena
Elikonas
Skala Oropou
Notios Evoikos Kolpos
Nea Makri
Rafina
Markopoulo
Keratea
Lavrio
Akra Sounio
Almiropotamos
Nea Stira
Stira
Ochi Oros
Kavo Doro
Karistos
Megalonisos
Andros
Gavrio
Paliaopoli
Ormos
Tinos
Panormos
Giaros
Kea
Kithnos
Driopida
Aghios Georgios
Syros
Ano Siros
Ermoupoli
Mykonos
Mikonos
Rinia
Dilos
Tragonhsi
Htapodia
Kiklades
Serifos
Sifnos
Apolonia
Kamares
Antiparos
Despotiko
Paros
Naoussa
Marpisa
Naxos
Koronos
Filotio
Donousa
Kastraki
Koufonisi
Schinousa
Keros
Iraklia
Amorgos
Katapola
Liadi
Kinaros
Kimolos
Poliegos
Milos
Adamas
Antimilos
Folegandros
Sikinos
Ios
Anidros
Thira
Santorini
Thirasia
Hristiana
Anafi
Pachia
Makra
Astipalea
Ofidousa
Velopoula
Falkonera
Karavia
MIRTOO PELAGOS
MIRTOO SEA
IONIO PELAGOS
IONION SEA
KRITIKO PELAGOS
SEA OF CRETE
Venézia 64:00
Samos
Patmos Laros Kalimnos
Kos Rhodes
Kasos Karpathos
Rhodes
Ikaria
Armenistis
Melissa Oros
Aghios Kirikos
Marat
Mesta
Akra Mesta
Pirgi
Nenita
Akra Oura
Alaçati
Hamili
Pori
Antikythira
Potamos
Kolpos Kissamos
Kriti
Crete
Akra Spatha
Akra Vouxa
Kasteli
Platanos
Kolpos Chanion
Chania
Souda
Chersonisos Akrotiri
Kandanos
Paleochora
Omalos
Lakki
Samaria
Lefka Oros
Chora Sfakion
Vamos
Ormos Almyrou
Rethimno
Perama
Psiloritis Oros
Spili
Aghia Galini
Timbaki
Mires
Matala
Paximadia
Kolpos Mesara
Akra Lithino
Gavdopoula
Gavdos
Iraklio
Heraklion
Knossos
Dia
Archanes
Aghios Mironas
Kastelli
Pirgos
Achentrias
Viannos
Limenas Chersonisou
Malia
Tzermiado
Dikti Oros
Avgo
Neapoli
Elounda
Aghios Nikolaos
Kolpos Mirabello
Akra Aghios Ioannis
Males
Ierapetra
Gaidouronisi
Sitia
Vai
Palekastro
Chandra
Dionisades
E
F
G
H
2
3
4
5
6
7
20°
22°
24°
26°
36°
38°
15
119

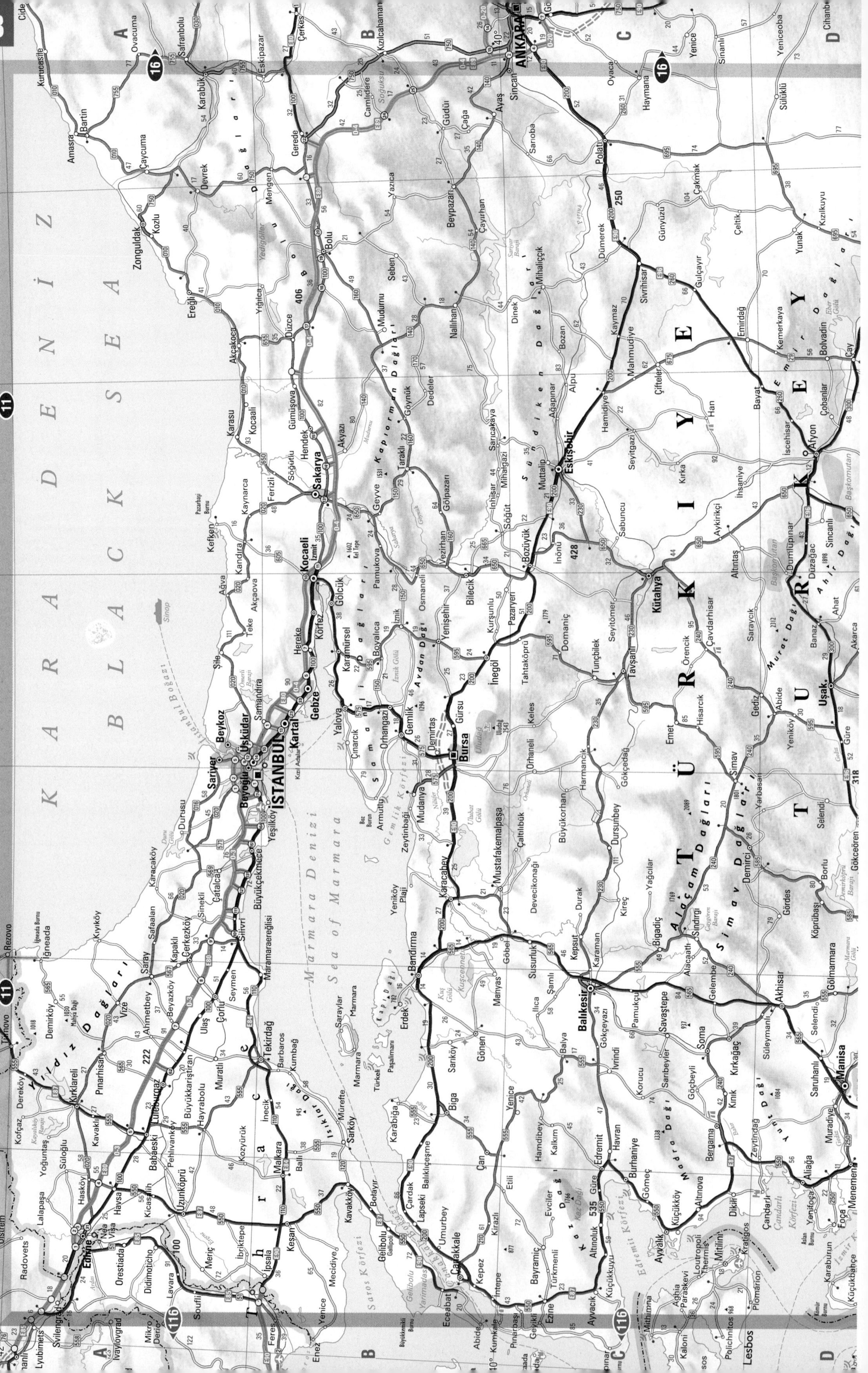
KARADENİZ
BLACK SEA
Marmara Denizi
Sea of Marmara
TÜRKİYE
İSTANBUL
ANKARA
Bursa
Eskişehir
Kocaeli
Sakarya
Balıkesir
Manisa
Kütahya
Afyon
Uşak
Edirne
Kırklareli
Tekirdağ
Çanakkale
Zonguldak
Karabük
Bartın
Düzce
Bolu
Yalova
Bilecik
Lesbos
İstanbul Boğazı
Saros Körfezi
Edremit Körfezi
Gemlik Körfezi
Uludağ
Sündiken Dağları
Yıldız Dağları
Kaz Dağı
Alaçam Dağları
Simav Dağları
Murat Dağı
Ahir Dağı
Köroğlu Dağları

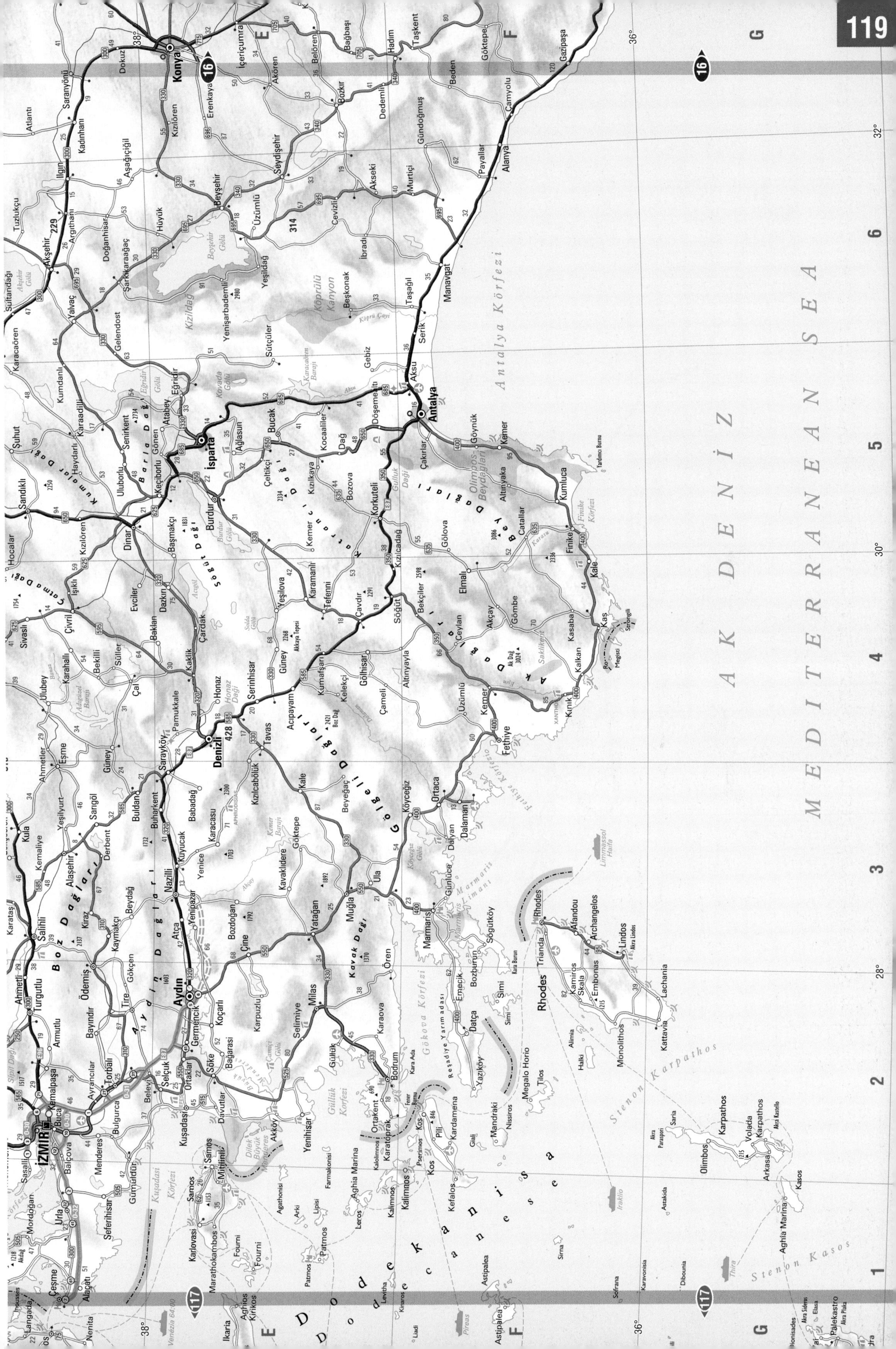
AKDENİZ
MEDITERRANEAN SEA
Antalya Körfezi
Dodecanisa
İZMİR
Aydın
Denizli
Konya
Isparta
Burdur
Antalya
Alanya
Manavgat
Kemer
Fethiye
Marmaris
Bodrum
Muğla
Milas
Kuşadası
Çeşme
Rhodes
Kos
Samos
Karpathos
Kalimnos
Patmos
Ikaria
Beyşehir
Eğirdir
Akşehir
Dinar
Finike
Kaş
Elmalı
Köprülü Kanyon
Boz Dağları
Aydın Dağları
Gölgeli Dağları
Beydağları
Olimbos-Beydağları
Ak Dağ
Kavak Dağı
Söğüt Dağı
Barla Dağı
Gökova Körfezi
Marmaris Limanı
Fethiye Körfezi
Stenon Karpathos
Stenon Kasos
Beyşehir Gölü
Burdur Gölü
Acıgöl
Salda Gölü
Köyceğiz Gölü
36°
30°
28°
32°
38°

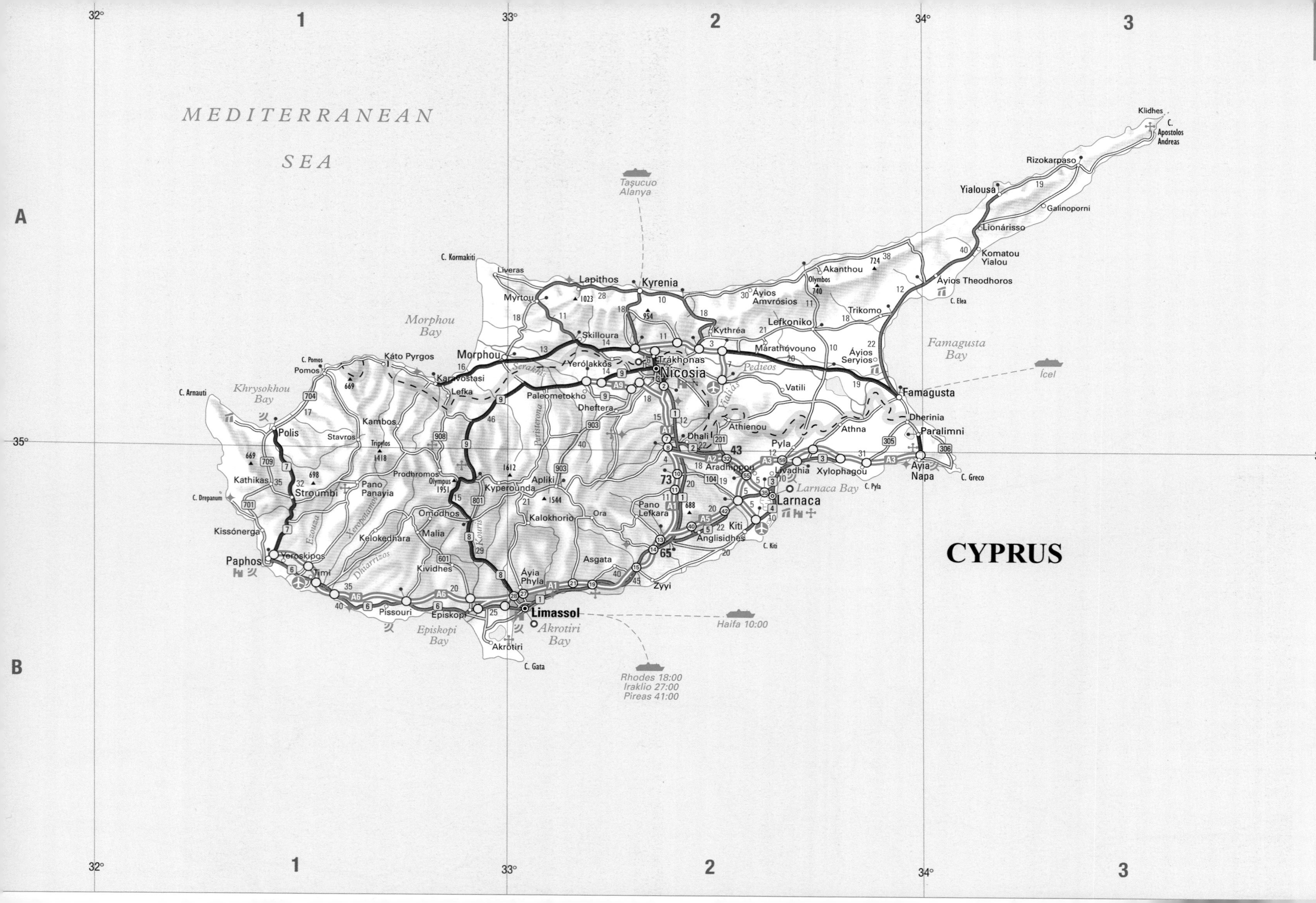

A B

3 3

2 2

1 1

34° 34°

33° 33°

32° 32°

35° 35°

CYPRUS

MEDITERRANEAN

SEA

C. Kildhes
Apóstolos Andréas
C. Aspóstolos Andréas
Rizokárpaso
19
Yialoúsa
40
Lionárisso
Galinopórni
Komátou Yialou
Ayios Theodhoros
C. Elea
Akanthou
724 38
Olymbos 740
12
Trikomo
18
22
Ayios Servios
Famagusta
Famagusta Bay
Dherinia
Paralimni
306
C. Greco
Ayia Napa
305
Xylophagou
C. Pyla
31
Ávdhia
Larnaca Bay
Athna
Pyla
Larnaca
3
Lefkoníko
21
Marathóvouno
Vatili
Athienou
Dhali
201
18 104
19
Aradhíppou
C. Kiti
Kiti
688
22
Anglisídhes
Ávios Amvrósios
30
Kythréa
7
Pedieos
Trakhónas
Nicosia
Dhali
73
Pano Lefkara
65
Zyví
Kyrenia
10
11
Serakhis
3
18
554
Skilloura
14
Yeroklakos
A9
9
Dhekélia
18
Oia
Ora
Asgata
40
19
Lapithos
1023 28
Myrtou
18
13
Paleometokho
Dheftera
903
40
Kalokhorio
Aplik
1544
21
Limassol
Akrotíri Bay
Liveras
C. Kormakiti
Morphou
16
Karavostasi
Lefka
Kyperounda
801
8
29
Ayia Phyla
25
Akrotíri
C. Gata
Morphou Bay
Xerolakas
Paristerona
908
15
Prodhromos
Olympus 1951
Malia
Omodhos
601
6
Kividhes
Episkopi
Episkopi Bay
Káto Pyrgos
Kambos
Tríploti
1418
Pano Panayia
Kelokedhara
Pissouri
Dhiarizos
Xeropotamos
Khrysokhou Bay
C. Pomos
Pomos
704
17
Stavros
Stroumbi
698
22
Yeroskipos
6
35
Tími
40
Pólis
7
709
7
669
Kathikas 35
701
Kissónerga
Paphos
C. Arnauti
C. Drepanum

Tasucu Alanya
Icel
Rhodes 18:00
Iraklio 27:00
Pireas 41:00
Haifa 10:00

City plans • Plans de villes
Stadtpläne • Piante di città

Motorway	Autoroute	Autobahn	Autostrada	
Major through route	Route principale majeur	Hauptstrecke	Strada di grande communicazione	
Through route	Route principale	Schnellstrasse	Strada d'importanza regionale	
Secondary road	Route secondaire	Nebenstrasse	Strada d'interesse locale	
Dual carriageway	Chaussées séparées	Zweispurig Schnellstrasse	Strada a carreggiate doppie	
Other road	Autre route	Nebenstrecke	Altra strada	
Tunnel	Tunnel	Tunnel	Galleria stradale	
Limited access / pedestrian road	Rue réglementée / rue piétonne	Beschränkter Zugang/ Fussgängerzone	Strada pedonale / a accesso limitato	
One-way street	Sens unique	Einbahnstrasse	Senso unico	
Parking	Parc de stationnement	Parkplatz	Parcheggio	
Motorway number	Numéro d'autoroute	Autobahnnummer	Numero di autostrada	
National road number	Numéro de route nationale	Nationalstrassen-nummer	Numero di strada nazionale	
European road number	Numéro de route européenne	Europäische Strassennummer	Numero di strada europea	
Destination	Destination	Ziel	Destinazione	
Car ferry	Bac passant les autos	Autofähre	Traghetto automobili	
Railway	Chemin de fer	Eisenbahn	Ferrovia	
Rail/bus station	Gare / gare routière	Bahnhof / Busstation	Stazione ferrovia / pullman	
Underground, metro station	Station de métro	U-Bahnstation	Metropolitano	
Cable car	Téléférique	Drahtseilbahn	Funivia	
Abbey, cathedral	Abbaye, cathédrale	Abtei, Kloster, Kathedrale	Abbazia, duomo	
Church of interest	Église intéressante	Interessante Kirche	Chiesa da vedere	
Synagogue	Synagogue	Synagoge	Sinagoga	
Hospital	Hôpital	Krankenhaus	Ospedale	
Police station	Police	Polizeiwache	Polizia	
Post office	Bureau de poste	Postamt	Ufficio postale	
Tourist information	Office de tourisme	Informationsbüro	Ufficio informazioni turistiche	
Place of interest	Autre curiosité	Sonstige Sehenswürdigkeit	Luogo da vedere	

Approach maps • Agglomérations
Carte régionale • Regionalkarte

Toll motorway – with motorway number	Autoroute à péage – avec numéro d'autoroute	Gebührenpflichtige Autobahn – mit Autobahnnummer	Autostrada a pedaggio – con numero
Toll-free motorway – with European road number	Autoroute – avec numéro de route européenne	Gebührenfreie Autobahn – Europäische Strassennummer	Autostrada – con numero di strada europea
Pre-pay motorway – vignette required	Autoroute – 'vignette'	Autobahn – 'vignette'	Autostrada – 'vignette'
Motorway services	Aire de service	Autobahnservice	Area di servizio autostradale
Motorway junction – full/restricted	Échangeur d'autoroute – accès libre/ accès reglémenté	Autobahnkreuz – voller/begrenzter Zugang	Raccordi autostradali – completo/parziali
Under construction	En construction	Im Bau	In construzione
Tunnel	Tunnel	Tunnel	Galleria stradale
Major route dual carriageway single carriageway	Route principale chausées séparées chausée sans séparation	Hauptstrecke	Strada di grande communicazione
Secondary route dual carriageway single carriageway	Route secondaire chausées séparées chausée sans séparation	zweispurige Schnellstrasse	carreggiata doppia carreggiata unica
Other road	Autre route	Nebenstrasse zweispurige Schnellstrasse	Strada d'interesse locale carreggiata doppia carreggiata unica
Car ferry	Bac passant les autos	Nebenstrecke	Altra strada
Destination	Destination	Autofähre	Traghetto automobili
Railway	Chemin de fer	Ziel	Destinazione
Railway station	Gare	Eisenbahn	Ferrovia
Height above sea level – in metres	Altitude – en mètres	Hauptbahnhof	Stazione ferrovia
Airport	Aéroport principal	Höhe über dem Meeresspiegel	Altezza in metri
Airfield	Autre aéroport	Flughafen	Aeroporto
City plan coverage area	Région de plan de ville	Flugplatz	Aerodromo/campo d'aviazione
		Vom Stadtplan abgedecktes Gebiet	Area della pianta della città

Alicante

0 km 0.5

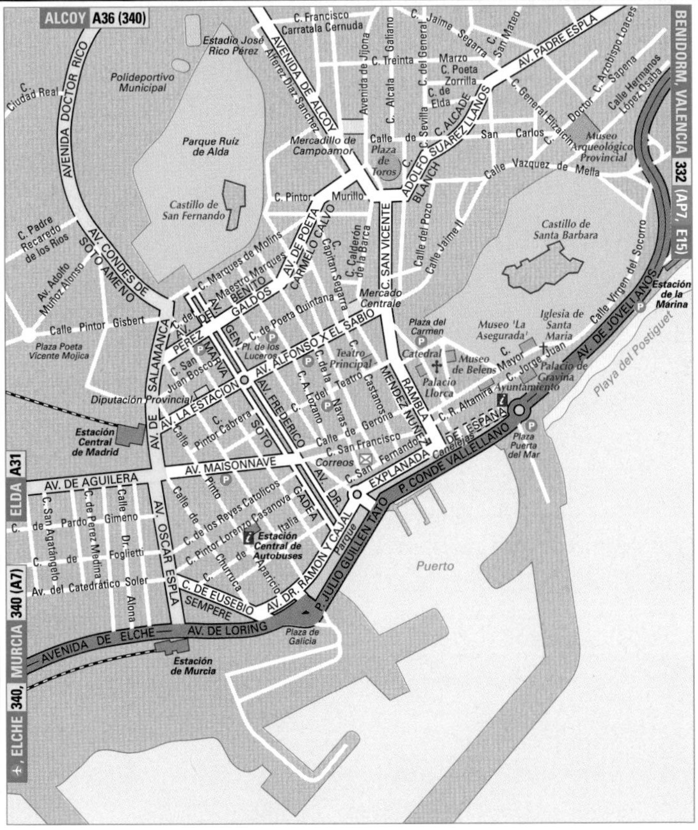

Antwerpen Antwerp

0 km 1

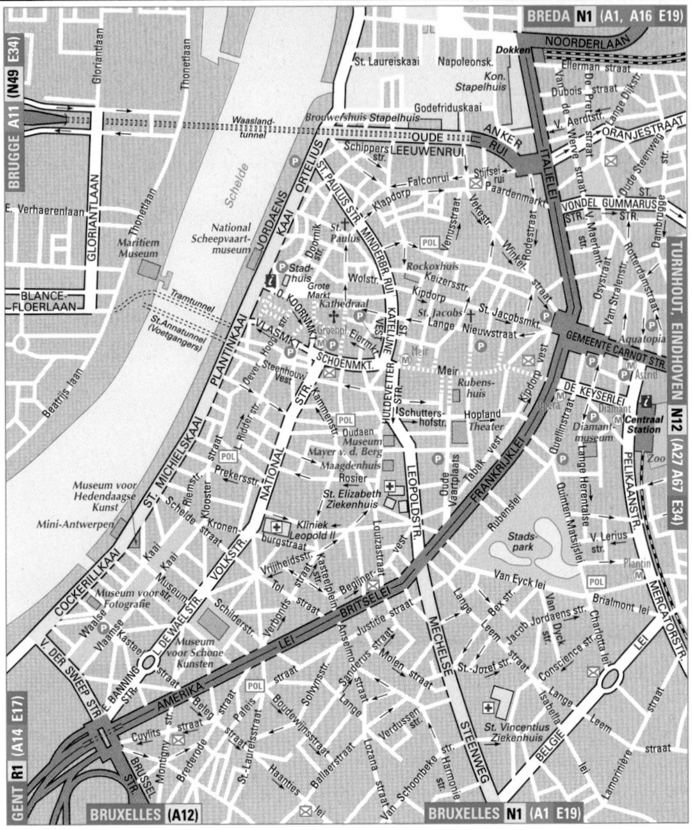

Amsterdam

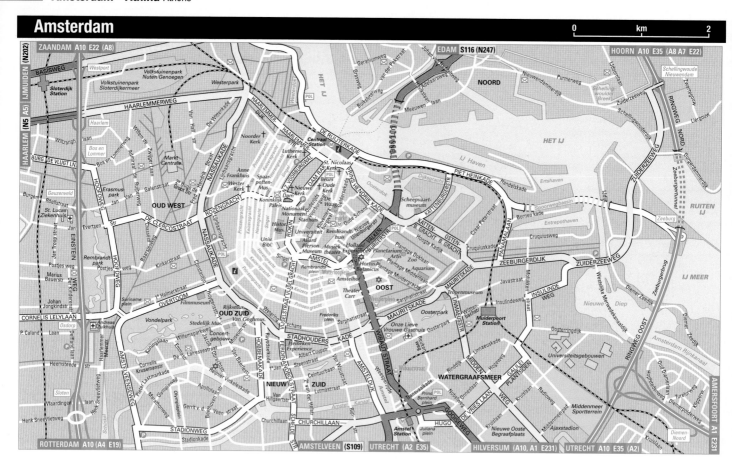

Athina Athens

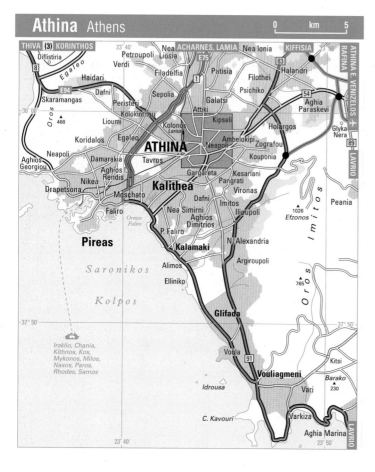

Athina Athens

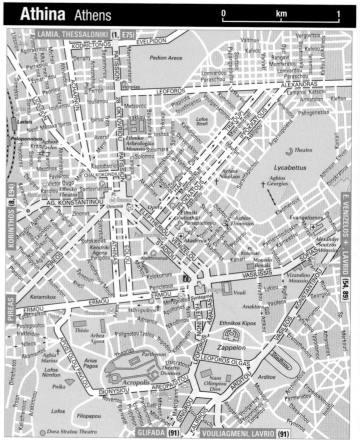

Barcelona

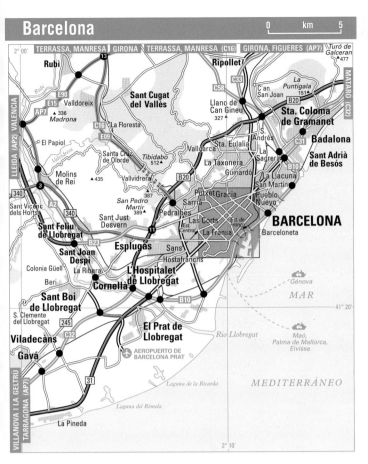

Barcelona

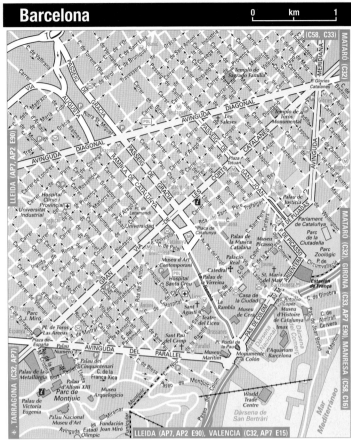

Bruxelles Brussels

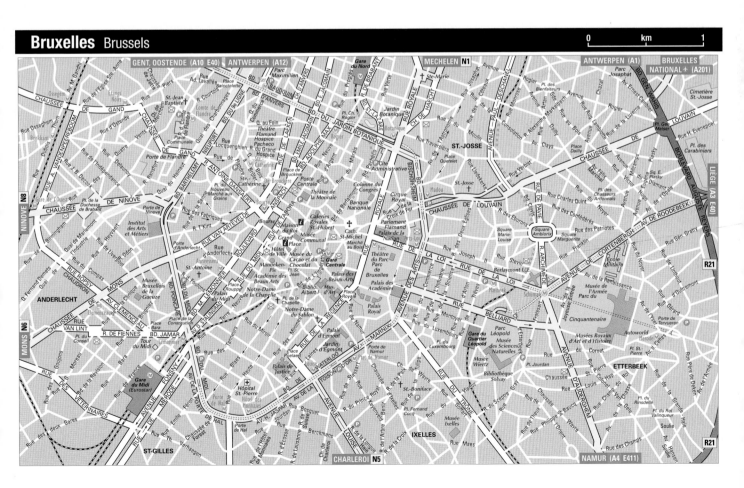

Berlin

0 km 5

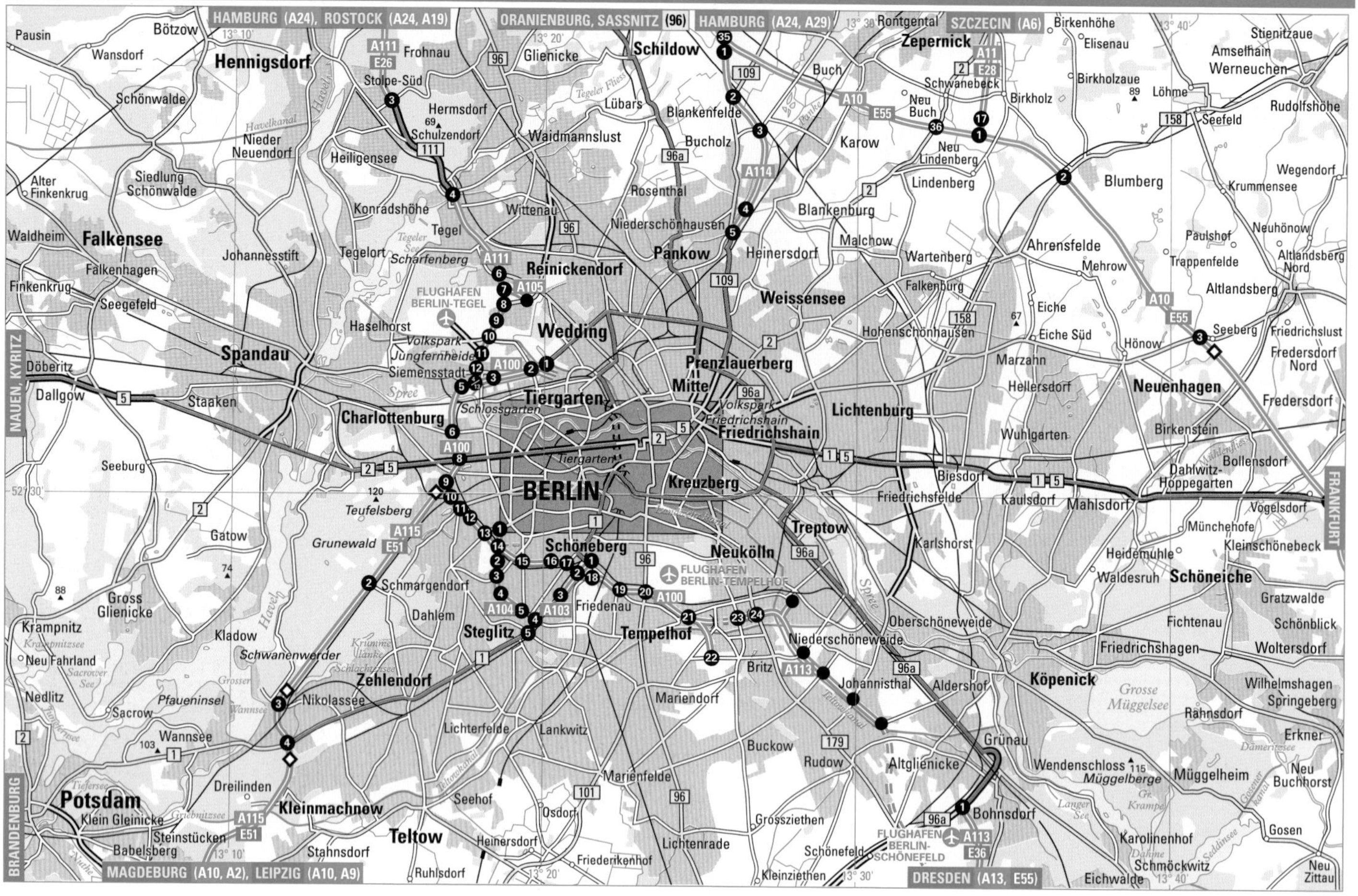
HAMBURG (A24), ROSTOCK (A24, A19)
ORANIENBURG, SASSNITZ (96)
HAMBURG (A24, A29)
SZCZECIN (A6)
NAUEN, KYRITZ
FRANKFURT
BRANDENBURG
MAGDEBURG (A10, A2), LEIPZIG (A10, A9)
DRESDEN (A13, E55)
Hennigsdorf
Schildow
Zepernick
Falkensee
Spandau
Reinickendorf
Wedding
Pankow
Weissensee
Prenzlauerberg
Mitte
Tiergarten
Charlottenburg
BERLIN
Friedrichshain
Lichtenburg
Kreuzberg
Treptow
Neukölln
Schöneberg
Steglitz
Tempelhof
Zehlendorf
Köpenick
Neuenhagen
Schöneiche
Potsdam
Kleinmachnow
Teltow
FLUGHAFEN BERLIN-TEGEL
FLUGHAFEN BERLIN-TEMPELHOF
FLUGHAFEN BERLIN-SCHÖNEFELD
Grunewald
Wannsee
Grosse Müggelsee

Berlin

0 km 1

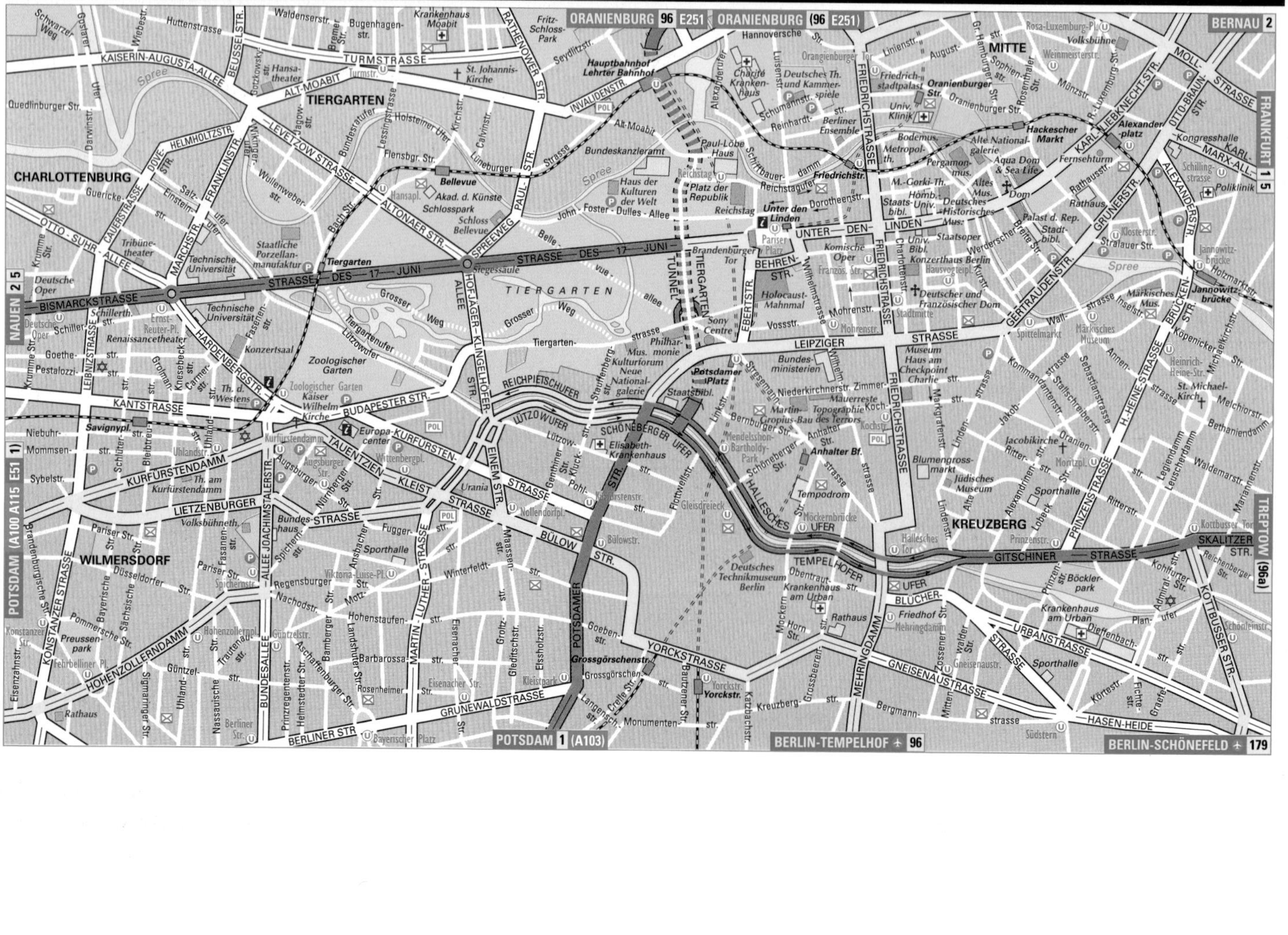
ORANIENBURG 96 E251
ORANIENBURG (96 E251)
BERNAU 2
FRANKFURT 1 5
TREPTOW (96a)
NAUEN 2 5
POTSDAM (A100 A115 E51 1)
POTSDAM 1 (A103)
BERLIN-TEMPELHOF 96
BERLIN-SCHÖNEFELD 179
TIERGARTEN
CHARLOTTENBURG
MITTE
WILMERSDORF
KREUZBERG
Hauptbahnhof Lehrter Bahnhof
Bundeskanzleramt
Reichstag
Brandenburger Tor
Potsdamer Platz
Alexanderplatz
Friedrichstr.
Unter den Linden
KANTSTRASSE
KURFÜRSTENDAMM
LEIPZIGER STRASSE
GITSCHINER STRASSE
YORCKSTRASSE
Zoologischer Garten
Anhalter Bf.
Deutsches Technikmuseum Berlin
Jüdisches Museum

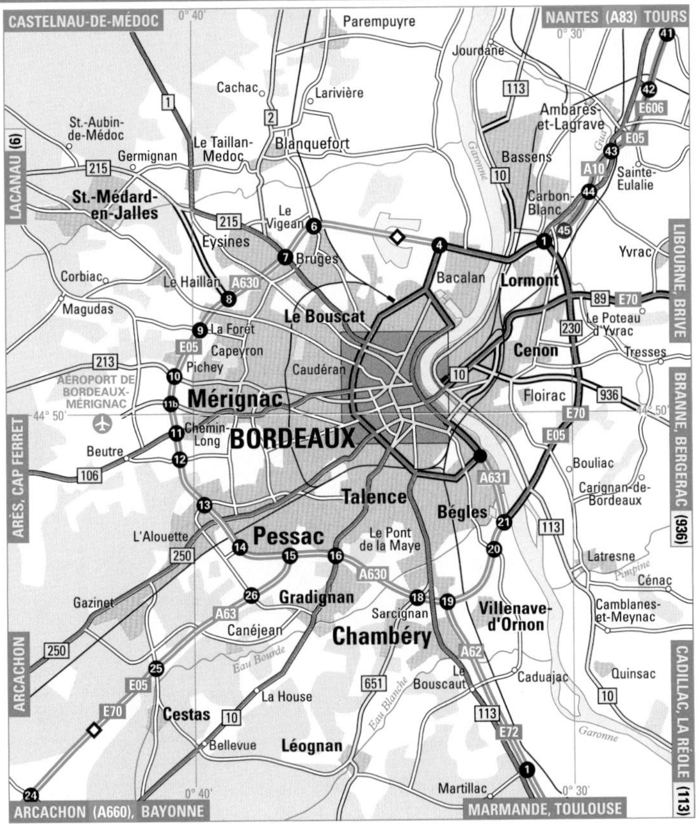

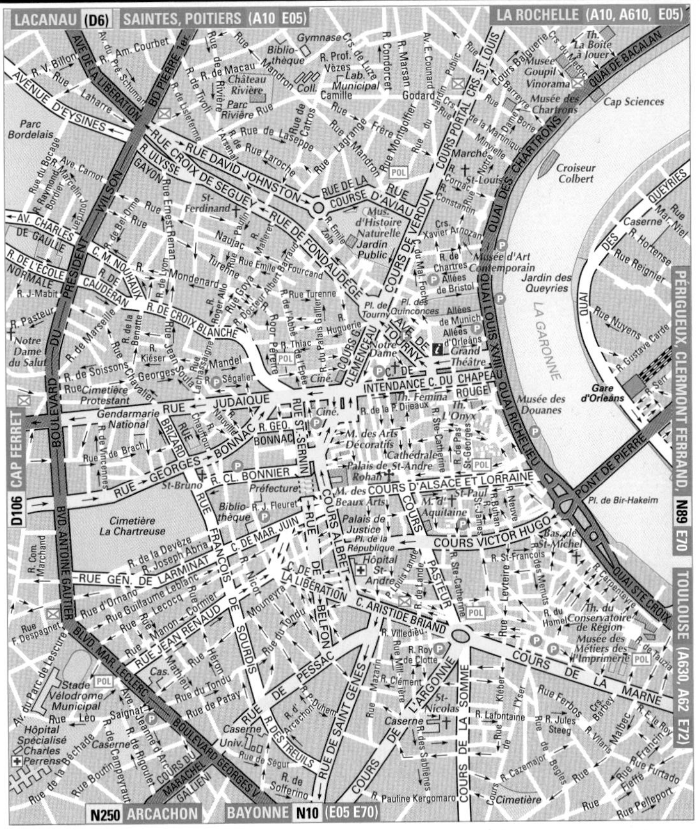

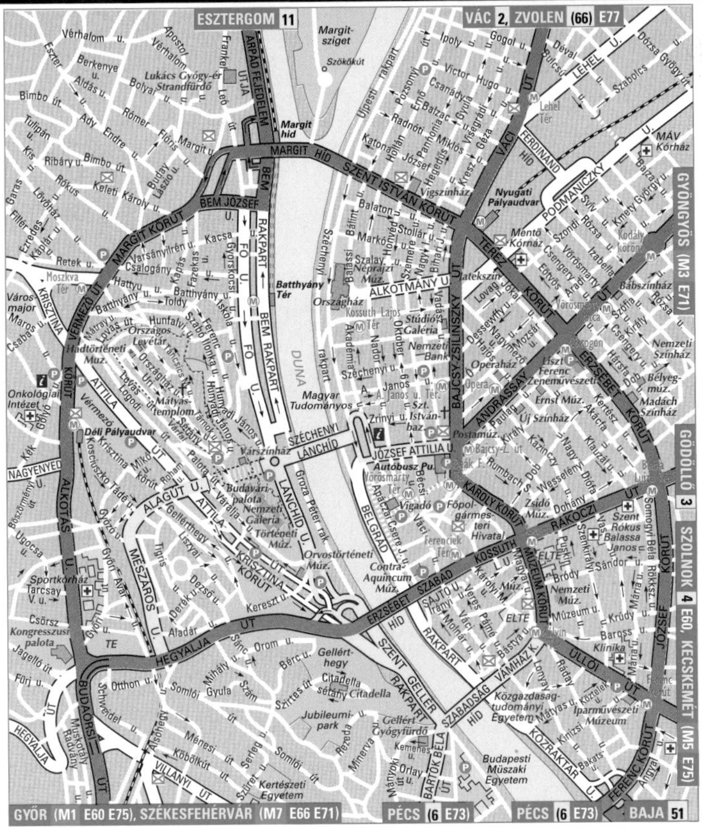

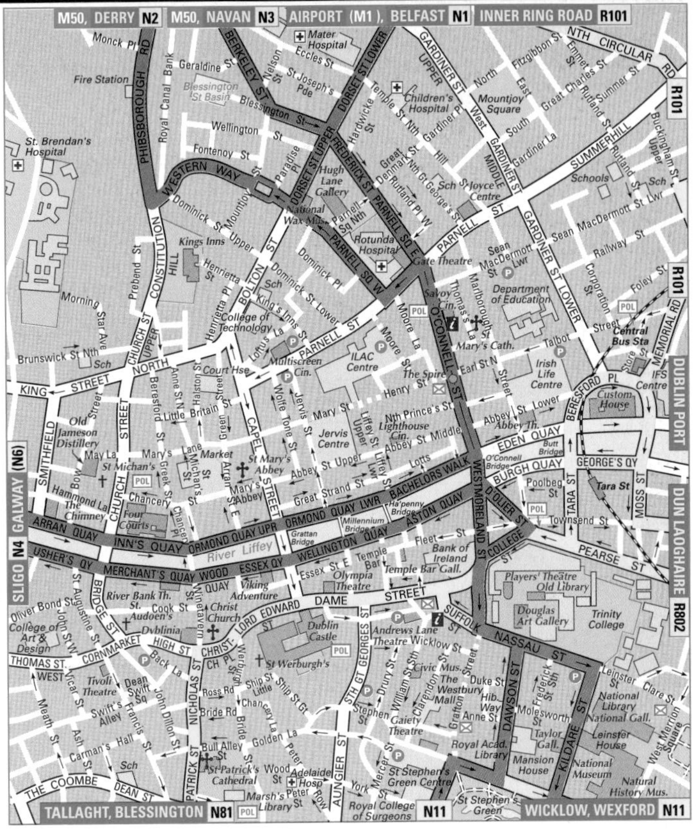

For **Cologne** see page 131

For **Copenhagen** see page 130

Düsseldorf (Ruhrgebiet)

0 km 5

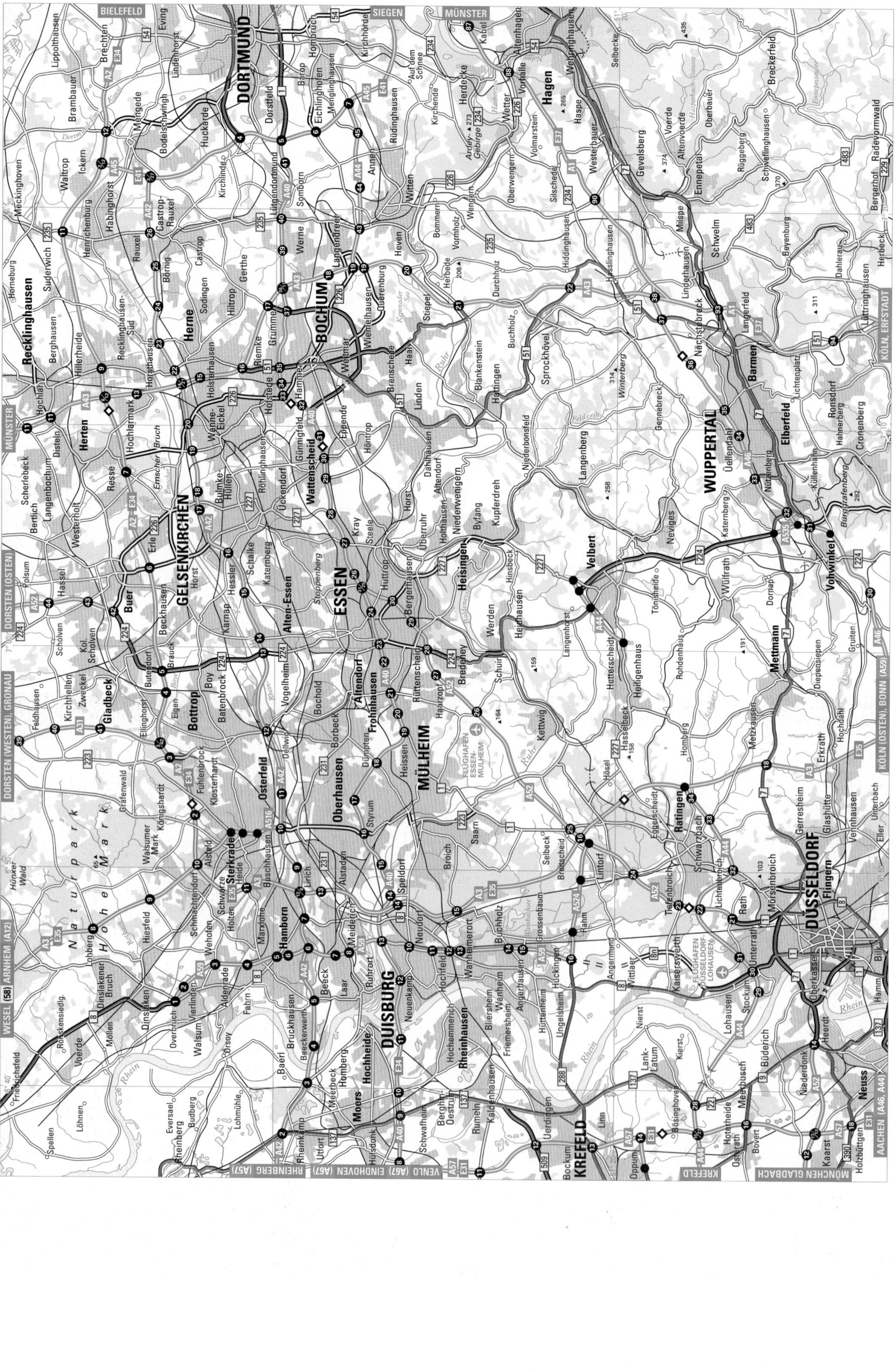
BIELEFELD
SIEGEN
MÜNSTER
DORTMUND
Recklinghausen
Herne
Herten
Bochum
Castrop-Rauxel
GELSENKIRCHEN
Buer
Gladbeck
Bottrop
Wattenscheid
Witten
Hagen
Herdecke
Wetter
ESSEN
Alten-Essen
Oberhausen
Sterkrade
Osterfeld
MÜLHEIM
DUISBURG
Hamborn
Rheinhausen
Moers
Homberg
KREFELD
Uerdingen
Velbert
Heisingen
Hattingen
Sprockhövel
Gevelsberg
Schwelm
WUPPERTAL
Barmen
Elberfeld
Vohwinkel
Mettmann
Ratingen
DÜSSELDORF
Flingern
Neuss
Dinslaken
FLUGHAFEN ESSEN-MÜLHEIM
FLUGHAFEN DÜSSELDORF-LOHAUSEN
Naturpark Hohe Mark
Rhein
Ruhr
DORSTEN (WESTEN), GRONAU
DORSTEN (OSTEN)
MÜNSTER
WESEL (58) ARNHEM (A12)
RHEINBERG (A57)
VENLO (A67) EINDHOVEN (A67)
KREFELD
MÖNCHEN GLADBACH
AACHEN (A46, A44)
KÖLN (OSTEN), BONN (A59)
KÖLN, ERFSTADT

Düsseldorf

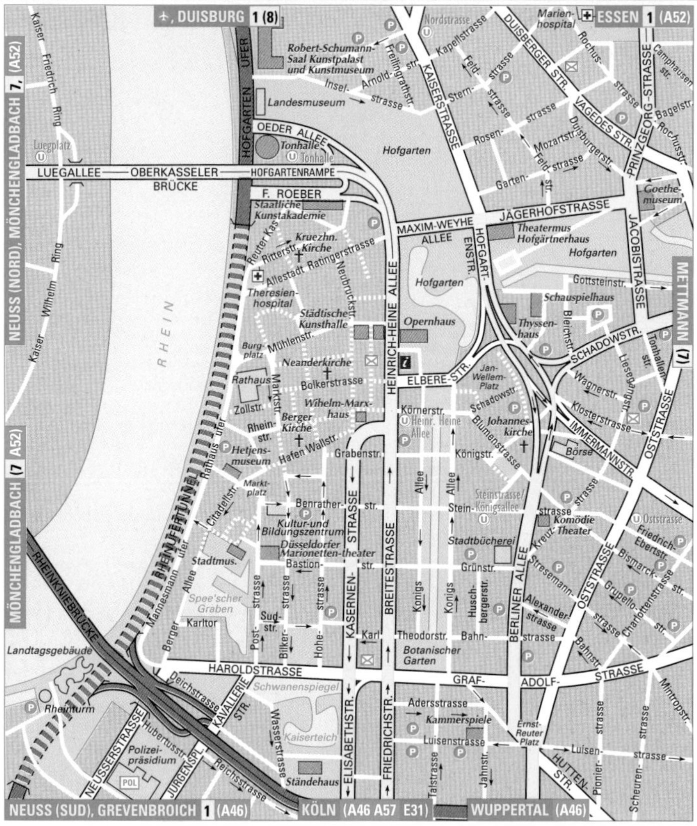

Edinburgh

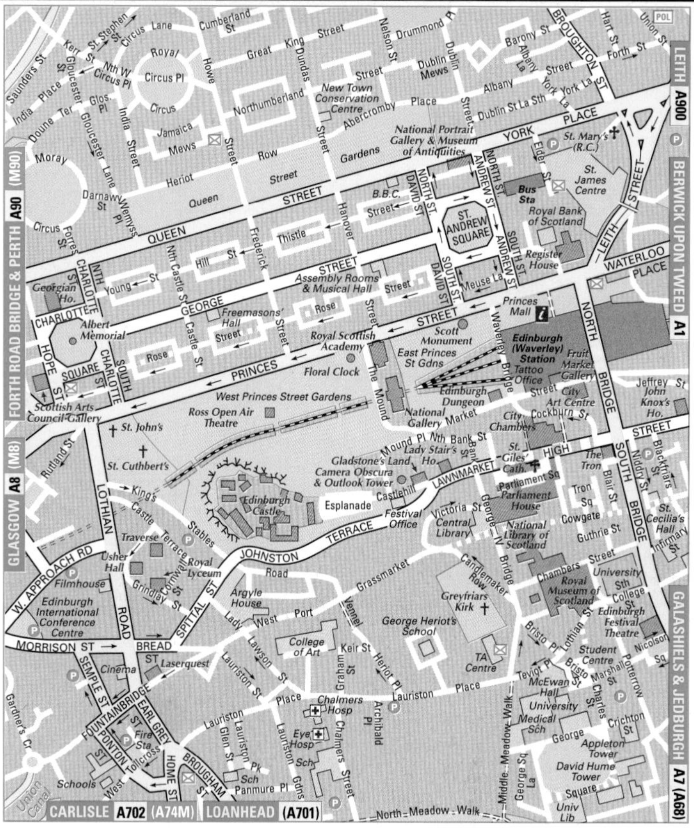

Firenze Florence

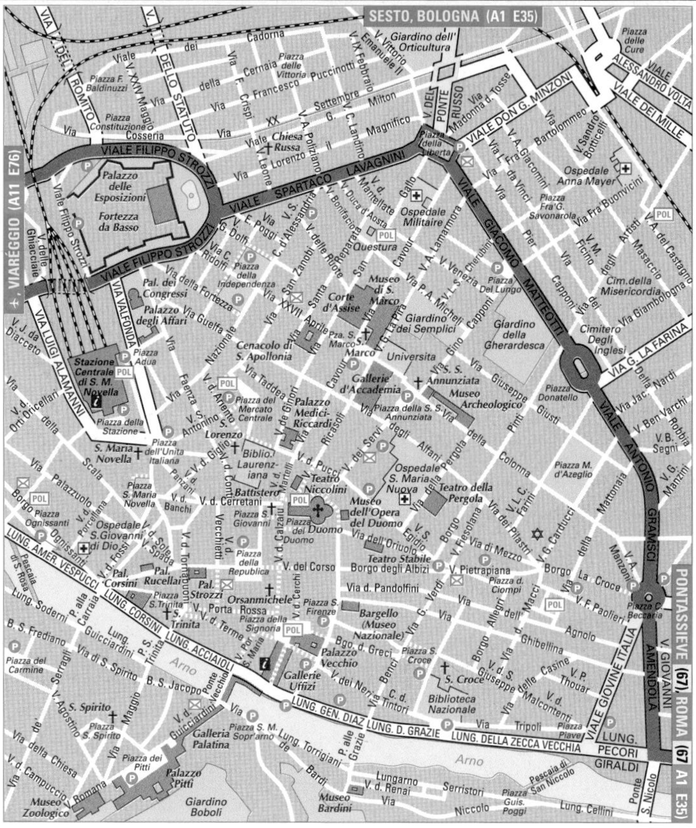

Frankfurt

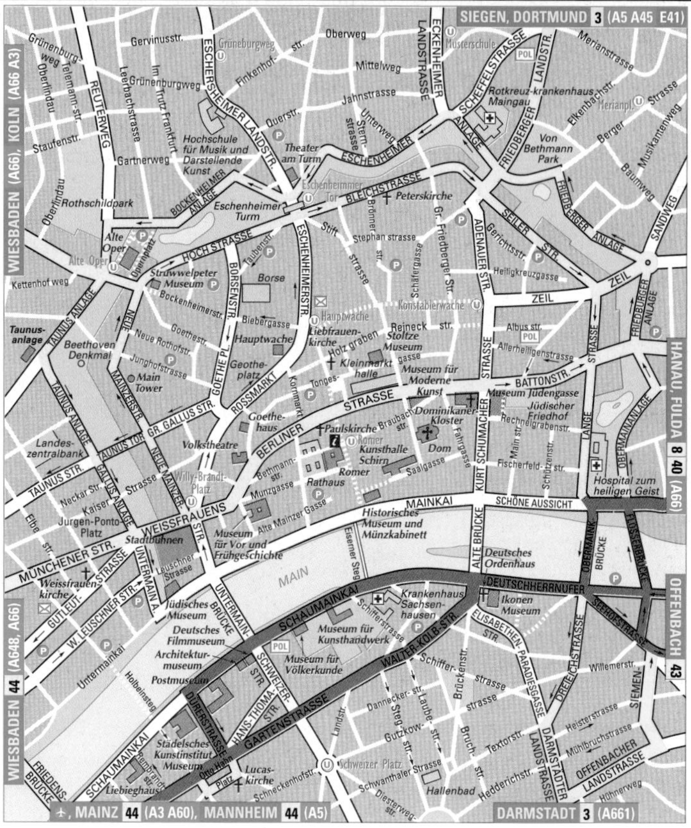

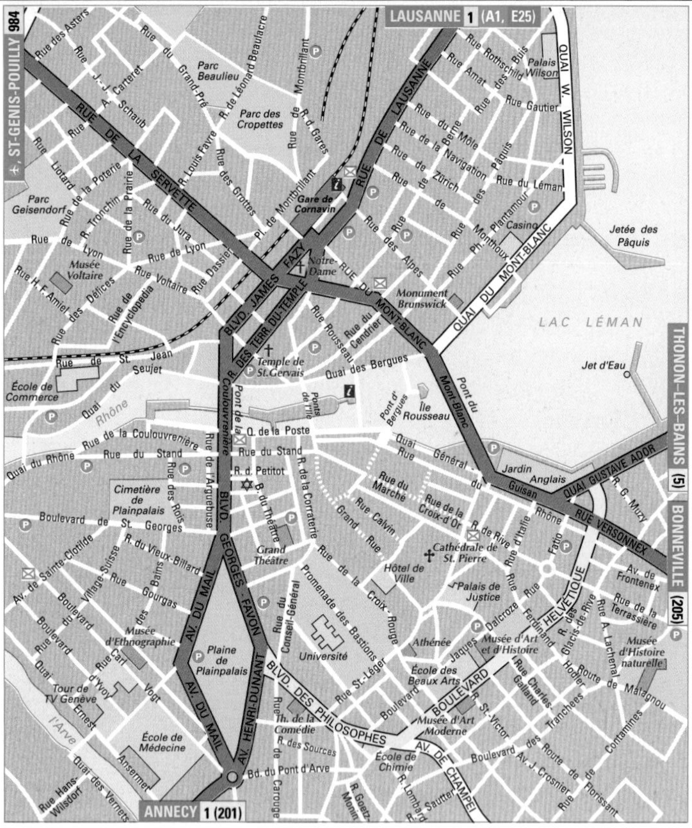

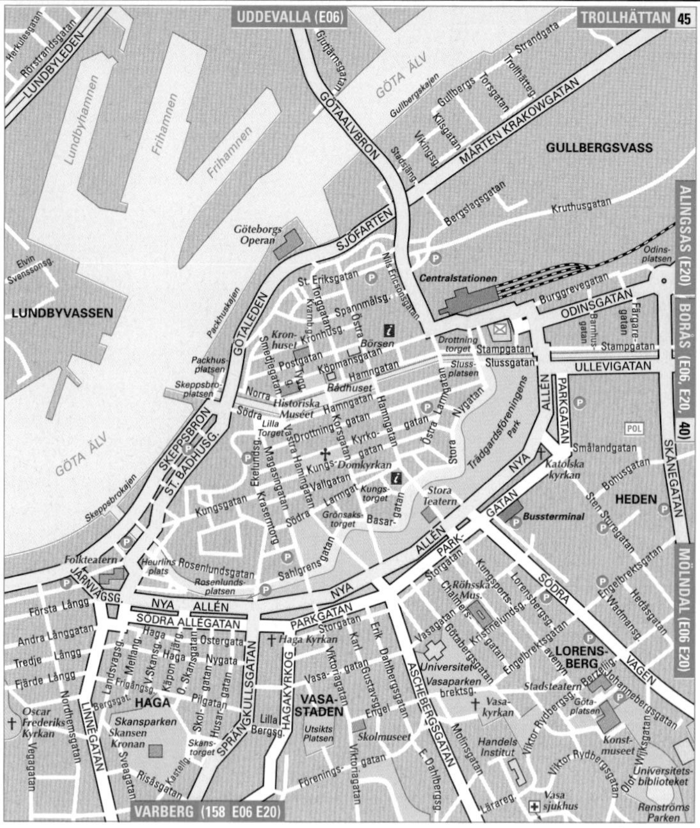

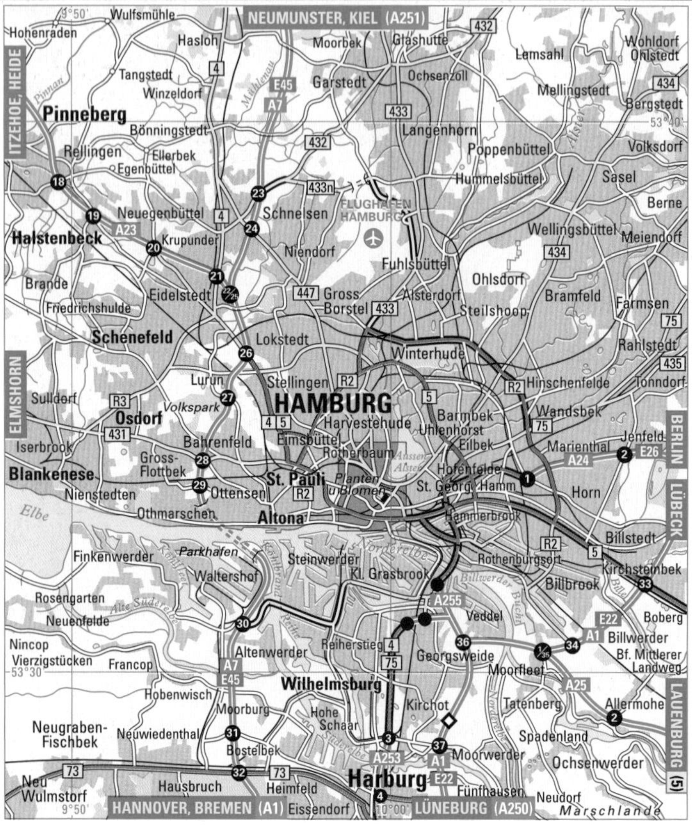

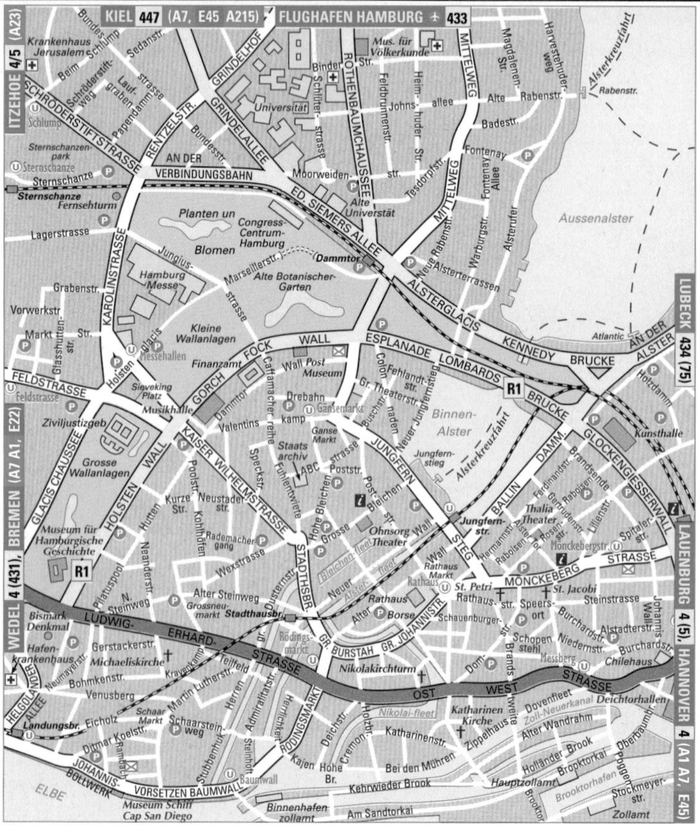

Helsinki

0 km 10

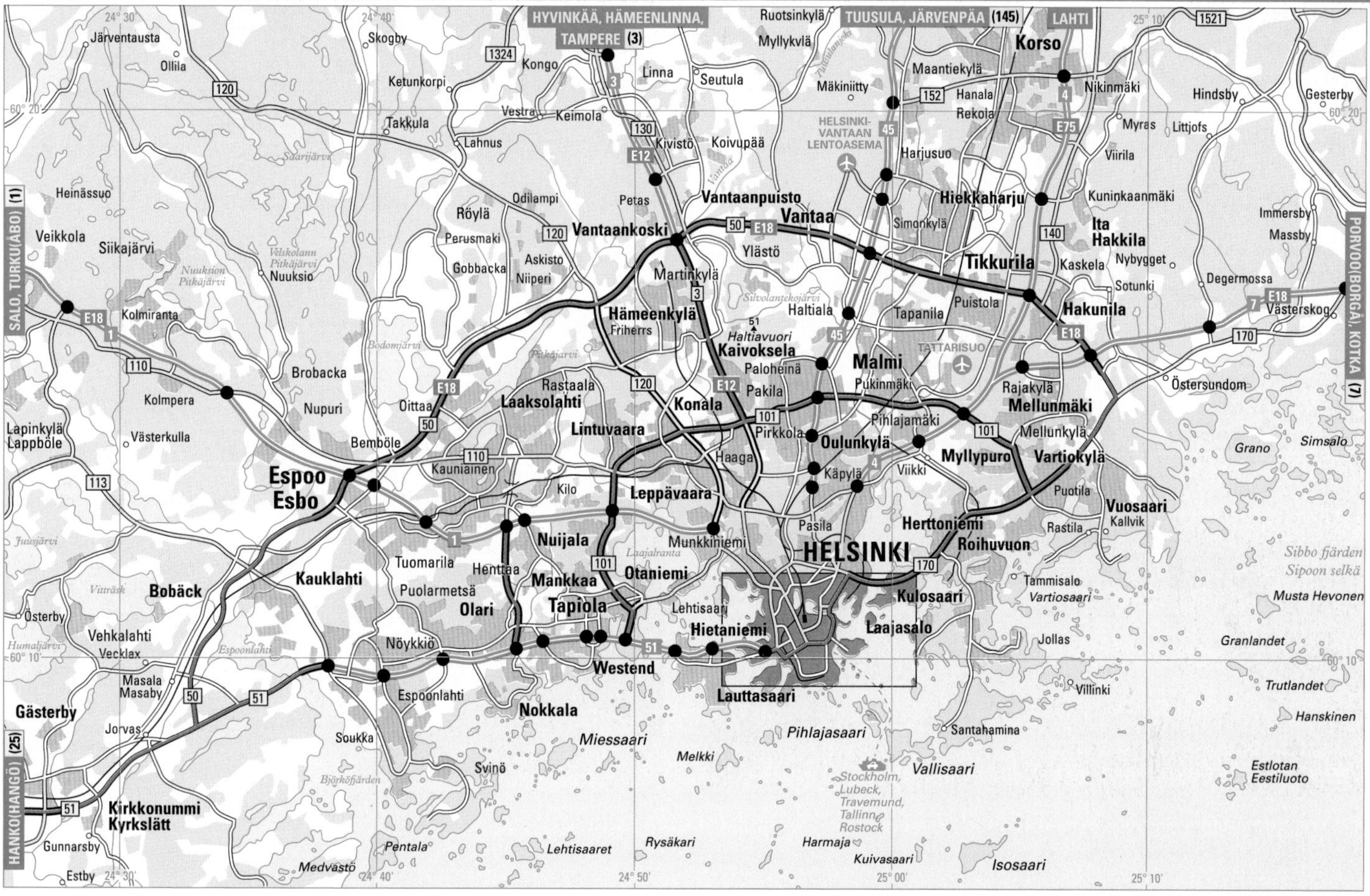

HYVINKÄÄ, HÄMEENLINNA, TAMPERE (3)
TUUSULA, JÄRVENPÄÄ (145)
LAHTI
SALO, TURKU(ÅBO) (1)
PORVOO(BORGÅ), KOTKA (7)
HANKO(HANGÖ) (25)
Järventausta
Ollila
Skogby
Kongo
Ketunkorpi
Linna
Seutula
Ruotsinkylä
Myllykvlä
Korso
Maantiekylä
Nikinmäki
Hindsby
Gesterby
Takkula
Vestra
Keimola
Mäkiniitty
Hanala
Rekola
Myras
Littjofs
Lahnus
Kivistö
Koivupää
HELSINKI-VANTAAN LENTOASEMA
Harjusuo
Viirila
Heinässuo
Odilampi
Petas
Vantaanpuisto
Hiekkaharju
Kuninkaanmäki
Röylä
Vantaa
Immersby
Massby
Veikkola
Siikajärvi
Perusmaki
Vantaankoski
Simonkylä
Ita Hakkila
Nuuksio
Askisto
Gobbacka
Niiperi
Ylästö
Tikkurila
Kaskela
Nybygget
Martinkylä
Sotunki
Degermossa
Kolmiranta
Hämeenkylä
Friherrs
Haltiala
Tapanila
Puistola
Hakunila
Västerskog
Haltiavuori
Kaivoksela
Paloheinä
Malmi
Pukinmäki
Brobacka
Rastaala
Laaksolahti
Konala
Pakila
Rajakylä
Mellunmäki
Östersundom
Kolmpera
Nupuri
Oittaa
Lintuvaara
Pirkkola
Pihlajamäki
Mellunkylä
Lapinkylä
Lappböle
Västerkulla
Bemböle
Oulunkylä
Myllypuro
Vartiokylä
Grano
Simsalo
Kauniainen
Haaga
Käpylä
Viikki
Espoo
Esbo
Kilo
Leppävaara
Puotila
Vuosaari
Kallvik
Pasila
Herttoniemi
Rastila
Nuijala
Munkkiniemi
Roihuvuori
Tuomarila
HELSINKI
Sibbo fjärden
Sipoon selkä
Henttaa
Otaniemi
Kauklahti
Bobäck
Puolarmetsä
Mankkaa
Tammisalo
Vartiosaari
Musta Hevonen
Olari
Tapiola
Lehtisaari
Kulosaari
Österby
Vehkalahti
Hietaniemi
Laajasalo
Jollas
Granlandet
Vecklax
Nöykkiö
Westend
Masala
Masaby
Lauttasaari
Villinki
Trutlandet
Gästerby
Espoonlahti
Nokkala
Jorvas
Hanskinen
Soukka
Miessaari
Pihlajasaari
Santahamina
Melkki
Svinö
Vallisaari
Estlotan
Eestiluoto
Kirkkonummi
Kyrkslätt
Stockholm, Lubeck, Travemund, Tallinn, Rostock
Gunnarsby
Pentala
Lehtisaaret
Rysäkari
Harmaja
Kuivasaari
Isosaari
Medvastö
Estby

Helsinki

0 km 1

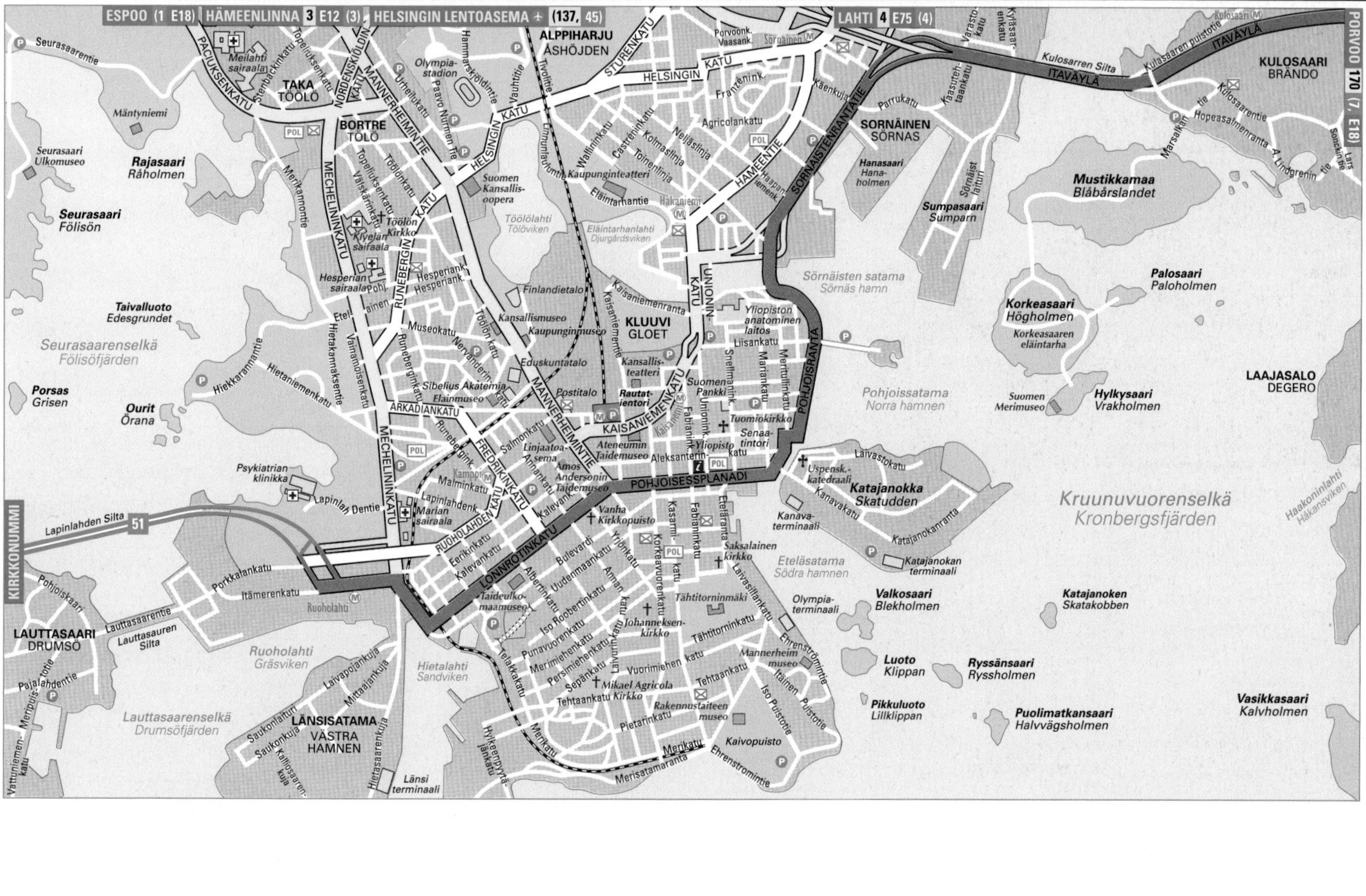

ESPOO (1 E18) HÄMEENLINNA 3 E12 (3) HELSINGIN LENTOASEMA (137, 45)
LAHTI 4 E75 (4)
PORVOO 170 (7, E18)
KIRKKONUMMI
Seurasaarentie
TAKA TÖÖLÖ
Olympia-stadion
ALPPIHARJU ÅSHÖJDEN
STURENKATU
HELSINGIN KATU
Mäntyniemi
BORTRE TÖLÖ
MANNERHEIMINTIE
Seurasaari Ulkomuseo
Rajasaari Råholmen
Seurasaari Fölisön
Suomen Kansallis-oopera
Kaupunginteatteri
Töölönlahti Tölöviken
Eläintarhanlahti Djurgårdsviken
SORNÄINEN SÖRNÄS
Hanasaari Hanaholmen
Sumpasaari Sumparn
Mustikkamaa Blåbärslandet
KULOSAARI BRÄNDÖ
Kulosaaren Silta
ITÄVÄYLÄ
Sörnäisten satama Sörnäs hamn
Palosaari Paloholmen
Korkeasaari Högholmen
Korkeasaaren eläintarha
Taivalluoto Edesgrundet
Seurasaarenselkä Fölisöfjärden
Finlandiatalo
Kansallismuseo
KLUUVI GLOET
Eduskuntatalo
Sibelius Akatemia
Yliopiston anatominen laitos
Porsas Grisen
Ourit Örana
ARKADIANKATU
Pohjoissatama Norra hamnen
Suomen Merimuseo
Hylkysaari Vrakholmen
LAAJASALO DEGERÖ
Tuomiokirkko
Senaatintori
Ateneumin Taidemuseo
Amos Andersonin Taidemuseo
POHJOISESPLANADI
Uspenskin katedraali
Katajanokka Skatudden
Psykiatrian klinikka
Lapinlahden Silta
Kruunuvuorenselkä Kronbergsfjärden
Vanha Kirkkopuisto
Kanavaterminaali
Eteläsatama Södra hamnen
Katajanokan terminaali
LÖNNROTINKATU
Porkkalankatu
Itämerenkatu
Ruoholahti
Taideteollisuusmuseo
Tähtitorninmäki
Johanneksen kirkko
Olympiaterminaali
Valkosaari Blekholmen
Katajanoken Skatakobben
LAUTTASAARI DRUMSÖ
Lauttasaaren Silta
Ruoholahti Gräsviken
Hietalahti Sandviken
Mannerheim museo
Luoto Klippan
Ryssänsaari Ryssholmen
Mikael Agricola Kirkko
Rakennustaiteen museo
Pikkuluoto Lillklippan
Puolimatkansaari Halvvägsholmen
Vasikkasaari Kalvholmen
Lauttasaarenselkä Drumsöfjärden
LÄNSISATAMA VÄSTRA HAMNEN
Kaivopuisto
Länsi terminaali
Merisatamaranta
Ehrenströmintie

Istanbul

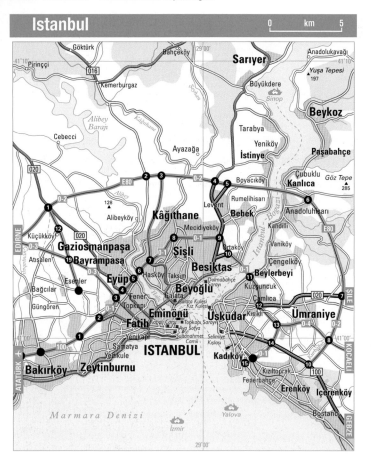

København Copenhagen

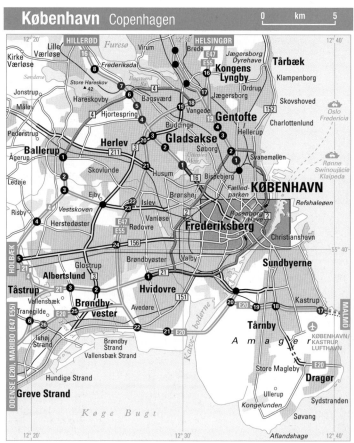

København Copenhagen

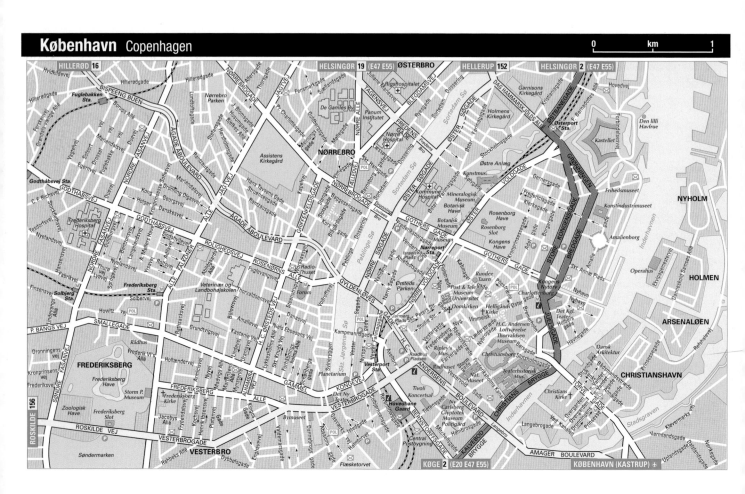

Köln Cologne

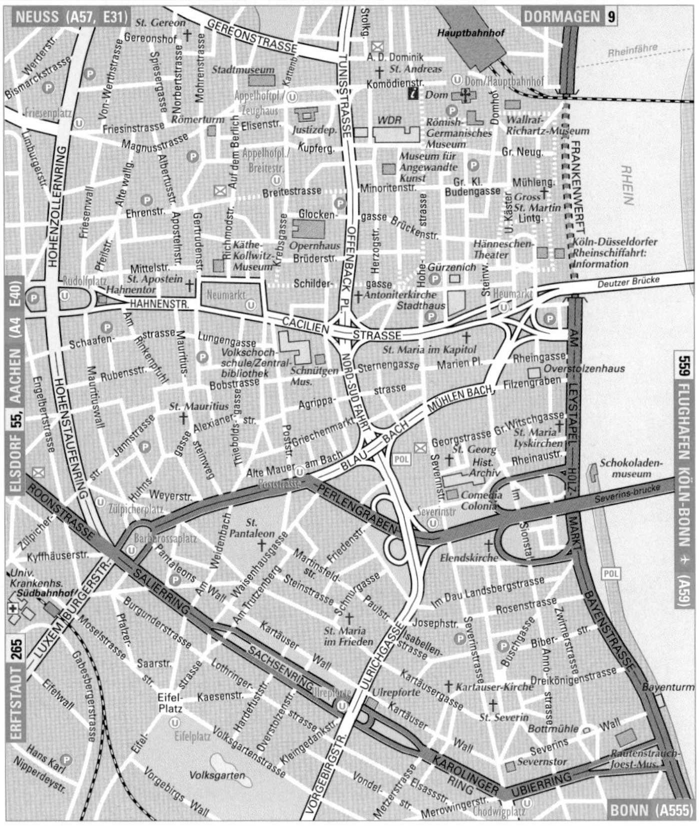

Luxembourg

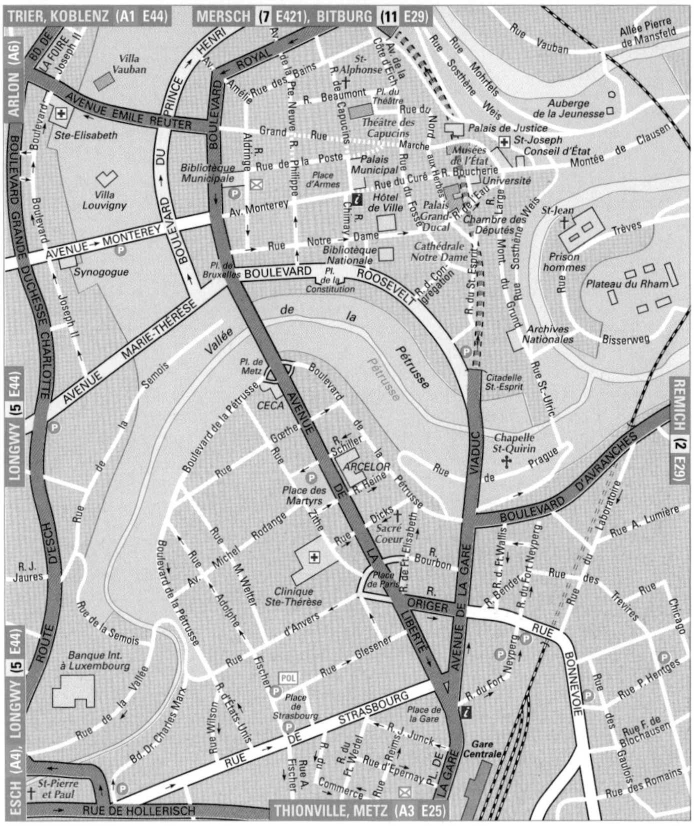

Lisboa Lisbon

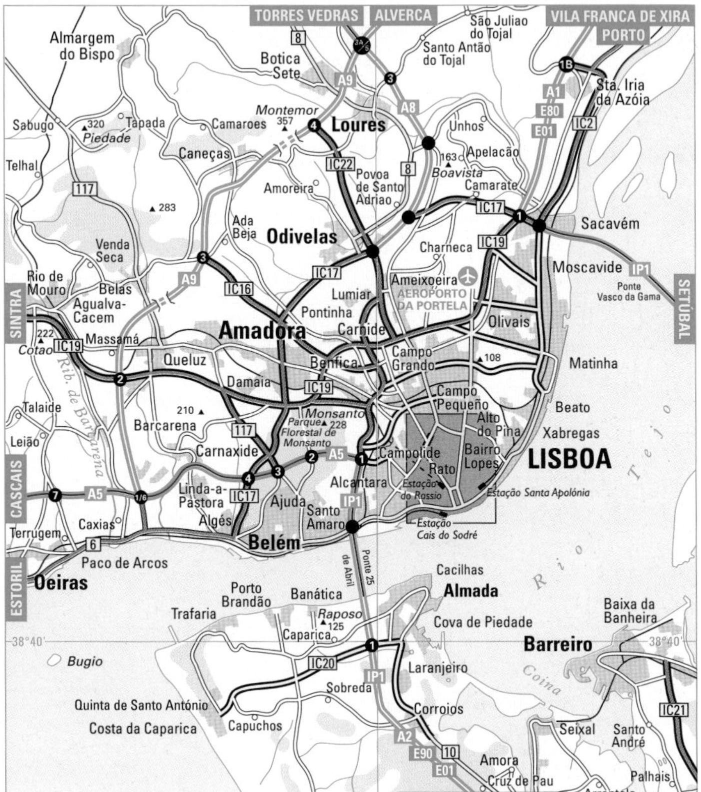

Lisboa Lisbon

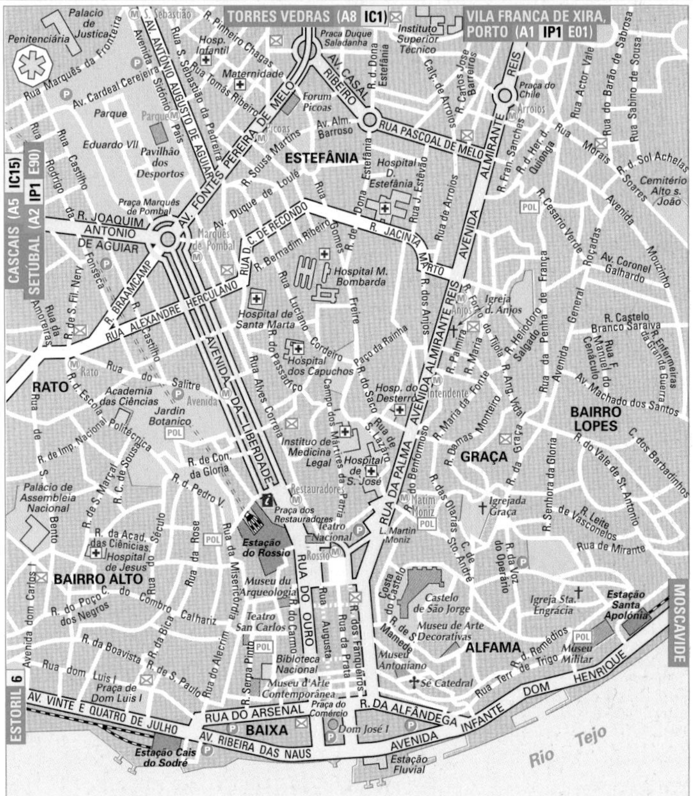

London

0 km 10

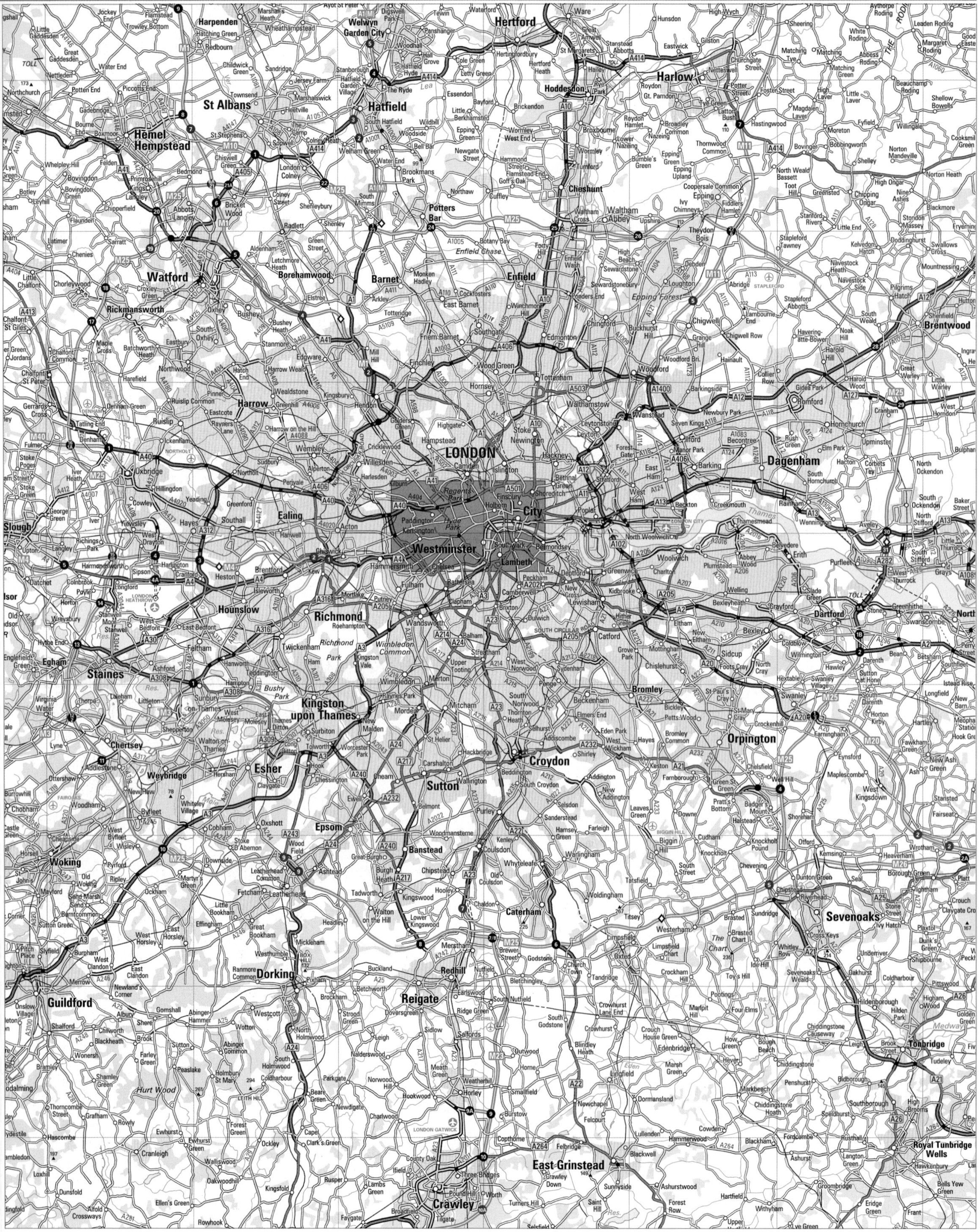

Hertford
Harpenden
Welwyn Garden City
St Albans
Hatfield
Hemel Hempstead
Harlow
Hoddesdon
Cheshunt
Waltham Abbey
Potters Bar
Watford
Borehamwood
Barnet
Enfield
Rickmansworth
Brentwood
Harrow
Romford
Dagenham
LONDON
City
Westminster
Lambeth
Ealing
Slough
Staines
Hounslow
Richmond
Kingston upon Thames
Croydon
Bromley
Orpington
Dartford
Esher
Weybridge
Chertsey
Egham
Woking
Epsom
Sutton
Caterham
Redhill
Reigate
Dorking
Guildford
Sevenoaks
Tonbridge
Royal Tunbridge Wells
East Grinstead
Crawley

London

0 km 2

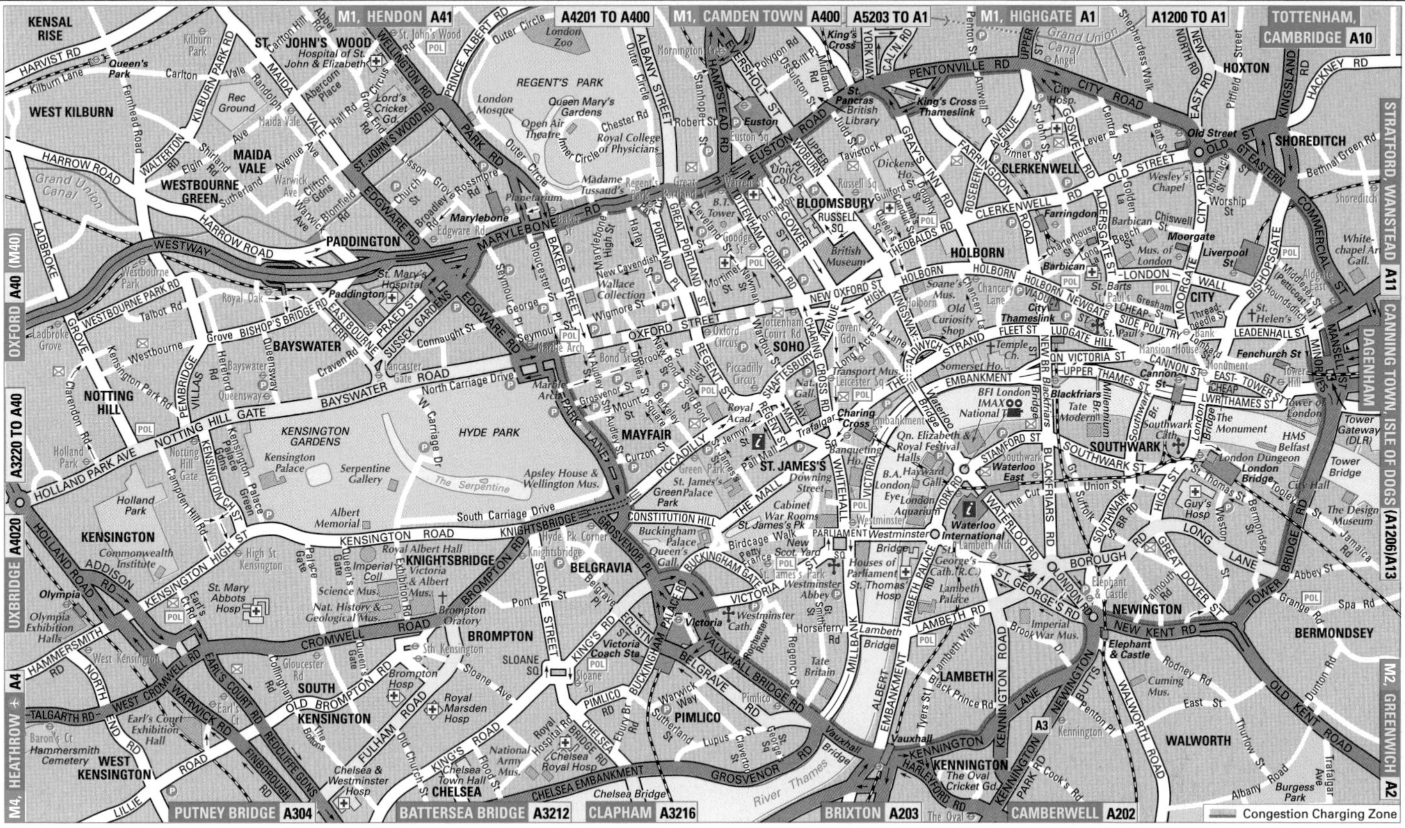
M1, HENDON A41
A4201 TO A400
M1, CAMDEN TOWN A400
A5203 TO A1
M1, HIGHGATE A1
A1200 TO A1
TOTTENHAM, CAMBRIDGE A10
STRATFORD, WANSTEAD A11
CANNING TOWN, ISLE OF DOGS (A1206) A13
DAGENHAM
M2, GREENWICH A2
CAMBERWELL A202
BRIXTON A203
CLAPHAM A3216
BATTERSEA BRIDGE A3212
PUTNEY BRIDGE A304
M4, HEATHROW A4
UXBRIDGE A4020
A3220 TO A40
OXFORD A40 (M40)
KENSAL RISE
WEST KILBURN
ST. JOHN'S WOOD
MAIDA VALE
WESTBOURNE GREEN
PADDINGTON
BAYSWATER
NOTTING HILL
KENSINGTON
KNIGHTSBRIDGE
BELGRAVIA
BROMPTON
SOUTH KENSINGTON
WEST KENSINGTON
CHELSEA
PIMLICO
MAYFAIR
ST. JAMES'S
SOHO
BLOOMSBURY
HOLBORN
CLERKENWELL
HOXTON
SHOREDITCH
CITY
SOUTHWARK
NEWINGTON
BERMONDSEY
LAMBETH
KENNINGTON
WALWORTH
REGENT'S PARK
HYDE PARK
KENSINGTON GARDENS
River Thames
Congestion Charging Zone

Lyon

0 km 5

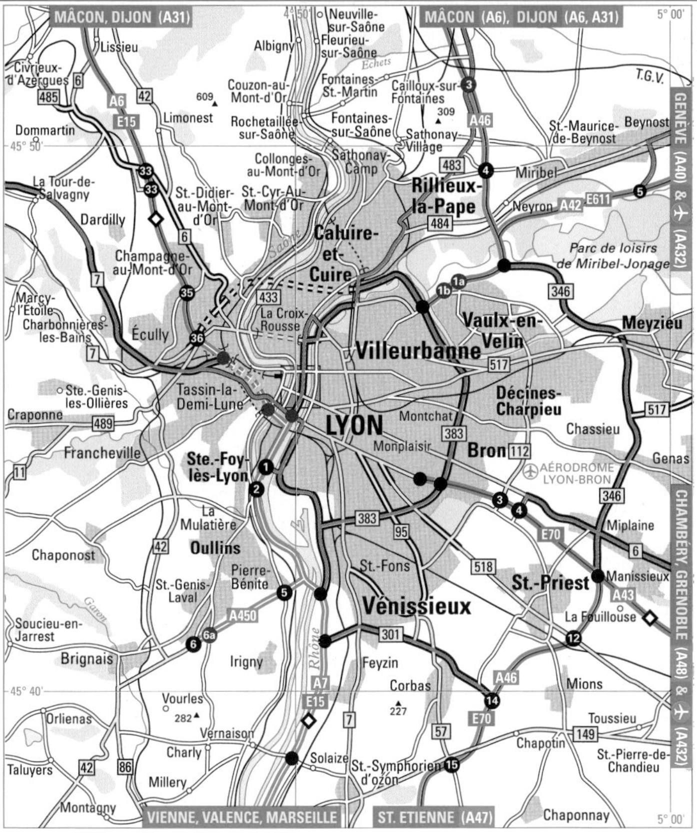
MÂCON, DIJON (A31)
MÂCON (A6), DIJON (A6, A31)
GENÈVE (A40) & ✈ (A432)
CHAMBERY, GRENOBLE (A48) & ✈ (A432)
VIENNE, VALENCE, MARSEILLE
ST. ETIENNE (A47)
LYON
Villeurbanne
Caluire-et-Cuire
Rillieux-la-Pape
Vaulx-en-Velin
Meyzieu
Décines-Charpieu
Bron
Vénissieux
St.-Priest
Oullins
Ste.-Foy-lès-Lyon
Écully
Tassin-la-Demi-Lune
Francheville
Craponne
Brignais
Irigny
Feyzin
Corbas
Mions
Chaponost
Limonest
Dardilly
Chassieu
Genas
Saône
Rhône

Lyon

0 km 1

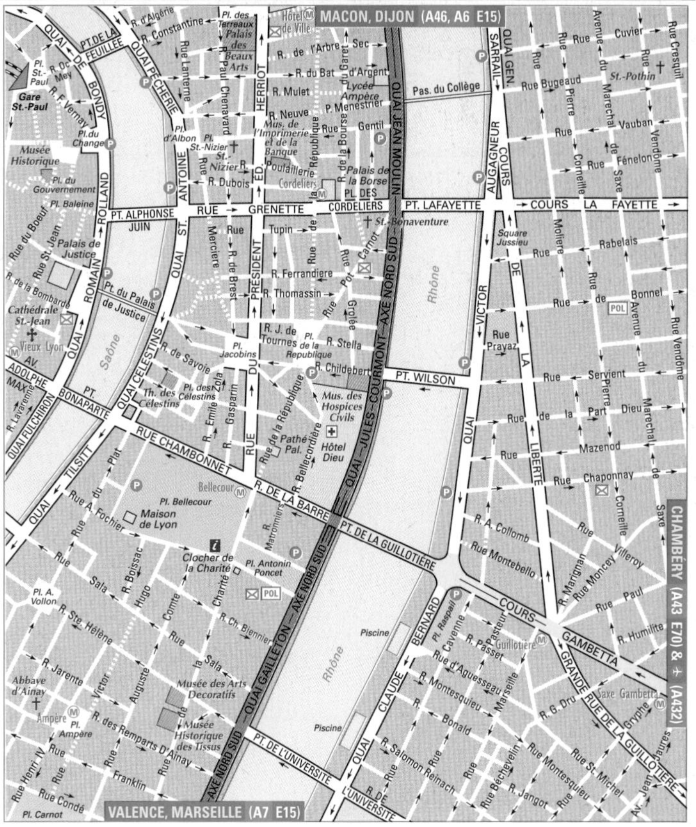
MACON, DIJON (A46, A6 E15)
CHAMBERY (A43 E70) & ✈ (A432)
VALENCE, MARSEILLE (A7 E15)
Saône
Rhône
QUAI JEAN MOULIN
COURS LA FAYETTE
COURS GAMBETTA
RUE DE LA BARRE
PT. LAFAYETTE
PT. WILSON
PT. BONAPARTE
Pl. Bellecour
Gare St.-Paul
Cathédrale St.-Jean
Hôtel Dieu
Musée des Arts Decoratifs

Madrid

0 km 5

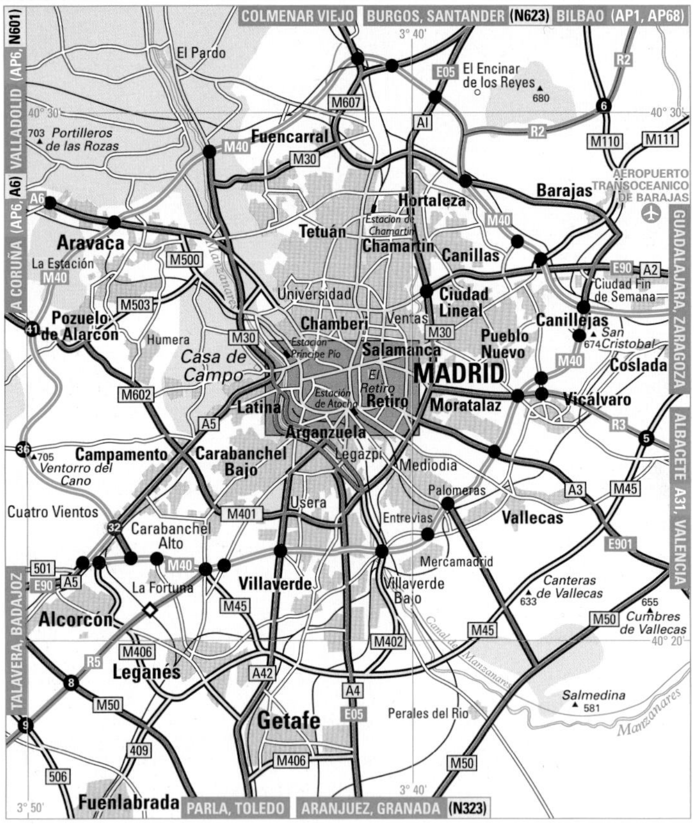

Marseille Marseilles

0 km 0.5

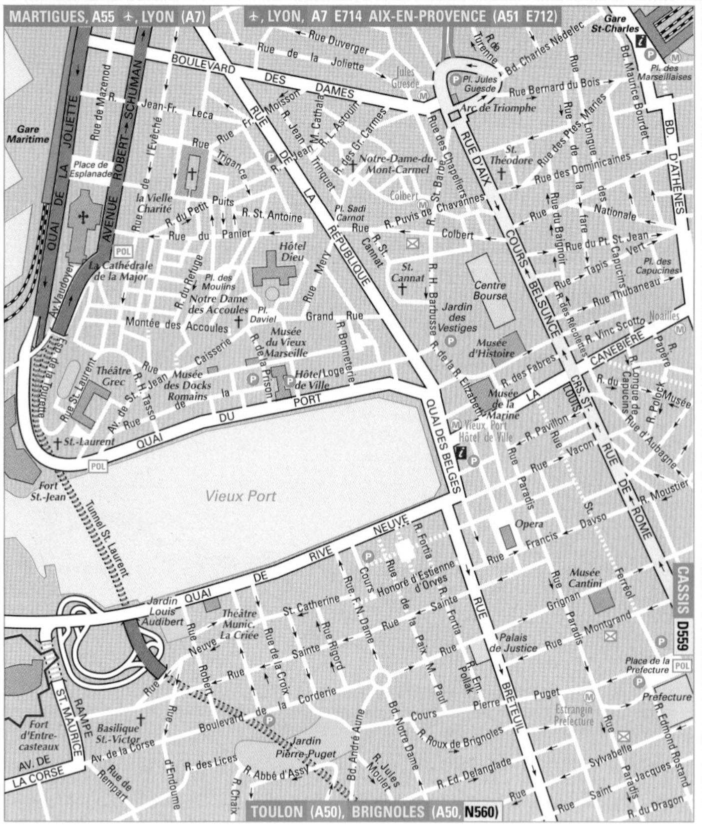

Madrid

0 km 1

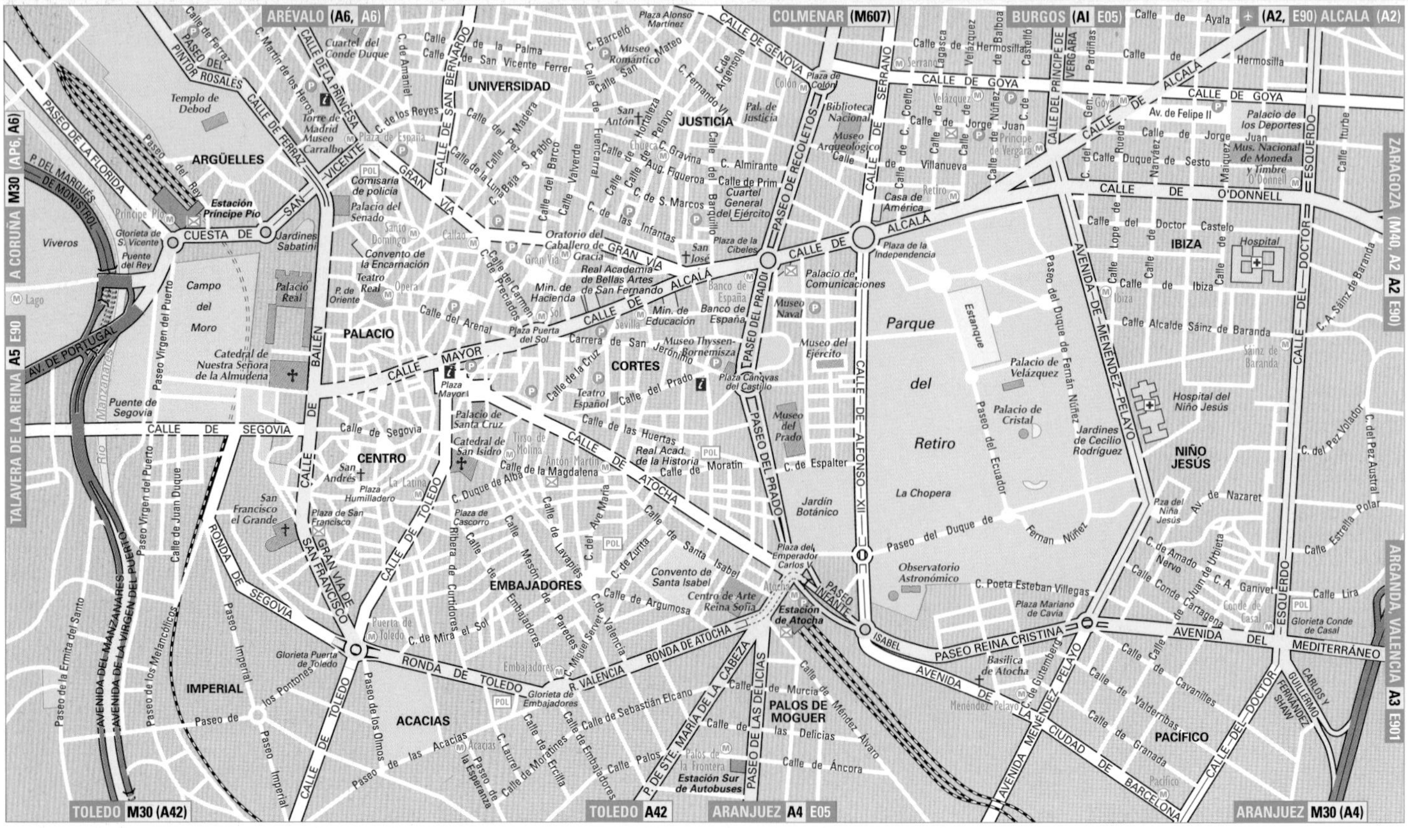

Milano Milan

0 km 5

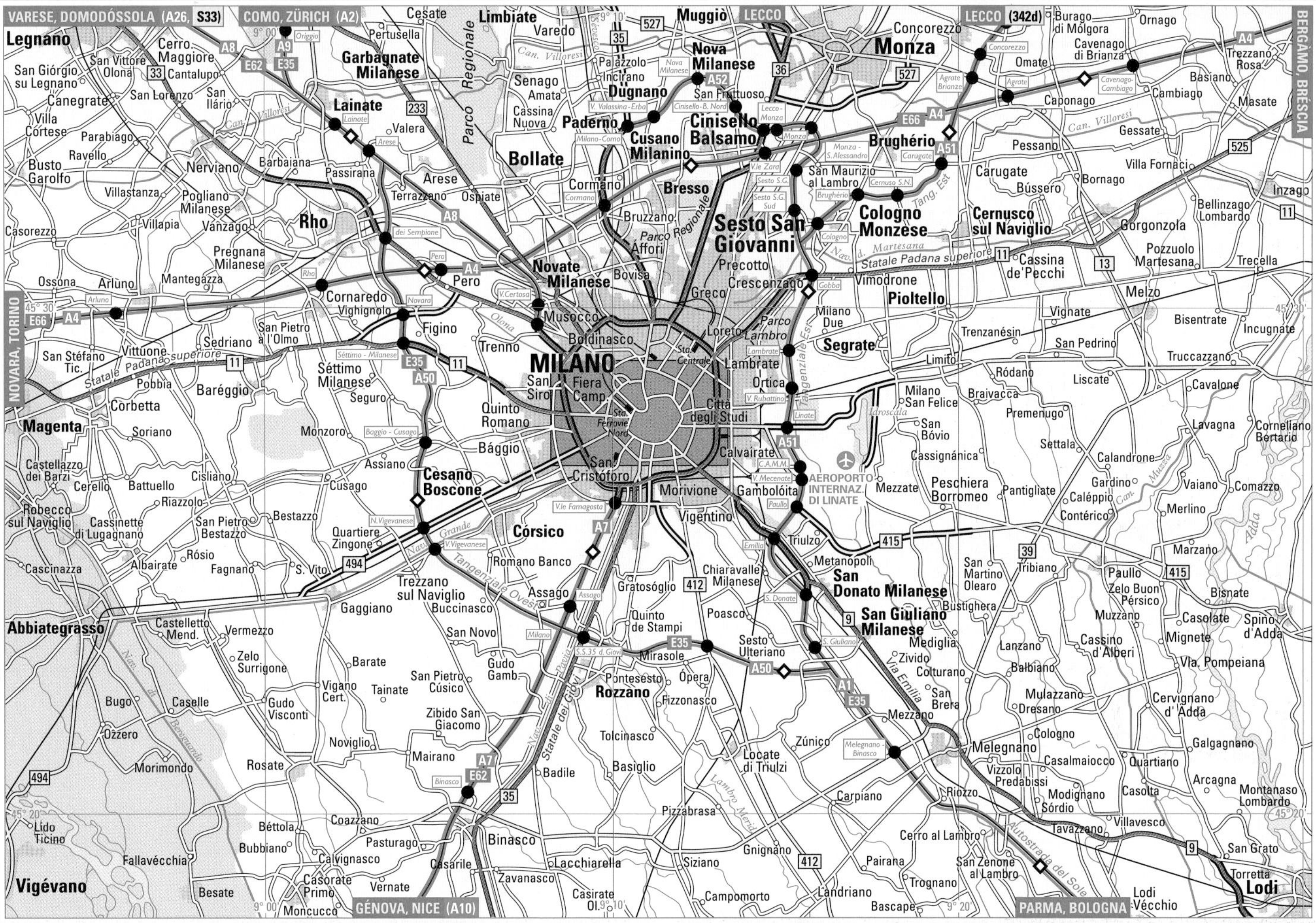

VARESE, DOMODÓSSOLA (A26, S33)
COMO, ZÜRICH (A2)
LECCO
LECCO (342d)
BERGAMO, BRESCIA
NOVARA, TORINO
GÉNOVA, NICE (A10)
PARMA, BOLOGNA
Legnano
Cerro Maggiore
Garbagnate Milanese
Lainate
Limbiate
Varedo
Muggiò
Nova Milanese
Concorezzo
Monza
Burago di Mólgora
Ornago
Cavenago di Brianza
Trezzano Rosa
Basiano
Masate
San Giórgio su Legnano
San Vittore Olona
Canegrate
San Lorenzo
Villa Cortese
Parabiago
Busto Garolfo
Nerviano
Pogliano Milanese
Vanzago
Pregnana Milanese
Rho
Arese
Bollate
Senago
Paderno
Dugnano
Cusano Milanino
Cinisello Balsamo
Bresso
Sesto San Giovanni
Brughério
Cologno Monzese
Carugate
Cernusco sul Naviglio
Gorgonzola
Pozzuolo Martesana
Inzago
Bellinzago Lombardo
Melzo
Trecella
Cassina de'Pecchi
Pioltello
Vimodrone
Segrate
Novate Milanese
Cormano
Bruzzano
Affori
Precotto
Crescenzago
Greco
Bovisa
Musocco
Pero
Cornaredo
Arluno
Ossona
Casorezzo
Mantegazza
Vittuone
Sedriano
San Pietro all'Olmo
Figino
Trenno
Séttimo Milanese
Baréggio
Magenta
Corbetta
MILANO
San Siro
Fiera Camp.
Quinto Romano
Bággio
Lambrate
Ortica
Città degli Studi
Milano San Felice
Limito
Rodano
Pantigliate
Settala
Liscate
Truccazzano
Cesano Boscone
San Cristóforo
Corsico
Calvairate
Morivione
Vigentino
Gamboloita
AEROPORTO INTERNAZ. DI LINATE
Mezzate
Peschiera Borromeo
Abbiategrasso
Castelletto Mend.
Vermezzo
Gaggiano
Trezzano sul Naviglio
Buccinasco
Romano Banco
Assago
Gratosóglio
Chiaravalle Milanese
San Donato Milanese
San Giuliano Milanese
Metanopoli
Rozzano
Opera
Mirasole
Sesto Ulteriano
Pieve Emanuele
Locate di Triulzi
Melegnano
Vizzolo Predabissi
Cerro al Lambro
Binasco
Lacchiarella
Siziano
Rosate
Bubbiano
Casorate Primo
Vigévano
Besate
Motta Visconti
San Zenone al Lambro
Lodi Vécchio
Lodi
Tavazzano
Villavesco
Paullo
Mulazzano
Casalmaiocco
Dresano
Montanaso Lombardo
Galgagnano

Milano Milan

0 km 1

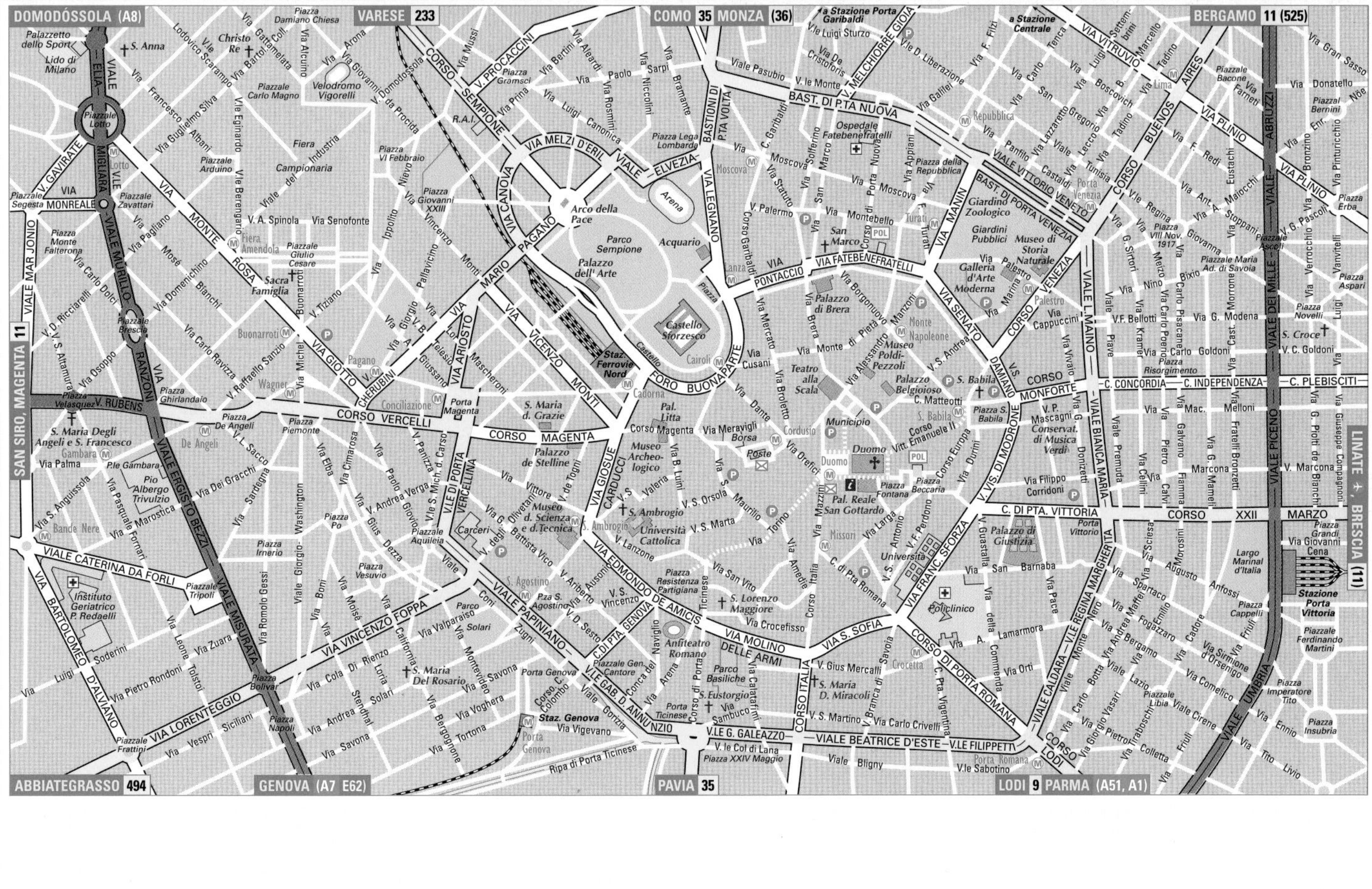

DOMODÓSSOLA (A8)
VARESE 233
COMO 35 MONZA (36)
BERGAMO 11 (525)
SAN SIRO, MAGENTA 11
LINATE, BRESCIA (11)
ABBIATEGRASSO 494
GENOVA (A7 E62)
PAVIA 35
LODI 9 PARMA (A51, A1)
a Stazione Porta Garibaldi
a Stazione Centrale
Piazzale Lotto
Lido di Milano
Velodromo Vigorelli
Piazzale Carlo Magno
Fiera Campionaria
CORSO SEMPIONE
Arco della Pace
Parco Sempione
Palazzo dell' Arte
Arena
Acquario
Castello Sforzesco
Staz. Ferrovie Nord
Cadorna
FORO BUONAPARTE
CORSO MAGENTA
S. Maria d. Grazie
Museo d. Scienza e d. Tecnica
S. Ambrogio
Università Cattolica
Palazzo di Brera
Teatro alla Scala
Museo Poldi-Pezzoli
Duomo
Pal. Reale
San Gottardo
Ospedale Fatebenefratelli
Piazza della Repubblica
Giardini Pubblici
Museo di Storia Naturale
Giardino Zoologico
Galleria d'Arte Moderna
VIALE VITTORIO VENETO
CORSO BUENOS AIRES
CORSO VENEZIA
CORSO MONFORTE
Palazzo di Giustizia
Policlinico
Università
S. Lorenzo Maggiore
Anfiteatro Romano
Parco Basiliche
Porta Ticinese
Staz. Genova
Porta Genova
Porta Romana
VIALE BEATRICE D'ESTE
VIALE PAPINIANO
VIALE MISURATA
VIALE ERGISTO BEZZI
VIA LORENTEGGIO
VIA VINCENZO FOPPA
CORSO VERCELLI
VIALE CATERINA DA FORLI
Istituto Geriatrico P. Redaelli
Stazione Porta Vittoria
CORSO XXII MARZO
VIALE UMBRIA
VIALE PICENO
Largo Marinai d'Italia

München Munich

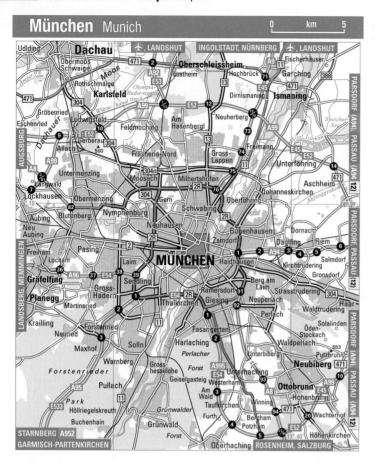

München Munich

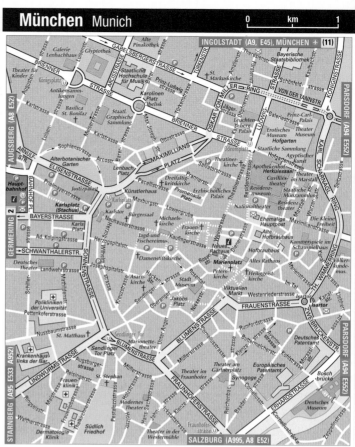

Nápoli Naples

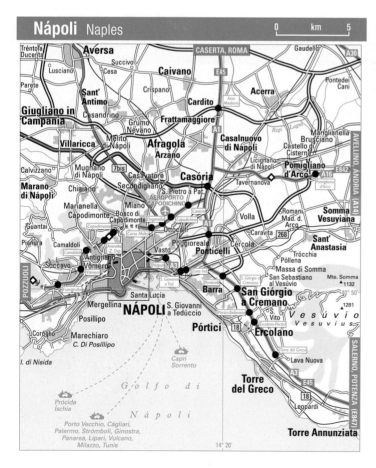

Nápoli Naples

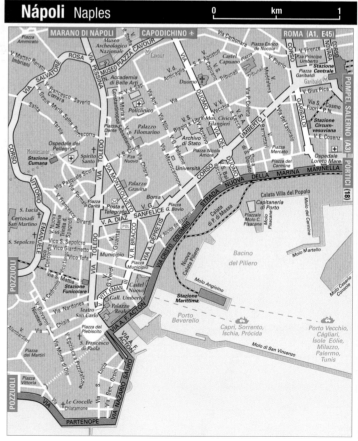

Oslo

0 km 5

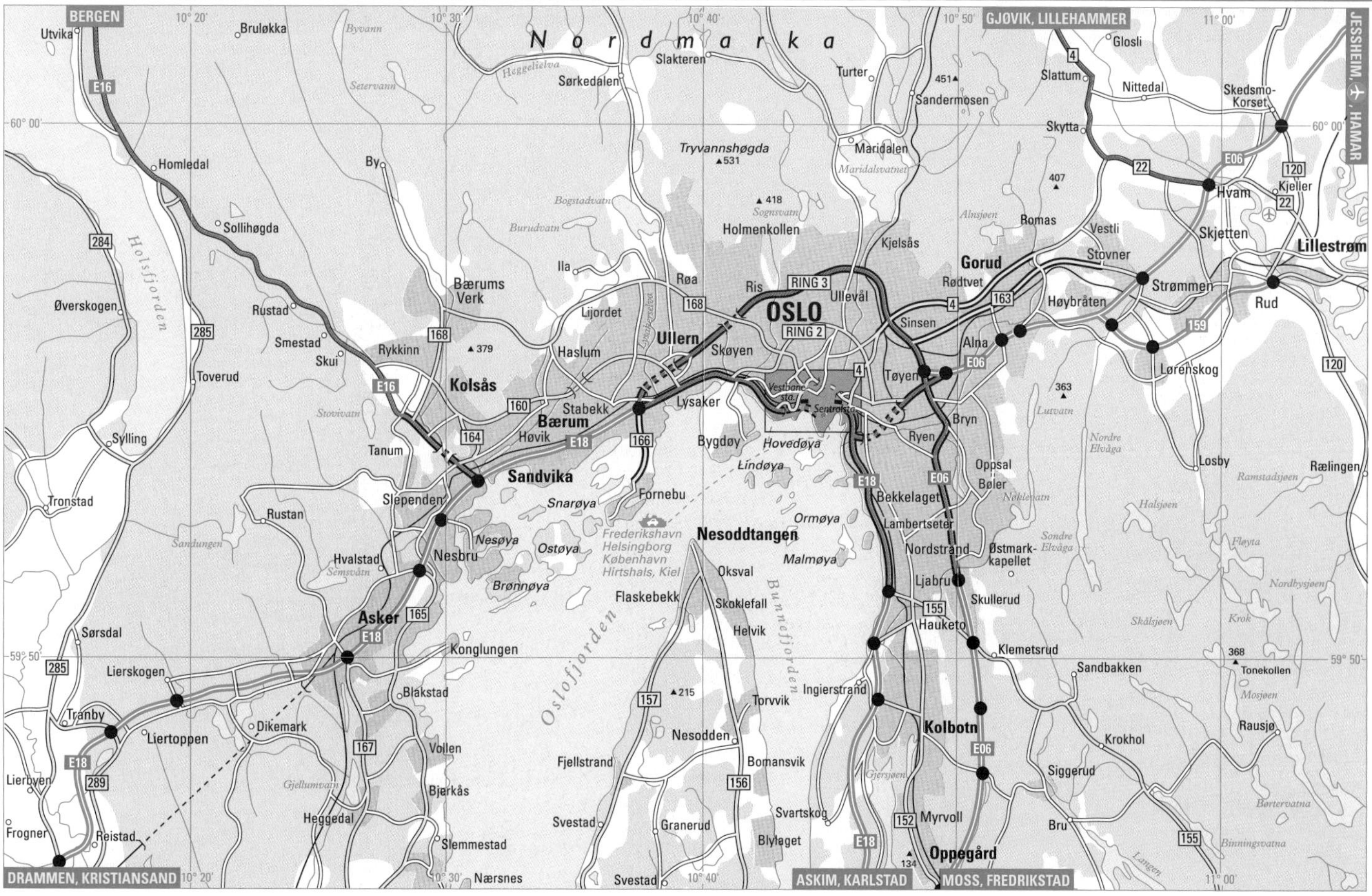

BERGEN
GJØVIK, LILLEHAMMER
JESSHEIM, HAMAR
DRAMMEN, KRISTIANSAND
ASKIM, KARLSTAD
MOSS, FREDRIKSTAD
N o r d m a r k a
Utvika
Brułøkka
Sørkedalen
Slakteren
Turter
Sandermosen
Slattum
Glosli
Nittedal
Skedsmo-Korset
Skytta
Homledal
By
Tryvannshøgda
Maridalen
Maridalsvatnet
Hvam
Kjeller
Sollihøgda
Holmenkollen
Bomas
Vestli
Skjetten
Lillestrøm
Kjelsås
Stovner
Gorud
Rødtvet
Strømmen
Rud
Øverskogen
Bærums Verk
Ila
Røa
Ris
OSLO
Ullevål
RING 3
RING 2
Høybråten
Rustad
Lijordet
Ullern
Sinsen
Alna
Smestad
Skui
Rykkinn
Haslum
Skøyen
Tøyen
Lørenskog
Toverud
Kolsås
Stabekk
Bærum
Høvik
Lysaker
Bryn
Sylling
Tanum
Bygdøy
Hovedøya
Ryen
Sandvika
Fornebu
Lindøya
Oppsal
Bøler
Losby
Rælingen
Tronstad
Slependen
Snarøya
Bekkelaget
Rustan
Nesøya
Frederikshavn
Helsingborg
København
Hirtshals, Kiel
Nesoddtangen
Ormøya
Lambertseter
Hvalstad
Nesbru
Østøya
Malmøya
Nordstrand
Østmark-kapellet
Brønnøya
Oksval
Ljabru
Flaskebekk
Skoklefall
Skullerud
Asker
Sørsdal
Helvik
Hauketo
Bunnefjorden
Oslofjorden
Konglungen
Klemetsrud
Sandbakken
Tonekollen
Lierskogen
Blakstad
Ingierstrand
Torvvik
Kolbotn
Tranby
Dikemark
Rausjø
Liertoppen
Nesodden
Krokhol
Lierbyen
Vollen
Fjellstrand
Bomansvik
Siggerud
Bjørkås
Frogner
Heggedal
Svestad
Granerud
Svartskog
Myrvoll
Bru
Reistad
Slemmestad
Blylaget
Oppegård
Nærsnes

Oslo

0 km 0,5

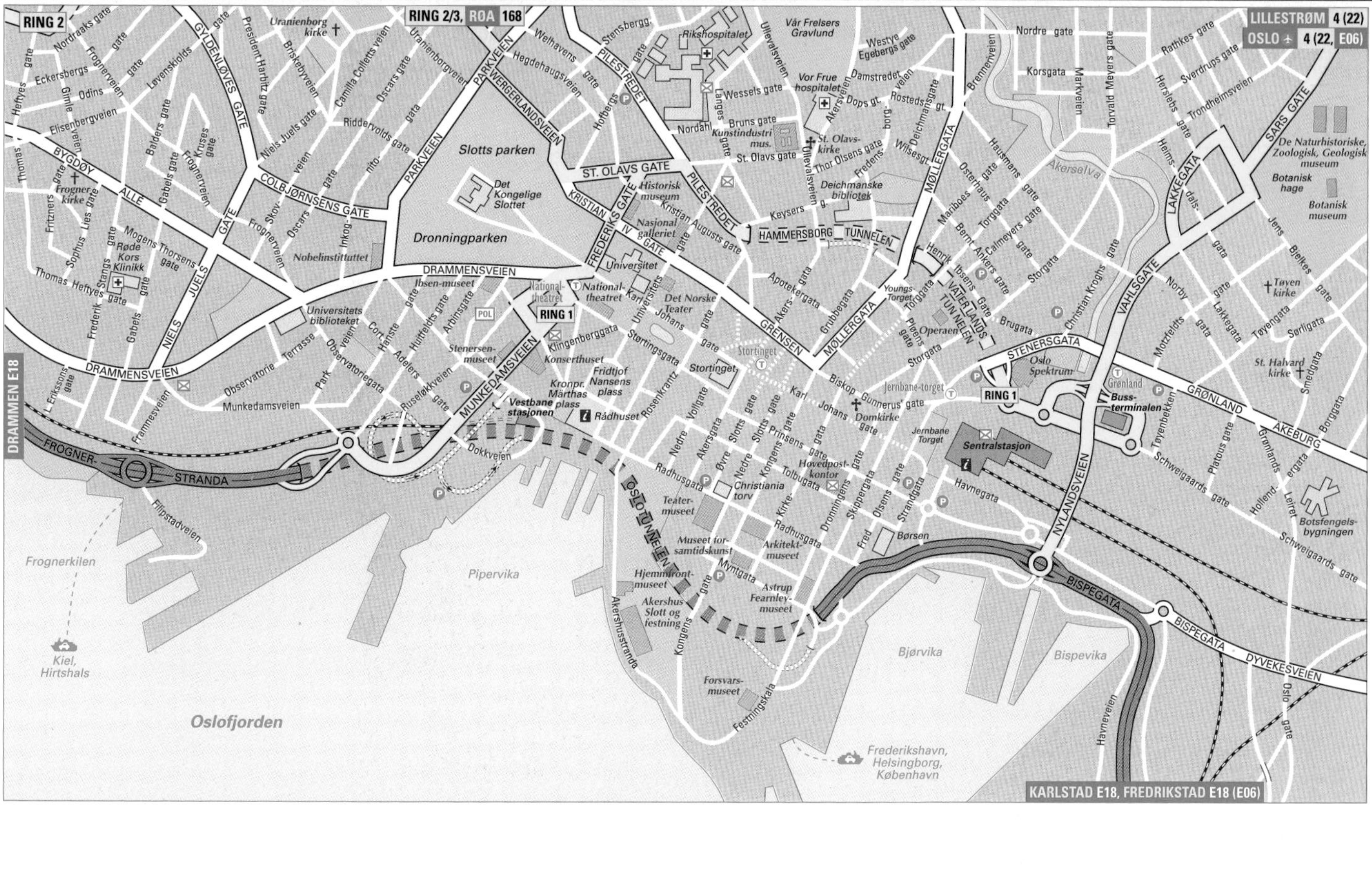

RING 2
RING 2/3, RØA 168
LILLESTRØM 4 (22)
OSLO ✈ 4 (22, E06)
DRAMMEN E18
KARLSTAD E18, FREDRIKSTAD E18 (E06)
Uranienborg kirke
Vår Frelsers Gravlund
Rikshospitalet
Slotts parken
Det Kongelige Slottet
Dronningparken
Frogner kirke
Nobelinstituttet
Universitets biblioteket
Nationaltheatret
Det Norske Teater
Historisk museum
Nasjonal galleriet
Universitet
Deichmanske bibliotek
Operaen
Oslo Spektrum
Grønland
Buss-terminalen
Sentralstasjon
Domkirke
Stortinget
Rådhuset
Vestbane stasjonen
Konserthuset
Stenersen-museet
Ibsen-museet
Kronpr. Märthas plass
Fridtjof Nansens plass
Christiania torv
Teater-museet
Museet for samtidskunst
Hjemmefront-museet
Akershus Slott og festning
Astrup Fearnley-museet
Arkitekt-museet
Forsvars-museet
Hovedpost-kontor
Børsen
De Naturhistoriske, Zoologisk, Geologisk museum
Botanisk hage
Botanisk museum
Tøyen kirke
St. Halvard kirke
Botsfengsels-bygningen
Vor Frue hospital
St. Olavs kirke
Frognerkilen
Kiel, Hirtshals
Pipervika
Bjørvika
Bispevika
Oslofjorden
Frederikshavn, Helsingborg, København
DRAMMENSVEIEN
BYGDØY ALLÉ
FROGNER-STRANDA
MUNKEDAMSVEIEN
OSLO TUNNELEN
BISPEGATA
DYVEKESVEIEN
NYLANDSVEIEN
VAHLSGATE
STENERSGATA
GRØNLAND
AKEBURG
HAMMERSBORG TUNNELEN
VATERLANDS TUNNELEN
GRENSEN
MØLLERGATA
PILESTREDET
ST. OLAVS GATE
PARKVEIEN
WERGELANDSVEIEN
COLBJØRNSENS GATE
GYLDENLØVES GATE
LAKKEGATA
SARS GATE
Akerselva

Paris

0 km 5

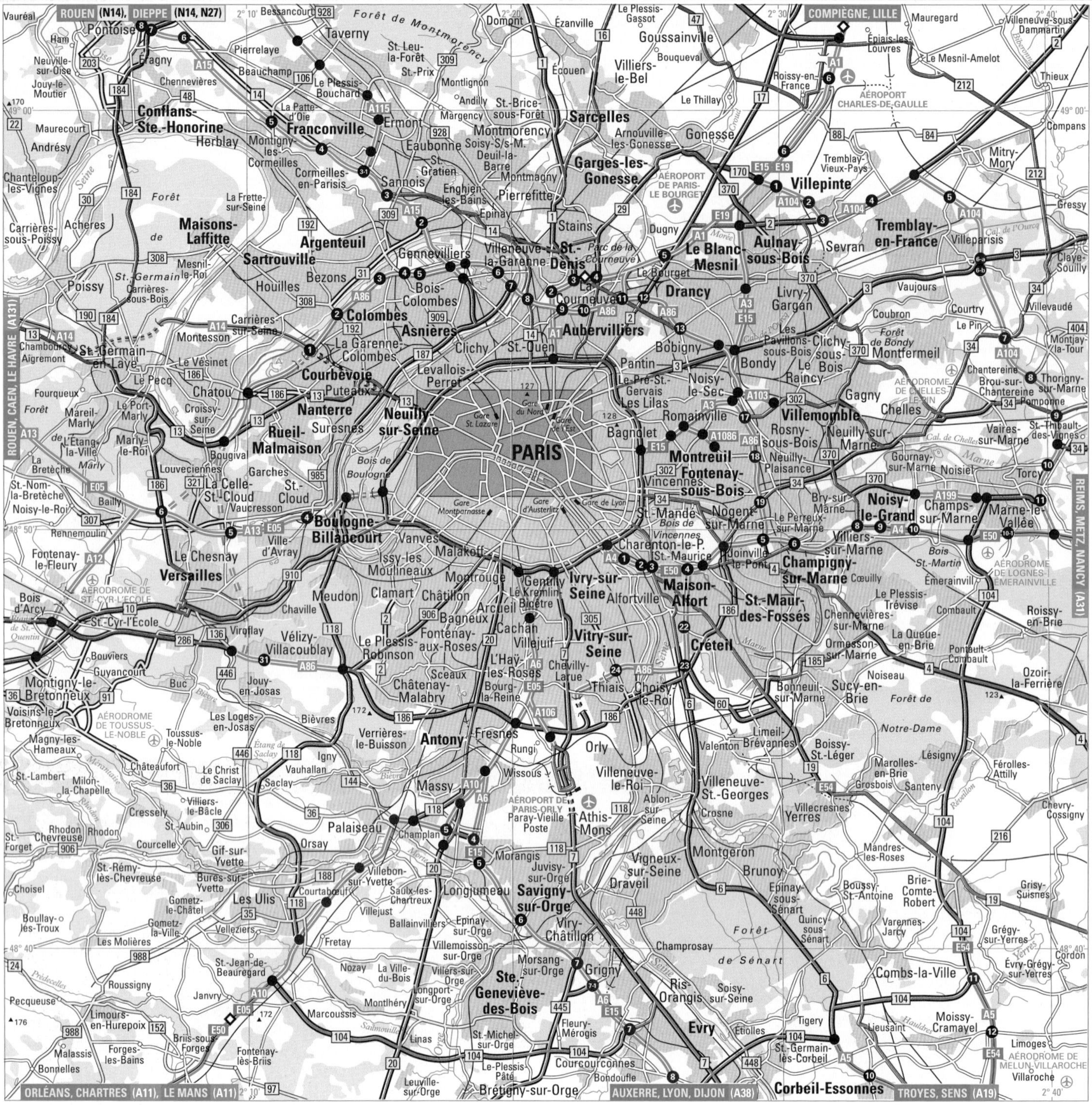
ROUEN (N14), DIEPPE (N14, N27)
COMPIÈGNE, LILLE
ROUEN, CAEN, LE HAVRE (A131)
REIMS, METZ, NANCY (A31)
ORLÉANS, CHARTRES (A11), LE MANS (A11)
AUXERRE, LYON, DIJON (A38)
TROYES, SENS (A19)
PARIS
Gare St. Lazare
Gare du Nord
Gare de l'Est
Gare Montparnasse
Gare d'Austerlitz
Gare de Lyon
AÉROPORT CHARLES-DE-GAULLE
AÉROPORT DE PARIS-LE BOURGET
AÉROPORT DE PARIS-ORLY
AÉRODROME DE ST.-CYR-L'ÉCOLE
AÉRODROME DE TOUSSUS-LE-NOBLE
AÉRODROME DE CHELLES-LE PIN
AÉRODROME DE LOGNES-EMERAINVILLE
AÉRODROME DE MELUN-VILLAROCHE
Forêt de Montmorency
Forêt de St.-Germain
Forêt de Sénart
Forêt de Notre-Dame
Forêt de Bondy
Bois de Boulogne
Bois de Vincennes
Pontoise
Cergy
Taverny
Conflans-Ste.-Honorine
Franconville
Sarcelles
Garges-lès-Gonesse
Goussainville
Villiers-le-Bel
Villepinte
Tremblay-en-France
Aulnay-sous-Bois
Le Blanc-Mesnil
Drancy
St.-Denis
Aubervilliers
Maisons-Laffitte
Sartrouville
Argenteuil
Colombes
Asnières
Courbevoie
Nanterre
Rueil-Malmaison
Neuilly-sur-Seine
Boulogne-Billancourt
Versailles
Montreuil
Fontenay-sous-Bois
Villemomble
Noisy-le-Grand
Champigny-sur-Marne
St.-Maur-des-Fossés
Maison-Alfort
Créteil
Ivry-sur-Seine
Vitry-sur-Seine
Antony
Massy
Savigny-sur-Orge
Ste. Geneviève-des-Bois
Evry
Corbeil-Essonnes
Marne-la-Vallée

Paris

0 km 1

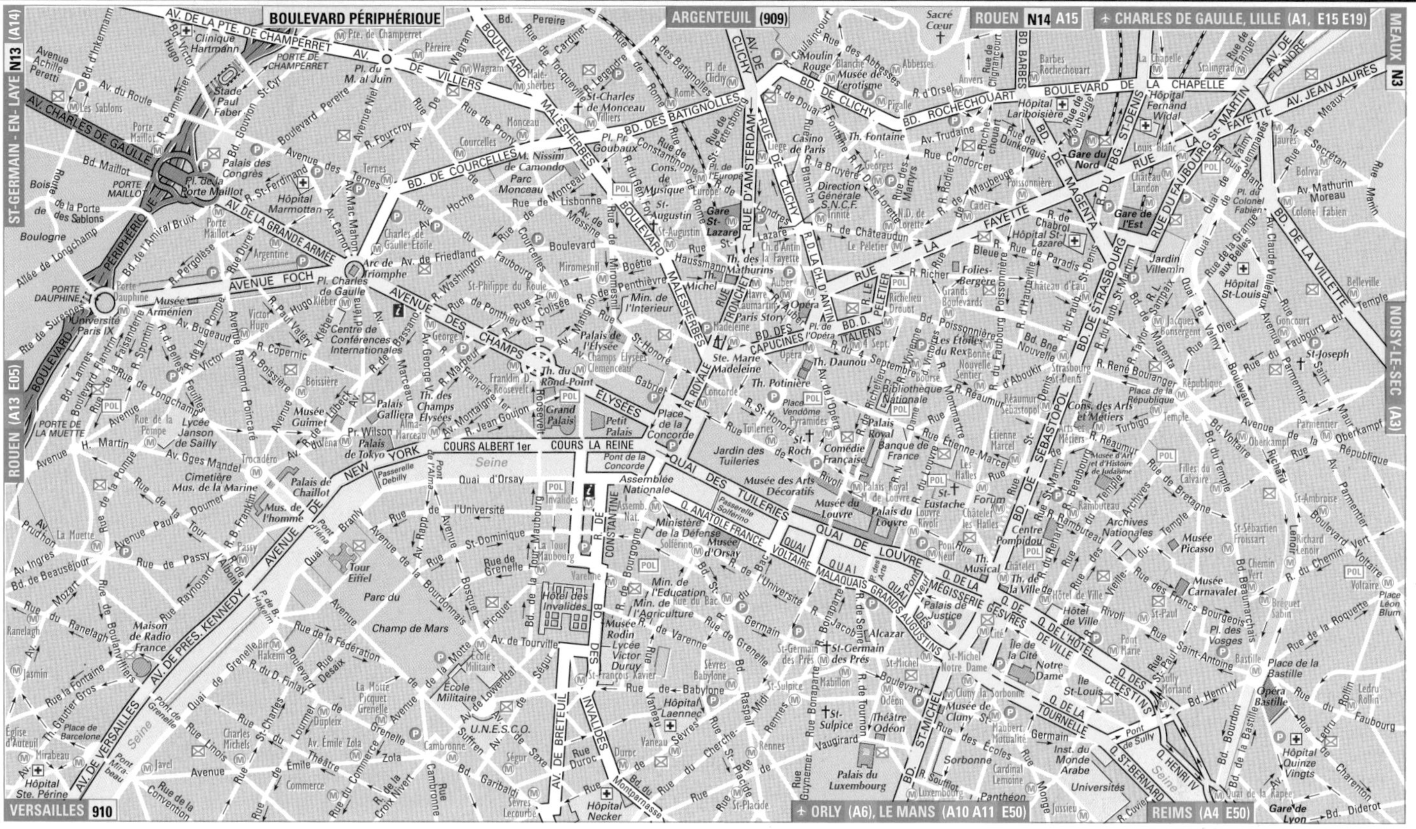
BOULEVARD PÉRIPHÉRIQUE
ARGENTEUIL (909)
ROUEN N14 A15
CHARLES DE GAULLE, LILLE (A1, E15 E19)
MEAUX N3
NOISY-LE-SEC (A3)
ORLY (A6), LE MANS (A10 A11 E50)
REIMS (A4 E50)
VERSAILLES 910
ROUEN (A13 E05)
ST-GERMAIN - EN - LAYE N13 (A14)

Praha Prague

0 km 5

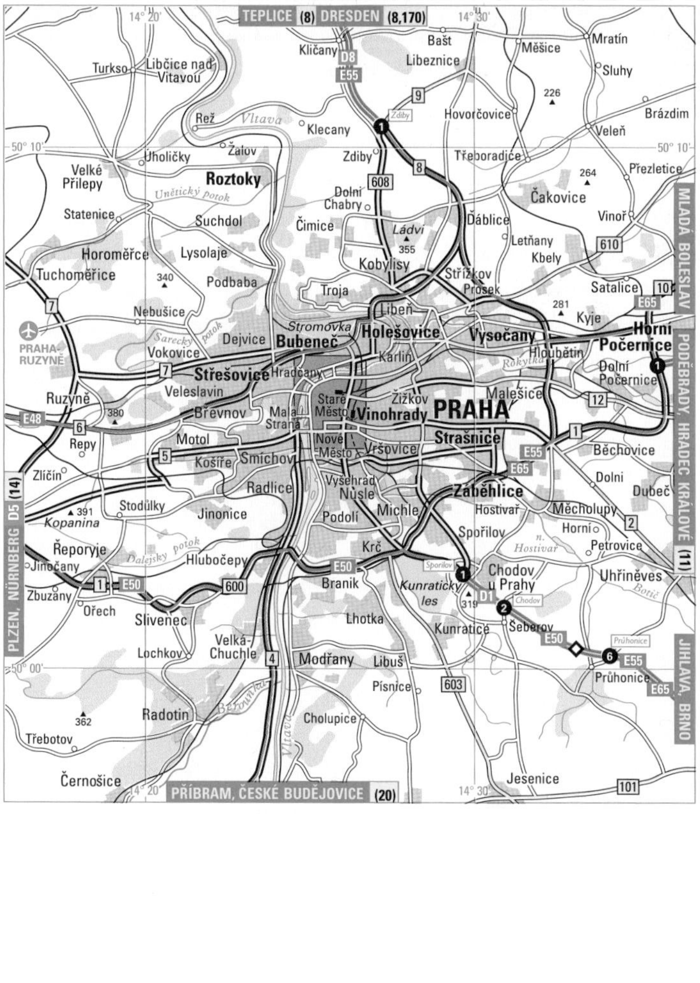
TEPLICE (8) DRESDEN (8,170)
MLADÁ BOLESLAV
PODĚBRADY HRADEC KRÁLOVÉ (11)
JIHLAVA, BRNO
PŘÍBRAM, ČESKÉ BUDĚJOVICE (20)
PLZEN, NÜRNBERG D5 (14)
PRAHA

Praha Prague

0 km 1

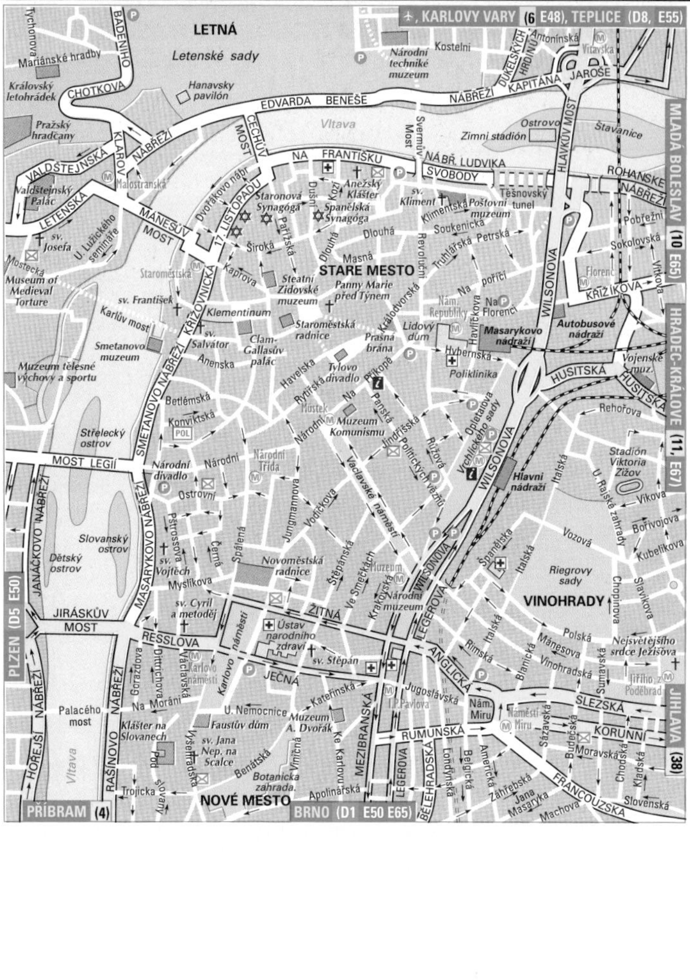
KARLOVY VARY (6 E48), TEPLICE (D8, E55)
MLADA BOLESLAV (10 E65)
HRADEC-KRÁLOVÉ (11, E67)
JIHLAVA (38)
BRNO (D1 E50 E65)
PŘÍBRAM (4)
PLZEN (D5 E50)
LETNÁ
STARE MESTO
NOVÉ MESTO
VINOHRADY

Roma Rome

0 km 5

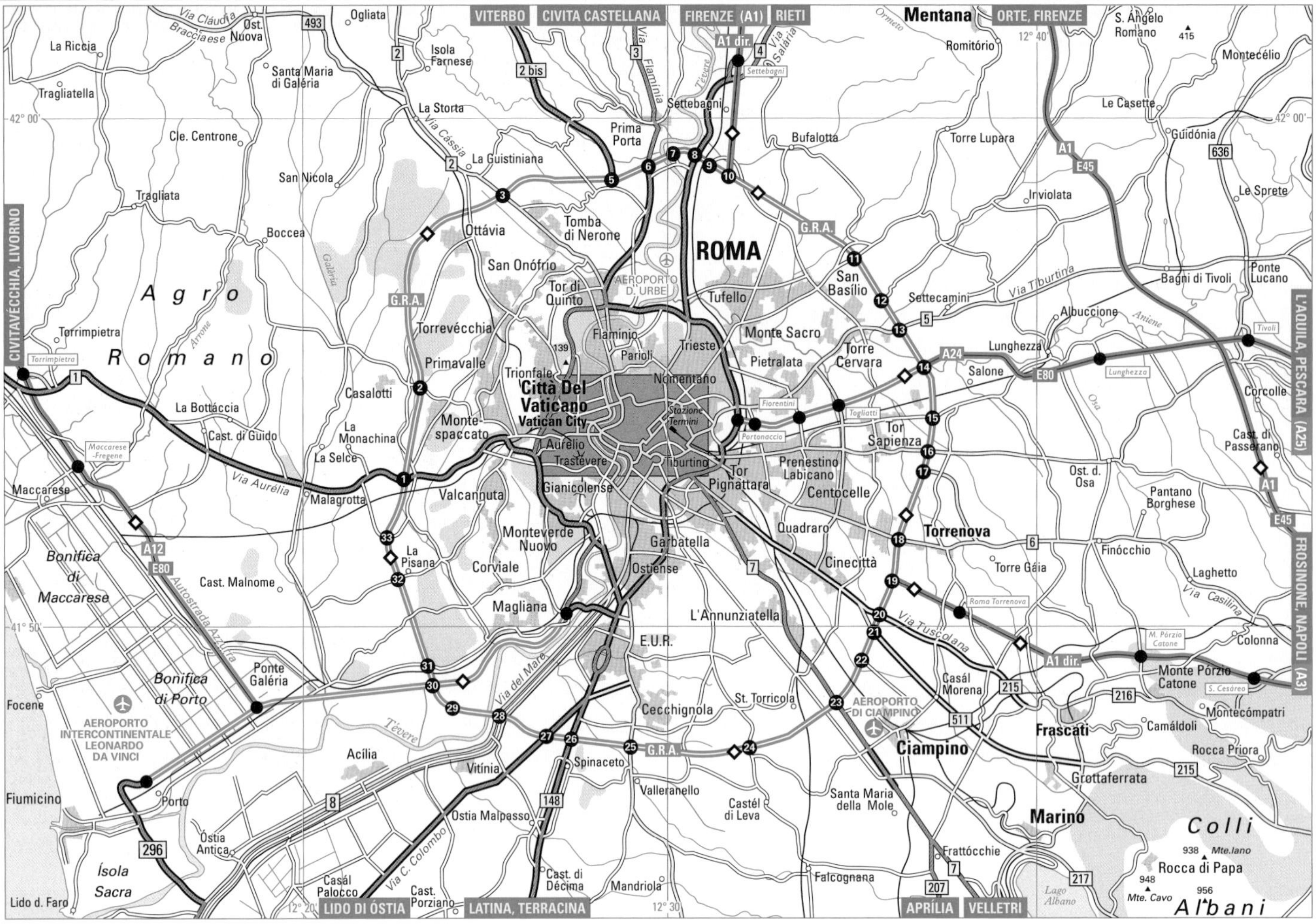
VITERBO
CIVITA CASTELLANA
FIRENZE (A1)
RIETI
Mentana
ORTE, FIRENZE
CIVITAVECCHIA, LIVORNO
L'AQUILA, PESCARA (A25)
FROSINONE, NAPOLI (A3)
LIDO DI ÓSTIA
LATINA, TERRACINA
APRÌLIA
VELLETRI
ROMA
Città Del Vaticano
Vatican City
La Riccia
Ogliata
Ost. Nuova
Isola Farnese
Santa Maria di Galèria
Tragliatella
La Storta
Prima Porta
Settebagni
Romitório
S. Angelo Romano
Montecélio
Le Casette
Guidònia
Cle. Centrone
La Giustiniana
Bufalotta
Torre Lupara
San Nicola
Tragliata
Irviolata
Le Sprete
Boccea
Ottávia
Tomba di Nerone
San Onófrio
Tor di Quinto
AEROPORTO D. URBE
Tufello
San Basílio
Settecamini
Bagni di Tivoli
Ponte Lucano
Agro Romano
Torrimpietra
Torrevécchia
Flaminio
Parioli
Trieste
Monte Sacro
Albuccione
Lunghezza
Primavalle
Pietralata
Torre Cervara
Salone
Casalotti
Trionfale
Nomentano
Corcolle
La Bottáccia
Monte-spaccato
La Monachina
Cast. di Guido
Stazione Termini
Tor Sapienza
Cast. di Passerano
La Selce
Aurelio
Trastévere
Tiburtino
Tor Pignattara
Prenestino Labicano
Ost. d. Osa
Maccarese
Malagrotta
Via Aurélia
Valcannuta
Gianicolense
Centocelle
Pantano Borghese
Quadraro
Torrenova
Monteverde Nuovo
Garbatella
La Pisana
Corviale
Ostiense
Cinecittà
Torre Gaia
Finócchio
Laghetto
Bonifica di Maccarese
Cast. Malnome
Magliana
L'Annunziatella
E.U.R.
Colonna
Monte Pórzio Catone
Ponte Galéria
Bonifica di Porto
Casál Morena
Focene
St. Torricola
AEROPORTO DI CIAMPINO
Cecchignola
Frascati
Camáldoli
Montecómpatri
AEROPORTO INTERCONTINENTALE LEONARDO DA VINCI
Acília
Spinaceto
Ciampino
Rocca Priora
Vitinia
Grottaferrata
Fiumicino
Porto
Valleranello
Castél di Leva
Santa Maria della Mole
Marino
Ostia Malpasso
Colli Albani
Óstia Antica
Frattócchie
Rocca di Papa
Mte. Iano
Mte. Cavo
Ísola Sacra
Cast. di Décima
Mandriola
Falcognana
Lago Albano
Lido d. Faro
Casál Palocco
Cast. Porziano
G.R.A.
A1
E45
A24
E80
A12
A1 dir.
Via Cássia
Via Flaminia
Via Salaria
Via Tiburtina
Via Casilina
Via Tuscolana
Via del Mare
Via C. Colombo
Autostrada Azzurra
Tevere
Via Cláudia Bracciaese

Roma Rome

0 km 1

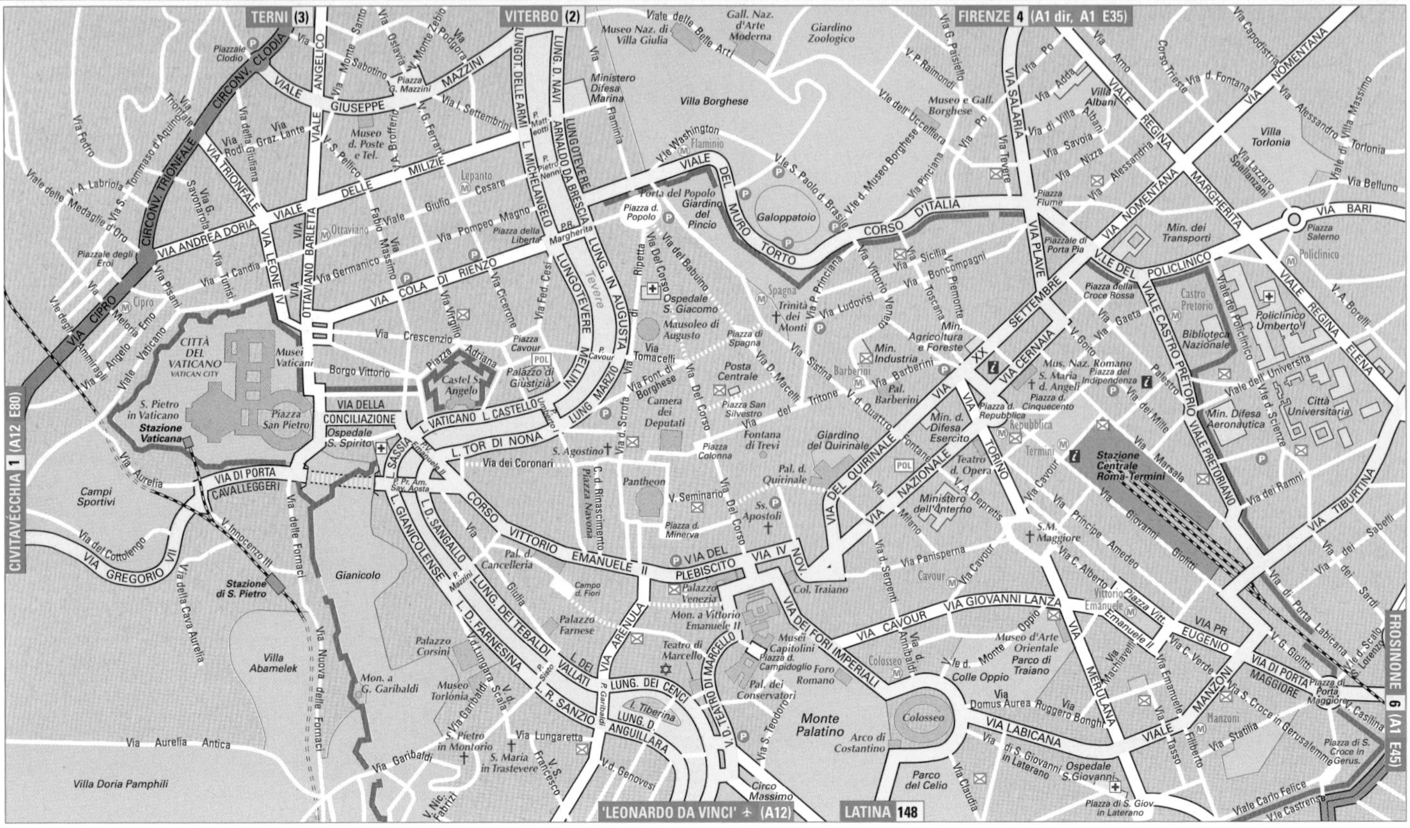
TERNI (3)
VITERBO (2)
FIRENZE 4 (A1 dir, A1 E35)
CIVITAVECCHIA 1 (A12 E80)
FROSINONE 6 (A1 E45)
'LEONARDO DA VINCI' (A12)
LATINA 148
Gall. Naz. d'Arte Moderna
Giardino Zoologico
Museo Naz. di Villa Giulia
Villa Borghese
Museo e Gall. Borghese
Villa Albani
Villa Torlonia
Piazzale Clodio
Viale Giuseppe Mazzini
Museo d. Poste e Tel.
Ministero Difesa Marina
Flaminio
Galoppatoio
Porta del Popolo
Piazza d. Popolo
Giardino del Pincio
Corso d'Italia
Via Nomentana
Piazza Fiume
Min. dei Trasporti
Piazzale di Porta Pia
Piazza Salerno
Policlinico
Lepanto
Ottaviano
Via Andrea Doria
Via Cola di Rienzo
Piazza della Libertà
Spagna
Trinità dei Monti
Ospedale S. Giacomo
Mausoleo di Augusto
Piazza di Spagna
Castro Pretorio
Biblioteca Nazionale
Policlinico Umberto I
Città del Vaticano
Vatican City
Musei Vaticani
Borgo Vittorio
Castel S. Angelo
Palazzo di Giustizia
Posta Centrale
Min. Industria e Foreste
Min. Agricoltura e Foreste
Pal. Barberini
Mus. Naz. Romano
S. Maria d. Angeli
Piazza d. Cinquecento
Città Universitaria
Min. Difesa Aeronautica
S. Pietro in Vaticano
Stazione Vaticana
Piazza San Pietro
Via della Conciliazione
Ospedale S. Spirito
Camera dei Deputati
Piazza Colonna
Fontana di Trevi
Giardino del Quirinale
Min. d. Difesa Esercito
Piazza d. Repubblica
Repubblica
Stazione Centrale Roma-Termini
Termini
Campi Sportivi
Via di Porta Cavalleggeri
Via dei Coronari
Pantheon
Pal. d. Quirinale
Teatro d. Opera
Ministero dell'Interno
S. M. Maggiore
Via Principe Amedeo
Via Giovanni Giolitti
Via Tiburtina
Stazione di S. Pietro
Gianicolo
Corso Vittorio Emanuele II
Pal. d. Cancelleria
Campo d. Fiori
Via del Plebiscito
Piazza Venezia
Col. Traiano
Via Cavour
Via Giovanni Lanza
Vittorio Emanuele
Via dei Fori Imperiali
Mon. a Vittorio Emanuele II
Musei Capitolini
Piazza del Campidoglio
Foro Romano
Colosseo
Palazzo Farnese
Palazzo Corsini
Museo Torlonia
Mon. a G. Garibaldi
Villa Abamelek
Teatro di Marcello
Pal. dei Conservatori
Monte Palatino
Arco di Costantino
Museo d'Arte Orientale
Parco di Traiano
Colle Oppio
Domus Aurea
Via Merulana
Via Labicana
Viale Manzoni
Via di S. Giovanni in Laterano
Ospedale S. Giovanni
Piazza di S. Giov. in Laterano
Piazza di S. Croce in Gerus.
Piazza di Porta Maggiore
Via di Porta Maggiore
Via Casilina
Manzoni
Villa Doria Pamphili
Via Aurelia Antica
Via Gregorio VII
Via Garibaldi
S. Pietro in Montorio
S. Maria in Trastevere
Via Lungaretta
Lung. d. Anguillara
I. Tiberina
Circo Massimo
Parco del Celio
Viale Carlo Felice
Via Marsala
Viale Regina Margherita
Viale Regina Elena
Via Bari
Via Bellano
Via XX Settembre
Via Cernaia
Via Nazionale
Via del Quirinale
Via Veneto
Via del Muro Torto
Via del Corso
Via Ripetta
Via del Babuino
Via del Tritone
Lung. in Augusta
Lungotevere Mellini
Via Crescenzio
Via Candia
Viale delle Milizie
Via Cipro
Circonv. Trionfale
Circonv. Clodia
Viale Angelico
Via Trionfale
Via Leone IV
Via Ottaviano
Piazza Navona
S. Agostino
Via Tor di Nona
Via Giulia
Lung. dei Tebaldi
Lung. d. Farnesina
Lung. d. Sangallo
Via Gianicolense
Via Arenula
Lung. d. Cenci
Via Nuova delle Fornaci
Via delle Fornaci
Viale Trastevere

Stockholm

0 km 5

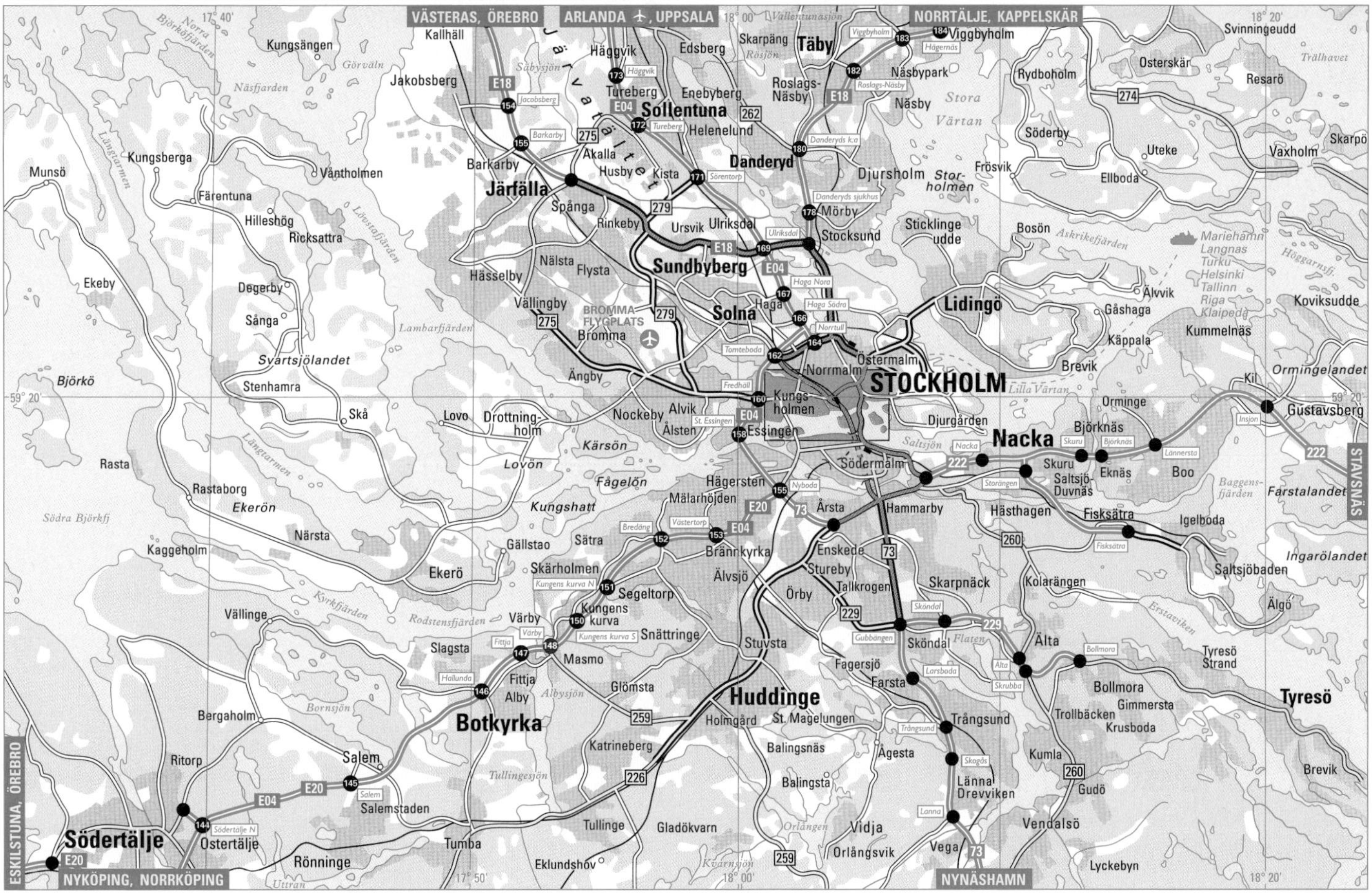
VÄSTERAS, ÖREBRO
ARLANDA, UPPSALA
NORRTÄLJE, KAPPELSKÄR
STAVSNÄS
NYNÄSHAMN
NYKÖPING, NORRKÖPING
ESKILSTUNA, ÖREBRO
STOCKHOLM
Järfälla
Sollentuna
Täby
Danderyd
Sundbyberg
Solna
Lidingö
Nacka
Huddinge
Botkyrka
Södertälje
Tyresö
Kungsängen
Jakobsberg
Kallhäll
Häggvik
Edsberg
Skarpäng
Viggbyholm
Näsbypark
Näsby
Roslags-Näsby
Rydboholm
Svinningeudd
Österskär
Resarö
Vaxholm
Tureberg
Enebyberg
Helenelund
Barkarby
Akalla
Husby
Kista
Spånga
Rinkeby
Ursvik
Ulriksdal
Mörby
Stocksund
Djursholm
Stora Värtan
Frösvik
Täby
Söderby
Uteke
Ellboda
Bosön
Sticklinge udde
Hässelby
Nälsta
Flysta
Vällingby
BROMMA FLYGPLATS
Bromma
Haga
Ängby
Östermalm
Norrmalm
Kungsholmen
Gåshaga
Käppala
Kummelnäs
Koviksudde
Älvvik
Brevik
Orminge
Gustavsberg
Kil
Ormingelandet
Djurgården
Saltsjön
Södermalm
Björknäs
Skuru
Saltsjö-Duvnäs
Eknäs
Boo
Farstalandet
Nockeby
Alvik
Ålsten
Essingen
Lovö
Drottningholm
Kärsön
Fågelön
Lovön
Kungshatt
Hägersten
Mälarhöjden
Årsta
Hammarby
Hästhagen
Fisksätra
Igelboda
Saltsjöbaden
Ingarölandet
Enskede
Stureby
Tallkrogen
Skarpnäck
Kolarängen
Älgö
Gällstad
Sätra
Skärholmen
Bredäng
Bränkyrka
Älvsjö
Örby
Segeltorp
Kungens kurva
Snättringe
Stuvsta
Sköndal
Älta
Fagersjö
Farsta
Tyresö Strand
Bollmora
Gimmersta
Trollbäcken
Krusboda
Ekerö
Ekerön
Närsta
Kaggeholm
Rastaborg
Rasta
Björkö
Munsö
Kungsberga
Vantholmen
Färentuna
Hilleshög
Ricksattra
Ekeby
Degerby
Sånga
Svartsjölandet
Stenhamra
Skå
Lovo
Vällinge
Värby
Slagsta
Fittja
Alby
Masmo
Glömsta
Holmgård
St. Magelungen
Balingsnäs
Trångsund
Ågesta
Balingsta
Katrineberg
Bergaholm
Ritorp
Salem
Salemstaden
Östertälje
Rönninge
Tumba
Tullinge
Gladökvarn
Eklundshov
Vidja
Orlångsvik
Vega
Lännа Drevviken
Vendalsö
Kumla
Gudö
Lyckebyn
Brevik
Mälaren
Görväln
Lambarfjärden
Södra Björkfj
Kyrkfjärden
Rodstensfjärden
Bornsjön
Tullingesjön
Albysjön
Orlången
Kvarnsjön
Uttran
Erstaviken
Askrikefjärden
Lilla Värtan
Trälhavet
Baggensfjärden
Mariehamn Langnas Turku Helsinki Tallinn Riga Klaipeda
E18
E04
E20
73
222
226
229
259
260
262
274
275
279

Stockholm

0 km 1

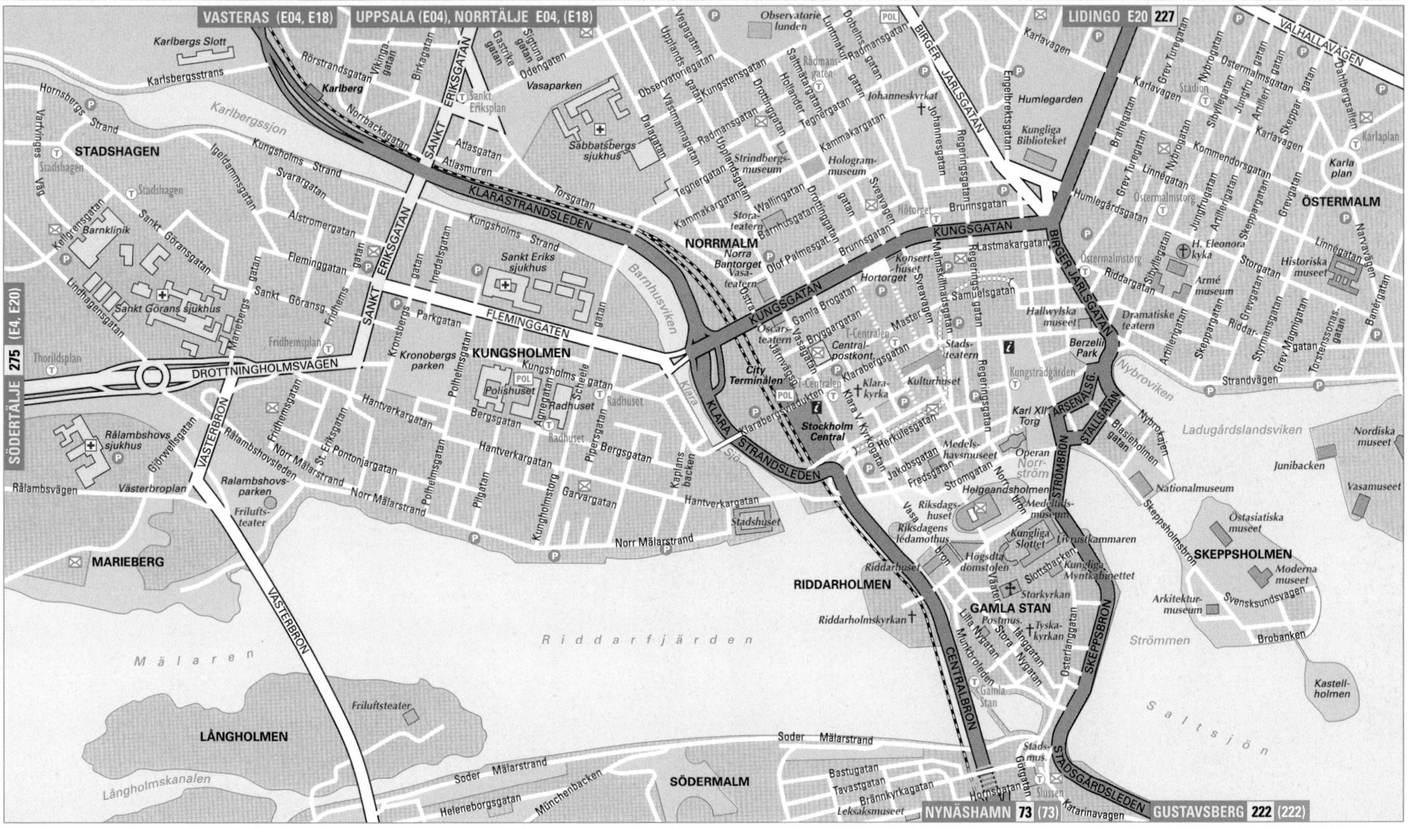
VÄSTERAS (E04, E18)
UPPSALA (E04), NORRTÄLJE E04, (E18)
LIDINGÖ E20 227
SÖDERTÄLJE 275 (E4, E20)
NYNÄSHAMN 73 (73)
GUSTAVSBERG 222 (222)
Karlbergs Slott
Karlbergsstrans
Karlberg
Karlbergssjön
STADSHAGEN
Stadshagen
Barnklinik
Sankt Görans sjukhus
Thorildsplan
DROTTNINGHOLMSVÄGEN
Rålambshovs sjukhus
Rålambsvägen
Västerbroplan
Rålambshovsparken
Friluftsteater
MARIEBERG
VÄSTERBRON
KUNGSHOLMEN
Kronobergs parken
Polishuset
Rådhuset
FLEMINGGATAN
Fridhemsplan
Sankt Eriks sjukhus
SANKT ERIKSGATAN
Barnhusviken
KLARASTRANDSLEDEN
Stadshuset
Norr Mälarstrand
Hantverkargatan
R i d d a r f j ä r d e n
M ä l a r e n
LÅNGHOLMEN
Friluftsteater
Långholmskanalen
Söder Mälarstrand
Heleneborgsgatan
Münchenbacken
SÖDERMALM
Sabbatsbergs sjukhus
Vasaparken
Observatorielunden
Strindbergsmuseum
Hologrammuseum
NORRMALM
Norra Bantorget
Vasateatern
KUNGSGATAN
Oscarsteatern
City Terminalen
Stockholm Central
Centralpostkont.
Konserthuset
Hötorget
Stadsteatern
Kulturhuset
Klarakyrka
Medelshavsmuseet
Riksdagshuset
Riksdagens fedamothus
Operan
Norrström
Karl XII Torg
Berzelii Park
Kungsträdgården
Hallwylska museet
Dramatiska teatern
Humlegarden
Kungliga Biblioteket
Johanneskyrkan
BIRGER JARLSGATAN
ÖSTERMALM
Karlaplan
Historiska museet
Armé museum
H. Eleonora kyrka
Strandvägen
Nybroviken
Ladugårdslandsviken
Nationalmuseum
Nordiska museet
Junibacken
Vasamuseet
Östasiatiska museet
SKEPPSHOLMEN
Moderna museet
Arkitekturmuseum
Kastellholmen
Skeppsholmsbron
Strömmen
S a l t s j ö n
RIDDARHOLMEN
Riddarholmskyrkan
Riddarhuset
GAMLA STAN
Kungliga Slottet
Livrustkammaren
Högsta domstolen
Storkyrkan
Tyska kyrkan
Kungliga Myntkabinettet
CENTRALBRON
SKEPPSBRON
STRÖMBRON
STADSGÅRDSLEDEN
Slussen
Stadsmus.
Katarinavägen
Hornsgatan
Götgatan
Bastugatan
Tavastgatan
Bränkyrkagatan
Leksaksmuseet
VALHALLAVÄGEN
Karlavägen
Engelbrektsgatan
Sveavägen
Drottninggatan
Vasagatan
Tegnérgatan
Kammakargatan
Brunnsgatan
Regeringsgatan
Hamngatan
Strandvägen
Fleminggatan
Kungsholmsgatan
Sankt Göransg.
Pontonjärgatan
Norr Mälarstrand
Polhemsgatan
Bergsgatan

Strasbourg

0 km 5

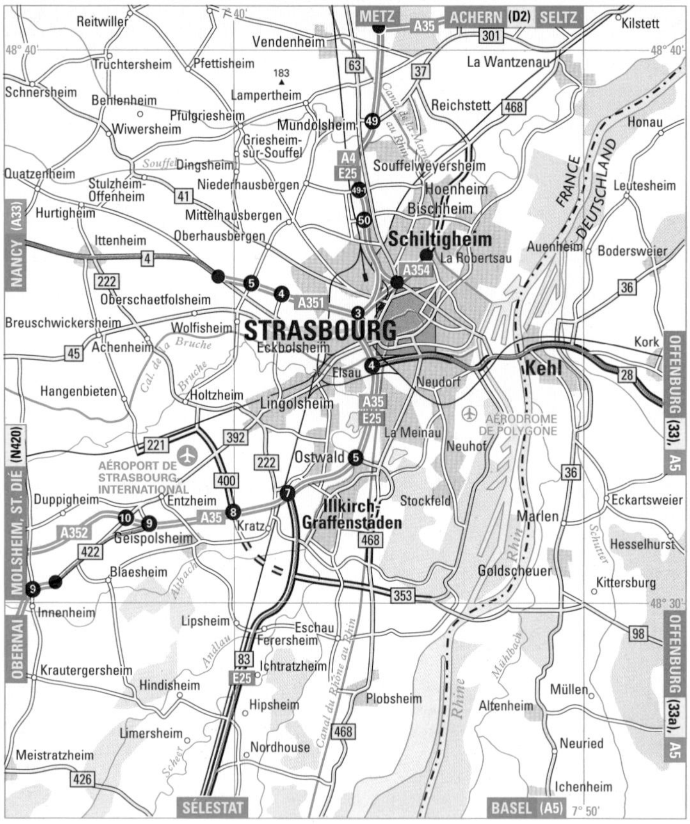

Strasbourg

0 km 0.5

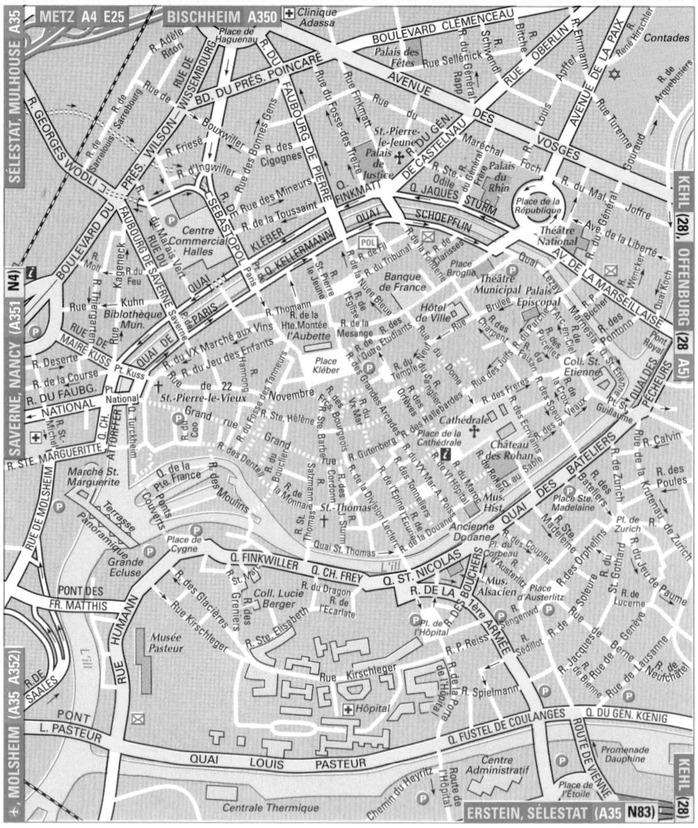

Sevilla Seville

0 km 0.5

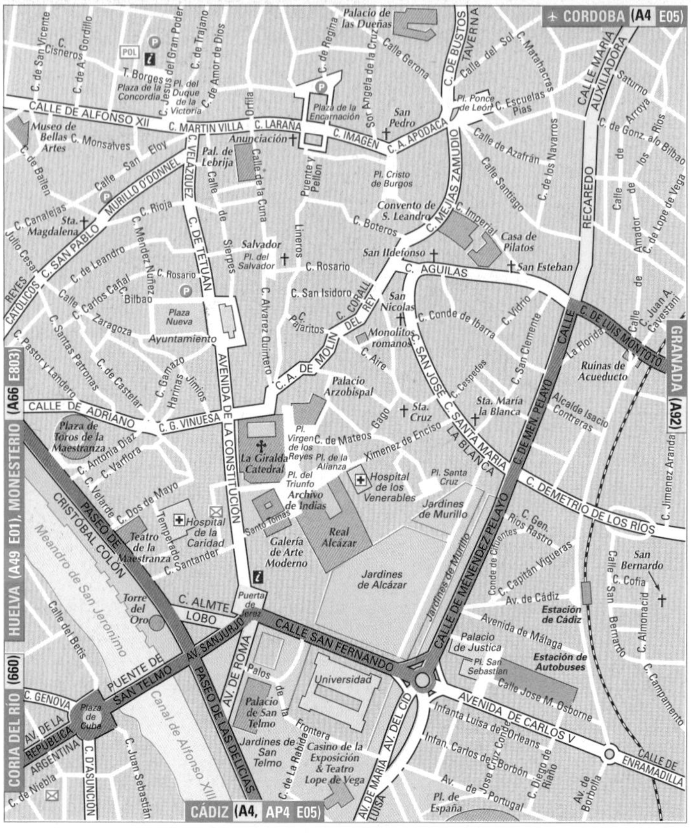

Stuttgart

0 km 0.5

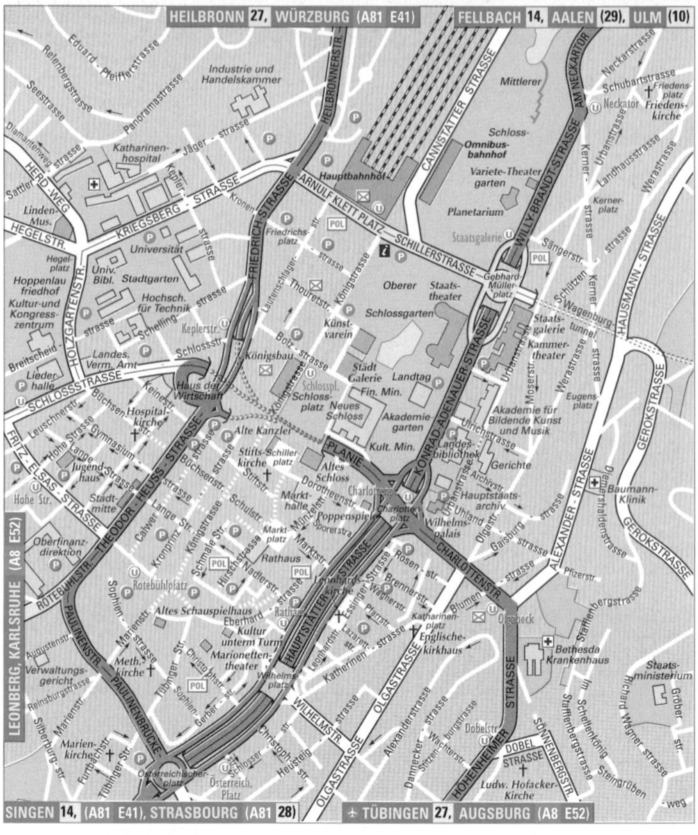

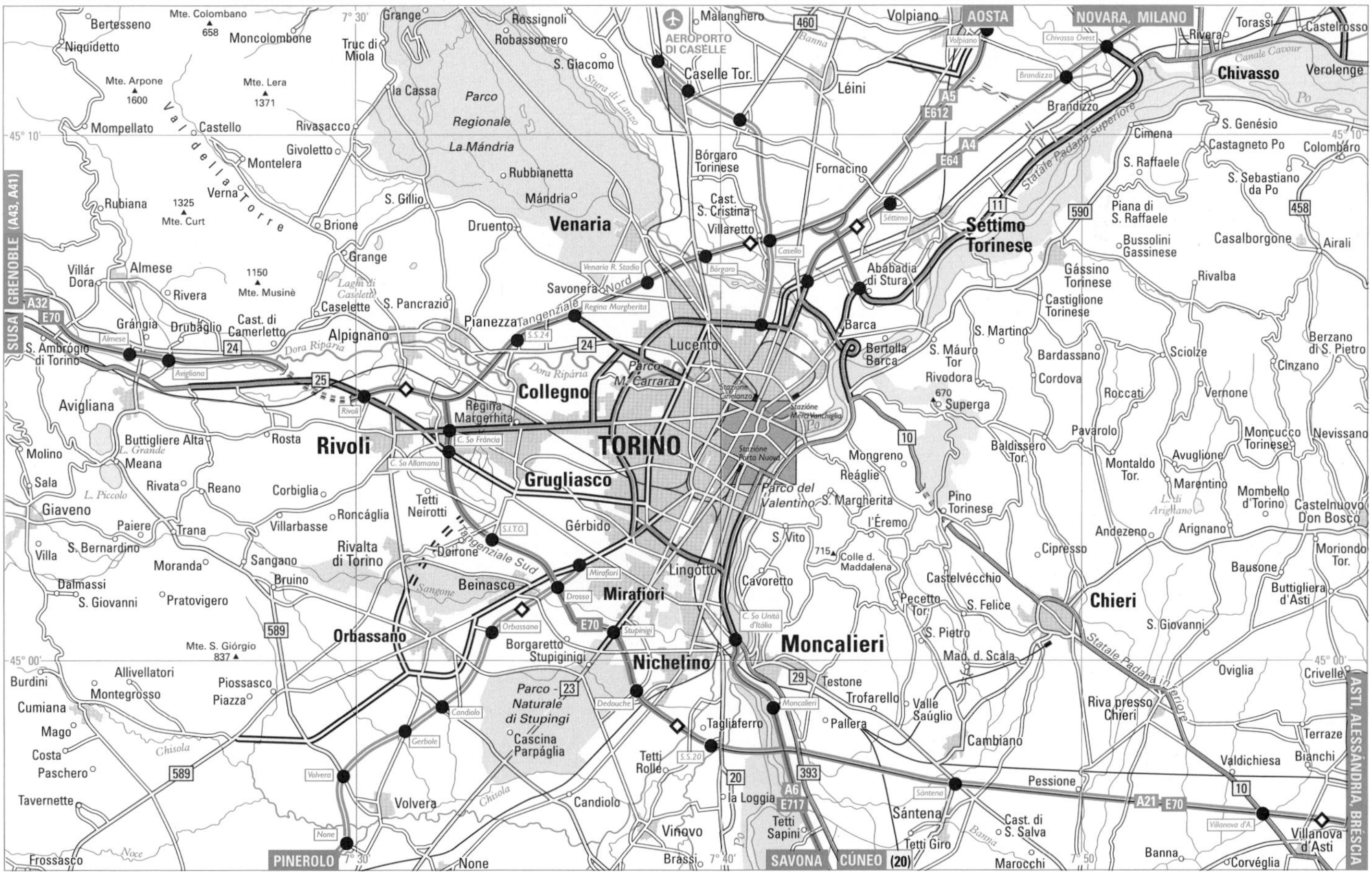

Torino Turin

0 km 5

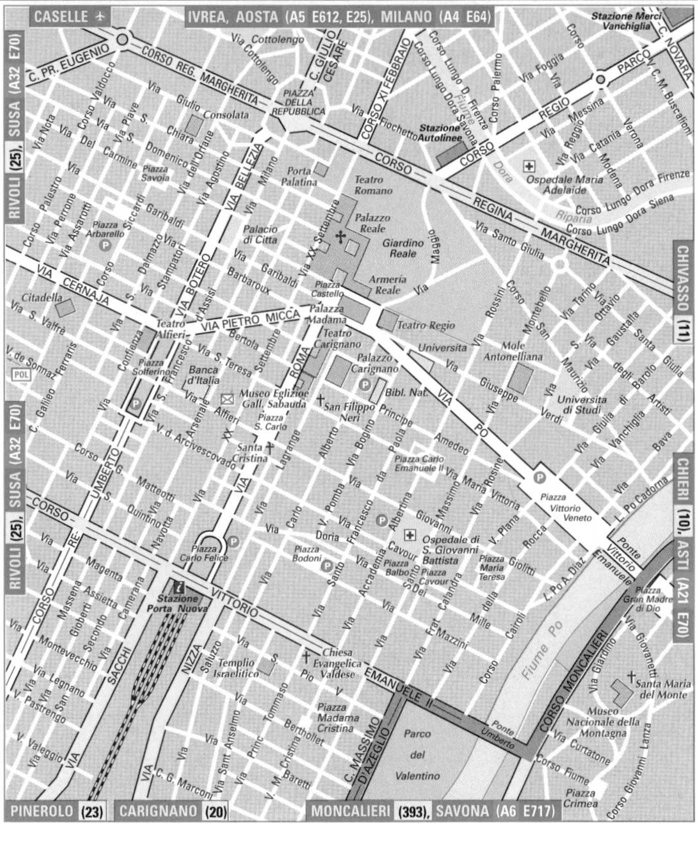

Torino Turin

0 km 1

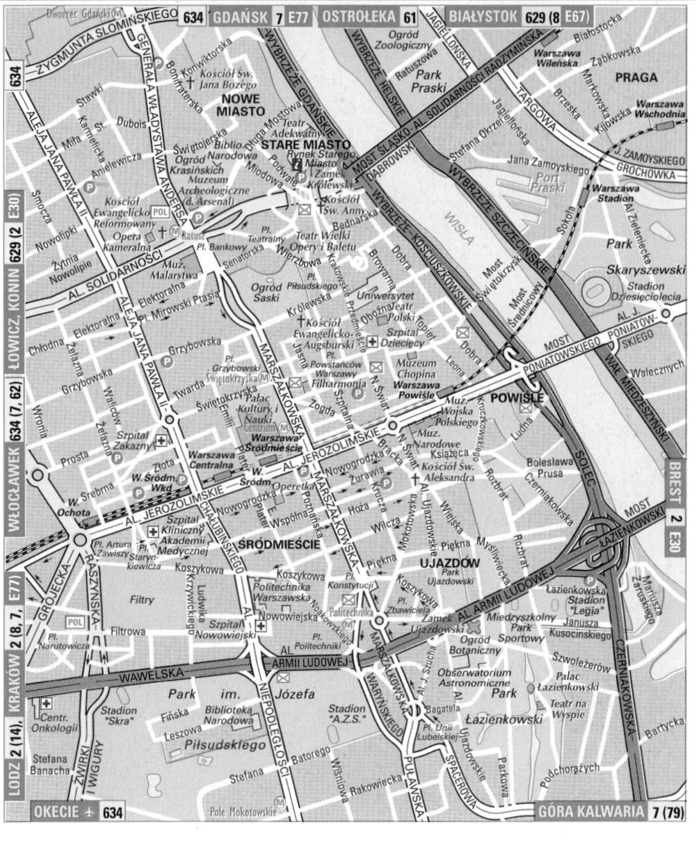

Warszawa Warsaw

0 km 1

For **Vienna** see page 144

Wien Vienna

0 km 1

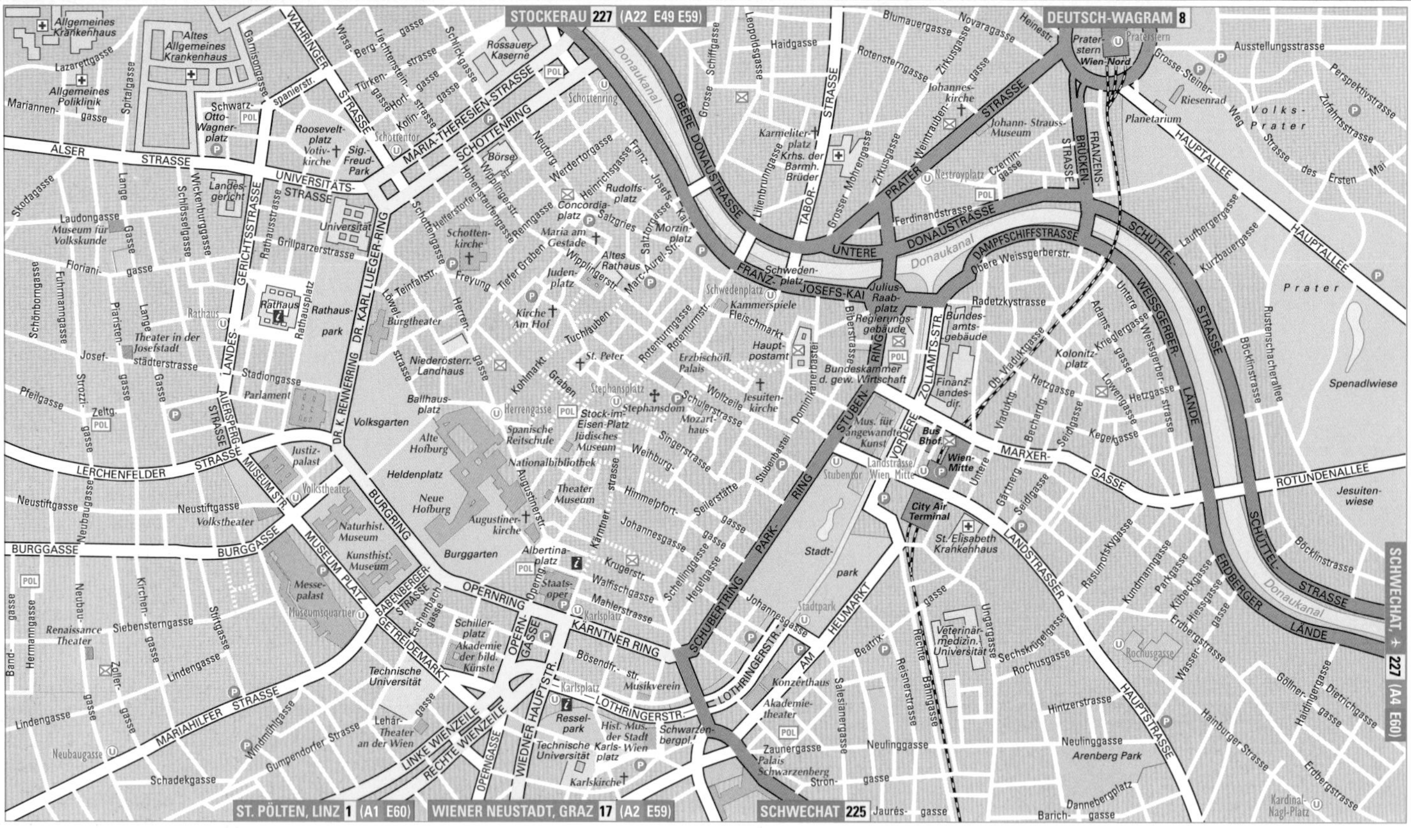
STOCKERAU 227 (A22 E49 E59)
DEUTSCH-WAGRAM 8
SCHWECHAT ✈ 227 (A4 E60)
ST. PÖLTEN, LINZ 1 (A1 E60)
WIENER NEUSTADT, GRAZ 17 (A2 E59)
SCHWECHAT 225
Allgemeines Krankenhaus
Altes Allgemeines Krankenhaus
Alser Strasse
Universitätsstrasse
Maria-Theresien-Strasse
Schottenring
Rossauer Kaserne
Donaukanal
Obere Donaustrasse
Untere Donaustrasse
Praterstern
Wien-Nord
Riesenrad
Planetarium
Volksprater
Hauptallee
Prater
Spenadlwiese
Jesuitenwiese
Rotundenallee
Schüttelstrasse
Weissgerberlände
Erdberger Lände
Praterstrasse
Franz-Josefs-Kai
Schwedenplatz
Landstrasser Hauptstrasse
Rathaus
Parlament
Universität
Burgtheater
Volksgarten
Heldenplatz
Neue Hofburg
Alte Hofburg
Burggarten
Nationalbibliothek
Spanische Reitschule
Stephansdom
Stephansplatz
Staatsoper
Opernring
Kärntner Ring
Schubertring
Parkring
Stubenring
Stadtpark
Karlsplatz
Karlskirche
Technische Universität
Musikverein
Konzerthaus
Akademietheater
Schwarzenbergplatz
Lothringerstrasse
Museumsquartier
Naturhist. Museum
Kunsthist. Museum
Mariahilfer Strasse
Linke Wienzeile
Rechte Wienzeile
Lerchenfelder Strasse
Burggasse
Neustiftgasse
Josefstädter Strasse
Landesgericht
Votivkirche
City Air Terminal
Wien Mitte
Bus Bhf.
St. Elisabeth Krankenhaus
Veterinärmedizin. Universität
Rochusgasse
Arenberg Park
Kardinal-Nagl-Platz
Ungargasse
Marxergasse
Radetzkystrasse
Rasumofskygasse

Wien Vienna

0 km 5

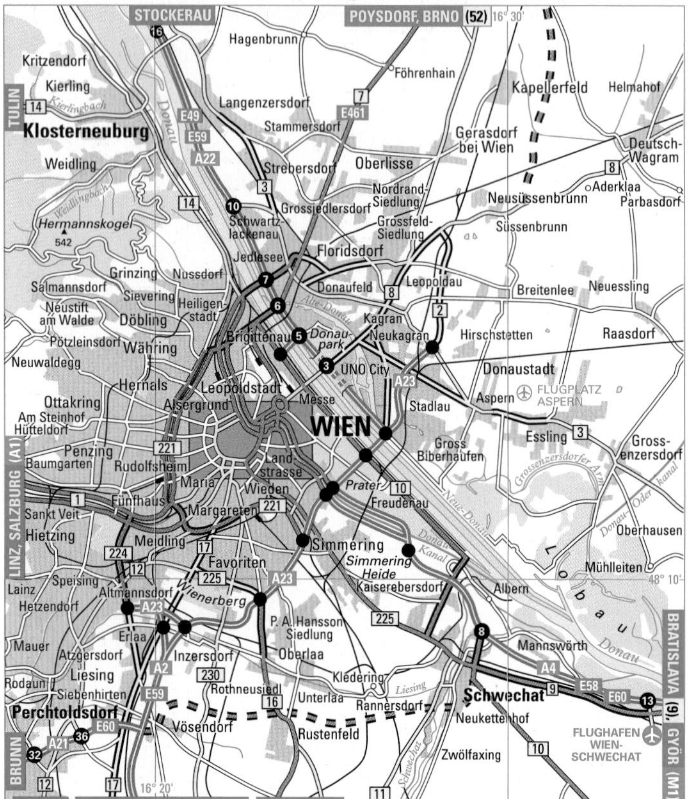
STOCKERAU
POYSDORF, BRNO (52)
TULLN
LINZ, SALZBURG (A1)
BRUNN
BADEN
WIENER NEUSTADT, GRAZ
EISENSTADT
BRUCK
BRATISLAVA (9), GYÖR (M1)
Klosterneuburg
Kritzendorf
Kierling
Weidling
Hermannskogel
Hagenbrunn
Föhrenhain
Langenzersdorf
Stammersdorf
Strebersdorf
Oberlisse
Kapellerfeld
Helmahof
Gerasdorf bei Wien
Deutsch-Wagram
Aderklaa
Parbasdorf
Nordrand-Siedlung
Neusüssenbrunn
Süssenbrunn
Grossjedlersdorf
Schwartz-lackenau
Grossfeld-Siedlung
Floridsdorf
Jedlesee
Grinzing
Nussdorf
Salmannsdorf
Sievering
Heiligenstadt
Neustift am Walde
Döbling
Pötzleinsdorf
Währing
Neuwaldegg
Hernals
Ottakring
Am Steinhof
Hütteldorf
Penzing
Baumgarten
Rudolfsheim
Sankt Veit
Hietzing
Lainz
Speising
Hetzendorf
Mauer
Atzgersdorf
Liesing
Rodaun
Siebenhirten
Perchtoldsdorf
Vösendorf
Brigittenau
Leopoldstadt
Alsergrund
Donaufeld
Leopoldau
Breitenlee
Neuessling
Kagran
Neukagran
Hirschstetten
Raasdorf
Donaupark
UNO City
Donaustadt
Messe
WIEN
Stadlau
Aspern
FLUGPLATZ ASPERN
Essling
Gross-Enzersdorf
Biberhaufen
Landstrasse
Maria
Fünfhaus
Wieden
Margareten
Prater
Freudenau
Meidling
Favoriten
Simmering
Simmeringer Heide
Kaiserebersdorf
Oberhausen
Mühlleiten
Albern
Altmannsdorf
Wienerberg
P. A. Hansson Siedlung
Erlaa
Inzersdorf
Oberlaa
Rothneusiedl
Unterlaa
Kledering
Rannersdorf
Schwechat
Mannswörth
Neukettenhof
Rustenfeld
Zwölfaxing
FLUGHAFEN WIEN-SCHWECHAT
Donau
Lobau
Neue Donau
Alte Donau
Donaukanal

Zürich

0 km 0.5

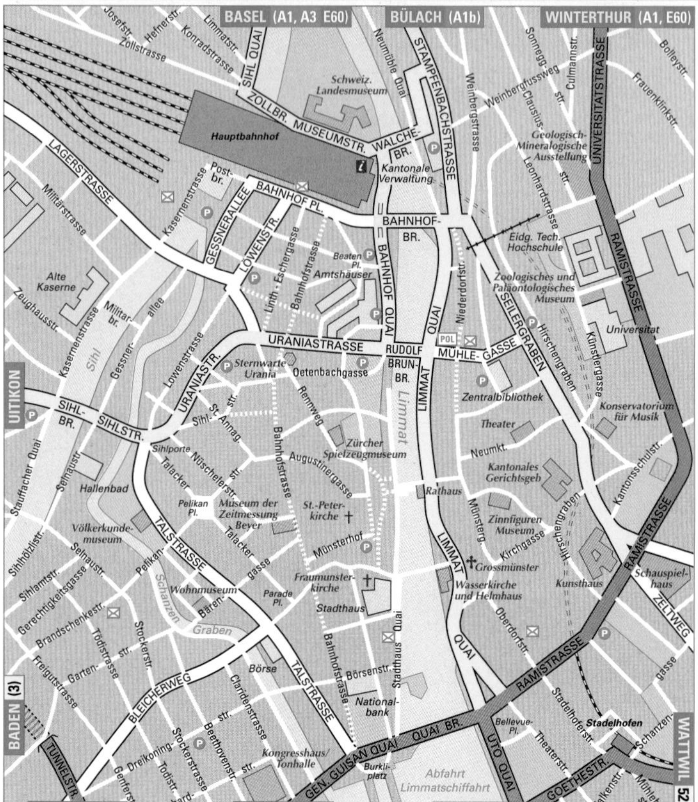
BASEL (A1, A3 E60)
BÜLACH (A1b)
WINTERTHUR (A1, E60)
UITIKON
BADEN (3)
CHUR (A3 A13)
RAPPERSWIL 17
WATTWIL 52 (8)
Hauptbahnhof
Schweiz. Landesmuseum
Museumstr.
Walchebr.
Kantonale Verwaltung
Bahnhofplatz
Bahnhofbrücke
Stampfenbachstrasse
Lagerstrasse
Gessnerallee
Löwenstrasse
Bahnhofstrasse
Bahnhofquai
Limmatquai
Uraniastrasse
Sternwarte Urania
Rudolf-Brun-Br.
Mühlegasse
Seilergraben
Universitätstrasse
Rämistrasse
Eidg. Tech. Hochschule
Zoologisches und Paläontologisches Museum
Geologisch-Mineralogische Ausstellung
Universität
Zentralbibliothek
Theater
Konservatorium für Musik
Kantonales Gerichtsgeb.
Kunsthaus
Schauspielhaus
Grossmünster
Wasserkirche und Helmhaus
Zinnfiguren Museum
Rathaus
Alte Kaserne
Sihl
Sihlstr.
Sihlporte
Zürcher Spielzeugmuseum
Museum der Zeitmessung Beyer
St.-Peter-kirche
Fraumünster-kirche
Stadthaus
Münsterhof
Paradeplatz
Nationalbank
Börse
Talstrasse
Hallenbad
Völkerkundemuseum
Wohnmuseum Bärengasse
Bleicherweg
Kongresshaus/ Tonhalle
Bürkliplatz
General-Guisan-Quai
Quaibrücke
Utoquai
Stadelhofen
Goethestr.
Abfahrt Limmatschiffahrt
Limmat
Schanzengraben

GB	F		D	I
Austria	Autriche	**A**	Österreich	Austria
Albania	Albanie	**AL**	Albanien	Albania
Andorra	Andorre	**AND**	Andorra	Andorra
Belgium	Belgique	**B**	Belgien	Belgio
Bulgaria	Bulgarie	**BG**	Bulgarien	Bulgaria
Bosnia-Herzegovina	Bosnia-Herzegovine	**BIH**	Bosnien-Herzegowina	Bosnia-Herzogovina
Belarus	Belarus	**BY**	Weissrussland	Bielorussia
Switzerland	Suisse	**CH**	Schweiz	Svizzera
Cyprus	Chypre	**CY**	Zypern	Cipro
Czech Republic	République Tchèque	**CZ**	Tschechische Republik	Repubblica Ceca
Germany	Allemagne	**D**	Deutschland	Germania
Denmark	Danemark	**DK**	Dänemark	Danimarca
Spain	Espagne	**E**	Spanien	Spagna
Estonia	Estonie	**EST**	Estland	Estonia
France	France	**F**	Frankreich	Francia
Finland	Finlande	**FIN**	Finnland	Finlandia
Liechtenstein	Liechtenstein	**FL**	Liechtenstein	Liechtenstein
Faeroe Islands	Îles Féroé	**FO**	Färoër-Inseln	Isole Faroe
United Kingdom	Royaume Uni	**GB**	Grossbritannien und Nordirland	Regno Unito
Gibraltar	Gibraltar	**GBZ**	Gibraltar	Gibilterra
Greece	Grèce	**GR**	Greichenland	Grecia
Hungary	Hongrie	**H**	Ungarn	Ungheria
Croatia	Croatie	**HR**	Kroatien	Croazia
Italy	Italie	**I**	Italien	Italia
Ireland	Irlande	**IRL**	Irland	Irlanda
Iceland	Islande	**IS**	Island	Islanda
Luxembourg	Luxembourg	**L**	Luxemburg	Lussemburgo
Lithuania	Lituanie	**LT**	Litauen	Lituania
Latvia	Lettonie	**LV**	Lettland	Lettonia
Malta	Malte	**M**	Malta	Malta
Monaco	Monaco	**MC**	Monaco	Monaco
Moldova	Moldavie	**MD**	Moldawien	Moldavia
Macedonia	Macédoine	**MK**	Makedonien	Macedonia
Norway	Norvège	**N**	Norwegen	Norvegia
Netherlands	Pays-Bas	**NL**	Niederlande	Paesi Bassi
Portugal	Portugal	**P**	Portugal	Portogallo
Poland	Pologne	**PL**	Polen	Polonia
Romania	Roumanie	**RO**	Rumanien	Romania
San Marino	Saint-Marin	**RSM**	San Marino	San Marino
Russia	Russie	**RUS**	Russland	Russia
Sweden	Suède	**S**	Schweden	Svezia
Serbia and Montenegro	Serbie et Monténégro	**SCG**	Serbien und Montenegro	Serbia e Montenegro
Slovak Republic	République Slovaque	**SK**	Slowak Republik	Repubblica Slovacca
Slovenia	Slovénie	**SLO**	Slowenien	Slovenia
Turkey	Turquie	**TR**	Türkei	Turchia
Ukraine	Ukraine	**UA**	Ukraine	Ucraina

A

A Baña E **86** B2
A Bola E **87** B3
A Cañiza E **87** B2
A Capela E **86** A2
A Coruña E **86** A2
A Estrada E **86** B2
A Fonsagrada E **86** A3
A Guarda E **87** C2
A Gudiña E **87** B3
A Merca E **87** B3
A Peroxa E **86** B3
A Pontenova E **86** A3
A Rúa E **87** B3
A Teixeira E **87** B3
A Veiga E **87** B3
A-Ver-o-Mar P **87** C2
Aabybro DK **38** B2
Aach D **71** A4
Aachen D **50** C2
Aalen D **61** B6
Aalsmeer NL **49** A5
Aalst B **49** C5
Aalten NL **50** B2
Aalter B **49** B4
Äänekoski FIN **3** E26
Aapajärvi FIN **113** E16
Aarau CH **70** A3
Aarberg CH **70** A2
Aarburg CH **70** A2
Aardenburg NL **49** B4
Aarschot B **49** C5
Aba H **74** A3
Abádanes E **95** B4
Abades E **94** B2
Abadin E **86** A3
Abádszalók H **75** A5
Abaliget H **74** B3
Abana TR **16** A7
Abanilla E **101** A4
Abano Terme I **72** C1
Abarán E **101** A4
Abasár H **65** C6
Abbadia San Salvatore I **81** D5
Abbaue D **45** B5
Abbehausen D **43** B5
Abbekås S **41** D3
Abbeville F **48** C2
Abbey IRL **20** A3
Abbey Town GB **25** D4
Abbeydorney IRL **20** B2
Abbeyfeale IRL **20** B2
Abbeyleix IRL **21** B4
Abbiategrasso I **70** C3
Abborrträsk S **115** B16
Abbots Bromley GB **27** C4
Abbotsbury GB **29** C5
Abda H **64** C3
Abejar E **89** C4
Abela P **98** B2
Abelvær N **114** C8
Abenberg D **62** A1
Abenójar E **100** A1
Åbenrå DK **39** D2
Abensberg D **62** B2
Aberaeron GB **28** A3
Abercarn GB **29** B4
Aberchirder GB **23** D6
Aberdare GB **29** B4
Aberdaron GB **26** C1
Aberdeen GB **23** D6
Aberdulais GB **28** B4
Aberdyfi GB **26** C1
Aberfeldy GB **25** B4
Aberffraw GB **26** B1
Aberfoyle GB **24** B3
Abergavenny GB **29** B4
Abergele GB **26** B2
Abergynolwyn GB **26** C2
Aberporth GB **28** A3
Abersoch GB **26** C1
Abertillery GB **29** B4
Abertura E **93** B5
Aberystwyth GB **26** C1
Abetone I **81** B4
Abfaltersbach A **72** B2
Abide, *Çanakkale* TR **118** B1
Abide, *Kütahya* TR **118** D4
Abiego E **90** A2
Abild DK **39** E1
Abingdon GB **31** C2
Abington GB **25** C4
Abisko S **112** D7
Abiul P **92** B2
Abla E **101** B3
Ablis F **58** B2
Abondance F **70** B1
Abony H **75** A5
Aboyne GB **23** D6
Abrantes P **92** B2
Abreiro P **87** C3
Abreschviller F **60** B3
Abrest F **68** B3
Abriès F **79** B5
Abrud RO **11** C7
Absdorf A **64** B1
Abtenau A **72** A3
Abtsgmünd D **61** B5
Abusejo E **93** A4
Åby, *Kronoberg* S **40** B4
Åby, *Östergötland* S **37** D3
Åbyggeby S **36** B4
Åbytorp S **37** C2
Acate I **109** B3
Accadia I **103** B8
Accéglio I **79** B5
Accettura I **104** C2
Acciaroli I **106** A2
Accous F **76** D2
Accrington GB **26** B3
Accúmoli I **82** D2
Acedera E **93** B5
Acehuche E **93** B4
Acered E **95** A5
Acerenza I **104** C1
Acerno I **103** C8
Acerra I **103** C7
Aceuchal E **93** C4
Acharacle GB **24** B2
Acharnes GR **117** D5
Achavanich GB **23** C5
Achene B **49** C6
Achenkirch A **72** A1
Achensee A **72** A1
Achenthal A **72** A1
Achentrias GR **117** H7
Achern D **61** B4
Acheux-en-Amienois F **48** C3
Achiltibuie GB **22** C3
Achim D **43** B6
Achladokambos GR **117** E4
Achnasheen GB **22** D3
Achnashellach GB **22** D3
Achosnich GB **24** B1
Aci Castello I **109** B4
Aci Catena I **109** B4
Acilia I **102** B5
Acıpayam TR **119** E4
Acireale I **109** B4
Acle GB **30** B5
Acqua Doria F **102** B1
Acquacadda I **110** C1
Acquanegra sul Chiese I **71** C5
Acquapendente I **81** D5
Acquasanta Terme I **82** D2
Acquasparta I **102** A5
Acquaviva I **81** C5
Acquaviva delle Fonti I **104** C2
Acquaviva Picena I **82** D2
Acqui Terme I **80** B2
Acquigny F **58** A2
Acri I **106** B3
Acs H **64** C4
Acsa H **65** C5
Ácsteszér H **74** A2
Acy-en-Multien F **59** A3
Ada SCG **75** C5
Adak S **115** B15
Ådalsbruk N **34** B3
Adamas GR **117** F6
Adamsfjord N **113** B15
Adamuz E **100** A1
Adana TR **16** C7
Ádánd H **74** B3
Adanero E **94** B2
Adare IRL **20** B3
Adaševci SCG **85** A4
Adeanueva de Ebro E **89** B5
Adelboden CH **70** B2
Adelebsen D **51** B5
Adélfia I **104** B2
Adelmannsfelden D **61** B6
Adelsheim D **61** A5
Adelsö S **37** C4
Ademuz E **96** A1
Adenau D **50** C2
Adendorf D **44** B2
Adinkerke B **48** B3
Adjud RO **11** C9
Adliswil CH **70** A3
Admont A **63** C5
Ådneram N **33** C3
Adolfsström S **115** A13
Adony H **74** A3
Adorf, *Hessen* D **51** B4
Adorf, *Sachsen* D **52** C2
Adra E **100** C2
Adradas E **89** C4
Adrall E **91** A4
Adrano I **109** B3
Ádria I **82** A1
Adrigole IRL **20** C2
Adwick le Street GB **27** B4
Adzaneta E **96** A2
Ærøskøbing DK **39** E3
Aesch CH **70** A2
Afandou GR **119** F3
Åfarnes N **114** E4
Affing D **62** B1
Affoltern CH **70** A3
Affric Lodge GB **22** D3
Åfjord N **114** D7
Aflenz Kurort A **73** A5
Afragóla I **103** C7
Afritz A **72** B3
Afyon TR **118** D5
Ağapınar TR **118** C5
Ágasegyháza H **75** B4
Agay F **79** C5
Agazzano I **80** B3
Agde F **78** C2
Agdenes N **114** D6
Agen F **77** B3
Ager E **90** B3
Agerbæk DK **39** D1
Agerskov DK **39** D2
Ageyevo RUS **7** D14
Agger DK **38** C1
Aggersund DK **38** B2
Ággius I **110** B2
Aggsbach Dorf A **63** B6
Aggsbach Markt A **63** B6
Aggtelek H **65** B6
Aghalee GB **19** B5
Aghia GR **116** C4
Aghia Anna GR **116** D5
Aghia Galini GR **117** G6
Aghia Marina, *Dodekanisa* GR **119** E1
Aghia Marina, *Dodekanisa* GR **119** G1
Aghia Paraskevi GR **118** C1
Aghia Pelagia GR **117** F4
Aghia Triada GR **117** E3
Aghio Theodori GR **117** E5
Aghiokambos GR **116** C4
Aghios Efstratios GR **116** C6
Aghios Kirikos GR **119** E1
Aghios Matheos GR **116** C1
Aghios Mironas GR **117** G7
Aghios Nikolaos GR **117** G7
Aghios Petros GR **116** D2
Agiči BIH **83** B5
Agira I **109** B3
Ağlasun TR **119** E5
Aglientu I **110** A2
Agnières F **79** B4
Agno CH **70** C3
Agnone I **103** B7
Agolada E **86** B2
Agon Coutainville F **57** A4
Ágordo I **72** B2
Agost E **96** C2
Agramón E **101** A4
Agramunt E **91** B4
Agreda E **89** C5
Agria GR **116** C5
Agrigento I **108** B2
Agrinio GR **116** D3
Agrón E **100** B2
Agrópoli I **103** C7
Agua Longa P **87** C2
Aguadulce, *Almería* E **101** C3
Aguadulce, *Sevilla* E **100** B1
Agualada E **86** A2
Aguarón E **89** C5
Aguas E **90** A2
Aguas Belas P **92** B2
Aguas de Busot E **96** C2
Aguas de Moura P **92** C2
Águas Frias P **87** C3
Aguas Santas P **87** C2
Aguaviva E **90** C2
Aguaviva de la Vega E **89** C4
Agudo E **94** D2
Águeda P **92** A2
Aguessac F **78** B2
Agugliano I **82** C2
Aguiar P **92** C3
Aguiàr da Beira P **87** D3
Aguilafuente E **94** A2
Aguilar de Campóo E **88** B2
Aguilar de la Frontera E **100** B1
Aguilas E **101** B4
Agunnaryd S **40** C4
Ağva TR **118** A4
Ahat TR **118** D4
Ahaus D **50** A2
Åheim N **114** E2
Ahigal E **93** A4
Ahigal de Villarino E **87** C4
Ahillones E **99** A5
Ahlbeck, *Mecklenburg-Vorpommern* D **45** B6
Ahlbeck, *Mecklenburg-Vorpommern* D **45** B6
Ahlen D **50** B3
Ahlhorn D **43** C5
Ahmetbey TR **118** A2
Ahmetler TR **119** D4
Ahmetli TR **119** D2
Ahoghill GB **19** B5
Ahrensbök D **44** A2
Ahrensburg D **44** B2
Ahrenshoop D **44** A4
Ahun F **68** B2
Åhus S **41** D4
Ahvenselkä FIN **113** F17
Aibar E **89** B5
Aich D **62** B3
Aicha D **63** B4
Aichach D **62** B2
Aidone I **109** B3
Aiello Cálabro I **106** B3
Aigen im Mühlkreis A **63** B4
Aigle CH **70** B1
Aignan F **76** C3
Aignay-le-Duc F **59** C5
Aigre F **67** C5
Aigrefeuille-d'Aunis F **66** B4
Aigrefeuille-sur-Maine F **66** A3
Aiguablava E **91** B6
Aiguebelle F **69** C6
Aigueperse F **68** B3
Aigues-Mortes F **78** C3
Aigues-Vives F **78** C1
Aiguilles F **79** B5
Aiguillon F **77** B3
Aigurande F **68** B1
Ailefroide F **79** B5
Aillant-sur-Tholon F **59** C4
Ailly-sur-Noye F **58** A3
Ailly-sur-Somme F **58** A3
Aimargues F **78** C3
Aime F **69** C6
Ainaži LV **6** C8
Ainet A **72** B2
Ainhoa F **76** C1
Ainsa E **90** A3
Airaines F **48** D2
Aird GB **24** B2
Aird Asaig Tairbeart GB **22** D2
Airdrie GB **25** C4
Aire-sur-la-Lys F **48** C3
Aire-sur-l'Adour F **76** C2
Airole I **80** C1
Airolo CH **70** B3
Airvault F **67** B4
Aisey-sur-Seine F **59** C5
Aïssey F **69** A6
Aisy-sur-Armançon F **59** C5
Aiterhofen D **62** B3
Aith, *Orkney* GB **23** B6
Aith, *Shetland* GB **22** A7
Aitona E **90** B3
Aitrach D **61** C6
Aiud RO **11** C7
Aix-en-Othe F **59** B4
Aix-en-Provence F **79** C4
Aix-les-Bains F **69** C5
Aixe-sur-Vienne F **67** C6
Aizenay F **66** B3
Aizkraukle LV **7** C8
Aizpute LV **6** C6
Ajac F **77** C5
Ajaccio F **102** B1
Ajain F **68** B1
Ajaureforsen S **115** B12
Ajdovščina SLO **72** C3
Ajka H **74** A2
Ajo E **89** A3
Ajofrin E **94** C3
Ajuda P **93** C3
Akanthou CY **120** A2
Akarca TR **118** D4
Akasztó H **75** B4
Akçakoca TR **118** A6
Akçaova TR **118** A4
Akçay TR **119** F4
Aken D **52** B2
Åkerby S **36** B4
Åkernes N **33** D4
Åkers styckebruk S **37** C4
Åkersberga S **37** C5
Åkervik N **115** B10
Akhisar TR **118** D2
Åkirkeby DK **41** D4
Akköy TR **119** E2
Akkrum NL **42** B2
Akören TR **119** E7
Åkra N **32** C3
Akranes IS **111** C3
Åkrehamn N **33** C2
Akrotiri CY **120** B1
Aksaray TR **16** B7
Akşehir TR **119** D6
Akseki TR **119** E6
Aksla N **32** A3
Aksu TR **119** F5
Aktsyabrski BY **7** E10
Akureyri IS **111** B7
Åkvåg N **33** D6
Akyazı TR **118** B5
Ål N **32** B5
Ala I **71** C6
Alà dei Sardi I **110** B2
Ala di Stura I **70** C2
Ala-Nampa FIN **113** F15
Alaca TR **16** A7
Alacaatlı TR **118** C3
Alaçam TR **16** A7
Alaçatı TR **119** D1
Alaejos E **88** C1
Alagna Valsésia I **70** C2
Alagón E **90** B1
Alaior E **97** B4
Alájar E **99** B4
Alakurtti RUS **3** C29
Alakylä FIN **113** E13
Alameda E **100** B1
Alameda de la Sagra E **94** B3
Alamedilla E **100** B2
Alamillo E **100** A1
Alaminos E **95** B4
Alanäs S **115** C12
Alandroal P **92** C3
Alange E **93** C4
Alanís E **99** A5
Alanno I **103** A6
Ålansbro S **115** E14
Alanya TR **119** F7
Alap H **74** B3
Alaquáso E **96** B2
Alar del Rey E **88** B2
Alaraz E **94** B1
Alarcón E **95** C4
Alaró E **97** B2
Alaşehir TR **119** D3
Alássio I **80** B2
Alatoz E **96** B1
Alatri I **103** B6
Alavus FIN **3** E25
Alba E **95** B5
Alba I **80** B2
Alba Adriática I **82** D2
Alba de Tormes E **94** B1
Alba de Yeltes E **93** A4
Alba-Iulia RO **11** C7
Albacete E **95** D5
Ålbæk DK **38** B3
Albaida E **96** C2
Albala del Caudillo E **93** B4
Albaladejo E **101** A3
Albalat E **96** B2
Albalate de Cinca E **90** B3
Albalate de las Nogueras E **95** B4
Albalate del Arzobispo E **90** B2
Albalete de Zorita E **95** B4
Alban F **77** C5
Albánchez E **101** B3
Albanchez de Ubeda E **100** B2
Albano Laziale I **102** B5
Albanyà E **91** A5
Albaredo d'Adige I **71** C6
Albares E **95** B3
Albarracín E **95** B5
Albatana E **101** A4
Albatarrec E **90** B3
Albatera E **101** A5
Albbruck D **61** C4
Albedin E **100** B1
Albelda de Iregua E **89** B4
Albenga I **80** B2
Albens F **69** C5
Ålberga, *Södermanland* S **37** C3
Ålberga, *Södermanland* S **37** D3
Albergaria-a-Nova P **87** D2
Albergaria-a-Velha P **92** A2
Albergaria dos Doze P **92** B2
Alberge P **92** C2
Alberic E **96** B2
Albernoa P **98** B3
Alberobello I **104** C3
Alberoni I **72** C2
Albersdorf D **43** A6
Albersloh D **50** B3
Albert F **48** C3
Albertirsa H **75** A4
Albertville F **69** C6
Alberuela de Tubo E **90** B2
Albi F **77** C5
Albidona I **106** B3
Albinia I **102** A4
Albino I **71** C4
Albinshof D **45** B5
Albires E **88** B1
Albisola Marina I **80** B2
Albocácer E **90** C3
Albolote E **100** B2
Albondón E **100** C2
Alborea E **96** B1
Ålborg DK **38** B2
Albox E **101** B3
Albrechtice nad Vitavou CZ **63** A5
Albstadt D **61** B5
Albufeira P **98** B2
Albuñol E **100** C2
Albuñuelas E **100** C2
Alburquerque E **93** B3
Alby, *Öland* S **41** C6
Alby, *Västernorrland* S **115** E12
Alcácer do Sal P **92** C2
Alcáçovas P **92** C2
Alcadozo E **101** A4
Alcafoces P **93** B3
Alcains P **92** B3
Alcalá de Guadaira E **99** B5
Alcalá de Gurrea E **90** A2
Alcalá de Henares E **95** B3
Alcalá de la Selva E **90** C2
Alcalá de los Gazules E **99** C5
Alcalá de Xivert E **90** C3
Alcalá del Júcar E **96** B1
Alcalá del Río E **99** B5
Alcalá del Valle E **99** C5
Alcalá la Real E **100** B2
Álcamo I **108** B1
Alcampell E **90** B3
Alcanadre E **89** B4
Alcanar E **90** C3
Alcanede P **92** B2
Alcanena P **92** B2
Alcañices E **87** C4
Alcántara E **93** B4
Alcantarilha P **98** B2
Alcantarilla E **101** B4
Alcañz E **90** B2
Alcara il Fusi I **109** A3
Alcaracejos E **100** A1
Alcaraz E **101** A3
Alcaria Ruiva P **98** B3
Alcarraz E **90** B3
Alcaudete E **100** B1
Alcaudete de la Jara E **94** C2
Alcázar de San Juan E **95** C3
Alcazarén E **88** C2
Alcester GB **29** A6
Alcoba E **94** C2
Alcobaça P **92** B2
Alcobendas E **94** B3
Alcocer E **95** B4
Alcochete P **92** C2
Alcoentre P **92** B2
Alcolea, *Almería* E **100** C3
Alcolea, *Córdoba* E **100** B1
Alcolea de Calatrava E **94** D2
Alcolea de Cinca E **90** B3
Alcolea de Tajo E **93** B5
Alcolea del Pinar E **95** A4
Alcolea del Rio E **99** B5
Alcollarin E **93** B5
Alconchel E **93** C3
Alconera E **93** C4
Alcontar E **101** B3
Alcora E **96** A2
Alcorcón E **94** B3
Alcorisa E **90** C2
Alcossebre E **96** A3
Alcoutim P **98** B3
Alcover E **91** B4
Alcoy E **96** C2
Alcsútdoboz H **74** A3
Alcubierre E **90** B2
Alcubilla de Avellaneda E **89** C3
Alcubilla de Nogales E **88** B1
Alcubillas E **100** A2
Alcublas E **96** B2
Alcúdia E **97** B3
Alcudia de Guadix E **100** B2
Alcuéscar E **93** B4
Aldbrough GB **27** B5
Aldea de Trujillo E **93** B5
Aldea del Cano E **93** B4
Aldea del Fresno E **94** B2
Aldea del Obispo E **87** D4
Aldea del Rey E **100** A2
Aldea Real E **94** A2
Aldeacentenera E **93** B5
Aldeadávila de la Ribera E **87** C4
Aldealcorvo E **94** A3
Aldealuenga de Santa Maria E **89** C3
Aldeamayor de San Martin E **88** C2
Aldeanueva de Barbarroya E **94** C1
Aldeanueva de San Bartolomé E **94** C1
Aldeanueva del Camino E **93** A5
Aldeanueva del Codonal E **94** A2
Aldeapozo E **89** C4
Aldeaquemada E **100** A2
Aldearrubia E **94** A1
Aldeaseca de la Frontera E **94** B1
Aldeasoña E **88** C2
Aldeatejada E **94** B1
Aldeavieja E **94** B2
Aldeburgh GB **30** B5
Aldehuela E **96** A1
Aldehuela de Calatañazor E **89** C4
Aldeia da Serra P **92** C3
Aldeia do Bispo P **93** A4
Aldeia do Mato P **92** B2
Aldeia Gavinha P **92** B1
Aldeire E **100** B2
Aldenhoven D **50** C2
Aldersbach D **62** B4
Aldershot GB **31** C3
Aldudes F **76** C1
Åled S **40** C2
Aledo E **101** B4
Alegria E **89** B4
Aleksa Šantić SCG **75** C4
Aleksandrovac, *Srbija* SCG **85** B6
Aleksandrovac, *Srbija* SCG **85** C6
Aleksandrów Kujawski PL **47** C4
Aleksandrów Łódźki PL **55** B4
Aleksin RUS **7** D14
Ålem S **40** C6
Alençon F **57** B6
Alenquer P **92** B1
Alenya F **91** A5
Aléria F **102** A2
Alès F **78** B3
Áles I **110** C1
Alessándria I **80** B2
Alessándria della Rocca I **108** B2
Alessano I **107** B5
Ålestrup DK **38** C2
Ålesund N **114** E3
Alet-les-Bains F **77** D5
Alexandria GB **24** C3
Alexandria GR **116** B4
Alexandria RO **11** E8
Alexandroupoli GR **116** B7
Aleyrac F **78** B3
Alézio I **107** A5
Alfacar E **100** B2
Alfaiates P **93** A4
Alfajarin E **90** B2
Alfambra E **90** C1
Alfambra P **98** B2
Alfândega da Fé P **87** C4
Alfarela de Jafes P **87** C3
Alfarelos P **92** A2
Alfarim P **92** C1
Alfarnate E **100** C1
Alfaro E **89** B5
Alfarrás E **90** B3
Alfaz del Pi E **96** C2
Alfedena I **103** B7
Alfeizarão P **92** B1
Alfeld, *Bayern* D **62** A2
Alfeld, *Niedersachsen* D **51** B5

Alfena P 87 C2
Alferce P 98 B2
Alfhausen D 43 C4
Alfonsine I 81 B6
Alford, *Aberdeenshire* GB 23 D6
Alford, *Lincolnshire* GB 27 B6
Alforja E 90 B3
Alfoz E 86 A3
Alfreton GB 27 B4
Alfta S 36 A3
Alfundão P 98 A2
Algaida E 97 B2
Algar E 99 C5
Älgarås S 35 D6
Ålgård N 33 D2
Algarinejo E 100 B1
Algarrobo E 100 C1
Algatocin E 99 C5
Algeciras E 99 C5
Algemesí E 96 B2
Algés P 92 C1
Algete E 95 B3
Alghero I 110 B1
Älghult S 40 B5
Alginet E 96 B2
Algodonales E 99 C5
Algodor E 94 C3
Algodor P 98 B3
Algora E 95 B4
Algoso P 87 C4
Algoz P 98 B2
Älgsjö S 115 C14
Alguaire E 90 B3
Alguazas E 101 A4
Algutsrum S 41 C6
Algyö H 75 B5
Alhama de Almería E 101 C3
Alhama de Aragón E 89 C5
Alhama de Granada E 100 C2
Alhama de Murcia E 101 B4
Alhambra E 100 A2
Alhandra P 92 C1
Alhaurin de la Torre E 100 C1
Alhaurín el Grande E 100 C1
Alhendin E 100 B2
Alhóndiga E 95 B4
Ali Terme I 109 A4
Alia E 93 B5
Ália I 108 B2
Aliaga E 90 C2
Aliağa TR 118 D1
Alibunar SCG 85 A5
Alicante E 96 C2
Alicún de Ortega E 100 B2
Alife I 103 B7
Alija del Infantado E 88 B1
Alijó P 87 C3
Alimena I 109 B3
Alingsås S 40 B2
Alinyà E 91 A4
Aliseda E 93 B4
Aliveri GR 116 D6
Alixan F 79 B4
Aljaraque E 99 B3
Aljezur P 98 B2
Aljorra E 101 B4
Aljubarrota P 92 B2
Aljucen E 93 B4
Aljustrel P 98 B2
Alken B 49 C6
Alkmaar NL 42 C1
Alkoven A 63 B5
Allaines F 58 B2
Allaire F 57 C3
Allanche F 68 C2
Alland A 64 B2
Allariz E 87 B3
Allassac F 67 C6
Allauch F 79 C4
Alleen N 33 D4
Allègre F 68 C3
Allemont F 69 C6
Allendale Town GB 25 D5
Allendorf D 51 C4
Allentsteig A 63 B6
Allepuz E 90 C2
Allersberg D 62 A2
Allershausen D 62 B2
Alles E 88 A2
Allevard F 69 C6
Allgunnen S 40 B5
Allihies IRL 20 C1
Allingåbro DK 38 C3
Allmannsdorf D 61 C5
Allo E 89 B4
Alloa GB 25 B4
Allogny F 68 A2
Ålloluokta S 112 E8
Allones, *Eure et Loire* F 58 B2
Allones, *Maine-et-Loire* F 67 A5
Allonnes F 57 C6
Allons F 76 B2
Allos F 79 B5
Allstedt D 52 B1
Alltwalis GB 28 B3
Allumiere I 102 A4
Almaceda P 92 B3
Almacelles E 90 B3
Almachar E 100 C1
Almada P 92 C1
Almadén E 100 A1
Almadén de la Plata E 99 B4
Almadenejos E 100 A1
Almadrones E 95 B4
Almagro E 100 A2
Almajano E 89 C4
Almansa E 96 C1
Almansil P 98 B2
Almanza E 88 B1
Almaraz E 93 B5
Almargen E 99 C5
Almarza E 89 C4
Almásfüzitő H 64 C4
Almassora E 96 B2
Almazán E 89 C4
Almazul E 89 C4
Alme D 51 B4
Almedina E 100 A3
Almedinilla E 100 B1
Almeida E 87 C4
Almeida P 93 A4
Almeirim P 92 B2
Almelo NL 42 C3
Almenar E 90 B3
Almenar de Soria E 89 C4
Almenara E 96 B2
Almendra P 87 D3
Almendral E 93 C4
Almendral de la Cañada E 94 B2
Almendralejo E 93 C4
Almenno San Bartolomeo I 71 C4
Almere NL 42 C2
Almería E 101 C3
Almerimar E 101 C3
Almese I 70 C2
Almexial P 98 B3
Älmhult S 40 C4
Almiropotamos GR 117 D6
Almiros GR 116 C4
Almodôvar P 98 B2
Almodóvar del Campo E 100 A1
Almodóvar del Pinar E 95 C5
Almodóvar del Río E 99 B5
Almofala P 87 D3
Almogia E 100 C1
Almoharin E 93 B4
Almonacid de la Sierra E 89 C5
Almonacid de Toledo E 94 C3
Almonaster la Real E 99 B4
Almondsbury GB 29 B5
Almonte E 99 B4
Almoradí E 101 A5
Almoraima E 99 C5
Almorox E 94 B2
Almoster P 92 B2
Almsele S 115 C14
Älmsta S 36 C5
Almudena E 101 A4
Almudévar E 90 A2
Almuñécar E 100 C2
Almunge S 36 C5
Almuradiel E 100 A2
Almussafes E 96 B2
Almvik S 40 B6
Alness GB 23 D4
Alnmouth GB 25 C6
Alnwick GB 25 C6
Åloppe S 36 C4
Álora E 100 C1
Alos d'Ensil E 91 A4
Alosno E 99 B3
Alozaina E 100 C1
Alpbach A 72 A1
Alpedrete de la Sierra E 95 B3
Alpedrinha P 92 A3
Alpen D 50 B2
Alpera E 96 C1
Alphen aan de Rijn NL 49 A5
Alpiarça P 92 B2
Alpignano I 70 C2
Alpirsbach D 61 B4
Alpu TR 118 C5
Alpuente E 96 B1
Alqueva P 98 A3
Alquézar E 90 A3
Als DK 38 C3
Alsasua E 89 B4
Alsdorf D 50 C2
Alselv DK 39 D1
Alsfeld D 51 C5
Alsike S 36 C4
Alskog S 37 E5
Alsleben D 52 B1
Alsónémedi H 75 A4
Alsótold H 65 C5
Alsóújlak H 74 A1
Alstad N 112 E4
Alstätte D 50 A2
Alsterbro S 40 C5
Alstermo S 40 C5
Alston GB 25 D5
Alsvåg N 112 D4
Alsvik N 112 E3
Alt Ruppin D 45 C4
Alta N 113 C12
Älta S 37 C5
Altamura I 104 C2
Altarejos E 95 C4
Altaussee A 63 C4
Altavilla Irpina I 103 B7
Altavilla Silentina I 103 C8
Altdöbern D 53 B4
Altdorf CH 70 B3
Altdorf D 62 B3
Altdorf bei Nürnberg D 62 A2
Alte P 98 B2
Altea E 96 C2
Altedo I 81 B5
Alten-weddingen D 52 A1
Altena D 50 B3
Altenau D 51 B6
Altenberg D 53 C3
Altenberge D 50 A3
Altenbruch D 43 B5
Altenburg D 52 C2
Altenfelden A 63 B4
Altengronau D 51 C5
Altenheim D 60 B3
Altenhundem D 50 B4
Altenkirchen, *Mecklenburg-Vorpommern* D 45 A5
Altenkirchen, *Radom* D 50 C3
Altenkunstadt D 52 C1
Altenmarkt A 63 C5
Altenmarkt D 62 B3
Altenmarkt im Pongall A 72 A3
Altensteig D 61 B4
Altentreptow D 45 B5
Altenwalde D 43 B5
Alter do Chão P 92 B3
Altfraunhofen D 62 B3
Altheim A 63 B4
Altheim D 61 A5
Althofen A 73 B4
Altinoluk TR 118 C1
Altinova TR 118 C1
Altıntaş TR 118 C5
Altınyaka TR 119 F5
Altınyayla TR 119 E4
Altkirch F 60 C3
Altlandsberg D 45 C5
Altlewin D 45 C6
Altmannstein D 62 B2
Altmorschen D 51 B5
Altmunster A 63 C4
Altnaharra GB 23 C4
Alto Campoó E 88 A2
Altofonte I 108 A2
Altomonte I 106 B3
Alton, *Hampshire* GB 31 C3
Alton, *Staffordshire* GB 27 C4
Altopáscio I 81 C4
Altötting D 62 B3
Altreichenau D 63 B4
Altshausen D 61 C5
Altstätten CH 71 A4
Altura E 96 B2
Altusried D 61 C6
Alüksne LV 7 C9
Alunda S 36 B5
Alustante E 95 B5
Alva GB 25 B4
Alvaiázere P 92 B2
Alvalade P 98 B2
Älvängen S 38 B5
Alvarenga P 87 D2
Alvares P 92 A2
Alvdal N 114 E7
Älvdalen S 34 A6
Alverca P 92 C1
Alversund N 32 B2
Alvesta S 40 C4
Alvignac F 77 B4
Alvignano I 103 B7
Ålvik N 32 B3
Alvik S 36 B1
Alvimare F 58 A1
Alviobeira P 92 B2
Alvito P 98 A3
Älvkarleby S 36 B4
Älvkarleö bruk S 36 B4
Alvor P 98 B2
Alvorge P 92 B2
Alvøy N 32 B2
Älvros S 115 E11
Alvsbacka S 35 C5
Älvsbyn S 3 D24
Älvsered S 40 B2
Alwernia PL 55 C4
Alwinton GB 25 C5
Alyth GB 25 B4
Alytus LT 6 D8
Alzénau D 51 C5
Alzey D 61 A4
Alzira E 96 B2
Alzonne F 77 C5
Amadora P 92 C1
Åmål S 35 C4
Amalfi I 103 C7
Amaliada GR 117 E3
Amance F 60 C2
Amancey F 69 A6
Amándola I 82 D2
Amantea I 106 B3
Amarante P 87 C2
Amareleja P 98 A3
Amares P 87 C2
Amaseno I 103 B6
Amasra TR 118 A7
Amasya TR 16 A8
Amatrice I 103 A6
Amay B 49 C6
Ambarnyy RUS 3 D30
Ambazac F 67 C6
Ambelonas GR 116 C4
Amberg D 62 A2
Ambérieu-en-Bugey F 69 C5
Ambérieux-en-Dombes F 69 B4
Ambert F 68 C3
Ambés F 76 A2
Ambjörby S 34 B5
Ambjörnarp S 40 B3
Amble GB 25 C6
Ambleside GB 26 A3
Ambleteuse F 48 C2
Amboise F 67 A5
Ambrières-les-Vallées F 57 B5
Amden CH 71 A4
Amel B 50 C2
Amélia I 102 A5
Amélie-les-Bains-Palalda F 91 A5
Amelinghausen D 44 B2
Amendoa P 92 B2
Amendoeira P 98 B3
Améndola I 104 B1
Amendolara I 106 B3
Amer E 91 A5
Amerongen NL 49 A6
Amersfoort NL 49 A6
Amersham GB 31 C3
Ames E 86 B2
Amesbury GB 29 B6
Amfiklia GR 116 D4
Amfilochia GR 116 D3
Amfipoli GR 116 B5
Amfissa GR 116 D4
Amieira, *Évora* P 98 A3
Amieira, *Portalegre* P 92 B3
Amieiro P 92 A2
Amiens F 58 A3
Amindeo GR 116 B3
Åminne S 40 B3
Åmli N 33 D5
Amlwch GB 26 B1
Ammanford GB 28 B4
Ammarnäs S 115 B13
Åmmeberg S 37 D1
Ammerbach D 61 A5
Amorebieta E 89 A4
Amorgos GR 117 F7
Amorosa P 87 C2
Amorosi I 103 B7
Åmot, *Buskerud* N 34 C1
Åmot, *Telemark* N 33 C4
Åmot S 36 B3
Åmotfors S 34 C4
Åmotsdal N 33 C5
Amou F 76 C2
Ampezzo I 72 B2
Ampfing D 62 B3
Ampflwang A 63 B4
Amplepuis F 69 C4
Amposta E 90 C3
Ampthill GB 30 B3
Ampudia E 88 C2
Ampuero E 89 A3
Amriswil CH 71 A4
Åmsele S 115 C16
Amstelveen NL 49 A5
Amsterdam NL 42 C1
Amstetten A 63 B5
Amtzell D 61 C5
Amulree GB 25 B4
Amurrio E 89 A4
Amusco E 88 B2
An t-Ob GB 22 D1
Åna-Sira N 33 D3
Anacapri I 103 C7
Anadia P 92 A2
Anadon E 90 C1
Anafi GR 117 F7
Anagni I 102 B6
Anamur TR 16 C6
Ananyiv UA 11 C10
Anascaul IRL 20 B1
Ånäset S 3 D24
Anastaźewo PL 47 C4
Anaya de Alba E 94 B1
Ança P 92 A2
Ancaster GB 27 C5
Ancede P 87 C2
Ancenis F 66 A3
Ancerville F 59 B6
Anchuras E 94 C2
Ancona I 82 C2
Ancora P 87 C2
Ancrum GB 25 C5
Ancy-le-Franc F 59 C5
Andalo I 71 B5
Åndalsnes N 114 E4
Andance F 69 C4
Andau A 64 C3
Andebu N 35 C2
Andeer CH 71 B4
Andelfingen CH 61 C4
Andelot F 59 B6
Andelot-en-Montagne F 69 B5
Andenes N 112 C5
Andenne B 49 C6
Anderlues B 49 C5
Andermatt CH 70 B3
Andernach D 50 C3
Andernos-les-Bains F 76 B1
Anderslöv S 41 D3
Anderstorp S 40 B3
Andijk NL 42 C2
Andoain E 89 A4
Andocs H 74 B2
Andolsheim F 60 B3
Andorra E 90 C2
Andorra La Vella AND 91 A4
Andosilla E 89 B5
Andover GB 31 C2
Andratx E 97 B2
Andreapol RUS 7 C12
Andreas GB 26 A1
Andréspol PL 55 B4
Andrest F 76 C3
Andretta I 103 C8
Andrezieux-Bouthéon F 69 C4
Ándria I 104 B2
Andrijevica SCG 85 D4
Andritsena GR 117 E3
Andros GR 117 E6
Andrychów PL 65 A5
Andselv N 112 C7
Andújar E 100 A1
Anduze F 78 B2
Åneby N 34 B2
Aneby S 40 B4
Añes E 89 A3
Anet F 58 B2
Anfo I 71 C5
Ang S 40 B4
Anga S 37 E5
Angaïs F 76 C2
Änge, *Jämtland* S 115 D11
Ånge, *Västernorrland* S 115 E12
Angeja P 92 A2
Ängelholm S 41 C2
Angeli FIN 113 D14
Ängelsberg S 36 C3
Anger A 73 A5
Angera I 70 C3
Angermünde D 45 B6
Angern A 64 B2
Angers F 67 A4
Angerville F 58 B3
Anghiari I 82 C1
Angle GB 28 B2
Anglès E 91 B5
Anglés, *Tarn* F 77 C5
Angles, *Vendée* F 66 B3
Angles sur l'Anglin F 67 B5
Anglesola E 91 B4
Anglet F 76 C1
Anglisidhes CY 120 B2
Anglure F 59 B4
Angoulême F 67 C5
Angoulins F 66 B3
Angsö S 37 C3
Angueira P 87 C4
Angües E 90 A2
Anguiano E 89 B4
Anguillara Sabazia I 102 A5
Anguillara Véneta I 72 C1
Anhée B 49 C5
Anholt DK 38 C4
Aniane F 78 C2
Aniche F 49 C4
Ånimskog S 35 D4
Anina RO 10 D6
Anixi GR 116 C3
Anizy-le-Château F 59 A4
Anjalankoski FIN 3 F27
Anjan S 115 D9
Ankara TR 118 C7
Ankaran SLO 72 C3
Ankarsrum S 40 B6
Ankerlia N 112 C9
Anklam D 45 B5
Ankum D 43 C4
Anlauftal A 72 A3
Anlezy F 68 B3
Ann S 115 D9
Annaberg A 63 C6
Annaberg-Buchholz D 52 C3
Annaberg im Lammertal A 72 A3
Annaburg D 52 B3
Annahütte D 53 B3
Annalong GB 19 B6
Annan GB 25 D4
Anndalsvågen N 115 B9
Anneberg, *Halland* S 38 B5
Anneberg, *Jönköping* S 40 B4
Annecy F 69 C6
Annelund S 40 B3
Annemasse F 69 B6
Annenskiy Most RUS 7 A14
Annerstad S 40 C3
Annestown IRL 21 B4
Annevoie-Rouillon B 49 C5
Annonay F 69 C4
Annot F 79 C5
Annweiler D 60 A3
Ano Poroia GR 116 A5
Ano Siros GR 117 E6
Añora E 100 A1
Anould F 60 B2
Anquela del Ducado E 95 B4
Anröchte D 51 B4
Ans DK 39 C2
Ansager DK 39 D1
Ansbach D 62 A1
Anse F 69 C4
Anserœul B 49 C4
Ansfelden A 63 B5
Ansião P 92 B2
Ansó E 76 D2
Ansoain E 76 D1
Anstruther GB 25 B5
Antalya TR 119 F5
Antas E 101 B4
Antegnate I 71 C4
Antequera E 100 B1
Anterselva di Mezzo I 72 B2
Antibes F 79 C6
Antigüedad E 88 C2
Antillo I 109 B4
Antirio GR 117 D3
Antoing B 49 C4
Antonin PL 54 B2
Antrain F 57 B4
Antrim GB 19 B5
Antrodoco I 102 A6
Antronapiana I 70 B3
Anttis S 113 E11
Antuzede P 92 A2
Antwerp = Antwerpen B 49 B5
Antwerpen = Antwerp B 49 B5
Anversa d'Abruzzi I 103 B6
Anvin F 48 C3
Anzat-le-Luguet F 68 C3
Anzi I 104 C1
Ánzio I 102 B5
Anzola d'Emilia I 81 B5
Anzón E 89 C5
Aoiz E 76 D1
Aosta I 70 C2
Apalhão P 92 B3
Apátfalva H 75 B5
Apatin SCG 75 C4
Apatity RUS 3 C30
Apc H 65 C5
Apécchio I 82 C1
Apeldoorn NL 50 A1
Apen D 43 B4
Apenburg D 44 C3
Apensen D 43 B6
Apiro I 82 C2
Apliki CY 120 B2
Apolda D 52 B1
Apolonia GR 117 F6
Apostag H 75 B3
Äppelbo S 34 B6
Appennino I 82 D2
Appenzell CH 71 A4
Appiano I 71 B6
Appingedam NL 42 B3
Appleby-in-Westmorland GB 26 A3
Applecross GB 22 D3
Appledore GB 28 B3
Appoigny F 59 C4
Apremont-la-Forêt F 60 B1
Aprica I 71 B5
Apricena I 103 B8
Aprigliano I 106 B3
Aprilia I 102 B5
Apt F 79 C4
Apúlia P 87 C2
Aquiléia I 72 C3
Aquilónia I 103 C8
Aquino I 103 B6
Ar S 37 E5
Arabayona E 94 A1
Arabba I 72 B1
Araç TR 16 A6
Aracena E 99 B4
Arachova GR 116 D4
Arad RO 75 B6
Aradac SCG 75 C5
Aradhippou CY 120 B2
Aragnouet F 76 D3
Aragona I 108 B2
Aramits F 76 C2
Aramon F 78 C3
Aranda de Duero E 88 C3
Aranda de Moncayo E 89 C5
Arandjelovac SCG 85 B5
Aranjuez E 95 B3
Arantzazu E 89 B4
Aranzueque E 95 B3
Aras de Alpuente E 96 B1
Arauzo de Miel E 89 C3
Arazede P 92 A2
Arbas F 77 D3
Árbatax I 110 C2
Arbeca E 90 B3
Arberg D 62 A1
Arbesbach A 63 B5
Arboga S 37 C2
Arbois F 69 B5
Arbon CH 71 A4
Arboréa I 110 C1
Arbório I 70 C3
Årbostad N 112 D6
Arbrå S 36 A3
Arbroath GB 25 B5
Arbùcies E 91 B5
Arbuniel E 100 B2
Arbus I 110 C1
Arc-en-Barrois F 59 C5
Arc-et-Senans F 69 A5
Arc-lès-Gray F 69 A5
Arc-sur-Tille F 69 A5
Arcachon F 76 B1
Arce I 103 B6
Arcen NL 50 B2
Arces-Dilo F 59 B4
Arcévia I 82 C1
Arcey F 70 A1
Archanes GR 117 G7
Archangelos GR 119 F3
Archena E 101 A4
Archez E 100 C2
Archiac F 67 C4
Archidona E 100 B1
Archiestown GB 23 D5
Archivel E 101 A4
Arcidosso I 81 D5
Arcille I 81 D5
Arcis-sur-Aube F 59 B5
Arco I 71 C5
Arcones E 94 A3
Arcos E 88 B3
Arcos de Jalón E 95 A4
Arcos de la Frontera E 99 C5
Arcos de la Sierra E 95 B4
Arcos de las Salinas E 96 B1
Arcos de Valdevez P 87 C2
Arcozelo P 92 A3
Arcusa E 90 A3
Arcy-sur-Cure F 59 C4
Ardagh IRL 20 B2
Årdal N 33 C3
Ardala S 35 D5
Ardales E 100 C1
Årdalstangen N 32 A4
Ardara I 110 B1
Ardara IRL 18 B3
Ardarroch GB 22 D3
Ardbeg GB 24 C1
Ardcharnich GB 22 D3
Ardchyle GB 24 B3
Ardee IRL 19 C5
Arden DK 38 C2
Ardentes F 68 B1
Ardenza I 81 C4
Ardersier GB 23 D4
Ardes F 68 C3
Ardessie GB 22 D3
Ardez CH 71 B5
Ardfert IRL 20 B2
Ardgay GB 23 D4
Ardglass GB 19 B6
Ardgroom IRL 20 C2
Ardhasig GB 22 D2
Ardino BG 116 A7
Ardisa E 90 A2
Ardkearagh IRL 20 C1
Ardlui GB 24 B3
Ardlussa GB 24 B2
Ardón E 88 B1
Ardooie B 49 C4
Ardore I 106 C3
Ardre S 37 E5
Ardres F 48 C2
Ardrishaig GB 24 B2
Ardrossan GB 24 C3
Are N 33 C2
Åre S 115 D10
Areia Branca P 92 B1
Aremark N 35 C3
Arenales de San Gregorio E 95 C3
Arenas E 100 C1
Arenas de Iguña E 88 A2
Arenas de San Juan E 95 C3
Arenas de San Pedro E 94 B1
Arenas del Rey E 100 C2
Arendal N 33 D5
Arendonk B 49 B6
Arengosse F 76 B2
Arentorp S 35 D4
Arenys de Mar E 91 B5
Arenys de Munt E 91 B5
Arenzano I 80 B2
Areo E 91 A4
Areopoli GR 117 F4
Ares E 86 A2
Arès F 76 B1
Ares del Maestrat E 90 C2
Aresvika N 114 D5
Arette F 76 C2
Aretxabaleta E 89 A4
Arevalillo E 93 A5
Arévalo E 94 A2
Arez P 92 B3
Arezzo I 81 C5
Arfeuilles F 68 B3
Argalasti GR 116 C5
Argallón E 99 A5
Argamasilla de Alba E 95 C3
Argamasilla de Calatrava E 100 A1
Arganda E 95 B3
Arganil P 92 A2
Argasion GR 117 E2
Argegno I 71 C4
Argelès-Gazost F 76 C2
Argelès-sur-Mer F 91 A6
Argent-sur-Sauldre F 68 A2
Argenta I 81 B5
Argentan F 57 B5
Argentat F 77 A4
Argentera I 79 B5
Argenteuil F 58 B3
Argenthal D 50 D3
Argentiera I 110 B1
Argenton-Château F 67 B4
Argenton-sur-Creuse F 67 B6
Argentona E 91 B5
Argentré F 57 B5
Argentré-du-Plessis F 57 B4
Argirades GR 116 C1
Argıthanı TR 119 D6
Argos GR 117 E4
Argos Orestiko GR 116 B3
Argostoli GR 117 D2
Argote E 89 B4
Arguedas E 89 B5
Argueil F 58 A2
Arholma S 36 C6
Århus DK 39 C3
Ariano Irpino I 103 B8
Ariano nel Polésine I 82 B1
Aribe E 76 D1
Aridea GR 116 B4
Arienzo I 103 B7
Arild S 41 C2
Arileod GB 24 B1
Arilje SCG 85 C5
Arinagour GB 24 B1
Ariño E 90 B2
Arinthod F 69 B5
Arisaig GB 24 B2
Arisgotas E 94 C3
Aritzo I 110 C2
Ariza E 89 C4
Årjäng S 35 C4
Arjeplog S 115 A14
Arjona E 100 B1
Arjonilla E 100 B1
Arkasa GR 119 G2
Arkelstorp S 41 C4
Arklow IRL 21 B5
Arkösund S 37 D3
Ärla S 37 C3
Arlanc F 68 C3
Arlanzón E 89 B3
Arlebosc F 78 A3
Arlena di Castro I 102 A4
Arles F 78 C3
Arles-sur-Tech F 91 A5
Arló H 65 B6
Arlon B 60 A1
Armação de Pera P 98 B2
Armadale, *Highland* GB 22 D3
Armadale, *West Lothian* GB 25 C4
Armagh GB 19 B5
Armamar P 87 C3
Armenistis GR 117 E8
Armeno I 70 C3
Armenteros E 93 A5
Armentières F 48 C3
Armilla E 100 B2
Armiñón E 89 B4
Armoy GB 19 A5
Armuña de Tajuña E 95 B3
Armutlu, *Bursa* TR 118 B3
Armutlu, *İzmır* TR 119 D2
Arnac-Pompadour F 67 C6
Arnafjord N 32 A3
Arnage F 57 C6
Arnas F 69 B4
Ärnäs S 35 D5
Arnay-le-Duc F 69 A4
Arnborg DK 39 C2
Arnbruck D 62 A3
Arnea GR 116 B5
Arneberg, *Hedmark* N 34 A2
Arneberg, *Hedmark* N 34 B4
Arneburg D 44 C4
Arnedillo E 89 B4
Arnedo E 89 B4
Arneguy F 76 C1
Arnés E 90 C3
Árnes IS 111 A4
Årnes, *Akershus* N 34 B3
Årnes, *Troms* N 112 C7
Arnfels A 73 B5
Arnhem NL 50 B1
Arnissa GR 116 B3
Arno S 37 D4
Arnold GB 27 B4
Arnoldstein A 72 B3
Arnsberg D 50 B4
Arnschwang D 62 A3
Arnsdorf D 53 B3
Årnset N 114 D6
Arnside GB 26 A3
Arnstadt D 51 C6
Arnstein D 51 D5
Arnstorf D 62 B3
Arnum DK 39 D1
Aroche E 99 B4
Arolla CH 70 B2
Arolsen D 51 B5
Arona I 70 C3
Åros N 35 C2
Arosa CH 71 B4
Arosa P 87 C2
Årøsund DK 39 D2
Arouca P 87 D2
Årøysund N 35 C2
Arpajon F 58 B3
Arpajon-sur-Cère F 77 B5
Arpino I 103 B6
Arquata del Tronto I 82 D2
Arques F 48 C3
Arques-la-Bataille F 58 A2
Arquillos E 100 A2
Arraia-Maeztu E 89 B4
Arraiolos P 92 C2
Arrancourt F 60 B2
Arras F 48 C3
Arrasate E 89 A4
Årre DK 39 D1
Arreau F 77 D3
Arredondo E 89 A3
Arrens-Marsous F 76 D2
Arriate E 99 C5
Arrifana P 98 B2
Arrigorriaga E 89 A4
Arriondas E 88 A1
Arroba de los Montes E 94 C2
Arrochar GB 24 B3
Arromanches-les-Bains F 57 A5
Arronches P 92 B3
Arroniz E 89 B4
Arrou F 58 B2
Arroya E 88 B2

Balugães P 87 C2
Balve D 50 B3
Balvi LV 7 C9
Balvicar GB 24 B2
Balya TR 118 C2
Balzo I 82 D2
Bamberg D 62 A1
Bamburgh GB 25 C6
Banatska Palanka SCG 85 B6
Banatski Brestovac SCG 85 B5
Banatski Despotovac SCG 75 C5
Banatski Dvor SCG 75 C5
Banatski-Karlovac SCG 85 A6
Banatsko Arandjelovo SCG 75 B5
Banatsko-Novo Selo SCG 85 B5
Banaz TR 118 D4
Banbridge GB 19 B5
Banbury GB 30 B2
Banchory GB 23 D6
Bande B 49 C6
Bande E 87 B3
Bandholm DK 39 E4
Bandırma TR 118 B2
Bandol F 79 C4
Bandon IRL 20 C3
Bañeres E 96 C2
Banff GB 23 D6
Bangor F 66 A1
Bangor, *Down* GB 19 B6
Bangor, *Gwynedd* GB 26 B1
Bangor IRL 18 B2
Bangsund N 114 C8
Banie PL 45 B6
Banja SCG 85 C4
Banja Koviljača SCG 85 B4
Banja Luka BIH 84 B2
Banja Vručica BIH 84 B2
Banjaloka SLO 73 C4
Banjani SCG 85 B4
Banje SCG 85 D5
Banjska SCG 85 D5
Banka SK 64 B3
Bankekind S 37 D2
Bankend GB 25 C4
Bankeryd S 40 B4
Bankfoot GB 25 B4
Banloc RO 75 C6
Bannalec F 56 C2
Bannes F 59 B4
Bannockburn GB 25 B4
Bañobárez E 87 D4
Bañon E 90 C1
Banon F 79 B4
Baños E 93 A5
Baños de Gigonza E 99 C5
Baños de la Encina E 100 A2
Baños de Molgas E 87 B3
Baños de Rio Tobia E 89 B4
Baños de Valdearados E 89 C3
Bánov CZ 64 B3
Banova Jaruga HR 74 C1
Bánovce nad Bebravou SK 64 B4
Banovići BIH 84 B3
Banoviči Selo BIH 84 B3
Bánréve H 65 B6
Bansin D 45 B6
Banská Belá SK 65 B4
Banská Bystrica SK 65 B5
Banská Štiavnica SK 65 B4
Banstead GB 31 C3
Banteer IRL 20 B3
Bantheville F 59 A6
Bantry IRL 20 C2
Bantzenheim F 60 C3
Banyalbufar E 97 B2
Banyoles E 91 A5
Banyuls-sur-Mer F 91 A6
Bapaume F 48 C3
Bar SCG 105 A5
Bar UA 11 B9
Bar-le-Duc F 59 B6
Bar-sur-Aube F 59 B5
Bar-sur-Seine F 59 B5
Barabhas GB 22 C2
Barači BIH 84 B1
Baracs H 74 B3
Baracska H 74 A3
Barahona E 89 C4
Barajes de Melo E 95 B4
Barakaldo E 89 A4
Baralla E 86 B3
Barañain E 76 D1
Baranavichy BY 7 E9
Báránd H 75 A6
Baranda SCG 85 A5
Baranello I 103 B7
Baranów Sandomierski PL 55 C6
Baraqueville F 77 B5
Barasoain E 89 B5
Barbacena P 92 C3
Barbadás E 87 B3
Barbadillo E 94 B1
Barbadillo de Herreros E 89 B3
Barbadillo del Mercado E 89 B3
Barbadillo del Pez E 89 B3
Barban HR 82 A3
Barbarano Vicento I 71 C6
Barbariga HR 82 B2
Barbaros TR 118 B2
Barbastro E 90 A3
Barbate de Franco E 99 C5
Barbatona E 95 A4
Barbâtre F 66 B2
Barbazan F 77 C3
Barbeitos E 86 A3
Barbentane F 78 C3
Barberino di Mugello I 81 B5
Barbezieux-St. Hilaire F 67 C4
Barbonne-Fayel F 59 B4
Barbotan-les-Thermes F 76 C2
Barby D 52 B1
Barca de Alva P 87 C4
Bárcabo E 90 A3
Barcarrota E 93 C4
Barcellona-Pozzo di Gotto I 109 A4
Barcelona E 91 B5
Barcelonette F 79 B5
Barcelos P 87 C2
Barcena de Pie de Concha E 88 A2
Bárcena del Monasterio E 86 A4
Barchfeld D 51 C6
Barcin PL 46 C3
Barcino PL 46 A2
Bárcis I 72 B2
Barco P 92 A3
Barcones E 89 C4
Barcs H 74 C2
Barcus F 76 C2
Barczewo PL 47 B6
Bardejov SK 10 B6
Bårdesø DK 39 D3
Bardi I 81 B3
Bardney GB 27 B5
Bardo PL 54 C1
Bardolino I 71 C5
Bardonécchia I 79 A5
Bardoňovo SK 65 B4
Barèges F 76 D3
Barenstein D 52 C3
Barentin F 58 A1
Barenton F 57 B5
Barevo BIH 84 B2
Barfleur F 57 A4
Barga I 81 B4
Bargas E 94 C2
Barge I 79 B6
Bargemon F 79 C5
Barghe I 71 C5
Bargoed GB 29 B4
Bargrennan GB 24 C3
Bargteheide D 44 B2
Barham GB 31 C5
Bari I 104 B2
Bari Sardo I 110 C2
Barič Draga HR 83 B4
Barilović HR 73 C5
Barisciano I 103 A6
Barjac F 78 B3
Barjols F 79 C4
Barjon F 59 C5
Bårkåker N 35 C2
Barkald N 114 F7
Barkowo, *Dolnośląskie* PL 54 B1
Barkowo, *Pomorskie* PL 46 B3
Bârlad RO 11 C9
Barles F 79 B5
Barletta I 104 B2
Barlinek PL 45 C7
Barmouth GB 26 C1
Barmstedt D 43 B6
Barnard Castle GB 27 A4
Barnarp S 40 B4
Bärnau D 62 A3
Bärnbach A 73 A5
Barneberg D 52 A1
Barnenitz D 45 C4
Barnet GB 31 C3
Barnetby le Wold GB 27 B5
Barneveld NL 49 A6
Barneville-Carteret F 57 A4
Barnoldswick GB 26 B3
Barnowko PL 45 C6
Barnsley GB 27 B4
Barnstädt D 52 B1
Barnstaple GB 28 B3
Barnstorf D 43 C5
Barntrup D 51 B5
Baron F 58 A3
Baronissi I 103 C7
Barqueiro P 92 B2
Barquinha P 92 B2
Barr F 60 B3
Barr GB 24 C3
Barra P 92 A2
Barracas E 96 A2
Barraco E 94 B2
Barrado E 93 A5
Barrafranca I 109 B3
Barranco do Velho P 98 B3
Barrancos P 99 A4
Barrax E 95 C4
Barrbaar D 62 B1
Barre-des-Cevennes F 78 B2
Barreiro P 92 C1
Barreiros E 86 A3
Barrême F 79 C5
Barret-le-Bas F 79 B4
Barrhead GB 24 C3
Barrhill GB 24 C3
Barrio de Nuesra Señora E 88 B1
Barrow-in-Furness GB 26 A2
Barrow upon Humber GB 27 B5
Barrowford GB 26 B3
Barruecopardo E 87 C4
Barruelo de Santullán E 88 B2
Barruera E 90 A3
Barry GB 29 B4
Bårse DK 39 D4
Barsinghausen D 51 A5
Barssel D 43 B4
Barth D 45 A4
Bartholomä D 61 B5
Bartin TR 118 A7
Barton upon Humber GB 27 B5
Bartoszyce PL 47 A6
Barúmini I 110 C1
Baruth D 52 A3
Barvaux B 49 C6
Barver D 43 C5
Barwałd PL 65 A5
Barwice PL 46 B2
Barysaw BY 7 D10
Barzana E 88 A1
Bârzava RO 10 C6
Bárzio I 71 C4
Bas E 91 A5
Bašaid SCG 75 C5
Basaluzzo I 80 B2
Basarabeasca MD 11 C10
Basauri E 89 A4
Baschi I 82 D1
Baschurch GB 26 C3
Basconcillos del Tozo E 88 B3
Bascones de Ojeda E 88 B2
Basécles B 49 C4
Basel CH 70 A2
Basélice I 103 B7
Basildon GB 31 C4
Basingstoke GB 31 C2
Baška CZ 65 A4
Baška HR 83 B3
Baška Voda HR 84 C1
Bäsksjö S 115 C14
Baslow GB 27 B4
Başmakçı TR 119 E5
Basovizza I 72 C3
Bassacutena I 110 A2
Bassano del Grappa I 72 C1
Bassano Romano I 102 A5
Bassecourt CH 70 A2
Bassella E 91 A4
Bassevuovdde N 113 D14
Bassou F 59 C4
Bassoues F 76 C3
Bassum D 43 C5
Båstad S 40 C2
Bastardo I 82 D1
Bastelica F 102 A2
Bastelicaccia F 102 B1
Bastia F 102 A2
Bastia I 82 C1
Bastogne B 50 C1
Baston GB 30 B3
Bastuträsk S 115 C17
Bata H 74 B3
Batajnica SCG 85 B5
Batalha P 92 B2
Bátaszék H 74 B3
Batea E 90 B3
Batelov CZ 63 A6
Bath GB 29 B5
Bathgate GB 25 C4
Batida H 75 B5
Batignano I 81 D5
Batina HR 74 C3
Bátka SK 65 B6
Batković BIH 85 B4
Batlava SCG 85 D6
Batley GB 27 B4
Batnfjordsøra N 114 E4
Batočina SCG 85 B6
Bátonyterenye H 65 C5
Batrina HR 74 C2
Båtsfjord N 113 B18
Battaglia Terme I 72 C1
Bätterkinden CH 70 A2
Battice B 50 C1
Battipáglia I 103 C7
Battle GB 31 D4
Battonya H 75 B6
Batuša SCG 85 B6
Bátya H 75 B3
Bau I 110 C1
Baud F 56 C2
Baudour B 49 C4
Baugé F 67 A4
Baugy F 68 A2
Bauma CH 70 A3
Baume-les-Dames F 69 A6
Baumholder D 60 A3
Baunatal D 51 B5
Baunei I 110 B2
Bauska LV 6 C8
Bautzen D 53 B4
Bavanište SCG 85 B5
Bavay F 49 C4
Bavilliers F 60 C2
Bavorov CZ 63 A5
Bawdsey GB 31 B5
Bawinkel D 43 C4
Bawtry GB 27 B4
Bayat TR 118 D5
Bayel F 59 B5
Bayeux F 57 A5
Bayındır TR 119 D2
Bayon F 60 B2
Bayonne F 76 C1
Bayons F 79 B5
Bayramiç TR 118 C1
Bayreuth D 52 D1
Bayrischzell D 62 C3
Baza E 101 B3
Bazas F 76 B2
Baziege F 77 C4
Bazoches-les-Gallerandes F 58 B3
Bazoches-sur-Hoëne F 58 B1
Bazzano I 81 B5
Beaconsfield GB 31 C3
Beade E 87 B2
Beadnell GB 25 C6
Beaminster GB 29 C5
Bearsden GB 24 C3
Beas E 99 B4
Beas de Segura E 100 A3
Beasain E 89 A4
Beattock GB 25 C4
Beaubery F 69 B4
Beaucaire F 78 C3
Beaufort F 69 C6
Beaufort IRL 20 B2
Beaufort-en Vallée F 67 A4
Beaugency F 58 C2
Beaujeu, *Alpes-de-Haute-Provence* F 79 B5
Beaujeu, *Rhône* F 69 B4
Beaulac F 76 B2
Beaulieu F 68 A2
Beaulieu GB 31 D2
Beaulieu-sous-la-Roche F 66 B3
Beaulieu-sur-Dordogne F 77 B4
Beaulieu-sur-Mer F 80 C1
Beaulon F 68 B3
Beauly GB 23 D4
Beaumaris GB 26 B1
Beaumesnil F 58 A1
Beaumetz-lès-Loges F 48 C3
Beaumont B 49 C5
Beaumont F 77 B3
Beaumont-de-Lomagne F 77 C3
Beaumont-du-Gâtinais F 58 B3
Beaumont-en-Argonne F 59 A6
Beaumont-Hague F 57 A4
Beaumont-la-Ronce F 58 C1
Beaumont-le-Roger F 58 A1
Beaumont-sur-Oise F 58 A3
Beaumont-sur-Sarthe F 57 B6
Beaune F 69 A4
Beaune-la-Rolande F 58 B3
Beaupréau F 66 A4
Beauraing B 49 C5
Beaurepaire F 69 C5
Beaurepaire-en-Bresse F 69 B5
Beaurières F 79 B4
Beauvais F 58 A3
Beauval F 48 C3
Beauville F 77 B3
Beauvoir-sur-Mer F 66 B2
Beauvoir-sur-Niort F 67 B4
Beba Veche RO 75 B5
Bebertal D 52 A1
Bebington GB 26 B2
Bebra D 51 C5
Bebrina HR 84 A2
Beccles GB 30 B5
Becedas E 93 A5
Beceite E 90 C3
Bečej SCG 75 C5
Becerreá E 86 B3
Becerril de Campos E 88 B2
Bécherel F 57 B4
Bechhofen D 61 A6
Bechyně CZ 63 A5
Bečići SCG 105 A4
Becilla de Valderaduey E 88 B1
Beckfoot GB 25 D4
Beckingham GB 27 B5
Beckum D 50 B4
Beco P 92 B2
Bécon-les-Granits F 66 A4
Bečov nad Teplou CZ 52 C2
Becsehely H 74 B1
Bedale GB 27 A4
Bedames E 89 A3
Bédar E 101 B4
Bédarieux F 78 C2
Bédarrides F 78 B3
Bedburg D 50 C2
Beddgelert GB 26 B1
Beddingestrand S 41 D3
Bédée F 57 B4
Bedegkér H 74 B3
Beden TR 119 F7
Bedford GB 30 B3
Będków PL 55 B4
Bedlington GB 25 C6
Bedlno PL 55 A4
Bedmar E 100 B2
Bédoin F 79 B4
Bedónia I 80 B3
Bedretto CH 70 B3
Bedsted DK 38 C1
Bedum NL 42 B3
Bedwas GB 29 B4
Bedworth GB 30 B2
Będzin PL 55 C4
Beek en Donk NL 49 B6
Beekbergen NL 50 A1
Beelen D 50 B4
Beelitz D 52 A2
Beer GB 29 C4
Beerfelde D 45 C6
Beerfelden D 61 A4
Beernem B 49 B4
Beeskow D 53 A4
Beetsterzwaag NL 42 B3
Beetzendorf D 44 C3
Beflelay CH 70 A2
Begaljica SCG 85 B5
Bégard F 56 B2
Begejci SCG 75 C5
Begijar E 100 B2
Begijnendijk B 49 B5
Begndal N 34 B1
Begues E 91 B4
Beguildy GB 26 C2
Begur E 91 B6
Beho B 50 C1
Behringen D 51 B6
Beilen NL 42 C3
Beilngries D 62 A2
Beine-Nauroy F 59 A5
Beinwil CH 70 A3
Beiseförth D 51 B5
Beith GB 24 C3
Beitostølen N 32 A5
Beiuş RO 11 C7
Beja P 98 A3
Béjar E 93 A5
Bekçiler TR 119 F4
Békés H 75 B6
Békéscsaba H 75 B6
Bekilli TR 119 D4
Bekkarfjord N 113 B16
Bela SK 65 A4
Bela Crkva SCG 85 B6
Belá nad Radbuzou CZ 62 A3
Bělá pod Bezdězem CZ 53 C4
Bělábre F 67 B6
Belalcázar E 93 C5
Belanovica SCG 85 B5
Bélapátfalva H 65 B6
Belcaire F 77 D4
Bełchatów PL 55 B4
Belchite E 90 B2
Bělčice CZ 63 A4
Belcoo GB 19 B4
Belecke D 51 B4
Beled H 74 A2
Belej HR 83 B3
Beleño E 88 A1
Bélesta F 77 D4
Belev RUS 7 E14
Belevi TR 119 D2
Belfast GB 19 B6
Belford GB 25 C6
Belfort F 60 C2
Belgentier F 79 C4
Belgern D 52 B3
Belgioioso I 71 C4
Belgodère F 102 A2
Belgooly IRL 20 C3
Belgorod RUS 7 F14
Belgrade = Beograd SCG 85 B5
Belhade F 76 B2
Beli Manastir HR 74 C3
Belica HR 74 B1
Belin-Bèliet F 76 B2
Belinchón E 95 B3
Belišće HR 74 C3
Bělkovice-Lašt'any CZ 64 A3
Bell-lloc d'Urgell E 90 B3
Bella I 104 C1
Bellac F 67 B6
Bellágio I 71 C4
Bellananagh IRL 19 C4
Bellano I 71 B4
Bellária I 82 B1
Bellavary IRL 18 C2
Belle-Isle-en-Terre F 56 B2
Belleau F 59 A4
Belleek GB 18 B3
Bellegarde, *Gard* F 78 C3
Bellegarde, *Loiret* F 58 C3
Bellegarde-en-Diois F 79 B4
Bellegarde-en-Marche F 68 C2
Bellegarde-sur-Valserine F 69 B5
Bellême F 58 B1
Bellenaves F 68 B3
Bellentre F 70 C1
Bellevaux F 69 B6
Bellevesvre F 69 B5
Belleville F 69 B4
Belleville-sur-Vie F 66 B3
Bellevue-la-Montagne F 68 C3
Belley F 69 C5
Bellheim D 61 A4
Bellinge DK 39 D3
Bellingham GB 25 C5
Bellinzago Novarese I 70 C3
Bellinzona CH 70 B4
Bello E 95 B5
Bellpuig d'Urgell E 91 B4
Bellreguart E 96 C2
Bellsbank GB 24 C3
Belltall E 91 B4
Belluno I 72 B2
Bellver de Cerdanya E 91 A4
Bellvis E 90 B3
Bélmez E 93 C5
Belmez de la Moraleda E 100 B2
Belmont GB 22 A8
Belmont-de-la-Loire F 69 B4
Belmont-sur-Rance F 78 C1
Belmonte, *Asturias* E 86 A4
Belmonte, *Cuenca* E 95 C4
Belmonte P 92 A3
Belmonte de San José E 90 C2
Belmonte de Tajo E 95 B3
Belmullet IRL 18 B2
Belobreşca RO 85 B6
Belœil B 49 C4
Belogradchik BG 11 E7
Belokorovichi UA 11 A10
Beloljin SCG 85 C6
Belorado E 89 B3
Belotič SCG 85 B4
Bělotin CZ 64 A3
Belozersk RUS 7 B14
Belp CH 70 B2
Belpasso I 109 B3
Belpech F 77 C4
Belper GB 27 B4
Belsay GB 25 C6
Belsh AL 105 C5
Belsk Duzy PL 55 B5
Beltinci SLO 73 B6
Beltra IRL 18 C2
Belturbet IRL 19 B4
Beluša SK 64 A4
Belušić SCG 85 C6
Belvedere Maríttimo I 106 B2
Belver de Cinca E 90 B3
Belver de los Montes E 88 C1
Belvès F 77 B3
Belvezet F 78 B2
Belvis de la Jara E 94 C2
Belvis de Monroy E 93 B5
Belyy RUS 7 D12
Belz F 56 C2
Bełżec PL 11 A7
Belzig D 52 A2
Bembibre E 86 B4
Bembridge GB 31 D2
Bemmel NL 50 B1
Bemposta, *Bragança* P 87 C4
Bemposta, *Santarém* P 92 B2
Benabarre E 90 A3
Benacazón E 99 B4
Benaguacil E 96 B2
Benahadux E 101 C3
Benalmádena E 100 C1
Benalúa de Guadix E 100 B2
Benalúa de las Villas E 100 B2
Benalup E 99 C5
Benamargosa E 100 C1
Benamaurel E 101 B3
Benameji E 100 B1
Benamocarra E 100 C1
Benaocaz E 99 C5
Benaoján E 99 C5
Benarrabá E 99 C5
Benasque E 90 A3
Benátky nad Jizerou CZ 53 C4
Benavente E 88 B1
Benavente P 92 C2
Benavides de Órbigo E 88 B1
Benavila P 92 B3
Bendorf D 50 C3
Bene Vagienna I 80 B1
Benedikt SLO 73 B5
Benejama E 101 A5
Benejúzar E 101 A5
Benešov CZ 63 A5
Bénestroff F 60 B2
Benet F 67 B4
Bénévent-l'Abbaye F 67 B6
Benevento I 103 B7
Benfeld F 60 B3
Benfica P 92 B2
Bengtsfors S 35 C4
Bengtsheden S 36 B2
Beničanci HR 74 C3
Benicarló E 90 C3
Benicássim E 96 A3
Benidorm E 96 C2
Benifaió E 96 B2
Beniganim E 96 C2
Benington GB 27 B6
Benisa E 96 C3
Benkovac HR 83 B4
Benllech GB 26 B1
Benneckenstein D 51 B6
Bénodet F 56 C1
Benquerencia de la Serena E 93 C5
Bensafrim P 98 B2
Bensdorf D 44 C4
Benshausen D 51 C6
Bensheim D 61 A4
Bentley GB 31 C3
Bentwisch D 44 A4
Beočin SCG 75 C4
Beograd = Belgrade SCG 85 B5
Beragh GB 19 B4
Berane SCG 85 D4
Beranga E 89 A3
Berat AL 105 C5
Bérat F 77 C4
Beratzhausen D 62 A2
Bérbaltavár H 74 A1
Berbegal E 90 B2
Berbenno di Valtellina I 71 B4
Berberana E 89 B3
Bercedo E 89 A3
Bercel H 65 C5
Bercenay-le-Hayer F 59 B4
Berceto I 81 B3
Berchem B 49 C4
Berchidda I 110 B2
Berching D 62 A2
Berchtesgaden D 62 C4
Bérchules E 100 C2
Bercianos de Aliste E 87 C4
Berck F 48 C2
Berclaire d'Urgell E 90 B3
Berdoias E 86 A1
Berducedo E 86 A4
Berdún E 90 A2
Berdychiv UA 11 B10
Bere Alston GB 28 C3
Bere Regis GB 29 C5
Bereguardo I 70 C4
Berehommen N 33 C4
Berehove UA 11 B7
Berek BIH 84 A2
Beremend H 74 C3
Berestechko UA 11 A8
Berettyóújfalu H 10 C6
Berezhany UA 11 B8
Berezivka UA 11 C11
Berezna UA 7 F11
Berg D 62 A2
Berg N 114 B9
Berg S 37 D3
Berg im Gau D 62 B2
Berga, *Sachsen-Anhalt* D 51 B7
Berga, *Thüringen* D 52 C2
Berga E 91 A4
Berga S 40 B6
Bergama TR 118 C2
Bérgamo I 71 C4
Bergara E 89 A4
Bergby S 36 B4
Berge, *Brandenburg* D 45 C4
Berge, *Niedersachsen* D 43 C4
Berge, *Telemark* N 33 C5
Berge, *Telemark* N 33 C5
Bergeforsen S 115 E14
Bergen, *Mecklenburg-Vorpommern* D 45 A5
Bergen, *Niedersachsen* D 44 C1
Bergen, *Niedersachsen* D 44 C2
Bergen N 32 B2
Bergen NL 42 C1
Bergen op Zoom NL 49 B5
Bergerac F 77 B3
Bergères-lés-Vertus F 59 B5
Bergeyk NL 49 B6
Berghausen D 61 B4
Bergheim D 50 C2
Berghem S 40 B2
Bergisch Gladbach D 50 C3
Bergkamen D 50 B3
Bergkvara S 41 C6
Berglern D 62 B2
Bergneustadt D 50 B3
Bergs slussar S 37 D2
Bergsäng S 34 B5
Bergshamra S 37 C5
Bergsjö S 115 F14
Bergtheim D 61 A6
Bergues F 48 C3
Bergum NL 42 B2
Bergün Bravuogn CH 71 B4
Bergwitz D 52 B2
Berhida H 74 A3
Beringel P 98 A3
Beringen B 49 B6
Berja E 100 C3
Berkåk N 114 E7
Berkeley GB 29 B5
Berkenthin D 44 B2
Berkhamsted GB 31 C3
Berkheim D 61 B6
Berkhof D 43 C6
Berkovići BIH 84 C3
Berkovitsa BG 11 E7
Berlanga E 99 A5
Berlanga de Duero E 89 C4
Berlevåg N 113 B18
Berlikum NL 42 B2
Berlin D 45 C5
Berlstedt D 52 B1
Bermeo E 89 A4
Bermillo de Sayago E 87 C4
Bern CH 70 B2
Bernalda I 104 C2
Bernardos E 94 A2
Bernartice, *Jihočeský* CZ 63 A5
Bernartice, *Vychodočeský* CZ 53 C5
Bernau, *Baden-Württemberg* D 61 C4
Bernau, *Bayern* D 62 C3
Bernau, *Brandenburg* D 45 C5
Bernaville F 48 C3
Bernay F 58 A1
Bernburg D 52 B1
Berndorf A 64 C2
Berne D 43 B5
Bernecebarati H 65 B4
Bernhardsthal A 64 B2
Bernkastel-Kues D 60 A3
Bernolakovo SK 64 B3
Bernsdorf D 53 B4
Bernstadt D 53 B4
Bernstein A 73 A6
Bernués E 90 A2
Beromünster CH 70 A3
Beroun CZ 53 D4
Berovo MK 116 A4
Berre-l'Etang F 79 C4
Berriedale GB 23 C5
Berriew GB 26 C2
Berrocal E 99 B4
Bersenbrück D 43 C4
Bershad' UA 11 B10
Berthåga S 36 C4
Berthelming F 60 B2
Bertincourt F 48 C3
Bertinoro I 82 B1
Bertogne B 49 C6
Bertrix B 59 A6
Berufjörður IS 111 C11
Berville-sur-Mer F 58 A1
Berwick-upon-Tweed GB 25 C5
Berzasca RO 10 D6
Berzence H 74 B2
Berzocana E 93 B5
Besalú E 91 A5
Besançon F 69 A6
Besenfeld D 61 B4
Besenyötelek H 65 C6
Besenyszög H 75 A5
Beshenkovichi BY 7 D10
Besigheim D 61 B5
Běšiny CZ 63 A4
Beška SCG 75 C5
Beşkonak TR 119 E6
Besle F 57 C4
Besnyö H 74 A3
Bessais-le-Fromental F 68 B2
Bessan F 78 C2
Besse-en-Chandesse F 68 C2
Bessé-sur-Braye F 58 C1
Bessèges F 78 B3
Bessines-sur-Gartempe F 67 B6
Best NL 49 B6
Bestorp S 37 D2
Betanzos E 86 A2
Betelu E 76 C1
Bétera E 96 B2
Beteta E 95 B4
Béthenville F 59 A5
Bethesda GB 26 B1
Béthune F 48 C3
Beton-Bazoches F 59 B4
Bettembourg L 60 A2
Betterdorf L 60 A2
Bettna S 37 D3
Béttola I 80 B3
Bettona I 82 C1
Bettyhill GB 23 C4
Betws-y-Coed GB 26 B2
Betxi E 96 B2
Betz F 59 A3
Betzdorf D 50 C3
Beuil F 79 B5
Beulah GB 29 A4
Beuzeville F 58 A1
Bevagna I 82 D1
Bevens-bruk S 37 C2
Beveren B 49 B5
Beverley GB 27 B5
Bevern D 51 B5
Beverstedt D 43 B5
Beverungen D 51 B5
Beverwijk NL 42 C1
Bex CH 70 B2
Bexhill GB 31 D4
Beyazköy TR 118 A2
Beychevelle F 76 A2
Beydağ TR 119 D3
Beyeğaç TR 119 E3
Beykoz TR 118 A4
Beynat F 68 C1
Beyoğlu TR 118 A4
Beypazarı TR 118 B6
Beyşehir TR 119 E6
Bezas E 95 B5
Bezau A 71 A4
Bezdan SCG 75 C3
Bèze F 69 A5

Bracadale GB 22 D2
Bracciano I 102 A5
Bracieux F 67 A6
Bräcke S 115 E12
Brackenheim D 61 A5
Brackley GB 30 B2
Bracklin IRL 19 C5
Bracknell GB 31 C3
Brackwede D 51 B4
Braco GB 25 B4
Brad RO 11 C7
Bradford GB 27 B4
Bradford on Avon GB 29 B5
Bradina BIH 84 C3
Brådland N 33 D3
Brae GB 22 A7
Brædstrup DK 39 D2
Braemar GB 23 D5
Braemore GB 22 D3
Braga P 87 C2
Bragança P 87 C4
Brăila RO 11 D9
Braine F 59 A4
Braine-le-Comte B 49 C5
Braintree GB 31 C4
Braives B 49 C6
Brake D 43 B5
Brakel B 49 C4
Brakel D 51 B5
Bräkne-Hoby S 41 C5
Brålanda S 35 D4
Bralin PL 54 B2
Brallo di Pregola I 80 B3
Bram F 77 C5
Bramafan F 79 C5
Bramberg am Wildkogel A 72 A2
Bramdrupdam DK 39 D2
Bramming DK 39 D1
Brampton GB 25 D5
Bramsche D 43 C4
Branca I 82 C1
Brancaleone Marina I 106 D3
Brancaster GB 30 B4
Brand, *Nieder Östereich* A 63 B6
Brand, *Vorarlberg* A 71 A4
Brand-Erbisdorf D 52 C3
Brandbu N 34 B2
Brande DK 39 D2
Brande-Hornerkirchen D 43 B6
Brandenberg A 72 A1
Brandenburg D 45 C4
Brandis D 52 B2
Brando F 102 A2
Brandomil E 86 A2
Brandon GB 30 B4
Brandshagen D 45 A5
Brandval N 34 B4
Brandýs nad Labem CZ 53 C4
Branice PL 54 C2
Braničevo SCG 85 B6
Braniewo PL 47 A5
Branik SLO 72 C3
Brankovina SCG 85 B4
Branky CZ 64 A3
Branne F 76 B2
Brannenburg-Degerndorf D 62 C3
Brantôme F 67 C5
Branzi I 71 B4
Bras d'Asse F 79 C5
Braskereidfoss N 34 B3
Braslaw BY 7 D9
Brașov RO 11 D8
Brasparts F 56 B2
Brassac, *Charente* F 67 C4
Brassac, *Tarn* F 77 C5
Brassac-les-Mines F 68 C3
Brasschaat B 49 B5
Brastad S 35 D3
Břasy CZ 63 A4
Brąszewice PL 54 B3
Brataj AL 105 C5
Bratislava SK 64 B3
Brattfors S 35 C6
Brattvåg N 114 E3
Bratunac BIH 85 B4
Braubach D 50 C3
Braunau A 62 B4
Braunfels D 51 C4
Braunlage D 51 B6
Braunsbedra D 52 B1
Braunschweig D 51 A6
Bray IRL 21 A5
Bray Dunes F 48 B3
Bray-sur-Seine F 59 B4
Bray-sur-Somme F 48 D3
Brazatortas E 100 A1
Brazey-en-Plaine F 69 A5
Brbinj HR 83 B4
Brčko BIH 84 B3
Brdani SCG 85 C5
Brdów PL 47 C4
Brea de Tajo E 95 B3
Brécey F 57 B4
Brechen D 50 C4
Brechin GB 25 B5
Brecht B 49 B5
Brecketfeld D 50 B3
Břeclav CZ 64 B2
Brecon GB 29 B4
Brécy F 68 A2
Breda E 91 B5
Breda NL 49 B5
Bredaryd S 40 B3
Bredbyn S 115 D15
Breddin D 44 C4
Bredebro DK 39 D1
Bredelar D 51 B4
Bredenfelde D 45 B5
Bredsjö S 36 C1
Bredstedt D 43 A5
Bredsten DK 39 D2
Bredträsk S 115 D15
Bredviken S 115 A11
Bree B 49 B6
Bregana HR 73 C5
Breganze I 72 C1
Bregenz A 71 A4
Bréhal F 57 B4
Brehna D 52 B2
Breidenbach F 60 A3
Breiðdalsvík IS 111 C11
Breil-sur-Roya F 80 C1
Breisach D 60 B3
Breitenbach CH 70 A2
Breitenbach D 51 C5
Breitenberg D 63 B4
Breitenfelde D 44 B2
Breitengussbach D 51 D6
Breivikbotn N 113 B11
Brejning DK 39 D2
Brekke N 32 A2
Brekken N 114 E8
Brekkestø N 33 D5
Brekkvasselv N 115 C10
Brekstad N 114 D6
Breland N 33 D4
Brem-sur-Mer F 66 B3
Bremanger N 114 F1
Bremen D 43 B5
Bremerhaven D 43 B5
Bremervörde D 43 B6
Bremgarten CH 70 A3
Bremsnes N 114 D4
Brenderup DK 39 D2
Brenes E 99 B5
Brengova SLO 73 B5
Brenna PL 65 A4
Breno I 71 C5
Brénod F 69 B5
Brensbach D 61 A4
Brentwood GB 31 C4
Brescello I 81 B4
Bréscia I 71 C5
Breskens NL 49 B4
Bresles F 58 A3
Bresnica SCG 85 C5
Bressana I 80 A3
Bressanone I 72 B1
Bressuire F 67 B4
Brest BY 6 E7
Brest F 56 B1
Brest HR 72 C3
Brestač SCG 85 B4
Brestanica SLO 73 B5
Brestova HR 82 A3
Brestovac HR 74 C2
Bretenoux F 77 B4
Breteuil, *Eure* F 58 B1
Breteuil, *Oise* F 58 A3
Brétigny-sur-Orge F 58 B3
Bretten D 61 A4
Bretteville-sur-Laize F 57 A5
Brettheim D 61 A6
Breuil-Cervinia I 70 C2
Breukelen NL 49 A6
Brevik N 35 C1
Brevik, *Stockholm* S 37 C5
Brevik, *Västra Götaland* S 37 D1
Breza BIH 84 B3
Brežice SLO 73 C5
Bréziers F 79 B5
Brezna SCG 85 C5
Breznica HR 73 B6
Breznica Našička HR 74 C3
Březnice CZ 63 A4
Brezno SK 65 B5
Brezojevice SCG 85 D4
Brezolles F 58 B2
Březová nad Svitavou CZ 64 A2
Brezová pod Bradlom SK 64 B3
Brezovica SK 65 A6
Brezovica SLO 73 B4
Brezovo Polje Selo BIH 84 B3
Briançon F 79 B5
Brianconnet F 79 C5
Briare F 58 C3
Briatexte F 77 C4
Briático I 106 C3
Briaucourt F 59 B6
Bribir HR 73 C4
Bricquebec F 57 A4
Bridge of Cally GB 25 B4
Bridge of Don GB 23 D6
Bridge of Earn GB 25 B4
Bridge of Orchy GB 24 B3
Bridgend, *Argyll & Bute* GB 24 C1
Bridgend, *Bridgend* GB 29 B4
Bridgnorth GB 26 C3
Bridgwater GB 29 B5
Břidličná CZ 64 A3
Bridlington GB 27 A5
Bridport GB 29 C5
Brie-Comte-Robert F 58 B3
Briec F 56 B1
Brienne-le-Château F 59 B5
Brienon-sur-Armançon F 59 C4
Brienz CH 70 B3
Brienza I 104 C1
Briesen D 45 C6
Brieskow Finkenheerd D 53 A4
Brietlingen D 44 B2
Brieva de Cameros E 89 B4
Briey F 60 A1
Brig CH 70 B3
Brigg GB 27 B5
Brighouse GB 27 B4
Brightlingsea GB 31 C5
Brighton GB 31 D3
Brignogan-Plage F 56 B1
Brignoles F 79 C5
Brigstock GB 30 B3
Brihuega E 95 B4
Brijuni HR 82 B2
Brillon-en-Barrois F 59 B6
Brilon D 51 B4
Brimnes N 32 B3
Brinches P 98 A3
Bríndisi I 105 C3
Brinje HR 83 A4
Brinon-sur-Beuvron F 68 A3
Brinon-sur-Sauldre F 68 A2
Brinyan GB 23 B5
Brión E 86 B2
Briones E 89 B4
Brionne F 58 A1
Brioude F 68 C3
Brioux-sur-Boutonne F 67 B4
Briouze F 57 B5
Briscous F 76 C1
Brisighella I 81 B5
Brissac-Quincé F 67 A4
Brissago CH 70 B3
Bristol GB 29 B5
Brive-la-Gaillarde F 67 C6
Briviesca E 89 B3
Brixham GB 29 C4
Brixlegg A 72 A1
Brjánslækur IS 111 B2
Brka BIH 84 B3
Brnaze HR 83 C5
Brněnec CZ 64 A2
Brno CZ 64 A2
Bro S 37 C4
Broad Haven GB 28 B2
Broadclyst GB 29 C4
Broadford GB 22 D3
Broadford IRL 20 B3
Broadstairs GB 31 C5
Broadstone GB 29 C5
Broadway GB 29 A6
Broager DK 39 E2
Broaryd S 40 B3
Broby S 41 C4
Brobyværk DK 39 D3
Bročanac BIH 84 C2
Broćanac SCG 84 D3
Brocas F 76 B2
Brock D 50 A3
Brockel D 43 B6
Brockenhurst GB 31 D2
Broczyno PL 46 B2
Brod MK 116 A3
Brod na Kupi HR 73 C4
Brodalen S 35 D3
Brodarevo SCG 85 C4
Broddbo S 36 C3
Brodek u Přerova CZ 64 A3
Broden-bach D 50 C3
Brodick GB 24 C2
Brodnica PL 47 B5
Brodnica Graniczna PL 47 A4
Brody, *Lubuskie* PL 53 A5
Brody, *Lubuskie* PL 53 B4
Brody, *Mazowieckie* PL 47 C6
Brody UA 11 A8
Broglie F 58 B1
Brójce PL 53 A5
Brokind S 37 D2
Brolo I 109 A3
Brome D 44 C2
Bromley GB 31 C4
Bromölla S 41 C4
Bromont-Lamothe F 68 C2
Brömsebro S 41 C5
Bromsgrove GB 29 A5
Bromyard GB 29 A5
Bronchales E 95 B5
Bronco E 93 A4
Brønderslev DK 38 B2
Broni I 80 A3
Brønnøysund N 114 B9
Brøns DK 39 D1
Bronte I 109 B3
Bronzani Mejdan BIH 84 B1
Bronzolo I 71 B6
Broons F 57 B3
Broquies F 78 B1
Brora GB 23 C5
Brørup DK 39 D2
Brösarp S 41 D4
Brostrud N 32 B5
Brotas P 92 C2
Brötjärna S 36 B2
Broto E 90 A2
Brottby S 37 C5
Brøttum N 34 A2
Brou F 58 B2
Brouage F 66 C3
Brough GB 26 A3
Broughshane GB 19 B5
Broughton GB 25 C4
Broughton-in-Furness GB 26 A2
Broumov CZ 53 C6
Broût-Vernet F 68 B3
Brouvelieures F 60 B2
Brouwershaven NL 49 B4
Brovary UA 11 A11
Brovst DK 38 B2
Brownhills GB 27 C4
Brozas E 93 B4
Brozzo I 71 C5
Brtnice CZ 63 A6
Brtonigla HR 72 C3
Bruay-la-Buissière F 48 C3
Bruchhausen-Vilsen D 43 C6
Bruchsal D 61 A4
Bruck, *Bayern* D 62 A3
Brück, *Brandenburg* D 52 A2
Bruck an der Grossglocknerstrasse A 72 A2
Bruck an der Leitha A 64 B2
Bruck an der Mur A 73 A5
Brückl A 73 B4
Bruckmühl D 62 C2
Brue-Auriac F 79 C4
Brüel D 44 B3
Bruen CH 70 B3
Bruère-Allichamps F 68 B2
Bruff IRL 20 B3
Bruflat N 32 B6
Brugg CH 70 A3
Brugge B 49 B4
Brüggen D 50 B2
Brühl D 50 C2
Bruinisse NL 49 B5
Brûlon F 57 C5
Brumano I 71 C4
Brumath F 60 B3
Brummen NL 50 A2
Brumov-Bylnice CZ 64 A4
Brumunddal N 34 B2
Brunau D 44 C3
Brunehamel F 59 A5
Brünen D 50 B2
Brunete E 94 B2
Brunflo S 115 D11
Brunico I 72 B1
Brunkeberg N 33 C5
Brunn D 45 B5
Brunnen CH 70 B3
Brunsbüttel D 43 B6
Brunssum NL 50 C1
Bruntál CZ 54 D2
Brus SCG 85 C6
Brušane HR 83 B4
Brusasco I 70 C3
Brusio CH 71 B5
Brusno SK 65 B5
Brusque F 78 C1
Brussels = Bruxelles B 49 C5
Brusson I 70 C2
Brüssow D 45 B6
Brusy PL 46 B3
Bruton GB 29 B5
Bruvno HR 83 B4
Bruvoll N 34 B3
Bruxelles = Brussels B 49 C5
Bruyères F 60 B2
Bruz F 57 B4
Bruzaholm S 40 B5
Brwinów PL 55 A5
Bryansk RUS 7 E13
Brynamman GB 28 B4
Bryncrug GB 26 C1
Bryne N 33 D2
Brynmawr GB 29 B4
Bryrup DK 39 C2
Brzeće SCG 85 C5
Brzeg PL 54 C2
Brzeg Dolny PL 54 B1
Brześć Kujawski PL 47 C4
Brzesko PL 55 D5
Brzeszcze PL 55 D4
Brzezie PL 46 B2
Brzeziny, *Łódzkie* PL 55 B4
Brzeziny, *Wielkopolskie* PL 54 B3
Brzeźnica PL 53 B5
Brzeźnica Nowa PL 55 B4
Brzeżno PL 46 B1
Brzotin SK 65 B6
Brzozie Lubawskie PL 47 B5
Bua S 40 B2
Buarcos P 92 A2
Buaveg N 33 C2
Bubbio I 80 B2
Bubry F 56 C2
Buca TR 119 D2
Bucak TR 119 E5
Bučany SK 64 B3
Buccheri I 109 B3
Buccino I 103 C8
Bucelas P 92 C1
Buch, *Bayern* D 61 B6
Buch, *Bayern* D 62 B3
Buchach UA 11 B8
Bucharest = Bucureşti RO 11 D9
Buchbach D 62 B3
Buchboden A 71 A4
Buchen, *Baden-Württemberg* D 61 A5
Büchen, *Schleswig-Holstein* D 44 B2
Buchenberg D 61 C6
Buchères F 59 B5
Buchholz D 44 B1
Buchloe D 62 B1
Buchlovice CZ 64 A3
Buchlyvie GB 24 B3
Bucholz D 44 B4
Buchs CH 71 A4
Buchy F 58 A2
Bückeburg D 51 A5
Buckfastleigh GB 28 C4
Buckhaven GB 25 B4
Buckie GB 23 D6
Buckingham GB 31 B3
Buckley GB 26 B2
Bückwitz D 44 C4
Bučovice CZ 64 A3
Bucsa H 75 A6
Bucureşti = Bucharest RO 11 D9
Bucy-lés-Pierreport F 59 A4
Buczek PL 55 B4
Bud N 114 E3
Budakalasz H 65 C5
Budakeszi H 75 A3
Budal N 114 E7
Budaörs H 75 A3
Budapest H 75 A4
Budča SK 65 B5
Buddusò I 110 B2
Bude GB 28 C3
Budeč CZ 63 A6
Büdelsdorf D 43 A6
Budens P 98 B2
Búðardalur IS 111 B4
Budia E 95 B4
Budimlić-Japra BIH 83 B5
Büdingen D 51 C5
Budinšćina HR 73 B6
Budišov CZ 64 A3
Budleigh Salterton GB 29 C4
Budmerice SK 64 B3
Budoni I 110 B2
Búdrio I 81 B5
Budva SCG 105 A4
Budyně nad Ohří CZ 53 C4
Budziszewice PL 55 B4
Budzyń PL 46 C2
Bue N 33 D2
Bueña E 95 B5
Buenache de Alarcón E 95 C4
Buenache de la Sierra E 95 B5
Buenaventura E 94 B2
Buenavista de Valdavia E 88 B2
Buendia E 95 B4
Bueu E 87 B2
Buezo E 89 B3
Bugac H 75 B4
Bugarra E 96 B2
Bugeat F 68 C1
Buggerru I 110 C1
Bugojno BIH 84 B2
Bugøyfjord N 113 C18
Bugøynes N 113 C18
Bugyi H 75 A4
Buharkent TR 119 E3
Bühl, *Baden-Württemberg* D 61 B4
Bühl, *Bayern* D 61 C6
Bühlertal D 61 B4
Bühlertann D 61 A5
Buia I 72 B3
Builth Wells GB 29 A4
Buin N 32 B6
Buis-les-Baronnies F 79 B4
Buitenpost NL 42 B3
Buitrago del Lozoya E 94 B3
Bujalance E 100 B1
Bujaraloz E 90 B2
Buje HR 72 C3
Bujedo E 89 B3
Bük H 74 A1
Buk PL 46 C2
Bükkösd H 74 B2
Bükkzsérc H 65 C6
Bukovci SLO 73 B5
Bukowiec PL 53 A6
Bukowina Tatrzańska PL 65 A6
Bukownica PL 54 B3
Bukowno PL 55 C4
Bülach CH 70 A3
Búland IS 111 D7
Buldan TR 119 D3
Bulgnéville F 60 B1
Bulgurca TR 119 D2
Bülkau D 43 B5
Bulken N 32 B3
Bulkowo PL 47 C6
Bullas E 101 A4
Bulle CH 70 B2
Büllingen B 50 C2
Bulqizë AL 116 A2
Buna BIH 84 C2
Bunahowen IRL 18 B2
Bunbeg IRL 18 A3
Bunclody IRL 21 B5
Buncrana IRL 19 A4
Bunde, *Niedersachsen* D 43 B4
Bünde, *Nordrhein-Westfalen* D 51 A4
Bundoran IRL 18 B3
Bunessan GB 24 B1
Bungay GB 30 B5
Bunge S 37 E6
Bunić HR 83 B4
Bunmahon IRL 21 B4
Bunnyconnellan IRL 18 B2
Buño E 86 A2
Buñol E 96 B2
Bunratty IRL 20 B3
Bunsbeek B 49 C5
Buñuel E 89 C5
Bünyan TR 16 B7
Bunyola E 97 B2
Buonabitácolo I 104 C1
Buonalbergo I 103 B7
Buonconvento I 81 C5
Buonvicino I 106 B2
Burano I 72 C2
Burbach D 50 C4
Burcei I 110 C2
Burdons-sur-Rognon F 59 B6
Burdur TR 119 E5
Bureå S 3 D24
Burela E 86 A3
Büren D 51 B4
Büren an der Aare CH 70 A2
Burford GB 29 B6
Burg, *Cottbus* D 53 B4
Burg, *Magdeburg* D 52 A1
Burg, *Schleswig-Holstein* D 43 B6
Burg auf Fehmarn D 44 A3
Burg Stargard D 45 B5
Burgas BG 11 E9
Burgau A 73 A6
Burgau D 61 B6
Burgau P 98 B2
Burgbernheim D 61 A6
Burgdorf CH 70 A2
Burgdorf D 44 C2
Burgebrach D 62 A1
Bürgel D 52 C1
Burgess Hill GB 31 D3
Burgh le Marsh GB 27 B6
Burghaslach D 61 A6
Burghausen D 62 B3
Burghead GB 23 D5
Burgheim D 62 B2
Búrgio I 108 B2
Burgkirchen D 62 B3
Burgkunstadt D 52 C1
Burglengenfeld D 62 A3
Burgo P 87 D2
Burgoberbach D 61 A6
Burgohondo E 94 B2
Burgos E 88 B3
Burgsinn D 51 C5
Burgstädt D 52 C2
Burgstall D 44 C3
Burgsvik S 37 E5
Burgui E 76 D2
Burguillos E 99 B5
Burguillos de Toledo E 94 C3
Burguillos del Cerro E 93 C4
Burhaniye TR 118 C1
Burhave D 43 B5
Burie F 67 C4
Burjassot E 96 B2
Burk D 61 A6
Burkhardtsdorf D 52 C2
Burlada E 76 D1
Burladingen D 61 B5
Burlage D 43 B4
Burness GB 23 B6
Burnham GB 31 C3
Burnham Market GB 30 B4
Burnham-on-Crouch GB 31 C4
Burnham-on-Sea GB 29 B5
Burniston GB 27 A5
Burnley GB 26 B3
Burntisland GB 25 B4
Burón E 88 A1
Buronzo I 70 C3
Burovac SCG 85 B6
Burow D 45 B5
Burravoe GB 22 A7
Burrel AL 105 B6
Burret F 77 D4
Burriana E 96 B2
Burry Port GB 28 B3
Bürs A 71 A4
Bursa TR 118 B4
Burseryd S 40 B3
Bürstadt D 61 A4
Burton GB 26 A3
Burton Agnes GB 27 A5
Burton Bradstock GB 29 C5
Burton Latimer GB 30 B3
Burton upon Stather GB 27 B5
Burton upon Trent GB 27 C4
Burujón E 94 C2
Burwell GB 30 B4
Burwick GB 23 C6
Bury GB 26 B3
Bury St. Edmunds GB 30 B4
Buryn UA 7 F12
Burzenin PL 54 B3
Busachi I 110 B1
Busalla I 80 B2
Busana I 81 B4
Busano I 70 C2
Busca I 80 B1
Busch D 44 C3
Buševec HR 73 C6
Bushat AL 105 B5
Bushey GB 31 C3
Bushmills GB 19 A5
Bušince SK 65 B5
Buskhyttan S 37 D3
Busko-Zdrój PL 55 C5
Busot E 96 C2
Busovača BIH 84 B2
Busquistar E 100 C2
Bussang F 60 C2
Busseto I 81 B4
Bussière-Badil F 67 C5
Bussière-Poitevine F 67 B5
Bussolengo I 71 C5
Bussoleno I 70 C2
Bussum NL 49 A6
Busto Arsízio I 70 C3
Büsum D 43 A5
Butera I 109 B3
Butgenbach B 50 C2
Butler's Bridge IRL 19 B4
Butryny PL 47 B6
Bütschwil CH 70 A4
Buttermere GB 26 A2
Buttevant IRL 20 B3
Buttle S 37 E5
Buttstädt D 52 B1
Butzbach D 51 C4
Bützfleth D 43 B6
Bützow D 44 B3
Buxières-les-Mines F 68 B2
Buxtehude D 43 B6
Buxton GB 27 B4
Buxy F 69 B4
Büyükçekmece TR 118 A3
Büyükkariştiran TR 118 A2
Büyükorhan TR 118 C3
Buzançais F 67 B6
Buzancy F 59 A5
Buzău RO 11 D9
Buzet HR 72 C3
Buzsák H 74 B2
Buzy F 76 C2
By S 36 B3
Byala BG 11 E8
Byaroza BY 6 E8
Byczyna PL 54 B3
Bydalen S 115 D10
Bydgoszcz PL 47 B4
Bygdin N 32 A5
Bygland N 33 D4
Byglandsfjord N 33 D4
Bygstad N 32 A2
Bykhaw BY 7 E11
Bykle N 33 C4
Bylderup-Bov DK 39 E2
Byrkjedal N 33 D3
Byrkjelo N 114 F3
Byrum DK 38 B3
Byšice CZ 53 C4
Byske S 3 D24
Býškovice CZ 64 A3
Bysław PL 46 B3
Bystré CZ 64 A2
Bystrice, *Středočeský* CZ 65 A4
Bystřice, *Středočeský* CZ 63 A5
Bystřice n Pernštejnem CZ 64 A2
Bystřice pod Hostýnem CZ 64 A3
Bystrzyca Kłodzka PL 54 C1
Bytča SK 65 A4
Bytnica PL 53 A5
Bytom PL 54 C3
Bytom Odrzański PL 53 B5
Bytów PL 46 A3
Byxelkrok S 41 B7
Bzenec CZ 64 B3
Bzince SK 64 B3

C

Cabacos P 92 B2
Cabaj-Čápor SK 64 B4
Cabana E 86 A2
Cabanac-et-Villagrains F 76 B2
Cabañaquinta E 88 A1
Cabanas P 98 B3
Cabañas de Yepes E 95 C3
Cabañas del Castillo E 93 B5
Cabanelles E 91 A5
Cabanes E 96 A3
Cabanillas E 89 B5
Čabar HR 73 C4
Cabasse F 79 C5
Cabdella E 91 A4
Cabeceiras de Basto P 87 C2
Cabeço de Vide P 92 B3
Cabella Ligure I 80 B3
Cabeza del Buey E 93 C5
Cabeza la Vaca E 99 A4
Cabezamesada E 95 C3
Cabezarados E 100 A1
Cabezarrubias del Puerto E 100 A1
Cabezas del Villar E 94 B1
Cabezas Rubias E 98 B3
Cabezón E 88 C2
Cabezón de la Sal E 88 A2
Cabezón de Liébana E 88 A2
Cabezuela E 94 A3
Cabezuela del Valle E 93 A5
Cabo de Gata E 101 C3
Cabo de Palos E 101 B5
Cabolafuenta E 95 A4
Cabourg F 57 A5
Cabra E 100 B1
Cabra P 92 A3
Cabra del Santo Cristo E 100 B2
Cabrach GB 23 D5
Cábras I 110 C1
Cabreiro P 87 C2
Cabreiros E 86 A3
Cabrejas E 95 B4
Cabrela P 92 C2
Cabrillas E 87 D4
Cabuna HR 74 C2
Cacabelos E 86 B4
Čačak SCG 85 C5
Cáccamo I 108 B2
Caccuri I 107 B3
Cacela P 98 B3
Cacém P 92 C1
Cáceres E 93 B4
Cachafeiro E 86 B2
Cachopo P 98 B3
Čachtice SK 64 B3
Cacin E 100 B2
Čačinci HR 74 C2
Cadafais P 92 C1
Cadalen F 77 C5
Cadalso E 93 A4
Cadaqués E 91 A6
Cadaval P 92 B1
Cadavedo E 86 A4
Čadavica BIH 84 B1
Čadca SK 65 A4
Cadéac F 77 D3
Cadelbosco di Sopra I 81 B4
Cadenazzo CH 70 B3
Cadenberge D 43 B6
Cadenet F 79 C4
Cadeuil F 66 C4
Cádiar E 100 C2
Cadillac F 76 B2
Cádiz E 99 C4
Čadjavica HR 74 C2
Cadouin F 77 B3
Cadours F 77 C4
Cadrete E 90 B2
Caen F 57 A5
Caerleon GB 29 B5
Caernarfon GB 26 B1
Caerphilly GB 29 B4
Caersws GB 26 C2
Cafede P 92 B3
Çağa TR 118 B7
Caggiano I 104 C1
Cagli I 82 C1
Cágliari I 110 C2
Čaglin HR 74 C2
Cagnano Varano I 104 B1
Cagnes-sur-Mer F 79 C6
Caher IRL 21 B4
Caherciveen IRL 20 C1
Caherdaniel IRL 20 C1
Cahors F 77 B4
Cahul MD 11 D10
Caiazzo I 103 B7
Caion E 86 A2
Cairndow GB 24 B3
Cairnryan GB 24 D2
Cairo Montenotte I 80 B2
Caister-on-Sea GB 30 B5
Caistor GB 27 B5
Caivano I 103 C7
Cajarc F 77 B4
Čajetina SCG 85 C4
Čajniče BIH 84 C4
Çakırlar TR 119 F5
Çakmak TR 118 C6
Čakovec HR 73 B6
Cakran AL 105 C5
Çal TR 119 D4
Cala E 99 B4
Cala d'Or E 97 B3
Cala Galdana E 97 B3
Cala Gonone I 110 B2
Cala Llonga E 97 C1
Cala Millor E 97 B3
Cala Morell E 97 A3
Cala Ratjada E 97 B3
Calabritto I 103 C8
Calaceite E 90 C3
Calacuccia F 102 A2
Calaf E 91 B4
Calafat RO 11 D7
Calafell E 91 B4
Calahonda, *Granada* E 100 C2
Calahonda, *Málaga* E 100 C1
Calahorra E 89 B5
Calais F 48 C2
Calalzo di Cadore I 72 B2
Calamocha E 95 B5
Calamonte E 93 C4
Calanais GB 22 C2
Calañas E 99 B4
Calanda E 90 C2
Calangiánus I 110 B2
Călărași RO 11 D9
Calascibetta I 109 B3
Calasetta I 110 C1
Calasparra E 101 A4

Dechtice SK 64 B3
Decima I 102 B5
Decimomannu I 110 C1
Děčín CZ 53 C4
Decize F 68 B3
Decollatura I 106 B3
Decs H 74 B3
Dedaj AL 105 A5
Deddington GB 31 C2
Dedeler TR 118 B5
Dedelow D 45 B5
Dedemli TR 119 E7
Dedemsvaart NL 42 C3
Dédestapolcsány H 65 B6
Dedovichi RUS 7 C10
Deeping St. Nicholas GB 30 B3
Dég H 74 B3
Degaña E 86 B4
Degeberga S 41 D4
Degerby FIN 36 B7
Degerfors S 37 C1
Degerhamn S 41 C6
Degernes N 35 C3
Deggendorf D 62 B3
Deggingen D 61 B5
Dego I 80 B2
Degolados P 93 B3
Dehesas de Guadix E 100 B2
Dehesas Viejas E 100 B2
Deia E 97 B2
Deining D 62 A2
Deinze B 49 C4
Déiva Marina I 80 B3
Dej RO 11 C7
Deje S 35 C5
Delabole GB 28 C3
Delary S 40 C3
Delbrück D 51 B4
Delden NL 50 A2
Deleitosa E 93 B5
Delekovec HR 74 B1
Delémont CH 70 A2
Delft NL 49 A5
Delfzijl NL 42 B3
Délia I 108 B2
Delianuova I 106 C2
Deliblato SCG 85 B6
Delice TR 16 B6
Deliceto I 103 B8
Delitzsch D 52 B2
Dellach A 72 B3
Delle F 70 A2
Delme F 60 B2
Delmen-horst D 43 B5
Delnice HR 73 C4
Delsbo S 115 F13
Delvin IRL 19 C4
Delvinë AL 116 C2
Demandice SK 65 B4
Demen D 44 B3
Demidov RUS 7 D11
Demigny F 69 B4
Demirci TR 118 C3
Demirköy TR 118 A2
Demirtaş TR 118 B4
Demmin D 45 B5
Demonte I 79 B6
Demyansk RUS 7 C12
Den Burg NL 42 B1
Den Ham NL 42 C3
Den Helder NL 42 C1
Den Oever NL 42 C2
Denain F 49 C4
Denbigh GB 26 B2
Dender-monde B 49 B5
Denekamp NL 42 C3
Denholm GB 25 C5
Denia E 96 C3
Denizli TR 119 E4
Denkendorf D 62 B2
Denklingen D 50 C3
Denny GB 25 B4
Denta RO 75 C6
Déols F 68 B1
Derbent TR 119 D3
Derby GB 27 C4
Dereköy TR 118 A2
Derenberg D 51 B6
Derinkuyu TR 16 B7
Dermbach D 51 C6
Dermulo I 71 B6
Deronje SCG 75 C4
Derrygonnelly GB 19 B4
Derrylin GB 19 B4
Derry/Londonderry GB 19 B4
Dersingham GB 30 B4
Deruta I 82 D1
Dervaig GB 24 B1
Derval F 57 C4
Derveni GR 117 D4
Derventa BIH 84 B2
Dervock GB 19 A5
Desana I 70 C3
Descartes F 67 B5
Desenzano del Garda I 71 C5
Deset N 34 A3
Deševa BIH 84 C3
Desfina GR 116 D4
Desimirovac SCG 85 B5
Désio I 71 C4
Deskati GR 116 C3
Deskle SLO 72 B3
Desná CZ 53 C5
Dešov CZ 64 B2
Despotovac SCG 85 B6
Despotovo SCG 75 C4
Dessau D 52 B2
Deštná CZ 63 A5
Destriana E 87 B4
Désulo I 110 B2
Desvres F 48 C2
Deszk H 75 B5
Deta RO 75 C6
Detmold D 51 B4
Dětřichov CZ 64 A3
Dettelbach D 61 A6
Dettingen, *Baden-Württemberg* D 61 B5
Dettingen, *Baden-Württemberg* D 61 C5
Dettwiller F 60 B3
Detva SK 65 B5
Deurne NL 50 B1
Deutsch Wagram A 64 B2
Deutschkreutz A 64 C2
Deutschlandsberg A 73 B5
Deva RO 11 D7
Dévaványa H 75 A5
Devecikonağı TR 118 C3
Devecser H 74 A2
Develi TR 16 B7
Deventer NL 50 A2
Devil's Bridge GB 28 A4
Devin BG 116 A6
Devinska Nova Ves SK 64 B2
Devizes GB 29 B6
Devonport GB 28 C3
Devrek TR 118 A6
Devrekâni TR 16 A6
Đevrske HR 83 C4
Dewsbury GB 27 B4
Deza E 89 C4
Dežanovac HR 74 C2
Dezzo I 71 C5
Dhali CY 120 A2
Dheftera CY 120 A2
Dherinia CY 120 A2
Dhërmi AL 105 C5
Diamante I 106 B2
Dianalund DK 39 D4
Diano d'Alba I 80 B2
Diano Marina I 80 C2
Dicomano I 81 C5
Didcot GB 31 C2
Didimoticho GR 118 A1
Die F 79 B4
Diebling F 60 A2
Dieburg D 61 A4
Diego del Carpio E 93 A5
Diekirch L 60 A2
Diélette F 57 A4
Diémoz F 69 C5
Dienten am Hochkönig A 72 A2
Diepenbeck B 49 C6
Diepholz D 43 C5
Dieppe F 58 A2
Dierberg D 45 B4
Dierdorf D 50 C3
Dieren NL 50 A2
Dierhagen D 44 A4
Diesdorf D 44 C2
Diessen D 62 C2
Diest B 49 C6
Dietenheim D 61 B6
Dietfurt D 62 A2
Dietikon CH 70 A3
Dietzenbach D 51 C4
Dieue-sur-Meuse F 60 A1
Dieulefit F 79 B4
Dieulouard F 60 B2
Dieuze F 60 B2
Diever NL 42 C3
Diez D 50 C4
Diezma E 100 B2
Differdange L 60 A1
Digermulen N 112 D4
Dignac F 67 C5
Dignano I 72 B2
Digne-les-Bains F 79 B5
Digny F 58 B2
Digoin F 68 B3
Dijon F 69 A5
Dikanäs S 115 B13
Dikili TR 118 C1
Diksmuide B 48 B3
Dilar E 100 B2
Dillenburg D 50 C4
Dillingen, *Bayern* D 61 B6
Dillingen, *Saarland* D 60 A2
Dilsen B 50 B1
Dimaro I 71 B5
Dimitrovgrad BG 11 E8
Dimitsana GR 117 E4
Dinami I 106 C3
Dinan F 57 B3
Dinant B 49 C5
Dinar TR 119 D5
Dinard F 57 B3
Dinek TR 118 C6
Dingden D 50 B2
Dingelstädt D 51 B6
Dingle IRL 20 B1
Dingle S 35 D3
Dingolfing D 62 B3
Dingtuna S 37 C3
Dingwall GB 23 D4
Dinkelsbühl D 61 A6
Dinkelscherben D 62 B1
Dinklage D 43 C5
Dinslaken D 50 B2
Dinxperlo NL 50 B2
Diö S 40 C4
Diósgyőr H 65 B6
Diósjenő H 65 C5
Diou F 68 B3
Dippen GB 24 C2
Dipperz D 51 C5
Dippoldiswalde D 53 C3
Dirdal N 33 D3
Dirksland NL 49 B5
Dirlewang D 61 C6
Dischingen D 61 B6
Disentis CH 70 B3
Diso I 107 A5
Diss GB 30 B5
Dissen D 50 A4
Distington GB 26 A2
Ditzingen D 61 B5
Ditzum D 43 B4
Divača SLO 72 C3
Dives-sur-Mer F 57 A5
Divín SK 65 B5
Divion F 48 C3
Divišov CZ 63 A5
Divjakë AL 105 C5
Divonne les Bains F 69 B6
Dixmont F 59 B4
Dizy-le-Gros F 59 A5
Djúpivogur IS 111 C11
Djupvasshytta N 114 E4
Djura S 36 B1
Djurås S 36 B2
Djurmo S 36 B2
Djursdala S 40 B5
Dlouhá Loucka CZ 64 A3
Długowola PL 55 B6
Dmitriyev Lgovskiy RUS 7 E13
Dmitrov RUS 7 C14
Dmitrovsk-Orlovskiy RUS 7 E13
Dno RUS 7 C10
Doade E 86 B3
Dobanovci SCG 85 B5
Dobbertin D 44 B4
Dobbiaco I 72 B2
Dobczyce PL 65 A6
Dobele LV 6 C7
Döbeln D 52 B3
Doberlug-Kirchhain D 52 B3
Dobern D 53 B4
Dobersberg A 63 B6
Dobiegniew PL 46 C1
Dobieszyn PL 55 B6
Doboj BIH 84 B3
Dobošnica BIH 84 B3
Doboz H 75 B6
Dobrá CZ 65 A4
Dobra, *Wielkopolskie* PL 54 B3
Dobra, *Zachodnio-Pomorskie* PL 45 B6
Dobra, *Zachodnio-Pomorskie* PL 45 B7
Dobrá Niva SK 65 B5
Dobřany CZ 63 A4
Dobre, *Kujawsko-Pomorskie* PL 47 C4
Dobre, *Mazowieckie* PL 55 A6
Dobre Miasto PL 47 B6
Dobreta-Turnu-Severin RO 11 D7
Dobri H 74 B1
Dobri Do SCG 85 D6
Dobrica SCG 75 C5
Dobrich BG 11 E9
Dobříš CZ 63 A5
Dobro E 89 B3
Dobrodzień PL 54 C3
Döbrököz H 74 B3
Dobromierz PL 53 C6
Dobrosołowo PL 47 C4
Dobroszyce PL 54 B2
Dobrota SCG 105 A4
Dobrovnik SLO 73 B6
Dobrush BY 7 E11
Dobruška CZ 53 C6
Dobrzany PL 46 B1
Dobrzen Wielki PL 54 C2
Dobrzyca, *Wielkopolskie* PL 46 B2
Dobrzyca, *Wielkopolskie* PL 54 B2
Dobrzyca, *Zachodnio-Pomorskie* PL 46 A1
Dobrzyń nad Wisłą PL 47 C5
Dobšiná SK 65 B6
Dobwalls GB 28 C3
Dochamps B 49 C6
Docking GB 30 B4
Docksta S 115 D15
Doddington GB 25 C5
Döderhult S 40 B6
Doesburg NL 50 A2
Doetinchem NL 50 B2
Doğanhisar TR 119 D6
Dogliani I 80 B1
Dogueno P 98 B3
Dois Portos P 92 B1
Doische B 49 C5
Dojč SK 64 B3
Dokka N 34 B2
Dokkedal DK 38 C3
Dokkum NL 42 B2
Dokležovje SLO 73 B6
Doksy CZ 53 C4
Dokuz TR 119 D7
Dol-de-Bretagne F 57 B4
Dolancourt F 59 B5
Dolceácqua I 80 C1
Dole F 69 A5
Dølemo N 33 D5
Dolenja vas SLO 73 C4
Dolenjske Toplice SLO 73 C5
Dolfor GB 26 C2
Dolgarrog GB 26 B2
Dolgellau GB 26 C2
Doliana GR 116 C2
Dolianova I 110 C2
Dolice PL 45 B7
Doljani HR 83 B5
Döllach im Mölltal A 72 B2
Dolle D 44 C3
Dollnstein D 62 B2
Dollot F 59 B4
Döllstadt D 51 B6
Dolná Strehová SK 65 B5
Dolné Saliby SK 64 B3
Dolni Benešov CZ 64 A4
Dolni Bousov CZ 53 C5
Dolni Kounice CZ 64 A2
Dolni Kralovice CZ 63 A6
Dolni Újezd CZ 64 A2
Dolni Žandov CZ 52 C2
Dolný Kubín SK 65 A5
Dolo I 72 C2
Dolores E 96 C2
Dolovo SCG 85 B5
Dölsach A 72 B2
Dolsk PL 54 B2
Dolwyddelan GB 26 B2
Dolynska UA 11 B12
Domaljevac BIH 84 A3
Domaniç TR 118 C4
Domaniža SK 65 A4
Domanovići BIH 84 C2
Domašov CZ 54 C2
Domaszék H 75 B4
Domaszków PL 54 C1
Domaszowice PL 54 B2
Domat-Ems CH 71 B4
Domažlice CZ 62 A3
Dombås N 114 E6
Dombasle-sur-Meurthe F 60 B2
Dombegyház H 75 B6
Dombóvár H 74 B3
Domène F 69 C5
Domérat F 68 B2
Domfessel F 60 B3
Domfront F 57 B5
Domfront-en-Champagne F 57 B6
Domingão P 92 B2
Domingo Pérez, *Granada* E 100 B2
Domingo Pérez, *Toledo* E 94 C2
Dömitz D 44 B3
Dommartin F 59 B5
Dommartin-le-Franc F 59 B5
Domme F 77 B4
Dommitzsch D 52 B2
Domodóssola I 70 B3
Domokos GR 116 C4
Domoszló H 65 C6
Dompaire F 60 B2
Dompierre-du-Chemin F 57 B4
Dompierre-sur-Besbre F 68 B3
Dompierre-sur-Mer F 66 B3
Domrémy-la-Pucelle F 60 B1
Dömsöd H 75 A4
Domsure F 69 B5
Dómus de Maria I 110 D1
Domusnóvas I 110 C1
Domvena GR 117 D4
Domžale SLO 73 B4
Don Alvaro E 93 C4
Don Benito E 93 C5
Doña Mencía E 100 B1
Donado E 87 B4
Donaghadee GB 19 B6
Donaueschingen D 61 C4
Donauwörth D 62 B1
Doncaster GB 27 B4
Donegal IRL 18 B3
Donestebe-Santesteban E 76 C1
Donges F 66 A2
Dongo I 71 B4
Donington GB 30 B3
Doniños E 86 A2
Donja Bebrina HR 84 A3
Donja Brela HR 84 C1
Donja Dubica BIH 84 A3
Donja Dubrava HR 74 B1
Donja Kupčina HR 73 C5
Donja Mutnica SCG 85 C6
Donja Šatornja SCG 85 B5
Donja Stubica HR 73 C5
Donje Brišnik BIH 84 C2
Donje Ljupče SCG 85 D6
Donje Stative HR 73 C5
Donji-Andrijevci HR 74 C3
Donji Kazanci BIH 83 C5
Donji Koričáni BIH 84 B2
Donji Lapac HR 83 B4
Donji Malovan BIH 84 C2
Donji Miholjac HR 74 C3
Donji Mosti HR 74 B1
Donji Poloj HR 73 C5
Donji-Rujani BIH 83 C5
Donji Srb HR 83 B5
Donji Svilaj BIH 84 A3
Donji Tovarnik SCG 85 B4
Donji Vakuf BIH 84 B2
Donnalucata I 109 C3
Donnemarie-Dontilly F 59 B4
Donnersbach A 73 A4
Donnersbachwald A 73 A4
Donnerskirchen A 64 C2
Donorático I 81 C4
Donostia-San Sebastián E 76 C1
Donovaly SK 65 B5
Donzenac F 67 C6
Donzère F 78 B3
Donzy F 68 A3
Doonbeg IRL 20 B2
Doorn NL 49 A6
Dor E 86 A1
Dorchester GB 29 C5
Dørdal N 33 D6
Dordrecht NL 49 B5
Dörenthe D 50 A3
Dores GB 23 D4
Dorf Mecklenburg D 44 B3
Dorfen D 62 B3
Dorfgastein A 72 A3
Dorfmark D 43 C6
Dorgali I 110 B2
Dorking GB 31 C3
Dormagen D 50 B2
Dormánd H 65 C6
Dormans F 59 A4
Dornava SLO 73 B5
Dornbirn A 71 A4
Dornburg D 52 B1
Dorndorf D 51 C6
Dornecy F 68 A3
Dornes F 68 B3
Dornhan D 61 B4
Dornie GB 22 D3
Dornoch GB 23 D4
Dornum D 43 B4
Dorog H 65 C4
Dorogobuzh RUS 7 D12
Dorohoi RO 11 C9
Dorotea S 115 C13
Dorotowo PL 47 B6
Dörpen D 43 C4
Dorsten D 50 B2
Dortan F 69 B5
Dortmund D 50 B3
Doruchów PL 54 B3
Dorum D 43 B5
Dörverden D 43 C6
Dörzbach D 61 A5
Dos Aguas E 96 B2
Dos Hermanas E 99 B5
Dos-Torres E 100 A1
Dosbarrios E 95 C3
Döşemealtı TR 119 E5
Dospat BG 116 A6
Dötlingen D 43 C5
Dottignies B 49 C4
Döttingen CH 70 A3
Douai F 49 C4
Douarnenez F 56 B1
Douchy F 59 C4
Douchy-les-Mines F 49 C4
Doucier F 69 B5
Doudeville F 58 A1
Doué-la-Fontaine F 67 A4
Douglas, *Isle of Man* GB 26 A1
Douglas, *South Lanarkshire* GB 25 C4
Doulaincourt F 59 B6
Doulevant-le-Château F 59 B5
Doullens F 48 C3
Dounby GB 23 B5
Doune GB 24 B3
Dounreay GB 23 C5
Dour B 49 C4
Dourdan F 58 B3
Dourgne F 77 C5
Dournazac F 67 C5
Douro Calvo P 87 D3
Douvaine F 69 B6
Douvres-la-Délivrande F 57 A5
Douzy F 59 A6
Dover GB 31 C5
Dovje SLO 72 B3
Dovre N 114 F6
Downham Market GB 30 B4
Downhill GB 19 A5
Downpatrick GB 19 B6
Dowra IRL 18 B3
Doxato GR 116 A6
Doyet F 68 B2
Dozule F 57 A5
Drača SCG 85 B5
Dračevo BIH 84 D3
Drachten NL 42 B3
Draga SLO 73 C4
Drăgăşani RO 11 D8
Dragatuš SLO 73 C5
Dragichyn BY 7 E8
Draginja SCG 85 B4
Dragobi AL 105 A6
Dragocvet SCG 85 C6
Dragolovci BIH 84 B2
Dragoni I 103 B7
Dragør DK 41 D2
Dragotina HR 73 C6
Dragotinja BIH 83 A5
Dragozetići HR 83 A3
Draguignan F 79 C5
Drahnsdorf D 52 B3
Drahonice CZ 63 A5
Drahovce SK 64 B3
Drama GR 116 A6
Drammen N 35 C2
Drangedal N 33 C6
Drangsnes IS 111 B4
Dransfeld D 51 B5
Dranske D 45 A5
Draperstown GB 19 B5
Drassburg A 64 C2
Drávaszabolcs H 74 C3
Dravograd SLO 73 B5
Drawno PL 46 B1
Drawsko Pomorskie PL 46 B1
Drayton GB 30 B5
Draženov CZ 62 A3
Draževac SCG 85 B5
Dražice HR 73 C4
Drebkau D 53 B4
Dreieich D 51 C4
Dreisen D 61 A4
Dren SCG 85 C5
Drenovac SCG 85 C6
Drenovci HR 84 B3
Drensteinfurt D 50 B3
Dresden D 53 B3
Dretyń PL 46 A2
Dreux F 58 B2
Dřevohostice CZ 64 A3
Drevsjø N 114 F9
Drewitz D 52 A2
Drezdenko PL 46 C1
Drežnica HR 83 A4
Drežnik-Grad HR 83 B4
Drietona SK 64 B3
Driffield GB 27 A5
Drimnin GB 24 B2
Drimoleague IRL 20 C2
Dringenberg D 51 B5
Drinić BIH 83 B5
Drinjača BIH 85 B4
Drinovci BIH 84 C2
Driopida GR 117 E6
Drivstua N 114 E6
Drlače SCG 85 B4
Drnholec CZ 64 B2
Drniš HR 83 C5
Drnje HR 74 B1
Drnovice CZ 64 A2
Dro I 71 C5
Drøbak N 35 C2
Drobin PL 47 C6
Drochia MD 11 B9
Drochtersen D 43 B6
Drogheda IRL 19 C5
Drohobych UA 11 B7
Droitwich Spa GB 29 A5
Drołtowice PL 54 B2
Dromahair IRL 18 B3
Dromcolliher IRL 20 B3
Dromore, *Down* GB 19 B5
Dromore, *Tyrone* GB 19 B4
Dromore West IRL 18 B3
Dronero I 79 B6
Dronfield GB 27 B4
Drongan GB 24 C3
Dronninglund DK 38 B3
Dronrijp NL 42 B2
Dronten NL 42 C2
Drosendorf A 63 B6
Drösing A 64 B2
Drottningholm S 37 C4
Droué F 58 B2
Drulingen F 60 B3
Drumbeg GB 22 C3
Drumcliff IRL 18 B3
Drumgask GB 23 D4
Drumkeeran IRL 18 B3
Drummore GB 24 D3
Drumnadrochit GB 23 D4
Drumquin GB 19 B4
Drumshanbo IRL 18 B3
Drumsna IRL 19 C4
Drunen NL 49 B6
Druskininkai LT 6 D7
Druten NL 49 B6
Druya BY 7 D9
Družetići SCG 85 B5
Drvar BIH 83 B5
Drvenik HR 84 C2
Drwalew PL 55 B6
Drymen GB 24 B3
Drynoch GB 22 D2
Drzewce PL 54 A2
Drzewiany PL 46 B2
Drzewica PL 55 B5
Dualchi I 110 B1
Duas Igrejas P 87 C4
Dub SCG 85 C4
Dubá CZ 53 C4
Dubăsari MD 11 C10
Duben D 53 B3
Dübendorf CH 70 A3
Dubí CZ 53 C3
Dubica HR 74 C1
Dublin IRL 21 A5
Dubna RUS 7 C14
Dubňany CZ 64 B3
Dubnica nad Váhom SK 64 B4
Dubnik SK 65 C4
Dubno UA 11 A8
Dubodiel SK 64 B4
Dubona SCG 85 B5
Dubovac SCG 85 B6
Dubovic BIH 83 B5
Dubranec HR 73 C5
Dubrava HR 74 C1
Dubrave BIH 84 B3
Dubravica HR 73 C5
Dubravica SCG 85 B6
Dubrovnik HR 84 D3
Dubrovytsya UA 7 F9
Ducey F 57 B4
Duchcov CZ 53 C3
Ducherow D 45 B5
Dučina SCG 85 B5
Duclair F 58 A1
Dudar H 74 A2
Duddington GB 30 B3
Duderstadt D 51 B6
Dudeştii Vechi RO 75 B5
Dudley GB 26 C3
Dueñas E 88 C2
Duesund N 32 B2
Dueville I 72 C1
Duffel B 49 B5
Duffield GB 27 C4
Dufftown GB 23 D5
Duga Poljana SCG 85 C5
Duga Resa HR 73 C5
Dugi Rat HR 83 C5
Dugny-sur-Meuse F 59 A6
Dugo Selo HR 73 C6
Dugopolje HR 83 C5
Duino I 72 C3
Duisburg D 50 B2
Dukat AL 105 C5
Dukhovshchina RUS 7 D12
Dukovany CZ 64 A2
Duleek IRL 19 C5
Dülken D 50 B2
Dülmen D 50 B3
Dulovo BG 11 E9
Dulpetorpet N 34 B4
Dulverton GB 29 B4
Dumbarton GB 24 C3
Dümerek TR 118 C6
Dumfries GB 25 C4
Dumlupinar TR 118 D4
Dümpelfeld D 50 C2
Dun Laoghaire IRL 21 A5
Dun-le-Palestel F 67 B6
Dun-les-Places F 68 A4
Dun-sur-Auron F 68 B2
Dun-sur-Meuse F 59 A6
Dunaalmás H 65 C4
Dunabogdány H 65 C5
Dunafalva H 74 B3
Dunaföldvár H 74 B3
Dunaharaszti H 75 A4
Dunajská Streda SK 64 C3
Dunakeszi H 65 C5
Dunakiliti H 64 C3
Dunakömlöd H 74 B3
Dunapataj H 75 B3
Dunaszekcsö H 74 B3
Dunaszentgyorgy H 74 B3
Dunatetétlen H 75 B4
Dunaújváros H 74 B3
Dunavecse H 75 B3
Dunbar GB 25 B5
Dunbeath GB 23 C5
Dunblane GB 25 B4
Dunboyne IRL 21 A5
Dundalk IRL 19 B5
Dundee GB 25 B5
Dundrennan GB 25 D4
Dundrum GB 19 B6
Dunfanaghy IRL 19 A4
Dunfermline GB 25 B4
Dungannon GB 19 B5
Dungarvan IRL 21 B4
Dungiven GB 19 B5
Dunglow IRL 18 B3
Dungourney IRL 20 C3
Duninowo PL 46 A2
Đunis SCG 85 C6
Dunkeld GB 25 B4
Dunker S 37 C3
Dunkerque = Dunkirk F 48 B3
Dunkineely IRL 18 B3
Dunkirk = Dunkerque F 48 B3
Dunlavin IRL 21 A5
Dunleer IRL 19 C5
Dunlop GB 24 C3
Dunloy GB 19 A5
Dunmanway IRL 20 C2
Dunmore IRL 18 C3
Dunmore East IRL 21 B5
Dunmurry GB 19 B5
Dunnet GB 23 C5
Dunningen D 61 B4
Dunoon GB 24 C3
Duns GB 25 C5
Dunscore GB 25 C4
Dunsford GB 29 C4
Dunshaughlin IRL 21 A5
Dunstable GB 31 C3
Dunster GB 29 B4
Dunvegan GB 22 D2
Duplek SLO 73 B5
Dupnitsa BG 11 E7
Durach D 61 C6
Durağan TR 16 A7
Durak TR 118 C3
Đurakovac SCG 85 D5
Durana E 89 B4
Durance F 76 B3
Durango E 89 A4
Durankulak BG 11 E10
Duras F 76 B3
Durban-Corbières F 78 D1
Dürbheim D 61 B4
Durbuy B 49 C6
Dúrcal E 100 C2
Đurdjenovac HR 74 C3
Đurdjevac HR 74 B2
Đurdjevik BIH 84 B3
Düren D 50 C2
Durham GB 25 D6
Đurinci SCG 85 B5
Durlach D 61 B4
Đurmanec HR 73 B5
Durness GB 22 C4
Dürnkrut A 64 B2
Dürrboden CH 71 B4
Dürrenboden CH 70 B3
Durrës AL 105 B5
Durrow IRL 21 B4
Durrus IRL 20 C2
Dursunbey TR 118 C3
Durtal F 57 C5
Durup DK 38 C1
Durusu TR 118 A3
Dusina BIH 84 C2
Dusnok H 75 B3
Dusocin PL 47 B4
Düsseldorf D 50 B2
Dusslingen D 61 B5
Duszniki PL 46 C2
Duszniki-Zdrój PL 54 C1
Dutovlje SLO 72 C3
Duvebo S 40 A4
Duved S 115 D9
Düzağac TR 118 D5
Düzce TR 118 B6
Dvärsätt S 115 D11
Dvor HR 83 A5
Dvorce CZ 64 A3
Dvorníky SK 64 B3
Dvory nad Žitavou SK 64 C4
Dvůr Králové nad Labem CZ 53 C5
Dyatkovo RUS 7 E13
Dybvad DK 38 B3
Dyce GB 23 D6
Dygowo PL 46 A1
Dykehead GB 25 B4
Dymchurch GB 31 C5
Dymer UA 11 A11
Dyrnes N 114 D4
Dywity PL 47 B6
Džanići BIH 84 C2
Dziadowa Kłoda PL 54 B2
Działdowo PL 47 B6
Działoszyce PL 55 C5
Działoszyn PL 54 B3
Dziemiany PL 46 A3
Dzierządnia PL 47 C6
Dzierzgoń PL 47 B5
Dzierzgowo PL 47 B6
Dzierżoniów PL 54 C1
Dzisna BY 7 D10
Dziwnów PL 45 A6
Dzyarzhynsk BY 7 E9
Dzyatlava BY 7 E8

E

Ea E 89 A4
Eaglesfield GB 25 C4
Ealing GB 31 C3
Eardisley GB 29 A4
Earl Shilton GB 30 B2
Earls Barton GB 30 B3
Earlston GB 25 C5
Easington GB 27 B6
Easky IRL 18 B3
East Calder GB 25 C4
East Dereham GB 30 B4
East Grinstead GB 31 C4
East Ilsley GB 31 C2
East Kilbride GB 24 C3
East Linton GB 25 C5
East Markham GB 27 B5
East Wittering GB 31 D3
Eastbourne GB 31 D4
Easter Skeld GB 22 A7
Eastleigh GB 31 D2
Easton GB 29 C5
Eaton Socon GB 30 B3
Eaux-Bonnes F 76 D2
Eauze F 76 C3
Ebberup DK 39 D2
Ebbs A 62 C3
Ebbw Vale GB 29 B4
Ebeleben D 51 B6
Ebeltoft DK 39 C3
Eben im Pongau A 72 A3
Ebene Reichenau A 72 B3
Ebensee A 63 C4
Ebensfeld D 51 C6
Eberbach D 61 A4
Ebergötzen D 51 B6
Ebermann-Stadt D 62 A2
Ebern D 51 C6
Eberndorf A 73 B4
Ebersbach D 53 B4
Ebersberg D 62 B2
Ebersdorf, *Bayern* D 52 C1
Ebersdorf, *Niedersachsen* D 43 B6
Eberstein A 73 B4
Eberswalde D 45 C5
Ebnat-Kappel CH 71 A4
Éboli I 103 C8
Ebrach D 61 A6
Ebreichsdorf A 64 C2
Ebreuil F 68 B3
Ebstorf D 44 B2
Ecclefechan GB 25 C4
Eccleshall GB 26 C3
Eceabat TR 118 B1
Echallens CH 69 B6
Echauri E 76 D1
Echinos GR 116 A7
Echiré F 67 B4
Échirolles F 69 C5
Echourgnac F 76 A3
Echt NL 50 B1
Echte D 51 B6
Echternach L 60 A2

F

Gaildorf D 61 B5
Gaillac F 77 C4
Gaillefontaine F 58 A2
Gaillon F 58 A2
Gainsborough GB 27 B5
Gairloch GB 22 D3
Gairlochy GB 24 B3
Gáiro I 110 C2
Gaj HR 74 C2
Gaj SCG 85 B6
Gaja-la-Selve F 77 C4
Gajanejos E 95 B4
Gajary SK 64 B2
Gajdobra SCG 75 C4
Galan F 77 C3
Galanta SK 64 B3
Galapagar E 94 B2
Galápagos E 95 B3
Galaroza E 99 B4
Galashiels GB 25 C5
Galatas GR 117 E5
Galaţi RO 11 D10
Galatina I 107 A5
Galatista GR 116 B5
Galátone I 107 A5
Galaxidi GR 117 D4
Galdakao E 89 A4
Galeata I 81 C5
Galende E 87 B4
Galera E 101 B3
Galéria F 102 A1
Galgamácsa H 65 C5
Galgate GB 26 B3
Galgon F 76 B2
Galices P 92 A3
Galinduste E 93 A5
Galinoporni CY 120 A3
Galisteo E 93 B4
Galków PL 55 B4
Gallarate I 70 C3
Gallardon F 58 B2
Gallegos de Argañán E 93 A4
Gallegos del Solmirón E 93 A5
Galleguillos de Campos E 88 B1
Galleno I 81 C4
Galliate I 70 C3
Gallicano I 81 B4
Gállio I 72 C1
Gallípoli I 107 A4
Gallipoli = Gelibolu TR 118 B1
Gällivare S 112 E9
Gallizien A 73 B4
Gallneukirchen A 63 B5
Gällö S 115 E12
Gallocanta E 95 B5
Gällstad S 40 B3
Gallur E 90 B1
Galmisdale GB 24 B1
Galmpton GB 29 C4
Galston GB 24 C3
Galta N 33 C2
Galtelli I 110 B2
Galten DK 39 C2
Galtür A 71 B5
Galve de Sorbe E 95 A3
Galveias P 92 B2
Gálvez E 94 C2
Galway IRL 20 A2
Gamaches F 48 D2
Gámbara I 71 C5
Gambárie I 106 C2
Gambassi Terme I 81 C4
Gambatesa I 103 B7
Gambolò I 70 C3
Gaming A 63 C6
Gamla Uppsala S 36 C4
Gamleby S 40 B6
Gamlingay GB 30 B3
Gammelgarn S 37 E5
Gammelstad S 3 D25
Gammertingen D 61 B5
Gams CH 71 A4
Gamvik, *Finnmark* N 113 A17
Gamvik, *Finnmark* N 113 B11
Gan F 76 C2
Gáname E 87 C4
Ganda di Martello I 71 B5
Gandarela P 87 C2
Ganddal N 33 D2
Ganderkesee D 43 B5
Gandesa E 90 B3
Gandía E 96 C2
Gandino I 71 C4
Gandrup DK 38 B3
Ganges F 78 C2
Gånghester S 40 B3
Gangi I 109 B3
Gangkofen D 62 B3
Gannat F 68 B3
Gannay-sur-Loire F 68 B3
Gänserdorf A 64 B2
Ganzlin D 44 B4
Gap F 79 B5
Gara H 75 B4
Garaballa E 96 B1
Garaguso I 104 C2
Garbayuela E 94 C1
Garbhallt GB 24 B2
Garbsen D 43 C6
Garching D 62 B3
Garciaz E 93 B5
Garcihernández E 94 B1
Garcillán E 94 B2
Garcinarro E 95 B4
Garcisobaco E 99 C5
Garda I 71 C5
Gardanne F 79 C4
Gärdås S 34 B5
Gårdby S 41 C6
Gardeja PL 47 B4
Gardelegen D 44 C3
Gardermoen N 34 B3
Gardiki GR 116 D3
Garding D 43 A5
Gardone Riviera I 71 C5
Gardone Val Trómpia I 71 C5
Gárdony H 74 A3
Gardouch F 77 C4
Gards Köpinge S 41 D4
Gårdsjö S 37 D1
Gårdskär S 36 B4
Garein F 76 B2
Garelochhead GB 24 B3
Garéoult F 79 C5
Garešnica HR 74 C1
Garéssio I 80 B2
Garforth GB 27 B4
Gargaliani GR 117 E3
Gargaligas E 93 B5
Gargallo E 90 C2
Garganta la Olla E 93 A5
Gargantiel E 100 A1
Gargellen A 71 B4
Gargilesse-Dampierre F 67 B6
Gargnano I 71 C5
Gargnäs S 115 B14
Gárgoles de Abajo E 95 B4
Gargrave GB 26 B3
Garitz D 52 B2
Garlasco I 70 C3
Garlieston GB 24 D3
Garlin F 76 C2
Garlitos E 94 D1
Garmisch-Partenkirchen D 71 A6
Garnat-sur-Engièvre F 68 B3
Garpenberg S 36 B3
Garphyttan S 37 C1
Garray E 89 C4
Garrel D 43 C5
Garriguella E 91 A6
Garrison GB 18 B3
Garrovillas E 93 B4
Garrucha E 101 B4
Gars-a-Kamp A 63 B6
Garsås S 36 B1
Garsdale Head GB 26 A3
Gärsnäs S 41 D4
Garstang GB 26 B3
Gartow D 44 B3
Gartz D 45 B6
Garvagh GB 19 B5
Garvão P 98 B2
Garve GB 22 D4
Garwolin PL 55 B6
Garz D 45 A5
Garzyn PL 54 B1
Gąsawa PL 46 C3
Gåsborn S 34 C6
Gaschurn A 71 B5
Gascueña E 95 B4
Gasny F 58 A2
Gąsocin PL 47 C6
Gastes F 76 B1
Gastouni GR 117 E3
Gastouri GR 116 C1
Gata E 93 A4
Gata HR 83 C5
Gata de Gorgos E 96 C3
Gatchina RUS 7 B11
Gatehouse of Fleet GB 24 D3
Gátér H 75 B4
Gateshead GB 25 D6
Gátova E 96 B2
Gattendorf A 64 B2
Gatteo a Mare I 82 B1
Gattinara I 70 C3
Gattorna I 80 B3
Gaucín E 99 C5
Gaulstad N 114 D9
Gaupne N 32 A4
Gautefall N 33 C5
Gauting D 62 B2
Gauto S 115 A13
Gava E 91 B5
Gavardo I 71 C5
Gavarnie F 76 D2
Gavi I 80 B2
Gavião P 92 B3
Gavirate I 70 C3
Gävle S 36 B4
Gavoi I 110 B2
Gavorrano I 81 D4
Gavray F 57 B4
Gavrio GR 117 E6
Gävunda S 34 B6
Gaweinstal A 64 B2
Gaworzyce PL 53 B5
Gawroniec PL 46 B2
Gaydon GB 30 B2
Gayton GB 30 B4
Gazipaşa TR 119 F7
Gazoldo degli Ippoliti I 71 C5
Gazzuolo I 81 A4
Gbelce SK 65 C4
Gdańsk PL 47 A4
Gdinj HR 84 C1
Gdov RUS 7 B9
Gdów PL 65 A6
Gdynia PL 47 A4
Gea de Albarracin E 95 B5
Geary GB 22 D2
Géaudot F 59 B5
Geaune F 76 C2
Gebesee D 51 B6
Gebiz TR 119 E5
Gebze TR 118 B4
Géderlak H 75 B3
Gedern D 51 C5
Gedinne B 49 D5
Gediz TR 118 D4
Gèdre F 76 D3
Gedser DK 44 A3
Gedsted DK 38 C2
Geel B 49 B5
Geesthacht D 44 B2
Geetbets B 49 C6
Gefell D 52 C1
Gehrden D 51 A5
Gehren D 52 C1
Geilenkirchen D 50 C2
Geilo N 32 B5
Geinsheim D 61 A4
Geisa D 51 C5
Geiselhöring D 62 B3
Geiselwind D 61 A6
Geisenfeld D 62 B2
Geisenhausen D 62 B3
Geisenheim D 50 D4
Geising D 53 C3
Geisingen D 61 C4
Geislingen D 61 B5
Geistthal A 73 A5
Geiteryggyhytta N 32 B4
Geithain D 52 B2
Geithus N 34 C1
Gela I 109 B3
Geldermalsen NL 49 B6
Geldern D 50 B2
Geldrop NL 49 B6
Geleen NL 50 C1
Gelembe TR 118 C2
Gelendost TR 119 D6
Gelibolu = Gallipoli TR 118 B1
Gelida E 91 B4
Gelnhausen D 51 C5
Gelnica SK 65 B6
Gelsa E 90 B2
Gelse H 74 B1
Gelsenkirchen D 50 B3
Gelsted DK 39 D2
Geltendorf D 62 B2
Gelterkinden CH 70 A2
Gelting D 39 E2
Gelu RO 75 B6
Gelves E 99 B4
Gembloux B 49 C5
Gemeaux F 69 A5
Gémenos F 79 C4
Gemerská Poloma SK 65 B6
Gemerská Ves SK 65 B6
Gemert NL 50 B1
Gemla S 40 C4
Gemlik TR 118 B4
Gemmenich B 50 C1
Gemona del Friuli I 72 B3
Gémozac F 67 C4
Gemund D 50 C2
Gemünden, *Bayern* D 51 C5
Gemünden, *Hessen* D 51 C4
Gemünden, *Rheinland-Pfalz* D 60 A3
Genappe B 49 C5
Génave E 101 A3
Genazzano I 102 B5
Gençay F 67 B5
Gencsapáti H 74 A1
Gendringen NL 50 B2
Genelard F 69 B4
Genemuiden NL 42 C3
Generalski Stol HR 73 C5
Geneva = Genève CH 69 B6
Genevad S 40 C3
Genève = Geneva CH 69 B6
Genevriéres F 60 C1
Gengenbach D 61 B4
Genillé F 67 A6
Genk B 49 C6
Genlis F 69 A5
Gennep NL 50 B1
Genner DK 39 D2
Gennes F 67 A4
Genoa = Génova I 80 B2
Genola I 80 B1
Génova = Genoa I 80 B2
Genowefa PL 54 A3
Gensingen D 60 A3
Gent = Ghent B 49 B4
Genthin D 44 C4
Gentioux F 68 C1
Genzano di Lucánia I 104 C2
Genzano di Roma I 102 B5
Georgenthal D 51 C6
Georgsmarienhütte D 50 A4
Gera D 52 C2
Geraards-bergen B 49 C4
Gerace I 106 C3
Geraci Sículo I 109 B3
Geraki GR 117 F4
Gérardmer F 60 B2
Geras A 63 B6
Gerbéviller F 60 B2
Gerbini I 109 B3
Gerbstedt D 52 B1
Gerði IS 111 C9
Gerede TR 118 B7
Gerena E 99 B4
Geretsried D 62 C2
Gérgal E 101 B3
Gergy F 69 B4
Gerindote E 94 C2
Gerjen H 74 B3
Gerlos A 72 A2
Germay F 59 B6
Germencik TR 119 E2
Germering D 62 B2
Germersheim D 61 A4
Gërmeç AL 105 C5
Gernika-Lumo E 89 A4
Gernrode D 52 B1
Gernsbach D 61 B4
Gernsheim D 61 A4
Geroda D 51 C5
Gerola Alta I 71 B4
Geroldsgrun D 52 C1
Gerolsbach D 62 B2
Gerolstein D 50 C2
Gerolzhofen D 61 A6
Gerovo HR 73 C4
Gerpinnes B 49 C5
Gerrards Cross GB 31 C3
Gerri de la Sal E 91 A4
Gersfeld D 51 C5
Gerstetten D 61 B6
Gersthofen D 62 B1
Gerstungen D 51 C6
Gerswalde D 45 B5
Gerzat F 68 C3
Gerze TR 16 A7
Gerzen D 62 B3
Gescher D 50 B3
Geseke D 51 B4
Geslau D 61 A6
Gespunsart F 59 A5
Gesté F 66 A3
Gestorf D 51 A5
Gesualda I 103 C8
Gesunda S 36 B1
Geta FIN 36 B6
Getafe E 94 B3
Getinge S 40 C2
Getxo E 89 A4
Geversdorf D 43 B6
Gevgelija MK 116 A4
Gevora del Caudillo E 93 C4
Gevrey-Chambertin F 69 A4
Gex F 69 B6
Gey D 50 C2
Geyikli TR 118 C1
Geysir IS 111 C5
Geyve TR 118 B5
Gföhl A 63 B6
Ghedi I 71 C5
Ghent = Gent B 49 B4
Gheorgheni RO 11 C8
Ghigo I 79 B6
Ghilarza I 110 B1
Ghisonaccia F 102 A2
Ghisoni F 102 A2
Gialtra GR 116 D4
Gianitsa GR 116 B4
Giardinetto Vécchio I 103 B8
Giardini Naxos I 109 B4
Giarratana I 109 B3
Giarre I 109 B4
Giat F 68 C2
Giaveno I 80 A1
Giazza I 71 C6
Giba I 110 C1
Gibellina Nuova I 108 B1
Gibostad N 112 C7
Gibraleón E 99 B4
Gibraltar GBZ 99 C5
Gic H 74 A2
Gideå S 115 D16
Gideåkroken S 115 C14
Gidle PL 55 C4
Giebelstadt D 61 A5
Gieboldehausen D 51 B6
Gielniów PL 55 B5
Gielow D 45 B4
Gien F 58 C3
Giengen D 61 B6
Giens F 79 C5
Giera RO 75 C5
Gieselwerder D 51 B5
Giessen D 51 C4
Gieten NL 42 B3
Giethoorn NL 42 C3
Giffaumont-Champaubert F 59 B5
Gifford GB 25 C5
Gifhorn D 44 C2
Gige H 74 B2
Giglio Porto I 102 A3
Gignac F 78 C2
Gijón E 88 A1
Gilena E 100 B1
Gilford GB 19 B5
Gillberga S 35 C4
Gilleleje DK 41 C2
Gilley F 69 A6
Gilley-sur-Loire F 68 B3
Gillingham, *Dorset* GB 29 B5
Gillingham, *Medway* GB 31 C4
Gilocourt F 59 A3
Gilserberg D 51 C5
Gilsland GB 25 D5
Gilze NL 49 B5
Gimåt S 115 D15
Gimo S 36 B5
Gimont F 77 C3
Ginasservis F 79 C4
Gingelom B 49 C6
Gingst D 45 A5
Ginosa I 104 C2
Ginzling A 72 A1
Giões P 98 B3
Gióia dei Marsi I 103 B6
Gióia del Colle I 104 C2
Gióia Sannitica I 103 B7
Gióia Táuro I 106 C2
Gioiosa Iónica I 106 C3
Gioiosa Marea I 109 A3
Giosla GB 22 C2
Giovinazzo I 104 B2
Girifalco I 106 C3
Giromagny F 60 C2
Girona E 91 B5
Gironcourt-sur-Vraine F 60 B1
Gironella E 91 A4
Gironville-sous-les-Côtes F 60 B1
Girvan GB 24 C3
Gislaved S 40 B3
Gislev DK 39 D3
Gisors F 58 A2
Gissi I 103 A7
Gistad S 37 D2
Gistel B 48 B3
Gistrup DK 38 C3
Giswil CH 70 B3
Githio GR 117 F4
Giugliano in Campania I 103 C7
Giulianova I 103 A6
Giulvăz RO 75 C5
Giurgiu RO 11 E8
Give DK 39 D2
Givet F 49 C5
Givors F 69 C4
Givry B 49 C5
Givry F 69 B4
Givry-en-Argonne F 59 B5
Givskud DK 39 D2
Giżalki PL 54 A2
Gizeux F 67 A5
Giżycko PL 6 D7
Gizzeria I 106 C3
Gizzeria Lido I 106 C3
Gjedved DK 39 D2
Gjegjan AL 105 B6
Gjendesheim N 32 A5
Gjerde N 32 B3
Gjerlev DK 38 C3
Gjermundshamn N 32 B2
Gjerrild DK 38 C3
Gjerstad N 33 D6
Gjesås N 34 B4
Gjesvær N 113 A14
Gjirokastër AL 116 B2
Gjøfjell N 35 C2
Gjøl DK 38 B2
Gjøra N 114 E6
Gjøvik N 34 B2
Gladbeck D 50 B2
Gladenbach D 51 C4
Gladstad N 114 B8
Glamis GB 25 B4
Glamoč BIH 84 B1
Glamsbjerg DK 39 D3
Gland CH 69 B6
Glandorf D 50 A3
Glanegg A 73 B4
Glanshammar S 37 C2
Glarus CH 70 A4
Glasgow GB 24 C3
Glashütte, *Bayern* D 62 C2
Glashütte, *Sachsen* D 53 C3
Glastonbury GB 29 B5
Glatzau A 73 B5
Glauchau D 52 C2
Glava S 35 C4
Glavatičevo BIH 84 C3
Glavičice BIH 85 B4
Glavnik SCG 85 D6
Gledica SCG 85 C5
Glein A 73 A4
Glein N 115 A9
Gleinstätten A 73 B5
Gleisdorf A 73 A5
Glenamoy IRL 18 B2
Glenarm GB 19 B6
Glenavy GB 19 B5
Glenbarr GB 24 C2
Glenbeigh IRL 20 B2
Glenbrittle GB 22 D2
Glencoe GB 24 B2
Glencolumbkille IRL 18 B3
Glendalough IRL 21 A5
Glenealy IRL 21 B5
Glenelg GB 22 D3
Glenfinnan GB 24 B2
Glengarriff IRL 20 C2
Glenluce GB 24 D3
Glennamaddy IRL 18 C3
Glenrothes GB 25 B4
Glenties IRL 18 B3
Glesborg DK 38 C3
Glesien D 52 B2
Gletsch CH 70 B3
Glewitz D 45 A4
Glifada GR 117 E5
Glimåkra S 41 C4
Glin IRL 20 B2
Glina HR 73 C6
Glinde D 44 B2
Glinojeck PL 47 C6
Glinsk IRL 20 A1
Gliwice PL 54 C3
Glödnitz A 73 B4
Gloggnitz A 64 C1
Głogoczów PL 65 A5
Glogonj SCG 85 B5
Glogovac SCG 85 D6
Głogów PL 53 B6
Głogówek PL 54 C2
Glomel F 56 B2
Glomfjord N 112 F2
Glommen S 40 C2
Glommersträsk S 115 B16
Glonn D 62 C2
Glorenza I 71 B5
Gloria P 92 B2
Glosa GR 116 C5
Glossop GB 27 B4
Gloucester GB 29 B5
Głowaczów PL 55 B6
Glówczyce PL 46 A3
Glöwen D 44 C4
Głowno PL 55 B4
Gložan SCG 75 C4
Głubczyce PL 54 C2
Głuchołazy PL 54 C2
Głuchów PL 55 B5
Głuchowo PL 54 A1
Glücksburg D 39 E2
Glückstadt D 43 B6
Glumina BIH 84 B4
Glumsø DK 39 D4
Glušci SCG 85 B4
Glusk BY 7 E10
Głuszyca PL 53 C6
Glyn Neath GB 29 B4
Glyngøre DK 38 C1
Gmünd, *Karnten* A 72 B3
Gmünd, *Nieder Östereich* A 63 B5
Gmund D 62 C2
Gmunden A 63 C4
Gnarp S 115 E14
Gnarrenburg D 43 B6
Gnesau A 72 B3
Gnesta S 37 C4
Gnięchowice PL 54 B1
Gniew PL 47 B4
Gniewkowo PL 47 C4
Gniezno PL 46 C3
Gnoien D 45 B4
Gnojnice BIH 84 C2
Gnojno PL 55 C5
Gnosall GB 26 C3
Gnosjö S 40 B3
Göbel TR 118 B3
Göçbeyli TR 118 C2
Goch D 50 B2
Gochsheim D 51 C6
Göd H 65 C5
Godalming GB 31 C3
Godby FIN 36 B6
Goddelsheim D 51 B4
Gódega di Sant'Urbano I 72 C2
Godegård S 37 D2
Godelheim D 45 B5
Goderville F 58 A1
Godiasco I 80 B3
Godič SLO 73 B4
Godkowo PL 47 A5
Godmanchester GB 30 B3
Gödöllö H 65 C5
Gödre H 74 B2
Godshill GB 31 D2
Godzikowice PL 54 C2
Godziszewo PL 47 A4
Goes NL 49 B4
Goetzenbrück F 60 B3
Góglio I 70 B3
Gogolin PL 54 C3
Göhren D 45 A5
Goirle NL 49 B6
Góis P 92 A2
Góito I 71 C5
Goizueta E 76 C1
Gojna Gora SCG 85 C5
Gójsk PL 47 C5
Gökçedağ TR 118 C3
Gökçen TR 119 D2
Gökçeören TR 119 D3
Gökçeyazı TR 118 C2
Göktepe TR 119 E3
Gol N 32 B5
Gola HR 74 B2
Gola N 34 A1
Gołańcz PL 46 C3
Gölbaşı TR 16 B6
Gölby FIN 36 B6
Gölcük, *Kocaeli* TR 118 B4
Gölcük, *Niğde* TR 16 B7
Golčův Jenikov CZ 63 A6
Gołczewo PL 45 B6
Goldach CH 71 A4
Goldbach D 51 C5
Goldbeck D 44 C3
Goldberg D 44 B4
Goldelund D 43 A6
Goldenstedt D 43 C5
Gołębiewo PL 47 A4
Golegã P 92 B2
Goleniów PL 45 B6
Golfo Aranci I 110 B2
Gölhisar TR 119 E4
Golina PL 54 A3
Gölle H 74 B3
Göllersdorf A 64 B2
Golling an der Salzach A 63 C4
Gölmarmara TR 118 D2
Golnice PL 53 B5
Golnik SLO 73 B4
Gölova TR 119 F5
Gölpazarı TR 118 B5
Gols A 64 C2
Golspie GB 23 D5
Golssen D 52 B3
Golub-Dobrzyń PL 47 B5
Golubac SCG 85 B6
Golubinci SCG 85 B5
Golubovci SCG 105 A5
Goluchów PL 54 B2
Golzow D 52 A2
Gomagoi I 71 B5
Gómara E 89 C4
Gomaringen D 61 B5
Gömbe TR 119 F4
Gömeç TR 118 C1
Gomel = Homyel BY 7 E11
Gomes Aires P 98 B2
Gómezserracin E 88 C2
Gommern D 52 A1
Gomulin PL 55 B4
Gonäs S 36 B2
Goncelin F 69 C5
Gończyce PL 55 B6
Gondomar E 87 B2
Gondomar P 87 C2
Gondrecourt-le-Château F 60 B1
Gondrin F 76 C3
Gönen, *Balıkesir* TR 118 B2
Gönen, *İsparta* TR 119 E5
Gonfaron F 79 C5
Goñi E 76 D1
Goni GR 116 C4
Goni I 110 C2
Gonnesa I 110 C1
Gonnosfanádiga I 110 C1
Gönyü H 64 C3
Gonzaga I 81 B4
Goodrich GB 29 B5
Goodwick GB 28 A2
Gooik B 49 C5
Goole GB 27 B5
Goor NL 50 A2
Göpfritz an der Wild A 63 B6
Goppenstein CH 70 B2
Göppingen D 61 B5
Gor E 100 B3
Góra, *Dolnośląskie* PL 54 B1
Góra, *Mazowieckie* PL 47 C6
Góra Kalwaria PL 55 B6
Gorafe E 100 B2
Gorawino PL 46 B1
Goražde BIH 84 C3
Gordaliza del Pino E 88 B1
Gördes TR 118 D3
Gørding DK 39 D1
Górdola CH 70 B3
Gordon GB 25 C5
Gordoncillo E 88 B1
Gorebridge GB 25 C4
Gorenja Vas SLO 73 B4
Gorenje Jelenje HR 73 C4
Gorey GB 57 A3
Gorey IRL 21 B5
Gorgonzola I 71 C4
Gorica HR 83 B4
Gorican HR 74 B1
Gorinchem NL 49 B5
Goring GB 31 C2
Goritsy RUS 7 C14
Göritz D 45 B5
Gorizia I 72 C3
Górki PL 47 C5
Gorleben D 44 B3
Gorleston-on-sea GB 30 B5
Gørlev DK 39 D4
Görlitz D 53 B4
Górliz E 89 A4
Görmin D 45 B5
Górna Grupa PL 47 B4
Gorna Oryakhovitsa BG 11 E8
Gornja Gorevnica SCG 85 C5
Gornja Klina SCG 85 D5
Gornja Ploča HR 83 B4
Gornja Radgona SLO 73 B5
Gornja Sabanta SCG 85 C6
Gornja Trešnjevica SCG 85 B5
Gornja Tuzla BIH 84 B3
Gornje Polje SCG 84 D3
Gornje Ratkovo BIH 84 B1
Gornji Grad SLO 73 B4
Gornji Humac HR 83 C5
Gornji Jasenjani BIH 84 C2
Gornji Kamengrad BIH 83 B5
Gornji Kneginec HR 73 B6
Gornji Kokoti SCG 105 A5
Gornji Kosinj HR 83 B4
Gornji Milanovac SCG 85 B5
Gornji Podgradci BIH 84 A2
Gornji Ravno BIH 84 C2
Gornji Sjenicak HR 73 C5
Gornji Vakuf BIH 84 C2
Górno PL 55 C5
Görömböly H 65 B6
Górowo Iławeckie PL 47 A6
Gorran Haven GB 28 C3
Gorredijk NL 42 B3
Gorron F 57 B5
Gorseinon GB 28 B3
Gort IRL 20 A3
Gortin GB 19 B4
Görzke D 52 A2
Gorzkowice PL 55 B4
Górzno, *Kujawsko-Pomorskie* PL 47 B5
Górzno, *Zachodnio-Pomorskie* PL 46 B1
Gorzów Śląski PL 54 B3
Gorzów Wielkopolski PL 45 C7
Górzyca PL 45 C6
Gorzyce PL 54 D3
Górzyn, *Lubuskie* PL 53 B4
Gorzyń, *Wielkopolskie* PL 46 C1
Gorzyno PL 46 A3
Gosaldo I 72 B1
Gosau A 63 C4
Gosberton GB 30 B3
Gościcino PL 47 A4
Gościęcin PL 54 C3
Gościm PL 46 C1
Gościno PL 46 A1
Gosdorf A 73 B5
Gosforth GB 26 A2
Goslar D 51 B6
Goslice PL 47 C5
Gospič HR 83 B4
Gosport GB 31 D2
Goss Ilsede D 51 A6
Gössäter S 35 D5
Gossau CH 71 A4
Gössnitz D 52 C2
Gössweinstein D 62 A2
Gostimë AL 105 C6
Gostkow PL 55 B4
Göstling an der Ybbs A 63 C5
Gostomia PL 46 B2
Gostycyn PL 46 B3
Gostyń PL 54 B2
Gostynin PL 47 C5
Goszczyn PL 55 B5
Göta S 35 D4
Göteborg = Gothenburg S 38 B4
Götene S 35 D5
Gotha D 51 C6
Gothem S 37 E5
Gothenburg = Göteborg S 38 B4
Gotse Delchev BG 116 A5
Gottersdorf D 62 B3
Göttingen D 51 B5
Gottne S 115 D15
Götzis A 71 A4
Gouarec F 56 B2
Gouda NL 49 A5
Goudhurst GB 31 C4
Goumenissa GR 116 B4
Goura GR 117 E4
Gourdon F 77 B4
Gourgançon F 59 B5
Gourin F 56 B2
Gournay-en-Bray F 58 A2
Gourock GB 24 C3
Gouveia P 92 A3
Gouvy B 50 C1
Gouzeacourt F 49 C4
Gouzon F 68 B2
Govedari HR 84 D2
Govérnolo I 81 A4
Gowarczów PL 55 B5
Gowerton GB 28 B3
Gowidlino PL 46 A3
Gowran IRL 21 B4
Goyatz D 53 A4
Göynük, *Antalya* TR 119 F5
Göynük TR 118 B5
Gozdnica PL 53 B5
Gozdowo PL 47 C5
Gozee B 49 C5
Graal-Müritz D 44 A4
Grab BIH 84 D3
Grabenstätt D 62 C3
Grabhair GB 22 C2
Gråbo S 38 B5
Grabovac HR 84 C1
Grabovac SCG 85 B5
Grabovci SCG 85 B4
Grabow D 44 B3
Grabów PL 55 A4
Grabów nad Pilicą PL 55 B6
Grabów nad Prosną PL 54 B3
Grabowno PL 46 B3
Grabs CH 71 A4
Gračac HR 83 B4
Gračanica BIH 84 B3
Gračanica SCG 85 D6
Graçay F 68 A1
Gracen AL 105 B5
Grad SLO 73 B6
Gradac BIH 84 D3
Gradac HR 84 C2
Gradac, *Crna Gora* SCG 85 C4
Gradac, *Srbija* SCG 85 C5
Gradačac BIH 84 B3
Gradec HR 74 C1
Gradefes E 88 B1
Grades A 73 B4
Gradil P 92 C1
Gradina HR 74 C2
Gradina SCG 85 C4
Gradisca d'Isonzo I 72 C3
Gradište HR 74 C3
Grado E 86 A4
Grado I 72 C3
Grærup Strand DK 39 D1
Græsted DK 41 C2
Grafenau D 63 B4
Gräfenberg D 62 A2
Gräfenhainichen D 52 B2
Grafenschlag A 63 B6

Grafenstein A 73 B4
Gräfenthal D 52 C1
Grafentonna D 51 B6
Grafenwöhr D 62 A2
Grafing D 62 B2
Grafling D 62 B3
Gräfsnäs S 40 A2
Gragnano I 103 C7
Grahovo SCG 84 D3
Grahovo SLO 72 B3
Graiguenamanagh IRL 21 B5
Grain GB 31 C4
Grainau D 71 A6
Graja de Iniesta E 95 C5
Grajera E 89 B4
Gram DK 39 D2
Gramais A 71 A5
Gramat F 77 B4
Gramatneusiedl A 64 B2
Grambow D 45 B6
Grammichele I 109 B3
Gramsh AL 116 B2
Gramzow D 45 B6
Gran N 34 B2
Granada E 100 B2
Granard IRL 19 C4
Grañas E 86 A3
Granátula de Calatrava E 100 A2
Grancey-le-Château F 59 C6
Grand-Champ F 56 C3
Grand Couronne F 58 A2
Grand-Fougeray F 57 C4
Grandas de Salime E 86 A4
Grandcamp-Maisy F 57 A4
Grândola P 98 A2
Grandpré F 59 A5
Grandrieu B 49 C5
Grandrieu F 78 B2
Grandson CH 70 B1
Grandvillars F 70 A1
Grandvilliers F 58 A2
Grañén E 90 B2
Grangärde S 36 B1
Grange IRL 18 B3
Grange-over-Sands GB 26 A3
Grangemouth GB 25 B4
Granges-de Crouhens F 77 D3
Granges-sur-Vologne F 60 B2
Grängesberg S 36 B1
Gräningen D 44 C4
Granitola-Torretta I 108 B1
Granja, *Évora* P 98 A3
Granja, *Porto* P 87 C2
Granja de Moreruela E 88 C1
Granja de Torrehermosa E 93 C5
Gränna S 40 A4
Grannäs, *Västerbotten* S 115 B13
Grannäs, *Västerbotten* S 115 B14
Granö S 115 C16
Granollers E 91 B5
Granowiec PL 54 B2
Granowo PL 54 A1
Gransee D 45 B5
Gransherad N 33 C6
Grantham GB 27 C5
Grantown-on-Spey GB 23 D5
Grantshouse GB 25 C5
Granville F 57 B4
Granvin N 32 B3
Gräsås S 40 C2
Grasbakken N 113 B17
Grasberg D 43 B6
Grasmere GB 26 A2
Gräsmyr S 115 D16
Grasö S 36 B5
Grassano I 104 C2
Grassau D 62 C3
Grasse F 79 C5
Grassington GB 27 A4
Gråsten DK 39 E2
Grästorp S 35 D4
Gratkorn A 73 A5
Gråträsk S 115 B16
Gratwein A 73 A5
Graulhet F 77 C4
Graus E 90 A3
Grávalos E 89 B5
Gravberget N 34 B4
Grave NL 50 B1
Gravedona I 71 B4
Gravelines F 48 B3
Gravellona Toce I 70 C3
Gravendal S 36 B1
's-Gravendeel NL 49 B5
's-Gravenhage = The Hague NL 49 A5
Gravens DK 39 D2
's-Gravenzande NL 49 B5
Gravesend GB 31 C4
Graveson F 78 C3
Gravina in Púglia I 104 C2
Gray F 69 A5
Grayrigg GB 26 A3
Grays GB 31 C4
Grayshott GB 31 C3
Grayvoron RUS 7 F13
Graz A 73 A5
Grazalema E 99 C5
Grążawy PL 47 B5
Grazzano Visconti I 80 B3
Greåker N 35 C3
Great Dunmow GB 31 C4
Great Malvern GB 29 A5
Great Torrington GB 28 C3
Great Waltham GB 31 C4
Great Yarmouth GB 30 B5
Grebbestad S 35 D3
Grebenstein D 51 B5
Grębocice PL 53 B5
Grębocin PL 47 B4
Greding D 62 A2
Gredstedbro DK 39 D1
Greenhead GB 25 D5
Greenisland GB 19 B6
Greenlaw GB 25 C5
Greenock GB 24 C3
Greenway GB 28 B3
Greenwich GB 31 C4
Grefrath D 50 B2
Greifenburg A 72 B3
Greiffenberg D 45 B5
Greifswald D 45 A5
Grein A 63 B5
Greipstad N 33 D4
Greiz D 52 C2
Grenaa DK 39 C3
Grenade F 77 C4
Grenade-sur-l'Adour F 76 C2
Grenchen CH 70 A2
Grendi N 33 D4
Grenivík IS 111 B7
Grenoble F 69 C5
Gréoux-les-Bains F 79 C4
Gresenhorst D 44 A4
Gressoney-la-Trinité I 70 C2
Gressoney-St.-Jean I 70 C2
Gressthal D 51 C6
Gressvik N 35 C2
Gresten A 63 C6
Gretna GB 25 D4
Greussen D 51 B6
Greve in Chianti I 81 C5
Greven, *Mecklenburg-Vorpommern* D 44 B2
Greven, *Nordrhein-Westfalen* D 50 A3
Grevena GR 116 B3
Grevenbroich D 50 B2
Grevenbrück D 50 B4
Grevenmacher L 60 A2
Grevesmühlen D 44 B3
Grevestrand DK 41 D2
Grevie S 41 C2
Greystoke GB 26 A3
Greystones IRL 21 A5
Grez-Doiceau B 49 C5
Grez-en-Bouère F 57 C5
Grèzec F 77 B4
Grezzana I 71 C6
Grgar SLO 72 B3
Grgurevci SCG 85 A4
Gries A 71 A6
Gries in Sellrain A 71 A6
Griesbach D 63 B4
Griesheim D 61 A4
Grieskirchen A 63 B4
Griffen A 73 B4
Grignan F 78 B3
Grignano I 72 C3
Grigno I 72 B1
Grignols F 76 B2
Grignon F 69 C6
Grijota E 88 B2
Grijpskerk NL 42 B3
Gril AL 105 A5
Grillby S 37 C4
Grimaud F 79 C5
Grimbergen B 49 C5
Grimma D 52 B2
Grimmen D 45 A5
Grimmialp CH 70 B2
Grimsås S 40 B3
Grimsby GB 27 B5
Grimslöv S 40 C4
Grímsstaðir IS 111 B9
Grimstad N 33 D5
Grimstorp S 40 B4
Grindavík IS 111 D3
Grindelwald CH 70 B3
Grindheim N 33 D4
Grindsted DK 39 D1
Griñón E 94 B3
Gripenberg S 40 B4
Gripsholm S 37 C4
Grisolles F 77 C4
Grisslehamn S 36 B5
Gritley GB 23 C6
Grizebeck GB 26 A2
Grndina BIH 84 B1
Gröbming A 72 A3
Gröbzig D 52 B1
Grocka SCG 85 B5
Gröditz D 52 B3
Gródki PL 47 B6
Grodków PL 54 C2
Grodziec PL 54 A3
Grodzisk Mazowiecki PL 55 A5
Groenlo NL 50 A2
Groesbeek NL 50 B1
Grohote HR 83 C5
Groitzsch D 52 B2
Groix F 56 C2
Grójec PL 55 B5
Grom PL 47 B6
Gromiljca BIH 84 C3
Grömitz D 44 A2
Gromnik PL 65 A6
Gromo I 71 C4
Gronau, *Niedersachsen* D 51 A5
Gronau, *Nordrhein-Westfalen* D 50 A3
Grønbjerg DK 39 C1
Grönenbach D 61 C6
Grong N 114 C9
Grönhögen S 41 C6
Groningen D 52 B1
Groningen NL 42 B3
Grønnestrand DK 38 B2
Grono CH 71 B4
Grönskåra S 40 B5
Grootegast NL 42 B3
Gropello Cairoli I 70 C3
Grorud N 34 C2
Grósio I 71 B5
Grošnica SCG 85 C5
Gross Beeren D 45 C5
Gross Berkel D 51 A5
Gross-botwar D 61 B5
Gross-Dölln D 45 B5
Gross-Gerau D 61 A4
Gross-hartmansdorf D 52 C3
Gross Kreutz D 45 C4
Gross Lafferde D 51 A6
Gross Leutheb D 53 A4
Gross Muckrow D 53 A4
Gross Oesingen D 44 C2
Gross Reken D 50 B3
Gross Sarau D 44 B2
Gross Särchen D 53 B4
Gross Schönebeck D 45 C5
Gross Umstadt D 61 A4
Gross Warnow D 44 B3
Gross-Weikersdorf A 64 B1
Gross-Welle D 44 B4
Gross Wokern D 44 B4
Grossalmerode D 51 B5
Grossarl A 72 A3
Grossbodungen D 51 B6
Grossburgwedel D 44 C1
Grosschönau D 53 C4
Grossenbrode D 44 A3
Grossenehrich D 51 B6
Grossengottern D 51 B6
Grossenhain D 52 B3
Grossenkneten D 43 C5
Grossenlüder D 51 C5
Grossensee D 44 B2
Grossenzersdorf A 64 B2
Grosseto I 81 D5
Grossgerungs A 63 B5
Grossglobnitz A 63 B6
Grosshabersdorf D 62 A1
Grossharras A 64 B2
Grosshöchstetten CH 70 B2
Grosskrut A 64 B2
Grosslohra D 51 B6
Grossmehring D 62 B2
Grossostheim D 61 A5
Grosspertholz A 63 B5
Grosspetersdorf A 73 A6
Grosspostwitz D 53 B4
Grossraming A 63 C5
Grossräschen D 53 B4
Grossrinderfeld D 61 A5
Grossröhrsdorf D 53 B4
Grossschirma D 52 C3
Grossschweinbarth A 64 B2
Grosssiegharts A 63 B6
Grosssölk A 72 A3
Grosswarasdorf A 74 A1
Grosswilfersdorf A 73 A5
Grostenquin F 60 B2
Grosuplje SLO 73 C4
Grotli N 114 E4
Grötlingbo S 37 E5
Grottáglie I 104 C3
Grottaminarda I 103 B8
Grottammare I 82 D2
Grotte di Castro I 81 D5
Grotteria I 106 C3
Gróttole I 104 C2
Grouw NL 42 B2
Grov N 112 D6
Grova N 33 C5
Grove E 86 B2
Grua N 34 B2
Grube D 44 A3
Grubišno Polje HR 74 C2
Gruda HR 105 A4
Grude BIH 84 C2
Grudovo BG 11 E9
Grudusk PL 47 B6
Grudziądz PL 47 B4
Grue N 34 B4
Gruissan F 78 C2
Grullos E 86 A4
Grumo Áppula I 104 B2
Grums S 35 C5
Grünau im Almtal A 63 C4
Grünberg D 51 C4
Grünburg A 63 C5
Grundarfjörður IS 111 C2
Gründau D 51 C5
Gründelhardt D 61 A5
Grundforsen S 34 A4
Grundlsee A 63 C4
Grundsund S 35 D3
Grunewald D 53 B3
Grungedal N 33 C4
Grunow D 53 A4
Grünstadt D 61 A4
Gruvberget S 36 A3
Gruyères CH 70 B2
Gruža SCG 85 C5
Grybów PL 65 A6
Grycksbo S 36 B2
Gryfice PL 45 B7
Gryfino PL 45 B6
Gryfów Śląski PL 53 B5
Gryllefjord N 112 C6
Grymyr N 34 B2
Gryt S 37 D3
Grytgöl S 37 D2
Grythyttan S 37 C1
Grytnäs S 37 D4
Grzmiąca PL 46 B2
Grzybno PL 45 B6
Grzywna PL 47 B4
Gschnitz A 71 A6
Gschwend D 61 B5
Gstaad CH 70 B2
Gsteig CH 70 B2
Guadahortuna E 100 B2
Guadalajara E 95 B3
Guadalaviar E 95 B5
Guadalcanal E 99 A5
Guadalcázar E 100 B1
Guadalix de la Sierra E 94 B3
Guadálmez E 100 A1
Guadalupe E 93 B5
Guadamur E 94 C2
Guadarrama E 94 B2
Guadiaro E 99 C5
Guadix E 100 B2
Guagnano I 105 C3
Guagno F 102 A1
Guajar-Faragüit E 100 C2
Gualchos E 100 C2
Gualdo Tadino I 82 C1
Gualtieri I 81 B4
Guarcino I 103 B6
Guarda P 92 A3
Guardamar del Segura E 96 C2
Guardão P 92 A2
Guardavalle I 106 C3
Guardea I 102 A5
Guárdia Sanframondi I 103 B7
Guardiagrele I 103 A7
Guardiarégia I 103 B7
Guardias Viejas E 100 C3
Guardiola de Bergueda E 91 A4
Guardo E 88 B2
Guareña E 93 C4
Guaro E 100 C1
Guarromán E 100 A2
Guasila I 110 C2
Guastalla I 81 B4
Gubbhögen S 115 C12
Gúbbio I 82 C1
Guben D 53 B4
Gubin PL 53 B4
Guča SCG 85 C5
Gudå N 114 D8
Gudavac BIH 83 B5
Guddal N 32 A2
Güderup DK 39 E2
Gudhem S 35 D5
Gudhjem DK 41 D4
Gudovac HR 74 C1
Gudow D 44 B2
Güdüı TR 118 B7
Gudvangen N 32 B3
Guebwiller F 60 C3
Guéjar-Sierra E 100 B2
Guéméné-Penfao F 57 C4
Guéméné-sur-Scorff F 56 B2
Güeñes E 89 A3
Guer F 57 C3
Guérande F 66 A2
Guéret F 68 B1
Guérigny F 68 A3
Guesa E 76 D1
Gueugnon F 68 B4
Guglionesi I 103 B7
Gühlen Glienicke D 45 B4
Guia P 92 B2
Guichen F 57 C4
Guidizzolo I 71 C5
Guidónia-Montecélio I 102 B5
Guiglia I 81 B4
Guignes F 58 B3
Guijo E 100 A1
Guijo de Coria E 93 A4
Guijo de Santa Bábera E 93 A5
Guijuelo E 93 A5
Guildford GB 31 C3
Guillaumes F 79 B5
Guillena E 99 B4
Guillestre F 79 B5
Guillos F 76 B2
Guilsfield GB 26 C2
Guilvinec F 56 C1
Guimarães P 87 C2
Guincho P 92 C1
Guînes F 48 C2
Guingamp F 56 B2
Guipavas F 56 B1
Guisborough GB 27 A4
Guiscard F 59 A4
Guiscriff F 56 B2
Guise F 59 A4
Guisona E 91 B4
Guitiriz E 86 A3
Guîtres F 76 A2
Gujan-Mestras F 76 B1
Gulbene LV 7 C9
Gülçayır TR 118 C6
Guldborg DK 39 E4
Gullabo S 40 C5
Gullane GB 25 B5
Gullbrå N 32 B3
Gullbrandstorp S 40 C2
Gulleråsen S 36 A2
Gullhaug N 35 C2
Gullringen S 40 B5
Gullspång S 35 D6
Gullstein N 114 D5
Güllük TR 119 E2
Gülnar TR 16 C6
Gülpınar TR 116 C8
Gülşehir TR 16 B7
Gulsvik N 34 B1
Gumiel de Hizán E 88 C3
Gummersbach D 50 B3
Gümüldür TR 119 D2
Gümüşhaciköy TR 16 A7
Gümüşova TR 118 B5
Gundel-fingen D 60 B3
Gundelfingen D 61 B6
Gundelsheim D 61 A5
Gunderschoffen F 60 B3
Gunderts-hausen A 62 B3
Gundinci HR 74 C3
Gündoğmuş TR 119 F7
Güney, *Burdur* TR 119 E4
Güney, *Denizli* TR 119 D4
Gunja HR 84 B3
Günlüce TR 119 F3
Gunnarn S 115 B14
Gunnarskog S 34 C4
Gunnebo S 40 B6
Gunnislake GB 28 C3
Günselsdorf A 64 C2
Guntersblum D 61 A4
Guntersdorf A 64 B2
Guntin E 86 B3
Günyüzü TR 118 C6
Günzburg D 61 B6
Gunzenhausen D 62 A1
Güre, *Balıkesir* TR 118 C1
Güre, *Uşak* TR 118 D4
Gurk A 73 B4
Gurrea de Gállego E 90 A2
Gürsu TR 118 B4
Gušće HR 74 C1
Gusev RUS 6 D7
Gusinje SCG 105 A5
Gusmar AL 105 C5
Gúspini I 110 C1
Gusselby S 37 C2
Güssing A 73 A6
Gusswerk A 63 C6
Gustav Adolf S 34 B5
Gustavsberg S 37 C5
Gustavsfors S 35 C4
Güstrow D 44 B4
Gusum S 37 D3
Gutcher GB 22 A7
Gutenstein A 64 C1
Gütersloh D 51 B4
Guttannen CH 70 B3
Guttaring A 73 B4
Guttau D 53 B4
Güttingen CH 61 C5
Gützkow D 45 B5
Guzów PL 55 A5
Gvardeysk RUS 6 D6
Gvarv N 33 C6
Gvozd SCG 85 D4
Gvozdansko HR 73 C6
Gwda Wielka PL 46 B2
Gwennap GB 28 C2
Gy F 69 A5
Gyál H 75 A4
Gyarmat H 74 A2
Gyé-sur-Seine F 59 B5
Gyékényes H 74 B2
Gylling DK 39 D3
Gyoma H 75 B5
Gyömöre H 74 A2
Gyömrö H 75 A4
Gyón H 75 A4
Gyöngyfa H 74 C2
Gyöngyös H 65 C5
Gyöngyöspata H 65 C5
Gyönk H 74 B3
Györ H 64 C3
Györszemere H 74 A2
Gypsera CH 70 B2
Gysinge S 36 B3
Gyttorp S 37 C1
Gyula H 75 B6
Gyulafirátót H 74 A2
Gyulaj H 74 B3

H

Haacht B 49 C5
Haag, *Nieder Östereich* A 63 B5
Haag, *Ober Östereich* A 63 B4
Haag D 62 B3
Haaksbergen NL 50 A2
Haamstede NL 49 B4
Haan D 50 B3
Haapajärvi FIN 3 E26
Haapsalu EST 6 B7
Haarlem NL 42 C1
Habas F 76 C2
Habay B 60 A1
Habo S 40 B4
Håbol S 35 D4
Habry CZ 63 A6
Habsheim F 60 C3
Hachenburg D 50 C3
Hacıbektaş TR 16 B7
Hacılar TR 16 B7
Hacinas E 89 C3
Hackås S 115 E11
Hacketstown IRL 21 B5
Hackthorpe GB 26 A3
Hadamar D 50 C4
Hädanberg S 115 D15
Haddington GB 25 C5
Hadersdorf am Kamp A 63 B6
Haderslev DK 39 D2
Haderup DK 39 C1
Hadım TR 119 F7
Hadleigh, *Essex* GB 31 C4
Hadleigh, *Suffolk* GB 30 B4
Hadlow GB 31 C4
Hadmersleben D 52 A1
Hadsten DK 39 C3
Hadsund DK 38 C3
Hadyach UA 7 F12
Hadžići BIH 84 C3
Hægebostad N 33 D4
Hægeland N 33 D4
Hafnarfjörður IS 111 C4
Hafnir IS 111 D3
Hafslo N 32 A4
Haganj HR 74 C1
Hagby S 40 C6
Hage D 43 B4
Hagen, *Niedersachsen* D 43 B5
Hagen, *Nordrhein-Westfalen* D 50 B3
Hagenbach D 61 A4
Hagenow D 44 B3
Hagetmau F 76 C2
Hagfors S 34 B5
Häggenås S 115 D11
Hagondange F 60 A2
Hagsta S 36 B4
Haguenau F 60 B3
Hahnbach D 62 A2
Hahnslätten D 50 C4
Hahót H 74 B1
Haiger D 50 C4
Haigerloch D 61 B4
Hailsham GB 31 D4
Hainburg A 64 B2
Hainfeld A 64 B1
Hainichen D 52 C3
Hajdúböszörmény H 10 C6
Hajdučica SCG 75 C5
Hajdúszoboszló H 75 A6
Hajnáčka SK 65 B5
Hajnówka PL 6 E7
Hajós H 75 B4
Håkafot S 115 C11
Hakkas S 113 F10
Håksberg S 36 B2
Halaszi H 64 C3
Halberstadt D 52 B1
Halberton GB 29 C4
Hald Ege DK 39 C2
Haldem D 43 C5
Halden N 35 C3
Haldensleben D 52 A1
Halenbeck D 44 B4
Halesowen GB 26 C3
Halesworth GB 30 B5
Halfing D 62 C3
Halhjem N 32 B2
Håliden S 34 B5
Halifax GB 27 B4
Häljelöt S 37 D3
Halkida GR 116 D5
Halkirk GB 23 C5
Hall S 37 E5
Hall in Tirol A 71 A6
Hälla S 115 D14
Hallabro S 41 C5
Hällabrottet S 37 C2
Halland GB 31 D4
Hällaryd, *Blekinge* S 41 C4
Hallaryd, *Kronoberg* S 40 C3
Hällberga S 37 C3
Hällbybrunn S 37 C3
Halle B 49 C5
Halle, *Nordrhein-Westfalen* D 51 A4
Halle, *Sachsen-Anhalt* D 52 B1
Hålleberga S 40 C5
Hällefors S 36 C1
Hälleforsnäs S 37 C3
Hallein A 62 C4
Hällekis S 35 D5
Hallen, *Jämtland* S 115 D11
Hållen, *Uppsala* S 36 B4
Hallenberg D 51 B4
Hällestad S 37 D2
Hällevadsholm S 35 D3
Hällevik S 41 C4
Hälleviksstrand S 35 D3
Hallingby N 34 B2
Hallingeberg S 40 B6
Hallingen N 32 B6
Hällnäs, *Norrbotten* S 115 A15
Hållnäs, *Uppsala* S 36 B4
Hällnäs, *Västerbotten* S 115 C16
Hallormsstaður IS 111 B11
Hallsberg S 37 C2
Hållsta S 37 C3
Hallstahammar S 37 C3
Hallstatt A 72 A3
Hallstavik S 36 B5
Halltorp S 40 C6
Halluin F 49 C4
Hallviken S 115 D12
Hallworthy GB 28 C3
Halmstad S 40 C2
Hals DK 38 B3
Halsa N 114 D5
Halstead GB 31 C4
Haltdalen N 114 E8
Haltern D 50 B3
Haltwhistle GB 25 D5
Halvarsgårdarna S 36 B2
Halver D 50 B3
Halvrimmen DK 38 B2
Ham F 59 A4
Hamar N 34 B3
Hamarhaug N 32 B2
Hamarøy N 112 D4
Hambach F 60 A3
Hambergen D 43 B5
Hambergsund S 35 D3
Hambledon GB 31 D2
Hambuhren D 44 C1
Hamburg D 44 B2
Hamdibey TR 118 C2
Hamdorf D 43 A6
Hämeenlinna FIN 3 F26
Hameln = Hamlin D 51 A5
Hamersleben D 52 A1
Hamidiye TR 118 C5
Hamilton GB 24 C3
Hamina FIN 7 A9
Hamlagrø N 32 B3
Hamlin = Hameln D 51 A5
Hamm D 50 B3
Hammar S 37 D1
Hammarland FIN 36 B6
Hammarö S 35 C5
Hammarstrand S 115 D13
Hamme B 49 B5
Hammel DK 39 C2
Hammelburg D 51 C5
Hammelspring D 45 B5
Hammenhög S 41 D4
Hammerdal S 115 D12
Hammerfest N 113 B12
Hammershøj DK 38 C2
Hammerum DK 39 C2
Hamminkeln D 50 B2
Hamnavoe GB 22 A7
Hamneda S 40 C3
Hamningberg N 113 B19
Hamoir B 49 C6
Hamont B 49 B6
Hámor H 65 B6
Hamra, *Gävleborg* S 115 F12
Hamra, *Gotland* S 37 F5
Hamrångefjärden S 36 B4
Hamstreet GB 31 C4
Hamsund N 112 D4
Han SCG 84 D3
Han TR 118 C5
Han i Hotit AL 105 A5
Han Knežica BIH 83 A5
Han Pijesak BIH 84 B3
Hanaskog S 41 C4
Hanau D 51 C4
Händelöp S 40 B6
Handlová SK 65 B4
Hanerau-Hademarschen D 43 A6
Hånger S 40 B3
Hanhimaa FIN 113 E14
Hanken S 37 D1
Hankensbüttel D 44 C2
Hanko FIN 6 B7
Hannover D 43 C6
Hannut B 49 C6
Hansnes N 112 C8
Hanstedt D 44 B2
Hanstholm DK 38 B1
Hantsavichy BY 7 E9
Hanušovice CZ 54 C1
Haparanda S 3 D26
Haradok BY 7 D10
Harads S 3 C24
Häradsbäck S 40 C4
Häradsbygden S 36 B2
Harbo S 36 B4
Harboør DK 38 C1
Harburg, *Bayern* D 62 B1
Harburg, *Hamburg* D 44 B1
Hårby DK 39 D3
Harc H 74 B3
Hardegarijp NL 42 B2
Hardegsen D 51 B5
Hardelot Plage F 48 C2
Hardenbeck D 45 B5
Hardenberg NL 42 C3
Harderwijk NL 42 C2
Hardheim D 61 A5
Hardt D 61 B4
Hareid N 114 E3
Haren D 43 C4
Haren NL 42 B3
Harestua N 34 B2
Harfleur F 57 A6
Harg S 36 B5
Hargicourt F 49 D4
Hargnies F 49 C5
Hargshamn S 36 B5
Härja S 40 A3
Harkány H 74 C3
Härkeberga S 37 C4
Härkebrügge D 43 B4
Harlech GB 26 C1
Harleston GB 30 B5
Hårlev DK 41 D2
Harlingen NL 42 B2
Harlösa S 41 D3
Harlow GB 31 C4
Harmancık TR 118 C4
Harmånger S 115 F14
Härnevi S 37 C4
Härnösand S 115 E14
Haro E 89 B4
Haroldswick GB 22 A8
Háromfa H 74 B2
Haroué F 60 B2
Harpenden GB 31 C3
Harplinge S 40 C2
Harpstedt D 43 C5
Harrogate GB 27 A4
Harrow GB 31 C3
Härryda S 40 B2
Harsefeld D 43 B6
Harsewinkel D 50 B4
Hârşova RO 11 D9
Harstad N 112 D5
Harsum D 51 A5
Harsvik N 114 C7
Harta H 75 B4
Hartberg A 73 A5
Hartburn GB 25 C6
Hartennes F 59 A4
Hartest GB 30 B4
Hartha D 52 B2
Hartland GB 28 C3
Hartlepool GB 27 A4
Hartmanice CZ 63 A4
Hartmannsdorf A 73 A5
Harvassdal N 115 B11
Harwell GB 31 C2
Harwich GB 31 C5
Harzgerode D 52 B1
Häselgehr A 71 A5
Haselünne D 43 C4
Hasköy TR 118 A1
Haslach D 61 B4
Haslach an der Mühl A 63 B5
Hasle DK 41 D4
Haslemere GB 31 C3
Haslev DK 39 D4
Hasloch D 61 A5
Hasparren F 76 C1
Hassela S 115 E13
Hasselfelde D 51 B6
Hasselfors S 37 C1
Hasselt B 49 C6
Hasselt NL 42 C3
Hassfurt D 51 C6
Hassleben D 45 B5
Hässleholm S 41 C3
Hasslö S 41 C5
Hassloch D 61 A4
Hästbo S 36 B4
Hastersboda FIN 36 B7
Hästholmen S 37 D1
Hastière-Lavaux B 49 C5
Hastigrow GB 23 C5
Hastings GB 31 D4
Hästveda S 41 C3
Hasvik N 113 B11
Hatfield, *Hertfordshire* GB 31 C3
Hatfield, *South Yorkshire* GB 27 B5
Hatherleigh GB 28 C3
Hathersage GB 27 B4
Hatlestrand N 32 B2
Hattem NL 42 C3
Hatten D 43 B5
Hatten F 60 B3
Hattfjelldal N 115 B10
Hatting DK 39 D2
Hattingen D 50 B3
Hattstadt F 60 B3
Hattstedt D 43 A6
Hatvan H 65 C5
Hatvik N 32 B2
Hau D 50 B2
Haudainville F 59 A6
Hauganes IS 111 B7
Haugastøl N 32 B4
Hauge N 33 D3
Haugesund N 33 C2
Haughom N 33 D3
Haugsdal N 32 B2
Haugsdorf A 64 B2
Haukedal N 32 A3
Haukeland N 32 B2
Haukeligrend N 33 C4
Haukeliseter N 33 C4
Haukipudas FIN 3 D26
Haulerwijk NL 42 B3
Haunersdorf D 62 B3
Haus N 32 B2
Hausach D 61 B4
Hausham D 62 C2
Hausmannstätten A 73 B5
Hausvik N 33 D3
Haut-Fays B 49 C6
Hautajärvi FIN 113 F18
Hautefort F 67 C6
Hauterives F 69 C5
Hauteville-Lompnès F 69 C5
Hautmont F 49 C4
Hautrage B 49 C4
Hauzenberg D 63 B4
Havant GB 31 D3
Havdhem S 37 E5
Havdrup DK 39 D5
Havelange B 49 C6
Havelberg D 44 C4
Havelte NL 42 C3
Haverfordwest GB 28 B3
Haverhill GB 30 B4
Havering GB 31 C4
Håverud S 35 D4
Havířov CZ 65 A4
Havixbeck D 50 B3

Hurstbourne Tarrant GB 31 C2
Hurstpierpoint GB 31 D3
Hürth D 50 C2
Hurum N 32 A5
Hurup DK 38 C1
Húsafell IS 111 C5
Húsavík IS 111 A8
Husbands Bosworth GB 30 B2
Husby D 39 E2
Husby DK 39 C1
Husey IS 111 B11
Huşi RO 11 C10
Husina BIH 84 B3
Husínec CZ 63 A4
Husinish GB 22 D1
Huskvarna S 40 B4
Husnes N 32 C2
Husøy N 112 C6
Hustad N 114 E4
Hüsten D 50 B3
Hustopeče CZ 64 B2
Hustopeče nad Bečvou CZ 64 A3
Husum D 43 A6
Husum S 115 D16
Husvika N 115 B9
Huta PL 46 C2
Hutovo BIH 84 D2
Hüttenberg A 73 B4
Hüttlingen D 61 B6
Huttoft GB 27 B6
Hutton Cranswick GB 27 B5
Hüttschlag A 72 A3
Huttwil CH 70 A2
Huy B 49 C6
Hüyük TR 119 E6
Hval N 34 B2
Hvåle N 32 B6
Hvaler N 35 C3
Hvalpsund DK 38 C2
Hvammstangi IS 111 B5
Hvammur IS 111 B6
Hvanneyri IS 111 C4
Hvar HR 83 C5
Hvarnes N 35 C1
Hveragerði IS 111 D4
Hvidbjerg DK 38 C1
Hvide Sande DK 39 D1
Hvittingfoss N 35 C2
Hvolsvöllur IS 111 D5
Hybe SK 65 A5
Hycklinge S 40 B5
Hydra GR 117 E5
Hyen N 114 F2
Hyères F 79 C5
Hyéres Plage F 79 C5
Hylestad N 33 C4
Hylke DK 39 D2
Hyllestad N 32 A2
Hyllstofta S 41 C3
Hyltebruk S 40 B3
Hynish GB 24 B1
Hynnekleiv N 33 D5
Hythe, *Hampshire* GB 31 D2
Hythe, *Kent* GB 31 C5
Hyvinkää FIN 3 F26

I

Iam RO 85 A6
Iaşi RO 11 C9
Iasmos GR 116 A7
Ibahernando E 93 B5
Iballë AL 105 A5
Ibarranguelua E 89 A4
Ibbenbüren D 50 A3
Ibeas de Juarros E 89 B3
Ibestad N 112 D6
Ibi E 96 C2
Ibiza = Eivissa E 97 C1
İbradı TR 119 E6
İbriktepe TR 118 A1
Ibros E 100 A2
Ibstock GB 27 C4
İçel TR 16 C7
Ichenhausen D 61 B6
Ichnya UA 11 A12
Ichtegem B 49 B4
Ichtershausen D 51 C6
Idanha-a-Novo P 93 B3
Idar-Oberstein D 60 A3
Idd N 35 C3
Idiazábal E 89 B4
Idivuoma S 113 D10
Idkerberget S 36 B2
Idön S 36 B5
Idre S 115 F9
Idrija SLO 73 C4
Idritsa RUS 7 C10
Idstein D 50 C4
Idvor SCG 75 C5
Iecca Mare RO 75 C5
Ielsi I 103 B7
Ieper = Ypres B 48 C3
Ierapetra GR 117 G7
Ierissos GR 116 B5
Iesi I 82 C2
Ifjord N 113 B16
Ig SLO 73 C4
Igal H 74 B2
Igalo SCG 105 A4
Igea E 89 B4
Igea Marina I 82 B1
Igelfors S 37 D2
Igersheim D 61 A5
Iggesund S 115 F14
Iglarevo SCG 85 D5
Iglesias E 88 B3
Iglésias I 110 C1
Igls A 71 A6
İğneada TR 118 A2
Igny-Comblizy F 59 A4
Igorre E 89 A4
Igoumenitsa GR 116 C2
Igries E 90 A2
Igualada E 91 B4
Igüeña E 86 B4
Iguerande F 68 B4
Iharosberény H 74 B2
Ihl'any SK 65 A6
Ihlienworth D 43 B5
Ihringen D 60 B3
Ihrlerstein D 62 B2
İhsaniye TR 118 C5
Ii FIN 3 D26
Iijärvi FIN 113 C16
Iisalmi FIN 3 E27
IJmuiden NL 42 C1
IJsselmuiden NL 42 C2
IJzendijke NL 49 B4
Ikast DK 39 C2
Ikervár H 74 A1
il Castagno I 81 C4
Ilandža SCG 75 C5
Ilanz CH 71 B4
Ilava SK 64 B4
Iława PL 47 B5
Ilche E 90 B3
Ilchester GB 29 C5
Ilfeld D 51 B6
Ilfracombe GB 28 B3
Ilgaz TR 16 A6
Ilgın TR 119 D6
Ílhavo P 92 A2
Ilıca TR 118 C2
Ilidža BIH 84 C3
Ilijaš BIH 84 C3
Ilirska Bistrica SLO 73 C4
Ilkeston GB 27 C4
Ilkley GB 27 B4
Illana E 95 B4
Illano E 86 A4
Illar E 101 C3
Illas E 88 A1
Illats F 76 B2
Ille-sur-Têt F 91 A5
Illertissen D 61 B6
Illescas E 94 B3
Illfurth F 60 C3
Illichivsk UA 11 C11
Illiers-Combray F 58 B2
Illkirch-Graffenstaden F 60 B3
Illmersdorf D 52 B3
Illmitz A 64 C2
Íllora E 100 B2
Illueca E 89 C5
Ilmajoki FIN 3 E25
Ilmenau D 51 C6
Ilminster GB 29 C5
Ilok HR 75 C4
Ilomantsi FIN 3 E29
Iłow PL 47 C6
Iłowa PL 53 B5
Iłowo-Osada PL 47 B6
Ilsenburg D 51 B6
Ilshofen D 61 A5
Ilz A 73 A5
Iłża PL 55 B6
İmamoğlu TR 16 C7
Imatra FIN 3 F28
Imielin PL 55 C4
Imingen N 32 B5
Immeln S 41 C4
Immenhausen D 51 B5
Immenstadt D 61 C6
Immingham GB 27 B5
Ímola I 81 B5
Imon E 95 A4
Imotski HR 84 C2
Impéria I 80 C2
Imphy F 68 B3
İmroz TR 116 B7
Imsland N 33 C2
Imst A 71 A5
Inagh IRL 20 B2
Inari FIN 113 D15
Inca E 97 B2
Inchnadamph GB 22 C4
Incinillas E 89 B3
Indal S 115 E14
Indjija SCG 85 A5
Indre Arna N 32 B2
Indre Billefjord N 113 B14
Indre Brenna N 113 B14
İnebolu TR 16 A6
İnecik TR 118 B2
İnegöl TR 118 B4
Inerthal CH 70 A3
Infiesto E 88 A1
Ingatorp S 40 B5
Ingedal N 35 C3
Ingelheim D 50 D4
Ingelmunster B 49 C4
Ingelstad S 40 C4
Ingleton GB 26 A3
Ingolfsland N 32 C5
Ingolstadt D 62 B2
Ingrandes, *Maine-et-Loire* F 66 A4
Ingrandes, *Vienne* F 67 B5
Ingwiller F 60 B3
Inhisar TR 118 B5
Inhulec UA 11 C12
Iniesta E 95 C5
Inishannon IRL 20 C3
Inishcrone IRL 18 B2
Inke H 74 B2
Inndyr N 112 E3
Innellan GB 24 C3
Innerleithen GB 25 C4
Innermessan GB 24 D3
Innertkirchen CH 70 B3
Innervillgraten A 72 B2
Innsbruck A 71 A6
Innset N 112 D7
Innvik N 114 F3
İnönü TR 118 C5
Inowłódz PL 55 B5
Inowrocław PL 47 C4
Ins CH 70 A2
Insch GB 23 D6
Insjön S 36 B2
Ińsko PL 46 B1
Instow GB 28 B3
İntepe TR 118 B1
Interlaken CH 70 B2
Intragna CH 70 B3
Introbio I 71 C4
Inverallochy GB 23 D7
Inveran GB 23 D4
Inveran IRL 20 A2
Inveraray GB 24 B2
Inverbervie GB 25 B5
Invergarry GB 22 D4
Invergordon GB 23 D4
Invergowrie GB 25 B4
Inverkeilor GB 25 B5
Inverkeithing GB 25 B4
Invermoriston GB 22 D4
Inverness GB 23 D4
Inveruno I 70 C3
Inverurie GB 23 D6
Ioannina GR 116 C2
Iolanda di Savoia I 81 B5
Ion Corvin RO 11 D9
Ióppolo I 106 C2
Ios GR 117 F7
Ipati GR 116 D4
İpsala TR 118 B1
Ipswich GB 30 B5
Iraklia GR 116 A5
Iraklio = Heraklion GR 117 G7
Irdning A 73 A4
Iregszemcse H 74 B3
Irgoli I 110 B2
Irig SCG 85 A4
Ironbridge GB 26 C3
Irpin UA 11 A11
Irrel D 60 A2
Irsina I 104 C2
Irthlingborough GB 30 B3
Iruela E 87 B4
Irún E 76 C1
Irurita E 76 C1
Irurzun E 76 D1
Irvine GB 24 C3
Irvinestown GB 19 B4
Is-sur-Tille F 69 A5
Isaba E 76 D2
Isabela E 100 A2
Ísafjörður IS 111 A2
Isane N 114 F2
Isaszeg H 75 A4
Isbister GB 22 A7
Íscar E 88 C2
İscehisar TR 118 D5
Ischgl A 71 A5
Íschia I 103 C6
Ischia di Castro I 102 A4
Ischitella I 104 B1
Isdes F 58 C3
Ise N 35 C3
Iselle I 70 B3
Iseltwald CH 70 B2
Isen D 62 B3
Isenbüttel D 44 C2
Iseo I 71 C5
Iserlohn D 50 B3
Isérnia I 103 B7
Isfjorden N 114 E4
Ishëm AL 105 B5
Isigny-sur-Mer F 57 A4
Işıklı TR 119 D4
Ísili I 110 C2
İskilip TR 16 A7
Isla Canela E 98 B3
Isla Cristina E 98 B3
Islares E 89 A3
Isle Of Whithorn GB 24 D3
Isleham GB 30 B4
Ismaning D 62 B2
Isna P 92 B3
Isnestoften N 113 B11
Isny D 61 C6
Isoba E 88 A1
Isokylä FIN 113 F16
Isokylä S 113 E11
Isola F 79 B6
Isola del Gran Sasso d'Itália I 103 A6
Ísola del Liri I 103 B6
Ísola della Scala I 71 C6
Isola delle Fémmine I 108 A2
Ísola di Capo Rizzuto I 107 C4
Isona E 91 A4
Ispagnac F 78 B2
Isparta TR 119 E5
Isperikh BG 11 E9
Íspica I 109 C3
Isselburg D 50 B2
Issigeac F 77 B3
Issogne I 70 C2
Issoire F 68 C3
Issoncourt F 59 B6
Issoudun F 68 B2
Issum D 50 B2
Issy-l'Evêque F 68 B3
Istán E 100 C1
İstanbul TR 118 A3
Istebna PL 65 A4
Ístia d'Ombrone I 81 D5
Istiea GR 116 D5
Istok SCG 85 D5
Istres, *Bouches du Rhône* F 78 C3
Istvándi H 74 B2
Itea GR 116 D4
Ithaki GR 117 D2
Itoiz E 76 D1
Ítrabo E 100 C2
Itri I 103 B6
Ittireddu I 110 B1
Íttiri I 110 B1
Itzehoe D 43 B6
Ivalo FIN 113 D16
Iván H 74 A1
Ivanava BY 7 E8
Ivančice CZ 64 A2
Ivančna Gorica SLO 73 C4
Iváncsa H 74 A3
Ivanec HR 73 B6
Ivanić Grad HR 73 C6
Ivanjica SCG 85 C5
Ivanjska BIH 84 B2
Ivanka SK 64 B4
Ivankovo HR 74 C3
Ivano-Frankivsk UA 11 B8
Ivanovice na Hané CZ 64 A3
Ivanska HR 74 C1
Ivatsevichy BY 7 E8
Ivaylovgrad BG 116 A8
Iveland N 33 D4
Ivoz Ramet B 49 C6
Ivrea I 70 C2
İvrindi TR 118 C2
Ivry-en-Montagne F 69 A4
Ivry-la-Bataille F 58 B2
Ivybridge GB 28 C4
Iwaniska PL 55 C6
Iwiny PL 53 B5
Iwuy F 49 C4
Ixworth GB 30 B4
Izarra E 89 B4
Izbica Kujawska PL 47 C4
Izbište SCG 85 A6
Izeda P 87 C4
Izegem B 49 C4
Izernore F 69 B5
Izmayil UA 11 D10
İzmir TR 119 D2
İzmit = Kocaeli TR 118 B4
Iznájar E 100 B1
Iznalloz E 100 B2
Iznatoraf E 100 A2
İznik TR 118 B4
Izola SLO 72 C3
Izsák H 75 B4
Izsófalva H 65 B6
Izyaslav UA 11 A9

J

Jabalquinto E 100 A2
Jablanac HR 83 B3
Jablanica BIH 84 C2
Jablonec nad Jizerou CZ 53 C5
Jablonec nad Nisou CZ 53 C5
Jablonica SK 64 B3
Jablonka PL 65 A5
Jabłonna PL 55 A5
Jablonné nad Orlicí CZ 54 C1
Jablonne Podještědi CZ 53 C4
Jablonov nad Turňou SK 65 B6
Jabłonowo Pomorskie PL 47 B5
Jablúnka CZ 64 A3
Jablunkov CZ 65 A4
Jabučje SCG 85 B5
Jabugo E 99 B4
Jabuka, *Srbija* SCG 85 C4
Jabuka, *Vojvodina* SCG 85 B5
Jabukovac HR 73 C6
Jaca E 90 A2
Jáchymov CZ 52 C2
Jacobidrebber D 43 C5
Jade D 43 B5
Jäderfors S 36 B3
Jädraås S 36 B3
Jadraque E 95 B4
Jægerspris DK 39 D4
Jaén E 100 B2
Jagare BIH 84 B2
Jagel D 43 A6
Jagenbach A 63 B6
Jagodina SCG 85 C6
Jagodnjak HR 74 C3
Jagodzin PL 53 B5
Jagstheim D 61 A6
Jagstzell D 61 A6
Jahodna SK 64 B3
Jajce BIH 84 B2
Ják H 74 A1
Jakabszálbs H 75 B4
Jäkkvik S 115 A14
Jaklovce SK 65 B6
Jakobsnes N 113 C19
Jakovlje HR 73 C5
Jakšic HR 74 C2
Jakubany SK 65 A6
Jalance E 96 B1
Jalasjärvi FIN 3 E25
Jalhay B 50 C1
Jaligny-sur-Besbre F 68 B3
Jallais F 66 A4
Jalón E 96 C2
Jâlons F 59 B5
Jamena SCG 84 B4
Jamilena E 100 B2
Jämjö S 41 C5
Jamnička Kiselica HR 73 C5
Jamno PL 46 A2
Jamoigne B 59 A6
Jämsä FIN 3 F26
Jämshög S 41 C4
Janakkala FIN 3 F26
Jandelsbrunn D 63 B4
Jänickendorf D 52 A3
Janikowo PL 47 C4
Janja BIH 85 B4
Janjina HR 84 D2
Janki, *Łódzkie* PL 55 B4
Janki, *Mazowieckie* PL 55 A5
Jankov CZ 63 A5
Jankowo Dolne PL 46 C3
Jánoshalma H 75 B4
Jánosháza H 74 A2
Jánoshida H 75 A5
Jánossomorja H 64 C3
Janovice nad Uhlavou CZ 63 A4
Janów PL 55 C4
Janowiec Wielkopolski PL 46 C3
Janowo PL 47 B6
Jänsmässholmen S 115 D10
Janville F 58 B2
Janzé F 57 C4
Jarabá SK 65 B5
Jaraczewo PL 54 B2
Jarafuel E 96 B1
Jaraicejo E 93 B5
Jaraíz de la Vera E 93 A5
Jarak SCG 85 B4
Jarandilla de la Vera E 93 A5
Jaray E 89 C4
Järbo S 36 B3
Jard-sur-Mer F 66 B3
Jaren N 34 B2
Jargeau F 58 C3
Jarkovac SCG 75 C5
Järlåsa S 36 C4
Jarmen D 45 B5
Järna S 37 C4
Jarnac F 67 C4
Järnäs S 115 D16
Järnforsen S 40 B5
Jarny F 60 A1
Jarocin PL 54 B2
Jaroměř CZ 53 C5
Jaroměřice nad Rokytnou CZ 64 A1
Jaroslav CZ 53 C6
Jaroslavice CZ 64 B2
Jarosław PL 11 A7
Jaroslawiec PL 46 A2
Jarošov nad Nežarkou CZ 63 A6
Järpås S 35 D4
Järpen S 115 D10
Jarrow GB 25 D6
Järso FIN 36 B6
Järvenpää FIN 7 A8
Jarvorník CZ 54 C1
Järvsö S 115 F13
Jarzé F 67 A4
Jaša Tomic SCG 75 C5
Jasenak HR 73 C5
Jasenica BIH 83 B5
Jasenice HR 83 B4
Jasenovac HR 74 C1
Jasenovo, *Srbija* SCG 85 C4
Jasenovo, *Vojvodina* SCG 85 B6
Jasień PL 53 B5
Jasienica PL 53 B4
Jasika SCG 85 C6
Jasło PL 10 B6
Jásova SK 65 C4
Jasseron F 69 B5
Jastarnia PL 47 A4
Jastrebarsko HR 73 C5
Jastrowie PL 46 B2
Jastrzębia-Góra PL 47 A4
Jastrzębie Zdrój PL 54 D3
Jászals-Lószentgyörgy H 75 A5
Jászapáti H 75 A5
Jászárokszállás H 65 C5
Jászberény H 75 A4
Jászdózsa H 65 C6
Jászfényszaru H 75 A4
Jászjakóhalma H 75 A5
Jászkarajenö H 75 A5
Jászkisér H 75 A5
Jászladány H 75 A5
Jászszentlászló H 75 B4
Jásztelek H 75 A5
Játar E 100 C2
Jättendal S 115 F14
Jatznick D 45 B5
Jaun CH 70 B2
Jausiers F 79 B5
Jávea E 96 C3
Jävenitz D 44 C3
Javerlhac F 67 C5
Javier E 90 A1
Javorani BIH 84 B2
Javorina SK 65 A6
Javron F 57 B5
Jawor PL 53 B6
Jaworzno PL 55 C4
Jaworzyna Śl. PL 54 C1
Jayena E 100 C2
Jaźow PL 53 B4
Jebel RO 75 C6
Jebjerg DK 38 C2
Jedburgh GB 25 C5
Jedlinsk PL 55 B6
Jedlnia PL 55 B6
Jedlnia Letnisko PL 55 B6
Jedovnice CZ 64 A2
Jędrychow PL 47 B5
Jędrzejów PL 55 C5
Jedwabno PL 47 B6
Jeesiö FIN 113 E15
Jegłownik PL 47 A5
Jegun F 77 C3
Jēkabpils LV 7 C8
Jektevik N 32 C2
Jektvik N 112 F2
Jelakci SCG 85 C5
Jelcz-Laskowice PL 54 B2
Jelenec SK 64 B4
Jelenia Góra PL 53 C5
Jelgava LV 6 C7
Jelka SK 64 B3
Jelling DK 39 D2
Jels DK 39 D2
Jelsa HR 83 C5
Jelsa N 33 C3
Jelšava SK 65 B6
Jemgum D 43 B4
Jemnice CZ 63 A6
Jena D 52 C1
Jenaz CH 71 B4
Jenbach A 72 A1
Jenikow PL 45 B7
Jennersdorf A 73 B6
Jenny S 40 B6
Jerchel D 44 C3
Jeres del Marquesado E 100 B2
Jerez de la Frontera E 99 C4
Jerez de los Caballeros E 99 A4
Jerica E 96 B2
Jerichow D 44 C4
Jerka PL 54 A1
Jermenovci SCG 75 C6
Jerslev DK 38 B3
Jerte E 93 A5
Jerup DK 38 B3
Jerxheim D 51 A6
Jerzmanowice PL 55 C4
Jerzu I 110 C2
Jerzwałd PL 47 B5
Jesberg D 51 C5
Jesenice, *Středočeský* CZ 52 C3
Jesenice, *Středočeský* CZ 53 D4
Jesenice SLO 73 B4
Jeseník CZ 54 C2
Jesenké SK 65 B6
Jésolo I 72 C2
Jessen D 52 B2
Jessenitz D 44 B3
Jessheim N 34 B3
Jessnitz D 52 B2
Jesteburg D 44 B1
Jeumont F 49 C5
Jeven-stedt D 43 A6
Jever D 43 B4
Jevičko CZ 64 A2
Jevišovice CZ 64 B1
Jevnaker N 34 B2
Jezerane HR 83 A4
Jezero BIH 84 B2
Jezero HR 83 A4
Jeziorany PL 47 B6
Jezów PL 55 B4
Jičín CZ 53 C5
Jičiněves CZ 53 C5
Jihlava CZ 63 A6
Jijona E 96 C2
Jilemnice CZ 53 C5
Jilové CZ 53 C4
Jílové u Prahy CZ 63 A5
Jimbolia RO 75 C5
Jimena E 100 B2
Jimena de la Frontera E 99 C5
Jimera de Libar E 99 C5
Jimramov CZ 64 A2
Jince CZ 63 A4
Jindřichovice CZ 52 C2
Jindřichův Hradec CZ 63 A6
Jirkov CZ 52 C3
Jistebnice CZ 63 A5
Joachimsthal D 45 C5
João da Loura P 92 C2
Jobbágyi H 65 C5
Jochberg A 72 A2
Jockfall S 113 F11
Jódar E 100 B2
Jodoigne B 49 C5
Joensuu FIN 3 E28
Joesjö S 115 B11
Jœuf F 60 A1
Jõgeva EST 7 B9
Johann-georgen-stadt D 52 C2
Johannishus S 41 C5
Johanniskirchen D 62 B3
Johansfors S 40 C5
John o'Groats GB 23 C5
Johnshaven GB 25 B5
Johnstone GB 24 C3
Johnstown IRL 21 B4
Jõhvi EST 7 B9
Joigny F 59 C4
Joinville F 59 B6
Jokkmokk S 112 F8
Jöllenbeck D 51 A4
Jomala FIN 36 B6
Jönåker S 37 D3
Jonava LT 6 D8
Jonchery-sur-Vesle F 59 A4
Jondal N 32 B3
Jondalen N 33 C6
Joniškis LT 6 C7
Jönköping S 40 B4
Jonkowo PL 47 B6
Jønnbu N 33 C6
Jonsberg S 37 D3
Jonsered S 38 B5
Jonstorp S 41 C2
Jonzac F 67 C4
Jorba E 91 B4
Jordanów PL 65 A5
Jordanów Ślaski PL 54 C1
Jordanowo PL 46 C1
Jordbro S 37 C5
Jordbrua N 115 A11
Jördenstorf D 45 B4
Jordet N 34 A4
Jordøse DK 39 D3
Jork D 43 B6
Jörlanda S 38 B4
Jormlien S 115 C10
Jormvattnet S 115 C11
Jörn S 115 B17
Jørpeland N 33 C3
Jorquera E 96 B1
Jošan HR 83 B4
Jošanička Banja SCG 85 C5
Jošavka BIH 84 B2
Josipdol HR 73 C5
Josipovac HR 74 C3
Jössefors S 35 C4
Josselin F 56 C3
Jøssund N 114 C7
Jostedal N 114 F4
Jósvafö H 65 B6
Jou P 87 C3
Jouarre F 59 B4
Joué-lès-Tours F 67 A5
Joué-sur-Erdre F 66 A3
Joure NL 42 C2
Joutseno FIN 3 F28
Joutsijärvi FIN 113 F16
Joux-la-Ville F 59 C4
Jouy F 58 B2
Jouy-le-Châtel F 59 B4
Jouy-le-Potier F 58 C2
Joyeuse F 78 B3
Joze F 68 C3
Józefów PL 55 A6
Juan-les-Pins F 79 C6
Juankoski FIN 3 E28
Juban AL 105 A5
Jübek D 43 A6
Jubera E 89 B4
Jubrique E 99 C5
Jüchsen D 51 C6
Judaberg N 33 C2
Judenburg A 73 A4
Juelsminde DK 39 D3
Jugon-les-Lacs F 56 B3
Juillac F 67 C6
Juillan F 76 C3
Juist D 43 B4
Jukkasjärvi S 112 E9
Jule N 115 C10
Julianadorp NL 42 C1
Julianstown IRL 19 C5
Jülich D 50 C2
Jullouville F 57 B4
Jumeaux F 68 C3
Jumièges F 58 A1
Jumilhac-le-Grand F 67 C6
Jumilla E 101 A4
Juncosa E 90 B3
Juneda E 90 B3
Jung S 35 D5
Jungingen D 61 B5
Junglingster L 60 A2
Juniville F 59 A5
Junosuando S 113 E11
Junqueira P 87 C3
Junsele S 115 D13
Juoksengi S 113 F12
Juoksenki FIN 113 F12
Juprelle B 49 C6
Jurata PL 47 A4
Jurbarkas LT 6 D7
Jurjevo HR 83 B3
Jūrmala LV 6 C7
Juromenha P 93 C3
Jursla S 37 D3
Jussac F 77 B5
Jussey F 60 C1
Jussy F 59 A4
Juta H 74 B2
Jüterbog D 52 B3
Juuka FIN 3 E28
Juvigny-le-Terte F 57 B4
Juvigny-sous-Andaine F 57 B5
Juzennecourt F 59 B5
Jyderup DK 39 D4
Jyväskylä FIN 3 E26

K

Kaamanen FIN 113 C16
Kaamasmukka FIN 113 C15
Kaaresuvanto FIN 113 D11
Kaarssen D 44 B3
Kaatsheuvel NL 49 B6
Kaba H 75 A6
Kåbdalis S 115 A17
Kačarevo SCG 85 B5
Kačikol SCG 85 D6
Kács H 65 C6
Kadan CZ 52 C3
Kadarkút H 74 B2
Kadınhanı TR 119 D7
Kaduy RUS 7 B14
Kåfalla S 37 C2
Kåfjord N 113 C12
Kåfjordbotn N 112 C9
Kågeröd S 41 D3
Kahl D 51 C5
Kahla D 52 C1
Kainach bei Voitsberg A 73 A5
Kaindorf A 73 A5
Kainulasjärvi S 113 F11
Kairala FIN 113 E16
Kaisepakte S 112 D8
Kaisersesch D 50 C3
Kaiserslautern D 60 A3
Kaisheim D 62 B1
Kajaani FIN 3 D27
Kajárpéc H 74 A2
Kajdacs H 74 B3
Kakanj BIH 84 B3
Kakasd H 74 B3
Kaklik TR 119 E4
Kakolewo PL 54 B1
Kál H 65 C6
Kalače SCG 85 D5
Kalajoki FIN 3 D25
Kalak N 113 B16
Kalamata GR 117 E4
Kalambaka GR 116 C3
Kalamria GR 116 B4
Kalandra GR 116 C5
Kälarne S 115 E13
Kalavrita GR 117 D4
Kalbe D 44 C3
Kalce SLO 73 C4
Káld H 74 A2
Kale, *Antalya* TR 119 F4
Kale, *Denizli* TR 119 E3
Kalecik TR 16 A6
Kalefeld D 51 B6
Kalenić SCG 85 C5
Kalesija BIH 84 B3
Kalety PL 54 C3
Kalevala RUS 3 D29
Kalhovd N 32 B5
Kalí HR 83 B4
Kalimnos GR 119 F2
Kaliningrad RUS 47 A6
Kalinkavichy BY 7 E10
Kalinovac HR 74 B2
Kalinovik BIH 84 C3
Kalinovo SK 65 B5
Kalirachi GR 116 B6
Kaliska, *Pomorskie* PL 47 A4
Kaliska, *Pomorskie* PL 47 B4
Kalisko PL 55 B4
Kalisz PL 54 B3
Kalisz Pomorski PL 46 B1
Kalix S 3 D25
Kaljord N 112 D4
Kalkan TR 119 F4
Kalkar D 50 B2
Kalkım TR 118 C2
Kall D 50 C2
Kall S 115 D10
Källby S 35 D5
Kållered S 38 B5
Kållerstad S 40 B3
Kallinge S 41 C5
Kallmeti i Madh AL 105 B5
Kallmünz D 62 A2
Kallo FIN 113 E13
Kallsedet S 115 D9
Källvik S 37 D4
Kalmar S 40 C6
Kalmthout B 49 B5
Kalná SK 65 B4
Kalo Nero GR 117 E3
Kalocsa H 75 B3
Kalokhorio CY 120 B2
Kaloni GR 116 C8
Káloz H 74 B3
Kals A 72 A2
Kalsdorf A 73 B5
Kaltbrunn CH 70 A4
Kaltenbach A 72 A1
Kaltenkirchen D 44 B1
Kaltennordheim D 51 C6
Kaluga RUS 7 D14
Kalundborg DK 39 D4
Kalush UA 11 B8
Kałuszyn PL 55 A6
Kalv S 40 B3
Kalvåg N 114 F1
Kalvehave DK 41 D2
Kalwang A 73 A4
Kalwaria-Zebrzydowska PL 65 A5
Kalyazin RUS 7 C14
Kam H 74 A1
Kaman TR 16 B6
Kamares GR 117 F6
Kambos CY 120 A1
Kamen D 50 B3
Kamenice CZ 64 A1
Kamenice nad Lipou CZ 63 A6
Kameničná SK 64 C4
Kamenný Most SK 65 C4
Kamenny Ujezd CZ 63 B5
Kamenska HR 74 C2
Kamensko HR 84 C1
Kamenz D 53 B4
Kamičak BIH 84 B1

La Puebla de Montalbán E 94 C2
La Puebla de Roda E 90 A3
La Puebla de Valdavia E 88 B2
La Puebla de Valverde E 96 A2
La Puebla del Río E 99 B4
La Pueblanueva E 94 C2
La Puerta de Segura E 101 A3
La Punt CH 71 B4
La Quintana E 100 B1
La Quintera E 99 B5
La Rábita, *Granada* E 100 C2
La Rábita, *Jaén* E 100 B1
La Rambla E 100 B1
La Reale I 110 A1
La Redondela E 98 B3
La Réole F 76 B2
La Riera E 86 A4
La Riera de Gaià E 91 B4
La Rinconada E 99 B4
La Rivière-Thibouville F 58 A1
La Robla E 88 B1
La Roca de la Sierra E 93 B4
La Roche CH 70 B2
La Roche-Bernard F 66 A2
La Roche-Canillac F 68 C1
La Roche-Chalais F 67 C5
La Roche Derrien F 56 B2
La Roche-des-Arnauds F 79 B4
La Roche-en-Ardenne B 49 C6
La Roche-en-Brénil F 69 A4
La Roche-Guyon F 58 A2
La Roche-Posay F 67 B5
La Roche-sur-Foron F 69 B6
La Roche-sur-Yon F 66 B3
La Rochebeaucourt-et-Argentine F 67 C5
La Rochefoucauld F 67 C5
La Rochelle F 66 B3
La Rochette F 79 B4
La Roda, *Albacete* E 95 C4
La Roda, *Oviedo* E 86 A4
La Roda de Andalucía E 100 B1
La Roque-Gageac F 77 B4
La Roque-Ste. Marguerite F 78 B2
La Roquebrussanne F 79 C4
La Rubia E 89 C4
La Sagrada E 87 D4
La Salceda E 94 A3
La Salle F 79 B5
la Salute di Livenza I 72 C2
La Salvetat-Peyralés F 77 B5
La Salvetat-sur-Agout F 78 C1
La Sarraz CH 69 B6
La Seca E 88 C2
La Selva del Camp E 91 B4
La Senia E 90 C3
La Serra E 91 B4
La Seu d'Urgell E 91 A4
La Seyne-sur-Mer F 79 C4
La Solana E 95 D3
La Souterraine F 67 B6
La Spézia I 81 B3
La Storta I 102 B5
La Suze-sur-Sarthe F 57 C6
La Teste F 76 B1
La Thuile I 70 C1
La Toba E 95 B5
La Toledana E 94 C2
La Torre de Cabdella E 90 A3
La Torre de Esteban Hambrán E 94 B2
La Torre del l'Espanyol E 90 B3
La Torresaviñán E 95 B4
La Tour d'Aigues F 79 C4
La Tour de Peilz CH 70 B1
La Tour-du-Pin F 69 C5
La Tranche-sur-Mer F 66 B3
La Tremblade F 66 C3
La Trimouille F 67 B6
La Trinité F 56 C2
La Trinité-Porhoët F 56 B3
La Turballe F 66 A2
La Uña E 88 A1
La Unión E 101 B5
La Vall d'Uixó E 96 B2
La Vecilla de Curueño E 88 B1
La Vega, *Asturias* E 88 A1
La Vega, *Asturias* E 88 A1
La Vega, *Cantabria* E 88 A2
La Velilla E 94 A3
La Velles E 94 A1
La Ventosa E 95 B4
La Victoria E 100 B1
La Vid E 89 C3
La Vilavella E 96 B2
La Vilella Baixa E 90 B3
La Villa de Don Fadrique E 95 C3
La Ville Dieu-du-Temple F 77 B4
La Villedieu F 67 B4
La Voulte-sur-Rhône F 78 B3
La Wantzenau F 60 B3
La Yesa E 96 B2
La Zubia E 100 B2
Laa an der Thaya A 64 B2
Laage D 44 B4
Laanila FIN 113 D16
Laatzen D 51 A5
Laban IRL 20 A3
Labastide-Murat F 77 B4
Labastide-Rouairoux F 77 C5
Labastide-St. Pierre F 77 C4
Lábatlan H 65 C4
Labenne F 76 C1
Labin HR 82 A3
Łabiszyn PL 46 C3
Lablachère F 78 B3
Lábod H 74 B2
Laboe D 44 A2
Labouheyre F 76 B2
Łabowa PL 65 A6
Labrit F 76 B2
Labros E 95 A5
Labruguière F 77 C5
Labrujo P 87 C2
L'Absie F 67 B4
Laç AL 105 B5
Lacalahorra E 100 B2
Lacanau F 76 B1
Lacanau-Océan F 76 A1
Lacanche F 69 A4
Lacapelle-Marival F 77 B4
Laćarak SCG 85 A4
Lacaune F 78 C1
Laceby GB 27 B5
Lacedónia I 103 B8
Láces I 71 B5
Lachania GR 119 G2
Lachen CH 70 A3
Lachendorf D 44 C2
Lachowice PL 65 A5
Łąck PL 47 C5
Läckeby S 40 C6
Läckö S 35 D5
Lacock GB 29 B5
Láconi I 110 C2
Lacq F 76 C2
Lacroix-Barrez F 77 B5
Lacroix-St. Ouen F 58 A3
Lacroix-sur-Meuse F 60 B1
Łącznik PL 54 C2
Lad H 74 B2
Ladbergen D 50 A3
Lądek-Zdrój PL 54 C1
Ladelund D 39 E2
Ladendorf A 64 B2
Ladignac-le-Long F 67 C6
Ladispoli I 102 B5
Ladoeiro P 93 B3
Ladon F 58 C3
Ladushkin RUS 47 A6
Ladybank GB 25 B4
Laer D 50 A3
Lærdalsøyri N 32 A4
Lafkos GR 116 C5
Lafnitz A 73 A6
Lafrançaise F 77 B4
Lagan S 40 C3
Laganadi I 109 A4
Lagarde F 77 C4
Lagares, *Coimbra* P 92 A3
Lagares, *Porto* P 87 C2
Lagaro I 81 B5
Lagartera E 93 B5
Lågbol S 36 B5
Lage D 51 B4
Lägerdorf D 43 B6
Lagg GB 24 C2
Laggan GB 22 D4
Laggartorp S 35 C6
Łagiewniki PL 54 C1
Láglio I 71 C4
Lagnieu F 69 C5
Lagny-sur-Marne F 58 B3
Lago, *Calabria* I 106 B3
Lago, *Veneto* I 72 C2
Lagôa P 98 B2
Lagoaça P 87 C4
Lagonegro I 106 A2
Lagos GR 116 A7
Lagos P 98 B2
Lagosanto I 82 B1
Łagów, *Lubuskie* PL 46 C1
Łagów, *Świętokrzyskie* PL 55 C6
Lagrasse F 77 C5
Laguardia E 89 B4
Laguarres E 90 A3
Laguenne F 68 C1
Laguépie F 77 B4
Laguiole F 78 B1
Laguna de Duera E 88 C2
Laguna de Negrillos E 88 B1
Laguna del Marquesado E 95 B5
Lagundo I 71 B6
Lagunilla E 93 A4
Laharie F 76 B2
Lahden D 43 C4
Laheycourt F 59 B6
Lahnstein D 50 C3
Laholm S 40 C3
Lahr D 60 B3
Lahti FIN 3 F26
Laichingen D 61 B5
L'Aigle F 58 B1
Laignes F 59 C5
Laiguéglia I 80 C2
L'Aiguillon-sur-Mer F 66 B3
Laimbach am Ostrong A 63 B6
Laina E 95 A4
Lainio S 113 E11
Lairg GB 23 C4
Laissac F 78 B1
Laisvall S 115 A14
Láives I 71 B6
Lajkovac SCG 85 B5
Lajoskomárom H 74 B3
Lajosmizse H 75 A4
Lak H 65 B6
Lakenheath GB 30 B4
Lakitelek H 75 B5
Lakki GR 117 G5
Lakolk DK 39 D1
Łąkorz PL 47 B5
Lakšárska Nová Ves SK 64 B3
Lakselv N 113 B13
Laksfors N 115 B10
Laktaši BIH 84 B2
Lalapaşa TR 118 A1
L'Albagès E 90 B3
Lalbenque F 77 B4
L'Alcudia E 96 B2
L'Aldea E 90 C3
Lalëz AL 105 B5
Lalín E 86 B2
Lalinde F 77 B3
Lalizolle F 68 B3
Lalley F 79 B4
Lalling D 62 B4
Lalm N 114 F6
L'Alpe-d'Huez F 79 A5
Laluque F 76 C1
Lam D 62 A4
Lama dei Peligni I 103 A7
Lama Mocogno I 81 B4
Lamadrid E 88 A2
Lamagistére F 77 B3
Lamarche F 60 B1
Lamarche-sur-Saône F 69 A5
Lamargelle F 69 A4
Lamarosa P 92 B2
Lamarque F 76 A2
Lamas P 92 A2
Lamas de Moaro P 87 B2
Lamastre F 78 B3
Lambach A 63 B4
Lamballe F 56 B3
Lamberhurst GB 31 C4
Lambesc F 79 C4
Lambia GR 117 E3
Lambley GB 25 D5
Lambourn GB 31 C2
Lamego P 87 C3
L'Ametlla de Mar E 90 C3
Lamia GR 116 D4
Lammhult S 40 B4
Lamothe-Cassel F 77 B4
Lamothe-Montravel F 76 B3
Lamotte-Beuvron F 58 C3
Lampaul F 56 B1
Lampertheim D 61 A4
Lampeter GB 28 A3
L'Ampolla E 90 C3
Lamprechtshausen A 62 C3
Lamsfeld D 53 B4
Lamspringe D 51 B6
Lamstedt D 43 B6
Lamure-sur-Azergues F 69 B4
Lana I 71 B6
Lanaja E 90 B2
Lanarce F 78 B2
Lanark GB 25 C4
Lancaster GB 26 A3
Lanchester GB 25 D6
Lanciano I 103 A7
Lancing GB 31 D3
Lancon-provence F 79 C4
Lancova Vas SLO 73 B5
Landau, *Bayern* D 62 B3
Landau, *Rheinland-Pfalz* D 61 A4
Landeck A 71 A5
Landen B 49 C6
Landerneau F 56 B1
Landeryd S 40 B3
Landesbergen D 43 C6
Landete E 96 B1
Landévant F 56 C2
Landévennec F 56 B1
Landivisiau F 56 B1
Landivy F 57 B4
Landl A 62 C3
Landön S 115 D11
Landos F 78 B2
Landouzy-le-Ville F 59 A5
Landquart CH 71 B4
Landrecies F 49 C4
Landreville F 59 B5
Landriano I 71 C4
Lands-berg D 52 B2
Landsberg D 62 B1
Landsbro S 40 B4
Landscheid D 50 D2
Landshut D 62 B3
Landskrona S 41 D2
Landstuhl D 60 A3
Lanesborough IRL 19 C4
Lanester F 56 C2
Lanestosa E 89 A3
Langå DK 39 C2
Langa de Duero E 89 C3
Langada GR 116 D8
Langadas GR 116 B5
Langadia GR 117 E4
Langangen N 35 C1
Långared S 40 A2
Långaröd S 41 D3
Långaryd S 40 B3
Långasjö S 40 C5
Langau A 63 B6
Langeac F 78 A2
Langeais F 67 A5
Langedijk NL 42 C1
Langeln D 51 B6
Langelsheim D 51 B6
Langemark-Poelkapelle B 48 C3
Langen, *Hessen* D 51 D4
Langen, *Niedersachsen* D 43 B5
Langenau D 61 B6
Langenberg D 50 B4
Langenbruck CH 70 A2
Langenburg D 61 A5
Längenfeld A 71 A5
Langenfeld D 50 B2
Langenhorn D 43 A5
Langenlois A 63 B6
Langenlonsheim D 60 A3
Langennaudorf D 52 B3
Langenneufnach D 62 B1
Langenthal CH 70 A2
Langenzenn D 62 A1
Langeoog D 43 B4
Langeskov DK 39 D3
Langesund N 35 C1
Langewiesen D 51 C6
Långflon S 34 A4
Langförden D 43 C5
Langhagen D 44 B4
Länghem S 40 B3
Langhirano I 81 B4
Langholm GB 25 C5
Langholt IS 111 D7
Långlöt S 41 C6
Langnau CH 70 B2
Langø DK 39 E4
Langogne F 78 B2
Langon F 76 B2
Langquaid D 62 B3
Långrådna S 37 D3
Langreo E 88 A1
Langres F 59 C6
Långsele S 115 D14
Långserud S 35 C4
Langset N 34 B3
Långshyttan S 36 B3
Langstrand N 113 B12
Långträsk S 115 B17
Langueux F 56 B3
Languidic F 56 C2
Längvik S 37 C5
Langwarden D 43 B5
Langwathby GB 26 A3
Langwedel D 43 C6
Langweid D 62 B1
Langwies CH 71 B4
Lanheses P 87 C2
Lanięta PL 47 C5
Lanildut F 56 B1
Lanjarón E 100 C2
Lanmeur F 56 B2
Lanna, *Jönköping* S 40 B3
Lanna, *Örebro* S 37 C1
Lännaholm S 36 C4
Lannavaara S 113 D10
Lannéanou F 56 B2
Lannemezan F 77 C3
Lanneuville-sur-Meuse F 59 A6
Lannilis F 56 B1
Lannion F 56 B2
Lanouaille F 67 C6
Lansjärv S 113 F11
Lanškroun CZ 64 A2
Lanslebourg-Mont-Cenis F 70 C1
Lanta F 77 C4
Lantadilla E 88 B2
Lanton F 76 B1
Lantosque F 79 C6
Lanusei I 110 C2
Lanúvio I 102 B5
Lanvollon F 56 B3
Lánycsók H 74 B3
Lanz D 44 B3
Lanza E 86 A2
Lanzada E 86 B2
Lanzahita E 94 B2
Lanžhot CZ 64 B2
Lanzo Torinese I 70 C2
Laole SCG 85 B6
Laon F 59 A4
Laons F 58 B2
Lapalisse F 68 B3
Łapczyna Wola PL 55 C4
Lapeyrade F 76 B2
Lapeyrouse F 68 B2
Lapford GB 28 C4
Lapithos CY 120 A2
Laplje Selo SCG 85 D6
Laplume F 77 B3
Lapoutroie F 60 B3
Lapovo SCG 85 B6
Läppe S 37 C2
Lappeenranta FIN 3 F28
Lappoluobbal N 113 C12
Lapseki TR 118 B1
Lapua FIN 3 E25
L'Áquila I 103 A6
Laracha E 86 A2
Laragh IRL 21 A5
Laragne-Montéglin F 79 B4
l'Arboç E 91 B4
L'Arbresle F 69 C4
Lärbro S 37 E5
Larceveau F 76 C1
Larche, *Alpes-de-Haute-Provence* F 79 B5
Larche, *Corrèze* F 77 A4
Lårdal N 33 C5
Lardosa P 92 B3
Laredo E 89 A3
Largentière F 78 B3
L'Argentière-la-Bessée F 79 B5
Largs GB 24 C3
Lari I 81 C4
Lariño E 86 B1
Larino I 103 B7
Larisa GR 116 C4
Larkhall GB 25 C4
Larkollen N 35 C2
Larmor-Plage F 56 C2
Larnaca CY 120 B2
Larne GB 19 B6
Larochette L 60 A2
Laroque d'Olmes F 77 D4
Laroque-Timbaut F 77 B3
Laroquebrou F 77 B5
Larouco E 87 B3
Larraga E 89 B5
Larrau F 76 C2
Larrazet F 77 C4
Larsnes N 114 E2
Laruns F 76 C2
Larva E 100 B2
Larvik N 35 C2
Las Arenas E 88 A2
Las Cabezadas E 95 A3
Las Cabezas de San Juan E 99 C5
Las Correderas E 100 A2
Las Cuevas de Cañart E 90 C2
Las Gabias E 100 B2
Las Herencias E 94 C2
Las Labores E 95 C3
Las Mesas E 95 C4
Las Minas E 101 A4
Las Navas E 100 B1
Las Navas de la Concepción E 99 B5
Las Navas del Marqués E 94 B2
Las Navillas E 94 C2
Las Negras E 101 C4
Las Pajanosas E 99 B4
Las Pedroñas E 95 C4
Las Planes d'Hostoles E 91 A5
Las Rozas, *Cantabria* E 88 B2
Las Rozas, *Madrid* E 94 B3
Las Uces E 87 C4
Las Veguillas E 94 B1
Las Ventas con Peña Aguilera E 94 C2
Las Ventas de San Julián E 93 A5
Las Villes E 96 A3
Lasalle F 78 B2
Lasarte E 89 A4
Låsby DK 39 C2
Łasin PL 47 B5
Lask PL 55 B4
Laska PL 46 B3
Łaskarzow PL 55 B6
Laško SLO 73 B5
Laskowice PL 47 B4
Laspaules E 90 A3
Laspuña E 90 A3
Lassan D 45 B5
Lassay-les-Châteaux F 57 B5
Lasseube F 76 C2
Lassigny F 58 A3
Lastovo HR 84 D1
Lastras de Cuéllar E 88 C2
Lästringe S 37 D4
Lastrup D 43 C4
Lastva BIH 84 D3
Latasa E 76 D1
Látera I 102 A4
Laterza I 104 C2
Lathen D 43 C4
Latheron GB 23 C5
Latiano I 105 C3
Latina I 102 B5
Latisana I 72 C3
Látky SK 65 B5
Latowicz PL 55 A6
Latrónico I 106 A3
Latronquière F 77 B5
Latterbach CH 70 B2
Laubach D 51 C4
Laubert F 78 B2
Laucha D 52 B1
Lauchhammer D 53 B3
Lauchheim D 61 B6
Lauda-Königshofen D 61 A5
Laudal N 33 D4
Lauder GB 25 C5
Lauenau D 51 A5
Lauenburg D 44 B2
Lauf D 62 A2
Laufach D 51 C5
Laufen CH 70 A2
Laufen D 62 C3
Lauffen D 61 A5
Laugar IS 111 B8
Laugarás IS 111 C5
Laugarbakki IS 111 B5
Laugarvatn IS 111 C5
Laugharne GB 28 B3
Lauingen D 61 B6
Laujar de Andarax E 100 C3
Laukaa FIN 3 E26
Lauker S 115 B16
Laukvik N 112 E3
Launceston GB 28 C3
Launois-sur-Vence F 59 A5
Laupheim D 61 B5
Lauragh IRL 20 C2
Laureana di Borrello I 106 C3
Laurencekirk GB 25 B5
Laurencetown IRL 20 A3
Laurenzana I 104 C1
Lauria I 106 A2
Laurière F 67 B6
Laurieston GB 24 D3
Laurino I 103 C8
Lausanne CH 69 B6
Laussonne F 78 B3
Lauta D 53 B4
Lautenthal D 51 B6
Lauterach A 71 A4
Lauterbach D 51 C5
Lauterbrunnen CH 70 B2
Lauterecken D 60 A3
Lauterhofen D 62 A2
Lautrec F 77 C5
Lauvsnes N 114 C7
Lauvvlk N 33 D3
Lauzerte F 77 B4
Lauzès F 77 B4
Lauzun F 77 B3
Lavagna I 80 B3
Laval F 57 B5
Lavamünd A 73 B4
Lavara GR 118 A1
Lavardac F 76 B3
Lavaris P 92 A2
Lavarone I 71 C6
Lavau F 59 C3
Lavaur F 77 C4
Lavelanet F 77 D4
Lavello I 104 B1
Lavelsloh D 43 C5
Lavenham GB 30 B4
Laveno I 70 C3
Lavezzola I 81 B5
Laviano I 103 C8
Lavik N 32 A2
Lavilledieu F 78 B3
Lavinio-Lido di Enea I 102 B5
Lavis I 71 B6
Lavit F 77 C3
Lavoncourt F 60 C1
Lavos P 92 A2
Lavoûter-Chilhac F 68 C3
Lavradio P 92 C1
Lavre P 92 C2
Lavrio GR 117 E6
Lawers GB 24 B3
Ławy PL 45 C6
Laxå S 37 D1
Laxamýri IS 111 B8
Laxe E 86 A2
Laxey GB 26 A1
Laxford Bridge GB 22 C3
Laxhall S 35 D5
Laxsjö S 115 D11
Laxtjarn S 34 B6
Laxvik S 40 C2
Laxviken S 115 D11
Laza E 87 B3
Lazarev Krst SCG 105 A5
Lazarevac SCG 85 B5
Lazarevo SCG 75 C5
Lazise I 71 C5
Łaziska Grn. PL 54 C3
Lazkao E 89 A4
Lázně Bělohrad CZ 53 C5
Lázně Bohdaneč CZ 53 C5
Lázně Kynžvart CZ 52 C2
Lazonby GB 26 A3
Łazy PL 46 A2
Lazzaro I 109 B4
Le Bar-sur-Loup F 79 C5
Le Barp F 76 B2
Le Béage F 78 B3
Le Beausset F 79 C4
Le Bessat F 69 C4
Le Blanc F 67 B6
Le Bleymard F 78 B2
Le Boullay-Mivoye F 58 B2
Le Boulou F 91 A5
Le Bourg F 77 B4
Le Bourg-d'Oisans F 79 A5
Le Bourget-du-Lac F 69 C5
Le Bourgneuf-la-Forêt F 57 B5
Le Bousquet d'Orb F 78 C2
Le Brassus CH 69 B6
Le Breuil F 68 B3
Le Breuil-en-Auge F 57 A6
Le Brusquet F 79 B5
Le Bry CH 70 B2
Le Bugue F 77 B3
Le Buisson F 77 B3
Le Caloy F 76 C2
Le Cap d'Agde F 78 C2
Le Cateau Cambrésis F 49 C4
Le Caylar F 78 C2
Le Cayrol F 78 B1
Le Chambon-Feugerolles F 69 C4
Le Chambon-sur-Lignon F 78 A3
Le Château d'Oléron F 66 C3
Le Châtelard F 69 C6
Le Châtelet F 68 B2
Le Chatelet-en-Brie F 58 B3
Le Chesne F 59 A5
Le Cheylard F 78 B3
Le Collet-de-Deze F 78 B2
Le Conquet F 56 B1
Le Creusot F 69 B4
Le Croisic F 66 A2
Le Crotoy F 48 C2
Le Deschaux F 69 B5
Le Donjon F 68 B3
Le Dorat F 67 B6
Le Faou F 56 B1
Le Faoüet F 56 B2
Le Folgoet F 56 B1
Le Fossat F 77 C4
Le Fousseret F 77 C4
Le Fugeret F 79 B5
Le Gault-Soigny F 59 B4
Le Grand-Bornand F 69 C6
Le-Grand-Bourg F 67 B6
Le Grand-Lucé F 58 C1
Le Grand-Pressigny F 67 B5
Le Grand-Quevilly F 58 A2
Le Grau-du-Roi F 78 C3
Le Havre F 57 A6
Le Hohwald F 60 B3
Le Houga F 76 C2
Le Lardin-St. Lazare F 67 C6
Le Lauzet-Ubaye F 79 B5
Le Lavandou F 79 C5
Le Lion-d'Angers F 57 C5
Le Locle CH 70 A1
Le Loroux-Bottereau F 66 A3
Le Louroux-Béconnais F 66 A4
Le Luc F 79 C5
Le Lude F 57 C6
Le Malzieu-Ville F 78 B2
Le Mans F 57 B6
Le Mas-d'Azil F 77 C4
Le Massegros F 78 B2
Le May-sur-Evre F 66 A4
Le Mayet-de-Montagne F 68 B3
Le Mêle-sur-Sarthe F 58 B1
Le Ménil F 60 B2
Le Merlerault F 57 B6
Le Mesnil-sur-Oger F 59 B5
Le Miroir F 69 B5
Le Molay-Littry F 57 A5
Le Monastier-sur-Gazeille F 78 B2
Le Monêtier-les-Bains F 79 B5
Le Mont-Dore F 68 C2
Le Mont-St. Michel F 57 B4
Le Montet F 68 B3
Le Muret F 76 B2
Le Muy F 79 C5
Le Neubourg F 58 A1
Le Nouvion-en-Thiérache F 49 C4
Le Palais F 66 A1
Le Parcq F 48 C3
Le Péage-de-Roussillon F 69 C4
Le Pellerin F 66 A3
Le Perthus F 91 A5
Le Pertuis F 78 A3
Le Petit-Bornand F 69 C6
Le Poët F 79 B4
Le Poirè-sur-Vie F 66 B3
Le Pont CH 69 B6
Le Pont-de-Montvert F 78 B2
Le Porge F 76 B1
Le Porge-Océan F 76 B1
Le Portel F 48 C2
Le Pouldu F 56 C2
Le Pouliguen F 66 A2
le Prese I 71 B5
Le Puy-en-Velay F 78 A2
Le Puy-Ste. Réparade F 79 C4
Le Quesnoy F 49 C4
Le Rayol F 79 C5
Le Rœulx B 49 C5
Le Rouget F 77 B5
Le Rozier F 78 B2
Le Russey F 70 A1
Le Sel-de-Bretagne F 57 C4
Le Sentier CH 69 B6
Le Souquet F 76 C1
Le Teil F 78 B3
Le Teilleul F 57 B5
Le Temple-de-Bretagne F 66 A3
Le Theil F 58 B1
Le Thillot F 60 C2
Le Touquet-Paris-Plage F 48 C2
Le Touvet F 69 C5
Le Translay F 48 D2
Le Tréport F 48 C2
Le Val F 79 C5
Le Val-André F 56 B3
Le Val-d'Ajol F 60 C2
Le Verdon-sur-Mer F 66 C3
Le Vernet F 79 B5
Le Vigan F 78 C2
le Ville I 82 C1
Le Vivier-sur-Mer F 57 B4
Lea GB 27 B5
Leadburn GB 25 C4
Leadhills GB 25 C4
Leap IRL 20 C2
Leatherhead GB 31 C3
Łeba PL 46 A3
Lebach D 60 A2
Lebedyn UA 7 F13
Lebekke B 49 B5
Lébény H 64 C3
Łebno PL 47 A4
Leboreiro E 87 B3
Lębork PL 46 A3
Lebrija E 99 C4
Lebring A 73 B5
Lebus D 45 C6
Lebusa D 52 B3
Leca da Palmeira P 87 C2
Lecce I 105 C4
Lecco I 71 C4
Lécera E 90 B2
Lećevica HR 83 C5
Lech A 71 A5
Lechbruck D 62 C1
Lechena GR 117 E3
Lechlade GB 29 B6
Lechovice CZ 64 B2
Leciñena E 90 B2
Leck D 39 E1
Lectoure F 77 C3
Łęczyca, *Łódzkie* PL 55 A4
Łęczyca, *Zachodnio-Pomorskie* PL 45 B7
Ledaña E 95 C5
Ledbury GB 29 A5
Lede B 49 C4
Ledeč nad Sazavou CZ 63 A6
Ledenice CZ 63 B5
Ledesma E 87 C4
Lédignan F 78 C3
Lédigos E 88 B2
Ledmore GB 22 C4
Lednice CZ 64 B2
Lednicke-Rovné SK 64 A4
Lędyczek PL 46 B2
Lędziny PL 55 C4
Leeds GB 27 B4
Leek GB 26 B3
Leek NL 42 B3
Leenaun IRL 18 C2
Leens NL 42 B3
Leer D 43 B4
Leerdam NL 49 B6
Leerhafe D 43 B4
Leese D 43 C6
Leeuwarden NL 42 B2
Leezen D 44 B2
Lefka CY 120 A1
Lefkada GR 116 D2
Lefkimis GR 116 C2
Lefkoniko CY 120 A2
Leganés E 94 B3
Legau D 61 C6
Legbąd PL 46 B3
Legé F 66 B3
Lège-Cap-Ferret F 76 B1
Legionowo PL 55 A5
Léglise B 60 A1
Legnago I 71 C6
Legnano I 70 C3
Legnaro I 72 C1
Legnica PL 53 B6
Łęgowo PL 47 A4
Legrad HR 74 B1
Léguevin F 77 C4
Legutiano E 89 B4
Lehesten D 52 C1
Lehnice SK 64 B3
Lehnin D 52 A2
Lehrberg D 61 A6
Lehre D 51 A6
Lehrte D 44 C1
Lehsen D 44 B3
Leibnitz A 73 B5
Leicester GB 30 B2
Leiden NL 49 A5
Leidschendam NL 49 A5
Leigh GB 26 B3
Leighlinbridge IRL 21 B5
Leighton Buzzard GB 31 C3

Leignon B 49 C6
Leikanger N 114 E2
Leimen D 61 A4
Leinefelde D 51 B6
Leinesfjord N 112 E4
Leintwardine GB 29 A5
Leipojärvi S 112 E10
Leipzig D 52 B2
Leira, *Nordland* N 115 A10
Leira, *Oppland* N 32 B6
Leiråmoen N 112 F3
Leiria P 92 B2
Leirvik, *Hordaland* N 32 C2
Leirvik, *Sogn og Fjordane* N 32 A2
Leisach A 72 B2
Leisnig D 52 B2
Leiston GB 30 B5
Leitholm GB 25 C5
Leitrim IRL 18 C3
Leitza E 76 C1
Leitzkau D 52 A1
Lejkowo PL 46 A2
Lekani GR 116 A6
Łękawa PL 55 B4
Łekawica PL 65 A5
Lekbibaj AL 105 A5
Lekeitio E 89 A4
Lekenik HR 73 C6
Lekeryd S 40 B4
Leknes N 112 D2
Łęknica PL 53 B4
Leksand S 36 B1
Leksvik N 114 D7
Lekunberri E 76 C1
Lekvattnet S 34 B4
Lelkowo PL 47 A6
Lelów PL 55 C4
Lelystad NL 42 C2
Lem, *Ringkøbing* DK 39 C1
Lem, *Viborg Amt.* DK 38 C1
Lembach F 60 A3
Lemberg F 60 A3
Lembèye F 76 C2
Lemelerveld NL 42 C3
Lemförde D 43 C5
Lemgo D 51 A4
Lemland FIN 36 B7
Lemmer NL 42 C2
Lempdes F 68 C3
Lemvig DK 38 C1
Lemwerder D 43 B5
Lena N 34 B2
Lenart SLO 73 B5
Lenartovce SK 65 B6
Lenauheim RO 75 C5
Lencloître F 67 B5
Lend A 72 A3
Lendalfoot GB 24 C3
Lendava SLO 73 B6
Lendery RUS 3 E29
Lendinara I 81 A5
Lendorf A 72 B3
Lendum DK 38 B3
Lengefeld D 52 C3
Lengerich, *Niedersachsen* D 43 C4
Lengerich, *Nordrhein-Westfalen* D 50 A3
Lenggries D 62 C2
Lengyeltóti H 74 B2
Lenhovda S 40 C5
Lenk CH 70 B2
Lennartsfors S 35 C3
Lennestadt D 50 B4
Lennoxtown GB 24 C3
Leno I 71 C5
Lénola I 103 B6
Lens B 49 C4
Lens F 48 C3
Lens Lestang F 69 C5
Lensahn D 44 A2
Lensvik N 114 D6
Lentellais E 87 B3
Lentföhrden D 44 B1
Lenti H 74 B1
Lentini I 109 B3
Lenungshammar S 35 C4
Lenzburg CH 70 A3
Lenzen D 44 B3
Lenzerheide CH 71 B4
Leoben A 73 A5
Leogang A 72 A2
Leominster GB 29 A5
León E 88 B1
Léon F 76 C1
Leonberg D 61 B5
Léoncel F 79 B4
Leonding A 63 B5
Leonessa I 102 A5
Leonforte I 109 B3
Leonidio GR 117 E4
Leopoldsburg B 49 B6
Leopoldsdorf im Marchfeld A 64 B2
Leopoldshagen D 45 B5
Leova MD 11 C10
Lepe E 98 B3
Lepenac, *Crna Gora* SCG 85 D4
Lepenac, *Srbija* SCG 85 C6
Lepenou GR 116 D3
Lephin GB 22 D2
L'Epine F 79 B4
Lepoglava HR 73 B6
Leppäjärvi FIN 113 D12
Leppävirta FIN 3 E27
Leppin D 44 C3
Lepsény H 74 B3
Léquile I 105 C4
Lercara Friddi I 108 B2
Lerdal S 35 D3
Leré F 68 A2
Lérici I 81 B3
Lerin E 89 B5
Lerm-et-Musset F 76 B2
Lerma E 88 B3
Lermoos A 71 A5
Lérouville F 60 B1
Lerum S 40 B2
Lervik N 35 C2
Lerwick GB 22 A7
Lés E 77 D3
Les Abrets F 69 C5
Les Aix-d'Angillon F 68 A2
Les Ancizes-Comps F 68 C2
Les Andelys F 58 A2
Les Arcs, *Savoie* F 70 C1
Les Arcs, *Var* F 79 C5
Les-Aubiers F 67 B4
Les Baux-de-Provence F 78 C3
Les Bézards F 58 C3
Les Bois CH 70 A1
Les Bordes F 58 C3
Les Borges Blanques E 90 B3
Les Borges del Camp E 91 B4
Les Brunettes F 68 B3
Les Cabannes F 77 D4
Les Contamines-Montjoie F 70 C1
les Coves de Vinroma E 90 C3
Les Déserts F 69 C5
Les Deux-Alpes F 79 B5
Les Diablerets CH 70 B2
Les Echelles F 69 C5
Les Escaldes AND 91 A4
Les Essarts F 66 B3
Les Estables F 78 B3
Les Eyzies-de-Tayac F 77 B4
Les Gets F 70 B1
Les Grandes-Ventes F 58 A2
Les Haudères CH 70 B2
Les Herbiers F 66 B3
Les Hôpitaux-Neufs F 69 B6
Les Lucs-sur-Boulogne F 66 B3
Les Mages F 78 B3
Les Mazures F 59 A5
Les Mées F 79 B4
Les Mureaux F 58 B2
Les Omergues F 79 B4
Les Ormes-sur-Voulzie F 59 B4
Les Orres F 79 B5
Les Pieux F 57 A4
Les Ponts-de-Cé F 67 A4
Les Ponts-de-Martel CH 70 B1
Les Praz F 70 C1
Les Riceys F 59 C5
Les Roches F 69 C4
Les Rosaires F 56 B3
Les Rosiers F 67 A4
Les Rousses F 69 B6
Les Sables-d'Olonne F 66 B3
Les Settons F 68 A4
Les Ternes F 78 A1
Les Thilliers en-Vexin F 58 A2
Les Touches F 66 A3
Les Trois Moûtiers F 67 A5
Les Vans F 78 B3
Les Verrières CH 69 B6
Les Vignes F 78 B2
Lešak SCG 85 D5
Lesaka E 76 C1
Lesbury GB 25 C6
L'Escala E 91 A6
Lescar F 76 C2
L'Escarène F 80 C1
Lesce SLO 73 B4
Lescheraines F 69 C6
Lesconil F 56 C1
Lesdins F 59 A4
Lesično SLO 73 B5
Lésina I 103 B8
Lesjaskog N 114 E5
Lesjöfors S 34 C6
Leskova Dolina SLO 73 C4
Leskovac SCG 10 E6
Leskovec CZ 64 A3
Leskovec SLO 73 C5
Leskovice CZ 63 A6
Leskovik AL 116 B2
Leslie GB 25 B4
Lesmahagow GB 25 C4
Lesmont F 59 B5
Leśna PL 53 B5
Lesneven F 56 B1
Leśnica PL 54 C3
Lešnica SCG 85 B4
Leśniów Wielkoplski PL 53 B5
Lesnoye RUS 7 B13
Lesparre-Médoc F 66 C4
l'Espérance F 59 A4
l'Esperou F 78 B2
Lesponne F 76 C3
L'Espunyola E 91 A4
Lessach A 72 A3
Lessay F 57 A4
Lessebo S 40 C5
Lessines B 49 C4
L'Estany E 91 B5
Lesterps F 67 B5
Leswalt GB 24 D2
Leszno, *Mazowieckie* PL 55 A5
Leszno, *Wielkopolskie* PL 54 B1
Leszno Górne PL 53 B5
Letchworth GB 31 C3
Letenye H 74 B1
Letino I 103 B7
Letohrad CZ 54 C1
Letovice CZ 64 A2
Letschin D 45 C6
Letterfrack IRL 18 C2
Letterkenny IRL 19 B4
Lettermacaward IRL 18 B3
Lettoch GB 23 D5
Letur E 101 A3
Letux E 90 B2
Letzlingen D 44 C3
Leucate F 78 D2
Leuchars GB 25 B5
Leuglay F 59 C5
Leuk CH 70 B2
Leukerbad CH 70 B2
Leumrabhagh GB 22 C2
Leuna D 52 B2
Leusden NL 49 A6
Leutenberg D 52 C1
Leuterschach D 61 C6
Leutershausen D 61 A6
Leutkirch D 61 C6
Leuven B 49 C5
Leuze-en-Hainaut B 49 C4
Levan AL 105 C5
Levanger N 114 D8
Levanjska Varoš HR 74 C3
Lévanto I 80 B3
Levaré F 57 B5
Levata I 71 C5
Leveld N 32 B5
Leven, *East Yorkshire* GB 27 B5
Leven, *Fife* GB 25 B5
Leverano I 105 C3
Leverkusen D 50 B2
Levern D 43 C5
Levet F 68 B2
Levice SK 65 B4
Lévico Terme I 71 B6
Levie F 102 B2
Levier F 69 B6
Lévignen F 59 A3
Levinovac HR 74 C2
Levoča SK 65 A6
Levroux F 67 B6
Lewes GB 31 D4
Lewin Brzeski PL 54 C2
Lewisham GB 31 C3
Leyburn GB 27 A4
Leyland GB 26 B3
Leysdown-on-Sea GB 31 C4
Leysin CH 70 B2
Lezajsk PL 11 A7
Lézardrieux F 56 B2
Lézat-sur-Léze F 77 C4
Lezay F 67 B4
Lezhë AL 105 B5
Lézignan-Corbières F 78 C1
Lezignan-la-Cèbe F 78 C2
Ležimir SCG 75 C4
Lézinnes F 59 C5
Lezoux F 68 C3
Lezuza E 95 D4
Lgov RUS 7 F13
Lhenice CZ 63 B5
Lherm F 77 C4
Lhommaizé F 67 B5
L'Hospitalet F 91 A4
L'Hospitalet de l'Infant E 90 C3
L'Hospitalet de Llobregat E 91 B5
L'Hospitalet-du-Larzac F 78 C2
Lhuître F 59 B5
Liancourt F 58 A3
Liart F 59 A5
Liatorp S 40 C4
Liatrie GB 22 D4
Libáň CZ 53 C5
Libceves CZ 53 C3
Liběchov CZ 53 C4
Liber E 86 B3
Liberec CZ 53 C5
Libiąż PL 55 C4
Libina CZ 64 A3
Libochovice CZ 53 C4
Libofshë AL 105 C5
Libohovë AL 116 B2
Libourne F 76 B2
Libramont B 59 A6
Librazhd AL 116 A2
Librilla E 101 B4
Libros E 96 A1
Licata I 108 B2
Licciana Nardi I 81 B4
Licenza I 102 A5
Liceros E 89 C3
Lich D 51 C4
Lichères-près-Aigremont F 59 C4
Lichfield GB 27 C4
Lichtenau A 63 B6
Lichtenau D 51 B4
Lichtenberg D 52 C1
Lichtenfels D 52 C1
Lichtensteig CH 71 A4
Lichtenstein D 52 C2
Lichtenvoorde NL 50 B2
Lichtervelde B 49 B4
Lička Jesenica HR 83 A4
Lickershamn S 37 E5
Lički Osik HR 83 B4
Ličko Lešce HR 83 B4
Licodia Eubéa I 109 B3
Licques F 48 C2
Lida BY 7 E8
Lidar N 32 A6
Lidečko CZ 64 A4
Liden S 115 E13
Lidhult S 40 C3
Lidköping S 35 D5
Lido I 72 C2
Lido Azzurro I 104 C3
Lido degli Estensi I 82 B1
Lido degli Scacchi I 82 B1
Lido della Nazioni I 82 B1
Lido di Camaiore I 81 C4
Lido di Casalbordino I 103 A7
Lido di Castél Fusano I 102 B5
Lido di Cincinnato I 102 B5
Lido di Classe I 82 B1
Lido di Fermo I 82 C2
Lido di Fondi I 103 B6
Lido di Jésolo I 72 C2
Lido di Licola I 103 C7
Lido di Metaponto I 104 C2
Lido di Óstia I 102 B5
Lido di Policoro I 106 A3
Lido di Pomposa I 82 B1
Lido di Savio I 82 B1
Lido di Scanzano I 104 C2
Lido di Siponto I 104 B1
Lido di Squillace I 106 C3
Lido di Volano I 82 B1
Lido Riccio I 103 A7
Lido Silvana I 104 C3
Lidoriki GR 116 D4
Lidsjöberg S 115 C12
Lidzbark PL 47 B5
Lidzbark Warmiński PL 47 A6
Liebenau A 63 B5
Liebenau D 43 C6
Liebenwalde D 45 C5
Lieberose D 53 B4
Liebling RO 75 C6
Lieboch A 73 B5
Liège B 49 C6
Lieksa FIN 3 E29
Lienen D 50 A3
Lienz A 72 B2
Liepāja LV 6 C6
Lier B 49 B5
Lierbyen N 34 C2
Liernais F 69 A4
Liesing A 72 B2
Liestal CH 70 A2
Liétor E 101 A4
Lieurac F 77 D4
Lieurey F 58 A1
Liévin F 48 C3
Liezen A 73 A4
Liffol-le-Grand F 60 B1
Lifford IRL 19 B4
Liffré F 57 B4
Ligardes F 77 B3
Lignano Sabbiadoro I 72 C3
Ligne F 66 A3
Lignières F 68 B2
Ligny-en-Barrois F 59 B6
Ligny-le-Châtel F 59 C4
Ligoła Polska PL 54 B2
Ligourio GR 117 E5
Ligowo PL 47 C5
Ligueil F 67 A5
Lijeva Rijeka SCG 85 D4
Likavka SK 65 A5
Likenäs S 34 B5
Likhoslavl RUS 7 C13
Lild Strand DK 38 B1
L'Île-Bouchard F 67 A5
l'Île-Rousse F 102 A1
Lilienfeld A 63 B6
Lilienthal D 43 B5
Lilla Edet S 35 D4
Lilla Tjärby S 40 C3
Lille B 49 B5
Lille F 49 C4
Lillebonne F 58 A1
Lillehammer N 34 A2
Lillerød DK 41 D2
Lillers F 48 C3
Lillesand N 33 D5
Lillestrøm N 34 C3
Lillhärdal S 115 F11
Lillkyrka S 37 C4
Lillo E 95 C3
Lillögda S 115 C14
Lima S 34 B5
Limanowa PL 65 A6
Limassol CY 120 B2
Limavady GB 19 A5
Limbach-Oberfrohna D 52 C2
Limbaži LV 6 C8
Limbourg B 50 C1
Limburg D 50 C4
Lime DK 39 C3
Limedsforsen S 34 B5
Limenaria GR 116 B6
Limenas Chersonisou GR 117 G7
Limerick IRL 20 B3
Limes I 71 C5
Liméy F 58 A1
Limmared S 40 B3
Limni GR 116 D5
Limoges F 67 C6
Limogne-en-Quercy F 77 B4
Limoise F 68 B3
Limone Piemonte I 80 B1
Limone sul Garda I 71 C5
Limons F 68 C3
Limours F 58 B3
Limoux F 77 C5
Linares E 100 A2
Linares de Mora E 90 C2
Linares de Riofrio E 93 A5
Linaria GR 116 D6
Linas de Broto E 90 A2
Lincoln GB 27 B5
Lind DK 39 C1
Lindås N 32 B2
Lindau D 71 A4
Lindberget N 34 A3
Lindelse DK 39 E3
Lindenberg D 53 A4
Lindenberg im Allgäu D 61 C5
Lindern D 43 C4
Linderöd S 41 D3
Lindesberg S 37 C2
Lindesnäs S 36 B1
Lindesnes N 33 E4
Lindholmen S 37 C5
Lindknud DK 39 D2
Lindlar D 50 B3
Lindö S 37 D3
Lindome S 38 B5
Lindos GR 119 F3
Lindoso P 87 C2
Lindow D 45 C4
Lindsdal S 40 C6
Lindshammar S 40 B5
Lindstedt D 44 C3
Lindved DK 39 D2
Líně CZ 63 A4
Lingbo S 36 A3
Lingen D 43 C4
Linghed S 36 B2
Linghem S 37 D2
Linguaglossa I 109 B4
Linia PL 46 A3
Linie PL 45 B6
Liniewo PL 47 A4
Linkenheim D 61 A4
Linköping S 37 D2
Linksness GB 23 C5
Linlithgow GB 25 C4
Linneryd S 40 C5
Linnes Hammarby S 36 C4
Linnich D 50 C2
Linsell S 115 E10
Linslade GB 31 C3
Linthal CH 70 B4
Linyola E 90 B3
Linz A 63 B5
Linz D 50 C3
Liomseter N 32 A6
Lion-sur-Mer F 57 A5
Lionárisso CY 120 A3
Lioni I 103 C8
Lipany SK 65 A6
Lipar SCG 75 C4
Lípari I 106 C1
Lipcani MD 11 B9
Liperi FIN 3 E28
Liphook GB 31 C3
Lipiany PL 45 B6
Lipik HR 74 C2
Lipka PL 46 B3
Lipki Wielkie PL 46 C1
Lipnica PL 46 B3
Lipnica Murowana PL 65 A6
Lipnik PL 55 C6
Lipník nad Bečvou CZ 64 A3
Lipno, *Kujawsko-Pomorskie* PL 47 C5
Lipno, *Łódzkie* PL 54 B3
Liposthey F 76 B2
Lipovac HR 84 A4
Lipovec CZ 64 A2
Lipovets UA 11 B10
Lipovljani HR 74 C1
Lipowina PL 47 A5
Lippborg D 50 B4
Lippó H 74 C3
Lippoldsberg D 51 B5
Lippstadt D 51 B4
Lipsko PL 55 B6
Liptál CZ 64 A3
Liptovská-Lúžna SK 65 B5
Liptovská Osada SK 65 B5
Liptovská-Teplička SK 65 B6
Liptovský Hrádok SK 65 A5
Liptovský Milkuláš SK 65 A5
Lipusz PL 46 A3
Lipůvka CZ 64 A2
Liré F 66 A3
Lis AL 105 B6
Lisa SCG 85 C5
Lisac BIH 84 B2
Lisbellaw GB 19 B4
Lisboa = Lisbon P 92 C1
Lisbon = Lisboa P 92 C1
Lisburn GB 19 B5
Liscannor IRL 20 B2
Lisdoonvarna IRL 20 A2
Lisewo PL 47 B4
Lisia Góra PL 55 C6
Lisięcice PL 54 C2
Lisieux F 57 A6
Lisjö S 37 C3
Liskeard GB 28 C3
L'Isle CH 69 B6
L'Isle-Adam F 58 A3
L'Isle-de-Noé F 77 C3
L'Isle-en-Dodon F 77 C3
L'Isle-Jourdain, *Gers* F 77 C4
L'Isle-Jourdain, *Vienne* F 67 B5
L'Isle-sur-la-Sorgue F 79 C4
L'Isle-sur-le Doubs F 69 A6
L'Isle-sur-Serein F 59 C5
Lisle-sur-Tarn F 77 C4
Lismore IRL 21 B4
Lisnaskea GB 19 B4
Lišov CZ 63 A5
Lisów, *Lubuskie* PL 45 C6
Lisów, *Śląskie* PL 54 C3
Lisse NL 49 A5
Lissycasey IRL 20 B2
List D 39 D1
Listerby S 41 C5
Listowel IRL 20 B2
Listrac-Médoc F 76 A2
Liszki PL 55 C4
Liszkowo PL 46 B3
Lit S 115 D11
Lit-et-Mixe F 76 B1
Litava SK 65 B5
Litcham GB 30 B4
Litija SLO 73 B4
Litke H 65 B5
Litlabø N 32 C2
Litochoro GR 116 B4
Litoměřice CZ 53 C4
Litomyšl CZ 64 A2
Litovel CZ 64 A3
Litschau A 63 B6
Little Walsingham GB 30 B4
Littlehampton GB 31 D3
Littleport GB 30 B4
Littleton IRL 21 B4
Litvinov CZ 52 C3
Livadero GR 116 B3
Livadhia CY 120 B2
Livadi GR 116 B4
Livadia GR 116 D4
Livarot F 57 B6
Liveras CY 120 A1
Livernon F 77 B4
Liverovici SCG 85 D4
Liverpool GB 26 B3
Livigno I 71 B5
Livingston GB 25 C4
Livno BIH 84 C1
Livold SLO 73 C4
Livorno I 81 C4
Livorno Ferraris I 70 C3
Livron-sur-Drôme F 78 B3
Livry-Louvercy F 59 A5
Lixheim F 60 B3
Lixouri GR 117 D2
Lizard GB 28 D2
Lizy-sur-Ourcq F 59 A4
Lizzano I 104 C3
Lizzano in Belvedere I 81 B4
Lješane SCG 85 D5
Ljig SCG 85 B5
Ljørdalen N 34 A4
Ljosland N 33 D4
Ljubija BIH 83 B5
Ljubinje BIH 84 D3
Ljubljana SLO 73 B4
Ljubno ob Savinji SLO 73 B4
Ljubovija SCG 85 B4
Ljubuški BIH 84 C2
Ljugarn S 37 E5
Ljung S 40 B3
Ljunga S 37 D3
Ljungaverk S 115 E13
Ljungby S 40 C3
Ljungbyhed S 41 C3
Ljungbyholm S 40 C6
Ljungdalen S 115 E9
Ljungsarp S 40 B3
Ljungsbro S 37 D2
Ljungskile S 35 D3
Ljusdal S 115 F13
Ljusfallshammar S 37 D2
Ljusne S 36 A4
Ljusterö S 37 C5
Ljutomer SLO 73 B6
Lladurs E 91 A4
Llafranc E 91 B6
Llagostera E 91 B5
Llanaelhaiarn GB 26 C1
Llanarth GB 28 A3
Llanbedr GB 26 C1
Llanbedrog GB 26 C1
Llanberis GB 26 B1
Llanbister GB 29 A4
Llanbrynmair GB 26 C2
Llançà E 91 A6
Llandeilo GB 28 B4
Llandissilio GB 28 B3
Llandovery GB 28 B4
Llandrillo GB 26 C2
Llandrindod Wells GB 29 A4
Llandudec F 56 B1
Llandudno GB 26 B2
Llandysul GB 28 A3
Llanelli GB 28 B3
Llanerchymedd GB 26 B1
Llanes E 88 A2
Llanfair Caereinion GB 26 C2
Llanfairfechan GB 26 B2
Llanfyllin GB 26 C2
Llangadog GB 28 B4
Llangefni GB 26 B1
Llangollen GB 26 C2
Llangrannog GB 28 A3
Llangurig GB 26 C2
Llanidloes GB 26 C2
Llanilar GB 28 A3
Llanrhystud GB 28 A3
Llanrwst GB 26 B2
Llansannan GB 26 B2
Llansawel GB 28 A3
Llanstephan GB 28 B3
Llanteno E 89 A3
Llanthony GB 29 B4
Llantrisant GB 29 B4
Llantwit-Major GB 29 B4
Llanuwchllyn GB 26 C2
Llanwddyn GB 26 C2
Llanwrda GB 28 B4
Llanwrtyd Wells GB 29 A4
Llanybydder GB 28 A3
Llanymynech GB 26 C2
Llavorsi E 91 A4
Lleida E 90 B3
Llera E 93 C4
Llerena E 99 A4
Lles E 91 A4
Llessui E 91 A4
Llinars E 91 A4
Lliria E 96 B2
Llivia E 91 A4
Llodio E 89 A4
Lloret de Mar E 91 B5
Llosa de Ranes E 96 B2
Lloseta E 97 B2
Llucena del Cid E 96 A2
Llucmajor E 97 B2
Llutxent E 96 C2
Llwyngwril GB 26 C1
Llyswen GB 29 A4
Lnáře CZ 63 A4
Lniano PL 47 B4
Lo Pagán E 101 B5
Loanhead GB 25 C4
Loano I 80 B2
Loarre E 90 A2
Löbau D 53 B4
Löbejün D 52 B1
Löberöd S 41 D3
Łobez PL 46 B1
Löbnitz D 45 A4
Lobón E 93 C4
Loburg D 52 A2
Łobżenica PL 46 B3
Locana I 70 C2
Locarno CH 70 B3
Loccum D 43 C6
Loče SLO 73 B5
Loch Baghasdail GB 22 D1
Loch nam Madadh GB 22 D1
Lochailort GB 24 B2
Lochaline GB 24 B2
Lochans GB 24 D2
Locharbriggs GB 25 C4
Lochau A 71 A4
Lochcarron GB 22 D3
Lochearnhead GB 24 B3
Lochem NL 50 A2
Loches F 67 A5
Lochgelly GB 25 B4
Lochgilphead GB 24 B2
Lochgoilhead GB 24 B3
Lochinver GB 22 C3
Lochranza GB 24 C2
Ločika SCG 85 C6
Lockenhaus A 73 A6
Lockerbie GB 25 C4
Löcknitz D 45 B6
Locmaria F 66 A1
Locmariaquer F 56 C3
Locminé F 56 C3
Locorotondo I 104 C3
Locquirec F 56 B2
Locri I 106 C3
Locronan F 56 B1
Loctudy F 56 C1
Lodares de Osma E 89 C4
Lodé I 110 B2
Lodeinoye Pole RUS 7 A12
Lodève F 78 C2
Lodi I 71 C4
Løding N 112 E3
Lødingen N 112 D4
Lodosa E 89 B4
Lödöse S 38 A5
Łódź PL 55 B4
Loeches E 95 B3
Løfallstrand N 32 B3
Lofer A 62 C3
Lofsdalen S 115 E10
Loftahammar S 40 B6
Lofthus N 32 B3
Loftus GB 27 A5
Loga N 33 D3
Logatec SLO 73 C4
Lögdeå S 115 D16
Lograto I 71 C5
Logroño E 89 B4
Logrosán E 93 B5
Løgstør DK 38 C2
Løgumgårde DK 39 D1
Løgumkloster DK 39 D1
Lohals DK 39 D3
Lohiniva FIN 113 E14
Lohja FIN 6 A8
Löhlbach D 51 B4
Lohmen, *Mecklenburg-Vorpommern* D 44 B4
Lohmen, *Sachsen* D 53 C4
Löhnberg D 50 C4
Lohne, *Niedersachsen* D 43 C5
Löhne, *Nordrhein-Westfalen* D 51 A4
Lohr D 51 D5
Lohra D 51 C4
Lohsa D 53 B4
Loiano I 81 B5
Loimaa FIN 3 F25
Lóiri I 110 B2
Loitz D 45 B5
Loivos P 87 C3
Loivos do Monte P 87 C3
Loja E 100 B1
Lojanice SCG 85 B4
Lojsta S 37 E5
Løjt Kirkeby DK 39 D2
Lok SK 65 B4
Lokca SK 65 A5
Løken N 34 C3
Lokeren B 49 B4
Loket CZ 52 C2
Lokhvitsa UA 11 A12
Lokka FIN 113 E16
Løkken DK 38 B2
Løkken N 114 D6
Loknya RUS 7 C11
Lökösháza H 75 B6
Lokot RUS 7 E13
Lokve SCG 75 C6
Lollar D 51 C4
L'Olleria E 96 C2
Lölling-Graben A 73 B4
Lom BG 11 E7
Lom N 114 F5
Lom SK 65 B5
Lombez F 77 C3
Lomello I 80 A2
Łomianki PL 55 A5
Lomma S 41 D3
Lommaryd S 40 B4
Lommatzsch D 52 B3
Lommel B 49 B6
Lommersum D 50 C2
Lomnice CZ 64 A2
Lomnice nad Lužnici CZ 63 A5
Lomnice-nad Popelkou CZ 53 C5
Lompolo FIN 113 D13
Łomża PL 6 E7
Lönashult S 40 C4
Lønborg DK 39 D1
Londerzeel B 49 B5
Londinières F 58 A2
London GB 31 C3
Lonevåg N 32 B2
Long Bennington GB 27 C5
Long Eaton GB 27 C4
Long Melford GB 30 B4
Long Preston GB 26 A3
Long Sutton GB 30 B4
Longa GR 117 F3
Longare I 72 C1
Longares E 90 B1
Longarone I 72 B2
Longastrino I 81 B6
Longbenton GB 25 C6
Longchamp-sur-Aujon F 59 B5
Longchaumois F 69 B5
Longeau F 59 C6
Longecourt-en-Plaine F 69 A5
Longeville-les-St. Avold F 60 A2
Longeville-sur-Mer F 66 B3
Longford IRL 19 C4
Longframlington GB 25 C6
Longhope GB 23 C5
Longhorsley GB 25 C6
Longhoughton GB 25 C6
Longi I 109 A3
Longny-au-Perche F 58 B1
Longobucco I 106 B3
Longré F 67 B4
Longridge GB 26 B3
Longroiva P 87 D3
Longtown, *Cumbria* GB 25 C5
Longtown, *Herefordshire* GB 29 B5
Longué-Jumelles F 67 A4
Longueau F 58 A3
Longuyon F 60 A1
Longvic F 69 A5
Longvilly B 50 C1
Longwy F 60 A1
Lonigo I 71 C6
Löningen D 43 C4
Lonja HR 74 C1
Lönneberga S 40 B5
Lons-le-Saunier F 69 B5
Lönsboda S 41 C4
Lønset N 114 E6
Lønstrup DK 38 B2
Looe GB 28 C3
Loon op Zand NL 49 B6
Loone-Plage F 48 B3
Loosdorf A 63 B6

Lopar HR 83 B3
Lopare BIH 84 B3
Lopera E 100 B1
Lopigna F 102 A1
Loppersum NL 42 B3
Łopuszna PL 65 A6
Łopuszno PL 55 C5
Lor F 59 A5
Lora N 114 E5
Lora de Estepa E 100 B1
Lora del Río E 99 B5
Loranca del Campo E 95 B4
Lörby S 41 C4
Lorca E 101 B4
Lorch D 50 C3
Lørenfallet N 34 B3
Lørenskog N 34 C2
Loreo I 82 A1
Loreto I 82 C2
Lorgues F 79 C5
Lorica I 106 B3
Lorient F 56 C2
Lorignac F 67 C4
Lörinci H 65 C5
Loriol-sur-Drôme F 78 B3
Lormes F 68 A3
Loro Ciuffenna I 81 C5
Lorqui E 101 A4
Lörrach D 60 C3
Lorrez-le-Bocage F 59 B3
Lorris F 58 C3
Lorup D 43 C4
Łoś PL 55 B5
Los S 115 F12
Los Alcázares E 101 B5
Los Arcos E 89 B4
Los Barios de Luna E 88 B1
Los Barrios E 99 C5
Los Caños de Meca E 99 C4
Los Cerricos E 101 B3
Los Corrales E 100 B1
Los Corrales de Buelna E 88 A2
Los Dolores E 101 B4
Los Gallardos E 101 B4
Los Hinojosos E 95 C4
Los Isidros E 96 B1
Los Molinos E 94 B2
Los Morales E 99 B5
Los Navalmorales E 94 C2
Los Navalucillos E 94 C2
Los Nietos E 101 B5
Los Palacios y Villafranca E 99 B5
Los Pozuelos de Calatrava E 100 A1
Los Rábanos E 89 C4
Los Santos E 93 A5
Los Santos de la Humosa E 95 B3
Los Santos de Maimona E 93 C4
Los Tijos E 88 A2
Los Villares E 100 B2
Los Yébenes E 94 C3
Losacino E 87 C4
Losar de la Vera E 93 A5
Losenstein A 63 C5
Losheim, *Nordrhein-Westfalen* D 50 C2
Losheim, *Saarland* D 60 A2
Losne F 69 A5
Løsning DK 39 D2
Lossburg D 61 B4
Losse F 76 B2
Losser NL 50 A3
Lossiemouth GB 23 D5
Lössnitz D 52 C2
Loštice CZ 64 A2
Lostwithiel GB 28 C3
Løten N 34 B3
Lotorp S 37 D2
Lottefors S 36 A3
Löttorp S 41 B7
Lotyń PL 46 B2
Lotzorai I 110 C2
Louargat F 56 B2
Loudéac F 56 B3
Loudun F 67 A5
Loué F 57 C5
Loughborough GB 27 C4
Loughbrickland GB 19 B5
Loughrea IRL 20 A3
Louhans F 69 B5
Louisburgh IRL 18 C2
Loukhi RUS 3 C30
Loulay F 67 B4
Loulé P 98 B2
Louny CZ 53 C3
Lourdes F 76 C2
Lourenzá E 86 A3
Loures P 92 C1
Loures-Barousse F 77 C3
Louriçal P 92 A2
Lourinhã P 92 B1
Lourmarin F 79 C4
Loury F 58 C3
Lousa, *Bragança* P 87 C3
Lousa, *Castelo Branco* P 92 B3
Lousã, *Coimbra* P 92 A2
Lousa, *Lisboa* P 92 C1
Lousada E 86 B3
Lousada P 87 C2
Louth GB 27 B5
Loutra Edipsou GR 116 D5
Loutraki GR 117 E4
Loutropoli Thermis GR 118 C1
Louverné F 57 B5
Louvie-Juzon F 76 C2
Louviers F 58 A2
Louvigné-du-Désert F 57 B4
Louvois F 59 A5
Lova I 72 C2
Lovasberény H 74 A3
Lövåsen S 34 C5
Lovászpatona H 74 A2
Lövberga S 115 D12
Lovech BG 11 E8
Lövenich D 50 B2
Lóvere I 71 C5
Lövestad S 41 D3
Loviisa FIN 7 A9
Lovikka S 113 E11
Lovinobaňa SK 65 B5
Loviste HR 84 C2
Lovke HR 73 C4
Lovnäs S 34 A6
Lövö H 74 A1
Lovosice CZ 53 C4
Lovozero RUS 3 C31
Lovran HR 73 C4
Lovreć HR 84 C1
Lovrenc na Pohorju SLO 73 B5
Lovrin RO 75 C5
Lövstabruk S 36 B4
Löwenberg D 45 C5
Löwenstein D 61 A5
Lowestoft GB 30 B5
Lowick GB 25 C6
Łowicz PL 55 A4
Loxstedt D 43 B5
Loyew BY 7 F11
Lož SLO 73 C4
Loza CZ 63 A4
Łozina PL 54 B2
Loznica SCG 85 B4
Lozničko Polje SCG 85 B4
Lozorno SK 64 B3
Lozovik SCG 85 B6
Lozoya E 94 B3
Lozoyuela E 94 B3
Lozzo di Cadore I 72 B2
Luanco E 88 A1
Luarca E 86 A4
Lubaczów PL 11 A7
Lubań PL 53 B5
Lubanie PL 47 C4
Lubanów PL 55 B4
Lubars D 52 A2
Lubasz PL 46 C2
Lubawa PL 47 B5
Lubawka PL 53 C6
Lübbecke D 51 A4
Lübben D 53 B3
Lübbenau D 53 B3
Lubczyna PL 45 B6
Lübeck D 44 B2
Lubenec CZ 52 C3
Lubersac F 67 C6
Lübesse D 44 B3
Lubia E 89 C4
Lubian E 87 B4
Lubiatowo PL 45 B7
Lubichowo PL 47 B4
Lubicz Dolny PL 47 B4
Lubień PL 65 A5
Lubień Kujawski PL 47 C5
Lubienia PL 55 B6
Lubieszewo PL 46 B1
Lubin, *Dolnosląskie* PL 53 B6
Lubin, *Zachodnio-Pomorskie* PL 45 B6
Lublin, *Lubelskie* PL 11 A7
Lubliniec PL 54 C3
Lubmin D 45 A5
Lubniewice PL 45 C7
Lubny UA 11 A12
Lubochnia PL 55 B5
Lubomierz, *Dolnosląskie* PL 53 B5
Lubomierz, *Małopolskie* PL 65 A6
Lubomino PL 47 A6
Luboń PL 54 A1
L'ubotín SK 65 A6
Lubowidz PL 47 B5
Łubowo, *Wielkopolskie* PL 46 C3
Łubowo, *Zachodnio-Pomorskie* PL 46 B2
Lubraniec PL 47 C4
Lubrin E 101 B3
Lubrza PL 54 C2
Lubsko PL 53 B4
Lübtheen D 44 B3
Lubuczewo PL 46 A3
Luby CZ 52 C2
Lübz D 44 B4
Luc F 78 B2
Luc-en-Diois F 79 B4
Luc-sur-Mer F 57 A5
Lucainena de las Torres E 101 B3
Lucan IRL 21 A5
Lučani SCG 85 C5
Lúcar E 101 B3
Luçay-le-Mâle F 67 A6
Lucca I 81 C4
Lucciana F 102 A2
Lucé F 58 B2
Luče SLO 73 B4
Lucena, *Córdoba* E 100 B1
Lucena, *Huelva* E 99 B4
Lucenay-les-Aix F 68 B3
Lucenay-l'Evêque F 69 A4
Lučenec SK 65 B5
Luceni E 90 B1
Lucens CH 70 B1
Lucera I 103 B8
Luceram F 80 C1
Lüchow D 44 C3
Luciana E 94 D2
Lucignano I 81 C5
Lucija SLO 72 C3
Lucka D 52 B2
Luckau D 53 B3
Luckenwalde D 52 A3
Lückstedt D 44 C3
Luco dei Marsi I 103 B6
Luçon F 66 B3
Ludanice SK 64 B4
Ludbreg HR 74 B1
Lüdenscheid D 50 B3
Lüderitz D 44 C3
Lüdersdorf D 44 B2
Ludgershall GB 31 C2
Ludgo S 37 D4
Lüdinghausen D 50 B3
Ludlow GB 29 A5
Ludomy PL 46 C2
Ludvika S 36 B2
Ludweiler Warndt D 60 A2
Ludwigsburg D 61 B5
Ludwigsfelde D 52 A3
Ludwigshafen D 61 A4
Ludwigslust D 44 B3
Ludwigsstadt D 52 C1
Ludza LV 7 C9
Luesia E 90 A1
Luftkurort Arendsee D 44 C3
Lug BIH 84 D3
Lug HR 74 C3
Luga RUS 7 B10
Lugagnano Val d'Arda I 81 B3
Lugano CH 70 B3
Lugau D 52 C2
Lugnas S 35 D5
Lúgnola I 102 A5
Lugny F 69 B4
Lugo E 86 A3
Lugo I 81 B5
Lugoj RO 10 D6
Lugones E 88 A1
Lugros E 100 B2
Luhačovice CZ 64 A3
Luhe D 62 A3
Luino I 70 C3
Luintra E 87 B3
Lújar E 100 C2
Luka nad Jihlavou CZ 63 A6
Lukavac BIH 84 B3
Lukavika BIH 84 B3
Lukovë AL 116 C1
Lukovica SLO 73 B4
Lukovit BG 11 E8
Lukovo HR 83 B3
Lukovo SCG 85 C6
Lukovo Šugorje HR 83 B4
Łuków PL 6 F7
Łukowice Brzeskie PL 54 C2
Luksefjell N 33 C6
Łukta PL 47 B6
Lula I 110 B2
Luleå S 3 D25
Lüleburgaz TR 118 A2
Lumbarda HR 84 D2
Lumbier E 90 A1
Lumbrales E 87 D4
Lumbreras E 89 B4
Lumbres F 48 C3
Lummelunda S 37 E5
Lummen B 49 C6
Lumparland FIN 36 B7
Lumpiaque E 90 B1
Lumsås DK 39 D4
Lumsden GB 23 D6
Lumsheden S 36 B3
Lun HR 83 B3
Luna E 90 A2
Lunamatrona I 110 C1
Lunano I 82 C1
Lunas F 78 C2
Lund N 114 C8
Lund, *Skåne* S 41 D3
Lund, *Västra Götaland* S 35 C4
Lundamo N 114 D7
Lunde DK 39 D1
Lunde, *Sogn og Fjordane* N 32 A3
Lunde, *Sogn og Fjordane* N 32 A3
Lunde, *Telemark* N 33 C6
Lunde S 115 E14
Lundebyvollen N 34 B4
Lunden D 43 A6
Lunderseter N 34 B4
Lunderskov DK 39 D2
Lundsberg S 35 C6
Lüneburg D 44 B2
Lunel F 78 C3
Lünen D 50 B3
Lunéville F 60 B2
Lungern CH 70 B3
Lungro I 106 B3
Luninyets BY 7 E9
Lünne D 43 C4
Lunner N 34 B2
Lunteren NL 49 A6
Lunz am See A 63 C6
Luogosanto I 110 A2
Łupawa PL 46 A3
Lupión E 100 A2
Lupoglav HR 73 C4
Luppa D 52 B2
Luque E 100 B1
Lurago d'Erba I 71 C4
Lúras I 110 B2
Lurcy-Lévis F 68 B2
Lure F 60 C2
Lurgan GB 19 B5
Luri F 102 A2
Lury-sur-Arnon F 68 A2
Lušci Palanka BIH 83 B5
Lusévera I 72 B3
Lushnjë AL 105 C5
Lusignan F 67 B5
Lusigny-sur-Barse F 59 B5
Lusnić BIH 84 C1
Luso P 92 A2
Lusówko PL 46 C2
Luspebryggan S 112 E8
Luss GB 24 B3
Lussac F 76 B2
Lussac-les-Châteaux F 67 B5
Lussac-les-Eglises F 67 B6
Lussan F 78 B3
Lüssow D 44 B4
Lustenau A 71 A4
Luštěnice CZ 53 C4
Luster N 32 A4
Lutago I 72 B1
Lutherstadt Wittenberg D 52 B2
Lütjenburg D 44 A2
Lutnes N 34 A4
Lutocin PL 47 C5
Lutomiersk PL 55 B4
Luton GB 31 C3
Lutry CH 70 B1
Lutry PL 47 A6
Lutsk UA 11 A8
Lutter am Barenberge D 51 B6
Lutterworth GB 30 B2
Lututów PL 54 B3
Lützen D 52 B2
Lutzow D 44 B3
Luusua FIN 113 F16
Luvos S 112 F7
Luxembourg L 60 A2
Luxeuil-les-Bains F 60 C2
Luxey F 76 B2
Luz, *Évora* P 92 C3
Luz, *Faro* P 98 B2
Luz, *Faro* P 98 B3
Luz-St. Sauveur F 76 D2
Luzarches F 58 A3
Luže CZ 64 A2
Luzech F 77 B4
Luzern CH 70 A3
Luzino PL 47 A4
Luzy F 68 B3
Luzzi I 106 B3
L'viv UA 11 B8
Lwówek PL 46 C2
Lwówek Śląski PL 53 B5
Lyakhavichy BY 7 E9
Lybster GB 23 C5
Lychen D 45 B5
Lychkova RUS 7 C12
Lyckeby S 41 C5
Lycksele S 115 C15
Lydd GB 31 D4
Lydford GB 28 C3
Lydney GB 29 B5
Lyepyel BY 7 D10
Lygna N 34 B2
Lykkja N 32 B5
Lykling N 33 C2
Lyme Regis GB 29 C5
Lymington GB 31 D2
Lympne GB 31 C5
Lyndhurst GB 31 D2
Lyneham GB 29 B6
Lyness GB 23 C5
Lyngdal, *Buskerud* N 32 C6
Lyngdal, *Vest-Agder* N 33 D4
Lyngør N 33 D6
Lyngsa DK 38 B3
Lyngseidet N 112 C9
Lyngsnes N 114 C8
Lynmouth GB 28 B4
Lynton GB 28 B4
Lyntupy BY 7 D9
Lyon F 69 C4
Lyons-la-Forêt F 58 A2
Lyozna BY 7 D11
Lyrestad S 35 D6
Lysá nad Labem CZ 53 C4
Lysá pod Makytou SK 64 A4
Lysebotn N 33 C3
Lysekil S 35 D3
Lysice CZ 64 A2
Lysomice PL 47 B4
Lysøysund N 114 D6
Lyss CH 70 A2
Lystrup DK 39 C3
Lysvik S 34 B5
Łyszkowice PL 55 B4
Lytham St. Anne's GB 26 B2
Lyuban RUS 7 B11
Lyubertsy RUS 7 D14
Lyuboml' UA 11 A8
Lyubytino RUS 7 B12
Lyudinovo RUS 7 E13

M

Maaninkavaara FIN 113 F17
Maarheeze NL 49 B6
Maaseik B 50 B1
Maastricht NL 50 C1
Mablethorpe GB 27 B6
Mably F 68 B4
Macael E 101 B3
Maçanet de Cabrenys E 91 A5
Mação P 92 B2
Macau F 76 A2
Maccagno-Agra I 70 B3
Maccarese I 102 B5
Macchiagódena I 103 B7
Macclesfield GB 26 B3
Macduff GB 23 D6
Maceda E 87 B3
Macedo de Cavaleiros P 87 C4
Maceira, *Guarda* P 92 A3
Maceira, *Leiria* P 92 B2
Macelj HR 73 B5
Macerata I 82 C2
Macerata Féltria I 82 C1
Machault F 59 A5
Machecoul F 66 B3
Machrihanish GB 24 C2
Machynlleth GB 26 C2
Macieira P 87 C2
Maciejowice PL 55 B6
Macinaggio F 102 A2
Mackenrode D 51 B6
Mačkovci SLO 73 B6
Macomer I 110 B1
Macon B 49 C5
Mâcon F 69 B4
Macotera E 94 B1
Macroom IRL 20 C3
Macugnaga I 70 C2
Madan BG 116 A6
Madängsholm S 35 D5
Madaras H 75 B4
Maddaloni I 103 B7
Made NL 49 B5
Madeley GB 26 C3
Maderuelo E 89 C3
Madetkoski FIN 113 E15
Madley GB 29 A5
Madocsa H 75 B3
Madona LV 7 C9
Madonna di Campíglio I 71 B5
Madrid E 94 B3
Madridejos E 95 C3
Madrigal de la Vera E 93 A5
Madrigal de las Altas Torres E 94 A1
Madrigalejo E 93 B5
Madrigalejo de Monte E 88 B3
Madriguera E 89 C3
Madrigueras E 95 C5
Madroñera E 93 B5
Maël-Carhaix F 56 B2
Maella E 90 B3
Maello E 94 B2
Maesteg GB 29 B4
Mafra P 92 C1
Magacela E 93 C5
Magallon E 89 C5
Magaluf E 97 B2
Magán E 94 C3
Magaña E 89 C4
Magasa I 71 C5
Magaz E 88 C2
Magdeburg D 52 A1
Magenta I 70 C3
Magescq F 76 C1
Maghera GB 19 B5
Magherafelt GB 19 B5
Maghull GB 26 B3
Magione I 82 C1
Maglaj BIH 84 B3
Maglehem S 41 D4
Magliano de'Marsi I 103 A6
Magliano in Toscana I 102 A4
Magliano Sabina I 102 A5
Maglić SCG 75 C4
Máglie I 107 A5
Maglód H 75 A4
Magnac-Bourg F 67 C6
Magnac-Laval F 67 B6
Magnieres F 60 B2
Magnor N 34 C4
Magnuszew PL 55 B6
Magny-Cours F 68 B3
Magny-en-Vexin F 58 A2
Mágocs H 74 B3
Magoute P 92 C1
Maguilla E 93 C5
Maguiresbridge GB 19 B4
Magyarbóly H 74 C3
Magyarkeszi H 74 B3
Magyarszék H 74 B3
Mahala SCG 105 A5
Mahide E 87 C4
Mahilyow BY 7 E11
Mahmudiye TR 118 C5
Mahora E 95 C5
Mahovo HR 73 C6
Mähring D 62 A3
Maia E 76 C1
Maia P 87 C2
Maiaelrayo E 95 A3
Maials E 90 B3
Maîche F 70 A1
Máida I 106 C3
Maiden Bradley GB 29 B5
Maiden Newton GB 29 C5
Maidenhead GB 31 C3
Maidstone GB 31 C4
Maienfeld CH 71 A4
Maignelay Montigny F 58 A3
Maijanen FIN 113 E14
Maillezais F 66 B4
Mailly-le-Camp F 59 B5
Mailly-le-Château F 59 C4
Mainar E 89 C5
Mainbernheim D 61 A6
Mainburg D 62 B2
Mainhardt D 61 A5
Maintal D 51 C4
Maintenon F 58 B2
Mainvilliers F 58 B2
Mainz D 50 C4
Maiorca P 92 A2
Mairena de Aljarafe E 99 B4
Mairena del Alcor E 99 B5
Maisach D 62 B2
Maishofen A 72 A2
Maison-Rouge F 59 B4
Maissau A 64 B1
Maisse F 58 B3
Maizières-lès-Vic F 60 B2
Maja HR 73 C6
Majadahonda E 94 B3
Majadas E 93 B5
Majavatn N 115 B10
Majs H 74 C3
Majšperk SLO 73 B5
Makarska HR 84 C2
Makkum NL 42 B2
Maklár H 65 C6
Makó H 75 B5
Makoszyce PL 54 C2
Makov SK 65 A4
Makovac SCG 85 D6
Maków Podhalański PL 65 A5
Mąkowarsko PL 46 B3
Makrakomi GR 116 D4
Malå S 115 B15
Mala Bosna SCG 75 B4
Mala Kladuša BIH 73 C5
Mala Krsna SCG 85 B6
Mala Lehota SK 65 B4
Mala Pijace SCG 75 B4
Mala Plana SCG 85 C6
Mala Subotica HR 74 B1
Mala Vyska UA 11 B11
Malacky SK 64 B3
Maladzyechna BY 7 D9
Málaga E 100 C1
Malagón E 94 C3
Malaguilla E 95 B3
Malahide IRL 21 A5
Malalbergo I 81 B5
Malanów PL 54 B3
Malaucène F 79 B4
Malaunay F 58 A2
Malaya Vishera RUS 7 B12
Malborghetto I 72 B3
Malbork PL 47 A5
Malborn D 60 A2
Malbuisson F 69 B6
Malcésine I 71 C5
Malchin D 45 B4
Malching D 63 B4
Malchow D 44 B4
Malcocinado E 99 A5
Malczyce PL 54 B1
Maldegem B 49 B4
Maldon GB 31 C4
Małdyty PL 47 B5
Malè I 71 B5
Malemort F 67 C6
Malente D 44 A2
Målerås S 40 C5
Males GR 117 G7
Malesherbes F 58 B3
Malesina GR 116 D5
Malestroit F 56 C3
Maletto I 109 B3
Malexander S 40 A5
Malfa I 106 C1
Malgrat de Mar E 91 B5
Malhadas P 87 C4
Mali Lošinj HR 83 B3
Malia CY 120 B1
Malia GR 117 G7
Malicorne-sur-Sarthe F 57 C5
Malijai F 79 B5
Malildjoš SCG 75 C4
Målilla S 40 B5
Malin IRL 19 A4
Málinec SK 65 B5
Malingsbo S 36 C2
Maliniec PL 54 A3
Malinska HR 83 A3
Maliq AL 116 B2
Maljevac HR 73 C5
Malkara TR 118 B1
Małki PL 47 B5
Malko Tŭrnovo BG 11 E9
Mallaig GB 22 D3
Mallaranny IRL 18 C2
Mallemort F 79 C4
Mallén E 89 C5
Malléon F 77 C4
Mallersdorf-Pfaffenberg D 62 B3
Málles Venosta I 71 B5
Malling DK 39 C3
Mallnitz A 72 B3
Mallow IRL 20 B3
Mallwyd GB 26 C2
Malm N 114 C8
Malmbäck S 40 B4
Malmberget S 112 E9
Malmby S 37 C4
Malmédy B 50 C2
Malmesbury GB 29 B5
Malmköping S 37 C3
Malmö S 41 D3
Malmon S 35 D3
Malmslätt S 37 D2
Malnate I 70 C3
Malo I 71 C6
Maloarkhangelsk RUS 7 E14
Małogoszcz PL 55 C5
Maloja CH 71 B4
Małomice PL 53 B5
Måløy N 114 F2
Maloyaroslovets RUS 7 D14
Malpartida E 93 B4
Malpartida de la Serena E 93 C5
Malpartida de Plasencia E 93 B4
Malpas E 90 A3
Malpas GB 26 B3
Malpica P 92 B3
Malpica de Bergantiños E 86 A2
Malpica de Tajo E 94 C2
Malsch D 61 B4
Malšice CZ 63 A5
Malta A 72 B3
Maltat F 68 B3
Maltby GB 27 B4
Malung S 34 B5
Malungsfors S 34 B5
Maluszów PL 45 C7
Maluszyn PL 55 C4
Malva E 88 C1
Malvaglia CH 70 B3
Malveira P 92 C1
Malvik N 114 D7
Malyn UA 11 A10
Mamarrosa P 92 A2
Mamer L 60 A2
Mamers F 58 B1
Mamirolle F 69 A6
Mammendorf D 62 B2
Mámmola I 106 C3
Mamoiada I 110 B2
Mamonovo RUS 47 A5
Mamurras AL 105 B5
Maňa SK 64 B4
Manacor E 97 B3
Manavgat TR 119 F6
Mancera de Abajo E 94 B1
Mancha Real E 100 B2
Manchester GB 26 B3
Manching D 62 B2
Manchita E 93 C4
Manciano I 102 A4
Manciet F 76 C3
Mandal N 33 D4
Mandanici I 109 A4
Mándas I 110 C2
Mandatoríccio I 107 B3
Mandayona E 95 B4
Mandelieu-la-Napoule F 79 C5
Mandello del Lário I 71 C4
Mandelsloh D 43 C6
Manderfeld B 50 C2
Manderscheid D 50 C2
Mandino Selo BIH 84 C2
Mandoudi GR 116 D5
Mandra GR 117 D5
Mandraki GR 119 F2
Mandúria I 104 C3
Mane, *Alpes-de-Haute-Provence* F 79 C4
Mane, *Haute-Garonne* F 77 C3
Manérbio I 71 C5
Mañeru E 89 B5
Manetin CZ 52 D3
Manfredónia I 104 B1
Mangalia RO 11 E10
Manganeses de la Lampreana E 88 C1
Manganeses de la Polvorosa E 88 B1
Mangen N 34 C3
Manger N 32 B2
Mangiennes F 60 A1
Mangotsfield GB 29 B5
Mångsbodarna S 34 A5
Mangualde P 92 A3
Maniago I 72 B2
Manilva E 99 C5
Manisa TR 118 D2
Manises E 96 B2
Mank A 63 B6
Månkarbo S 36 B4
Manlleu E 91 B5
Manna DK 38 B2
Männedorf CH 70 A3
Mannersdorf am Leithagebirge A 64 C2
Mannheim D 61 A4
Manningtree GB 31 C5
Manoppello I 103 A7
Manorbier GB 28 B3
Manorhamilton IRL 18 B3
Manosque F 79 C4
Manowo PL 46 A2
Manresa E 91 B4
Månsarp S 40 B4
Månsåsen S 115 D11
Manschnow D 45 C6
Mansfeld D 52 B1
Mansfield GB 27 B4
Mansilla de Burgos E 88 B3
Mansilla de las Mulas E 88 B1
Manskog S 35 C4
Mansle F 67 C5
Manso F 102 A1
Manteigas P 92 A3
Mantel D 62 A3
Mantes-la-Jolie F 58 B2
Mantes-la-Ville F 58 B2
Manthelan F 67 A5
Mantorp S 37 D2
Mántova I 71 C5
Mänttä FIN 3 E26
Manuel E 96 B2
Manyas TR 118 B2
Manzanal de Arriba E 87 B4
Manzanares E 95 C3
Manzanares el Real E 94 B3
Manzaneda, *León* E 87 B4
Manzaneda, *Orense* E 87 B3
Manzanedo E 88 B3
Manzaneque E 94 C3
Manzanera E 96 A2
Manzanilla E 99 B4
Manzat F 68 C2
Manziana I 102 A5
Manziat F 69 B4
Maó E 97 B4
Maoča BIH 84 B3
Maqueda E 94 B2
Mara E 89 C5
Maramaraereğlisi TR 118 B2
Maraña E 88 A1
Maranchón E 95 A4
Maranello I 81 B4
Marano I 103 C7
Marano Lagunare I 72 C3
Marans F 66 B3
Maratea I 106 B2
Marateca P 92 C2
Marathokambos GR 119 E1
Marathonas GR 117 D5
Marathóvouno CY 120 A2
Marazion GB 28 C2
Marbach, *Baden-Württemberg* D 61 B5
Marbach, *Hessen* D 51 C5
Marbach F 60 B2
Marbäck S 40 B3
Mårbacka S 34 C5
Marbella E 100 C1
Marboz F 69 B5
Marburg D 51 C4
Marcali H 74 B2
Marčana HR 82 B2
Marcaria I 81 A4
Marcelová SK 64 C4
Marcenat F 68 C2
March GB 30 B4
Marchamalo E 95 B3
Marchaux F 69 A6
Marche-en-Famenne B 49 C6
Marchegg A 64 B2
Marchena E 99 B5
Marchenoir F 58 C2
Marcheprime F 76 B2
Marciac F 76 C3
Marciana Marina I 81 D4
Marcianise I 103 B7
Marcigny F 68 B4
Marcilla E 89 B5
Marcillac-la-Croisille F 68 C2
Marcillac-Vallon F 77 B5
Marcillat-en-Combraille F 68 B2
Marcille-sur-Seine F 59 B4
Marcilloles F 69 C5
Marcilly-le-Hayer F 59 B4
Marcinkowice PL 46 B2
Marciszów PL 53 C6
Marck F 48 C2
Marckolsheim F 60 B3
Marco de Canevezes P 87 C2
Mårdsele S 115 C16
Mårdsjö S 115 D12
Mareham le Fen GB 27 B5
Marek S 40 B5
Marennes F 66 C3
Maresquel F 48 C2
Mareuil F 67 C5
Mareuil-en-Brie F 59 B4
Mareuil-sur-Arnon F 68 B2
Mareuil-sur-Lay F 66 B3
Mareuil-sur-Ourcq F 59 A4
Margam GB 28 B4
Margariti GR 116 C2
Margate GB 31 C5
Margaux F 76 A2
Margerie-Hancourt F 59 B5
Margès F 69 C5
Margherita di Savóia I 104 B2
Margita SCG 75 C6
Margone I 70 C2
Margonin PL 46 C3

Marguerittes F 78 C3
Margut F 59 A6
Maria E 101 B3
Maria Neustift A 63 C5
Maria Saal A 73 B4
Mariager DK 38 C2
Mariana E 95 B4
Mariannelund S 40 B5
Marianópoli I 108 B2
Mariánské Lázně CZ 52 D2
Mariapfarr A 72 A3
Mariazell A 63 C6
Maribo DK 39 E4
Maribor SLO 73 B5
Marieberg S 37 C2
Mariefred S 37 C4
Mariehamn FIN 36 B6
Marieholm S 41 D3
Mariembourg B 49 C5
Marienbaum D 50 B2
Marienberg D 52 C3
Marienheide D 50 B3
Mariental D 51 A6
Mariestad S 35 D5
Marieux F 48 C3
Marigliano I 103 C7
Marignane F 79 C4
Marigny, *Jura* F 69 B5
Marigny, *Manche* F 57 A4
Marigny-le-Châtel F 59 B4
Marija Bistrica HR 73 B6
Marijampolė LT 6 D7
Marín E 87 B2
Marina HR 83 C5
Marina del Cantone I 103 C7
Marina di Acquappesa I 106 B2
Marina di Alberese I 81 D5
Marina di Amendolara I 106 B3
Marina di Árbus I 110 C1
Marina di Campo I 81 D4
Marina di Carrara I 81 B4
Marina di Castagneto-Donorático I 81 C4
Marina di Cécina I 81 C4
Marina di Gáiro I 110 C2
Marina di Ginosa I 104 C2
Marina di Gioiosa Iónica I 106 C3
Marina di Grosseto I 81 D4
Marina di Léuca I 107 B5
Marina di Massa I 81 B4
Marina di Novāglie I 107 B5
Marina di Pisa I 81 C4
Marina di Ragusa I 109 C3
Marina di Ravenna I 82 B1
Marina di Torre Grande I 110 C1
Marina Romea I 82 B1
Marinaleda E 100 B1
Marine de Sisco F 102 A2
Marinella I 108 B1
Marinella di Sarzana I 81 B4
Marineo I 108 B2
Marines F 58 A2
Maringues F 68 C3
Marinha das Ondas P 92 A2
Marinha Grande P 92 B2
Marinhas P 87 C2
Marino I 102 B5
Marjaliza E 94 C3
Markabygd N 114 D8
Markaryd S 40 C3
Markdorf D 61 C5
Markelo NL 50 A2
Market Deeping GB 30 B3
Market Drayton GB 26 C3
Market Harborough GB 30 B3
Market Rasen GB 27 B5
Market Warsop GB 27 B4
Market Weighton GB 27 B5
Markethill GB 19 B5
Markgröningen D 61 B5
Markhausen D 43 C4
Marki PL 55 A6
Markina-Xemein E 89 A4
Markinch GB 25 B4
Märkische Buchholz D 53 A3
Markitta S 113 E10
Markkleeberg D 52 B2
Marklohe D 43 C6
Marknesse NL 42 C2
Markneukirchen D 52 C2
Markopoulo GR 117 E5
Markovac SCG 85 B6
Markowice PL 54 C3
Markranstädt D 52 B2
Marksuhl D 51 C6
Markt Allhau A 73 A6
Markt Bibart D 61 A6
Markt Erlbach D 62 A1
Markt-heidenfeld D 61 A5
Markt Indersdorf D 62 B2
Markt Rettenbach D 61 C6
Markt Schwaben D 62 B2
Markt-Übelbach A 73 A5
Marktbreit D 61 A6
Marktl D 62 B3
Marktleuthen D 52 C1
Marktoberdorf D 62 C1
Marktredwitz D 52 C2
Markusica HR 74 C3
Markušovce SK 65 B6
Marl D 50 B3
Marlborough, *Devon* GB 28 C4
Marlborough, *Wiltshire* GB 29 B6
Marle F 59 A4
Marlieux F 69 B5
Marlow D 45 A4
Marlow GB 31 C3
Marma S 36 B4
Marmagne F 69 B4
Marmande F 76 B3
Marmara TR 118 B2
Marmaris TR 119 F3
Marmelete P 98 B2
Marmolejo E 100 A1
Marmoutier F 60 B3
Marnay F 69 A5
Marne D 43 B6
Marnheim D 61 A4
Marnitz D 44 B3
Maroldsweisach D 51 C6
Marolles-les-Braults F 58 B1
Maromme F 58 A2
Marone I 71 C5
Maronia GR 116 B7
Maroslele H 75 B5
Maróstica I 72 C1
Marotta I 82 C2
Marpisa GR 117 E7
Marquion F 49 C4
Marquise F 48 C2
Marradi I 81 B5
Marrasjärvi FIN 113 F14
Marraskoski FIN 113 F14
Marratxi E 97 B2
Marrúbiu I 110 C1
Marrum NL 42 B2
Marrupe E 94 B2
Mars-la-Tours F 60 A1
Marsac F 77 C5
Marsac-en-Livradois F 68 C3
Marságlia I 80 B3
Marsala I 108 B1
Marsberg D 51 B4
Marsciano I 82 D1
Marseillan F 78 C2
Marseille = Marseilles F 79 C4
Marseille en Beauvaisis F 58 A2
Marseilles = Marseille F 79 C4
Mársico Nuovo I 104 C1
Marske-by-the-Sea GB 27 A4
Marsliden S 115 B12
Marson F 59 B5
Märsta S 37 C4
Marstal DK 39 E3
Marstrand S 38 B4
Marta I 102 A4
Martano I 107 A5
Martel F 77 B4
Martelange B 60 A1
Martfeld D 43 C6
Martfű H 75 A5
Martham GB 30 B5
Marthon F 67 C5
Martiago E 93 A4
Martigné-Briand F 67 A4
Martigné-Ferchaud F 57 C4
Martigne-sur-Mayenne F 57 B5
Martigny CH 70 B2
Martigny-les-Bains F 60 B1
Martigues F 79 C4
Martim-Longo P 98 B3
Martin SK 65 A4
Martin de la Jara E 100 B1
Martin Muñoz de las Posadas E 94 A2
Martina CH 71 B5
Martina Franca I 104 C3
Martinamor E 94 B1
Martinengo I 71 C4
Martinsberg A 63 B6
Martinšćica HR 82 B3
Martinshöhe D 60 A3
Martinsicuro I 82 D2
Martinszell D 61 C6
Mártis I 110 B1
Martofte DK 39 D3
Martonvásár H 74 A3
Martorell E 91 B4
Martos E 100 B2
Martres Tolosane F 77 C3
Martti FIN 113 E17
Marugán E 94 B2
Marúggio I 104 C3
Marvão P 92 B3
Marvejols F 78 B2
Marville F 60 A1
Marwałd PL 47 B5
Marykirk GB 25 B5
Marypark GB 23 D5
Maryport GB 26 A2
Marytavy GB 28 C3
Marzabotto I 81 B5
Marzahna D 52 B2
Marzahne D 45 C4
Marzamemi I 109 C4
Marzocca I 82 C2
Mas-Cabardès F 77 C5
Mas de Barberáns E 90 C3
Mas de las Matas E 90 C2
Masa E 88 B3
Máscali I 109 B4
Mascaraque E 94 C3
Mascarenhas P 87 C3
Mascioni I 103 A6
Masegoso E 101 A3
Masegoso de Tajuña E 95 B4
Masera I 70 B3
Masevaux F 60 C2
Masfjorden N 32 B2
Masham GB 27 A4
Masi N 113 C12
Maside E 87 B2
Maslacq F 76 C2
Maslinica HR 83 C5
Maslovare BIH 84 B2
Masone I 80 B2
Massa I 81 B4
Massa Fiscáglia I 81 B6
Massa Lombarda I 81 B5
Massa Lubrense I 103 C7
Massa Maríttima I 81 C4
Massa Martana I 82 D1
Massafra I 104 C3
Massamagrell E 96 B2
Massanassa E 96 B2
Massarosa I 81 C4
Massat F 77 D4
Massay F 68 A1
Massbach D 51 C6
Masseret F 67 C6
Masseube F 77 C3
Massiac F 68 C3
Massignac F 67 C5
Massing D 62 B3
Massmechelen B 50 C1
Masterud N 34 B4
Mästocka S 40 C3
Masty BY 6 E8
Masúa I 110 C1
Masueco E 87 C4
Masugnsbyn S 113 E11
Mašun SLO 73 C4
Maszewo, *Lubuskie* PL 53 A4
Maszewo, *Zachodnio-Pomorskie* PL 45 B7
Mata de Alcántara E 93 B4
Matala GR 117 H6
Matalebreras E 89 C4
Matallana de Torio E 88 B1
Matamala E 89 C4
Mataporquera E 88 B2
Matapozuelos E 88 C2
Mataró E 91 B5
Matarocco I 108 B1
Mataruge SCG 85 C4
Mataruška Banja SCG 85 C5
Matélica I 82 C2
Matera I 104 C2
Mateševo SCG 85 D4
Mátészalka H 11 C7
Matet E 96 B2
Matfors S 115 E14
Matha F 67 C4
Mathay F 70 A1
Matignon F 57 B3
Matilla de los Caños del Rio E 94 B1
Matlock GB 27 B4
Matosinhos P 87 C2
Matour F 69 B4
Mátrafüred H 65 C5
Mátraterenye H 65 B5
Matre, *Hordaland* N 32 B2
Matre, *Hordaland* N 32 C2
Matrei am Brenner A 71 A6
Matrei in Osttirol A 72 A2
Matrice I 103 B7
Matsdal S 115 B12
Mattarello I 71 B6
Mattersburg A 64 C2
Mattighofen A 62 B4
Mattinata I 104 B2
Mattos P 92 B2
Mattsee A 62 C4
Mattsmyra S 36 A2
Matulji HR 73 C4
Maubert-Fontaine F 59 A5
Maubeuge F 49 C4
Maubourguet F 76 C3
Mauchline GB 24 C3
Maud GB 23 D6
Mauer-kirchen A 62 B4
Mauern D 62 B2
Mauguio F 78 C3
Maulbronn D 61 B4
Maule F 58 B2
Mauléon F 67 B4
Mauléon-Barousse F 77 D3
Mauléon-Licharre F 76 C2
Maulévrier F 67 A4
Maum IRL 18 C2
Maurach A 72 A1
Maure-de-Bretagne F 57 C4
Maureilhan F 78 C2
Mauriac F 68 C2
Mauron F 57 B3
Maurs F 77 B5
Maury F 77 D5
Maussane-les-Alpilles F 78 C3
Mautern A 63 B6
Mautern im Steiermark A 73 A4
Mauterndorf A 72 A3
Mauthausen A 63 B5
Mauthen A 72 B3
Mauvezin F 77 C3
Mauzé-sur-le-Mignon F 67 B4
Maxent F 57 C3
Maxey-sur-Vaise F 60 B1
Maxial P 92 B1
Maxieira P 92 B2
Maxwellheugh GB 25 C5
Mayalde E 88 C1
Maybole GB 24 C3
Mayen D 50 C3
Mayenne F 57 B5
Mayet F 58 C1
Maylough IRL 18 C3
Mayorga E 88 B1
Mayres F 78 B3
Mayrhofen A 72 A1
Mazagón E 99 B4
Mazaleón E 90 B3
Mazamet F 77 C5
Mazan F 79 B4
Mazara del Vallo I 108 B1
Mazarambroz E 94 C2
Mazarete E 95 B4
Mazaricos E 86 B2
Mazarrón E 101 B4
Mažeikiai LT 6 C7
Mazères F 77 C4
Mazères-sur-Salat F 77 C3
Mazières-en-Gâtine F 67 B4
Mazin HR 83 B4
Mazuelo E 88 B3
Mazyr BY 7 E10
Mazzarino I 109 B3
Mazzarrà Sant'Andrea I 109 A4
Mazzo di Valtellina I 71 B5
Mchowo PL 47 B6
Mdzewo PL 47 C6
Mealabost GB 22 C2
Mealhada P 92 A2
Méan B 49 C6
Meana Sardo I 110 C2
Meaulne F 68 B2
Meaux F 59 B3
Mebonden N 114 D8
Mecerreyes E 89 B3
Mechelen B 49 B5
Mechernich D 50 C2
Mechnica PL 54 C3
Mechowo PL 45 B7
Mechterstädt D 51 C6
Mecidiye TR 118 B1
Mecikal PL 46 B3
Mecina-Bombarón E 100 C2
Mecitözü TR 16 A7
Meckenbeuren D 61 C5
Meckenheim, *Rheinland-Pfalz* D 50 C3
Meckenheim, *Rheinland-Pfalz* D 61 A4
Meckesheim D 61 A4
Mecseknádasd H 74 B3
Meda I 71 C4
Meda P 87 D3
Medak HR 83 B4
Mede I 80 A2
Medebach D 51 B4
Medelim P 93 A3
Medemblik NL 42 C2
Medena Selista BIH 84 B1
Medesano I 81 B4
Medevi S 37 D1
Medgidia RO 11 D10
Medgyesháza H 75 B6
Medhamn S 35 C5
Mediaș RO 11 C8
Medicina I 81 B5
Medina de las Torres E 93 C4
Medina de Pomar E 89 B3
Medina de Ríoseco E 88 C1
Medina del Campo E 88 C2
Medina Sidonia E 99 C5
Medinaceli E 95 A4
Medinilla E 93 A5
Medja SCG 75 C5
Medjedja BIH 85 C4
Medulin HR 82 B2
Meduno I 72 B2
Medveda SCG 85 B6
Medvedja SCG 85 C6
Medvedov SK 64 C3
Medvide HR 83 B4
Medvode SLO 73 B4
Medzev SK 65 B6
Medžitlija MK 116 B3
Meerane D 52 C2
Meerle B 49 B5
Meersburg D 61 C5
Meeuwen B 49 B6
Megalo Horio GR 119 F2
Megalopoli GR 117 E4
Megara GR 117 D5
Megève F 69 C6
Meggenhofen A 63 B4
Megra RUS 7 A14
Mehamn N 113 A16
Mehedeby S 36 B4
Méhkerék H 75 B6
Mehun-sur-Yèvre F 68 A2
Meigle GB 25 B4
Meijel NL 50 B1
Meilen CH 70 A3
Meilhan F 76 C2
Meimôa P 93 A3
Meina I 70 C3
Meine D 44 C2
Meinersen D 44 C2
Meinerzhagen D 50 B3
Meiningen D 51 C6
Meira E 86 A3
Meiringen CH 70 B3
Meisenheim D 60 A3
Meissen D 52 B3
Meitingen D 62 B1
Meix-devant-Virton B 60 A1
Męka PL 54 B3
Meka Gruda BIH 84 C3
Mel I 72 B2
Melbu N 112 D3
Melč CZ 64 A3
Meldal N 114 D6
Méldola I 82 B1
Meldorf D 43 A6
Melegnano I 71 C4
Melenci SCG 75 C5
Melendugno I 105 C4
Melfi I 104 C1
Melfjordbotn N 112 F2
Melgaço P 87 B2
Melgar de Arriba E 88 B1
Melgar de Fernamental E 88 B2
Melgar de Yuso E 88 B2
Melhus N 114 D7
Meliana E 96 B2
Melide CH 70 C3
Melide E 86 B2
Melides P 98 A2
Meligales GR 117 E3
Melilli I 109 B4
Melinovac HR 83 B4
Melisenda I 110 C2
Melisey F 60 C2
Mélito di Porto Salvo I 109 B4
Melk A 63 B6
Melksham GB 29 B5
Mellanström S 115 B15
Mellbystrand S 40 C2
Melle B 49 B4
Melle D 50 A4
Melle F 67 B4
Mellendorf D 43 C6
Mellerud S 35 D4
Mellieha M 107 C5
Mellösa S 37 C3
Mellrichstadt D 51 C6
Mělnické Vtelno CZ 53 C4
Mělník CZ 53 C4
Melón E 87 B2
Melrose GB 25 C5
Mels CH 71 A4
Melsungen D 51 B5
Meltaus FIN 113 F14
Meltham GB 27 B4
Melton Mowbray GB 30 B3
Meltosjärvi FIN 113 F13
Melun F 58 B3
Melvaig GB 22 D3
Melvich GB 23 C5
Mélykút H 75 B4
Melzo I 71 C4
Memaliaj AL 116 B1
Membrilla E 95 D3
Membrio E 93 B3
Memer F 77 B4
Memmelsdorf D 51 D6
Memmingen D 61 C6
Memoria P 92 B2
Mena UA 7 F12
Menággio I 71 B4
Menai Bridge GB 26 B1
Menasalbas E 94 C2
Menat F 68 B2
Mendavia E 89 B4
Mendaza E 89 B4
Mende F 78 B2
Menden D 50 B3
Menderes TR 119 D2
Mendig D 50 C3
Mendiga P 92 B2
Mendrisio CH 70 C3
Ménéac F 56 B3
Menemen TR 118 D2
Menen B 49 C4
Menesjärvi FIN 113 D15
Menetou-Salon F 68 A2
Menfi I 108 B1
Ménfőcsanak H 64 C3
Mengamuñoz E 94 B2
Mengen D 61 B5
Mengen TR 118 B7
Mengeš SLO 73 B4
Mengibar E 100 B2
Mengkofen D 62 B3
Menou F 68 A3
Mens F 79 B4
Menslage D 43 C4
Mensträsk S 115 B16
Mentana I 102 A5
Menton F 80 C1
Méntrida E 94 B2
Méobecq F 67 B6
Méounes-les-Montrieux F 79 C4
Meppel NL 42 C3
Meppen D 43 C4
Mequinenza E 90 B3
Mer F 58 C2
Mera, *Coruña* E 86 A2
Mera, *Coruña* E 86 A3
Meråker N 114 D8
Merano I 71 B6
Merate I 71 C4
Mercadillo E 89 A3
Mercatale I 82 C1
Mercatino Conca I 82 C1
Mercato San Severino I 103 C7
Mercato Saraceno I 82 C1
Merching D 62 B1
Merchtem B 49 C5
Merdrignac F 56 B3
Merdžanići BIH 84 C2
Meré E 88 A2
Mere GB 29 B5
Meréville F 58 B3
Merfeld D 50 B3
Méribel F 69 C6
Méribel Motraret F 69 C6
Meriç TR 118 A1
Mérida E 93 C4
Mérignac F 76 B2
Měřín CZ 64 A1
Mering D 62 B1
Merkendorf D 62 A1
Merklin CZ 63 A4
Merksplas B 49 B5
Merlånna S 37 C3
Merlimont Plage F 48 C2
Mern DK 39 D5
Mernye H 74 B2
Mers-les-Bains F 48 C1
Mersch L 60 A2
Merseburg D 52 B1
Merthyr Tydfil GB 29 B4
Mertingen D 62 B1
Mértola P 98 B3
Méru F 58 A3
Merufe P 87 B2
Mervans F 69 B5
Merville F 48 C3
Méry-sur-Seine F 59 B4
Merzen D 43 C4
Merzifon TR 16 A7
Merzig D 60 A2
Mesagne I 105 C3
Mesão Frio P 87 C3
Mesas de Ibor E 93 B5
Meschede D 50 B4
Meschers-sur-Gironde F 66 C4
Meshchovsk RUS 7 D13
Meslay-du-Maine F 57 C5
Mesna N 34 A2
Mesnalien N 34 A2
Mesocco CH 71 B4
Mésola I 82 B1
Mesologi GR 116 D3
Mesopotamo GR 116 C2
Mesoraca I 107 B3
Messac F 57 C4
Messancy B 60 A1
Messdorf D 44 C3
Messei F 57 B5
Messejana P 98 B2
Messelt N 34 A3
Messina I 109 A4
Messingen D 43 C4
Messini GR 117 E4
Messkirch D 61 C5
Messlingen S 115 E9
Messtetten D 61 B4
Mesta GR 117 D7
Mestanza E 100 A1
Městec Králové CZ 53 C5
Mestlin D 44 B3
Město Albrechtice CZ 54 C2
Město Libavá CZ 64 A3
Město Touškov CZ 63 A4
Mestre I 72 C2
Mesvres F 69 B4
Mesztegnyő H 74 B2
Meta I 103 C7
Metajna HR 83 B4
Metelen D 50 A3
Methana GR 117 E5
Methlick GB 23 D6
Methven GB 25 B4
Methwold GB 30 B4
Metković HR 84 C2
Metlika SLO 73 C5
Metnitz A 73 B4
Metslawier NL 42 B3
Metsovo GR 116 C3
Metten D 62 B3
Mettendorf D 50 D2
Mettet B 49 C5
Mettingen D 50 A3
Mettlach D 60 A2
Mettlen CH 70 B2
Mettmann D 50 B2
Metz F 60 A2
Metzervisse F 60 A2
Metzingen D 61 B5
Meulan F 58 A2
Meung-sur-Loire F 58 C2
Meuselwitz D 52 B2
Meuzac F 67 C6
Mevagissey GB 28 C3
Mexborough GB 27 B4
Meximieux F 69 C5
Mey GB 23 C5
Meyenburg D 44 B4
Meyerhöfen D 43 C5
Meylan F 69 C5
Meymac F 68 C2
Meyrargues F 79 C4
Meyrueis F 78 B2
Meyssac F 77 A4
Meysse F 78 B3
Meyzieu F 69 C4
Mèze F 78 C2
Mézériat F 69 B5
Mežica SLO 73 B4
Mézidon-Canon F 57 A5
Mézières-en-Brenne F 67 B6
Mézières-sur-Issoire F 67 B5
Mézilhac F 78 B3
Mézilles F 59 C4
Mézin F 76 B3
Mezőberény H 75 B6
Mezőcsát H 65 C6
Mezőfalva H 74 B3
Mezőhegyes H 75 B5
Mezőkeresztes H 65 C6
Mezőkomárom H 74 B3
Mezőkovácsháza H 75 B5
Mezőkövesd H 65 C6
Mezőörs H 74 A2
Mézos F 76 B1
Mezőszilas H 74 B3
Mezőtúr H 75 A5
Mezquita de Jarque E 90 C2
Mezzano, *Emilia Romagna* I 81 B6
Mezzano, *Trentino Alto Adige* I 72 B1
Mezzojuso I 108 B2
Mezzoldo I 71 B4
Mezzolombardo I 71 B6
Mgarr M 107 C5
Mglin RUS 7 E12
Miajadas E 93 B5
Miały PL 46 C2
Mianowice PL 46 A3
Miasteczko Krajeńskie PL 46 B3
Miasteczko Sł. PL 54 C3
Miastko PL 46 A2
Michalovce SK 10 B6
Michałowice PL 55 C4
Michelau D 61 A6
Michelbach D 61 A6
Micheldorf A 63 C5
Michelhausen A 64 B1
Michelsneukirchen D 62 A3
Michelstadt D 61 A5
Michendorf D 52 A3
Michurin BG 11 E9
Mickleover GB 27 C4
Mid Yell GB 22 A7
Midbea GB 23 B6
Middelburg NL 49 B4
Middelfart DK 39 D2
Middelharnis NL 49 B5
Middelkerke B 48 B3
Middelstum NL 42 B3
Middlesbrough GB 27 A4
Middleton GB 24 B1
Middleton Cheney GB 30 B2
Middleton-in-Teesdale GB 26 A3
Middletown GB 19 B5
Middlewich GB 26 B3
Middlezoy GB 29 B5
Midhurst GB 31 D3
Midleton IRL 20 C3
Midlum D 43 B5
Midsomer Norton GB 29 B5
Midtgulen N 114 F2
Midtskogberget N 34 A4
Midwolda NL 43 B4
Miechów PL 55 C5
Miedes de Aragón E 89 C5
Miedes de Atienza E 95 A3
Międzybodzie Bielskie PL 65 A5
Międzybórz PL 54 B2
Międzychód PL 46 C1
Międzylesie PL 54 C1
Międzyrzec Podlaski PL 6 F7
Międzyrzecz PL 46 C1
Międzywodzie PL 45 A6
Międzyzdroje PL 45 B6
Miejska Górka PL 54 B1
Miélan F 76 C3
Mielec PL 55 C6
Mielęcin PL 45 B6
Mielno, *Warmińsko-Mazurskie* PL 47 B6
Mielno, *Zachodnio-Pomorskie* PL 46 A2
Miengo E 88 A3
Mieraslompolo FIN 113 C16
Miercurea Ciuc RO 11 C8
Mieres, *Asturias* E 88 A1
Mieres, *Girona* E 91 A5
Mieroszów PL 53 C6
Mierzyn PL 55 B4
Miesau D 60 A3
Miesbach D 62 C2
Mieścisko PL 46 C3
Mieste D 44 C3
Miesterhorst D 44 C3
Mieszków PL 54 A2
Mieszkowice PL 45 C6
Mietków PL 54 C1
Migennes F 59 C4
Miggiano I 107 B5
Migliánico I 103 A7
Migliarino I 81 B5
Migliónico I 104 C2
Mignano Monte Lungo I 103 B6
Migné F 67 B6
Miguel Esteban E 95 C3
Miguelturra E 94 D3
Mihajlovac SCG 85 B5
Miháld H 74 B2
Mihalgazi TR 118 B5
Mihalıççık TR 118 C6
Mihályi H 74 A2
Mihla D 51 B6
Mihohnić HR 83 A3
Miholjsko HR 73 C5
Mihovljan HR 73 B5
Mijares E 94 B2
Mijas E 100 C1
Mijoska SCG 85 D4
Mike H 74 B2
Mikhnevo RUS 7 D14
Mikines GR 117 E4
Mikkeli FIN 3 F27
Mikkelvik N 112 B8
Mikleuš HR 74 C2
Mikołajki Pomorskie PL 47 B5
Mikołów PL 54 C3
Mikonos GR 117 E7
Mikorzyn PL 54 B3
Mikro Derio GR 116 A8
Mikstat PL 54 B2
Mikulášovice CZ 53 C4
Mikulov CZ 64 B2
Mikulovice CZ 54 C2
Milagro E 89 B5
Miłakowo PL 47 A6
Milan = Milano I 71 C4
Miland N 32 C5
Milano = Milan I 71 C4
Milano Marittima I 82 B1
Milas TR 119 E2
Milazzo I 109 A4
Mildenhall GB 30 B4
Milejewo PL 47 A5
Milelín CZ 53 C5
Miletić SCG 75 C4
Miletićevo SCG 75 C6
Mileto I 106 C3
Milevsko CZ 63 A5
Milford IRL 19 A4
Milford Haven GB 28 B2
Milford on Sea GB 31 D2
Milhão P 87 C4
Milići BIH 84 B4
Miličín CZ 63 A5
Milicz PL 54 B2
Milín CZ 63 A5
Militello in Val di Catánia I 109 B3
Miljevina BIH 84 C3
Milkowice PL 53 B6
Millançay F 68 A1
Millares E 96 B2
Millas F 91 A5
Millau F 78 B2
Millesimo I 80 B2
Millevaches F 68 C2
Millom GB 26 A2
Millport GB 24 C3
Millstatt A 72 B3
Millstreet, *Cork* IRL 20 B2
Millstreet, *Waterford* IRL 21 B4
Milltown, *Galway* IRL 18 C3
Milltown, *Kerry* IRL 20 B1
Milltown Malbay IRL 20 B2
Milly-la-Forêt F 58 B3
Milmarcos E 95 A5
Milmersdorf D 45 B5
Milna HR 83 C5
Milnthorpe GB 26 A3
Miločaj SCG 85 B5
Milogórze PL 47 A6
Miłomłyn PL 47 B5
Milos GR 117 F6
Miloševo SCG 85 B6
Miłosław PL 54 A2
Milot AL 105 B5
Milówka PL 65 A5
Miltach D 62 A3
Miltenberg D 61 A5
Milton Keynes GB 31 B3
Miltzow D 45 A5
Milutovac SCG 85 C6
Milverton GB 29 B4
Milzyn PL 47 C4
Mimice HR 84 C1
Mimizan F 76 B1
Mimizan-Plage F 76 B1
Mimoň CZ 53 C4
Mina de Juliana P 98 B2
Mina de São Domingos P 98 B3
Minas de Riotinto E 99 B4
Minateda E 101 A4
Minaya E 95 C4
Minde P 92 B2
Mindelheim D 61 B6
Mindelstetten D 62 B2
Minden D 51 A4
Mindszent H 75 B5
Minehead GB 29 B4
Mineo I 109 B3
Minerbe I 71 C6
Minérbio I 81 B5
Minervino Murge I 104 B2
Minglanilla E 95 C5
Mingorria E 94 B2

Minnesund N 34 B3
Miño E 86 A2
Miño de San Esteban E 89 C3
Minsen D 43 B4
Minsk BY 7 E9
Mińsk Mazowiecki PL 55 A6
Minsterley GB 26 C3
Mintlaw GB 23 D6
Minturno I 103 B6
Mionica BIH 84 B3
Mionica SCG 85 B5
Mios F 76 B2
Mira E 96 B1
Mira I 72 C2
Mira P 92 A2
Mirabel E 93 B4
Mirabel-aux-Baronnies F 79 B4
Mirabella Eclano I 103 B8
Mirabella Imbáccari I 109 B3
Mirabello I 81 B5
Miradoux F 77 B3
Miraflores de la Sierra E 94 B3
Miralrio E 95 B4
Miramar P 87 C2
Miramare I 82 B1
Miramas F 78 C3
Mirambeau F 67 C4
Miramont-de-Guyenne F 77 B3
Miranda de Arga E 89 B5
Miranda de Ebro E 89 B4
Miranda do Corvo P 92 A2
Miranda do Douro P 87 C4
Mirande F 77 C3
Mirandela P 87 C3
Mirandilla E 93 C4
Mirándola I 81 B5
Miranje HR 83 B4
Mirano I 72 C2
Miras AL 116 B2
Miravet E 90 B3
Miré F 57 C5
Mirebeau F 67 B5
Mirebeau-sur-Bèze F 69 A5
Mirecourt F 60 B2
Mirepoix F 77 C4
Mires GR 117 G6
Miribel F 69 C4
Miričina BIH 84 B3
Mirina GR 116 C7
Mirna SLO 73 C5
Miroslav CZ 64 B2
Mirosławice PL 54 C1
Mirosławiec PL 46 B2
Mirošov CZ 63 A4
Mirotice CZ 63 A5
Mirovice CZ 63 A5
Mirow D 45 B4
Mirsk PL 53 C5
Mirzec PL 55 B6
Misi FIN 113 F15
Misilmeri I 108 A2
Miske H 75 B4
Miskolc H 65 B6
Mislinja SLO 73 B5
Missanello I 104 C2
Missillac F 66 A2
Mistelbach A 64 B2
Mistelbach D 62 A2
Misten N 112 E3
Misterbianco I 109 B4
Misterhult S 40 B6
Mistretta I 109 B3
Misurina I 72 B2
Mitchelstown IRL 20 B3
Mithimna GR 116 C8
Mithoni GR 117 F3
Mitilini GR 118 C1
Mitilinii GR 119 E1
Mittelberg, *Tirol* A 71 B5
Mittelberg, *Vorarlberg* A 71 A5
Mittenwald D 71 A6
Mittenwalde D 52 A3
Mitter-Kleinarl A 72 A3
Mitterback A 63 C6
Mitterdorf im Mürztal A 73 A5
Mittersheim F 60 B2
Mittersill A 72 A2
Mitterskirchen D 62 B3
Mitterteich D 62 A3
Mitton F 76 B2
Mittweida D 52 C2
Mitwitz D 52 C1
Mizhhir'ya UA 11 B7
Mjällby S 41 C4
Mjåvatn N 33 D5
Mjöbäck S 40 B2
Mjölby S 37 D2
Mjølfjell N 32 B3
Mjøndalen N 35 C2
Mjørlund N 34 B2
Mladá Boleslav CZ 53 C4
Mladá Vožice CZ 63 A5
Mladé Buky CZ 53 C5
Mladenovac SCG 85 B5
Mladenovo SCG 75 C4
Mladikovine BIH 84 B2
Mława PL 47 B6
Mlinište BIH 84 B1
Młodzieszyn PL 55 A5
Młogoszyn PL 55 A4
Młynary PL 47 A5
Mnichóvice CZ 63 A5
Mnichovo Hradiště CZ 53 C4
Mniów PL 55 B5
Mnisek nad Hnilcom SK 65 B6
Mnišek pod Brdy CZ 63 A5
Mniszek PL 55 B5
Mniszków PL 55 B5
Mo, *Hedmark* N 34 B3
Mo, *Hordaland* N 32 B2
Mo, *Møre og Romsdal* N 114 E5
Mo, *Telemark* N 33 C4
Mo, *Gävleborg* S 36 A3
Mo, *Västra Götaland* S 35 D3
Mo i Rana N 115 A11
Moaña E 87 B2
Moate IRL 21 A4
Mocejón E 94 C3
Močenok SK 64 B3
Mochales E 95 A4
Mochowo PL 47 C5
Mochy PL 53 A6
Mockern D 52 A1
Mockfjärd S 36 B1
Möckmühl D 61 A5
Mockrehna D 52 B2
Moclin E 100 B2
Mocsa H 64 C4
Möcsény H 74 B3
Modane F 70 C1
Modbury GB 28 C4
Módena I 81 B4
Möðrudalur IS 111 B10
Módica I 109 C3
Modigliana I 81 B5
Modlin PL 47 C6
Mödling A 64 B2
Modliszewice PL 55 B5
Modliszewko PL 46 C3
Modogno I 104 B2
Modra SK 64 B3
Modran BIH 84 B2
Modriča BIH 84 B3
Modrý Kamen SK 65 B5
Moëlan-sur-Mer F 56 C2
Moelfre GB 26 B1
Moelv N 34 B2
Moen N 112 C7
Moena I 72 B1
Moerbeke B 49 B4
Moers D 50 B2
Móes P 87 D3
Moffat GB 25 C4
Mogadouro P 87 C4
Mogata S 37 D3
Móggio Udinese I 72 B3
Mogielnica PL 55 B5
Mogilany PL 65 A5
Mogilno PL 46 C3
Mogliano I 82 C2
Mogliano Véneto I 72 C2
Mogor E 87 B2
Mógoro I 110 C1
Moguer E 99 B4
Mohács H 74 C3
Moheda S 40 B4
Mohedas E 93 A4
Mohedas de la Jara E 93 B5
Mohelnice CZ 64 A2
Mohill IRL 19 C4
Möhlin CH 70 A2
Moholm S 35 D6
Mohorn D 52 B3
Mohyliv-Podil's'kyy UA 11 B9
Moi N 33 D3
Moià E 91 B5
Móie I 82 C2
Moimenta da Beira P 87 D3
Moirans F 69 C5
Moirans-en-Montagne F 69 B5
Moisaküla EST 7 B8
Moisdon-la-Rivière F 57 C4
Moissac F 77 B4
Moita, *Coimbra* P 92 A2
Moita, *Guarda* P 93 A3
Moita, *Santarém* P 92 B2
Moita, *Setúbal* P 92 C1
Moita dos Ferreiros P 92 B1
Moixent E 101 A5
Mojacar E 101 B4
Mojados E 88 C2
Mojkovac SCG 85 D4
Mojmírovce SK 64 B4
Mojtin SK 65 B4
Möklinta S 36 B3
Mokošica HR 84 D3
Mokra Gora SCG 85 C4
Mokro Polje HR 83 B5
Mokronog SLO 73 C5
Mokrzyska PL 55 C5
Møkster N 32 B2
Mol B 49 B6
Mol SCG 75 C5
Mola di Bari I 104 B3
Molai GR 117 F4
Molare I 80 B2
Molaretto I 70 C2
Molas F 77 C3
Molassano I 80 B2
Molbergen D 43 C4
Mold GB 26 B2
Molde N 114 E4
Møldrup DK 38 C2
Moledo do Minho P 87 C2
Molfetta I 104 B2
Molfsee D 44 A2
Moliden S 115 D15
Molières F 77 B4
Molina de Aragón E 95 B5
Molina de Segura E 101 A4
Molinar E 89 A3
Molinaseca E 86 B4
Molinella I 81 B5
Molinet F 68 B3
Molini di Tures I 72 B1
Molinicos E 101 A3
Molinos de Duero E 89 C4
Molins de Rei E 91 B5
Moliterno I 104 C1
Molkom S 35 C5
Mollas AL 105 C6
Möllbrücke A 72 B3
Mölle S 41 C2
Molledo E 88 A2
Möllenbeck D 45 B5
Mollerussa E 90 B3
Mollet de Perelada E 91 A5
Mollina E 100 B1
Mölln D 44 B2
Molló E 91 A5
Mollösund S 35 D3
Mölltorp S 37 D1
Mölnbo S 37 C4
Mölndal S 38 B5
Mölnlycke S 38 B5
Molompize F 68 C3
Moloy F 69 A4
Molsheim F 60 B3
Moltzow D 45 B4
Molve HR 74 B2
Molveno I 71 B5
Molvizar E 100 C2
Molzbichl A 72 B3
Mombaróccio I 82 C1
Mombeltrán E 94 B1
Mombris D 51 C5
Mombuey E 87 B4
Momchilgrad BG 116 A7
Mommark DK 39 E3
Momo I 70 C3
Monaghan IRL 19 B5
Monar Lodge GB 22 D4
Monasterace Marina I 106 C3
Monasterevin IRL 21 A4
Monasterio de Rodilla E 89 B3
Monastir I 110 C2
Monbahus F 77 B3
Monbazillac F 77 B3
Moncada E 96 B2
Moncalieri I 80 A1
Moncalvo I 80 A2
Monção P 87 B2
Moncarapacho P 98 B3
Moncel-sur-Seille F 60 B2
Monchegorsk RUS 3 C30
Mönchen-gladbach = Munchen-Gladbach D 50 B2
Mónchio della Corti I 81 B4
Monchique P 98 B2
Monclar-de-Quercy F 77 C4
Moncofa E 96 B2
Moncontour F 56 B3
Moncoutant F 67 B4
Monda E 100 C1
Mondariz E 87 B2
Mondavio I 82 C1
Mondéjar E 95 B3
Mondello I 108 A2
Mondim de Basto P 87 C3
Mondolfo I 82 C2
Mondoñedo E 86 A3
Mondorf-les-Bains L 60 A2
Mondoubleau F 58 C1
Mondovì I 80 B1
Mondragon F 78 B3
Mondragone I 103 B6
Mondsee A 63 C4
Monéglia I 80 B3
Monegrillo E 90 B2
Monein F 76 C2
Monemvasia GR 117 F5
Mónesi I 80 B1
Monesiglio I 80 B2
Monesterio E 99 A4
Monestier-de-Clermont F 79 B4
Monestiés F 77 B5
Monéteau F 59 C4
Moneygall IRL 21 B4
Moneymore GB 19 B5
Monfalcone I 72 C3
Monfero E 86 A2
Monflanquin F 77 B3
Monflorite E 90 A2
Monforte P 92 B3
Monforte da Beira E 92 B3
Monforte da Beira P 92 B3
Monforte d'Alba I 80 B1
Monforte de Lemos E 86 B3
Monforte de Moyuela E 90 B1
Monforte del Cid E 96 C2
Monghidoro I 81 B5
Mongiana I 106 C3
Monguelfo I 72 B2
Monheim D 62 B1
Moniaive GB 25 C4
Monifieth GB 25 B5
Monikie GB 25 B5
Monistrol-d'Allier F 78 B2
Monistrol de Montserrat E 91 B4
Monistrol-sur-Loire F 68 C4
Mönkebude D 45 B5
Monkton GB 24 C3
Monmouth GB 29 B5
Monnaie F 67 A5
Monnerville F 58 B3
Monnickendam NL 42 C2
Monolithos GR 119 F2
Monópoli I 104 C3
Monor H 75 A4
Monóvar E 101 A5
Monpazier F 77 B3
Monreal D 50 C3
Monreal E 76 D1
Monreal del Campo E 95 B5
Monreale I 108 A2
Monroy E 93 B4
Monroyo E 90 C2
Mons B 49 C4
Monsaraz P 92 C3
Monschau D 50 C2
Monségur F 76 B3
Monsélice I 72 C1
Mønshaug N 32 B3
Monster NL 49 A5
Mönsterås S 40 B6
Monsummano Terme I 81 C4
Mont-de-Marsan F 76 C2
Mont-Louis F 91 A5
Mont-roig del Camp E 90 B3
Mont-St. Aignan F 58 A2
Mont-St. Vincent F 69 B4
Mont-sous-Vaudrey F 69 B5
Montabaur D 50 C3
Montafia I 80 B2
Montagnac F 78 C2
Montagnana I 71 C6
Montaigu F 66 B3
Montaigu-de-Quercy F 77 B4
Montaiguët-en-Forez F 68 B3
Montaigut F 68 B2
Montaigut-sur-Save F 77 C4
Montainville F 58 B2
Montalbán E 90 C2
Montalbán de Córdoba E 100 B1
Montalbano Elicona I 109 A4
Montalbano Iónico I 104 C2
Montalbo E 95 C4
Montalcino I 81 C5
Montaldo di Cósola I 80 B3
Montalegre P 87 C3
Montalieu-Vercieu F 69 C5
Montalivet-les-Bains F 66 C3
Montallegro I 108 B2
Montalto delle Marche I 82 D2
Montalto di Castro I 102 A4
Montalto Pavese I 80 B3
Montalto Uffugo I 106 B3
Montalvão P 92 B3
Montamarta E 88 C1
Montana BG 11 E7
Montana-Vermala CH 70 B2
Montánchez E 93 B4
Montanejos E 96 A2
Montano Antilia I 106 A2
Montans F 77 C4
Montargil P 92 B2
Montargis F 58 C3
Montastruc-la-Conseillère F 77 C4
Montauban F 77 B4
Montauban-de-Bretagne F 57 B3
Montbard F 59 C5
Montbarrey F 69 A5
Montbazens F 77 B5
Montbazon F 67 A5
Montbéliard F 70 A1
Montbenoit F 69 B6
Montbeugny F 68 B3
Montblanc E 91 B4
Montbozon F 69 A6
Montbrison F 68 C4
Montbron F 67 C5
Montbrun-les-Bains F 79 B4
Montceau-les-Mines F 69 B4
Montcenis F 69 B4
Montchanin F 69 B4
Montcornet F 59 A5
Montcuq F 77 B4
Montdardier F 78 C2
Montdidier F 58 A3
Monte-Carlo MC 80 C1
Monte Clara P 92 B3
Monte Clérigo P 98 B2
Monte da Pedra P 92 B3
Monte de Goula P 92 B3
Monte do Trigo P 92 C3
Monte Gordo P 98 B3
Monte Juntos P 92 C3
Monte Porzio I 82 C2
Monte Real P 92 B2
Monte Redondo P 92 B2
Monte Romano I 102 A4
Monte San Giovanni Campano I 103 B6
Monte San Savino I 81 C5
Monte Sant'Ángelo I 104 B1
Monte Vilar P 92 B1
Monteagudo E 101 A4
Monteagudo de las Vicarias E 89 C4
Montealegre E 88 C2
Montealegre del Castillo E 101 A4
Montebello Iónico I 109 B4
Montebello Vicentino I 71 C6
Montebelluna I 72 C2
Montebourg F 57 A4
Montebruno I 80 B3
Montecarotto I 82 C2
Montecassiano I 82 C2
Montecastrilli I 102 A5
Montecatini Terme I 81 C4
Montécchio I 82 C1
Montécchio Emilia I 81 B4
Montécchio Maggiore I 71 C6
Montech F 77 C4
Montechiaro d'Asti I 80 A2
Montecórice I 103 C7
Montecorvino Rovella I 103 C7
Montederramo E 87 B3
Montedoro I 108 B2
Montefalco I 82 D1
Montefalcone di Val Fortore I 103 B8
Montefalcone nel Sánnio I 103 B7
Montefano I 82 C2
Montefiascone I 102 A5
Montefiorino I 81 B4
Montefortino I 82 D2
Montefranco I 102 A5
Montefrío E 100 B2
Montegiordano Marina I 106 A3
Montegiórgio I 82 C2
Montegranaro I 82 C2
Montehermoso E 93 A4
Montejicar E 100 B2
Montejo de la Sierra E 95 A3
Montejo de Tiermes E 89 C3
Montel-de-Gelat F 68 C2
Monteleone di Púglia I 103 B8
Monteleone di Spoleto I 102 A5
Monteleone d'Orvieto I 81 D6
Montelepre I 108 A2
Montelibretti I 102 A5
Montelier F 79 B4
Montélimar F 78 B3
Montella E 91 A4
Montella I 103 C8
Montellano E 99 B5
Montelupo Fiorentino I 81 C5
Montemaggiore Belsito I 108 B2
Montemagno I 80 B2
Montemayor E 100 B1
Montemayor de Pinilla E 88 C2
Montemésola I 104 C3
Montemilleto I 103 B7
Montemilone I 104 B1
Montemolin E 99 A4
Montemónaco I 82 D2
Montemor-o-Novo P 92 C2
Montemor-o-Velho P 92 A2
Montemurro I 104 C1
Montendre F 67 C4
Montenegro de Cameros E 89 B4
Montenero di Bisáccia I 103 B7
Monteneuf F 57 C3
Monteparano I 104 C3
Montepescali I 81 D5
Montepiano I 81 B5
Montepulciano I 81 C5
Montereale I 103 A6
Montereale Valcellina I 72 B2
Montereau-Faut-Yonne F 59 B3
Monterénzio I 81 B5
Monteroni d'Arbia I 81 C5
Monteroni di Lecce I 105 C4
Monterosso al Mare I 80 B3
Monterosso Almo I 109 B3
Monterosso Grana I 79 B6
Monterotondo I 102 A5
Monterotondo Maríttimo I 81 C4
Monterrey E 87 C3
Monterroso E 86 B3
Monterrubio de la Serena E 93 C5
Monterubbiano I 82 C2
Montes Velhos P 98 B2
Montesa E 96 C2
Montesalgueiro E 86 A2
Montesano sulla Marcellana I 104 C1
Montesárchio I 103 B7
Montescaglioso I 104 C2
Montesclaros E 94 B2
Montesilvano I 103 A7
Montespértoli I 81 C5
Montesquieu-Volvestre F 77 C4
Montesquiou F 77 C3
Montestruc-sur-Gers F 77 C3
Montevarchi I 81 C5
Montéveglio I 81 B5
Montfaucon F 66 A3
Montfaucon-d'Argonne F 59 A6
Montfaucon-en-Velay F 69 C4
Montferrat, *Isère* F 69 C5
Montferrat, *Var* F 79 C5
Montfort-en-Chalosse F 76 C2
Montfort-l'Amaury F 58 B2
Montfort-le-Gesnois F 58 B1
Montfort-sur-Meu F 57 B4
Montfort-sur-Risle F 58 A1
Montgai E 90 B3
Montgaillard F 76 C3
Montgenèvre F 79 B5
Montgiscard F 77 C4
Montgomery GB 26 C2
Montguyon F 67 C4
Monthermé F 59 A5
Monthey CH 70 B1
Monthois F 59 A5
Monthureux-sur-Saône F 60 B1
Monti I 110 B2
Monticelli d'Ongina I 81 A3
Montichiari I 71 C5
Monticiano I 81 C5
Montiel E 100 A3
Montier-en-Der F 59 B5
Montieri I 81 C5
Montiglio I 80 A2
Montignac F 77 A4
Montigny-le-Roi F 60 C1
Montigny-lès-Metz F 60 A2
Montigny-sur-Aube F 59 C5
Montijo E 93 C4
Montijo P 92 C2
Montilla E 100 B1
Montillana E 100 B2
Montilly F 68 B3
Montivilliers F 57 A6
Montjaux F 78 B1
Montjean-sur-Loire F 66 A4
Montlhéry F 58 B3
Montlieu-la-Gard F 67 C4
Montlouis-sur-Loire F 67 A5
Montluçon F 68 B2
Montluel F 69 C5
Montmarault F 68 B2
Montmartin-sur-Mer F 57 B4
Montmédy F 59 A6
Montmélian F 69 C6
Montmeyan F 79 C5
Montmeyran F 78 B3
Montmirail, *Marne* F 59 B4
Montmirail, *Sarthe* F 58 B1
Montmiral F 69 C5
Montmirat F 78 C3
Montmirey-le-Château F 69 A5
Montmoreau-St. Cybard F 67 C5
Montmorency F 58 B3
Montmorillon F 67 B5
Montmort-Lucy F 59 B4
Montoir-de-Bretagne F 66 A2
Montoire-sur-le-Loir F 58 C1
Montoito P 92 C3
Montolieu F 77 C5
Montório al Vomano I 103 A6
Montoro E 100 A1
Montpellier F 78 C2
Montpezat-de-Quercy F 77 B4
Montpezat-sous-Bouzon F 78 B3
Montpon-Ménestérol F 76 A3
Montpont-en-Bresse F 69 B5
Montréal, *Aude* F 77 C5
Montréal, *Gers* F 76 C3
Montredon-Labessonnié F 77 C5
Montréjeau F 77 C3
Montrésor F 67 A6
Montresta I 110 B1
Montret F 69 B5
Montreuil, *Pas de Calais* F 48 C2
Montreuil, *Seine St. Denis* F 58 B3
Montreuil-aux-Lions F 59 A4
Montreuil-Bellay F 67 A4
Montreux CH 70 B1
Montrevault F 66 A3
Montrevel-en-Bresse F 69 B5
Montrichard F 67 A6
Montricoux F 77 B4
Montrond-les-Bains F 69 C4
Montrose GB 25 B5
Montroy E 96 B2
Monts-sur-Guesnes F 67 B5
Montsalvy F 77 B5
Montsauche-les-Settons F 68 A4
Montseny E 91 B5
Montsoreau F 67 A5
Montsûrs F 57 B5
Montuenga E 94 A2
Montuïri E 97 B3
Monturque E 100 B1
Monza I 71 C4
Monzón E 90 B3
Monzón de Campos E 88 B2
Moorbad Lobenstein D 52 C1
Moordorf D 43 B4
Moorslede B 49 C4
Moos D 61 C4
Moosburg D 62 B2
Moosburg im Kärnten A 73 B4
Mór H 74 A3
Mora E 94 C3
Móra P 92 C2
Mora S 36 A1
Mora de Rubielos E 96 A2
Mòra d'Ebre E 90 B3
Mòra la Nova E 90 B3
Moraby S 36 B2
Moradillo de Roa E 88 C3
Morąg PL 47 B5
Mórahalom H 75 B4
Moraime E 86 A1
Morais P 87 C4
Moral de Calatrava E 100 A2
Moraleda de Zafayona E 100 B2
Moraleja E 93 A4
Moraleja del Vino E 88 C1
Morales de Toro E 88 C1
Morales de Valverde E 88 C1
Morales del Vino E 88 C1
Moralina E 87 C4
Morano Cálabro I 106 B3
Mörarp S 41 C2
Morasverdes E 93 A4
Morata de Jalón E 89 C5
Morata de Jiloca E 89 C5
Morata de Tajuña E 95 B3
Moratalla E 101 A4
Moravče SLO 73 B4
Moravec CZ 64 A2
Moraviţa RO 75 C6
Morávka CZ 65 A4
Moravská Třebová CZ 64 A2
Moravské Budějovice CZ 64 A1
Moravské Lieskové SK 64 B3
Moravske Toplice SLO 73 B6
Moravský-Beroun CZ 64 A3
Moravský Krumlov CZ 64 A2
Moravský Svätý Ján SK 64 B3
Morawica PL 55 C5
Morawin PL 54 B3
Morbach D 60 A3
Morbegno I 71 B4
Morbier F 69 B6
Mörbisch am See A 64 C2
Mörbylånga S 41 C6
Morcenx F 76 B2
Morciano di Romagna I 82 C1
Morcone I 103 B7
Morcuera E 89 C3
Mordelles F 57 B4
Mordoğan TR 119 D1
Moréac F 56 C3
Morebattle GB 25 C5
Morecambe GB 26 A3
Moreda, *Granada* E 100 B2
Moreda, *Oviedo* E 88 A1
Morée F 58 C2
Moreles de Rey E 88 B1
Morella E 90 C2
Moreruela de los Infanzones E 88 C1
Morés E 89 C5
Móres I 110 B1
Morestel F 69 C5
Moret-sur-Loing F 58 B3
Moreton-in-Marsh GB 29 B6
Moretonhampstead GB 28 C4
Moretta I 80 B1
Moreuil F 58 A3
Morez F 69 B6
Mörfelden D 51 D4
Morgat F 56 B1
Morges CH 69 B6
Morgex I 70 C2
Morgongåva S 36 C3
Morhange F 60 B2
Morhet B 49 D6
Mori I 71 C5
Morialmé B 49 C5
Morianes P 98 B3
Moriani Plage F 102 A2
Mórichida H 74 A2
Moriles E 100 B1
Morille E 94 B1
Moringen D 51 B5
Morjärv S 3 C25
Morkarla S 36 B4
Morke DK 39 C3
Mørkøv DK 39 D4
Morkovice-Slížany CZ 64 A3
Morlaàs F 76 C2
Morlaix F 56 B2
Morley F 59 B6
Mörlunda S 40 B5
Mormanno I 106 B2
Mormant F 59 B3
Mornant F 69 C4
Mornay-Berry F 68 A2
Morokovo SCG 85 D4
Morón de Almazán E 89 C4
Morón de la Frontera E 99 B5
Morović SCG 85 A4
Morozzo I 80 B1
Morpeth GB 25 C6
Morphou CY 120 A1
Mörrum S 41 C4
Morsbach D 50 C3
Mörsch D 61 B4
Mörsil S 115 D10
Morsum D 39 E1
Mørsvikbotn N 112 E4
Mortagne-au-Perche F 58 B1
Mortagne-sur-Gironde F 66 C4
Mortagne-sur-Sèvre F 66 B4
Mortágua P 92 A2
Mortain F 57 B5
Mortara I 70 C3
Morteau F 69 A6
Mortegliano I 72 C3
Mortelle I 109 A4
Mortemart F 67 B5
Mortimer's Cross GB 29 A5
Mortrée F 57 B6
Mörtschach A 72 B2
Mortsel B 49 B5
Morud DK 39 D3
Morwenstow GB 28 C3
Moryń PL 45 C6
Morzeszczyn PL 47 B4
Morzewo PL 47 B5
Morzine F 70 B1
Mosalsk RUS 7 D13
Mosbach D 61 A5
Mosbjerg DK 38 B3
Mosby N 33 D4
Mosca P 87 C4
Moscavide P 92 C1
Moščenica HR 73 C6
Mošćenice HR 73 C4
Moščenička Draga HR 73 C4
Mosciano Sant'Ángelo I 82 D2
Mościsko PL 54 C1
Moscow = Moskva RUS 7 D14
Mosina PL 54 A1
Mosjøen N 115 B10
Moskog N 32 A3
Moskorzew PL 55 C4
Moskosel S 115 B16
Moskuvarra FIN 113 E15
Moskva = Moscow RUS 7 D14
Moslavina Podravska HR 74 C2
Moșnița Nouă RO 75 C6
Moso in Passiria I 71 B6
Mosonmagyaróvár H 64 C3
Mošorin SCG 75 C5
Mošovce SK 65 B4
Mosqueruela E 90 C2
Moss N 35 C2
Mossfellsbær IS 111 C4
Mössingen D 61 B5
Møsstrand N 32 C5
Most CZ 52 C3
Most na Soči SLO 72 B3
Mosta M 107 C5
Mostar BIH 84 C2
Mosterhamn N 33 C2
Mostki PL 53 A5

Newtown Cunningham IRL 19 B4
Newtown Hamilton GB 19 B5
Newtown St. Boswells GB 25 C5
Newtown Sands IRL 20 B2
Newtownabbey GB 19 B6
Newtownards GB 19 B6
Newtownbutler GB 19 B4
Newtownmountkennedy IRL 21 A5
Newtownshandrum IRL 20 B3
Newtownstewart GB 19 B4
Nexon F 67 C6
Neyland GB 28 B3
Nibbiano I 80 B3
Nibe DK 38 C2
Nicaj-Shalë AL 105 A5
Nicastro I 106 C3
Niccone I 82 C1
Nice F 80 C1
Nickelsdorf A 64 C3
Nicolosi I 109 B4
Nicosia CY 120 A2
Nicosia I 109 B3
Nicótera I 106 C2
Nidda D 51 C5
Nidzica PL 47 B6
Niebla E 99 B4
Nieborów PL 55 A5
Niebüll D 39 E1
Niechanowo PL 46 C3
Niechorze PL 45 A7
Niedalino PL 46 A2
Nieder-Olm D 61 A4
Niederaula D 51 C5
Niederbipp CH 70 A2
Niederbronn-les-Bains F 60 B3
Niederfischbach D 50 C3
Niedergörsdorf D 52 B2
Niederkrüchten D 50 B2
Niederndorf A 62 C3
Niedersachswerfen D 51 B6
Niederstetten D 61 A5
Niederurnen CH 70 A4
Niederwölz A 73 A4
Niedoradz PL 53 B5
Niedzica PL 65 A6
Niegosławice PL 53 B5
Nieheim D 51 B5
Niemcza PL 54 C1
Niemegk D 52 A2
Niemodlin PL 54 C2
Nienburg, *Niedersachsen* D 43 C6
Nienburg, *Sachsen-Anhalt* D 52 B1
Niepołomice PL 55 C5
Nierstein D 61 A4
Niesky D 53 B4
Niestronno PL 46 C3
Nieświń PL 55 B5
Nieszawa PL 47 C4
Nieul-le-Dolent F 66 B3
Nieul-sur-Mer F 66 B3
Nieuw-Amsterdam NL 42 C3
Nieuw-Buinen NL 42 C3
Nieuw-Weerdinge NL 42 C3
Nieuwe Niedorp NL 42 C1
Nieuwe-Pekela NL 42 B3
Nieuwe-schans NL 43 B4
Nieuwegein NL 49 A6
Nieuwerkerken B 49 C6
Nieuwolda NL 42 B3
Nieuwpoort B 48 B3
Niğde TR 16 C7
Nigrita GR 116 B5
Nigüelas E 100 C2
Níjar E 101 C3
Nijemci HR 75 A4
Nijkerk NL 49 A6
Nijlen B 49 B5
Nijmegen NL 50 B1
Nijverdal NL 42 C3
Nikel RUS 113 C19
Nikinci SCG 85 B4
Nikiti GR 116 B5
Nikitsch A 74 A1
Nikkaluokta S 112 E8
Nikla H 74 B2
Niklasdorf A 73 A5
Nikolayev = Mykolayiv UA 11 C12
Nikšić SCG 84 D3
Nilivaara S 113 E10
Nîmes F 78 C3
Nimis I 72 B3
Nimtofte DK 39 C3
Nin HR 83 B4
Nindorf D 43 A6
Ninemilehouse IRL 21 B4
Ninove B 49 C5
Niort F 67 B4
Niš SCG 10 E6
Nisa P 92 B3
Niscemi I 109 B3
Nissafors S 40 B3
Nissan-lez-Ensérune F 78 C2
Nissedal N 33 C5
Nissumby DK 38 C1
Nisterud N 33 C6
Niton GB 31 D2
Nitra SK 64 B4
Nitrianske-Pravno SK 65 B4
Nitrianske Rudno SK 65 B4
Nitry F 59 C4
Nittedal N 34 B2
Nittenau D 62 A3
Nittendorf D 62 A2
Nivala FIN 3 E26
Nivelles B 49 C5
Nivenskoye RUS 47 A6
Nivnice CZ 64 B3
Nizhyn UA 11 A11
Nižná SK 65 A5
Nižná Boca SK 65 B5
Nižne Repaše SK 65 A6
Nizza Monferrato I 80 B2
Njarðvík IS 111 D3
Njegůsevo SCG 75 C4
Njivice HR 73 C4
Njurundabommen S 115 E14
Njutånger S 115 F14
Noailles F 58 A3
Noain E 76 D1
Noale I 72 C2
Noalejo E 100 B2
Noblejas E 95 C3
Noceda E 86 B4
Nocera Inferiore I 103 C7
Nocera Terinese I 106 B3
Nocera Umbra I 82 C1
Noceto I 81 B4
Noci I 104 C3
Nociglia I 107 A5
Nodeland N 33 D4
Nödinge S 38 B5
Nods F 69 A6
Noé F 77 C4
Noépoli I 106 A3
Noeux-les-Mines F 48 C3
Noez E 94 C2
Nogales E 93 C4
Nogara I 71 C6
Nogarejas E 87 B4
Nogaro F 76 C2
Nogent F 59 B6
Nogent l'Artaud F 59 B4
Nogent-le-Roi F 58 B2
Nogent-le-Rotrou F 58 B1
Nogent-sur-Seine F 59 B4
Nogent-sur-Vernisson F 58 C3
Nogersund S 41 C4
Noguera E 95 B5
Noguerones E 100 B1
Nohfelden D 60 A3
Nohn D 50 C2
Noia E 86 B2
Noicáttaro I 104 B2
Noirétable F 68 C3
Noirmoutier-en-l'Île F 66 A2
Noja E 89 A3
Nojewo PL 46 C2
Nokia FIN 3 F25
Nol S 38 B5
Nola I 103 C7
Nolay F 69 B4
Noli I 80 B2
Nolnyra S 36 B4
Nombela E 94 B2
Nomeny F 60 B2
Nomexy F 60 B2
Nonancourt F 58 B2
Nonant-le-Pin F 57 B6
Nonántola I 81 B5
Nonaspe E 90 B3
None I 80 B1
Nontron F 67 C5
Nonza F 102 A2
Noordhorn NL 42 B3
Noordwijk NL 49 A5
Noordwijkerhout NL 49 A5
Noordwolde NL 42 C3
Noppikoski S 36 A1
Nora S 37 C2
Nørager DK 38 C2
Norberg S 36 B2
Norboda S 36 B5
Nórcia I 82 D2
Nord-Odal N 34 B3
Nordagutu N 33 C6
Nordanås S 115 C15
Nordausques F 48 C3
Nordborg DK 39 D2
Nordby, *Aarhus Amt.* DK 39 D3
Nordby, *Ribe Amt.* DK 39 D1
Norddeich D 43 B4
Norddorf D 43 A5
Norden D 43 B4
Nordenham D 43 B5
Norderhov N 34 B2
Norderney D 43 B4
Norderstapel D 43 A6
Norderstedt D 44 B2
Nordfjord N 113 B19
Nordfjordeid N 114 F3
Nordfold N 112 E4
Nordhalben D 52 C1
Nordhausen D 51 B6
Nordheim vor der Rhön D 51 C6
Nordholz D 43 B5
Nordhorn D 43 C4
Nordingrå S 115 E15
Nordkjosbotn N 112 C8
Nordli N 115 C10
Nördlingen D 61 B6
Nordmaling S 115 D16
Nordmark S 34 C6
Nordmela N 112 C4
Nordre Osen N 34 A3
Nordsinni N 34 B1
Nørdstedalsseter N 114 F4
Nordstemmen D 51 A5
Nordvågen N 113 B15
Nordwalde D 50 A3
Noreña E 88 A1
Noresund N 34 B1
Norg NL 42 B3
Norheimsund N 32 B3
Norie S 41 C4
Norma I 102 B5
Nornäs S 34 A5
Norra Vi S 40 B5
Norrahammar S 40 B4
Norråker S 115 C12
Norrala S 36 A3
Nørre Åby DK 39 D2
Nørre Alslev DK 39 E4
Nørre Lyndelse DK 39 D3
Nørre Nebel DK 39 D1
Nørre Snede DK 39 D2
Nørre Vorupør DK 38 C1
Norrent-Fontes F 48 C3
Nørresundby DK 38 B2
Norrhult Klavreström S 40 B5
Norrköping S 37 D3
Norrskedika S 36 B5
Norrsundet S 36 B4
Norrtälje S 36 C5
Nors DK 38 B1
Norsbron S 35 C5
Norsholm S 37 D2
Norsjö S 115 C16
Nort-sur-Erdre F 66 A3
Nörten-Hardenberg D 51 B5
North Berwick GB 25 B5
North Charlton GB 25 C6
North Frodingham GB 27 B5
North Kessock GB 23 D4
North Molton GB 28 B4
North Petherton GB 29 B4
North Somercotes GB 27 B6
North Tawton GB 28 C4
North Thoresby GB 27 B5
North Walsham GB 30 B5
Northallerton GB 27 A4
Northampton GB 30 B3
Northeim D 51 B6
Northfleet GB 31 C4
Northleach GB 29 B6
Northpunds GB 22 B7
Northwich GB 26 B3
Norton GB 27 A5
Nortorf D 44 A1
Nörvenich D 50 C2
Norwich GB 30 B5
Norwick GB 22 A8
Nøsen N 32 B5
Nosivka UA 11 A11
Nossa Senhora do Cabo P 92 C1
Nossebro S 35 D4
Nössemark S 35 C3
Nossen D 52 B3
Notaresco I 103 A6
Noto I 109 C4
Notodden N 33 C6
Nottingham GB 27 C4
Nottuln D 50 B3
Nouan-le-Fuzelier F 68 A2
Nouans-les-Fontaines F 67 A6
Nougaroulet F 77 C3
Nouvion F 48 C2
Nouzonville F 59 A5
Nova H 74 B1
Nová Baňa SK 65 B4
Nová Bystrica SK 65 A5
Nová Bystřice CZ 63 A6
Nova Crnja SCG 75 C5
Nova Gorica SLO 72 C3
Nova Gradiška HR 74 C2
Nova Levante I 71 B6
Nova Odesa UA 11 C11
Nová Paka CZ 53 C5
Nova Pazova SCG 85 B5
Nová Pec CZ 63 B4
Nova Siri I 106 A3
Nova Topola BIH 84 A2
Nova Varoš SCG 85 C4
Nova Zagora BG 11 E8
Novafeltria I 82 C1
Nováky SK 65 B4
Novalaise F 69 C5
Novales E 90 A2
Novalja HR 83 B3
Novara I 70 C3
Novara di Sicília I 109 A4
Novate Mezzola I 71 B4
Novaya Ladoga RUS 7 A12
Nové Hrady CZ 63 B5
Nové Mesto SK 64 B3
Nové Město na Moravě CZ 64 A2
Nové Město nad Metují CZ 53 C6
Nové Město pod Smrkem CZ 53 C5
Nové Mitrovice CZ 63 A4
Nové Sady SK 64 B3
Nové Strašeci CZ 53 C3
Nové Zámky SK 64 C4
Novelda E 101 A5
Novellara I 81 B4
Noventa di Piave I 72 C2
Noventa Vicentina I 71 C6
Novés E 94 B2
Noves F 78 C3
Novés de Segre E 91 A4
Novgorod RUS 7 B11
Novohrad-Siverskyy UA 7 F12
Novi Bečej SCG 75 C5
Novi di Módena I 81 B4
Novi Kneževac SCG 75 B5
Novi Lígure I 80 B2
Novi Marof HR 73 B6
Novi Pazar BG 11 E9
Novi Pazar SCG 85 C5
Novi Sad SCG 75 C4
Novi Slankamen SCG 75 C5
Novi Travnik BIH 84 B2
Novi Vinodolski HR 83 A3
Novigrad, *Istarska* HR 72 C3
Novigrad, *Zadarsko-Kninska* HR 83 B4
Novigrad Podravski HR 74 B1
Noville B 50 C1
Novion-Porcien F 59 A5
Novo Brdo SCG 85 D6
Novo Mesto SLO 73 C5
Novo Miloševo SCG 75 C5
Novo Selo BIH 84 A2
Novo Selo, *Kosovo* SCG 85 D5
Novo Selo, *Srbija* SCG 85 C5
Novohrad-Volynskyy UA 11 A9
Novomirgorod UA 11 B11
Novorzhev RUS 7 C10
Novoselë AL 105 C5
Novoselytsya UA 11 B9
Novosil RUS 7 E14
Novosokolniki RUS 7 C10
Novoukrayinka UA 11 B11
Novoveská Huta SK 65 B6
Novovolynsk UA 11 A8
Novozybkov RUS 7 E11
Novska HR 74 C1
Nový Bor CZ 53 C4
Nový Bydžov CZ 53 C5
Novy-Chevrières F 59 A5
Novy Dwór Mazowiecki PL 47 C6
Nový-Hrozenkov CZ 64 A4
Nový Jičín CZ 64 A4
Novy Knin CZ 63 A5
Novyy Buh UA 11 C12
Nowa Cerekwia PL 54 C2
Nowa Karczma PL 47 A4
Nowa Kościoł PL 53 B5
Nowa Ruda PL 54 C1
Nowa Słupia PL 55 C6
Nowa Sól PL 53 B5
Nowa Wieś PL 47 B5
Nowa-Wieś Wielka PL 47 C4
Nowe PL 47 B4
Nowe Brzesko PL 55 C5
Nowe Grudze PL 55 A4
Nowe Miasteczko PL 53 B5
Nowe Miasto, *Mazowieckie* PL 47 C6
Nowe Miasto, *Mazowieckie* PL 55 B5
Nowe Miasto Lubawskie PL 47 B5
Nowe Miasto nad Wartą PL 54 A2
Nowe Skalmierzyce PL 54 B3
Nowe Warpno PL 45 B6
Nowica PL 47 A5
Nowogard PL 45 B7
Nowogród Bobrzanski PL 53 B5
Nowogrodziec PL 53 B5
Nowosolna PL 55 B4
Nowy Dwór Gdański PL 47 A5
Nowy Korczyn PL 55 C5
Nowy Sącz PL 65 A6
Nowy Staw PL 47 A5
Nowy Targ PL 65 A6
Nowy Tomyśl PL 46 C2
Nowy Wiśnicz PL 65 A6
Noyal-Pontivy F 56 B3
Noyalo F 56 C3
Noyant F 67 A5
Noyelles-sur-Mer F 48 C2
Noyen-sur-Sarthe F 57 C5
Noyers F 59 C4
Noyers-sur-Cher F 67 A6
Noyers-sur-Jabron F 79 B4
Noyon F 59 A3
Nozay F 66 A3
Nuaillé F 66 A4
Nuaillé-d'Aunis F 66 B4
Nuars F 68 A3
Nubledo E 88 A1
Nuéno E 90 A2
Nuestra Señora Sa Verge des Pilar E 97 C1
Nueva E 88 A2
Nueva Carteya E 100 B1
Nuevalos E 95 A5
Nuits F 59 C5
Nuits-St. Georges F 69 A4
Nule I 110 B2
Nules E 96 B2
Nulvi I 110 B1
Numana I 82 C2
Numansdorp NL 49 B5
Nümbrecht D 50 C3
Nunchritz D 52 B3
Nuneaton GB 30 B2
Nunnanen FIN 113 D13
Nuñomoral E 93 A4
Nunspeet NL 42 C2
Nuorgam FIN 113 B16
Núoro I 110 B2
Nurallao I 110 C2
Nuremberg = Nürnberg D 62 A2
Nurmes FIN 3 E28
Nürnberg = Nuremberg D 62 A2
Nurri I 110 C2
Nürtingen D 61 B5
Nus I 70 C2
Nusnäs S 36 B1
Nusplingen D 61 B4
Nuštar HR 74 C3
Nyåker S 115 D16
Nyáregyháza H 75 A4
Nyarlörinc H 75 B4
Nyasvizh BY 7 E9
Nybble S 35 C6
Nybergsund N 34 A4
Nybøl DK 39 E2
Nyborg DK 39 D3
Nybro S 40 C5
Nybster GB 23 C5
Nyby DK 39 E5
Nye S 40 B5
Nyékládháza H 65 C6
Nyergesujfalu H 65 C4
Nyhammar S 36 B1
Nyhyttan S 37 C1
Nyirád H 74 A2
Nyirbátor H 11 C7
Nyíregyháza H 10 C6
Nyker DK 41 D4
Nykil S 37 D2
Nykirke N 34 B2
Nykøbing, *Falster* DK 39 E4
Nykøbing, *Vestsjællands Amt.* DK 39 D4
Nykøbing M DK 38 C1
Nyköping S 37 D3
Nykroppa S 35 C6
Nykvarn S 37 C4
Nykyrke S 37 D1
Nyland S 115 D14
Nylars DK 41 D4
Nymburk CZ 53 C5
Nynäshamn S 37 D4
Nyon CH 69 B6
Nyons F 79 B4
Nýřany CZ 63 A4
Nýrsko CZ 63 A4
Nyrud N 113 C18
Nysa PL 54 C2
Nysäter S 35 C4
Nyseter N 114 E5
Nyskoga S 34 B4
Nysted DK 44 A3
Nystrand N 35 C1
Nyúl H 64 C3
Nyvoll N 113 B12

O

O Barco E 86 B4
O Bolo E 87 B3
O Carballiño E 86 B2
O Corgo E 86 B3
Ö Lagnö S 37 C5
O Näsberg S 34 B5
O Páramo E 86 B3
O Pedrouzo E 86 B2
O Pino E 86 B2
O Porriño E 87 B2
O Rosal E 87 C2
Oadby GB 30 B2
Oakengates GB 26 C3
Oakham GB 30 B3
Oanes N 33 D3
Obalj BIH 84 C3
Oban GB 24 B2
Obdach A 73 A4
Obejo E 100 A1
Ober Grafendorf A 63 B6
Ober-Morlen D 51 C4
Oberammergau D 62 C2
Oberasbach D 62 A1
Oberau D 62 C2
Oberaudorf D 62 C3
Oberbruck F 60 C2
Oberdiessbach CH 70 B2
Oberdorf CH 70 A2
Oberdrauburg A 72 B2
Obere Stanz A 73 A5
Oberelsbach D 51 C6
Obergünzburg D 61 C6
Obergurgl A 71 B6
Oberhausen D 50 B2
Oberhof D 51 C6
Oberkirch D 61 B4
Oberkirchen D 51 B4
Oberkochen D 61 B6
Obermassfeld-Grimmenthal D 51 C6
Obermünchen D 62 B2
Obernai F 60 B3
Obernberg A 63 B4
Obernburg D 61 A5
Oberndorf D 61 B4
Oberndorf bei Salzburg A 62 C3
Obernkirchen D 51 A5
Oberort A 73 A5
Oberpullendorf A 74 A1
Oberriet CH 71 A4
Oberröblingen D 52 B1
Oberrot D 61 A5
Oberstaufen D 61 C6
Oberstdorf D 71 A5
Obertauern A 72 A3
Obertilliach A 72 B2
Obertraubling D 62 B3
Obertraun A 72 A3
Obertrubach D 62 A2
Obertrum A 62 C4
Oberursel D 51 C4
Obervellach A 72 B3
Oberviechtach D 62 A3
Oberwart A 73 A6
Oberwesel D 50 C3
Oberwinter D 50 C3
Oberwölzstadt A 73 A4
Oberzell D 63 B4
Obice PL 55 C5
Óbidos P 92 B1
Obilić SCG 85 D6
Obing D 62 C3
Objat F 67 C6
Objazda PL 46 A3
Öblarn A 73 A4
Obninsk RUS 7 D14
Oborniki PL 46 C2
Oborniki Śląskie PL 54 B1
Obornjača SCG 75 C4
Oboyan RUS 7 F14
Obrenovac SCG 85 B5
Obrež, *Srbija* SCG 85 B5
Obrež, *Vojvodina* SCG 85 B4
Obrigheim D 61 A5
Obrov SLO 73 C4
Obrovac HR 83 B4
Obrovac SCG 75 C4
Obrovac Sinjski HR 83 C5
Obruk TR 16 B6
Obrzycko PL 46 C2
Obudovac BIH 84 B3
Ocaña E 95 C3
Occhiobello I 81 B5
Occimiano I 80 A2
Očevlja BIH 84 B3
Ochagavía E 76 D1
Ochakiv UA 11 C11
Ochiltree GB 24 C3
Ochla PL 53 B5
Ochotnica-Dolna PL 65 A6
Ochotnica-Górna PL 65 A6
Ochsenfurt D 61 A6
Ochsenhausen D 61 B5
Ochtendung D 50 C3
Ochtrup D 50 A3
Ocieka PL 55 C6
Ockelbo S 36 B3
Öckerö S 38 B4
Ocniţa MD 11 B9
Očová SK 65 B5
Ócsa H 75 A4
Öcseny H 74 B3
Öcsöd H 75 B5
Octeville F 57 A4
Ocypel PL 47 B4
Ödåkra S 41 C2
Odby DK 38 C1
Odda N 32 B3
Odder DK 39 D3
Ödeborg S 35 D3
Odeceixe P 98 B2
Odechów PL 55 B6
Odeleite P 98 B3
Odemira P 98 B2
Ödemiş TR 119 D2
Ödensbacken S 37 C2
Odense DK 39 D3
Odensjö, *Jönköping* S 40 B4
Odensjö, *Kronoberg* S 40 C3
Oderberg D 45 C6
Oderzo I 72 C2
Odesa = Odessa UA 11 C11
Ödeshög S 37 D1
Odessa = Odesa UA 11 C11
Odiáxere P 98 B2
Odie GB 23 B6
Odiham GB 31 C3
Odintsovo RUS 7 D14
Odivelas P 98 A2
Odolanów PL 54 B2
Odón E 95 B5
Odorheiu Secuiesc RO 11 C8
Odoyevo RUS 7 E14
Odrowaz PL 55 B5
Odry CZ 64 A3
Odrzywół PL 55 B5
Ødsted DK 39 D2
Odžaci SCG 75 C4
Odžak BIH 84 A3
Oebisfelde D 44 C2
Oederan D 52 C3
Oeding D 50 B2
Oegstgeest NL 49 A5
Oelde D 50 B4
Oelsnitz D 52 C2
Oer-Erkenschwick D 50 B3
Oerlinghausen D 51 B4
Oettingen D 62 B1
Oetz A 71 A5
Oeventrop D 50 B4
Offanengo I 71 C4
Offenbach D 51 C4
Offenburg D 60 B3
Offida I 82 D2
Offingen D 61 B6
Offranville F 58 A2
Ofir P 87 C2
Ofte N 33 C5
Ofterschwang D 71 A5
Oggiono I 71 C4
Ogihares E 100 B2
Ogliastro Cilento I 103 C8
Ogliastro Marina I 103 C7
Ogmore-by-Sea GB 29 B4
Ogna N 33 D2
Ogre LV 6 C8
Ogrodzieniec PL 55 C4
Ogulin HR 73 C5
Ögur IS 111 A3
Ohanes E 101 B3
Ohey B 49 C6
Ohlstadt D 62 C2
Ohrdorf D 44 C2
Ohrdruf D 51 C6
Ohrid MK 116 A2
Öhringen D 61 A5
Oia E 87 B2
Oiã P 92 A2
Oiartzun E 76 C1
Oilgate IRL 21 B5
Oimbra E 87 C3
Oiselay-et-Grachoux F 69 A5
Oisemont F 48 D2
Oisterwijk NL 49 B6
Öja S 37 E5
Öje S 34 B5
Ojén E 100 C1
Ojrzeń PL 47 C6
Ojuelos Altos E 99 A5
Okalewo PL 47 B5
Okány H 75 B6
Okehampton GB 28 C3
Okhtyrka UA 7 F13
Oklaj HR 83 C5
Økneshamn N 112 D4
Okoč SK 64 C3
Okoličné SK 65 A5
Okonek PL 46 B2
Okonin PL 47 B4
Okřisky CZ 64 A1
Oksa PL 55 C5
Oksbøl DK 39 D1
Oksby DK 39 D1
Øksfjord N 113 B11
Øksna N 34 B3
Okučani HR 74 C2
Okulovka RUS 7 B12
Ólafsfjörður IS 111 A7
Ólafsvík IS 111 C2
Olagüe E 76 D1
Oland N 33 D5
Olargues F 78 C1
Oława PL 54 C2
Olazagutia E 89 B4
Olbernhau D 52 C3
Ólbia I 110 B2
Olching D 62 B2
Old Deer GB 23 D6
Oldbury GB 29 B5
Oldcastle IRL 19 C4
Oldeberkoop NL 42 C3
Oldeboorn NL 42 B2
Olden N 114 F3
Oldenbrok D 43 B5
Oldenburg, *Niedersachsen* D 43 B5
Oldenburg, *Schleswig-Holstein* D 44 A2
Oldenzaal NL 50 A2
Olderdalen N 112 C9
Olderfjord N 113 B14
Oldersum D 43 B4
Oldervik N 112 C7
Oldham GB 26 B3
Oldisleben D 52 B1
Oldmeldrum GB 23 D6
Olea E 88 B2
Oleby S 34 B5
Olechów PL 55 B6
Oledo P 92 B3
Oléggio I 70 C3
Oleiros, *Coruña* E 86 A2
Oleiros, *Coruña* E 86 B1
Oleiros P 92 B3
Oleksandriya, *Kirovohrad* UA 11 B12
Oleksandriya, *Rivne* UA 11 A9
Oleksandrovka UA 11 B12
Olen B 49 B5
Ølen N 33 C2
Olenegorsk RUS 3 B30
Olenino RUS 7 C12
Olesa de Montserrat E 91 B4
Oleśnica PL 54 B2
Olešnice CZ 64 A2
Olesno PL 54 C3
Oletta F 102 A2
Olette F 91 A5
Olevsk UA 11 A9
Olfen D 50 B3
Olgiate Comasco I 70 C3
Olginate I 71 C4
Ølgod DK 39 D1
Olgrinmore GB 23 C5
Olhão P 98 B3
Olhavo P 92 B1
Oliana E 91 A4
Olias del Rey E 94 C3
Oliena I 110 B2
Oliete E 90 C2
Olimbos GR 119 G2
Olite E 89 B5
Oliva E 96 C2
Oliva de la Frontera E 99 A4
Oliva de Mérida E 93 C4
Oliva de Plasencia E 93 A4
Olivadi I 106 C3
Olival P 92 B2
Olivar E 100 C2
Olivares E 99 B4
Olivares de Duero E 88 C2
Olivares de Júcar E 95 C4
Oliveira de Azeméis P 87 D2
Oliveira de Frades P 87 D2
Oliveira do Conde P 92 A3
Oliveira do Douro P 87 C2
Oliveira do Hospital P 92 A3
Olivenza E 93 C3
Olivet F 58 C2
Olivone CH 70 B3
Öljehult S 41 C5
Olkusz PL 55 C4
Ollerton GB 27 B4
Ollerup DK 39 D3
Olliergues F 68 C3
Ölmbrotorp S 37 C2
Ölme S 35 C5
Olmedilla de Alarcón E 95 C4
Olmedillo de Roa E 88 C3
Olmedo E 88 C2
Olmedo I 110 B1
Olmeto F 102 B1
Olmillos de Castro E 87 C4
Olmos de Ojeda E 88 B2
Olney GB 30 B3
Ołobok PL 54 B3
Olocau del Rey E 90 C2
Olofström S 41 C4
Olomouc CZ 64 A3
Olonets RUS 3 F30
Olonne-sur-Mer F 66 B3
Olonzac F 78 C1
Oloron-Ste. Marie F 76 C2
Olost E 91 B5
Olot E 91 A5
Olovo BIH 84 B3
Olpe D 50 B3
Olsberg D 51 B4
Olsene B 49 C4
Olserud S 35 C5
Olshammar S 37 D1
Olshanka UA 11 B11
Olszanica PL 53 B5
Olsztyn, *Śląskie* PL 55 C4
Olsztyn, *Warmińsko-Mazurskie* PL 47 B6
Olsztynek PL 47 B6
Olszyna PL 53 B5
Oltedal N 33 D3
Olten CH 70 A2
Olteniţa RO 11 D9
Olula del Rio E 101 B3
Ølve N 32 B2
Olvega E 89 C5
Olvera E 99 C5
Olympia GR 117 E3
Olzai I 110 B2
Omagh GB 19 B4
Omalos GR 117 G5
Omegna I 70 C3
Omiš HR 83 C5
Omišalj HR 73 C4
Ommen NL 42 C3
Omodhos CY 120 B1
Omoljica SCG 85 B5
On B 49 C6
Oña E 89 B3
Onano I 81 D5
Oñati E 89 A4
Onda E 96 B2
Ondara E 96 C3
Ondarroa E 89 A4
Onesse-et-Laharie F 76 B1
Oneşti RO 11 C9
Onhaye B 49 C5
Onich GB 24 B2
Onil E 96 C2
Onis E 88 A2
Önnestad S 41 C4
Onsala S 38 B5
Ontinyent E 96 C2
Ontur E 101 A4
Onzain F 67 A6
Onzonilla E 88 B1
Oost-Vlieland NL 42 B2
Oostburg NL 49 B4
Oostende B 48 B3
Oosterend NL 42 B2
Oosterhout NL 49 B5
Oosterwolde NL 42 C3
Oosterzele B 49 C4
Oosthuizen NL 42 C2
Oostkamp B 49 B4
Oostmalle B 49 B5
Oostvoorne NL 49 B5
Ootmarsum NL 42 C3
Opalenica PL 54 A1
Opařany CZ 63 A5
Oparić SCG 85 C6
Opatija HR 73 C4
Opatów, *Śląskie* PL 54 C3
Opatów, *Świętokrzyskie* PL 55 C6
Opatów, *Wielkopolskie* PL 54 B3

Opatówek PL 54 B3
Opatowiec PL 55 C5
Opava CZ 64 A3
Opeinde NL 42 B3
Oper Thalkirchdorf D 61 C6
Opglabbeek B 49 B6
Opicina I 72 C3
Oplotnica SLO 73 B5
Opmeer NL 42 C1
Opochka RUS 7 C10
Opočno CZ 53 C6
Opoczno PL 55 B5
Opole PL 54 C2
Oporów PL 55 A4
Opovo SCG 85 A5
Oppach D 53 B4
Oppdal N 114 E6
Oppeby, *Östergötland* S 40 A5
Oppeby, *Södermanland* S 37 D3
Oppedal N 32 A2
Oppegård N 34 C2
Oppenau D 61 B4
Oppenberg A 73 A4
Oppenheim D 61 A4
Óppido Lucano I 104 C1
Óppido Mamertina I 106 C2
Opponitz A 63 C5
Oppstad N 34 B3
Oprtalj HR 72 C3
Opsaheden S 34 B5
Ópusztaszer H 75 B5
Opuzen HR 84 C2
Ora CY 120 B2
Ora I 71 B6
Orada P 92 C3
Oradea RO 10 C6
Oradour-sur-Glane F 67 C6
Oradour-sur-Vayres F 67 C5
Oragonja SLO 72 C3
Orah BIH 84 D3
Orahova BIH 84 B2
Orahovica HR 74 C2
Orahovo BIH 74 C2
Oraison F 79 C4
Orajärvi FIN 113 F13
Orange F 78 B3
Orani I 110 B2
Oranienbaum D 52 B2
Oranienburg D 45 C5
Oranmore IRL 20 A3
Orašac SCG 85 B5
Orašje BIH 84 A3
Oravská Lesná SK 65 A5
Oravská Polhora SK 65 A5
Oravské Veselé SK 65 A5
Oravsky-Podzámok SK 65 A5
Orba E 96 C2
Orbacém P 87 C2
Ørbæk DK 39 D3
Orbais F 59 B4
Orbassano I 80 A1
Orbe CH 69 B6
Orbec F 58 A1
Orbetello I 102 A4
Orbetello Scalo I 102 A4
Orbigny F 67 A6
Ørby DK 39 C3
Örbyhus S 36 B4
Orce E 101 B3
Orcera E 101 A3
Orchamps-Vennes F 69 A6
Orches F 67 B5
Orchete E 96 C2
Orchies F 49 C4
Orchowo PL 47 C4
Orcières F 79 B5
Ordes E 86 A2
Ordhead GB 23 D6
Ordino AND 91 A4
Ordizia E 89 A4
Orduña E 89 B4
Ore S 36 A2
Orea E 95 B5
Orebić HR 84 D2
Örebro S 37 C2
Öregcsertő H 75 B4
Öregrund S 36 B5
Orehoved DK 39 E4
Orel RUS 7 E14
Orellana E 93 B5
Orellana de la Sierra E 93 B5
Ören TR 119 E2
Örencik TR 118 C4
Orestiada GR 118 A1
Organyà E 91 A4
Orgaz E 94 C3
Orgelet F 69 B5
Ørgenvika N 34 B1
Orgères-en-Beauce F 58 B2
Orgibet F 77 D3
Orgnac-l'Aven F 78 B3
Orgon F 79 C4
Orgósolo I 110 B2
Orhaneli TR 118 C3
Orhangazi TR 118 B4
Orhei MD 11 C10
Orhomenos GR 116 D4
Oria E 101 B3
Ória I 104 C3
Origny-Ste. Benoite F 59 A4
Orihuela E 101 A5
Orihuela del Tremedal E 95 B5
Orikum AL 105 C5
Oriola P 92 C3
Oriolo I 106 A3
Oriovac HR 74 C2
Orissaare EST 6 B7
Oristano I 110 C1
Öriszentpéter H 73 B6
Ørje N 35 C3
Orjiva E 100 C2
Orkanger N 114 D6
Örkelljunga S 41 C3
Örkény H 75 A4
Orlamünde D 52 C1
Orlane SCG 85 D6
Orléans F 58 C2
Orlová CZ 65 A4
Orlovat SCG 75 C5
Ormea I 80 B1
Ormelet N 35 C2
Ormemyr N 33 C6
Ormilia GR 116 B5
Ormos GR 117 E6
Ormož SLO 73 B6
Ormskirk GB 26 B3
Ornans F 69 A6
Ornäs S 36 B2
Ørnes N 112 F2
Orneta PL 47 A6
Ørnhøj DK 39 C1
Ornö S 37 C5
Örnsköldsvik S 115 D15
Orolik HR 75 C3
Orom SCG 75 C4
Oron-la-Ville CH 70 B1
Oronsko PL 55 B5
Oropa I 70 C2
Oropesa, *Castellón de la Plana* E 96 A3
Oropesa, *Toledo* E 93 B5
Orosei I 110 B2
Orosháza H 75 B5
Oroslavje HR 73 C5
Oroszlány H 74 A3
Oroszlo H 74 B3
Orotelli I 110 B2
Orozko E 89 A4
Orphir GB 23 C5
Orpington GB 31 C4
Orreaga-Roncesvalles E 76 C1
Orrefors S 40 C5
Orrviken S 115 D11
Orsa S 36 A1
Orsara di Púglia I 103 B8
Orsay F 58 B3
Orscholz D 60 A2
Orsennes F 67 B6
Orserum S 40 A4
Orsha BY 7 D11
Orsières CH 70 B2
Örsjö S 40 C5
Ørslev DK 39 D4
Örslösa S 35 D4
Orsogna I 103 A7
Orsomarso I 106 B2
Orşova RO 11 D7
Ørsta N 114 E3
Ørsted DK 38 C3
Örsundsbro S 37 C4
Orta Nova I 104 B1
Ortaca TR 119 F3
Ortakent TR 119 E2
Ortaklar TR 119 E2
Ortaköy TR 16 B7
Orte I 102 A5
Ortenburg D 63 B4
Orth A 64 B2
Orthez F 76 C2
Ortigueira E 86 A3
Ortilla E 90 A2
Ortisei I 72 B1
Orţişoara RO 75 C6
Ortnevik N 32 A3
Orton GB 26 A3
Ortona I 103 A7
Ortrand D 53 B3
Orubica HR 74 C2
Ørum DK 38 C2
Orune I 110 B2
Orusco E 95 B3
Orvalho P 92 A3
Orvault F 66 A3
Ørvella N 33 C6
Orvieto I 82 D1
Orvínio I 102 A5
Oryakhovo BG 11 E7
Orzesze PL 54 C3
Orzinuovi I 71 C4
Orzivécchi I 71 C4
Os, *Hedmark* N 114 E8
Os, *Hedmark* N 34 B3
Os Peares E 86 B3
Osann-Monzelo D 60 A2
Osaonica SCG 85 C5
Osbruk S 40 B4
Øsby DK 39 D2
Osby S 41 C3
Oščadnica SK 65 A4
Oschatz D 52 B3
Oschersleben D 52 A1
Óschiri I 110 B2
Osciłowo PL 47 C6
Osdorf D 44 A2
Osečina SCG 85 B4
Osečná CZ 53 C4
Oseja de Sajambre E 88 A1
Osek CZ 53 C3
Osen N 114 C7
Osera de Ebro E 90 B2
Osidda I 110 B2
Osie PL 47 B4
Osieck PL 55 B6
Osieczna, *Pomorskie* PL 47 B4
Osieczna, *Wielkopolskie* PL 54 B1
Osieczno PL 46 B1
Osiek, *Kujawsko-Pomorskie* PL 47 B5
Osiek, *Kujawsko-Pomorskie* PL 47 C4
Osiek, *Pomorskie* PL 47 B4
Osiek, *Świętokrzyskie* PL 55 C6
Osiek nad Notecią PL 46 B3
Osielsko PL 47 B4
Osijek HR 74 C3
Osilnica SLO 73 C4
Ósilo I 110 B1
Ósimo I 82 C2
Osinja BIH 84 B2
Osintorf BY 7 D11
Osipaonica SCG 85 B6
Osjaków PL 54 B3
Oskamull GB 24 B1
Oskarshamn S 40 B6
Oskarström S 40 C2
Oslany SK 65 B4
Oslavany CZ 64 A2
Ošlje HR 84 D2
Oslo N 34 C2
Øsløs DK 38 B1
Osmancık TR 16 A7
Osmaneli TR 118 B4
Ösmo S 37 D4
Osmolin PL 55 A4
Osnabrück D 50 A4
Ośno Lubuskie PL 45 C6
Osoblaha CZ 54 C2
Osor HR 83 B3
Osorno E 88 B2
Øsoyra N 32 A2
Osøyro N 32 B2
Óspakseyri IS 111 B4
Ospedaletti I 80 C1
Ospitaletto I 71 C5
Oss NL 49 B6
Ossa de Montiel E 95 D4
Ossi I 110 B1
Ossjøen N 32 B5
Ossun F 76 C2
Ostanå S 41 C4
Ostanvik S 36 A2
Ostashkov RUS 7 C12
Östavall S 115 E12
Ostbevern D 50 A3
Østborg N 115 C10
Østby N 34 A4
Osted DK 39 D4
Ostenfeld D 43 A6
Oster UA 11 A11
Øster Assels DK 38 C1
Øster Hornum DK 38 C2
Øster Hurup DK 38 C3
Øster Jølby DK 38 C1
Øster-marie DK 41 D5
Øster Tørslev DK 38 C3
Øster Vrå DK 38 B3
Osterburg D 44 C3
Osterburken D 61 A5
Österbybruk S 36 B4
Osterbyhavn DK 38 B4
Österbymo S 40 B5
Ostercappeln D 43 C5
Österfärnebo S 36 B3
Osterfeld D 52 B1
Österforse S 115 D14
Osterhever D 43 A5
Osterhofen D 62 B4
Osterholz-Scharmbeck D 43 B5
Østerild DK 38 B1
Österlövsta S 36 B4
Ostermiething A 62 B3
Osterode am Harz D 51 B6
Ostersiel D 43 A5
Östersund S 115 D11
Östervåla S 36 B4
Östervallskog S 35 C3
Osterwieck D 51 B6
Osterzell D 62 C1
Östffyasszonyfa H 74 A2
Östfora S 36 C4
Östhammar S 36 B5
Ostheim F 60 B3
Ostheim vor der Rhön D 51 C6
Osthofen D 61 A4
Ostiano I 71 C5
Ostíglia I 81 A5
Ostiz E 76 D1
Östmark S 34 B4
Östnor S 36 A1
Ostojićevo SCG 75 C5
Ostra I 82 C2
Östra Amtervik S 35 C5
Östra Husby S 37 D3
Östra Ljungby S 41 C3
Östra Ryd S 37 D3
Östraby S 41 D3
Ostrach D 61 C5
Ostrau D 52 B3
Ostrava CZ 64 A4
Østre Halsen N 35 C2
Ostrhauderfehn D 43 B4
Ostritz D 53 B4
Ostróda PL 47 B5
Ostroh UA 11 A9
Ostrołęka PL 6 E6
Ostropole PL 46 B2
Ostroróg PL 46 C2
Ostros SCG 105 A5
Ostrošovac BIH 83 B4
Ostrov CZ 52 C2
Ostrov RUS 7 C10
Ostrov nad Oslavou CZ 64 A1
Ostrów Mazowiecka PL 6 E6
Ostrów Wielkopolski PL 54 B2
Ostrówek PL 54 B3
Ostrowiec PL 46 A2
Ostrowiec-Świętokrzyski PL 55 C6
Ostrowite PL 47 B5
Ostrowo PL 47 C4
Ostrožac BIH 84 C2
Ostrzeszów PL 54 B2
Ostseebad Kühlungsborn D 44 A3
Ostuni I 104 C3
Osuna E 99 B5
Osvětimany CZ 64 A3
Oswestry GB 26 C2
Oświęcim PL 55 C4
Osztopán H 74 B2
Oteiza E 89 B5
Otelec RO 75 C5
Oteo E 89 A3
Oterbekk N 35 C2
Otero de Herreros E 94 B2
Otero de O Bodas E 87 C4
Othem S 37 E5
Otley GB 27 B4
Otmuchów PL 54 C2
Otočac HR 83 B4
Otok, *Splitsko-Dalmatinska* HR 83 C5
Otok, *Vukovarsko-Srijemska* HR 74 C3
Otoka BIH 83 B5
Otrić HR 83 B5
Otrícoli I 102 A5
Otrokovice CZ 64 A3
Otta N 114 F6
Ottana I 110 B2
Ottaviano I 103 C7
Ottenby S 41 C6
Ottendorf-Okrilla D 53 B3
Ottenhöfen D 61 B4
Ottenschlag A 63 B6
Ottensheim A 63 B5
Otter Ferry GB 24 B2
Otterbach D 60 A3
Otterbäcken S 35 D6
Otterberg D 60 A3
Otterburn GB 25 C5
Otterndorf D 43 B5
Ottersburg D 43 B6
Ottersweier D 61 B4
Otterup DK 39 D3
Ottery St. Mary GB 29 C4
Ottignies B 49 C5
Ottmarsheim F 60 C3
Ottobeuren D 61 C6
Öttömös H 75 B4
Ottone I 80 B3
Ottsjö S 115 D10
Ottweiler D 60 A3
Ötvöskónyi H 74 B2
Otwock PL 55 A6
Ouanne F 59 C4
Ouarville F 58 B2
Oucques F 58 C2
Oud-Beijerland NL 49 B5
Oud Gastel NL 49 B5
Ouddorp NL 49 B4
Oude-Pekela NL 43 B4
Oude-Tonge NL 49 B5
Oudemirdum NL 42 C2
Oudenaarde B 49 C4
Oudenbosch NL 49 B5
Oudenburg B 48 B3
Oudewater NL 49 A5
Oudon F 66 A3
Oughterard IRL 20 A2
Ouguela P 93 B3
Ouistreham F 57 A5
Oulainen FIN 3 D26
Oulchy-le-Château F 59 A4
Oullins F 69 C4
Oulmes F 67 B4
Oulton GB 30 B5
Oulton Broad GB 30 B5
Oulu FIN 3 D26
Oulx I 79 A5
Oundle GB 30 B3
Ouranopoli GR 116 B6
Ourense E 87 B3
Ourique P 98 B2
Ourol E 86 A3
Ouroux-en-Morvan F 68 A3
Ousdale GB 23 C5
Oust F 77 D4
Outakoski FIN 113 C15
Outeiro P 92 A2
Outeiro de Rei E 86 A3
Outes E 86 B2
Outokumpu FIN 3 E28
Outreau F 48 C2
Outwell GB 30 B4
Ouzouer-le-Marché F 58 C2
Ouzouer-sur-Loire F 58 C3
Ovada I 80 B2
Ovar P 87 D2
Ove DK 38 C2
Ovelgönne D 43 B5
Over-jerstal DK 39 D2
Overath D 50 C3
Overbister GB 23 B6
Øverbygd N 112 D8
Overdinkel NL 50 A3
Överenhörna S 37 C4
Överhalla N 114 C8
Overijse B 49 C5
Överkalix S 3 C25
Overlade DK 38 C2
Överlida S 40 B2
Överö FIN 36 B7
Overpelt B 49 B6
Overton GB 26 C3
Övertorneå S 3 C25
Överum S 40 B6
Ovidiopol UA 11 C11
Oviedo E 88 A1
Oviglio I 80 B2
Ovíndoli I 103 A6
Ovodda I 110 B2
Øvre Årdal N 32 A4
Øvre Rendal N 114 F8
Øvre Sirdal N 33 D3
Övre Soppero S 113 D10
Övre Ullerud S 35 C5
Øvrebygd N 33 D3
Ovruch UA 7 F10
Ovtrup DK 39 D1
Owińska PL 46 C2
Oxaback S 40 B2
Oxberg S 34 A6
Oxelösund S 37 D4
Oxenholme GB 26 A3
Oxford GB 31 C2
Oxie S 41 D3
Oxilithos GR 116 D6
Oxted GB 31 C4
Oyaca TR 118 C7
Øye N 32 A5
Øyenkilen N 35 C2
Øyer N 34 A2
Øyeren N 34 B4
Oyfiell N 33 C5
Øygärdslia N 33 D5
Oykel Bridge GB 22 D4
Øymark N 35 C3
Oyonnax F 69 B5
Øyslebø N 33 D4
Øystese N 32 B3
Oyten D 43 B6
Øyuvsbu N 33 C4
Ozaeta E 89 B4
Ozalj HR 73 C5
Ożarów PL 55 C6
Ożarów Maz PL 55 A5
Ožbalt SLO 73 B5
Ózd H 65 B6
Ožďany SK 65 B5
Ozieri I 110 B2
Ozimek PL 54 C3
Ozimica BIH 84 B3
Ozora H 74 B3
Ozorków PL 55 B4
Ozzano Monferrato I 80 A2

P

Paal B 49 B6
Pabianice PL 55 B4
Pacanów PL 55 C6
Paceco I 108 B1
Pachino I 109 C4
Pačir SCG 75 C4
Pack A 73 A5
Paços de Ferreira P 87 C2
Pacov CZ 63 A6
Pacsa H 74 B2
Pacy-sur-Eure F 58 A2
Paczków PL 54 C2
Padany RUS 3 E30
Padborg DK 39 E2
Padej SCG 75 C5
Padene HR 83 B5
Paderborn D 51 B4
Paderne P 98 B2
Padiham GB 26 B3
Padina SCG 75 C5
Padinska Skela SCG 85 B5
Padornelo P 87 C2
Pádova I 72 C1
Padragkút H 74 A2
Padria I 110 B1
Padrón E 86 B2
Padru I 110 B2
Padstow GB 28 C3
Padul E 100 B2
Padula I 104 C1
Paduli I 103 B7
Paesana I 79 B6
Paese I 72 C2
Pag HR 83 B4
Pagani I 103 C7
Pagánica I 103 A6
Pagánico I 81 D5
Paglieta I 103 A7
Pagny-sur-Moselle F 60 B2
Páhi H 75 B4
Pahkakumpu FIN 113 F17
Pahl D 62 C2
Paide EST 7 B8
Paignton GB 29 C4
Pailhès F 77 C4
Paimboeuf F 66 A2
Paimpol F 56 B2
Paimpont F 57 B3
Painswick GB 29 B5
Painten D 62 B2
Paisley GB 24 C3
Pajala S 113 E12
Pajares E 88 A1
Pajares de los Oteros E 88 B1
Pajęczno PL 54 B3
Páka H 74 B1
Pakość PL 47 C4
Pakosławice PL 54 C2
Pakoštane HR 83 C4
Pakrac HR 74 C2
Paks H 74 B3
Palacios de la Sierra E 89 C3
Palaciòs de la Valduerna E 88 B1
Palacios de Sanabria E 87 B4
Palacios del Sil E 86 B4
Palaciosrubios E 94 A1
Palafrugell E 91 B6
Palagiano I 104 C3
Palagonia I 109 B3
Paláia I 81 C4
Palaiseau F 58 B3
Palaj AL 105 A5
Palamas GR 116 C4
Palamós E 91 B6
Palanga LT 6 D6
Palanzano I 81 B4
Palárikovo SK 64 B4
Palas de Rei E 86 B3
Palata I 103 B7
Palatna SCG 85 C6
Palau I 110 A2
Palavas-les-Flots F 78 C2
Palazuelos de la Sierra E 89 B3
Palazzo Adriano I 108 B2
Palazzo del Pero I 81 C5
Palazzo San Gervásio I 104 C1
Palazzolo Acréide I 109 B3
Palazzolo sull Oglio I 71 C4
Palazzuolo sul Senio I 81 B5
Paldiski EST 6 B8
Pale BIH 84 C3
Palekastro GR 117 G8
Palena I 103 B7
Palencia E 88 B2
Palenciana E 100 B1
Paleochora GR 117 G5
Paleometokho CY 120 A2
Palermo I 108 A2
Paleros GR 116 D2
Palestrina I 102 B5
Pálfa H 74 B3
Palfau A 63 C5
Palhaça P 92 A2
Palheiros da Tocha P 92 A2
Palheiros de Quiaios P 92 A2
Paliaopoli GR 117 E6
Palić SCG 75 B4
Palidoro I 102 B5
Palinuro I 106 A2
Paliouri GR 116 C5
Paliseul B 59 A6
Pallanza I 70 C3
Pallares E 99 A4
Pallaruelo de Monegros E 90 B2
Pallas Green IRL 20 B3
Pallerols E 91 A4
Palling D 62 B3
Palluau F 66 B3
Palma P 92 C2
Palma Campánia I 103 C7
Palma de Mallorca E 97 B2
Palma del Río E 99 B5
Palma di Montechiaro I 108 B2
Palma Nova E 97 B2
Palmádula I 110 B1
Palmanova I 72 C3
Palmela P 92 C2
Palmerola E 91 A5
Palmi I 106 C2
Pálmonostora H 75 B4
Palo del Colle I 104 B2
Palojärvi FIN 113 D12
Palojoensuu FIN 113 D12
Palomares E 101 B4
Palomares del Campo E 95 C4
Palomas E 93 C4
Palombara Sabina I 102 A5
Palos de la Frontera E 99 B4
Palotabozsok H 74 B3
Palotás H 65 C5
Pals E 91 B6
Pålsboda S 37 C2
Paluzza I 72 B3
Pamhagen A 64 C2
Pamiers F 77 C4
Pamiętowo PL 46 B3
Pampaneira E 100 C2
Pamparato I 80 B1
Pampilhosa, *Aveiro* P 92 A2
Pampilhosa, *Coimbra* P 92 A3
Pampliega E 88 B3
Pamplona E 76 D1
Pampow D 44 B3
Pamukçu TR 118 C2
Pamukkale TR 119 E4
Pamukova TR 118 B5
Panagyurishte BG 11 E8
Pancalieri I 80 B1
Pančevo SCG 85 B5
Pancey F 59 B6
Pancorvo E 89 B3
Pancrudo E 90 C1
Pandino I 71 C4
Pandrup DK 38 B2
Panenský-Týnec CZ 53 C3
Panes E 88 A2
Panevėžys LT 6 D8
Pangbourne GB 31 C2
Panissières F 69 C4
Panki PL 54 C3
Pannes F 58 B3
Panningen NL 50 B1
Pannonhalma H 74 A2
Pano Lefkara CY 120 B2
Pano Panayia CY 120 B1
Panormos GR 117 E7
Panschwitz-Kuckau D 53 B4
Pansdorf D 44 B2
Pantano de Cíjara E 94 C2
Pantelleria I 108 C1
Panticosa E 76 D2
Pantín E 86 A2
Pantoja E 94 B3
Pantón E 86 B3
Panxon E 87 B2
Páola I 106 B3
Paola M 107 C5
Pápa H 74 A2
Papasídero I 106 B2
Pápateszér H 74 A2
Papenburg D 43 B4
Paphos CY 120 B1
Pappenheim D 62 B1
Paprotnia PL 55 A5
Parábita I 107 A5
Paraćin SCG 85 C6
Parád H 65 C6
Parada, *Bragança* P 87 C4
Parada, *Viseu* P 92 A2
Paradas E 99 B5
Paradela E 86 B3
Parades de Rubiales E 94 A1
Paradinas de San Juan E 94 B1
Paradiso di Cevadale I 71 B5
Paradyż PL 55 B5
Parainen FIN 6 A7
Parakhino Paddubye RUS 7 B12
Parakka S 113 E10
Paralimni CY 120 A2
Parallo Astros GR 117 E4
Paramé F 57 B4
Paramithia GR 116 C2
Páramo E 86 A4
Páramo del Sil E 86 B4
Parandaça P 87 C3
Paravadella E 86 A3
Paray-le-Monial F 68 B4
Parceiros P 92 B2
Parcey F 69 A5
Parchim D 44 B3
Parcice PL 54 B3
Pardilla E 88 C3
Pardubice CZ 53 C5
Paredes E 95 B4
Paredes P 87 C2
Paredes de Coura P 87 C2
Paredes de Nava E 88 B2
Paredes de Siguenza E 95 A4
Pareja E 95 B4
Parennes F 57 B5
Parenti I 106 B3
Parentis-en-Born F 76 B1
Parey D 44 C3
Parfino RUS 7 C11
Parga GR 116 C2
Pargny-sur-Saulx F 59 B5
Pari-Gagné F 69 B4
Parigné-l'Évêque F 58 C1
Parikkala FIN 3 F28
Paris F 58 B3
Parisot F 77 B4
Parkalompolo S 113 E11
Parkano FIN 3 E25
Parknasilla IRL 20 C2
Parla E 94 B3
Parlavà E 91 A6
Parma I 81 B4
Parndorf A 64 C2
Párnica SK 65 A5
Parnu EST 6 B8
Parolis E 101 A3
Paros GR 117 E7
Parrillas E 94 B1
Parsberg D 62 A2
Parstein D 45 C6
Partakko FIN 113 C16
Partanna I 108 B1
Parthenay F 67 B4
Partinico I 108 A2
Partizani SCG 85 B5
Partizánske SK 65 B4
Partney GB 27 B6
Påryd S 40 C5
Parysów PL 55 B6
Parzymiechy PL 54 B3
Paşcani RO 11 C9
Pasewalk D 45 B5
Pašina Voda SCG 85 C4
Påskallavik S 40 B6
Pasłęk PL 47 A5
Pašman HR 83 C4
Passage East IRL 21 B5
Passage West IRL 20 C3
Passail A 73 A5
Passais F 57 B5
Passau D 63 B4
Passegueiro P 92 A2
Passignano sul Trasimeno I 82 C1
Passo di Tréia I 82 C2
Passopisciaro I 109 B4
Passow D 45 B6
Passy F 70 C1
Pastavy BY 7 D9
Pástena I 103 B7
Pastrana E 95 B4
Pastrengo I 71 C5
Pasym PL 47 B6
Pásztó H 65 C5
Pata SK 64 B3
Patay F 58 B2
Pateley Bridge GB 27 A4
Paterek PL 46 B3
Paterna E 96 B2
Paterna de Rivera E 99 C5
Paterna del Campo E 99 B4
Paterna del Madera E 101 A3
Paternion A 72 B3
Paternò I 109 B3
Paternópoli I 103 C8
Patersdorf D 62 A3
Patersdwolde NL 42 B3
Patitiri GR 116 C5
Patmos GR 119 E1
Patna GB 24 C3
Patnow PL 54 A3
Patoniva FIN 113 C16
Patopirtti FIN 113 E18
Patos AL 105 C5
Patra = Patras GR 117 D3
Patras = Patra GR 117 D3
Patreksfjörður IS 111 B2
Patrickswell IRL 20 B3
Patrimonio F 102 A2
Patrington GB 27 B5
Pattada I 110 B2
Pattensen, *Niedersachsen* D 44 B2
Pattensen, *Niedersachsen* D 51 A5
Patterdale GB 26 A3
Patti I 109 A3
Páty H 74 A3
Pau F 76 C2
Pauillac F 66 C4
Paularo I 72 B3
Paulhaguet F 68 C3
Paulhan F 78 C2
Paulilátino I 110 B1
Paulström S 40 B5
Paullo I 71 C4
Paulstown IRL 21 B4
Pausa D 52 C1
Pauträsk S 115 C14
Pavia I 71 C4
Pavia P 92 C2
Pavias E 96 B2
Pavilly F 58 A1
Pāvilosta LV 6 C6
Pavino Polje SCG 85 C4
Pavullo nel Frignano I 81 B4
Pawłowice, *Opolskie* PL 54 B2
Pawlowice, *Śląskie* PL 54 D3
Paxi GR 116 C2
Payallar TR 119 F6
Payerne CH 70 B1
Paymogo E 98 B3
Payrac F 77 B4
Pazardzhik BG 11 E8
Pazaryeri TR 118 B4
Pazin HR 72 C3
Paziols F 78 D1
Pčelić HR 74 C2
Peal de Becerro E 100 B2
Peasmarsh GB 31 D4
Peć SCG 85 D5
Péccioli I 81 C4
Pécel H 75 A4
Pechao P 98 B3
Pechenga RUS 3 B29
Pechenizhyn UA 11 B8
Pecica RO 75 B6
Pećinci SCG 85 B4
Pecka SCG 85 B4
Peckelsheim D 51 B5
Pečory RUS 7 C9
Pécs H 74 B3
Pécsvárad H 74 B3
Pečurice SCG 105 A5
Peczniew PL 54 B3
Pedaso I 82 C2
Pedavena I 72 B1
Pedérobba I 72 C1
Pedersker DK 41 D4
Pedescala I 71 C6
Pedrafita E 86 B3
Pedrajas de San Esteban E 88 C2
Pedralba E 96 B2
Pedralba de la Praderia E 87 B4
Pedraza E 94 A3

Pedreguer E 96 C3
Pedrera E 100 B1
Pedro Abad E 100 B1
Pedro Bernardo E 94 B2
Pedro-Martinez E 100 B2
Pedro Muñoz E 95 C4
Pedroche E 100 A1
Pedrógão, *Beja* P 98 A3
Pedrogao, *Castelo Branco* P 92 A3
Pedrógão, *Leiria* P 92 B2
Pedrógão Grande P 92 B2
Pedrola E 90 B1
Pedrosa de Tobalina E 89 B3
Pedrosa del Rey E 88 C1
Pedrosa del Rio Urbel E 88 B3
Pedrosillo de los Aires E 94 B1
Pedrosillo el Ralo E 94 A1
Pędzewo PL 47 B4
Peebles GB 25 C4
Peel GB 26 A1
Peenemünde D 45 A5
Peer B 49 B6
Pega P 93 A3
Pegalajar E 100 B2
Pegau D 52 B2
Peggau A 73 A5
Pegli I 80 B2
Pegnitz D 62 A2
Pego E 96 C2
Pegões-Estação P 92 C2
Pegões Velhos P 92 C2
Pęgów PL 54 B1
Pegswood GB 25 C6
Peguera E 97 B2
Pehlivanköy TR 118 A1
Peine D 51 A6
Peisey-Nancroix F 70 C1
Peissenberg D 62 C2
Peiting D 62 C1
Peitz D 53 B4
Péjo I 71 B5
Pelagićevo BIH 84 B3
Pelahustán E 94 B2
Pełczyce PL 46 B1
Pelhřimov CZ 63 A6
Pélissanne F 79 C4
Pelkosenniemi FIN 113 E16
Pellegrino Parmense I 81 B3
Pellegrue F 76 B3
Pellérd H 74 B3
Pellestrina I 72 C2
Pellevoisin F 67 B6
Pellizzano I 71 B5
Pello FIN 113 F13
Pello S 113 F12
Peloche E 93 B5
Pelplin PL 47 B4
Pelussin F 69 C4
Pély H 75 A5
Pembroke GB 28 B3
Pembroke Dock GB 28 B3
Peña de Cabra E 94 B1
Peñacerrada E 89 B4
Penacova P 92 A2
Peñafiel E 88 C2
Penafiel P 87 C2
Peñaflor E 99 B5
Peñalba de Santiago E 86 B4
Peñalsordo E 93 C5
Penalva do Castelo P 92 A3
Penamacôr P 93 A3
Peñaparda E 93 A4
Peñaranda de Bracamonte E 94 B1
Peñaranda de Duero E 89 C3
Peñarroya de Tastavins E 90 C3
Peñarroya-Pueblonuevo E 93 C5
Peñarrubla E 86 B3
Penarth GB 29 B4
Peñas de San Pedro E 101 A4
Peñascosa E 101 A3
Peñausende E 88 C1
Penc H 65 C5
Pencoed GB 29 B4
Pendalofos GR 116 B3
Pendeen GB 28 C2
Pendine GB 28 B3
Pendueles E 88 A2
Penedono P 87 D3
Penela P 92 A2
Penhas Juntas P 87 C3
Peniche P 92 B1
Penicuik GB 25 C4
Penig D 52 C2
Penilhos P 98 B3
Peñíscola E 90 C3
Penistone GB 27 B4
Penkridge GB 26 C3
Penkun D 45 B6
Penmarch F 56 C1
Pennabilli I 82 C1
Penne I 103 A6
Penne-d'Agenais F 77 B3
Pennes I 71 B6
Pennyghael GB 24 B1
Peno RUS 7 C12
Penpont GB 25 C4
Penrhyndeudraeth GB 26 C1
Penrith GB 26 A3
Penryn GB 28 C2
Pentraeth GB 26 B1
Penybontfawr GB 26 C2
Penygroes, *Carmarthenshire* GB 28 B3
Penygroes, *Gwynedd* GB 26 B1
Penzance GB 28 C2
Penzberg D 62 C2
Penzlin D 45 B5
Pepeljevac SCG 85 C6
Pepinster B 50 C1
Peqin AL 105 B5
Pér H 64 C3
Pera Boa P 92 A3
Perachora GR 117 D4
Perafita P 87 C2
Peraleda de la Mata E 93 B5
Peraleda de San Román E 93 B5
Peraleda del Zaucejo E 93 C5
Perales de Alfambra E 90 C1
Perales de Tajuña E 95 B3
Perales del Puerto E 93 A4
Peralta E 89 B5
Peralta de la Sal E 90 B3
Peralva P 98 B3
Peralveche E 95 B4
Perama GR 117 G6
Perast SCG 105 A4
Perbál H 65 C4
Perchtoldsdorf A 64 B2
Percy F 57 B4
Perdasdefogu I 110 C2
Perdiguera E 90 B2
Peredo P 87 C4
Peregu Mare RO 75 B5
Pereiro, *Faro* P 98 B3
Pereiro, *Guarda* P 87 D3
Pereiro, *Santarém* P 92 B2
Pereiro de Aguiar E 87 B3
Perelada E 91 A6
Perelejos de las Truchas E 95 B5
Pereña E 87 C4
Pereruela E 88 C1
Pereyaslav-Khmelnytskyy UA 11 A11
Pérfugas I 110 B1
Perg A 63 B5
Pérgine Valsugana I 71 B6
Pérgola I 82 C1
Pergusa I 109 B3
Periam RO 75 B5
Periana E 100 C1
Périers F 57 A4
Périgueux F 67 C5
Perino I 80 B3
Perjasica HR 73 C5
Perkáta H 74 A3
Perković HR 83 C5
Perleberg D 44 B3
Perlez SCG 75 C5
Përmet AL 116 B2
Pernarec CZ 62 A4
Pernek SK 64 B3
Pernes P 92 B2
Pernes-les-Fontaines F 79 B4
Pernik BG 11 E7
Pernink CZ 52 C2
Pernitz A 64 C1
Pero Pinheiro P 92 C1
Peroguarda P 98 A2
Pérols F 78 C2
Péronne F 59 A3
Péronnes B 49 C5
Perorrubio E 94 A3
Perosa Argentina I 79 B6
Perozinho P 87 C2
Perpignan F 91 A5
Perranporth GB 28 C2
Perranzabuloe GB 28 C2
Perrecy-les-Forges F 69 B4
Perrero I 79 B6
Perrignier F 69 B6
Perros-Guirec F 56 B2
Persan F 58 A3
Persberg S 34 C6
Persenbeug A 63 B6
Pershore GB 29 A5
Perstorp S 41 C3
Perth GB 25 B4
Pertisau A 72 A1
Pertoča SLO 73 B6
Pertuis F 79 C4
Perućac SCG 85 C4
Perúgia I 82 C1
Perušić HR 83 B4
Péruwelz B 49 C4
Pervomaysk UA 11 B11
Perwez B 49 C5
Pesadas de Burgos E 89 B3
Pesaguero E 88 A2
Pésaro I 82 C1
Pescantina I 71 C5
Pescara I 103 A7
Pescasséroli I 103 B6
Peschici I 104 B2
Peschiera del Garda I 71 C5
Péscia I 81 C4
Pescina I 103 A6
Pesco Sannita I 103 B7
Pescocostanzo I 103 B7
Pescopagano I 103 C8
Peshkopi AL 116 A2
Pesmes F 69 A5
Pesnica SLO 73 B5
Peso da Régua P 87 C3
Pesquera de Duero E 88 C2
Pessac F 76 B2
Pestovo RUS 7 B13
Petalidi GR 117 F3
Pétange L 60 A1
Petas GR 116 C3
Peteranec HR 74 B1
Peterborough GB 30 B3
Peterculter GB 23 D6
Peterhead GB 23 D7
Peterlee GB 25 D6
Petersfield GB 31 C3
Petershagen, *Brandenburg* D 45 C5
Petershagen, *Brandenburg* D 45 C6
Petershagen, *Nordrhein-Westfalen* D 43 C5
Petershausen D 62 B2
Peterswell IRL 20 A3
Pétervására H 65 B6
Petília Policastro I 107 B3
Petín E 87 B3
Pětipsy CZ 52 C3
Petkus D 52 B3
Petlovac HR 74 C3
Petlovača SCG 85 B4
Petőfiszallás H 75 B4
Petra E 97 B3
Petralia Sottana I 109 B3
Petrčane HR 83 B4
Petrelë AL 105 B5
Petrella Tifernina I 103 B7
Petrer E 101 A5
Petreto-Bicchisano F 102 B1
Petrich BG 116 A5
Petrijevci HR 74 C3
Petrinja HR 73 C6
Petrodvorets RUS 7 B10
Pétrola E 101 A4
Petronà I 107 B3
Petronell A 64 B2
Petroşani RO 11 D7
Petrovac, *Crna Gora* SCG 105 A4
Petrovac, *Serbia* SCG 85 B6
Petrovaradin SCG 75 C4
Petrovice BIH 84 B3
Petrovice CZ 53 C3
Pettenbach A 63 C5
Pettigo IRL 19 B4
Petworth GB 31 D3
Peuerbach A 63 B4
Peuntenansa E 88 A2
Peurasuvanto FIN 113 E15
Pevensey Bay GB 31 D4
Peveragno I 80 B1
Pewsey GB 29 B6
Pewsum D 43 B4
Peyrat-le-Château F 68 C1
Peyrehorade F 76 C1
Peyriac-Minervois F 77 C5
Peyrins F 79 A4
Peyrissac F 67 C6
Peyrolles-en-Provence F 79 C4
Peyruis F 79 B4
Pézarches F 59 B3
Pézenas F 78 C2
Pezinok SK 64 B3
Pezuls F 77 B3
Pfaffenhausen D 61 B6
Pfaffenhofen, *Bayern* D 61 B6
Pfaffenhofen, *Bayern* D 62 B2
Pfaffenhoffen F 60 B3
Pfäffikon CH 70 A3
Pfarrkirchen D 62 B3
Pfeffenhausen D 62 B2
Pfetterhouse F 70 A2
Pforzheim D 61 B4
Pfreimd D 62 A3
Pfronten D 61 C6
Pfullendorf D 61 C5
Pfullingen D 61 B5
Pfunds A 71 B5
Pfungstadt D 61 A4
Pfyn CH 61 C4
Phalsbourg F 60 B3
Philippeville B 49 C5
Philippsreut D 63 B4
Philippsthal D 51 C5
Piacenza I 81 A3
Piacenza d'Adige I 72 C1
Piádena I 71 C5
Piana F 102 A1
Piana Crixia I 80 B2
Piana degli Albanesi I 108 B2
Piana di Monte Verna I 103 B7
Piancastagnáio I 81 D5
Piandelagotti I 81 B4
Pianella, *Abruzzi* I 103 A7
Pianella, *Toscana* I 81 C5
Pianello Val Tidone I 80 B3
Piano I 80 B2
Pianoro I 81 B5
Pians A 71 A5
Pías E 87 B4
Pias P 98 A3
Piaseczno PL 55 A6
Piasek PL 45 C6
Piaski PL 47 A5
Piastów PL 55 A5
Piaszcyna PL 46 A3
Piątek PL 55 A4
Piatra Neamţ RO 11 C9
Piazza al Sérchio I 81 B4
Piazza Armerina I 109 B3
Piazza Brembana I 71 C4
Piazze I 81 D5
Piazzola sul Brenta I 72 C1
Picassent E 96 B2
Piccione I 82 C1
Picerno I 104 C1
Picher D 44 B3
Pickering GB 27 A5
Pico I 103 B6
Picón E 94 C2
Picquigny F 58 A3
Piechowice PL 53 C5
Piecnik PL 46 B2
Piedicavallo I 70 C2
Piedicroce F 102 A2
Piedimonte Etneo I 109 B4
Piedimonte Matese I 103 B7
Piedimulera I 70 B3
Piedipaterno I 82 D1
Piedrabuena E 94 C2
Piedraescrita E 94 C2
Piedrafita E 88 A1
Piedrahita E 93 A5
Piedralaves E 94 B2
Piedras Albas E 93 B4
Piedras Blancas E 88 A1
Piegaro I 82 D1
Piekary Śl. PL 54 C3
Piekoszów PL 55 C5
Pieksämäki FIN 3 E27
Pielenhofen D 62 A2
Pielgrzymka PL 53 B5
Pieniężno PL 47 A6
Pieńsk PL 53 B5
Pienza I 81 C5
Piera E 91 B4
Pieranie PL 47 C4
Pierowall GB 23 B6
Pierre-Buffière F 67 C6
Pierre-de-Bresse F 69 B5
Pierrecourt F 60 C1
Pierrefeu-du-Var F 79 C5
Pierrefitte-Nestalas F 76 D2
Pierrefitte-sur-Aire F 59 B6
Pierrefonds F 59 A3
Pierrefontaine-les-Varans F 69 A6
Pierrefort F 78 B1
Pierrelatte F 78 B3
Pierrepont, *Aisne* F 59 A4
Pierrepont, *Meurthe-et-Moselle* F 60 A1
Piesendorf A 72 A2
Pieštany SK 64 B3
Pieszkowo PL 47 A6
Pieszyce PL 54 C1
Pietarsaari FIN 3 E25
Pietra Ligure I 80 B2
Pietragalla I 104 C1
Pietralunga I 82 C1
Pietramelara I 103 B7
Pietraperzia I 109 B3
Pietrasanta I 81 C4
Pietravairano I 103 B7
Pieve del Cáiro I 80 A2
Pieve di Bono I 71 C5
Pieve di Cadore I 72 B2
Pieve di Cento I 81 B5
Pieve di Soligo I 72 C2
Pieve di Teco I 80 B1
Pieve Santo Stefano I 82 C1
Pieve Torina I 82 C2
Pievepélago I 81 B4
Piges GR 116 C3
Píglio I 102 B6
Pigna I 80 C1
Pignan F 78 C2
Pignataro Maggiore I 103 B7
Pijnacker NL 49 A5
Pikalevo RUS 7 B13
Piła PL 46 B2
Pilar de la Horadada E 101 B5
Pilas E 99 B4
Pilastri I 81 B5
Piława PL 55 B6
Piława Górna PL 54 C1
Piławki PL 47 B5
Pilchowice PL 54 C3
Pilea GR 116 B5
Pilgrimstad S 115 E12
Pili, *Dodekanisa* GR 119 F2
Pili, *Trikala* GR 116 C3
Pilica PL 55 C4
Pilis H 75 A4
Piliscaba H 65 C4
Pilisszántó H 65 C4
Pilisvörösvár H 65 C4
Pilos GR 117 F3
Pilsting D 62 B3
Pilszcz PL 54 C2
Pilterud N 34 C2
Pilu RO 75 B6
Pilzno PL 55 D6
Pina de Ebro E 90 B2
Piñar E 100 B2
Pınarbaşı TR 118 C1
Pınarhisar TR 118 A2
Pinas F 77 C3
Pincehely H 74 B3
Pinchbeck GB 30 B3
Pińczów PL 55 C5
Pineda de la Sierra E 89 B3
Pineda de Mar E 91 B5
Pinerella I 82 B1
Pinerolo I 79 B6
Pineta Grande I 103 C6
Pineto I 103 A7
Piney F 59 B5
Pinggau A 73 A6
Pinhal Novo P 92 C2
Pinhão P 87 C3
Pinheiro, *Aveiro* P 87 C2
Pinheiro, *Aveiro* P 87 D2
Pinheiro Grande P 92 B2
Pinhel P 87 D3
Pinhoe GB 29 C4
Pinilla E 101 A4
Pinilla de Toro E 88 C1
Pinkafeld A 73 A6
Pinneberg D 43 B6
Pinnow D 53 B4
Pino F 102 A2
Pino de Val E 86 B2
Pino del Rio E 88 B2
Pinofranqueado E 93 A4
Pinols F 78 A2
Piñor E 86 B2
Pinos del Valle E 100 C2
Pinos Puente E 100 B2
Pinoso E 101 A4
Pinsk BY 7 E9
Pinto E 94 B3
Pinzano al Tagliamento I 72 B2
Pinzio P 93 A3
Pinzolo I 71 B5
Pióbbico I 82 C1
Piombino I 81 D4
Pionki PL 55 B6
Pionsat F 68 B2
Pióraco I 82 C1
Piornal E 93 A5
Piotrków-Kujawski PL 47 C4
Piotrków Trybunalski PL 55 B4
Piotrkowice PL 55 C5
Piotrowice PL 55 A6
Piotrowo PL 46 C2
Piove di Sacco I 72 C2
Piovene I 71 C6
Piperskärr S 40 B6
Pipriac F 57 C4
Piraeus = Pireas GR 117 E5
Piran SLO 72 C3
Piré-sur-Seiche F 57 B4
Pireas = Piraeus GR 117 E5
Pirgi GR 117 D7
Pirgos, *Ilia* GR 117 E3
Pirgos, *Kriti* GR 117 G7
Piriac-sur-Mer F 66 A2
Piringsdorf A 73 A6
Pirmasens D 60 A3
Pirna D 53 C3
Pirnmill GB 24 C2
Pirot SCG 11 E7
Pirovac HR 83 C4
Pirttivuopio S 112 E8
Pisa I 81 C4
Pisany F 66 C4
Pisarovina HR 73 C5
Pischelsdorf in der Steiermark A 73 A5
Pişchia RO 75 C6
Pisciotta I 106 A2
Písek CZ 63 A5
Pisogne I 71 C5
Pissos F 76 B2
Pissouri CY 120 B1
Pisticci I 104 C2
Pistóia I 81 C4
Piteå S 3 D24
Piteşti RO 11 D8
Pithiviers F 58 B3
Pitigliano I 102 A4
Pitkyaranta RUS 3 F29
Pitlochry GB 25 B4
Pitomača HR 74 C2
Pitres E 100 C2
Pittentrail GB 23 D4
Pitvaros H 75 B5
Pivka SLO 73 C4
Pivnice SCG 75 C4
Piwniczna PL 65 A6
Pizarra E 100 C1
Pizzano I 71 B5
Pizzighettone I 71 C4
Pizzo I 106 C3
Pízzoli I 103 A6
Pizzolungo I 108 A1
Pjätteryd S 40 C4
Plabennec F 56 B1
Placencia E 89 A4
Plaffeien CH 70 B2
Plaisance, *Gers* F 76 C3
Plaisance, *Haute-Garonne* F 77 C4
Plaisance, *Tarn* F 77 C5
Plaka GR 116 C7
Plan E 90 A3
Plan-de-Baix F 79 B4
Plan-d'Orgon F 78 C3
Planá CZ 62 A3
Planá nad Lužnici CZ 63 A5
Plaňany CZ 53 C5
Planchez F 68 A4
Plancoët F 57 B3
Plancy-l'Abbaye F 59 B4
Plandište SCG 75 C6
Plánice CZ 63 A4
Planina SLO 73 B5
Planina SLO 73 C4
Plankenfels D 62 A2
Plasencia E 93 A4
Plasenzuela E 93 B4
Plaški HR 83 A4
Plassen, *Buskerud* N 32 B4
Plassen, *Hedmark* N 34 A4
Plášť'ovce SK 65 B5
Plasy CZ 63 A4
Plat HR 84 D3
Platamona Lido I 110 B1
Platania I 106 B3
Platanos GR 117 G5
Platí I 106 C3
Platičevo SCG 85 B4
Platja d'Aro E 91 B6
Plattling D 62 B3
Plau D 44 B4
Plaue, *Brandenburg* D 44 C4
Plaue, *Thüringen* D 51 C6
Plauen D 52 C2
Plav SCG 85 D4
Plavecký Mikuláš SK 64 B3
Plavinas LV 7 C8
Plavna SCG 75 C4
Plavnica SK 65 A6
Plavno HR 83 B5
Plavsk RUS 7 E14
Playben F 56 B2
Pléaux F 68 C2
Pleine-Fourgères F 57 B4
Pleinfeld D 62 A1
Pleinting D 62 B4
Plélan-le-Grand F 57 C3
Plémet F 56 B3
Pléneuf-Val-André F 56 B3
Plentzia E 89 A4
Plérin F 56 B3
Plešivec SK 65 B6
Plessa D 52 B3
Plessé F 66 A3
Plestin-les-Grèves F 56 B2
Pleszew PL 54 B2
Pleternica HR 74 C2
Plettenberg D 50 B3
Pleubian F 56 B2
Pleumartin F 67 B5
Pleumeur-Bodou F 56 B2
Pleurs F 59 B4
Pleven BG 11 E8
Plevlja SCG 85 C4
Plevnik-Drienové SK 65 A4
Pleyber-Christ F 56 B2
Pliego E 101 B4
Pliešovce SK 65 B5
Plitvička Jezera HR 83 B4
Plitvički Ljeskovac HR 83 B4
Ploaghe I 110 B1
Ploče HR 84 C2
Plochingen D 61 B5
Płock PL 47 C5
Ploemeur F 56 C2
Ploërmel F 56 C3
Plœuc-sur-Lie F 56 B3
Plogastel St. Germain F 56 C1
Plogoff F 56 B1
Ploieşti RO 11 D9
Plomari GR 118 D1
Plombières-les-Bains F 60 C2
Plomin HR 82 A3
Plön D 44 A2
Plonéour-Lanvern F 56 C1
Płonia PL 45 B6
Płońsk PL 47 C6
Płoskinia PL 47 A5
Plössberg D 62 A3
Płoty PL 45 B7
Plouagat F 56 B2
Plouaret F 56 B2
Plouarzel F 56 B1
Plouay F 56 C2
Ploubalay F 57 B3
Ploubazlanec F 56 B2
Ploudalmézeau F 56 B1
Ploudiry F 56 B1
Plouescat F 56 B1
Plouézec F 56 B3
Plougasnou F 56 B2
Plougastel-Daoulas F 56 B1
Plougonven F 56 B2
Plougonver F 56 B2
Plougrescant F 56 B2
Plouguenast F 56 B3
Plouguerneau F 56 B1
Plouha F 56 B3
Plouhinec F 56 B1
Plouigneau F 56 B2
Ploumanach F 56 B2
Plounévez-Quintin F 56 B2
Plouray F 56 B2
Plouzévédé F 56 B1
Plovdiv BG 11 E8
Plozévet F 56 C1
Plumbridge GB 19 B4
Pluméliau F 56 C3
Plumlov CZ 64 A3
Plungė LT 6 D6
Pluty PL 47 A6
Pluvigner F 56 C3
Plužine BIH 84 C3
Plužine SCG 84 C3
Płużnica PL 47 B4
Plymouth GB 28 C3
Plymstock GB 28 C3
Płytnica PL 46 B2
Plyusa RUS 7 B10
Plzeň CZ 63 A4
Pniewy PL 46 C2
Pobes E 89 B4
Poběžovice CZ 62 A3
Pobiedziska PL 46 C3
Pobierowo PL 45 A6
Pobla de Segur E 90 A3
Pobla-Tornesa E 96 A3
Pobladura del Valle E 88 B1
Pobra de Trives E 87 B3
Pobra do Brollón E 86 B3
Pobra do Caramiñal E 86 B2
Pobudje BIH 85 B4
Počátky CZ 63 A6
Poceirão P 92 C2
Pochep RUS 7 E12
Pochinok RUS 7 D12
Pöchlarn A 63 B6
Pociecha PL 55 B5
Pockau D 52 C3
Pocking D 63 B4
Pocklington GB 27 B5
Poda SCG 85 D4
Podbořany CZ 52 C3
Podbrdo SLO 72 B3
Podbrezová SK 65 B5
Podčetrtek SLO 73 B5
Poddębice PL 54 B3
Poděbrady CZ 53 C5
Podence P 87 C4
Podensac F 76 B2
Podenzano I 80 B3
Podersdorf am See A 64 C2
Podgaje PL 46 B2
Podgora HR 84 C2
Podgóra PL 55 B6
Podgorač HR 74 C3
Podgorica SCG 105 A5
Podgorie AL 116 B2
Podgrad SLO 73 C4
Podhájska SK 65 B4
Podkova BG 116 A7
Podlapača HR 83 B4
Podlejki PL 47 B6
Podlužany SK 65 B4
Podnovlje BIH 84 B3
Podolie SK 64 B3
Podolínec SK 65 A6
Podolsk RUS 7 D14
Podporozhy RUS 7 A13
Podromanija BIH 84 C3
Podturen HR 74 B1
Podujevo SCG 85 D6
Podvín CZ 64 B2
Podwilk PL 65 A5
Poetto I 110 C2
Poggendorf D 45 A5
Poggiardo I 107 A5
Poggibonsi I 81 C5
Póggio a Caiano I 81 C5
Poggio Imperiale I 103 B8
Póggio Mirteto I 102 A5
Póggio Moiano I 102 A5
Póggio Renatico I 81 B5
Póggio Rusco I 81 B5
Pöggstall A 63 B6
Pogny F 59 B5
Pogorzela PL 54 B2
Pogorzelice PL 46 A3
Pogradec AL 116 B2
Pogrodzie PL 47 A5
Pohorelá SK 65 B6
Pohořelice CZ 64 B2
Pohronská Polhora SK 65 B5
Poiares P 92 A2
Poio E 86 B2
Poirino I 80 B1
Poisson F 68 B4
Poissons F 59 B6
Poissy F 58 B3
Poitiers F 67 B5
Poix-de-Picardie F 58 A2
Poix-Terron F 59 A5
Pokka FIN 113 D14
Pokój PL 54 C2
Pokupsko HR 73 C5
Pol E 86 A3
Pol a Charra GB 22 D1
Pola RUS 7 C11
Pola de Allande E 86 A4
Pola de Laviana E 88 A1
Pola de Lena E 88 A1
Pola de Siero E 88 A1
Pola de Somiedo E 86 A4
Polaincourt-et-Clairefontaine F 60 C2
Połajewo PL 46 C2
Polán E 94 C2
Polanica-Zdrój PL 54 C1
Połaniec PL 55 C6
Polanów PL 46 A2
Polatlı TR 118 C7
Polatsk BY 7 D10
Polch D 50 C3
Polczno PL 46 A3
Połczyn-Zdrój PL 46 B2
Polegate GB 31 D4
Poleñino E 90 B2
Polesella I 81 B5
Polessk RUS 6 D6
Polgárdi H 74 A3
Polhov Gradec SLO 73 B4
Police PL 45 B6
Police nad Metují CZ 53 C6
Polichnitos GR 116 C8
Polička CZ 64 A2
Poličnik HR 83 B4
Policoro I 106 A3
Policzna PL 55 B6
Poligiros GR 116 B5
Polignano a Mare I 104 C3
Poligny F 69 B5
Polis CY 120 A1
Polistena I 106 C3
Polizzi Generosa I 109 B3
Poljana SCG 85 B6
Poljanák HR 83 B4
Poljčane SLO 73 B5
Polje BIH 84 B2
Poljice BIH 83 B5
Poljice BIH 84 B3
Poljna SCG 85 C6
Polkowice PL 53 B6
Polla I 104 C1
Pollas E 88 C1
Pöllau A 73 A5
Polleben D 52 B1
Pollença E 97 B3
Pollenfeld D 62 B2
Pollfoss N 114 F4
Póllica I 106 A2
Polminhac F 77 B5
Polná CZ 63 A6
Polna RUS 7 B10
Polne PL 46 B2
Polomka SK 65 B5
Polonne UA 11 A9
Polperro GB 28 C3
Polruan GB 28 C3
Pöls A 73 A4
Polska Cerekiew PL 54 C3
Poltár SK 65 B5
Põltsamaa EST 7 B8
Polyarny RUS 3 B30
Polyarnyye Zori RUS 3 C30
Polzela SLO 73 B5
Pomarance I 81 C4
Pomarez F 76 C2
Pomárico I 104 C2
Pomáz H 65 C5
Pombal P 92 B2
Pomeroy GB 19 B5
Pomézia I 102 B5
Pomichna UA 11 B11
Pommard F 69 A4
Pommelsbrunn D 62 A2
Pomonte I 81 D4
Pomorie BG 11 E9
Pomos CY 120 A1
Pompei I 103 C7
Pompey F 60 B2
Pomposa I 82 B1
Poncin F 69 B5
Pondorf D 62 B2
Ponferrada E 86 B4
Pongoma RUS 3 D31
Poniec PL 54 B1
Ponikva SLO 73 B5
Poniky SK 65 B5
Pons F 67 C4
Ponsacco I 81 C4
Pont I 70 C2
Pont-a-Celles B 49 C5
Pont-a-Marcq F 49 C4
Pont-à-Mousson F 60 B2
Pont-Audemer F 58 A1
Pont-Aven F 56 C2
Pont Canavese I 70 C2
Pont-Croix F 56 B1
Pont-d'Ain F 69 B5
Pont-de-Beauvoisin F 69 C5
Pont-de-Buis-lès-Quimerch F 56 B1
Pont-de-Chéruy F 69 C5
Pont de Dore F 68 C3
Pont-de-Labeaume F 78 B3
Pont-de-l'Arche F 58 A2
Pont de Molins E 91 A5
Pont-de-Roide F 70 A1
Pont-de-Salars F 78 B1
Pont de Suert E 90 A3
Pont-de-Vaux F 69 B4
Pont-de-Veyle F 69 B4
Pont d'Espagne F 76 D2
Pont d'Ouilly F 57 B5
Pont-du-Château F 68 C3
Pont-du-Navoy F 69 B5
Pont-en-Royans F 79 A4
Pont Farcy F 57 B4
Pont-l'Abbé F 56 C1
Pont-l'Évêque F 57 A6
Pont-Remy F 48 C2
Pont-St. Esprit F 78 B3
Pont-St. Mamet F 77 B3
Pont-St. Martin F 66 A3
Pont-St. Martin I 70 C2
Pont-St. Vincent F 60 B2
Pont-Ste. Maxence F 58 A3
Pont-Scorff F 56 C2
Pont-sur-Yonne F 59 B4
Pontacq F 76 C2
Pontailler-sur-Saône F 69 A5
Pontão P 92 B2
Pontardawe GB 28 B4
Pontarddulais GB 28 B3

Roquebilière F 79 B6
Roquebrun F 78 C2
Roquecourbe F 77 C5
Roquefort F 76 B2
Roquemaure F 78 B3
Roquesteron F 79 C6
Roquetas de Mar E 101 C3
Roquetes E 90 C3
Roquevaire F 79 C4
Røra N 114 D8
Rörbäcksnäs S 34 A4
Rørbæk DK 38 C2
Rore BIH 83 B5
Röro S 38 B4
Røros N 114 E8
Rorschach CH 71 A4
Rørvig DK 39 D4
Rørvik N 114 C8
Rörvik S 40 B4
Rosà I 72 C1
Rosa Marina I 104 C3
Rosal de la Frontera E 98 B3
Rosalina Mare I 72 C2
Rosans F 79 B4
Rosário P 98 B2
Rosarno I 106 C2
Rosbach D 50 C3
Rosche D 44 C2
Rościszewo PL 47 C5
Roscoff F 56 B2
Roscommon IRL 18 C3
Roscrea IRL 21 B4
Rosdorf D 51 B5
Rose I 106 B3
Rosegg A 73 B4
Rosehall GB 22 D4
Rosehearty GB 23 D6
Rosel GB 57 A3
Rosell E 90 C3
Roselló E 90 B3
Rosendal N 32 C3
Rosenfeld D 61 B4
Rosenfors S 40 B5
Rosenheim D 62 C3
Rosenow D 45 B5
Rosenthal D 51 B4
Rosersberg S 37 C4
Roses E 91 A6
Roseto degli Abruzzi I 103 A7
Roseto Valfortore I 103 B8
Rosheim F 60 B3
Rosia I 81 C5
Rosice CZ 64 A2
Rosières-en-Santerre F 58 A3
Rosignano Maríttimo I 81 C4
Rosignano Solvay I 81 C4
Roşiori-de-Vede RO 11 D8
Roskhill GB 22 D2
Roskilde DK 39 D5
Roskovec AL 105 C5
Röslau D 52 C1
Roslavl RUS 7 E12
Roslev DK 38 C1
Rosmaninhal P 93 B3
Rosmult IRL 21 B4
Rosnowo PL 46 A2
Rosolini I 109 C3
Rosova SCG 85 C4
Rosoy F 59 B4
Rosporden F 56 C2
Rosquete P 92 B2
Rosrath D 50 C3
Ross-on-Wye GB 29 B5
Rossa CH 71 B4
Rossano I 106 B3
Rossas, *Aveiro* P 87 D2
Rossas, *Braga* P 87 C2
Rossdorf D 51 C6
Rossett GB 26 B3
Rosshaupten D 62 C1
Rossiglione I 80 B2
Rossignol B 60 A1
Rossla D 52 B1
Rosslare IRL 21 B5
Rosslare Harbour IRL 21 B5
Rosslau D 52 B2
Rosslea GB 19 B4
Rossleben D 52 B1
Rossön S 115 D13
Rossoszyca PL 54 B3
Rosswein D 52 B3
Röstånga S 41 C3
Roštár SK 65 B6
Rostock D 44 A4
Rostrenen F 56 B2
Røsvik N 112 E4
Rosyth GB 25 B4
Röszke H 75 B5
Rot S 34 A6
Rot am See D 61 A6
Rota E 99 C4
Rota Greca I 106 B3
Rotberget N 34 B4
Rotella I 82 D2
Rotenburg, *Hessen* D 51 C5
Rotenburg, *Niedersachsen* D 43 B6
Roth, *Bayern* D 62 A2
Roth, *Rheinland-Pfalz* D 50 C3
Rothbury GB 25 C6
Rothemühl D 45 B5
Rothenkempenow D 45 B6
Röthenbach D 62 A2
Rothenburg D 53 B4
Rothenburg ob der Tauber D 61 A6
Rothéneuf F 57 B4
Rothenstein D 62 B2
Rotherham GB 27 B4
Rothes GB 23 D5
Rothesay GB 24 C2
Rothwell GB 30 B3
Rotnes N 34 B2
Rotonda I 106 B3
Rotondella I 106 A3
Rotova E 96 C2
Rott, *Bayern* D 62 C1
Rott, *Bayern* D 62 C3
Rottach-Egern D 62 C2
Röttenbach D 62 A2
Rottenbuch D 62 C1
Rottenburg, *Baden-Württemberg* D 61 B4
Rottenburg, *Bayern* D 62 B3
Rottenmann A 73 A4
Rotterdam NL 49 B5
Rotthalmünster D 63 B4
Rottingdean GB 31 D3
Röttingen D 61 A5
Rottleberode D 51 B6
Rottne S 40 B4
Rottneros S 34 C5
Rottofreno I 80 A3
Rottweil D 61 B4
Rötz D 62 A3
Roubaix F 49 C4
Roudnice nad Labem CZ 53 C4
Roudouallec F 56 B2
Rouen F 58 A2
Rouffach F 60 C3
Rougé F 57 C4
Rougemont F 69 A6
Rougemont le-Château F 60 C2
Rouillac F 67 C4
Rouillé F 67 B5
Roujan F 78 C2
Roulans F 69 A6
Roundwood IRL 21 A5
Rousínov CZ 64 A2
Roussac F 67 B6
Roussennac F 77 B5
Rousses F 78 B2
Roussillon F 69 C4
Rouvroy-sur-Audry F 59 A5
Rouy F 68 A3
Rovanieman maalaiskunta FIN 113 F14
Rovaniemi FIN 113 F14
Rovato I 71 C4
Rovensko pod Troskami CZ 53 C5
Roverbella I 71 C5
Rovereto I 71 C6
Rövershagen D 44 A4
Roverud N 34 B4
Rovigo I 81 A5
Rovinj HR 82 A2
Rovišce HR 74 C1
Rów PL 45 C6
Rowy PL 46 A3
Royal Leamington Spa GB 30 B2
Royal Tunbridge Wells GB 31 C4
Royan F 66 C3
Royat F 68 C3
Roybon F 69 C5
Roybridge GB 24 B3
Roye F 58 A3
Royère-de-Vassivière F 68 C1
Røykenvik N 34 B2
Royos E 101 B3
Røyrvik N 115 C10
Royston GB 30 B3
Rozadas E 86 A4
Rožaj SCG 85 D5
Rozalén del Monte E 95 C4
Różańsko PL 45 C6
Rožanstvo SCG 85 C4
Rozay-en-Brie F 59 B3
Roždalovice CZ 53 C5
Rozdilna UA 11 C11
Rozental PL 47 B5
Rozhyshche UA 11 A8
Rožmitál pod Třemšínem CZ 63 A4
Rožňava SK 65 B6
Rožnov pod Radhoštěm CZ 64 A4
Rozoy-sur-Serre F 59 A5
Rozprza PL 55 B4
Roztoky CZ 53 C4
Rozvadov CZ 62 A3
Rozzano I 71 C4
Rranxë AL 105 B5
Rrëshen AL 105 B5
Rrogozhinë AL 105 B5
Ruanes E 93 B5
Rubbestadnesset N 32 C2
Rubi E 91 B5
Rubiá E 86 B4
Rubiacedo de Abajo E 89 B3
Rubielos Bajos E 95 C4
Rubielos de Mora E 96 A2
Rubiera I 81 B4
Rubik AL 105 B5
Rucandio E 89 B3
Rud, *Akershus* N 34 B3
Rud, *Buskerud* N 34 B2
Ruda PL 54 B3
Ruda S 40 B6
Ruda Maleniecka PL 55 B5
Ruda Pilczycka PL 55 B5
Ruda Śl. PL 54 C3
Rudabánya H 65 B6
Ruddervorde B 49 B4
Ruden A 73 B4
Rudersberg D 61 B5
Rudersdorf A 73 A6
Rüdersdorf D 45 C5
Ruderting D 63 B4
Rüdesheim D 50 D3
Rudkøbing DK 39 E3
Rudmanns A 63 B6
Rudna CZ 53 C4
Rudna PL 53 B6
Rudnik, *Kosovo* SCG 85 D5
Rudnik, *Srbija* SCG 85 B5
Rudniki, *Opolskie* PL 54 B3
Rudniki, *Śląskie* PL 55 C4
Rudno, *Dolnośląskie* PL 54 B1
Rudno, *Pomorskie* PL 47 B4
Rudnya RUS 7 D11
Rudo BIH 85 C4
Rudolstadt D 52 C1
Rudowica PL 53 B5
Rudozem BG 116 A6
Ruds Vedby DK 39 D4
Rudskoga S 35 C6
Rudston GB 27 A5
Rudy PL 54 C3
Rue F 48 C2
Rueda E 88 C2
Rueda de Jalón E 90 B1
Ruelle-sur-Touvre F 67 C5
Ruerrero E 88 B3
Ruffano I 107 B5
Ruffec F 67 B5
Rufina I 81 C5
Rugby GB 30 B2
Rugeley GB 27 C4
Ruggstrop S 40 C6
Rugles F 58 B1
Rugozero RUS 3 D30
Rühen D 44 C2
Ruhla D 51 C6
Ruhland D 53 B3
Ruhle D 43 C4
Ruhpolding D 62 C3
Ruhstorf D 63 B4
Ruidera E 95 D4
Ruillé-sur-le-Loir F 58 C1
Ruinen NL 42 C3
Ruiselede B 49 B4
Rulles B 60 A1
Rülzheim D 61 A4
Rum H 74 A1
Ruma SCG 85 A4
Rumboci BIH 84 C2
Rumburk CZ 53 C4
Rumenka SCG 75 C4
Rumia PL 47 A4
Rumigny F 59 A5
Rumilly F 69 C5
Rumma S 37 D3
Rumney GB 29 B4
Rumont F 59 B6
Rumy PL 47 B6
Runa P 92 B1
Runcorn GB 26 B3
Rundmoen N 115 A11
Rungsted DK 41 D2
Runhällen S 36 B3
Runowo PL 47 A6
Ruokojärvi FIN 113 E13
Ruokolahti FIN 3 F28
Ruokto S 112 E8
Ruoms F 78 B3
Ruoti I 104 C1
Rupa HR 73 C4
Ruppichteroth D 50 C3
Rupt-sur-Moselle F 60 C2
Rus E 100 A2
Ruse BG 11 E9
Ruše SLO 73 B5
Rusele S 115 C15
Ruševo HR 74 C3
Rush IRL 21 A5
Rushden GB 30 B3
Rusiec PL 54 B3
Rusinowo, *Zachodnio-Pomorskie* PL 46 B1
Rusinowo, *Zachodnio-Pomorskie* PL 46 B2
Ruskele S 115 C15
Ruski Krstur SCG 75 C4
Ruskington GB 27 B5
Rusovce SK 64 B3
Rüsselsheim D 51 D4
Russelv N 112 C9
Russi I 81 B6
Rust A 64 C2
Rustefjelbma N 113 B17
Rustrel F 79 C4
Ruszki PL 55 A5
Ruszów PL 53 B5
Rute E 100 B1
Rüthen D 51 B4
Rutherglen GB 24 C3
Ruthin GB 26 B2
Ruthven GB 23 D4
Ruthwell GB 25 D4
Rüti CH 70 A3
Rutigliano I 104 B3
Rutledal N 32 A2
Rutoši SCG 85 C4
Rutuna S 37 D4
Ruurlo NL 50 A2
Ruuvaoja FIN 113 E17
Ruvo del Monte I 104 C1
Ruvo di Púglia I 104 B2
Ruynes-en-Margeride F 78 B2
Ružic HR 83 C5
Ružomberok SK 65 A5
Ruzsa H 75 B4
Ry DK 39 C2
Rybany SK 64 B4
Rybina PL 47 A5
Rybinsk RUS 7 B15
Rybnik PL 54 C3
Rychliki PL 47 B5
Rychlocice PL 54 B3
Rychnov nad Kněžnou CZ 53 C6
Rychnowo PL 47 B6
Rychtal PL 54 B2
Rychwał PL 54 A3
Ryczywół, *Mazowieckie* PL 55 B6
Ryczywół, *Wielkopolskie* PL 46 C2
Ryd S 40 C4
Rydaholm S 40 C4
Rydal S 40 B2
Rydbo S 37 C5
Rydboholm S 40 B2
Ryde GB 31 D2
Rydöbruk S 40 C3
Rydsgård S 41 D3
Rydsnäs S 40 B5
Rydultowy PL 54 C3
Rydzyna PL 54 B1
Rye GB 31 D4
Rygge N 35 C2
Ryjewo PL 47 B4
Rykene N 33 D5
Rylsk RUS 7 F13
Rymań PL 46 B1
Rýmařov CZ 64 A3
Rynarzewo PL 46 B3
Ryomgård DK 39 C3
Rypefjord N 113 B12
Rypin PL 47 B5
Rysjedalsvika N 32 A2
Ryssby S 40 C4
Rytel PL 46 B3
Rytro PL 65 A6
Rywociny PL 47 B6
Rzeczenica PL 46 B3
Rzeczniów PL 55 B6
Rzeczyca PL 55 B5
Rzęgnowo PL 47 B6
Rzejowice PL 55 B4
Rzemień PL 55 C6
Rzepin PL 45 C6
Rzesznikowo PL 46 B1
Rzeszów PL 10 A6
Rzgów PL 55 B4
Rzhev RUS 7 C13

S

Sa Pobla E 97 B3
Sa Savina E 97 C1
Saal, *Bayern* D 51 C6
Saal, *Bayern* D 62 B2
Saalbach A 72 A2
Saalburg D 52 C1
Saales F 60 B3
Saalfeld D 52 C1
Saalfelden am Steinernen Meer A 72 A2
Saanen CH 70 B2
Saarbrücken D 60 A2
Saarburg D 60 A2
Saarijärvi FIN 3 E26
Saarlouis D 60 A2
Saas-Fee CH 70 B2
Šabac SCG 85 B4
Sabadell E 91 B5
Sabáudia I 102 B6
Sabbioneta I 81 B4
Sabero E 88 B1
Sabiñánigo E 90 A2
Sabiote E 100 A2
Sablé-sur-Sarthe F 57 C5
Sables-d'Or-les-Pins F 56 B3
Sabóia P 98 B2
Saborsko HR 83 A4
Sabres F 76 B2
Sabrosa P 87 C3
Sabugal P 93 A3
Sabuncu TR 118 C5
Săcălaz RO 75 C6
Sacecorbo E 95 B4
Saceda del Rio E 95 B4
Sacedón E 95 B4
Săcele RO 11 D8
Saceruela E 94 D2
Sachsenburg A 72 B3
Sachsenhagen D 43 C6
Sacile I 72 C2
Sacramenia E 88 C3
Sada E 86 A2
Sádaba E 90 A1
Saddell GB 24 C2
Sadernes E 91 A5
Sadki PL 46 B3
Sadkowice PL 55 B5
Sadlinki PL 47 B4
Sadów PL 53 A4
Sadská CZ 53 C4
Sæbøvik N 32 C2
Sæby DK 38 B3
Saelices E 95 C4
Saelices de Mayorga E 88 B1
Saerbeck D 50 A3
Særslev DK 39 D3
Sætre N 35 C2
Saeul L 60 A1
Sævareid N 32 B2
Sævråsvåg N 32 B2
Safaalan TR 118 A3
Safara P 98 A3
Säffle S 35 C4
Saffron Walden GB 31 B4
Safonovo RUS 7 D12
Safranbolu TR 16 A6
Säfsnäs S 36 B1
Şag RO 75 C6
Sagard D 45 A5
S'Agaro E 91 B6
Sågmyra S 36 B2
Sagone F 102 A1
Sagres P 98 C2
Ságújfalu H 65 B5
Sagunt E 96 B2
Sagvåg N 32 C2
Ságvár H 74 B3
Sagy F 69 B5
Sahagún E 88 B1
Šahy SK 65 B4
Saignelégier CH 70 A1
Saignes F 68 C2
Saija FIN 113 E17
Saillagouse F 91 A5
Saillans F 79 B4
Sains F 59 A4
St. Abb's GB 25 C5
St. Affrique F 78 C1
St. Agnan F 68 B3
St. Agnant F 66 C4
St. Agnes GB 28 C2
St. Agrève F 78 A3
St. Aignan F 67 A6
St. Aignan-sur-Roë F 57 C4
St. Alban-sur-Limagnole F 78 B2
St. Albans GB 31 C3
St. Amand-en-Puisaye F 68 A3
St. Amand-les-Eaux F 49 C4
St. Amand-Longpré F 58 C2
St. Amand-Montrond F 68 B2
St. Amans F 78 B2
St. Amans-Soult F 77 C5
St. Amant-Roche-Savine F 68 C3
St. Amarin F 60 C2
St. Ambroix F 78 B3
St. Amé F 60 B2
St. Amour F 69 B5
St. André-de-Corcy F 69 C4
St. André-de-Cubzac F 76 B2
St. André-de-l'Eure F 58 B2
St. André-de-Roquepertuis F 78 B3
St. André-de-Sangonis F 78 C2
St. Andre-de-Valborgne F 78 B2
St. André-les-Alpes F 79 C5
St. Andrews GB 25 B5
St. Angel F 68 C2
St. Anthème F 68 C3
St. Antoine F 102 A2
St. Antoine-de-Ficalba F 77 B3
St. Antönien CH 71 B4
St. Antonin-Noble-Val F 77 B4
St. Août F 68 B1
St. Armant-Tallende F 68 C3
St. Arnoult F 58 B2
St. Asaph GB 26 B2
St. Astier F 67 C5
St. Athan GB 29 B4
St. Auban F 79 C5
St. Aubin CH 70 B1
St. Aubin F 69 A5
St. Aubin GB 57 A3
St. Aubin-d'Aubigné F 57 B4
St. Aubin-du-Cormier F 57 B4
St. Aubin-sur-Aire F 60 B1
St. Aubin-sur-Mer F 57 A5
St. Aulaye F 67 C5
St. Austell GB 28 C3
St. Avit F 68 C2
St. Avold F 60 A2
St. Aygulf F 79 C5
St. Bauzille-de-Putois F 78 C2
St. Béat F 77 D3
St. Beauzély F 78 B1
St. Bees GB 26 A2
St. Benim-d'Azy F 68 B3
St. Benoît-du-Sault F 67 B6
St. Benoit-en-Woëvre F 60 B1
St. Berthevin F 57 B5
St. Blaise-la-Roche F 60 B3
St. Blazey GB 28 C3
St. Blin F 59 B6
St. Bonnet F 79 B5
St. Bonnet Briance F 67 C6
St. Bonnet-de-Joux F 69 B4
St. Bonnet-le-Château F 68 C4
St. Bonnet-le-Froid F 69 C4
St. Brévin-les-Pins F 66 A2
St. Briac-sur-Mer F 57 B3
St. Brice-en-Coglès F 57 B4
St. Brieuc F 56 B3
St. Bris-le-Vineux F 59 C4
St. Broladre F 57 B4
St. Calais F 58 C1
St. Cannat F 79 C4
St. Cast-le-Guildo F 57 B3
St. Céré F 77 B4
St. Cergue CH 69 B6
St. Cergues F 69 B6
St. Cernin F 77 A5
St. Chamant F 68 C1
St. Chamas F 79 C4
St. Chamond F 69 C4
St. Chély-d'Apcher F 78 B2
St. Chély-d'Aubrac F 78 B1
St. Chinian F 78 C1
St. Christol F 79 B4
St. Christol-lès-Alès F 78 B3
St. Christoly-Médoc F 66 C4
St. Christophe-du-Ligneron F 66 B3
St. Christophe-en-Brionnais F 69 B4
St. Ciers-sur-Gironde F 67 C4
St. Clair-sur-Epte F 58 A2
St. Clar F 77 C3
St. Claud F 67 C5
St. Claude F 69 B5
St. Clears GB 28 B3
St. Columb Major GB 28 C3
St. Come-d'Olt F 78 B1
St. Cosme-en-Vairais F 58 B1
St. Cyprien, *Dordogne* F 77 B4
St. Cyprien, *Pyrenées-Orientales* F 91 A6
St. Cyr-sur-Loire F 67 A5
St. Cyr-sur-Mer F 79 C4
St. Cyr-sur-Methon F 69 B4
St. David's GB 28 B2
St. Denis F 58 B3
St. Denis-d'Oléron F 66 B3
St. Denis d'Orques F 57 B5
St. Didier F 69 B4
St. Didier-en-Velay F 69 C4
St. Dié F 60 B2
St. Dier-d'Auvergne F 68 C3
St. Dizier F 59 B5
St. Dizier-Leyrenne F 68 B1
St. Dogmaels GB 28 A3
St. Efflam F 56 B2
St. Égrève F 69 C5
St. Eloy-les-Mines F 68 B2
St. Emiland F 69 B4
St. Émilion F 76 B2
St. Enoder GB 28 C3
St. Esteben F 76 C1
St. Estèphe F 66 C4
St. Étienne F 69 C4
St. Etienne-de-Baigorry F 76 C1
St. Étienne-de-Cuines F 69 C6
St. Etienne-de-Fursac F 67 B6
St. Etienne-de-Montluc F 66 A3
St. Etienne-de-St. Geoirs F 69 C5
St. Étienne-de-Tinée F 79 B5
St. Étienne-du-Bois F 69 B5
St. Étienne-du-Rouvray F 58 A2
St. Etienne-les-Orgues F 79 B4
St. Fargeau F 59 C4
St. Félicien F 78 A3
St. Felix-de-Sorgues F 78 C1
St. Félix-Lauragais F 77 C4
St. Fillans GB 24 B3
St. Firmin F 79 B5
St. Florent F 102 A2
St. Florent-le-Vieil F 66 A3
St. Florent-sur-Cher F 68 B2
St. Florentin F 59 C4
St. Flour F 78 A2
St. Flovier F 67 B6
St. Fort-sur-le-Né F 67 C4
St. Fulgent F 66 B3
St. Galmier F 69 C4
St. Gaudens F 77 C3
St. Gaultier F 67 B6
St. Gély-du-Fesc F 78 C2
St. Genest-Malifaux F 69 C4
St. Gengoux-le-National F 69 B4
St. Geniez F 79 B5
St. Geniez-d'Olt F 78 B1
St. Genis-de-Saintonge F 67 C4
St. Genis-Pouilly F 69 B6
St. Genix-sur-Guiers F 69 C5
St. Georges Buttavent F 57 B5
St. Georges-d'Aurac F 68 C3
St. Georges-de-Commiers F 79 A4
St. Georges-de-Didonne F 66 C4
St. Georges-de-Luzençon F 78 B1
St. Georges-de Mons F 68 C2
St. Georges-de-Reneins F 69 B4
St. Georges d'Oléron F 66 C3
St. Georges-en-Couzan F 68 C3
St. Georges-lès-Baillargeaux F 67 B5
St. Georges-sur-Loire F 66 A4
St. Georges-sur-Meuse B 49 C6
St. Geours-de-Maremne F 76 C1
St. Gérand-de-Vaux F 68 B3
St. Gérand-le-Puy F 68 B3
St. Germain F 60 C2
St. Germain-Chassenay F 68 B3
St. Germain-de-Calberte F 78 B2
St. Germain-de-Confolens F 67 B5
St. Germain-de-Joux F 69 B5
St. Germain-des-Fossés F 68 B3
St. Germain-du-Bois F 69 B5
St. Germain-du-Plain F 69 B4
St. Germain-du Puy F 68 A2
St. Germain-en-Laye F 58 B3
St. Germain-Laval F 68 C4
St. Germain-Lembron F 68 C3
St. Germain-les-Belles F 67 C6
St. Germain-Lespinasse F 68 B3
St. Germain-l'Herm F 68 C3
St. Gervais-d'Auvergne F 68 B2
St. Gervais-les-Bains F 70 C1
St. Gervais-sur-Mare F 78 C2
St. Gildas-de-Rhuys F 66 A2
St. Gildas-des-Bois F 66 A2
St. Gilles, *Gard* F 78 C3
St. Gilles, *Ille-et-Vilaine* F 57 B4
St. Gilles-Croix-de-Vie F 66 B3
St. Gingolph F 70 B1
St. Girons, *Ariège* F 77 D4
St. Girons, *Landes* F 76 C1
St. Girons-Plage F 76 C1
St. Gobain F 59 A4
St. Gorgon-Main F 69 A6
St. Guénolé F 56 C1
St. Harmon GB 29 A4
St. Helens GB 26 B3
St. Helier GB 57 A3
St. Herblain F 66 A3
St. Hilaire, *Allier* F 68 B3
St. Hilaire, *Aude* F 77 C5
St. Hilaire-de-Riez F 66 B3
St. Hilaire-de-Villefranche F 67 C4
St. Hilaire-des-Loges F 67 B4
St. Hilaire-du-Harcouët F 57 B4
St. Hilaire-du-Rosier F 79 A4
St. Hippolyte, *Aveyron* F 77 B5
St. Hippolyte, *Doubs* F 70 A1
St. Hippolyte-du-Fort F 78 C2
St. Honoré-les-Bains F 68 B3
St. Hubert B 49 C6
St. Imier CH 70 A2
St. Issey GB 28 C3
St. Ives, *Cambridgeshire* GB 30 B3
St. Ives, *Cornwall* GB 28 C2
St. Izaire F 78 C1
St. Jacques-de-la-Lande F 57 B4
St. Jacut-de-la-Mer F 57 B3
St. James F 57 B4
St. Jaume d'Enveja E 90 C3
St. Jean-Brévelay F 56 C3
St. Jean-d'Angély F 67 C4
St. Jean-de-Belleville F 69 C6
St. Jean-de-Bournay F 69 C5
St. Jean-de-Braye F 58 C2
St. Jean-de-Côle F 67 C5
St. Jean-de-Daye F 57 A4
St. Jean de Losne F 69 A5
St. Jean-de-Luz F 76 C1
St. Jean-de-Maurienne F 69 C6
St. Jean-de-Monts F 66 B2
St. Jean-d'Illac F 76 B2
St. Jean-du-Bruel F 78 B2
St. Jean-du-Gard F 78 B2
St. Jean-en-Royans F 79 A4
St. Jean-la-Riviere F 79 C6
St. Jean-Pied-de-Port F 76 C1
St. Jean-Poutge F 77 C3
St. Jeoire F 69 B6
St. Joachim F 66 A2
St. Johnstown IRL 19 B4
St. Jorioz F 69 C6
St. Joris Winge B 49 C5
St. Jouin-de-Marnes F 67 B4
St. Juéry F 77 C5
St. Julien F 69 B5
St. Julien-Chapteuil F 78 A3
St. Julien-de-Vouvantes F 57 C4
St. Julien-du-Sault F 59 B4
St. Julien-du-Verdon F 79 C5
St. Julien-en-Born F 76 B1
St. Julien-en-Genevois F 69 B6
St. Julien la-Vêtre F 68 C3
St. Julien-l'Ars F 67 B5
St. Julien-Mont-Denis F 69 C6
St. Julien-sur-Reyssouze F 69 B5
St. Junien F 67 C5
St. Just F 78 B3
St. Just GB 28 C2
St. Just-en-Chaussée F 58 A3
St. Just-en-Chevalet F 68 C3
St. Just-St. Rambert F 69 C4
St. Justin F 76 C2
St. Keverne GB 28 C2
St. Lary-Soulan F 77 D3
St. Laurent-d'Aigouze F 78 C3
St. Laurent-de-Chamousset F 69 C4
St. Laurent-de-Condel F 57 A5
St. Laurent-de-la-Cabrerisse F 78 C1
St. Laurent-de-la-Salanque F 78 D1
St. Laurent-des-Autels F 66 A3
St. Laurent-du-Pont F 69 C5
St. Laurent-en-Caux F 58 A1
St. Laurent-en-Grandvaux F 69 B5
St. Laurent-Médoc F 76 A2
St. Laurent-sur-Gorre F 67 C5
St. Laurent-sur-Mer F 57 A5
St. Laurent-sur-Sèvre F 66 B4

St. Leger B 60 A1
St. Léger-de-Vignes F 68 B3
St. Léger-sous-Beuvray F 68 B4
St. Léger-sur-Dheune F 69 B4
St. Léonard-de-Noblat F 67 C6
St. Leonards GB 31 D4
St. Lô F 57 A4
St. Lon-les-Mines F 76 C1
St. Louis F 60 C3
St. Loup F 68 B3
St. Loup-de-la-Salle F 69 B4
St. Loup-sur-Semouse F 60 C2
St. Lunaire F 57 B3
St. Lupicin F 69 B5
St. Lyphard F 66 A2
St. Lys F 77 C4
St. Macaire F 76 B2
St. Maclou F 58 A1
St. Maixent-l'École F 67 B4
St. Malo F 57 B3
St. Mamet-la-Salvetat F 77 B5
St. Mandrier-sur-Mer F 79 C4
St. Marcel, *Drôme* F 78 B3
St. Marcel, *Saône-et-Loire* F 69 B4
St. Marcellin F 69 C5
St. Marcellin sur Loire F 68 C4
St. Marcet F 77 C3
St. Mards-en-Othe F 59 B4
St. Margaret's-at-Cliffe GB 31 C5
St. Margaret's Hope GB 23 C6
St. Mars-la-Jaille F 66 A3
St. Martin-d'Ablois F 59 B4
St. Martin-d'Auxigny F 68 A2
St. Martin-de-Belleville F 69 C6
St. Martin-de-Bossenay F 59 B4
St. Martin-de-Crau F 78 C3
St. Martin-de-Londres F 78 C2
St. Martin-de-Queyrières F 79 B5
St. Martin-de-Ré F 66 B3
St. Martin-de-Valamas F 78 B3
St. Martin-d'Entraunes F 79 B5
St. Martin des Besaces F 57 A5
St. Martin-d'Estreaux F 68 B3
St. Martin-d'Hères F 69 C5
St. Martin-du-Frêne F 69 B5
St. Martin-en-Bresse F 69 B5
St. Martin-en-Haut F 69 C4
St. Martin-la-Méanne F 68 C1
St. Martin-sur-Ouanne F 59 C4
St. Martin-Valmeroux F 77 A5
St. Martin-Vésubie F 79 B6
St. Martory F 77 C3
St. Mary's GB 23 C6
St. Mathieu F 67 C5
St. Mathieu-de-Tréviers F 78 C2
St. Maurice CH 70 B1
St. Maurice-Navacelles F 78 C2
St. Maurice-sur-Moselle F 60 C2
St. Mawes GB 28 C2
St. Maximin-la-Ste. Baume F 79 C4
St. Méard-de-Gurçon F 76 B3
St. Médard-de-Guizières F 76 A2
St. Médard-en-Jalles F 76 B2
St. Méen-le-Grand F 57 B3
St. Menges F 59 A5
St. Merløse DK 39 D4
St. Město CZ 54 C1
St. M'Hervé F 57 B4
St. Michel, *Aisne* F 59 A5
St. Michel, *Gers* F 77 C3
St. Michel-Chef-Chef F 66 A2
St. Michel-de-Castelnau F 76 B2
St. Michel-de-Maurienne F 69 C6
St. Michel-en-Grève F 56 B2
St. Michel-en-l'Herm F 66 B3
St. Michel-Mont-Mercure F 66 B4
St. Mihiel F 60 B1
St. Monance GB 25 B5
St. Montant F 78 B3
St. Moritz CH 71 B4
St. Nazaire F 66 A2
St. Nazaire-en-Royans F 79 A4
St. Nazaire-le-Désert F 79 B4
St. Nectaire F 68 C2
St. Neots GB 30 B3
St. Nicolas-de-Port F 60 B2
St. Nicolas-de-Redon F 57 C3
St. Nicolas-du-Pélem F 56 B2
St. Niklaas B 49 B5
St. Omer F 48 C3
St. Pair-sur-Mer F 57 B4
St. Palais F 76 C1
St. Palais-sur-Mer F 66 C3
St. Pardoux-la-Rivière F 67 C5
St. Paul-Cap-de-Joux F 77 C4
St. Paul-de-Fenouillet F 77 D5
St. Paul-de-Varax F 69 B5
St. Paul-le-Jeune F 78 B3
St. Paul-lès-Dax F 76 C1
St. Paul-Trois-Châteaux F 78 B3
St. Paulien F 68 C3
St. Pé-de-Bigorre F 76 C2
St. Pée-sur-Nivelle F 76 C1
St. Péravy-la-Colombe F 58 C2
St. Péray F 78 B3
St. Père-en-Retz F 66 A2
St. Peter Port GB 56 A3
St. Petersburg = Sankt-Peterburg RUS 7 B11
St. Philbert-de-Grand-Lieu F 66 A3
St. Pierre F 78 C1
St. Pierre-d'Albigny F 69 C6
St. Pierre-d'Allevard F 69 C6
St. Pierre-de-Chartreuse F 69 C5
St. Pierre-de-Chignac F 77 A3
St. Pierre-de-la-Fage F 78 C2
St. Pierre-d'Entremont F 69 C5
St. Pierre-d'Oléron F 66 C3
St. Pierre-Eglise F 57 A4
St. Pierre-en-Port F 58 A1
St. Pierre-le-Moûtier F 68 B3
St. Pierre Montlimart F 66 A3
St. Pierre-Quiberon F 66 A1
St. Pierre-sur-Dives F 57 A5
St. Pierreville F 78 B3
St. Pieters-Leeuw B 49 C5
St. Plancard F 77 C3
St. Poix F 57 C4
St. Pol-de-Léon F 56 B2
St. Pol-sur-Ternoise F 48 C3
St. Polgues F 68 C3
St. Pons-de-Thomières F 78 C1
St. Porchaire F 66 C4
St. Pourçain-sur-Sioule F 68 B3
St. Priest F 69 C4
St. Privat F 68 C2
St. Quay-Portrieux F 56 B3
St. Quentin F 59 A4
St. Quentin-la-Poterie F 78 B3
St. Quentin-les-Anges F 57 C5
St. Rambert-d'Albon F 69 C4
St. Rambert-en-Bugey F 69 C5
St. Raphaël F 79 C5
St. Rémy-de-Provence F 78 C3
St. Rémy-du-Val F 57 B6
St. Remy-en-Bouzemont F 59 B5
St. Renan F 56 B1
St. Révérien F 68 A3
St. Riquier F 48 C2
St. Romain-de-Colbosc F 58 A1
St. Rome-de-Cernon F 78 B1
St. Rome-de-Tarn F 78 B1
St. Sadurní d'Anoia E 91 B4
St. Saëns F 58 A2
St. Sampson GB 56 A3
St. Samson-la-Poterie F 58 A2
St. Saturnin-de-Lenne F 78 B2
St. Saturnin-lès-Apt F 79 C4
St. Sauflieu F 58 A3
St. Saulge F 68 A3
St. Sauveur, *Finistère* F 56 B2
St. Sauveur, *Haute-Saône* F 60 C2
St. Sauveur-de-Montagut F 78 B3
St. Sauveur-en-Puisaye F 59 C4
St. Sauveur-en-Rue F 69 C4
St. Sauveur-le-Vicomte F 57 A4
St. Sauveur-Lendelin F 57 A4
St. Sauveur-sur-Tinée F 79 B6
St. Savin, *Gironde* F 76 A2
St. Savin, *Vienne* F 67 B5
St. Savinien F 67 C4
St. Savournin F 79 C4
St. Seine-l'Abbaye F 69 A4
St. Sernin-sur-Rance F 77 C5
St. Sevan-sur-Mer F 57 B3
St. Sever F 76 C2
St. Sever-Calvados F 57 B4
St. Sorlin-d'Arves F 69 C6
St. Soupplets F 58 A3
St. Sulpice F 77 C4
St. Sulpice-Laurière F 67 B6
St. Sulpice-les-Feuilles F 67 B6
St. Symphorien F 76 B2
St. Symphorien-de-Lay F 69 C4
St. Symphorien d'Ozon F 69 C4
St. Symphorien-sur-Coise F 69 C4
St. Teath GB 28 C3
St. Thégonnec F 56 B2
St. Thiébault F 60 B1
St. Trivier-de-Courtes F 69 B5
St. Trivier sur-Moignans F 69 B4
St. Trojan-les-Bains F 66 C3
St. Tropez F 79 C5
St. Truiden B 49 C6
St. Vaast-la-Hougue F 57 A4
St. Valérien F 59 B4
St. Valery-en-Caux F 58 A1
St. Valéry-sur-Somme F 48 C2
St. Vallier, *Drôme* F 69 C4
St. Vallier, *Saône-et-Loire* F 69 B4
St. Varent F 67 B4
St. Vaury F 68 B1
St. Venant F 48 C3
St. Véran F 79 B5
St. Vincent I 70 C2
St. Vincent-de-Tyrosse F 76 C1
St. Vit F 69 A5
St. Vith B 50 C2
St. Vivien-de-Médoc F 66 C3
St. Yan F 68 B4
St. Ybars F 77 C4
St. Yorre F 68 B3
St. Yrieix-la-Perche F 67 C6
Ste. Adresse F 57 A6
Ste. Anne F 58 B1
Ste. Anne-d'Auray F 56 C3
Ste. Croix CH 69 B6
Ste. Croix-Volvestre F 77 C4
Ste. Engrâce F 76 C2
Ste. Enimie F 78 B2
Ste. Foy-de-Peyrolières F 77 C4
Ste. Foy-la-Grande F 76 B3
Ste. Foy l'Argentiere F 69 C4
Ste. Gauburge-Ste. Colombe F 58 B1
Ste. Gemme la Plaine F 66 B3
Ste. Geneviève F 58 A3
Ste. Hélène F 76 B2
Ste. Hélène-sur-Isère F 69 C6
Ste. Hermine F 66 B3
Ste. Jalle F 79 B4
Ste. Livrade-sur-Lot F 77 B3
Ste. Marie-aux-Mines F 60 B3
Ste. Marie-du-Mont F 57 A4
Ste. Maure-de-Touraine F 67 A5
Ste. Maxime F 79 C5
Ste. Ménéhould F 59 A5
Ste. Mère-Église F 57 A4
Ste. Ode B 49 C6
Ste. Savine F 59 B5
Ste. Sévère-sur-Indre F 68 B2
Ste. Sigolène F 69 C4
Ste. Suzanne F 57 B5
Ste. Tulle F 79 C4
Sainteny F 57 A4
Saintes F 67 C4
Stes. Maries-de-la-Mer F 78 C3
Saintfield GB 19 B6
Saissac F 77 C5
Saja E 88 A2
Sajan SCG 75 C5
Šajkaš SCG 75 C5
Sajókaza H 65 B6
Sajószentpéter H 65 B6
Sajóvámos H 65 B6
Sakarya TR 118 B5
Šakiai LT 6 D7
Sakskøbing DK 39 E4
Sakule SCG 75 C5
Sala S 36 C3
Šal'a SK 64 B3
Sala Baganza I 81 B4
Sala Consilina I 104 C1
Salakovac SCG 85 B6
Salamanca E 94 B1
Salamina GR 117 E5
Salandra I 104 C2
Salaparuta I 108 B1
Salar E 100 B1
Salardú E 90 A3
Salas E 86 A4
Salas de los Infantes E 89 B3
Salau F 77 D4
Salavaux CH 70 B2
Salbertrand I 79 A5
Salbohed S 36 C3
Salbris F 68 A2
Salbu N 32 A2
Salce E 86 B4
Salching D 62 B3
Salcombe GB 28 C4
Saldaña E 88 B2
Saldus LV 6 C7
Sale I 80 B2
Saleby S 35 D5
Salem D 61 C5
Salemi I 108 B1
Salen, *Highland* GB 24 B2
Salen, *Highland* GB 24 B2
Salen N 114 C8
Sälen S 34 A5
Salernes F 79 C5
Salerno I 103 C7
Salers F 68 C2
Salford GB 26 B3
Salgótarján H 65 B5
Salgueiro P 92 B3
Salhus N 32 B2
Sali HR 83 C4
Sálice Salentino I 105 C3
Salientes E 86 B4
Salies-de-Béarn F 76 C2
Salies-du-Salat F 77 C3
Salignac-Eyvigues F 77 B4
Saligney-sur-Roudon F 68 B3
Salihli TR 119 D3
Salihorsk BY 7 E9
Salinas, *Alicante* E 101 A5
Salinas, *Huesca* E 90 A3
Salinas de Medinaceli E 95 A4
Salinas de Pisuerga E 88 B2
Salindres F 78 B3
Saline di Volterra I 81 C4
Salins-les-Bains F 69 B5
Salir P 98 B2
Salisbury GB 29 B6
Salla A 73 A4
Salla FIN 113 F17
Sallachy GB 23 C4
Sallanches F 70 C1
Sallent E 91 B4
Sallent de Gállego E 76 D2
Salles F 76 B2
Salles-Curan F 78 B1
Salles-sur-l'Hers F 77 C4
Sallins IRL 21 A5
Sällsjö S 115 D10
Salmerón E 95 B4
Salmiech F 77 B5
Salmivaara FIN 113 F17
Salmoral E 94 B1
Salo FIN 6 A7
Salò I 71 C5
Salobreña E 100 C2
Salon-de-Provence F 79 C4
Salonica = Thessaloniki GR 116 B4
Salonta RO 10 C6
Salorino E 93 B3
Salornay-sur-Guye F 69 B4
Salorno I 71 B6
Salou E 91 B4
Šalovci SLO 73 B6
Salsbruket N 114 C8
Salses-le-Chateau F 78 D1
Salsomaggiore Terme I 81 B3
Salt E 91 B5
Saltara I 82 C1
Saltash GB 28 C3
Saltburn-by-the-Sea GB 27 A5
Saltcoats GB 24 C3
Saltfleet GB 27 B6
Salto P 87 C3
Saltrød N 33 D5
Saltsjöbaden S 37 C5
Saltvik FIN 36 B7
Saltvik S 40 B6
Saludécio I 82 C1
Salussola I 70 C3
Saluzzo I 80 B1
Salvacañete E 95 B5
Salvada P 98 B3
Salvagnac F 77 C4
Salvaleon E 93 C4
Salvaterra de Magos P 92 B2
Salvaterra do Extremo P 93 B4
Salvatierra, *Avila* E 89 B4
Salvatierra, *Badajoz* E 93 C4
Salvatierra de Santiago E 93 B4
Salviac F 77 B4
Salz-hemmendorf D 51 A5
Salzburg A 62 C4
Salzgitter D 51 A6
Salzgitter Bad D 51 A6
Salzhausen D 44 B2
Salzkotten D 51 B4
Salzmünde D 52 B1
Salzwedel D 44 C3
Samadet F 76 C2
Samandıra TR 118 B4
Samassi I 110 C1
Samatan F 77 C3
Sambiase I 106 C3
Sambir UA 11 B7
Samborowo PL 47 B5
Sambuca di Sicilia I 108 B2
Samedan CH 71 B4
Samer F 48 C2
Sami GR 117 D2
Şamlı TR 118 C2
Sammichele di Bari I 104 C2
Samnaun CH 71 B5
Samobor HR 73 C5
Samoëns F 70 B1
Samogneux F 59 A6
Samokov BG 11 E7
Samora Correia P 92 C2
Šamorín SK 64 B3
Samos E 86 B3
Samos GR 119 E1
Samoš SCG 75 C5
Samothraki GR 116 B7
Samper de Calanda E 90 B2
Sampéyre I 79 B6
Sampieri I 109 C3
Sampigny F 60 B1
Samplawa PL 47 B5
Samproniano I 81 D5
Samtens D 45 A5
Samugheo I 110 C1
San Adrián E 89 B5
San Agustín E 101 C3
San Agustin de Guadalix E 94 B3
San Alberto I 82 B1
San Amaro E 87 B2
San Andrés del Rabanedo E 88 B1
San Antanio di Santadi I 110 C1
San Antolín de Ibias E 86 A4
San Arcángelo I 104 C2
San Asensio E 89 B4
San Bartolomé de la Torre E 99 B3
San Bartolomé de las Abiertas E 94 C2
San Bartolomé de Pinares E 94 B2
San Bartolomeo in Galdo I 103 B8
San Benedetto del Tronto I 82 D2
San Benedetto in Alpe I 81 C5
San Benedetto Po I 81 A4
San Benito E 100 A1
San Benito de la Contienda E 93 C3
San Biágio Plátani I 108 B2
San Biágio Saracinisco I 103 B6
San Bonifacio I 71 C6
San Calixto E 99 B5
San Cándido I 72 B2
San Carlo CH 70 B3
San Carlo I 108 B2
San Carlos del Valle E 100 A2
San Casciano dei Bagni I 81 D5
San Casciano in Val di Pesa I 81 C5
San Cataldo, *Puglia* I 105 C4
San Cataldo, *Sicilia* I 108 B2
San Cebrián de Castro E 88 C1
San Cesário di Lecce I 105 C4
San Chírico Raparo I 106 A3
San Cibrao das Viñas E 87 B3
San Cipirello I 108 B2
San Ciprián E 86 A3
San Clemente E 95 C4
San Clodio E 86 B3
San Colombano al Lambro I 71 C4
San Costanzo I 82 C2
San Crisóbal de Entreviñas E 88 B1
San Cristóbal de la Polantera E 88 B1
San Cristóbal de la Vega E 94 A2
San Cristovo E 87 C3
San Damiano d'Asti I 80 B2
San Damiano Macra I 79 B6
San Daniele del Friuli I 72 B3
San Demétrio Corone I 106 B3
San Demétrio né Vestini I 103 A6
San Donà di Piave I 72 C2
San Dónaci I 105 C3
San Donato Val di Comino I 103 B6
San Emiliano E 86 B5
San Enrique E 99 C5
San Esteban E 86 A4
San Esteban de Gormaz E 89 C3
San Esteban de la Sierra E 93 A5
San Esteban de Litera E 90 B3
San Esteban de Valdueza E 86 B4
San Esteban del Molar E 88 C1
San Esteban del Valle E 94 B2
San Fele I 104 C1
San Felice Circeo I 102 B6
San Felice sul Panaro I 81 B5
San Felices E 88 B3
San Felices de los Gallégos E 87 D4
San Ferdinando di Púglia I 104 B2
San Fernando E 99 C4
San Fernando de Henares E 95 B3
San Fili I 106 B3
San Foca I 105 C4
San Fratello I 109 B3
San Gavino Monreale I 110 C1
San Gémini Fonte I 102 A5
San Germano Vercellese I 70 C3
San Giácomo, *Trentino Alto Adige* I 72 B1
San Giácomo, *Umbria* I 82 D1
San Gimignano I 81 C5
San Ginésio I 82 C2
San Giórgio a Liri I 103 B6
San Giórgio del Sánnio I 103 B7
San Giorgio della Richinvelda I 72 B2
San Giórgio di Lomellina I 70 C3
San Giórgio di Nogaro I 72 C3
San Giorgio di Piano I 81 B5
San Giórgio Iónico I 104 C3
San Giovanni a Piro I 106 A2
San Giovanni Bianco I 71 C4
San Giovanni di Sinis I 110 C1
San Giovanni in Croce I 81 A4
San Giovanni in Fiore I 106 B3
San Giovanni in Persiceto I 81 B5
San Giovanni Reatino I 102 A5
San Giovanni Rotondo I 104 B1
San Giovanni Suérgiu I 110 C1
San Giovanni Valdarno I 81 C5
San Giuliano Terme I 81 C4
San Giustino I 82 C1
San Godenzo I 81 C5
San Gregorio Magno I 103 C8
San Guiseppe Jato I 108 B2
San Javier E 101 B5
San Jorge P 92 B2
San José E 101 C3
San Juan E 89 B3
San Juan de Alicante E 96 C2
San Juan de la Nava E 94 B2
San Justo de la Vega E 86 B4
San Lazzaro di Sávena I 81 B5
San Leo I 82 C1
San Leonardo de Yagüe E 89 C3
San Leonardo in Passiria I 71 B6
San Lorenzo a Merse I 81 C5
San Lorenzo al Mare I 80 C1
San Lorenzo Bellizzi I 106 B3
San Lorenzo de Calatrava E 100 A2
San Lorenzo de El Escorial E 94 B2
San Lorenzo de la Parrilla E 95 C4
San Lorenzo di Sebato I 72 B1
San Lorenzo in Campo I 82 C1
San Lorenzo Nuovo I 81 D5
San Lourenco P 98 A2
San Luca I 106 C3
San Lúcido I 106 B3
San Marcello I 82 C2
San Marcello Pistoiese I 81 B4
San Marcial E 88 C1
San Marco I 103 C7
San Marco Argentano I 106 B3
San Marco dei Cavoti I 103 B7
San Marco in Lámis I 104 B1
San Marino RSM 82 C1
San Martin de Castañeda E 87 B4
San Martín de la Vega E 95 B3
San Martin de la Vega del Alberche E 93 A5
San Martín de Luiña E 86 A4
San Martin de Montalbán E 94 C2
San Martin de Oscos E 86 A4
San Martin de Pusa E 94 C2
San Martin de Unx E 89 B5
San Martín de Valdeiglesias E 94 B2
San Martín del Tesorillo E 99 C5
San Martino di Campagna I 72 B2
San Martino di Castrozza I 72 B1
San-Martino-di-Lota F 102 A2
San Martino in Pénsilis I 103 B8
San Mateo de Gallego E 90 B2
San Máuro Forte I 104 C2
San Michele all'Adige I 71 B6
San Michele di Ganzaria I 109 B3
San Michele Mondovì I 80 B1
San Miguel de Aguayo E 88 A2
San Miguel de Bernuy E 88 C3
San Miguel de Salinas E 101 B5
San Miguel del Arroyo E 88 C2
San Millán de la Cogolla E 89 B4
San Miniato I 81 C4
San Muñoz E 87 D4
San Nicola del'Alto I 107 B3
San Nicolás del Puerto E 99 B5
San Nicolò I 81 B5
San Nicolò Gerrei I 110 C2
San Pablo de los Montes E 94 C2
San Pancrázio Salentino I 105 C3
San Pantaleo I 110 A2
San Pàolo di Civitate I 103 B8
San Pawl il-Bahar M 107 C5
San Pedro, *Albacete* E 101 A3
San Pedro, *Oviedo* E 86 A4
San Pedro de Alcántara E 100 C1
San Pedro de Cadeira P 92 B1
San Pedro de Ceque E 87 B4
San Pedro de Latarce E 88 C1
San Pedro de Merida E 93 C4
San Pedro de Valderaduey E 88 B2
San Pedro del Arroyo E 94 B2
San Pedro del Pinatar E 101 B5
San Pedro del Romeral E 88 A3
San Pedro Manrique E 89 B4
San Pellegrino Terme I 71 C4
San Piero a Sieve I 81 C5
San Piero in Bagno I 81 C5
San Piero Patti I 109 A3
San Pietro I 109 B3
San Pietro in Casale I 81 B5
San Pietro in Gu I 72 C1
San Pietro in Palazzi I 81 C4
San Pietro in Volta I 72 C2
San Pietro Vara I 80 B3
San Pietro Vernótico I 105 C3
San Polo d'Enza I 81 B4
San Quírico d'Órcia I 81 C5
San Rafael del Rio E 90 C3
San Remo I 80 C1
San Román de Cameros E 89 B4
San Roman de Hernija E 88 C1
San Román de la Cuba E 88 B2
San Roman de los Montes E 94 B2
San Romao P 92 C3
San Roque E 99 C5
San Roque de Riomera E 88 A3
San Rufo I 104 C1
San Sebastián de los Ballesteros E 100 B1
San Salvador de Cantamuda E 88 B2
San Salvo I 103 A7
San Salvo Marina I 103 A7
San Sebastián de los Reyes E 94 B3
San Sebastiano Curone I 80 B3
San Secondo Parmense I 81 B4
San Serverino Marche I 82 C2
San Severino Lucano I 106 A3
San Severo I 103 B8
San Silvestre de Guzmán E 98 B3
San Sosti I 106 B3
San Stéfano di Cadore I 72 B2
San Stino di Livenza I 72 C2
San Telmo E 99 B4
San Tirso de Abres E 86 A3
San Valentino alla Muta I 71 B5
San Venanzo I 82 D1
San Vicente de Alcántara E 93 B3
San Vicente de Arana E 89 B4
San Vicente de la Barquera E 88 A2
San Vicente de la Sonsierra E 89 B4
San Vicente de Toranzo E 88 A3
San Vietro E 87 C4
San Vigilio I 72 B1
San Vincente del Raspeig E 96 C2
San Vincenzo I 81 C4
San Vito I 110 C2
San Vito al Tagliamento I 72 C2
San Vito Chietino I 103 A7
San Vito dei Normanni I 104 C3
San Vito di Cadore I 72 B2
San Vito lo Capo I 108 A1
San Vito Romano I 102 B5
Sanaigmore GB 24 C1
Sânandrei RO 75 C6
Sanary-sur-Mer F 79 C4
Sancergues F 68 A2
Sancerre F 68 A2
Sancey-le-Long F 69 A6
Sanchiorian E 94 B2

Sanchonuño E 88 C2
Sancoins F 68 B2
Sancti-Petri E 99 C4
Sancti-Spiritus E 87 D4
Sand, *Hedmark* N 34 B3
Sand, *Rogaland* N 33 C3
Sanda S 37 E5
Sandane N 114 F3
Sandanski BG 116 A5
Sandared S 40 B2
Sandarne S 36 A4
Sandau D 44 C4
Sandbach D 63 B4
Sandbach GB 26 B3
Sandbank GB 24 C3
Sandbanks GB 29 C6
Sandbukt N 112 C10
Sandby DK 39 E4
Sande D 43 B5
Sande, *Sogn og Fjordane* N 32 A2
Sande, *Vestfold* N 35 C2
Sandefjord N 35 C2
Sandeid N 33 C2
Sandersleben D 52 B1
Sanderstølen N 32 B6
Sandes N 33 D4
Sandesneben D 44 B2
Sandhead GB 24 D3
Sandhem S 40 B3
Sandhorst D 43 B4
Sandhurst GB 31 C3
Sandıklı TR 119 D5
Sandillon F 58 C3
Sandl A 63 B5
Sandnes N 33 D2
Sandness GB 22 A7
Sandnessjøen N 115 A9
Sando E 87 D4
Sandomierz PL 55 C6
Sándorfalva H 75 B5
Sandown GB 31 D2
Sandøysund N 35 C2
Sandrigo I 72 C1
Sandsele S 115 B14
Sandset N 112 D3
Sandsjöfors S 40 B4
Sandstad N 114 D6
Sandvatn N 33 D3
Sandvig-Allinge DK 41 D4
Sandvika, *Akershus* N 34 C2
Sandvika, *Hedmark* N 34 B3
Sandvika, *Nord-Trøndelag* N 114 D9
Sandviken S 36 B3
Sandvikvåy N 32 C2
Sandwich GB 31 C5
Sandy GB 30 B3
Sangatte F 48 C2
Sangerhausen D 52 B1
Sangineto Lido I 106 B2
Sangonera la Verde E 101 B4
Sangüesa E 90 A1
Sanguinet F 76 B1
Sanica BIH 83 B5
Sanitz D 44 A4
Sankt Aegyd am Neuwalde A 63 C6
Sankt Andrä A 73 B4
Sankt Andreasberg D 51 B6
Sankt Anna S 37 D3
Sankt Anna am Aigen A 73 B5
Sankt Anton am Arlberg A 71 A5
Sankt Anton an der Jessnitz A 63 C6
Sankt Augustin D 50 C3
Sankt Blasien D 61 C4
Sankt Englmar D 62 A3
Sankt Gallen A 63 C5
Sankt Gallen CH 71 A4
Sankt Gallenkirch A 71 A4
Sankt Georgen A 63 B5
Sankt Georgen D 61 B4
Sankt Georgen am Reith A 63 C5
Sankt Georgen ob Judenburg A 73 A4
Sankt Georgen ob Murau A 73 A4
Sankt Gilgen A 63 C4
Sankt Goar D 50 C3
Sankt Goarshausen D 50 C3
Sankt Ingbert D 60 A3
Sankt Jacob A 73 B4
Sankt Jakob in Defereggen A 72 B2
Sankt Johann am Tauern A 73 A4
Sankt Johann am Wesen A 63 B4
Sankt Johann im Pongau A 72 A3
Sankt Johann in Tirol A 72 A2
Sankt Katharein an der Laming A 73 A5
Sankt Kathrein am Hauenstein A 73 A5
Sankt Lambrecht A 73 A4
Sankt Leonhard am Forst A 63 B6
Sankt Leonhard im Pitztal A 71 A5
Sankt Lorenzen A 72 B2
Sankt Marein, *Steiermark* A 73 A5
Sankt Marein, *Steiermark* A 73 A5
Sankt Margarethen im Lavanttal A 73 B4
Sankt Margrethen CH 71 A4
Sankt Michael A 73 A5
Sankt Michael im Burgenland A 73 A6
Sankt Michael im Lungau A 72 A3
Sankt Michaelisdonn D 43 B6
Sankt Niklaus CH 70 B2
Sankt Nikolai im Sölktal A 73 A4
Sankt Olof S 41 D4
Sankt Oswald D 63 B4
Sankt Paul A 73 B4
Sankt Paul F 79 B5
Sankt Peter D 61 B4
Sankt Peter am Kammersberg A 73 A4
Sankt Peter-Ording D 43 A5
Sankt-Peterburg = St. Petersburg RUS 7 B11
Sankt Pölten A 63 B6
Sankt Radegund A 73 A5
Sankt Ruprecht an der Raab A 73 A5
Sankt Salvator A 73 B4
Sankt Stefan A 73 B4
Sankt Stefan an der Gail A 72 B3
Sankt Stefan im Rosental A 73 B5
Sankt Valentin A 63 B5
Sankt Veit an der Glan A 73 B4
Sankt Veit an der Gölsen A 63 B6
Sankt Veit in Defereggen A 72 B2
Sankt Wendel D 60 A3
Sankt Wolfgang A 63 C4
Sankt Wolfgang D 62 B3
Sanlúcar de Barrameda E 99 C4
Sanlúcar de Guadiana E 98 B3
Sanlúcar la Mayor E 99 B4
Sanluri I 110 C1
Sânmihaiu Roman RO 75 C6
Sänna S 37 D1
Sannazzaro de'Burgondi I 80 A2
Sanne D 44 C3
Sannicandro di Bari I 104 B2
Sannicandro Gargánico I 104 B1
Sânnicolau Mare RO 75 B5
Sannidal N 33 D6
Sanniki PL 47 C5
Sanok PL 11 B7
Sanquhar GB 25 C4
Sansepolcro I 82 C1
Sanski Most BIH 83 B5
Sant Agustí de Lluçanès E 91 A5
Sant Antoni Abat E 97 C1
Sant Antoni de Calonge E 91 B6
Sant Boi de Llobregat E 91 B5
Sant Carles de la Ràpita E 90 C3
Sant Carlos E 97 B1
Sant Celoni E 91 B5
Sant Climent E 97 B4
Sant Feliu E 91 B5
Sant Feliu de Codines E 91 B5
Sant Feliu de Guíxols E 91 B6
Sant Feliu Sasserra E 91 B5
Sant Ferran E 97 C1
Sant Francesc de Formentera E 97 C1
Sant Francesc de ses Salines E 97 C1
Sant Hilari Sacalm E 91 B5
Sant Hipòlit de Voltregà E 91 A5
Sant Jaume dels Domenys E 91 B4
Sant Joan Baptista E 97 B1
Sant Joan de les Abadesses E 91 A5
Sant Jordi E 90 C3
Sant Josep E 97 C1
Sant Julià de Loria AND 91 A4
Sant Llorenç de Morunys E 91 A4
Sant Llorenç des Carctassar E 97 B3
Sant Llorenç Savall E 91 B5
Sant Luis E 97 B4
Sant Martí de Llemaná E 91 A5
Sant Martí de Maldá E 91 B4
Sant Martí Sarroca E 91 B4
Sant Mateu E 90 C3
Sant Miquel E 97 B1
Sant Pau de Seguries E 91 A5
Sant Pere de Riudebitles E 91 B4
Sant Pere Pescador E 91 A6
Sant Pere Sallavinera E 91 B4
Sant Quirze de Besora E 91 A5
Sant Rafel E 97 C1
Sant Ramon E 91 B4
Sant Vincenç de Castellet E 91 B4
Santa Agnès E 97 B1
Santa Amalia E 93 B4
Santa Ana, *Cáceres* E 93 B5
Santa Ana, *Jaén* E 100 B2
Santa Ana de Pusa E 94 C2
Santa Barbara E 90 C3
Santa Bárbara P 98 B2
Santa Barbara de Casa E 98 B3
Santa Bárbara de Padrões P 98 B3
Santa Catarina P 98 B3
Santa Caterina di Pittinuri I 110 B1
Santa Caterina Villarmosa I 109 B3
Santa Cesárea Terme I 107 A5
Santa Clara-a-Nova P 98 B2
Santa Clara-a-Velha P 98 B2
Santa Clara de Louredo P 98 B3
Santa Coloma de Farners E 91 B5
Santa Coloma de Gramenet E 91 B5
Santa Coloma de Queralt E 91 B4
Santa Colomba de Curueño E 88 B1
Santa Colomba de Somoza E 86 B4
Santa Comba E 86 A2
Santa Comba Dão P 92 A2
Santa Comba de Rossas P 87 C4
Santa Cristina I 71 C4
Santa Cristina de la Polvorosa E 88 B1
Santa Croce Camerina I 109 C3
Santa Croce di Magliano I 103 B7
Santa Cruz E 86 A2
Santa Cruz P 92 B1
Santa Cruz de Alhama E 100 B2
Santa Cruz de Campezo E 89 B4
Santa Cruz de Grio E 89 C5
Santa Cruz de la Salceda E 89 C3
Santa Cruz de la Sierra E 93 B5
Santa Cruz de la Zarza E 95 C3
Santa Cruz de Moya E 96 B1
Santa Cruz de Mudela E 100 A2
Santa Cruz de Paniagua E 93 A4
Santa Cruz del Retamar E 94 B2
Santa Cruz del Valle E 94 B1
Santa Doménica Talao I 106 B2
Santa Doménica Vittória I 109 B3
Santa Elena E 100 A2
Santa Elena de Jamuz E 88 B1
Santa Eufemia E 100 A1
Santa Eufémia d'Aspromonte I 106 C2
Santa Eulalia E 95 B5
Santa Eulália P 92 C3
Santa Eulalia de Oscos E 86 A3
Santa Eulàlia des Riu E 97 C1
Santa Fe E 100 B2
Santa Fiora I 81 D5
Santa Gertrude I 71 B5
Santa Giustina I 72 B2
Santa Iria P 98 B3
Santa Leocadia P 87 C2
Santa Lucia-de-Porto-Vecchio F 102 B2
Santa Lucia del Mela I 109 A4
Santa Luzia P 98 B2
Santa Maddalena Vallalta I 72 B2
Santa Magdalena de Polpis E 90 C3
Santa Margalida E 97 B3
Santa Margarida P 92 B2
Santa Margarida do Sado P 98 A2
Santa Margaridao de Montbui E 91 B4
Santa Margherita I 110 D1
Santa Margherita di Belice I 108 B2
Santa Margherita Ligure I 80 B3
Santa Maria CH 71 B5
Santa Maria E 90 A2
Santa Maria al Bagno I 107 A4
Santa Maria Cápua Vétere I 103 B7
Santa Maria da Feira P 87 D2
Santa Maria de Cayón E 88 A3
Santa Maria de Corco E 91 A5
Santa Maria de Huerta E 95 A4
Santa Maria de la Alameda E 94 B2
Santa Maria de las Hoyas E 89 C3
Santa Maria de Mercadillo E 89 C3
Santa Maria de Nieva E 101 B4
Santa Maria de Trassierra E 100 B1
Santa Maria del Camí E 97 B2
Santa Maria del Campo E 88 B3
Santa Maria del Campo Rus E 95 C4
Santa Maria del Páramo E 88 B1
Santa Maria del Taro I 80 B3
Santa Maria della Versa I 80 B3
Santa Maria di Licodia I 109 B3
Santa Maria-di-Rispéscia I 81 D5
Santa Maria la Palma I 110 B1
Santa María la Real de Nieva E 94 A2
Santa Maria Maggiore I 70 B3
Santa Maria Ribarredonda E 89 B3
Santa Marina del Rey E 88 B1
Santa Marinella I 102 A4
Santa Marta, *Albacete* E 95 C4
Santa Marta, *Badajoz* E 93 C4
Santa Marta de Magasca E 93 B4
Santa Marta de Penaguião P 87 C3
Santa Marta de Tormes E 94 B1
Santa Ninfa I 108 B1
Santa Olalla, *Huelva* E 99 B4
Santa Olalla, *Toledo* E 94 B2
Santa Pau E 91 A5
Santa Pola E 96 C2
Santa Ponça E 97 B2
Santa Severa F 102 A2
Santa Severa I 102 A4
Santa Severina I 107 B3
Santa Sofia I 81 C5
Santa Suzana, *Évora* P 92 C3
Santa Suzana, *Setúbal* P 92 C2
Santa Teresa di Riva I 109 B4
Santa Teresa Gallura I 110 A2
Santa Uxía E 86 B2
Santa Valburga I 71 B5
Santa Vittória in Matenano I 82 C2
Santacara E 89 B5
Santadi I 110 C1
Santaella E 100 B1
Sant'Ágata dei Goti I 103 B7
Sant'Ágata di Ésaro I 106 B2
Sant'Ágata di Puglia I 103 B8
Sant'Agata Feltria I 82 C1
Sant'Ágata Militello I 109 A3
Santana, *Évora* P 92 C2
Santana, *Setúbal* P 92 C1
Santana da Serra P 98 B2
Sant'Ana de Cambas P 98 B3
Santana do Mato P 92 C2
Sant'Anastasia I 103 C7
Santander E 88 A3
Sant'Andrea Frius I 110 C2
Sant'Ángelo dei Lombardi I 103 C8
Sant'Angelo in Vado I 82 C1
Sant'Angelo Lodigiano I 71 C4
Sant'Antioco I 110 C1
Sant'Antonio-di-Gallura I 110 B2
Santanyí E 97 B3
Santarcángelo di Romagna I 82 B1
Santarém P 92 B2
Santas Martas E 88 B1
Sant'Caterina I 81 D5
Santed E 95 A5
Sant'Egidio alla Vibrata I 82 D2
Sant'Elia a Pianisi I 103 B7
Sant'Elia Fiumerapido I 103 B6
Santelices E 88 A3
Sant'Elpídio a Mare I 82 C2
Santéramo in Colle I 104 C2
Santervas de la Vega E 88 B2
Santhià I 70 C3
Santiago de Alcántara E 92 B3
Santiago de Calatrava E 100 B1
Santiago de Compostela E 86 B2
Santiago de la Espade E 101 A3
Santiago de la Puebla E 94 B1
Santiago de la Ribera E 101 B5
Santiago de Litem P 92 B2
Santiago del Campo E 93 B4
Santiago do Cacém P 98 B2
Santiago do Escoural P 92 C2
Santiago Maior P 92 C3
Santibáñez de Béjar E 93 A5
Santibáñez de la Peña E 88 B2
Santibáñez de Murias E 88 A1
Santibáñez de Vidriales E 87 B4
Santibáñez el Alto E 93 A4
Santibáñez el Bajo E 93 A4
Santillana E 88 A2
Santiponce E 99 B4
Santisteban del Puerto E 100 A2
Santiuste de San Juan Bautiste E 94 A2
Santiz E 94 A1
Sant'Ilario d'Enza I 81 B4
Santo Aleixo P 98 A3
Santo Amado P 98 A3
Santo Amaro P 92 C3
Santo André P 98 A2
Santo Domingo E 93 C3
Santo Domingo de la Calzada E 89 B4
Santo Domingo de Silos E 89 C3
Santo Estêvão, *Faro* P 98 B3
Santo Estêvão, *Santarém* P 92 C2
Santo-Pietro-di Tenda F 102 A2
Santo Spirito I 104 B2
Santo Stefano d'Aveto I 80 B3
Santo Stéfano di Camastra I 109 B3
Santo Stefano di Magra I 81 B3
Santo Stéfano Quisquina I 108 B2
Santo Tirso P 87 C2
Santo Tomé E 100 A2
Santok PL 46 C1
Santomera E 101 A4
Santoña E 89 A3
Sant'Oreste I 102 A5
Santotis E 88 A2
Santovenia, *Burgos* E 89 B3
Santovenia, *Zamora* E 88 C1
Santpedor E 91 B4
Santu Lussurgiu I 110 B1
Santutzi E 89 A3
Sanxenxo E 86 B2
Sanza I 104 C1
São Aleixo P 92 C3
São Barnabé P 98 B2
São Bartolomé da Serra P 98 A2
São Bartolomeu de Messines P 98 B2
São Bento P 87 C2
São Brás P 98 B3
São Brás de Alportel P 98 B3
São Braz do Reguedoura P 92 C2
São Cristóvão P 92 C2
São Domingos P 98 B2
São Geraldo P 92 C2
São Jacinto P 92 A2
São João da Madeira P 87 D2
São João da Pesqueira P 87 C3
São João da Ribeira P 92 B2
São João da Serra P 87 D2
São João da Venda P 98 B3
São João dos Caldeireiros P 98 B3
São Julião P 92 B3
São Leonardo P 92 C3
São Luis P 98 B2
São Manços P 92 C3
São Marcos da Ataboeira P 98 B3
Saõ Marcos da Serra P 98 B2
São Marcos de Campo P 92 C3
São Martinho da Cortiça P 92 A2
São Martinho das Amoreiras P 98 B2
São Martinho do Porto P 92 B1
São Matias, *Beja* P 98 A3
São Matias, *Évora* P 92 C2
São Miguel d'Acha P 92 A3
São Miguel de Machede P 92 C3
São Pedro da Torre P 87 C2
São Pedro de Muel P 92 B1
São Pedro de Solis P 98 B3
São Pedro do Sul P 87 D2
São Romão P 92 C2
São Sebastião dos Carros P 98 B3
São Teotónio P 98 B2
São Torcato P 87 C2
Saorge F 80 C1
Sapataria P 92 C1
Sapes GR 116 A7
Sapiãos P 87 C3
Sappada I 72 B2
Sappen N 112 C10
Sapri I 106 A2
Sarajevo BIH 84 C3
Saramon F 77 C3
Sarandë AL 116 C2
Saranovo SCG 85 B5
Saraorci SCG 85 B6
Saray TR 118 A2
Saraycık TR 118 C4
Sarayköy TR 119 E3
Saraylar TR 118 B2
Sarayönü TR 119 D7
Sarbia PL 46 C2
Sarbinowo, *Zachodnio-Pomorskie* PL 45 C6
Sarbinowo, *Zachodnio-Pomorskie* PL 46 A1
Sárbogárd H 74 B3
Sarcelles F 58 A3
Sarche I 71 B5
Sardara I 110 C1
Sardoal P 92 B2
Sardón de Duero E 88 C2
Sare F 76 C1
S'Arenal E 97 B2
Šarengrad HR 75 C4
Sarentino I 71 B6
Sarezzo I 71 C5
Sargans CH 71 A4
Sári H 75 A4
Sari-d'Orcino F 102 A1
Sarıbeyler TR 118 C2
Sarıcakaya TR 118 B5
Sarıgöl TR 119 D3
Sarıkaya TR 16 B7
Sarıköy TR 118 B2
Sarilhos Grandes P 92 C2
Sariñena E 90 B2
Sarıoba TR 118 C7
Sárisáp H 65 C4
Sariyer TR 118 A4
Sarkad H 75 B6
Sárkeresztes H 74 A3
Sárkeresztúr H 74 A3
Särkijärvi FIN 113 E12
Şarkikaraağaç TR 119 D6
Şarköy TR 118 B2
Sarlat-la-Canéda F 77 B4
Sarliac-sur-l'Isle F 67 C5
Sármellék H 74 B2
Särna S 115 F10
Sarnadas P 92 B3
Sarnano I 82 C2
Sarnen CH 70 B3
Sarnesfield GB 29 A5
Sárnico I 71 C4
Sarno I 103 C7
Sarnonico I 71 B6
Sarnow D 45 B5
Sarny UA 11 A9
Särö S 38 B4
Saronno I 70 C4
Sárosd H 74 A3
Šarovce SK 65 B4
Sarpoil F 68 C3
Sarpsborg N 35 C3
Sarracín E 88 B3
Sarral E 91 B4
Sarralbe F 60 A3
Sarrancolin F 77 D3
Sarras F 69 C4
Sarre I 70 C2
Sarre-Union F 60 B3
Sarreaus E 87 B3
Sarrebourg F 60 B3
Sarreguemines F 60 A3
Sárrétudvari H 75 A6
Sarria E 86 B3
Sarrià de Ter E 91 A5
Sarrión E 96 A2
Sarroca de Lleida E 90 B3
Sarroch I 110 C2
Sarron F 76 C2
Sársina I 82 C1
Sarstedt D 51 A5
Sárszentlőrinc H 74 B3
Sárszentmihaly H 74 B3
Sárszentmiklós H 74 B3
Sarteano I 81 D5
Sartène F 102 B1
Sartilly F 57 B4
Sartirana Lomellina I 80 A2
Saruhanlı TR 118 D2
Sárvár H 74 A1
Sarvisvaara S 113 F10
Sarzana I 81 B3
Sarzeau F 66 A2
Sarzedas P 92 B3
Sas van Gent NL 49 B4
Sasalli TR 119 D1
Sasamón E 88 B2
Sásd H 74 B3
Sasino PL 46 A3
Sássari I 110 B1
Sassello I 80 B2
Sassenberg D 50 B4
Sassetta I 81 C4
Sassnitz D 45 A5
Sasso d'Ombrone I 81 D5
Sasso Marconi I 81 B5
Sassocorvaro I 82 C1
Sassoferrato I 82 C1
Sassoleone I 81 B5
Sassuolo I 81 B4
Sástago E 90 B2
Šaštinske Stráže SK 64 B3
Såtåhaugen N 114 E7
Satão P 87 D3
Såtenäs S 35 D4
Säter S 36 B2
Sätila S 40 B2
Satillieu F 69 C4
Satnica Đakovačka HR 74 C3
Sátoraljaújhely H 10 B6
Satow D 44 B3
Sätra-brunn S 36 C3
Satrup D 43 A6
Satteins A 71 A4
Satu Mare RO 11 C7
Saturnia I 102 A4
Saucats F 76 B2
Saucelle E 87 C4
Sauda N 33 C3
Saudasjøen N 33 C3
Sauðarkrókur IS 111 B6
Sauerlach D 62 C2
Saugues F 78 B2
Sauherad N 33 C6
Saujon F 66 C4
Sauland N 33 C5
Saulces Monclin F 59 A5
Saulgau D 61 B5
Saulgrub D 62 C2
Saulieu F 69 A4
Saulnot F 60 C2
Sault F 79 B4
Sault-Brénaz F 69 C5
Sault-de-Navailles F 76 C2
Saulx F 60 C2
Saulxures-sur-Moselotte F 60 C2
Saulzais-le-Potier F 68 B2
Saumos F 76 B1
Saumur F 67 A4
Saunavaara FIN 113 E16
Saundersfoot GB 28 B3
Saurat F 77 D4
Saurbær, *Borgarfjarðarsýsla* IS 111 C4
Saurbær, *Dalasýsla* IS 111 B4
Saurbær, *Eyjafjarðarsýsla* IS 111 B7
Sáuris I 72 B2
Sausset-les-Pins F 79 C4
Sauteyrargues F 78 C2
Sauvagnat F 68 C2
Sauve F 78 C2
Sauveterre-de-Béarn F 76 C2
Sauveterre-de-Guyenne F 76 B2
Sauviat-sur-Vige F 67 C6
Sauxillanges F 68 C3
Sauzé-Vaussais F 67 B5
Sauzet, *Drôme* F 78 B3
Sauzet, *Lot* F 77 B4
Sauzon F 66 A1
Sava I 104 C3
Savarsin RO 11 C7
Savaştepe TR 118 C2
Savci SLO 73 B6
Säve S 38 B4
Savelletri I 104 C3
Savelli I 107 B3
Savenay F 66 A3
Saverdun F 77 C4
Saverne F 60 B3
Savières F 59 B4
Savigliano I 80 B1
Savignac-les-Eglises F 67 C5
Savignano Irpino I 103 B8
Savignano sul Rubicone I 82 B1
Savigny-sur-Braye F 58 C1
Saviñán E 89 C5
Savines-le-lac F 79 B5
Savino Selo SCG 75 C4
Savio I 82 B1
Sävja S 36 C4
Šavnik SCG 85 D4
Savognin CH 71 B4
Savona I 80 B2
Savonlinna FIN 3 F28
Savournon F 79 B4
Sävsjö S 40 B4
Savsjön S 36 C1
Sävsjöström S 40 B5
Savudrija HR 72 C3
Savukoski FIN 113 E17
Sawbridgeworth GB 31 C4
Sawtry GB 30 B3
Sax E 101 A5
Saxdalen S 36 B1
Saxilby GB 27 B5
Saxmundham GB 30 B5
Saxnäs S 115 C12
Saxthorpe GB 30 B5
Sayalonga E 100 C1
Sayatón E 95 B4
Sayda D 52 C3
Säytsjärvi FIN 113 C16
Sázava, *Jihomoravský* CZ 64 A1
Sázava, *Středočeský* CZ 63 A5
Scaër F 56 B2
Scafa I 103 A7
Scalasaig GB 24 B1
Scalby GB 27 A5
Scalea I 106 B2
Scaletta Zanclea I 109 A4
Scalloway GB 22 A7
Scamblesby GB 27 B5
Scandale I 107 B3
Scandiano I 81 B4
Scandicci I 81 C5
Scandolara Ravara I 81 A4
Scanno I 103 B6
Scansano I 81 D5
Scanzano Jónico I 104 C2
Scarborough GB 27 A5
Scardovari I 82 B1
Scardoy GB 22 D4
Scarinish GB 24 B1
Scarperia I 81 C5
Scarriff IRL 20 B3
Scey-sur-Saône et St. Albin F 60 C1
Sch-en-feld D 62 A3
Schachendorf A 73 A6
Schaffhausen CH 61 C4
Schafstädt D 52 B1
Schafstedt D 43 A6
Schäftlarn D 62 C2
Schagen NL 42 C1
Schalkau D 51 C7
Schangnau CH 70 B2
Schapbach D 61 B4
Scharbeutz D 44 A2
Schärding A 63 B4
Scharnitz A 71 A6
Scharrel D 43 B4
Schattendorf A 64 C2
Scheemda NL 42 B3
Scheessel D 43 B6
Schéggia I 82 C1
Scheibbs A 63 B6
Scheibenberg D 52 C2
Scheidegg D 61 C5
Scheifling A 73 A4
Scheinfeld D 61 A6
Schelklingen D 61 B5
Schenefeld, *Schleswig-Holstein* D 43 A6
Schenefeld, *Schleswig-Holstein* D 44 B1
Schenklengsfeld D 51 C5
Scherfede D 51 B5
Schermbeck D 50 B2
Scherpenzeel NL 49 A6
Schesslitz D 52 D1
Scheveningen NL 49 A5
Schiedam NL 49 B5
Schieder-Schwalenberg D 51 B5
Schierling D 62 B3
Schiers CH 71 B4
Schildau D 52 B2
Schillingen D 60 A2
Schillingsfürst D 61 A6
Schilpário I 71 B5
Schiltach D 61 B4
Schiltigheim F 60 B3
Schio I 71 C6
Schirmeck F 60 B3
Schirnding D 52 C2
Schkeuditz D 52 B2
Schkölen D 52 B1

Skognes N 112 C8
Skogstorp, *Halland* S 40 C2
Skogstorp, *Södermanland* S 37 C3
Skoki PL 46 C3
Skokloster S 37 C4
Sköldinge S 37 C3
Skole UA 11 B7
Skollenborg N 35 C1
Sköllersta S 37 C2
Skomlin PL 54 B3
Skonseng N 115 A11
Skopelos GR 116 C5
Skopje MK 10 E6
Skoppum N 35 C2
Skórcz PL 47 B4
Skorogoszcz PL 54 C2
Skoroszów PL 54 B2
Skorovatn N 115 C10
Skorped S 115 D14
Skørping DK 38 C2
Skotfoss N 33 C6
Skotniki PL 55 B4
Skotselv N 34 C1
Skotterud N 34 C4
Skottorp S 40 C2
Skovby DK 39 E2
Skövde S 35 D5
Skovsgård DK 38 B2
Skrad HR 73 C4
Skradin HR 83 C4
Skradnik HR 73 C5
Skråmestø N 32 B1
Škrdlovice CZ 64 A1
Skrea S 40 C2
Skreia N 34 B2
Skrolsvik N 112 C5
Skruv S 40 C5
Skrwilno PL 47 B5
Skrydstrup DK 39 D2
Skucani BIH 84 C1
Skudeneshavn N 33 C2
Skui N 34 C2
Skulsk PL 47 C4
Skultorp S 35 D5
Skultuna S 37 C3
Skuodas LT 6 C6
Skurup S 41 D3
Skute N 34 B2
Skuteč CZ 64 A1
Skutskär S 36 B4
Skutvik N 112 D4
Skvyra UA 11 B10
Skwierzyna PL 46 C1
Skýcov SK 65 B4
Skyllberg S 37 D1
Skyttmon S 115 D12
Skyttorp S 36 B4
Sládkovičovo SK 64 B3
Slagelse DK 39 D4
Slagharen NL 42 C3
Slagnäs S 115 B15
Slaidburn GB 26 B3
Slane IRL 19 C5
Slangerup DK 41 D2
Slano HR 84 D2
Slantsy RUS 7 B10
Slaný CZ 53 C4
Slap SLO 72 B3
Šlapanice CZ 64 A2
Slåstad N 34 B3
Slatina BIH 84 C2
Slatina HR 74 C2
Slatina RO 11 D8
Slatina SCG 85 C5
Slatiňany CZ 64 A1
Slatinice CZ 64 A3
Slättberg S 36 A1
Slattum N 34 C2
Slavičin CZ 64 A3
Slavkov CZ 64 B3
Slavkov u Brna CZ 64 A2
Slavkovica SCG 85 B5
Slavonice CZ 63 B6
Slavonski Brod HR 74 C3
Slavonski Kobas HR 84 A2
Slavošovce SK 65 B6
Slavskoye RUS 47 A6
Slavuta UA 11 A9
Sława, *Lubuskie* PL 53 B6
Sława, *Zachodnio-Pomorskie* PL 46 B1
Slawharad BY 7 E11
Sławków PL 55 C4
Sławno, *Wielkopolskie* PL 46 C3
Sławno, *Zachodnio-Pomorskie* PL 46 A2
Sławoborze PL 46 B1
Sl'ažany SK 64 B4
Sleaford GB 27 C5
Sleðbrjótur IS 111 B11
Sledmere GB 27 A5
Sleights GB 27 A5
Slemmestad N 34 C2
Ślesin PL 47 C4
Sliač SK 65 B5
Sliema M 107 C5
Sligo IRL 18 B3
Slite S 37 E5
Slitu N 35 C3
Sliven BG 11 E9
Śliwice PL 47 B4
Slobozia RO 11 D9
Slochteren NL 42 B3
Slöinge S 40 C2
Słomniki PL 55 C5
Slonim BY 7 E8
Słońsk PL 45 C6
Slootdorp NL 42 C1
Slottsbron S 35 C5
Slough GB 31 C3
Slövag N 32 B2
Slovenj Gradec SLO 73 B5
Slovenska Bistrica SLO 73 B5
Slovenská L'upča SK 65 B5
Slovenská-Ves SK 65 A6
Slovenské Darmoty SK 65 B5
Slovenske Konjice SLO 73 B5
Słubice PL 45 C6
Sluderno I 71 B5
Sluis NL 49 B4
Šluknov CZ 53 B4
Slunj HR 83 A4
Słupca PL 54 A2
Słupia PL 55 B4
Słupiec PL 54 C1
Słupsk PL 46 A3
Slutsk BY 7 E9
Smålandsstenar S 40 B3
Smalåsen N 115 B10
Smardzewo PL 53 A5
Smarhon BY 7 D9
Smarje SLO 73 B5
Šmarjeta SLO 73 C5
Šmartno SLO 73 B4
Smečno CZ 53 C4
Smedby S 40 C6
Smědec CZ 63 B5
Smederevo SCG 85 B5
Smederevska Palanka SCG 85 B5
Smedjebacken S 36 B2
Smęgorzów PL 55 C6
Smeland N 33 D5
Smidary CZ 53 C5
Śmigiel PL 54 A1
Smila UA 11 B11
Smilde NL 42 C3
Smiřice CZ 53 C5
Smithfield GB 25 D5
Śmitowo PL 46 B2
Smögen S 35 D3
Smogulec PL 46 B3
Smołdzino PL 46 A3
Smolenice SK 64 B3
Smolensk RUS 7 D12
Smolník SK 65 B6
Smolyan BG 116 A6
Smuka SLO 73 C4
Smygehamn S 41 D3
Smykow PL 55 B5
Snainton GB 27 A5
Snaith GB 27 B4
Snaptun DK 39 D3
Snarby N 112 C8
Snarum N 34 B1
Snåsa N 115 C9
Snedsted DK 38 C1
Sneek NL 42 B2
Sneem IRL 20 C2
Snejbjerg DK 39 C1
Snihurivka UA 11 C12
Snillfjord N 114 D6
Šnjegotina BIH 84 B2
Snøde DK 39 D3
Snøfjord N 113 B13
Snogebaek DK 41 D5
Snyatyn UA 11 B8
Soave I 71 C6
Sober E 86 B3
Sobernheim D 60 A3
Soběslav CZ 63 A5
Sobienie Jeziory PL 55 B6
Sobota, *Dolnośląskie* PL 53 B5
Sobota, *Łódzkie* PL 55 A4
Sobotište SK 64 B3
Sobotka CZ 53 C5
Sobótka, *Dolnośląskie* PL 54 C1
Sobótka, *Wielkopolskie* PL 54 B2
Sobra HR 84 D2
Sobrado, *Coruña* E 86 A2
Sobrado, *Lugo* E 86 B3
Sobral da Adica P 98 A3
Sobral de Monte Argraço P 92 C1
Sobreira Formosa P 92 B3
Søby DK 39 E3
Soca SLO 72 B3
Sočanica SCG 85 C5
Sochaczew PL 55 A5
Sochos GR 116 B5
Socodor RO 75 B6
Socol RO 85 B6
Socovos E 101 A4
Socuéllamos E 95 C4
Sodankylä FIN 113 E15
Soderåkra S 40 C6
Söderala S 36 A3
Söderås S 36 B2
Söderbärke S 36 B2
Söderby-Karl S 36 C5
Söderfors S 36 B4
Söderhamn S 36 A4
Söderköping S 37 D3
Söderö S 40 A5
Södertälje S 37 C4
Södingberg A 73 A5
Södra Finnö S 37 D3
Södra Ny S 35 C5
Södra Råda S 35 C6
Södra Sandby S 41 D3
Södra Vi S 40 B5
Sodražica SLO 73 C4
Sodupe E 89 A3
Soengas P 87 C2
Soest D 50 B4
Soest NL 49 A6
Sofades GR 116 C4
Sofia = Sofiya BG 11 E7
Sofikon GR 117 E5
Sofiya = Sofia BG 11 E7
Şofronea RO 75 B6
Sögel D 43 C4
Sogliano al Rubicone I 82 B1
Sogndalsfjøra N 32 A4
Søgne N 33 D4
Söğüt, *Bilecik* TR 118 B5
Söğüt, *Burdur* TR 119 E4
Söğütköy TR 119 F3
Söğütlu TR 118 B5
Soham GB 30 B4
Sohland D 53 B4
Sohren D 60 A3
Soignies B 49 C5
Soissons F 59 A4
Söjtör H 74 B1
Sokal' UA 11 A8
Söke TR 119 E2
Sokna N 34 B1
Sokndal N 33 D3
Soknedal N 114 E7
Soko BIH 84 B3
Sokolac BIH 84 C3
Sokółka PL 6 E7
Sokolov CZ 52 C2
Sokołów Podlaski PL 6 E7
Sokołowo PL 54 A3
Sola N 33 D2
Solana de los Barros E 93 C4
Solana del Pino E 100 A1
Solánas I 110 C2
Solares E 88 A3
Solarino I 109 B4
Solarussa I 110 C1
Solas GB 22 D1
Solber-gelva N 34 C2
Solberg S 115 D14
Solberga S 40 B4
Solbjørg N 32 B2
Solčany SK 64 B4
Solčava SLO 73 B4
Solda I 71 B5
Sölden A 71 B6
Solec Kujawski PL 47 B4
Solec nad Wisłą PL 55 B6
Soleils F 79 C5
Solenzara F 102 B2
Solera E 100 B2
Solesmes F 49 C4
Soleto I 107 A5
Solgne F 60 B2
Solheim N 32 B2
Solheimsvik N 33 C3
Solignac F 67 C6
Solihull GB 27 C4
Solin HR 83 C5
Solingen D 50 B3
Solivella E 91 B4
Solkan SLO 72 C3
Söll A 72 A2
Sollana E 96 B2
Sollebrunn S 35 D4
Sollefteå S 115 D14
Sollen-tuna S 37 C4
Sollenau A 64 C2
Sóller E 97 B2
Sollerön S 36 B1
Søllested DK 39 E4
Solliès-Pont F 79 C5
Sollihøgda N 34 C2
Solnechnogorsk RUS 7 C14
Solnice CZ 53 C6
Solofra I 103 C7
Solomiac F 77 C3
Solopaca I 103 B7
Solórzano E 89 A3
Solothurn CH 70 A2
Solre-le-Château F 49 C5
Solsona E 91 B4
Solsvik N 32 B1
Solt H 75 B4
Soltau D 44 C1
Soltsy RUS 7 B11
Soltszentimre H 75 B4
Soltvadkert H 75 B4
Solumsmoen N 34 C1
Solund N 32 A1
Solva GB 28 B2
Sölvesborg S 41 C4
Solymár H 65 C4
Soma TR 118 C2
Somain F 49 C4
Somberek H 74 B3
Sombernon F 69 A4
Sombor SCG 75 C4
Sombreffe B 49 C5
Someren NL 50 B1
Somero FIN 6 A7
Somersham GB 30 B3
Somerton GB 29 B5
Sominy PL 46 A3
Somma Lombardo I 70 C3
Sommariva del Bosco I 80 B1
Sommarøy N 112 C7
Sommarset N 112 E4
Sommatino I 109 B3
Somme-Tourbe F 59 A5
Sommeilles F 59 B5
Sommen S 37 D1
Sommepy-Tahure F 59 A5
Sömmerda D 52 B1
Sommerfeld D 45 C5
Sommersted DK 39 D2
Sommesous F 59 B5
Sommières F 78 C3
Sommières-du-Clain F 67 B5
Somo E 88 A3
Somogyfajsz H 74 B2
Somogyjád H 74 B2
Somogysámson H 74 B2
Somogysárd H 74 B2
Somogyszil H 74 B3
Somogyszob H 74 B2
Somogyvár H 74 B2
Somontin E 101 B3
Somosiero E 95 A3
Somosköújifalu H 65 B5
Sompolno PL 47 C4
Sompuis F 59 B5
Son N 35 C2
Son Bou E 97 B4
Son en Breugel NL 49 B6
Son Servera E 97 B3
Sonceboz CH 70 A2
Soncillo E 88 B3
Soncino I 71 C4
Sondalo I 71 B5
Søndeled N 33 D6
Sønder Bjert DK 39 D2
Sønder Felding DK 39 D1
Sønder Hygum DK 39 D1
Sønder Omme DK 39 D1
Sønderborg DK 39 E2
Sønderby DK 39 E2
Sønderho DK 39 D1
Sondershausen D 51 B6
Søndersø DK 39 D3
Søndervig DK 39 C1
Søndre Enningdal Kappel N 35 D3
Sóndrio I 71 B4
Soneja E 96 B2
Songe N 33 D6
Songeons F 58 A2
Sonkamuotka FIN 113 D12
Sonkovo RUS 7 C14
Sönnarslöv S 41 D4
Sonneberg D 52 C1
Sonnefeld D 52 C1
Sonnewalde D 52 B3
Sonnino I 102 B6
Sonogno CH 70 B3
Sonsbeck D 50 B2
Sonseca E 94 C3
Sønsterud N 34 B4
Sonstorp S 37 D2
Sonta SCG 75 C4
Sontheim D 61 B6
Sonthofen D 71 A5
Sontra D 51 B5
Sopelana E 89 A4
Sopje HR 74 C2
Šoporňa SK 64 B3
Sopot PL 47 A4
Sopot SCG 85 B5
Sopotnica MK 116 A3
Sopron H 64 C2
Šor SCG 85 B4
Sora I 103 B6
Soragna I 81 B4
Söråker S 115 E14
Sorano I 81 D5
Sorbara I 81 B5
Sorbas E 101 B3
Sórbolo I 81 B4
Sörbygden S 115 E13
Sordal N 33 D4
Sordale GB 23 C5
Sore F 76 B2
Sörenberg CH 70 B3
Soresina I 71 C4
Sorèze F 77 C5
Sörforsa S 115 F14
Sorges F 67 C5
Sórgono I 110 B2
Sorgues F 78 B3
Sorgun TR 16 B7
Soria E 89 C4
Soriano Cálabro I 106 C3
Soriano nel Cimino I 102 A5
Sorihuela del Guadalimar E 100 A2
Sorisdale GB 24 B1
Sørkjosen N 112 C9
Sørli N 115 C10
Sormás H 74 B1
Sörmjöle S 115 D17
Sørmo N 112 D7
Sornac F 68 C2
Sorø DK 39 D4
Soroca MD 11 B10
Sørreisa N 112 C7
Sorrento I 103 C7
Sorsele S 115 B14
Sörsjön S 34 A5
Sorso I 110 B1
Sort E 91 A4
Sortavala RUS 3 F29
Sortino I 109 B4
Sortland N 112 D4
Sørum N 34 B2
Sørumsand N 34 C3
Sorunda S 37 C4
Sörup D 44 A1
Sørvær N 113 B11
Sørvågen N 112 E1
Sorvik S 36 B2
Sørvika N 114 E8
Sos F 76 B3
Sos del Rey Católico E 90 A1
Sösdala S 41 C3
Sošice HR 73 C5
Sośnica PL 46 B2
Sośnicowice PL 54 C3
Sośno PL 46 B3
Sosnovyy Bor RUS 7 B10
Sosnowiec PL 55 C4
Sospel F 80 C1
Šoštanj SLO 73 B5
Sotaseter N 114 F4
Sotillo de Adrada E 94 B2
Sotillo de la Ribera E 88 C3
Sotin HR 75 C4
Sotkamo FIN 3 D28
Soto de la Marina E 88 A3
Soto de los Infantes E 86 A4
Soto de Real E 94 B3
Soto de Ribera E 88 A1
Soto del Barco E 86 A4
Soto y Amío E 88 B1
Sotobañado y Priorato E 88 B2
Sotoserrano E 93 A4
Sotresgudo E 88 B2
Sotrondio E 88 A1
Sotta F 102 B2
Sottomarina I 72 C2
Sottrum D 43 B6
Sottunga FIN 36 B7
Sotuelamos E 95 C4
Souain F 59 A5
Soual F 77 C5
Soucy F 59 B4
Souda GR 117 G6
Soudron F 59 B5
Souesmes F 68 A2
Souffleinheim F 60 B3
Soufli GR 116 A8
Souillac F 77 B4
Souilly F 59 A6
Soulac-sur-Mer F 66 C3
Soulaines-Dhuys F 59 B5
Soulatgé F 77 D5
Soultz-Haut-Rhin F 60 C3
Soultz-sous-Forêts F 60 B3
Soumagne B 50 C1
Soumoulou F 76 C2
Souppes-sur-Loing F 58 B3
Souprosse F 76 C2
Sourdeval F 57 B5
Soure P 92 A2
Sournia F 77 D5
Souro Pires P 87 D3
Sourpi GR 116 C4
Sours F 58 B2
Sousceyrac F 77 B5
Sousel P 92 C3
Soustons F 76 C1
Soutelo de Montes E 86 B2
South Brent GB 28 C4
South Cave GB 27 B5
South Hayling GB 31 D3
South Molton GB 28 B4
South Ockendon GB 31 C4
South Petherton GB 29 C5
South Shields GB 25 D6
South Tawton GB 28 C4
South Woodham Ferrers GB 31 C4
Southam GB 30 B2
Southampton GB 31 D2
Southborough GB 31 C4
Southend GB 24 C2
Southend-on-Sea GB 31 C4
Southport GB 26 B2
Southwell GB 27 B5
Southwold GB 30 B5
Souto P 92 A3
Souto da Carpalhosa P 92 B2
Soutochao E 87 C3
Souvigny F 68 B3
Souzay-Champigny F 67 A4
Soverato I 106 C3
Soveria Mannelli I 106 B3
Sövestad S 41 D3
Sovetsk RUS 6 D6
Sovići BIH 84 C2
Sovicille I 81 C5
Søvik N 114 E3
Sowerby GB 27 A4
Soyaux F 67 C5
Søyland N 33 D2
Spa B 50 C1
Spadafora I 109 A4
Spaichingen D 61 B4
Spakenburg NL 49 A6
Spalding GB 30 B3
Spálené Poříčí CZ 63 A4
Spalt D 62 A1
Spangenberg D 51 B5
Spangereid N 33 D4
Spantekow D 45 B5
Sparanise I 103 B7
Sparbu N 114 D8
Sparkær DK 38 C2
Sparkford GB 29 B5
Sparreholm S 37 C3
Sparta = Sparti GR 117 E4
Spartà I 109 A4
Sparti = Sparta GR 117 E4
Spas-Demensk RUS 7 D13
Spean Bridge GB 24 B3
Speicher D 60 A2
Speichersdorf D 62 A2
Speke GB 26 B3
Spello I 82 D1
Spenge D 51 A4
Spennymoor GB 25 D6
Spentrup DK 38 C3
Sperenberg D 52 A3
Sperlinga I 109 B3
Sperlonga I 103 B6
Spetalen N 35 C2
Spetses GR 117 E5
Speyer D 61 A4
Spézet F 56 B2
Spezzano Albanese I 106 B3
Spezzano della Sila I 106 B3
Spiddle IRL 20 A2
Spiegelau D 63 B4
Spiekeroog D 43 B4
Spiez CH 70 B2
Spigno Monferrato I 80 B2
Spijk NL 42 B3
Spijkenisse NL 49 B5
Spilamberto I 81 B5
Spili GR 117 G6
Spilimbergo I 72 B2
Spilsby GB 27 B6
Spinazzola I 104 C2
Spincourt F 60 A1
Spind N 33 D3
Spindleruv-Mlyn CZ 53 C5
Spinoso I 104 C1
Špišjć Bukovica HR 74 C2
Spišská Belá SK 65 A6
Spišská Nová Ves SK 65 B6
Spisská Stará Ves SK 65 A6
Spišské-Hanušovce SK 65 A6
Spišské Podhradie SK 65 B6
Spišské Vlachy SK 65 B6
Spišský-Štvrtok SK 65 B6
Spital A 63 C5
Spital am Semmering A 63 C6
Spittal an der Drau A 72 B3
Spittle of Glenshee GB 25 B4
Spitz A 63 B6
Spjærøy N 35 C2
Spjald DK 39 C1
Spjelkavik N 114 E3
Spjutsbygd S 41 C5
Split HR 83 C5
Splügen CH 71 B4
Spodsbjerg DK 39 E3
Spofforth GB 27 B4
Spohle D 43 B5
Spoleto I 82 D1
Spoltore I 103 A7
Spondigna I 71 B5
Sponvika N 35 C3
Spornitz D 44 B3
Spotorno I 80 B2
Spraitbach D 61 B5
Sprakensehl D 44 C2
Spręcowo PL 47 B6
Spremberg D 53 B4
Spresiano I 72 C2
Sprimont B 49 C6
Springe D 51 A5
Sproatley GB 27 B5
Spuž SCG 105 A5
Spydeberg N 35 C3
Spytkowice PL 55 D4
Squillace I 106 C3
Squinzano I 105 C4
Sračinec HR 73 B6
Srbac BIH 84 A2
Srbica SCG 85 D5
Srbobran SCG 75 C4
Srebrenica BIH 85 B4
Srebrenik BIH 84 B3
Središče SLO 73 B6
Śrem PL 54 A2
Sremska Mitrovica SCG 85 B4
Sremski Karlovci SCG 75 C4
Srní CZ 63 A4
Srnice Gornje BIH 84 B3
Srock PL 55 B4
Środa Śląska PL 54 B1
Środa Wielkopolski PL 54 A2
Srpska Crnja SCG 75 C5
Srpski Itebej SCG 75 C5
Srpski Miletić SCG 75 C4
Staatz A 64 B2
Stabbursnes N 113 B13
Staberdorf D 44 A3
Stabroek B 49 B5
Stachy CZ 63 A4
Stade D 43 B6
Staden B 49 C4
Staðarfell IS 111 B3
Stadl an der Mur A 72 A3
Stadskanaal NL 42 C3
Stadtallendorf D 51 C5
Stadthagen D 51 A5
Stadtilm D 52 C1
Stadtkyll D 50 C2
Stadtlauringen D 51 C6
Stadtlengsfeld D 51 C6
Stadtlohn D 50 B2
Stadtoldendorf D 51 B5
Stadtroda D 52 C1
Stadtsteinach D 52 C1
Stäfa CH 70 A3
Staffanstorp S 41 D3
Staffelstein D 51 C6
Staffin GB 22 D2
Stafford GB 26 C3
Stainach A 73 A4
Staindrop GB 27 A4
Staines GB 31 C3
Stainville F 59 B6
Stainz A 73 B5
Staithes GB 27 A5
Staïti I 106 D3
Stäket S 37 C4
Stakroge DK 39 D1
Stalać SCG 85 C6
Štalcerji SLO 73 C4
Stalden CH 70 B2
Stalham GB 30 B5
Stalheim N 32 B3
Stallarholmen S 37 C4
Ställberg S 36 C1
Ställdalen S 36 C1
Stallhofen A 73 A5
Stalon S 115 C12
Stalowa Wola PL 11 A7
Stamford GB 30 B3
Stamford Bridge GB 27 B5
Stamnes N 32 B2
Stams A 71 A5
Stamsried D 62 A3
Stamsund N 112 D2
Stanford le Hope GB 31 C4
Stånga S 37 E5
Stange N 34 B3
Stanghella I 72 C1
Stanhope GB 25 D5
Stanišić SCG 75 C4
Stanisławów PL 55 A6
Staňkov CZ 62 A4
Stankovci HR 83 C4
Stanley GB 25 D6
Stans CH 70 B3
Stansted Mountfitchet GB 31 C4
Stanzach A 71 A5
Stapar SCG 75 C4
Staphorst NL 42 C3
Staplehurst GB 31 C4
Staporków PL 55 B5
Stara Baška HR 83 B3
Stara Fužina SLO 72 B3
Stara Kamienica PL 53 C5
Stara Kiszewa PL 47 B4
Stará L'ubovňa SK 65 A6
Stara Moravica SCG 75 C4
Stara Novalja HR 83 B3
Stara Pazova SCG 85 B5
Stará Turá SK 64 B3
Stara Zagora BG 11 E8
Starachowice PL 55 B6
Staraya Russa RUS 7 C11
Stärbsnäs S 36 C6
Starčevo SCG 85 B5
Stare Dłutowo PL 47 B5
Staré Hamry CZ 65 A4
Stare Jablonki PL 47 B6
Staré Město CZ 64 A3
Stare Pole PL 47 A5
Stare Sedlo CZ 63 A5
Stare Strącze PL 53 B6
Stargard Szczeciński PL 45 B7
Stårheim N 114 F2
Stari Banovci SCG 85 B5
Stari Bar SCG 105 A5
Stari Gradac HR 74 C2
Stari Jankovci HR 75 C3
Stari Majdan BIH 83 B5
Stari-Mikanovci HR 74 C3
Stari Raušić SCG 85 D5
Starigrad, *Ličko-Senjska* HR 83 B3
Starigrad, *Splitsko-Dalmatinska* HR 83 C5
Starigrad-Paklenica HR 83 B4
Staritsa RUS 7 C13
Starkenbach A 71 A5
Starnberg D 62 C2
Staro Petrovo Selo HR 74 C2
Staro Selo HR 73 C5
Staro Selo SCG 85 B6
Starodub RUS 7 E12
Starogard PL 46 B1
Starogard Gdański PL 47 B4
Starokonstyantyniv UA 11 B9
Stary Brzozów PL 55 A5
Stary Dzierzgoń PL 47 B5
Starý Hrozenkov CZ 64 B3
Stary Jaroslaw PL 46 A2
Stary Plzenec CZ 63 A4
Stary Sącz PL 65 A6
Starý Smokovec SK 65 A6
Staryy Chartoriysk UA 11 A8
Staškov SK 65 A4
Stassfurt D 52 B1
Staszów PL 55 C6
Stathelle N 35 C1
Staufen D 60 C3
Staunton GB 29 B5
Štavalj SCG 85 C5
Stavang N 32 A2
Stavanger N 33 D2
Stavåsnäs S 34 B4
Stavby S 36 B5
Staveley GB 27 B4
Stavelot B 50 C1
Stavenisse NL 49 B5
Stavern N 35 D2
Stavnäs S 35 C4
Stavoren NL 42 C2
Stavros CY 120 A1
Stavros GR 116 B5
Stavroupoli GR 116 A6
Stavseng N 32 A6
Stavsiø N 34 B2
Stavsnäs S 37 C5
Stawiszyn PL 54 B3
Steane N 33 C5
Steblevë AL 116 A2
Stechelberg CH 70 B2
Štěchovice CZ 63 A5
Stechow D 44 C4
Steckborn CH 61 C4
Stede Broek NL 42 C2
Steeg A 71 A5
Steenbergen NL 49 B5
Steenvoorde F 48 C3
Steenwijk NL 42 C3
Štefanje HR 74 C1
Steffisburg CH 70 B2
Stegaurach D 62 A1
Stege DK 41 E2
Stegelitz D 45 B5
Stegersbach A 73 A6
Stegna PL 47 A5
Steimbke D 43 C6
Stein GB 22 D2
Stein an Rhein CH 61 C4
Steinach A 71 A6
Steinach, *Baden-Württemberg* D 61 B4
Steinach, *Bayern* D 51 C6
Steinach, *Thüringen* D 52 C1
Steinau, *Bayern* D 51 C5
Steinau, *Niedersachsen* D 43 B5
Steinbeck D 45 C5
Steinberg am Rofan A 72 A1
Steindorf A 73 B4
Steine N 32 B2
Steinen D 60 C3
Steinfeld A 72 B3
Steinfeld D 43 C5
Steinfurt D 50 A3
Steingaden D 62 C1
Steinhagen D 51 A4
Steinheid D 52 C1
Steinheim, *Bayern* D 61 B6
Steinheim, *Nordrhein-Westfalen* D 51 B5
Steinhöfel D 45 C6
Steinhorst D 44 C2
Steinigtwolmsdorf D 53 B4
Steinkjer N 114 C8
Steinsholt N 35 C1
Stekene B 49 B5
Stelle D 44 B2
Stellendam NL 49 B5
Stenåsa S 41 C6
Stenay F 59 A6
Stenberga S 40 B5
Stendal D 44 C3
Stenhammar S 35 D5
Stenhamra S 37 C4
Stenhousemuir GB 25 B4
Stenlose DK 41 D2
Stensätra S 36 B3
Stensele S 115 B14
Stenstorp S 35 D5
Stenstrup DK 39 D3
Stenudden S 112 F6
Stenungsund S 38 A4
Štěpánov CZ 64 A3
Stephanskirchen D 62 C3
Stepnica PL 45 B6
Stepojevac SCG 85 B5
Stepping DK 39 D2
Sterbfritz D 51 C5
Sternberg D 44 B3
Šternberk CZ 64 A3
Sterup D 44 A1
Stęszew PL 54 A1
Štěti CZ 53 C4
Stevenage GB 31 C3
Stewarton GB 24 C3
Steyerburg D 43 C6
Steyning GB 31 D3
Steyr A 63 B5
Stężyca PL 46 A3
Stezzano I 71 C4
Stia I 81 C5
Stibb Cross GB 28 C3
Sticciano Scalo I 81 D5
Stidsvig S 41 C3
Stiens NL 42 B2
Stige DK 39 D3
Stigen S 35 D4
Stigliano I 104 C2
Stigtomta S 37 D3
Stilida GR 116 D4
Stilla N 113 C12
Stillington GB 27 A4
Stilo I 106 C3
Stintino I 110 B1
Stio I 103 C8
Štip MK 116 A4
Stira GR 117 D6
Stirling GB 25 B4
Štítnik SK 65 B6
Štíty CZ 54 D1
Stjärnhov S 37 C4
Stjärnsund S 36 B3
Stjørdalshalsen N 114 D7

Stobnica PL 55 B4
Stobno PL 46 B2
Stobreč HR 83 C5
Stochov CZ 53 C3
Stockach D 61 C5
Stöckalp CH 70 B3
Stockaryd S 40 B4
Stockbridge GB 31 C2
Stockerau A 64 B2
Stockheim D 52 C1
Stockholm S 37 C5
Stockport GB 26 B3
Stocksbridge GB 27 B4
Stockton-on-Tees GB 27 A4
Stod CZ 62 A4
Stöde S 115 E13
Stöðvarfjörður IS 111 C12
Stødi N 112 F4
Stoer GB 22 C3
Stoholm DK 38 C2
Stoke Ferry GB 30 B4
Stoke Fleming GB 29 C4
Stoke Mandeville GB 31 C3
Stoke-on-Trent GB 26 B3
Stokesley GB 27 A4
Stokke N 35 C2
Stokkemarke DK 39 E4
Stokken N 33 D5
Stokkseyri IS 111 D4
Stokkvågen N 115 A10
Stokmarknes N 112 D3
Štoky CZ 63 A6
Stolac BIH 84 C2
Stølaholmen N 32 A3
Stolberg D 50 C2
Stolin BY 7 F9
Stollberg D 52 C2
Stöllet S 34 B5
Stollhamm D 43 B5
Stolno PL 47 B4
Stolpen D 53 B4
Stolzenau D 43 C6
Stompetoren NL 42 C1
Ston HR 84 D2
Stonařov CZ 63 A6
Stone GB 26 C3
Stonehaven GB 25 B5
Stonehouse GB 25 C4
Stongfjorden N 32 A2
Stonndalen N 32 B4
Stony Stratford GB 30 B3
Stopanja SCG 85 C6
Stopnica PL 55 C5
Storå S 37 C2
Storås N 114 D6
Storby FIN 36 B6
Stordal, Møre og Romsdal N 114 E4
Stordal, Nord-Trøndelag N 114 D8
Store GB 23 B6
Store Damme DK 41 E2
Store Heddinge DK 41 D2
Store Herrestad S 41 D3
Store Levene S 35 D4
Store Molvik N 113 B17
Store Skedvi S 36 B2
Store Vika S 37 D4
Storebø N 32 B2
Storebro S 40 B5
Storelv N 113 B11
Støren N 114 D7
Storfjellseter N 114 F7
Storfjord N 112 C8
Storfjorden N 114 E3
Storfors S 35 C6
Storforshei N 112 F3
Storhøliseter N 32 A6
Storjord N 112 F4
Storkow, Brandenburg D 53 A3
Storkow, Mecklenburg-Vorpommern D 45 B6
Storli N 114 E6
Storlien S 114 D9
Stornara I 104 B1
Stornoway GB 22 C2
Storo I 71 C5
Storozhynets UA 11 B8
Storrington GB 31 D3
Storseleby S 115 C13
Storsjön S 36 A3
Storslett N 112 C10
Storsteinnes N 112 C8
Storuman S 115 B14
Störvattnet S 115 E9
Storvik N 112 F2
Storvik S 36 B3
Storvreta S 36 C4
Štos SK 65 B6
Stössen D 52 B1
Stotel D 43 B5
Stötten D 62 C1
Stotternheim D 52 B1
Stouby DK 39 D2
Stourbridge GB 26 C3
Stourport-on-Severn GB 29 A5
Støvring DK 38 C2
Stow GB 25 C5
Stow-on-the-Wold GB 29 B6
Stowbtsy BY 7 E9
Stowmarket GB 30 B5
Straach D 52 B2
Strabane GB 19 B4
Strachan GB 23 D6
Strachur GB 24 B2
Strackholt D 43 B4
Stradbally IRL 20 B1
Stradella I 80 A3
Straelen D 50 B2
Stragari SCG 85 B5
Strakonice CZ 63 A4
Strålsnäs S 37 D2
Stralsund D 45 A5
Strand N 34 A3
Stranda, Møre og Romsdal N 114 E3
Strandby DK 38 B3
Strandebarm N 32 B3
Strandhill IRL 18 B3
Strandlykkja N 34 B3
Strandvik N 32 B2
Strangford GB 19 B6
Strängnäs S 37 C4
Strångsjö S 37 D3
Stráni CZ 64 B3
Stranice SLO 73 B5
Stranorlar IRL 19 B4
Stranraer GB 24 D2
Strasatti I 108 B1
Strasbourg F 60 B3
Strasburg D 45 B5
Strašice CZ 63 A4
Strass im Steiermark A 73 B5
Stråssa S 37 C2
Strassburg A 73 B4
Strasskirchen D 62 B3
Strasswalchen A 63 C4
Stratford-upon-Avon GB 29 A6
Strathaven GB 24 C3
Strathdon GB 23 D5
Strathkanaird GB 22 D3
Strathpeffer GB 23 D4
Strathy GB 23 C5
Strathyre GB 24 B3
Stratinska BIH 84 B1
Stratton GB 28 C3
Straubing D 62 B3
Straulas I 110 B2
Straume N 33 C6
Straumen, Nord-Trøndelag N 114 D8
Straumen, Nordland N 112 E4
Straumsjøen N 112 D3
Straumsnes N 112 E4
Straupitz D 53 B4
Strausberg D 45 C5
Straussfurt D 51 B7
Strawczyn PL 55 C5
Straž nad Nezárkou CZ 63 A5
Stráž Pod Ralskem CZ 53 C4
Straža SCG 85 B6
Straža SLO 73 C5
Strážnice CZ 64 B3
Strážný CZ 63 B4
Štrbské Pleso SK 65 A6
Strečno SK 65 A4
Street GB 29 B5
Strehla D 52 B3
Strekov SK 65 C4
Strem A 73 A6
Stremska-Rača SCG 85 B4
Strengberg A 63 B5
Strengelvåg N 112 D4
Streoci SCG 85 D5
Stresa I 70 C3
Streufdorf D 51 C6
Strib DK 39 D2
Striberg S 37 C1
Střibro CZ 62 A3
Strichen GB 23 D6
Strigno I 71 B6
Štrigova HR 73 B6
Strijen NL 49 B5
Strizivojna HR 74 C3
Strmica HR 83 B5
Strmilov CZ 63 A6
Ströhen D 43 C5
Strokestown IRL 18 C3
Stromberg, Nordrhein-Westfalen D 50 B4
Stromberg, Rheinland-Pfalz D 60 A3
Stromeferry GB 22 D3
Strömnäs S 115 C13
Stromness GB 23 C5
Strömsberg S 36 B4
Strömsbruk S 115 F14
Strömsfors S 37 D3
Strömsnäsbruk S 40 C3
Strömstad S 35 D3
Strömsund, Jämtland S 115 D12
Strömsund, Västerbotten S 115 B13
Stronachlachar GB 24 B3
Stróngoli I 107 B4
Stronie Ślaskie PL 54 C1
Strontian GB 24 B2
Stroppiana I 70 C3
Stroud GB 29 B5
Stroumbi CY 120 B1
Stróża PL 65 A5
Strücklingen D 43 B4
Struer DK 38 C1
Struga MK 116 A2
Strugi Krasnyye RUS 7 B10
Strumica MK 116 A4
Strumien PL 65 A4
Struy GB 22 D4
Stružec HR 74 C1
Stryków PL 55 B4
Stryn N 114 F3
Stryy UA 11 B7
Strzałkowo PL 54 A2
Strzegocin PL 47 C6
Strzegom PL 54 C1
Strzegowo PL 47 C6
Strzelce PL 55 A4
Strzelce Krajeńskie PL 46 C1
Strzelce Kurowo PL 46 C1
Strzelce Opolskie PL 54 C3
Strzelin PL 54 C2
Strzelno PL 47 C4
Strzepcz PL 47 A4
Strzybnica PL 54 C3
Strzygi PL 47 B5
Stubal SCG 85 C5
Stubbekøbing DK 39 E5
Stuben A 71 A5
Stubenberg A 73 A5
Stubline SCG 85 B5
Studená CZ 63 A6
Studenci HR 84 C2
Studenica SCG 85 C5
Studenka CZ 64 A4
Studenzen A 73 A5
Studienka SK 64 B3
Studland GB 29 C6
Studley GB 29 A6
Studzienice PL 46 A3
Stuer D 44 B4
Stugudal N 114 E8
Stugun S 115 D12
Stuhr D 43 B5
Stukenbrock D 51 B4
Stülpe D 52 A3
Stupava SK 64 B3
Stupnik HR 73 C5
Stupsk PL 47 B6
Sturkö S 41 C5
Sturminster Newton GB 29 C5
Štúrovo SK 65 C4
Sturton GB 27 B5
Stuttgart D 61 B5
Stvolny CZ 52 C3
Stykkishólmur IS 111 B3
Styri N 34 B3
Stysö S 38 B4
Suances E 88 A2
Subbiano I 81 C5
Subiaco I 102 B6
Subotica SCG 75 B4
Subotište SCG 85 B4
Sučany SK 65 A4
Suceava RO 11 C9
Sucha-Beskidzka PL 65 A5
Suchacz PL 47 A5
Suchań PL 46 B1
Suchdol nad Lužnice CZ 63 B5
Suchedniów PL 55 B5
Suchorze PL 46 A3
Suchteln D 50 B2
Sucina E 101 B5
Suckow D 44 B3
Sućuraj HR 84 C2
Sudbury GB 30 B4
Suddesjaur S 115 B16
Suden D 43 A5
Süderbrarup D 44 A1
Süderlügum D 39 E1
Súðavík IS 111 A3
Suðureyri IS 111 A2
Sudoměřice u Bechyně CZ 63 A5
Sudovec HR 73 B6
Sudzha RUS 7 F13
Sueca E 96 B2
Suelli I 110 C2
Sugenheim D 61 A6
Sugères F 68 C3
Sugny B 59 A5
Suhl D 51 C6
Suhlendorf D 44 C2
Suho Polje BIH 85 B4
Suhopolje HR 74 C2
Şuhut TR 119 D5
Šuica BIH 84 C2
Suippes F 59 A5
Sukhinichi RUS 7 D13
Sukobin SCG 105 A5
Sukošan HR 83 B4
Sükösd H 75 B3
Suków PL 55 C5
Šul'a SK 65 B5
Suldalsosen N 33 C3
Suldrup DK 38 C2
Sulechów PL 53 A5
Sulęcin PL 45 C7
Sulęczyno PL 46 A3
Sulejów PL 55 B4
Sulejówek PL 55 A6
Süleymanlı TR 118 D2
Sulgen CH 71 A4
Sulibórz PL 46 B1
Sulina RO 11 D10
Sulingen D 43 C5
Suliszewo PL 46 B1
Sulitjelma N 112 E5
Sułkowice PL 65 A5
Süller TR 119 D4
Sully-sur-Loire F 58 C3
Sulmierzyce, Łódzkie PL 55 B4
Sulmierzyce, Wielkopolskie PL 54 B2
Sulmona I 103 A6
Süloğlu TR 118 A1
Sułoszowa PL 55 C4
Sulów PL 54 B2
Sulsdorf D 44 A3
Sultandağı TR 119 D6
Sülüklü TR 118 D7
Suluova TR 16 A7
Sulvik S 35 C4
Sülysáp H 75 A4
Sülz D 61 B4
Sulzbach, Baden-Württemberg D 61 A5
Sulzbach, Baden-Württemberg D 61 B5
Sulzbach, Bayern D 61 A5
Sulzbach, Saarland D 60 A3
Sulzbach-Rosenberg D 62 A2
Sülze D 44 C2
Sulzfeld D 51 C6
Sumartin HR 84 C1
Sumburgh GB 22 B7
Sümeg H 74 B2
Sumiswald CH 70 A2
Šumná CZ 64 B1
Šumperk CZ 54 D1
Šumvald CZ 64 A3
Sumy UA 7 F13
Sunbilla E 76 C1
Sünching D 62 B3
Sund FIN 36 B7
Sund S 35 C3
Sundborn S 36 B2
Sundby DK 38 C1
Sunde N 32 C2
Sunde bru N 33 D6
Sunderland GB 25 D6
Sundern D 50 B4
Sundhultsbrunn S 40 B4
Sundnäs S 115 A14
Sunds DK 39 C2
Sundsfjord N 112 F3
Sundsvall S 115 E14
Sungurlu TR 16 A7
Suni I 110 B1
Sunja HR 74 C1
Sunnansjö S 36 B1
Sunnaryd S 40 B3
Sunndalsøra N 114 E5
Sunne S 34 C5
Sunnemo S 34 C5
Sunnersberg S 35 D5
Suolovuopmio N 113 C12
Suomussalmi FIN 3 D28
Suoyarvi RUS 3 E30
Super Sauze F 79 B5
Supetar HR 83 C5
Supetarska Draga HR 83 B3
Supino I 102 B6
Šuplja Stijena SCG 84 C4
Surahammar S 37 C3
Šurany SK 64 B4
Surazh BY 7 D11
Surazh RUS 7 E12
Surbo I 105 C4
Surčin SCG 85 B5
Surgères F 66 B4
Surhuisterveen NL 42 B3
Súria E 91 B4
Surin F 67 B5
Surka N 34 B2
Surnadalsøra N 114 E5
Sursee CH 70 A3
Surte S 38 B5
Surwold D 43 C4
Sury-le-Comtal F 69 C4
Susa I 70 C2
Šušara SCG 85 B6
Susch CH 71 B5
Susegana I 72 C2
Süsel D 44 A2
Sušice CZ 63 A4
Šušnjevica HR 73 C4
Sussen D 61 B5
Susurluk TR 118 C3
Susz PL 47 B5
Sütçüler TR 119 E5
Sutivan HR 83 C5
Sutjeska SCG 75 C5
Sutomore SCG 105 A5
Sutri I 102 A5
Sutton GB 31 C3
Sutton Coldfield GB 27 C4
Sutton-in-Ashfield GB 27 B4
Sutton-on-Sea GB 27 B6
Sutton-on-Trent GB 27 B5
Sutton Scotney GB 31 C2
Sutton Valence GB 31 C4
Suvaja BIH 83 B5
Suvereto I 81 C4
Suvorov RUS 7 D14
Suwałki PL 6 D7
Suze-la-Rousse F 78 B3
Suzzara I 81 B4
Svabensverk S 36 A2
Svalbarð IS 111 A10
Svalöv S 41 D3
Svanabyn S 115 C13
Svanberga S 36 C5
Svaneke DK 41 D5
Svanesund S 35 D3
Svängsta S 41 C4
Svannäs S 115 A15
Svanskog S 35 C4
Svanstein S 113 F12
Svappavaara S 112 E10
Svärdsjö S 36 B2
Svarstad N 35 C1
Svartå, Örebro S 37 C1
Svärta, Södermanland S 37 D4
Svartå, Värmland S 34 C5
Svärtinge S 37 D3
Svartnäs S 36 B3
Svartnes N 112 E3
Svarttjärn S 115 B13
Svatsum N 34 A1
Svätý Jur SK 64 B3
Svätý Peter SK 64 C4
Svedala S 41 D3
Sveg S 115 E11
Sveindal N 33 D4
Sveio N 33 C2
Svejbæk DK 39 C2
Svelgen N 114 F2
Svelvik N 35 C2
Svendborg DK 39 D3
Svene N 32 C6
Svenljunga S 40 B3
Svennevad S 37 C2
Svenstavik S 115 E11
Svenstrup DK 38 C2
Švermov CZ 53 C4
Sveti Ivan Zabno HR 74 C1
Sveti Ivan Zelina HR 73 C6
Sveti Nikola SCG 105 B5
Sveti Rok HR 83 B4
Sveti Stefan SCG 105 A4
Světla nad Sázavou CZ 63 A6
Svetlyy RUS 47 A6
Svetvinčenat HR 82 A2
Švica HR 83 B4
Svidník SK 10 B6
Švihov CZ 63 A4
Svilajnac SCG 85 B6
Svilengrad BG 11 F9
Svindal N 35 C3
Svinhult S 40 B5
Svinna SK 64 B4
Svinninge DK 39 D4
Svinninge S 37 C5
Sviritsa RUS 7 A12
Svishtov BG 11 E8
Svislach BY 6 E8
Svit SK 65 A6
Svitavy CZ 64 A2
Svitlovodsk UA 11 B12
Svodin SK 65 C4
Svolvær N 112 D3
Svortemyr N 32 A2
Svortland N 32 C2
Svratka CZ 64 A2
Svrčinovec SK 65 A4
Svullrya N 34 B4
Svyetlahorsk BY 7 E10
Swadlincote GB 27 C4
Swaffham GB 30 B4
Swanage GB 29 C6
Swanley GB 31 C4
Swanlinbar IRL 19 B4
Swansea GB 28 B4
Swarzędz PL 46 C3
Swatragh GB 19 B5
Świątki PL 47 B6
Świdnica, Dolnośląskie PL 54 C1
Świdnica, Lubuskie PL 53 B5
Świdnik PL 11 A7
Świdwin PL 46 B1
Świebodzice PL 53 C6
Świebodzin PL 53 A5
Świecie PL 47 B4
Świedziebnia PL 47 B5
Świeradów Zdrój PL 53 C5
Świerki PL 54 C1
Świerzawa PL 53 B5
Świerzno PL 45 B6
Święta PL 45 B6
Święta Anna PL 55 C4
Świętno PL 53 A6
Swifterbant NL 42 C2
Swindon GB 29 B6
Swineshead GB 30 B3
Swinford IRL 18 C3
Świnoujście PL 45 B6
Swinton GB 25 C5
Swobnica PL 45 B6
Swords IRL 21 A5
Swornegacie PL 46 B3
Sya S 37 D2
Syasstroy RUS 7 A12
Sycewice PL 46 A2
Sychevka RUS 7 D13
Syców PL 54 B2
Sycowice PL 53 A5
Sydnes N 33 C2
Syfteland N 32 B2
Syke D 43 C5
Sykkylven N 114 E3
Sylling N 34 C2
Sylte N 114 E4
Symbister GB 22 A7
Symington GB 25 C4
Symonds Yat GB 29 B5
Sypniewo, Kujawsko-Pomorskie PL 46 B3
Sypniewo, Wielkopolskie PL 46 B2
Sysserum S 40 B6
Sysslebäck S 34 B4
Syväjärvi FIN 113 E14
Szabadbattyán H 74 A3
Szabadegyháza H 74 A3
Szabadszállás H 75 B4
Szadek PL 54 B3
Szajol H 75 A5
Szakály H 74 B3
Szakcs H 74 B3
Szakmár H 75 B4
Szalánta H 74 C3
Szałas PL 55 B5
Szalkszentmárton H 75 B4
Szalonna H 65 B6
Szamocin PL 46 B3
Szamotuły PL 46 C2
Szany H 74 A2
Szarvas H 75 B5
Szarvaskö H 65 C6
Szászvár H 74 B3
Százhalombatta H 74 A3
Szczawa PL 65 A6
Szczawnica PL 65 A6
Szczecin PL 45 B6
Szczecinek PL 46 B2
Szczekociny PL 55 C4
Szczerców PL 55 B4
Szczucin PL 55 C6
Szczuczarz PL 46 B2
Szczurkowo PL 47 A6
Szczurowa PL 55 C5
Szczyrk PL 65 A5
Szczytna PL 54 C1
Szczytno PL 6 E6
Szczyty PL 54 B3
Szécsény H 65 B5
Szederkény H 74 C3
Szedres H 74 B3
Szeged H 75 B5
Szeghalom H 75 A6
Szegvár H 75 B5
Székesfehérvár H 74 A3
Székkutas H 75 B5
Szekszárd H 74 B3
Szemplino Czarne PL 47 B6
Szemud PL 47 A4
Szendehely H 65 C5
Szendrö H 65 B6
Szentendre H 65 C5
Szentes H 75 B5
Szentgotthárd H 73 B6
Szentlászló H 74 B2
Szentlörinc H 74 B2
Szentmártonkáta H 75 A4
Szenyér H 74 B2
Szeremle H 74 B3
Szerep H 75 A6
Szigetszentmiklós H 75 A4
Szigetvár H 74 B2
Szikáncs H 75 B5
Szikszó H 65 B6
Szil H 74 A2
Szilvásvárad H 65 B6
Szklarska Poreba PL 53 C5
Szlichtyngowa PL 53 B6
Szob H 65 C4
Szolnok H 75 A5
Szombathely H 74 A1
Szorosad H 74 B3
Szpetal Graniczny PL 47 C5
Szprotawa PL 53 B5
Szreńsk PL 47 B6
Sztum PL 47 B5
Sztutowo PL 47 A5
Szubin PL 46 B3
Szücsi H 65 C5
Szulmierz PL 47 C6
Szulok H 74 B2
Szumanie PL 47 C5
Szwecja PL 46 B2
Szydłów, Łódzkie PL 55 B4
Szydłów, Świętokrzyskie PL 55 C6
Szydłowiec PL 55 B5
Szydlowo, Mazowieckie PL 47 B6
Szydłowo, Wielkopolskie PL 46 B2
Szymanów PL 55 A5
Szynkielów PL 54 B3
Szynwałd PL 55 D6

T

Tab H 74 B3
Tabanera la Luenga E 94 A2
Tabaqueros E 96 B1
Tábara E 88 C1
Tabenera de Cerrato E 88 B2
Taberg S 40 B4
Tabernas E 101 B3
Tabiano Bagni I 81 B4
Taboada E 86 B3
Taboadela E 87 B3
Tábor CZ 63 A5
Táborfalva H 75 A4
Taborište HR 73 C6
Tábua P 92 A2
Tabuaco P 87 C3
Tabuenca E 89 C5
Tabuyo del Monte E 87 B4
Täby S 37 C5
Tác H 74 A3
Tachov CZ 62 A3
Tadcaster GB 27 B4
Tadley GB 31 C2
Tafalla E 89 B5
Tafjord N 114 E4
Taganheira P 98 B2
Tågarp S 41 D2
Tággia I 80 C1
Tagliacozzo I 102 A6
Táglio di Po I 82 A1
Tagnon F 59 A5
Tahal E 101 B3
Tahitótfalu H 65 C5
Tahtaköprü TR 118 C4
Tailfingen D 61 B5
Taillis F 57 B4
Tain GB 23 D4
Tain-l'Hermitage F 78 A3
Taipadas P 92 C2
Taivalkoski FIN 3 D28
Takene S 35 C5
Takovo SCG 85 B5
Taksony H 75 A4
Tal E 86 B2
Tal-Y-Llyn GB 26 C2
Talachyn BY 7 D10
Talamello I 82 C1
Talamone I 102 A4
Talant F 69 A4
Talarrubias E 93 B5
Talas TR 16 B7
Talaván E 93 B4
Talavera de la Reina E 94 C2
Talavera la Real E 93 C4
Talayuela E 93 B5
Talayuelas E 96 B1
Talgarth GB 29 B4
Talgje N 33 C2
Talhadas P 92 A2
Táliga E 93 C3
Talizat F 78 A2
Tálknafjörður IS 111 B2
Talla I 81 C5
Talladale GB 22 D3
Tallaght IRL 21 A5
Tallard F 79 B5
Tällberg S 36 B1
Tallinn EST 6 B8
Talloires F 69 C6
Tallow IRL 21 B4
Tallsjö S 115 C15
Talmay F 69 A5
Talmont-St. Hilaire F 66 B3
Talmont-sur-Gironde F 66 C4
Talne UA 11 B11
Talsano I 104 C3
Talsi LV 6 C7
Talvik N 113 B11
Talybont GB 26 C2
Tamajón E 95 B3
Tamame E 88 C1
Tamames E 93 A4
Tamarit de Mar E 91 B4
Tamarite de Litera E 90 B3
Tamariu E 91 B6
Tamási H 74 B3
Tambach-Dietharz D 51 C6
Tameza E 86 A4
Tammisaari FIN 6 A7
Tampere FIN 3 F25
Tamsweg A 72 A3
Tamurejo E 94 D2
Tamworth GB 27 C4
Tana bru N 113 B17
Tañabueyes E 89 B3
Tanakajd H 74 A1
Tananger N 33 D2
Tanaunella I 110 B2
Tancarville F 58 A1
Tandsjöborg S 115 F11
Tånga S 41 C2
Tangelic H 74 B3
Tangen N 34 B3
Tangerhütte D 44 C3
Tangermünde D 44 C3
Tanhua FIN 113 E16
Taninges F 69 B6
Tankavaara FIN 113 D16
Tann D 51 C6
Tanna D 52 C1
Tannadice GB 25 B5
Tannåker S 40 C3
Tännäs S 115 E9
Tannay, Ardennes F 59 A5
Tannay, Nièvre F 68 A3
Tannenbergsthal D 52 C2
Tännesberg D 62 A3
Tannheim A 71 A5
Tanowo PL 45 B6
Tanum S 35 D3
Tanumshede S 35 D3
Tanus F 77 B5
Tanvald CZ 53 C5
Taormina I 109 B4
Tapa EST 7 B8
Tapfheim D 62 B1
Tapia de Casariego E 86 A4
Tapio F 77 C4
Tápióbicske H 75 A4
Tápiógyörgye H 75 A4
Tápióság H 75 A4
Tápiószecsö H 75 A4
Tápiószele H 75 A4
Tápiószentmárton H 75 A4
Tapolca H 74 B2
Tapolcafö H 74 A2
Tar HR 72 C3
Tarabo S 40 B2
Taradell E 91 B5
Taraklı TR 118 B5
Taramundi E 86 A3
Tarancón E 95 B3
Táranto I 104 C3
Tarare F 69 C4
Tarascon F 78 C3
Tarascon-sur-Ariège F 77 D4
Tarashcha UA 11 B11
Tarazona E 89 C5
Tarazona de la Mancha E 95 C5
Tarbena E 96 C2
Tarbert GB 24 C2
Tarbert IRL 20 B2
Tarbes F 76 C3
Tarbet GB 24 B3
Tarbolton GB 24 C3
Tarcento I 72 B3
Tarčin BIH 84 C3
Tarczyn PL 55 B5
Tardajos E 88 B3
Tardelcuende E 89 C4
Tardets-Sorholus F 76 C2
Tardienta E 90 B2
Tärendö S 113 E11
Targon F 76 B2
Târgovişte RO 11 D8
Târgu-Jiu RO 11 D7
Târgu Mureş RO 11 C8
Târgu Ocna RO 11 C9
Târgu Secuiesc RO 11 D9
Tarifa E 99 C5
Tariquejas E 98 B3
Tarján H 65 C4
Tárkany H 64 C4
Tarland GB 23 D6
Tarłów PL 55 B6
Tarm DK 39 D1
Tarmstedt D 43 B6
Tärnaby S 115 B12
Tarnalelesz H 65 B6
Tarnaörs H 65 C6
Târnăveni RO 11 C8
Tårnet N 113 C19
Tarnobrzeg PL 55 C6
Tarnos F 76 C1
Tarnów, Lubuskie PL 45 C6
Tarnów, Małopolskie PL 55 C5
Tarnowo Podgórne PL 46 C2
Tarnowskie Góry PL 54 C3
Tärnsjö S 36 B3
Tårnvik N 112 E4
Tarouca P 87 C3
Tarp D 43 A6
Tarquínia I 102 A4
Tarquínia Lido I 102 A4
Tarragona E 91 B4
Tàrrega E 91 B4
Tarrenz A 71 A5
Tårs, Nordjyllands DK 38 B3
Tårs, Storstrøms DK 39 E4
Tarsia I 106 B3
Tarsus TR 16 C7
Tartas F 76 C2
Tartu EST 7 B9
Tarussa RUS 7 D14
Tarves GB 23 D6
Tarvísio I 72 B3
Taşağıl TR 119 F6
Täsch CH 70 B2
Taşköprü TR 16 A7
Tasov CZ 64 A2
Tasovčići BIH 84 C2
Tåstrup DK 41 D2
Taşucuo TR 16 C6
Tát H 65 C4
Tata H 65 C4
Tatabánya H 74 A3
Tataháza H 75 B4
Tatarbunary UA 11 D10
Tatárszentgyörgy H 75 A4
Tatranská-Lomnica SK 65 A6
Tau N 33 C2
Tauber-bischofsheim D 61 A5
Taucha D 52 B2
Taufkirchen D 62 B3
Taufkirchen an der Pram A 63 B4
Taulé F 56 B2
Taulignan F 78 B3
Taulov DK 39 D2
Taunton GB 29 B4
Taunusstein D 50 C4
Tauragė LT 6 D7
Taurianova I 106 C3
Taurisano I 107 B5
Tauste E 90 B1
Tauves F 68 C2
Tavankut SCG 75 B4
Tavannes CH 70 A2
Tavarnelle val di Pesa I 81 C5
Tavas TR 119 E4
Tavaux F 69 A5
Tävelsås S 40 C4
Taverna I 106 B3
Taverne CH 70 B3
Tavernelle I 82 C1
Tavernes de la Valldigna E 96 B2
Tavérnola Bergamasca I 71 C5
Taverny F 58 A3
Tavescan E 91 A4
Taviano I 107 B5
Tavira P 98 B3
Tavistock GB 28 C3
Tavnik SCG 85 C5
Tavşanlı TR 118 C4
Tayinloan GB 24 C2
Taynuilt GB 24 B2

Tricárico I 104 C2
Tricase I 107 B5
Tricésimo I 72 B3
Trie-sur-Baïse F 77 C3
Trieben A 73 A4
Triebes D 52 C2
Triepkendorf D 45 B5
Trier D 60 A2
Trieste I 72 C3
Triggiano I 104 B2
Triglitz D 44 B4
Trignac F 66 A2
Trigueros E 99 B4
Trigueros del Valle E 88 C2
Trijebine SCG 85 C4
Trikala GR 116 C3
Trikeri GR 116 C5
Trikomo CY 120 A2
Trilj HR 83 C5
Trillo E 95 B4
Trilport F 59 B3
Trim IRL 21 A5
Trimdon GB 25 D6
Trindade, *Beja* P 98 B3
Trindade, *Bragança* P 87 C3
Třinec CZ 65 A4
Tring GB 31 C3
Trinità d'Agultu I 110 B1
Trinitápoli I 104 B2
Trino I 70 C3
Trinta P 92 A3
Triora I 80 C1
Tripoli GR 117 E4
Triponzo I 82 D1
Triptis D 52 C1
Triste E 90 A2
Trittau D 44 B2
Trivento I 103 B7
Trivero I 70 C3
Trivigno I 104 C1
Trn BIH 84 B2
Trnava HR 74 C3
Trnava SK 64 B3
Trnovec SK 64 B3
Trnovo BIH 84 C3
Trnovska vas SLO 73 B5
Troarn F 57 A5
Trochtelfingen D 61 B5
Trödje S 36 B4
Trœnse DK 39 D3
Trofa P 87 C2
Trofaiach A 73 A5
Trofors N 115 B10
Trogir HR 83 C5
Trøgstad N 35 C3
Tróia I 103 B8
Troia P 92 C2
Troina I 109 B3
Trois-Ponts B 50 C1
Troisdorf D 50 C3
Troisvierges L 50 C2
Trojane SLO 73 B4
Trojanów PL 55 B6
Troldhede DK 39 D1
Trollhättan S 35 D4
Trolog BIH 84 C1
Tromello I 70 C3
Tromøy N 33 D5
Tromsø N 112 C8
Trondheim N 114 D7
Tronget F 68 B3
Trönninge S 40 C2
Trönningeby S 40 B2
Trönö S 36 A3
Tronzano-Vercellese I 70 C3
Trôo F 58 C1
Troon GB 24 C3
Tropea I 106 C2
Tropojë AL 105 A6
Tropy Sztumskie PL 47 B5
Trosa S 37 D4
Trösken S 36 B3
Trosly-Breuil F 59 A4
Trossingen D 61 B4
Trostberg D 62 B3
Trostyanets UA 7 F13
Trouville-sur-Mer F 57 A6
Trowbridge GB 29 B5
Troyes F 59 B5
Trpanj HR 84 C2
Trpezi SCG 85 D5
Trpinja HR 74 C3
Tršće HR 73 C4
Tršice CZ 64 A3
Trstená SK 65 A5
Trstenci BIH 84 A2
Trstenik, *Kosovo* SCG 85 D5
Trstenik, *Srbija* SCG 85 C6
Trsteno HR 84 D2
Trstice SK 64 B3
Trstín SK 64 B3
Trubchevsk RUS 7 E12
Trubia E 88 A1
Trubjela SCG 84 D3
Truchas E 87 B4
Trujillanos E 93 C4
Trujillo E 93 B5
Trumieje PL 47 B5
Trun CH 70 B3
Trun F 57 B6
Truro GB 28 C2
Trusetal D 51 C6
Truskavets' UA 11 B7
Trustrup DK 39 C3
Trutnov CZ 53 C5
Tryserum S 37 D3
Trysil N 34 A4
Tryszczyn PL 46 B3
Trzcianka PL 46 B2
Trzciel PL 46 C1
Trzcińsko Zdrój PL 45 C6
Trzebiatów PL 45 A7
Trzebiel PL 53 B4
Trzebielino PL 46 A3
Trzebień PL 53 B5
Trzebiez PL 45 B6
Trzebinia PL 55 C4
Trzebnica PL 54 B2
Trzebnice PL 53 B6
Trzeciewiec PL 47 B4
Trzemeszno PL 46 C3
Trzemeszno-Lubuskie PL 46 C1
Trzetrzewina PL 65 A6
Tržič SLO 73 B4
Tsamandas GR 116 C2
Tschagguns A 71 A4
Tschernitz D 53 B4
Tsebrykove UA 11 C11
Tsvetkovo UA 11 B11
Tsyelyakhany BY 7 E8
Tua P 87 C3
Tuam IRL 20 A3
Tubbergen NL 42 C3
Tubilla del Lago E 89 C3
Tübingen D 61 B5
Tubize B 49 C5
Tučapy CZ 63 A5
Tučepi HR 84 C2
Tuchan F 78 D1
Tüchen D 44 B4
Tuchola PL 46 B3
Tuchomie PL 46 A3
Tuchów PL 65 A7
Tuczno PL 46 B2
Tuddal N 32 C5
Tudela E 89 B5
Tudela de Duero E 88 C2
Tudweiliog GB 26 C1
Tuejar E 96 B1
Tuffé F 58 B1
Tufsingdalen N 114 E8
Tuhaň CZ 53 C4
Tui E 87 B2
Tukums LV 6 C7
Tula I 110 B1
Tula RUS 7 D14
Tulcea RO 11 D10
Tul'chyn UA 11 B10
Tulette F 78 B3
Tuliszków PL 54 A3
Tulla IRL 20 B3
Tullamore IRL 21 A4
Tulle F 68 C1
Tullins F 69 C5
Tulln A 64 B2
Tullow IRL 21 B5
Tułowice PL 54 C2
Tulppio FIN 113 E18
Tulsk IRL 18 C3
Tumba S 37 C4
Tummel Bridge GB 24 B3
Tun S 35 D5
Tuna, *Kalmar* S 40 B6
Tuna, *Uppsala* S 36 B5
Tuna Hästberg S 36 B2
Tunçbilek TR 118 C4
Tunes P 98 B2
Tungelsta S 37 C5
Tunje AL 105 C6
Tunnerstad S 40 A4
Tunnhovd N 32 B5
Tunstall GB 30 B5
Tuohikotti FIN 3 F27
Tuoro sul Trasimeno I 82 C1
Tupadły PL 47 C4
Tupanari BIH 84 B3
Tupik RUS 7 D12
Tuplice PL 53 B4
Tura H 65 C5
Turanj HR 83 C4
Turany SK 65 A5
Turbe BIH 84 B2
Turbenthal CH 70 A3
Turcia E 88 B1
Turčianske Teplice SK 65 B4
Turcifal P 92 B1
Turckheim F 60 B3
Turda RO 11 C7
Turégano E 94 A3
Turek PL 54 A3
Tŭrgovishte BG 11 E9
Turgutlu TR 119 D2
Turi I 104 C3
Turin = Torino I 80 A1
Turis E 96 B2
Türje H 74 B2
Turka UA 11 B7
Túrkeve H 75 A5
Türkheim D 62 B1
Türkmenli TR 118 C1
Turku FIN 6 A7
Turleque E 94 C3
Turňa nad Bodvou SK 65 B6
Turnberry GB 24 C3
Turnhout B 49 B5
Türnitz A 63 C6
Turnov CZ 53 C5
Turnu RO 75 B6
Turnu Măgurele RO 11 E8
Turón E 100 C2
Turoszów PL 53 C4
Turowo PL 47 B6
Turquel P 92 B1
Turri I 110 C1
Turries F 79 B5
Turriff GB 23 D6
Tursi I 104 C2
Turtmann CH 70 B2
Turtola FIN 113 F12
Turze PL 54 B2
Turzovka SK 65 A4
Tusa I 109 B3
Tuscánia I 102 A4
Tušilovic HR 73 C5
Tuszyn PL 55 B4
Tutin SCG 85 D5
Tutow D 45 B5
Tutrakan BG 11 D9
Tuttlingen D 61 C4
Tutzing D 62 C2
Tuzi SCG 105 A5
Tuzla BIH 84 B3
Tuzla TR 16 C7
Tuzlukçu TR 119 D6
Tvååker S 40 B2
Tvärålund S 115 C16
Tvärskog S 40 C6
Tvedestrand N 33 D5
Tveit, *Hordaland* N 32 B4
Tveit, *Rogaland* N 33 C3
Tver RUS 7 C13
Tverrelvmo N 112 D8
Tversted DK 38 B3
Tving S 41 C5
Tvrdošin SK 65 A5
Tvrdošovce SK 64 B4
Twardogóra PL 54 B2
Twatt GB 23 B5
Twello NL 50 A2
Twimberg A 73 B4
Twist D 43 C4
Twistringen D 43 C5
Tworóg PL 54 C3
Twyford, *Hampshire* GB 31 C2
Twyford, *Wokingham* GB 31 C3
Tyachiv UA 11 B7
Tychówka PL 46 B2
Tychowo PL 46 B2
Tychy PL 54 C3
Tydal N 114 D8
Týec nad Labem CZ 53 C5
Tyfors S 34 B6
Tygelsjö S 41 D2
Tylldal N 114 E7
Tylstrup DK 38 B2
Tymbark PL 65 A6
Tymowa PL 65 A6
Týn nad Vltavou CZ 63 A5
Tyndrum GB 24 B3
Týnec nad Sázavou CZ 63 A5
Tynemouth GB 25 C6
Tyngsjö S 34 B5
Týniště nad Orlicí CZ 53 C6
Tynset N 114 E7
Tyresö S 37 C5
Tyringe S 41 C3
Tyrislöt S 37 D3
Tyristrand N 34 B2
Tyrrellspass IRL 21 A4
Tysnes N 32 B2
Tysse N 32 B2
Tyssebotn N 32 B2
Tyssedal N 32 B3
Tystberga S 37 D4
Tysvær N 33 C2
Tywyn GB 26 C1
Tzermiado GR 117 G7
Tzummarum NL 42 B2

U

Ub SCG 85 B5
Ubby DK 39 D4
Úbeda E 100 A2
Überlingen D 61 C5
Ubidea E 89 A4
Ubli HR 84 D1
Ubli SCG 105 A5
Ubrique E 99 C5
Ucero E 89 C3
Uchaud F 78 C3
Uchte D 43 C5
Uckerath D 50 C3
Uckfield GB 31 D4
Ucklum S 38 A4
Uclés E 95 C4
Ucria I 109 A3
Udbina HR 83 B4
Uddebo S 40 B3
Uddeholm S 34 B5
Uddevalla S 35 D3
Uddheden S 34 C4
Uden NL 49 B6
Uder D 51 B6
Udiča SK 65 A4
Údine I 72 B3
Udvar H 74 C3
Ueckermünde D 45 B6
Uelsen D 42 C3
Uelzen D 44 C2
Uetendorf CH 70 B2
Uetersen D 43 B6
Uetze D 44 C2
Uffculme GB 29 C4
Uffenheim D 61 A6
Ugarana E 89 A4
Ugento I 107 B5
Ugerldse DK 39 D4
Uggerby DK 38 B3
Uggerslev DK 39 D3
Uggiano la Chiesa I 107 A5
Ugíjar E 100 C2
Ugine F 69 C6
Uglejevik BIH 84 B4
Uglenes N 32 B2
Uglich RUS 7 C15
Ugljane HR 84 C1
Ugod H 74 A2
Uherské Hradiště CZ 64 A3
Uherský Brod CZ 64 A3
Uherský Ostroh CZ 64 B3
Uhingen D 61 B5
Uhliřské-Janovice CZ 63 A6
Uhřiněves CZ 53 C4
Uhyst D 53 B4
Uig GB 22 D2
Uitgeest NL 42 C1
Uithoorn NL 49 A5
Uithuizen NL 42 B3
Uithuizermeeden NL 42 B3
Uivar RO 75 C5
Ujazd, *Łódzkie* PL 55 B4
Ujazd, *Opolskie* PL 54 C3
Ujezd u Brna CZ 64 A2
Ujhartyán H 75 A4
Újkígyós H 75 B6
Ujpetre H 74 C3
Ujście PL 46 B2
Ujsolt H 75 B4
Újszász H 75 A5
Ujué E 89 B5
Ukanc SLO 72 B3
Ukmergė LT 6 D8
Ukna S 40 A6
Ula TR 119 E3
Ul'anka SK 65 B5
Ulaş TR 118 A2
Ulássai I 110 C2
Ulbjerg DK 38 C2
Ulbster GB 23 C5
Ulceby GB 27 B5
Ulcinj SCG 105 B5
Uldum DK 39 D2
Ulefoss N 33 C6
Uleila del Campo E 101 B3
Ulëz AL 105 B5
Ulfborg DK 39 C1
Uljma SCG 85 A6
Ullånger S 115 D15
Ullapool GB 22 D3
Ullared S 40 B2
Ullatti S 113 E10
Ullatun N 33 C3
Ulldecona E 90 C3
Ulldemolins E 90 B3
Ullerslev DK 39 D3
Ullervad S 35 D5
Üllés H 75 B4
Üllo H 75 A4
Ullvi S 37 C3
Ulm D 61 B5
Ulme P 92 B2
Ulmen D 50 C2
Ulnes N 32 B6
Ulog BIH 84 C3
Ulricehamn S 40 B3
Ulrichstein D 51 C5
Ulrika S 37 D2
Ulriksfors S 115 D12
Ulrum NL 42 B3
Ulsberg N 114 E6
Ulsta GB 22 A7
Ulsted DK 38 B3
Ulsteinvik N 114 E2
Ulstrup, *Vestsjællands Amt.* DK 39 D3
Ulstrup, *Viborg Amt.* DK 39 C2
Ulsvåg N 112 D4
Ulubey TR 119 D4
Uluborlu TR 119 D5
Ulukışla TR 16 C7
Ulverston GB 26 A2
Ulvik N 32 B3
Umag HR 72 C3
Uman UA 11 B11
Umba RUS 3 C31
Umbértide I 82 C1
Umbriático I 107 B3
Umčari SCG 85 B5
Umeå S 3 E24
Umgransele S 115 C15
Umhausen A 71 A5
Umka SCG 85 B5
Umljanovic HR 83 C5
Umnäs S 115 B13
Umurbey TR 118 B1
Unaðsdalur IS 111 A3
Unapool GB 22 C3
Unari FIN 113 E14
Uncastillo E 90 A1
Undenäs S 37 D1
Undersaker S 115 D10
Undredal N 32 B4
Unecha RUS 7 E12
Unešić HR 83 C5
Úněšov CZ 62 A4
Ungheni MD 11 C9
Unhais da Serra P 92 A3
Unhošť CZ 53 C4
Unichowo PL 46 A3
Uničov CZ 64 A3
Uniejów PL 54 B3
Unisław PL 47 B4
Unkel D 50 C3
Unken A 62 C3
Unna D 50 B3
Unnaryd S 40 C3
Unquera E 88 A2
Unter Langkampfen A 72 A2
Unter-steinbach D 61 A6
Unterach A 63 C4
Unterägeri CH 70 A3
Unterammergau D 62 C2
Unterhaching D 62 B2
Unteriberg CH 70 A3
Unterkochen D 61 B6
Unterlaussa A 63 C5
Unterlüss D 44 C2
Untermünkheim D 61 A5
Unterschächen CH 70 B3
Unterschleissheim D 62 B2
Unterschwaningen D 62 A1
Untersiemau D 51 C6
Unterweissenbach A 63 B5
Unterzell D 62 A3
Upavon GB 29 B6
Úpice CZ 53 C6
Upiłka PL 46 B3
Upphärad S 35 D4
Uppingham GB 30 B3
Upplands-Väsby S 37 C4
Uppsala S 36 C4
Uppsjøhytta N 34 A1
Upton-upon-Severn GB 29 A5
Ur F 91 A4
Ura e Shtrenjte AL 105 A5
Ura-Vajgurorë AL 105 C5
Uras I 110 C1
Uraz PL 54 B1
Urbánia I 82 C1
Urbino I 82 C1
Urçay F 68 B2
Urda E 94 C3
Urdax E 76 C1
Urdilde E 86 B2
Urdos F 76 D2
Urk NL 42 C2
Úrkút H 74 A2
Urla TR 119 D1
Urlingford IRL 21 B4
Urnäsch CH 71 A4
Urnes N 32 A4
Uroševac SCG 10 E6
Urracal E 101 B3
Urries E 90 A1
Urroz E 76 D1
Ursensollen D 62 A2
Urshult S 40 C4
Uršna Sela SLO 73 C5
Urszulewo PL 47 C5
Ury F 58 B3
Urziceni RO 11 D9
Urzulei I 110 B2
Usagre E 93 C4
Uşak TR 118 D4
Ušće SCG 85 C5
Usedom D 45 B5
Useldange L 60 A1
Uséllus I 110 C1
Ushakovo RUS 47 A6
Usingen D 51 C4
Usini I 110 B1
Usk GB 29 B5
Uskedal N 32 C2
Üsküdar TR 118 A4
Uslar D 51 B5
Úsov CZ 64 A3
Usquert NL 42 B3
Ussássai I 110 C2
Ussé F 67 A5
Usséglio I 70 C2
Ussel, *Cantal* F 78 A1
Ussel, *Corrèze* F 68 C2
Usson-du-Poitou F 67 B5
Usson-en-Forez F 68 C3
Usson-les-Bains F 77 D5
Ust Luga RUS 7 B10
Ustaoset N 32 B5
Ustaritz F 76 C1
Úštěk CZ 53 C4
Uster CH 70 A3
Ústí CZ 64 A3
Ústí nad Labem CZ 53 C4
Ústí nad Orlicí CZ 54 D1
Ustibar BIH 85 C4
Ustikolina BIH 84 C3
Ustiprača BIH 84 C4
Ustka PL 46 A2
Ustroń PL 65 A4
Ustronie Morskie PL 46 A1
Ustyuzhna RUS 7 B14
Uszód H 74 B3
Utåker N 32 C2
Utansjö S 115 E14
Utebo E 90 B2
Utena LT 7 D8
Utery CZ 62 A4
Uthaug N 114 D6
Utiel E 96 B1
Utne N 32 B3
Utö S 37 D5
Utrecht NL 49 A6
Utrera E 99 B5
Utrillas E 90 C2
Utsjoki FIN 113 C16
Utstein kloster N 33 C2
Uttendorf A 72 A2
Uttenweiler D 61 B5
Utterslev DK 39 E4
Uttoxeter GB 27 C4
Utvälinge S 41 C2
Utvorda N 114 C7
Uusikaarlepyy FIN 3 E25
Uusikaupunki FIN 3 F24
Uvac BIH 85 C4
Uvaly CZ 53 C4
Uvdal N 32 B5
Uza F 76 B1
Uzdin SCG 75 C5
Uzdowo PL 47 B6
Uzein F 76 C2
Uzel F 56 B3
Uzerche F 67 C6
Uzès F 78 B3
Uzhhorod UA 11 B7
Uzhok UA 11 B7
Užice SCG 85 C4
Uznach CH 70 A3
Uznovë AL 105 C6
Üzümlü, *Konya* TR 119 E6
Üzümlü, *Muğla* TR 119 F4
Uzunköprü TR 118 A1

V

Vaalajärvi FIN 113 E15
Vaas F 58 C1
Vaasa FIN 3 E24
Vaasen NL 50 A1
Vabre F 77 C5
Vác H 65 C5
Vacha D 51 C6
Váchartyán H 65 C5
Väckelsång S 40 C4
Vacqueyras F 78 B3
Vad S 36 B2
Vada I 81 C4
Väddö S 36 C5
Väderstad S 37 D1
Vadheim N 32 A2
Vadillo de la Sierra E 93 A5
Vadillos E 95 B4
Vadla N 33 C3
Vado I 81 B5
Vado Lígure I 80 B2
Vadsø N 113 B18
Vadstena S 37 D1
Vadum DK 38 B2
Vaduz FL 71 A4
Væggerløse DK 44 A3
Vafos N 33 D6
Vág H 74 A2
Vågåmo N 114 F6
Vaggeryd S 40 B4
Vaghia GR 117 D5
Vaglia I 81 C5
Váglio Basilicata I 104 C1
Vagney F 60 B2
Vagnhärad S 37 D4
Vagnsunda S 37 C5
Vagos P 92 A2
Vai GR 117 G8
Vaiano I 81 C5
Vaiges F 57 B5
Vaihingen D 61 B4
Vaillant F 59 C6
Vailly-sur-Aisne F 59 A4
Vailly-sur Sauldre F 68 A2
Vairano Scalo I 103 B7
Vaison-la-Romaine F 79 B4
Vaite F 60 C1
Väjern S 35 D3
Vajszló H 74 C2
Vaksdal N 32 B2
Vál H 74 A3
Val de San Lorenzo E 86 B4
Val de Santo Domingo E 94 B2
Val d'Esquières F 79 C5
Val-d'Isère F 70 C1
Val-Suzon F 69 A4
Val Thorens F 69 C6
Valaam RUS 3 F29
Valada P 92 B2
Vålådalen S 115 D10
Valadares P 87 C2
Valado P 92 B1
Valandovo MK 116 A4
Valaská SK 65 B5
Valaská Belá SK 65 B4
Valaská Dubová SK 65 A5
Valašská Polanka CZ 64 A3
Valašské Klobouky CZ 64 A4
Valašské Meziříčí CZ 64 A3
Valberg F 79 B5
Vålberg S 35 C5
Valbo S 36 B4
Valbom P 87 C2
Valbondione I 71 B5
Valbonë AL 105 A5
Valbonnais F 79 B4
Valbuena de Duero E 88 C2
Vâlcani RO 75 C5
Valdagno I 71 C6
Valdahon F 69 A6
Valdaracete E 95 B3
Valday RUS 7 C12
Valdealgorfa E 90 C2
Valdecaballeros E 93 B5
Valdecabras E 95 B4
Valdecarros E 94 B1
Valdeconcha E 95 B4
Valdeflores E 99 B4
Valdefresno E 88 B1
Valdeganga E 95 C5
Valdelacasa E 93 A5
Valdelacasa de Tajo E 93 B5
Valdelarco E 99 B4
Valdelosa E 94 A1
Valdeltormo E 90 C3
Valdelugeros E 88 B1
Valdemanco de Esteras E 94 D2
Valdemarsvik S 37 D3
Valdemorillo E 94 B2
Valdemoro E 94 B3
Valdemoro Sierra E 95 B5
Valdenoceda E 89 B3
Valdeobispo E 93 A4
Valdeolivas E 95 B4
Valdepeñas E 100 A2
Valdepeñas de Jaén E 100 B2
Valdepiélago E 88 B1
Valdepolo E 88 B1
Valderas E 88 B1
Valdérice I 108 A1
Valderrobres E 90 C3
Valderrueda E 88 B2
Valdestillas E 88 C2
Valdetorres E 93 C4
Valdetorres de Jarama E 95 B3
Valdeverdeja E 93 B5
Valdevimbre E 88 B1
Valdieri I 80 B1
Valdilecha E 95 B3
Valdobbiádene I 72 C1
Valdocondes E 89 C3
Valdoviño E 86 A2
Vale de Açor, *Beja* P 98 B3
Vale de Açor, *Portalegre* P 92 B3
Vale de Agua P 98 B2
Vale de Cambra P 87 D2
Vale de Lobo P 98 B2
Vale de Prazeres P 92 A3
Vale de Reis P 92 C2
Vale de Rosa P 98 B3
Vale de Santarém P 92 B2
Vale de Vargo P 98 B3
Vale do Peso P 92 B3
Valea lui Mihai RO 11 C7
Valega P 87 D2
Valéggio sul Mincio I 71 C5
Valeiro P 92 C2
Valença P 87 B2
Valençay F 67 A6
Valence, *Charente* F 67 C5
Valence, *Drôme* F 78 B3
Valence d'Agen F 77 B3
Valence-d'Albigeois F 77 B5
Valence-sur-Baise F 77 C3
Valencia E 96 B2
Valencia de Alcántara E 93 B3
Valencia de Don Juan E 88 B1
Valencia de las Torres E 93 C4
Valencia de Mombuey E 99 A3
Valencia del Ventoso E 99 A4
Valenciennes F 49 C4
Valensole F 79 C4
Valentano I 102 A4
Valentigney F 70 A1
Valentine F 77 C3
Valenza I 80 A2
Valenzuela E 100 B1
Valenzuela de Calatrava E 100 A2
Våler, *Hedmark* N 34 B3
Våler, *Østfold* N 35 C2
Valera de Abajo E 95 C4
Valeria E 95 C4
Valestrand N 33 C2
Valestrandsfossen N 32 B2
Valevåg N 33 C2
Valfabbrica I 82 C1
Valflaunes F 78 C2
Valga EST 7 C9
Valgorge F 78 B3
Valgrisenche I 70 C2
Valguarnera Caropepe I 109 B3
Valhelhas P 92 A3
Valjevo SCG 85 B4
Valka LV 7 C8
Valkeakoski FIN 3 F26
Valkenburg NL 50 C1
Valkenswaard NL 49 B6
Valkó H 75 A4
Vall d'Alba E 96 A2
Valla S 37 C3
Vallada E 96 C2
Vallado E 86 A4
Valladolid E 88 C2
Vallåkra S 41 D2
Vallata I 103 B8
Vallberga S 40 C3
Valldemossa E 97 B2
Valle N 33 C4
Valle Castellana I 82 D2
Valle de Abdalajís E 100 C1
Valle de Cabuérniga E 88 A2
Valle de la Serena E 93 C5
Valle de Matamoros E 93 C4
Valle de Santa Ana E 93 C4
Valle Mosso I 70 C3
Valledolmo I 108 B2
Valledoria I 110 B1
Vallelado E 88 C2
Vallelunga Pratameno I 108 B2
Vallendar D 50 C3
Vallentuna S 37 C5
Vallerås S 34 B5
Valleraugue F 78 B2
Vallermosa I 110 C1
Vallet F 66 A3
Valletta M 107 C5
Valley GB 26 B1
Vallfogona de Riucorb E 91 B4
Valli del Pasúbio I 71 C6
Vallo della Lucánia I 103 C8
Valloire F 69 C6
Vallombrosa I 81 C5
Vallon-Pont-d'Arc F 78 B3
Vallorbe CH 69 B6
Vallouise F 79 B5
Valls E 91 B4
Vallset N 34 B3
Vallsta S 36 A3
Vallstena S 37 E5
Valmadrid E 90 B2
Valmiera LV 7 C8
Valmojado E 94 B2
Valmont F 58 A1
Valmontone I 102 B5
Valö S 36 B5
Valognes F 57 A4
Valonga P 92 A2
Valongo P 87 C2
Válor E 100 C2
Valoria la Buena E 88 C2
Valøy N 114 C7
Valozhyn BY 7 D9
Valpaços P 87 C3
Valpelline I 70 C2
Valpiana I 81 C4
Valpovo HR 74 C3
Valras-Plage F 78 C2
Valréas F 78 B3
Vals CH 71 B4
Vals-les-Bains F 78 B3
Valsavarenche I 70 C2
Vålse DK 39 E4
Valsequillo E 93 C5
Valsjöbyn S 115 C11
Valsonne F 69 C4
Valstagna I 72 C1
Valtablado del Rio E 95 B4
Valþjofsstaður IS 111 B11
Valtice CZ 64 B2
Valtiendas E 88 C3
Valtierra E 89 B5
Valtopina I 82 C1
Valtorta I 71 C4
Valtournenche I 70 C2
Valverde E 89 C5
Valverde de Burguillos E 93 C4
Valverde de Júcar E 95 C4
Valverde de la Vera E 93 A5
Valverde de la Virgen E 88 B1
Valverde de Llerena E 99 A5
Valverde de Mérida E 93 C4
Valverde del Camino E 99 B4
Valverde del Fresno E 93 A4
Vamberk CZ 53 C6
Vamdrup DK 39 D2
Våmhus S 34 A6
Vamlingbo S 37 F5
Vammala FIN 3 F25
Vamos GR 117 G6
Vámosmikola H 65 C4
Vámosszabadi H 64 C3
Vanault-les-Dames F 59 B5
Vandel DK 39 D2
Vandenesse F 68 B3
Vandenesse-en-Auxois F 69 A4
Vandóies I 72 B1
Väne-Åsaka S 35 D4
Vänersborg S 35 D4
Vänersnäs S 35 D4
Vang N 32 A5
Vänge S 36 C4
Vangsnes N 32 A3
Vänjaurbäck S 115 C15
Vännacka S 35 C4
Vannareid N 112 B8
Vännäs S 115 D16
Vannes F 56 C3
Vannsätter S 36 A3
Vannvåg N 112 B8
Vansbro S 34 B6
Vanse N 33 D3
Vantaa FIN 6 A8
Vanviken, *Nord-Trøndelag* N 114 D7
Vanyarc H 65 C5
Vaour F 77 B4
Vapnyarka UA 11 B10
Vaprio d'Adda I 71 C4
Vaqueiros P 98 B3
Vara S 35 D4
Varacieux F 69 C5
Varades F 66 A3
Varages F 79 C4
Varaldsøy N 32 B2
Varallo I 70 C3
Varangerbotn N 113 B17

Varano de'Melegari I 81 B4
Varaždin HR 73 B6
Varaždinske Toplice HR 73 B6
Varazze I 80 B2
Varberg S 40 B2
Vardal N 34 B2
Varde DK 39 D1
Vårdö FIN 36 B7
Vardø N 113 B20
Vardomb H 74 B3
Varel D 43 B5
Varėna LT 6 D8
Vårenes N 33 C2
Varengeville-sur-Mer F 58 A1
Varenna I 71 B4
Varennes-en-Argonne F 59 A6
Varennes-le-Grand F 69 B4
Varennes-St. Sauveur F 69 B5
Varennes-sur-Allier F 68 B3
Varennes-sur-Amance F 60 C1
Vareš BIH 84 B3
Varese I 70 C3
Varese Ligure I 80 B3
Vârfurile RO 11 C7
Vårgårda S 40 A2
Vargas E 88 A3
Vargas P 92 B2
Vargön S 35 D4
Varhaug N 33 D2
Variaş RO 75 B5
Variaşu Mic RO 75 B6
Varilhes F 77 C4
Varin SK 65 A4
Väring S 35 D5
Váriz P 87 C4
Varkaus FIN 3 E27
Varmahlíð IS 111 B6
Varmaland IS 111 C4
Värmlands Bro S 35 C5
Värmskog S 35 C4
Varna BG 11 E9
Varna SCG 85 B4
Värnamo S 40 B4
Varnhem S 35 D5
Varnsdorf CZ 53 C4
Värö S 40 B2
Varoška Rijeka BIH 83 A5
Városlöd H 74 A2
Várpalota H 74 A3
Varreddes F 59 B3
Vars F 79 B5
Varsi I 81 B3
Varsseveld NL 50 B2
Vårsta S 37 C4
Vartdal N 114 E3
Vartofta S 40 A3
Varvarin SCG 85 C6
Vårvik S 35 C4
Várvölgy H 74 B2
Varzi I 80 B3
Varzjelas P 92 A2
Varzo I 70 B3
Varzy F 68 A3
Vasad H 75 A4
Väse S 35 C5
Vašica SCG 85 A4
Vasilevichi BY 7 E10
Väskinde S 37 E5
Vaskút H 75 B3
Vaslui RO 11 C9
Vassbotn N 33 D5
Vassenden N 32 A6
Vassieux-en-Vercors F 79 B4
Vassmolösa S 40 C6
Vassy F 57 B5
Västansjö S 115 B12
Västanvik S 36 B1
Västerås S 37 C3
Västerby S 36 B2
Västerfärnebo S 36 C3
Västergarn S 37 E5
Västerhaninge S 37 C5
Västervik S 40 B6
Vasto I 103 A7
Västra Ämtervik S 35 C5
Västra-Bodarne S 40 B2
Västra Karup S 41 C2
Vasvár H 74 A1
Vasylkiv UA 11 A11
Vát H 74 A1
Vatan F 68 A1
Väte S 37 E5
Vathia GR 117 F4
Vatican City = Città del Vaticano I 102 B5
Vatili CY 120 A2
Vatin SCG 75 C6
Vatland N 33 D4
Vatnar N 33 C6
Vatnås N 32 C6
Vatne N 33 D4
Vatnestrøm N 33 D5
Vätö S 36 C5
Vatra-Dornei RO 11 C8
Vatry F 59 B5
Vattholma S 36 B4
Vättis CH 71 B4
Vauchamps F 59 B4
Vauchassis F 59 B4
Vaucouleurs F 60 B1
Vaudoy-en-Brie F 59 B4
Vaulen N 33 D2
Vaulruz CH 70 B1
Vaulx Vraucourt F 48 C3
Vaumas F 68 B3
Vausseroux F 67 B4
Vauvenargues F 79 C4
Vauvert F 78 C3
Vauvillers F 60 C2
Vaux-sur-Sure B 60 A1
Vawkavysk BY 6 E8
Vaxholm S 37 C5
Växjö S 40 C4
Våxtorp S 41 C3
Vayrac F 77 B4
Važec SK 65 A5
Veberöd S 41 D3
Vechelde D 51 A6
Vechta D 43 C5
Vecinos E 94 B1
Vecsés H 75 A4
Vedavågen N 33 C2
Veddige S 40 B2
Vedersø DK 39 C1
Vedeseta I 71 C4
Vedevåg S 37 C2
Vedra E 86 B2
Vedum S 35 D4
Veendam NL 42 B3
Veenendaal NL 49 A6
Vega, *Asturias* E 88 A1
Vega, *Asturias* E 88 A1
Vega de Espinareda E 86 B4
Vega de Infanzones E 88 B1
Vega de Pas E 88 A3
Vega de Valcarce E 86 B4
Vega de Valdetronco E 88 C1
Vegadeo E 86 A3
Vegårshei N 33 D5
Vegas de Coria E 93 A4
Vegas del Condado E 88 B1
Vegby S 40 B3
Vegger DK 38 C2
Veggli N 32 B6
Veghel NL 49 B6
Veglast D 45 A4
Véglie I 105 C3
Veguillas E 95 B3
Vegusdal N 33 D4
Veidholmen N 114 D4
Veidnes N 113 B15
Veikåker N 34 B1
Veinge S 40 C3
Vejbystrand S 41 C2
Vejen DK 39 D2
Vejer de la Frontera E 99 C5
Vejle DK 39 D2
Vejprty CZ 52 C3
Vela Luka HR 83 D5
Velada E 94 B2
Velayos E 94 B2
Velbert D 50 B3
Velburg D 62 A2
Velde N 114 C8
Velden, *Bayern* D 62 B3
Velden, *Bayern* D 62 B3
Velden am Worther See A 73 B4
Velefique E 101 B3
Velen D 50 B2
Velenje SLO 73 B5
Veles MK 116 A3
Velesevec HR 73 C6
Velešin CZ 63 B5
Velestino GR 116 C4
Velez Blanco E 101 B3
Vélez de Benaudalla E 100 C2
Vélez-Málaga E 100 C1
Vélez Rubio E 101 B3
Veli Lošinj HR 83 B3
Veliki Radinci SCG 85 A4
Velika HR 74 C2
Velika SCG 85 D4
Velika Drenova SCG 85 C6
Velika Gorica HR 73 C6
Velika Grdevac HR 74 C2
Velika Greda SCG 75 C6
Velika Ilova BIH 84 B2
Velika Kladuša BIH 73 C5
Velika Kopanica HR 74 C3
Velika Krsna SCG 85 B5
Velika Obarska BIH 85 B4
Velika Pisanica HR 74 C2
Velika Plana, *Serbia* SCG 85 B6
Velika Plana, *Serbia* SCG 85 C6
Velika Zdenci HR 74 C2
Velike Lašče SLO 73 C4
Veliki Gaj SCG 75 C6
Veliki Popović SCG 85 B6
Veliki Šiljegovac SCG 85 C6
Velikiye Luki RUS 7 C11
Veliko Gradište SCG 85 B6
Veliko Orašje SCG 85 B6
Veliko Selo SCG 85 B6
Veliko Tŭrnovo BG 11 E8
Velilla de San Antonio E 95 B3
Velilla del Río Carrió E 88 B2
Velipojë AL 105 B5
Velizh RUS 7 D11
Veljun HR 73 C5
Velká Bíteš CZ 64 A2
Velká Hleďsebe CZ 52 D2
Velká Lomnica SK 65 A6
Velká nad Veličkou CZ 64 B3
Velké Bystřice CZ 64 A3
Velké Heraltice CZ 54 D2
Velké Karlovice CZ 64 A4
Veľké Leváre SK 64 B3
Velké Losiny CZ 54 C2
Velké Meziříčí CZ 64 A2
Velké Pavlovice CZ 64 B2
Veľké Rovné SK 65 A4
Veľké Uherce SK 65 B4
Veľké Zálužie SK 64 B3
Veľke'Kostoľany SK 64 B3
Veľký Blahovo SK 65 B6
Velky Bor CZ 63 A4
Veľký Cetin SK 64 B4
Veľký Krtiš SK 65 B5
Veľký Meder SK 64 C3
Velky Ujezd CZ 64 A3
Vellahn D 44 B2
Vellberg D 61 A5
Velles F 67 B6
Velletri I 102 B5
Vellinge S 41 D3
Vellisca E 95 B4
Velliza E 88 C2
Vellmar D 51 B5
Velp NL 50 A1
Velten D 45 C5
Velvary CZ 53 C4
Velvendos GR 116 B4
Vemb DK 39 C1
Vemdalen S 115 E10
Veme N 34 B2
Véménd H 74 B3
Vemmedrup DK 39 D5
Vena S 40 B5
Venaco F 102 A2
Venafro I 103 B7
Venarey-les-Laumes F 69 A4
Venaría I 70 C2
Venasca I 80 B1
Venčane SCG 85 B5
Vence F 79 C6
Venda Nova, *Coimbra* P 92 A2
Venda Nova, *Leiria* P 92 B2
Vendas Novas P 92 C2
Vendays-Montalivet F 66 C3
Vendel S 36 B4
Vendelso S 37 C5
Vendeuil F 59 A4
Vendeuvre-sur-Barse F 59 B5
Vendœuvres F 67 B6
Vendôme F 58 C2
Venelles F 79 C4
Veness GB 23 B6
Venézia = Venice I 72 C2
Venialbo E 88 C1
Venice = Venézia I 72 C2
Vénissieux F 69 C4
Venjan S 34 B5
Venlo NL 50 B2
Venn Green GB 28 C3
Vennesla N 33 D4
Vennesund N 114 B9
Vennezey F 60 B2
Venosa I 104 C1
Venray NL 50 B1
Vent A 71 B5
Venta de Baños E 88 C2
Venta de los Santos E 100 A2
Venta del Moro E 96 B1
Venta las Ranas E 88 A1
Ventanueva E 86 A4
Ventas de Huelma E 100 B2
Ventas de Zafarraya E 100 C1
Ventavon F 79 B4
Ventimíglia I 80 C1
Ventnor GB 31 D2
Ventosa de la Sierra E 89 C4
Ventosilla E 89 C4
Ventspils LV 6 C6
Venturina I 81 C4
Venzolasca F 102 A2
Venzone I 72 B3
Vép H 74 A1
Vera E 101 B4
Vera N 115 D9
Vera Cruz P 98 A3
Vera de Bidasoa E 76 C1
Vera de Moncayo E 89 C5
Verbánia I 70 C3
Verberie F 58 A3
Verbicaro I 106 B2
Verbier CH 70 B2
Vercel-Villedieu-le-Camp F 69 A6
Vercelli I 70 C3
Verchen D 45 B4
Vercheny F 79 B4
Verclause F 79 B4
Verdalsøra N 114 D8
Verden D 43 C6
Verdens Ende N 35 C2
Verdikoussa GR 116 C3
Verdille F 67 C4
Verdú E 91 B4
Verdun F 59 A6
Verdun-sur-Garonne F 77 C4
Verdun-sur-le-Doubs F 69 B5
Veresegyház H 65 C5
Verfeil F 77 C4
Vergato I 81 B5
Vergel E 96 C3
Vergeletto CH 70 B3
Verges E 91 A6
Vergiate I 70 C3
Vergt F 77 A3
Veria GR 116 B4
Verín E 87 C3
Veringenstadt D 61 B5
Verkhovye RUS 7 E14
Verl D 51 B4
Verma N 114 E5
Vermand F 59 A4
Vermelha P 92 B1
Vermenton F 59 C4
Vermosh AL 85 D4
Vern-d'Anjou F 57 C5
Vernago I 71 B5
Vernante I 80 B1
Vernantes F 67 A5
Vernár SK 65 B6
Vernasca I 81 B3
Vernayaz CH 70 B2
Vernazza I 81 B3
Verneřice CZ 53 C4
Vernet F 77 C4
Vernet-les-Bains F 91 A5
Verneuil F 59 A4
Verneuil-sur-Avre F 58 B1
Vernier CH 69 B6
Vérnio I 81 B5
Vérnole I 105 C4
Vernon F 58 A2
Vernoux-en-Vivarais F 78 B3
Veróce H 65 C5
Verolanuova I 71 C5
Véroli I 103 B6
Verona I 71 C6
Verpelét H 65 C6
Verrabotn N 114 D7
Verrès I 70 C2
Verrey-sous-Salmaise F 69 A4
Verrières F 67 B5
Versailles F 58 B3
Versam CH 71 B4
Verseg H 65 C5
Versmold D 50 A4
Versoix CH 69 B6
Verteillac F 67 C5
Vértesacsa H 74 A3
Vertou F 66 A3
Vertus F 59 B4
Verviers B 50 C1
Vervins F 59 A4
Verwood GB 29 C6
Veryan GB 28 C3
Veržej SLO 73 B6
Verzuolo I 80 B1
Verzy F 59 A5
Vescovato F 102 A2
Vése H 74 B2
Veselí nad Lužnicí CZ 63 A5
Veselí nad Moravou CZ 64 B3
Veseliy BG 11 E9
Vésime I 80 B2
Veskoniemi FIN 113 D16
Vesoul F 60 C2
Vespolate I 70 C3
Vessigebro S 40 C2
Vestbygd N 33 D3
Vestenanova I 71 C6
Vester Husby S 37 D3
Vester Nebel DK 39 D2
Vester Torup DK 38 B2
Vester Vedsted DK 39 D1
Vesterøhavn DK 38 B3
Vestervig DK 38 C1
Vestfossen N 35 C1
Vestmannaeyjar IS 111 D5
Vestmarka N 34 C3
Vestnes N 114 E4
Vestone I 71 C5
Vestre Gausdal N 34 A2
Vestre Jakobselv N 113 B18
Vestre Slidre N 32 A5
Vesyegonsk RUS 7 B14
Veszprém H 74 A2
Veszprémvarsány H 74 A2
Vésztő H 75 B6
Vetlanda S 40 B5
Vetovo HR 74 C2
Vetralla I 102 A5
Větrný Jeníkov CZ 63 A6
Vétroz CH 70 B2
Vetschau D 53 B4
Vettasjärvi S 113 E10
Vetto I 81 B4
Vetulónia I 81 D4
Veules-les-Roses F 58 A1
Veulettes-sur-Mer F 58 A1
Veum N 33 C5
Veurne B 48 B3
Veverská Bítýška CZ 64 A2
Vevey CH 70 B1
Vevi GR 116 B3
Vevring N 32 A2
Vex CH 70 B2
Veynes F 79 B4
Veyre-Monton F 68 C3
Veyrier F 69 C6
Vézelay F 68 A3
Vézelise F 60 B2
Vézenobres F 78 B3
Vezins F 67 A4
Vézins-de-Lévézou F 78 B1
Vezirhan TR 118 B5
Vezirköprü TR 16 A7
Vezza di Óglio I 71 B5
Vezzani F 102 A2
Vezzano I 71 B6
Vezzano sul Cróstolo I 81 B4
Vi S 115 E14
Via Gloria P 98 B3
Viadana I 81 B4
Viana E 89 B4
Viana do Alentejo P 92 C2
Viana do Bolo E 87 B3
Viana do Castelo P 87 C2
Vianden L 60 A2
Viannos GR 117 G7
Viaréggio I 81 C4
Viator E 101 C3
Vibble S 37 E5
Vibo Valéntia I 106 C3
Viborg DK 38 C2
Vibraye F 58 B1
Vic E 91 B5
Vic-en-Bigorre F 76 C3
Vic-Fézensac F 76 C3
Vic-le-Comte F 68 C3
Vic-sur-Aisne F 59 A4
Vic-sur-Cère F 77 B5
Vícar E 101 C3
Vicarello I 81 C4
Vicari I 108 B2
Vicchio I 81 C5
Vicdesses F 77 D4
Vicenza I 71 C6
Vichy F 68 B3
Vickan S 38 B5
Vickerstown GB 26 A2
Vico F 102 A1
Vico del Gargano I 104 B1
Vico Equense I 103 C7
Vicopisano I 81 C4
Vicosoprano CH 71 B4
Vicovaro I 102 A5
Victoria = Rabat, Gozo M 107 C5
Vidago P 87 C3
Vidauban F 79 C5
Vide P 92 A3
Videbæk DK 39 C1
Videm SLO 73 C4
Videseter N 114 F4
Vidigueira P 98 A3
Vidin BG 11 E7
Vidlin GB 22 A7
Vidzy BY 7 D9
Viechtach D 62 A3
Vieille-Brioude F 68 C3
Vieira P 92 B2
Vieira do Minho P 87 C2
Vieiros P 92 C3
Vielha E 90 A3
Vielle-Aure F 77 D3
Viellespesse F 68 C3
Viellevigne F 66 B3
Vielmur-sur-Agout F 77 C5
Viels Maison F 59 B4
Vielsalm B 50 C1
Vienenburg D 51 B6
Vienna = Wien A 64 B2
Vienne F 69 C4
Vieritz D 44 C4
Viernheim D 61 A4
Vierraden D 45 B6
Viersen D 50 B2
Vierville-sur-Mer F 57 A5
Vierzon F 68 A2
Vieselbach D 52 C1
Vieste I 104 B2
Vietas S 112 E7
Vieteren B 48 C3
Vietri di Potenza I 104 C1
Vietri sul Mare I 103 C7
Vieux-Boucau-les-Bains F 76 C1
Vif F 79 A4
Vig DK 39 D4
Vigásio I 71 C5
Vigaun A 63 C4
Vigeland N 33 D4
Vigeois F 67 C6
Vigévano I 70 C3
Viggianello I 106 B3
Viggiano I 104 C1
Vigliano I 102 A6
Vigmostad N 33 D4
Vignale I 80 A2
Vignanello I 102 A5
Vigneulles-lès-Hattonchâtel F 60 B1
Vignevieille F 77 D5
Vignola I 81 B5
Vignory F 59 B6
Vignoux-sur-Barangeon F 68 A2
Vigo E 87 B2
Vigo di Fassa I 72 B1
Vigone I 80 B1
Vigrestad N 33 D2
Vihiers F 67 A4
Viitasaari FIN 3 E26
Vik IS 111 D6
Vik, *Nordland* N 114 B9
Vik, *Rogaland* N 33 D2
Vik, *Sogn og Fjordane* N 32 A3
Vik S 41 D4
Vika S 36 B2
Vikajärvi FIN 113 F15
Vikane N 35 C2
Vikarbyn S 36 B2
Vike N 32 B2
Vikedal N 33 C2
Vikeland N 33 D4
Viken, *Jämtland* S 115 C10
Viken, *Skåne* S 41 C2
Viker N 34 B2
Vikersund N 34 C1
Vikeså N 33 D3
Vikevåg N 33 C2
Vikingstad S 37 D2
Vikmanshyttan S 36 B2
Vikna N 114 C7
Vikøy N 32 B3
Vikran, *Troms* N 112 C7
Vikran, *Troms* N 112 D5
Viksjö S 115 E14
Viksøyri N 32 A3
Viksta S 36 B4
Vila Boim P 92 C3
Vila Chã de Ourique P 92 B2
Vila de Cruces E 86 B2
Vila de Rei P 92 B2
Vila do Bispo P 98 B2
Vila do Conde P 87 C2
Vila Flor P 87 C3
Vila Franca das Navas P 87 D3
Vila Franca de Xira P 92 C1
Vila Fresca P 92 C1
Vila Nogueira P 92 C1
Vila Nova da Baronia P 98 A2
Vila Nova de Cerveira P 87 C2
Vila Nova de Famalicão P 87 C2
Vila Nova de Foz Côa P 87 C3
Vila Nova de Gaia P 87 C2
Vila Nova de Milfontes P 98 B2
Vila Nova de Ourém P 92 B2
Vila Nova de Paiva P 87 D3
Vila Nova de São Bento P 98 B3
Vila Pouca de Aguiar P 87 C3
Vila Praja de Ancora P 87 C2
Vila Real P 87 C3
Vila-real de los Infantes E 96 B2
Vila Real de Santo António P 98 B3
Vila-Rodona E 91 B4
Vila Ruiva P 98 A3
Vila Seca P 92 A2
Vila Velha de Ródão P 92 B3
Vila Verde, *Braga* P 87 C2
Vila Verde, *Lisboa* P 92 B1
Vila Verde de Filcalho P 98 B3
Vila Viçosa P 92 C3
Viladamat E 91 A6
Viladrau E 91 B5
Vilafranca del Maestrat E 90 C2
Vilafranca del Penedès E 91 B4
Vilagarcía de Arousa E 86 B2
Vilajuiga E 91 A6
Vilamarin E 86 B3
Vilamartín de Valdeorras E 86 B3
Vilanova de Castelló E 96 B2
Vilanova de Sau E 91 B5
Vilanova i la Geltrú E 91 B4
Vilapedre E 86 A3
Vilar de Santos E 87 B3
Vilar Formosa P 93 A4
Vilarandelo P 87 C3
Vilardevós E 87 C3
Vilasantar E 86 A2
Vilaseca E 91 B4
Vilassar de Mar E 91 B5
Vilasund S 115 A11
Vilches E 100 A2
Vildbjerg DK 39 C1
Vilémov CZ 63 A6
Vileyka BY 7 D9
Vilhelmina S 115 C13
Vilia GR 117 D5
Viljandi EST 7 B8
Villa Castelli I 104 C3
Villa Cova de Lixa P 87 C2
Villa de Peralonso E 87 C4
Villa del Prado E 94 B2
Villa del Rio E 100 B1
Villa di Chiavenna I 71 B4
Villa Minozzo I 81 B4
Villa San Giovanni I 109 A4
Villa Santa Maria I 103 B7
Villa Santina I 72 B2
Villabáñez E 88 C2
Villablanca E 98 B3
Villablino E 86 B4
Villabona E 89 A4
Villabragima E 88 C1
Villabuena del Puente E 88 C1
Villacadima E 95 A3
Villacañas E 95 C3
Villacarriedo E 88 A3
Villacarrillo E 100 A2
Villacastín E 94 B2
Villach A 72 B3
Villacidro I 110 C1
Villaconejos E 95 B3
Villaconejos de Trabaque E 95 B4
Villada E 88 B2
Villadangos del Páramo E 88 B1
Villadecanes E 86 B4
Villadepera E 87 C4
Villadiego E 88 B2
Villadompardo E 100 B1
Villadóssola I 70 B3
Villaeles de Valdavia E 88 B2
Villaescusa de Haro E 95 C4
Villafáfila E 88 C1
Villafeliche E 95 A5
Villaflores E 94 A1
Villafrades de Campos E 88 B2
Villafranca, *Avila* E 93 A5
Villafranca, *Navarra* E 89 B5
Villafranca de Córdoba E 100 B1
Villafranca de los Barros E 93 C4
Villafranca de los Caballeros E 95 C3
Villafranca del Bierzo E 86 B4
Villafranca di Verona I 71 C5
Villafranca in Lunigiana I 81 B3
Villafranca-Montes de Oca E 89 B3
Villafranca Tirrena I 109 A4
Villafranco del Campo E 95 B5
Villafranco del Guadalquivir E 99 B4
Villafrati I 108 B2
Villafrechós E 88 C1
Villafruela E 88 C3
Villagarcia de las Torres E 93 C4
Villaggio Mancuso I 106 B3
Villagonzalo E 93 C4
Villagotón E 86 B4
Villagrains F 76 B2
Villaharta E 100 A1
Villahermosa E 100 A3
Villaherreros E 88 B2
Villahoz E 88 B3
Villaines-la-Juhel F 57 B5
Villajoyosa E 96 C2
Villalago I 103 B6
Villalba E 86 A3
Villalba I 108 B2
Villalba de Calatrava E 100 A2
Villalba de Guardo E 88 B2
Villalba de la Sierra E 95 B4
Villalba de los Alcores E 88 C2
Villalba de los Barros E 93 C4
Villalba del Alcor E 99 B4
Villalba del Rey E 95 B4
Villalcampo E 87 C4
Villalcázar de Sirga E 88 B2
Villalengua E 89 C5
Villalgordo del Júcar E 95 C4
Villalgordo del Marquesado E 95 C4
Villalmóndar E 89 B3
Villalón de Campos E 88 B1
Villalonga E 96 C2
Villalonso E 88 C1
Villalpando E 88 C1
Villaluenga E 94 B3
Villalumbroso E 88 B2
Villálvaro E 89 C3
Villamalea E 95 C5
Villamanán E 88 B1
Villamanín E 88 B1
Villamanrique E 100 A3
Villamanrique de la Condesa E 99 B4
Villamanta E 94 B2
Villamantilla E 94 B2
Villamar I 110 C1
Villamartín E 99 C5
Villamartín de Campos E 88 B2
Villamartin de Don Sancho E 88 B1
Villamassárgia I 110 C1
Villamayor E 88 A1
Villamayor de Calatrava E 100 A1
Villamayor de Campos E 88 C1
Villamayor de Santiago E 95 C4
Villamblard F 77 A3
Villamejil E 86 B4
Villamesias E 93 B5
Villaminaya E 94 C3
Villamor de los Escuderos E 88 C1
Villamoronta E 88 B2
Villamuelas E 94 C3
Villamuriel de Cerrato E 88 C2
Villandraut F 76 B2
Villanova I 104 C3
Villanova d'Asti I 80 B1
Villanova del Battista I 103 B8
Villanova Mondovì I 80 B1
Villanova Monteleone I 110 B1
Villante E 88 B3
Villantério I 71 C4
Villanubla E 88 C2
Villanueva de Alcardete E 95 C3
Villanueva de Alcorón E 95 B4
Villanueva de Algaidas E 100 B1
Villanueva de Argaña E 88 B3
Villanueva de Bogas E 95 C3
Villanueva de Córdoba E 100 A1
Villanueva de Gállego E 90 B2
Villanueva de la Concepcion E 100 C1
Villanueva de la Fuente E 101 A3
Villanueva de la Jara E 95 C5
Villanueva de la Reina E 100 A2
Villanueva de la Serena E 93 C5
Villanueva de la Sierra E 93 A4
Villanueva de la Vera E 93 A5
Villanueva de las Manzanas E 88 B1
Villanueva de las Peras E 88 C1
Villanueva de las Torres E 100 B2
Villanueva de los Castillejos E 98 B3
Villanueva de los Infantes E 100 A3
Villanueva de Mesia E 100 B2
Villanueva de Nía E 88 B2
Villanueva de Oscos E 86 A4
Villanueva de San Carlos E 100 A2
Villanueva de San Juan E 99 B5
Villanueva de Tapia E 100 B1
Villanueva de Valdegovia E 89 B3
Villanueva del Aceral E 94 A2
Villanueva del Arzobispo E 100 A3
Villanueva del Campo E 88 C1
Villanueva del Duque E 100 A1
Villanueva del Fresno E 93 C3
Villanueva del Huerva E 90 B1
Villanueva del Rey E 99 A5
Villanueva del Rio E 99 B5
Villanueva del Rio y Minas E 99 B5
Villanueva del Rosario E 100 C1
Villanueva del Trabuco E 100 B1
Villány H 74 C3
Villaputzu I 110 C2
Villaquejida E 88 B1
Villaquilambre E 88 B1
Villaquiran de los Infantes E 88 B2
Villar de Barrio E 87 B3
Villar de Cañas E 95 C4
Villar de Chinchilla E 96 C1
Villar de Ciervo E 87 D4
Villar de Domingo Garcia E 95 B4
Villar de los Navarros E 90 B1
Villar de Rena E 93 B5
Villar del Arzobispo E 96 B2
Villar del Buey E 87 C4
Villar del Cobo E 95 B5
Villar del Humo E 95 C5
Villar del Pedroso E 93 B5
Villar del Rey E 93 B4
Villar del Rio E 89 B4
Villar del Saz de Navalón E 95 B4

Wheatley GB 31 C2
Whickham GB 25 D6
Whipsnade GB 31 C3
Whitburn GB 25 C4
Whitby GB 27 A5
Whitchurch, *Hampshire* GB 31 C2
Whitchurch, *Herefordshire* GB 29 B5
Whitchurch, *Shropshire* GB 26 C3
White Bridge GB 23 D4
Whitegate IRL 20 C3
Whitehaven GB 26 A2
Whitehead GB 19 B6
Whithorn GB 24 D3
Whitley Bay GB 25 C6
Whitstable GB 31 C5
Whittington GB 26 C3
Whittlesey GB 30 B3
Wiązów PL 54 C2
Wiązowna PL 55 A6
Wick GB 23 C5
Wickede D 50 B3
Wickford GB 31 C4
Wickham GB 31 D2
Wickham Market GB 30 B5
Wicklow IRL 21 B5
Wicko PL 46 A3
Widawa PL 54 B3
Widdrington GB 25 C6
Widecombe in the Moor GB 28 C4
Widemouth GB 28 C3
Widnes GB 26 B3
Widuchowo PL 45 B6
Więcbork PL 46 B3
Wiefelstede D 43 B5
Wiehe D 52 B1
Wiehl D 50 C3
Wiek D 45 A5
Większyce PL 54 C2
Wiele PL 46 B3
Wieleń PL 46 C2
Wielgie, *Kujawsko-Pomorskie* PL 47 C5
Wielgie, *Łódzkie* PL 54 B3
Wielgie, *Mazowieckie* PL 55 B6
Wielgomłyny PL 55 B4
Wielichowo PL 54 A1
Wieliczka PL 55 D5
Wielka Łąka PL 47 B4
Wielowies PL 54 C3
Wieluń PL 54 B3
Wien = Vienna A 64 B2
Wiener Neustadt A 64 C2
Wiepke D 44 C3
Wierden NL 42 C3
Wieren D 44 C2
Wieruszów PL 54 B3
Wierzbica PL 55 B6
Wierzbie PL 54 B3
Wierzbięcin PL 45 B7
Wierzbno PL 55 A6
Wierzchowo PL 46 B2
Wierzchucino PL 47 A4
Wierzchy PL 54 B3
Wies A 73 B5
Wiesau D 62 A3
Wiesbaden D 50 C4
Wieselburg A 63 B6
Wiesen CH 71 B4
Wiesenburg D 52 A2
Wiesenfelden D 62 A3
Wiesensteig D 61 B5
Wiesentheid D 61 A6
Wiesloch D 61 A4
Wiesmath A 64 C2
Wiesmoor D 43 B4
Wietmarschen D 43 C4
Wietze D 44 C1
Wigan GB 26 B3
Wiggen CH 70 B2
Wigston GB 30 B2
Wigton GB 25 D4
Wigtown GB 24 D3
Wijchen NL 50 B1
Wijhe NL 42 C3
Wijk bij Duurstede NL 49 B6
Wil CH 70 A4
Wilamowice PL 65 A5
Wilczęta PL 47 A5
Wilczkowice PL 55 A4
Wilczna PL 54 A3
Wilczyn PL 47 C4
Wildalpen A 63 C5
Wildbad D 61 B4
Wildberg, *Baden-Württemberg* D 61 B4
Wildberg, *Brandenburg* D 45 C4
Wildegg CH 70 A3
Wildendürnbach A 64 B2
Wildeshausen D 43 C5
Wildon A 73 B5
Wilfersdorf A 64 B2
Wilga PL 55 B6
Wilhelmsburg A 63 B6
Wilhelmsburg D 45 B5
Wilhelmsdorf D 61 C5
Wilhelmshaven D 43 B5
Wilków PL 47 C6
Willebadessen D 51 B5
Willebroek B 49 B5
Willgottheim F 60 B3
Willhermsdorf D 62 A1
Willich D 50 B2
Willingen D 51 B4
Willington GB 25 D6
Willisau CH 70 A3
Wilmslow GB 26 B3
Wilsdruff D 52 B3
Wilster D 43 B6
Wilsum D 42 C3
Wilton GB 29 B6
Wiltz L 50 D1
Wimborne Minster GB 29 C6
Wimereux F 48 C2
Wimmenau F 60 B3
Wimmis CH 70 B2
Wincanton GB 29 B5
Winchcombe GB 29 B6
Winchelsea GB 31 D4
Winchester GB 31 C2
Windermere GB 26 A3
Windischeschenbach D 62 A3
Windischgarsten A 63 C5
Windorf D 63 B4
Windsbach D 62 A1
Windsor GB 31 C3
Windygates GB 25 B4
Wingene B 49 B4
Wingham GB 31 C5
Winkleigh GB 28 C4
Winklern A 72 B2
Winnenden D 61 B5
Winnigstedt D 51 A6
Winnweiler D 60 A3
Winschoten NL 43 B4
Winsen, *Niedersachsen* D 44 B2
Winsen, *Niedersachsen* D 44 C1
Winsford GB 26 B3
Wińsko PL 54 B1
Winslow GB 31 C3
Winsum, *Friesland* NL 42 B2
Winsum, *Groningen* NL 42 B3
Winterberg D 51 B4
Winterfeld D 44 C3
Winterswijk NL 50 B2
Winterthur CH 70 A3
Wintzenheim F 60 B3
Winzer D 62 B4
Wipperdorf D 51 B6
Wipperfürth D 50 B3
Wirksworth GB 27 B4
Wisbech GB 30 B4
Wischhafen D 43 B6
Wishaw GB 25 C4
Wisła PL 65 A4
Wisła Wielka PL 54 D3
Wislica PL 55 C5
Wismar D 44 B3
Wisniewo PL 47 B6
Wiśniowa PL 65 A6
Wissant F 48 C2
Wissembourg F 60 A3
Wissen D 50 C3
Witanowice PL 65 A5
Witham GB 31 C4
Withern GB 27 B6
Withernsea GB 27 B6
Witkowo PL 46 C3
Witmarsum NL 42 B2
Witney GB 31 C2
Witnica PL 45 C6
Witonia PL 55 A4
Witry-les-Reims F 59 A5
Wittdün D 43 A5
Wittelsheim F 60 C3
Witten D 50 B3
Wittenberge D 44 B3
Wittenburg D 44 B3
Wittenheim F 60 C3
Wittichenau D 53 B4
Wittighausen D 61 A5
Wittingen D 44 C2
Wittislingen D 61 B6
Wittlich D 50 D2
Wittmannsdorf A 73 B5
Wittmund D 43 B4
Wittorf D 43 B6
Wittstock D 44 B4
Witzenhausen D 51 B5
Wiveliscombe GB 29 B4
Wivenhoe GB 31 C4
Władysławowo PL 47 A4
Wleń PL 53 B5
Włocławek PL 47 C5
Włodawa PL 6 F7
Włodzimierzów PL 55 B4
Włosień PL 53 B5
Włostow PL 55 C6
Włoszakowice PL 54 B1
Włoszczowa PL 55 C4
Wöbbelin D 44 B3
Woburn GB 31 C3
Wodzisław PL 55 C5
Wodzisław Śląski PL 54 D3
Woerden NL 49 A5
Wœrth F 60 B3
Wohlen CH 70 A3
Woippy F 60 A2
Wojciechy PL 47 A6
Wojcieszow PL 53 C5
Wojkowice Kościelne PL 55 C4
Wojnicz PL 55 D5
Woking GB 31 C3
Wokingham GB 31 C3
Wola Jachowa PL 55 C5
Wola Niechcicka PL 55 B4
Wolbórz PL 55 B4
Wolbrom PL 55 C4
Wołczyn PL 54 B3
Woldegk D 45 B5
Wolfach D 61 B4
Wolfegg D 61 C5
Wolfen D 52 B2
Wolfenbüttel D 51 A6
Wolfersheim D 51 C4
Wolfhagen D 51 B5
Wolfratshausen D 62 C2
Wolf's Castle GB 28 B3
Wolfsberg A 73 B4
Wolfsburg D 44 C2
Wolfshagen D 45 B5
Wolfstein D 60 A3
Wolfurt A 71 A4
Wolgast D 45 A5
Wolhusen CH 70 A3
Wolin PL 45 B6
Wolka PL 55 B5
Wolkenstein D 52 C3
Wolkersdorf A 64 B2
Wöllersdorf A 64 C2
Wollin D 52 A2
Wöllstadt D 51 C4
Wolmirstedt D 52 A1
Wolnzach D 62 B2
Wołomin PL 55 A6
Wołów PL 54 B1
Wolsztyn PL 53 A6
Wolvega NL 42 C2
Wolverhampton GB 26 C3
Wolverton GB 30 B3
Wombwell GB 27 B4
Woodbridge GB 30 B5
Woodhall Spa GB 27 B5
Woodstock GB 31 C2
Wookey Hole GB 29 B5
Wool GB 29 C5
Woolacombe GB 28 B3
Wooler GB 25 C5
Woolwich GB 31 C4
Wooperton GB 25 C6
Worb CH 70 B2
Worbis D 51 B6
Worcester GB 29 A5
Wördern A 64 B2
Wörgl A 72 A2
Workington GB 26 A2
Worksop GB 27 B4
Workum NL 42 C2
Wörlitz D 52 B2
Wormer NL 42 C1
Wormhout F 48 C3
Wormit GB 25 B5
Worms D 61 A4
Worpswede D 43 B5
Wörrstadt D 61 A4
Wörschach A 73 A4
Worsley GB 26 B3
Wörth, *Bayern* D 61 A5
Wörth, *Bayern* D 62 A3
Wörth, *Bayern* D 62 B3
Wörth, *Rheinland-Pfalz* D 61 A4
Worthing GB 31 D3
Woudsend NL 42 C2
Woumen B 48 B3
Woźniki PL 55 C4
Wragby GB 27 B5
Wrangle GB 27 B6
Wręczyca Wlk. PL 54 C3
Wredenhagen D 44 B4
Wremen D 43 B5
Wrentham GB 30 B5
Wrexham GB 26 B2
Wriedel D 44 B2
Wriezen D 45 C6
Wrist D 43 B6
Wróblewo, *Mazowieckie* PL 47 C6
Wróblewo, *Wielkopolskie* PL 46 C2
Wrocki PL 47 B5
Wrocław PL 54 B2
Wronki PL 46 C2
Wroxham GB 30 B5
Września PL 54 A2
Wrzosowo PL 46 A1
Wschowa PL 53 B6
Wulfen, *Nordrhein-Westfalen* D 50 B3
Wülfen, *Sachsen-Anhalt* D 52 B1
Wulkau D 44 C4
Wünnenberg D 51 B4
Wünsdorf D 52 A3
Wunsiedel D 52 C2
Wunstorf D 43 C6
Wuppertal D 50 B3
Wurmannsquick D 62 B3
Würselen D 50 C2
Wurzbach D 52 C1
Würzburg D 61 A5
Wurzen D 52 B2
Wust D 45 C4
Wusterhausen D 44 C4
Wusterwitz D 44 C4
Wustrau-Altfriesack D 45 C4
Wustrow D 44 A4
Wuustwezel B 49 B5
Wye GB 31 C4
Wyględów PL 55 B6
Wyk D 43 A5
Wykroty PL 53 B5
Wylye GB 29 B6
Wymiarki PL 53 B5
Wymondham GB 30 B5
Wyrzysk PL 46 B3
Wyśmierzyce PL 55 B5
Wysoka, *Dolnośląskie* PL 53 B5
Wysoka, *Wielkopolskie* PL 46 B3
Wyszanów PL 54 B3
Wyszogród PL 47 C6

X

Xanten D 50 B2
Xanthi GR 116 A6
Xarrë AL 116 C2
Xátiva E 96 C2
Xeraco E 96 B2
Xert E 90 C3
Xerta E 90 C3
Xertigny F 60 B2
Xilagani GR 116 B7
Xilokastro GR 117 D4
Xinzo de Limia E 87 B3
Xove E 86 A3
Xubia E 86 A2
Xunqueira de Ambía E 87 B3
Xunqueira de Espadañedo E 87 B3
Xylophagou CY 120 B2

Y

Y Felinheli GB 26 B1
Yablanitsa BG 11 E8
Yağcılar TR 118 C3
Yahotyn UA 11 A11
Yahyalı TR 16 B7
Yalova TR 118 B4
Yalvaç TR 119 D6
Yambol BG 11 E9
Yampil UA 11 B10
Yaniskoski RUS 113 D17
Yarbasan TR 118 D3
Yarcombe GB 29 C4
Yaremcha UA 11 B8
Yarm GB 27 A4
Yarmouth GB 31 D2
Yarrow GB 25 C4
Yartsevo RUS 7 D12
Yasinya UA 11 B8
Yatağan TR 119 E3
Yate GB 29 B5
Yatton GB 29 B5
Yavoriv UA 11 B7
Yaxley GB 30 B3
Yazıca TR 118 B6
Yazıköy TR 119 F2
Ybbs A 63 B6
Ybbsitz A 63 C5
Ydby DK 38 C1
Yddal N 32 B2
Yealmpton GB 28 C4
Yebra de Basa E 90 A2
Yecla E 101 A4
Yecla de Yeltes E 87 D4
Yelnya RUS 7 D12
Yelsk BY 7 F10
Yelverton GB 28 C3
Yenice, *Ankara* TR 16 B6
Yenice, *Aydın* TR 119 E3
Yenice, *Çanakkale* TR 118 C2
Yenice, *Edirne* TR 116 B8
Yenifoça TR 118 D1
Yenihisar TR 119 E2
Yeniköy TR 118 D4
Yeniköy Plaji TR 118 B3
Yenipazar TR 119 E3
Yenişarbademli TR 119 E6
Yenişehir TR 118 B4
Yenne F 69 C5
Yeovil GB 29 C5
Yepes E 95 C3
Yerköy TR 16 B7
Yerólakkos CY 120 A2
Yeroskipos CY 120 B1
Yerseke NL 49 B5
Yerville F 58 A1
Yeşildağ TR 119 E6
Yeşilhisar TR 16 B7
Yeşilköy TR 118 B3
Yeşilova TR 119 E4
Yeşilyurt TR 119 D3
Yesnogorsk RUS 7 D14
Yeste E 101 A3
Yezerishche BY 7 D10
Ygos-St. Saturnin F 76 C2
Ygrande F 68 B2
Yialousa CY 120 A3
Yığılca TR 118 B6
Yiñuela E 100 C1
Yli-Muonia FIN 113 D12
Ylitornio FIN 3 C25
Ylivieska FIN 3 D26
Ylläsjärvi FIN 113 E13
Ymonville F 58 B2
Yngsjö S 41 D4
Yoğuntaş TR 118 A2
York GB 27 B4
Youghal IRL 21 C4
Yozgat TR 16 B7
Yport F 58 A1
Ypres = Ieper B 48 C3
Yssingeaux F 68 C4
Ystad S 41 D3
Ystalyfera GB 28 B4
Ystebrød N 33 D2
Ystradgynlais GB 28 B4
Ytre Arna N 32 B2
Ytre Enebakk N 35 C3
Ytre Rendal N 114 F8
Ytteran S 115 D11
Ytterhogdal S 115 E11
Yttermalung S 34 B5
Yukhnov RUS 7 D13
Yumurtalık TR 16 C7
Yunak TR 118 D6
Yuncos E 94 B3
Yunquera E 100 C1
Yunquera de Henares E 95 B3
Yushkozero RUS 3 D30
Yverdon-les-Bains CH 70 B1
Yvetot F 58 A1
Yvignac F 57 B3
Yvoir B 49 C5
Yvonand CH 70 B1
Yxnerum S 37 D3
Yzeure F 68 B3

Z

Zaamslag NL 49 B4
Zaanstad NL 42 C1
Žabalj SCG 75 C5
Zabar H 65 B6
Žabari SCG 85 B6
Zabiče SLO 73 C4
Zabierzów PL 55 C4
Ząbki PL 55 A6
Ząbkowice Śląskie PL 54 C1
Zablaće HR 83 C4
Zablače SCG 85 C5
Žabljak SCG 85 C4
Żabno PL 55 C5
Zabok HR 73 B5
Žabokreky SK 64 B4
Zabor PL 53 B5
Żabowo PL 45 B7
Zabrdje BIH 84 B3
Zábřeh CZ 64 A2
Zabrežje SCG 85 B5
Ząbrowo PL 46 B1
Zabrze PL 54 C3
Zabrzeź PL 65 A6
Zacharo GR 117 E3
Zadar HR 83 B4
Zadzim PL 54 B3
Zafarraya E 100 C1
Zafferana Etnea I 109 B4
Zafra E 93 C4
Žaga SLO 72 B3
Zagajica SCG 85 B6
Żagań PL 53 B5
Zaglav HR 83 C4
Zaglavak SCG 85 C4
Zagnanśk PL 55 C5
Zagora GR 116 C5
Zagorc SLO 73 B5
Zagoričani BIH 84 C2
Zagorje SLO 73 B4
Zagórów PL 54 A2
Zagradje SCG 85 B5
Zagreb HR 73 C5
Zagrilla E 100 B1
Zagvozd HR 84 C2
Zagwiździe PL 54 C2
Zagyvarekas H 75 A5
Zagyvaróna H 65 B5
Zahara E 99 C5
Zahara de los Atunes E 99 C5
Zahinos E 93 C4
Zahna D 52 B2
Záhoři CZ 63 A5
Zahrádka CZ 63 A6
Zahrensdorf D 44 B2
Zaidin E 90 B3
Zaječar SCG 11 E7
Zákamenné SK 65 A5
Zákány H 74 B1
Zákányszék H 75 B4
Zakliczyn PL 65 A6
Zakopane PL 65 A5
Zakroczym PL 47 C6
Zakrzew PL 55 B6
Zakrzewo PL 47 C4
Zakupy CZ 53 C4
Zakynthos GR 117 E2
Zalaapáti H 74 B2
Zalabaksa H 74 B1
Zalaegerszeg H 74 B1
Zalakomár H 74 B2
Zalakoppány H 74 B2
Zalalövő H 74 B1
Zalamea de la Serena E 93 C5
Zalamea la Real E 99 B4
Zalaszentgrót H 74 B2
Zalaszentiván H 74 B1
Zalău RO 11 C7
Zalavár H 74 B2
Zalcsie PL 55 B4
Zaldibar E 89 A4
Žalec SLO 73 B5
Zalesie PL 47 B6
Zalewo PL 47 B5
Zalishchyky UA 11 B8
Zalla E 89 A3
Zaltbommel NL 49 B6
Zamárdi H 74 B2
Zamarte PL 46 B3
Zamberk CZ 54 C1
Zambra E 100 B1
Zambugueira do Mar P 98 B2
Zámoly H 74 A3
Zamora E 88 C1
Zamość PL 11 A7
Zamoście PL 55 B4
Zams A 71 A5
Zandhoven B 49 B5
Žandov CZ 53 C4
Zandvoort NL 42 C1
Zangliveri GR 116 B5
Zánka H 74 B2
Zaorejas E 95 B4
Zaovine SCG 85 C4
Zapadnaya Dvina RUS 7 C12
Zapfend D 51 C6
Zapole PL 54 B3
Zapolyarnyy RUS 3 B29
Zapponeta I 104 B1
Zaprešić HR 73 C5
Zaragoza E 90 B2
Zarasai LT 7 D9
Zarautz E 89 A4
Zarcilla de Ramos E 101 B4
Żarki PL 55 C4
Zarko GR 116 C4
Žarnovica SK 65 B4
Zarnow PL 55 B5
Zarnowiec PL 47 A4
Zarošice CZ 64 A2
Żarów PL 54 C1
Zarren B 48 B3
Zarrentin D 44 B2
Żary PL 53 B5
Zarza Capilla E 93 C5
Zarza de Alange E 93 C4
Zarza de Granadilla E 93 A4
Zarza de Tajo E 95 B3
Zarza la Mayor E 93 B4
Zarzadilla de Totana E 101 B4
Zarzuela del Monte E 94 B2
Zarzuela del Pinar E 88 C2
Zas E 86 A2
Zasavica SCG 85 B4
Zasieki PL 53 B4
Zásmuky CZ 53 D5
Žatec CZ 52 C3
Zaton HR 84 D3
Zatonie PL 53 B5
Zator PL 55 C4
Zauchwitz D 52 A3
Zavala BIH 84 D2
Zavalje BIH 83 B4
Zavattarello I 80 B3
Zavidovići BIH 84 B3
Zavlaka SCG 85 B4
Zawady PL 55 B5
Zawadzkie PL 54 C3
Zawdy PL 54 B3
Zawidów PL 53 B5
Zawidz PL 47 C5
Zawiercie PL 55 C4
Zawoja PL 65 A5
Zawonia PL 54 B2
Žažina HR 73 C6
Zázrivá SK 65 A5
Zbarazh UA 11 B8
Zbąszyń PL 53 A5
Zbąszynek PL 53 A5
Zbehy SK 64 B4
Zbiersk PL 54 B3
Zbiroh CZ 63 A4
Zblewo PL 47 B4
Zbójno PL 47 B5
Zbrachlin PL 47 B4
Zbraslav CZ 53 D4
Zbraslavice CZ 63 A6
Ždala HR 74 B2
Ždánice CZ 64 A3
Ždár nad Sázavou CZ 64 A1
Zdbice PL 46 B2
Zdenci HR 74 C2
Ždiar SK 65 A6
Zdice CZ 63 A4
Zdirec nad Doubravou CZ 64 A1
Zdolbuniv UA 11 A9
Zdounky CZ 64 A3
Zdravinje SCG 85 C6
Ždrelo SCG 85 B6
Zduńska Wola PL 54 B3
Zduny, *Łódzkie* PL 55 A4
Zduny, *Wielkopolskie* PL 54 B2
Żdżary PL 55 B5
Zdziechowice, *Opolskie* PL 54 B3
Zdziechowice, *Wielkopolskie* PL 54 A2
Zdziszowice PL 54 C3
Zeberio E 89 A4
Žebrák CZ 63 A4
Zebreira P 93 B3
Zebrzydowa PL 53 B5
Zechlin D 45 B4
Zechlinerhütte D 45 B4
Zederhaus A 72 A3
Žednik SCG 75 C4
Zeebrugge B 49 B4
Zehdenick D 45 C5
Zehren D 52 B3
Zeil D 51 C6
Zeilarn D 62 B3
Zeist NL 49 A6
Zeithain D 52 B3
Zeitz D 52 B2
Želatava CZ 63 A6
Želazno, *Dolnośląskie* PL 54 C1
Želazno, *Pomorskie* PL 46 A3
Zele B 49 B5
Zelenoborskiy RUS 3 C30
Zelenogorsk RUS 7 A10
Zelenograd RUS 7 C14
Zelenogradsk RUS 6 D6
Železná Ruda CZ 63 A4
Železnice CZ 53 C5
Železnik SCG 85 B5
Zelezniki SLO 73 B4
Železny Brod CZ 53 C5
Zelhem NL 50 A2
Želiezovce SK 65 B4
Żelkowo PL 46 A3
Zell CH 70 A2
Zell, *Baden-Württemberg* D 60 C3
Zell, *Baden-Württemberg* D 61 B4
Zell, *Rheinland-Pfalz* D 50 C3
Zell am See A 72 A2
Zell am Ziller A 72 A1
Zell an der Pram A 63 B4
Zell bei Zellhof A 63 B5
Zella-Mehlis D 51 C6
Zellerndorf A 64 B1
Zellingen D 61 A5
Želovce SK 65 B5
Zelów PL 55 B4
Zeltweg A 73 A4
Zelzate B 49 B4
Zemberovce SK 65 B4
Zembrzyce PL 65 A5
Zemianske-Kostol'any SK 65 B4
Zemitz D 45 B5
Zemné SK 64 C3
Zemst B 49 C5
Zemun SCG 85 B5
Zemunik Donji HR 83 B4
Zenica BIH 84 B2
Zennor GB 28 C2
Žepa BIH 85 C4
Žepče BIH 84 B3
Zepponami I 102 A5
Zerbst D 52 B2
Zerf D 60 A2
Żerków PL 54 A2
Zermatt CH 70 B2
Zernez CH 71 B5
Zerpen-schleuse D 45 C5
Zestoa E 89 A4
Zetel D 43 B4
Zeulenroda D 52 C1
Zeven D 43 B6
Zevenaar NL 50 B2
Zevenbergen NL 49 B5
Zévio I 71 C6
Zeytinbaği TR 118 B3
Zeytindağ TR 118 D2
Zgierz PL 55 B4
Zgorzelec PL 53 B5
Zgošća BIH 84 B3
Zhabinka BY 6 E8
Zharkovskiy RUS 7 D12
Zhashkiv UA 11 B11
Zheleznogorsk RUS 7 E13
Zhizdra RUS 7 E13
Zhlobin BY 7 E11
Zhmerynka UA 11 B10
Zhodzina BY 7 D10
Zhovti Vody UA 11 B12
Zhovtneve UA 11 C12
Zhukovka RUS 7 E12
Zhytomyr UA 11 A10
Žiar nad Hronom SK 65 B4
Zicavo F 102 B2
Zickhusen D 44 B3
Zidani Most SLO 73 B5
Ziddorf D 45 B4
Židlochovice CZ 64 A2
Ziębice PL 54 C2
Ziegendorf D 44 B3
Ziegenrück D 52 C1
Zieleniec, *Dolnośląskie* PL 54 C1
Zieleniec, *Zachodnio-Pomorskie* PL 46 B1
Zielona PL 47 B5
Zielona Góra PL 53 B5
Zielonka PL 55 A6
Zieluń-Osada PL 47 B5
Ziemetshausen D 61 B6
Zierenberg D 51 B5
Zierikzee NL 49 B4
Ziersdorf A 64 B1
Zierzow D 44 B3
Ziesar D 52 A2
Ziesendorf D 44 B4
Ziethen D 45 C5
Žihle CZ 52 C3
Zile TR 16 A7
Žilina SK 65 A4
Ziltendorf D 53 A4
Zimandu Nou RO 75 B6
Zimna Woda PL 47 B6
Zimnicea RO 11 E8
Zinal CH 70 B2
Zinasco I 70 C4
Zingst D 45 A4
Zinkgruvan S 37 D2
Žinkovy CZ 63 A4
Zinnowitz D 45 A5
Zirc H 74 A2
Žiri SLO 73 B4
Zirl A 71 A6
Zirndorf D 62 A1
Žirovnica SCG 85 B6
Žirovnice CZ 63 A6
Zisterdorf A 64 B2
Žitište SCG 75 C5
Zitsa GR 116 C2
Zittau D 53 C4
Živaja HR 74 C1
Živinice BIH 84 B3
Zlatar HR 73 B6
Zlatar Bistrica HR 73 B6
Zlate Hory CZ 54 C2
Zlaté Klasy SK 64 B3
Zlaté Moravce SK 65 B4
Zlatná na Ostrove SK 64 C3
Zlatniky SK 64 B4
Zlatograd BG 116 A7
Žlebič SLO 73 C4
Zlín CZ 64 A3
Złocieniec PL 46 B2
Złoczew PL 54 B3
Zlonice CZ 53 C4
Złotniki Kujawskie PL 47 C4
Złotoryja PL 53 B5
Złotów PL 46 B3
Złoty Stok PL 54 C1
Zlutice CZ 52 C3
Zmajevac BIH 83 B5
Zmajevo SCG 75 C4
Żmigród PL 54 B1
Zmijavci HR 84 C2
Žminj HR 72 C3
Znamyanka UA 11 B12
Żnin PL 46 C3
Znojmo CZ 64 B2
Zöblitz D 52 C3
Zocca I 81 B4
Zoetermeer NL 49 A5
Zofingen CH 70 A2
Zogno I 71 C4
Zohor SK 64 B2
Zolling D 62 B2
Zolochiv UA 11 B8
Zolotonosha UA 11 B12
Zomba H 74 B3
Zomergem B 49 B4
Zoñán E 86 A3
Zonguldak TR 118 A6
Zonhoven B 49 C6
Zonza F 102 B2
Zörbig D 52 B2
Zorita E 93 B5
Żory PL 54 C3
Zossen D 52 A3
Zottegem B 49 C4
Zoutkamp NL 42 B3
Zovi Do BIH 84 C3
Zreče SLO 73 B5
Zrenjanin SCG 75 C5
Žrnovica HR 83 C5
Zruč nad Sázavou CZ 63 A6
Zsámbék H 65 C4
Zsámbok H 75 A4
Zsana H 75 B4
Zschopau D 52 C3
Zuberec SK 65 A5
Zubieta E 76 C1
Zubin Potok SCG 85 D5
Zubiri E 76 D1
Zubtsov RUS 7 C13
Zucaina E 96 A2
Zudar D 45 A5
Zuera E 90 B2
Zufre E 99 B4
Zug CH 70 A3
Zuheros E 100 B1
Zuidhorn NL 42 B3
Zuidlaren NL 42 B3
Zuidwolde NL 42 C3
Zújar E 101 B3
Żukowo PL 47 A4
Žuljana HR 84 D2
Žulová CZ 54 C2
Zülpich D 50 C2
Zumaia E 89 A4
Zumárraga E 89 A4
Zundert NL 49 B5
Županja HR 84 A3
Zurgena E 101 B3
Zürich CH 70 A3
Żuromin PL 47 B5
Zurzach CH 70 A3
Zusmarshausen D 62 B1
Zusow D 44 B3
Züssow D 45 B5
Žuta Lovka HR 83 B4
Zutphen NL 50 A2
Žužemberk SLO 73 C4
Zvečan SCG 85 D5
Zvenyhorodka UA 11 B11
Zvikovské Podhradí CZ 63 A5
Zvolen SK 65 B5
Zvolenská Slatina SK 65 B5
Zvornik BIH 85 B4
Zwartsluis NL 42 C3
Zweibrücken D 60 A3
Zweisimmen CH 70 B2
Zwettl A 63 B6
Zwettl an der Rodl A 63 B5
Zwickau D 52 C2
Zwiefalten D 61 B5
Zwieryn PL 46 C1
Zwierzno PL 47 A5
Zwiesel D 63 A4
Zwieselstein A 71 B6
Zwoleń PL 55 B6
Zwolle NL 42 C3
Zwönitz D 52 C2
Żychlin PL 55 A4
Zydowo, *Wielkopolskie* PL 46 C3
Zydowo, *Zachodnio-Pomorskie* PL 46 A2
Żyrardów PL 55 A5
Żytno PL 55 C4
Żywiec PL 65 A5
Zyyi CY 120 B2